D0588546

Oxford
Essential
English
Dictionary

OXFORD
UNIVERSITY PRESS

Editors: Morven Dooner, Mary O'Neill
Robert Allen, Andrew Delahunty

OXFORD
UNIVERSITY PRESS

Great Clarendon Street, Oxford OX2 6DP

Oxford University Press is a department of the University of Oxford.
It furthers the University's objective of excellence in research,
scholarship, and education by publishing worldwide in

Oxford   New York

Auckland   Cape Town   Dar es Salaam   Hong Kong   Karachi
Kuala Lumpur   Madrid   Melbourne   Mexico City   Nairobi
New Delhi   Shanghai   Taipei   Toronto

with offices in

Argentina   Austria   Brazil   Chile   Czech Republic   France   Greece
Guatemala   Hungary   Italy   Japan   Poland   Portugal   Singapore
South Korea   Switzerland   Thailand   Turkey   Ukraine   Vietnam

Oxford is a registered trade mark of Oxford University Press
in the UK and in certain other countries

© Oxford University Press 2011
Database right Oxford University Press (maker)
First published for The Book People 2011

British Library Cataloguing in Publication Data
Data available

ISBN: 978-0-19-279281-5

10 9 8 7 6 5 4 3 2

Printed in India by Nutech Print Services

Contents

Oxford Essential English Dictionary

Preface

The *Essential English Dictionary* is a dictionary that will help you with all your language queries and, with its special binding and slipcase, it is also a dictionary to cherish.

It has been created to be a helpful source of key information about the words you will meet today. It is compiled using the latest language data available, so you can be confident that the information is completely up to date and the focus is on contemporary words and meanings.

The meanings of words are explained in straightforward language, and example sentences and phrases are included where some context helps to make a meaning more clear or distinguish between different meanings of the same word. Words and phrases containing the entry word appear alongside that word, making them easy to find.

Pronunciations are given using a simple system that spells out how you would say the word. Extra notes highlight tricky spellings and words that can be confused with one another, and give pointers to using English well.

Whether you are at school, in the office, or at home, the *Essential English Dictionary* will quickly provide vital answers to your questions about English and will become a treasured possession.

Abbreviations used in this dictionary

n	noun	*Gram*	Grammar
v	verb	*N. Am.*	North American
adj	adjective	*Mus*	Music
adv	adverb	*Biol*	Biology
prep	preposition	*Chem*	Chemistry
abbr	abbreviation	*Phys*	Physics
hist	historical		
ICT	Information and Communication Technology		

Using this dictionary

headword

pronunciation guide

definition

subject label

numbered meanings

usage label

idioms and phrases

noteworthy verb forms or plurals

numbered headword (homograph)

word class (part of speech)

derived words

usage note

example of a word in use

abhor (say əb-**hor**) v **abhorred, abhorring** to detest something **abhorrence** n **abhorrent** adj

abstract¹ (say **ab**-strakt) adj **1** not having any physical existence ♦ *Truth is an abstract quality.* **2** theoretical rather than practical **3** (said about a painting or sculpture) using designs that show the creator's ideas without attempting to show a real person or thing **abstract** n **1** an abstract quality or idea **2** a summary of a long book or article **3** an abstract painting or sculpture **abstraction** n **abstractly** adv **abstractness** n

abstracted adj having your mind on other things, not paying attention

accelerate v **1** to move steadily faster **2** to happen earlier or more quickly **3** to cause something to happen more quickly **acceleration** n **accelerator** n **accelerometer** n *Phys* an instrument for measuring acceleration or vibrations

accept v **1** to take something offered to you **2** to undertake a responsibility **3** to treat someone as welcome ♦ *They were never really accepted by their neighbours.* **4** to be willing to agree to a suggestion or idea ♦ *I accept that I may have been wrong.* **acceptable** adj **1** worth accepting, welcome **2** tolerable or adequate ♦ *The quality was barely acceptable.* **acceptability** n **acceptably** adj **acceptance** n **acceptor** Physics an atom or molecule able to receive an extra electron or proton etc. n ◊ Do not confuse this word with *except*.

acclaim (say ə-**klaym**) v to welcome someone with shouts of approval **acclaim** n applause or praise **acclamation** n

accord n consent or agreement **accord** v **1** to be in harmony or consistent with something **2** *formal* to give or grant something to someone ♦ *We were accorded a rare privilege.* **accordance** n **according** adv

according to 1 as stated by a person or book ♦ *According to the encyclopedia light bulbs give out more heat than light.* **2** in a manner corresponding to or in proportion to ♦ *The eggs are classed according to size.* **accordingly** adv

Aa

A the first letter of the English alphabet

A *abbr* ampere(s)

Å *abbr* ångström(s)

a-¹ *prefix* (changing to **an-** before a vowel sound) not or without (as in *asymmetrical, anarchy*)

a-² *prefix* **1** on or towards (as in *ashore, aside*) **2** in the process of doing something (as in *go a-hunting*)

aardvark (say **ahd**-vark) *n* an African animal with a large heavy body like a pig, which feeds on termites

ab- *prefix* (changing to **abs-** before c and t) away; from (as in *abduct, abnormal, abstract*)

aback *adv* **to be taken aback** to be upset or disconcerted by something that happens

abacus (say **ab**-ə-kəs) *n pl* **abacuses** a frame with beads that slide along rods, used for counting

abandon *v* **1** to leave a person or place without intending to return to them **2** to stop working on something ♦ *We decided to abandon the attempt.* **abandon** *n* a careless or reckless freedom of manner ♦ *They acted with carefree abandon.* **abandoned** *adj* **abandonment** *n*

abase *v* to humiliate or degrade someone **abasement** *n*

abashed *adj* embarrassed or ashamed

abate *v* to become less ♦ *At last the storm abated.* **abatement** *n*

abattoir (say **ab**-ə-twar) *n* a slaughterhouse

abbess (say **ab**-ess) *n* a woman who is the head of an abbey of nuns

abbey *n pl* **abbeys 1** a building occupied by monks or nuns living as a community, or the community itself **2** a church or house that was once an abbey

abbot *n* a man who is the head of an abbey of monks

abbreviate *v* to shorten a word or title **abbreviation** *n*

ABC *n* **1** the alphabet **2** the basic facts that you learn about a subject ♦ *the ABC of music*

abdicate *v* to give up a high office, especially the throne **abdication** *n*

abdomen (say **ab**-dəm-ən) *n* **1** the part of the body below the chest and diaphragm **2** the hindmost section of the body of an insect, spider, or crustacean **abdominal** *adj* **abdominally** *adv*

abduct *v* to carry off a person illegally by force **abduction** *n* **abductor** *n*

aberration (say ab-er-**ay**-shən) *n* **1** a deviation from what is normal **2** a mental or moral lapse **3** a distortion **aberrant** *adj*

abet *v* **abetted, abetting** to encourage or assist someone to commit an offence **abetment** *n* **abetter, abettor** *n*

abeyance (say ə-**bay**-əns) *n* **in abeyance** (said about a right, rule, problem, etc.) not in force or in use for a time

abhor (say əb-**hor**) *v* **abhorred, abhorring** to detest something **abhorrence** *n* **abhorrent** *adj*

abide *v* **1** to bear or endure ♦ *I can't abide wasps.* **2** *old use* to remain or dwell in a place **abiding** *adj* **to abide by** to act in accordance with a rule or decision

ability *n pl* **abilities 1** the capacity or power to do something **2** cleverness or talent

abject (say **ab**-jekt) *adj* **1** wretched and degrading ♦ *They lived for years in abject poverty.* **2** having no pride ♦ *He gave her an abject apology.* **abjectly** *adv*

ablaze *adj* burning fiercely

able *adj* **1** having the ability to do something **2** having a lot of ability **ably** *adv*

-able *suffix* forming adjectives meaning 'that can be done' (as in *readable*)

able-bodied *adj* physically fit and strong

abnormal *adj* different from what is normal **abnormality** *n* **abnormally** *adv*

aboard *adv, prep* on or into a ship or aircraft or train

abode *n old use* a place where someone lives, a home

abolish *v* to put an end to a practice or institution **abolition** *n* **abolitionist** *n*

A-bomb *n* an atomic bomb

abominable *adj* horrible or loathsome **abominably** *adv* **Abominable Snowman** *n* a large animal like a bear, said to exist in the Himalayas

abominate v to detest or loathe something **abomination** n

aboriginal adj (said about a people or about plants) living or growing in a land from the earliest times or from before the arrival of colonists **aboriginal** n an aboriginal inhabitant **Aboriginal** n an aboriginal inhabitant of Australia **aborigine** n pl **aborigines**

abort (say ə-**bort**) v 1 to carry out the abortion of a fetus 2 to end a scheme or activity because of a fault or failure **abortion** n the expulsion of a fetus from the womb before it is able to survive **abortionist** n **abortive** adj **abortively** adv

abound v 1 to be plentiful ♦ Ferns abound on the hillside. 2 to have in large quantities ♦ The river abounds in fish.

about prep 1 approximately, roughly ♦ about £100 2 in connection with, on the subject of ♦ What is the film about? 3 all around ♦ round about the town **about** adv 1 somewhere near, not far away ♦ The children are somewhere about. 2 in various places or directions ♦ lying about ♦ running about 3 on the move, active ♦ She will soon be about again. **about-face** n 1 a turning movement to face the opposite direction 2 a complete change of opinion or policy

above adv 1 at or to a higher point ♦ See the stars above. 2 earlier in a book or article ♦ The picture is shown above. **above** prep 1 higher than ♦ There is a sign above the door. 2 more than ♦ Don't pay above £20. **above-board** adj honest, done honestly or openly

abracadabra (say abrə-kə-**dab**-rə) n a formula supposed to be magical

abrasive (say ə-**bray**-siv) adj 1 suitable for polishing surfaces by rubbing or grinding them 2 having a harsh or rough manner **abrasive** n a substance used to polish surfaces by rubbing

abreast adv side by side and facing the same way **to keep abreast of** to be up to date with information or news about something

abridge v to shorten a story by using fewer words **abridgement** n

abroad adv 1 in or to a foreign country 2 over a large area ♦ They scattered the seeds abroad.

abrogate (say **ab**-rə-gayt) v to cancel or repeal a law or agreement **abrogation** n

abrupt adj 1 sudden ♦ The car came to an abrupt stop. 2 curt and almost rude **abruptly** adv **abruptness** n

abscess (say **ab**-sis) n a swollen area that contains pus

abscond (say əb-**skond**) v to leave or escape secretly and without permission **absconder** n

abseil (say **ab**-sayl) v to descend a rock-face using a doubled rope that is fixed at a higher point

absence n 1 the state of being away 2 a lack or non-existence ♦ in the absence of proof

absent[1] (say **ab**-sənt) adj 1 not present 2 non-existent 3 having your mind on other things **absentee** n **absenteeism** n **absently** adv **absent-minded** adj having your mind on other things, forgetful

absent[2] (say əb-**sent**) v to absent yourself to be absent or stay away

absolute adj 1 complete ♦ The holiday was absolute bliss. 2 without any limits ♦ The dictators enjoyed absolute power. 3 independent, not relative ♦ There is no absolute standard for beauty. **absolutely** adv **absolution** n a priest's formal declaration that a person's sins are forgiven **absolutism** n the principle of having a rule, etc. that must apply in all cases **absolute majority** n a majority of votes or seats in a parliament over all rivals combined **absolute temperature** n temperature measured in kelvins from absolute zero **absolute zero** n the lowest temperature that is theoretically possible (-273.15°C)

absolve v to clear a person of blame or guilt

absorb v 1 to soak up liquid or other substances 2 to learn and remember information 3 to reduce the effect of something unwelcome ♦ The buffers absorbed the impact. **absorbable** adj **absorbency** n **absorbent** adj **absorber** n **absorbing** adj **absorption** n **absorptive** adj

abstain v 1 to make yourself not do something you would like to 2 to decide not to use your vote in an election **abstainer** n **abstention** n **abstinence** n abstaining, especially going without food or alcohol **abstinent** adj

abstemious (say əb-**steem**-iəs) adj not eating or drinking much **abstemiously** adv **abstemiousness** n

abstract[1] (say **ab**-strakt) adj 1 not having any physical existence ♦ *Truth is an abstract quality.* 2 theoretical rather than practical 3 (said about a painting or sculpture) using designs that show the creator's ideas without attempting to show a real person or thing **abstract** n 1 an abstract quality or idea 2 a summary of a long book or article 3 an abstract painting or sculpture **abstraction** n **abstractly** adv **abstractness** n

abstract[2] (say əb-**strakt**) v formal 1 to take something out 2 to get information or data from a resource 3 to make a written summary of a story or text **abstractor** n

abstracted adj having your mind on other things, not paying attention

abstruse (say əb-**strooss**) adj hard to understand **abstruseness** n

absurd adj ridiculous or foolish **absurdity** n pl **absurdities absurdly** adv

abundance n a large amount of something, more than enough **abundant** adj **abundantly** adv

abuse (say ə-**bewss**) n 1 a misuse of something 2 treating someone cruelly 3 an unjust or corrupt practice 4 offensive or insulting language **abusive** adj **abusively** adv

abut (say ə-**but**) v **abutted**, **abutting** to be next to or touching something ♦ *Their land abuts ours.* **abutment** n

abysmal (say ə-**biz**-məl) adj 1 extremely bad ♦ *Their taste is abysmal.* 2 very deep ♦ *He shows abysmal ignorance.* **abysmally** adv

abyss (say ə-**biss**) n 1 a very deep hole or chasm 2 disaster seen as likely to happen

AC, ac abbr alternating current

acacia (say ə-**kay**-shə) n a tree with small yellow or white flowers

academy n pl **academies** 1 a school, especially for specialized training 2 in Scotland, a secondary school **Academy** n a

society of scholars or artists **academic** adj 1 to do with a school, college, or university 2 scholarly as opposed to technical or practical ♦ *academic subjects* 3 having theoretical interest only **academic** n a scholar or academic person **academically** adv **academician** n a member of an Academy

acanthus n a Mediterranean plant with bold spikes of flowers and large spiny leaves

ACAS (say **ay**-kass) abbr Advisory, Conciliation, and Arbitration Service

accede (say ək-**seed**) v to take office, to become king or queen

accelerate v 1 to move steadily faster 2 to happen earlier or more quickly 3 to cause something to happen more quickly **acceleration** n **accelerator** n **accelerometer** n Phys an instrument for measuring acceleration or vibrations

accent (say **ak**-sənt) n 1 a particular way of pronouncing words, associated with a country, area, or social class 2 the emphasis put on a syllable or word when pronouncing it 3 a mark indicating an emphasis or the quality of a vowel sound 4 the importance given to something ♦ *The accent is on quality.* **accent** (say ək-**sent**) v 1 to pronounce a word with an accent 2 to emphasize something **accentuate** v to emphasize something or make it important **accentuation** n

accept v 1 to take something offered to you 2 to undertake a responsibility 3 to treat someone as welcome ♦ *They were never really accepted by their neighbours.* 4 to be willing to agree to a suggestion or idea ♦ *I accept that I may have been wrong.* **acceptable** adj 1 worth accepting, welcome 2 tolerable or adequate ♦ *The quality was barely acceptable.* **acceptability** n **acceptably** adj **acceptance** n **acceptor** Phys an atom or molecule able to receive an extra electron or proton etc. n ◊ Do not confuse this word with except.

access (say **ak**-sess) n 1 a means of approaching or entering a place 2 the right or opportunity of reaching or using something ♦ *Students need access to books.* 3 an attack of emotion ♦ *a sudden access of* rage **access** v to retrieve information stored in a computer **accessible** adj **accessibly** adv

accessibility n **accession** n **1** reaching a rank or position, especially that of king or queen ♦ *the Queen's accession to the throne* **2** an addition to a library or other collection

accessory (say ək-**sess**-er-i) n pl **accessories 1** an extra or decorative thing that is added to something to make it more useful or attractive **2** *Law* a person who helps someone to commit a crime, without taking part in it

accident n **1** an unexpected or unwelcome event, especially one causing injury or damage **2** chance or fortune ♦ *We met by accident.* **accidental** adj **accidentally** adv

acclaim (say ə-**klaym**) v to welcome someone with shouts of approval **acclaim** n applause or praise **acclamation** n

acclimatize v to become used to a new climate or new conditions **acclimatization** n

accolade (say ak-ə-**layd**) n **1** a special honour conferred as praise or approval **2** a ceremonial touch of the shoulder with a sword, given when conferring a knighthood

accommodate v **1** to provide lodging or a room for someone **2** to provide what someone wants or needs ♦ *The bank will accommodate you with a loan.* **accommodating** adj willing to do what someone else wants **accommodation** n **1** a room or building in which someone can live **2** the process of adapting to what someone else needs

accompany v **accompanies, accompanied, accompanying 1** to go to a place with someone **2** to be present with someone **3** to provide a thing in addition to something **4** *Mus* to play an accompaniment to a singer or soloist **accompaniment** n **1** *Mus* an instrumental part which supports a solo instrument or voice or a choir **2** something that goes with something else **accompanist** n a person who plays a musical accompaniment

accomplice (say ə-**kum**-plis) n a person who helps someone to commit a crime

accomplish (say ə-**kum**-plish) v to succeed in doing something **accomplished** adj **accomplishment** n

accord n consent or agreement **accord** v **1** to be in harmony or consistent with something **2** *formal* to give or grant something to someone ♦ *We were accorded a rare privilege.* **accordance** n **according** adv **according to 1** as stated by a person or book ♦ *According to the encyclopedia light bulbs give out more heat than light.* **2** in a manner corresponding to or in proportion to ♦ *The eggs are classed according to size.* **accordingly** adv

accordion n a musical instrument played by squeezing and stretching a set of bellows, and making the melody on keys or buttons **accordionist** n

accost (say ə-**kost**) v to approach and speak to someone in a bold or challenging way

account n **1** a description or report of something that happened **2** an arrangement with a bank or firm to hold a customer's money or provide goods or services on credit **3** a statement of money paid or owed for goods or services, or a bill stating the amount owed **4** importance or value ♦ *Money is of no account to him.* **account** v to regard or consider someone in a special way ♦ *A person is accounted innocent until proved guilty.* **accountable** adj **accountability** n **on account** to be paid for fully at a later date **on account of** because of something, for a stated reason **to account for 1** to give or be an explanation of something **2** to describe how you have used something, e.g. money

accounting n the business of keeping or inspecting accounts, accountancy **accountancy** n **accountant** n

accoutrements (say ə-**koo**-trə-mənts) pl n a soldier's equipment other than weapons and uniform

accredited (say ə-**kred**-itid) adj **1** officially recognized or appointed to a position ♦ *our accredited representative in New York* **2** generally accepted or believed **3** certified as being of a prescribed quality

accretion (say ə-**kree**-shən) n **1** a growth or increase resulting from gradual additions **2** the growing of separate things into one

accrue (say ə-**kroo**) v **accrues**, **accrued**, **accruing** (said about a sum of money or a benefit) to be received at regular intervals, to accumulate ♦ *Interest on investments accrues annually.* **accrual** n

accumulate v **1** to acquire an increasing quantity of something **2** to increase in quantity or amount **accumulation** n **accumulative** adj

accumulator n **1** a large rechargeable electric battery **2** a series of bets, with the winnings from each bet placed on the next

accurate adj **1** true or conforming to a standard **2** precise or correct in all its details **accuracy** n **accurately** adv

accursed (say ə-**ker**-sid) adj **1** under a curse **2** detestable, hateful

accuse v to make a statement putting the blame for a crime or wrongdoing, etc. on a named person **the accused** the person accused in a court of law **accusation** n **accuser** n **accusingly** adv

accustom v to make someone become used to something **accustomed** adj

ace n **1** a playing card with one spot **2** a person who is very good at something ♦ *an ace pilot* **3** (in tennis) a service that is so good that the other player cannot return it **ace** adj informal extremely good, excellent

acerbic (say ə-**serb**-ik) n having a sharp manner of speaking **acerbity** n

acetate (say **ass**-it-ayt) n **1** a compound derived from acetic acid **2** a fabric made from cellulose acetate

acetic acid n the acid that gives vinegar its special taste and smell

acetone (say **ass**-i-tohn) n a colourless liquid used as a solvent

acetylene (say ə-**set**-i-leen) n a gas that burns with a bright flame, used in cutting and welding metal

ache v **1** to suffer a dull continuous physical or mental pain **2** to yearn **ache** n a dull continuous pain **achy** adj

achieve v to gain or reach something by an effort **achievable** adj **achievement** n

Achilles' heel (say ə-**kil**-eez) n a weak or vulnerable point

Achilles' tendon n the tendon connecting the heel with the calf muscles

acid n **1** any of a class of substances containing hydrogen that can be replaced by a metal to form a salt **2** a sour substance **acid** adj **1** sour or sharp-tasting **2** looking or sounding bitter ♦ *He made some acid remarks.* **acidic** adj **acidify** v **acidifies**, **acidified**, **acidifying**, **acidity** n **acidly** adv

acid rain n rain made acid by contamination

acid test n a conclusive test to see whether something is right or genuine

acknowledge v **1** to admit that something is true or genuine **2** to confirm that you have received something, or to express thanks for receiving it **3** to show that you have noticed or recognized someone **acknowledgement** n

acme (say **ak**-mi) n the highest point or achievement, the peak of perfection

acne (say **ak**-ni) n inflammation of the oil-glands of the skin, producing red pimples

acolyte (say **ak**-ə-liyt) n **1** a person who assists a priest in certain religious services **2** an attendant

aconite n a perennial plant of the buttercup family, with a poisonous root

acorn n the fruit of the oak tree, with a base like a cup

acoustic (say ə-**koo**-stik) adj **1** to do with sound or the sense of hearing **2** (said about a musical instrument) amplifying the sound by natural means, such as a sound box; not electrically amplified **acoustics** pl n the properties of sound; the qualities of a hall, etc. that make it good or bad for carrying sound **acoustically** adv

acquaint v to make someone aware of something or familiar with it ♦ *You had better acquaint us with the facts.*

acquaintance n **1** being acquainted **2** a person you know slightly **to be acquainted with** to know someone slightly

acquiesce (say akwi-**ess**) v to agree willingly **acquiescent** adj willing to agree to something **acquiescence** n

acquire v to get possession of something **acquirement** n **acquisition** n **acquired taste** n something that you gradually get to like over time

acquisitive (say ə-**kwiz**-itiv) adj wanting to have a lot of new things **acquisitively** adv

acquisitiveness *n*

acquit *v* **acquitted**, **acquitting** in a court of law, to declare a person not guilty of the crime they were charged with **acquittal** *n* **to acquit oneself** to conduct oneself or perform in a certain way ♦ *She acquitted herself well in the test.*

acre (say **ay-ker**) *n* a measure of land, equal to 4840 sq. yds **acreage** *n*

acrid (say **ak-**rid) *adj* **1** having a bitter smell or taste **2** having a sharp temper or manner **acridity** *n*

acrimony (say **ak-**ri-məni) *n* bitterness of manner or words **acrimonious** *adj* (said about a person or remark) unpleasant or bad-tempered **acrimoniously** *adv*

acrobatics *pl* *n* spectacular gymnastic exercises and movements **acrobat** *n* **acrobatic** *adj* **acrobatically** *adv*

acronym (say **ak-**rə-nim) *n* a word formed from the initial letters of other words and pronounced as a word in its own right, e.g. *Aids*, *Nato*

acropolis (say a-**krop-**ə-lis) *n* the citadel or upper fortified part of an ancient Greek city, especially (**Acropolis**) Athens

across *prep, adv* **1** from one side of a thing to the other **2** to or on the other side of **3** so as to be understood or accepted ♦ *He got his points across to the audience.* **4** so as to form a cross or intersect ♦ *They were laid across each other.* **across the board** applying to all members or groups

acrostic (say ə-**kros-**tik) *n* a word puzzle or poem in which the first or last letters of each line form a word or phrase

acrylic (say ə-**kril-**ik) *adj* **1** of a synthetic material made from an organic acid **2** *Art* a type of thick paint used by artists **acrylic** *n* an acrylic fibre, plastic, or resin

act *n* **1** something someone does **2** the process of doing something ♦ *The thieves were caught in the act.* **3** a pose or pretence ♦ *His show of concern was just an act.* **4** each of a series of short performances in a programme ♦ *The next act will be the clowns.* **5** each of the main divisions of a play **6** a decree or law made by a parliament **act** *v* **1** to behave or perform actions in a certain way ♦ *You have acted wisely.* **2** to function or

do what is required ♦ *Will you act as referee?* ♦ *The brakes were slow to act.* **3** to have an effect on something ♦ *Acid acts on metal.* **4** to perform a part in a play ♦ *Stephen was chosen to act Hamlet.* **5** to portray by actions as though taking part in a play ♦ *act the fool*

acting *adj* serving for a time as a substitute or replacement ♦ *the acting manager*

actor *n* someone who performs in a stage play or a film **actress** *n* a female actor

action *n* **1** the process of doing something to achieve a purpose **2** the exertion of energy or influence ♦ *the action of acid on metal* **3** a thing that someone has done ♦ *Their prompt action prevented an accident.* **4** a series of events in a story or play ♦ *The action is set in China.* **5** the mechanism or movements by which a machine or device works **6** a lawsuit **7** fighting in a war ♦ *Her brother was killed in action.* **actionable** *adj* **1** (said about an act) of a kind against which legal action could be taken **2** able to be done or put into practice; useful, practical

action replay *n* a playback of a piece of action in the broadcast of a sports event

active *adj* **1** moving about, characterized by energetic action **2** taking part in many activities **3** (said about a machine) working or in operation **4** (said about a volcano) erupting occasionally **5** having an effect ♦ *the active ingredients* **6** radioactive **7** *Gram* denoting the form of a verb used when the subject of the sentence is the person or thing that performs the action, e.g. *saw* in *We saw him* and *stops* in *When the train stops* **active** *n* *Gram* the active form of a verb **activate** *v* to make something active **activation** *n* **activator** *n* **actively** *adv* **activity** *n* *pl* **activities**

activist *n* someone who is very active and energetic, especially in politics **activism** *n*

actual *adj* existing in fact, real **actuality** *n* what is real or happening **actually** *adv*

actuary (say **ak-**tew-er-i) *n* *pl* **actuaries** an expert in statistics who calculates insurance risks and premiums **actuarial** *adj*

actuate *v* **1** to start or activate a movement or process **2** to be a motive for a person's actions **actuator** *n*

acuity (say ə-**kew-**iti) *n* sharpness or

acuteness

acumen (say **ak**-yoo-men) *n* shrewdness or sharpness of mind

acupuncture (say **ak**-yoo-punk-cher) *n* a form of alternative medicine in which the tissues of the body are pricked with fine needles at special points **acupuncturist** *n*

acute *adj* **1** shrewd and perceptive **2** sharp or severe in its effect ♦ *She felt an acute pain in her arm.* **3** (said about an illness) coming sharply or quickly to a crisis **acutely** *adv* **acuteness** *n* **acute accent** *n* a mark put over a vowel in some languages, for example é in *café* **acute angle** *n* an angle of less than 90°

AD *abbr* (in dates) anno Domini: denoting the Christian era, placed after a date to indicate the number of years after the traditional date of the birth of Christ

ad- *prefix* (changing to **ac-, af-, ag-, al-, an-, ap-, ar-, as-, at-** before certain consonants) to; towards (as in *adapt, admit*)

adagio (say ə-**dahj**-yoh) *adv Mus* to be played in slow time **adagio** *n pl* **adagios** a movement to be played in this way

adamant (say **ad**-ə-mənt) *adj* refusing to change your mind, determined

Adam's apple *n* the projection of cartilage at the front of the neck, especially in men

adapt *v* **1** to make something suitable for a new use or situation **2** to become used to a new situation **adaptable** *adj* **adaptability** *n* **adaptation** *n* **adaptor** *n* **1** a device used to connect different pieces of equipment **2** a device allowing several electrical plugs to be put in one socket

add *v* **1** to join one thing to another to make it larger in size or quantity **2** (also **add up**) to put numbers or amounts together to reach a total **3** to reach a total **4** to make an extra remark ♦ *She added that it was time to leave anyway.*

addenda *pl n* extra text added at the end of a book or pamphlet

adder *n* a small poisonous snake

addict (say **ad**-ikt) *n* a person who is addicted to something **addicted** *adj* **addiction** *n* **addictive** *adj*

addition *n* **1** the process of adding or being added **2** something added to something else **additional** *adj* **additionally** *adv*

additive (say **ad**-it-iv) *n* a substance added in small amounts to something, especially to colour or flavour food or to preserve it

addle *v* to muddle or confuse ♦ *The din has addled my brains.*

address *n* **1** the details of where a person lives or an organization is situated **2** a formal speech delivered to an audience **3** *ICT* the part of a computer instruction that specifies the location of a piece of stored information **address** *v* **1** to write the details of a person's or organization's address on an envelope or package **2** to make a formal speech to an audience **3** to direct a remark or statement to someone ♦ *At this point Jennifer addressed her brother.* **4** to use a particular style in speaking or writing to an important person ♦ *Do you know how to address an archbishop?* **5** (in golf) to take aim at the ball **addressee** *n*

adduce (say ə-**dewss**) *v* to mention or state something as an example or proof **adducible** *adj*

adenoids (say **ad**-in-oidz) *pl n* a piece of spongy tissue between the back of the nose and the throat **adenoidal** *adj*

adept (say **ad**-ept) *adj* very able or skilful **adept** *n* a skilful person

adequate *adj* **1** sufficient or satisfactory **2** good enough but not outstanding **adequacy** *n* **adequately** *adv*

adhere (say əd-**heer**) *v* **1** to stick fast to a surface ♦ *There was something pink and gloopy adhering to the underside of his left shoe.* **2** to continue to believe in something or to follow a course ♦ *Every effort has been made to adhere to the literal meaning of the original writing.* **adherent** *n* someone who supports a political party or religious doctrine **adherence** *n* **adhesion** *n* the state of sticking fast

adhesive *adj* causing things to adhere, sticky **adhesive** *n* an adhesive substance **adhesiveness** *n*

ad hoc *adj, adv* done or meant for a special purpose ♦ *They set up an ad hoc committee.*

adieu (say ə-**dew**) *interjection, n pl* **adieus** goodbye

Adi Granth (say ah-di **grunt**) *n* the sacred

writings of Sikhism

ad infinitum (say in-fin-**iy**-təm) *adv* without limit, for ever

adipose (say **ad**-i-pohs) *adj* of animal fat, fatty **adiposity** *n*

adjacent *adj* **1** lying near or adjoining something else **2** *Mathematics* (said about a pair of angles) formed on the same side of a straight line when crossed by another line.

adjective (say **aj**-ik-tiv) *n* a word added to a noun to describe it or change its meaning, e.g. *old, tall, Swedish, my, this* **adjectival** *adj* **adjectivally** *n*

adjoin *v* to be next or nearest to something

adjourn (say ə-**jern**) *v* **1** to break off a meeting for a time **2** to stop doing something and go somewhere else **adjournment** *n*

adjudge *v* to decide or award something formally ♦ *He was adjudged to be guilty.* **adjudicate** *v* **adjudication** *n* **adjudicator** *n*

adjunct (say **ad**-junkt) *n* something added or attached but subordinate

adjust *v* **1** to arrange something or put it into the right position **2** to alter a machine or device by a small amount to make it right for use ♦ *The steering needs adjusting.* **3** (said about a person) to be able to adapt to new circumstances **4** *Law* to assess loss or damage in settlement of an insurance claim **adjustable** *adj* **adjuster** *n* **adjustment** *n*

adjutant (say **aj**-oo-tənt) *n* an army officer who assists a superior officer with administrative work

ad lib *adv* as you want, without restraint **ad-lib** *adj* said or done impromptu **ad-lib** *v* **ad-libbed, ad-libbing** to speak impromptu, to improvise remarks or actions

admin (say **ad**-min) *n* *informal* administration

administer *v* **1** to manage business affairs **2** to provide something or hand it out formally ♦ *They administered much comfort to the victims.* **3** to listen officially to someone taking an oath

administrate *v* to act as an administrator **administration** *n* **administrative** *adj* **administrator** *n*

admiral *n* a naval officer of high rank, usually a commander of a fleet or squadron

admire *v* **1** to regard someone or something with pleasure or satisfaction **2** to look at something with enjoyment ♦ *to admire the view* **admirable** *adj* **admirably** *adv* **admiration** *n* **admirer** *n*

admissible *adj* valid or allowed to be included ♦ *admissible evidence* **admissibility** *n*

admission *n* **1** the act of admitting someone to a place **2** a charge made to admit someone **3** a statement admitting something

admit *v* **admitted, admitting 1** to allow someone to enter a place **2** to accept someone into somewhere, such as a hospital or school **3** to accept something as true or valid ♦ *The judge agreed to admit the new evidence.* **4** to state something reluctantly ♦ *We have to admit that we were wrong.* **admittance** *n* permission to enter a place **admittedly** *adv* as you have to admit ♦ *It is admittedly rather late but I'd still like some tea.*

admixture *n* something added as an ingredient

admonish (say əd-**mon**-ish) *v* **1** to advise or urge someone seriously to do something **2** to reprimand someone gently but firmly **admonition** *n* **admonitory** *adj*

ad nauseam (say **naw**-si-am) *adv* to a sickening extent

ado (say ə-**doo**) *n* fuss or excitement

adobe (say ə-**doh**-bi) *n* sun-dried clay brick

adolescent (say ad-ə-**less**-ənt) *adj* at a time of life between childhood and adulthood **adolescent** *n* an adolescent person **adolescence** *n*

adopt *v* **1** to take another person's child into your own family as the legal guardian **2** to follow a decision or course of action **3** to choose a person to be a candidate in an election **4** to take a position or attitude ♦ *He adopted a standing position.* **adoption** *n* **adoptive** *adj*

adorable *adj* **1** very lovable **2** *informal* delightful **adorably** *adv*

adore *v* **1** to love someone deeply **2** to worship a divine being **3** *informal* to like something or someone very much **adoration** *n* **adorer** *n*

1 a strong natural liking or attraction **2** a similarity, a close resemblance or connection **3** the tendency of some substances to combine with others

affirm v **1** to assert something or state it as a fact **2** Law to make an affirmation instead of an oath **affirmation** n **1** stating something as a fact **2** a solemn declaration that a person makes in a law court instead of an oath **affirmative** adj affirming or agreeing, giving the answer 'yes' ♦ an affirmative reply **affirmative** n an affirmative word or statement **affirmatively** adv

affix[1] (say **af**-iks) n Gram a prefix or suffix

affix[2] (say ə-**fiks**) v **1** to stick or attach something to something else **2** to add something in writing

afflict v to cause someone physical or mental pain or discomfort ♦ He has been afflicted with rheumatism for years. **affliction** n

affluent (say **af**-loo-ənt) adj (usually said about groups of people) rich or wealthy **affluence** n **affluently** adv

afford v **1** to have enough money or time for something **2** to be able to do something without a risk ♦ You can't afford to be critical. **3** formal to provide something ♦ The trees afforded some protection against the rain. **affordable** adj

afforest v to plant an area with trees to make a forest **afforestation** n

affray (say ə-**fray**) n old use a breach of the peace by fighting or rioting in public

affront (say ə-**frunt**) v to insult deliberately, to offend or embarrass **affront** n a deliberate insult or show of disrespect

Afghan (say **af**-gan) n **1** a person born in Afghanistan **2** the language spoken in Afghanistan, Pashto **Afghan** adj to do with or coming from Afghanistan

aficionado (say ə-fis-yon-**ah**-doh) n pl **aficionados** someone who is very keen on ▪▪ particular sport or pastime

ld adv at or to a large distance, far away ▪ n home

▪▪ ▪ adv, adj in flames, burning
▪▪▪▪▪▪ adj **1** floating, especially on the ▪▪▪▪▪▪ nger or difficulty
▪▪▪▪▪▪ happening or in progress

♦ There's a scheme afoot to improve the roads.

aforementioned, **aforesaid** adj formal mentioned or said previously

afraid adj feeling fear

afresh adv anew

African adj to do with or coming from Africa **African** n a person born in Africa or descended from people born there, especially a black person

Afrikaans (say af-ri-**kahns**) n a language developed from Dutch and used in South Africa **Afrikaner** n a White person in South Africa whose first language is Afrikaans

Afro- combining form African ♦ Afro-Caribbean.

aft adv in or towards the stern of a ship or the tail of an aircraft

after prep **1** at a later time ♦ I won't arrive until after eight. **2** behind in place or order ♦ The police cars followed on after the procession. **3** in spite of something ♦ After all our help they still left without a word. **4** as a result of something ♦ After what she said, I can hardly like her. **5** in pursuit or search of someone ♦ I'd better run after him. **6** about or concerning someone ♦ Daphne was asking after you. **7** in imitation of someone or in honour of them ♦ They named their daughter Sibyl after her grandmother. **after** adv **1** behind ♦ Jill came tumbling after. **2** later ♦ They met again twenty years after. **after** conjunction at or in a time later than ♦ They arrived after we had left. **afters** pl n informal a course following the main course at a meal

afterbirth n the placenta and foetal membrane discharged from the womb after childbirth

aftercare n **1** extra care or treatment of a patient who has left hospital **2** extra support given to someone who has just left prison

after-effect n an effect that happens or arises after whatever caused it has stopped or gone away

afterglow n light still glowing in the sky after sunset

afterlife n (in some beliefs) a life that follows after death

aftermath n events or circumstances that come after something bad or unpleasant ♦ *Disease was the aftermath of war.*

afternoon n the time from midday to early evening

aftershave n a soothing lotion for use on the skin after shaving

afterthought n something thought of or added later

afterwards adv at a later time

Ag abbr Chem the symbol for silver

again adv 1 another time, once more ♦ *We decided to try again.* 2 as before, in an original place or condition ♦ *The doctor says you'll soon be well again.* 3 what is more, besides ♦ *Then again, she could have asked if she wanted help.* 4 on the other hand ♦ *I might, and again I might not.*

against prep 1 touching or hitting something ♦ *Lean your bicycle against the wall.* 2 in opposition to something ♦ *We are against fox-hunting.* 3 in contrast to something ♦ *The picture looked beautiful against a dark background.* 4 in preparation for ♦ *You'll need a warm coat to protect you against the cold.*

agape (say ə-**gayp**) adj gaping, open-mouthed

agate (say ag-ət) n a very hard stone with patches or concentric bands of colour

age n 1 the length of time a person has lived or a thing has existed 2 the later part of life 3 a period of history, with special characteristics or events ♦ *the Elizabethan Age* 4 a very long time ♦ *It took ages.* **age** v **aged, ageing** 1 to grow old and show signs of age 2 (said about wine, cheese, etc.) to become mature 3 to make someone seem old **aged** adj 1 (say ayjd) having the age of ♦ *a girl aged 10* 2 (say **ay**-jid) very old ♦ *He still lived at home with his aged mother.* **ageless** adj never ageing or seeming to be old **age-old** adj very old **age group** n all the people of the same age **age of consent** n the age at which a person may legally agree to have sexual intercourse

agency n pl **agencies** 1 a business or place of business that provides a special service ♦ *a travel agency* ♦ *The Child Support Agency.* 2 the action that is done to achieve something ♦ *Flowers are fertilized by the agency of bees.*

agenda (say ə-**jen**-də) n pl **agendas** a list of items of business to be dealt with at a meeting ◊ Although it is originally a Latin plural, *agenda* is normally used with a singular verb ♦ *The agenda is rather long.*

agent n 1 someone who organizes the business side of the work of a writer, actor, etc. 2 someone who acts on behalf of another person or organization ♦ *The Company has an agent in Paris.* 3 something that produces an effect or change ♦ *Soda is the active agent.* **agent provocateur** (say azh-ahn prə-vok-ə-**ter**) a person employed to prove that suspects are guilty by encouraging them to do something illegal

agglomerate (say ə-**glom**-er-ayt) v to collect things or become collected into a mass **agglomerate** (say ə-**glom**-er-ət) n a collection or mass of things **agglomeration** n

aggrandize (say ə-**gran**-diyz) v to increase the power, wealth, or importance of a person or organization **aggrandizement** n

aggravate v to make something worse or more serious **aggravation** n

aggregate (say **ag**-ri-gət) n 1 a mass or amount made by combining several parts 2 a mixture of hard substances, such as sand, gravel, broken stone, mixed with cement to make concrete **aggregate** adj combined or total ♦ *the aggregate amount* **aggregate** (say **ag**-ri-gayt) v to collect something or form into an aggregate, to unite **aggregation** n

aggression n 1 the act of attacking someone without being provoked 2 a hostile action **aggressive** adj 1 tending to make unprovoked attacks 2 assertive or forceful ♦ *an aggressive salesman* **aggressively** adv **aggressiveness** n **aggressor** n a person or country th‍ attacks first or begins hostilities

aggrieved (say ə-**greevd**) adj ups‍ resentful because of unfair treatm‍

aghast (say ə-**gahst**) adj filled ‍ dismay

agile adj able to move a

nimbly **agilely** adv **agility** n

agitate v **1** to stir up public interest or concern about something **2** to shake or move something briskly **3** to disturb someone or cause them anxiety **agitated** adj **agitation** n **agitator** n

aglow adj glowing brightly

AGM abbr annual general meeting

agnostic (say ag-**nos**-tik) n a person who believes that we can know nothing about the existence of God **agnosticism** n

ago adv in the past, before now ♦ It happened ten days ago.

agog (say ə-**gog**) adj eager or expectant

agonize v to worry a lot about something **agonizing** adj **agonizingly** adv

agony n pl **agonies** great physical or mental pain or suffering

agoraphobia (say ag-er-ə-**foh**-biə) n an abnormal fear of being in public places or open spaces **agoraphobic** n, adj

AGR abbr advanced gas-cooled reactor

agrarian (say ə-**grair**-iən) adj to do with agriculture and the cultivation of land

agree v **agrees**, **agreed**, **agreeing** **1** to have the same opinion as someone else ♦ I'm afraid I don't agree with you. **2** to say that you are willing to do something ♦ The boy agreed to come and help. **3** to authorize or approve something ♦ The Bank Manager has agreed an overdraft. **4** to come to a decision about something ♦ Can we agree a time to meet? **5** to get on well together **6** to be consistent with something else ♦ Your story agrees with his. **7** to be good for you or not harm you ♦ I'm afraid curry doesn't agree with me. **agreeable** adj **1** pleasant or enjoyable ♦ We had an agreeable time. **2** willing to agree to something ♦ I'll go if you are agreeable. **agreeably** adv **agreement** n **1** agreeing with someone **2** having the same opinion or feeling **3** an arrangement, such as a treaty or contract

agriculture n the process of cultivating land on a large scale and rearing livestock **agricultural** adj **agriculturally** adv

agrochemical n a chemical used in agriculture

agronomy (say ə-**gron**-əmi) n the scientific study of soil management and crop production

aground adv, adj on or touching the bottom in shallow water ♦ The ship has run aground.

ague (say **ay**-gew) n malaria or another illness involving a fit of shivering

AH abbr (in dates) of the Muslim era

ah interjection an exclamation of surprise, pity, admiration, etc.

ahead adv **1** further forward in space or time **2** having made more progress

ahimsa (say ə-**him**-sə) n (in Hinduism, Buddhism, Jainism) the doctrine of non-violence or non-killing

ahoy interjection a cry used by seamen to call attention

AI abbr **1** artificial insemination **2** artificial intelligence

aid v to help someone or support an activity **aid** n **1** help **2** something that helps you ♦ a hearing aid **3** food, money, etc., sent to a country to help it

aide n an assistant or aide-de-camp

Aids n a condition caused by the HIV virus

ail v old use to make someone feel ill or uneasy

ailing adj sick or unwell

ailment n a slight illness

aim v **1** to point or send a weapon towards its target; to direct (a blow, missile, remark, etc.) towards a specified object or goal **2** to attempt or try ♦ aim to please **aim** n **1** the act of aiming a weapon ♦ The marksman took aim and fired. **2** a purpose or intention ♦ What are your aims in life?

aimless adj without any purpose **aimlessly** adv **aimlessness** n

air n **1** the mixture of gases (mainly oxygen and nitrogen) surrounding the earth **2** the open space above the surface of the earth **3** the earth's atmosphere, especially as a medium for transmitting radio waves **4** a light wind or breeze **5** an impression you get about a place ♦ The house had an air of mystery. **6** a tune or melody **air** v **1** to express an opinion publicly **2** to broadcast on a radio or television programme **3** to expose a place to the air **4** to put clothes or laundry in a warm place to finish drying

air bag n a safety device in a vehicle, which inflates to protect occupants

airborne *adj* **1** carried in the air or by aircraft **2** in flight after taking off

air brake *n* a brake worked by compressed air

airbrush *n* a device for spraying paint by means of compressed air **airbrush** *v* to paint over a surface with an airbrush

air-conditioned *adj* equipped with air conditioning

air conditioning *n* a system for controlling the humidity and temperature of the air in a room or building

aircraft *n pl* **aircraft** an aeroplane, helicopter, or other flying machine

aircraft carrier *n* a ship that carries and acts as a base for aeroplanes

aircraftman, aircraftwoman *n* the lowest rank in the RAF

Airedale *n* a large black-and-tan dog with a rough coat

airfield *n* an area of open level ground on which aircraft land and take off

airflow *n* a flow of air past a vehicle or aircraft

air force *n* the branch of a country's armed forces that uses aircraft as the main means of fighting and defence

airgun *n* a gun which fires lead pellets by means of compressed air

air hostess *n* a female flight attendant in a passenger aircraft

airless *adj* **1** stuffy **2** calm and still, with no wind **airlessness** *n*

air letter *n* a sheet of light paper that is folded and sent as a letter by airmail

airlift *n* large-scale transport of troops or supplies by aircraft **airlift** *v* to transport troops or supplies in this way

airline *n* an organization that provides a regular service of air transport for the public

air line *n* a pipe for supplying air

airliner *n* a large passenger aircraft

airlock *n* **1** a stoppage of the flow in a pump or pipe, caused by an air bubble **2** a compartment with controlled pressure and a set of airtight doors at each end, allowing movement between areas having different pressures

airmail *n* a system of sending overseas mail by air transport **airmail** *v* to send mail by airmail

airman *n pl* **airmen** a male aviator or member of an air force

air pocket *n* an area of low pressure that causes an aircraft flying through it to lose height suddenly

airport *n* an area with hangars and runways for aircraft to land and take off, and passenger terminals and other buildings

air quality *n* the quality of the air in the immediate environment

air raid *n* an attack by aircraft dropping bombs on targets on the ground

airship *n* a power-driven aircraft containing helium or another gas that is lighter than air

airspace *n* the air above a country and subject to its control

airstrip *n* a strip of ground for aircraft to land and take off on

airtight *adj* not allowing air to enter or escape

airtime *n* the time during which a radio or television programme is being broadcast

air traffic control *n* an organization of people and equipment that monitors and controls the movement of aircraft in its area

airway *n* **1** a regular route used by aircraft **2** the passage by which air goes into the lungs

airwoman *n pl* **airwomen** a female aviator or member of an air force

airworthy *adj* (said about an aircraft) fit and safe to fly **airworthiness** *n*

airy *adj* **airier**, **airiest** **1** having plenty of space and fresh air **2** light as air, delicate **3** careless and light-hearted ♦ *an airy manner* **airily** *adv* **airiness** *n*

aisle (rhymes with *mile*) *n* **1** a passage between rows of pews in a church, seats in a theatre or cinema, or shelves in a supermarket **2** a side part of a church

ajar *adv*, *adj* (said about a door) slightly open

akimbo (say a-kim-boh) *adv* with the hands on the hips and the elbows pointed outwards

akin *adj* related or similar ♦ *I had a feeling akin to jealousy.*

alabaster (say **al**-ə-bah-stər) n a form of stone that is white and translucent

à la carte (say ah lah **kart**) adj (said about a restaurant meal) ordered as separate items from a menu

alacrity (say ə-**lak**-riti) n eager willingness to do or take something

à la mode (say ah lah **mohd**) adj fashionable or up to date

alarm n 1 sudden fear caused by expectation of danger 2 a warning sound or signal, or a device that makes this 3 an alarm clock **alarm** v to frighten someone suddenly

alarm clock n a clock with a device that can be set to ring or bleep at a certain time

alarmist n someone who raises unnecessary or excessive alarm

alas interjection an exclamation of pity or sorrow

albatross n a large seabird with long narrow wings

albeit (say awl-**bee**-it) conjunction literary although

albino (say al-**bee**-noh) n pl **albinos** a person or animal with no colouring pigment in the skin and hair (which are white) and the eyes (which are normally pink)

album n 1 a blank book for keeping a collection of autographs, photographs, postage stamps, etc. 2 a CD or LP with recordings of several items

albumen (say **al**-bew-min) n the white of an egg

albumin (say **al**-bew-min) n a protein found in egg white, milk, and blood

alchemy (say **al**-kəmi) n a form of chemistry in the Middle Ages, concerned mainly with attempts to turn ordinary metals into gold **alchemist** n

alcohol n 1 a colourless liquid which is the intoxicant in wine, beer, and spirits 2 a drink containing this 3 a chemical compound of this type

alcoholic adj containing alcohol or relating to the drinking of alcohol **alcoholic** n a person suffering from alcoholism

alcoholism n an illness caused by continual heavy drinking of alcohol

alcove n 1 a recess in the wall of a room 2 a recess forming an extension of a room, etc.

aldehyde (say **al**-di-hiyd) n a fluid with a suffocating smell, obtained from alcohol

alder (say **awl**-der) n a tree of the birch family with toothed leaves

alderman (say **awl**-der-mən) n pl **aldermen** a co-opted member of an English county or borough council, next in dignity to the mayor

ale n beer other than lager or stout

alert adj watchful and ready to act **alert** n 1 a state of watchfulness or readiness 2 a warning of danger **alert** v to warn someone of danger **alertly** adv **alertness** n **on the alert** watchful and ready to act

A level n Advanced level in GCE

alfalfa (say al-**fal**-fə) n a plant with leaves like clover and blue flowers

alfresco (say al-**fres**-koh) adj, adv in the open air

alga (say **al**-gə) pl **algae** (say **al**-jee) n a water plant with no true stems or leaves

algebra (say **al**-jib-rə) n the branch of mathematics in which letters and symbols are used to represent quantities in formulae and equations **algebraic** adj **algebraically** adv

Algol n a high-level computer language using algebra

algorithm (say **al**-ger-ithəm) n a process or set of rules for solving a problem, especially by a computer

alias (say **ay**-li-əs) n pl **aliases** a false or assumed name **alias** adv also known as ♦ Norma Jean Baker, alias Marilyn Monroe.

alibi (say **al**-i-biy) n pl **alibis** a claim or piece of evidence that an accused person was not at the scene of a crime when it was committed

alien (say **ay**-li-ən) n 1 a person from another country, a foreigner 2 a being from another world **alien** adj 1 not your own, foreign or unfamiliar 2 not a part of something ♦ Cruelty is alien to her character.

alienate (say **ay**-li-ən-ayt) v to make someone become unfriendly or not willing to help you **alienation** n

alight[1] adj on fire, lit up

alight[2] v formal 1 to get down from a vehicle 2 to rest or settle on something ♦ A bird had *alighted on a branch.*

align (say ə-**liyn**) *v* **1** to arrange a number of things in their right positions in relation to each other **2** to join a person or group as an ally **alignment** *n*

alike *adj, adv* like one another, in the same way

alimentary canal (say ali-**ment**-er-i) *n* the long passage through which food passes through the body

alimony (say **al**-i-məni) *n* N. Am an allowance that a person has to pay to a spouse after a separation or divorce ◊ In Britain this is called *maintenance.*

aliquot (say **al**-i-kwot) *n* **1** *Chem* a portion of a substance, especially a sample used for chemical analysis **2** *Mathematics* a number that can be divided into a larger number without producing a fraction in the quotient

alive *adj* **1** living, not dead **2** aware of something and able to deal with it ♦ *She seems alive to all the possible dangers.* **3** active or lively **4** full of living or moving things ♦ *The forest was alive with wildlife.*

alkali (say **al**-kə-liy) *n pl* **alkalis** a substance which neutralizes acids and is neutralized by them, turns litmus blue, and forms caustic or corrosive solutions in water **alkaline** *adj* **alkalinity** *n*

alkaloid (say **al**-kə-loid) *n* a substance that contains nitrogen, is derived from plants, and is often used in medicine, for example morphine and quinine

all *adj* the whole amount or number of something ♦ *all day* ♦ *all people* **all** *n* **1** all people ♦ *All were agreed that we should wait.* **2** everything ♦ *All is lost.* **all** *adv* **1** completely **2** (in scores) on both sides

Allah (say **al**-ə) the Muslim name for God

allay (say ə-**lay**) *v* **allayed, allaying** to calm or reduce someone's fear or suspicion

all-clear *n* a signal that a danger is over

allegation (say ali-**gay**-shən) *n* an accusation made without any proof to support it

allege (say ə-**lej**) *v* to say something without being able to prove that it is true

alleged *adj* said to be, without any proof ♦ *The alleged culprit was a doctor.*

allegedly *adv*

allegiance (say ə-**lee**-jəns) *n* loyalty or support someone gives to a government, sovereign, or cause

allegory (say **al**-ig-er-i) *n pl* **allegories** a story, poem, or play in which the characters and events are made to represent a deeper underlying meaning **allegorical** *n* **allegorically** *adv*

alleluia *interjection, n* an exclamation of praise to God

allergic (say ə-**ler**-jik) *adj* **1** having an allergy ♦ *She is allergic to onions.* **2** caused by an allergy ♦ *She has had an allergic reaction.*

allergy (say **al**-er-ji) *n pl* **allergies** a condition producing an unfavourable reaction to certain foods, pollens, or other substances

alleviate (say ə-**lee**-vi-ayt) *v* to lessen something unpleasant or make it less severe ♦ *The pills will alleviate the pain.* **alleviation** *n*

alley *n pl* **alleys** **1** a narrow passage or street between houses or other buildings **2** a path bordered by hedges or shrubbery **3** a long channel along which balls are rolled in bowling and skittles

alliance *n* a union or association formed by people, countries, or organizations who want to support each other

allied see *ally*[2] **allied** *adj* of the same kind, related

alligator *n* a reptile of the crocodile family, found especially in the rivers of tropical America and China

alliteration (say ə-lit-er-**ay**-shən) *n* the occurrence of the same letter or sound at the beginning of a group of words for special effect, e.g. *sing a song of sixpence* **alliterative** *adj*

allocate (say **al**-ə-kayt) *v* to give resources or duties to various people or groups, to allot things **allocable** *adj* **allocation** *n* **allocator** *n*

allot (say ə-**lot**) *v* **allotted, allotting** to give resources or duties as a share to various people or groups

allotment *n* **1** a small area of public land let out to people for growing vegetables or flowers **2** the process of allotting things, or a share allotted

allotrope (say **al-ə-trohp**) n one of the physical forms in which an element can exist, for example charcoal, diamond, and graphite are allotropes of carbon

allotropy (say ə-**lot**-rə-pi) n the existence of a chemical element in different forms with different physical or chemical properties **allotropic** adj

allow v 1 to let someone do something, to give someone permission or authority 2 to give someone something as their amount or share 3 to take account of something in making calculations ♦ You should allow 10% for inflation. 4 to agree that something is true or acceptable ♦ They did allow that we might be right. 5 to authorize something ♦ The tax inspector allowed their claim for expenses. **allowable** adj

allowance n 1 allowing 2 an amount or sum allowed to someone, especially a sum of money paid regularly to them **to make allowances for something** to be lenient towards someone for a reason ♦ We have to make allowances for his inexperience.

alloy¹ (say **al**-oi) n 1 a metal made by mixing other metals or by mixing a metal and another substance 2 an inferior metal mixed with one of greater value

alloy² (say ə-**loi**) v **alloyed, alloying** 1 to mix metals to form an alloy 2 to weaken or spoil something by adding something that reduces its value

all right adj 1 feeling healthy or well 2 satisfactory or in good condition 3 allowed **all right** adv fairly well, reasonably ♦ It seemed to work all right.

all-round adj having many abilities or uses

all-rounder n someone who has a wide range of talents or abilities

allspice n a spice made from the dried and ground berries of the pimento, a West Indian tree

all-time adj not improved on up to now ♦ an all-time long-jump record

allude (say ə-**lewd**) v to refer to something indirectly, without actually naming it ◊ Do not confuse this word with elude.

allure (say əl-**yoor**) n attractiveness or appeal **allurement** n

alluring adj attractive or appealing

allusion n a reference made to something without actually naming it

allusive (say ə-**loo**-siv) adj containing allusions or indirect references to something **allusively** adv

alluvium (say ə-**loo**-viəm) n a deposit of soil and sand left by rivers or floods and usually very fertile **alluvial** adj

ally¹ (say **al**-iy) n pl **allies** a person, organization, or country that has agreed to help and support another **the Allies** the nations opposed to Germany in each of the two World Wars

ally² (say əl-**iy**) v **allies, allied, allying** to become an ally, or make someone an ally

almanac (say **awl**-mən-ak) n 1 an annual publication containing a calendar with important dates, astronomical data, and other information 2 an annually published handbook for a sport or other activity ◊ Some publications use the older spelling almanack in their titles, e.g. Whitaker's Almanac.

almighty adj 1 all-powerful 2 informal very great ♦ Then there was an almighty crash. **the Almighty** a name for God

almond (say **ah**-mənd) n 1 the nut-like kernel of the fruit of a tree related to the peach 2 this tree

almost adv very close to

alms (say ahmz) n old use gifts of money and food given to the poor

almshouse n a house founded by charity for poor elderly people

aloe n a tropical plant with thick sharp-pointed leaves and bitter juice **aloes** n this juice

aloft adv high up, up in or into the air

alone adj not with others, on your own **alone** adv only, exclusively ♦ You alone can help me.

along adv 1 forward or onward ♦ Push it along. 2 accompanying somebody, in addition ♦ I've brought my brother along. **along** prep following or close to the length of something

alongside adv close to the side of something **alongside** prep beside

aloof adj unfriendly and keeping a distance

from people **aloofly** *adv* **aloofness** *n*

aloud *adv* in a voice loud enough to be heard

alp *n* a high mountain **the Alps** *pl n* a high range of mountains in Switzerland and neighbouring countries

alpha (say **al**-fə) *n* the first letter of the Greek alphabet, equivalent to Roman *A*, *a*

alphabet *n* the set of letters used in writing a language, especially when arranged in a fixed order

alphabetical *adj* **1** following the order of the letters of the alphabet **2** to do with the alphabet **alphabetically** *adv*

alphanumeric (say al-fə-new-**merrik**) *adj* using or containing letters of the alphabet and numerals

alpine *adj* to do with or growing on high mountains **Alpine** *adj* to do with the Alps

already *adv* **1** before this time ♦ *They had already gone.* **2** as early as this ♦ *Is she back already?*

alright *adv* another spelling of *all right* ◊ Some people regard this spelling as incorrect.

Alsatian (say al-**say**-shən) *n* a large strong brown or black dog with smooth hair (also called *German shepherd dog*)

also *adv* in addition, besides

also-ran *n* someone who is not among the winners or leaders in an activity

altar *n* **1** the table on which bread and wine are consecrated in the Communion service **2** any structure on which offerings are made to a god

alter *v* **1** to make something different **2** to become changed or different **alteration** *n*

altercation (say ol-ter-**kay**-shən) *n* a noisy argument or quarrel

alternate (say ol-**ter**-nət) *adj* happening or following one after the other in turns ♦ *We have to buy milk on alternate days.*
alternate (say ol-**ter**-nayt) *v* **1** to occur or do something one after the other in turn **2** to change repeatedly between two conditions **alternately** *adv* **alternation** *n* ◊ See the note at *alternative*.

alternating current *n* an electric current that reverses its direction many times a second at regular intervals

alternative (say ol-**ter**-nə-tiv) *adj* available instead of something else
alternative *n* one of two or more possibilities **alternatively** *adv* ◊ Do not confuse *alternative* with *alternate*. If there are *alternative colours* there is a choice of several colours, whereas *alternate colours* means that there is first one colour then another.

alternative energy *n* energy using fuels that do not harm the environment

alternative medicine *n* unconventional forms of medical treatment

alternative technology *n* technology using resources and methods that cause the least possible damage to the environment

although *conjunction* though

altitude *n* **1** the height of an object above sea level or ground level **2** the distance of a star or other heavenly object above the horizon, measured as an angle **3** *Geometry* the height of a triangle as measured by a line drawn from a vertex at right angles to the opposite side

alto (say **al**-toh) *n pl* **altos** **1** the highest adult male singing voice **2** the lowest female singing voice, a contralto **3** a musical instrument having the second or third highest pitch in its family ♦ *an alto saxophone*

altogether *adv* **1** entirely, totally **2** on the whole ◊ Do not confuse this word with *all together*. If you say *thirty people altogether* you mean a total of thirty people, whereas if you say *thirty people all together* you mean thirty people in one place.

altruism (say **al**-troo-izm) *n* concern for other people rather than yourself **altruist** *n* an unselfish person **altruistic** *adj* **altruistically** *adv*

aluminium *n* a strong lightweight silvery metal that is free of corrosion, a chemical element (symbol A1)

always *adv* **1** at all times, on all occasions **2** whatever the circumstances ♦ *You can always sleep on the floor.* **3** constantly, repeatedly ♦ *He is always complaining.*

Alzheimer's disease *n* a brain disease of middle age or old age, causing mental deterioration and senility

am a form of *be*, used with *I*

a.m. *abbr* before noon

amalgam *n* **1** an alloy of mercury and another metal, as used for dental fillings **2** a soft pliable mixture

amalgamate *v* to mix or combine ingredients **amalgamation** *n*

amass (say ə-**mass**) *v* to heap things up, to collect things ♦ *Over the years the family amassed a large fortune.*

amateur (say **am**-ə-ter) *n* a person who does something, especially a sport or one of the performing arts, without pay rather than as a profession

amateurish (say **am**-ə-ter-ish) *adj* showing the limited ability of an amateur **amateurishly** *adv* **amateurishness** *n*

amaze *v* to surprise someone greatly **amazement** *n*

amazing *adj* surprising or highly remarkable

Amazon *Greek Mythology* a woman of a race of female warriors **amazon** *n* a tall and strong or athletic woman **amazonian** *adj*

ambassador *n* **1** a diplomat sent by one country as its representative or on a special mission to another **2** someone who actively promotes a cause ♦ *an ambassador for peace*

amber *n* **1** a hard clear yellowish resin used for making ornaments **2** a yellow traffic light shown as a cautionary signal between red for 'stop' and green for 'go' **amber** *adj* made of amber or having the colour of amber

ambergris (say **am**-ber-grees) *n* a wax-like substance from the intestines of the sperm whale, used in making perfumes

ambidextrous (say ambi-**deks**-trəs) *adj* able to use the right and left hands equally well

ambience (say **am**-bi-əns) *n* **1** the character a place has from its immediate surroundings **2** the quality given to a sound recording by the acoustics in which it is made **ambient** *adj*

ambiguous (say am-**big**-yoo-əs) *adj* **1** having more than one possible meaning **2** doubtful or uncertain **ambiguity** *n* **ambiguously** *adv*

ambit *n* the scope, extent, or limit of something

ambition *n* **1** a strong desire to achieve success **2** something successful you want to achieve

ambitious (say am-**bish**-əs) *adj* **1** having a lot of ambition **2** (said about a plan or idea) difficult or demanding **ambitiously** *adv*

ambivalent (say am-**biv**-ələnt) *adj* with mixed feelings or conflicting ideas about something or someone **ambivalence** *n* **ambivalently** *adv*

amble *v* to walk at a slow gentle pace **amble** *n* a slow gentle pace **ambler** *n*

ambrosia (say am-**broh**-ziə) *n* **1** *Greek and Roman Mythology* the food of the gods, which made them immortal **2** something very pleasant to taste or smell **ambrosial** *adj*

ambulance *n* a vehicle equipped to carry sick or injured people to and from hospital

ambulatory (say **am**-bew-lə-ter-i) *adj* **1** relating to or made for walking **2** (said of a person or animal) able to walk

ambush *n* a surprise attack by troops or bandits from a hidden position on an approaching enemy or victim **ambush** *v* to lie in wait for someone, to attack someone from an ambush

ameliorate (say ə-**mee**-li-er-ayt) *v formal* to make something better or to become better **amelioration** *n*

amen (say ah-**men** or say ay-**men**) *interjection* (said at the end of a prayer) so be it

amenable (say ə-**meen**-əbəl) *adj* willing to respond to advice or guidance ♦ *He was not amenable to persuasion.* **amenability** *n* **amenably** *adv*

amend *v* to correct an error in something or to make minor alterations in it **amendment** *n* **to make amends** to compensate or make up for something

amenity (say ə-**meen**-iti) *n pl* **amenities 1** a useful or pleasant feature that a place has **2** pleasantness of a place or circumstance

American *adj* to do with or coming from the continent of America, or the USA **American** *n* **1** a person born in America or descended from people born there **2** a citizen of the USA

Americanism n a word or phrase mainly used or originally used in American English

Amerindian n an American Indian

amethyst (say **am**-i-thist) n a precious stone formed from purple or violet quartz

Amharic (say am-**ha**-rik) n the official language of Ethiopia

amiable (say **aym**-i-əbəl) adj friendly and good-tempered **amiability** n **amiably** adv

amicable (say **am**-ik-əbəl) adj pleasant and friendly **amicability** n **amicably** adv

amid, amidst prep in the middle of, during ♦ The team arrived amid loud cheers.

amidships adv in the middle of a ship

amino acid (say ə-**mee**-noh) n an organic acid found in proteins

amir (say ə-**meer**) n another spelling of emir

amiss adj wrong or out of order **amiss** adv wrongly or faultily **to take something amiss** to be offended by a remark or comment

amity n friendship, friendly relations

ammeter (say **am**-it-er) n an instrument that measures electric current

ammo n informal ammunition

ammonia n 1 a colourless gas with a strong smell 2 a solution of this in water, used as a cleaning fluid

ammonite (say **am**-ə-niyt) n the fossil of an extinct mollusc with a flat spiral shell

ammunition n 1 a supply of bullets and shells for use in guns and other weapons 2 useful or persuasive facts and reasoning used in an argument

amnesia (say am-**nee**-ziə) n complete or partial loss of memory **amnesiac** adj, n

amnesty (say **am**-nis-ti) n pl **amnesties** an official pardon for people who have committed a crime, especially those convicted of political offences

amniocentesis (say amni-ə-sen-**tee**-sis) n the inserting of a hollow needle into the womb of a pregnant woman and withdrawing a sample of amniotic fluid

amniotic fluid n the fluid surrounding a fetus in the womb

amoeba (say ə-**mee**-bə) n pl **amoebae** (say ə-**mee**-bee) pl **amoebas** a microscopic organism consisting of a single cell which changes shape constantly

amok adv **to run amok** to behave wildly, to cause damage or confusion

among, amongst prep 1 in or surrounded by ♦ Poppies were growing amongst the corn. 2 in the number of ♦ This is reckoned among her best works. 3 within the limits of, between ♦ We only have £5 amongst us.

amoral (say ay-**mo**-rəl) adj having or showing no moral standards, not concerned with morality

amorous (say **am**-er-əs) adj feeling or showing sexual love **amorously** adv **amorousness** n

amorphous (say ə-**mor**-fəs) adj not having any definite shape or form

amount n 1 the total of something in number or size 2 a quantity ♦ Add a small amount of salt. **amount** v **to amount to** 1 to add up to a total 2 to be equivalent to something ♦ Their behaviour amounts to fraud.

amp n 1 short for ampere 2 informal short for amplifier

ampere (say **am**-pair) n a unit for measuring electric current (symbol A) **amperage** n

ampersand n the sign & (= and)

amphetamine (say am-**fet**-ə-min) n a drug used as a stimulant or to relieve congestion

amphibian (say am-**fib**-iən) n 1 an animal able to live both on land and in water, such as a frog, toad, newt, and salamander 2 a vehicle that can move on both land and water

amphibious (say am-**fib**-iəs) adj 1 able to live or operate both on land and in water 2 (said of a military operation) involving both sea and land forces

amphitheatre n an oval or circular Roman theatre without a roof and with tiers of seats surrounding a central arena, used mainly for sports and gladiator contests

ample adj 1 plentiful, quite enough ♦ They have ample supplies. 2 (said about a person) large or stout **amply** adv

amplifier n an electronic device that increases the loudness of sounds or the power of audio or radio signals

amplify v **amplifies, amplified, amplifying**

1 to increase the strength of a sound **2** to explain something more clearly or add details to it **amplification** n

amputate v to cut off a part of the body by surgical operation **amputation** n

amuck adv another spelling of *amok*

amulet (say **am**-yoo-lit) n a small ornament or piece of jewellery worn as a charm against evil or danger

amuse v **1** to cause someone to laugh or smile **2** to entertain someone

amusement n **1** the process of amusing someone or of being amused **2** something that amuses or entertains people

amusement arcade n an indoor area with slot machines and electronic games

amusing adj making people laugh or smile, entertaining **amusingly** adv

an adj the form of *a* used before vowel sounds ♦ *an egg* ♦ *an hour* (but *a unicorn*)

anabolic steroid (say an-ə-**bol**-ik) n a steroid hormone used to build up muscle tissue and sometimes (illegally) to improve athletic performance

anabolism (say ə-**nab**-əl-izm) n Biochemistry a process in living organisms in which complex molecules are formed from simpler ones using energy **anabolic** adj

anachronism (say ən-**ak**-rən-izm) n **1** the placing of something, especially in fiction and drama, in a historical period to which it does not belong **2** something put in the wrong time **3** a person, idea, or institution that is regarded as out of date **anachronistic** adj

anaemia (say ə-**nee**-miə) n Medicine a lack of red corpuscles, or of their haemoglobin in blood

anaemic (say ə-**nee**-mik) adj **1** suffering from anaemia **2** pale or weak in colour **3** lacking vigour or positive characteristics

anaerobic (say an-air-**oh**-bik) adj not needing or using oxygen from the air ♦ *anaerobic bacteria* **anaerobically** adv

anaesthesia (say anis-**theez**-iə) n loss of physical sensation induced by use of anaesthetics

anaesthetic (say anis-**thet**-ik) n a substance that produces loss of sensation and of ability to feel pain **anaesthetic** adj

causing a loss of physical sensation **anaesthetize** v **anaesthetization** n

anaesthetist (say ən-**ees**-thət-ist) n a medical specialist who administers anaesthetics

anagram (say **an**-ə-gram) n a word or phrase formed from the rearranged letters of another word or phrase (e.g. *carthorse* is an anagram of *orchestra*)

analgesia (say an-əl-**jees**-iə) n loss of ability to feel pain while still conscious **analgesic** adj

analogous (say ə-**nal**-əgəs) adj similar in certain respects **analogously** adv

analogue (say **an**-ə-log) n something that is analogous to something else **analogue** adj (said about a clock, watch, or other instrument) showing the time or information by using hands or a pointer. (Compare *digital*.)

analogy (say ə-**nal**-əji) n pl **analogies** partial likeness between two things which are compared ♦ *the analogy between the human brain and a computer*

analysis n pl **analyses** (say ə-**nal**-i-seez) **1** the process of examining a substance or its structure by separating it into parts **2** a statement of the result of analysing something **3** psychoanalysis **analysable** adj **analyse** v **analyst** n **analytical** adj **analytically** adv

anarchy (say **an**-er-ki) n **1** disorder or lawlessness caused by a lack of government or control **2** a political system based on lack of government **anarchic** adj **anarchical** adj **anarchism** n **anarchist** n **anarchistic** adj

anathema (say ən-**ath**-imə) n something you detest ♦ *Blood sports are anathema to them.*

anatomy n **1** the branch of medicine concerned with the study of the structure of the body **2** the bodily structure of an animal or plant **anatomical** adj **anatomically** adv

ANC abbr African National Congress

ancestor n any of the people from whom someone is descended **ancestral** adj **ancestry** n

anchor n **1** a heavy metal object, usually with a shank and curved pieces (called flukes) at one end at right angles to the shank, used to moor a ship to the sea bottom or a balloon, etc. to the ground **2** something that gives stability or security **anchor** v **1** to make a ship or balloon, etc. secure with an anchor **2** (said about a ship) to be moored by an anchor **3** to fix something firmly **anchorage** n

anchovy (say **an**-chəvi) n pl **anchovies** a small fish of the herring family, having a strong flavour

ancient adj **1** belonging to times in the distant past **2** having lived or existed for a long time **ancient history** n the history of the period before the end of the Western Roman Empire in AD 476 **the ancients** the people who lived in ancient times, especially ancient Greeks and Romans

ancillary (say an-**sil**-er-i) adj providing extra support to a main activity or organization

and conjunction a word used to link words, phrases, and parts of sentences ♦ fish and chips ♦ Go away and don't come back.

andiron (say **and**-iy-ern) n a metal support, usually one of two, for burning wood in a fireplace

android n (in science fiction) a robot having the appearance of a human

anecdote (say **an**-ik-doht) n a short entertaining story about a real person or event

anemometer (say anim-**om**-it-er) n an instrument for measuring the force of the wind

anemone (say ə-**nem**-əni) n a plant related to the buttercup, with white, red, or purple flowers and divided leaves

anew adv again, or in a different way

angel n **1** in some beliefs, an attendant or messenger of God that is usually pictured as a being in human form with wings and dressed in long white robes **2** an extremely beautiful or kind person **angelic** adj **angelically** adv **angel fish** n a fish with a flat upright body and large fins like wings

angelica (say an-**jel**-ikə) n a fragrant plant with stalks that are candied and used in cookery

angelus (say **an**-jil-əs) n **1** in the Roman Catholic Church, a prayer to the Virgin Mary commemorating the Incarnation, said at morning, noon, and sunset **2** a bell rung as a signal for this prayer

anger n a strong feeling of displeasure or hostility **anger** v to make someone angry

angina, **angina pectoris** (say an-**jiy**-nə **pek**-ter-iss) n a diseased condition of the heart, causing a sharp pain in the chest

angle¹ n **1** the space between two lines or surfaces that meet **2** a point of view **angle** v **1** to move or place something in a slanting position **2** to present news or information from a particular point of view

angle² v **1** to fish with a hook and bait **2** to try to get something you want by hinting ♦ He was clearly angling for an invitation to the party. **angler** n

Anglican adj to do with the Church of England or a Church in communion with it **Anglican** n a member of the Anglican Church **Anglicanism** n

anglicize (say **ang**-li-siyz) v to make something English in form or character

Anglo- prefix English or British (and) ♦ an Anglo-French agreement

Anglo-Indian adj **1** to do with England and India **2** (said about a person) of British descent but having lived for a long time in India **3** of mixed British and Indian parentage **Anglo-Indian** n an Anglo-Indian person

Anglo-Saxon n **1** an English person of the period between the 5th century and the Norman Conquest in the 11th century **2** the English language of this period, also called Old English **3** a person of English descent **Anglo-Saxon** adj to do with the Anglo-Saxons or their language

angora n **1** a long haired variety of cat, goat, or rabbit **2** a yarn or fabric made from the hair of angora goats or rabbits

angry adj **angrier**, **angriest 1** feeling or showing anger **2** (said about a wound or sore place) red and inflamed **angrily** adv

angst n a feeling of anxious guilt or remorse

ångström (say **ang**-strəm) n a unit of length for measuring wavelengths

anguish n severe mental or physical suffering **anguished** adj

angular adj **1** having angles or sharp corners

2 (said about a person) having a lean build with prominent bones **3** measured by an angle **angularity** n

animal n **1** a living organism that can feel, respond to stimuli, and move of its own accord **2** a living organism of this kind other than a human being **3** a four-footed animal as distinct from a bird, fish, reptile, or insect **4** a cruel or uncivilized person **animal** adj to do with or relating to animal life **animal liberation** n

animate (say **an**-im-ət) adj living, having life **animate** (say **an**-im-ayt) v **1** to make something active or lively ♦ A few anecdotes animated the discussion. **2** to motivate someone ♦ She was animated mainly by a feeling of loyalty. **3** to produce as an animated cartoon **animated** adj **animation** n **animator** n

animism n the belief that natural things such as rocks, rivers, and winds, as well as living beings, have a living soul **animistic** adj

animosity (say anim-**os**-iti) n a feeling of strong hostility towards someone

animus (say **an**-iməs) n strong hostility shown in speech or action

aniseed n the seed of the plant called anise, having a sweet smell and used for flavouring and in herbal medicine

ankle n **1** the joint connecting the foot with the leg **2** the narrow part of the leg between the ankle and the calf

anklet n an ornamental chain or band worn around the ankle

annals (say **an**-əlz) pl n a history of events year by year, a set of historical records

anneal (say ə-**neel**) v to toughen glass or metal by heating it and then cooling it slowly

annelid (say **an**-il-id) n a worm having a segmented body, for example an earthworm

annex (say ən-**eks**) v **1** to add or join something to a larger thing **2** to take possession of territory belonging to another country **annexation** n

annexe (say **an**-eks) n a building attached to a larger building or associated with it in some way

annihilate (say ə-**niy**-hil-ayt) v to destroy something completely **annihilation** n **annihilator** n

anniversary n pl **anniversaries 1** the date on which an important event took place in a previous year **2** a celebration of this

Anno Domini (say an-oh **dom**-in-iy) in the year of Our Lord (usually shortened to AD and put before a date, as in AD 1066)

annotate (say **an**-oh-tayt) v to add notes giving a comment or explanation to a text, piece of writing, or diagram **annotation** n

announce v **1** to make a formal statement about an event, plan, or intention **2** to make known the arrival of a guest at a formal social occasion **announcement** n **announcer** n

annoy v **1** to make someone slightly angry **2** to be troublesome to someone or harass them **annoyance** n

annual adj **1** happening once every year **2** calculated or reckoned by the year ♦ Our annual income has increased. **3** (said about a plant) lasting only one year or season **annual** n **1** a plant that lives for one year or one season **2** a book or periodical belonging to a series published once a year **annually** adv

annuity (say ə-**new**-iti) n pl **annuities** a fixed annual allowance, usually provided by a form of investment

annul (say ə-**nul**) v **annulled, annulling** to make a contract or agreement invalid or void

annular (say **an**-yoo-ler) adj having the form of a ring

Annunciation n **1** in Christian belief, the announcement by the angel Gabriel to the Virgin Mary that she was to be the mother of Christ **2** the festival commemorating this on 25 March (also called Lady Day)

anode (say **an**-ohd) n a positively charged electrode, by which electric current enters a device. (Compare cathode.)

anodize (say **an**-ə-diyz) v to coat metal with a protective layer by means of electrolysis

anodyne (say **an**-ə-diyn) n a drug that relieves pain **anodyne** adj **1** relieving pain **2** feebly dull or unexciting

anoint v to rub a person with ointment

or oil, especially as part of a religious ceremony

anomaly (say ə-**nom**-əli) n pl **anomalies** something that deviates from what is normal or expected ♦ *the many anomalies in our tax system* **anomalous** adj

anon (say ə-**non**) adv old use soon or presently ♦ *I will say more of this anon.*

anon. abbr anonymous (with reference to an author)

anonymity (say an-ən-**im**-iti) n being anonymous

anonymous (say ə-**non**-im-əs) adj **1** having a name that is not known **2** written or given by a person whose name is not known **anonymously** adv

anorak (say an-er-ak) n a waterproof jacket with a hood attached

anorexia, anorexia nervosa (say an-er-**eks**-iə) n a psychological condition involving an obsession with reducing weight by not eating **anorexic** adj

another adj **1** additional, one more ♦ *Have another biscuit.* **2** different ♦ *If this one doesn't work I'll give you another.* **another** pronoun another person or thing

answer n **1** something said, written, or done to deal with a question, accusation, or situation **2** something needed to resolve a problem or difficulty **answer** v **1** to make an answer to someone **2** to be suitable or enough for something ♦ *This will answer the purpose.* **answerable** adj **answering machine** n a machine that answers telephone calls by playing a recorded message and recording the caller's reply

ant n a small insect of which there are many species mostly without wings, which live in highly organized groups

antacid (say ant-**ass**-id) n a substance that prevents or corrects acidity

antagonism (say an-**tag**-ən-izm) n active opposition or hostility **antagonist** n **antagonistic** adj **antagonistically** adv **antagonize** v

Antarctic n **1** the regions round the South Pole **2** the Antarctic Ocean, the sea surrounding Antarctica **Antarctic** adj relating to these regions **Antarctic Circle** n an imaginary line round the Antarctic regions at a latitude of 66° 30' S

ante (say **an**-ti) n a stake put up by a poker player before drawing new cards

ante- prefix before (as in *ante-room*)

anteater n an animal with a long nose and a sticky tongue, which feeds on ants and termites

antecedent (say **ant**-i-seedənt) n **1** something that happened before something else ♦ *We discussed the Great War and its antecedents.* **2** Gram a noun, clause, or sentence to which a following pronoun refers (in *the book which I have*, 'book' is the antecedent of 'which') **antecedent** adj previous **antecedents** pl n a person's ancestors and social background

antechamber n a small room leading to a larger one, an ante-room

antedate v to put an earlier date on a document than the date on which it was issued

antediluvian (say anti-di-**loo**-viən) adj **1** of the time before Noah's Flood as recounted in the Bible **2** completely out of date

antelope n a fast-running animal like a deer, found especially in Africa, for example a chamois or gazelle

antenatal adj before birth or during a pregnancy ♦ *an antenatal clinic*

antenna n **1** pl **antennae** (say an-**ten**-ee) each of a pair of thin flexible extensions on the heads of insects and some other invertebrate animals, used as feelers **2** pl **antennas** an aerial

antepenultimate (say anti-pin-**ult**-imət) adj last but two in a series

anterior adj coming before something in position or time

ante-room n a small room leading to a larger one, an antechamber

anthem n **1** a short musical composition for singing in religious services **2** short for *national anthem* **3** a rousing song sung by a large group of people, such as supporters of a sport

anther n the part of a flower's stamen that contains pollen

anthology (say an-**thol**-əji) n pl **anthologies** a collection of poems or other pieces of literature

anthracite n a hard form of coal that burns with little flame or smoke

anthrax n a disease of sheep and cattle that can be transmitted to people

anthropoid (say **an**-thrəp-oid) adj like a human being in form, especially with reference to the higher primates **anthropoid** n an anthropoid ape such as a gorilla or chimpanzee

anthropology (say anthrə-**pol**-əji) n the study of humankind, especially of human societies and cultures **anthropological** adj **anthropologically** adv **anthropologist** n

anthropomorphic (say an-thrəp-ə-**mor** -fik) adj attributing human forms or characteristics to a god, animal, or object **anthropomorphism** n

anti prep opposed to, against

anti- prefix (changing to **ant-** before a vowel) **1** against or opposed to ♦ anti-abortion **2** preventing or counteracting

anti-aircraft adj (said about a gun or missile) used against enemy aircraft

antibiotic (say anti-biy-**ot**-ik) n a medicine that destroys bacteria or prevents their growth **antibiotic** adj acting in this way

antibody (say **an**-ti-bodi) n pl **antibodies** a protein formed in the blood as a defence against certain substances which it then attacks and destroys

anticipate v **1** to take action in advance about something you are aware of ♦ A good teacher learns to anticipate what students will ask. **2** to make use of something before the proper time **3** to take action before someone else has had a chance to do so **4** to expect **anticipation** n **anticipatory** adj ◊ Some people regard meaning **4** as incorrect. It is better to avoid it and use expect instead.

anticlimax n a disappointing ending to a series of events that seemed to be leading to a climax

anticlockwise adv, adj moving in a curve in the opposite direction to the hands of a clock

antics pl n foolish or amusing behaviour

anticyclone n a weather system in which atmospheric pressure is high, usually producing fine settled weather

antidote (say **an**-ti-doht) n **1** a medicine that counteracts the effects of a poison or a disease **2** anything that counteracts unpleasant effects

antifreeze n a liquid added to water, especially in the radiator of a motor vehicle, to lower its freezing point and make it less likely to freeze

antigen (say **an**-ti-jən) n a substance (e.g. a toxin) that the body recognizes as alien and that causes the body to produce antibodies

anti-hero n a central character in a story or drama who lacks the usual characteristics of a hero

antihistamine (say anti-**hist**-ə-min) n a drug or other substance that counteracts the effects of histamine, used in treating allergies

antimony (say **an**-ti-məni) n a brittle silvery metal used in alloys, a chemical element (symbol Sb)

antipasto (say an-ti-**pah**-stoh) n pl **antipasti** an Italian appetizer

antipathy (say an-**tip**-ə-thi) n a strong feeling of dislike for someone or something

antiperspirant (say anti-**per**-spi-rənt) n a substance that prevents or reduces perspiration

antipodes (say an-**tip**-ə-deez) pl n places on opposite sides of the earth **Antipodes** Australia and New Zealand, as regarded by people in the northern hemisphere **antipodean** adj

antiquary (say an-tik-wer-i) n pl **antiquaries** a person who studies or collects antiques or antiquities

antiquated (say **an**-ti-kway-tid) adj old-fashioned or out of date

antique (say an-**teek**) adj **1** belonging to the distant past **2** made in the style of past times **antique** n an object, especially a piece of furniture or a decorative object, that has value because of its age

antiquity (say an-**tik**-witi) n ancient times, especially the classical civilizations before the Middle Ages **antiquities** pl n objects dating from ancient times

anti-Semitic (say anti-sim-**it**-ik) adj hostile to or prejudiced against Jews **anti-Semitism** n

antiseptic adj **1** preventing the growth of micro-organisms that cause disease **2** completely clean and free from germs **antiseptic** n an antiseptic substance **antiseptically** adv

antisocial adj **1** opposed to normal social institutions and conventions **2** inconsiderate towards other people **3** not sociable, keeping away from the company of others **antisocially** adv

anti-static adj preventing the build-up of static electricity or reducing its effects

antithesis (say an-tith-i-sis) n pl **antitheses** **1** someone or something that is the direct opposite of something or someone else **2** in literature, the expression of a contrast of ideas **antithetic** adj **antithetical** adj **antithetically** adv

antitoxin n an antibody that neutralizes a toxin and prevents it from having a harmful effect **antitoxic** adj

antler n a branched horn, one of a pair on a stag or other deer **antlered** adj

antonym (say ant-ən-im) n a word that is opposite in meaning to another word

anus (say ay-nəs) n the opening at the lower end of the alimentary canal, through which solid waste matter is passed out of the body **anal** adj

anvil n a large block of iron on which a blacksmith hammers metal into shape

anxiety n pl **anxieties** **1** a feeling of being anxious **2** something that causes this feeling

anxious adj **1** troubled and worried **2** causing worry ♦ A few anxious moments followed. **3** eager ♦ They are always anxious to please. **anxiously** adv

any adj **1** used to refer to one or some of a thing, or a number of things (usually more than two) when it is not important which are meant ♦ Have you any bread? **2** every, whichever one you choose ♦ Any fool knows that. **3** in a significant amount ♦ They did not stay any length of time. **any** pronoun any person, thing, or amount ♦ I can't see any of them. **any** adv at all, to some extent ♦ Is that any better?

anybody n, pronoun **1** any person **2** a person of importance ♦ Is she anybody?

anyhow adv **1** anyway **2** in a careless or disorderly way ♦ They just did the work anyhow.

any more adv any further, from now or then on ♦ She didn't love him any more.

anyone n, pronoun anybody

anything n, pronoun a thing, no matter which ♦ Anything will do.

anyway adv in any case

anywhere adv in or to any place **anywhere** pronoun any place

Anzac n **1** a soldier in the Australian and New Zealand Army Corps (1914-18) **2** a person from Australia or New Zealand

AOB abbr any other business

aorta (say ay-or-tə) n the main artery of the body, through which blood is pumped into the circulatory system **aortic** adj

apart adv **1** separately or by themselves ♦ The children lived apart for many years. **2** to or at a distance ♦ Keep the tables apart. **3** into pieces ♦ I'll have to take it apart. **apart from** excluding, other than

apartheid (say ə-part-hayt) n the political policy that used to be followed in South Africa, of keeping Europeans and non-Europeans apart

apartment n a set of rooms, a flat

apathy (say ap-ə-thi) n a feeling of not caring or not being interested **apathetic** adj **apathetically** adv

ape n any of the four primates (gorilla, chimpanzee, orang-utan, gibbon) most closely related to man **ape** v to imitate or mimic someone **apeman** n pl **apemen** an extinct being believed to have features of both apes and humans

aperitif (say ə-pe-ri-teef) n an alcoholic drink taken before a meal as an appetizer

aperture n an opening, especially one that admits light into a camera

apex (say ay-peks) n pl **apexes** the tip or highest point of something, especially when it forms a point

aphid (say ay-fid) n a small bug, such as a greenfly or blackfly, that feeds off the sap of plants

aphorism (say af-er-izm) n a short saying that states a truth, a maxim

aphrodisiac (say afrə-diz-iak) n a food or

drink that arouses sexual desire

apiary (say **ay**-pi-er-i) *n pl* **apiaries** a place with a number of hives where bees are kept

apiece *adv* for or by each one of a group
♦ *They cost a pound apiece.*

aplomb (say ə-**plom**) *n* confident self-assurance

apocalypse (say ə-**pok**-ə-lips) *n* an event of great destruction or disaster **Apocalypse** *n* the last book in the New Testament (also called the *Revelation of St John the Divine*), which includes a prophecy about the end of the world **apocalyptic** *adj* **apocalyptically** *adv*

Apocrypha (say ə-**pok**-rif-ə) *n* the books of the Old Testament that were not accepted by Jews as part of the Hebrew Scriptures and are omitted from some versions of the Bible **apocryphal** *adj* **apocryphally** *adv*

apogee (say **ap**-ə-jee) *n* **1** the point in the orbit of the moon or a satellite when it is furthest from the earth. (Compare *perigee*.) **2** a climax

apolitical (say ay-pə-**lit**-ikəl) *adj* not political, not interested in politics

apology *n pl* **apologies 1** a statement of regret for having done wrong or caused offence **2** an explanation or defence of beliefs **3** a poor example of something ♦ *this feeble apology for a meal* **apologetic** *adj* wanting to apologize for something **apologetically** *adv* **apologetics** *pl n* a set of arguments that justify a doctrine, especially Christianity **apologist** *n* a person who defends a doctrine by presenting an argument **apologize** *v* to express regret for a wrongdoing or offence

apoplexy (say **ap**-ə-plek-si) *n* sudden inability to feel and move, caused by blockage or rupture of an artery in the brain **apoplectic** *adj* **apoplectically** *adv*

apostate (say ə-**poss**-tayt) *n* a person who renounces a religious belief or political principle **apostasy** *n* **apostatize** *v*

Apostle *n* each of Christ's twelve disciples **apostle** *n* a teacher or supporter of a new idea or cause **apostolic** *adj*

apostrophe (say ə-**pos**-trə-fi) *n* **1** a punctuation mark (') used to show that letters or numbers have been omitted (as

in *didn't* = did not; *'05* = 2005) or showing the possessive case (as in *Rachel's book, their parents' house*) **2** a part of a speech or a poem addressed to an absent person or an abstract idea **apostrophize** *v*

apothecary (say ə-**poth**-ik-eri) *n pl* **apothecaries** *old use* a person who prepared medicines

apotheosis (say ə-poth-ee-**oh**-sis) *n* **1** making a person divine **2** the highest point of perfection something reaches

appal (say ə-**pawl**) *v* **appalled**, **appalling** to make someone feel horrified, to shock someone deeply **appalling** *adj*

apparatus *n* **1** the equipment needed for doing something, especially the instruments, devices, and containers used in scientific experiments **2** a complex piece of organization

apparel *n formal* clothing

apparent (say ə-**pa**-rənt) *adj* **1** clearly seen or understood **2** seeming to be true or real **apparently** *adv*

apparition (say apə-**rish**-ən) **1** something remarkable or unexpected that appears suddenly **2** a ghost

appeal *v* **appealed**, **appealing 1** to make a serious or formal request ♦ *The police appealed for calm.* **2** to go or speak to someone with authority for an opinion **3** *Law* to take a case to a higher court for review of the decision of a lower court **4 appeal to** to be attractive or pleasing to someone ♦ *Air travel doesn't appeal to me.* **appeal** *n* **1** the act of appealing **2** attraction or pleasantness **3** *Law* the process of appealing to a higher court

appear *v* **1** to become visible **2** to start to exist or be used **3** to give a certain impression ♦ *You appear to have forgotten.* **4** to give a public performance, especially on stage ♦ *Olivier appeared as Hamlet.* **5** to act as counsel in a law court ♦ *I appear for the defendant.* **6** to be published ♦ *Her new novel will appear next month.* **appearance** *n* **1** the act of appearing **2** an outward sign, what something appears to be

appease *v* to make someone feel calm or quiet by giving them what they want **appeasement** *n*

appellant (say ə-pel-ənt) *n* a person who appeals against the ruling of a law court

appellation (say ap-əl-**ay**-shən) *n formal* a name or title

append *v formal* 1 to attach something 2 to add something at the end of a text or document **appendage** *n*

appendix *n* 1 *pl* **appendices** a part at the end of a book or document, giving extra information 2 *pl* **appendixes** a small tube of tissue closed at one end, attached to the lower end of the intestine **appendicitis** *n* inflammation of the appendix

appertain (say ap-er-**tayn**) *v* to relate to something or be appropriate to it

appetite *n* 1 a physical desire, especially for food 2 a desire or liking ♦ *They have an appetite for power.* **appetizer** *n* a small amount of food or drink taken before a meal to stimulate the appetite **appetizing** *adj* stimulating the appetite ♦ *an appetizing smell* **appetizingly** *adv*

applaud *v* 1 to show approval of something or someone by clapping the hands 2 to praise something ♦ *We all applaud your decision.* **applause** *n* clapping by people to show approval

apple *n* 1 a round fruit with green or red skin and a firm juicy flesh 2 the tree that bears this

appliance *n* a device or instrument

applicable (say ap-**lik**-əbəl) *adj* able to be applied, relevant, or appropriate **applicability** *n*

application *n* 1 a formal request for something ♦ *His application has been refused.* 2 the action of putting something on a surface ♦ *The ointment is for external application only.* 3 putting something into effect or to practical use 4 the ability to concentrate on a task 5 a computer program or piece of software designed for a particular purpose **applicant** *n*

appliqué (say ə-**plee**-kay) *n* needlework in which pieces of material are sewn to a fabric background **appliqué** *v*

apply *v* **applies**, **applied**, **applying** 1 to put one thing into contact with another 2 to bring into use or action ♦ *The United Nations voted to apply economic sanctions.*

3 (**apply to**) to be relevant to someone ♦ *The rules apply to everyone.* 4 to make a formal request ♦ *I am applying for a job.* **applicator** *n* a device for putting a substance on a surface **applied** *adj* (said about a subject of study) used for a practical purpose

appoint *v* 1 to choose a person for a job or special purpose 2 to decide or arrange something officially **appointment** *n* 1 an arrangement to meet at a particular time and place 2 a job or position, or the act of appointing someone to it

apportion (say ə-**por** -shən) *v* to share something out **apportionment** *n*

apposite (say ap-ə-zit) *adj* (said about a remark) very apt or appropriate **appositely** *adv*

appraise *v* to estimate the value or quality of something **appraisal** *n*

appreciable (say ə-**pree**-shə-bəl) *adj* enough to be noticed or felt, considerable **appreciably** *adv*

appreciate *v* 1 to value something highly, to be grateful for something 2 to enjoy something intelligently ♦ *It is good that they appreciate good singing.* 3 to understand ♦ *We appreciate their reluctance to give details.* 4 to increase in value ♦ *The value of the house has appreciated over the years.* **appreciation** *n* **appreciative** *adj* **appreciatively** *adv*

apprehend (say apri-**hend**) *v* 1 to seize or arrest someone who is doing wrong 2 to understand something 3 to expect something with fear or anxiety

apprehension (say apri-**hen**-shən) *n* 1 a feeling of fear about a danger or difficulty 2 understanding 3 the act of arresting someone **apprehensive** *adj* **apprehensively** *adv* **apprehensiveness** *n*

apprentice *n* someone who is learning a craft from an employer **apprentice** *v* to bind someone legally as an apprentice **apprenticeship** *n*

apprise (say ə-**priyz**) *v formal* to inform someone of something

approach *v* 1 to come near or nearer to a place or time 2 to set about doing a task 3 to go to someone with a request or offer

4 to be similar to something **approach** n **1** the action of approaching **2** a way of reaching a place **3** a method of doing or tackling something **4** an effort to establish an agreement or friendly relations **approachable** adj **approachability** n

approbation (say aprə-**bay**-shən) n approval

appropriate (say ə-**proh**-pri-ayt) v **1** to take and use something without permission as your own **2** to set money aside for a special purpose **appropriation** n **appropriator** n

approve v **1** (often **approve of**) to say or feel that something is good or suitable **2** to agree formally to something **approval** n

approximate (say ə-**prok**-sim-ət) adj nearly but not completely exact or correct **approximate** (say ə-prok-sim-ayt) v **1** to be almost the same as something ♦ His remarks approximated to an apology. **2** to make something approximately the same **approximately** adv **approximation** n

APR abbr annual or annualized percentage rate, with reference to the rate of interest on a credit arrangement

apricot n **1** a juicy fruit containing a stone, related to the plum and peach **2** the tree on which this grows **3** the orange-pink colour of an apricot

April n the fourth month of the year **April Fool's Day** n 1 April, by tradition a day for playing practical jokes on people

apron n **1** a garment you wear over the front part of the body to protect your clothes **2** an extra area next to a larger one, for example a part of a theatre stage reaching in front of the curtain **3** an area on an airfield used for loading or manoeuvring aircraft

apropos (say aprə-**poh**) adv appropriately, to the point **apropos** adj suitable or relevant to what someone is saying or doing **apropos of** concerning or with reference to

apse n a recess in a church, usually with an arched or domed roof

apt adj **1** suitable or appropriate ♦ an apt quotation **2** having a certain tendency, likely ♦ They are apt to be careless. **3** quick at learning **aptly** adv **aptness** n

aptitude n a natural ability or skill

aqualung n a portable breathing apparatus used by divers and consisting of cylinders of compressed air connected to a mask with a mouthpiece

aquamarine (say akwə-mə-**reen**) n **1** a bluish-green variety of beryl **2** a bluish-green colour

aquaplane n a board for riding on water pulled by a speedboat **aquaplane** v **1** to ride on an aquaplane **2** (said about a road vehicle) to slide out of control on the wet surface of a road

aquarium (say ə-**kwair**-iəm) n pl **aquariums 1** a glass tank for keeping living fish and other water animals **2** a building containing a collection of fish in tanks

Aquarius (say ə-**kwair**-iəs) (the Water-carrier) the sign of the zodiac which the sun enters about 21 January **Aquarian** adj, n

aquatic (say ə-**kwat**-ik) adj **1** growing in water or living in or near water ♦ aquatic plants **2** taking place in or on water ♦ aquatic sports

aqueduct (say **ak**-wi-dukt) n an artificial water channel, especially a bridge carrying water across a valley or low ground

aqueous (say **ay**-kwi-əs) adj **1** like water, or containing water **2** produced by water

aquiline (say **ak**-wi-liyn) adj (said about a person's nose) hooked like an eagle's beak

Arab n **1** a member of a Semitic people living in parts of the Middle East and North Africa **2** a horse of a breed originating in Arabia **Arab** adj to do with the Arabs **Arabian** adj **Arabic** adj to do with the Arabs or their language **Arabic** n the language of the Arabs **Arabic numeral** n any of the numerals 0, 1, 2, 3, 4, 5, 6, 7, 8, and 9 (see also Roman numeral)

arabesque (say a-rə-**besk**) n **1** an elaborate design with intertwined leaves, branches, and scrolls **2** a ballet position

arable (say **a**-rə-bəl) adj (said about land) suitable for growing crops **arable** n arable land

arachnid (say ə-**rak**-nid) n a member of the class of animals including spiders, scorpions, and mites

Aramaic (say a-rə-**may**-ik) *n* a Semitic language spoken in Syria and Palestine in New Testament times

arbiter (say **ar**-bit-er) *n* **1** a person who has a strong influence over public opinion ♦ *the arbiters of fashion* **2** a person given the power to settle a dispute, an arbitrator

arbitrary (say **ar**-bit-rer-i) *adj* **1** based on random choice or impulse ♦ *an arbitrary selection* **2** unrestrained or autocratic ♦ *arbitrary powers* **arbitrarily** *adv* **arbitrariness** *n*

arbitrator *n* an independent person or group of people chosen to settle a dispute **arbitrate** *v* **arbitration** *n*

arboreal (say ar-**bor**-iəl) *adj* to do with trees, or living in trees

arbour (say **ar**-ber) *n* a shady alcove in a garden, formed with climbing plants growing over a framework **arboretum** *n pl* **arboreta** a botanical garden where trees are grown for study and display

arc *n* **1** a curve forming part of the circumference of a circle or other figure **2** a luminous electric current passing across a gap between two terminals **arc** *v* **arced**, **arcing 1** to form an arc or curve **2** to form an electrical arc

arcade *n* **1** a covered passage or walk with shops on one or both sides **2** a series of arches along a wall

arcane (say ar-**kayn**) *adj* mysterious or secret

arch[1] *n* **1** a curved structure built across an opening and supporting the weight above it **2** a curve shaped like an arch **3** the curved underside of the foot **arch** *v* to form an arch, or to make something form an arch

arch[2] *adj* self-consciously playful or mischievous ♦ *an arch smile* **archly** *adv* **archness** *n*

arch- *prefix* **1** chief (as in *archbishop*) **2** extreme (as in *arch-enemy*)

archaeology (say ar-ki-**ol**-əji) *n* the study of ancient civilizations by digging for their physical remains and examining them **archaeological** *adj* **archaeologist** *n*

archaic (say ar-**kay**-ik) *adj* **1** belonging to ancient times **2** old or old-fashioned **archaism** *n*

archangel *n* an angel of high rank

archbishop *n* the chief bishop of a region

archdeacon *n* a senior priest, ranking next below a bishop **archdeaconry** *n*

archduke *n* a chief duke, especially formerly as the title of a son of an Austrian emperor

arch-enemy *n pl* **arch-enemies** a chief or major enemy

archery *n* the sport of shooting with bows and arrows **archer** *n*

archetype (say **ar**-ki-tiyp) *n* **1** an original model from which others are copied **2** a typical example of something **archetypal** *adj*

archipelago (say arki-**pel**-ə-goh) *n pl* **archipelagos** a large group of islands, or a sea containing such a group

architecture *n* **1** the art or science of designing and constructing buildings **2** the design or style of a building or buildings **architect** *n* **architectural** *adj* **architecturally** *adv*

architrave (say **ar**-ki-trayv) *n* **1** a horizontal beam resting along the top of a row of columns **2** the surround of a doorway or window

archive (say **ar**-kiyv) *n* **1** a collection of the records or historical documents of an institution or community **2** *ICT* a set of computer files that are stored and no longer in active use **archive** *v ICT* to put computer files into an archive

archivist (say **ar**-kiv-ist) *n* a person qualified to organize and manage an archive

archway *n* a passageway under an arch

arc lamp, arc light *n* an artificial light using an electric arc

Arctic *n* the regions round the North Pole **Arctic** *adj* relating to these regions **arctic** *adj informal* extremely cold **Arctic Circle** *n* an imaginary line round the Arctic regions at a latitude of 66° 30′ N

ardent (say **ar**-dənt) *adj* very enthusiastic, full of ardour **ardently** *adv*

ardour (say **ar**-der) *n* great enthusiasm or feeling

arduous (say **ar**-dew-əs) *adj* very difficult and needing much effort **arduously** *adv*

are[1] a form of *be*, used with plural nouns and with *we*, *you*, and *they*

are² (say ar) *n* a former unit of area equal to 100 square metres

area *n* **1** the extent or measurement of a surface **2** a region or district **3** a space set aside for a purpose **4** the scope or range of an activity **5** a sunken enclosure in front of the basement of a house

arena (say ə-ree-nə) *n* the level area in the centre of a sports stadium or amphitheatre

aren't *informal* are not

arête (say a-rayt) *n* a sharp ridge on a mountain

argon *n* a chemical element (symbol Ar), an inert gas used in electric lamps

argue *v* **1** to express disagreement; to exchange opposite views, especially with anger **2** to give reasons for or against something, to discuss an issue **arguable** *adj* **1** able to be stated as a possibility **2** open to doubt or discussion **arguably** *adv*

argument *n* **1** a discussion involving disagreement, a quarrel **2** a reason or set of reasons in support of something **3** *Mathematics* an independent variable determining the value of a function **argumentation** *n* systematic reasoning in support of something **argumentative** *adj* arguing a lot **argumentatively** *adv*

aria (say ah-riə) *n* a song for one voice in an opera or oratorio

arid (say a-rid) *adj* **1** (said about a region) dry and parched **2** dull and uninteresting **aridity** *n* **aridly** *adv* **aridness** *n*

Aries (say air-eez) (the Ram) the sign of the zodiac which the sun enters about 20 March **Arian** *adj*, *n*

arise *v* **arose**, **arisen 1** to happen or come into existence ♦ *Some confusion arose about what happened next.* **2** *old use* to get up or stand up ♦ *Arise, Sir Francis.*

aristocracy (say a-ri-stok-rəsi) *n pl* **aristocracies 1** the upper classes of people in a society **2** a form of government in which these people have power **aristocrat** *n* a member of the aristocracy, a noble **aristocratic** *adj* **1** to do with the aristocracy **2** noble in style **aristocratically** *adv*

arithmetic (say ə-rith-mə-tik) *n* **1** the part of mathematics concerned with numbers **2** using numbers to count and calculate

arithmetical *adj* **arithmetically** *adv*

ark *n* **1** the boat built by Noah at the time of the Flood, according to the Bible **2** a model of Noah's boat

arm¹ *n* **1** each of the two upper limbs of the human body from the shoulder to the hand **2** a sleeve of a piece of clothing **3** something shaped like an arm or projecting from the main part of something **4** each of the raised parts of a chair, supporting the arms of the person sitting in it **armband** *n* **1** a band worn round the upper part of an arm or sleeve **2** an inflatable plastic band worn round each arm as a support in swimming **armchair** *n* **1** a chair with arms or raised sides **2** (used with a noun) taking an interest in an activity without any practical experience of it ♦ *an armchair traveller* **armful** *n pl* **armfuls** as much as you can hold in your arms **armpit** *n* a hollow under the arm below the shoulder

arm² *v* **1** to supply people with weapons **2** to fit weapons to a vehicle or piece of equipment **3** to make a bomb ready to explode **arm** *n* each of the kinds of troops that make up an army ♦ *the Fleet Air Arm* **arms** *pl n* **1** weapons **2** an emblem or heraldic device **armed forces** *pl n* a country's army, navy, and air force **up in arms** protesting very strongly about something

armada (say ar-mah-də) *n* a fleet of warships **the Armada, the Spanish Armada** the armada sent from Spain to invade England in 1588

armadillo (say ar-mə-dil-oh) *n pl* **armadillos** a small burrowing animal of South America with large claws and a body covered in bony plates

Armageddon (say ar-mə-ged-ən) *n* **1** (in the Bible) the scene of the final conflict between good and evil at the end of the world **2** a decisive or catastrophic conflict

armament *n* **1** the weapons and equipment used by an army **2** the process of equipping armed forces for war

armature (say ar-mə-choor) *n* **1** the rotating coil of a dynamo or electric motor **2** a bar placed across the poles of a magnet to preserve its power or transmit force to support a load **3** a framework round which a clay or plaster sculpture is modelled

armistice *n* an agreement during a war or battle to stop fighting for a time

armour *n* **1** a metal covering formerly worn to protect the body in fighting **2** a set of tough metal plates covering a warship or military vehicle to protect it from attack **3** armoured fighting vehicles collectively **armorial** *adj* **armoured** *adj* **armoury** *n pl* **armouries**

army *n pl* **armies 1** an organized military force equipped for fighting on land **2** something compared to an army in being large or hostile ♦ *an army of locusts* **3** a large group of people organized for a particular purpose ♦ *an army of helpers*

aroma (say ə-**roh**-mə) *n* a pleasant or special smell **aromatic** *adj* **aromatherapy** *n* the use of aromatic plant extracts and natural oils for medicinal and cosmetic purposes

around *adv, prep* **1** all round, on every side, in every direction **2** close at hand ♦ *She's somewhere around.* **3** about, approximately at ♦ *I'll be there around eight o'clock.*

arouse *v* **1** to waken from sleep **2** to stir up feelings

arpeggio (say ar-**pej**-i-oh) *n pl* **arpeggios** *Mus* the notes of a chord played in succession instead of together

arrange *v* **1** to put things into the right order or position **2** to form plans or settle the details of something **3** to adapt a piece of music for voices or instruments other than those for which it was originally written, or to adapt a story or drama for broadcasting **arrangement** *n* **arranger** *n*

arrant (say **a**-rənt) *adj* downright, out-and-out ♦ *What arrant nonsense!*

arras (say **a**-rəs) *n* a richly decorated tapestry or wall-hanging

array *v* **1** to arrange something in order ♦ *The army was arrayed along the river.* **2** to dress or clothe ♦ *She was arrayed in her finest ball gown.* **array** *n* **1** an impressive display of things ♦ *There was a fine array of tools on the garage wall.* **2** *Mathematics* an arrangement of figures or symbols in a grid or matrix **3** *ICT* an arrangement of data in a computer

arrears *pl n* money that is owed and should have been paid earlier **in arrears** behind with a payment ♦ *They are still in arrears with their rent.*

arrest *v* **1** to seize someone suspected of having committed a crime and hold them by legal authority **2** to stop or check a process or movement **arrest** *n* **1** the act of arresting someone **2** a stoppage

arrive *v* **1** to reach a place you are going towards ♦ *Some of the guests arrived early.* **2** to come at last ♦ *The day of the party arrived.* **3** (said about a person) to be recognized as having achieved success in the world **arrival** *n*

arrogant (say **a**-rə-gant) *adj* proud and overbearing **arrogance** *n* **arrogantly** *adv*

arrogate (say **a**-rə-gayt) *v* to claim or seize something for yourself without having the right to do so **arrogation** *n*

arrow *n* **1** a straight thin pointed stick for shooting from a bow **2** a symbol of the outline of an arrow, used to show direction or position on a chart **arrowhead** *n* the pointed end of an arrow

arsenal *n* a store of weapons and ammunition

arsenic (say **ar**-sən-ik) *n* **1** a brittle steel-grey chemical element (symbol As) **2** a highly poisonous white compound made from this **arsenical** *adj*

arson *n* the criminal act of deliberately setting fire to a house or other property **arsonist** *n*

art *n* **1** the use of creative skill and imagination to produce something beautiful **2** works such as paintings or sculptures produced by this skill **3** any practical skill or ability ♦ *the art of sailing* **4** cunning or artfulness **arts** *pl n* subjects such as languages, literature, and history, dealing with human activity and creativity, as opposed to the sciences **artful** *adj* crafty, cunningly clever **artfully** *adv* **artfulness** *n* **artisan** *n* a skilled worker or craftsman who makes things **artist** *n* **artiste** *n* **artistic** *adj* **artistically** *adv* **artistry** *n* **artless** *adj* not artful, simple and natural **artlessly** *adv* **artlessness** *n* **the arts** creative activity including painting, sculpture, music, literature, and dance **arty** *adj* **artier**, **artiest**, **artiness** *n*

artefact (say **ar**-ti-fakt) *n* an object made by a human, especially a simple prehistoric tool or weapon

artery *n pl* **arteries** **1** any of the tubes carrying blood away from the heart to all parts of the body **2** an important route in a traffic system **arterial** *adj* **arteriole** *n* a small artery **arterial road** *n* an important main road

arthritis (say arth-**riy**-tiss) *n* a disease causing pain and stiffness in the joints **arthritic** *adj*, *n*

arthropod (say **arth**-rə-pod) *n* an animal of the group that includes insects, spiders, and crustaceans, having divided bodies and limbs with joints

artichoke *n* a plant with a large flower consisting of thick scales like leaves, used as a vegetable

article *n* **1** a particular or separate object ♦ *Articles of clothing lay on the floor.* **2** a piece of writing in a newspaper or magazine **3** a separate clause or item in a contract or agreement **4** *Gram* a word, such as *a* or *the*, used before a noun to show what it refers to **article** *v* to bind an apprentice by the terms of an apprenticeship

articulate[1] (say ar-**tik**-yoo-lət) *adj* **1** (said about a person) able to express ideas clearly, good with words **2** (said about language) spoken clearly, well expressed **articulately** *adv*

articulate[2] (say ar-**tik**-yoo-layt) *v* **1** to say something clearly and distinctly ♦ *Articulate each word with care.* **2** to form a joint ♦ *This bone articulates with the next.* **articulated** *adj* (said about a vehicle, especially a large one) having sections connected by flexible joints **articulation** *n*

artifice (say **ar**-ti-fiss) *n* a clever trick that is meant to mislead someone **artificer** *n* a skilled craftsman or mechanic

artificial *adj* **1** made or done by human skill or effort as a copy of something natural **2** contrived or pretentious **artificiality** *n* **artificially** *adv* **artificial insemination** *n* the injection of semen into the womb

artificially **artificial intelligence** *n* the performance by computers of tasks normally needing human intelligence **artificial respiration** *n* a process of stimulating natural breathing by forcing air into and out of the lungs

artillery *n* **1** large guns used in fighting on land **2** the part of an army that uses large guns **artillerist** *n*

Aryan (say **air**-iən) *n* **1** a member of a people who settled in northern India in the second millennium BC and spoke an Indo-European language **2** (in Nazi Germany) a person of Caucasian and not Jewish descent **Aryan** *adj* to do with the Aryans or their language

as *adv* equally, in the same way ♦ *This one is just as good.* **as** *prep* in the function or role of ♦ *She was dressed up as an angel.* **as** *conjunction* **1** at the same time that, when or while ♦ *We reached the platform as the train was leaving.* **2** because ♦ *As it's late we'd better go home now.* **3** in the way in which ♦ *Just leave it as it is.* **as** *relative pronoun* that, who, or which ♦ *I had the same problem as you did.*

asbestos (say ass-**best**-oss) *n* a soft fibrous mineral substance that is made into fireproof material and used for heat insulation **asbestosis** *n* a lung disease caused by inhaling asbestos particles

Asbo (say **az**-boh) *n* in Britain, an antisocial behaviour order, a court order for a person to stop behaving in a way that harasses or distresses other people

ascend *v* to go up or come up **ascendancy** *n* the state of having great influence or being in control **ascendant** *adj* **ascension** *n* an ascent or going up **Ascension** in Christian belief, the ascent of Christ into heaven as witnessed by the Apostles and recorded in the New Testament **ascent** *n* **1** ascending or going up **2** a way up, an upward slope or path ascending or rising **in the ascendant** having greater control or influence **to ascend the throne** to become king or queen

ascertain (say ass-er-**tayn**) *v* to find something out by asking or making enquiries **ascertainable** *adj*

ascetic (say ə-**set**-ik) adj not allowing yourself any pleasures or physical comforts **ascetic** n a person who leads a simple life without ordinary pleasures, often for religious reasons **ascetically** adv **asceticism** n

ascorbic acid (say ə-**skor** -bik) n vitamin C, found in citrus fruits and vegetables

ascribe (say ə-**skriyb**) v to regard something as belonging to something else or caused by it ♦ She ascribes her success to hard work. **ascribable** adj **ascription** n

aseptic (say ay-**sep**-tik) adj clean and free from bacteria that cause things to become septic **aseptically** adv

asexual (say ay-**seks**-yoo-əl) adj not having a sex or sex organs **asexually** adv

ash[1] n the powder that is left after something has been burned **the Ashes** a cricket trophy which England and Australia compete to win **ashen** adj (said about a person's face) pale like ashes **ashtray** n a small dish for putting tobacco ash into while smoking **ashy** adj

ash[2] **1** a tree with a silver-grey bark and leaves divided into several parts **2** the hard pale wood of this tree

ashamed adj feeling great shame or guilt

ashore adv to or on the shore

ashram n a religious place in India where people go to learn and be restful, or a place modelled on this

Asian (say **ay**-shən) adj to do with Asia, the continent extending from Europe to the Pacific Ocean **Asian** n a person from Asia **Asiatic** adj situated in Asia, or coming from Asia ◊ Use Asian when referring to people.

aside adv **1** to or on one side ♦ Please step aside. **2** away, in reserve **aside** n (especially in acting) words spoken so that only certain people will hear them **aside from** apart from

asinine (say **ass**-i-niyn) adj very silly or foolish **asininity** n

ask v **1** to address a question to someone **2** to try to get something from someone ♦ He has a favour to ask you. **3** to invite someone ♦ I'm not going to ask him to the party.

askance (say ə-**skanss**) adv to look askance

at to regard someone or something with distrust or disapproval

askew adv, adj slightly crooked

asleep adv, adj **1** in or into a state of sleep **2** (said about a limb) numbed

asp n a small poisonous snake

asparagus (say ə-**spa**-rə-gəs) n a plant with tender shoots that are cooked and eaten as a vegetable

aspect n **1** one part or feature of a situation or event ♦ The violence was the worst aspect of the crime. **2** the look or appearance that a person or thing has ♦ The forest had a sinister aspect. **3** the direction a thing faces, or a side facing this way ♦ The house has a southern aspect.

asperity (say ə-**spe**-riti) n a harsh or severe manner or tone

aspersions (say ə-**sper**-shənz) pl n **to cast aspersions** to attack someone's reputation or honesty

asphalt (say **ass**-falt) n a black sticky substance like coal tar, used to make surfaces for roads **asphalt** v to cover a surface with asphalt

asphyxia (say ə-**sfiks**-iə) n suffocation caused by lack of air in the lungs **asphyxiate** v **asphyxiation** n

aspic n a clear savoury jelly used for coating meat, eggs, etc.

aspirate[1] (say **ass**-pər-ət) n the sound of 'h'

aspirate[2] (say **ass**-per-ayt) v to pronounce a sound with an h

aspire v to have a strong hope or ambition about something ♦ He aspires to become president. ♦ She aspires to the presidency. **aspirant** n **aspiration** n

aspirin n pl **aspirins** or **aspirin** a medicinal drug used to relieve pain and reduce fever

ass n **1** an animal of the horse family, smaller than a horse and with longer ears **2** a foolish person

assail (say ə-**sayl**) v **1** to attack someone violently **2** to begin a task with determination **assailant** n

assassinate v to kill an important person by violent means, usually from political or religious motives **assassin** n **assassination** n

assault n **1** a violent attack **2** Law an act that

threatens another person **assault** v to make an assault on someone

assay (say ə-**say**) n a test of metal or ore (especially of gold or silver used for coin or bullion) for quality **assay** v to make an assay of something

assegai (say **ass**-ig-iy) n a light spear with an iron tip, used by South African peoples

assemble v 1 to bring people or things together into a group 2 to come together into a group 3 to fit or put parts together to make something **assemblage** n **assembly** n pl **assemblies** 1 the process of assembling 2 a group of people who have come together for a purpose **assembly language** n ICT a low-level computer language for translation by an assembler **assembly line** n in a factory, a sequence of workers and machines that assemble a product in successive stages

assent v to consent or express agreement **assent** n formal consent or approval

assert v 1 to state something firmly ♦ They asserted their innocence. 2 to make other people recognize a claim or right ♦ The country began to assert its independence. **assertion** n **assertive** adj **assertively** adv **assertiveness** n **to assert yourself** to behave in a confident or forceful way; to insist on your rights

assess v 1 to decide the value or quality of something 2 to set the amount of a tax or fine for a person or property **assessment** n

asset (say **ass**-et) n 1 a piece of property that has money value 2 a useful or valuable quality or skill 3 a useful or helpful person

assiduous (say ə-**sid**-yoo-əs) adj hard-working and conscientious **assiduity** n **assiduously** adv

assign v 1 to give or allot something to someone ♦ Rooms were assigned to us on the first floor. 2 to appoint a person to perform a task ♦ The police assigned a team of detectives to the case. 3 to regard something as correct or suitable ♦ We cannot assign an exact date to Stonehenge. **assignable** adj **assignation**(say ass-ig-**nay**-shən) n an arrangement to meet, especially a secret one **assignment** n 1 a task or piece of work that is assigned to someone, especially as

part of a course of study 2 the process of assigning

assimilate v 1 to absorb nourishment into the body 2 to take in and understand information or ideas 3 to absorb something into a system or organization **assimilation** n

assist v to help someone **assistance** n **assistant** n 1 a person who serves customers in a shop 2 a person who assists in a task, a helper **assistant** adj ranking next below a senior person and helping them in their work ♦ an assistant manager

associate[1] (say ə-**soh**-si-ayt) v 1 to spend a lot of time with certain people 2 to have regular dealings with a group of people 3 to connect things in the mind ♦ I always associate forests with Germany.

associate[2] n 1 a partner or colleague in business 2 someone who has limited membership of an association or organization **associate** adj 1 associated 2 having limited membership of an organization **association** n 1 a group of people organized for a special purpose 2 being associated with other people 3 a mental connection between ideas **associative** adj 1 involving association 2 Mathematics (said about a mathematical operation) producing the same result regardless of the way the elements are grouped, e.g. $(4 + 5) + 6 = 15$, and $4 + (5 + 6) = 15$

assonance (say **ass**-ən-əns) n similarity of vowel sounds in words that do not completely rhyme, as in vermin and furnish

assorted adj including different sorts put together ♦ assorted chocolates **assortment** n a collection made up of several sorts of things

assuage (say ə-**swayj**) v 1 to soothe an unpleasant feeling or make it less severe 2 to satisfy a thirst or appetite

assume v 1 to accept without proof that something is true or sure to happen ♦ We assume that you will be coming tomorrow. 2 to take on a duty or responsibility 3 to begin to show a particular facial expression ♦ Then she assumed a stern look. **assumption** n 1 assuming something

2 something that is accepted without proof **Assumption** in Roman Catholic belief, the reception of the Virgin Mary in bodily form into heaven, or the festival commemorating this on 15 August

assure (say ə-**shoor**) v **1** to declare that something is true or will happen ♦ *I assure you there is no danger.* **2** to make something certain ♦ *The medicine will assure a complete recovery.* **3** to insure a life by means of a policy of assurance **assurance** n **1** a formal declaration or promise that something is true or will happen **2** a kind of life insurance **3** confidence in yourself ♦ *She acted with great assurance.* **assured** adj **assuredly** adv(say ə-**shoor**-idli)

aster n a garden plant with flowers of various colours like daisies

astern adv **1** at or towards the back (or stern) of a ship or the tail of an aircraft **2** (said of a ship's engine) backwards

asteroid (say **ass**-ter-oid) n **1** any of several small planets revolving round the sun **2** a starfish

asthma (say **ass**-mə) n a disease that is often caused by allergies and leads to coughing and difficulties in breathing **asthmatic** adj **asthmatically** adv

astir adv, adj moving about excitedly

astonish v to surprise someone very much **astonishment** n

astound v to surprise someone so they feel shocked

astral (say **ass**-trəl) adj to do with the stars, or like stars

astray adv, adj away from the right path or direction

astride adj having the legs wide apart, or on either side of something **astride** prep with a leg on each side of ♦ *She sat astride a horse.*

astringent (say ə-**strin**-jənt) adj **1** causing skin or body tissue to contract **2** harsh or severe **astringent** n an astringent lotion, used to treat minor damage to the skin **astringency** n

astrology (say ə-**strol**-əji) n the study of the movements of stars **astrologer** n **astrological** adj **astrologically** adv

astronaut n a person trained to travel in a spacecraft **astronautics** n

astronomy (say ə-**stron**-əmi) n the study of the stars and planets and their movements **astronomer** n **astronomical** adj **1** to do with astronomy **2** huge, enormous ♦ *We won an astronomical sum of money.* **astronomically** adv

astute (say ə-**stewt**) adj able to judge people and situations well, shrewd **astutely** adv **astuteness** n

asunder (say ə-**sun**-der) adv apart or into pieces ♦ *torn asunder*

asylum n **1** refuge and safety offered by one country to political refugees from another **2** a place of refuge

asymmetry (say ay-**sim**-ət-ri) n lack of symmetry **asymmetrical** adj **asymmetrically** adv

asymptote (say **as**-im-toht) n a straight line that continuously approaches a curve but does not touch it **asymptotic** adj

at prep **1** expressing position ♦ *at the top of the hill* **2** expressing time ♦ *Come at six o'clock.* **3** expressing a state or occupation ♦ *We felt at ease.* **4** indicating a price, amount, or age ♦ *They are sold at £5 each.* **5** expressing a reason or cause ♦ *I was annoyed at losing.* **6** expressing direction towards something ♦ *He drove straight at us.*

atavistic (say at-ə-**vis**-tik) adj following or imitating something done by a remote ancestor **atavism** n

ate past tense of *eat*

atheist (say **ayth**-ee-ist) n a person who believes there is no God **atheism** n **atheistic** adj

athlete n a person who takes part in athletic sports **athletic** adj **athletically** adv **athleticism** n

athwart adv, prep across from side to side

Atlantic n the Atlantic Ocean, the ocean separating the Americas from Europe and Africa **Atlantic** adj to do with the Atlantic Ocean

atlas n a book of maps

atman n (in Hinduism) the human soul or individual self, the supreme principle of life in the universe, identified with Brahman

atmosphere n **1** the mixture of gases surrounding the earth or other planets

2 the air in a place **3** a feeling or tone conveyed by something ♦ *The room had an atmosphere of peace and calm.* **4** a unit of pressure, equal to the pressure of the atmosphere at sea level **atmospheric** *adj* **atmospherics** *pl n*

atoll (say **at**-ol) *n* a ring-shaped coral reef around a lagoon

atom *n* **1** the smallest particle of a chemical element **2** this particle as a source of atomic energy **3** an extremely small quantity or thing ♦ *There's not an atom of truth in it.* **atomic** *adj* **atomize** *v* **atomization** *n* **atomizer** *n* **atom bomb** *n* a bomb in which the rapid release of atomic energy creates immense destructive power **atomic energy** *n* energy obtained from nuclear fission **atomic number** *n* the number of protons in the nucleus of an atom, as a characteristic of a chemical element **atomic weight** *n* the ratio between the mass of an atom of one element or isotope and one-twelfth the weight of an atom of the isotope carbon-12

atonal (say ay-**toh**-nəl) *adj* (said about music) not written in a particular key and using all the notes of the chromatic scale

atone *v* to make amends, to make up for an error or deficiency **atonement** *n*

atrium (say **ay**-tri-əm) *n pl* **atria** or **atriums** **1** the central court, with an open roof, of a building **2** each of the two upper cavities in the heart that receive blood from the veins

atrocious (say ə-**troh**-shəs) *adj* **1** extremely wicked or cruel ♦ *an atrocious act of vandalism* **2** *informal* very bad or unpleasant ♦ *The weather has been atrocious.* **atrociously** *adv* **atrocity** *n pl* **atrocities**

atrophy (say **at**-rə-fi) *n* the process of wasting away through undernourishment or lack of use **atrophy** *v* **atrophies**, **atrophied**, **atrophying** to undergo this process, to waste away

attach *v* **1** to fix or join something to something else **2** to appoint someone to a particular group or to do a particular job **3** to associate a quality with something ♦ *We attach little importance to the report's conclusions.* **4** to be ascribed to something or associated with it ♦ *No blame attaches to*

the company. **attachable** *adj* **attached** *adj* **attachment** *n*

attaché (say ə-**tash**-ay) *n* a person who is attached to the staff of an ambassador with a special area of responsibility ♦ *The cultural attaché at the British Embassy.*

attack *v* **1** to act violently against someone **2** to criticize someone strongly **3** to have a harmful effect on something ♦ *Rust attacks most metals.* **4** to start on a task with energy **attack** *n* **1** an act of attacking someone or something **2** a piece of strong or hostile criticism **3** a sudden onset of an illness ♦ *an attack of jaundice* **attacker** *n*

attain *v* to succeed in doing or getting something **attainable** *adj* **attainment** *n*

attar (say **at**-er) *n* a fragrant oil made from flowers ♦ *attar of roses*

attempt *v* to make an effort to achieve something ♦ *I was attempting to finish my letters.* **attempt** *n* **1** an effort to achieve something **2** an attack or an effort to overcome something

attend *v* **1** to be present at a place, especially on a regular basis ♦ *Children attend school from the age of 5.* **2** (**attend to**) to give care and thought to something ♦ *I will attend to the matter immediately.* **3** to take care of someone or look after them ♦ *Which doctor is attending you?* **4** to accompany someone as an attendant **attendance** *n* **attendant** *n*

attention *n* **1** the act of applying the mind to something, mental concentration **2** awareness ♦ *Try not to attract attention.* **3** consideration or care ♦ *She will get every attention.* **4** (**attentions**) things you do for someone out of kindness or romantic interest **5** a position of readiness taken by a soldier ♦ *to stand to attention* **attentive** *adj* **attentively** *adv* **attentiveness** *n*

attenuate (say ə-**ten**-yoo-ayt) *v* **1** to make something slender or thin **2** to make something weaker or reduce its force or value **attenuation** *n*

attest (say ə-**test**) *v* **1** to provide clear proof of something **2** to declare that something is true or genuine **attestation** *n*

attic *n* a room or space below the roof of a building

attire *n formal* clothes **attire** *v formal* to

be attired to be dressed in clothes of a particular kind ♦ *The old man was attired in a tweed jacket.*

attitude *n* **1** a position of the body or its parts **2** a way of thinking or behaving, especially one you have for quite a long time

attorney (say ə-ter-ni) *n pl* **attorneys 1** a person, usually a lawyer, who is appointed to act on behalf of someone else in business or legal matters **2** N. Am a lawyer who is qualified to act for clients in a law court

attract *v* **1** to make someone interested or pleased ♦ *They were attracted by the colourful stalls in the market.* **2** to bring people in by offering something interesting ♦ *The game attracted a large crowd.* **3** to draw something by means of a physical force (the opposite of *repel*) ♦ *Magnets attract metals.*

attraction *n* **1** the process of attracting, or the ability to attract **2** something that attracts people by arousing their interest or pleasure **attractive** *adj* having a pleasing appearance or effect **attractively** *adv* **attractiveness** *n*

attribute[1] (say ə-trib-yoot) *v* to say that something was made or done by a certain person or group of people ♦ *The painting is attributed to Rembrandt.* **attributable** *adj* **attribution** *n*

attribute[2] (say at-rib-yoot) *n* **1** a quality that is characteristic of a person or thing ♦ *Kindness is one of his attributes.* **2** an object that is regularly associated with a person or thing

attrition (say ə-trish-ən) *n* **1** wearing something away by rubbing **2** a process of wearing down someone's strength or stamina by constant attack or pressure ♦ *a war of attrition*

atypical (say ay-tip-ikəl) *adj* not typical

aubergine (say oh-ber-zheen) *n* **1** the purple fruit of a tropical plant, used as a vegetable **2** the colour of an aubergine

auburn (say aw-bern) *n* a reddish-brown colour **auburn** *adj* having this colour

auction *n* a public sale in which items are sold to the highest bidder **auction** *v* to sell goods by auction **auctioneer** *n*

audacious (say aw-day-shəs) *adj* bold or daring **audaciously** *adv* **audacity** *n*

audible *adj* loud enough to be heard **audibility** *n* **audibly** *adv*

audience *n* **1** the people who have come to hear or watch something **2** the people watching a television programme **3** people who can hear what is being said **4** the people for whom a book or speech is intended **5** a formal interview with a distinguished person

audio *n* the reproduction of sound by electronic means **audio-visual** *adj* involving both sight and sound, especially video

audit *n* an official scrutiny of financial accounts to see that they are in order **audit** *v* **audited**, **auditing** to examine a set of accounts **auditor** *n*

audition *n* a practical demonstration given by an actor, musician, or other performer to test whether they are suitable for a particular role or job **audition** *v* **1** to test someone with an audition **2** to be tested in an audition

auditorium (say awdit-or -iəm) *n pl* **auditoriums** the part of a theatre or hall in which an audience sits

auditory (say aw-dit-er-i) *adj* to do with hearing

au fait (say oh fay) *adj* knowing a subject well

augment (say awg-ment) *v* to add to something or to increase it **augmentation** *n* **augmented** *adj*

augur (say awg-er) *v* to foretell a result or outcome ♦ *This augurs well for the future.*

August *n* the eighth month of the year

august (say aw-gust) *adj* deserving honour or respect

aunt *n* the sister of your father or mother, or your uncle's wife

auntie *n* informal an aunt

au pair (say oh pair) *n* a young person from abroad, usually a woman, who helps with housework and the care of children in exchange for board and lodging

aura (say or -ə) *n* the atmosphere associated with a person or place ♦ *an aura of happiness*

aural (say or -əl) *adj* to do with the ear

or hearing **aurally** *adv* ◊ Do not confuse this word with *oral*, which has a different meaning.

aureole (say aw-ri-**oh**-l), **aureola** (say aw-ri-**oh**-lə) *n* **1** a halo round the head of a figure in a painting, to indicate holiness **2** a corona round the sun or moon

au revoir (say oh rə-**vwar**) *interjection* goodbye for the moment

auricle (say **or** -i-kəl) *n* **1** the part of the ear that is outside the head **2** an atrium of the heart

aurora (say aw-**ror** -ə) *n* bands of coloured light appearing in the sky at night and probably caused by electrical radiation from the north and south magnetic poles **aurora australis** *n* the southern lights, an aurora in the southern hemisphere **aurora borealis** *n* the northern lights, an aurora in the northern hemisphere

auspices (say **aw**-spis-iz) *pl n* patronage or protection ♦ *under the auspices of the Red Cross*

auspicious (say aw-**spish**-əs) *adj* showing signs that indicate success **auspiciously** *adv*

austere (say aw-**steer**) *adj* **1** severe in manner or appearance **2** simple and lacking any comforts **austerely** *adv* **austerity** *n*

authentic *adj* genuine, known to be true ♦ *an authentic signature* **authentically** *adv* **authenticate** *v* **authentication** *n* **authenticator** *n* **authenticity** *n*

author *n* **1** the writer of a book, article, or report **2** someone who develops a plan or policy **authoress** *n* **authorship** *n*

authority *n* *pl* **authorities 1** the power or right to give orders and make people obey **2** the power to take action **3** a person or group having power or authority **4** a person or book that can provide reliable information **authoritarian** *adj* **authoritarianism** *n* **authoritative** *adj* **authoritatively** *adv* **authorize** *v* **authorization** *n*

autistic (say aw-**tist**-ik) *adj* having a disability that means someone has difficulty responding to their surroundings or communicating with other people **autism** *n*

auto- *prefix* (changing to **aut-** before

a vowel) **1** yourself, your own (as in *autobiography*) **2** by yourself or itself, automatic (as in *automobile*)

autobahn (say **aw**-tə-bahn) *n* a German, Austrian, or Swiss motorway

autobiography *n* *pl* **autobiographies** the story of a person's life written by that person **autobiographical** *adj*

autocracy (say aw-**tok**-rə-si) *n* government by one person with total power **autocrat** *n* **autocratic** *adj* **autocratically** *adv*

autocross *n* the sport of motor racing over rough country and unmade roads

Autocue *n* *trademark* a device which displays a text for a television presenter to read on air

autofocus *n* a device in a camera that sets the correct focus automatically

autograph *n* **1** the signature of a famous person **2** a literary or musical manuscript written in the author's or composer's own handwriting **3** a document signed by its author **autograph** *v* to write a signature on something, especially a book or document

automated *adj* controlled or operated by automation ♦ *The process is fully automated.*

automatic *adj* **1** (said about a machine or device) working by itself without direct human control **2** (said about a gun) firing repeatedly until pressure on the trigger is released **3** done without thought or from habit **automatic** *n* **1** an automatic machine or device **2** a motor vehicle with an automatic gearbox **automatically** *adv* **automatic pilot** *n* a device in an aircraft to keep it on its course

automation *n* the use of automatic equipment in factories and other processes

automaton (say aw-**tom**-ə-tən) *n* **1** a mechanical device made in imitation of a human being, a robot **2** someone who acts mechanically or without thinking

automobile (say **aw**-təm-ə-beel) *n N. Am* a motor car **automotive** *adj*

autonomy (say aw-**tonn**-ə-mi) *n* **1** independence or self-government **2** the freedom to act as you want to **autonomous** *adj*

autopilot *n* an automatic pilot in an aircraft

autopsy (say **aw**-top-si) *n* *pl* **autopsies** a

post-mortem examination of a body to find out the cause of death

autostrada (say **aw**-tə-strah-də) *n pl* **autostradas** an Italian motorway

autumn *n* the season between summer and winter **autumnal** *adj* **autumnally** *adv*

auxiliary (say awg-**zil**-yər-i) *adj* providing extra help or support **auxiliary** *n* a helper **auxiliaries** *pl n* foreign or allied troops used by a country in wartime

avail *v* to be of help or advantage ♦ *Nothing availed against the storm.* **avail** *n* **of** or **to no avail** having no use or benefit

available *adj* ready to be obtained or used **availability** *n*

avalanche (say av-ə-lahnsh) *n* 1 a mass of snow or rock falling rapidly down a mountainside 2 a large number of things coming at once ♦ *We've had an avalanche of letters.*

avant-garde (say av-ahn gard) *adj* using a new style or approach, especially in art or literature **avant-garde** *n* an avant-garde group, or set of ideas

avarice (say av-er-iss) *n* greed for wealth or gain **avaricious** *adj* **avariciously** *adv*

avatar (say **av**-ə-tar) *n* (in Hinduism) the appearance on earth of a deity in human, animal, or superhuman form

Ave Maria (say **ah**-vay mə-**ree**-ə) *n* a prayer to the Virgin Mary in Catholic worship, a Hail Mary

avenge *v* to take vengeance for a wrong that someone has done **avenger** *n*

avenue *n* 1 a wide street or road, often one lined with trees 2 a way of achieving something or making progress ♦ *There are other avenues to fame.*

aver (say ə-**ver**) *v* **averred**, **averring** to state something definitely

average *n* 1 a number obtained by adding several quantities together and dividing the total by the number of quantities 2 the standard or level regarded as usual **average** *adj* 1 found by making an average 2 ordinary or usual ♦ *people of average intelligence* 3 not very good, mediocre **average** *v* 1 to have as an average ♦ *The car averaged 40 miles to the gallon.* 2 to calculate the average of several quantities

averse (say ə-**verss**) *adj* opposed to doing something ♦ *They seem averse to hard work.* **aversion** *n*

avert (say ə-**vert**) *v* 1 to turn something away ♦ *People averted their eyes.* 2 to prevent something bad or unwelcome ♦ *They managed to avert a disaster.*

Avesta (say ə-**vest**-ə) *n* the sacred writings of Zoroastrianism

aviary (say **ay**-vi-er-i) *n pl* **aviaries** a large enclosure or building for keeping birds

aviation (say ay-vi-**ay**-shən) *n* the practice or business of flying aircraft **aviator** *n*

avid (say **av**-id) *adj* eager or greedy **avidity** *n* **avidly** *adv*

avocado (say av-ə-**kah**-doh) *n pl* **avocados** a pear-shaped tropical fruit with a rough skin and thick smooth flesh

avoid *v* 1 to keep yourself away from something or someone dangerous or undesirable 2 to refrain from doing something ♦ *Try to avoid making them angry.* **avoidable** *adj* **avoidance** *n*

avoirdupois (say av-er-dew-**poiz**) *n* a system of weights based on the pound of 16 ounces or 7,000 grains

avow *v formal* to admit something or declare it openly **avowal** *n* **avowedly** *adv*

avuncular (say ə-**vunk**-yoo-ler) *adj* kind and friendly towards someone younger, like an uncle

await *v* 1 to wait for something ♦ *I await your reply.* 2 to be about to happen to someone ♦ *A surprise awaited us.*

awake *v* **awoke**, **awoken** 1 to wake up, to stop sleeping 2 to become active 3 to rouse someone from sleep **awake** *adj* 1 not yet asleep, or no longer asleep 2 alert or aware

awaken *v* 1 to wake up 2 to rouse someone from sleep 3 to make someone experience a feeling ♦ *The sound awakened fears in all of them.* **awakening** *n*

award *v* to give someone an amount of money, a prize, or a penalty by an official decision **award** *n* something given in this way, such as a sum of money or a prize

aware *adj* knowing or realizing something **awareness** *n*

awash *adj* washed over by water or waves

away *adv* 1 to or at a distance, not at

the usual place **2** out of existence ♦ *The water had boiled away.* **3** constantly or continuously ♦ *We worked away at it.*

away *adj* (said about a sports event) played at the opponent's ground ♦ *an away match*

awayday *n* a day away from normal work

awe *n* a mixed feeling of respect and fear or wonder **awe** *v* to fill someone with awe **awesome** *adj* inspiring awe **awestricken** *adj* filled with awe or wonder

awful *adj* **1** very bad or unpleasant ♦ *There has been an awful accident.* **2** *informal* extreme, very great ♦ *This is an awful nuisance.* **awfully** *adv*

awhile *adv* for a short time

awkward *adj* **1** difficult to do or deal with **2** (said about a person) clumsy **3** inconvenient or unsuitable ♦ *They arrived at a very awkward time.* **4** slightly embarrassed ♦ *I feel awkward about it.* **awkwardly** *adv* **awkwardness** *n*

awl *n* a small pointed tool for making holes in leather or wood

awning *n* a sheet of canvas or plastic stretched over a frame and fixed over a doorway or shop window

awry (say ə-**riy**) *adv* **1** twisted towards one side **2** not as you intended, amiss ♦ *Our plans have gone awry.* **awry** *adj* crooked or wrong

axe *n* **1** a large chopping tool with a heavy blade **2** *informal* dismissal or redundancy ♦ *Thirty staff are facing the axe.* **axe** *v* to dismiss people or end a project suddenly

axillary (say **aks**-il-er-i) *adj* **1** in the armpit **2** *Botany* growing from an axil

axiom (say **aks**-i-əm) *n* a truth or principle that is obviously true and that everyone accepts **axiomatic** *adj*

axis *n* *pl* **axes** **1** an imaginary line through the centre of an object, round which the object rotates **2** a line about which a regular figure is symmetrically arranged **3** a reference line for measuring coordinates **axial** *adj* **axially** *adv* **the Axis** the alliance between Germany and Italy in the Second World War

axle *n* a bar or rod on which a wheel or set of wheels turns

ayatollah (say iy-ə-**tol**-ə) *n* a Shiite Muslim religious leader in Iran

aye (say iy) *adv* old or dialect use yes **aye** *n* a vote in favour of a proposal **the ayes have it** those voting in favour are in a majority

azalea (say ə-**zay**-liə) *n* a flowering shrub with brightly coloured flowers

azimuth (say **az**-i-məth) *n* **1** an arc of the sky from the zenith to the horizon **2** the angle between this arc and the meridian **3** the angle or direction of a compass bearing

Aztec *n* **1** a member of an Indian people of Mexico before the Spanish conquest of the 16th century **2** the language of this people **Aztec** *adj* relating to the Aztecs or their language

azure (say **az**-yoor) *n* a bright sky blue **azure** *adj* having this colour

Bb

B the second letter of the English alphabet

b. & b. *abbr* bed and breakfast

BA *abbr* Bachelor of Arts

baa *n* the cry of a sheep or lamb

babble *v* **1** to talk quickly without making sense **2** to make a continuous murmuring sound ♦ *a babbling brook* **babble** *n* babbling talk or sound

babe *n* **1** a baby **2** *informal* an attractive young woman

babel (say **bay**-bəl) *n* a confused noise made by a lot of people talking at the same time

baboon *n* a large African or Asian monkey with a long snout and large teeth

baby *n* *pl* **babies** **1** a very young child or animal **2** a timid or childish person **3** (used before a noun) small of its kind ♦ *a baby helicopter* **baby** *v* **babies, babied, babying** to treat someone like a baby, to pamper them **babyhood** *n* **babyish** *adj* **babysit** *v* to look after a child in its home while its parents are out **babysitter** *n* a person who looks after a child in its home while its parents are out

bachelor *n* a man who has not married

Bachelor n a person who has taken a first degree at a university or college ♦ *Bachelor of Arts.*

back¹ n 1 the part or surface of something that is furthest from the front 2 the rear surface of the human body from the shoulders to the buttocks 3 the corresponding part of an animal's body 4 the part of a chair, etc. that your back rests against when you sit down 5 the part of a piece of clothing that covers the back 6 a defending player near the goal in football, hockey, rugby, etc. **back** adj 1 situated at or near the back ♦ *the back teeth;* ♦ *back streets* 2 to do with your back ♦ *back pain* 3 to do with a time in the past ♦ *back pay* **back** adv 1 at or towards the back, away from the front or centre 2 to the place you have come from ♦ *Go back home.* 3 in or to an earlier time or position ♦ *I'll be back at six.* ♦ *Put the clocks back one hour.* 4 in return or in reply ♦ *Can you ring me back?*

backbencher n a Member of Parliament who does not hold an important position **backbiting** n saying unkind or nasty things about a person who is not present **backbone** n 1 the column of small bones down the centre of the back, the spine 2 the people who give most support to an organization or institution ♦ *They are the backbone of the choral society.* 3 strength of character, courage **backfire** v 1 (said about a car or its engine) to make a loud noise because of an explosion in the exhaust pipe 2 (said about a plan or action) to go wrong and produce an undesired effect on the people who originated it **backgammon** n a game played with draughts and dice on a double board marked with 24 triangular points **background** n 1 the back part of a scene or picture, the setting for the main objects or people 2 a person's family, upbringing, education, experience, etc. ♦ *She comes from a farming background.* 3 the circumstances and events surrounding and influencing something ♦ *Let me give you the background to this case.* **background** adj (said about sounds, music, etc.) not very noticeable, used as an accompaniment to a play or film,

etc. **backhander** n a bribe **backing** n 1 support for something ♦ *This campaign has the backing of the major political parties.* 2 a musical accompaniment to a pop singer 3 material used to line the back of something **backlash** n a strong and hostile reaction by a lot of people to some event or development **backless** adj 1 without a back 2 (said about a dress) cut low at the back **backlog** n an amount of work that should have been finished but is still waiting to be dealt with **back-up** adj kept in reserve in case it is needed **back-up** n in computing, a spare copy of a file, disk, etc. made to be stored in safety separately from the original **backward** adj 1 directed behind you or towards the back ♦ *a backward glance* 2 having made less than normal progress 3 diffident, lacking confidence ♦ *She's not backward in expressing herself in class.* 4 slow at learning or developing **backward** adv backwards, away from the front **backwardness** n **backwards** adv 1 away from the front, towards the back 2 with the back facing forwards 3 in reverse order **backpack** n 1 a rucksack 2 a package of equipment carried on the back **back seat** n a seat at the back, especially in a car **back-seat driver** n 1 a passenger in a car who keeps giving advice to the driver in an annoying way 2 a person who has no responsibility but is eager to give orders to someone who has **backside** n the buttocks **backspace** v to move a computer cursor one space back **backspace** n the key on a computer keyboard used to move the cursor backwards **backstage** adv behind the stage of a theatre, in the wings or dressing-rooms **backstage** adj to do with this area in a theatre **backtrack** v 1 to go back the same way that you came 2 to reverse your previous position or opinion **backwoods** n 1 remote uncleared forest, as in North America 2 a remote or backward area **backwoodsman** n **backyard** n a yard at the back of a house **to take a back seat** to allow someone else to be in charge

back² v 1 to go or move backwards ♦ *I backed slowly out of the room.* 2 to make something move backwards ♦ *She backed the car into* the garage. **3** to give your support or help to someone **4** to give financial support to something ♦ *He is backing the play.* **5** to put a bet on a horse, team, etc. ♦ *Did any of you back the winner?* **6** to cover the back of something ♦ *The rug is backed with canvas.* **7** (said about the wind) to change gradually in an anticlockwise direction (Compare *veer*) **backer** *n*

bacon *n* salted or smoked meat from the back or sides of a pig

bad *adj* **worse, worst 1** of poor quality or a low standard ♦ *The roads are bad round here.* **2** unpleasant or upsetting ♦ *I have some bad news.* **3** serious or severe ♦ *a bad accident* **4** wicked or evil **5** guilty or ashamed ♦ *I feel bad about forgetting to invite you.* **6** unhealthy or harmful ♦ *Too much cholesterol is bad for you.* **7** in ill health, diseased ♦ *bad teeth* **8** decayed or rotten ♦ *This meat has gone bad.* **9** (said about a debt) not able to be repaid **baddy** *n pl* **baddies** a villain in a film, book, etc. **badly** *adv* **badness** *n* **bad blood** *n* ill feeling or enmity **bad form** *n* behaviour that offends against social conventions **bad luck** *n* **1** misfortune **2** an expression of real or mock sympathy at someone's misfortune **bad-tempered** *adj* having or showing bad temper

bade past tense of *bid²*

badge *n* a piece of metal, cloth, plastic, etc. with a design on it that you wear

badger *n* an animal of the weasel family that burrows in the ground and has a black and white head **badger** *v* to keep asking someone to do something, to pester them

badminton *n* a game in which players use rackets to hit a light object called a shuttlecock across a high net

baffle *v* to puzzle or bewilder someone **baffle** *n* a screen placed in order to block or control the passage of sound, light, or fluid **bafflement** *n*

bag *n* **1** a container made of flexible material with an opening at the top, used for holding or carrying things **2** the contents of a bag, or the amount it contains **3** the amount of game shot by a hunter **bag** *v* **bagged, bagging 1** to put something into a bag

or bags **2** to kill or catch a bird or animal ♦ *They each bagged a pheasant.* **3** *informal* to get something or stake a claim to it before anyone else can **bagful** *n pl* **bagfuls bags** *pl n* **1** folds of loose skin under the eyes **2** *informal* plenty ♦ *There's bags of room upstairs.*

bagel (say **bay**-gəl) *n* a ring-shaped bread roll

baggage *n* all the suitcases and bags you take on a journey

baggy *adj* **baggier, baggiest** (said about clothes) hanging in loose folds **baggily** *adv* **bagginess** *n*

bagpipe, bagpipes *n* a musical instrument with air stored in a bag and pressed out through pipes

Baha'i (say bah-hah-i) *n* **1** a religion founded in Persia in the 19th century by Baha'ullah (1817-92) and his son, whose quest is for world peace and the unification of mankind **2** a follower of this religion **Baha'ism** *n*

bail¹ *n* **1** money that is paid or promised as a guarantee that a person accused of a crime will return to stand trial, if he or she is released temporarily **2** permission for a person's release if this money is paid or promised **bail** *v* to provide bail for a person

bail² *v* to scoop water out of a boat

bailiff *n* **1** a law officer who helps a sheriff by serving writs and performing arrests **2** an official who takes people's property when they owe money

Bairam (say biy-**rahm**) *n* either of two annual Muslim festivals, **Lesser Bairam** (which follows Ramadan) in the tenth month and **Greater Bairam** in the twelfth month of the Islamic year

bairn *n* Scottish a child

Baisakhi (say **biy**-sa-ki) *n* a major Sikh festival, commemorating the formation of the Khalsa in 1699

bait *n* **1** food that is placed on a hook or in a trap to help catch fish or animals **2** something that is meant to tempt or entice someone **bait** *v* **1** to place bait on or in something ♦ *You will need to bait the trap.* **2** to torment a person or animal by jeering at them

bake v **1** to cook food by dry heat, usually in an oven **2** to make something hard by heating it ♦ *The clay pots are now baked in a kiln.* **3** *informal* to become extremely hot ♦ *I'm baking in this heat!* **baker** n a person who bakes and sells bread **bakery** n pl **bakeries** a place where bread is baked for sale **baking** adj (said about weather, etc.) extremely hot **baker's dozen** n thirteen

bakelite (say bay-kə-liyt) n a kind of plastic

Balaclava (say bal-ə-klah-və) n a woollen hood covering the head and neck and part of the face

balance n **1** a steady position, with the weight or amount evenly distributed **2** your ability to keep steady and not fall over ♦ *She has learned how to keep her balance on a bicycle.* **3** the amount of one thing in excess of another ♦ *The balance of the evidence suggests she is guilty.* **4** a device for weighing things, with two scales or pans hanging from a crossbar **5** the difference between money paid into an account and money taken out of it **6** the money that remains to be paid after something has been partly paid for **balance** v **1** to keep steady and not fall over ♦ *Can you balance an egg on its end?* **2** to consider something by comparing two things; to compare the value of one thing with another **3** to be or put or keep something in a state of balance ♦ *a balanced diet* **4** to compare the debits and credits of an account and make the entry needed to make these equal **5** to have the debits and credits of an account equal ♦ *The cash account doesn't balance.*

balcony (say bal-kəni) n pl **balconies 1** a platform with a rail or parapet, sticking out from an outside wall of a building **2** an upper floor of seats in a cinema or above the dress circle in a theatre **balconied** adj

bald adj **1** having little or no hair on the top of the head **2** (said about animals) lacking the usual hair or feathers of the species **3** (said about tyres) with the tread worn away **4** bare, without details ♦ *a bald statement* **balding** adj **baldly** adv **baldness** n

balderdash n nonsense

bale[1] n a large bundle of hay, straw, paper, etc. tied up tightly **bale** v to make something into a bale or bales **baler** n

bale[2] v **to bale out** to make a parachute descent from an aircraft in an emergency

baleful adj menacing or harmful ♦ *a baleful influence* **balefully** adv

balk (say bawlk) v, n another spelling of **baulk**

ball[1] n **1** a solid or hollow sphere, especially one used in games **2** material that has been gathered or wound into a round mass ♦ *a ball of string* **3** a single delivery of the ball by the bowler in cricket or by the pitcher in baseball **ball** v to squeeze or wind something so that it forms into a ball **ball bearing** n **1** a bearing using small steel balls **2** one of these balls **ballcock** n a device with a floating ball that controls the water level in a cistern **ballpark** n N. Am a baseball ground

ball[2] n a formal party where people dance **ballroom** n a large room where dances are held

ballad n **1** a song or poem that tells a story **2** a slow romantic pop song

ballast (say bal-əst) n **1** heavy material placed in a ship's hold to make it more stable **2** gravel or coarse stone used to form the bed of a railway or road

ballet (say bal-ay) n **1** a form of dancing and mime to music, usually telling a story **2** a performance of this **ballerina** n a female ballet dancer

ballistic (say bə-lis-tik) adj to do with objects that are fired through the air (*projectiles*) such as bullets and missiles **ballistics** pl n the scientific study of objects that are fired through the air (*projectiles*) and of firearms **ballistic missile** n a missile that is initially powered and guided and then falls under gravity on to its target

balloon n **1** a small inflatable rubber pouch with a neck, used as a child's toy or a decoration **2** a large usually round bag inflated with hot air or light gases to make it rise in the air, often carrying a basket in which passengers may ride **3** a balloon-shaped line enclosing the words or thoughts of a character in a comic strip or cartoon **balloon** v **1** to swell like a balloon

2 to kick or hit a ball or other object high in the air **3** to travel by balloon **balloonist** n a person who travels by balloon

ballot n **1** a secret method of voting, usually by making a mark on a piece of paper **2** a piece of paper on which a vote is made **3** the number of such votes recorded **ballot** v **balloted**, **balloting** to invite and arrange for people to vote for something by ballot ♦ *The union is to ballot its members on this issue.* **ballot box** n a sealed container for ballot papers **ballot paper** n a paper used in voting by ballot, usually having the names of candidates, etc. printed on it

balm (say bahm) n **1** a sweet-scented ointment used to soothe or heal the skin **2** something that soothes or heals you **balmy** adj **balmier**, **balmiest**

balti (say **bawl**-ti) n a type of Pakistani curry, cooked in a bowl-shaped pan

bamboo (say bam-**boo**) n a giant tropical grass with hollow stems, used for making furniture

bamboozle v informal to mystify or trick someone

ban v **banned**, **banning** to forbid something officially ♦ *She is banned from driving for a year.* **ban** n an order that bans something ♦ *a ban on exporting beef*

banal (say bə-**nahl**) adj so familiar or obvious that it is uninteresting ♦ *a banal remark* **banality** n

banana n **1** a long curved fruit with a yellow or green skin and whitish flesh **2** the tropical tree which bears this fruit

band¹ n **1** a narrow strip or loop of something ♦ *a rubber band* ♦ *a band of cloud* **2** a range of values, wavelengths, etc. within a series **band** v to put a band on or round something

band² n **1** a small group of musicians who play pop, rock, or jazz music **2** a group of musicians who play brass, wind, or percussion instruments **3** an organized group of people doing something together **band** v to join together in an organized group ♦ *We all banded together to buy her a present.* **bandmaster** n the conductor of a brass band **bandstand** n a covered platform for a musical band to play outdoors, usually in a park

bandage n a strip of material for binding up a wound **bandage** v to bind up a wound with a bandage

bandanna (say ban-**dan**-ə) n a large coloured handkerchief or neckerchief

bandeau (say **ban**-doh) n pl **bandeaux** (say **ban**-doh) a strip of material worn round the head to hold the hair in place

bandit n a member of a gang of robbers who attack travellers **banditry** n

bandwagon n **to jump on the bandwagon** to seek to join something that has suddenly become successful or popular

bandwidth n a range of frequencies used to transmit radio or television signals

bandy¹ v **bandies**, **bandied**, **bandying** to pass a name, story, etc. from one person to another ♦ *The story has been bandied about for weeks.*

bandy² adj **bandier**, **bandiest** (said about legs) curving apart at the knees **bandiness** n

bane n a cause of trouble, worry, or annoyance ♦ *Traffic jams are the bane of my life!*

bang n **1** a sudden loud noise like that of an explosion **2** a sharp blow or knock ♦ *a nasty bang on the head* **bang** v **1** to shut or hit something noisily ♦ *Don't bang the door!* **2** to hit something sharply against something else, especially by accident ♦ *I banged my head on the door frame.* **3** to make a sudden loud noise like an explosion **bang** adv exactly ♦ *We arrived bang on time.* **banger** n

bangle n a bracelet of rigid material

banish v **1** to send someone away from a country as a punishment **2** to dismiss something from your mind ♦ *You must banish all thoughts of failure.* **banishment** n

banister n the uprights and handrail at the side of a staircase

banjo (say **ban**-joh) n pl **banjos** a stringed instrument rather like a guitar with a round body

bank¹ n **1** a financial organization that looks after people's money, pays money out on a customer's order, makes loans, etc. **2** a place for storing a reserve supply of something ♦ *a blood bank* **3** the store of money used in some board games **bank** *v* **1** to put money into a bank **2** to have a bank account ♦ *Where do you bank?* **banker** *n* **banking** *n* the business of running a bank **bankrupt** *adj* declared by a law court to be unable to pay your debts **bankrupt** *n* someone who has been declared bankrupt **bankrupt** *v* to make someone bankrupt **bankruptcy** *n* **bank holiday** *n* a day on which banks are officially closed, usually kept as a public holiday **banknote** *n* a piece of paper money issued by a bank **to bank on** to base your hopes on something ♦ *We are banking on your support.*

bank² *n* **1** the land at the side of a river or canal **2** a raised mass of earth, sand, etc. **3** a long mass of cloud, snow, or some other soft substance **4** a set of lights, switches, etc. arranged in a line **bank** *v* **1** to build or form a bank **2** to tilt sideways while making a turn ♦ *The plane banked as it prepared to land.* **3** to cover a fire with coal so that it keeps burning slowly

banner *n* **1** a strip of cloth with an emblem or slogan on it, hung up or carried in a crossbar or between two poles in a procession, etc. **2** a flag

banns *pl n* a public announcement in a Christian church of a forthcoming marriage between two named people

banquet *n* an elaborate formal meal for a lot of people **banquet** *v* **banqueted**, **banqueting** to give or take part in a banquet

banter *n* good-humoured teasing **banter** *v* to joke in a good-humoured way

bap *n* a soft flat bread roll

baptism *n* the Christian ceremony in which a person is sprinkled with or immersed in water to symbolize purification and admission to the Christian Church **baptismal** *adj* **baptistery** *n* *pl* **baptisteries 1** the part of a church used for baptism **2** a tank used in a Baptist chapel for baptism by immersion **baptize** *v* to perform baptism on someone

Baptist *n* a member of a Protestant Christian Church believing that baptism should be by immersion and performed at an age when the person is old enough to affirm his or her own faith before witnesses

bar¹ *n* **1** a long piece of something hard, especially metal ♦ *the bars of a cage* **2** a block of something ♦ *a bar of soap* ♦ *a chocolate bar* **3** a narrow strip or band ♦ *bars of colour* **4** a barrier or obstacle ♦ *a bar to promotion* **5** one of the small equal units into which a piece of music is divided, shown on a score by vertical lines across the stave ♦ *three beats to the bar* **6** a room or counter where alcoholic drinks are served **7** a place where drinks and snacks are served across a counter ♦ *a coffee bar* **8** a small shop or stall selling a single type of commodity or service **9** (**the Bar**) barristers thought of collectively, or the profession of being a barrister **10** a sandbank **11** a strip of silver given as an additional award of the same honour ♦ *DSO and bar.* **bar** *v* **barred**, **barring 1** to fasten something with a bar or bars ♦ *The door was barred.* **2** to forbid someone from doing something or going somewhere ♦ *He was barred from the club for a month.* **3** to block or obstruct something ♦ *Two large men barred the way.* **bar** *prep* except for ♦ *It's all over bar the shouting.* **barring** *prep* except for; if not for ♦ *We should arrive on time, barring accidents.*

bar chart *n* a graph on which quantities are represented by bars of equal width but varying height **bar code** *n* a pattern of black stripes printed on goods, library books, etc. containing information that can be read by a computer **barmaid** *n* a woman who serves behind a bar, especially in a pub **barman** *n* *pl* **barmen** a man who serves behind a bar, especially in a pub **bartender** *n* a barman or barmaid

bar² *n* a unit of pressure used in meteorology, equivalent to 100,000 newtons per square metre

barb *n* **1** the backward-pointing part of an arrow, fish hook, etc. that is designed to make it difficult to pull out **2** a deliberately hurtful remark **3** a small pointed projecting part or filament **barbed** *adj* **barbed wire** *n* wire with short sharp spikes at intervals, used to make fences

barbarian *n* **1** in ancient times, a member

of a people not belonging to the Greek, Roman, or Christian civilizations **2** an uncivilized or brutal person **barbaric** adj extremely cruel or brutal **barbarically** adv **barbarism** n **1** an uncivilized condition or practice **2** extreme cruelty or brutality **barbarity** n pl **barbarities** savage cruelty, or a savagely cruel act **barbarous** adj uncivilized or cruel **barbarously** adv

barbecue (say bar-bi-kew) n **barbecues 1** a metal frame for grilling food over a charcoal fire outdoors **2** an outdoor party at which food is cooked in this way **barbecue** v **barbecued**, **barbecuing** to cook food on a barbecue

barber n a men's hairdresser **barbershop** n

barbican n an outer defence of a castle or city, especially a double tower over a gate or bridge

barcarole (say bar-kə-**rol** or -**rohl**) n **1** a song traditionally sung by Venetian gondoliers **2** a piece of music with a steady lilting rhythm

bard n literary a poet **bardic** adj

bare adj **1** not covered by clothes ♦ She walked home in her bare feet. **2** without the usual or natural covering ♦ bare floorboards **3** plain, without details ♦ the bare facts **4** empty of stores ♦ The cupboard was bare. **5** only just enough ♦ a bare majority **bare** v to uncover or reveal something ♦ The dog bared its teeth in a snarl. **barely** adv **1** scarcely, only just ♦ I barely knew him. **2** plainly or scantily ♦ The room was barely furnished. **bareness** n **bareback** adj, adv on a horse without a saddle **barefaced** adj shameless or undisguised ♦ That's a barefaced lie. **barefoot** adj, adv wearing nothing on the feet **bareheaded** adj not wearing a hat

bargain n **1** an agreement between two or more people about what each one will do for the other **2** something that you buy cheaply **bargain** v to discuss the terms of an agreement

barge n a large flat-bottomed boat used for carrying goods on canals or rivers **barge** v to push or knock against someone roughly or clumsily

baritone n **1** a male singing voice between tenor and bass **2** a singer with such a voice

bark[1] n the sharp harsh sound made by a dog, fox, or seal **bark** v **1** (said about a dog, fox, or seal) to give a bark **2** to speak in a sharp commanding voice ♦ The sergeant barked out his orders.

bark[2] n the outer layer of a tree's trunk and branches **bark** v **1** to peel bark from a tree **2** to scrape the skin off part of your body accidentally ♦ I barked my shin on the gate.

barley n a kind of cereal plant, used to make malt

bar mitzvah (say **mits**-və) n the ceremony at which a Jewish boy who has reached the age of 13 takes on the responsibilities of an adult under Jewish law

barmy adj **barmier**, **barmiest** informal crazy or foolish

barn n a large farm building used for storing grain, hay, etc. or for housing livestock **barn dance** n **1** an informal gathering for country dancing **2** a kind of country dance **barn owl** n an owl with a heart-shaped face, often breeding and roosting in farm buildings **barnyard** n a yard beside a barn

barnacle n a kind of shellfish that attaches itself to underwater surfaces, such as rocks and the bottoms of ships

barometer (say bə-**rom**-it-er) n **1** an instrument that measures atmospheric pressure, used for forecasting the weather **2** something that indicates change ♦ The housing market is a barometer of the economy. **barometric** adj

baron n **1** a member of the lowest rank of the British nobility **2** in the Middle Ages, a person who held lands or property from the king **3** a powerful owner of an industry or business ♦ a press baron **baroness** n a female baron or a baron's wife **baronet** n a British nobleman with a knighthood inherited from his father **baronetcy** n **baronial** adj to do with or suitable for a baron ♦ a grand baronial hall **barony** n pl **baronies** the rank or lands of a baron

baroque (say bə-**rok**) adj to do with an ornate style of European architecture, art, and music of the 17th and 18th centuries **baroque** n the baroque style or period

barrack v to jeer at someone while they are

performing or speaking

barracks *n* a large building or group of buildings for soldiers to live in

barrage (say **ba-rahzh**) *n* **1** heavy continuous gunfire **2** a large number of questions, complaints, or criticisms all coming at the same time **3** an artificial barrier across a river, used especially to prevent flooding

barre *n* a horizontal bar that ballet dancers use to steady themselves while exercising

barrel *n* **1** a large round container with flat ends, used for liquids **2** a metal tube of a gun, through which the shot is fired **3** a measure of mineral oil equal to about 192 litres (35 gallons or 42 US gallons) **barrel** *v* **barrelled, barrelling** to put something into barrels

barren *adj* **1** (said about land) not fertile enough to produce crops **2** (said about a plant or tree) not producing fruit or seeds **3** (said about a woman or female animal) not able to bear young **barrenness** *n*

barricade *n* a barrier, especially one that is put up hastily across a door or street **barricade** *v* to block a door or street with a barricade

barrier *n* **1** a fence or wall that prevents people or animals getting past **2** an obstacle that prevents people communicating, making progress, or understanding something **barrier reef** *n* a coral reef close to the shore but separated from it by a channel of deep water

barrister (say **ba-ris-ter**) *n* a lawyer entitled to represent clients in the higher courts

barrow[1] *n* **1** a wheelbarrow **2** a two-wheeled cart pulled or pushed by hand

barrow[2] *n* a mound of earth built over a prehistoric grave

barter *v* to trade by exchanging goods or services for other goods or services, not for money **barter** *n* trading by exchanging goods and services, not by buying and selling ◊ This word does not mean 'to bargain'.

basal (say **bay-səl**) *adj* forming or belonging to the base or the lowest level of something

base[1] *n* **1** the lowest part of something, the part on which it stands or is supported **2** a starting point **3** the main place where someone works or stays **4** a place from which an expedition, military operation, etc. is directed and where its supplies are stored **5** a substance which can combine with an acid to form a salt **6** the number on which a system of counting and calculation is based. 10 is the base of the decimal system and 2 is the base of the binary system **7** a substance into which other things are mixed ♦ *Some paints have an oil base.* **8** a cream or liquid applied to the skin as a foundation for make-up **9** each of the four corners that must be reached by a runner in baseball **base** *v* **1** to use one thing as the foundation for something else ♦ *The film is based on a true incident.* **2** to put someone somewhere as the main place where they work or stay ♦ *Where are you based now?* **baseless** *adj* without foundation in fact ♦ *baseless rumours* **basement** *n* the lowest storey of a building, below ground level **baseball** *n* a team game in which runs are scored by hitting a ball and running round a series of four bases **base jump** *n* a parachute jump from a fixed point such as the top of a high building **baseline** *n* **1** a line used as a base or starting point **2** the line at each end of a tennis court **base metal** *n* a common metal that is not considered precious **base rate** *n* the rate of interest that a bank uses as a basis for fixing the rates it charges to borrowers or pays to investors

base[2] *adj* **1** dishonourable or despicable ♦ *base motives* **2** not made of precious metal ♦ *base coins* **basely** *adv* **baseness** *n*

bash *v informal* **1** to strike someone or something violently ♦ *We bashed into the back of another car.* **2** to criticize someone severely **bash** *n* **1** a violent blow or knock **2** a party

bashful *adj* shy and easily embarrassed **bashfully** *adv* **bashfulness** *n*

basic *adj* **1** forming a base or starting point ♦ *basic principles* **2** being the minimum that is needed or offered, with no extras ♦ *basic rates of pay* **basically** *adv* at the simplest or most fundamental level **basics** *pl n* the essential facts or principles of a subject or skill

basil n a sweet-smelling herb

basin n **1** a large bowl for holding liquids or soft substances or for mixing food **2** a washbasin **3** the area from which water drains into a river ♦ *the Amazon basin* **4** a sheltered area of water for mooring boats ♦ *a yacht basin* **basinful** n **basinfuls**

basis n pl **bases 1** a foundation or support for an idea, belief, etc. **2** the way that something is arranged or organized ♦ *You will be paid on a weekly basis.*

bask v **1** to sit or lie comfortably warming yourself in the sun **2** to enjoy someone's approval

basket n **1** a container for holding or carrying things, made of strips of flexible material or wire woven together **2** the hoop through which players try to throw the ball in basketball, or a point scored in this way **3** an assorted set of things ♦ *a basket of currencies* **basketry** n **basketball** n **1** a game in which goals are scored by throwing a ball through high nets at each end of the court **2** the ball used in this game **basketwork** n **1** material woven in the style of a basket **2** the art of making this

basmati (say baz-**mahh**-ti) n a kind of long-grain Indian rice

Basque (say bahsk) n **1** a member of a people living in the western Pyrenees **2** their language

bass¹ (say bayss) n **1** the lowest male singing voice, or a singer with such a voice **2** the lowest-pitched member of a group of similar musical instruments **3** a bass guitar or double bass **bass** adj of the lowest pitch in music **bassist** n

bass² (say bas) n pl **bass** an edible fish of the perch family

bassoon (say bə-**soon**) n a woodwind instrument with a deep tone **bassoonist** n

bastard n **1** an illegitimate child **2** *informal* an unpleasant or difficult person or thing **bastard** adj *old use* **1** of illegitimate birth **2** no longer in its pure or original form **bastardy** n

baste (say bayst) v to moisten meat with fat or juices during cooking

bastion (say **bas**-ti-ən) n **1** a projecting part of a fortification **2** something that protects a belief or way of life ♦ *a bastion of democracy*

bat¹ n **1** a shaped piece of wood used to hit the ball in games such as cricket and baseball **2** a turn at batting ♦ *Have you had a bat yet?* **bat** v **batted**, **batting 1** (in cricket) to have a turn at hitting the ball with a bat **2** to hit something with a bat or as if with a bat **batsman** n pl **batsmen** a player who is batting in cricket

bat² n a flying nocturnal mammal with membranous wings

bat³ v **batted**, **batting** to flutter ♦ *She batted her eyelashes at him.*

batch n **1** a number of people or things dealt with or produced at one time **2** *ICT* a group of records processed as a single unit **batch** v **1** to arrange things in sets or groups **2** *ICT* to group items for processing as a batch

bated (say **bay**-tid) adj **with bated breath** anxiously; hardly daring to speak

bath n **1** a large container for water, in which you sit to wash your whole body **2** washing the whole of your body while sitting in water ♦ *I need a bath.* **3** water for this ♦ *My bath is getting cold.* **4** a liquid in which something is immersed, or its container ♦ *an eye bath* **bath** v to wash someone or yourself in a bath **baths** pl n **1** a public swimming pool **2** a building with rooms where baths may be taken **bathe** v **1** to take a swim ♦ *We bathed in the sea every day.* **2** to wash something gently in liquid to clean or soothe it ♦ *You should immediately bathe your eyes in water.* **3** to make something bright all over ♦ *The fields were bathed in sunlight.* **bathe** n a swim **bather** n

bathroom n a room containing a bath

batholith (say **ba**-thə-lith) n a huge mass of igneous rock extending from near the earth's surface to an unknown depth, e.g. Dartmoor

batik (say **bat**-ik or ba-**teek**) n a method of printing coloured designs on textiles by waxing the parts that are not to be dyed, originating in Java

bat mitzvah (say **mits**-və) n pl **bat mitzvahs** a religious ceremony for Jewish girls aged 13, after which they take on the responsibilities of an adult under Jewish law

baton (say bat-ən) n 1 a thin stick used by the conductor of an orchestra or choir for beating time and giving instructions 2 a short stick passed from runner to runner in a relay race 3 a police officer's truncheon

battalion n an army unit made up of several companies and forming part of a regiment

batten n a strip of wood or metal that fastens or holds something in place **batten** v to fasten something down securely by fixing battens across it **to batten down the hatches** to prepare for a difficult time ahead

batter v 1 to hit someone or something hard and often ♦ *Our ship was being battered by the waves.* 2 to subject someone to repeated violence ♦ *battered wives* **batter** n a beaten mixture of flour, eggs, and milk, used for making pancakes or for coating food before frying it **battering ram** n 1 a heavy object rammed against a door to break it down 2 a heavy iron-headed beam formerly used in war to break down walls or gates

battery n pl **batteries** 1 a device consisting of one or more electric cells, used for storing and supplying electricity 2 a set of similar or connected units of equipment 3 a series of cages in which poultry or animals are kept close together ♦ *battery farming* 4 a group of heavy guns on land or on a warship 5 *Law* the crime of inflicting unlawful blows or a menacing touch on another person ♦ *assault and battery*

battle n 1 a fight between organized armed forces 2 a difficult contest or struggle ♦ *a battle of wits* **battle** v to fight or struggle with someone or to achieve something **battlements** pl n a wall built along the top of a castle wall (*parapet*) with gaps at intervals, originally for firing from **battleaxe** n 1 a heavy axe used as a weapon in ancient times 2 *informal* a formidable aggressive woman **battle cry** n a cry or slogan used in a battle or contest **battlefield** n a piece of ground on which a battle is or was fought

battleship n a heavily armed warship

batty adj **battier**, **battiest** *informal* crazy **battiness** n

bauble n 1 a bright, showy but cheap ornament 2 a decorative ball hung on a Christmas tree

baulk (say bawlk) v 1 to hesitate to do something difficult ♦ *She baulked at the idea of confronting him.* 2 (said about a horse) to stop and refuse to go on ♦ *The horse baulked at the fence.* 3 to prevent someone from doing or getting something **baulk** n 1 the area of a billiard table within which the cue balls are placed at the start of a game 2 a roughly squared timber beam

bawdy adj **bawdier**, **bawdiest** referring to sex in a humorous way **bawdily** adv **bawdiness** n

bawl v 1 to shout at someone 2 to cry noisily

bay[1] n a place where the coastline curves inwards

bay[2] n 1 an area or compartment used for a particular purpose ♦ *a parking bay* 2 a window area that sticks outwards from a wall

bay[3] v (said about a dog) to make a deep drawn-out cry, especially in pursuit of a hunted animal **bay** n the sound of baying

bayonet (say bay-ən-it) n a long blade that can be fixed to the muzzle of a rifle and used in hand-to-hand fighting **bayonet** v **bayoneted**, **bayoneting** to stab someone with a bayonet

bazaar n 1 a market place in a Middle-Eastern country 2 a sale of goods to raise money for charity

BBC *abbr* British Broadcasting Corporation

BC *abbr* 1 (in dates) before Christ 2 British Columbia

BCG *abbr* Bacillus Calmette-Guérin, an anti-tuberculosis vaccine

be v **am**, **are**, **is**, **was**, **were**, **been** 1 to exist or occupy a position ♦ *The shop is on the corner.* 2 to take place ♦ *The wedding is tomorrow.* 3 to have a certain nature, quality, or condition ♦ *This is a very scary film.* 4 to become ♦ *He wants to be a pilot.* **be** *auxiliary verb* used to form parts of other verbs ♦ *She is studying electronics.* ♦ *They were all killed.*

be- *prefix* used to form verbs (as in *befriend,*

belittle) or to strengthen their meaning (as in *begrudge*)

beach *n* the part of the shore at the edge of the sea, covered with sand or pebbles

beach *v* **1** to bring something on to a beach from out of the water **2** (said about a whale) to become stranded on a beach **beachcomber** *n* a person who searches beaches for articles of value **beachcombing** *n* **beachhead** *n* a fortified position established on a beach by an invading army

beacon *n* **1** a fire lit on the top of a hill as a signal **2** a light used as a signal or warning **3** a radio transmitter signalling the position of a ship, aircraft, etc.

bead *n* **1** a small shaped piece of glass, stone, plastic, etc. pierced for threading with others on a string or wire, or for sewing on to fabric **2** a drop of liquid on a surface ◆ *beads of sweat* **beaded** *adj* **beady** *adj* **beadier, beadiest, beadily** *adv* **beading** *n* **beads** *pl n* a necklace or rosary of beads

beagle *n* a small short-legged hound, sometimes used for hunting hares **beagling** *n* hunting hares with beagles

beak *n* **1** the hard horny part of a bird's mouth **2** a part of something that resembles a bird's beak, such as the projecting part at the prow of an ancient warship **3** *informal* a magistrate **beaked** *adj* **beaker** *n*

beam *n* **1** a long thick piece of squared timber or other solid material, supported at both ends and carrying the weight of part of a building or other structure **2** a ray or shaft of light or other radiation **3** a happy smile **4** a narrow length of wood used for balancing exercises in gymnastics **beam** *v* **1** to send out a beam of light or other radiation **2** to transmit a radio signal or broadcast **3** to smile happily

bean *n* **1** a kidney-shaped seed growing in long pods on certain plants. The seeds, and sometimes the pods, can be eaten as a vegetable **2** a plant bearing beans **3** a similar seed of coffee, cocoa, and certain other plants **beanbag** *n* **1** a small bag filled with dried beans and used for throwing

or carrying in games **2** a large cushion filled with plastic granules and used as a seat **beanpole** *n* a tall thin person **bean sprout** *n* a sprout of a bean seed that can be eaten either cooked or raw **beanstalk** *n* the stem of a bean plant

bear[1] *n* **1** a large heavy mammal with thick fur **2** a rough ill-mannered person

bear[2] *v* **bore, borne 1** to carry or support something ◆ *They arrived bearing gifts.* ◆ *She knew her ankle wouldn't bear her weight.* **2** to have or show a certain mark, characteristic, or feature ◆ *He still bears the scar.* **3** to manage to tolerate something ◆ *He could hardly bear the pain.* **4** to be fit for something ◆ *His language doesn't bear repeating.* **5** to give birth to a child ◆ *She had borne him two sons.* **6** (said about land, trees, or plants) to produce flowers, fruit, etc. **7** to turn in a particular direction ◆ *Bear right when the road forks.* **bearable** *adj* **bearably** *adv* **bearer** *n* **to bear down on** to move rapidly or purposefully towards

beard *n* **1** hair growing on a man's chin and cheeks **2** a similar hairy or bristly growth of hair on an animal or plant **beard** *v* to confront or challenge someone boldly **bearded** *adj*

bearing *n* **1** a person's way of standing, walking, or behaving ◆ *his soldierly bearing* **2** relevance to a situation ◆ *These events have no bearing on the case.* **3** a compass direction or position **4** a device for reducing friction in a part of a machine where another part moves in contact with it

bear market *n* (on the Stock Exchange) a situation where share prices are falling rapidly

beast *n* **1** any large four-footed animal **2** a cruel or vicious person **beastly** *adj* **beastlier, beastliest**

beat *v* **beat, beaten 1** to hit a person or animal repeatedly to hurt or punish them, especially using a stick **2** to hit something repeatedly to make a noise, or to be hit like this ◆ *The rain was beating against the roof.* **3** to defeat someone or do better than them ◆ *They beat us in the final.* **4** to shape or flatten something by hitting it with a hammer **5** to stir cooking ingredients vigorously to a frothy or smooth consistency ♦ *Now beat the eggs.* **6** (said about the heart) to expand and contract with a regular rhythm **7** (said about a bird or insect) to move its wings up and down **8** to sail towards the direction from which the wind is blowing, by tacking in alternate directions **beat** *n* **1** a regular repeated stroke, or a sound of this ♦ *the beat of your heart* **2** recurring emphasis marking rhythm in music or poetry **3** the strongly marked rhythm of pop music **4** the regular route of a police officer, or the area covered by this **beater** *n* **to beat someone up** to assault someone violently and severely injure them

beatify (say bee-**at**-i-fiy) *v* **beatifies**, **beatified**, **beatifying** in the Roman Catholic Church, to honour a person who has died by declaring that he or she is among the Blessed, the first step towards declaring that person a saint **beatification** *n*

Beaufort scale (say **boh**-fert) *n* a scale and description of wind velocity ranging from 0 (calm) to 12 (hurricane)

beauty *n pl* **beauties 1** a combination of qualities that give pleasure to the sight or other senses or to the mind **2** a beautiful woman **3** a fine specimen or example **4** an attractive feature or advantage of something ♦ *That's the beauty of the scheme - it doesn't cost you a penny.* **beautician** *n* a person whose job is to give people beauty treatments **beautiful** *adj* **1** attractive to look at ♦ *a beautiful girl* **2** giving pleasure to the senses or the mind ♦ *beautiful music* **3** of a high standard ♦ *a beautiful shot* **beautifully** *adv* **beautify** *v* **beautifies**, **beautified**, **beautifying** to make someone or something beautiful **beautification** *n* **beauty parlour** *n* an establishment for giving hairdressing, make-up, and other cosmetic treatments to the face and body **beauty spot** *n* **1** a place with beautiful scenery **2** a small natural or artificial mark on the face, said to heighten a person's beauty

beaver *n* **1** an animal with soft fur, a broad tail, and strong teeth that lives both on land and in water **2** the soft brown fur of this animal **Beaver** *n* a member of a junior branch of the Scout Association **beaver** *v informal* to work hard ♦ *He's beavering away on the computer.*

becalmed (say bi-**kahmd**) *adj* (said about a sailing ship) unable to move because there is no wind

became past tense of *become*

because *conjunction* for the reason that ♦ *I failed because I didn't do enough work.* **because of** by reason of ♦ *He missed most of the season because of injury.*

beck *n old use* a gesture **beckon** *v* **beckoned**, **beckoning at someone's beck and call** always ready and waiting to obey his or her orders

become *v* **became**, **become 1** to come or grow to be, to begin to be ♦ *She became a doctor.* ♦ *It became dark.* **2** to suit or look well on someone ♦ *That hairstyle becomes you.* **becoming** *adj* **becomingly** *adv*

bed *n* **1** a piece of furniture that you sleep or rest on, especially one with a mattress and coverings **2** an area of ground in a garden or park where flowers and plants are grown **3** a flat base on which something rests, a foundation **4** the bottom of the sea or a river **5** a layer of rock, soil, etc. ♦ *a bed of clay* **bed** *v* **bedded**, **bedding 1** to provide someone with a place to sleep, or to go to bed ♦ *I found somewhere to bed down for the night.* **2** to plant seeds, plants, etc. in a garden bed ♦ *He was bedding out seedlings.* **3** to place or fix something in a foundation ♦ *The bricks are bedded in concrete.* **bedding** *n* mattresses and bedclothes **bedclothes** *pl n* **bedfellow** *n* a person or thing that is closely connected with another, often in an unexpected way ♦ *Charity and rock music are no longer such strange bedfellows.* **bedpan** *n* a pan used instead of a toilet by a person confined to bed **bedpost** *n* one of the upright supports of a bedstead **bedridden** *n* too ill or weak to get out of bed **bedroom** *n* a room for sleeping in **bedside** *n* the space beside a bed **bedsitter** *n* a rented room used for both living and sleeping in **bedsore** *n* a sore caused by pressure, developed by lying in bed for a long time **bedspread** n a decorative covering spread over a bed during the day **bedstead** n a framework supporting the springs and mattress of a bed

bedevil v **bedevilled**, **bedevilling** to constantly trouble someone or something ♦ *The project has been bedevilled with problems.*

bedlam (say bed-ləm) n a scene of uproar ♦ *Upstairs it was bedlam.*

Bedouin (say bed-oo-in) n pl **Bedouin** a member of an Arab people living in tents in the desert

bedraggled (say bi-**drag**-əld) adj very untidy or messy

bedrock n **1** solid rock beneath loose soil **2** the fundamental facts or principles on which an idea or belief is based

bee n a four-winged stinging insect that produces wax and honey after gathering nectar from flowers **beehive** n a box or other container in which bees are kept **beeswax** n a yellowish substance produced by bees, used for polishing wood **beeline** n **to make a beeline for somewhere** to go there quickly and directly

beech n **1** a kind of tree with smooth bark and glossy leaves **2** the wood of this tree

beef n **1** meat from an ox, bull, or cow **2** informal muscular strength **3** informal a grumble or complaint **beef** v informal to grumble or complaint **beefy** adj **beefier**, **beefiest** having a solid muscular body **beefiness** n **beefburger** n a flat round cake of minced beef, served fried or grilled **beefeater** n a guard at the Tower of London, wearing Tudor dress as uniform **beefsteak** n a slice of beef for grilling or frying

been past participle of be

beep n a short high-pitched sound made by electronic equipment or a car horn **beep** v to produce this sound **beeper** n

beer n an alcoholic drink made from malt and flavoured with hops **beery** adj

beet n pl **beet** or **beets** a plant with a fleshy root used as a vegetable or for making sugar

beetle n an insect with hard wing covers

beetle-browed adj with eyebrows that stick out

beetroot n the dark red root of a type of beet, used as a vegetable

before adv, prep, conjunction **1** at an earlier time; earlier than ♦ *Have you been here before?* ♦ *I was here before you.* **2** ahead of ♦ *You can go before me.* **3** in front of, in the presence of ♦ *He had to appear before the magistrate.* **4** rather than, in preference to ♦ *Death before dishonour!* **beforehand** adv in advance, in readiness

befriend v to make friends with someone

befuddled adj muddled or confused

beg v **begged**, **begging 1** to ask for money or food as charity **2** to ask for something earnestly or humbly **3** to ask for something formally ♦ *I beg to differ.* **4** (said about a dog) to sit up expectantly, as it has been trained, with its front paws off the ground

beggar n **1** a person who lives by begging for food or money **2** informal a person ♦ *You lucky beggar!* **beggar** v to reduce someone to poverty **to beggar belief** or **description** to be too extraordinary to be believed or described ♦ *The scenery simply beggars description.*

begin v **began**, **begun**, **beginning 1** to do the earliest or first part of an activity **2** to come into or bring something into existence **3** to be the first to do something ♦ *Who would like to begin?* **4** to start speaking **5** to have something as its first element or starting point ♦ *The word begins with the letter B.* **beginner** n **beginning** n

begone (say bi-gon) interjection old use go away at once ♦ *Begone dull care!*

begrudge v to resent the fact that someone has something ♦ *I hope you don't begrudge me my success.*

beguile (say bi-**giyl**) v **1** to enchant or amuse someone **2** to trick someone into doing something **beguiling** adj

begun past participle of begin

behalf n **on behalf of** for the benefit of someone else or as their representative ♦ *a lawyer speaking on behalf of his client*

behave v **1** to act in a particular way ♦ *He has been behaving strangely all week.* **2** to show good manners ♦ *The children must learn to*

behave. ♦ *I wish you would behave yourself.*
behaviour *n* **behavioural** *adj*

behead *v* to cut a person's head off,
especially as a form of execution

beheld past tense and past participle of
behold

behest *n formal* a command or request **at a
person's behest** done because they have
asked or commanded you to do it ♦ *We
attended the funeral at the behest of the
family.*

behind *prep* **1** at or to the back of, on the
further side of ♦ *She had been hiding behind
the curtain.* **2** responsible for or causing
♦ *What's behind all this trouble?* **3** supporting
♦ *We are all behind you.* **4** having made less
progress than ♦ *Some countries are behind
others in development.* **5** later than ♦ *We
are a month behind schedule.* **behind** *adv*
1 remaining after others have gone ♦ *Would
you stay behind for a few minutes?* **2** at a
place you have left ♦ *Don't leave your coat
behind.* **3** not making good progress; late
♦ *I'm behind with my rent.* **behind** *n informal*
a person's bottom

behold *v* past tense and past participle
beheld *old use* to see or observe
beholden *adj* **beholder** *n* **to be beholden
to someone** *n* to be indebted to someone
for something they have done

beige (say bayzh) *n* a very light brown
colour **beige** *adj* of this colour

being *n* **1** existence ♦ *When did the European
Union come into being?* **2** the essence
or nature of a person or thing **3** a living
creature ♦ *alien beings*

bejewelled *adj* decorated with jewels

belated (say bi-lay-tid) *adj* coming very late
or too late **belatedlyy** *adv*

belch *v* **1** to send out wind from the stomach
noisily through the mouth **2** to send out a
large amount of smoke or flames ♦ *The front
of the car was belching smoke.* **belch** *n* an act
or sound of belching

beleaguered (say bi-leeg-erd) *adj*
1 experiencing a lot of difficulties or
criticism ♦ *the country's beleaguered
government* **2** under siege

belfry *n pl* **belfries** a tower or part of a tower
in which bells hang

belie *v* **belies**, **belied**, **belying** **1** to give a
false idea of something ♦ *The quality of
her writing belies her youth.* **2** to show that
something is untrue ♦ *His actions seem to
belie these fine words.*

belief *n pl* **beliefs** **1** the feeling that
something exists or is true **2** trust
or confidence ♦ *I have belief in you.*
3 something that a person believes
4 acceptance of the teachings of a religion
believe *v* **to believe in** **1** to have faith in
the existence of something ♦ *Do you believe
in ghosts?* **2** to feel sure that something
or someone is good or can be relied on
believable *adj* **believer** *n*

belittle *v* to suggest that something is
unimportant or of little value ♦ *I don't want
to belittle their achievement.* **belittlement** *n*

bell *n* **1** a cup-shaped metal instrument
that makes a ringing sound when it is
struck by the clapper hanging inside it **2** a
device making a ringing or buzzing sound
to attract attention **3** the sound of a bell,
especially when used as a signal **4** a bell-
shaped object **bell-bottomed** *adj* (said
about trousers) widening from knee to
ankle **to ring a bell** to sound familiar

belle (say bel) *n* a beautiful girl or woman
♦ *the belle of the ball*

belligerent (say bi-lij-er-ənt) *adj* **1** hostile
and aggressive ♦ *a belligerent reply* **2** taking
part in a war ♦ *the belligerent nations*
belligerence *n* **belligerently** *adv*

bellow *n* **1** the loud deep sound made by a
bull **2** a loud deep shout **bellow** *v* to utter
a bellow

belly *n pl* **bellies** **1** a person's stomach or
abdomen **2** the underside of an animal's
body **3** a bulging or rounded part of
something **belly** *v* **bellies**, **bellied**, **bellying**
to swell out, or to make something swell
out **bellyful** *n* **to have a bellyful** *informal* to
have more than enough of something **belly
dance** *n* a style of dance originating in the
Middle East **belly dancer** *n* **belly dancing** *n*

belong *v* **1** to be the property of someone
♦ *The house belongs to me now.* **2** to rightly
go with something else or be part of
it ♦ *That lid belongs to this jar.* **3** to be a
member of something ♦ *I belong to the*

local chess club. **4** to fit in ♦ *I don't really belong here.* **5** to have a proper or usual place ♦ *The pans belong in the top cupboard.* **belongings** *pl n*

beloved (say bi-**luvd** or bi-**luv**-id) *adj* dearly loved ♦ *my beloved wife* **beloved** (say bi-**luv**-id) *n* a much loved person

below *adv* **1** at or to a lower position **2** mentioned further down ♦ *See chapter 6 below.* **below** *prep* lower in position, amount, or rank, etc. than; under ♦ *It was ten degrees below zero.*

belt *n* **1** a strip of cloth or leather, etc. worn round the waist **2** a continuous moving strap passing over pulleys and so driving machinery ♦ *a fan belt* **3** a long narrow region or strip ♦ *A belt of rain will move eastwards.* **4** *informal* a heavy blow **belt** *v* **1** to fasten something with a belt **2** *informal* to hit or beat someone **3** *informal* to rush along

bemused (say bi-**mewzd**) *adj* puzzled or confused

bench *n* **1** a long seat of wood or stone **2** a long table for working at in a workshop or laboratory **3** the place where judges and magistrates sit **4** the judges or magistrates hearing a case **benchmark** *n* **1** a standard or point of reference against which things can be compared or assessed **2** a surveyor's mark indicating a point in a line of levels

bend *v* past tense and past participle **bent** **1** to make something curved or angular and no longer straight **2** to move the top part of your body downwards, to stoop ♦ *She bent to pick it up.* **3** to turn in a new direction ♦ *The river bends ahead.* **bend** *n* a place where something bends, a curve or turn **bends** *pl n* sickness due to too rapid decompression, e.g. after diving

beneath *adv, prep* **1** below or underneath **2** not worthy of ♦ *Cheating is beneath you.*

benediction (say ben-i-**dik**-shən) *n* a spoken blessing **benedictory** *adj*

benefactor *n* a person who gives money or other help **benefactress** *n*

beneficiary (say ben-i-**fish**-er-i) *n pl* **beneficiaries** **1** a person who receives a benefit from something **2** a person who is left a legacy under someone's will

beneficial *adj* **beneficially** *adv*

benefit *n* **1** an advantage that something brings **2** a payment to which a person is entitled from an insurance policy or government funds **3** a performance or game held in order to raise money for a particular player or for charity ♦ *a benefit match* **benefit** *v* **benefited**, **benefiting** to receive or to bring an advantage

benevolent *adj* **1** wishing to do good to others; kindly and helpful **2** formed for charitable purposes ♦ *a benevolent fund* **benevolence** *n* **benevolently** *adv*

benighted *adj* intellectually or morally ignorant

benign (say bi-**niyn**) *adj* **1** kindly **2** mild or favourable ♦ *a benign climate* **3** (said about a tumour) not malignant **benignly** *adv*

bent *adj* **1** curved or crooked **2** *informal* dishonest or corrupt **bent** *n* a natural talent or skill ♦ *She has a bent for photography.* **bent on** determined to do or have something ♦ *He was bent on mischief.*

bequeath (say bi-**kweeth**) *v* to leave something to a person, especially in a will

bequest (say bi-**kwest**) *n* something left to a person, especially in a will

berate (say bi-**rayt**) *v* to scold someone angrily

bereaved *adj formal* having recently suffered the death of a close relative **bereavement** *n*

bereft *adj* deprived of something ♦ *They were bereft of hope.*

beret (say **be**-ray) *n* a round flat cap with no peak

berry *n pl* **berries** **1** a small round juicy fruit without a stone **2** (in botanical use) a fruit with seeds enclosed in a pulp, such as a banana or tomato

berserk (say ber-**zerk**) *adj* frenzied **to go berserk** to go into an uncontrollable and destructive rage

berth *n* **1** a place for a ship to tie up at a wharf or dock **2** a bunk or sleeping place on a ship or train **berth** *v* to moor at a berth **to give someone or something a wide berth** to stay well away from them

beseech *v* past tense and past participle **beseeched** or **besought** to ask someone earnestly for something; to implore

beset v **beset, besetting** to surround or attack someone from all sides ♦ *We are beset with problems.*

beside prep **1** by the side of, close to **2** compared with ♦ *His work looks poor beside yours.* **to be beside yourself** to be very excited or upset

besides prep in addition to, other than ♦ *He has no income besides his pension.* **besides** adv also, in addition ♦ *And besides, it's the wrong colour.*

besiege v **1** to surround a place in order to capture it **2** to crowd round someone with requests or questions ♦ *Fans besieged the singer after the concert.* **besieger** n

besotted (say bi-**sot**-id) adj foolishly infatuated

bespeak v **bespoke, bespoken, bespeaking 1** to be evidence of something **2** to order or reserve goods in advance **bespoke** adj **1** (said about clothes or other goods) made to order ♦ *a bespoke suit* **2** (said about a computer program) written or adapted for a specific user

best adj of the most excellent kind; most satisfactory **best** adv **1** in the best manner, to the greatest degree ♦ *I like this one best.* **2** most usefully or wisely ♦ *We had best go.* **best** n **1** that which is best ♦ *The best is yet to come.* **2** victory in a contest, especially by winning the majority of games, etc. ♦ *Let's make it the best of three.* **best** v informal to defeat or outwit someone **best man** n the bridegroom's chief attendant at a wedding **best-seller** n a book that sells in large numbers

bestial (say **best**-iəl) adj like a beast, especially by being cruel or disgusting **bestiality** n

bestow v to present something to someone as a gift **bestowal** n

bet n **1** an agreement that you will pay money if you are wrong in forecasting the result of a race, game, etc. and receive money if you are right **2** the money that you agree to pay in this way **3** a person or thing thought to be likely to be successful ♦ *She's a good bet to win the title.* **4** a prediction or opinion ♦ *My bet is that he won't come.* **bet** v

bet or **betted, betting 1** to make a bet ♦ *I bet you £10 they lose.* **2** to predict, to think most likely ♦ *I bet it rains tomorrow.* **betting shop** n a bookmaker's office

beta (say **bee**-tə) n **1** the second letter of the Greek alphabet, equivalent to Roman B, b **2** a second-class mark given for a piece of work

beta blocker n a drug used to prevent increased heart activity

bête noire (say bayt **nwar**) n pl **bêtes noires** (say bayt **nwar**) a thing or person that you particularly dislike

betray v **1** to hand someone over to an enemy or give information to your country's enemy ♦ *During the war he betrayed his country.* **2** to be disloyal to someone ♦ *She felt betrayed.* **3** to reveal something unintentionally ♦ *His shaking hand betrayed his nervousness.* **betrayal** n **betrayer** n

betroth (say bi-**trohth**) v formal **to be betrothed** to be engaged to be married **betrothal** n

better[1] adj **1** more excellent, satisfactory, or desirable ♦ *It would be better to start again.* **2** partly or fully recovered from an illness ♦ *Are you feeling better?* **better** adv **1** in a better manner, to a greater degree ♦ *I like this one better.* **2** more usefully or wisely ♦ *We had better go.* **better** n that which is better **better** v to improve on or do better than something ♦ *See if you can better that score.* **betterment** n **betters** pl n people who are of higher status than yourself **to better yourself** to get a better social position or status

better[2] n a person who bets

between prep, adv **1** in the space separating two or more points, lines, or objects **2** connecting two or more people, places, or things ♦ *the great love between them* ♦ *The train runs between London and Glasgow.* **3** more than one amount or level and less than another **4** in the period separating two points in time ♦ *We'll arrive between 6.00 and 6.30.* **5** separating ♦ *the difference between right and wrong* **6** shared by ♦ *Divide the money between you.* **7** taking one and rejecting the other ♦ *It is difficult to* *choose between them.*

bevel (say **bev**-əl) n **1** a sloping edge or surface **2** a tool for making such slopes **bevel** v **bevelled**, **bevelling** to give a sloping edge to something

beverage (say **bev**-er-ij) n any drink

bevy (say **bev**-i) n pl **bevies** a large group ♦ *a bevy of beauties*

bewail v to express great sorrow about something ♦ *refugees bewailing their fate*

beware v to be on your guard ♦ *Beware of pickpockets.*

bewilder v to puzzle or confuse someone completely **bewilderment** n

bewitch v **1** to put someone under a magic spell **2** to delight someone very much

beyond adv, prep **1** at or to the further side of; further on ♦ *They live beyond those hills.* **2** outside the scope or limits of ♦ *His bike is beyond repair.* ♦ *This is beyond a joke.*

Bhagavadgita (say bah-gə-vahd-**gee**-tə) n the 'Song of the Lord' (i.e. Krishna), the most famous religious text of Hinduism

bhaji (say **bah**-ji) n pl **bhajis** a ball of vegetables fried in batter, served as an appetizer in Indian cooking

bhangra n a style of music that combines traditional Punjabi music with Western rock music

bi- prefix **1** two (as in bicycle) **2** twice (as in biannual)

biannual adj appearing or happening twice a year **biannually** adv ◊ Do not confuse this word with biennial.

bias n pl **biases 1** an opinion or feeling that strongly favours one side in preference to another **2** a distortion in statistical information because of a factor or influence that has not been taken account of **3** the tendency of a ball in the game of bowls to swerve because of the way it is weighted **bias** v **biased**, **biasing** to give a bias to something, to influence something unfairly

biased adj inclined to favour one side rather than another

bib n **1** a cloth or plastic covering put under a young child's chin to protect the front of its clothes while eating **2** the front part of an apron, above the waist

Bible n the sacred book of the Jews (the Old Testament) and of the Christians (the Old and New Testament) **bible** n **1** a copy of either of these **2** a book regarded as authoritative ♦ *This should be every gardener's bible.* **biblical** adj

bibliography (say bibli-**og**-rəfi) n pl **bibliographies 1** a list of books or articles about a particular subject or by a particular author **2** the study of the history of books and their production **bibliographer** n **bibliographical** adj

bicentenary (say biy-sen-**teen**-er-i) n pl **bicentenaries** a 200th anniversary **bicentennial** adj

biceps (say **biy**-seps) n the large muscle at the front of the upper arm, which bends the elbow

bicker v to quarrel constantly over unimportant things

bicycle n a two-wheeled vehicle driven by pedals **bicycle** v to ride on a bicycle **bicyclist** n

bid[1] n **1** an offer of an amount you are willing to pay for something, especially at an auction **2** a statement of the number of tricks a player proposes to win in a card game **3** an effort to obtain something ♦ *an unsuccessful bid for the title* **bid** v **bid**, **bidding** to make a bid **biddable** adj **bidder** n **bidding** n

bid[2] v **bid** or **bade** (say bad) **bid**, **bidding 1** to say something as a greeting or farewell ♦ *I bid you all good night.* **2** to command someone to do something ♦ *Do as you are bid.*

bide v old use to wait **to bide your time** to wait for a good opportunity to do something

bidet (say **bee**-day) n a low oval washbasin that you can sit astride for washing the lower part of your body

biennial (say biy-**en**-iəl) adj **1** lasting or living for two years **2** happening once every two years **biennial** n a plant that lives for two years, flowering and dying in the second **biennially** adv ◊ Do not confuse this word with biannual.

biff v informal to hit someone or something **biff** n a blow

bifocals (say biy-**foh**-kəlz) pl n spectacles

with lenses made in two sections, an upper part for looking at distant objects and a lower part for reading

big adj **bigger**, **biggest 1** large in size, amount, or intensity **2** more grown up, elder ♦ *my big sister* **3** important ♦ *the big match* **4** boastful or pretentious ♦ *big talk* **5** informal generous ♦ *That's big of you.*

big bang n the theory that the universe originated when a fireball of radiation expanded suddenly and then cooled **Big Brother** n a person or organization that exercises close supervision and control of people's lives **big-head** n informal a conceited person **big-headed** adj **big-hearted** adj very kind, generous **big shot** n an important person **big top** n the main tent at a circus

bigamy (say **big-a-mee**) n the crime of marrying a person when you are already married to someone else **bigamist** n **bigamous** adj **bigamously** adv

bigot (say **big-ət**) n a person who holds an opinion or belief obstinately and is intolerant of other people's opinions **bigoted** adj narrow-minded and intolerant **bigotry** n being a bigot or bigoted

bijou (say **bee-zhoo**) adj small and elegant ♦ *a bijou flat*

bike n informal a bicycle or motorcycle **bike** v informal to ride a bicycle or motorcycle **biker** n **biking** n

bikini n a woman's two-piece swimsuit

bilateral (say **biy-lat-erəl**) adj **1** having or to do with two sides **2** between two people or groups ♦ *a bilateral agreement* **bilaterally** adv

bile n **1** a bitter yellowish liquid produced by the liver and stored in the gall bladder, helping the digestion of fats **2** anger or bad temper

bilingual (say **biy-ling-gwəl**) adj **1** able to speak two languages **2** written in two languages

bilious (say **bil-yəs**) adj **1** feeling sick **2** of a sickly yellowish colour or shade ♦ *a bilious green* **3** spiteful or bad-tempered **biliousness** n

bilk v to avoid paying your debts to someone; to defraud someone

bill[1] n **1** a written statement of charges for goods or services supplied **2** the draft of a proposed law to be discussed by parliament **3** N. Am a banknote ♦ *a ten-dollar bill* **4** a programme of entertainment at a theatre, cinema, etc. ♦ *Who's on the bill?* **5** a poster or notice **bill** v **1** to send a bill to someone **2** to announce or advertise something ♦ *This has been billed as the match of the century.* **bill of exchange** n a written order to pay a specified sum of money on a particular date to a named person or to the bearer **to fit** or **fill the bill** to be suitable for what is needed

bill[2] n a bird's beak **bill** v (said about doves) to stroke each other with their bills

billboard n a hoarding for advertisements

billet n a temporary lodging for soldiers, especially in a private house **billet** v **billeted**, **billeting** to house soldiers in a billet

billiards n a game played with cues and three balls on a cloth-covered table

billion n **1** a thousand million **2** old use a million million **billionaire** n **billionth** adj, n

billow n a large rolling mass of cloud, smoke, or steam **billow** v **1** to fill with air and swell outwards ♦ *His cloak billowed out behind him.* **2** to flow upwards and outwards ♦ *Smoke billowed forth.*

bimbo n pl **bimbos** an attractive but unintelligent young woman

bimonthly adj **1** happening every two months **2** happening twice a month

bin n **1** a container for rubbish or litter **2** a large container used for storing grain, flour, wine, etc. **bin** v **binned**, **binning** to throw something away by putting it in a bin

binary (say **biy-ner-i**) adj **1** involving sets of two; consisting of two parts **2** Mathematics using two as a base **binary** n pl **binaries** a binary star **binary code** n ICT a coding system using the two digits 0 and 1 **binary digit** n one of the two digits 0 and 1 used in the binary system **binary number** n a number expressed in the binary system **binary star** n two stars that revolve round each other **binary system** n a system of numbers using only the two digits 0 and 1, used in computing

bind v past tense and past participle **bound** **1** to tie or fasten something tightly **2** to fasten a strip of material round something ♦ *Help me bind up the wound.* **3** to tie someone up **4** to hold things together; to unite them ♦ *We are bound by ties of friendship.* **5** to fasten the pages of a book into a cover **6** to stick ingredients together in a solid mass ♦ *Now bind the mixture with egg yolk.* **7** to cover the edge of a piece of material in order to strengthen it or as a decoration **8** to make someone agree to do something or place them under an obligation **bind** n *informal* **1** a difficult or annoying situation **2** a situation in which you cannot act freely **binding** n **1** the covering, glue, etc. that hold the pages of a book together **2** fabric used for binding the edges of a piece of material **binding** *adj* (said about a promise or agreement) that must be carried out or obeyed ♦ *The agreement is binding on both parties.*

binder n **1** a cover for holding magazines or loose papers together **2** a bookbinder **3** a machine that binds harvested corn into sheaves or straw into bales

bindi (say **bin**-dee) n pl **bindis 1** a coloured dot traditionally worn by Hindu girls and women on their forehead **2** a decorative jewel or tattoo worn on the forehead

binge (say binj) n *informal* a time spent eating or drinking too much **binge** v to spend time eating to excess **binge drinking** n excessive drinking over a short period **binge drinker** n

bingo n a gambling game with cards on which numbered squares are crossed out as the numbers are called out at random

binocular (say bin-**ok**-yoo-ler) *adj* for or using both eyes ♦ *binocular vision* **binoculars** pl n an instrument with lenses for both eyes, making distant objects seem nearer

bio- *prefix* life (as in *biology*)

biochemistry n the study of the chemical composition and processes of living organisms **biochemical** *adj* **biochemist** n

biodegradable (say biy-oh-di-**gray**-də-bəl) *adj* able to be broken down by bacteria in the environment ♦ *All our packaging is biodegradable.* **biodegradability** n **biodegradation** n

biodiversity n the variety of plant and animal life in an area

bioengineering n the application of engineering techniques to biological processes

biography n pl **biographies** the story of a person's life written by someone else **biographer** n **biographical** *adj*

biology n the scientific study of the life and structure of living things **biological** *adj* **1** to do with biology **2** (said about a parent) related to a child by blood **3** (said about a detergent) containing enzymes **biologically** *adv* **biologist** n **biological clock** n an innate mechanism that an organism has for controlling regular functions **biological warfare** n the deliberate use of organisms to spread disease among an enemy

bionics n the study of mechanical systems that function like parts of living beings **bionic** *adj*

biopsy (say **biy**-op-si) n pl **biopsies** an examination of tissue cut from a living body, to find out the cause or extent of a disease

biosphere n pl **biospheres** all the parts of the Earth which contain living things

biotechnology n the use of living micro-organisms and biological processes in industrial and commercial production

bipartisan (say biy-parti-**zan**) *adj* to do with or involving two political or other parties

bipartite (say biy-**par**-tiyt) *adj* **1** involving or made by two groups ♦ *a bipartite agreement* **2** having two parts

biped (say **biy**-ped) n a two-footed animal

biplane (say **biy**-playn) n a type of aircraft with two sets of wings, one above the other

bipolar disorder (say biy-**poh**-lə) n a form of manic depression

birch n **1** a deciduous tree with smooth bark and slender branches **2** the wood of this tree **3** a bundle of birch twigs used in the past for flogging people **birch** v to beat someone with a bundle of birch twigs

bird n **1** a feathered animal with two wings and two legs **2** *informal* a young woman

bird's-eye view n a general view from above **bird of prey** n a bird, such as an eagle or hawk, that kills animals for food **birdseed** n special seed used as food for caged birds

biriani (say bi-ri-**ah**-ni) n an Indian dish made with rice and meat, fish, or vegetables

birth n 1 the process by which a baby or young animal comes out from its mother's body 2 the beginning of something ♦ *the birth of rock and roll* 3 a person's ancestry or parentage ♦ *He is of noble birth.* **birth certificate** n an official document giving the date and place of a person's birth **birth control** n using contraception and other ways of avoiding conceiving a baby **birthday** n the anniversary of the day of your birth **birthmark** n a coloured mark that has been on a person's skin since birth **birthplace** n the house or district where you were born **birth rate** n the number of children born in one year for every 1,000 people **birthright** n a right or privilege to which a person is entitled through being born into a particular family or country **to give birth** to bear a baby or young

biscuit (say **bis**-kit) n 1 a small flat kind of cake that has been baked until it is crisp 2 a light brown colour

bisect (say biy-**sekt**) v to divide something into two equal parts **bisection** n **bisector** n

bisexual (say biy-**seks**-yoo-əl) adj 1 sexually attracted to both men and women 2 having both male and female sexual organs in one individual **bisexual** n a person who is sexually attracted to both men and women

bishop n 1 a high-ranking member of the Christian clergy with authority over the work of the church in a city or district (called *diocese*) 2 a chess piece shaped like a bishop's mitre **bishopric** n

bison (say **biy**-sən) n pl **bison** a shaggy haired wild ox of Europe and North America

bistro (say **bee**-stroh) n pl **bistros** a small restaurant

bit[1] n 1 a small piece or quantity ♦ *a bit of cheese* 2 a fair amount ♦ *He took a bit of persuading.* **bit part** n **bitty** adj **bittier, bittiest**

bit[2] n 1 a metal bar forming the mouthpiece of a horse's bridle 2 the part of a drill used for boring 3 the part of a tool that cuts or grips when twisted

bit[3] past tense of *bite*

bitch n 1 a female dog, fox, wolf, or otter 2 *informal* a spiteful woman **bitchy** adj **bitchily** adv **bitchiness** n

bite v **bit, bitten** 1 to cut or take something with the teeth 2 to be in the habit of biting people ♦ *Does your dog bite?* 3 (said about an insect or snake) to pierce the skin with its sting or fangs 4 (said about fish) to accept bait 5 to grip or take hold on a surface ♦ *Tyres don't bite so well on a wet road.* 6 to have an unpleasant effect ♦ *The education cuts were beginning to bite.* **bite** n 1 an act of biting, or a mouthful cut off by biting ♦ *He took a bite of the pie.* 2 a wound or mark made by biting ♦ *She was covered in insect bites.* 3 a quick snack ♦ *Have we got time for a bite to eat?* 4 an attempt by a fish to take the bait 5 the way the teeth close in biting **biter** n **biting** adj **bitten**

bitmap n pl **bitmaps** ICT a digital image made up of rows and columns of dots

bitter adj 1 having a sharp unpleasant taste, like quinine or aspirin 2 showing or feeling angry hurt or resentment ♦ *He still feels bitter about the way he was treated.* 3 causing sorrow ♦ *a bitter disappointment* 4 very cold ♦ *a bitter wind* **bitter** n beer that is strongly flavoured with hops and has a bitter taste **bitterly** adv **bitterness** n **bittersweet** adj 1 sweet but with a bitter aftertaste 2 pleasant but with a mixture of something sad or unpleasant

bivouac (say **biv**-oo-ak) n a temporary camp without tents or other cover **bivouac** v **bivouacs, bivouacked, bivouacking** to camp in a bivouac

biweekly adj 1 happening every two weeks 2 happening twice a week

bizarre (say biz-**ar**) adj strikingly odd in appearance or effect

blab v **blabbed, blabbing** to let out a secret

black adj 1 of the very darkest colour, like coal or soot 2 having a dark skin 3 to do with dark-skinned people or with their culture 4 (said about coffee or tea) without milk **5** very dirty **6** not hopeful ♦ *The outlook is black.* **7** involving tragedy or disaster ♦ *This has been a black day in our history.* **8** (said about humour) presenting a tragic theme or situation in comic terms **9** hostile or disapproving ♦ *He gave me a black look.* **black** n **1** a black colour **2** black clothes ♦ *She was dressed in black.* **3** a person with a dark skin, especially a person with African or Australian Aboriginal ancestry **4** the black ball in snooker **5** the player using the black pieces in chess **black** v **1** to make something black **2** to polish something with blacking **3** to refuse to handle goods as a form of industrial action **blacken** v **blackened, blackening, blackly** adv **blackness** n **blackball** v to prevent a person from being elected as a member of a club by voting against him or her at a secret ballot **blackberry** n pl **blackberries 1** the bramble **2** its small sweet dark berry **blackberrying** n picking blackberries **blackbird** n a European songbird, the male of which is black **blackboard** n a dark board for writing on with chalk **black box** n an aircraft's flight recorder **black eye** n an eye with the skin round it darkened by a bruise **blackhead** n a small black spot blocking a pore in the skin **black hole** n a region in outer space with a gravitational field so intense that no matter or radiation can escape from it **black ice** n hard thin transparent ice on roads **blacklist** n a list of people who are disapproved of **blacklist** v to put someone on a blacklist **black magic** n magic involving the summoning of evil spirits **blackmail** v to demand payment or action from a person by threatening to do something, especially to reveal a secret which will damage their reputation **blackmail** n the crime of demanding payment or using threats in this way **blackmailer** n **black mark** n a record of the fact that someone has done something to earn disapproval or criticism **black market** n the illegal buying and selling of goods or currencies **black marketeer** n someone who trades in the black market **blackout** n **1** a period of darkness when no light must be shown; the extinguishing

of all lights **2** a temporary loss of consciousness **3** prevention of the release of information ♦ *a total news blackout* **black pudding** n a large dark sausage containing blood, suet, etc. **black sheep** n a member of a family or other group who is seen as a disgrace to it **blacksmith** n a person who makes and repairs iron things, especially someone who makes and fits horseshoes **black spot** n a dangerous place **black tie** n a man's black bow tie worn with a dinner jacket **black widow** n a poisonous spider found in tropical and subtropical regions **bladder** n **1** the bag-like part of the body in which urine collects **2** the inflatable bag inside a football **blade** n **1** the flat cutting edge of a knife, sword, chisel, etc. **2** the flat wide part of an oar, spade, propeller, etc. **3** a flat narrow leaf ♦ *blades of grass* **4** a broad flattish bone ♦ *the shoulder blade* **blame** v **1** to hold someone responsible for causing what is wrong ♦ *Police are blaming him for the accident.* **2** to find fault with someone ♦ *I don't blame you for feeling angry.* **blame** n responsibility for what is wrong **blameless** adj **blanch** v **1** to make or become white or pale ♦ *He blanched with fear.* **2** to immerse fruit or vegetables briefly in boiling water **bland** adj **1** lacking flavour ♦ *bland foods* **2** polite but dull ♦ *a bland reply* **blandly** adv **blandness** n **blandishments** pl n flattering or coaxing words **blank** adj **1** not written, printed, recorded on, or decorated ♦ *Just leave a blank space.* ♦ *a blank cheque* **2** showing no expression ♦ *a blank look* **3** empty ♦ *a blank cartridge* **4** empty of thoughts ♦ *My mind's gone blank.* **blank** n **1** an empty space ♦ *In this puzzle you have to fill in the blanks.* **2** a blank cartridge **blank** v **blankly** adv **blankness** n **to blank something out 1** to cross something out or obscure it **2** to deliberately try to forget something **to draw a blank** to fail to find what you are looking for **blanket** n **1** a thick covering made of woollen or other fabric **2** a thick soft mass of something that completely covers a place ♦ *a blanket of snow* **blanket** *adj* covering all cases or instances ♦ *a blanket ban on tobacco advertising* **blanket** *v* **blanketed, blanketing** to cover something completely with a thick layer

blare *v* to make a loud harsh sound like that of a horn or trumpet **blare** *n* a loud harsh sound

blarney *n* smooth talk that flatters and deceives people

blasé (say **blah**-zay) *adj* bored or unimpressed by things because you have already experienced or seen them so often

blasphemy (say **blas**-femi) *n* *pl* **blasphemies** contemptuous or irreverent talk about God and sacred things **blaspheme** *v* **blasphemer** *n* **blasphemous** *adj* **blasphemously** *adv*

blast *n* **1** a sudden strong rush of wind or air **2** a wave of air from an explosion **3** a single loud note from a trumpet, whistle, car horn, etc. **blast** *v* **1** to blow something up with explosives **2** to kick or hit a ball hard **3** to cause a plant to wither or shrivel **blast-off** *n* the launching of a rocket or spacecraft **to blast off** to launch by the firing of rockets **at full blast** at maximum power

blatant (say **blay**-tent) *adj* very obvious and unashamed ♦ *a blatant lie* **blatantly** *adv*

blaze¹ *n* **1** a large hot fire **2** a bright display of light or colour ♦ *The garden was a blaze of colour.* **3** an impressive show of something ♦ *The film opened in a blaze of publicity.* **blaze** *v* **1** to burn or shine strongly and brightly **2** to have an outburst of intense feeling or anger ♦ *He was blazing with anger.*

blaze² *n* **1** a white mark on an animal's face **2** a mark chipped in the bark of a tree to mark a route **blaze** *v* to mark a tree or route with blazes

blazer *n* a type of jacket, often in the colours or bearing the badge of a school, club, or team

bleach *v* to make something turn white by sunlight or chemicals **bleach** *n* a chemical used to bleach things and kill germs

bleak *adj* **1** cold and bare ♦ *a bleak landscape* **2** not at all hopeful ♦ *The future looks bleak.* **bleakly** *adv* **bleakness** *n*

bleary *adj* (said about eyes) watery and not

seeing clearly **blearily** *adv* **bleariness** *n*

bleat *v* **1** to make the cry of a sheep, goat, or calf **2** to speak or complain in a weak or foolish way ♦ *What are they bleating about now?* **bleat** *n* a bleating sound

bleed *v* past tense and past participle **bled** **1** to lose blood **2** to come out in water ♦ *Some dyes bleed.* **3** to draw blood from someone **4** to take money away from someone ♦ *Local gangsters were bleeding him dry.*

bleep *v* to make the high-pitched sound of an electronic device **bleep** *n* a bleeping sound **bleeper** *n*

blemish *n* a flaw that prevents something from being perfect **blemish** *v* to spoil something with a blemish ♦ *These allegations have blemished his reputation.*

blend *v* **1** to mix things together, or to become a mixture **2** to combine well with something ♦ *Their voices blend well.* **3** to join together so that nothing stands out from the rest ♦ *The sea and the sky seemed to blend into each other.* **blend** *n* a mixture of different sorts ♦ *a blend of tea* **blender** *n*

bless *v* **1** (said about a priest) to ask for a person or thing to receive God's favour and protection, e.g. by making the sign of the cross over them **2** to praise God or call God holy **blessed** *adj* **blessedness** *n* **blessing** *n* **to be blessed with** to be fortunate in having something ♦ *She is blessed with good health.*

blew past tense of *blow*¹

blight *n* **1** a disease that withers plants, especially one caused by a fungus **2** a thing that spoils or damages something ♦ *Poverty is a blight on their community.* **3** an unsightly area or landscape **blight** *v* **1** to affect something with blight **2** to spoil or damage something ♦ *Scandal has blighted his career.*

blind *adj* **1** without the ability to see **2** without thought or understanding ♦ *blind obedience* ♦ *She was in a blind rage.* **3** (said about a corner or bend) impossible to see round **4** (said about a tube, passage, or road) closed at one end **5** (said about a plant) failing to produce a flower **blind** *adv* without being able to see clearly **blind** *v* **1** to make someone blind **2** to dazzle someone with bright light **3** to prevent you from realizing something ♦ *Her loyalty blinded her to his faults.* **blind** *n* **1** a screen, especially on a roller, for a window **2** something used to hide your real intentions **blinding** *adj* (said about light) so bright that it hurts your eyes ♦ *a blinding flash* **blindingly** *adv* **blindly** *adv* **blindness** *n* **blind alley** *n* **1** an alley that is closed at one end **2** a course of action that leads nowhere **blind date** *n* a date between people who have not met before **blindfold** *n* a strip of cloth tied round someone's eyes so that they cannot see **blindfold** *v* to cover someone's eyes with a blindfold **blindfold** *adv* with a blindfold covering the eyes **blind spot** *n* **1** a point on the eye that is insensitive to light **2** an area cut off from a motorist's vision **3** a subject that you do not understand or know much about ♦ *I've got a blind spot about modern art.*

bling *n informal* flashy or ostentatious jewellery

blink *v* **1** to open and shut your eyes rapidly **2** to shine unsteadily ♦ *a blinking light* **blink** *n* **1** an act of blinking **2** a quick gleam of light **blinker** *v* **blinkered**, **blinkering** **blinkered** *adj*

blip *n* **1** a very short high-pitched sound made by an electronic device **2** a spot of light on a radar screen **blip** *v* **blipped**, **blipping** to make a blip

bliss *adj* perfect happiness **blissful** *adj* **blissfully** *adv*

blister *n* **1** a bubble-like swelling on the skin, filled with watery liquid **2** a raised swelling, e.g. on a painted surface **blister** *v* **blistered**, **blistering** to cause a blister on the skin, or to be affected with blisters **blistering** *adj*

blithe (say *bliyth*) *adj* casual and carefree **blithely** *adv*

blitz *n* **1** a sudden violent attack, especially from aircraft **2** a burst of busy activity **blitz** *v* to attack or damage a place in a blitz

blizzard *n* a severe snowstorm

bloated *adj* **1** swollen with fat, gas, or liquid **2** puffed up with pride or excessive wealth

bloater *n* a salted smoked herring

blob *n* **1** a drop of thick liquid **2** a round mass or spot

bloc *n* a group of parties or countries who have formed an alliance

block *n* **1** a solid piece of wood, stone, or other hard substance **2** a large building divided into separate flats or offices **3** a group of buildings with streets on all sides ♦ *I went for a walk round the block.* **4** a large piece of wood on which condemned people were beheaded in the past **5** the main part of a petrol engine, consisting of the cylinders **6** a pad of paper for drawing or writing on **7** an obstacle or obstruction ♦ *I've got a mental block about her name.* **8** a starting block in a race **block** *v* **1** to obstruct something so that nothing can get through ♦ *The pipe is blocked.* ♦ *A fallen tree was blocking the road.* **2** to prevent something happening ♦ *The opposition will try to block the new proposals.* **3** (in cricket) to stop a bowled ball with the bat **blockade** *n* **blockage** *n* **blockbuster** *n informal* a film or book that is extremely successful **block capitals** *pl n* plain capital letters

blog *n ICT* a weblog **blogger** *n* **blogging** *n*

bloke *n informal* a man **blokeish** *adj*

blonde, **blond** *adj* **1** (said about hair) fair **2** fair-haired **blonde** *n* a woman with blonde hair

blood *n* **1** the red oxygen-bearing liquid circulating in the bodies of animals **2** violence involving bloodshed **3** family background, descent, or parentage ♦ *Do you have any Irish blood?* **4** temper or passion **blood** *v* **1** to initiate someone in a new activity **2** to give a first taste of blood to a hound **bloodily** *adv* **bloodiness** *n* **bloodless** *adj* **1** looking pale, drained of blood **2** without violence or killing ♦ *a bloodless coup* **3** without vitality, feeble **bloody** *adj* **bloodier**, **bloodiest 1** covered in blood **2** involving much killing and wounding ♦ *a bloody battle* **3** *informal* used as a mild swear word **bloody** *v* **bloodies**, **bloodied**, **bloodying** to stain something with blood **blood bank** *n* a place where supplies of blood and plasma for transfusions are stored **bloodbath** *n* a massacre **blood-curdling** *adj* horrifying **blood group** *n* any of the classes or types of human blood **bloodhound** n a large dog with a very keen sense of smell, formerly used in tracking **blood money** n money paid as compensation to the family of someone who has been killed **blood poisoning** n the condition that results when the bloodstream is infected with harmful micro-organisms that have entered the body **blood pressure** n the pressure of blood within the arteries and veins **bloodshed** n the killing or wounding of people **bloodshot** adj (said about the eyes) streaked with red, usually because of tiredness **blood sport** n a sport involving wounding or killing animals **bloodstain** n a stain made by blood **bloodstained** adj **bloodstream** n the blood circulating in the body **bloodsucker** n an animal or insect that sucks blood **blood sugar** n the proportion of glucose in the blood **bloodthirsty** adj eager to use or watch violence **blood vessel** n a vein, artery, or capillary tube carrying blood **bloody-minded** adj deliberately awkward and unhelpful

bloom n 1 a flower 2 a state of youthful beauty or health 3 the fine powder on fresh ripe grapes, etc. **bloom** v 1 to bear flowers, to be in bloom 2 to be in full beauty or health

blossom n a flower or mass of flowers on a tree **blossom** v 1 to produce blossom 2 to develop and flourish ♦ *She has blossomed into a fine singer.*

blot n 1 a spot of ink 2 a thing that spoils something ♦ *a blot on his reputation* **blot** v **blotted**, **blotting** 1 to make a blot or blots on something 2 to dry something with blotting paper, to soak up

blotch n a large irregular mark or patch **blotch** v to mark something with blotches **blotchy** adj

blouse n 1 a woman's piece of clothing like a shirt 2 a waist-length coat forming part of a military uniform

blow[1] v **blew**, **blown** 1 to move or flow as a current of air does ♦ *The wind was blowing hard.* 2 to move something by sending out a current of air ♦ *A gust of wind blew his wig off.* 3 to be moved or carried by air

or the wind ♦ *The door blew open.* 4 to send out a current of air from your mouth, or to make or sound something by doing this ♦ *The kids were blowing bubbles.* 5 to shape molten glass by blowing into it 6 to melt with too strong an electric current ♦ *A fuse must have blown.* 7 to break something with explosives ♦ *The thieves blew the safe.* 8 informal to make a mess of something ♦ *You've completely blown it!* 9 informal to reveal something ♦ *The spy's cover was blown.* 10 informal to spend money recklessly ♦ *He blew the lot on the horses.* **blow** n 1 an act of blowing 2 exposure to fresh air **blower** n **blowy** adj **blowier**, **blowiest**, **blow-by-blow** adj telling all the details of an event in the order in which they occurred **blow-dry** v **blow-dries**, **blow-dried**, **blow-drying** to use a hand-held dryer to style washed hair while drying it **blowhole** n the nostril of a whale or dolphin on the top of its head **blowlamp** n a blowtorch **blowout** n 1 a burst tyre 2 a melted fuse 3 a rapid uncontrolled upward rush of oil or gas from a well **blowpipe** n 1 a tube for sending out darts or pellets by blowing 2 a tube through which air or gas is blown **blowtorch** n a portable burner producing a very hot flame that can be directed on a selected spot **blow-up** n an enlargement of a photograph

blow[2] n 1 a hard knock or hit with the hand or a weapon 2 a sudden shock or disappointment

blub v **blubbed**, **blubbing** to weep noisily

blubber n whale fat **blubber** v to weep noisily

bludgeon (say **bluj**-ən) n a short stick with a thickened end, used as a weapon **bludgeon** v 1 to beat someone with a heavy stick or other object 2 to bully someone into doing something

blue adj **bluer**, **bluest** 1 of the colour of a cloudless sky 2 unhappy or depressed 3 indecent or obscene ♦ *blue films* **blue** n 1 blue colour 2 blue clothes ♦ *She was dressed all in blue.* 3 (**the blue**) the sky or sea 4 a person who has represented Oxford or Cambridge University in a sport **blue** v **blues**, **blued**, **blueing** to make something blue, or to become blue **blueness** n **blues** n 1 a slow sad jazz song or tune, of black American folk origin 2 (**the blues**) feelings of sadness or depression **bluebell** n a plant with blue bell-shaped flowers **blueberry** n pl **blueberries** 1 a shrub with edible blue berries 2 the fruit of this shrub **blue blood** n aristocratic descent **blue-blooded** adj **bluebottle** n a large fly with a bluish body **blue cheese** n cheese with veins of blue mould **blue-chip** adj (said about companies or their shares) fairly reliable as an investment though less secure than gilt-edged **blue-collar** adj (said about a worker) involved in manual work, especially in industry **blueprint** n 1 a design plan or technical drawing 2 a detailed plan or scheme

bluff[1] v to try to deceive someone into believing that you are in a stronger position than you really are or that you are able to do something **bluff** n an attempt to bluff someone, a threat that you make but do not intend to carry out

bluff[2] adj frank and direct, but in a good-natured way **bluff** n a headland or cliff with a broad steep front **bluffness** n

bluish adj having a blue tinge

blunder n a mistake made especially through ignorance or carelessness **blunder** v 1 to make a blunder 2 to move clumsily and uncertainly ♦ I could hear him blundering about upstairs. **blunderer** n

blunt adj 1 with no sharp edge or point, not sharp 2 speaking or expressed in plain terms ♦ a blunt refusal **blunt** v to make something blunt, or to become blunt **bluntly** adv **bluntness** n

blur n something that you cannot see, hear, or remember clearly ♦ Without his glasses on, everything was a blur. **blur** v **blurred**, **blurring** to make something less clear or distinct, or to become less clear or distinct **blurred** adj 1 not clear in outline, out of focus ♦ a blurred photograph 2 difficult to distinguish ♦ The boundary between right and wrong had become blurred.

blurb n a description of something praising it, e.g. on the back of a book

blurt v to say something abruptly or tactlessly ♦ He blurted it out before he had time to think.

blush v to become red in the face because you are ashamed or embarrassed **blush** n a reddening of the face **blusher** n a cosmetic used to add red colour to the cheeks

bluster v 1 to talk aggressively, especially with empty threats 2 (said about the wind or rain) to blow strongly in gusts **bluster** n blustering talk **blustery** adj

boa, **boa constrictor** (say boh-ə) n a large non-poisonous South American snake that squeezes its prey in order to suffocate it

boar n 1 a wild pig 2 an uncastrated domestic male pig

board n 1 a long thin flat piece of sawn timber 2 a flat piece of wood or stiff material for a special purpose ♦ a chopping board ♦ a chess board 3 a committee, the group of people who make the decisions in an organization 4 daily meals obtained in return for payment or work ♦ board and lodging **board** v 1 to get on or into a ship, aircraft, etc. 2 to receive meals and accommodation for payment **boarder** n 1 a resident pupil at a boarding school 2 a lodger who receives meals **board game** n a game in which you move pieces around a board **boarding house** n a private house where people obtain meals and lodging for payment **boarding school** n a school where pupils live during the term **boardroom** n a room where the meetings of the board of a company are held

boast v 1 to speak with great pride about yourself in order to impress people 2 to have something to be proud of ♦ The town boasts a fine park. **boast** n 1 a boastful statement 2 something you are proud of **boaster** n **boastful** adj boasting frequently **boastfully** adv **boastfulness** n

boat n 1 a small vessel for travelling on water, propelled by paddle, oars, sails, or an engine 2 a ship **boathouse** n a shed at the water's edge for housing boats **boatman** n pl **boatmen** a man who rows or sails boats or who rents out boats **boat people** pl n refugees leaving a country by sea **boatswain** (say boh-sen) n a ship's officer in charge of rigging, boats, anchors, etc.

bob v bobbed, bobbing 1 to make a jerky movement, to move quickly up and down 2 to cut hair short so that it hangs loosely and evenly all round the head **bob** n 1 a quick short movement up and down 2 the style of bobbed hair

bobble n a small ball made of strands of wool, e.g. on a woolly hat

bobsleigh (say **bob**-slay), **bobsled** n a sledge with two sets of runners and mechanical steering, used for racing down an ice-covered run **bobsleighing** n

bode v to be a sign or omen of what is to come ♦ It doesn't bode well for their future.

bodice (say **bod**-iss) n 1 the upper part of a woman's dress, down to the waist 2 a woman's piece of underclothing like a vest

body n pl **bodies** 1 the structure of bones, flesh, etc., of a human being or animal, living or dead 2 the main part of the body apart from the head and limbs 3 a corpse or carcass 4 the main or central part of something ♦ the body of a concert hall 5 a group or quantity of people, things, or matter, regarded as a unit ♦ the school's governing body 6 a distinct piece of matter, or an object in space 7 a thick texture or full flavour ♦ This wine has no body. 8 another word for bodysuit **bodily** adj **body blow** n 1 a heavy punch 2 a severe setback **bodybuilder** n **bodybuilding** n strengthening and enlarging your muscles by exercise such as weightlifting **bodyguard** n a personal guard employed to protect an important person **body language** n movements by which you communicate your feelings or moods **body piercing** n the piercing of parts of the body for decoration **body shop** n a garage that deals with repairs to the bodywork of vehicles **bodysuit** n a tight-fitting piece of clothing worn by women on the upper part of the body **bodywork** n the outer shell of a motor vehicle

boffin n informal a person involved in scientific or technical research

bog n an area of ground that is permanently wet and spongy **to be bogged down** to be stuck and unable to make progress

boggy adj

bogey n pl **bogeys** 1 an evil spirit 2 something that frightens people **bogeyman** n pl **bogeymen** an imaginary man feared by children

boggle v informal to be amazed or puzzled ♦ The mind boggles at the idea.

bogus adj not genuine or true

Bohemian adj not conventional in your way of living **Bohemian** n a person who does not live in a socially conventional way

boil¹ v 1 (said about a liquid) to bubble up and change into vapour through being heated 2 to heat a liquid or its container so that the liquid boils 3 to cook or wash something in boiling water, to be heated or cooked in this way 4 to be seething with anger 5 informal to be very hot ♦ I'm boiling! **boil** n boiling point ♦ Bring the milk to the boil. **boiler** n boiling point n 1 the temperature at which a liquid boils 2 a state of great anger or excitement

boil² n an inflamed swelling under the skin, filled with pus

boisterous adj 1 noisy and lively ♦ boisterous children 2 wild and stormy ♦ boisterous weather **boisterously** adv

bold adj 1 confident and courageous 2 (said about colours, designs, etc.) strong and vivid 3 without feelings of shame, impudent 4 printed in thick black type **boldly** adv **boldness** n **boldface** n a type face with thick strokes

bollard (say **bol**-erd) n 1 a short post for keeping traffic off a road or part of a road 2 a short thick post on a quayside or ship to which a ship's rope may be tied

bolshie adj informal rebellious or uncooperative **bolshiness** n

bolster n a long pillow for placing across a bed under other pillows **bolster** v to add extra strength or support to something ♦ Winning the prize has really bolstered her confidence.

bolt n 1 a sliding bar for fastening a door or window 2 a strong metal pin that screws into a nut, used for fastening things together 3 the sliding bar that opens and closes the breech of a rifle 4 an arrow shot from a crossbow 5 a shaft of lightning

bolt v **1** to fasten something with a bolt or bolts ♦ *We bolted all the windows.* **2** to escape or run away **3** (said about plants) to run to seed **4** to gulp down food quickly **bolt hole** n a place where someone can escape or hide

bomb n **1** a container filled with explosive or incendiary material to be set off by impact or by a timing device **2** (**the bomb**) nuclear weapons **3** *informal* a large sum of money ♦ *He must be making a bomb these days.* **bomb** v **1** to attack a place with bombs **2** *informal* to fail badly **bombproof** adj built to withstand the impact of a bomb **bombshell** n something that comes as a great shock or disappointment

bombard v **1** to attack a place with many missiles, especially from big guns **2** to attack someone with constant questions or criticism **3** to send a stream of high-energy particles against something **bombardier** n **bombardment** n

bombast (say bom-bast) n pompous words or speech **bombastic** adj

bomber n **1** an aircraft that carries and drops bombs **2** a person who plants bombs

bona fide (say boh-nə fiy-di) genuine or real ♦ *bona fide customers*

bonanza (say bə-nan-zə) n a source of sudden great wealth or luck

bonbon n a sweet

bond n **1** a close friendship or connection between two or more people ♦ *We hope to strengthen the bonds between our two countries.* **2** (**bonds**) ropes or chains used to tie up a prisoner **3** the strong force of attraction that holds atoms together in a molecule **4** a document issued by a government or public company acknowledging that money has been lent to it and will be repaid **5** a binding agreement, or a document containing this ♦ *My word is my bond.* **bond** v **1** to become closely linked or connected **2** to establish a close relationship with someone ♦ *He has bonded well with his girlfriend's children.* **bonded** adj

bondage n slavery or captivity

bone n **1** one of the hard whitish parts that make up the skeleton of an animal's body **2** the substance from which these parts are made **bone** v to remove the bones from fish or meat **bony** adj **bonier, boniest 1** having large or prominent bones, having bones with little flesh on them **2** like or containing bones **boniness** n **bone china** n fine china made of clay mixed with bone ash **bone dry** adj extremely dry **bonehead** n a stupid person **bone idle** adj very lazy

bonfire n a large fire built in the open air to destroy rubbish or as a celebration

bongo n pl **bongos** each of a pair of small drums held between the knees and played with the fingers

bonhomie (say bon-ə-mi) n a good-natured friendly manner

bonk v *informal* **1** to hit someone **2** to have sexual intercourse with someone **bonk** n a hit or thud

bonkers adj *informal* crazy

bonnet n **1** a woman's or child's hat with strings that tie under the chin **2** a Scottish cap like a beret **3** a hinged cover over a car engine

bonny adj **bonnier, bonniest 1** healthy-looking **2** *Scottish N. England* good-looking

bonsai (say bon-siy) n **1** a tree or shrub grown in miniature form **2** the art of growing trees and shrubs like this

bonus n pl **bonuses 1** an extra payment in addition to a person's normal wages **2** an extra benefit

bon voyage (say bon voi-yahzh) *interjection* an expression of good wishes to someone starting a journey

bonze (say bonz) n a Buddhist priest in Japan or China

boo *interjection* **1** a sound made to show disapproval or contempt **2** an exclamation used to startle someone 'boo' **boo** v to show disapproval by shouting 'boo'

boob[1] n *informal* an embarrassing mistake **boob** v to make an embarrassing mistake **booby** n pl **boobies booby prize** n a prize given as a joke to the competitor who comes last **booby trap** n a hidden bomb placed so that it will explode when some apparently harmless object is touched or moved

boob[2] n a woman's breast

book n 1 a set of sheets of paper, usually with printing or writing on them, fastened together at one edge and enclosed in a cover 2 each of the main divisions of a written work ♦ *the Books of the Bible* 3 a number of cheques, stamps, tickets, matches, etc. fastened together in the shape of a book 4 a libretto 5 (**books**) a set of records or accounts **book** v 1 to reserve a seat on a train, room in a hotel, etc.; to buy tickets in advance 2 to enter a person in a police record ♦ *The police booked him for speeding.* 3 (said about a referee) to make a note of the name of a player who has committed a foul **bookable** adj **bookie** n a bookmaker **bookish** adj **booklet** n a small thin book with paper covers **bookbinding** n binding books professionally **bookbinder** n **bookcase** n a piece of furniture with shelves for books **book club** n a society for members who can buy books at a reduced price **bookends** pl n a pair of supports for keeping a row of books upright **booking office** n an office where tickets are sold **bookkeeping** n keeping records of the money that is spent and received by a business **bookkeeper** n **bookmaker** n a person whose business is taking bets **bookmark** n 1 something placed between the pages of a book to mark a place 2 ICT a record of the address of a file, web page, etc., enabling you to find it again quickly **bookmark** v ICT to make a record of a file, web page, etc., so as to find it again easily **bookseller** n a person whose business is selling books **bookshop** n a shop selling books **bookstall** n a stall or kiosk at which books and newspapers are sold **book token** n a voucher for a specified amount which can be exchanged for books to that value **bookworm** n 1 informal a person who enjoys reading 2 a grub that eats holes in books

boom[1] v 1 to make a hollow deep resonant sound 2 to be growing and prospering ♦ *The economy is booming.* **boom** n 1 a deep hollow sound 2 a period of increased growth or prosperity

boom[2] n 1 a long pole used to keep the bottom of a sail stretched 2 a floating barrier or a heavy chain across a river or a harbour entrance 3 a long pole carrying a microphone or film camera

boomerang n a curved wooden missile, especially one that can be thrown so that it returns to the thrower

boon n something very useful or practical

boor n a rough and bad-mannered person **boorish** adj **boorishly** adv **boorishness** n

boost v to help something to increase in strength or value ♦ *Winning last night really boosted the team's morale.* **boost** n 1 an increase in something ♦ *a boost in sales* 2 help or encouragement ♦ *That gave my confidence a boost.* **booster** n

boot n 1 a shoe that covers the foot and ankle or lower leg 2 a compartment for luggage in a car 3 informal a hard kick **boot** v 1 to kick something hard 2 to start a computer and prepare it for use **bootee** n a baby's knitted or crocheted boot **booty** n valuable goods taken away by soldiers after a battle **boot camp** n a prison for young offenders, run on military lines **bootleg** v **bootlegged, bootlegging** 1 to smuggle alcohol 2 to make and sell something illegally **bootleg** adj sold or distributed illegally ♦ *a bootleg recording* **bootlegger** n

booth n 1 a small temporary shelter at a market or fair 2 an enclosed compartment for a public telephone, for voting at elections, etc.

booze n informal alcoholic drink **booze** v informal to drink large quantities of alcohol **boozer** n **boozy** adj

bop v **bopped, bopping** informal to dance to pop music **bop** n informal a dance to pop music

border n 1 the line dividing two countries or other areas 2 something placed round an edge to strengthen or decorate it 3 a strip of ground round a garden or a part of it **border** v 1 to form a border around or along something 2 (said about a country or area) to be next to another

borderline n the line that marks a boundary, especially between two countries **borderline** adj only just belonging to a particular group or category ♦ *You're a borderline pass.*

bore[1] v to make a hole or well with a drill or other tool **bore** n the width of the inside of a gun barrel or engine cylinder

bore[2] v to make a person feel uninterested by being dull or tedious **bore** n a dull and uninteresting person or thing **bored** adj **boredom** n **boring** adj

bore[3] n a tidal wave with a steep front that moves up an estuary ♦ the Severn bore

bore[4] past tense of bear[2]

born adj 1 having a certain order, status, or place of birth ♦ first-born ♦ well-born ♦ French-born. 2 having a certain natural quality or ability ♦ a born leader **born** past participle of bear in some meanings **born-again** adj having experienced a revival of Christian faith **born of** existing as a result of something ♦ Their courage was born of despair. **to be born** to be brought forth by birth

borne past participle of bear[2] ◊ The word borne is used as part of the verb to bear when it comes before by or after have, has, or had, e.g. children (who were) borne by Eve. She bore him a son. The word born is used in a son was born.

boron (say bor -on) n a chemical element (symbol B) that is very resistant to high temperatures, used in metalwork and in nuclear reactors

borough (say bu-rə) n 1 a town or part of a city that has its own council 2 an administrative area of Greater London or of New York City

borrow v 1 to get something to use for a time, with the intention of giving it back afterwards 2 to obtain money as a loan 3 to copy something ♦ We should borrow their methods. **borrower** n

borscht (say borsht) n a Russian soup made with beetroot

borstal n a type of prison to which young offenders were formerly sent

bosom (say buu-zəm) n 1 a woman's breast 2 the centre of care or emotion ♦ He returned to the bosom of his family. **bosom** adj (said about a friend) very close

boss[1] n informal a person who controls or gives orders to workers **boss** v **bossy** adj **bossier**, **bossiest**, **bossily** adv **bossiness** n

boss[2] n a round raised knob or stud

botany n the scientific study of plants **botanical** adj **botanist** n **botanical garden** n a garden where plants and trees are grown for scientific study

botch v informal to spoil something by poor or clumsy work ♦ a botched job **botch** n a piece of work that has been badly done ♦ He made a botch of the tiling.

both adj, pronoun the two, not only the one ♦ Are both films good? **both** adv **both... and...** not only...but also... ♦ The house is both small and ugly.

bother v 1 to cause someone trouble, worry, or annoyance ♦ Does the noise bother you? 2 to take the trouble to do something, to feel concern ♦ You really shouldn't have bothered. **bother** interjection an exclamation of annoyance **bother** n 1 trouble or worry 2 a person or thing causing this **bothersome** adj

Botox n a drug made from botulin, used to treat certain muscular conditions, remove wrinkles from the skin, etc.

bottle n 1 a narrow-necked glass or plastic container for storing liquid 2 a baby's feeding bottle 3 a hot-water bottle 4 informal courage **bottle** v 1 to store liquid in bottles 2 to preserve something in glass jars ♦ bottled fruit **bottle bank** n a place where used glass bottles are deposited for recycling **bottleneck** n 1 a narrow stretch of road where traffic cannot flow freely 2 something that obstructs progress

bottom n 1 the lowest part of something, the lowest place 2 the part furthest away ♦ the bottom of the garden 3 a person's buttocks 4 the ground under a stretch of water 5 a ship's keel or hull **bottom** adj lowest in position, rank, or degree ♦ the bottom shelf **bottom** v to reach or touch bottom **bottomless** adj **bottom line** n 1 the final total of an account or balance sheet after profit and loss, etc. have been calculated 2 the basic and most important requirement **bottom-up** adj (said about plans or theories) developed from basic facts or details

boudoir (say boo-dwar) n a woman's private room

bough (say bow) n a large branch coming from the trunk of a tree

bought past tense and past participle of *buy*

bouillon (say boo-yawn) n clear soup, broth

boulder (say bohl-der) n a large rock

boulevard (say boo-lə-vard) n a wide street, often with trees on each side

bounce v 1 to spring back after hitting a hard surface 2 to make something do this ♦ *A boy was bouncing a ball against the wall.* 3 to jump suddenly, to move up and down repeatedly 4 *informal* (said about a cheque) to be sent back by the bank because there is not enough money in the account 5 *informal* to coerce someone into doing something **bounce** n 1 an act of bouncing a ball, etc. 2 a strongly self-confident manner **bouncer** n a person employed to stand at the door of a club, etc. and stop unwanted people coming in or make troublemakers leave **bouncing** adj **bouncy** adj **bouncier**, **bounciest**

bound¹ v to move or run with large leaps **bound** n a large leap

bound² past tense and past participle of *bind* **bound** adj obstructed or hindered by something ♦ *The airport was fog-bound.* **bound to** certain to ♦ *He is bound to fail.*

bound³ v 1 to form the boundary of something ♦ *Their land is bounded by the river.* 2 to limit or restrict something **bounds** pl n limits ♦ *This was beyond the bounds of possibility.* **boundary** n pl **boundaries**, **boundless** adj

bound⁴ adj going or heading towards ♦ *We are bound for Spain.* ♦ *northbound traffic*

bounty n pl **bounties** 1 a reward paid for capturing or killing someone 2 *literary* a generous gift or supply ♦ *the bounty of nature* **bountiful** adj

bouquet (say boo-kay) n 1 a bunch of flowers 2 the scent of wine **bouquet garni** n pl **bouquets garnis** a bunch of herbs used for flavouring

bourbon (say ber-bən) n 1 an American whisky made mainly from maize 2 a kind of chocolate-flavoured biscuit

bourgeois (say boor -zhwah) adj to do with the middle class, especially in having conventional ideas and tastes **bourgeoisie** n

bout n 1 a boxing or wrestling contest 2 a period of exercise or work or illness ♦ *a bout of flu*

boutique (say boo-teek) n a small shop selling fashionable clothes

bovine (say boh-viyn) adj 1 to do with or like cattle 2 dull and stupid

bow¹ (say boh) n 1 a knot made with two loops and two loose ends 2 a piece of wood curved by a tight string joining its ends, used as a weapon for shooting arrows 3 a rod with horsehair stretched between its ends, used for playing the violin, etc. **bow tie** n a man's necktie tied into a bow

bow² (say bow) v 1 to bend your body forwards to show respect or as a greeting 2 to bend downwards under a weight 3 to submit or give in ♦ *We must bow to the inevitable.* **bow** n a bending of the head or body in greeting, respect, agreement, etc.

bow³ (say bow) n the front end of a ship

bowel n the intestine **bowels** pl n the deepest inner parts of something

bowl¹ n 1 a rounded usually deep container for food or liquid 2 the hollow rounded part of a spoon, tobacco pipe, etc. 3 a stadium for sporting or musical events ♦ *the Hollywood Bowl*

bowl² n 1 a ball used in the game of bowls 2 a ball used in tenpin bowling or skittles 3 a period of bowling in cricket ♦ *Have you had a bowl yet?* **bowls** n a game played by rolling heavy balls that are weighted so that they roll in a curve **bowl** v 1 to send a ball, etc. rolling along the ground 2 (in cricket) to send a ball to be played by a batsman 3 to go along quickly and smoothly ♦ *The cart was bowling along the road.* **bowling** n

bowler¹ n a person who bowls in cricket 2 a person who plays at bowls

bowler² **bowler hat** n a man's stiff felt hat with a rounded top

box¹ n 1 a container with a flat base and usually a lid 2 a rectangular space to be filled in on a form, computer screen, etc. 3 a compartment in a theatre where several people can sit together, or one for the jury or witnesses in a law court ♦ *the*

box 71 **bran**

witness box **4** a small hut or shelter ♦ *a sentry box* **5** a facility at a newspaper office for receiving replies to an advertisement **6** (**the box**) *informal* television **box** *v* to put something into a box **box junction** *n* a road junction marked with a grid, which vehicles may only enter if the exit is clear **box number** *n* a number used to identify a box in a newspaper office or post office to which letters to an advertiser may be sent **box office** *n* a place at a theatre, cinema, etc. where tickets are sold **box room** *n* a very small room

box² *v* to fight with the fists as a sport **box** *n* a slap on the side of someone's head **boxer** *n* **1** a person who boxes as a sport **2** a dog resembling a bulldog **boxing** *n* the sport of fighting with the fists **boxer shorts** *pl n* men's underpants that look like shorts **Boxing Day** *n* a public holiday on the first weekday after Christmas Day

boy *n* a male child or youth **boyfriend** *n* a person's usual male companion in a romantic relationship **boyhood** *n* **boyish** *adj* **boyishly** *adv* **boyishness** *n*

boycott (say boy-kot) *v* to refuse to use, buy, or have anything to do with something ♦ *Customers have been boycotting these products.* **boycott** *n* an act of boycotting something ♦ *an Olympic boycott*

bra *n* a piece of underwear worn by women to support their breasts

brace *n* **1** a device that clamps things together or holds them in place **2** a wire device fitted in the mouth to straighten the teeth **3** *pl n* a pair of birds or animals killed in hunting ♦ *a brace of pheasants* **braces** *pl n* straps used to hold trousers up, fastened to the waistband and passing over the shoulders **brace** *v* to support or give firmness to something **bracing** *adv* **to brace yourself** to prepare yourself for something unpleasant

bracelet *n* an ornamental band or chain worn on the arm

bracken *n* a large fern that grows on waste land, or a mass of such ferns

bracket *n* **1** any of the marks used in pairs for enclosing words or figures, e.g. (), [] **2** a support attached to a wall or other upright surface **3** a group or range between certain limits ♦ *a high income bracket* **bracket** *v* **bracketed, bracketing 1** to enclose or join something by brackets **2** to put a number of things together in a group because they are similar

brae (say bray) *n Scottish* a hillside

brag *v* **bragged, bragging** to boast **brag** *n* a card game **braggart** *n*

Brahman, Brahmin (say brah-mən) *n* a member of the highest Hindu class, originally priests **Brahmanism** *n*

braid *n* **1** a plait of hair **2** a strip of cloth with a woven decorative pattern, used as a trimming **braid** *v* **1** to plait hair **2** to trim something with braid

Braille (say brayl) *n* a system of representing letters, etc. by patterns of raised dots which blind people can read by touch

brain *n* **1** the organ that is the centre of the nervous system in animals, a mass of soft grey matter in the skull **2** a person's mind or intelligence ♦ *She's got both beauty and brains.* **brain** *v informal* to hit someone hard on the head **brainless** *adj* unintelligent or stupid **brainy** *adj* **brainier, brainiest, braininess** *n* **brainchild** *n* a person's invention or plan **brain drain** *n* the loss from a country of clever and skilled people by emigration **brainpower** *n* mental ability or intelligence **brainstorm** *n* **1** a moment of mental confusion **2** a spontaneous group discussion organized to try to think of new ideas **brainstorm** *v* to try to think of new ideas by having a spontaneous group discussion **brainwash** *v* to use mental pressure to force someone to reject old beliefs and accept new ones **brainwave** *n* **1** an electrical impulse in the brain **2** a sudden clever idea

braise *v* to cook food slowly with very little liquid in a closed container

brake *n* **1** a device for slowing down or stopping a moving vehicle **2** the pedal or lever that operates this device **brake** *v* to slow down a moving vehicle by using a brake

bramble *n* a rough shrub with long prickly shoots, a blackberry bush

bran *n* ground-up inner husks of grain, sifted

out from flour

branch n **1** an arm-like part of a tree **2** a part of a river, road, or railway that leads off from the main part **3** a local shop or office, etc. belonging to a larger organization **4** a subdivision of a family or a group of languages or a subject **branch** v **1** (said about a road, river, etc.) to divide into branches **2** (said about a tree or plant) to send out branches

brand n **1** a particular make of goods **2** a company's trademark or label **3** a characteristic kind of something ♦ *his strange brand of humour* **4** a mark of identification made on livestock with a hot iron **5** a piece of burning wood **brand** v **1** to mark livestock with a hot iron to identify them **2** to sell goods under a particular trademark **3** to give a bad name to someone ♦ *He has been branded a liar.* **brand name** n a name given to a product or range of products **brand new** adj completely new

brandish v to wave something about

brandy n pl **brandies** a strong alcoholic spirit distilled from wine or from fermented fruit juice

brash adj rudely or aggressively self-assertive **brashly** adv **brashness** n

brass n **1** a yellow alloy of copper and zinc **2** a brass ornament **3** the brass wind instruments in an orchestra **4** a brass memorial tablet in a church **5** informal money **6** informal high-ranking officers or officials ♦ *the top brass* **brass** adj made of brass **brassy** adj **brassier, brassiest, brassiness** n **brass band** n a band playing brass and percussion instruments only

brasserie (say bras-er-i) n an inexpensive restaurant, especially one serving French food

brassiere (say bras-i-air) n a woman's bra

brat n informal a badly behaved child

brave adj having or showing courage **brave** v to face and endure something unpleasant or dangerous with courage ♦ *Are you ready to brave the elements?* **bravado** n a display of boldness intended to impress people **bravely** adv **bravery** n

bravo interjection, n pl **bravos** a cry meaning 'well done!'

bravura (say brə-voor -ə) n great skill and brilliance

brawl n a noisy quarrel or fight **brawl** v to take part in a brawl

brawn n **1** physical strength, in contrast to intelligence **2** meat from a pig's or calf's head boiled, chopped, and pressed in a mould **brawny** adj **brawnier, brawniest**

bray v to make the loud harsh cry of a donkey **bray** n a braying sound

brazen (say bray-zən) adj **1** bold and shameless **2** made of brass or like brass **brazen** v **to brazen it out** to behave, after doing wrong, as if you have nothing to be ashamed of

brazier (say bray-zi-er) n a basket-like stand for holding burning coals

breach n **1** the breaking or neglect of a rule, agreement, etc. ♦ *a breach of contract* **2** a gap in a wall or barrier, especially one made by an attacking army **breach** v **1** to make a gap in a wall or barrier **2** to break a rule, agreement, etc. ♦ *The company has breached the code of conduct.*

bread n **1** a food made of flour, water, and yeast mixed together and baked **2** informal money **breaded** adj coated with breadcrumbs **breadboard** n **1** a board for cutting bread on **2** a board for making an experimental model of an electric circuit **breadcrumb** n a small fragment of bread **breadline** n **breadwinner** n the member of a family who earns the money to support the others

breadth n **1** the distance or measurement from side to side **2** a wide range ♦ *She brings a breadth of experience to the job.*

break v **broke, broken 1** to fall into pieces, or to cause something to do this, especially as a result of a blow or pressure ♦ *My sister broke her leg skiing.* **2** to stop working properly, or to damage something so that it no longer works properly **3** to fail to keep a promise, rule, or law **4** to end or interrupt something ♦ *She finally broke her silence.* **5** to reveal news to someone, to become publicly known ♦ *When will you break the news to them?* **6** to make a rush or dash ♦ *The player broke clear with only the goalkeeper to beat.* **7** to surpass ♦ *He hopes* to break the world record. **8** to emerge or appear suddenly ♦ *Dawn had broken.* **9** to change suddenly ♦ *The weather broke.* **10** to find the solution to a code **11** to destroy a person's spirit ♦ *The scandal broke him.* **12** to make the first stroke in a game of snooker, pool, etc. **13** (said about a voice) to change its even tone, either with emotion or (in the case of a boy's voice) by becoming suddenly deeper at puberty **14** (said about waves) to fall in foam **15** (said about a ball) to change direction after touching the ground **break** *n* **1** an instance of breaking, or the place where something is broken **2** a sudden rush or dash **3** a gap in something **4** a short period during which you rest or do something different **5** a short holiday **6** a number of points scored continuously in snooker or billiards **7** (in tennis) the winning of a game against your opponent's serve **8** *informal* a piece of luck or an opportunity ♦ *a lucky break* **break off 1** to bring something to an end ♦ *The union announced it was breaking off negotiations.* **2** to suddenly stop speaking **break out 1** to begin suddenly ♦ *A fight broke out between rival supporters.* **2** to force your way out **3** to develop something unpleasant such as a rash ♦ *The whole family have broken out in spots.* **to break down 1** to stop working properly because of mechanical failure **2** to end or collapse because of disagreements or problems ♦ *The negotiations have broken down.* **3** to start crying **4** to act upon something chemically and reduce it to its constituent parts **to break even** to make gains and losses that balance exactly **to break in 1** to force your way into a building **2** to interrupt **3** to accustom a horse to being ridden **to break into** to suddenly start doing something ♦ *He broke into a run.* **breakable** *adj* **breakage** *n* **breakaway** becoming separate from a larger group **breakaway** *adj* separated from a large group **break-dancing** *n* an energetic style of street dancing **breakdown** *n* **1** mechanical failure, especially of a car ♦ *We had a breakdown on the motorway.* **2** failure or collapse ♦ *the breakdown of law and order* **3** a period of mental illness

caused by anxiety or depression **4** an analysis of accounts or statistics **break-in** *n* a forcible entry, especially by a thief **breakneck** *adj* (said about speed) dangerously fast **breakthrough** *n* a major advance in knowledge **break-up** *n* the disintegration or dispersal of something **breakwater** *n* a wall built out into the sea to protect a harbour or coast against heavy waves

breakfast *n* the first meal of the day **breakfast** *v* to eat breakfast

breast (say brest) *n* **1** either of the two fleshy parts on the upper front of a woman's body that produce milk to feed a baby **2** the upper front part of the human body or of a piece of clothing covering this **3** the corresponding part in animals, especially a joint of poultry cut from here **breast** *v* to face and move forwards against something ♦ *We swam out, breasting the waves.* **breastbone** *n* the flat vertical bone in the chest or breast, joined to the ribs **breastfeed** *v* past tense and past participle **breastfed** *v* to feed a baby with milk from the mother's breast **breastfed** *adj* **breastplate** *n* a piece of armour covering the chest **breaststroke** *n* a swimming stroke performed on your front, with sweeping movements of the arms

breath (say breth) *n* **1** air drawn into the lungs and sent out again **2** breathing in ♦ *Take six deep breaths.* **3** a gentle blowing ♦ *a breath of wind* **4** a hint or slight rumour ♦ *There was not a breath of scandal.* **breathe** *v* **1** to draw air into the lungs and send it out again **2** (said about plants) to respire **3** (said about wine) to be exposed to fresh air **4** to speak or utter ♦ *Don't breathe a word of this.* **breather** *n* a pause for rest ♦ *Let's take a breather.* **breathless** *adj* **1** out of breath, panting **2** holding your breath with excitement **breathlessly** *adv* **breathlessness** *n* **breathy** *adj* **breathier**, **breathiest** with a noticeable sound of breathing **breathalyse** *v* to test someone with a breathalyser **breathalyser** *n* a device used by police for measuring the amount of alcohol in a person's breath **breathing space** *n* a pause to recover from effort and decide what to do next **breathtaking** adj very exciting, spectacular

bred past tense and past participle of breed

breech n the back part of a gun barrel, where the bullets are put in **breech birth** n

breeches (say **brich**-iz) pl n trousers reaching to just below the knees, worn for riding or as part of ceremonial dress

breed v past tense and past participle **bred** 1 (said about animals) to produce offspring 2 to keep animals for the purpose of producing young 3 to train someone or to bring them up 4 to give rise to something ♦ Familiarity breeds contempt. **breed** n a variety of animals within a species, especially one that has been deliberately developed **breeder** n **breeding** n

breeze n a gentle wind **breeze** v informal to move in a casual or lively manner ♦ They breezed in halfway through the meal. **breezy** adj **breezier**, **breeziest**, **breezily** adv **breeziness** n

Breton (say **bret**-ən) adj to do with Brittany or its people or language **Breton** n 1 a native of Brittany 2 the Celtic language of Brittany

brew v 1 to make beer by boiling and fermentation 2 to make tea or coffee by mixing it with hot water 3 (said about tea or coffee) to be prepared in this way ♦ The tea is brewing. 4 to begin to develop ♦ Trouble is brewing. **brew** n 1 a kind of beer 2 a drink of tea **brewer** n **brewery** n pl **breweries**

briar n a thorny bush, especially the wild rose

bribe n something, especially money, offered to someone to influence them to act in favour of the giver **bribe** v to persuade someone to do something by offering them a bribe **bribable** adj **bribery** n

bric-a-brac (say **brik**-ə-brak) n odd items of furniture, ornaments, etc., of no great value

brick n 1 a block of baked or dried clay or other substance used to build walls 2 bricks considered as a building material ♦ Our garden shed is built of brick. 3 informal a kind-hearted person **brick** v to block something with bricks ♦ We bricked up the

fireplace. **bricklayer** n a person whose job is building with bricks **brick red** n a deep brownish red **brickwork** n a structure made of bricks

bride n a woman on her wedding day, or a newly married woman **bridal** adj **bridegroom** n a man on his wedding day, or a newly married man **bridesmaid** n a woman or girl attending the bride at a wedding

bridge[1] n 1 a structure providing a way across something or carrying a road or railway, etc. across 2 the raised platform on a ship from which the captain and officers direct its course 3 the bony upper part of the nose **bridge** v to make or form a bridge over something **bridgehead** n a fortified area established in enemy territory, especially on the far side of a river

bridge[2] n a card game rather like whist

bridle n the part of a horse's harness that fits over its head **bridle** v 1 to put a bridle on a horse 2 to bring something under control 3 to show you are offended by something **bridleway** n a path suitable for horses but not for vehicles

brief[1] adj 1 lasting only for a short time ♦ a brief visit 2 concise, using few words ♦ a brief summary ♦ I'll be brief. 3 short in length ♦ a brief skirt **briefs** pl n very short knickers or underpants **brevity** n **briefly** adv **briefness** n

brief[2] n 1 a summary of the facts of a case, drawn up for a barrister 2 a case given to a barrister 3 a set of instructions given to someone before they start a piece of work **brief** v 1 to give someone all the instructions and information they need before starting a piece of work 2 to give a brief to a barrister **briefing** n **briefcase** n a flat case for carrying documents

brigade n 1 an army unit forming part of a division 2 a group of people organized for a particular purpose ♦ the fire brigade **brigadier** n

brigand (say **brig**-ənd) n a member of a band of robbers

bright adj 1 giving out much light, or filled with light ♦ a bright room 2 (said about colours) vivid and bold 3 quick-witted

and clever **4** cheerful ♦ *a bright smile*
bright *adv* brightly **brighten** *v* **brightly** *adv*
brightness *n*
brilliant *adj* **1** very bright or sparkling **2** very
clever or talented **3** excellent, marvellous
brilliant *n* a cut diamond with many facets
brilliance *n* **brilliancy** *n* **brilliantly** *adv*
brim *n* **1** the edge of a cup, bowl, or other
container ♦ *The bucket was filled to the
brim.* **2** the bottom part of a hat that
sticks out **brim** *v* **brimmed, brimming**
to fill something to the brim, or to be full
to the brim ♦ *Her eyes brimmed with tears.*
brimful *adj* **brimstone** *n* sulphur
brindled (say brin-dəld) *adj* brown with
streaks of other colour ♦ *a brindled cow*
brine *n* salt water **briny** *adj* **brinier, briniest**
bring *v* past tense and past participle
brought **1** to cause a person or thing to
come, especially by carrying or leading
them **2** to result in or cause something
♦ *War brought famine.* **3** to cause something
to arrive at a particular state ♦ *I managed to
bring them to their senses.* **4** to put forward
charges, etc. in a law court ♦ *They brought
an action for libel.*
brink *n* **1** the edge of a steep place or of a
stretch of water **2** the point beyond which
something will happen ♦ *We were on the
brink of war.*
brisk *adj* **1** active, moving quickly ♦ *a brisk
walk* **2** (said about a person's manner)
dealing with people quickly and in a
businesslike way, perhaps slightly rudely
briskly *adv* **briskness** *n*
brisket (say brisk-it) *n* a joint of beef cut
from the breast
bristle (say briss-əl) *n* **1** a short stiff hair
2 any of the stiff pieces of hair, wire, or
plastic in a brush **bristle** *v* **1** (said about an
animal's hair or fur) to stand upright as a
sign of anger or fear **2** to show indignation
or irritation **bristly** *adj*
Britain *n* the island made up of England,
Scotland, and Wales, with the small
adjacent islands; Great Britain ◊ Note
the difference in use between the terms
Britain, *Great Britain*, the *United Kingdom*,
and the *British Isles*. Great Britain (or
Britain) is used to refer to the island made

up of England, Scotland, and Wales. The
United Kingdom includes Great Britain and
Northern Ireland. The British Isles refers
to the whole of the island group which
includes Great Britain, Ireland, and all the
smaller nearby islands. **Britannic** *adj* to do
with Britain ♦ *Her Britannic Majesty.* **Briton** *n*
a person born or living in Britain, especially
an inhabitant of southern Britain before the
Roman conquest
British Isles *pl n* the island group which
includes Great Britain, Ireland, and all the
smaller nearby islands ◊ See the note at
Britain.
brittle *adj* hard but easy to break or snap
broach *v* **1** to raise a subject for discussion
2 to make a hole in something and draw
out liquid
broad *adj* **1** large across, wide **2** measuring
from side to side ♦ *50 ft. broad* **3** large in
scope ♦ *She has broad tastes in music.* **4** in
general terms, not detailed ♦ *We were in
broad agreement.* **5** clear and unmistakable
♦ *a broad hint* **6** (said about a regional
accent) very noticeable and strong **7** rather
coarse ♦ *broad humour* **broaden** *v* to make
something broad, or to become broad
broadly *adv* **1** in a broad way **2** in a general
way ♦ *Broadly speaking, I agree with you.*
broadband *n* ICT a broadband Internet
connection is a continuous connection
that uses signals over a wide range of
frequencies **broad bean** *n* an edible
bean with large flat seeds **broadcast** *v*
broadcast, **broadcast**, or **broadcasted**
1 to send out a programme on television or
radio **2** to make a piece of news generally
known **3** to sow seed by scattering, not in
drills **broadcast** *n* a programme sent out on
television or radio **broadcast** *adv* scattered
freely **broadcaster** *n* **broad-minded** *adj*
having tolerant views, not easily shocked
broadsheet *n* a newspaper with a large
format, thought of as more serious than
the tabloids
brocade (say brə-kayd) *n* a rich fabric
woven with raised patterns **brocaded** *adj*
broccoli (say brok-əli) *n* a kind of
cauliflower with greenish flower heads
brochure (say broh-shə) *n* a booklet or

pamphlet containing information

brogue[1] (say brohg) n a strong shoe with ornamental perforated bands

brogue[2] n a dialectal accent, especially Irish

broil v 1 to cook meat over direct heat 2 to become very hot, especially from sunshine

broiler n a young chicken suitable or specially reared for broiling or roasting

broke past tense of break **broke** adj informal having run out of money **broken** adj **brokenly** adv **broken-hearted** adj overwhelmed by grief or disappointment **broken home** n a family in which the parents are divorced or separated

broker n a person who buys and sells things on behalf of others **broker** v to arrange or negotiate a deal or plan

brolly n pl **brollies** informal an umbrella

bronze n 1 a brown alloy of copper and tin 2 something made of bronze 3 a bronze medal, awarded as third prize 4 a yellowish-brown colour **bronze** adj 1 made of bronze 2 yellowish-brown **bronze** v to make someone suntanned **Bronze Age** n the period when weapons and tools were made of bronze

brooch (say brohch) n an ornamental hinged pin fastened with a clasp

brood n the young birds or other animals that were hatched or born together **brood** v 1 to keep thinking deeply or resentfully about something ♦ I've been brooding over what you said last night. 2 to sit on eggs to hatch them **brooding** adj **broody** adj **broodier, broodiest**

brook n a small stream

broom n 1 a long-handled brush for sweeping floors 2 a shrub with yellow or white flowers

broomstick n a broom handle

Bros (say bross) abbr Brothers

broth n a kind of thin soup

brothel (say broth-əl) n a house where women work as prostitutes

brother n 1 a son of the same parents as another person 2 a man who is a fellow member of a trade union, Christian Church, or other association 3 a member of a religious order of men **brotherly** adj **brotherhood** n 1 the relationship of

brothers 2 friendliness and companionship between men, or between people in general 3 a society or association of men, or its members **brother-in-law** n pl **brothers-in-law** the brother of a married person's husband or wife, or the husband of a person's sister

brought past tense and past participle of bring

brow n 1 a person's forehead 2 an eyebrow 3 the top of a hill **browbeat** v browbeat, **browbeaten** to intimidate someone, especially with words

brown adj 1 of a colour between orange and black, like the colour of dark wood 2 dark-skinned or suntanned 3 (said about bread) brown in colour, especially through being made with wholemeal flour **brown** n 1 brown colour 2 brown clothes **brown** v to make something brown, or to become brown **browning** n **brown sugar** n

brownie n 1 a small square of chocolate cake 2 a friendly elf **Brownie** n a member of a junior branch of the Guides, for girls between about 7 and 10

browse v 1 to look through a book, or examine items for sale, in a casual leisurely way ♦ I'm just browsing, thank you. 2 ICT to search files on a network 3 (said about animals) to feed on leaves or grass

bruise (say brooz) n 1 an injury caused by a blow or by pressure that makes a dark mark on the skin without breaking it 2 a similar area of damage on a fruit or vegetable **bruise** v 1 to cause a bruise or bruises to appear on a person's skin 2 to be susceptible to bruises ♦ I bruise easily.

brunch n informal a late-morning meal combining breakfast and lunch

brunette (say broo-**net**) n a woman with dark brown hair

brunt n the chief impact of something bad ♦ They bore the brunt of the attack.

brush n 1 an implement with bristles of hair, wire, or nylon set in a solid base, used for cleaning, smoothing, or painting things 2 an act of brushing ♦ Give your hair a good brush. 3 a brief unpleasant encounter ♦ We had a brush with a group of hooligans. 4 a fox's bushy tail 5 a brush-like piece of carbon or metal for making a good electrical connection **6** each of a pair of elastic sticks with long wire bristles for striking a drum or cymbal **brush** v **1** to clean something or make something tidy with a brush ♦ *I'll just brush my teeth.* **2** to touch something lightly in passing ♦ *Her hand brushed my cheek.* **brush-off** n a curt rejection **brushwood** n **1** undergrowth **2** cut or broken twigs **brushwork** n the style of the strokes made with a painter's brush

brusque (say bruusk) adj abrupt and offhand in manner **brusquely** adv **brusqueness** n

Brussels sprout n one of the edible buds growing thickly on the stem of a kind of cabbage

brutal adj cruel and violent ♦ *a brutal attack* **brutality** n **brutalization** n **brutalize** v **brutally** adv **brute** n **1** a brutal person **2** an unpleasant or difficult person or thing **3** an animal in contrast to a human being **brute** adj merely physical ♦ *We had to use brute force to get the door open.* **brutish** adj

BSc abbr Bachelor of Science

BSE abbr bovine spongiform encephalopathy; a fatal disease of cattle that affects the nervous system and causes staggering

BST abbr British Summer Time

Bt abbr Baronet ♦ *Sir John Davis, Bt.*

bubble n **1** a thin ball of liquid enclosing air or gas **2** a small ball of air in a liquid or in a solidified liquid, such as glass **3** a transparent domed cover **bubble** v **1** to send up or rise in bubbles **2** to make the sound of bubbles rising in liquid ♦ *The soup was bubbling away in the kitchen.* **3** to show great liveliness or excitement ♦ *She was bubbling with anticipation.* **bubbly** adj **bubblier, bubbliest 1** full of bubbles **2** cheerful and lively **bubbly** n informal champagne or sparkling wine **bubblegum** n chewing gum that can be blown into large bubbles **bubble wrap** n plastic packaging in the form of sheets which contain lots of small air cushions, used to protect whatever it is wrapped around

bubonic plague (say bew-bon-ik) n a contagious disease, transmitted by rat fleas, producing inflamed swellings (called *buboes*) in the groin or armpit

buccaneer n hist **1** a pirate **2** an unscrupulous adventurer **buccaneering** adj

buck¹ n a male deer, hare, or rabbit **buck** v **1** (said about a horse) to jump with its back arched and kick out its back legs **2** informal to resist or oppose something ♦ *We are bucking the trend.*

buck² n N. Am Austral. informal a dollar

buck³ n **to pass the buck** informal to shift the responsibility or blame for something to someone else

bucket n **1** a round open container with a handle, used for holding or carrying liquids or substances that are in small pieces **2** the amount of liquid in a bucket ♦ *You'll need three buckets to fill the bath.* **buckets** pl n informal large quantities of rain or tears ♦ *I cried buckets at the end of the film.* **bucket** v **bucketed, bucketing** to pour down heavily ♦ *Rain was bucketing down.* **bucketful** n **bucketfuls**

buckle n a device usually with a hinged tongue, through which a belt or strap is threaded to secure it **buckle** v **1** to fasten something with a buckle ♦ *He buckled on his sword.* **2** to bend and give way under pressure or intense heat ♦ *My legs buckled and I fell to the floor.* **to buckle down to** to start working at something with determination

bucolic (say bew-kol-ik) adj to do with country life

bud n **1** a small knob that will develop into a branch, flower, or cluster of leaves **2** a flower or leaf before it opens **bud** v **budded, budding** to produce buds **budding** adj **in bud** forming buds

Buddha (say buud-ə) n **1** the title (often treated as a name) of the Indian philosopher Gautama (5th century BC), and of a series of teachers of Buddhism **2** a statue or carving representing Gautama Buddha **Buddhism** n an Asian religion based on the teachings of the Buddha **Buddhist** adj, n

budge v **1** to move or make something move slightly ♦ *The window wouldn't budge.* **2** to alter a position or opinion, or to make someone do this ♦ *She refused to budge on the matter.*

budgerigar (say **buj-er-i-gar**) *n* a kind of Australian parakeet, often kept as a pet

budget *n* **1** an estimate or plan of income and expenditure in a given period **2** the amount of money set aside for a particular purpose ♦ *I have a budget of £30 for their present.* **3** (**the Budget**) a regular statement made by the Chancellor of the Exchequer about plans for government spending and raising revenue **budget** *v* **budgeted**, **budgeting** to allow for an expense in a budget ♦ *I didn't budget for staying in a hotel.* **budget** *adj* inexpensive ♦ *budget fares* **budgetary** *adj*

budgie *n informal* a budgerigar

buff[1] *n* **1** strong velvety dull-yellow leather **2** the colour of this **buff** *adj* dull yellow **buff** *v* to polish something with soft material **in the buff** naked

buff[2] *n informal* a person who is interested in and knows a lot about a particular subject ♦ *a film buff*

buffalo *n pl* **buffaloes** or **buffalo 1** a kind of domesticated ox found in Asia; a rather similar wild ox found in Africa **2** an American bison

buffer *n* **1** something that reduces the effect of an impact or forms a barrier between two opposing sides **2** *ICT* a temporary store in a system, used when editing text or transferring data **3** *informal* an elderly or strange person ♦ *Who's the old buffer over there?* **buffer** *v* to lessen the impact of something

buffet[1] (say **buu-fay**) *n* **1** a meal where guests serve themselves ♦ *a buffet lunch* **2** a room or counter selling light meals or snacks ♦ *the station buffet*

buffet[2] (say **buff-it**) *v* **buffeted**, **buffeting** to hit or knock something ♦ *Our aircraft was buffeted by strong winds.*

buffoon (say buf-**oon**) *n* a person who acts like a fool **buffoonery** *n*

bug *n* **1** an insect, especially one that infests dirty houses and beds **2** *informal* a harmful micro-organism, or an illness caused by one ♦ *a stomach bug* **3** *informal* an error in a computer program or system that

prevents it working properly **4** *informal* an enthusiasm for something ♦ *They've caught the skiing bug.* **5** a very small hidden microphone installed secretly **bug** *v* **bugged**, **bugging** *informal* **1** to fit a room with a hidden microphone secretly so that conversations, etc. can be overheard from a distance **2** to annoy someone ♦ *What's bugging you?* **bugbear** *n* something you fear or dislike **bug-eyed** *adj* having bulging eyes

buggy *n pl* **buggies 1** a small sturdy motor vehicle with an open top ♦ *a beach buggy* **2** a light collapsible pushchair

bugle *n* a brass instrument like a small trumpet, used for sounding military signals **bugler** *n*

build *v* past tense and past participle **built 1** to construct something by putting parts or material together **2** to develop something gradually ♦ *We first need to build trust.* **3** to accumulate or increase ♦ *Traffic has been building all morning.* **build** *n* the shape of a person's body ♦ *He is of slender build.* **builder** *n* **building** *n* **built** *adj* **building society** *n* a financial organization that accepts deposits and lends out money for mortgages to people wishing to buy or build a house, etc. **build-up** *n* **1** a gradual increase in something ♦ *the build-up of nuclear weapons* **2** a favourable description in advance of a person's appearance, or a period of preparation before an event **built-in** *adj* forming an integral part of a structure ♦ *a built-in wardrobe*

built-up *adj* (said about a place) filled in with buildings ♦ *a built-up area*

bulb *n* **1** a thick rounded mass of scale-like leaves from which a stem grows up and roots grow down **2** a plant grown from this, such as a daffodil **3** a bulb-shaped object ♦ *the bulb of a thermometer* **4** a glass globe that produces electric light **bulbous** *adj*

bulge *n* a rounded swelling **bulge** *v* to swell outwards

bulimia, **bulimia nervosa** (say **bew-lim**-ia) *n* a psychological condition causing someone to alternately overeat and fast, often making themselves vomit after eating

bulk n 1 the size of something, especially when it is large 2 the greater part, the majority ♦ *The bulk of the population agree with this view.* 3 a large shape, body, or person ♦ *He raised his bulk from the armchair.*
bulk v to increase the size or thickness of something ♦ *Use thicker paper to bulk it out.*
bulky adj **bulkier, bulkiest, in bulk** in large quantities

bull¹ n 1 an uncastrated male of any animal of the ox family 2 the male of the whale, elephant, and other large animals 3 the bullseye of a target **bullock** n a young castrated bull **bullfight** n **bullfighter** n **bullfighting** n the sport of baiting and killing bulls for public entertainment, as in Spain **bullring** n an arena for bullfights **bullseye** n 1 the centre of a target 2 a large hard round peppermint sweet

bull² n an official edict issued by the pope

bulldoze v 1 to clear an area with a bulldozer 2 *informal* to force someone to do something ♦ *He bulldozed them into accepting it.* **bulldozer** n

bullet n a small round or conical missile shot from a rifle or revolver **bulletproof** adj able to keep out bullets

bulletin n 1 a short official statement giving news 2 a regular newsletter or report **bulletin board** n ICT an information storage system that people can access via a network

bullet point n D & T a short piece of information with a small black blob in front of it, usually in a displayed list

bullion n bars of gold or silver, before coining or manufacture

bully n pl **bullies** a person who tries to hurt or frighten people who are weaker **bully** v **bullies, bullied, bullying** to use strength or power to hurt or frighten a weaker person

bum¹ n *informal* the buttocks

bum² n N. Am *informal* a tramp or lazy person

bumble v 1 to move or act in a clumsy way 2 to ramble when speaking **bumblebee** n a large bee with a loud hum

bump v 1 to knock against something with a jolt ♦ *Our cars bumped into each other.* 2 to move along with a jolting movement ♦ *We bumped along the road.* **bump** n 1 a bumping sound, knock, or movement 2 a swelling or lump on a surface **bumper** n **bumpy** adj **bumpier, bumpiest, bumpiness** n **to bump into** to meet someone by chance **to bump someone off** *informal* to kill someone

bumpkin n a country person with awkward manners

bumptious (say bump-shəs) n annoyingly loud and conceited **bumptiously** adv **bumptiousness** n

bun n 1 a small cake or bread roll 2 hair twisted into a round bunch at the back of the head

bunch n 1 a cluster ♦ *a bunch of grapes* 2 a number of small similar things held or fastened together ♦ *a bunch of keys* 3 a group of people **bunch** v to come or bring things together into a bunch

bundle n 1 a number of things loosely fastened or wrapped together 2 a set of sticks or rods tied together 3 a large amount of money **bundle** v 1 to make a number of things into a bundle 2 to put something away hastily and untidily ♦ *She bundled the letters into a drawer.* 3 to push someone hurriedly or carelessly ♦ *We bundled him into a taxi.*

bung n a stopper for closing a hole in a barrel or jar **bung** v 1 to close something with a bung 2 *informal* to throw or toss something carelessly ♦ *Bung it over here.* **bunged up** blocked

bungalow n a house with only one storey

bungee jumping (say bun-jee) n the sport of jumping from a height with a long piece of elastic (called a *bungee*) tied to your legs to stop you from hitting the ground

bungle v to make a mess of doing something **bungle** n a mistake or failure **bungler** n

bunion n a swelling at the side of the joint where the big toe joins the foot

bunk¹ n a bed built like a shelf, e.g. on a ship **bunker** n **bunk beds** pl n a pair of single beds mounted one above the other as a unit

bunk² v *informal* to leave school or work when you should be there

bunny n pl **bunnies** *informal* a child's name

Bunsen burner n a small gas burner used in laboratories

bunting n flags and streamers for decorating streets and buildings

buoy (say boi) n an anchored floating object marking a navigable channel or showing the position of submerged rocks, etc. **buoy** v 1 to keep something afloat 2 to mark something with a buoy or buoys **buoyancy** n **buoyant** adj **buoyantly** adv **to buoy someone up** to encourage someone or cheer them up ♦ They were now buoyed up with new hope.

burble v 1 to make a gentle murmuring sound 2 to speak in a confused way and at length

burden n 1 a heavy load that has to be carried 2 something difficult that you have to bear ♦ the heavy burden of taxation 3 the main theme of a speech, book, etc. **burden** v 1 to load someone heavily ♦ She staggered in, burdened with shopping. 2 to cause someone worry or hardship ♦ I'm sorry to burden you with my troubles. **burdensome** adj

bureau (say **bewr**-oh) n pl **bureaux** 1 a writing desk with drawers and a hinged flap for use as a writing surface 2 an office or department ♦ a travel bureau ♦ an information bureau

bureaucracy (say bewr-ok-rəsi) n pl **bureaucracies** 1 the use of too many rules and forms by officials, especially in government departments 2 government by state officials, not by elected representatives **bureaucrat** n **bureaucratic** adj

burgeon (say ber-jən) v to begin to grow rapidly ♦ the country's burgeoning tourist industry

burger n a hamburger or similar type of food

burgh (say bu-rə) n a borough in Scotland

burgle v to break into a building and steal things ♦ We've been burgled! **burglar** n **burglary** n

burgundy n pl **burgundies** 1 a rich red or white wine from Burgundy in France, or a similar wine from elsewhere 2 a dark purplish red

burlesque (say ber-lesk) n a mocking imitation

burly adj **burlier, burliest** having a strong heavy body **burliness** n

burn[1] v past tense and past participle **burned** or **burnt** 1 to be on fire, to blaze or glow 2 to damage, hurt, or destroy something by fire, heat, or the action of acid ♦ You should burn that letter. 3 to use something as fuel ♦ The stove burns wood. 4 to char or scorch food you are cooking ♦ Sorry, I've burnt the chops. 5 to feel very hot ♦ My face was burning. 6 (said about the skin) to become red and painful from too much sunlight 7 to feel great emotion ♦ He was burning with desire. **burn** n 1 a mark or sore made by burning 2 the firing of a spacecraft's rockets **burner** n **burning** adj **burnt**

burn[2] n Scottish a brook

burnish v to polish something by rubbing

burp n informal a belch **burp** v informal 1 to belch 2 to make a baby bring up wind from the stomach after feeding

burr n 1 a whirring sound 2 the strong pronunciation of the letter 'r', as in some regional accents 3 a prickly seed case or flower head that clings to hair or clothing 4 a small drill **burr** v to make a whirring sound

burrow n a hole or tunnel dug by a rabbit, fox, etc. as a dwelling **burrow** v 1 to make a burrow 2 to dig into or through something solid 3 to push your way through or into something, to search deeply ♦ She burrowed in her handbag.

bursary (say ber-ser-i) n pl **bursaries** a grant given to a student **bursar** n

burst v past tense and past participle **burst** 1 to break suddenly and violently apart, or to make something do this ♦ One of my tyres has burst. 2 to be very full ♦ My wardrobe is bursting with clothes. 3 to enter loudly or suddenly ♦ Three men burst into the room. 4 to let out a strong and noisy expression of feeling ♦ We all burst out laughing. **burst** n 1 a bursting, a split 2 a brief outbreak of something violent or noisy ♦ a burst of gunfire 3 a period of continuous effort **to**

be bursting to do something to be very eager to do it ♦ *The kids are bursting to tell you the news.* **to burst into flame** to catch fire **to burst into something** to suddenly start doing something ♦ *She burst into song.* ♦ *The boy burst into tears.*

bury *v* **buries**, **buried**, **burying** 1 to place a dead body in the earth, a tomb, or the sea 2 to put something in a hole in the ground and cover it up 3 to cover something up ♦ *She buried her face in her hands.* **burial** *n*

bus *n pl* **buses** 1 a large vehicle carrying passengers on a fixed route 2 *ICT* a set of conductors in a system, to which pieces of equipment can be connected in parallel **bus** *v* **bussed**, **bussing** 1 to travel or transport someone by bus 2 to take children to a distant school by bus in order to counteract racial segregation **bus station** *n* an area where a number of buses stop **bus stop** *n* a regular stopping place on a bus route

bush[1] *n* 1 a shrub 2 wild uncultivated land, especially in Africa and Australia **bushy** *adj* **bushier**, **bushiest**, **bushiness** *n* **bushman** *n pl* **bushmen** a dweller or traveller in the Australian bush **Bushman** *n pl* **Bushmen** a member of an aboriginal people of southern Africa, especially of the Kalahari Desert

bush[2] *n* 1 a metal lining for a round hole in which something fits or revolves 2 a sleeve that protects an electric cable

bushel *n* a measure for grain and fruit equal to 8 gallons (36.4 litres)

business (say *biz*-nis) *n* 1 a person's regular trade or profession 2 buying and selling things, trade ♦ *We always do a lot of business at Christmas.* 3 a shop or firm ♦ *a grocery business* 4 a thing you are concerned about or need to deal with ♦ *I have urgent business to see to.* 5 a matter or affair ♦ *I'm sick of the whole business.* **businesslike** *adj* efficient and practical **businessman**, **businesswoman** *n pl* **businessmen**, **businesswomen** a person working in commerce, especially at a senior level **business studies** *pl n* the study of economics and management

busker *n* an entertainer who performs in the street for money **busking** *n*

bust[1] *n* 1 a sculpture of a person's head, shoulders, and chest 2 a woman's breasts 3 the measurement round a woman's body at the bosom **bustier** *n* a tight-fitting top without straps, worn by women

bust[2] *v past tense and past participle* **busted or bust** *informal* 1 to break or burst something ♦ *Who's bust my radio?* 2 to arrest someone **bust** *n informal* 1 a period of economic difficulty or depression 2 a police raid **bust** *adj informal* 1 damaged or broken 2 bankrupt **bust-up** *n informal* a serious quarrel

bustle *v* 1 to hurry in a busy or excited way 2 (said about a place) to be full of activity ♦ *a bustling market town* **bustle** *n* hurried or excited activity

busy *adj* **busier**, **busiest** 1 working or occupied, having much to do ♦ *Look, I'm a bit busy at the moment.* 2 full of activity ♦ *a busy day* ♦ *It was busy in town today.* 3 (said about a telephone line) engaged 4 (said about a picture or design) too full of detail **busy** *v* **busies**, **busied**, **busying** to keep someone busy ♦ *He busied himself in the kitchen.* **busily** *adv* **busyness** *n* **busybody** *n pl* **busybodies** a person who meddles or interferes

but *conjunction* however, nevertheless ♦ *I wanted to go, but I couldn't.* **but** *prep* except, other than ♦ *There's no one here but me.* **but** *adv* only, no more than ♦ *We can but try.* **but** *n* an objection ♦ *You're coming, and no buts.*

butch *adj informal* masculine in appearance or behaviour

butcher *n* 1 a person who cuts up and sells meat in a shop 2 a brutal or murderous person **butcher** *v* 1 to slaughter or cut up an animal for meat 2 to kill someone needlessly or brutally **butchery** *n*

butler *n* the chief manservant of a household

butt[1] *n* a large cask or barrel

butt[2] *n* 1 the thicker end of a tool or weapon 2 a short remnant, a stub ♦ *a cigar butt*

butt[3] *n* 1 a person or thing that is a target for ridicule or teasing ♦ *She was sick of being the butt of their jokes.* 2 the mound of earth behind the targets on a shooting range **butts** pl n a shooting range

butt⁴ v **1** (said about a ram or goat) to hit something with the head or horns **2** to meet or place something edge to edge ♦ *The shop butted up against the row of houses.* ♦ *The strips should be butted against each other, not overlapping.* **butt** n **1** a rough push with the head **2** a butted join

butter n **1** a fatty food substance made from cream by churning **2** a similar substance made from other materials ♦ *peanut butter* **butter** v to spread, cook, or serve something with butter **buttery** adj

buttercup n a wild plant with bright yellow cup-shaped flowers **butterfingers** n a person who often drops things or fails to hold a catch **butterfly** n pl **butterflies 1** an insect with four often brightly coloured wings and knobbed feelers **2** a swimming stroke in which both arms are lifted forwards at the same time **buttermilk** n the liquid left after butter has been churned from milk **butterscotch** n a kind of hard toffee

buttock n either of the two fleshy rounded parts at the lower or rear end of the back of the human or an animal body

button n **1** a knob or disc sewn on a piece of clothing as a fastener or ornament **2** a knob pressed to operate a piece of electrical or electronic equipment **button** v **buttoned, buttoning** to fasten a piece of clothing with a button or buttons **buttonhole** n **1** a slit through which a button is passed to fasten clothing **2** a flower worn in the buttonhole of a coat lapel **buttonhole** v informal to come up to someone and talk to them for a long time

buttress n **1** a support built against a wall **2** a thing that supports or reinforces something **buttress** v **1** to support something with buttresses **2** to support or strengthen something

butty n pl **butties** informal a sandwich

buxom adj (said about a woman) plump and having large breasts

buy v past tense and past participle **bought 1** to obtain something in exchange for money ♦ *I'll buy you lunch.* **2** to get

something by great effort or sacrifice ♦ *This victory was dearly bought.* **3** informal to believe or accept the truth of something ♦ *No one would buy that excuse.* **buy** n informal something that is bought ♦ *That suit was a good buy.* **buyer** n

buzz n **1** a vibrating humming sound **2** informal a telephone call **3** informal a thrill **4** informal a rumour **buzz** v **1** to make or be filled with a humming sound ♦ *My ears are buzzing.* **2** to signal with a buzzer ♦ *Buzz when you know the answer.* **3** to go about quickly and busily **4** to threaten an aircraft by flying close to it **buzzer** n **buzzword** n informal a piece of fashionable jargon

buzzard n a kind of hawk

by prep **1** near to, beside ♦ *She stood by the door.* **2** going past ♦ *We drove by your house today.* **3** through the agency or means of ♦ *I persuaded him by flattery.* **4** (said about numbers or measurements) taking it together with ♦ *Multiply six by four.* ♦ *It measures ten metres by eight.* **5** not later than ♦ *Can you finish this by Friday?* **6** according to ♦ *You shouldn't judge by appearances.* ♦ *They pay by the hour.* **7** to the extent of ♦ *He missed it by inches.* **8** during ♦ *They came by night.* **by** adv so as to go past ♦ *The soldiers marched by.* **by** adj additional, less important ♦ *a by-road* **bygone** adj belonging to the past **by-law** n a law that applies only to a particular town or district **byline** n a line in a newspaper, etc. naming the writer of an article **bypass** n **1** a road taking traffic round a city or congested area **2** a secondary channel allowing something to flow when the main route is blocked **3** an operation to make an alternative passage to help the circulation of the blood ♦ *a heart bypass* **bypass** v **4** to avoid a place by means of a bypass **5** to omit or ignore procedures, regulations, etc. in order to act quickly **by-product** n a substance produced during the making of something else **byroad** n a minor road **bystander** n a person standing near but taking no part when something happens **byway** n a minor road or path **byword** n **1** a person or thing spoken of as a notable example ♦ *The firm became a byword for mismanagement.* **2** a word or

phrase that sums up a person's principles
♦ *Punctuality is my byword.*

bye *n* **1** (in cricket) a run scored when the ball goes past the batsman without being touched **2** the status of having no opponent for one round in a tournament and so going on to the next round as if you had won **3** (in golf) a hole or holes remaining unplayed when a match is ended

bye-bye *interjection informal* goodbye

by-election *n* an election to replace an MP who has died or resigned

byre *n* a cowshed

byte *n* a fixed number of bits (binary digits) in a computer, often representing a single character

Byzantine (say bi-**zan**-tiyn) *adj* **1** to do with Byzantium or the Eastern Roman Empire **2** extremely complicated and detailed **3** devious or underhand

Cc

C¹ 1 the third letter of the English alphabet **2** *Mus* the first note of the diatonic scale of C major **3** the Roman numeral for 100

C² *abbr* **1** Celsius or centigrade **2** *Chem* the symbol for carbon

c. *abbr* **1** cent or cents **2** century **3** (used before a date) about ♦ *c.1776*

(c) *symbol* copyright

cab *n* **1** a taxi **2** a compartment for the driver of a train, bus, lorry, or crane **cabby** *n pl* **cabbies** a taxi driver

cabal (say kə-**bal**) *n* a group of people involved in a plot

cabaret (say kab-ə-ray) *n* an entertainment provided for customers in a restaurant or nightclub

cabbage *n* a vegetable with green or purple leaves usually forming a round head

caber (say **kay**-ber) *n* a roughly-trimmed tree trunk thrown as a sport at Highland Games

cabin *n* **1** a small wooden house or shelter **2** a compartment in a ship or spacecraft **3** the part of an aircraft in which passengers sit

cabinet *n* a cupboard or container with drawers or shelves for storage **Cabinet** *n* the group of government ministers who meet regularly to discuss government policy

cable *n* **1** a thick rope of fibre or wire, or a thick chain **2** (as a nautical measure) a length of 200 yards (183 metres) **3** a set of insulated wires for carrying electricity or transmitting electrical signals **4** a telegram sent abroad **cable** *v* to send a telegram to someone abroad **cable car** *n* a small cabin suspended from a moving cable driven by a motor at one end **cable television** *n* a television service that transmits programmes by cable

caboodle (say kə-**boo**-dəl) *n informal* **the whole caboodle** the whole lot

cacao (say kə-**kay**-oh) *n pl* **cacaos 1** a tropical tree producing a seed from which cocoa and chocolate are made **2** the seed of this tree

cache (say kash) *n* **1** a hidden store of things, especially valuable things **2** *ICT* an extra store of memory allowing high-speed access to data **cache** *v* to store something in a cache

cachet (say **kash**-ay) *n* **1** distinction or prestige **2** a distinguishing mark or seal

cackle *n* **1** the loud clucking noise a hen makes after laying **2** noisy laughter or talk **cackle** *v* **1** to give a cackle **2** to talk or laugh noisily

cacophony (say kə-**kof**-əni) *n pl* **cacophonies** a harsh unpleasant mixture of sounds **cacophonous** *adj*

cactus *n pl* **cacti** (say **kak**-tiy) a fleshy desert plant, usually with prickles and no leaves

CAD *abbr* computer-assisted design

cad *n old use* a person who behaves in a dishonourable way **caddish** *adj*

cadaver (say kad-**av**-er) *n technical* a dead body; a corpse **cadaverous** *adj*

caddie, caddy *n pl* **caddies** a person who carries a golfer's clubs and gives other help during a game **caddie** *v* **caddies, caddied, caddying** to act as a caddie

caddy *n pl* **caddies** a small box for holding

tea

cadence (say **kay**-dəns) n **1** the rise and fall of the voice in speaking **2** Mus a sequence of notes or chords ending a musical phrase **3** rhythm

cadenza (say kə-**den**-zə) n an elaborate passage for a solo instrument or voice

cadet (say kə-**det**) n a young person being trained for the armed forces or the police

cadge v informal to get something you are not really entitled to, by asking repeatedly for it **cadger** n

cadmium (say **kad**-miəm) n a metal that looks like tin, a chemical element (symbol Cd)

cadre (say **kah**-dər) n a small group of trained people who can form the core of a military or political unit

caecum (say **see**-kəm) n pl **caeca** a tubular pouch forming the first part of the large intestine

Caesarean, Caesarian section (say siz-**air**-iən) n a surgical operation for delivering a baby by cutting through the wall of the mother's abdomen and into the womb

caesium (say **see**-zi-əm) n a soft silver-white metallic element (symbol Cs)

café (say **kaf**-ay) n a small restaurant that sells drinks and light meals

cafeteria (say kaf-i-**teer**-iə) n a café where customers serve themselves from a counter

caffeine (say **kaf**-een) n a stimulant substance found in tea and coffee

cage n **1** a container having a frame of wires or bars for keeping birds or animals **2** an open framework forming the moving part of a lift **cage** v to put or keep birds or animals in a cage

cagey adj **cagier, cagiest** informal cautious about giving information, secretive **cagily** adv **caginess** n

cagoule (say kə-**gool**) n a light waterproof jacket with a hood

caiman n pl **caimans** a kind of alligator found in South America

cairn n a pile of loose stones set up as a landmark or monument

caisson (say **kay**-sən) n a watertight box or chamber inside which construction work can be carried out underwater

cajole (say kə-**johl**) v to coax or flatter someone into doing something **cajolery** n

cake n **1** a baked sweet food made from a mixture of flour, fats, sugar, eggs, etc. **2** a savoury food baked or fried in a round flat shape ♦ fish cakes **3** a shaped or hardened mass of something ♦ a cake of soap **cake** v **1** to harden a mixture into a compact mass **2** to encrust something with a hardened mass

CAL abbr computer-assisted learning

calamine n a pink powder, chiefly zinc carbonate or oxide, used in skin lotions

calamity n pl **calamities** a disaster **calamitous** adj

calcify (say **kal**-si-fiy) v **calcifies, calcified, calcifying** to harden something by a deposit of calcium salts **calcification** n

calcium n a greyish-white chemical element (symbol Ca), present in bones and teeth and forming the basis of lime

calculate v **1** to get an answer by using mathematics, to count figures or values **2** to plan something deliberately **calculable** adj **calculated** adj (said about an action) done with knowledge of the consequences **calculating** adj (said about a person) shrewd or scheming **calculation** n **1** a process of getting an answer by using mathematics **2** an assessment of the risks and benefits involved in a course of action

calculator n a small electronic device with a keyboard and display, used to make calculations

calculus (say **kal**-kew-ləs) n a branch of mathematics that deals with problems involving rates of variation

caldera (say kahl-**dair**-ə) n a large bowl-shaped depression formed where part of a volcano has collapsed

Caledonian (say kali-**doh**-niən) adj to do with Scotland

calendar n **1** a chart or set of pages showing the days, weeks, and months of a particular year **2** a device that displays the date **3** a list of dates or events relating to a special activity ♦ the Racing Calendar **4** the system by which time is divided into fixed periods ♦ the Gregorian calendar

calender n a machine with rollers for pressing cloth or paper to glaze or smooth it **calender** v to press cloth or paper in a calender

calends pl n the first day of the month in the ancient Roman calendar

calf[1] n pl **calves** 1 a young cow or bull, or the young of the elephant, seal, whale, and certain other animals 2 calfskin **calfskin** n

calf[2] n pl **calves** the back of the leg below the knee

calibrate (say **kal**-i-brayt) v 1 to mark a gauge or instrument with a scale of measurements 2 to measure the calibre of a gun barrel **calibration** n **calibrator** n

calibre (say **kal**-i-ber) n 1 the diameter of the inside of a gun barrel, or of a bullet or shell fired from it 2 ability or importance ♦ We need a person of your calibre.

calico n a kind of plain white cotton cloth

caliph (say **kal**-if or **kay**-lif) n hist a Muslim civil and religious leader, regarded as a successor to Muhammad **caliphate** n

call n 1 a shout or cry made to attract someone's attention 2 a short visit 3 a summons or invitation 4 an act of telephoning 5 the particular cry a bird makes 6 a demand or claim ♦ There's little call for this style of clothes now. 7 a need or occasion ♦ There's no call for you to be angry. 8 a shout made by an official in a game to show that a rule has been broken **call** v 1 to shout or speak loudly in order to attract someone's attention 2 to pay a short visit to someone ♦ I'll call on them this afternoon. 3 to give someone a name, or use their name when addressing them ♦ Why did you call your cat Albert? 4 to describe someone or something in a certain way ♦ I would certainly call her a friend. 5 to summon someone or ask them to come to you ♦ We'd better call the doctor. 6 to telephone someone 7 (said about a bird) to make its cry **caller** n **calling** n an occupation, a profession or trade **callback** n a telephone call made to someone in reply to a call made by them **call girl** n a female prostitute who accepts appointments by telephone **call sign** n a tune or message transmitted by a radio station to identify itself or a particular broadcaster

calligraphy (say kə-**lig**-rə-fi) n the art of elegant or decorative handwriting **calligrapher** n

calliper (say **kal**-i-per) n a support for a weak or injured leg **callipers** pl n compasses for measuring the width of tubes or round objects

callous (say **kal**-əs) adj 1 unfeeling or cruel 2 Medicine having calluses **callously** adv **callousness** n

callow adj immature and inexperienced **callowly** adv **callowness** n

callus (say **kal**-əs) n pl **calluses** Medicine an area of thick hardened skin or tissue

calm adj 1 (said about a person) not excited or agitated 2 quiet and still, not windy **calm** n 1 a state or period of being calm 2 a lack of strong winds or of rough sea **calm** v (also **calm down**) to make someone or something calm, or to become calm **calmly** adv **calmness** n

Calor gas n trademark liquefied butane stored under pressure in containers and used instead of mains gas or in camping

calorie n 1 a unit for measuring a quantity of heat 2 a unit for measuring the energy produced by food **caloric** adj **calorific** adj

calumny (say **kal**-əm-ni) n pl **calumnies** the act of making an untrue statement that harms someone's reputation, a slander

Calvinism n the teachings of the French Protestant religious reformer John Calvin (1509-64), and his followers **Calvinist** n **Calvinistic** adj

calypso n pl **calypsos** a West Indian song with a variable rhythm and with lyrics improvised on a topical theme

calyx (say **kay**-liks) n pl **calyces** a ring of leaves (called sepals) that surrounds an unopened flower bud

CAM abbr computer-assisted manufacturing

cam n a projecting part on a rotating wheel or shaft, which makes another part move up and down or back and forth

camaraderie (say kamə-**rah**-der-i) n trust and friendship between people

camber n a slight arched shape or upward curve given to a surface, especially of a road **cambered** adj

cambric n a thin linen or cotton cloth

camcorder n a combined video camera and sound recorder

came v past tense of *come*

camel n 1 a large animal with a long neck and either one or two humps on its back 2 the fawn colour of a camel

camellia (say kə-mel-iə) n an evergreen flowering shrub from China and Japan, related to the tea plant

cameo (say kam-i-oh) n pl **cameos** 1 a small piece of hard stone carved with a raised design in a contrasting colour 2 a short but vivid description in a novel, or a short part in a play or film

camera n a device for taking photographs, films, or television pictures **cameraman** n pl **cameramen** a person whose job is to operate a film camera or television camera **in camera** (said about the hearing of evidence or lawsuits) in the judge's private room; in private, in secret

camisole (say kam-i-sohl) n a woman's loose-fitting piece of underwear for the top of the body

camomile (say kam-ə-miyl) n another spelling of *chamomile*

camouflage (say kam-ə-flahzh) n 1 an animal's natural colouring which enables it to blend in with its surroundings 2 a way of disguising or hiding objects by covering them so that they look like part of their surroundings **camouflage** v to disguise objects in this way

camp[1] n 1 a place where people live temporarily in tents, huts, or caravans 2 a group of buildings for people on holiday to live in 3 a place where soldiers are lodged or trained 4 a group of people sharing the same ideas or plans **camp** v 1 to make a camp 2 to live in a camp, especially while on holiday **camper** n **camp bed** n a folding bed used in camping **campsite** n a camping site

camp[2] adj informal 1 (said about a man) openly effeminate 2 exaggerated in style, especially for humorous effect

campaign n 1 a series of battles or military operations with the same purpose 2 an organized series of activities to achieve a purpose ♦ *an advertising campaign* **campaign** v to take part in a campaign **campaigner** n

campanology (say kamp-ən-ol-əji) n the study of the making and use of bells **campanologist** n

camphor n a strong-smelling white substance used in medicine and mothballs and in making plastics **camphorated** adj

campus n pl **campuses** the grounds and buildings of a university or college

can[1] auxiliary verb past tense **could** 1 to have the ability or power to do something ♦ *Can you play the piano?* 2 to be allowed to do something ♦ *You can go if you promise to be back before dark.* ◊ Some people insist on using *may* for meaning 2 (*You may go if you promise to be back before dark.*), but *can* is common in this meaning in ordinary speech and there is nothing wrong with it.

can[2] n 1 a sealed tin in which food or drink is preserved 2 a metal or plastic container for liquids **can** v **canned**, **canning** to preserve food or drink in a sealed can **canned** adj **canner** n **cannery** n pl **canneries**

canal n 1 an artificial river cut through land for boats to pass along or to irrigate an area of land 2 a tube through which food or air passes in a plant or animal body ♦ *the alimentary canal*

canapé (say kan-əpi) n a small piece of bread or pastry with a savoury topping, served with drinks

canary (say kə-nair-i) n pl **canaries** a small yellow songbird, often kept as a cage bird

canasta (say kə-nas-tə) n a card game played with two packs of 52 cards

cancan n a lively stage dance with high kicking

cancel v **cancelled**, **cancelling** 1 to say that something already decided on will not after all take place ♦ *Tomorrow's match has been cancelled.* 2 to say that something is no longer valid, to revoke something ♦ *Her permit has been cancelled.* 3 to mark a stamp or ticket so that it can no longer be used 4 to order a thing to be discontinued 5 to neutralize the effect of something 6 to cross out something written down **cancellation** n

Cancer n (the Crab) the sign of the zodiac which the sun enters about 21 June **tropic of Cancer** see *tropic* **Cancerian** adj, n

cancer n 1 a tumour, especially a malignant one 2 a disease in which malignant growths form in the body 3 something bad or harmful that spreads rapidly ♦ *Racism is a cancer in our society.* **cancerous** adj

candelabrum (say kandi-lahb-rəm) n pl **candelabra** a large branched candlestick or holder for lights

candid adj open and truthful, not hiding one's thoughts **candidly** adv **candidness** n

candidate n 1 a person who is applying for a job or is trying to get elected to a public office such as MP 2 a person who is taking an examination **candidacy** n **candidature** n

candle n a stick of wax with a wick through it, which gives out light when it burns **candlelight** n the light given out by a candle or candles **Candlemas** n a Christian feast held on 2 February, commemorating the Purification of the Virgin Mary, when candles are blessed **candlestick** n a holder for one or more candles **candlewick** n a thick cotton fabric

candour (say kan-dər) n being open and honest in what you say

candy n pl **candies** 1 crystallized sugar 2 N. Am sweets or a sweet **candied** adj **candyfloss** n a fluffy pink or white mass of spun sugar eaten on a stick **candy-striped** adj having alternate stripes of white and pink (or sometimes another colour)

cane n 1 the hollow jointed stem of tall reeds and grasses 2 the material of these plants used for making furniture and basketwork 3 a piece of cane used as a walking stick 4 a stem of raspberry plant **cane** v 1 to punish someone by beating them with a cane 2 to weave cane into a piece of furniture

canine (say kay-niyn) adj to do with dogs **canine** n 1 a dog 2 a strong pointed tooth next to the front teeth (called *incisors*)

canister n a metal box or other container

canker n 1 a disease that causes ulcers 2 a bad or corrupting influence

cannabis (say kan-ə-bis) n a drug obtained from the hemp plant

cannibal n 1 a person who eats human flesh 2 an animal that eats animals of its own kind **cannibalism** n **cannibalistic** adj **cannibalize** v to take a machine to pieces to provide spare parts for other machines **cannibalization** n

cannon n 1 pl **cannon** an old type of large heavy gun that fired solid metal balls 2 an automatic gun used in a military aircraft for firing shells 3 a shot in billiards in which a ball hits two other balls in succession **cannon** v **cannoned**, **cannoning** 1 to collide heavily with something 2 to make a cannon at billiards ◊ Do not confuse this word with *canon*. **cannonade** n continuous heavy gunfire **cannonball** n a solid metal ball fired from a cannon **cannon fodder** n soldiers regarded merely as material to be used up in a war

cannot v can not

canny adj **cannier**, **canniest** shrewd and clever **cannily** adv **canniness** n

canoe n a light narrow boat with pointed ends, moved forwards with paddles **canoe** v **canoes**, **canoed**, **canoeing** to paddle or travel in a canoe **canoeist** n

canon n 1 a general rule or principle 2 a set of writings by a particular author that are regarded as genuine 3 a member of the clergy who is on the staff of a cathedral 4 the central unchanging part of the Roman Catholic mass 5 Mus a passage or piece of music in which a theme is taken up by two or more parts that overlap ◊ Do not confuse this word with *cannon*. **canonical** adj **canonically** adv **canonize** v **canonization** n

canopy n pl **canopies** 1 a hanging cover forming a shelter above a bed, etc. 2 any similar covering, such as the high branches and foliage of a forest 3 the part of a parachute that opens out like an umbrella **canopied** adj

cant[1] n 1 insincere talk 2 the language or jargon associated with a particular group of people ♦ *thieves' cant*

cant[2] v to slope or tilt **cant** n a tilted or sloping position

can't v informal cannot

cantaloupe (say kan-tə-loop) n a small

round melon with orange-coloured flesh

cantankerous (say kan-**tank**-er-əs) adj bad-tempered and quarrelsome **cantankerously** adv **cantankerousness** n

canteen n 1 a restaurant for the employees of a factory, office, etc. 2 a case or box containing a set of cutlery 3 a small flask of water, carried by soldiers or campers

canter n a horse's slow gentle gallop **canter** v to ride at a canter, to gallop gently

canticle (say kan-ti-kəl) n a song or chant with words taken from the Bible, for example the Magnificat

cantilever (say kan-ti-lee-ver) n a beam or girder fixed at one end only and supporting a bridge, balcony, or similar structure

canto n pl **cantos** each of the sections into which some long poems are divided

canton n a division or district of a country, especially Switzerland

Cantonese adj to do with or coming from the city of Canton in China **Cantonese** n 1 pl **Cantonese** a person born or living in Canton 2 a Chinese language spoken in southern China and Hong Kong

cantor n 1 a singer in a Christian service who sings solo verses to which the choir or congregation responds 2 in Jewish worship, the leader of the prayers in a synagogue

canvas n 1 a strong coarse cloth used for making tents and sails, etc. 2 a piece of canvas as a surface for an oil painting

canvass v 1 to visit people to ask for their votes, opinions, etc. 2 to suggest a plan **canvass** n an act of canvassing **canvasser** n

canyon (say kan-yən) n a deep valley gorge, usually with a river flowing through it

CAP abbr Common Agricultural Policy (of the European Union)

cap n 1 a soft covering for the head 2 a particular covering for the head worn for special reasons ♦ a shower cap 3 a cover or top like a cap 4 a small amount of explosive in a paper or metal covering, a percussion cap **cap** v **capped, capping** 1 to put a cap on something, to cover the top or end of something 2 to award a sports cap to someone chosen to be in a team 3 to reply to someone's story, joke, etc. with a better one ♦ Can you cap that? 4 to set a limit to

the amount of something, especially the money available for spending

capable adj 1 able to do things well, competent 2 having the ability or capacity to do something ♦ They are quite capable of lying. **capability** n **capably** adv

capacity n pl **capacities** 1 the amount that a building, room, or container can hold 2 ability or capability 3 a position or function **capacious** adj **capaciously** adv **capaciousness** n **capacitor** n a device for storing an electric charge

cape¹ n 1 a short cloak, usually without sleeves 2 the top part of a longer coat or cloak

cape² n a large piece of high land that extends into the sea, a promontory

caper¹ v to jump or run about playfully **caper** n 1 capering 2 informal an activity or adventure

caper² n 1 a bud from a shrub used in cooking 2 the shrub from which these buds are taken

capillary (say kə-**pil**-er-i) n pl **capillaries** any of the very fine branching blood vessels that connect veins and arteries **capillary** adj

capital adj 1 (said about a crime) involving the death penalty ♦ a capital offence 2 (said about a letter) having the form and size used to begin a name or a sentence ♦ Athens begins with a capital A. 3 principal or most important ♦ a capital city **capital** n 1 the most important city of a country or region, usually the centre of government 2 a capital letter 3 Architecture the top part of a column or pillar 4 money or property that is used to start a business or invested to earn interest **capitalism** n an economic system in which trade and industry are controlled by private owners for profit, and not by the state **capitalist** n 1 someone who has a lot of wealth invested, a rich person 2 someone who supports or favours capitalism **capitalist** adj relating to or favouring capitalism **capitalistic** adj **capitalize** v 1 to write or print words in capital letters 2 to convert something into capital **capitalization** n **capital gain** n a profit made from the sale of investments or property

capitation n a payment or fee calculated from the number of people involved

Capitol n 1 the building in Washington DC in which the Congress of the USA meets 2 the temple of Jupiter in ancient Rome

capitulate v to give in to a demand, to surrender **capitulation** n

cappuccino (say kah-poo-**chee**-noh) n pl **cappuccinos** milky coffee made frothy with steam

caprice (say kə-**prees**) n 1 a whim or impulse 2 Mus a piece of music played in a lively fanciful style **capricious** adj **capriciously** adv **capriciousness** n

Capricorn (the Goat) the sign of the zodiac which the sun enters about 21 December **tropic of Capricorn** see tropic **Capricornian** adj, n

capsicum (say **kap**-si-kəm) n 1 a hot-tasting seed from a tropical plant 2 the plant from which these seeds are taken

capsize v to overturn ♦ A wave capsized the boat.

capstan (say **kap**-stən) n 1 a thick post that can be turned to pull in a rope or cable that winds round it 2 a small wheel that guides the tape in a tape recorder 3 a revolving device for holding tools in a lathe, so that they can be used in turn

capsule n 1 a small soluble case containing a dose of medicine for swallowing 2 a plant's seed-case that splits open when ripe 3 a compartment of a spacecraft that can be separated from the main part

captain n 1 a person who has authority over a sports team or other group of people 2 the person commanding a ship 3 the pilot of a civil aircraft 4 an army officer ranking below a major and above a lieutenant 5 a naval officer ranking below a commodore and above a commander **captain** v to act as the captain of a sports team or other group of people **captaincy** n

caption (say **kap**-shən) n 1 a group of words printed next to a picture to describe or explain it 2 words shown on a cinema or television screen

captivate v to charm someone or capture their fancy **captivation** n

captive n a person or animal that has been captured **captive** adj 1 taken or kept as a prisoner 2 unable to escape or choose an alternative ♦ a captive audience **captivity** n

captor n someone who has captured a person or animal

capture v 1 to take hold of a person or animal and keep them by force 2 to take possession of a place by force, especially in war ♦ The castle was captured after a long siege. 3 to succeed in attracting or securing something ♦ The film managed to capture the public's imagination. 4 ICT to put data in a form that can be stored in a computer 5 in board games, to remove another player's piece when you have made a move that allows this **capture** n 1 the act of capturing someone or something 2 a person or thing that has been captured

car n 1 a vehicle with a motor that can carry a small number of people 2 a railway carriage of a particular type ♦ a dining car 3 the passenger compartment of an airship, balloon, cable railway, or lift **car park** n an area or building for parking cars

carafe (say kə-**raf**) n a glass bottle for serving wine or water at a meal

caramel n 1 a kind of toffee tasting like burnt sugar 2 burnt sugar used for colouring and flavouring food **caramelization** n **caramelize** v

carapace (say **ka**-rə-payss) n the shell on the back of a tortoise or a crab or other crustacean

carat (say **ka**-rət) n 1 a unit of weight for precious stones 2 a measure of the purity of gold, up to 24 carats for pure gold

caravan n 1 an enclosed carriage for living in, towed by a motor vehicle 2 a group of people travelling together across country **caravanning** n

caraway n a plant with spicy seeds that are used for flavouring food

carbohydrate n an organic compound, such as the sugars and starches, which can be broken down to release energy in the body

carbolic n a kind of disinfectant made from carbon

carbon n a chemical element (symbol C)

that is present in all living matter and occurs in its pure form as diamond and graphite **carbonate** *n* a compound that releases carbon dioxide when mixed with acid **carbonated** *adj* (said about a drink) mixed with carbon dioxide to make it gassy or fizzy **carbonation** *n* **carboniferous** *adj* producing coal **Carboniferous** *adj Geology* of the period in the Palaeozoic era when many coal deposits were created **Carboniferous** *n* this period **carbonize** *v* **1** to convert a substance that contains carbon into carbon alone **2** to coat something with carbon **carbonization** *n* **carbon copy** *n* **1** a copy of a letter or document made with carbon paper **2** an exact copy of a thing or person ♦ *She is a carbon copy of her mother.* **carbon dating** *n* a method of finding the age of organic objects by measuring the decay of radiocarbon in them **carbon dioxide** *n* a colourless gas that is formed by the burning of carbon or breathed out by animals in respiration **carbon fibre** *n* a material consisting of carbon filaments **carbon footprint** *n* the effect that the carbon emissions involved in an activity have on the environment **carbonic acid** *n* a weak acid formed from carbon dioxide and water **carbon monoxide** *n* a poisonous gas formed when carbon burns incompletely **carbon neutral** *adj* not causing an increase in the amount of carbon dioxide in the atmosphere **carbon paper** *n* thin paper with a coloured coating, put between sheets of paper to make copies **carbon tax** *n* a tax on petrol and other fossil fuels **carbuncle** *n* **1** a severe abscess in the skin **2** a bright red round gem **carburettor** *n* a device for mixing fuel and air in an internal-combustion engine **carcass** *n* **1** the dead body of an animal, especially one prepared for cutting up as meat **2** the framework of a building or ship **carcinogen** (say kar-sin-ə-jin) *n* a substance that produces cancer **carcinogenic** *adj* **carcinoma** *n pl* **carcinomas** or **carcinomata**

card¹ *n* **1** thick stiff paper or thin cardboard **2** a small piece of this for writing or printing on **3** a small flat rectangular piece of plastic with machine-readable information on it, e.g. a bank card or credit card **4** a playing card **5** a card used for recording scores in games **6** a programme of events at a race meeting **7** *ICT* a circuit board with extra facilities **cards** *pl n* a game using playing cards **cardboard** *n* a type of thin board made of layers of paper or wood fibre **card game** *n* a game using playing cards **card index** *n* an index in which each item is entered on a separate card

card² *v* to clean or comb wool **card** *n* a wire brush or toothed instrument for doing this

cardiac (say kar-di-ak) *adj* to do with the heart

cardigan *n* a woollen jumper fastened with buttons at the front

cardinal *n* **1** a senior dignitary of the Roman Catholic Church **2** a deep scarlet colour like that of a cardinal's habit **cardinal** *adj* chief or most important, fundamental

cardinal number *n* a number that denotes an amount or quantity (*one, five, twenty,* etc.), as distinct from the ordinal numbers (*first, fifth, twentieth,* etc.)

cardinal point *n* each of the four main points of the compass, North, East, South, and West

cardiograph (say kar-di-ə-grahf) *n* an instrument that records the heart's movements **cardiogram** *n*

care *n* **1** serious attention and thought ♦ *The trip was planned with care.* **2** caution to avoid damage or loss ♦ *Handle with care.* **3** the protection or supervision of a person ♦ *We left the child in her sister's care.* **4** worry or anxiety ♦ *freedom from care* **care** *v* **1** to feel concerned or interested in something ♦ *I care very much about the environment.* **2** to feel affection or liking ♦ *His actions show that he cares.* **3** to be willing to do something ♦ *Would you care to come with us?* **carefree** *adj* **careful** *adj* **carefully** *adv* **carefulness** *n* **careless** *adj* **carelessly** *adv* **carelessness** *n* **carer** *n* **caretaker** *n* **1** a person employed to look after a house or building **2** used to mean a person or group of people who hold office temporarily until a successor is appointed

♦ *a caretaker president* **careworn** *adj* tired or unwell because of prolonged worry

care of to the address of someone who will deliver or forward post ♦ *Write to him care of his bank.* **in care** taken into the care of a local authority **to care for 1** to look after someone **2** to like someone or something **to take care** to be cautious

careen (say kə-**reen**) *v* to swerve, or tilt or lean to one side

career *n* **1** an occupation or way of making a living that a person follows ♦ *She is taking up accountancy as a career.* **2** (used before a noun) ambitious or keen to do well in a profession ♦ *a career politician* **career** *v* to rush wildly or recklessly **careerist** *n*

caress (say kə-**ress**) *n* a loving touch or stroke **caress** *v* to touch or stroke someone lovingly

caret (say **ka**-rit) *n* a mark (^) put in a piece of writing or printing to show that something should be added

cargo *n pl* **cargoes** goods carried on a ship or aircraft

Carib (say **ka**-rib) *n* **1** a member of a people living in the northern coastal regions of South America **2** the language spoken by them

Caribbean, **Caribbean Sea** (say ka-ri-**bee**-ən) *n* the part of the Atlantic Ocean off Central America and including the West Indies and other islands **Caribbean** *adj* relating to this region

caribou (say **ka**-ri-boo) *n pl* **caribou** a North American reindeer

caricature (say **ka**-rik-ə-choor) *n* a picture or description of a person or thing that exaggerates their well-known characteristics for comic effect **caricature** *v* to make a caricature of someone or something **caricaturist** *n*

carillon (say kə-**ril**-yən) *n* **1** a set of bells sounded either from a keyboard or mechanically **2** a tune played on bells

carmine (say **kar**-min) *adj*, *n* deep red

carnage (say **kar**-nij) *n* the killing of many people

carnal (say **kar**-nəl) *adj* to do with the body's physical, especially sexual, needs **carnally** *adv*

carnation *n* a garden flower with dark green leaves and showy pink, white, or red flowers

carnival *n* a festival, usually with a procession in fancy dress

carnivore (say **kar**-niv-or) *n* an animal that feeds on the flesh of other animals **carnivorous** *adj*

carol *n* a joyful song, especially a Christmas hymn **carol** *v* **carolled**, **carolling 1** to sing carols **2** to sing joyfully

carotene (say **ka**-rə-teen) *n* an orange or red substance in plants, a source of vitamin A

carotid artery (say kə-**rot**-id) *n* either of the two great arteries, one on each side of the neck, that carry blood to the head

carouse (say kə-**rowz**) *v* to have drinks and enjoy yourself with other people **carousal** *n*

carousel (say ka-roo-**sel**) *n* **1** a merry-go-round at a fair **2** a conveyor belt or system that goes round in a circle, e.g. at an airport for passengers to collect their luggage

carp¹ *n pl* **carp** an edible freshwater fish that lives in lakes and ponds

carp² *v* to keep complaining or finding fault

carpal (say **kar**-pəl) *adj* to do with the wrist joint (called *carpus*) **carpal** *n* any of the bones in the wrist

carpel (say **kar**-pəl) *n* the pistil of a flower, in which the seeds develop

carpenter *n* a person who makes or repairs wooden objects and structures **carpentry** *n*

carpet *n* **1** a thick soft covering for a floor, usually made from a woven material **2** a thick layer of something on the ground **carpet** *v* **carpeted**, **carpeting** to cover a floor with a carpet **carpeting** *n*

carriage *n* **1** a four-wheeled passenger vehicle pulled by horses **2** a passenger vehicle forming part of a railway train **3** the transporting of goods from place to place, or the cost of this **4** a support with wheels for moving a large gun or other heavy object **5** a moving part for carrying or holding other parts in a machine, e.g. the roller of a typewriter **6** the posture of the body when walking **carriageway** *n* the part of the road on which vehicles travel

carrier n 1 a person or thing that carries something 2 a business that transports goods or people for payment 3 a person or animal that transmits a disease to others without being affected by it **carrier bag** n a paper or plastic bag with handles, for carrying shopping **carrier pigeon** n a homing pigeon trained to carry messages tied to its leg or neck

carrion (say **ka-ri-ən**) n the decaying flesh of dead animals

carrot n 1 a tapering orange-coloured root eaten as a vegetable 2 the plant from which this root comes 3 something used to entice someone to do something, as distinct from the 'stick' or punishment **carroty** adj

carry v **carries, carried, carrying** 1 to take something or someone from one place to another 2 to have something with you constantly ♦ The police now carry guns. 3 to conduct or transmit ♦ The cables carry a powerful electric current. 4 to support the weight of something 5 to involve or entail a consequence ♦ The crime carries a life sentence. 6 to extend or develop an idea or feeling ♦ Don't carry the joke too far. 7 to take an amount into the next column when adding figures 8 to approve a proposed measure by a winning vote ♦ The motion was carried by a large majority. 9 to publish or broadcast something ♦ The Sunday papers all carried the story. 10 to hold and move the body in a certain way ♦ She carried herself with dignity. 11 to be transmitted clearly ♦ The sound carried far across the valley. **to carry off** 1 to take something or someone by force 2 to cause the death of someone ♦ The plague carried off half the population. 3 to win a prize 4 to deal with a situation successfully **to carry on** 1 to continue doing something 2 to take part in a conversation 3 to manage or conduct a business or activity 4 informal to behave excitedly **to carry out** to achieve something or put it into practice

cart n an open vehicle used for carrying loads, pulled by a horse or by hand **cart** v 1 to carry something in a cart, to transport a load 2 to carry something heavy or tiring ♦ We've carted these stones right across the field. **carthorse** n a strong horse used for pulling heavy loads **cartwheel** n 1 the wheel of a cart 2 a handstand in which the body turns with the arms and legs spread like spokes of a wheel, balancing on each hand in turn **cartwright** n someone who makes carts

carte blanche (say kart **blahnsh**) n freedom or authority to act as you think best

cartel (say kar-**tel**) n an agreement between business firms of the same kind to control the market and keep prices high

Cartesian (say kar-**tee**-ziən) adj relating to the 17th-century French philosopher Descartes or his theories

cartilage n tough white flexible tissue attached to a bone **cartilaginous** adj

cartography (say kar-**tog**-rəfi) n the science of planning and drawing maps **cartographer** n **cartographic** adj

carton n a light cardboard or plastic container

cartoon n 1 an amusing drawing, especially one intended as a comment on a topical matter 2 a sequence of drawings that tell a story 3 an animated film 4 a full-size drawing made by an artist as a preliminary sketch for a painting, mural, or other work of art **cartoon** v to show someone or something in a cartoon **cartoonist** n

cartouche (say kar-**toosh**) n 1 Architecture an ornament or feature in the shape of a scroll 2 Archaeology an oval emblem containing the name in hieroglyphs of an ancient Egyptian king

cartridge n 1 a tube or case containing explosive for a bullet or shell 2 a sealed case holding a length of film or recording tape, or an amount of ink, ready for insertion into a machine or pen, etc. **cartridge paper** n thick strong paper for drawing

carve v 1 to cut into solid material to make a design, inscription, etc. 2 to cut cooked meat into slices **carver** n **carving** n

caryatid (say ka-ri-**at**-id) n a sculpture of a female figure used as a supporting pillar in a building

Casanova (say kas-ə-**noh**-və) n a man with

a reputation for having many love affairs

cascade (say kas-**kayd**) n **1** a small waterfall or series of waterfalls **2** a mass of something falling or hanging **cascade** v to fall like a cascade

case[1] n **1** an instance or example of something existing or occurring **2** a condition of disease or injury, or a person suffering from this ♦ *two cases of measles* **3** something being investigated by the police or other authorities ♦ *a murder case* **4** a legal action in a court of law **5** a set of facts or arguments used to support something **6** *Gram* the form of a noun or pronoun that shows how it is related to other words. For example in *Tony's car*, *Tony's* is in the possessive case, and in *We saw him*, *him* is in the objective case

casework n social work that involves dealing directly with people who have problems **caseworker** n **in case** because something might happen ♦ *Take your umbrella in case.* **in case of** if something should occur ♦ *In case of fire leave by the staircase.*

case[2] n **1** a container or protective covering **2** a piece of luggage **case** v **1** to enclose something in a case **2** *informal* to check over a place before carrying out a robbery **casement** n a window that opens on hinges at the side, like a door **casing** n

cash n **1** money in the form of notes and coins **2** immediate payment for things bought, as opposed to credit **3** *informal* money or wealth ♦ *We're short of cash at the moment.* **cash** v to give or get cash for something ♦ *May I cash a cheque here?* **cashable** *adj* **cashier** n a person employed to receive and pay out money in a bank or to receive payments in a shop or business **cash card** n a plastic card used to withdraw cash from a cash dispenser **cash desk** n a desk for making payments in a shop or restaurant **cash dispenser** n a machine from which customers of a bank can withdraw cash by using a cash card **cash flow** n the movement of money out of and into a business as goods are bought and sold, which affects its ability to make cash payments **cash register** n a machine in a

shop that holds cash received and records the amount of each sale

cashew (say **kash**-oo) n **1** the small kidney-shaped edible nut of a tropical tree **2** the tree from which these nuts come

cashier v to dismiss someone in disgrace from the armed forces

cashmere n **1** a very fine soft wool, especially that from the Kashmir goat **2** a fabric made from this

casino n pl **casinos** a public building or room for gambling games

cask n a large barrel for holding liquid, especially alcoholic drinks

casket n a small usually ornamental box for holding valuables, etc.

Caspian n the Caspian Sea, a land-locked sea between SE Europe and Asia

Cassandra (say kə-**san**-drə) n a person who predicts disaster

cassata (say kə-**sah**-tə) n an ice cream containing fruit and nuts

cassava (say kə-**sah**-və) n a tropical plant with starchy roots used for food

casserole n **1** a covered dish for cooking food slowly in an oven **2** food cooked in a casserole **casserole** v to cook food in a casserole

cassette (say kə-**set**) n a small sealed case containing a length of film or magnetic tape

cassock n a long garment worn by Christian clergy and members of church choirs

cassowary (say **kas**-ə-wer-i) n pl **cassowaries** a large bird that is unable to fly, found mainly in New Guinea

cast v past tense and past participle **cast** **1** to throw something hard in a particular direction ♦ *The fishermen cast a net into the sea.* **2** to shed or discard something **3** to make a shadow fall **4** to direct your eye or your mind towards something ♦ *You'd better cast your eye over this letter.* **5** to record or register a vote **6** to make an object by pouring metal or plaster into a mould and leaving it to harden **7** to choose the actors for a play or film **cast** n **1** an act of casting or throwing something **2** an object made by putting soft material into a mould to harden **3** the actors taking part in a play or film **4** a tinge of colour **castaway** n a person who has been shipwrecked and washed up in a deserted place **casting vote** n a vote that decides which side will win when the votes on each side are equal **cast iron** a hard alloy of iron made by casting in a mould **cast-iron** adj **1** made of cast iron **2** very strong or effective ♦ a cast-iron excuse **cast-offs** pl n clothes that someone no longer uses

castanets (say kast-ə-**nets**) pl n a pair of shell-shaped pieces of wood, held in the hands and struck together with the fingers as an accompaniment to a Spanish dance

caste (say kahst) n in India, each of the hereditary social groups into which Hindus are born

caster n another spelling of castor

caster sugar n fine white sugar

castigate (say **kas**-ti-gayt) v to criticize someone harshly **castigation** n **castigator** n

castle n **1** a large fortified building or group of buildings **2** a piece in chess

castor n **1** a small container for sugar or salt **2** a small swivelled wheel fixed to each leg of a piece of furniture **castor oil** n oil from the seeds of a tropical plant, used as a purgative and as a lubricant **castor sugar** n another spelling of caster sugar

castrate (say kas-**trayt**) v to remove the testicles of a male animal, to geld an animal **castration** n

casual adj **1** happening by chance ♦ a casual meeting **2** made or done lightly and without much care or thought ♦ a casual remark **3** informal or meant for informal occasions ♦ casual clothes **4** available for a short time, not permanent ♦ He found some casual work. **casuals** pl n clothes or shoes for everyday use **casually** adv **casualness** n

casualty n pl **casualties 1** a person who has been killed or injured in war or in an accident **2** a thing that has been lost or destroyed **3** the casualty department of a hospital

cat n **1** a small furry domesticated animal often kept as a pet **2** a wild animal of the same family as a domestic cat, e.g. a lion, tiger, or leopard **3** informal a spiteful or malicious woman **cattery** n pl **catteries** a place where cats are bred or boarded **cattily** adv **cattiness** n **catty** adj **cattier**, **cattiest** spiteful, speaking spitefully

catfish n pl **catfishes** or **catfish** a large fish

catgut n a fine strong cord used for the strings of musical instruments **catkin** n a spike of small soft flowers hanging from the willow and other trees **catnap** n a short sleep during the day **catnap** v **catnapped**, **catnapping** to have a catnap **Catseye** n trademark each of a line of reflector studs marking the centre or edge of a road **catwalk** n **1** a raised narrow pathway **2** a long platform that models walk along at a fashion show

catabolism (say kə-**tab**-ə-lizm) n the breaking down of complex substances in the body to form simpler ones **catabolic** adj

cataclysm (say **kat**-ə-klizm) n a violent upheaval or disaster **cataclysmic** adj

catacombs (say **kat**-ə-koomz) pl n a series of underground galleries with recesses on each side for tombs

Catalan adj to do with or coming from Catalonia in NE Spain **Catalan** n **1** a person from Catalonia **2** the Romance language of Catalonia

catalogue n a list of items arranged in a systematic order **catalogue** v **catalogues**, **catalogued**, **cataloguing** to list items in a catalogue **cataloguer** n

catalysis (say kə-**tal**-i-sis) n pl **catalyses** the process of producing or accelerating a chemical reaction **catalyse** v **catalyst** n **1** a substance that produces or accelerates a chemical reaction while remaining unchanged itself **2** a person or thing that brings about a change **catalytic** adj **catalytic converter** n a device in the exhaust system of a motor vehicle, with a catalyst that converts polluting gases into harmless products

catamaran (say **kat**-ə-mə-ran) n a boat with twin hulls parallel to each other

catapult n **1** a device with elastic for shooting small stones **2** an ancient military weapon for hurling stones **3** a device for launching a glider, or for launching an aircraft from the deck of a carrier **catapult** v 1 to hurl a stone or other object from a catapult 2 to rush violently

cataract n 1 a large waterfall or rush of water 2 a cloudy area that forms on the lens of the eye and obscures sight

catarrh (say kǝ-**tar**) n an inflammation of the nose and throat that causes a discharge of watery mucus **catarrhal** adj

catastrophe (say kǝ-**tas**-trǝfi) n a sudden event that causes great damage or harm **catastrophic** adj **catastrophically** adv

catch v past tense and past participle **caught** 1 to grasp something moving and hold it 2 to arrest or capture (someone) 3 to come unexpectedly on someone or take them by surprise ♦ The boys were caught leaving school early. 4 to hear and understand something ♦ I'm afraid I didn't catch what you said. 5 in cricket, to get a batsman out by catching the ball before it hits the ground 6 to capture an animal in a net or snare or after a chase 7 to be in time to get on a train, bus, or other form of public transport 8 to reach or overtake someone moving ahead of you 9 to become infected with an illness 10 informal to manage to see a film or television programme or hear a radio broadcast 11 to become or make something become trapped or entangled ♦ I caught my dress in the lift doors. 12 to hit someone lightly or unexpectedly ♦ A twig caught him on the nose. 13 to begin to burn **catch** n 1 the act of catching something ♦ That was a good catch. 2 something caught or worth catching 3 someone thought to be worth having as a spouse or partner 4 a difficulty or disadvantage that is hidden or not obvious 5 a device for fastening something such as a door or window 6 Mus a round for singing by three or more voices **catcher** n **catching** adj **catchy** adj **catchier**, **catchiest**, **catch-22** n a dilemma from which a person cannot escape, because the condition needed to escape cannot be fulfilled **catchment area** n 1 the area from which a school takes pupils 2 the area from which rainfall drains into a river or reservoir **catchphrase** n a sentence or phrase that people use often

catchword n a memorable word or phrase that people often use

catechize (say **kat**-i-kiyz) v to teach someone by a series of questions and answers **catechism** n a summary of the principles of a religion in the form of questions and answers

categorical (say kat-ig-**o**-ri-kǝl) adj absolute or unconditional ♦ She gave a categorical refusal. **categorically** adv

category (say **kat**-ig-eri) n pl **categories** a class of things having the same features or characteristics **categorize** v **categorization** n

cater (say **kay**-ter) v 1 to provide food or entertainment at a social occasion ♦ We have to cater for 100 people. 2 to provide what is needed ♦ We cannot cater for all tastes. **caterer** n

caterpillar n the larva of a butterfly or moth **Caterpillar**, **Caterpillar track** n trademark a steel band passing round the wheels of a tractor or tank for travel over rough ground

caterwaul v to make a shrill wailing sound

catharsis (say kǝ-**thar**-sis) n the process of relieving strong feelings or tension through drama or art, etc. **cathartic** adj

cathedral n the principal church of an area

catheter (say **kath**-it-er) n a flexible tube that can be inserted into a body cavity to drain off fluid

cathode (say **kath**-ohd) n a negatively charged electrode, by which electric current leaves a device. (Compare anode.)

Catholic adj 1 short for Roman Catholic 2 relating to all Churches or all Christians **Catholic** n a Roman Catholic **Catholicism** n

cattle pl n large animals kept by farmers for their milk or meat **cattle grid** n a grid covering a ditch allowing vehicles to pass but not animals

Caucasian (say kaw-**kay**-ziǝn) adj 1 relating to the Caucasus, a mountainous region in SE Europe 2 relating to the light-skinned race of humankind **Caucasian** n a Caucasian person

caucus (say **kaw**-kǝs) n 1 a small group within a political party or other organization, with its own concerns and plans **2** a meeting of party leaders to decide policy or choose candidates

caudal (say **kaw**-dəl) *adj* **1** of or like a tail **2** at or near the tail of an animal

caught *v* past tense and past participle of *catch*

cauldron *n* a large deep pot for boiling things

cauliflower *n* a cabbage with a large white flower head

caulk (say kawk) *v* to make a boat or container watertight by filling its seams or joints with waterproof material

cause *n* **1** a person or thing that makes something happen or produces an effect **2** a reason ♦ *There is no cause to worry.* **3** a purpose or aim for which people do work **4** a lawsuit or case **cause** *v* to be the cause of something or make it happen **causal** *adj* **causality** *n* the relationship between cause and effect **causally** *adv* **causation** *n* **causative** *adj* **cause célèbre** *n pl* **causes célèbres** a controversial issue that causes great public interest **causeway** *n* a raised road or track across low or wet ground

caustic *adj* **1** able to burn or corrode organic tissue by chemical action **2** severely sarcastic **caustic** *n* a caustic substance **caustically** *adv* **causticity** *n*

cauterize *v* to burn the surface of flesh to destroy infection or stop bleeding **cauterization** *n*

caution *n* **1** care taken to avoid danger or difficulty **2** a warning ♦ *She let him off with a caution.* **caution** *v* to give someone a warning **cautionary** *adj* serving as a warning **cautious** *adj* **cautiously** *adv* **cautiousness** *n*

cavalcade (say kav-əl-**kayd**) *n* a procession of people on horseback or in vehicles

Cavalier *n* a supporter of Charles I in the English Civil War of 1642-9 **cavalier** *adj* offhand or unconcerned ♦ *He showed a cavalier attitude to punctuality.*

cavalry *n* soldiers who fight on horseback or in armoured vehicles

cave *n* a natural hollow underground or in the side of a hill or cliff **cave** *v* **to cave in 1** to fall inwards or collapse **2** to give way in an argument **caving** *n* **caveman** *n pl*

cavemen

caveat (say **kav**-i-at) *n* a warning, especially about a snag or exception

cavern *n* a large cave or chamber in a cave **cavernous** *adj*

caviar (say **kav**-i-ar) *n* the pickled roe of sturgeon or other large fish

cavity *n pl* **cavities** a hollow or hole in a solid body **cavity wall** *n* a wall made of two thicknesses of bricks or blocks with a cavity between

cavort (say kə-**vort**) *v* to caper about excitedly

caw *n* the harsh cry of a rook, raven, or crow **caw** *v* to make this sound

cayenne (say kay-**en**) *n* a hot red powdered pepper

cayman *n* another spelling of *caiman*

CB *abbr* Citizens' Band (radio)

CBE *abbr* Commander of the Order of the British Empire

CBI *abbr* Confederation of British Industry

cc *abbr* **1** cubic centimetre(s) **2** carbon copy (put on a letter or email to show that it has also been sent to someone else)

CCTV *abbr* closed-circuit television

CD *abbr* compact disc

CD-ROM *n* a compact disc storing data as a read-only device for use in a computer

CDT *abbr* craft, design, and technology

cease *v* to bring something to an end, or come to an end **cease** *n* **ceaseless** *adj* **ceaselessly** *adv* **cessation** *n* **ceasefire** *n* a signal to stop firing guns in war, a truce **without cease** without stopping

cedar (say **see**-der) *n* an evergreen tree with hard sweet-smelling wood **cedarwood** *n* the wood of a cedar tree

cede (say seed) *v* to give up rights to territory or possession of it **cession** *n*

cedilla (say si-**dil**-ə) *n* a mark written under *c* in some languages to show that it is pronounced as *s*, as in ♦ *façade*

ceilidh (say **kay**-li) *n* a social gathering with traditional Scottish or Irish music and dancing

ceiling *n* **1** the flat surface of the top of a room **2** an upper limit or level to prices, wages, etc. **3** the maximum altitude at which a particular aircraft can fly

celebrate v **1** to mark the importance of a day or event by doing something enjoyable or special **2** to perform a religious ceremony **celebrated** adj **celebration** n

celebrity (say si-**leb**-riti) n pl **celebrities 1** a famous person **2** fame, being famous

celeriac (say si-**le**-ri-ak) n a kind of celery with a swollen root like a turnip

celery n a garden plant with crisp white or green stems used in salads or as a vegetable

celestial adj **1** to do with the sky; in the sky ♦ celestial bodies **2** to do with heaven, divine

celibate (say **sel**-ib-ət) adj remaining unmarried or not having sexual intercourse **celibacy** n

cell n **1** a small room in which a prisoner is locked up **2** a small room for a monk in a monastery **3** a microscopic unit of living matter **4** a compartment of a honeycomb **5** a device for producing electric current by chemical action **6** a small group of people forming the core of an organization

cellar n **1** a room below ground level used for storage **2** a stock of wine stored in a cellar

cello (say **chel**-oh) n pl **cellos** a musical instrument like a large violin, played upright by a seated player who holds it between the knees **cellist** n

Cellophane (say **sel**-ə-fayn) n trademark a thin tough transparent wrapping material

cellular (say **sel**-yoo-ler) adj **1** to do with cells, composed of cells **2** (said about a fabric) woven with an open mesh that traps air and provides insulation ♦ cellular blankets

cellulite (say **sel**-yoo-liyt) n a lumpy form of fat on the hips, thighs, and buttocks, producing puckering of the skin

celluloid (say **sel**-yoo-loid) n a kind of plastic made from nitrocellulose and camphor, formerly used for making cinema film

cellulose (say **sel**-yoo-lohz) n **1** an organic substance forming the main part of plant tissues and textile fibres derived from these tissues **2** a paint or lacquer made from this

Celsius (say **sel**-si-əs) adj relating to or using a temperature scale in which water

freezes at 0° and boils at 100°

Celt (say kelt) n **1** a member of a group of ancient European peoples living in Britain and much of mainland Europe before the Roman period **2** someone who lives in a region in which a Celtic language is spoken **Celtic** adj

cement n **1** a grey mixture of lime and clay that is used for building **2** a glue that hardens when it sets **cement** v **1** to put cement on something, to join something with cement **2** to join things firmly together

cemetery n pl **cemeteries** a large piece of ground where dead people are buried

cenotaph (say **sen**-ə-tahf) n a monument like a tomb to honour people, especially soldiers, who are buried somewhere else

censer (say **sen**-ser) n a container in which incense is burnt in religious ceremonies

censor (say **sen**-ser) n an official who examines films, books, etc., and removes or bans anything regarded as harmful **censor** v to examine a film or other material and remove or ban harmful material **censorious** adj **censoriously** adv **censoriousness** n **censorship** n ◊ Do not confuse this word with censure.

censure (say **sen**-sher) n strong criticism or disapproval of something **censure** v to blame or rebuke someone ◊ Do not confuse this word with censor.

census (say **sen**-səs) n **1** an official count or survey of the population of a country or area **2** an official survey of other things, e.g. the amount of traffic

cent n a unit or coin worth one hundredth of a dollar or of certain other metric units of currency

centaur (say **sen**-tor) n a creature in Greek mythology with the upper body, head, and arms of a man and the lower body of a horse

centenary (say sən-**teen**-eri) n pl **centenaries** a hundredth anniversary **centenarian** n **centennial** adj

centi- prefix one hundredth **centigrade** adj relating to or using a temperature scale divided into 100 degrees, 0° being the freezing point of water and 100° the boiling point of water **centigram** n one hundredth of a gram **centilitre** n one hundredth of a litre **centimetre** n one hundredth of a metre (about 0.4 inch) **centipede** n a small crawling creature with a long thin body and many legs

centre n 1 the middle point or part of something 2 a place from which an activity or process is controlled 3 a place or group of buildings devoted to certain activities or facilities ♦ a shopping centre 4 a political party or group holding moderate opinions between two extremes 5 a player in the middle of the field in some games **centre** adj to do with or at the centre of something **centre** v **centres**, **centred**, **centring** 1 to place something in or at the centre 2 to concentrate something or be concentrated at one point 3 to kick or hit the ball from the wing towards the centre **centralism** n a policy of concentrating power or authority in one place **central** adj 1 at the centre of something or forming the centre 2 chief or most important **centralist** n **centrality** n **centralization** n **centralize** v to concentrate power or control in one central authority **centrally** adv **centric** adj in or at the centre of something, central **centricity** n being central or a centre **centrifugal** adj moving away from a centre or axis **centrifugally** adv **central heating** n a system of heating a building **central nervous system** n the brain and spinal cord, which together control the activities of the body **central processor** n the part of a computer that controls the activities of other units **centre back** n the middle player in the half-back line in some games **centre forward** n the player in the middle of the forward line in football or hockey **centre of gravity** n the point in a body about which its mass is evenly balanced **centrifugal force** n a force that appears to act on a body that is travelling round a centre and make it fly outwards away from its circular path **centripetal** adj moving towards a centre or axis

centrifuge (say sen-tri-fewj) n a machine that uses centrifugal force to separate substances, e.g. milk and cream **centrifuge** v to subject something to the action of a centrifuge

centurion (say sen-tewr-iən) n an officer in the ancient Roman army, originally one commanding a hundred foot soldiers

century n pl **centuries** 1 a period of a hundred years 2 a hundred runs made by a batsman in one innings at cricket 3 a unit of a hundred men in the ancient Roman army

cephalic (say si-fal-ik) adj to do with the head

cephalopod (say sef-əl-ə-pod) n a mollusc (such as an octopus or squid) that has a distinct head with a ring of tentacles round the mouth

ceramic (say si-ram-ik) adj made of pottery or to do with pottery **ceramics** pl n pottery, or the making of pottery

cereal n 1 a grass that produces a grain 2 the grain produced by this grass 3 a breakfast food made from this grain ◊ Do not confuse this word with serial.

cerebellum (say se-ri-bel-əm) n a part of the brain

cerebral (say se-ri-brəl) adj 1 to do with the brain 2 intellectual

cerebrum (say se-ri-brəm) n the main part of the brain

ceremonial adj to do with a ceremony or used in ceremonies **ceremonial** n 1 a ceremony or set of rites 2 the formalities or behaviour that is suited to an occasion **ceremonially** adv

ceremonious adj full of ceremony, elaborately performed **ceremoniously** adv

ceremony n pl **ceremonies** 1 the formal actions carried out at a public event or at a religious act of worship 2 formal politeness

cerise (say sər-eez) n, adj light clear red

certain adj 1 feeling sure or convinced about something 2 known without any doubt 3 that can be relied on to happen or be true 4 that is bound to happen ♦ A rise in prices now seems certain. 5 specific but not named or stated for various reasons 6 able to be recognized without being obvious or important ♦ The house has a certain charm. 7 not known to the hearer or reader ♦ A certain John Smith then arrived. **certainly** adv **certainty** n pl **certainties**

certitude n a feeling of certainty

certificate n an official written or printed statement giving information about a fact or event, or about someone's achievement **certificated** adj

certify v **certifies**, **certified**, **certifying** to declare something formally **certifiable** adj **certifiably** adv **certification** n

cervix (say **ser**-viks) n pl **cervices** 1 the passage forming the entrance to the womb 2 a technical term for the neck **cervical** adj

cesspit, **cesspool** n a covered pit where liquid waste or sewage is stored temporarily

cf. abbr compare

CFC abbr chlorofluorocarbon

CFE abbr College of Further Education

chador (say **chah**-dor) n a cloak worn by Muslim women in some countries, consisting of a large piece of cloth that is wrapped round the head and upper body leaving only the face exposed

chafe (say chayf) v 1 to make a part of the body sore from rubbing, or to become sore 2 to warm a part of the body by rubbing 3 to become irritated or impatient

chaff n husks of grain separated from the seed by threshing **chaff** v to joke or tease someone in a good-humoured way

chaffinch n a common European finch

chagrin (say **shag**-rin) n a feeling of embarrassed annoyance or disappointment at a failure **chagrined** adj

chain n 1 a series of connected metal links 2 a connected series or sequence of things ♦ a mountain chain ♦ a chain of events 3 a number of shops, hotels, or other businesses owned by the same company 4 a unit of length for measuring land equal to 66 feet **chain** v to secure or restrain something with a chain or chains **chain mail** n armour made of metal rings linked together **chain reaction** n 1 a chemical or other change forming products that themselves cause more changes 2 a series of events each of which causes or influences the next **chainsaw** n a powered saw with teeth set on a continuous rotating chain **chain-smoke** v to smoke continuously **chain-smoker** n **chain store** n one of a number of similar shops owned by the same firm

chair n 1 a movable seat with a back 2 the person in charge at a meeting, a chairperson 3 a university professorship **chair** v to be in charge of a meeting **chairlift** n a series of chairs hung from a moving cable, for carrying people up and down the side of a mountain **chairperson** n a person in charge of a meeting

chairman, **chairwoman** n pl **chairmen** or **chairwomen** 1 a person in charge of a meeting or a committee 2 a person who takes charge of a board of directors in a business **chairmanship** n ◊ The word chairman can be used about a man or a woman, but chairperson is now common to refer to a person of either gender.

chaise longue (say shayz lawng) n a chair with a backrest at one end and a long seat for resting the legs

chalet (say **shal**-ay) n a wooden house with eaves that overhang, found especially in the Swiss Alps

chalice (say **chal**-iss) n a large goblet for holding wine, especially one from which consecrated wine is drunk at the Christian Eucharist

chalk n 1 a soft white limestone 2 a white or coloured piece of a similar substance (calcium sulphate) used for drawing or writing **chalk** v to write or draw something with chalk, to mark or rub something with chalk **chalky** adj

challenge n 1 a call to someone to take part in a contest or to show their ability or strength 2 a task or undertaking that is new and exciting but also difficult or demanding 3 a call to someone to respond, especially a sentry's call for someone approaching to identify themselves 4 a formal objection, especially to the inclusion of a person in a jury **challenge** v 1 to issue a challenge to someone 2 to raise a formal objection to a decision or proposal 3 to question the truth or rightness of something **challenged** adj **challenger** n **challenging** adj

chamber n 1 old use a room or bedroom 2 a large room used for the meetings of a parliament or for other public events 3 the group or body of people using a chamber **4** a compartment in the body of an animal or plant, or in a machine **chamberlain** *n* an official who manages the household of a sovereign or member of the nobility **chambermaid** *n* a woman who cleans bedrooms in a hotel **chamber music** *n* music written for a small number of players

chameleon (say kə-mee-li-ən) *n* a small lizard that can change its colour to match its surroundings, as camouflage

chamfer (say **cham**-fer) *v* **chamfered**, **chamfering** to cut away a sharp edge or corner to make a rounded edge **chamfer** *n* an edge or corner that has been chamfered

chamois *n pl* **chamois 1** (say **sham**-wah) a small wild mountain antelope of Europe and Asia **2** (say **sham**-i) a piece of soft yellow leather made from the skin of sheep, goats, or deer and used for washing and polishing

chamomile (say **kam**-ə-miyl) *n* a plant with sweet-smelling flowers like daisies, which are dried and used as a tonic

champ[1] *v* **1** to munch food noisily **2** to show impatience

champ[2] *n informal* a champion

champagne *n* a sparkling white wine from Champagne in France

champion *n* **1** a person or thing that has defeated all the others in a sport or competition **2** a person who speaks or acts in support of another person or a cause **champion** *adj informal* splendid, excellent **champion** *v* to be active in supporting a person or cause **championship** *n*

chance *n* **1** the way things happen without being planned or intended, luck, or fate **2** a possibility or likelihood **3** an opportunity ♦ *Now is our chance to escape.* **4** (used before a noun) coming or happening without being planned ♦ *a chance meeting* **chance** *v* **1** to happen without plan or intention **2** *informal* to risk something ♦ *Let's chance it.* **chancy** *adj* **chancier**, **chanciest**

chancellor *n* **1** a senior state or legal official of various kinds **2** the head of government in some European countries **3** the honorary head of a university **chancellery** *n pl* **chancelleries chancellorship** *n* **Chancery** *n*

the Lord Chancellor's court, a division of the High Court of Justice **Chancellor of the Exchequer** *n* the chief finance minister of the British government

chandelier (say shan-də-leer) *n* a large ornamental fixture hanging from a ceiling

chandler *n* someone who deals in supplies for ships

change *v* **1** to make something different, or to become different **2** to pass from one form or phase into another **3** to take or use one thing instead of another **4** to put on fresh clothes or coverings ♦ *I'd better change before I go out.* **5** to go from one to another ♦ *We have to change trains at Crewe.* **6** to give smaller units of money, or money in another currency, for an amount of money ♦ *Can you change £20?* **change** *n* **1** the process of changing or becoming different **2** a substitution of one thing for another **3** a fresh occupation or surroundings ♦ *I feel in need of a change.* **4** coins and notes in small units **5** an amount of money given back to the payer as the balance when the price is less than the amount offered in payment **changeable** *adj* **changeling** *n* a child who is believed to have been substituted secretly for another, especially by fairies in stories **change of heart** *n* a change in attitude or feelings about something **changeover** *n* a change from one system or situation to another

channel *n* **1** a passage along which a liquid can flow, a sunken course or line along which something can move **2** a stretch of water wider than a strait, connecting two seas **3** the bed of a stream of water below normal ground level **4** the part of a waterway in which ships can travel, deeper than the parts on each side **5** any course by which news or information, etc. may travel **6** a band of frequencies used by a particular broadcasting station **7** an electrical circuit for transmitting a signal **the Channel** *n* the English Channel, between Britain and mainland Europe **channel** *v* **channelled**, **channelling 1** to direct something through the right channel or route **2** to make a channel in something

chant *n* **1** a tune to which words with an

irregular rhythm are fitted by singing several syllables or words to the same note **2** a rhythmic call or shout by a crowd **3** a monotonous or repetitive song **chant** v **1** to sing a chant **2** to call or shout repeatedly or monotonously **chanter** n **chantry** n pl **chantries** a chapel founded for priests to sing masses for the soul of its founder

Chanukkah n another spelling of *Hanukkah*

chaos (say **kay**-oss) n great confusion or disorder **chaotic** adj **chaotically** adv **chaos theory** n the branch of science concerned with the possible widespread effects on complex systems of very small changes within them

chap¹ n informal a man or boy

chap² v **chapped**, **chapping** (said about the skin) to crack and become sore

chapatti (say cha-**pah**-ti) n pl **chapattis** a flat cake of unleavened bread, used in Indian cookery

chapel n **1** a small building or room used for Christian worship **2** a service in a chapel ♦ *They were on their way to chapel.* **3** a room or area with a separate altar within a larger church

chaperone (say **shap**-er-ohn) n an older woman in charge of a girl or young unmarried woman on social occasions **chaperone** v to act as chaperone to a girl or young woman

chaplain (say **chap**-lin) n a member of the clergy attached to a private chapel, institution, or military unit

chaps pl n long leather leggings worn over ordinary trousers by cowboys

chapter n **1** a main division of a book, often numbered **2** a distinct period of a person's life **3** the canons of a cathedral or members of a monastic order

char¹ n informal a charwoman **char** v **charred**, **charring** to work as a charwoman

char² v **charred**, **charring** to make something black, or to become black, by burning

char³ n informal tea

charabanc (say **sha**-rə-bang) n an early form of bus with bench seats

character n **1** all the distinct qualities that a person or thing has **2** a person's good reputation **3** strength and purpose in a person's nature **4** an interesting or amusing person **5** a person in a novel, play, or film **6** a description of a person's qualities, a testimonial **7** a letter, sign, or mark used in a system of writing or printing or appearing on a computer screen **8** a physical characteristic of a plant or animal **characteristic** adj **characteristically** adv **characterize** v **characterization** n **characterless** adj

charade (say shə-**rahd**) n **1** a scene acted out in a game of *charades* as a clue to a word that the players have to guess **2** an absurd pretence that is meant to impress someone

charcoal n a black substance used in drawing, and made by burning wood slowly in an oven with little air

charge n **1** the price a seller asks for goods or services **2** an accusation that someone has done wrong or has committed a crime **3** a rush forward, especially to attack **4** the amount of explosive needed to fire a gun or make an explosion **5** the amount of material that a device can hold at one time **6** the electricity contained in a substance, or the electrical property (positive or negative) of a particle of matter **7** energy stored chemically for conversion into electricity **8** a task or duty, especially the care or custody of a person or thing **9** a person or thing entrusted to someone's care **10** formal instructions about a person's duty or responsibility **charge** v **1** to ask a certain amount as a price for something **2** to record an amount as a debt ♦ *Please charge it to my account.* **3** to accuse someone formally of having done wrong or committed a crime **4** to rush forward in attack **5** to load or fill a device with whatever it holds **6** to give an electric charge to something, to store energy in a device **7** to entrust someone with a task or duty **chargeable** adj **charger** n **charge card** n a type of credit card **chargé d'affaires** n pl **chargés d'affaires** **1** an ambassador's deputy **2** a state's representative in a small country

chariot n a two-wheeled carriage drawn by

horses **charioteer** n

charisma (say kə-**riz**-mə) n the ability a person has to inspire devotion and enthusiasm **charismatic** adj

charity n pl **charities** 1 loving kindness towards others 2 thinking well about people or what they do 3 help given freely to people in need 4 an organization or fund set up to help people in need **charitable** adj **charitably** adv

charlady n pl **charladies** a charwoman

charlatan (say **shar**-lə-tən) n a person who falsely claims to have special knowledge or ability

charm n 1 the power a person has of arousing love or admiration 2 an object or set of words that is believed to have magic power or bring good luck 3 a small ornament worn on a chain or bracelet 4 Phys a property that some elementary particles have **charm** v 1 to give pleasure or delight to people 2 to influence someone by personal charm 3 to control something as if by magic **charmer** n **charming** adj

chart n 1 a map designed for people sailing ships or flying aircraft 2 an outline map for showing special information ♦ a weather chart 3 a diagram, list, or table giving information in an orderly form **the charts** pl n a published list of the best-selling pop records **chart** v 1 to make a map of an area 2 to put information into a chart

charter n 1 an official document giving certain rights to a person or organization 2 the chartering of an aircraft, ship, or vehicle **charter** v 1 to grant a charter to someone 2 to hire an aircraft, ship, or vehicle for a particular journey **chartered** adj **charterer** n **charter flight** n a flight by an aircraft that has been chartered for that journey, as distinct from an airline's scheduled flights

chartreuse (say shar-**trerz**) n 1 a fragrant green or yellow liqueur made from brandy and herbs 2 a pale green colour 3 a dish of fruit set in jelly

charwoman n pl **charwomen** a woman employed as a cleaner in a house or office

chary (say **chair**-i) adj **charier**, **chariest** cautious or wary

chase v 1 to go quickly after a person or thing in order to capture them or catch them up, or to drive them away 2 to hurry 3 informal to try to get or achieve something **chase** n 1 an act of chasing, a pursuit 2 hunting animals for sport 3 a steeplechase 4 a piece of unenclosed parkland, originally used for hunting **chaser** n

chasm (say **kaz**-əm) n 1 a deep opening in the ground 2 a wide difference in people's opinions or feelings

chassis (say **sha**-see) n pl **chassis** (say **sha**-seez) 1 the base frame of a vehicle, on which other parts are mounted 2 the framework of a piece of computer or audio equipment

chaste (say chayst) adj 1 not having sexual intercourse at all, or only with the person you are married to 2 simple in style, without decoration **chastely** adv **chastity** n

chasten (say **chay**-sən) v to make someone realize they have done something wrong

chastise (say chas-**tyz**) v to punish or reprimand someone severely **chastisement** n

chat n an informal or casual conversation **chat** v **chatted**, **chatting** to talk in a friendly or informal way **chatter** v **chatterer** n **chat room** n an area on the Internet or other network in which users can exchange information in real time **chat show** n a television or radio programme in which celebrities are invited to talk informally **chatterbox** n a talkative person

chateau (say **shat**-oh) n pl **chateaux** (say **shat**-ohz) a castle or large country house in France

chatty adj **chattier**, **chattiest** 1 fond of chatting 2 friendly and lively **chattily** adv **chattiness** n

chauffeur (say **shoh**-fer) n a person employed to drive a car **chauffeur** v to drive someone about in a car

chauvinism (say **shoh**-vin-izm) n an exaggerated belief that your own country or sex is superior to others **chauvinist** n **chauvinistic** adj

chav n informal a young person of low social background who typically wears designer-style clothes and behaves brashly or aggressively

cheap *adj* **1** low in price, not expensive **2** charging low prices ♦ *We are looking for a cheap hotel.* **3** poor in quality, of low value **4** unfair or in bad taste ♦ *a cheap remark* **cheap** *adv* cheaply ♦ *We got it cheap.* **cheapen** *v* **cheaply** *adv* **cheapness** *n*

cheat *v* **1** to act dishonestly or unfairly in order to gain an advantage **2** to break the rules in a game or examination in order to be successful **3** to trick or deceive someone **cheat** *n* **1** a person who cheats, an unfair player **2** an act of cheating, a piece of deception

check[1] *v* **1** to make sure that something is correct or in good condition **2** to stop someone or something or make them go slower **3** to make a sudden stop **4** (in chess) to make a move that threatens the opponent's king **check** *n* **1** an act of checking that something is correct or in good condition **2** a stopping or slowing; a pause or restraint **3** N. Am a bill in a restaurant **checker** *n* **in check** in chess, a position in which the king is threatened by an opposing piece **to check in** to register on arrival at a hotel or an airport **to check out** to settle a hotel bill when leaving **to check up on** to make sure something or someone is all right

check[2] *n* a pattern of squares or crossing lines **checked** *adj* having a check pattern **checkmate** *n* **1** a position in chess in which the king is in check and cannot escape **2** a complete defeat **checkmate** *v* (in chess) to put the opposing king into checkmate **checkout** *n* a place where customers pay for goods in a supermarket **checkpoint** *n* a place at a frontier between countries where documents are checked **check-up** *n* a routine medical or dental examination

cheek *n* **1** the side of the face below the eye **2** rude or disrespectful talk or behaviour **cheek** *v* to address someone in a cheeky manner **cheeky** *adj* **cheekier**, **cheekiest** rather rude or disrespectful **cheekily** *adv* **cheekiness** *n* **cheekbone** *n* the bone below your eye

cheep *v* to make the weak shrill cry of a

young bird **cheep** *n* this cry

cheer *n* **1** a shout of encouragement or applause **2** cheerfulness ♦ *full of good cheer* **cheer** *v* **1** to encourage or applaud with cheers **2** to comfort or gladden someone **cheerful** *adj* **cheerfully** *adv* **cheerfulness** *n* **cheerless** *adj* *n* **cheery** *adj* **cheerier**, **cheeriest**, **cheerily** *adv*

cheerio *interjection informal* goodbye

cheese *n* a solid or soft food made from curds of milk **cheesy** *adj* **1** tasting of cheese **2** *informal* tawdry or sentimental **3** *informal* (said about a smile) broad and exaggerated, as though saying 'cheese' in posing for a photograph **cheeseburger** *n* a hamburger with cheese in or on it **cheesecake** *n* a tart with a filling of cream and soft cheese **cheesecloth** *n* a thin loosely-woven cotton fabric

cheetah (say **chee**-tə) *n* a large spotted cat that can run extremely fast

chef (say shef) *n* a professional cook

chemical *adj* to do with chemistry, or produced by chemistry **chemical** *n* a substance obtained by or used in chemistry **chemically** *adv* **chemical engineering** *n* engineering concerned with processes that involve chemical change and with the equipment needed for these **chemical warfare** *n* warfare using poison gas and other chemicals

chemise (say shəm-**eez**) *n* **1** a loose-fitting piece of underwear formerly worn by women, hanging straight from the shoulders **2** a dress of this shape

chemistry *n* **1** the study of substances and the ways in which they react with one another **2** chemical structure, properties, and reactions **3** the way in which two people react to each other emotionally and psychologically **chemist** *n*

chemotherapy (say keem-ə-the-rə-pi) *n* the treatment of disease, especially cancer, by medicinal drugs and other chemical substances

cheque *n* an order to a bank to pay out money from an account, written on a specially printed form **cheque book** *n* a book of printed cheques **cheque card** *n* a card guaranteeing payment of a bank customer's cheques

chequers (say **chek**-erz) n a pattern of squares of alternate colours **chequered** adj 1 marked with a pattern of squares 2 having alternating periods of success and failure ♦ a chequered career

cherish v 1 to look after a person or thing lovingly 2 to be fond of someone or something 3 to have a deep feeling about something ♦ We cherish hopes of their return.

cherry n pl **cherries** 1 a small soft round fruit, usually bright or dark red 2 the tree from which this comes 3 a deep red colour **cherry-pick** v to pick out the best items from those available and reject the rest

cherub (say **cher**-əb) n 1 pl **cherubim** or **cherubs** a winged angel, often represented in art as a chubby baby with wings 2 a beautiful or angelic child **cherubic** adj

chess n a game for two players having 16 pieces each, played on a chequered board of 64 squares **chessboard** n

chest n 1 a large strong box for storing or transporting things 2 the front part of the body between the neck and the waist **chest of drawers** n

chestnut n 1 a shiny hard brown nut that grows in a prickly green case 2 the large tree from which this comes 3 a deep reddish-brown colour 4 a horse of reddish-brown or yellowish-brown colour 5 (often **old chestnut**) an old joke or story

chevalier (say shev-ə-**leer**) n a member of certain orders of knighthood

chevron (say **shev**-rən) n a bent line or stripe

chew v to bite or grind food between the teeth **chew** n 1 the act of chewing 2 something suitable for chewing **chewy** adj **chewier**, **chewiest**, **chewing gum** n a sweetened and flavoured gum for chewing

chic (say sheek) adj stylish and elegant **chic** n stylishness and elegance

chicane (say shi-**kayn**) n an artificial barrier or obstacle on a motor-racing track

chicanery (say shi-**kayn**-er-i) n trickery used to get something you want

chick n 1 a young bird, especially one that

has just hatched 2 informal a young woman

chicken n 1 a domestic fowl, kept for its eggs or meat 2 the flesh of a domestic fowl used as food 3 informal a coward **chicken** adj informal afraid to do something, cowardly **chicken out** informal to be too afraid to take part in something **chickenpox** n an infectious disease that produces itchy red spots on the skin

chicory n a blue-flowered plant grown for its leaves

chief n 1 a leader or ruler of a people 2 a person with the highest authority **chief** adj 1 highest in rank or authority 2 most important ♦ the chief reason **chiefly** adv **chieftain** n the leader of a people or of a group of people **chief constable** n the head of the police force of an area **chief of staff** n the most senior staff officer

chiffon (say **shif**-on) n a very thin almost transparent fabric, usually of silk or nylon

chihuahua (say chi-**wah**-wə) n a very small smooth haired dog from a breed originating in Mexico

chilblain n a painful swelling on the hand or foot

child n pl **children** 1 a young human being before he or she has fully developed; a boy or girl 2 a son or daughter of any age **childhood** n the time or state of being a child **childish** adj **childishly** adv **childishness** n **childless** adj **child's play** n something that is very easy or straightforward to do **childbirth** n the process of giving birth to a child **childlike** adj (said about an adult) having the good qualities of a child, simple and innocent **childminder** n someone who looks after children in their own home for payment **child-minding** n

chill n 1 an unpleasant feeling of coldness 2 a mild illness with feverish shivering **chill** adj unpleasantly cold **chill** v 1 to keep food or drink at a low temperature 2 to make someone feel cold **chilly** adj **chillier**, **chilliest**, **chilliness** n

chilli n pl **chillies** a dried hot-tasting pod of red pepper used in sauces or as a seasoning

chime n a series of notes sounded by a set of

bells or tuned metal bars or tubes **chimes** *pl n* a set of bells or metal bars or tubes that make musical sounds **chime** *v* 1 (said about bells) to ring 2 (said about a clock) to show the hour by chiming

chimera (say ki-**meer**-ə) *n* a creature in Greek mythology with the head of a lion, the body of a goat, and the tail of a serpent

chimney *n pl* **chimneys** a tall pipe or structure that carries smoke or gases away from a fire **chimney pot** *n* **chimney stack** *n* **chimney sweep** *n*

chimpanzee, **chimp** *n* an African ape, smaller than a gorilla

chin *n* the front part of the lower jaw

china *n* 1 a fine earthenware porcelain 2 objects made from this ♦ *household china*

chine *n* 1 an animal's backbone, or a joint of meat containing part of this 2 a mountain ridge **chine** *v* to cut a joint of meat along the backbone

Chinese *adj* to do with or coming from China **Chinese** *n* 1 *pl* **Chinese** a person born in China or descended from people born there 2 the language of China

chink¹ *n* a narrow opening or slit

chink² *v* to make a sound like glasses or coins being struck together **chink** *n* this sound

chintz *n* a shiny cotton cloth with a printed pattern

chip *n* 1 a thin piece cut or broken off something hard 2 a part of an object where a thin piece has been broken off 3 a fried oblong strip of potato 4 *Amer.* a potato crisp 5 a counter used to represent money in gambling games 6 short for *microchip* **chip** *v* **chipped**, **chipping** 1 to cut or break something at its surface or edge 2 to cut potatoes into chips **chippings** *pl n* **chip and PIN** *n* a system of authorizing payment with a credit or debit card **chipboard** *n* thin board made of wood chips pressed together with resin **to chip in** 1 *informal* to interrupt a conversation with a remark 2 *informal* to give money to a collection **to have a chip on your shoulder** to feel bitter or resentful about something

chipmunk *n* a small North American animal like a squirrel, with light and dark stripes down its body

chiropody (say ki-**rop**-ədi) *n* medical treatment of the feet **chiropodist** *n*

chiropractic *n* **chiropractor** *n*

chirp *v* to make the short sharp note of a small bird or a grasshopper **chirp** *n* this sound **chirpy** *adj* **chirpier**, **chirpiest** lively and cheerful

chirrup *v* **chirruped**, **chirruping** to make a series of chirps **chirrup** *n* a series of chirps

chisel *n* a tool with a long blade ending in a bevelled edge **chisel** *v* **chiselled**, **chiselling** to cut or shape something with a chisel **chiseller** *n*

chit¹ *n* an impudent young woman

chit², **chitty** *n* a short written note, especially one recording an amount of money owed

chit-chat *n* chat or gossip

chivalry (say **shiv**-əl-ri) *n* courtesy and considerate behaviour **chivalrous** *adj*

chive *n* a small herb with leaves tasting like onion

chivvy *v* **chivvies**, **chivvied**, **chivvying** *informal* to keep urging someone to hurry

chlorine (say **klor** -een) *n* a chemical element (symbol Cl), a poisonous gas used in sterilizing water and in industry **chloride** *n* a compound of chlorine and one other element ♦ *sodium chloride* **chlorinate** *v* **chlorination** *n*

chlorofluorocarbon *n* see *CFC*

chloroform (say **klo**-rə-form) *n* a liquid that gives off vapour which causes unconsciousness when breathed in

chlorophyll (say **klo**-rə-fil) *n* the substance that makes plants green

chock *n* a block or wedge used to prevent something heavy from moving **chock** *v* to secure something with a chock or chocks

chock-a-block *adj informal* crammed or crowded together

chock-full *adj informal* crammed full

chocolate *n* 1 a drink made by mixing milk or water with chocolate powder 2 a sweet made of chocolate or covered with chocolate 3 a dark-brown colour **chocoholic** *n*

choice *n* 1 the act of choosing 2 the right to choose ♦ *Do we have a choice?* 3 a range of things from which to choose ♦ *There is a* good choice of meals every day. **4** a person or thing that has been chosen ♦ *This is my choice.* **choice** *adj* (said about food) of very high quality

choir (say **kwiy**-ər) *n* **1** an organized group of singers, especially in a church **2** the part of the church where these singers sit **choral** *adj* **chorale** *n* **chorally** *adv* **chorister** *n* **choirboy** *n*

choke *v* **1** to stop someone breathing properly by squeezing or blocking their windpipe **2** to be unable to breathe properly **3** to make someone unable to speak from emotion **4** to clog or smother ♦ *The garden has become choked with weeds.* **choke** *n* a device controlling the flow of air into a petrol engine

cholera (say **kol**-er-ə) *n* an serious infectious disease that causes severe vomiting and diarrhoea **choleric** *adj*

cholesterol (say kəl-**est**-er-əl) *n* a fatty substance in body tissue that can harden the arteries

choose *v* **chose**, **chosen** to take or decide on something or someone from a larger number that is available **chooser** *n* **choosy** *adj*

chop¹ *v* **chopped**, **chopping 1** to cut something with one or more blows with an axe or knife **2** to hit something or someone with a short downward stroke or blow **chop** *n* **1** a heavy cutting stroke with an axe or knife **2** a chopping blow **3** a small thick slice of meat, usually including a rib **chopper** *n*

chop² *v* **chopped**, **chopping**; **to chop and change** *informal* to keep changing your mind or the way you behave

choppy *adj* **choppier**, **choppiest** (said about the sea) slightly rough with a lot of short broken waves **choppiness** *n*

chopsticks *pl n* a pair of small thin sticks used to lift Chinese and Japanese food to the mouth

chord (say kord) *n* **1** *Mus* a group of three or more musical notes sounded together in harmony **2** *Mathematics* a straight line joining two points on a curve ◊ Do not confuse this word with cord, which has a different meaning.

chore (say chor) *n* a tedious or routine task

choreography (say ko-ri-**og**-rəfi) *n* an arrangement of the sequence of steps in dance **choreographer** *n* **choreographic** *adj*

chortle *v* to laugh in a gleeful way **chortle** *n* a chortling sound

chorus (say **kor**-əs) *n* **1** a part of a poem or song that is repeated after each of the main parts **2** a group of singers **3** a piece of music written for a group of singers **4** something said by a lot of people at once ♦ *There was a chorus of approval for the idea.* **chorus** *v* **choruses**, **chorused**, **chorusing** to sing or speak together **in chorus** speaking or singing together

choux pastry (say shoo) very light pastry made with eggs

chowder *n* a thick soup of fish or clams with vegetables

christen (say **kri**-sən) *v* **1** to admit someone to a Christian Church by baptism **2** to give a name to someone or something **christening** *n*

Christendom (say **kris**-ən-dəm) *n* Christians all over the world

Christian *n* a person who believes in Christianity or has been baptized in a Christian Church **Christian** *adj* to do with Christians or their beliefs **Christianity** *n* a religion based on the teachings of Christ **Christian era** *n* the period from the traditional date of Christ's birth **Christian name** *n* a name given at a christening, a person's given name **Christian Science** *n* a religious system claiming that health and healing can be achieved through faith and prayer **Christian Scientist** *n*

Christmas *n pl* **Christmases 1** a Christian festival held on 25 December, commemorating Christ's birth **2** the period just before and after this **Christmassy** *adj* **Christmas Day** *n* 25 December **Christmas Eve** *n* the day before Christmas, 24 December **Christmas tree** *n* an evergreen or artificial tree decorated with lights and baubles at Christmas

chromatic (say krə-**mat**-ik) *adj* to do with colour

chromium, **chrome** (say **kroh**-mi-əm) *n* a

hard shiny metal used in making stainless steel and for coating other metals, a chemical element (symbol Cr)

chromosome (say kroh-mə-sohm) *n* a tiny thread-like part of an animal or plant cell, carrying genes

chronic *adj* 1 (said about a disease) affecting a person for a long time 2 (said about a person) having had an illness or a habit for a long time ♦ *a chronic invalid* **chronically** *adv*

chronicle (say kron-ikəl) *n* a record of important events in the order in which they happened **chronicle** *v* to record events in a chronicle **chronicler** *n*

chronology (say krən-ol-əji) *n pl* **chronologies** 1 the study of the records of past events to decide when they occurred 2 the arrangement of events in the order in which they occurred **chronological** *adj* **chronologically** *adv* **chronometer** *n*

chrysalis (say kris-ə-lis) *n pl* **chrysalises** an insect at a stage when it changes from a grub to an adult insect

chubby *adj* **chubbier**, **chubbiest** round and plump **chubbiness** *n*

chuck *v* 1 *informal* to throw something carelessly or casually 2 to touch someone playfully under the chin **chuck** *n* a playful touch

chuckle *n* a quiet or suppressed laugh **chuckle** *v* to laugh quietly

chuffed *adj informal* pleased

chug *v* **chugged**, **chugging** to make a repeated muffled explosive sound, like an engine running slowly **chug** *n* a sound of this kind

chum *n informal, old use* a close friend

chump *n informal* a foolish person

chunk *n* 1 a thick solid piece of something 2 a large amount **chunky** *adj* **chunkier**, **chunkiest**

church *n* 1 a building used for public worship by Christians 2 a religious service in a church ♦ *I will see you after church.* **Church** *n* a Christian organization having its own doctrines and forms of worship **churchman**, **churchwoman** *n pl* **churchmen**, **churchwomen** a member of the Christian clergy **Church of England** *n* the English branch of the Western Christian

Church, rejecting the pope's supremacy and having the monarch at its head **Church of Scotland** *n* the national (Presbyterian) Church of Scotland **churchwarden** *n* a representative of a parish who helps with the business of the church **churchyard** *n* the ground round a church, often used as a graveyard

churlish *adj* ill-mannered and unfriendly **churlishly** *adv* **churlishness** *n*

churn *n* 1 a large container for milk 2 a machine in which milk is beaten to make butter **churn** *v* 1 to make butter from milk 2 to stir or swirl something vigorously

chute (say shoot) *n* 1 a steep channel for people or things to slide down 2 *informal* a parachute

chutney *n pl* **chutneys** a strong-flavoured mixture of fruit, peppers, vinegar, and spices, eaten with meat or cheese

CIA *abbr* (in the USA) Central Intelligence Agency

cicada (say sik-ah-də) *n* an insect like a grasshopper, which makes a shrill chirping sound

CID *abbr* (in Britain) Criminal Investigation Department

cider *n* an alcoholic drink made from apples

cigar *n* a roll of tobacco leaves for smoking

cigarette *n* a roll of shredded tobacco in thin paper for smoking

cilium (say sil-i-əm) *n pl* **cilia** 1 each of the minute hairs fringing a leaf, an insect's wing, etc. 2 a hair-like vibrating organ on animal or vegetable tissue **ciliary** *adj*

cinch (say sinch) *n informal* something that is easy to do or certain to happen

cinder *n* a small piece of partly burnt coal or wood

cinema *n* 1 a theatre where films are shown 2 making films as an art-form or an industry **cinematic** *adj* **cinematographic** *adj* used for taking or projecting cinema films **cinematography** *n*

cinnamon (say sin-a-mən) *n* a yellowish-brown spice made from the inner bark of a south-east Asian tree

cipher (say siy-fer) *n* 1 the symbol 0, representing nought or zero 2 a set of letters or symbols used as a code 3 a person or thing of no importance

circa (say **ser**-kə) *prep* (used with dates) about, approximately ♦ *circa 1050*

circle *n* **1** a perfectly round flat figure or shape **2** the line enclosing it, every point on which is the same distance from the centre **3** something shaped like a circle, a ring **4** a series of curved rows of seats above the lowest level in a theatre or cinema **5** a number of people associated by similar interests ♦ *artistic circles* **circle** *v* **1** to move in a circle **2** to form a circle round something **circular** *adj* **circularity** *n* **circularize** *v*

circuit (say **ser**-kit) *n* **1** a line, route, or distance that goes in a circle round a place **2** a track for motor racing **3** a path for an electric current, or an apparatus through which an electric current passes **circuitous** *adj* **circuitously** *adv* **circuitry** *n* **circuit-breaker** *n* a safety device for stopping an electric current in a circuit

circulate *v* **1** to go round continuously ♦ *Blood circulates in the body.* **2** to pass from place to place **3** to mix with people at a party and talk to them **4** to give or send something to a large number of people ♦ *We will circulate your letter.* **circulation** *n* **circulatory** *adj*

circum- *prefix* around (as in *circumference*) **circumcise** *v* to cut off the foreskin of a man or boy or the clitoris of a girl or woman **circumcision** *n* **circumference** *n* **1** the line round a circle **2** the distance round something **circumlocution** *n* a roundabout expression, using many words where a few would do, e.g. *at this moment in time* instead of *now* **circumnavigate** *v* to sail completely round something **circumnavigation** *n*

circumflex accent (say **ser**-kəm-fleks) *n* a mark put over a vowel in some languages, e.g. *e* in ♦ *fête*

circumscribe *v* **1** to draw a line round something **2** to limit or restrict an activity **circumscription** *n*

circumspect (say **ser**-kəm-spekt) *adj* cautious and watchful, wary **circumspection** *n*

circumstance *n* a condition or fact that is connected with an event, person, or action or influences it **circumstances** *pl n* the conditions of a person's life, and how much money they have **circumstantial** *adj* **circumstantially** *adv*

circumvent (say ser-kəm-**vent**) *v* to find a way round a difficulty **circumvention** *n*

circus *n* **1** a travelling show usually performed in a tent, with clowns, acrobats, and sometimes trained animals **2** *informal* a scene of lively or noisy activity **3** (in place names) an open space in a town, where several streets meet ♦ *Piccadilly Circus.* **4** (in ancient Rome) a round or oval arena used for chariot races and other sports

cirrhosis (say si-**roh**-sis) *n* a chronic disease in which the liver hardens

cirrus (say **si**-rus) *n pl* **cirri** cloud made up of light wispy streaks

CIS Commonwealth of Independent States

cistern (say **sis**-tern) *n* a tank or other container for storing water, especially as part of a flushing toilet

citadel (say **sit**-ə-dəl) *n* **1** a fortress protecting or overlooking a city **2** a meeting hall of the Salvation Army

cite *v* to quote or mention an author or piece of writing as an example or in support of an argument **citation** *n*

citizen *n* **1** a person who has full rights in a country or commonwealth by birth or by naturalization **2** a person who lives in a particular city or town **citizenry** *n* **citizenship** *n*

citrus (say **sit**-rəs) *n* any of a group of related trees including lemon, orange, and grapefruit **citric acid** *n* the sharp-tasting acid in the juice of lemons, limes, etc. **citrus fruit** *n* the fruit of a citrus tree

city *n pl* **cities** a large and important town **cityscape** *n* a city landscape

civic (say **siv**-ik) *adj* to do with or belonging to a city or town, or to do with the citizens of a town **civics** *pl n* the study of the rights and duties of citizens

civil *adj* **1** polite and helpful **2** to do with or belonging to citizens **3** to do with civilians and not the armed forces or the Church ♦ *civil aviation* ♦ *a civil marriage* **4** involving civil law and not criminal law ♦ *a civil dispute* **civilian** *n* an ordinary citizen, a person who is not serving in the armed forces

civility n pl **civilities** politeness, or an act of politeness **civilization** n **1** the process of becoming civilized or making people civilized **2** a stage in the development of human society ♦ *ancient civilizations* **3** civilized conditions or social activity ♦ *far from civilization* **civilize** v **1** to bring a primitive society to a more advanced stage of development **2** to improve the behaviour of a person **civilized** adj **civilly** adv **civil law** n law dealing with the private rights of citizens, not with criminal acts **civil servant** n someone who works in the civil service **civil service** n people employed by the government to run the state's affairs, other than the police and the armed forces **civil war** n war between groups of citizens of the same country

CJD abbr Creutzfeldt-Jakob disease

cl abbr centilitre(s)

clack v to make a short sharp sound like plates being struck together **clack** n a sound of clacking

clad adj **1** clothed ♦ *He arrived clad in a heavy business suit.* **2** covered in cladding **cladding** n

claim v **1** to state that something is true or has happened, without being able to prove it **2** to request something as a right or debt **3** to cause people to die ♦ *The earthquake claimed over a thousand lives.* **claim** n **1** a statement claiming that something is true **2** a request for something as a right **3** the right to something ♦ *A widow has a claim on her dead husband's estate.* **4** something that a person claims, especially land **claimant** n

clairvoyant (say klair-**voy**-ənt) n a person who claims to have the power of knowing about future events **clairvoyance** n

clam n a large shellfish with a hinged shell **clam** v **clammed, clamming clam up** *informal* to refuse to talk

clamber v to climb slowly and with difficulty

clammy adj **clammier, clammiest** unpleasantly damp and sticky **clammily** adv **clamminess** n

clamour n **1** a loud confused noise, especially of shouting **2** a loud protest or demand **clamour** v to make a loud protest

or demand **clamorous** adj

clamp n a device for holding things tightly **clamp** v to grip or fix something with a clamp

clan n **1** a group of related families, especially in the Scottish Highlands **2** a large family forming a close group **clannish** adj **clansman** n pl **clansmen** a male member of a clan

clandestine (say klan-**dest**-in) adj done secretly, kept secret **clandestinely** adv

clang v to make a loud ringing sound **clang** n a clanging sound **clangour** n

clanger n informal a bad or obvious mistake

clank v to make a dull metallic sound **clank** n a clanking sound

clap v **clapped, clapping 1** to strike the palms of the hands together repeatedly, especially as applause **2** (said about a bird) to flap its wings audibly **3** to slap someone in a friendly way **4** to impose a penalty abruptly on someone **clap** n **1** the sudden sharp noise of thunder **2** the sound of a person clapping; applause **3** a friendly slap ♦ *Jem gave him a clap on the shoulder.* **clapped out** adj worn out, exhausted

clarify v **clarifies, clarified, clarifying 1** to make something clear or easier to understand, or to become easier to understand **2** to remove impurities from fats **clarification** n

clarinet (say kla-rin-**et**) n a woodwind musical instrument with finger-holes and keys **clarinettist** n

clash v **1** (said about two groups of people) to come together and attack or fight one another **2** to disagree or quarrel **3** to strike cymbals together to make a loud harsh sound **4** to happen inconveniently at the same time as something else ♦ *Tomorrow's party clashes with my birthday.* **5** (said about colours) to look unpleasant together **clash** n **1** a sound of clashing **2** a disagreement or quarrel **3** a clashing of colours

clasp n **1** a device for fastening things **2** a grasp or handshake **clasp** v **1** to fasten something or join it with a clasp **2** to grasp something or someone

class n **1** a set of children or students taught

together, or a session when they are taught **2** a group or set of similar people, animals, or things **3** people of a particular social or economic level ♦ *the middle class* **4** a level of service or quality ♦ *first class* ♦ *tourist class* **5** distinction or high quality ♦ *a tennis player with class* **class** v to place something in a class or category, to classify things **classless** adj **classy** adj **classier, classiest, classily** adv **classiness** n **classroom** n a room where a class of pupils or students is taught

classic adj **1** generally recognized as important or outstanding ♦ *a classic novel* **2** noticeably typical ♦ *the classic symptoms of cholera* **3** simple and elegant in style ♦ *classic clothes* **classic** n a book or work of art of outstanding value or importance **classics** pl n the study of ancient Greek and Roman literature and history **classical** adj **1** to do with ancient Greek and Roman art, literature, and culture **2** simple and harmonious in style **3** serious or conventional in form or style ♦ *classical music* **classically** adv **classicism** n **classicist** n

classify v **classifies, classified, classifying** to arrange things systematically in classes or groups, or to put a single thing into a particular class **classifiable** adj **classification** n **classified** adj

clatter v to make a sound like hard objects rattling together **clatter** n a clattering noise

clause n **1** a single part in a treaty, law, or contract **2** *Gram* a part of a sentence, with its own verb

claustrophobia (say klaw-strə-**foh**-biə) n abnormal fear of being in an enclosed space **claustrophobic** adj

clavichord (say klav-i-kord) n a rectangular keyboard instrument with a very soft tone

clavicle (say klav-ikəl) n a technical term for the collarbone

clavier (say klav-i-er) n a musical instrument played from a keyboard

claw n **1** a sharp or pointed nail on an animal's or bird's foot **2** the pincers of a lobster or other shellfish **3** a device like a claw, used for grappling and holding things

claw v to grasp, pull, or scratch something with a claw or with the hands

clay n stiff sticky earth that becomes hard when baked, used for making bricks and pottery **clayey** adj

-cle suffix forming nouns that were once diminutives (as in *article*)

clean adj **1** without any dirt or impurities, not soiled **2** fresh, not yet used **3** morally pure, not indecent **4** honourable and keeping to the rules ♦ *a clean fight* **5** without projections or roughness **clean** adv completely or entirely ♦ *I clean forgot their wedding anniversary.* **clean** v to make something clean **clean** n an act of cleaning ♦ *I'll give the table a clean.* **cleaner** n **cleanliness** n **cleanly** adv **cleanness** n

cleanse v to make something thoroughly clean **cleanser** n something used for cleansing **clean-cut** adj (usually said about a person's features) having a sharp outline **clean-shaven** adj

clear adj **1** transparent, not muddy or cloudy ♦ *clear glass* **2** easy to see or hear or understand **3** free from obstructions or from anything unwanted ♦ *The streets are clear of traffic.* **4** not feeling guilt or regret ♦ *I have a clear conscience.* **5** evident or obvious ♦ *It was a clear case of cheating.* **6** not having any doubt, not confused ♦ *Are you clear about what you have to do?* **7** complete, without deductions ♦ *You have to give three clear days' notice.* **8** not touching something ♦ *One wheel was clear of the ground.* **clear** adv **1** clearly or distinctly ♦ *We can hear you loud and clear.* **2** completely ♦ *They got clear away.* **3** apart, not in contact ♦ *Stand clear of the doors!* **clear** v **1** to make something clear, or to become clear **2** to get past or over an obstacle without touching it **3** to get approval or authorization for something ♦ *We'll have to clear the goods through customs.* **4** to pass a cheque through a clearing house **5** to make an amount of money as a net gain or profit **clarity** n **clearance** n **clearing** n **clearly** adv **clearness** n **clear-cut** adj easy to see or understand, very distinct **clearing bank** n a bank which is a member of a clearing house **clearing house** n **1** an office at which banks exchange cheques and settle the balances **2** an agency that collects and distributes information **clearway** *n* (in Britain) a main road other than a motorway on which vehicles must not stop on the carriageway

cleat *n* **1** a short piece of wood or metal with projecting ends for fastening a rope **2** one of several small studs on the sole of a boot or shoe, to make it grip better **3** a wedge on a spar or tool to prevent it slipping

cleave *v* past tense **clove**, **cleaved**, or **cleft**; past participle **cloven**, **cleaved**, or **cleft 1** to split something or divide it by chopping, or to become split **2** to make a way through something ♦ *We saw a bird cleave the clear water.* **cleaver** *n*

cleft past tense and past participle of *cleave* **cleft** *adj* split or partly divided **cleft** *n* a split in something

clematis (say **klem**-ə-tiss or klim-**ay**-tiss) *n* a climbing plant with white, pink, or purple flowers

clemency (say **klem**-ən-si) *n* gentleness or mildness, mercy **clement** *adj*

clementine (say **klem**-ən-tiyn) *n* a deep-coloured citrus fruit like a small orange

clench *v* **1** to close the teeth or fingers tightly **2** to grasp something tightly **clench** *n* a clenching action, or a clenched state

clerestory (say **kleer**-stor-i) *n pl* **clerestories** the upper part of the main body of a large church, with a row of windows admitting light to the nave

clergy *n pl* **clergies** the people who have been ordained as priests or ministers of the Christian Church

cleric (say **kle**-rik) *n* a member of the clergy **clerical** *adj*

clerk (say klark) *n* **1** a person who keeps records or accounts in an office **2** an official who keeps the records of a court or council, etc.

clever *adj* **1** quick at learning and understanding **2** showing intelligent thought or skill ♦ *It's a clever idea.* **cleverly** *adv* **cleverness** *n*

cliché (say **klee**-shay) *n* a phrase or idea that is used so often that it has little meaning

click *n* a short sharp sound like two plastic objects coming abruptly into contact **click** *v* **1** to make a click, or cause something to make a click **2** to fasten something with a click **3** *ICT* to press a button on a mouse in order to perform a task **4** *informal* to become friendly, to get on well together **5** *informal* to become understood **clicky** *adj*

client *n* **1** a person who uses the services of a professional or organization **2** a customer of a shop or bank **3** *ICT* a computer or workstation that gets information from a server in a network **clientele** *n*

cliff *n* a steep rock face, especially on a coast **cliffhanger** *n* a tense and exciting ending to an episode of a story, leaving the audience anxious to know what happens next

climate *n* **1** the regular weather conditions of an area **2** an area with certain weather conditions ♦ *We enjoyed living in a warm climate.* **3** a general attitude or feeling ♦ *a climate of hostility* **climatic** *adj*

climax *n* the event or point in a series of events that reaches the greatest interest or excitement **climax** *v* to reach a climax, or bring something to a climax **climactic** *adj*

climb *v* **1** to go up or over something with an effort **2** to move upwards or go higher **3** (said about a plant) to grow up a wall or other support ♦ *a climbing rose* **climb** *n* climbing or going upwards **climber** *n* **to climb down 1** to go down something with an effort **2** to change your mind about something important and admit that you have been wrong

clinch *v* **1** to settle something definitely ♦ *Their new offer clinched the deal.* **2** to fasten something securely **3** to fight or grapple at close quarters **clinch** *n* **1** a fight at close quarters **2** an embrace

cling *v* past tense and past participle **clung 1** to hold on tightly to something **2** to become attached to something **3** to be emotionally dependent on someone ♦ *She continued to cling to her mother.* **4** to continue to believe in or hope for something ♦ *People often cling to their childhood ambitions.*

clinic *n* **1** a place where patients can get specialized medical treatment or advice

2 a session at which a hospital doctor sees patients **clinical** adj **1** relating to the treatment of patients ♦ clinical medicine **2** used for treating patients ♦ a clinical thermometer **3** based on observed signs and symptoms ♦ clinical death **4** (said about a place) looking bare and hygienic **5** (said about a person or behaviour) unemotional, cool and detached **clinically** adv

clink[1] v to make a thin sharp sound like glasses striking together **clink** n a clinking sound

clink[2] n informal prison ♦ in clink

clip[1] n **1** a fastener for holding things together **2** a piece of jewellery fastened by a clip **3** a holder containing cartridges for an automatic weapon **clip** v **clipped, clipping** to fix or fasten something with a clip

clip[2] v **clipped, clipping 1** to cut or trim something with scissors or shears **2** to punch a small piece from a ticket to show that it has been used **3** informal to hit someone sharply **clip** n **1** a short piece shown from a cinema or television film **2** the act or process of clipping something, or a piece clipped off **3** the wool cut from a sheep or flock at one shearing **4** informal a sharp blow **5** a fast pace ♦ The car was moving at quite a clip.

clipper n an old type of fast sailing ship

clipping n a piece clipped from something, especially from a newspaper

clique (say kleek) n a small group of people who support each other and keep others out **cliquey** adj **cliquish** adj

clitoris (say **klit-er-iss**) n a small sensitive piece of flesh near the opening of a woman's vagina **clitoral** adj

cloak n **1** a sleeveless piece of outdoor clothing that hangs loosely from the shoulders **2** something that hides or covers ♦ the cloak of secrecy **cloak** v to cover or conceal something **cloakroom** n **1** a room in a public building where outdoor clothes and bags may be left for a time **2** a toilet in a house or public building

clobber[1] n informal clothing and personal belongings

clobber[2] v informal **1** to hit someone hard or repeatedly **2** to defeat someone heavily

cloche (say klosh or klohsh) n **1** a small glass or plastic cover for outdoor plants **2** a close-fitting bell-shaped hat worn by women

clock n **1** a device that measures the time and shows it with a dial and hands, or through a digital display **2** any measuring device with a dial or digital display, such as a speedometer **3** the downy seed head of a dandelion **clock** v **1** to achieve or record a particular time, distance, or speed **2** informal to hit someone **clockwise** adv, adj moving in a curve in the same direction as the hands of a clock **clockwork** n a mechanism with a spring and toothed wheels, like that of a clock **like clockwork** precisely and easily **to clock in** or **out** to register the time you arrive at work or leave work **to clock something up** to reach a certain speed ♦ He clocked up 10 seconds for the 100 metres.

clod n a lump of earth or clay

clog n a shoe with a heavy wooden sole **clog** v **clogged, clogging** to make something blocked, or to become blocked

cloister n **1** a covered walk along the side of a church or other building, round a courtyard **2** a monastery or convent **cloistered** adj

clone n an animal or plant made from the cells of another animal or plant and therefore exactly like it **clone** v to produce a plant or animal as a clone of another

close[1] (say klohs) adj **1** only a short distance apart in space or time **2** belonging to the immediate family ♦ a close relative of my father **3** fond or affectionate ♦ They became close friends. **4** detailed or concentrated ♦ Pay close attention. **5** strong or noticeable ♦ There is a close resemblance between the two girls. **6** in which the competitors are nearly equal ♦ It proved a close match. **7** dense or compact ♦ The carpet has a close texture. **8** (said about information) closely guarded ♦ The code was a close secret. **9** (said about a person) stingy or mean **10** (said about the weather) stuffy or humid **close** adv at a point not far away ♦ My cousin lives close by. **close** n **1** a street that is closed at one end, a cul-de-sac **2** the grounds round a cathedral or abbey **closely** adv

closeness n **close-up** n a photograph or piece of film taken at close range, with a lot of detail **a close shave** a narrow escape from danger or difficulty **at close quarters** very close together

close² (say klohz) v **1** to move something so as to cover or block an opening, to shut something **2** to move or be moved into this position ♦ The door closed with a bang. **3** to finish business at the end of a day, or for a longer period, at a shop or office ♦ The shops close early on Wednesdays. **4** to end something, or come to an end **5** to bring two parts of something together ♦ She closed the book and put out the light. **6** to make an electric circuit continuous **7** to come within fighting or striking distance **close** n a conclusion or end **to close in** to surround someone or something gradually, especially to trap them or shut them in

closure (say kloh-zher) n **1** the act of closing something, or the state of being closed **2** a parliamentary procedure for ending a debate and taking a vote **3** a sense of emotional fulfilment or satisfaction, especially after a traumatic experience

clot n a small mass of blood or other liquid that has become solid **clot** v **clotted**, **clotting** to form clots

cloth n **1** woven material or felt **2** a piece of material used for a special purpose, such as a dishcloth or tablecloth **the cloth** the clergy

clothe v past tense and past participle **clothed** or **clad** to put clothes on someone **clothes** pl n things worn to cover the body and limbs **clothing** n

cloud n **1** a mass of condensed water vapour floating in the sky **2** a mass of smoke or dust in the air **3** a mass of things moving in the air ♦ a cloud of insects **4** a state of gloom or suspicion **cloud** v **1** to cover or darken with clouds or gloom or trouble **2** to become overcast or indistinct or gloomy **cloudless** adj **cloudy** adj **cloudier**, **cloudiest**, **cloudiness** n

clout n informal **1** a heavy blow **2** power or influence **clout** v informal to hit someone hard

clove¹ n the dried bud of a tropical tree, used as a spice

clove² n each of the small bulbs in a compound bulb ♦ a clove of garlic

clove³ past tense of cleave

cloven past participle of cleave

cloven hoof n a divided hoof, like those of cattle or sheep

clover n a small plant, usually with three leaves on each stalk

clown n **1** a performer who performs comical tricks and actions, especially in a circus **2** a person who does silly things **clown** v to do silly things to amuse other people **clownish** adj

cloy v to sicken or disgust with too much sweetness or pleasure **cloying** adj

club n **1** a heavy stick with one end thicker than the other, used as a weapon **2** (in golf) an implement for hitting the ball **3** a playing card of the suit (called clubs) marked with black clover leaves **4** a group of people who meet to enjoy a particular interest or activity, or the building where they meet **5** an organization offering certain benefits to its subscribers ♦ a book club **club** v **clubbed**, **clubbing 1** to hit someone with a club **2** to join with other people in doing something, especially paying money ♦ We clubbed together to buy a boat. **3** to visit night clubs ♦ to go clubbing **clubhouse** n the building used by a club

clue n **1** a fact or idea that helps to solve a problem or mystery **2** a word or phrase that gives a hint about what to put in a crossword puzzle **clueless** adj **clued-up** adj informal well informed about something

clump n **1** a cluster or mass of things **2** a clumping sound **clump** v **1** to form a cluster or mass **2** to walk with a heavy tread

clumsy adj **clumsier**, **clumsiest 1** heavy and ungraceful in movement **2** large and difficult to handle or use **3** done without much tact or skill ♦ a clumsy apology **clumsily** adv **clumsiness** n

clung past tense and past participle of cling

clunk v to make a dull sound like thick metal objects hitting each other **clunk** n this sound

cluster n a small close group of things **cluster** v to bring things together, or come together, in a cluster **cluster bomb** n a bomb that sprays metal pellets when it explodes

clutch v to grasp something tightly **clutch** n **1** a tight grasp **2** a device for connecting and disconnecting the engine and gears of a motor vehicle **to clutch at** to try to get hold of something

clutter n **1** things lying about untidily **2** a crowded untidy state **clutter** v to fill a place with clutter, or make it untidy

cm abbr centimetre(s)

Co. abbr **1** Company ♦ Briggs & Co. **2** County ♦ Co. Durham.

co- prefix together with, jointly ♦ co-author ♦ co-driver

c/o abbr care of (used in addresses)

coach n **1** a well equipped single-decker bus used for long journeys **2** a railway carriage **3** a large four-wheeled carriage drawn by horses **4** an instructor in sports **5** a teacher giving private specialized tuition **coach** v to train or teach someone

coagulate (say koh-**ag**-yoo-layt) v to change from liquid to semi-solid, to clot **coagulation** n

coal n **1** a hard black mineral used for burning to supply heat **2** a piece of this, especially one that is burning **collier** n **colliery** n pl **collieries coalface** n the exposed surface of coal in a mine **coalfield** n an area where there is coal underground **coal mine** n a mine where coal is dug **coal miner** n someone who mines coal

coalesce (say koh-ə-**less**) v to combine and form one whole thing **coalescence** n

coalition (say koh-ə-**lish**-ən) n a temporary alliance, especially between political parties forming a joint government

coarse adj **1** composed of large particles **2** rough or loose in texture **3** (said about a person) rough or crude in manner or behaviour, not refined **4** inferior or common **coarsely** adv **coarsen** v **coarseness** n

coast n the seashore and the land close to it **coast** v **1** to sail along a coast **2** to move easily without using power **coastal** adj **coastguard** n an official who keeps watch on the coast to assist ships in danger **coastline** n the shape or outline of a coast

coat n **1** a piece of clothing with sleeves, worn outdoors over other clothes **2** the hair or fur covering an animal's body **3** a covering layer, especially of paint **coat** v **1** to cover something with a layer **2** to form a covering to something **coat of arms** n a design on a shield, used as an emblem by a family, city, or institution

coating n a thin covering layer

coax v to persuade someone gently or gradually

cob n **1** the central part of an ear of maize, on which the corn grows **2** a male swan **3** a sturdy horse for riding **4** a loaf of bread with a rounded top **5** a large kind of hazelnut

cobalt (say **koh**-bollt) n **1** a hard silvery-white metal used in many alloys and with radioactive forms used in medicine and industry, a chemical element (symbol Co) **2** colouring-matter made from this; its deep-blue colour

cobble[1], **cobblestone** n a small rounded stone used for paving roads **cobble** v to pave a surface with cobblestones **cobbled** adj

cobble[2] v to put together or mend something roughly **cobbler** n

COBOL (say **koh**-bol) n a computer programming language designed for use in business

cobra (say **koh**-brə or **kob**-rə) n pl **cobras** a poisonous Indian or African snake

cobweb n a spider's web, especially an old one covered in dust **cobwebby** adj

coca (say **koh**-kə) n a tropical American shrub with leaves that are the source of cocaine

cocaine (say kə-**kayn**) n an addictive drug made from coca, used in medicine as a local anaesthetic or illegally as a stimulant

coccyx (say **kok**-siks) n a small triangular bone at the base of the spine

cochineal (say koch-in-**eel**) n a bright red dye used for colouring food

cochlea (say **kok**-liə) n the spiral cavity of the inner ear

cock n **1** a male bird **2** a lever in the firing mechanism of a gun **3** a tap or spout for controlling the flow of a liquid **cock** v to raise the cock of a gun ready for firing

cockerel n a young domestic cock

cock-eyed adj informal **1** crooked or slanting **2** (said about an idea or plan) absurd or impractical

cockle n **1** an edible shellfish **2** a small shallow boat

cockney n pl **cockneys 1** a native of the East End of London **2** the dialect or accent of this area

cockpit n **1** the compartment of an aircraft for the pilot and crew **2** the driver's compartment in a racing car

cockroach n an insect like a beetle with long legs and antennae

cocksure adj arrogantly confident or positive

cocktail n **1** an alcoholic drink made of a spirit mixed with other spirits or fruit juice **2** a small dish of shellfish or fruit, served as an appetizer ♦ prawn cocktail **3** a mixture of dangerous or unpleasant substances

cocky adj **cockier, cockiest** slightly over-confident or arrogant **cockily** adv **cockiness** n

cocoa n **1** a powder made from crushed cacao seeds **2** a drink made from this powder

coconut n **1** the large nut of the coco palm, with a hard shell containing a sweet milky juice **2** the flaky white lining of this nut, used in sweets and cookery

cocoon (say kə-**koon**) n **1** the silky covering round a chrysalis **2** a protective wrapping **cocoon** v to protect something by wrapping it completely

COD abbr cash on delivery

cod n pl **cod** a large sea fish used for food

coddle v **1** to be too protective towards someone **2** to cook eggs in water just below boiling point

code n **1** a pre-arranged word or phrase representing a message, for secrecy **2** a system of words, letters, or symbols used to represent others, either for secrecy or for transmitting by machine as in Morse code **3** a set of rules or laws ♦ the Highway Code **4** a set of numbers that represents an area in telephoning ♦ Do you know the code for Southampton? **5** ICT a set of programming instructions **code** v to put something into code

codeine (say koh-**deen**) n a white medicine made from morphine, used to relieve pain or induce sleep

codger n informal an elderly man

codify (say **koh**-di-fiy) v **codifies, codified, codifying** to organize laws or rules into a code **codification** n **codifier** n

co-education n education of pupils of both sexes together **co-educational** adj

coequal adj equal to one another

coerce (say koh-**erss**) v to compel someone by threats or force **coercion** n **coercive** adj

coeval (say koh-**ee**-vəl) adj having the same age or date of origin

coexist v to exist at the same time **coexistence** n **coexistent** adj

C. of E. abbr Church of England

coffee n **1** a hot drink made from the roasted and ground seeds of a tropical shrub **2** the seeds of this shrub **3** a light-brown colour **coffee bar** n a place serving coffee and light refreshments **coffee table** n a small low table, normally used in a living room

coffer n a large strong box for holding money and valuables **coffers** pl n the funds or financial resources of an organization

coffin n a long box in which a dead body is buried or cremated

cog n **1** each of a series of teeth on the edge of a wheel, fitting into and pushing those on another wheel **2** a wheel with a series of cogs round it

cogent (say **koh**-jənt) adj logical and convincing ♦ a cogent argument **cogency** n **cogently** adv

cogitate (say **koj**-i-tayt) v to think deeply about something **cogitation** n

cognac (say **kon**-yak) n French brandy

cognate (say **kog**-nayt) adj having the same source or origin **cognate** n **1** a relative **2** a word that has the same origin as another ♦ Die and death are cognates.

cognition (say kog-**ni**-shən) n the faculty of knowing or perceiving things **cognitive** adj **cognizant** adj **cognizance** n

cohabit v **cohabited, cohabiting** to live together and have a sexual relationship without being married **cohabitation** n

cohere (say koh-**heer**) v **1** to stick together

or form a united mass **2** to be logical or consistent **coherent** adj **coherence** n **coherently** adv **cohesion** n **cohesive** adj

cohort n **1** a division of the ancient Roman army, one-tenth of a legion **2** a group of people working together

coiffure (say kwah-**yoor**) n a hairstyle

coil n **1** a length of something wound into a series of joined rings **2** a length of wire wound in a spiral to conduct electric current **3** a contraceptive device for insertion into the womb **coil** v to wind something into a coil

coin n **1** a small round stamped piece of metal used for money **2** money in the form of coins **coin** v **1** to make coins by stamping metal **2** informal to make a large amount of money as profit **3** to invent a word or phrase **coinage** n

coincide (say koh-in-**siyd**) v **1** to happen at the same time as something else ♦ His holidays don't coincide with hers. **2** to be in the same place or area **3** to agree or be the same ♦ We found that our tastes coincided. **coincidence** n **coincident** adj **coincidental** adj **coincidentally** adv

coke[1] n the solid fuel left after gas and tar have been extracted from coal

coke[2] n informal cocaine

col n **1** a depression in a range of mountains **2** Meteorology a region of low pressure between two anticyclones

colander (say **kul**-en-der) n a bowl-shaped container with holes for straining water from food after cooking

cold adj **1** having or at a low temperature **2** not heated, having cooled after being heated or cooked ♦ cold meat **3** informal unconscious ♦ The blow knocked him cold. **4** unfriendly or unwelcoming ♦ We got a cold reception. **cold** n **1** lack of heat or warmth; a low temperature **2** an infectious illness that can cause catarrh, a sore throat, and sneezing **coldish** adj **coldly** adv **coldness** n **cold-blooded** adj **1** having a body temperature that changes with the temperature of surroundings, as fish have **2** unfeeling, deliberately ruthless ♦ a cold-blooded killer **cold war** n a state of hostility between nations without actual

fighting **in cold blood** deliberately and ruthlessly **to get cold feet** to have doubts about doing something bold or ambitious **to give someone the cold shoulder** to be deliberately unfriendly

coleslaw n a salad of finely shredded raw cabbage mixed with mayonnaise

colic n severe pain in the abdomen, caused by wind **colicky** adj

collaborate v **1** to work together on a piece of work **2** to help your country's enemy **collaboration** n **collaborator** n

collage (say kol-**ahzh**) n a piece of art made by fixing bits of paper, cloth, string, etc. to a surface

collagen (say **kol**-ə-jin) n a protein substance found in bone and tissue

collapse v **1** to fall down or give way suddenly **2** to lose strength or force suddenly ♦ Enemy resistance collapsed. **3** (said about a person) to fall down because of illness or physical breakdown **4** to fold into a smaller size **collapse** n **1** the collapsing of something **2** a sudden breakdown or failure **collapsible** adj

collar n **1** a band of material round the neck **2** a band put round the neck of an animal **3** a band, ring, or pipe holding part of a machine **4** a cut of bacon from near the head **collar** v **collared**, **collaring** informal to seize or catch someone **collarbone** n the bone joining the breastbone and shoulder blade, the clavicle

collate (say kə-**layt**) v **1** to collect and arrange something systematically **2** to compare things in detail **collateral** adj **1** additional but less important ♦ collateral evidence **2** side by side, parallel **3** descended from the same ancestor but by a different line ♦ a collateral branch of the family **collateral** n money or property that is pledged as security for repayment of a loan **collation** n **collator** n **collateral damage** n accidental damage to civilian areas in a war

colleague n a person you work with, especially in a business or profession

collect (say kə-**lekt**) v **1** to bring people or things together from several places **2** to come together **3** to get money or other contributions from a number of people

4 to look for and acquire examples of particular things as a hobby or for study ♦ *I've started collecting stamps.* **5** to fetch or go and get something ♦ *Will you collect my cleaning on your way home?* **6** to gather one's thoughts into systematic order or control **collected** *adj* (said about a person) calm and self-controlled **collectedly** *adv*

collective *adj* to do with a group taken as a whole ♦ *Our collective response to the idea.* **collective** *n* a collective enterprise **collectively** *adv* **collector** *n* **collective bargaining** *n* negotiation about pay and working conditions by an organized group of employees

collection *n* **1** the process of collecting **2** things collected systematically **3** a number of things that have come together or been placed together **4** money collected for a charity or at a church service

college *n* **1** a place of education providing courses in higher or specialized forms of education for adults **2** an independent part of a university with its own teachers and students **3** (in names) a school ♦ *Eton College.* **4** an organized body of professional people ♦ *the Royal College of Surgeons* **collegiate** *adj*

collide *v* **1** (said about a moving object) to strike violently against something **2** (said about interests or opinions) to conflict

collie *n* a dog with a long pointed nose and shaggy hair

collision *n* the act of colliding

collocate *v* to bring things together to compare them **collocation** *n* **collocator** *n*

colloquial (say kə-loh-kwee-əl) *adj* (said about a word or piece of language) suitable for ordinary conversation but not for formal speech or writing **colloquialism** *n* **colloquially** *adv*

collusion (say kə-loo-zhən) *n* a secret agreement between two or more people who are trying to deceive or cheat someone **collusive** *adj*

cologne (say kə-lohn) *n* eau de cologne or other lightly scented liquid used on the skin

colon[1] (say koh-lən) *n* the main part of the large intestine **colonic** *adj*

colon[2] (say koh-lən) *n* **1** the punctuation mark (:), used to introduce a list or summary of what has gone before, or an elaboration or explanation **2** the same mark used in mathematics, especially in statements of proportion (as in 1:3 = 2:6)

colonel (say ker-nəl) *n* an army officer commanding a regiment

colonnade (say kol-ən-ayd) *n* a row of columns

colony *n pl* **colonies 1** an area of land in one country that people from another country settle in and control **2** the people who live in a colony **3** a group of people sharing the same background or interest ♦ *a nudist colony* **4** a group of animals or plants of the same kind living close together **colonial** *adj* **colonialism** *n* **colonist** *n* **colonization** *n* **colonize** *v*

colossus (say kə-los-əs) *n pl* **colossi** (say kə-los-l) **1** a huge statue, much larger than life-size **2** a person of great importance and influence **colossal** *adj* **colossally** *adv*

colour *n* **1** the property an object has of producing a particular sensation on the eye by the way it reflects rays of light of different wavelengths **2** a particular effect produced in this way ♦ *Which colour did you choose for the bedroom?* **3** the use of all colours in photography or television **4** the redness of a person's complexion **5** the pigmentation of the skin, especially as an indication of racial origin **6** a pigment, paint, or dye **7** the flag of a ship or regiment **colour** *v* **1** to put colour on something; to paint, stain, or dye something **2** to change colour **3** (said about a person) to blush **4** to give a special character or bias to something ♦ *His political opinions colour his writings.* **coloration** *n* **colourant** *n* **coloured** *adj* **1** having colour **2** wholly or partly of non-white descent **Coloured** *adj* (in South Africa) of mixed white and non-white descent **coloured** *n* a coloured person ◊ The word *coloured*, used to describe people, is often considered to be insulting. It is better to use *black*. **colourful** *adj* **colourfully** *adv* **colouring** *n* **colourless** *adj* **colours** *pl n* an award given to regular or leading members of a sports team **colour-blind** *adj* unable to see the difference between certain colours

colt n a young male horse

column n 1 a round pillar 2 something long or tall and narrow ♦ *a column of smoke* 3 a section of printing or text down a page, especially in a newspaper or reference book 4 a regular feature in a newspaper ♦ *Who writes the gardening column?* 5 a long narrow formation of troops or vehicles **columnar** adj **columnist** n

com- prefix (changing to **col-** before *l*, **cor-** before *r*, **con-** before many other consonants) with; together (as in **combine**, **connect**)

coma (say **koh-**mə) n a state of deep unconsciousness

comatose (say **koh-**mə-tohs) adj 1 in a coma 2 very tired or inactive

comb n 1 a strip of plastic or wood or other hard material with teeth, used for tidying the hair or holding it in place 2 something shaped or used like this, e.g. to separate strands of wool or cotton 3 the fleshy crest of a fowl 4 a honeycomb **comb** v 1 to tidy hair with a comb 2 to search a place thoroughly

combat n a fight or contest **combat** v **combated**, **combating** to take action to reduce the effects of something ♦ *to combat the effects of alcohol* **combatant** n **combative** adj

combine[1] (say kəm-**biyn**) v 1 to join things to form a set, group, or mixture 2 to come together; to unite or merge **combination** n 1 the process of combining things, or of being combined 2 a number of people or things that are combined 3 a sequence of numbers or letters used in opening a combination lock **combine harvester** n a machine that reaps and threshes grain in one operation

combine[2] (say **kom-**biyn) n a group of people or firms acting together in business

combustion (say kəm-**bus-**chən) n the process of burning, a chemical process (accompanied by heat) in which substances combine with oxygen in air **combustible** adj **combustibility** n

come v **came**, **come** 1 to move or be brought towards the speaker or to a place

or point the speaker has in mind 2 to arrive, to be happening ♦ *When spring comes we can have a holiday.* 3 to reach a result ♦ *Have you come to a decision yet?* 4 to take or occupy a specified position ♦ *The picture comes on the next page.* 5 to be available ♦ *The paint comes in a wide range of colours.* 6 to happen ♦ *How did you come to lose it?* 7 to occur as a result ♦ *That's what comes of being careless.* 8 to have as a home or origin ♦ *The teacher came from France.* ♦ *Where did that car come from?* **coming** adj **comeback** n a return to former fame or success **comedown** n 1 a loss of importance or status 2 a disappointment or anticlimax **to come by** to obtain something, often by chance **to come in** to finish a race or competition in a certain position ♦ *In the end we came in third.* **to come in for** to receive a share of something **to come into** to inherit money or property **to come out** 1 to become known 2 to be published 3 to say what you think about something ♦ *They came out in favour of the idea.*

comedian n 1 someone who entertains people by making them laugh 2 a writer of comic plays

comedienne (say kə-mee-di-en) n a female comedian

comedy n pl **comedies** 1 entertainment that is meant to make people laugh 2 humour 3 a play or film that makes people laugh

comely (say **kum-**li) adj **comelier**, **comeliest** handsome or good-looking **comeliness** n

comet (say **kom-**it) n an object that moves round the sun, with a tail pointing away from the sun

comeuppance n informal a punishment or rebuke that someone deserves

comfort n 1 a state of ease and contentment 2 relief of suffering or grief 3 a person or thing that gives comfort **comfort** v to give comfort to someone **comfortable** adj **comfortably** adv **comforter** n

comfy adj **comfier**, **comfiest** informal comfortable

comic adj 1 meant to make people laugh, amusing 2 to do with comedy ♦ *a comic actor* **comic** n 1 a comedian 2 a children's paper containing comic strips **comical** adj **comically** adv

comma n the punctuation mark (,), used to mark a slight pause or break between parts of a sentence, or separating words or figures in a list

command n **1** a statement, based on authority, that some action must be performed **2** the right to control others, authority **3** knowledge or ability to use something ♦ a good command of languages **4** a body of troops or staff **5** an instruction to a computer to perform a function **command** v **1** to give a command or order to someone **2** to have authority over someone **3** to have something at your disposal ♦ The firm commands international resources. **4** to deserve and get something ♦ They command our respect. **5** to look down over or dominate someone **commandant** n a military officer in charge of a military establishment **commandeer** v **1** to take or seize something for military use **2** to take something for your own use

commander n **1** the person in command of a group of people **2** a naval officer ranking next below a captain **3** a senior police officer **commander-in-chief** n pl **commanders-in-chief** the overall commander

commandment n a divine command

commando n pl **commandos** a member of a military unit specially trained for making raids and assaults

commemorate v **1** to keep a past event or person in the memory by means of a celebration or ceremony **2** to be a memorial to a past event or person ♦ A plaque commemorates the victory. **commemoration** n **commemorative** adj

commence v formal to begin **commencement** n

commend v **1** to praise a person or their actions **2** to recommend someone **3** to entrust something ♦ We commend him to your care. **commendable** adj **commendably** adv **commendation** n

commensurable (say kə-men-sher-əbəl) adj able to be measured by the same standard

commensurate (say kə-men-sher-ət) adj **1** of the same size or extent **2** proportionate

comment n an opinion given about an event or to explain something **comment** v to make a comment or comments **commentary** n pl **commentaries** **1** a series of comments, especially describing a sports event while it is happening **2** a book of explanatory comments on a text **commentate** v to act as commentator **commentator** n

commerce (say kom-erss) n trade and the services that assist trading, such as banking and insurance **commercial** adj **commercialism** n **commercialization** n **commercialized** adj **commercially** adv

commiserate (say kə-miz-er-ayt) v to express pity, to sympathize **commiseration** n

commissariat (say kom-i-sair-iət) n a military department supplying food and equipment

commission n **1** a task formally given to someone ♦ a commission to paint a portrait **2** a body of people who are given a task **3** an appointment to be an officer in the armed forces **4** the act of committing something ♦ the commission of a crime **5** a payment made to an agent for selling goods or services **commission** v to give a commission to someone or for a task to be done **in commission** (said about military equipment) ready for service **out of commission** not in working order

commissionaire (say kə-mish-ən-air) n a uniformed attendant at the entrance to a hotel, theatre, or other large building

commissioner n **1** a person appointed to do a job or task by commission **2** a member of a commission **3** a government official in charge of a district abroad

commit v **committed**, **committing** **1** to do or perform something ♦ to commit a crime **2** to entrust someone or something for safe keeping or treatment **3** to send a person for trial in a law court **4** to agree to use time, money, or other resources for a particular purpose **commitment** n **committal** n **committed** adj

committee n a group of people appointed to deal with special business or to manage the business of a club or other organization

commode (say kə-mohd) n 1 a chair or covered box with a chamber pot fitted in it 2 an ornamental chest of drawers

commodious (say kə-moh-di-əs) adj spacious and comfortable

commodity n pl **commodities** something useful or valuable, a product or article of trade

commodore (say kom-ə-dor) n 1 a naval officer ranking above a captain and below a rear admiral 2 the commander of a squadron or other division of a fleet

common adj 1 occurring frequently, usual or ordinary ♦ Street crime is becoming more common. 2 to do with most people or with the whole community 3 belonging to or shared by two or more people or things 4 without special distinction, ordinary ♦ the common sparrow 5 having no taste or refinement, vulgar **common** n an area of land that everyone can use **commons** pl n hist the common people regarded as a political force **commoner** n **commonly** adv **commonness** n **common denominator** n 1 Mathematics a number that is a multiple of each of the denominators of two or more fractions 2 a feature shared by members of a group **common ground** n views or opinions shared by all the people involved **common law** n unwritten law based on custom and on former court decisions **Common Market** n a former name for the European Union **common or garden** adj of the ordinary or usual type **commonplace** adj ordinary or usual **commonplace** n something commonplace ♦ Air travel is now a commonplace. **common sense** n ordinary good sense and judgement in practical matters **commonwealth** n 1 an independent state or community 2 a federal association of states ♦ the Commonwealth of Australia 3 **Commonwealth** an association of the UK and its dependencies together with independent states that were formerly part of the British Empire

commotion n uproar or disturbance

communal (say kom-yoo-nəl) adj shared between the members of a group or community ♦ a communal kitchen **communally** adv

commune¹ (say kom-yoon) n 1 a group of people living together and sharing certain possessions and domestic responsibilities 2 a district of local government in France and some other European countries

commune² (say kə-mewn) v to share intimate thoughts or feelings

communicate v 1 to give or share information ♦ We will communicate the news to our friends. 2 to transfer or transmit ♦ There is a danger of communicating the disease to others. 3 to exchange news or have social dealings 4 to be connected ♦ The passage communicates with the hall and stairs. **communicable** adj **communication** n **communicative** adj

communion n 1 religious fellowship, sharing beliefs or ideas 2 social dealings between people 3 a body of Christians belonging to the same denomination ♦ the Anglican communion **Communion, Holy Communion** n the Christian sacrament in which bread and wine are consecrated and given to worshippers

communiqué (say kə-mew-ni-kay) n an official message or announcement

communism n a political and social system in which property is owned by the community **Communism** n a political doctrine or movement based on Marxist principles, including state control of the means of production **communist** n **communistic** adj

community n pl **communities** 1 the people living in one place or country and considered as a whole 2 a group with similar interests or origins ♦ the farming community 3 the state of having interests in common

commutator n a device for reversing the direction of flow of an electrical current

commute v 1 to travel regularly for some distance to and from work in a city 2 to exchange one thing for another 3 to change a punishment into something less severe **commutation** n **commuter** n

compact[1] (say **kom**-pakt) n 1 an agreement or contract 2 a small flat container for face powder

compact[2] (say kəm-**pakt**) adj 1 closely or neatly packed together 2 concise or brief **compact** v to make something compact; to join or press things firmly together or into a small space **compactly** adv **compactness** n

compact disc n a small plastic disc on which music or computer data is stored and can be read by a laser beam

companion n 1 a person you spend time with or travel with 2 the title given to a member of certain official orders ♦ Companion of Honour. 3 a person employed to live with and support someone who is old or unwell 4 each of two things that match or go together **companionable** adj **companionably** adv **companionship** n

company n pl **companies** 1 being with other people, companionship 2 a number of people who have come together for a social occasion 3 the people you spend a lot of time with ♦ He has got into bad company. 4 a business organization or firm 5 a ship's officers and crew 6 a subdivision of an infantry battalion

compare v to judge how two or more things or people are similar and different **comparable** adj **comparability** n **comparably** adv **comparative** adj **comparatively** adv

comparison n the act of comparing things or people

compartment n 1 one of the spaces into which a structure or other object is divided, a separate room or enclosed space 2 a division of a railway carriage, separated by partitions **compartmental** adj **compartmentalize** v

compass n 1 a device that shows direction, with a needle pointing to the magnetic north 2 the range or scope of something **compasses** pl n an instrument for drawing circles, with two arms joined at one end

compassion n a feeling of pity that makes you want to help or show mercy **compassionate** adj **compassionately** adv

compatible (say kəm-**pat**-ibəl) adj 1 able to exist or be used together ♦ The printer is not compatible with all types of computer. 2 (said about people) able to live together harmoniously **compatibility** n **compatibly** adv

compatriot (say kəm-**pat**-ri-ət) n a person from the same country as another

compel v **compelled**, **compelling** to use force or influence to make someone do something **compelling** adj

compendium (say kəm-**pen**-di-əm) n pl **compendiums** or **compendia** 1 a concise and comprehensive summary of information about a subject 2 a collection of board games in one box **compendious** adj

compensate v 1 to give someone money or something else, to make up for a loss or injury 2 to serve as a counterbalance ♦ Our recent victory compensates for earlier defeats. **compensation** n **compensatory** adj

compère (say **kom**-pair) n a person who introduces the performers in a variety show or broadcast **compère** v to act as compère to a show, etc.

compete v 1 to take part in a competition or other contest 2 to try to be more successful than your rivals **competition** n **competitor** n

competent (say **kom**-pit-ənt) adj 1 having the ability or authority to do a particular job or task 2 adequate or satisfactory ♦ He has a competent knowledge of Russian. **competence** n **competently** adv

competitive adj 1 involving competition ♦ competitive sports 2 as good as or better than others of the same kind ♦ competitive prices **competitively** adv **competitiveness** n

compile v 1 to collect and arrange information into a list or book 2 to make up a book of information in this way 3 ICT (said about a computer program) to translate instructions into a form which can be understood by the computer **compilation** n **compiler** n

complacent (say kəm-**play**-sənt) adj smug or self-satisfied **complacency** n **complacently** adv ◊ Do not confuse this word with complaisant, which has a different meaning.

complain v to say that you are unhappy about something or that something is wrong **complaint** n

complaisant (say kəm-**play**-zənt) adj willing to do what pleases other people **complaisance** n ◊ Do not confuse this word with *complacent*, which has a different meaning.

complement (say **kom**-pli-mənt) n 1 something that makes a thing complete 2 the number or quantity that fills something ♦ *The aircraft had its full complement of passengers.* 3 *Gram* a word or words used after verbs such as *be*, *become*, and *make*, which completes what is said about the subject or object of the verb, e.g. *happy* in the sentence *We are happy* and *king of England* in the sentence *They made him king of England* 4 *Geometry* the amount by which an angle is less than 90° **complement** v to make something complete; to form a complement to something ♦ *The hat complements the outfit.* ◊ Do not confuse this word with *compliment*, which has a different meaning.

complementary adj **complementary medicine** n medical methods that are not officially recognized but are used as an alternative to conventional methods, e.g. acupuncture and homoeopathy

complete adj 1 having all its parts, not lacking anything 2 finished ♦ *The work is now complete.* 3 thorough, in every way ♦ *The man is a complete stranger.* **complete** v 1 to add what is lacking to something to make it complete 2 to finish a task or piece of work 3 to give the information asked for in a document ♦ *Please complete the questionnaire and return it in the envelope provided.* **completely** adv **completeness** n **completion** n

complex (say **kom**-pleks) adj 1 made up of several parts 2 complicated **complex** n 1 a set of buildings made up of related parts ♦ *a sports complex* 2 a connected group of feelings or ideas that influence a person's behaviour or mental attitude ♦ *an inferiority complex* **complexity** n

complexion n 1 the colour, texture, and appearance of the skin of the face 2 the way things seem ♦ *That puts a different complexion on the matter.*

compliant (say kəm-**pliy**-ənt) adj 1 (said about a person) willing to comply or obey 2 meeting a standard or requirement **compliance** n

complicate v to make something complex or complicated **complicated** adj **complication** n

complicity (say kəm-**plis**-iti) n being involved in a crime or wrongdoing

compliment n something you say or do to show that you approve of a person or thing **compliment** v to pay a compliment to someone; to congratulate someone **compliments** pl n formal greetings conveyed in a message ◊ Do not confuse this word with *complement*, which has a different meaning. **complimentary** adj

comply (say kəm-**pliy**) v **complies, complied, complying** to do what you are asked or ordered to do

component (say kəm-**poh**-nənt) n each of the parts of which a machine or other thing is made **component** adj forming a component of something

compose v 1 to form or make up a whole ♦ *The class is composed of 20 students.* 2 to write or create a work of art, especially music or poetry 3 to arrange things into good order **composed** adj **composedly** adv **composer** n **composition** n

composite (say **kom**-pə-zit) adj 1 made up of a number of different parts or styles 2 (said about a plant) having a flower head of individual flowers forming one bloom 3 *Mathematics* (said about a number) able to be divided exactly by one or more whole numbers as well as by itself and 1

compos mentis adj in your right mind, sane

compost n 1 decayed leaves, grass, and other organic matter used as a fertilizer 2 a mixture of soil and other ingredients for growing seedlings, cuttings, etc. **compost** v to treat something with compost; to make things into compost

composure n the state of having a calm mind or manner

compound[1] (say **kom**-pownd) adj made up

of several parts or ingredients **compound** n a compound thing or substance

compound[2] (say kəm-**pownd**) v 1 to put things together to form a whole 2 to make something that is already bad worse

compound[3] (say **kom**-pownd) n a fenced area, often containing buildings

comprehend v 1 to understand something 2 to include something **comprehensible** adj **comprehensibility** n **comprehensibly** adv **comprehension** n

comprehensive adj 1 including all or most of something ♦ The new textbooks seem to be comprehensive. 2 including all or many kinds of people or things **comprehensive** n a comprehensive school **comprehensively** adv **comprehensiveness** n **comprehensive school** n a secondary school providing an education for children of all abilities in an area

compress (say kəm-**press**) v to press things together or into a smaller space **compress** (say **kom**-press) n a soft pad or cloth pressed on the body to stop bleeding or to relieve inflammation **compressible** adj **compression** n **compressor** n

comprise (say kəm-**priyz**) v 1 to include or consist of several things ♦ The pentathlon comprises five events. 2 to form or make up a whole ♦ These three rooms comprise the apartment.

compromise (say **kom**-prə-miyz) n 1 settling a disagreement by each side accepting less than it originally demanded 2 a settlement made in this way 3 something that is halfway between opposite opinions or courses of action **compromise** v 1 to settle a dispute by a compromise 2 to expose someone to danger or suspicion by indiscreet or unwise behaviour

compulsion n 1 a strong and uncontrollable desire to do something 2 the process of compelling someone to do something **compulsive** adj **compulsively** adv

compulsory adj that must be done, required by a rule or law **compulsorily** adv ◊ Do not confuse this word with compulsive, which has a different meaning.

compunction n a feeling of slight guilt or regret

compute v to calculate or reckon an amount mathematically **computable** adj **computation** n

computer n an electronic machine for making calculations, storing and analysing information put into it, or controlling machinery automatically **computerize** v **computerization** n **computer-assisted** adj using computers to control or support a process ♦ computer-assisted learning **computer graphics** pl n data displayed or printed out as graphics by a computer **computer science** n the study of the principles and use of computers

comrade n 1 a companion who shares your activities or is a fellow member of an organization 2 a fellow socialist or communist **comradeship** n

con[1] v **conned**, **conning** informal to persuade or swindle someone after winning their confidence **con** n informal a confidence trick

con[2] see pro and con

concatenate (say kən-**kat**-in-ayt) v to link things together in a chain or series **concatenation** n

concave adj curved like the inside surface of a ball **concavity** n

conceal v to keep something secret or hidden **concealment** n

concede (say kən-**seed**) v 1 to admit that something is true 2 to grant or allow something ♦ The farmer conceded us the right to cross his land. 3 to admit defeat in a contest **concession** n 1 something that you agree to concede to someone 2 a reduction in price for a certain category of person 3 a right given by the owners of land to use it for a special purpose ♦ an oil concession 4 a commercial operation set up in the premises of a larger one, such as a hairdresser in a department store **concessionary** adj

conceit n too much pride in yourself **conceited** adj **conceitedly** adv

conceive v 1 to become pregnant 2 to form an idea or plan, etc. in the mind, to imagine or think of something **conceivable** adj conceivably *adv* conception *n*

concentrate *v* **1** to give all your thought or attention or effort to something **2** to bring people or things together or to come together to one place **3** to make a liquid less dilute **concentrate** *n* a concentrated form of a substance, especially of food

concentration *n* **1** the process of concentrating **2** the ability to concentrate on something **3** the mass or amount of a substance contained in a specified amount of a solvent or in a mixture **concentration camp** *n* a place where political prisoners are kept together

concentric (say kən-**sen**-trik) *adj* having the same centre ♦ *concentric circles*

concept (say **kon**-sept) *n* an idea or general notion ♦ *the concept of liberty*

concern *v* **1** to be about something, or to have something as its subject ♦ *The story concerns a family in wartime.* **2** to be of importance to someone, or to affect someone ♦ *What I am saying concerns everyone.* **3** to worry someone ♦ *It concerned them that their son had not contacted them for several weeks.* **concern** *n* **1** something of interest or importance, a responsibility ♦ *That is not our concern.* **2** a worry or anxiety **3** a business or firm ♦ *a printing concern* **concerned** *adj*

concerning *prep* about, to do with

concert *n* a musical entertainment given in public **concertina** *n* a portable musical instrument with bellows **concertina** *v* **concertinas**, **concertinaed**, **concertinaing** to fold or collapse like the bellows of a concertina **concerto** *n pl* **concertos** or **concerti** a piece of music for one or more solo instruments and an orchestra **in concert** **1** acting together **2** giving a concert

concerted (say kən-**sert**-id) *adj* **1** done in cooperation with others ♦ *We made a concerted effort to finish on time.* **2** (said about music) arranged in parts, of equal importance, for voices or instruments

conch (say kongk or konch) *n* the spiral shell of a kind of shellfish

conciliate *v* **1** to make someone less angry or hostile by being friendly or pleasant

to them **2** to reconcile people who disagree **conciliation** *n* **conciliator** *n* **conciliatory** *adj*

concise (say kən-**siyss**) *adj* brief, giving much information in few words **concisely** *adv*

conclude *v* **1** to bring something to an end, or to come to an end **2** to arrange or settle something finally ♦ *The two countries then concluded a treaty.* **3** to arrive at a belief or opinion by reasoning ♦ *The inquiry concluded that the crash was caused by human error.* **conclusion** *n* **conclusive** *adj* **conclusively** *adv*

concoct (say kən-**kokt**) *v* **1** to make something by putting various ingredients together **2** to invent something to say ♦ *We'll have to concoct an excuse.* **concoction** *n*

concord *n* friendly agreement or harmony **concordant** *adj*

concourse (say **kon**-korss) *n* **1** a crowd or gathering **2** an open area through which people pass

concrete[1] (say **kon**-kreet) *n* a mixture of cement with sand and gravel, used in building **concrete** *adj* **1** existing in a physical form, able to be touched and felt **2** definite or positive ♦ *The police need concrete evidence.*

concrete[2] (say **kon**-kreet) *v* to cover a surface or area with concrete

concubine (say **konk**-yoo-biyn) *n* a woman who lives with a man but has a lower role than his wife **concubinage** *n*

concur (say kən-**ker**) *v* **concurred**, **concurring** **1** to agree **2** to happen together **concurrence** *n* **concurrent** *adj* **concurrently** *adv*

concussion (say kən-**kush**-ən) *n* injury to the brain caused by a hard blow **concuss** *v*

condemn *v* **1** to express strong disapproval of someone or something **2** to pronounce someone guilty of a crime **3** to sentence a criminal to a punishment ♦ *The murderer was condemned to death.* **4** to destine someone to an unhappy fate **5** to declare a building unfit for use **condemnation** *n*

condense *v* **1** to make a liquid denser or more concentrated **2** to change a substance from gas or vapour into liquid, or to be changed in this way ♦ *Steam was condensing on the windows.* **3** to express a thought or idea in fewer words **condenser** *n*

condescend *v* **1** to behave in a way that shows you feel superior **2** to agree to do something even though you think it is beneath your dignity ♦ *In the end they condescended to come with us.* **condescension** *n*

condiment (say **kon**-di-mənt) *n* a seasoning for food, such as salt or pepper

condition *n* **1** the state in which a person or thing is ♦ *My bicycle is not in good condition.* **2** a state of physical fitness or fitness for use ♦ *I'm trying to get into condition.* **3** an illness or medical problem ♦ *a heart condition* **4** something required as part of an agreement **conditions** *pl n* the situation or surroundings that affect something ♦ *They wanted to improve their working conditions.* **condition** *v* **1** to bring something into the right condition needed for use **2** to make someone physically fit **3** to have a strong effect or influence on someone or something **4** to train or accustom someone **conditional** *adj* **conditionally** *adv* **conditioner** *n* **on condition that** only if; on the understanding that a certain thing will be done

condole (say kən-**dohl**) *v* to express sympathy **condolence** *n*

condom (say **kon**-dəm) *n* a rubber sheath worn on the penis during sexual intercourse as a contraceptive or to prevent infection

condone (say kən-**dohn**) *v* to forgive or overlook a wrongdoing ♦ *We should not condone violence.* **condonation** *n*

condor *n* a large vulture of South America

conducive (say kən-**dew**-siv) *adj* helping to cause or produce something ♦ *We need an atmosphere that is conducive to work.*

conduct[1] (say kən-**dukt**) *v* **1** to lead or guide someone **2** to direct the performance of an orchestra or choir **3** to manage or direct an undertaking or business operation **4** to have the property of allowing heat, light, sound, or electricity to pass along or through itself **conductance** *n* **conduction** *n*

conductive *adj* **conductivity** *n* **conductor** *n*

conduct[2] (say **kon**-dukt) *n* **1** a person's behaviour **2** the directing or managing of affairs

conduit (say **kon**-dit or **kon**-dwit) *n* **1** a pipe or channel for carrying liquids **2** a tube or trough protecting insulated electric wires

cone *n* **1** an object with a round flat base, tapering to a point at the other end **2** something shaped like this **3** the dry fruit of certain evergreen trees, having woody scales arranged in a cone-like shape **conic** *adj* **conical** *adj* **conically** *adv* **conifer** *n* a tree that bears cones **coniferous** *adj* (said about a tree) bearing cones **conoid** *adj*

confection *n* **1** a dish made from various sweet ingredients **2** something made of various things put together **confectioner** *n* **confectionery** *n*

confederate *adj* allied, joined by an agreement or treaty **confederate** *n* **1** a member of a confederacy **2** an ally or accomplice **confederacy** *n* **confederated** *adj* **confederation** *n*

confer *v* **conferred**, **conferring** **1** to grant or bestow something **2** to hold a discussion before deciding something **conference** *n* **1** a meeting for holding a discussion or a series of discussions **2** a linking of telephones or computers so that several people can hold a discussion **conferrable** *adj*

confess *v* **1** to state openly that you have done wrong or have a weakness **2** to say something cautiously or reluctantly ♦ *I must confess that I am surprised.* **3** to declare your sins formally to a priest **confession** *n* **confessional** *n* **confessor** *n*

confetti *n* small pieces of coloured paper thrown over the bride and bridegroom at a wedding

confide *v* **1** to tell something to someone confidentially ♦ *Gemma decided to confide in her sister.* **2** to entrust something to someone

confidence *n* **1** firm trust ♦ *I have a lot of confidence in you.* **2** a feeling of certainty or self-assurance about what you can do ♦ *Does he have the confidence to do the task?*

3 something told confidentially ♦ *May I tell you a confidence?* **confidant** *n* a person you confide in **confident** *adj* **confidential** *adj* **1** meant to be kept secret **2** entrusted with private information ♦ *a confidential secretary* **confidentiality** *n* **confidentially** *adv* **confidently** *adv* **in confidence** as a secret **to take someone into your confidence** to trust them with a secret

configuration *n* **1** a method of arrangement of the parts of a machine or system **2** a shape or outline

confine (say kən-**fiyn**) *v* **1** to keep or restrict someone or something within certain limits **2** to keep someone shut up **confined** *adj* **confinement** *n* **1** the state of being confined or shut up **2** when a woman is giving birth to a baby **confines** *pl n* the limits or boundaries of an area

confirm *v* **1** to show that something is true or correct **2** to establish a feeling or idea more firmly ♦ *The incident confirmed his fear of dogs.* **3** to make something definite ♦ *Please write to confirm your reservation.* **4** to administer the Christian rite of confirmation to someone **confirmation** *n* **confirmatory** *adj*

confiscate (say **kon**-fis-kayt) *v* to take or seize something with authority, especially as a punishment **confiscation** *n*

conflagration (say kon-flə-**gray**-shən) *n* a large and destructive fire

conflict[1] (say **kon**-flikt) *n* **1** a fight or struggle **2** a disagreement between people having different ideas or beliefs

conflict[2] (say kən-**flikt**) *v* **1** to fight or struggle **2** to have a disagreement

confluence (say **kon**-floo-əns) *n* the place where two rivers unite

conform *v* **1** to keep to accepted rules or customs ♦ *They find it hard to conform.* **2** to be consistent or similar in type **conformation** *n* **conformism** *n* **conformist** *n* **conformity** *n*

confound *v* **1** to surprise or confuse someone **2** to prove someone to be wrong **3** to defeat a plan or hope **to be confounded with** to be mixed up or confused with someone or something else

confront (say kən-**frunt**) *v* **1** to face and challenge an opponent or enemy **2** to be present as something you have to deal with ♦ *There are many problems confronting us.* **3** to face up to a problem and deal with it ♦ *There are too many problems to confront all at once.* **4** to bring opponents face to face ♦ *They confronted him with his accusers.* **confrontation** *n*

confuse *v* **1** to make someone bewildered or muddled **2** to mistake one person or thing for another **3** to make something unclear **confusable** *adj* **confused** *adj* **confusion** *n*

confute (say kən-**fewt**) *v informal* to prove a person or argument to be wrong **confutation** *n*

conga *n* **1** a Latin American dance in which people form a long winding line, one behind the other **2** a tall narrow drum beaten with the hands

congeal (say kən-**jeel**) *v* (said about a liquid) to become jelly-like, especially when it cools after being hot

congenial (say kən-**jeen**-iəl) *adj* **1** pleasant through being similar to you or suiting your tastes ♦ *a congenial companion* **2** suited or agreeable to you ♦ *a congenial climate*

congenital (say kən-**jen**-itəl) *adj* existing in a person from birth ♦ *a congenital deformity* **congenitally** *adv*

conger (say **kong**-gər) *n* a large sea eel

congested *adj* **1** too full or crowded **2** (said about an organ or tissue of the body) abnormally full of blood **congestion** *n*

conglomerate[1] (say kən-**glom**-er-ət) *adj* gathered into a mass **conglomerate** *n* **1** a number of things gathered together to form a whole while keeping their individual identities **2** a commercial group formed by merging several different firms

conglomerate[2] (say kən-**glom**-er-ayt) *v* to gather things into a mass, or to form a mass **conglomeration** *n*

congratulate *v* to tell someone that you are pleased about their achievement or success **congratulation** *n* **congratulatory** *adj*

congregate *v* to come together, to form a crowd **congregation** *n* a group of people who have come together to take part in religious worship **congregational** *adj* **Congregationalism** *n* a form of church organization in which each local church is independent **Congregational** adj **Congregationalist** n

congress n a formal meeting of representatives for a discussion or series of discussions **Congress** n the law-making body of a country **congressional** adj

congruent (say **kong**-groo-ənt) adj **1** suitable or consistent **2** Geometry (said about two or more figures) having the same shape and size **congruence** n

conjecture v to form a conclusion based on incomplete information, to guess **conjecture** n a conclusion formed by conjecturing, a guess **conjectural** adj

conjoined adj (said about twins) born with their bodies joined together. See also Siamese twins

conjugal (say **kon**-jəg-əl) adj to do with marriage or the relationship between a husband and wife

conjugate (say **kon**-jəg-ayt) v **1** Gram to give the different forms of a verb, e.g. get, gets, got **2** to unite or become fused **conjugation** n

conjunction n **1** Gram a word that joins words or phrases or sentences, such as and, but, or **2** a combination or union ♦ The four countries acted in conjunction. **3** the happening of things at the same time

conjunctivitis n an eye infection

conjure (say **kun**-jer) v **1** to perform tricks which appear to be magical **2** to summon a spirit to appear **3** to produce something as if from nothing ♦ Meg managed to conjure up a meal. **conjuror** n **to conjure something up** to produce an image or memory in the mind ♦ Mention of the desert conjures up visions of sand and sun.

conk n informal the nose

conker n informal the hard shiny brown nut of the horse chestnut tree **conkers** pl n a game played with conkers on a string

connect v **1** to join one thing to another, or to be joined **2** (said about a train, bus, etc.) to arrive at a time that allows passengers to continue their journey on another train or bus, etc. **3** to put someone into communication with another person by telephone **4** to think of things or people

as being associated with each other **connection** n **1** the process of connecting or being connected **2** a place or point where things connect; a connecting part **3** a train, bus, etc. that leaves shortly after another arrives, so that passengers can change from one to the other **4** ICT an electrical or electronic link between telephones or computers **5** a link or relationship ♦ There is a connection between smoking and lung cancer. **6** people you have contact with, either personally or in business **connector** n

connective adj connecting or linking things **connective** n Gram a word that joins words or phrases or sentences, a conjunction

connoisseur (say kon-ə-ser) n a person with a lot of experience and appreciation of something ♦ a connoisseur of wine

connote (say kə-noht) v (said about a word) to imply or suggest something in addition to the main meaning (Compare denote.) **connotation** n

conquer v **1** to defeat or overcome an opponent or enemy in war **2** to overcome something with an effort ♦ I must learn to conquer my fear of heights. **conqueror** n **conquest** n

conscience n a person's sense of what is right and wrong in what they do **conscience-stricken** adj feeling deep remorse about a wrong you have done

conscientious (say kon-shi-en-shəs) adj showing care and attention **conscientiously** adv **conscientiousness** n **conscientious objector** n someone who refuses to serve in the armed forces because they believe it is morally wrong

conscious adj **1** awake and aware of your surroundings **2** aware of something ♦ We are conscious of the need for a quick answer. **3** intentional ♦ She spoke with conscious firmness. **consciously** adv **consciousness** n

conscript[1] (say kən-skript) v (said about a state or government) to make someone join the armed forces **conscription** n

conscript[2] (say kon-skript) n someone who has been made to join the armed forces

consecrate v **1** to make or declare something sacred **2** to dedicate a place to the service or worship of God **consecration** n

consecutive (say kən-**sek**-yoo-tiv) adj following one after the other **consecutively** adv

consensus (say kən-**sen**-səs) n general agreement

consent v to say that you are willing to do or allow what someone wishes **consent** n agreement to what someone wishes, permission

consequence n 1 something that happens as a result of some event or action 2 importance ♦ a person of consequence **consequent** adj **consequential** adj **consequentially** adv **consequently** adv

conservatism n conservative principles, especially in politics

conservative adj 1 liking established ways and opposed to change 2 moderate, avoiding extremes ♦ a conservative estimate **Conservative** adj to do with the Conservative Party **conservative** n a conservative person **Conservative** n someone who supports the Conservative Party **conservatively** adv

conservatory n pl **conservatories** a room with a glass roof and large windows

conserve (say kən-**serv**) v to keep something valuable or useful from being harmed or changed **conservancy** n pl **conservancies** official conservation of natural resources **conservation** n 1 the process of conserving or being conserved 2 preservation, especially of the natural environment **conservationist** n

consider v 1 to think carefully about something 2 to make allowances for something ♦ Please consider people's feelings. 3 to think a person or thing to be something **considerable** adj fairly great in amount or extent, etc. **considerably** adv **considerate** adj taking care not to inconvenience or hurt other people **considerately** adv **consideration** n 1 careful thought or attention 2 being considerate, kindness 3 a fact that must be kept in mind ♦ Time is now an important consideration. 4 a payment given as a reward ♦ I will do it for a small consideration.

considering prep taking something into consideration ♦ It's very warm, considering the time of year.

consign v 1 to hand something over or deliver it formally 2 to entrust something to someone's care **consignment** n

consist v **to consist of** to be made up of ♦ The house consists of 3 floors.

consistency n pl **consistencies** 1 the thickness or firmness of a liquid or soft mixture 2 the state of being consistent **consistent** adj **consistently** adv

console¹ (say kən-**sohl**) v to comfort someone who has suffered a loss or disappointment **consolable** adj **consolation** n **consolation prize** n a prize given to a competitor who has just missed winning one of the main prizes

console² (say **kon**-sohl) n a panel or unit containing a set of controls for electrical or other equipment

consolidate v 1 to make something secure and strong ♦ The team consolidated their lead with a second goal. 2 to combine two or more funds of money, organizations, etc. into one **consolidation** n

consonant n 1 a letter of the alphabet that is not a vowel, in English b, c, d, f, g, h, j, k, l, m, n, p, q, r, s, t, v, w, x, y (as in yoke), z 2 the speech sound represented by any of these letters **consonant** adj consistent or harmonious

consort¹ (say **kon**-sort) n 1 a husband or wife, especially of a monarch 2 a ship sailing in company with another

consort² (say kən-**sort**) v to keep regular company with someone ♦ He was often seen consorting with criminals. **consortium** n pl **consortia** a combination of countries, companies, or other groups acting together

conspicuous adj 1 easily seen, noticeable 2 attracting attention **conspicuously** adv **conspicuousness** n

conspire v 1 to plan secretly with others, especially to do something illegal 2 (said about events or circumstances) to seem to be acting together with unfortunate results ♦ Events conspired to bring about their downfall. **conspiracy** n pl **conspiracies**

conspirator n **conspiratorial** adj **conspiratorially** adv

constable n a police officer of the lowest rank **constabulary** n pl **constabularies** a police force

constant adj 1 happening or continuing all the time, or happening repeatedly 2 unchanging, faithful ♦ He always remained constant to his principles. **constant** n 1 something that is constant and does not vary 2 Mathematics a number that expresses a physical property or relationship and remains the same in all circumstances or for the same substance in the same conditions **constancy** n **constantly** adv

constellation n a group of stars forming a pattern

consternation n great surprise causing anxiety or dismay

constipated v unable to empty the bowels easily or regularly

constipation n difficulty in emptying the bowels

constituent adj forming part of a whole **constituent** n 1 one of the parts that forms a whole thing 2 a member of a constituency **constituency** n pl **constituencies** 1 a district that is represented by a Member of Parliament elected by its voters 2 the body of voters in this district

constitute v 1 to make up or form a whole ♦ 12 months constitute a year 2 to establish or be something ♦ This does not constitute a precedent. **constitution** n 1 a set of rules and principles which state how a country is to be organized and governed 2 the general condition and health of a person's body ♦ She has a strong constitution. **constitutional** adj 1 to do with a country's constitution ♦ constitutional reform 2 permitted by a country's constitution 3 to do with a person's physical or mental constitution ♦ a constitutional weakness **constitutionally** adv

constrain v to force someone to act in a certain way **constraint** n

constrict v to tighten something by making it narrower; to squeeze something **constriction** n **constrictor** n

construct v to make something by putting its parts together; to build something **construction** n 1 the process of constructing or being constructed 2 something constructed 3 two or more words put together to form a phrase, clause, or sentence 4 an explanation or interpretation ♦ They have put a bad construction on our refusal. **constructional** adj **constructive** adj offering helpful suggestions **constructively** adv **constructor** n

construe (say kən-**stroo**) v **construes**, **construed**, **construing** to interpret or explain what someone has said

consul n 1 an official supporting the state's interests in a foreign country 2 either of the two chief magistrates in ancient Rome **consular** adj

consulate n the office or building where a consul works

consult v 1 to seek information or advice from someone 2 to confer with someone **consultant** n **consultation** n **consultative** adj

consume v 1 to use something up ♦ Much time was consumed in waiting. 2 to eat or drink something 3 to destroy something completely ♦ Fire has consumed the buildings. **consumable** adj **consumer** n **consumerism** n **consuming** adj **consumption** n 1 the process of consuming or destroying something 2 the amount of something consumed **consumer goods** pl n goods that are bought and used by individual consumers

consummate[1] (say **kon**-səm-ayt) v 1 to make something complete or perfect 2 to complete a marriage by having sexual intercourse **consummation** n

consummate[2] (say kən-**sum**-ət) adj highly skilled ♦ a consummate artist

contact (say **kon**-takt) n 1 the act of touching or coming together 2 the state of being in touch 3 a connection for an electric current 4 someone who has recently been near a person with a contagious disease and who may carry the infection 5 someone you can communicate with when you need information or help **contact** v to get in touch with someone **contact lens** n a thin plastic lens worn directly on the surface of the eye to correct faulty vision

contagion (say kən-**tay**-jən) *n* the spreading of disease from one person to another by close contact **contagious** *adj*

contain *v* 1 to have inside it ♦ *The atlas contains 100 maps.* 2 to consist of something and amount or be equal to it ♦ *A kilometre contains 1,000 metres.* 3 to restrain something ♦ *We found it hard to contain our laughter.* 4 to keep something within limits ♦ *The enemy troops were contained in the valley.* **container** *n* **containerize** *v* **containerization** *n* **containment** *n*

contaminate *v* to make a thing dirty or impure **contaminant** *n* **contamination** *n* **contaminator** *n*

contemplate (say **kon**-təm-playt) *v* 1 to gaze at something or someone thoughtfully 2 to consider something ♦ *I contemplated going out.* 3 to intend something or have it in mind as a possibility ♦ *We are contemplating a trip to New York.* 4 to meditate **contemplation** *n* **contemplative** *adj*

contemporary (say kən-**tem**-per-er-i) *adj* 1 living in or belonging to the same period 2 modern or up to date ♦ *contemporary designs* **contemporary** *n pl* **contemporaries** a person living at the same time as someone else or who is about the same age ♦ *Jan and Sarah were contemporaries at college.* **contemporaneous** *adj*

contempt *n* a feeling of despising a person or thing intensely **contemptibility** *n* **contemptible** *adj* **contemptibly** *adv* **contemptuous** *adj* **contemptuously** *adv* **contemptuousness** *n*

contend *v* 1 to struggle in a fight or battle, or against difficulties 2 to argue or assert something ♦ *The defendant contends that he is innocent.* **contender** *n*

content[1] (say kən-**tent**) *adj* happy, satisfied with what one has **content** *n* being contented, satisfaction **content** *v* to make someone feel content or satisfied **contented** *adj* **contentedly** *adv* **contentment** *n*

content[2] (say **kon**-tent) *n* **contents** *pl n* what something contains

contention *n* 1 the act of quarrelling or arguing 2 an assertion made in arguing

contentious (say kən-**ten**-shəs) *adj* 1 likely to cause disagreement or argument 2 (said about a person) fond of argument, quarrelsome **contentiously** *adv*

contest[1] (say **kon**-test) *n* 1 a competition, a test in which rivals try to obtain something or do best 2 a struggle for superiority or victory **contestant** *n*

contest[2] (say kən-**test**) *v* 1 to compete in something ♦ *to contest an election* 2 to dispute or challenge a decision or ruling

context *n* 1 the words that come before and after a particular word or phrase and help to clarify its meaning 2 the circumstances or background in which something happens

continent[1] *n* any of the earth's main land masses, Europe, Asia, Africa, North and South America, Australia, and Antarctica **continental** *adj* **the Continent** the mainland of Europe as distinct from the British Isles

continent[2] *adj* able to control the bladder and bowels **continence** *n*

contingent (say kən-**tin**-jənt) *adj* 1 depending on something that may or may not happen 2 likely to occur but not certain **contingent** *n* a group forming part of a larger group, especially a body of troops or police **contingency** *n pl* **contingencies**

continue *v* **continues**, **continued**, **continuing** 1 to keep doing an action, to do something without stopping ♦ *They continued to quarrel all evening.* 2 to remain in a certain place or condition ♦ *She will continue as manager.* 3 to go further ♦ *The road continues beyond the village.* 4 to begin again after stopping ♦ *Play will continue this afternoon.* **continual** *adj* **continually** *adv* **continuance** *n* **continuation** *n* **continuity** *n* 1 the state of being continuous 2 the uninterrupted existence of something or succession of events 3 the process of maintaining continuous action with consistent details in a film or broadcast **continuous** *adj* continuing or happening without a break ♦ *There is a continuous hum of traffic from the bypass.* **continuously** *adv* **continuum** *n pl* **continua** something that extends or changes gradually and continuously

contort (say kən-**tort**) v to force or twist something out of its usual shape **contortion** n **contortionist** n a performer who can twist their body into strange and unusual positions

contour (say **kon**-toor) n 1 a line on a map joining the points that are the same height above sea level 2 an outline

contra- prefix against

contraband n goods that have been smuggled or imported illegally

contraception (say kon-trə-**sep**-shən) n preventing pregnancy **contraceptive** adj

contract[1] (say **kon**-trakt) n 1 a formal agreement to do something, made between people, organizations, or countries 2 a document stating the terms of an agreement **contractor** n **contractual** adj **contractually** adv

contract[2] (say kən-**trakt**) v 1 to make something smaller, or to become smaller 2 to undertake something by the terms of a contract ♦ The company has contracted to supply parts to the factory. 3 to catch an illness **contractable** adj (said about a disease) able to be caught **contraction** n 1 the act of contracting 2 a shortened form of a word, such as can't for cannot

contradict v 1 to state that something said is untrue or that someone is wrong 2 to state the opposite of something already said ♦ These opinions contradict previous ones. **contradiction** n **contradictory** adj

contraflow n a temporary arrangement of traffic in which vehicles from one carriageway use one of the lanes of the opposite carriageway

contraption n a strange or ingenious gadget or machine

contrary[1] (say **kon**-trə-ri) adj 1 having an opposite nature or effect ♦ They came, contrary to expectation. 2 opposite in direction ♦ a contrary wind **contrary** n the opposite **contrary** adv against or in opposition ♦ They were clearly acting contrary to instructions.

contrary[2] (say kon-**trair**-i) adj (said about a person) doing the opposite of what is usual

or advisable **contrariness** n

contrast[1] (say **kon**-trahst) n 1 a difference clearly seen when things are compared or seen together 2 something showing a clear difference 3 the degree of difference between tones or colours

contrast[2] (say kən-**trahst**) v 1 to compare or oppose two things to show their differences 2 to show a clear difference when compared

contravene (say kon-trə-**veen**) v to act against a rule or law **contravention** n

contretemps (say **kon**-trə-tahn) n a trivial disagreement or dispute

contribute (say kən-**trib**-yoot) v 1 to give money or help jointly with others 2 to write an article for a newspaper, magazine, or book 3 to help to bring something about ♦ Drink contributed to his ruin. **contribution** n **contributor** n **contributory** adj

contrite (say **kon**-triyt) adj feeling guilty or sorry for what you have done **contritely** adv **contrition** n

contrive v to plan something cleverly or effectively **contrivance** n **contriver** n

control n 1 the power to make people do things or to make things happen 2 a means of restraining or regulating something, especially a device for operating a machine 3 restraint or self-restraint ♦ He needed all his control to avoid losing his temper. 4 something or someone used as a standard of comparison for checking the results of an experiment or survey 5 a place from which an operation is directed or where something is checked or verified **control** v **controlled**, **controlling** 1 to have the power to make people do things or to make things happen 2 to operate a machine or direct an activity 3 to restrain someone or something **controllable** adj **controller** n **control key** n a key on a computer keyboard which changes the function of another key when both are pressed together **control tower** n a tall building from which air traffic is controlled at an airport **control unit** n that part of a computer which controls the operation of the other units

controversy (say **kon**-trə-ver-si or kən-**trov**-er-si) *n pl* **controversies** a long argument or disagreement **controversial** *adj*

contusion (say kən-**tew**-zhən) *n* a technical term for a bruise

conundrum (say kə-**nun**-drəm) *n pl* **conundrums** a difficult question or riddle

conurbation (say kon-er-**bay**-shən) *n* a large urban area where towns have spread into each other

convalesce *v* to regain health after illness **convalescence** *n* **convalescent** *adj*

convection *n* the transmission of heat within a liquid or gas by circulation of the heated parts **convective** *adj* **convector** *n*

convene *v* to summon or assemble people for a meeting **convener** *n*

convenient *adj* **1** suiting a person's plans or intentions ♦ *Would it be convenient to call tomorrow?* **2** easy to use or deal with, not causing any difficulty **3** easy to find or reach ♦ *The house is convenient for the station and shops.* **convenience** *n* **conveniently** *adv*

convent *n* **1** a place where nuns live and work **2** a school run by nuns from a convent

convention *n* **1** an accepted way of doing things **2** a formal assembly **3** a formal agreement between countries ♦ *the Geneva Convention* **conventional** *adj* **conventionality** *n* **conventionally** *adv*

converge *v* to come to or towards the same point from different directions **convergence** *n* **convergent** *adj*

conversant (say kən-**ver**-sənt) *adj formal* familiar with something ♦ *I am not conversant with the rules of this game.*

converse[1] (say kən-**verss**) *v* to talk informally with someone **conversation** *n* informal talk between people **conversational** *adj* **conversationalist** *n* **conversationally** *adv*

converse[2] (say **kon**-verss) *adj* opposite or contrary **converse** *n* an idea or statement that is the opposite of another **conversely** *adv*

convert[1] (say kən-**vert**) *v* **1** to change from one form, character, or use to another **2** to be made in such a way that its use can be changed ♦ *The sofa converts into a bed.* **3** to cause or influence someone to change their attitude or beliefs **4** (in rugby football) to gain extra points after a try by kicking the ball over the bar **conversion** *n* **converter** *n*

convert[2] (say **kon**-vert) *n* someone who has changed their beliefs, especially in religion

convertible *adj* designed so that its use can be changed **convertible** *n* a car with a roof that can be folded down or removed

convex (say **kon**-veks) *adj* curved like the outside surface of a ball **convexity** *n* **convexly** *adv*

convey *v* **conveyed**, **conveying** **1** to transport or transmit something or somebody **2** to communicate something as an idea or meaning **conveyable** *adj* **conveyance** *n* **1** the process of conveying something or someone **2** a means of transporting people, a vehicle **3** the transfer of the legal ownership of land or property, or a document bringing this about **conveyancing** *n* **conveyor** *n*

convict[1] (say kən-**vikt**) *v* to prove or declare that a certain person is guilty of a crime

convict[2] (say **kon**-vikt) *n* a convicted person who is in prison

conviction *n* **1** the process of convicting a person of a crime **2** the process of being convinced of something **3** a firm opinion or belief

convince *v* to make someone feel certain that something is true

convivial (say kən-**viv**-iəl) *adj* sociable and lively **conviviality** *n* **convivially** *adv*

convocation *n* **1** the process of calling people together for a meeting **2** an assembly called together

convolution (say kon-və-**loo**-shən) *n* **1** a coil or twist **2** a complexity or difficulty **convoluted** *adj* **1** coiled or twisted **2** complicated or involved

convoy (say **kon**-voi) *n* a group of ships or vehicles travelling together **convoy** *v* (said about a warship or armed troops) to escort and protect a group of ships or vehicles

convulse *v* to make someone have sudden or violent movements, especially with laughter **convulsion** *n* **convulsive** *adj* **convulsively** *adv*

coo *v* **coos**, **cooed**, **cooing** to make the

soft murmuring sound of a dove **coo** n a cooing sound **coo** interjection informal an exclamation of surprise

cook v 1 to prepare food for eating by heating it 2 to undergo this preparation ♦ Our meal is just cooking. 3 informal to alter accounts or other information falsely ♦ They were accused of cooking the books. **cook** n a person who cooks food, especially as a job **cooker** n **cookery** n **cookie** n 1 Amer. a sweet biscuit 2 ICT a set of data that an Internet server sends to a browser on a user's computer **cookbook** n **cookery book** n

cool adj 1 fairly cold, not hot or warm 2 (said about colours) suggesting coolness 3 (said about a person) calm and confident ♦ He seemed quite cool about the whole thing. 4 not enthusiastic or friendly ♦ We got a cool reception. 5 informal good or fashionable 6 full, complete ♦ It cost me a cool thousand. **cool** n 1 coolness; cool air or a cool place ♦ in the cool of the evening 2 informal calmness or composure ♦ Try to keep your cool. **cool** v to make something cool, or to become cool **coolant** n **coolly** adv **coolness** n

coop n a cage for poultry **coop** v **to coop up** to confine people or animals or shut them in

cooper n a person who makes and repairs barrels and tubs

cooperate v to work helpfully with another person or with other people **cooperation** n **cooperative** adj **cooperatively** adv **cooperator** n

co-opt v to invite someone to become a member of a committee or other group of people **co-option** n **co-optive** adj

coordinate¹ (say koh-**ord**-in-ət) n each of a set of numbers or letters used to fix the position of a point on a graph or map **coordinate** adj equal in importance **co-ordinately** adv

coordinate² (say koh-**ord**-in-ayt) v to organize people or things to work properly together **coordination** n **coordinator** n

coot n a waterbird with a horny white patch on its forehead

cop v **copped**, **copping** informal to catch or arrest someone **cop** n informal 1 a police officer 2 an arrest or capture ♦ It's a fair cop.

cop-out the act of avoiding a commitment or responsibility **to cop it** to get into trouble or be punished **to cop out** to back out of an agreement or responsibility

cope v to manage or deal with something successfully

co-pilot n a second pilot in an aircraft

copious adj in large amounts, plentiful **copiously** adv

copper¹ n 1 a reddish-brown metal used to make pipes, wire, coins, etc.; a chemical element (symbol Cu) 2 a coin made of copper or a copper alloy 3 a reddish-brown colour **copper** adj 1 made of copper 2 reddish-brown

copper² n informal a police officer

coppice n a group of trees and undergrowth

copra n dried coconut kernels

copulate (say **kop**-yoo-layt) v to have sexual intercourse **copulation** n

copy n pl **copies** 1 a thing made to look like another 2 something written or printed out again from its original form 3 one of a number of specimens of the same book, newspaper, or magazine 4 material for printing **copy** v **copies**, **copied**, **copying** 1 to make a copy of something 2 to try to do the same as someone, to imitate someone **copier** n **copycat** n a person who slavishly copies someone else **copyright** n the exclusive legal right owned by a person or organization to print or publish a book or article, to reproduce a picture or film, or to perform or record a piece of music **copyright** adj (said about a book, piece of music, etc.) protected by copyright

coquettish (say kə-**ket**-ish) adj (said about a woman) often flirting

coral n 1 a hard red, pink, or white substance formed from the skeletons of tiny sea creatures massed together 2 a reddish-pink colour **coral** adj reddish-pink **coralline** adj

cord n 1 a long thin flexible strip of twisted strands, or a piece of this 2 a structure like a cord in the body ♦ the spinal cord 3 corduroy material 4 a measure of cut wood **cords** pl n corduroy trousers ◊ Do not confuse this word with chord, which has a different meaning. **cordless** adj (said about a telephone or piece of electrical equipment) not connected by a flex to a central unit or mains supply

cordial n a fruit-flavoured drink **cordial** adj warm and friendly ♦ They sent cordial greetings. **cordiality** n **cordially** adv

cordite (say **kor** -diyt) n a smokeless explosive used in bullets and shells

cordon n a line of soldiers, police, or vehicles placed round an area to guard it or control the movement of people into and out of it **cordon** v to enclose an area with a cordon

cordon bleu (say kor-dawn **bler**) adj of the highest class in cookery

corduroy n cotton cloth with velvety ridges

core n 1 the hard central part of an apple, pear, or other fruit, containing the seeds 2 the central or most important part of something 3 ICT a unit in the structure of a computer memory storing one bit of data 4 the part of a nuclear reactor that contains the fissile material 5 a piece of soft iron along the middle of an electromagnet or induction coil **core** v to remove the core from a fruit **corer** n

co-respondent (say koh-ri-**spon**-dənt) n a person who is named as having allegedly committed adultery with a person (in law called the respondent) being divorced

corgi n pl **corgis** a small dog of a Welsh breed with short legs and upright ears

coriander (say ko-ri-**and**-er) n an aromatic plant with leaves and seeds used for flavouring

Corinthian (say kə-**rinth**-iən) adj 1 to do with Corinth, a city of ancient Greece 2 denoting a style of architecture, the most ornate of the five classical orders of architecture

cork n 1 a light tough substance made from the bark of a south European oak 2 a bottle stopper made of cork or a similar material 3 a piece of this substance used as a float **cork** v to close or seal a bottle with a cork **corkscrew** n

cormorant n a large black seabird

corn[1] n 1 the seed of wheat and similar plants 2 a plant, such as wheat, grown for its grain 3 Amer. maize

corn[2] n a small area of hardened skin on the foot

cornea (say **korn**-iə) n the transparent layer over the front of the eyeball **corneal** adj

corner n 1 the angle or area where two lines or sides or walls meet or where two streets join 2 a difficult position, or one with no escape 3 a hidden or remote place 4 a free hit or kick from the corner of the field in hockey or football 5 a situation in which one person or organization dominates the supply of a certain product or service, and can control its price **corner** v 1 to drive a person or animal into a corner 2 to obtain all or most of something for yourself; to establish a monopoly of a product or service 3 to move round a corner ♦ The car was cornering much too fast. **cornerstone** n 1 a stone built into the corner at the base of a building 2 a vital or important feature on which an idea or activity is based

cornet n 1 a brass musical instrument 2 a cone-shaped wafer for holding ice cream

cornice (say **korn**-iss) n a band of ornamental moulding round the wall of a room

Cornish adj to do with Cornwall or its people or language **Cornish** n the ancient language of Cornwall **Cornish pasty** n a small pie containing a mixture of meat and potato or other vegetables

cornucopia (say kor-new-**koh**-piə) n a plentiful supply of good things

corny adj **cornier**, **corniest** informal repeated so often that people are tired of it ♦ a corny joke **corniness** n

corollary (say kə-**rol**-er-i) n pl **corollaries** 1 a fact or proposition that follows as a logical consequence or result from something that has been proved 2 a direct result or consequence

corona (say kə-**roh**-nə) n pl **coronas** a circle or glow of light round something, especially round the sun or a star

coronary (say **ko**-rən-er-i) adj to do with the arteries supplying blood to the heart **coronary** n pl **coronaries** a coronary artery

coronation n the ceremony of crowning a king or queen

coroner (say **ko**-rən-er) *n* a public official who holds an inquiry into the cause of a death

coronet *n* 1 a small crown 2 an ornamental band of gold or jewels for the head

corporal¹ *adj* to do with the body **corporality** *n* **corporal punishment** *n* punishment on the body

corporal² *n* a non-commissioned soldier ranking below a sergeant and above a private

corporate (say **kor** -per-ət) *adj* 1 shared by members of a group ♦ *corporate responsibility* 2 united in one group ♦ *a corporate body* **corporation** *n* 1 a group of people or group of companies legally authorized to act as one entity, especially in business 2 a group of people elected to govern a town or borough **corporation tax** *n*

corps (say kor) *n pl* **corps** (say korz) 1 a military force or army unit 2 a body of people working in the same activity ♦ *the diplomatic corps*

corpse *n* a dead body, especially of a human

corpulent (say **kor** -pew-lənt) *adj* having a bulky body, fat **corpulence** *n*

corpus *n pl* **corpora** or **corpuses** a large collection of writings or written texts

corral (say kə-**rahl**) *n Amer.* an enclosure for horses or cattle **corral** *v* **corralled**, **corralling** *Amer.* to put animals into a corral

correct *adj* 1 true or accurate 2 proper, done or said in the approved way **correct** *v* 1 to make something correct by altering or adjusting it 2 to mark the errors in a piece of work 3 to point out the faults in a person, or to punish them **correctable** *adj* **correction** *n* **corrective** *adj* **correctly** *adv* **correctness** *n*

correlate (say **ko**-rəl-ayt) *v* 1 to compare or connect things systematically 2 to have a systematic connection **correlation** *n* **correlative** *adj*

correspond *v* 1 to match or be in agreement ♦ *Your story corresponds with what I've been told.* 2 to be similar or equivalent to something else ♦ *They have an official that corresponds to our mayor.* 3 to write letters to one other ♦ *Sarah and*

her cousin corresponded for many years. **correspondence** *n*

correspondent *n* 1 a person who writes letters to someone else 2 a person who works for a newspaper or radio station to gather news or write reports for them

corridor *n* a long narrow passage from which doors open into rooms

corroborate (say kə-**rob**-er-ayt) *v* to help to confirm a statement or theory **corroboration** *n* **corroborative** *adj*

corrode *v* to destroy a substance gradually by chemical action ♦ *Rust corrodes metal.* **corrodible** *adj* **corrosion** *n* **corrosive** *adj*

corrugated *adj* shaped into alternating ridges and grooves ♦ *corrugated iron* **corrugation** *n*

corrupt *adj* 1 willing to act dishonestly or accept bribes 2 immoral or wicked 3 (said about a text or computer data) unreliable because of errors **corrupt** *v* 1 to make someone corrupt or dishonest 2 to introduce errors into a text or computer data **corruptible** *adj* **corruption** *n*

corset *n* a close-fitting piece of underwear worn to shape or support the body

cortège (say kor-**tayzh**) *n* a funeral procession

cortex *n pl* **cortices** (say **kor** -ti-seez) 1 an outer layer of tissue on an organ 2 the outer grey matter of the brain **cortical** *adj*

cosh *n* a heavy weapon used for hitting people **cosh** *v* to hit someone with a cosh

cosmetic *n* a substance such as a cream or liquid used on the skin to make it look more attractive **cosmetic** *adj* used to improve the appearance ♦ *cosmetic surgery*

cosmopolitan *adj* 1 to do with or coming from many parts of the world ♦ *a cosmopolitan population* 2 including people from many parts of the world ♦ *a cosmopolitan city* 3 interested in all parts of the world and not just your own country ♦ *a cosmopolitan outlook* **cosmopolitan** *n* a cosmopolitan person

cosmos (say **koz**-moss) *n* the universe **cosmic** *adj* **cosmonaut** *n* a Russian astronaut

Cossack (say **koss**-ak) *n* a member of a people of southern Russia and neighbouring regions, famous as horsemen

cosset (say koss-it) v **cosseted, cosseting** to pamper someone

cost n **1** an amount you charge or have to pay for something **2** the effort or loss needed to achieve something ♦ *They shut the factory at a cost of 500 jobs.* **costs** pl n the expenses involved in a law case **cost** v past tense and past participle **cost 1** to have a certain amount as its price or charge **2** to need a certain effort or loss to achieve something **3** to estimate the cost of something **costly** adj **costlier, costliest, costliness** n **cost-effective** adj effective or beneficial enough to justify its cost **cost of living** the general level of prices ◊ In meaning 3 the past tense and past participle is *costed*.

co-star n a stage or cinema star appearing with another or others of equal importance **co-star** v **co-starred, co-starring 1** to appear as a co-star **2** (said about a film, etc.) to have a performer as a co-star

costume n **1** a set or style of clothes belonging to a particular place or time, or worn for a particular activity **2** *Drama* the clothes worn by an actor playing a particular role

cosy adj **cosier, cosiest** warm and comfortable **cosy** n pl **cosies** a cover put over a teapot or boiled egg to keep it hot **cosily** adv **cosiness** n

cot n a small bed having high sides with bars, for a baby or young child **cot death** n an unexplained death of a baby while sleeping

cottage n a small simple house, especially in the country **cottager** n

cotton n **1** a soft white substance covering the seeds of a tropical plant, or the plant itself **2** a thread made from this substance **3** a cloth made from cotton thread **cotton** v **to cotton on** *informal* to begin to understand something **cotton wool** n soft fluffy wadding of a kind originally made from cotton

couch n **1** a long soft seat like a sofa but with the back extending along half its length and only one raised end **2** a sofa or settee **3** a bed-like platform on which a doctor's patient can lie to be examined **couch** v to

express something in words of a certain kind ♦ *The request was couched in polite terms.*

cough v to send out air from the lungs with a sudden sharp sound **cough** n **1** an act or sound of coughing **2** an illness that makes you cough a lot

could auxiliary verb **1** the past tense of *can*² **2** to feel that you want to do something ♦ *I could laugh for joy.* **couldn't** v could not

coulomb (say koo-lom) n a unit of electric charge

council n a group of people chosen or elected to organize or discuss something, especially those elected to run the affairs of a town or county ◊ Do not confuse this word with *counsel*, which has a different meaning. **councillor** n **council house** n a house owned by a local council and let out to tenants

counsel n **1** advice or suggestions ♦ *to give counsel* **2** a barrister or group of barristers representing someone in a lawsuit **counsel** v **counselled, counselling 1** to advise or recommend something **2** to give professional guidance to a person about personal or social problems ◊ Do not confuse this word with *council*, which has a different meaning. **counsellor** n

count¹ v **1** to find the total of something by using numbers **2** to say numbers in the right order **3** to include something in a total ♦ *There were six of us, counting the dog.* **4** to be important ♦ *It's what you do that counts.* **5** to be a factor ♦ *I'm afraid his mistake will count against him.* **6** to regard or consider something in a certain way ♦ *I should count it an honour to be invited.* **count** n **1** the process of counting, a calculation **2** a number reached by counting, a total **3** any of the points being considered, e.g. in accusing someone of crimes ♦ *He was found guilty on all counts.* **countable** adj **countless** adj **countdown** n the process of counting numbers backwards to zero before a precisely timed event

count² n a foreign nobleman

countenance n **1** a person's face, or the expression on it **2** *formal* an appearance of approval ♦ *Their support lends countenance* to the plan. **countenance** v to allow something as acceptable or possible

counter¹ n 1 a flat surface over which customers are served in a shop, bank, etc. 2 a small round playing piece used in some board games 3 a token representing a coin 4 a device for counting things

counter² adv opposite or contrary ♦ This is counter to what we want. **counter** adj opposed **counter** v 1 to oppose or contradict someone or something 2 to return an opponent's attack by hitting back

counter- prefix 1 against or opposing; done in return (as in counter-attack) 2 corresponding (as in countersign) **counteract** v to take action against something and reduce or prevent its effects **counteraction** n **counter-attack** n an attack to oppose or return an enemy's attack **counter-attack** v to make a counter-attack on an enemy **counterbalance** n a weight or influence that balances another **counterbalance** v to act as a counterbalance to something **counterblast** n a strongly worded reply **counter-espionage** n action taken to uncover and counteract spying by an enemy **counter-intelligence** n counter-espionage **countermand** v to cancel a command or order already given **countermand** n a command or order cancelling an earlier one **countermeasure** n an action taken to counteract a threat or danger **counter-offensive** n a large-scale counter-attack **counterpart** n a person or thing that corresponds to another ♦ Their President is the counterpart of our Prime Minister. **counterpoise** n a counterbalance **counterpoise** v to counterbalance something **counterproductive** adj having the opposite of the effect that is wanted **countersign** v to add another signature to a document to give it authority **countersignature** n **countertenor** n a male singing voice higher than tenor, or a singer with this voice **counterweight** n a counterbalancing weight or influence **counterfeit** (say **cownt**-er-feet) adj fake **counterfeit** n a fake **counterfeit** v to fake

something, especially money

counterfoil n a section of a cheque or receipt that is torn off and kept by the sender as a record

counterpane n a bedspread

countess n 1 the wife or widow of a count or earl 2 a woman holding the rank of count or earl

country n pl **countries** 1 a nation or state, or the land it occupies 2 land away from a town, with fields and woods and few buildings 3 an area of land with certain features ♦ hill country **countrified** adj **countryside** n **country-and-western** n a form of popular music based on American rural or cowboy songs sung to a guitar **country dance** n a traditional English dance, often with couples face to face in long lines **countryman**, **countrywoman** n pl **countrymen**, **countrywomen** 1 a man or woman living in the country, not in a town 2 a man or woman from the same country as another person

county n pl **counties** 1 each of the main areas that a country is divided into for local government 2 N. Am a division of a state for administrative purposes **county court** n a local court where civil cases are heard

coup d'état (say koo day-**tah**) n pl **coups d'état** the sudden overthrow of a government by force or by unconstitutional means

couple n 1 two people or things considered together, a pair 2 a man and woman who are married to each other or romantically associated 3 a pair of partners in a dance **couple** v 1 to fasten or link things together; to join things with a coupling 2 to have sexual intercourse **couplet** n two successive lines of rhyming verse in the same metre **coupling** n

coupon n a small printed piece of paper that gives you the right to receive something or that can be used as an application form or an entry form for a competition

courage n the ability to face danger, difficulty, or pain even when you are afraid; bravery **courageous** adj **courageously** adv

courgette (say koor-**zhet**) n a kind of small vegetable marrow

courier (say **koor** -i-er) *n* **1** a messenger carrying news or important papers **2** a person employed to guide and help a group of tourists

course *n* **1** the route or direction taken or intended ♦ *Follow the course of the river.* **2** a movement forward or onward in space or time ♦ *in the ordinary course of events* **3** a series of events or actions that can achieve something ♦ *Your best course is to start again.* **4** each part of a meal **5** a series of lessons or talks in a particular subject **6** a series of medical treatments or medicines given for a particular ailment or illness **7** a stretch of land or water over which a race takes place **8** a continuous layer of brick or stone in a wall **course** *v* (said about something liquid) to move or flow freely ♦ *Tears coursed down his cheeks.* **coursework** *n*

court *n* **1** the household and staff of a king or queen **2** a yard surrounded by houses and opening off a street **3** a courtyard **4** an enclosed area for games **5** a law court, or the judges in a law court **court** *v* **1** to try to win the favour or support of someone **2** *old use* to try to win the love of someone **3** (said about animals) to try to attract a mate **4** to behave as though trying to bring about something harmful ♦ *The climbers were courting danger.* **courtly** *adj* **courtlier**, **courtliest**, **courtliness** *n* **courtship** *n* **1** a period of courting, especially for marriage **2** the mating ritual of some birds and animals **court martial** *n pl* **courts martial** **1** a court for trying offences against military law **2** a trial in this court **court-martial** *v* **court-martialled**, **court-martialling** to try someone by a court martial **courtyard** *n* a space enclosed by walls or buildings

courteous (say **ker**-ti-əs) *adj* polite and helpful **courteously** *adv* **courtesy** *n pl* **courtesies**

courtesan (say kor-ti-**zan**) *n old use* a prostitute having wealthy or upper-class clients

cousin (say **kuz**-ən) *n* a son or daughter of your uncle or aunt **cousinly** *adv*

couture (say koo-**tewr**) *n* the design and making of high-quality fashionable clothes

couturier *n*

cove *n* **1** a small bay or inlet on a coast **2** a curved moulding where a ceiling and wall meet

coven (say **kuv**-ən) *n* a gathering of witches

covenant (say **kuv**-ən-ənt) *n* a formal agreement or contract **covenant** *v* to agree to something by covenant **covenanter** *n*

cover *v* **1** to place one thing over or in front of another in order to protect or conceal it **2** to spread something over a surface ♦ *Cover the wall with new paint.* **3** to lie or extend over a certain area ♦ *The grounds cover six acres.* **4** to travel over a distance ♦ *The marching soldiers covered thirty miles a day.* **5** to guard or protect a place by dominating the approach to it **6** to have a target within a gun's range **7** to protect someone or something by providing insurance or a guarantee ♦ *The policy covers you against fire or theft.* **8** to be enough money to pay for something ♦ *£20 should cover the fare* **9** to include or deal with a subject ♦ *The book covers many aspects of modern art.* **cover** *n* **1** a thing that covers something, such as a lid, wrapper, or envelope **2** the binding of a book **3** a place or area that gives shelter or protection ♦ *There was no cover from the sun's heat.* **4** a military force that gives protection ♦ *The ground troops needed air cover.* **5** a screen or pretence ♦ *They acted under cover of friendship.* **6** insurance against a risk such as loss or damage **7** a place laid at a table in a restaurant **coverage** *n* **cover-up** *n*

covert (say **kuv**-ert or **koh**-vert) *adj* concealed or done secretly ♦ *There were many covert glances across the table.* **covertly** *adv* **covert** (say **kuv**-ert) *n* **1** an area of thick bushes and undergrowth in which animals hide **2** a bird's feather covering the base of another

covet (say **kuv**-it) *v* **coveted**, **coveting** to want very much to have something belonging to someone else **covetous** *adj* **covetously** *adv* **covetousness** *n*

cow[1] *n* the fully-grown female of cattle or of some other large animals, such as an elephant, whale, or seal **cowboy** *n* **1** a man in charge of grazing cattle on a ranch in the western USA **2** *informal* a person who uses unscrupulous methods in trade or business **cowhide** *n* the skin of a cow, or leather made from this

cow² *v* to subdue someone by frightening or bullying them

coward *n* a person who has no courage and shows fear in a shameful way **cowardice** *n* **cowardly** *adj*

cower *v* to crouch or shrink back in fear

cowl *n* **1** a monk's hood or hooded robe **2** a hood-shaped covering for a chimney or ventilation shaft

cox *n* a person who steers a boat with oars, a coxswain **cox** *v* to act as cox of a racing boat **coxswain** *n* **1** a person who steers a boat with oars **2** a sailor with special duties

coy *adj* pretending to be shy or modest; bashful **coyly** *adv* **coyness** *n*

coyote (say koi-oh-ti) *n pl* **coyotes** or **coyote** a wild dog like a wolf, found in North America

CPS *abbr* (in Britain) Crown Prosecution Service

crab *n* **1** a shellfish with ten legs, the first pair being a set of pincers **2** the flesh of a crab used for food

crack *n* **1** a narrow line or opening on the surface of something where it is broken but has not come completely apart **2** a sudden sharp or explosive noise **3** a sharp blow or knock ♦ *a crack on the head* **4** *informal* a joke or wisecrack **5** a narrow gap or chink **6** a strong drug made from cocaine **crack** *adj* first-class, excellent ♦ *a crack shot* **crack** *v* **1** to break without coming completely apart **2** to make a sudden sharp or explosive sound **3** to break with a sharp sound **4** *informal* to break into a safe **5** *informal* to find the solution to a code or problem **6** (said about a voice) to become suddenly harsh, especially with emotion **7** (said about a person or group of people) to collapse under strain, to stop resisting **8** *Chem* to break down heavy oils in order to produce lighter ones **cracking** *adj* **crackle** *v* **crackling** *n* the crisp fatty skin on roast pork **crackdown** *n* a series of severe measures taken against something illegal or forbidden **cracked wheat** *n* grains of wheat

crushed into small pieces **crackpot** *adj* crazy or impractical **crackpot** *n* a person with crazy or impractical ideas

cracker *n* **1** a small paper toy that makes a bang and releases a small novelty when the ends are pulled **2** a firework that explodes with a sharp crack **3** a thin dry biscuit

-cracy *suffix* forming nouns meaning 'ruling' or 'government' (as in *democracy*)

cradle *n* **1** a small bed or cot for a baby **2** a supporting framework or structure **3** a place where something begins ♦ *the cradle of civilization* **cradle** *v* to hold or support something gently

craft *n* **1** a job or occupation that needs skill **2** a skill or technique **3** cunning or deceit **4** *pl* **craft** a ship or boat; an aircraft or spacecraft **crafty** *adj* **craftier**, **craftiest**, **craftily** *adv* **craftiness** *n* **craftsman**, **craftswoman** *n pl* **craftsmen**, **craftswomen craftsmanship** *n*

crag *n* a steep or rugged rock face or cliff **craggy** *adj* **craggier**, **craggiest**, **cragginess** *n*

cram *v* **crammed**, **cramming 1** to force too many things or people into something so that it is very full **2** to study intensively just before an examination **crammer** *n*

cramp *n* **1** a sudden painful tightening of a muscle **2** a metal bar with bent ends for holding masonry together **3** a clamp **cramp** *v* **1** to hinder someone's freedom or growth **2** to suffer from cramp **3** to fasten something with a cramp **cramped** *adj*

crampon (say **kram**-pon) *n* an iron plate with spikes, worn on boots for walking or climbing on ice

cranberry *n pl* **cranberries 1** a small sour red berry, used for making jelly and sauce **2** the shrub that produces this berry

crane *n* **1** a machine for lifting and moving heavy objects, usually by suspending them from a jib by ropes or chains **2** a large wading bird with long legs, neck, and bill **crane** *v* to stretch out your neck in order to see something **crane fly** *n pl* **crane flies** a flying insect with very long thin legs

cranium (say **kray**-ni-əm) *n pl* **craniums** or **crania** the skull, especially the part enclosing the brain

crank¹ *n* an L-shaped part used for converting to-and-fro motion into circular motion **crank** *v* to move something by means of a crank **crankshaft** *n* a shaft turned by a crank

crank² *n* a person with very strange or fanatical ideas **cranky** *adj* **crankier, crankiest, crankiness** *n*

cranny *n pl* **crannies** a small narrow space or opening **crannied** *adj*

crash *n* 1 the sudden violent noise of something breaking or banging together ♦ *The tree fell to the ground with a loud crash.* 2 an accident in which a car, train, aircraft, etc. violently collides with something 3 the sudden failure of a business, economy, etc. ♦ *a stock market crash* **crash** *v* 1 to collide violently with something 2 (said about an aircraft) to fall from the sky and hit the ground or the sea 3 to make a crash, or to move or go with a crash ♦ *The whole pile of tins crashed to the floor.* 4 ICT (said about a computer system) to stop working suddenly 5 (said about a company's shares) to fall suddenly in value, leading to financial ruin 6 *informal* to enter a party without permission, to gatecrash it ♦ *We decided to crash the party.* **crash** *adj* involving intense effort to achieve something rapidly ♦ *a crash course in Japanese* **crash barrier** *n* a protective fence erected where there is danger of vehicles leaving a road **crash dive** *n* a sudden diving by an aircraft or submarine in an emergency **crash-dive** *v* to dive in this way **crash helmet** *n* a padded helmet worn to protect the head in case of a crash **crash landing** *n* an emergency landing of an aircraft, especially causing damage to it

crass *adj* stupidly insensitive or tactless **crassly** *adv* **crassness** *n*

crate *n* 1 a packing case made of strips of wood 2 a divided container for carrying bottles **crate** *v* to pack something into a crate

crater *n* 1 a bowl-shaped cavity or hollow caused by an explosion or impact 2 the mouth of a volcano

cravat (say krə-**vat**) *n* a short wide scarf worn by men round the neck and tucked into an open-necked shirt

crave *v* to have a strong desire for something **craving** *n* **craven** *adj* cowardly **cravenly** *adv*

crawl *v* 1 to move forward on your hands and knees 2 to move with the body close to the ground or other surface ♦ *A snake was crawling towards him.* 3 to move slowly or with difficulty ♦ *The train crawled into the station.* 4 *informal* to seek favour from someone by behaving in a servile way 5 (said about the skin) to feel as if it is covered with crawling things **crawl** *n* 1 a crawling movement 2 a very slow pace ♦ *The line of cars had slowed to a crawl.* 3 a swimming stroke **crawler** *n*

crayfish *n pl* **crayfish** a freshwater shellfish like a very small lobster

crayon *n* a stick or pencil of coloured wax or chalk, used for drawing **crayon** *v* to draw or colour something with crayons

craze *n* 1 a widespread but short-lived enthusiasm for something ♦ *a craze for yo-yos* 2 the object of this **crazed** *adj* **crazy** *adj* **crazier, craziest, crazily** *adv* **craziness** *n*

creak *n* a harsh squeak like that of a stiff door hinge **creak** *v* to make a sound like this ♦ *The door creaked open.* **creaky** *adj*

cream *n* 1 the fatty part of milk 2 a yellowish-white colour 3 a soft cream-like substance, especially one used as a cosmetic or for medical purposes ♦ *face cream* 4 a food containing or like cream ♦ *chocolate cream* 5 the very best part of something ♦ *the cream of British society* **cream** *adj* yellowish-white **cream** *v* 1 to make something creamy ♦ *Now cream the butter.* ♦ *creamed potatoes* 2 to rub a cosmetic cream into the skin **creamery** *n pl* **creameries** **creamy** *adj* **creamier, creamiest, creaminess** *n* **cream cheese** *n* a soft rich cheese made from unskimmed milk and cream **cream of tartar** *n* a compound of potassium used in cookery **to cream something off** to remove the best part of something

crease *n* 1 a line made on cloth or paper by folding, crushing, or pressing it 2 a wrinkle or furrow on the skin 3 (in cricket) a line on the pitch marking the limit of the bowler's or batsman's position **crease** v **1** to make a crease or creases in something **2** to develop creases ♦ *This linen jacket creases easily.*

create v **1** to bring something into existence ♦ *God is said to have created the world in six days.* **2** to produce something as a result of what you do ♦ *He was anxious to create a good impression.* **3** to give a new rank or position to someone ♦ *He was created Earl of Wessex.* **4** *informal* to make a fuss, to grumble **creative** adj **creatively** adv **creativity** n **the Creation** n the creating of the universe, especially when thought of as the work of God **creator** n **the Creator** God

creature n **1** a living being, especially an animal **2** a person ♦ *Who is this poor creature?*

crèche (say kresh) n a place where babies and young children are looked after while their parents are at work

credence (say **kree**-dəns) n willingness to believe in something ♦ *I don't give this story any credence.* ◊ Do not confuse this word with *credibility*, which has a different meaning.

credentials (say kri-**den**-shəlz) pl n **1** a person's qualifications and past achievements that make them suitable for something ♦ *Her credentials for the job are impeccable.* **2** documents that prove a person's identity or qualifications ♦ *May I see your credentials?*

credible adj able to be believed, convincing ♦ *I find it scarcely credible that she could have stolen the money.* **credibility** n **credibly** adv ◊ Do not confuse this word with *creditable*, which has a different meaning.

credit n **1** an arrangement trusting a person to pay at a later date for goods or services supplied **2** the amount of money you are allowed to owe or the length of time you are allowed to pay under this arrangement ♦ *We can offer you six months' credit.* **3** the amount of money in a person's bank account or entered in a financial account as paid in **4** praise or acknowledgement given for some achievement or good quality ♦ *How come I did all the work and you got all the credit?* **5** a source of pride

♦ *Your children are a credit to you.* **6** a grade above a pass in an examination **credits** pl n a list of the people who have helped to produce a film, television programme, or record **credit** v **credited**, **crediting 1** to say that someone has done or achieved something ♦ *Columbus is usually credited with the discovery of America.* **2** to enter an amount as a credit in a financial account **3** to believe something that seems unlikely ♦ *You would hardly credit it, but she's been voted Best Singer of the Year.* **creditable** adj **creditably** adv **creditor** n **credit card** n a plastic card authorizing a person to buy things on credit

credo (say **kree**-doh) n pl **credos** a statement of a person's beliefs or principles

credulous (say **kred**-yoo-ləs) adj too ready to believe things **credulity** n **credulously** adv

creed n **1** a person's religion **2** a formal summary of Christian beliefs **3** a statement of a person's beliefs or principles

creek n **1** a narrow inlet of water, especially on the coast **2** *N. Am., Austral.* a stream or minor tributary of a river

creel n a fisherman's wicker basket for carrying fish

creep v past tense and past participle **crept 1** to move quietly or stealthily ♦ *She crept across the landing.* **2** to move along with the body close to the ground **3** to move or progress very slowly ♦ *The tide was creeping up the beach.* **4** (said about a plant) to grow along the ground or other surface **creep** n *informal* someone you dislike, especially because they are always flattering people to try to become popular **creeper** n **creepy** adj **creepier**, **creepiest**, **creepily** adv **creepiness** n **creepy-crawly** n pl **creepy-crawlies** a crawling insect, spider, or worm **to give you the creeps** *informal* to produce a feeling of revulsion or fear

cremate v to burn a dead person's body to ashes **cremation** n **crematorium** n pl **crematoria** a place where the bodies of dead people are cremated

crème de menthe (say krem də mahnt) n a green liqueur flavoured with peppermint

crème fraiche (say krem **fresh**) *n* a type of thick sour cream

Creole (say **kree**-ohl) *n* **1** a descendant of European settlers in the West Indies or Central or South America; a white descendant of French settlers in the southern USA **2** a person of mixed European and African descent, especially one living in the West Indies **3** a language formed from the contact of a European language (especially English, French, or Portuguese) with a local language (especially an African one) **Creole** *adj* to do with a Creole or Creoles

creosote (say **kree**-ə-soht) *n* a thick brown oily liquid obtained from coal tar, used to prevent wood from rotting **creosote** *v* to treat a fence, etc. with creosote

crêpe (say **krayp**) *n* **1** a thin fabric with a wrinkled surface **2** rubber with a wrinkled texture, used for the soles of shoes **3** a thin pancake **crêpe paper** *n*

crept past tense and past participle of *creep*

crescendo (say kri-**shen**-doh) *n pl* **crescendos** a gradual increase in loudness

crescent *n* **1** a narrow curved shape tapering to a point at each end, such as the waxing moon **2** a curved street or terrace of houses

cress *n* any of various plants with hot-tasting leaves used in salads

crest *n* **1** a tuft of feathers, fur, or skin on the top of a bird's or animal's head **2** a plume of feathers on a helmet **3** the highest part of a hill or wave **4** the highest point in one cycle of an electromagnetic or sound wave **5** a design above the shield on a coat of arms, or used separately on a seal or notepaper ♦ *their family crest* **crested** *adj* **crestfallen** *adj* downcast or disappointed

cretin (say **kret**-in) *n* a stupid person **cretinism** *n* **cretinous** *adj*

crevasse (say kri-**vass**) *n* a deep open crack, especially in the ice of a glacier

crevice (say **krev**-iss) *n* a narrow opening or crack, especially in a rock or wall

crew[1] *n* **1** the group of people working in a ship, boat, or aircraft **2** all these people except the officers **3** a group of people working together ♦ *the camera crew* **crew** *v* **1** to act as a member of a crew for a ship,

boat, or aircraft **2** to provide a ship, boat, or aircraft with a crew

crew[2] past tense of *crow*[2]

crib *n* **1** a baby's cot **2** a wooden framework from which animals can pull out fodder **3** something copied from another person's work **4** a literal translation of something written in a foreign language, for use by students **crib** *v* **cribbed**, **cribbing** *informal* to copy someone else's work

crick *n* a painful stiffness in the neck or back **crick** *v* to cause a crick in your neck or back, especially by twisting it

cricket[1] *n* a game played on a large grass field with a ball, bats, and wickets **cricketer** *n*

cricket[2] *n* a brown grasshopper-like insect that makes a shrill chirping sound

crime *n* **1** a serious offence, especially one that breaks the law **2** such offences in general ♦ *the detection of crime* **3** *informal* a pity or shame ♦ *It would be a crime to waste these tickets now.* **criminal** *n* **criminologist** *n* **criminology** *n*

crimp *v* to press material into small folds or ridges **2** to make waves in hair with a hot iron

crimson *n* a deep red colour ♦ *He went crimson with embarrassment.*

cringe *v* **1** to shrink back or crouch down in fear **2** to feel extremely embarrassed or ashamed ♦ *My mother's rudeness made me cringe.*

crinkle *v* to make something wrinkled, or to become wrinkled **crinkle** *n* a wrinkle or crease **crinkly** *adj*

cripple *n* *old use* a person who is permanently lame through disability or injury **cripple** *v* **1** to make someone lame **2** to weaken or damage something seriously ♦ *The project was crippled by lack of money.*

crisis *n pl* **crises** (say **kriy**-seez) a time of danger or great difficulty ♦ *a political crisis*

crisp *adj* **1** firm but brittle, breaking with a snap ♦ *crisp pastry* **2** (said about paper) slightly stiff and crackling ♦ *a crisp £10 note* **3** pleasantly cold and bracing ♦ *a crisp winter morning* **4** brisk and decisive ♦ *She has a crisp manner.* **crisp** *n* a thin fried slice of potato, sold in packets and eaten as a snack **crisp** v to make something crisp, or to become crisp **crisply** adv **crispness** n **crispy** adj **crispier, crispiest**

criss-cross n a pattern of crossing lines **criss-cross** adj with crossing lines **criss-cross** v **1** to move around a place by repeatedly going back and forth **2** to form a criss-cross pattern

criterion (say kriy-**teer**-iən) n pl **criteria** a standard or principle by which something is judged

criticize v **1** to say that a person or thing has faults **2** to examine a book, piece of music, etc., and express judgements about it ♦ We were asked to criticize a poem by Blake. **critic** n **critical** adj **critically** adv **criticism** n **critique** n

croak v to make a deep hoarse cry or sound like that of a frog **croak** n a croaking sound

Croat (say **kroh**-at) n **1** a person born in Croatia in SE Europe, or descended from people born there **2** the language of Croatia, close to Serbian but written in the Roman alphabet **Croat** adj to do with or coming from Croatia

crochet (say **kroh**-shay) n a kind of needlework **crochet** v **crocheted**, **crocheting** to make something in this way

crock[1] n **1** an earthenware pot or jar **2** a broken piece of this **crockery** n

crock[2] n informal **1** someone who suffers from bad health or injury, especially an old person **2** an old and worn-out vehicle

crocodile n **1** a large tropical reptile **2** its skin, used especially to make bags and shoes **3** a long line of schoolchildren walking in pairs

croft n a small rented farm in Scotland **croft** v to farm a croft **crofter** n

croissant (say **krwass**-ahn) n a crescent-shaped roll made of flaky pastry

crone n an ugly old woman

crony n pl **cronies** informal someone's close friend or supporter

crook n **1** informal a person who is dishonest or a criminal **2** a shepherd's hooked stick or staff **3** a bend in something ♦ She carried the kitten in the crook of her arm. **crook** v to bend your finger or arm ♦ He crooked his

finger to beckon us over. **crook** adj Austral. NZ informal unwell, not working properly, or unsatisfactory **crooked** adj **crookedly** adv **crookedness** n

croon v to sing softly and gently **crooner** n

crop n **1** plants that are grown for food or other use, especially cereals **2** the harvest from such plants ♦ We had a good crop of barley this season. **3** a group or quantity appearing or produced at one time ♦ Who do you most admire among the current crop of players? **4** a very short haircut **5** the bag-like part of a bird's throat where food is broken up for digestion **6** the handle of a whip, or a whip with a loop instead of a lash **crop** v **cropped**, **cropping 1** to cut something or bite it off ♦ Sheep were cropping the grass. **2** to cut hair very short **3** to trim off the edges of a photograph **4** (said about land or a plant) to produce a crop **cropper** n **to come a cropper** informal **1** to fall heavily **2** to fail badly

croquet (say **kroh**-kay) n a game played on a lawn with wooden balls that you drive through hoops with mallets

croquette (say krə-**ket**) n a ball or roll of potato, meat, or fish, fried in breadcrumbs

cross n **1** a mark made by drawing one line across another, x or + **2** an upright post with another piece of wood across it, used in ancient times for crucifixion **3** (**the Cross**) the cross on which Christ was crucified, used as a symbol of Christianity **4** a cross-shaped medal, emblem, or monument ♦ the Victoria Cross **5** an annoying or distressing thing that someone has to bear **6** an animal or plant produced by cross-breeding **7** a mixture of two different things **8** (in football) a pass of the ball across the field from the side towards the centre **cross** v **1** to go across or to the other side of something **2** to intersect ♦ The roads cross near a little bridge. **3** to pass a person or vehicle going in a different direction ♦ The two planes crossed only a few metres apart. **4** to place one thing across another in the shape of a cross ♦ She crossed her arms. ♦ Cross your fingers for luck. **5** to draw a line across something or mark something with a cross **6** (in football) to pass the ball across the field from the side towards the centre **7** to frustrate or oppose someone ♦ *Don't cross me.* **8** to cross-breed animals or cross-fertilize plants **cross** adj annoyed or bad-tempered **crossing** n **crossly** adv **crossness** n **cross-legged** adj, adv with the ankles crossed and knees bent outwards **cross-pollinate** v to pollinate a flower or plant with pollen from another **cross-pollination** n **cross reference** n a note telling the reader to look at another part of a book, index, etc. for further information **crossroads** n a place where two or more roads cross one another **cross section** n **1** a diagram showing the internal structure of something as though it has been cut through **2** a representative sample ♦ *We interviewed a cross section of the local community.* **cross stitch** n a stitch formed by two crossing stitches **crossways** adv, adj in the form of a cross, with one thing crossing another **crosswind** n a wind blowing across the direction of travel **crossword** n a puzzle in which intersecting words have to be worked out from clues and then written into the blank squares in a diagram

cross- prefix **1** across, crossing something (as in *cross-channel, crossbar*) **2** from two different kinds (as in *cross-breed*) **crossbar** n a horizontal bar between two uprights **crossbow** n a powerful bow with a mechanism for pulling and releasing the string **cross-breed** v past tense and past participle **cross-bred** to produce an animal by mating an animal with one of a different kind **cross-breed** n an animal produced in this way **cross-country** adj, adv **1** across fields or open country ♦ *cross-country running* **2** not keeping to main roads or to a direct road **cross-examine** v to question a witness closely in a court of law in order to test answers given to previous questions **cross-examination** n **cross-eyed** adj having one or both eyes turned towards the nose **cross-fertilize** v to fertilize a plant using pollen from another plant of the same species **cross-fertilization** n **crossfire** n gunfire from two or more points so that the lines of fire cross **cross-grained** adj (said

about wood) with the grain running across the regular grain

crotch n the part of the body or of a piece of clothing between the tops of the legs

crotchety adj bad-tempered

crouch v to lower your body with your legs bent and close to your chest **crouch** n a crouching position

croup (say kroop) n a throat disease in children

croupier (say kroop-i-er) n a person who works at a gambling table

croûton (say kroo-tawn) n a small piece of fried or toasted bread served with soup

crow¹ n a large black bird of a family that includes the jackdaw, raven, and rook

crow² v past tense and past participle **crowed** or **crew 1** (said about a cock) to make a loud shrill cry **2** to boast about something or express great triumph **crow** n a crowing cry or sound

crowbar n a heavy iron bar with a flattened end, used as a lever

crowd n **1** a large number of people gathered together **2** the spectators at a sporting event **crowd** v **1** to gather together in a crowd ♦ *People crowded round to listen to her.* **2** to fill a space almost completely so that there is little room to move ♦ *Shoppers crowded the streets.* **crowded** adj

crown n **1** an ornamental headdress worn by a king or queen as a symbol of authority **2** (**the Crown**) the monarchy or sovereign ♦ *This land belongs to the Crown.* **3** a wreath worn on the head, especially as a symbol of victory **4** in sport, the achievement of being world champion, winning a major competition, etc. ♦ *Bailey took the 100m crown in a thrilling race.* **5** the top part of something such as the head or a hat **6** the highest part of something arched or curved ♦ *the crown of the road* **7** the part of a tooth above the gum, or an artificial covering for this **8** an old British coin with a value of five shillings (25p) **crown** v **1** to place a crown on someone as a symbol of royal power or victory **2** to declare someone to be the best at a sport ♦ *He was crowned world champion.* **3** to form, cover, or decorate the top part of something **4** to reward something or end it successfully ♦ *Our efforts were crowned with success.* **5** to put an artificial top on a tooth **6** *informal* to hit someone on the head

crow's-nest *n* a platform high on the mast of a ship for a lookout to watch from

crucial (say **kroo**-shəl) *adj* **1** of the greatest importance in deciding what will happen ♦ *The next few days will be crucial.* **2** *informal* excellent **crucially** *adv*

crucible (say **kroo**-si-bəl) *n* a pot in which metals are melted

crucifix *n* a model of a cross with a figure of Christ on it **cruciform** *adj*

crucify *v* **crucifies**, **crucified**, **crucifying** **1** to put a person to death by nailing or binding their hands and feet to a cross **2** to torment someone, or criticize or punish them severely **crucifixion** *n* **the Crucifixion** that of Christ

crude *adj* **1** in a natural state, not refined ♦ *crude oil* **2** not well finished or worked out, rough ♦ *a crude carving* **3** vulgar or indecent ♦ *a crude gesture* **crude** *n* crude oil **crudely** *adv* **crudity** *n*

cruel *adj* **crueller**, **cruellest** **1** deliberately causing suffering or pain to other people or animals ♦ *cruel remarks* **2** causing pain or suffering ♦ *this cruel war* **cruelly** *adv* **cruelty** *n*

cruet *n* a stand holding small containers for salt, pepper, mustard, etc. for use at the table

cruise *v* **1** to sail about from place to place for pleasure **2** (said about a vehicle or aircraft) to travel at a constant moderate speed **3** to achieve something with ease ♦ *Chelsea cruised to a 3-0 victory.* **cruise** *n* a voyage on a ship taken as a holiday **cruiser** *n* **cruise missile** *n* a missile that is able to fly at low altitude and is guided to its target by an on-board computer

crumb *n* **1** a small fragment of bread, cake, or other food **2** a small amount of something ♦ *a crumb of comfort* **3** the soft inner part of bread **crumb** *v* to cover food with breadcrumbs **crumble** *v* **crumbly** *adj* **crumblier**, **crumbliest**, **crumby** *adj*

crumpet *n* a soft flat cake made from a yeast mixture, eaten toasted with butter

crumple *v* to crush something or become crushed into creases

crunch *v* **1** to crush something noisily with the teeth **2** to walk over snow, gravel, etc. with a sound of crushing; to make a sound like this **crunch** *n* **1** a crunching sound **2** (**the crunch**) *informal* a decisive event or turning point

Crusade (say kroo-**sayd**) *n* any of the military expeditions made by European Christians in the Middle Ages to recover the Holy Land from the Muslims **crusade** *n* a campaign against something believed to be bad ♦ *her crusade against TV violence* **crusade** *v* to take part in a crusade **crusader** *n*

crush *v* **1** to press or squeeze something so that it becomes broken, injured, or wrinkled **2** to pound something into small fragments **3** to defeat or subdue someone completely ♦ *The rebellion was swiftly crushed.* **crush** *n* **1** a crowd of people pressed closely together **2** a drink made from the juice of crushed fruit **3** *informal* an infatuation that lasts only a short time **crushable** *adj*

crust *n* **1** the hard outer layer of something, especially bread **2** the rocky outer layer of the earth **crusty** *adj* **crustier**, **crustiest**, **crustily** *adv* **crustiness** *n*

crustacean (say krus-**tay**-shən) *n* an animal that has a hard shell, e.g. a crab, lobster, or shrimp

crutch *n* **1** a support for helping a lame person to walk **2** something used to support or reassure a person **3** the crotch of the body or of a piece of clothing

crux *n* *pl* **cruces** (say **kroo**-seez) the vital part of a problem ♦ *This is the crux of the matter.*

cry *v* **cries**, **cried**, **crying** **1** to shed tears **2** to shout or scream loudly ♦ *He cried out for help.* **3** (said about an animal) to utter its cry **cry** *n* *pl* **cries** **1** a loud shout or scream **2** the call of a bird or animal **3** a spell of weeping ♦ *Go on, have a good cry.* **4** an urgent appeal or demand **crybaby** *n* *pl* **crybabies** a person who weeps easily without good cause **to cry off** to go back on a promise or fail to keep to an arrangement **to cry out for** to clearly need something very much ♦ *The team is crying out for a decent striker.*

cryogenics (say kriy-ə-**jen**-iks) *n* the scientific study of very low temperatures and their effects

crypt (say kript) *n* a room or vault below the floor of a church, used as a chapel or burial place

cryptic (say **krip**-tik) *adj* hiding its meaning in a puzzling way ♦ *a cryptic remark* **cryptically** *adv* **cryptogram** *n* **cryptography** *n* **cryptographer** *n*

crystal *n* **1** a clear transparent colourless mineral, such as quartz **2** a piece of this **3** very clear glass of high quality **4** each of the tiny symmetrical pieces into which certain substances solidify ♦ *ice crystals* **crystal** *adj* as clear as crystal ♦ *the crystal waters of the Aegean Sea* **crystalline** *adj* **1** having the structure and form of a crystal **2** transparent, very clear **crystallize** *v* **crystallization** *n* **crystal ball** *n* a globe of glass used by fortune tellers for crystal-gazing

cu. *abbr* cubic

cub *n* a young animal, especially a fox, bear, or lion **Cub** or **Cub Scout** *n* a member of the junior branch of the Scout Association **cub** *v* **cubbed**, **cubbing 1** to give birth to cubs **2** to hunt fox cubs

cubbyhole *n* a very small room or snug space

cube *n* **1** a solid body with six equal square faces **2** a block shaped like this ♦ *an ice cube* **3** *Mathematics* the product of a number multiplied by itself twice ♦ *The cube of 3 is 27.* **cube** *v* **1** to cut food into small cubes **2** to multiply a number by itself twice **cubic** *adj* **cubicle** *n* a small enclosed space, screened off for privacy ♦ *a toilet cubicle* **cuboid** *adj* **cube root** *n* the number that produces a given number when it is cubed ♦ *The cube root of 27 is 3.*

cuckold (say **kuk**-əld) *n* a man whose wife has committed adultery during their marriage

cuckoo *n* a bird with a call that is like its name **cuckoo clock** *n* a clock that strikes the hour with a sound like a cuckoo's call

cucumber *n* a long green-skinned fleshy fruit eaten raw or pickled

cud *n* half-digested food that a cow, sheep, etc. brings back from the stomach into the mouth and chews again

cuddle *v* to hold someone closely and lovingly in your arms **cuddle** *n* an affectionate hug **cuddly** *adj* **cuddlier**, **cuddliest**

cudgel (say **kuj**-əl) *n* a short thick stick used as a weapon **cudgel** *v* **cudgelled**, **cudgelling** to beat someone with a cudgel

cue[1] *n* something said or done which acts as a signal for something else to be done **cue** *v* **cues**, **cued**, **cueing** to give a cue to someone

cue[2] *n* a long stick for striking the ball in snooker, billiards, and similar games

cuff[1] *n* the end part of a sleeve that fits round the wrist **cuffs** *pl n informal* handcuffs **cufflink** *n* each of a pair of fasteners for shirt cuffs

cuff[2] *v* to strike someone with an open hand **cuff** *n* a slap

cuisine (say kwi-**zeen**) *n* a style of cooking ♦ *Italian cuisine.*

cul-de-sac (say **kul**-də-sak) *n pl* **culs-de-sac** a street or passage that is closed at one end

culinary (say **kul**-in-er-i) *adj* to do with cooking or the kitchen ♦ *culinary herbs*

cull *v* **1** to select or gather things from a wide variety of sources ♦ *I've culled lines from several poems.* **2** to pick out and kill surplus wild animals from a herd **cull** *n* a selective killing of wild animals, done to reduce the population ♦ *a seal cull*

culminate *v* to reach its highest or final point **culmination** *n*

culpable (say **kul**-pə-bəl) *adj* deserving blame **culpability** *n* **culpably** *adv*

culprit *n* the person who has done something wrong

cult *n* **1** a religious sect **2** religious worship of a person or object, involving special rituals **3** a film, TV programme, rock group, etc. that is popular only with a small group of people

cultivate *v* **1** to prepare and use land for growing crops **2** to produce crops by tending them **3** to spend time trying to develop something **cultivated** adj **cultivation** n **cultivator** n

culture n **1** the appreciation and understanding of literature, art, music, etc. **2** the customs, traditions, and civilization of a particular society or group of people **3** Biol a quantity of bacteria or cells grown for study **4** the cultivating of plants **culture** v to grow bacteria or cells for study **cultural** adj **culturally** adv **cultured** adj

cumbersome (say **kum**-ber-səm) adj heavy and awkward to carry or use

cumin (say **kum**-in) n a plant with fragrant seeds that are used for flavouring

cummerbund n a sash worn round the waist

cumulative (say **kew**-mew-lə-tiv) adj increasing in amount by one addition after another **cumulatively** adv

cumulonimbus (say kew-mew-lə-**nim**-bəs) n a tall dense mass of cloud present during thunderstorms

cumulus n pl **cumuli** a form of cloud consisting of rounded masses heaped on a horizontal base

cunning adj **1** skilled at deceiving people **2** cleverly designed or planned ♦ a cunning device **cunning** n **1** skill in deceiving people **2** skill or ingenuity

cup n **1** a small container for drinking from **2** the amount a cup contains, used as a measure in cookery **3** something shaped like a cup **4** a goblet-shaped vessel awarded as a prize **5** a sports competition in which the winners receive a cup **6** either of the two cup-shaped parts of a bra **cup** v **cupped**, **cupping 1** to form something into the shape of a cup **2** to hold something as if in a cup **cupful** n **cupfuls**

cupboard (say **kub**-əd) n a piece of furniture or recess with a door, used for storing things

curate n a member of the clergy who assists a vicar or parish priest **curacy** n pl **curacies**

curator (say kewr-**ay**-ter) n a person in charge of a museum or other collection

curb n something that restrains ♦ The government has put a curb on spending. **curb** v to restrain something ♦ Try to curb your impatience. ◊ Do not confuse this word

with kerb, which has a different meaning.

curd n (often **curds**) the thick soft substance formed when milk turns sour **curdle** v

cure v **1** to bring someone back to health **2** to get rid of a disease or illness **3** to stop something bad **4** to preserve meat, fruit, tobacco, or skins by salting, drying, or smoking **cure** n **1** a substance or treatment that cures a disease or illness, a remedy **2** being cured of a disease or illness ♦ We cannot guarantee a cure. **curable** adj **curative** adj

curfew n a signal or time after which people must remain indoors until the next day

curie n a unit of radioactivity

curio n pl **curios** an object that is interesting because it is rare or unusual

curious adj **1** eager to learn or know something **2** strange or unusual ♦ Then a curious thing happened. **curiosity** n pl **curiosities**, **curiously** adv

curl v **1** to form a curved or spiral shape, or to make something do this ♦ The snake curled itself round a branch. **2** to move in a curve or spiral ♦ Smoke curled upwards. **curl** n **1** a piece of hair that curves round ♦ His hair is a mass of red curls. **2** something in a curved or spiral shape ♦ a curl of smoke **3** a curling movement **curly** adj **curlier**, **curliest**, **curliness** n **curling** n a game played with large flat round stones which are sent along ice

currant n **1** the dried fruit of a small seedless grape **2** a small round red, white, or black berry ◊ Do not confuse this word with current, which has a different meaning.

currency n pl **currencies 1** the money in use in a particular country **2** the state of being in common or general use ♦ The rumour soon gained currency.

current adj **1** belonging to the present time, happening now ♦ See the current issue of the magazine. **2** in general circulation or use ♦ This term is no longer current. **current** n **1** water or air flowing or moving in a certain direction **2** the flow of electricity through something or along a wire or cable ◊ Do not confuse this word with currant, which has a different meaning. **currently** adv **current affairs** pl n political events in the news at the present time

curriculum (say kə-**rik**-yoo-ləm) *n pl* **curricula** a course of study in a school or university **curriculum vitae** *n pl* **curricula vitae** a brief account of someone's education, qualifications, previous jobs, etc.

curried *adj* (said about food) flavoured with hot-tasting spices

curry¹ *n pl* **curries** a dish of meat, vegetables, etc. cooked in a sauce made with hot-tasting spices **curry powder** *n* a mixture of ground-up spices, used for making curry

curry² *v* **curries, curried, currying to curry favour** to try to win favour by flattering someone

curse *n* **1** a prayer or appeal to a supernatural power for someone to be harmed **2** the harm resulting from this **3** something very unpleasant or harmful ♦ *the curse of poverty* **4** a swear word **curse** *v* **1** to put a curse on someone **2** to use swear words **cursed** *adj*

cursor *n* an indicator, usually a flashing light or line, on a computer screen

cursory (say **ker**-ser-i) *adj* hasty and not thorough ♦ *a cursory inspection* **cursorily** *adv*

curt *adj* noticeably or rudely brief ♦ *a curt reply* **curtly** *adv* **curtness** *n*

curtail *v* to cut something short, to reduce something ♦ *I had to curtail my visit.* **curtailment** *n*

curtain *n* **1** a piece of cloth hung up at a window **2** the large cloth screen hung at the front of a stage **curtain** *v* to provide or shut something off with a curtain or curtains **curtain call** *n* applause calling for an actor, singer, etc. to take a bow after a performance

curtsy *n pl* **curtsies** a movement of respect made by a woman or girl, putting one foot behind the other and bending the knees **curtsy** *v* **curtsies, curtsied, curtsying** to make a curtsy

curve *n* **1** a line or surface of which no part is straight or flat **2** a line on a graph showing how one quantity varies in relation to another **curve** *v* **1** to have a curved shape or move in a curve ♦ *The road curves to the left.* **2** to bend something so that it forms a curve **curvaceous** *adj* (said about a woman) having an attractively curved figure **curvature** *n* the state of being curved; the curved shape that something has ♦ *the curvature of the earth* **curvy** *adj*

cushion *n* **1** a bag of cloth filled with soft material, used to make a seat more comfortable **2** anything soft or springy that supports something or protects against jarring ♦ *A hovercraft travels on a cushion of air.* **3** the elastic border round a billiard table **cushion** *v* **1** to lessen the effect of an impact or blow ♦ *Luckily a pile of boxes cushioned his fall.* **2** to protect something from the effects of something harmful

cushy *adj* **cushier, cushiest** *informal* easy and pleasant ♦ *a cushy job*

cusp *n* **1** a pointed end where two curves meet, e.g. the tips of a crescent moon **2** (in astrology) the time when one sign of the zodiac ends and the next begins **3** the point at which one state ends and another begins

cuss *v* *informal* to swear or curse **cuss** *n* *informal* **1** a swear word or curse **2** a difficult person ♦ *an awkward cuss*

custard *n* **1** a sweet yellow sauce made with milk **2** a pudding made with beaten eggs and milk

custody *n* **1** the right or duty of taking care of something, guardianship ♦ *in safe custody* **2** the legal responsibility to look after a child, given to one or other of the parents following a divorce ♦ *Custody was awarded to the mother.* **3** imprisonment **custodial** *adj* **custodian** *n*

custom *n* **1** an activity, ceremony, etc. that is traditional and part of the way of life of a particular society ♦ *Our customs can seem strange to foreigners.* **2** something that you usually do ♦ *It was his custom to take a walk every morning.* **3** the regular business from customers ♦ *We've lost a lot of custom since the hypermarket opened.* **customs** *pl n* taxes (called *duties*) charged by the government on goods imported from other countries **Customs** *pl n* **1** the government department dealing with taxes on goods imported from other countries **2** the area at a port or airport where Customs officials examine goods and baggage brought into a country **customary** adj **customarily** adv **customer** n **1** a person who buys goods or services from a shop or business **2** a person you have to deal with ♦ *He's a tough customer.* **customize** v **custom-built** adj made according to a customer's order

cut v past tense and past participle **cut**, **cutting 1** to divide, shorten, or remove something with a knife, scissors, or other sharp instrument ♦ *I'll cut some bread.* **2** to wound or puncture something ♦ *She cut her finger on a piece of glass.* **3** to be able to cut or to be cut easily ♦ *The cake cut beautifully.* ♦ *The knife doesn't cut.* **4** to reduce something or remove part of it ♦ *The government has promised to cut taxes.* **5** to cross or intersect something ♦ *The line cuts the circle at two points.* **6** to go by a shorter route ♦ *They reached the gate by cutting across the grass.* **7** to switch off an engine or machine, or a source of power **8** to lift and turn up part of a pack of cards, often to decide which player will deal **9** in computing and word-processing, to delete part of a file or document **10** in a film, to move to another shot or scene ♦ *The camera cut to a view of the mountains.* **11** to offend someone, or to ignore someone you know **12** to miss an event or commitment deliberately ♦ *She cut all her classes that morning.* **13** in cricket and other games, to hit the ball with a chopping movement **cut** n **1** an act of cutting **2** a division or wound made by cutting **3** a reduction or stoppage ♦ *There will be cuts in the local bus service.* ♦ *Did you have a power cut?* **4** the removal of part of a play, film, piece of music, or other work **5** *informal* a share of money or profits **6** a piece of meat cut from the carcass of an animal **7** the style in which clothes have been made **8** a stroke with a sword, whip, or cane **9** a hurtful or insulting remark **10** (in cricket and other games) a stroke made by cutting the ball **cutter** n **cutting** n **cuttingly** adv **cutlet** n a piece of meat **cutaway** adj (said about a diagram or plan) having some parts left out to show the interior construction or workings **cutback** n a reduction or saving ♦ *There*

have been cutbacks in library services. **cut glass** n glass with designs cut into it after it has been blown and has hardened **cut-off** n the point at which something is cut off or is no longer valid or permitted **cut-out** n **1** a shape or figure that has been cut out of something ♦ *a cardboard cut-out* **2** a device that cuts off a supply or stops a machine working, usually for safety reasons **cut-price** adj for sale at a reduced price ♦ *cut-price holiday deals* **cut and dried** already decided, and difficult to change **to cut and paste** (in computing and word-processing) to delete part of a file or document and insert it at another point **to cut in 1** to interrupt a conversation **2** in driving a vehicle, to return too soon to your own side of the road after overtaking another vehicle **to cut something back 1** to reduce something **2** to remove parts of something that is growing **to cut something down 1** to reduce something or use less of it **2** to remove or destroy something that is growing

cute adj **1** attractive in a pretty or quaint way ♦ *What a cute little dog.* **2** clever or ingenious **cutely** adv **cuteness** n

cuticle (say **kyoo**-ti-kəl) n the dead skin at the lower part of a fingernail or toenail

cutlass (say **kut**-ləs) n a short sword with a slightly curved blade, like those once used by sailors

cutlery (say **kut**-lə-ri) n knives, forks, and spoons used for eating at a meal

CV abbr curriculum vitae

cyan (say **siy**-ən) n a greenish-blue colour

cyanide (say **siy**-ə-niyd) n a highly poisonous chemical which is a salt or ester of hydrocyanic acid

cyber- (say **siy**-ber) combining form relating to the Internet and virtual reality **cybernetics** n the science of communication and control in machines (e.g. computers) and in animals (e.g. by the nervous system) **cybernetic** adj **cyberspace** n the imagined world in which communication between computers and on the Internet is described as occurring

cybercafe (say **siy**-bə-ka-fay) n ICT an Internet cafe

cycle *n* **1** a series of events that are regularly repeated in the same order ♦ *the cycle of the seasons* **2** one complete occurrence of a continually recurring process **3** a complete set or series, e.g. of songs or poems **4** short for *bicycle* **cycle** *v* to ride a bicycle **cyclic** *adj* **cyclical** *adj* **cyclically** *adv* **cyclist** *n*

cycloid (say **siy**-kloid) *n* the curve traced by a point on a circle rolling along a straight line

cyclone (say siy-**klohn**) *n* **1** a system of winds rotating round a calm central area; a depression **2** a violent tropical storm **cyclonic** *adj*

cygnet (say **sig**-nit) *n* a young swan

cylinder *n* **1** a solid or hollow object with straight sides and circular ends **2** a machine part shaped like this, especially the chamber in which a piston moves in an engine **3** a cylindrical container for gas in liquid form under pressure **cylindrical** *adj*

cymbal *n* a percussion instrument consisting of a metal plate that is hit to make a ringing sound ◊ Do not confuse this word with *symbol*, which has a different meaning.

cynic (say **sin**-ik) *n* a person who believes that people's reasons for doing things are always selfish and dishonest, and shows this by sneering at them **cynical** *adj* **cynically** *adv* **cynicism** *n* ◊ See the note at *sceptic.*

cypress *n* a coniferous evergreen tree with dark feathery leaves

cyst (say sist) *n* an abnormal swelling formed in or on the body, containing fluid or soft matter **cystic** *adj*

cytology (say siy-**tol**-əji) *n* the scientific study of biological cells **cytological** *adj*

czar (say zar) *n* another spelling of *tsar*

Czech (say chek) *adj* to do with or coming from the Czech Republic or the former country of Czechoslovakia **Czech** *n* **1** a person born in the Czech Republic or Czechoslovakia or descended from people born there **2** the language of Czechoslovakia or the Czech Republic

Dd

D 1 the fourth letter of the English alphabet **2** *Mus* the second note of the diatonic scale of C major **3** the Roman numeral for 500

dab *n* **1** a quick gentle touch, usually with something wet **2** a small amount of a soft substance applied to a surface ♦ *a dab of paint* **dab** *v* **dabbed, dabbing 1** to touch something lightly or quickly **2** to apply something to a surface with quick light strokes

dabble *v* **1** to splash in water **2** (said about a duck or water bird) to move its bill around in shallow water **dabbler** *n* **dab hand** *n* a person who is an expert at doing something **to dabble in** to study or work at something casually ♦ *I dabble in astronomy.*

dachshund (say **daks**-huund) *n* a small dog with a long body and very short legs

dad *n informal* father

Dada (say **dah**-dah) *n* an international movement in art and literature in the early 20th century

daddy *n pl* **daddies** *informal* father **daddy-long-legs** *n* a crane fly

dado (say **day**-doh) *n pl* **dados** the lower part of the wall of a room or corridor when it is coloured or decorated differently from the upper part

daffodil *n* a yellow flower with a trumpet-shaped central part

daft *adj informal* silly or foolish

dagger *n* a short pointed two-edged knife used as a weapon

daguerreotype (say də-**ge**-rə-tiyp) *n* an early kind of photograph taken on a silver-coated copper plate

dahlia (say **day**-liə) *n* a garden plant with large brightly-coloured flowers

Dáil (say doil) *n* (in full **Dáil éireann** (say doil **air**-ən)) the lower House of Parliament in the Republic of Ireland

dainty *adj* **daintier, daintiest 1** small, delicate, and pretty **2** fastidious, especially about food **daintily** *adv* **daintiness** *n*

dairy *n pl* **dairies 1** a room or building

where milk, butter, etc. are processed **2** a shop where these are sold **dairy** adj **1** containing or made from milk **2** to do with the production of milk ♦ *dairy farming*

dairymaid n a woman employed in a dairy

dais (say **day**-iss) n a low platform, especially at one end of a room or hall

daisy n pl **daisies** a flower with many white petal-like rays surrounding a yellow centre

Dalai Lama (say dal-iy **lah**-mə) n the spiritual leader of Tibetan Buddhists

dale n a valley, especially in north England

dally v **dallies**, **dallied**, **dallying 1** to dawdle or waste time **2** to show a casual interest in something **3** to flirt **dalliance** n

Dalmatian (say dal-**may**-shən) n a large white dog with dark spots

dam[1] n **1** a barrier built across a river, etc. to hold back water **2** a barrier of branches in a stream made by a beaver to provide a deep pool and a lodge **dam** v **dammed**, **damming 1** to hold water back with a dam **2** to obstruct a flow

dam[2] n the mother of a four-footed animal

damage n something done or suffered that reduces the value or usefulness of a thing or spoils its appearance **damages** pl n a sum of money paid as compensation for an injury or loss **damage** v to cause damage to something

dame n **1** (**Dame**) the title of a woman who has been awarded an order of knighthood (corresponding to the title of *Sir* for a knight) **2** a comic female character in pantomime, usually played by a man **3** *informal* a woman

damn v **1** to condemn someone to eternal punishment in hell **2** to condemn something as a failure **3** to swear at someone or curse them **damn** interjection an exclamation of anger or annoyance **damnable** adj hateful or annoying **damnably** adv **damnation** n **damned** adj

damp adj slightly wet, not quite dry **damp** n moisture in the air, on a surface, or throughout something **damp** v **1** to make something slightly wet **2** to discourage or reduce the strength of something ♦ *The defeat damped their enthusiasm.* **3** to reduce the vibration of the strings of a

musical instrument **dampen** v **1** to ~~something damp **2** to reduce the str~~ of something **damper** n **1** a felt pad that presses against a piano string to stop it vibrating **2** a metal plate that can be moved to increase or decrease the flow of air into the fire in a stove or furnace **damply** adv **dampness** n **damp course** n a layer of waterproof material built into a wall near the ground to prevent damp from rising

damsel (say **dam**-zəl) n old use a young unmarried woman

damson n a small dark purple plum, and the tree that bears it

dance v **1** to move with rhythmical steps or movements, usually to music **2** to perform a particular dance ♦ *We learnt to dance the tango.* **3** to move in a quick or lively way **dance** n **1** a piece of dancing **2** a piece of music for dancing to **3** a party or gathering where people dance **dancer** n

dandelion n a wild plant with bright yellow flowers and jagged leaves

dandle v to move a baby or young child up and down on your knee

dandruff n tiny white flakes of dead skin on the scalp and in the hair

dandy n pl **dandies** a man who pays too much attention to his appearance **dandy** adj **dandier**, **dandiest** informal excellent

Dane n a person born in Denmark or descended from people born there **Danish** adj to do with or coming from Denmark **Danish** n the Scandinavian language of Denmark **Danish pastry** n a cake of sweet yeast pastry filled or topped with fruit or icing

danger n **1** the possibility of suffering harm or death **2** something that is not safe or could harm you **3** the possibility of something unpleasant happening ♦ *There's a danger they might be sold out.* **dangerous** adj likely to kill or harm you **dangerously** adv

dangle v **1** to hang or swing loosely **2** to hold or carry something so that it swings loosely

dank adj unpleasantly damp, cold, and musty

dapper adj dressed neatly and smartly ♦ *a*

dapper little man

dapple v to mark something with spots or patches of shade or a different colour

dare v 1 to be brave enough to do something ♦ *He didn't dare go.* 2 to challenge a person to do something risky **dare** n a challenge to do something risky **daren't** v dare not

daring adj **daringly** adv **daredevil** n a person who enjoys doing dangerous things

dark adj 1 with little or no light 2 (said about a colour) of a deep shade closer to black than to white ♦ *dark grey* 3 (said about people) having a brown or black skin; having dark hair 4 involving misery or suffering ♦ *the long dark years of the war* 5 mysterious ♦ *a dark secret* 6 remote and unexplored 7 evil or sinister ♦ *dark deeds* **dark** n 1 absence of light 2 a time of darkness, night or nightfall ♦ *Don't stay out after dark.* 3 a dark colour **darken** v **darkly** adv **darkness** n **Dark Ages** pl n the early part of the Middle Ages in Europe (about 500-1100) **darkroom** n a room kept dark for developing photographs

dark horse n someone who might do surprisingly well, e.g. in a race or competition, because they have unexpected abilities

darling n someone who is loved very much **darling** adj 1 dearly loved 2 pretty or charming

darn v to mend a hole by weaving threads across it **darn** n a place mended by darning **darning** n

dart n 1 a small metal-tipped object thrown in the game of darts 2 a small pointed missile thrown or fired as a weapon 3 a darting movement 4 a tapering stitched tuck in a piece of clothing **darts** n an indoor game in which darts are thrown at a dartboard **dart** v 1 to move suddenly or rapidly 2 to send something out rapidly ♦ *She darted an angry look at him.* **dartboard** n

Darwinism n the theory of the evolution of species by natural selection, put forward by the English naturalist Charles Darwin (1809-82)

dash v 1 to run rapidly 2 to knock or throw a thing with great force against something

♦ *He dashed the plate to the floor.* 3 to destroy or frustrate something ♦ *Our hopes were dashed.* **dash** n 1 a short rapid run, a rush ♦ *We made a dash for the door.* 2 a small amount of liquid or flavouring added ♦ *Add a dash of cream.* 3 the punctuation mark (-) used to mark a pause or to show that letters or words are missing 4 a dashboard 5 confidence and style ♦ *She plays with real dash.* 6 the longer of the two signals used in Morse code **dashing** adj **dashboard** n a panel with instruments and controls in front of the driver of a vehicle

dastardly adj old use wicked and cruel

DAT abbr digital audiotape

data (say **day-t**ə) pl n facts or information used as a basis for discussing or deciding something, or prepared for being processed by a computer, etc. ◊ Strictly speaking, this word is a plural noun (the singular is *datum*), so it should be used with a plural verb: *Here are the data.* However, the word is widely used nowadays as if it were a singular noun and most people do not regard this as wrong: *Here is the data.*

datum n pl **data** 1 an item of information, a unit of data 2 the starting point from which something is measured or calculated

data processing n the performance of operations on data, especially using a computer, to obtain or classify information

data protection n the process of ensuring that data stored in computers cannot be accessed except by people who are legally authorized to do so **databank** n a large store of computerized data **database** n a structured store of computerized data

data capture n the process of putting data into a form that is accessible by computer

datum line n a set horizontal line from which measurements are taken

date¹ n 1 the day of the month or year expressed by a number 2 a day or year when something happened or will happen ♦ *We don't know the exact date of the battle.* 3 the period to which something belongs ♦ *What date are these ruins?* 4 informal an appointment to meet someone socially 5 informal a person you have a date with **date** v 1 to mark something with a date

♦ *Is the letter dated?* **2** to give a date to something ♦ *Experts have been trying to date the fossil.* **3** to have existed from a particular date ♦ *The custom dates from Victorian times.* **4** to show signs of becoming out of date ♦ *Some fashions date quickly.* **5** *informal* to go on a date with someone **datable** *adj* able to be dated to a particular time **dated** *adj* **Date Line** *n* a line from north to south roughly along the meridian 180° from Greenwich, to the east of which the date is a day earlier than it is to the west

date[2] *n* the small brown sweet edible fruit of the **date palm**, a palm-tree of North Africa and SW Asia

daub *v* to coat, paint, or smear something roughly with a thick substance **daub** *n* **1** a clumsily-painted picture **2** a covering or smear of a thick substance

daughter *n* **1** a female child in relation to her parents **2** a female descendant ♦ *daughters of Eve* **daughter-in-law** *v pl* **daughters-in-law** a son's wife

daunt *v* to make someone afraid or discouraged ♦ *She didn't seem daunted by the challenge ahead.* **daunting** *adj* **dauntless** *adj* **dauntlessly** *adv*

dauphin (say **daw-**fin) *n* eldest son of the king of France

dawdle *v* to walk slowly and idly, to take your time **dawdler** *n*

dawn *n* **1** the first light of the day just before sunrise **2** the beginning of something ♦ *the dawn of civilization* **dawn** *v* **1** to begin to grow light in the morning **2** to begin to appear or become evident ♦ *The truth dawned on them.* **dawning** *n*

day *n* **1** the time during which the sun is above the horizon **2** a period of 24 hours, especially from one midnight to the next **3** the hours given to work ♦ *She works an eight-hour day.* **4** a period of time in the past or in a person's life ♦ *in Queen Victoria's day* **daily** *adj* **daybreak** *n* the first light of day, dawn **day centre** *n* a place where facilities are provided for elderly or handicapped people during the day **daydream** *n* pleasant thoughts of something you would like to happen **daydream** *v* past tense and past participle **daydreamed** to have a daydream

daylight *n* **1** the natural light of day **2** dawn **day return** *n* a ticket sold at a reduced rate for a return journey in one day **day room** *n* a shared living room in a school, hospital, etc. **daytime** *n* the time of daylight

daze *v* to make someone feel stunned or bewildered **daze** *n* a dazed state ♦ *in a daze*

dazzle *v* **1** to make someone unable to see clearly because of too much bright light **2** to amaze and impress or confuse someone by a splendid display **dazzle** *n* blinding brightness

dB *abbr* decibel(s)

DBE *abbr* Dame Commander of the Order of the British Empire

DC *abbr* direct current

D-Day *n* **1** the day (6 June 1944) on which British and American forces invaded northern France in the Second World War **2** the date on which an important operation is planned to begin

DDT *n* an insecticide

de- *prefix* **1** removing (as in *defrost*) **2** down, away (as in *descend*) **3** completely (as in *denude*)

deacon *n* **1** a member of the clergy ranking below a priest **2** a lay person attending to church business in Nonconformist Churches

deaconess *n* a woman with duties similar to those of a deacon

deactivate *v* to make a machine or device stop working ♦ *had forgotten to deactivate the alarm*

dead *adj* **1** no longer alive **2** numb, without feeling ♦ *My fingers have gone dead.* **3** no longer used ♦ *a dead language* **4** no longer active or functioning ♦ *The microphone went dead.* **5** not lively or interesting ♦ *The town is dead on Sundays.* **6** (said about a ball in games) out of play **7** complete, abrupt, exact ♦ *dead silence* ♦ *a dead stop* **dead** *adv* **1** completely, exactly ♦ *dead drunk* ♦ *dead level* **2** *informal* very ♦ *I'm dead sorry.* **deaden** *v* **deadly** *adj* **deadlier, deadliest 1** likely to kill ♦ *a deadly poison* **2** extremely accurate or effective ♦ *He has a deadly right foot.* **3** *informal* very boring **deadly** *adv* **1** as if dead ♦ *deadly pale* **2** extremely ♦ *I'm deadly serious.* **deadliness** *n* **dead**

end n the closed end of a road or passage
dead-end job n a job with no prospects of advancement **dead heat** n the result of a race in which two or more competitors finish exactly level **dead leg** n an injury caused by a numbing blow to a person's upper leg **deadline** n the latest time or date by which something should be completed **deadlock** n a situation in which no progress can be made **deadlock** v to reach a deadlock; to cause something to do this ♦ *The negotiations are deadlocked.* **deadly nightshade** n a plant with poisonous black berries **dead march** n a funeral march **deadpan** adj, adv with an expressionless face **dead weight** n a heavy inert weight
deaf adj 1 wholly or partly without the sense of hearing 2 refusing to listen ♦ *He was deaf to all advice.* **deafen** v **deafening** adj **deafness** n **deaf aid** n a hearing aid **deaf mute** n a person who is deaf and unable to speak ◊ This term can cause offence and should be avoided. Use *profoundly deaf* instead.
deal[1] v past tense and past participle **dealt** 1 to give out cards to players in a card game 2 to hand something out to several people 3 to do business, to trade in something ♦ *He deals in scrap metal.* 4 to give or inflict something ♦ *His father's death dealt him a severe blow.* **deal** n 1 a business transaction or other agreement ♦ *The deal fell through.* 2 treatment ♦ *Working mothers don't get a fair deal.* 3 a player's turn to deal at cards ♦ *Whose deal is it?* **dealer** n **dealings** pl n
deal[2] n sawn fir or pine timber
dean n 1 a member of the clergy who is head of a cathedral chapter 2 a member of the clergy with authority over a group of parishes 3 the head of a university, college, or department **deanery** n pl **deaneries**
dear adj 1 loved very much 2 a polite greeting in letters ♦ *Dear Sir.* 3 expensive **dear** n a dear person **dear** adv at a high cost ♦ *It cost us dear.* **dear** interjection an exclamation of surprise, sympathy, or distress **dearly** adv **dearness** n
dearth (say derth) n a scarcity or lack of something
death n 1 the process of dying, the end of

life 2 the state of being dead 3 the ending or destruction of something ♦ *the death of our hopes* **deathless** adj immortal **deathly** adj, adv like death ♦ *a deathly hush* ♦ *deathly pale* **deathbed** n the bed on which a person dies or is dying **death certificate** n an official statement of the date, place, and cause of a person's death **death duty** n tax levied on property after the owner's death. It is now called *inheritance tax* **death penalty** n punishment for a crime by being put to death **death rate** n the number of deaths in one year for every 1000 people **death row** n a prison area housing prisoners sentenced to death **death toll** n the number of deaths resulting from a particular cause **death trap** n a dangerous place or situation
debacle (say day-bahkl) n an utter failure or disaster
debar v **debarred**, **debarring** to forbid or ban someone from doing something ♦ *He was debarred from the contest.*
debark v to leave a ship or aircraft **debarkation** n
debase v to reduce the quality or value of something **debasement** n
debate n 1 a formal discussion 2 an argument **debate** v 1 to hold a debate about a subject 2 to discuss or consider something **debatable** adj **debatably** adv
debauch (say di-bawch) v to destroy a person's moral purity, to lead them into debauchery **debauched** adj **debauchery** n
debility n weakness of the body **debilitate** v
debit n 1 an entry in an account of a sum owed 2 the sum itself **debit** v **debited**, **debiting** to enter something as a debit in an account, to remove money from an account **debit card** n a card that allows you to pay for things electronically
debonair (say deb-ən-air) adj having a carefree self-confident manner
debrief v to question someone in order to obtain information about a mission just completed **debriefing** n
debris (say deb-ree) n scattered broken pieces or remains
debt (say det) n something owed by one person to another **debtor** n **in debt** owing

money **to be in someone's debt** to owe gratitude to someone for a favour

debug v **debugged**, **debugging** 1 ICT to remove errors from a program or system 2 to remove concealed listening devices from a room 3 Amer. to remove insects from something

debunk v to show up a claim or theory, or a person's reputation, as exaggerated or false

debut (say **day**-bew) n the first public appearance of an actor or other performer **debutant** n **debutante** n

Dec. abbr December

deca- prefix ten (as in decathlon)

decade (say **dek**-ayd) n a period of ten years

decadent (say **dek**-ə-dənt) adj 1 falling to a lower standard of morality 2 luxuriously self-indulgent **decadence** n

decaffeinated (say di-**kaf**-in-ayt-id) adj (said about coffee or tea) with the caffeine removed

decagon n a geometric figure with ten sides **decagonal** adj

decamp v to go away suddenly or secretly

decant (say di-**kant**) v to pour liquid gently from one container into another **decanter** n

decapitate (say di-**kap**-it-ayt) v to cut someone's head off **decapitation** n

decarbonize v to remove the carbon deposit from an engine, etc. **decarbonization** n

decathlon (say dik-**ath**-lən) n an athletic contest in which each competitor takes part in ten events

decay v 1 to rot or cause something to rot 2 to lose quality or strength **decay** n 1 the state or process of decaying 2 decayed matter or tissue 3 radioactive change

decease (say di-**seess**) n formal death **deceased** adj **the deceased** the person who died recently

deceive v 1 to make someone believe something that is not true 2 to give someone a mistaken impression **deceit** n **deceitful** adj **deceitfully** adv **deceitfulness** n **deceiver** n

decelerate (say dee-**sel**-er-ayt) v to decrease your speed **deceleration** n

December n the twelfth month of the year

decent adj 1 conforming to the accepted standards of what is moral or proper, not immodest or obscene 2 respectable and honest ♦ ordinary decent people 3 quite good, satisfactory ♦ She earns a decent salary. 4 informal kind and generous ♦ That's very decent of you. **decency** n **decently** adv

decentralize v to divide and distribute powers, etc. from a central authority **decentralization** n

deception n 1 deceiving; being deceived 2 something that deceives people **deceptive** adj **deceptively** adv

deci- prefix one tenth part, as in decigram, decilitre

decibel (say **dess**-i-bəl) n a unit for measuring the loudness of sound

decide v 1 to make up your mind; to come to a decision 2 to settle a contest or argument by giving victory to one side ♦ A late goal decided the match. 3 to cause someone to reach a decision ♦ These letters of support decided me. **decided** adj **decidedly** adv **decider** n

deciduous (say di-**sid**-yoo-əs) adj (said about a tree) shedding its leaves annually

decimal (say **dess**-im-əl) adj expressed or calculated in tens or tenths **decimal** n a decimal fraction **decimalize** v **decimalization** n **decimal currency** n a currency in which each unit is ten or one hundred times the value of the one next below it **decimal fraction** n a fraction whose denominator is a power of 10 **decimal point** n the dot in a decimal fraction **decimal system** n a system of weights and measures with each unit ten times that immediately below it

decimal place n the position of a digit to the right of the decimal point in a decimal fraction

decimate (say **dess**-im-ayt) v 1 to kill or destroy a large proportion of something 2 to reduce the strength of something drastically **decimation** n

decipher (say di-**siy**-fer) v 1 to make out the meaning of a coded message 2 to succeed in understanding something that is unclear **decipherment** n

decision n 1 deciding, making a reasoned judgement about something 2 what you have decided 3 the ability to form clear opinions and act on them **decisive** adj **decisively** adv

deck n 1 any of the horizontal floors in a ship 2 a similar floor or platform, especially one of two or more ♦ the top deck of a bus 3 a pack of playing cards 4 a platform for a record or cd player **deck** v to decorate something with bright and colourful decorations, to dress something up ♦ The house was decked out with balloons. **deckchair** n

declaim (say di-**klaym**) v to speak or say something impressively or dramatically **declamation** n **declamatory** adj

declare v 1 to say something clearly or firmly ♦ He declares that he is innocent. 2 to tell customs officials that you have goods on which you ought to pay duty ♦ Do you have anything to declare? 3 to announce something openly, formally, or explicitly **declaration** n **declarative** adj **declaratory** adj

decline v 1 to politely refuse ♦ She reluctantly declined the offer. 2 to become weaker or smaller ♦ in her declining years 3 (said about the sun) to move downwards 4 Gram to give the forms of a noun, pronoun, or adjective that correspond to its cases, number, and gender **decline** n a gradual decrease or loss of strength **declination** n 1 the angle between the true north and the magnetic north 2 (in astronomy) the angle between the direction of a star, etc. and the celestial equator

decode v 1 to put a coded message into plain language 2 to translate coded characters in a computer **decoder** n

decommission v to take a ship or piece of equipment out of service

decompose v 1 to decay, or to make something decay 2 to separate a substance into its elements **decomposition** n

decompress v 1 ICT to expand compressed data to the normal size 2 to subject a diver to decompression **decompression** n

decongestant (say dee-kən-**jest**-ənt) n a medicinal substance that relieves a blocked nose

decontaminate v to get rid of poisonous chemicals or radioactive material from a place, clothes, etc. **decontamination** n

decor (say **day**-kor) n the style of furnishings and decoration used in a room

decorate v 1 to make something look more attractive or colourful by adding objects or details to it 2 to put fresh paint or wallpaper on walls 3 to give someone a medal or other award **decoration** n **decorative** adj **decoratively** adv **decorator** n

decorum (say di-**kor**-əm) n polite and dignified behaviour **decorous** adj polite and dignified **decorously** adv

decoy[1] (say **dee**-koi) n a person or thing used to lure a person or animal into a trap or into danger

decoy[2] (say di-**koi**) v to lure a person or animal by means of a decoy

decrease v to make something or become shorter, smaller, or fewer **decrease** n 1 decreasing 2 the amount by which something decreases

decree n 1 an order given by a government or other authority 2 a judgement or decision of certain law courts **decree** v **decreed**, **decreeing** to order something by decree

decrepit (say di-**krep**-it) adj 1 old and weak 2 worn out by long use **decrepitude** n

decriminalize v to stop treating something as a crime **decriminalization** n

decry (say di-**kriy**) v **decries**, **decried**, **decrying** to disparage something

dedicate v 1 to devote your time, energy, and loyalty to a special purpose ♦ She has dedicated her life to animals. 2 to devote a church or other building to a sacred person or use ♦ This church is dedicated to St Peter. 3 to address a book or piece of music, etc. to a person **dedicated** adj **dedication** n **dedicator** n

deduce (say di-**dewss**) v to work something out by reasoning from observed facts **deducible** adj **deductive** adj

deduct v to take away an amount or quantity, to subtract something **deductible** adj **deduction** n

deed n 1 something that someone has

done, an act **2** a legal document, especially one giving ownership or rights

deem v formal to consider or judge something ♦ The concert was deemed a great success.

deep adj **1** going or situated far down or back or in ♦ a deep well ♦ a deep cut **2** measured from top to bottom or front to back ♦ a hole six feet deep **3** intense or strong ♦ a deep sleep **4** (said about colour) dark and intense ♦ deep blue **5** low-pitched and resonant, not shrill ♦ a deep voice **6** fully absorbed or overwhelmed ♦ deep in thought **7** difficult to understand, obscure ♦ That's too deep for me. **8** (in cricket) distant from the batsman **deep** adv deeply, far down or in **deep** n (the deep) a deep place, especially the sea **deepen** v **deeply** adv **deepness** n **deep freeze** n a freezer **deep-freeze** v **deep-froze**, **deep-frozen** to store or freeze something in a deep freeze **deep-fry** v **deep-fries**, **deep-fried**, **deep-frying** to fry food in fat that covers it **deep-seated** adj firmly established, not superficial ♦ a deep-seated distrust **deep space** n the far distant regions beyond the earth's atmosphere or those beyond the solar system

deer n pl **deer** a fast-running graceful animal, the male of which usually has antlers

deface v to spoil or damage the surface of something, e.g. by scribbling on it **defacement** n

de facto (say dee **fak**-toh) adj existing in fact, whether by right or not ♦ a de facto ruler

defame (say di-**faym**) v to attack or damage a person's good reputation **defamation** n **defamatory** adj

default v to fail to do what you have agreed to do, especially to pay back a loan **default** n **1** failure to do something, especially to pay back a loan **2** a pre-selected option adopted by a computer program when no alternative is specified **defaulter** n

defeat v **1** to win a victory over someone **2** to baffle someone or be too difficult for them ♦ The problem completely defeated me. **3** to prevent something from being

achieved ♦ This defeats the object of the exercise. **defeat** n **1** defeating someone **2** being defeated; a lost battle or contest **defeatism** n **defeatist** n

defecate (say **def**-ik-ayt) v formal to get rid of waste matter from your body **defecation** n

defect[1] (say di-**fekt** or **dee**-fekt) n a flaw or deficiency **defective** adj **defectively** adv **defectiveness** n

defect[2] (say di-**fekt**) v to abandon your country or cause in favour of another one **defection** n **defector** n

defence n **1** defending something from or resistance against attack **2** something that defends or protects against attack **3** a justification put forward in response to an accusation **4** the defendant's case in a lawsuit **5** the lawyers representing an accused person **6** the players in a defending position in a game **defenceless** adj **defend** v **defendant** n **defender** n **defensible** adj **defensibly** adv **defensive** adj **defensively** adv

defer[1] v **deferred**, **deferring** to put something off to a later time, to postpone something **deferment** n

defer[2] v **deferred**, **deferring** to give way to a person's wishes, judgement, or authority **deference** n **deferential** adj **deferentially** adv **in deference to** out of respect for

defiance n open disobedience, bold resistance **defiant** adj **defiantly** adv

deficient (say di-**fish**-ənt) adj **1** not having enough of a quality or ingredient ♦ This diet is deficient in vitamin B. **2** insufficient or inadequate **deficiency** n pl **deficiencies**

deficit (say **def**-i-sit) n the amount by which a total is smaller than what is required

defile (say di-**fiyl**) v to make something dirty or impure, to pollute something **defilement** n

define v **1** to give the meaning of a word or phrase **2** to state or explain the scope of something ♦ Customers' rights are defined by law. **3** to show clearly the outline of something ♦ a well-defined image **4** to mark out the boundary or limits of something **definable** adj **definite** adj **definitely** adv

definition n **1** a statement of what a word or phrase means or what a thing is **2** clearness of outline, especially of a photographic image ♦ *The faces lack definition.* **definitive** adj **1** finally fixing or settling something, decisive ♦ *a definitive answer* **2** the most authoritative of its kind, not able to be bettered ♦ *the definitive history of French cinema* **definite article** n the word 'the'

deflate v **1** to let air or gas out of an inflated tyre, balloon, etc. **2** to make someone lose confidence or self-esteem **3** to reduce or reverse inflation in a country's economy, e.g. by reducing the amount of money in circulation **deflation** n **deflationary** adj

deflect v to make something turn aside **deflection** n **deflector** n

deforest v to clear away the trees from an area **deforestation** n

deform v to spoil the form or appearance of something, to put it out of shape **deformation** n **deformed** adj **deformity** n pl **deformities**

defraud v to get money from someone by fraud

defray v to provide money to pay costs or expenses **defrayal** n

defrost v **1** to thaw something out from frozen ♦ *The pie needs to be defrosted.* **2** to remove frost or ice from something ♦ *I've been defrosting the fridge.*

deft adj skilful and quick, handling things neatly **deftly** adv **deftness** n

defunct (say di-**funkt**) adj no longer existing or functioning

defuse v **1** to remove the fuse from a bomb so that it cannot explode **2** to make a situation less dangerous or tense

defy v **defies**, **defied**, **defying** **1** to resist something openly, to refuse to obey someone **2** to challenge a person to try and do something that you believe cannot be done ♦ *I defy you to prove this.* **3** to offer difficulties that cannot easily be overcome ♦ *The door defied all attempts to open it.*

degenerate[1] (say di-**jen**-er-ayt) v to become worse or lower in standard; to lose good qualities **degeneration** n

degenerate[2] (say di-**jen**-er-ət) adj having

become immoral or bad **degenerate** n a morally degenerate person **degeneracy** n

degrade v **1** to humiliate or dishonour someone **2** *Chem* to cause something to break down chemically or to decompose **3** *Phys* to reduce energy to a less easily convertible form **degradable** adj **degradation** n **degrading** adj

degree n **1** a stage in intensity or amount ♦ *a high degree of skill* **2** a unit for measuring temperature **3** a unit for measuring angles or arcs, indicated by the symbol °, e.g. 45° **4** a stage in a scale or series ♦ *third-degree burns* **5** an academic rank awarded to a person who has successfully completed a course of study at a university or college

dehumanize v to take away human qualities from someone

dehydrated adj **1** (said about a person) having lost a large amount of water **2** with all moisture removed **dehydration** n

de-ice v to remove ice from a windscreen or other surface **de-icer** n

deign (say dayn) v to do something that you think is below your dignity ♦ *She did not deign to reply.*

deity (say **dee**-iti or **day**-iti) n pl **deities** **1** a god or goddess ♦ *Roman deities.* **2** divine status or nature **deify** v **deifies**, **deified**, **deifying**, **deification** n **deism** n belief in the existence of a god arising from reason **deist** n

déjà vu (say day-zha **vew**) n the feeling that you have already experienced what is happening now

dejected adj sad or depressed **dejectedly** adv **dejection** n

delay v **1** to make someone or something late, or to be late **2** to put something off until later **3** to wait or linger ♦ *Don't delay!* **delay** n **1** delaying, being delayed **2** the amount of time for which something is delayed ♦ *a two-hour delay*

delectation (say dee-lek-**tay**-shən) n formal pleasure or delight ♦ *an evening of song for your delectation* **delectable** adj **delectably** adv

delegate[1] (say **del**-i-gət) n a person who represents others and acts on their instructions **delegation** n

delegate[2] (say **del**-i-gayt) *v* 1 to entrust a task, power, or responsibility to someone else ♦ *I'm going to delegate this job to one of my assistants.* 2 to appoint or send someone as a representative ♦ *James was delegated to meet the visitors.* **delegation** *n*

delete (say di-**leet**) *v* 1 to strike out something written or printed 2 to remove a product from the catalogue of those available to be bought 3 *ICT* to remove data or files stored on a computer **deletion** *n*

deliberate[1] (say di-**lib**-er-ət) *adj* 1 done on purpose, intentional 2 slow and careful, unhurried ♦ *She entered the room with deliberate steps.* **deliberately** *adv*

deliberate[2] (say di-**lib**-er-ayt) *v* to think over or discuss something carefully before reaching a decision **deliberation** *n* **deliberative** *adj*

delicate *adj* 1 fine in texture, slender 2 of exquisite quality or workmanship ♦ *delicate embroidery* 3 (said about colour or flavour) pleasant and subtle 4 becoming ill easily 5 fragile and easily damaged 6 needing tact and careful handling ♦ *a delicate situation* 7 skilful and sensitive ♦ *a player with a delicate touch* **delicacy** *n pl* **delicacies** **delicately** *adv* **delicateness** *n*

delicatessen (say del-i-kə-**tess**-ən) *n* a shop selling cooked meats, cheeses, salads, etc.

delicious *adj* tasting or smelling very pleasant **deliciously** *adv*

delight *v* 1 to please someone greatly 2 to take great pleasure in something ♦ *She delights in giving parties.* **delight** *n* 1 great pleasure 2 a cause of great pleasure **delightful** *adj* **delightfully** *adv*

delimit (say dee-**lim**-it) *v* **delimited**, **delimiting** to fix the limits or boundaries of something **delimitation** *n*

delineate (say di-**lin**-i-ayt) *v* to show something by drawing or describing it **delineation** *n*

delinquent (say di-**link**-wənt) *adj* 1 guilty of committing minor crimes 2 failing to perform a duty **delinquent** *n* a delinquent person, especially a young person who breaks the law **delinquency** *n*

delirium (say di-**li**-ri-əm) *n* 1 a state of mental confusion and agitation, especially during feverish illness 2 wild excitement or emotion **delirious** *adj* **deliriously** *adv*

deliver *v* 1 to take letters, goods, etc. to the person they are addressed to or to the person who has bought them 2 to give a speech or lecture 3 to aim or launch a blow or an attack 4 to rescue someone or set them free 5 to provide something you have promised 6 to help with the birth of a baby 7 to give birth to a child **deliverance** *n* **deliverer** *n* **delivery** *n pl* **deliveries**

dell *n* a small wooded valley

delta *n* 1 the fourth letter of the Greek alphabet, equivalent to Roman *D, d* 2 a fourth-class mark in an examination 3 a triangular area at the mouth of a river where it splits into two or more branches ♦ *the Nile Delta* **deltaic** *adj*

delude (say di-**lood**) *v* to deceive or mislead someone **delusion** *n* **delusional** *adj* **delusive** *adj*

deluge (say **del**-yooj) *n* 1 a great flood 2 a heavy fall of rain 3 anything coming in great numbers or a heavy rush ♦ *a deluge of questions* **the Deluge** the flood in Noah's time **deluge** *v* 1 to come down on someone like a deluge ♦ *The company was deluged with complaints.* 2 to flood a place or region

de luxe *adj* of very high quality, luxurious

delve *v* 1 to reach inside a bag, drawer, etc. and search for something 2 to search deeply for information

demagnetize *v* to remove the magnetic properties from something **demagnetization** *n*

demand *n* 1 a firm or forceful request 2 a desire to have or buy something ♦ *an increase in demand for mobile phones* 3 an urgent claim ♦ *There are many demands on my time.* **demand** *v* 1 to ask for something firmly or forcefully 2 to need something ♦ *The work demands great skill.* **demanding** *adj*

demarcation (say dee-mar-**kay**-shən) *n* fixing the boundary or limits of something

demean *v* to lower a person's dignity ♦ *I wouldn't demean myself to ask for it.*

demeanour *n* the way a person behaves

demented *adj* driven mad, crazy

dementia (say di-**men**-shə) *n* a serious mental disorder that is characterized by memory loss

demerara (say dem-er-**air**-ə) *n* brown raw cane sugar

demerit *n* a fault or defect

demi- *prefix* half (as in *demisemiquaver*)

demigod *n* a partly divine being

demilitarize *v* to remove all military forces from an area ♦ *a demilitarized zone* **demilitarization** *n*

demise (say di-**miyz**) *n* 1 the end or failure of something 2 a person's death

demist *v* to clear misty condensation from a windscreen, etc. **demister** *n*

demo *n pl* **demos** *informal* a demonstration

demobilize *v* to release soldiers, etc. from military service **demob** *v* **demobbed**, **demobbing**, **demobilization** *n*

democracy *n pl* **democracies** 1 government of a country by representatives elected by the whole people 2 a country governed in this way **democrat** *n* **democratic** *adj* **democratically** *adv* **democratize** *v* **democratization** *n*

demography (say di-**mog**-rəfi) *n* the study of statistics of births, deaths, diseases, etc. **demographic** *adj*

demolish *v* 1 to pull or knock down a building 2 to destroy something completely, especially a person's argument or theory, etc. 3 *informal* to eat food up **demolition** *n*

demon (say **dee**-mən) *n* 1 a devil or evil spirit 2 (also **daemon**) a person's spirit or genius 3 a forceful or skilful person ♦ *a demon on the squash court* 4 a naughty, cruel, or destructive person ♦ *She can be a little demon!* **demoniac** *adj* **demonic** *adj* **demonize** *v*

demonstrate *v* 1 to show evidence of something, to prove it 2 to show someone how to do something or how something works 3 to take part in a public demonstration **demonstrable** *adj* **demonstrably** *adv* **demonstration** *n* **demonstrative** *adj* **demonstratively** *adv* **demonstrativeness** *n* **demonstrator** *n*

demoralize *v* to weaken someone's confidence or morale **demoralization** *n*

demote (say dee-**moht**) *v* to give someone a less senior position **demotion** *n*

demure (say di-**mewr**) *adj* shy and modest **demurely** *adv* **demureness** *n*

demystify *v* **demystifies**, **demystified**, **demystifying** to make a subject easier to understand **demystification** *n*

den *n* 1 a wild animal's lair 2 a small room in which a person works or relaxes privately 3 a place where people gather for some illegal activity ♦ *an opium den*

denationalize *v* to transfer an industry from public to private ownership **denationalization** *n*

denigrate (say **den**-i-grayt) *v* to blacken the reputation of someone or something **denigration** *n*

denim *n* a kind of strong, usually blue, cotton cloth used to make jeans, etc. **denims** *pl n* trousers made of denim

denomination *n* 1 a branch of a church or religion ♦ *Baptists and other Protestant denominations.* 2 a unit of money ♦ *coins of small denomination* **denominational** *adj*

denominator *n* the number written below the line in a fraction, e.g. 4 in ¼, showing how many parts the whole is divided into

denote (say di-**noht**) *v* 1 to be the sign of something, to mean or indicate something ♦ *In road signs,* P *denotes a parking place.* 2 (said about a word) to have as its literal or basic meaning, without additional implications. (Compare *connote*.) **denotation** *n*

dénouement (say day-**noo**-mahn) *n* the final part of a play or story in which the complications of the plot are cleared up

denounce *v* 1 to speak strongly against someone or something 2 to give information against someone ♦ *They denounced him as a spy.*

dense *adj* 1 thick, not easy to see through ♦ *dense fog* 2 crowded or packed closely together ♦ *dense crowds* 3 *informal* stupid **densely** *adv* **denseness** *n* **density** *n pl* **densities**

dent *n* a hollow in a surface where something has pressed or hit it **dent** *v* 1 to make a dent in something 2 to have a bad effect on something ♦ *The experience has* *dented his confidence.*

dental *adj* **1** to do with the teeth **2** to do with dentistry ♦ *a dental practice* **dentist** *n* **dentistry** *n*

denude *v* **1** to make something bare or naked, to strip the cover from something ♦ *The trees were denuded of their leaves.* **2** to take all of something away from a person ♦ *Creditors denuded him of every penny.* **denudation** *n*

denunciation (say di-nun-si-ay-shən) *n* the act of denouncing someone or something **denunciatory** *adj*

deny *v* **denies**, **denied**, **denying 1** to say that something is not true or does not exist **2** to refuse to give or allow something ♦ *She doesn't deny her children anything.* **deniable** *adj* **denial** *n*

deodorant (say dee-oh-der-ənt) *n* a substance that removes or conceals unwanted smells **deodorize** *v*

deoxygenate *v* to remove oxygen from something

depart *v* **1** to go away, to leave **2** (said about trains or buses) to start, to begin a journey **3** to stop following a particular course ♦ *Today we will depart from our normal procedure.* **departed** *adj* **the departed** a dead person or dead people

department *n* one of the sections into which a business, shop, or organization is divided ♦ *the hardware department* **departmental** *adj* **departmentally** *adv* **department store** *n*

departure *n* **1** departing, going away **2** a new course of action or thought ♦ *Acting is a departure for me.*

depend *v* **dependable** *adj* **dependability** *n* **dependably** *adv* **dependant** *n* **dependence** *n* **dependency** *n* *pl* **dependencies dependent** *adj* **depend on 1** to be controlled or determined by something ♦ *It all depends on the weather.* **2** to be unable to do without something ♦ *She depends on my help.* **3** to rely on someone or something ♦ *I'm depending on you to come.*

depict *v* **1** to show something in the form of a picture **2** to describe something in words **depiction** *n*

depilatory (say di-pil-ə-ter-i) *adj* used to remove unwanted hair **depilatory** *n* *pl* **depilatories** a substance that removes unwanted hair

deplete (say di-pleet) *v* to reduce the supply of something by using up large quantities of it ♦ *Fish stocks are severely depleted.* **depletion** *n*

deplore *v* to feel or express strong disapproval of something ♦ *We deplore racism in any form.* **deplorable** *adj* **deplorably** *adv*

deploy *v* **1** to place troops or weapons in position so that they are ready to be used effectively **2** to bring something into effective action ♦ *He deployed his arguments well.* **deployment** *n*

depopulate *v* to reduce the population of a place **depopulation** *n*

deport *v* to send an unwanted foreign person out of a country **deportation** *n* **deportee** *n*

deportment *n* a person's way of standing and walking

depose *v* to remove someone from power or office ♦ *The king was deposed in a military coup.* **deposition** *n* **1** a written piece of evidence, given under oath **2** the act of deposing someone from power or office **3** (**the Deposition**) the taking down of Christ from the Cross, especially as a theme in art

deposit *n* **1** a sum of money paid into a bank or other account **2** a sum of money paid as a guarantee or a first instalment **3** a layer of solid matter deposited or accumulated naturally ♦ *New deposits of copper were found.* **deposit** *v* **deposited**, **depositing 1** to put something down ♦ *She deposited the books on the desk.* **2** to store or entrust something for safe keeping, to pay money into a bank **3** to pay money as a guarantee or first instalment **4** to leave something as a layer or covering ♦ *Floods deposited mud on the land.* **depositor** *n* **depository** *n* *pl* **depositories**

depot (say dep-oh) *n* **1** a place where things are stored, especially one used for military supplies **2** a place where buses, trains, or other vehicles are kept and maintained

3 the headquarters of a regiment

deprave (say di-**prayv**) v to make someone morally corrupt **depraved** adj **depravity** n pl **depravities**

deprecate (say **dep**-ri-kayt) v to feel and express disapproval of something **deprecation** n **deprecatory** adj

depreciate (say di-**pree**-shi-ayt) v **1** to make or become lower in value over a period of time **2** to disparage or belittle something **depreciation** n **depreciatory** adj

depredation (say dep-ri-**day**-shən) n the act of plundering or damaging something

depress v **1** to make someone sad or dispirited **2** to make something less active or lower the value of something ♦ The stock market is depressed. **3** to press something down ♦ Now depress the lever. **depressant** n **depressing** adj **depressingly** adv **depression** n **depressive** adj **depressurize** v

deprive v to prevent someone from using or enjoying something ♦ The prisoner had been deprived of food. **deprival** n **deprivation** n

deprived adj **1** suffering from the effects of a poor or loveless home ♦ a deprived child **2** with inadequate housing, employment, etc. ♦ a deprived area

Dept. abbr Department

depth n **1** how deep something is, the distance from the top down, from the surface inwards, or from the front to the back **2** being deep **3** deep learning or thought or feeling ♦ The poem has great depth. **4** intensity of colour or darkness **5** lowness of pitch in a voice or sound **6** the deepest or most central part ♦ living in the depths of the country **depth charge** n a bomb that will explode under water, for use against submarines, etc.

deputation n a group of people sent as representatives of others

depute (say di-**pewt**) v **1** to appoint a person to do something on your behalf or as your representative ♦ We deputed John to take the message. **2** to delegate a task to someone ♦ We deputed the task to him. **deputize** v **deputy** n pl **deputies 1** a person appointed to act as substitute for another

2 a member of a parliament in certain countries ♦ the Chamber of Deputies

derail v to make a train leave the tracks **derailment** n

deranged adj insane **derangement** n

Derby (say **dar**-bi) n **1** an annual flat race for three-year-old horses, run on Epsom Downs in Surrey **2** a similar race or other important sporting contest **derby** n pl **derbies** a sports match between two rival teams from the same area

deregulate v to free something from regulations or controls **deregulation** n

derelict adj abandoned and left to fall into ruin **derelict** n **1** a person who is destitute **2** an abandoned ship or other piece of property **dereliction** n

derestrict v to remove restrictions, especially speed limits, from something ♦ a derestricted road **derestriction** n

deride (say di-**riyd**) v to laugh at someone with contempt or scorn **derision** n **derisive** adj **derisively** adv **derisory** adj

derive v **1** to obtain something from a source ♦ He derived great satisfaction from his work. **2** to form or originate from something ♦ Some English words are derived from Latin. **derivation** n **derivative** adj

dermatology (say der-ma-**tol**-əji) n the scientific study of the skin and its diseases **dermatologist** n **dermatitis** n

derogatory (say di-**rog**-ə-ter-i) adj scornful or disparaging

dervish n a member of a Muslim religious order, vowed to live a life of poverty

descale v to remove scale from a kettle or boiler, etc.

descant n a melody sung or played in accompaniment to the main melody

descend v **1** to come or go down **2** to slope or lead downwards **3** to make a sudden attack or visit **4** to sink to immoral or unworthy behaviour ♦ I never thought he would descend to violence. **5** to be passed down by inheritance ♦ The title descended to his son. **descendant** n **descent** n

describe v **1** to say what something is like ♦ How would you describe your sister? **2** to give an account of something ♦ Can you describe what happened? **3** to draw the outline of something, to move in a certain pattern ♦ *The orbit of the Earth around the Sun describes an ellipse.* **description** n **descriptive** adj

desecrate (say **dess**-i-krayt) v to treat a sacred thing with irreverence or disrespect **desecration** n **desecrator** n

desert[1] (say **dez**-ert) n a large area of dry often sand-covered land **desert island** n

desert[2] (say di-**zert**) v 1 to abandon a person or place without intending to return 2 to leave service in the armed forces without permission **deserted** adj **deserter** n **desertion** n

deserve v to be worthy of or entitled to something **deservedly** adv **deserving** adj

desiccate (say **dess**-i-kayt) v to remove the moisture from something ♦ *desiccated coconut* **desiccation** n **desiccator** n

design n 1 a drawing that shows how something is to be made or built 2 the art of making such drawings ♦ *She studied design.* 3 the way something is made or arranged ♦ *The design of the building is good.* 4 a combination of lines and shapes that form a decoration 5 a mental plan or scheme **design** v 1 to prepare a drawing or design showing how something is to be made 2 to intend something for a specific purpose ♦ *The book is designed for students.* **designer** n

designate[1] (say **dez**-ig-nayt) v 1 to give a name or title to something ♦ *It has been designated an area of outstanding natural beauty.* 2 to mark or point something out clearly, to specify something ♦ *The river was designated as the western boundary.* 3 to appoint someone to a position ♦ *He designated Smith as his successor.* **designation** n

designate[2] (say **dez**-ig-nət) adj appointed to a job or office but not yet doing it ♦ *the bishop designate*

desire n 1 a feeling of wanting something very much 2 a request or wish ♦ *He expressed a desire to rest.* 3 something that you want very much ♦ *She has achieved her heart's desire.* **desire** v 1 to have a desire for something 2 to want someone sexually **desirable** adj **desirability** n **desirably** adv

desirous adj

desist (say di-**zist**) v to stop doing something

desk n 1 a piece of furniture with a flat top, used when writing or doing work 2 a counter in a hotel, bank, airport, etc. ♦ *Ask at the information desk.* 3 the section of a news organization dealing with specified topics ♦ *the sports desk* **desktop publishing** n the production of high-quality printed matter using a computer and printer

desolate (say **dess**-ə-lət) adj 1 uninhabited or barren ♦ *a desolate moor* 2 forlorn and unhappy **desolation** n

despair n complete loss or lack of hope **despair** v to lose all hope ♦ *I despaired of ever seeing her again.* **despairing** adj **despairingly** adv **desperate** adj **desperately** adv **desperation** n

despatch n, v another spelling of *dispatch*

despicable (say di-**spik**-ə-bəl or **dess**-pik-ə-bəl) adj deserving hatred and contempt **despicably** adv

despise v to regard someone as inferior or worthless, to feel disrespect for someone

despite prep in spite of

despoil v to plunder or rob a place **despoliation** n

despondent adj in low spirits, dejected **despondency** n **despondently** adv

despot (say **dess**-pot) n a tyrant, a ruler who has unrestricted power **despotic** adj **despotically** adv **despotism** n

dessert (say di-**zert**) n the sweet course of a meal

destination n the place to which a person or thing is going or being sent

destine (say **dess**-tin) v **to be destined** to be chosen or set apart for a purpose ♦ *He was destined to become President.*

destiny n pl **destinies** 1 fate considered as a power 2 what will happen or has happened to a person or thing

destitute adj 1 living in extreme poverty, without food, shelter, etc. 2 lacking in something ♦ *a landscape destitute of trees* **destitution** n

destroy v 1 to damage something so much that it is completely spoiled or made useless **2** to put an end to something ♦ *It destroyed our chances.* **3** to kill an animal by humane means ♦ *The dog had to be destroyed.* **destroyer** *n*

destruction *n* **1** destroying or being destroyed **2** a cause of destruction or ruin **destructive** *adj*

desultory (say dess-əl-ter-i) *adj* doing something without enthusiasm or a definite plan **desultorily** *adv*

detach *v* to release or remove one thing from something else or from a group **detachable** *adj* **detached** *adj* **detachment** *n*

detail *n* **1** a small individual item or feature **2** the minor decoration in a building or picture, etc. ♦ *Look at the detail in the carvings.* **3** a small detachment of soldiers or police officers given a special duty **detail** *v* **1** to describe something fully, item by item **2** to give soldiers, etc. a special duty **detailed** *adj* **in detail** describing the individual parts or events, etc. fully

detain *v* **1** to keep someone waiting or delay them **2** to keep someone at a police station, prison, etc. **detainee** *n*

detect *v* **1** to discover the existence or presence of something **2** to find a person doing something bad or secret **detectable** *adj* **detection** *n* **detective** *n* **detector** *n*

detention *n* **1** detaining or being detained **2** being kept in school after hours as a punishment **3** being kept in custody **detention centre** *n*

deter *v* **deterred**, **deterring** to discourage or prevent someone from doing something through fear or dislike of the consequences

detergent *n* a substance used for cleaning or washing things **detergent** *adj* having a cleansing effect

deteriorate (say di-teer-ior-ayt) *v* to become worse **deterioration** *n*

determine *v* **1** to find out or calculate something precisely ♦ *Can you determine the height of the mountain?* **2** to firmly decide to do something ♦ *He determined to confront her.* **3** to be the decisive factor or influence on something ♦ *Income determines your standard of living.* **determinable** *adj*

determinant *n* **determinate** *adj* **determination** *n* **determined** *adj* **determinedly** *adv* **determinism** *n* **determinist** *n* **deterministic** *adj*

deterrent (say di-te-rənt) *adj* able or intended to deter people **deterrent** *n* something that may deter people, such as a nuclear weapon that deters countries from attacking the one that has it **deterrence** *n*

detest *v* to dislike something intensely, to loathe something **detestable** *adj* **detestably** *adv* **detestation** *n*

dethrone *v* to remove someone from a throne, to depose someone **dethronement** *n*

detonate (say det-ən-ayt) *v* to explode or cause something to explode **detonation** *n* **detonator** *n*

detour (say dee-toor) *n* a roundabout route instead of the normal one ♦ *We had to make a detour.*

detoxify (say dee-toks-i-fiy) *v* **detoxifies**, **detoxified**, **detoxifying** to remove poison or harmful substances from something or someone **detoxification** *n*

detract *v* **detract from** to take away a part or amount from something, to make something seem less valuable or impressive ♦ *It will not detract from our pleasure.* **detraction** *n* **detractor** *n*

detriment (say det-ri-mənt) *n* harm or damage ♦ *She worked long hours, to the detriment of her health.* **detrimental** *adj* **detrimentally** *adv*

detritus (say di-triy-təs) *n* **1** loose pieces of gravel, silt, sand, etc. produced by erosion **2** rubbish or debris

deuce *n* (in tennis) a score in which both sides have 40 points and must win two consecutive points to win

devalue *v* **1** to reduce the value of something **2** to reduce the value of a country's currency in relation to other currencies or to gold **devaluation** *n*

devastate *v* **1** to ruin or cause great destruction to something **2** to overwhelm someone with shock or grief **devastating** *adj* **devastation** *n*

develop *v* **developed**, **developing 1** to make or become larger or more advanced

2 to bring or come gradually into existence ♦ *A storm developed.* **3** to begin to exhibit or suffer from something ♦ *They developed bad habits.* **4** to use an area of land for building houses, shops, factories, etc. **5** to treat a photographic film or plate, etc. with chemicals so that the picture becomes visible **developer** *n* **development** *n* **developing country** *n* a poor agricultural country that is developing better economic and social conditions

deviant (say **dee**-vi-ənt) *adj* deviating from what is accepted as normal or usual **deviant** *n* a person who deviates from accepted standards in beliefs or behaviour

deviate (say **dee**-vi-ayt) *v* to turn aside from a course or from what is usual or true **deviation** *n* **deviator** *n*

device *n* **1** a thing that is made or used for a particular purpose ♦ *a device for opening tins* **2** a plan or scheme for achieving something **3** a design used as a decoration or emblem **to leave someone to their own devices** to leave them to do as they wish without help or advice

devil *n* **1** (**the Devil**) in Jewish and Christian belief, the supreme spirit of evil and enemy of God **2** an evil spirit **3** a wicked or cruel person **4** a clever or mischievous person ♦ *You cunning devil!* **5** something difficult or hard to manage **6** *informal* a person ♦ *The lucky devil!* **devilish** *adj* **devilment** *n* **devilry** *n* **devil's advocate** *n*

devious (say **dee**-vi-əs) *adj* **1** not straightforward, underhand **2** (said about a route or journey) winding or roundabout **deviously** *adv* **deviousness** *n*

devise (say di-**viyz**) *v* to plan or invent something

devoid (say di-**void**) *adj* lacking or free from something ♦ *His work is devoid of merit.*

devolve *v* **1** to hand over power to a lower level, especially from central government to local or regional government **2** to pass or be passed on to a deputy or successor ♦ *This work will devolve on the new manager.* **devolution** *n*

devote *v* to give something completely for a particular activity or purpose ♦ *He devoted all his time to sport.* **devoted** *adj*

devotedly *adv* **devotee** *n* **devotional** *adj* used in religious worship

devotion *n* **1** great love, loyalty, or enthusiasm for someone or something **2** religious worship **devotions** *pl n* prayers

devour *v* **1** to eat something hungrily or greedily **2** to destroy something completely, to consume something ♦ *Fire devoured the forest.* **3** to take something in greedily with the eyes or ears ♦ *They devoured the story.* **4** to absorb the attention of someone ♦ *She was devoured by curiosity.*

devout *adj* **1** deeply religious **2** earnest or sincere ♦ *a devout supporter* **devoutly** *adv* **devoutness** *n*

dew *n* **1** small drops of moisture that condense on cool surfaces during the night from water vapour in the air **2** moisture in small drops on a surface **dewy** *adj* **dewier**, **dewiest**, **dewy-eyed** *adj* with eyes moist with tears because of sentimentality or nostalgia

dexterity (say deks-**te**-riti) *n* skill in using your hands or mind **dexterous** *adj* **dexterously** *adv*

dextrose (say **deks**-trohs) *n* the most common naturally occurring form of glucose

DfES *abbr* (in Britain) Department for Education and Skills

DfT *abbr* (in Britain) Department for Transport

dhal *n* an Indian dish made from split pulses

dharma (say **dar**-mə) *n* in Indian religion, the eternal law of the Hindu cosmos, what is and what should be

dhobi *n pl* **dhobis** (in the Indian subcontinent) a person who washes clothes for a living

dhoti (say **doh**-ti) *n pl* **dhotis** a loincloth worn by male Hindus

dhow (say dow) *n* a ship of the Arabian Sea, with a triangular sail on a slanting yard

di- *prefix* two or double (as in *dioxide*)

dia- *prefix* through or across (as in *diagonal*)

diabetes (say diy-ə-**bee**-teez) *n* a disease in which sugar and starch are not properly absorbed by the body **diabetic** *adj*

diabolical (say diy-ə-**bol**-ikəl) *adj* **1** like a devil, very cruel or wicked **2** very

clever or annoying ♦ *a diabolical puzzle*
diabolically *adv*

diagnose (say **diy-**əg-nohz) *v* to find out
what disease a person has or what is wrong
♦ *Typhoid fever was diagnosed in six patients.*
diagnosis *n pl* **diagnoses diagnostic** *adj*

diagonal (say diy-**ag-**ən-əl) *adj* slanting,
crossing from corner to corner **diagonal** *n*
a straight line joining two opposite corners
diagonally *adv*

diagram *n* **1** an outline drawing that shows
the parts of something or how it works **2** a
drawing explaining the course of a process
or representing a series of quantities
diagrammatic *adj* **diagrammatically** *adv*

dial *n* **1** a disc marked with a scale for
measuring something and having a
movable pointer that indicates the amount
registered **2** a disc on a radio or television
set, turned to choose a wavelength or
channel **3** the face of a clock or watch
4 a disc with finger-holes on an old type
of telephone, turned in order to make a
call **dial** *v* **dialled**, **dialling** to telephone
a number by turning a telephone dial or
pressing numbered buttons ♦ *He dialled the
operator.*

dialect (say **diy-**ə-lekt) *n* the words and
pronunciations that are used in a particular
area

dialogue (say **diy-**ə-log) *n* **1** *Drama* the
words spoken by characters in a play,
film, or story **2** *Language* a conversation
or discussion **3** *ICT* information and
commands that a user puts into a computer
◊ In Computing, it is usual to use the
American spelling *dialog*, as in *dialog box*.

dialysis (say diy-**al**-i-sis) *n pl* **dialyses**
purification of the blood by causing it to
flow through a suitable membrane

diamanté (say dee-ə-**mahn**-tay) *adj*
decorated with fragments of crystal or
another sparkling substance

diameter (say diy-**am**-it-er) *n* **1** a line
drawn straight across a circle or sphere and
passing through its centre **2** the length of
this line

diametrical (say diy-ə-**met**-rik-əl) *adj*
1 (said about opposites) complete or
absolute ♦ *He is the diametrical opposite*
of my last boss. **2** to do with or along a
diameter **diametrically** *adv*

diamond *n* **1** a very hard brilliant precious
stone of pure crystallized carbon **2** a figure
or shape with four equal sides and with
angles that are not right angles **3** a playing
card of the suit marked with red diamond
shapes on it **diamonds** *pl n* in cards, the
suit marked with red diamond shapes on it
diamond *adj* made of or set with diamonds
diamond jubilee *n* the 60th anniversary
of an event **diamond wedding** *n* the 60th
anniversary of a wedding

diaphanous (say diy-**af**-ən-əs) *adj* (said
about fabric) light, delicate, and almost
transparent

diaphragm (say **diy**-ə-fram) *n* **1** the
muscular layer inside the body that
separates the chest from the abdomen
and is used in breathing **2** a dome-shaped
contraceptive cap fitting over the neck of
the womb

diarrhoea (say diy-ə-**ree**-ə) *n* a condition in
which bowel movements are very frequent
and watery

diary *n pl* **diaries 1** a book for keeping a daily
record of events **2** a book for noting future
appointments **diarist** *n*

diaspora (say diy-**ass**-pər-ə) *n* **1** the
dispersion of any people originally of one
nation **2** the dispersing of the Jews beyond
Israel in the 8th to 6th centuries BC and
later

diatribe (say **diy**-ə-triyb) *n* a strong and
bitter verbal attack

dice *n* **1** (strictly the plural of *die*², but often
used as a singular) *pl* **dice** a small cube
marked on each side with a number of spots
(1-6), used in games **2** a game played with
these **dice** *v* to cut meat, vegetables, etc.
into small cubes ♦ *diced carrots* **dicey** *adj*
dicier, **diciest** risky or unreliable **to dice
with death** to take dangerous risks

dichotomy (say diy-**kot**-əmi) *n pl*
dichotomies a division into two entirely
different parts or kinds ♦ *a dichotomy
between his public and private lives*

dictate *v* **1** to say or read something aloud
for someone else to type or write down
2 to state or order something with the

force of authority ♦ *We are in a strong enough position to dictate terms.* **3** to give orders in a bossy way ♦ *I will not be dictated to.* **dictates** *pl n* commands or principles that must be obeyed ♦ *the dictates of conscience* **dictation** *n* **dictator** *n* **1** a ruler who has unlimited power, especially one who has taken control by force **2** a person with supreme authority in any sphere **3** a domineering person **dictatorial** *adj* **dictatorship** *n*

diction (say **dik**-shən) *n* **1** a person's way of speaking or pronouncing words ♦ *clear diction* **2** the choice of words used by a writer or poet

dictionary *n pl* **dictionaries** a book that lists and explains the words of a language or the words and topics of a particular subject, or that gives their equivalents in another language, usually in alphabetical order

dictum *n pl* **dicta** or **dictums** **1** a formal expression of an opinion **2** a saying or maxim

did past tense of *do*

didactic (say diy-**dak**-tik) *adj* **1** meant to teach or give instruction **2** having the manner of someone who is lecturing people **didactically** *adv*

diddle *v informal* to cheat or swindle someone

didn't *v informal* did not

die[1] *v* **dies**, **died**, **dying** **1** to stop living or existing **2** to cease to function, to stop working ♦ *The engine sputtered and died.* **3** (said about a fire or flame) to go out **4** to be forgotten ♦ *Her name will never die.* **5** to want to do or have something very much ♦ *We are all dying to see you.* ♦ *I'm dying for a drink.* **diehard** *n* a person who stubbornly resists change

die[2] *n* **1** a dice (see *dice*) **2** a device for stamping a design on coins or medals or for stamping, cutting, or moulding material into a particular shape

dielectric *adj* that does not conduct electricity, insulating **dielectric** *n* an insulator

diesel (say **dee**-zəl) *n* **1** an engine that works by burning oil in compressed air **2** fuel for a diesel engine

diet[1] *n* **1** the sort of foods that a person or animal usually eats ♦ *a healthy diet* **2** a selection of food to which a person is restricted, especially for medical reasons or because they are trying to lose weight **diet** *v* **dieted**, **dieting** to keep to a diet, especially in order to control your weight **dietary** *adj* **dieter** *n* **dietetic** *adj* **dietitian** *n*

diet[2] *n* the parliament of certain countries, e.g. Japan

differ *v* **1** to be unlike something else ♦ *The two accounts differ in some important details.* **2** to disagree in opinion **difference** *n* **1** the state of being different or unlike **2** the way in which things are different ♦ *There's a big difference between borrowing and stealing.* **3** the remainder left after subtracting one number from another ♦ *The difference between 8 and 5 is 3.* **4** a disagreement in opinion, a quarrel **differential** *adj* **1** of, showing, or depending on a difference **2** *Mathematics* relating to infinitesimal differences **differential** *n* **1** an agreed difference in wages between industries or between different classes of workers in the same industry **2** a differential gear **differentiate** *v* **1** to recognize differences between things, to distinguish things ♦ *I don't differentiate between them.* **2** to be a difference between things, to make one thing different from another ♦ *What are the features that differentiate one breed from another?* **3** to develop differences, to become different **4** *Mathematics* to calculate the derivative of a function **differentiation** *n* **different** *adj* **1** unlike, not the same ♦ *Your hair looks different.* ♦ *Her attitude is different from the others.* **2** separate or distinct ♦ *I called on three different occasions.* **3** unusual or novel ♦ *Try Finland for a holiday that's a bit different.* **differently** *adv*

difficult *adj* **1** needing a lot of effort or skill to do or understand **2** full of problems or hardships ♦ *These are difficult times.* **3** not easy to please or satisfy ♦ *a difficult employer* **difficulty** *n pl* **difficulties**

diffident (say **dif**-i-dənt) *adj* shy and lacking self-confidence, hesitating to put yourself or your ideas forward **diffidence** *n*

diffidently adv

diffuse[1] (say di-**fewss**) adj 1 spread widely, not concentrated ♦ diffuse light 2 wordy, not concise ♦ a diffuse style **diffusely** adv **diffuseness** n

diffuse[2] (say dif-**fewz**) v 1 to spread or make something spread over a wide area ♦ The Internet is being used to diffuse knowledge. ♦ diffused sunlight 2 to mix liquids or gases slowly, to become intermingled ♦ Let the milk diffuse in the water. **diffuser** n **diffusible** adj **diffusion** n

dig v past tense and past participle **dug**; **digging** 1 to break up and move ground with a tool or machine or claws, etc.; to make a hole or tunnel by doing this 2 to obtain something from the ground by digging ♦ I spent the morning digging potatoes. 3 to excavate an archaeological site 4 to seek or discover something by investigation ♦ We dug up some useful information. 5 to poke or jab something sharply ♦ Its claws dug into my hand. **dig** n 1 a piece of digging 2 an archaeological excavation 3 a thrust or poke ♦ a dig in the ribs 4 a cutting remark ♦ That was a dig at me. **digs** pl n lodgings **digger** n 1 someone who digs 2 a mechanical excavator

digest[1] (say diy-**jest**) v 1 to dissolve food in the stomach and intestines so that the body can absorb it 2 to take information into your mind and think it over ♦ I need time to digest this news. 3 to summarize information methodically **digestible** adj **digestion** n **digestive** adj

digest[2] (say **diy**-jest) n 1 a methodical summary 2 a periodical publication

digit (say **dij**-it) n 1 any numeral from 0 to 9, especially when forming part of a number 2 a finger or toe

digital (say **dij**-it-əl) adj 1 representing data as a series of binary digits ♦ a digital computer 2 (said about a clock, watch, or other instrument) showing the time or information by displaying a row of figures. (Compare analogue.) 3 to do with or using fingers **digitally** adv **digitize** v **digitizer** n

digitalis (say dij-i-**tay**-lis) n a drug prepared from dried foxglove leaves, used to stimulate the heart **digitalin** n a

drug containing the active ingredients of digitalis

dignify v **dignifies**, **dignified**, **dignifying** to give dignity to someone or something **dignified** adj

dignity n 1 a calm and serious manner or style, showing suitable formality or indicating that you deserve respect 2 the quality of being worthy of respect ♦ the dignity of labour **dignitary** n pl **dignitaries** a person holding a high rank or position

digress (say diy-**gress**) v to depart from the main subject **digression** n

dike n another spelling of dyke

dilapidation n a state of disrepair; bringing or being brought into this state **dilapidated** adj

dilate (say diy-**layt**) v 1 to make something wider or larger, or to become wider or larger ♦ dilated pupils 2 to speak or write at length on a subject **dilation** n **dilator** n

dilatory (say **dil**-ə-ter-i) adj 1 slow in doing something, not prompt ♦ a dilatory response 2 intended to cause delay **dilatorily** adv **dilatoriness** n

dilemma (say dil-**em**-ə) n 1 a situation in which a difficult choice has to be made between two or more alternatives 2 informal a difficult situation or problem

dilettante (say dili-**tan**-ti) n a person who dabbles in a subject for enjoyment and without serious study

diligent (say **dil**-i-jənt) adj 1 hard-working, putting care and effort into what you do 2 done with care and effort ♦ a diligent search **diligence** n **diligently** adv

dill n a yellow-flowered herb with spicy seeds used for flavouring pickles

dilly-dally v **dilly-dallies**, **dilly-dallied**, **dilly-dallying** informal to dawdle, to waste time by not making up your mind

dilute (say diy-**lewt**) v 1 to make a liquid weaker or less concentrated by adding water or some other liquid 2 to weaken or reduce the force or strength of something **dilute** adj diluted ♦ a dilute acid **dilution** n

dim adj **dimmer**, **dimmest** 1 only faintly lit, not bright 2 indistinct, not clearly seen, heard, or remembered 3 not able to see clearly ♦ eyes dim with tears 4 informal stupid **dim** v **dimmed**, **dimming** to make something dim, or to become dim **dimmer** n **dimly** adv **dimness** n

dime n N. Am a ten-cent coin

dimension (say diy-**men**-shən) n 1 a measurement such as length, breadth, thickness, area, or volume ♦ What are the dimensions of the room? 2 size or extent ♦ a structure of huge dimensions 3 an aspect or feature of something ♦ His passing adds a new dimension to the team. **dimensional** adj

diminish v to make something smaller or less, or to become smaller or less **diminuendo** adj, adv Mus gradually becoming quieter **diminution** n 1 diminishing or being diminished 2 a decrease **diminutive** adj very small **diminutive** n a word for a small specimen of something (e.g. booklet, duckling), or an affectionate form of a name, etc. (e.g. dearie, Johnnie)

dimple n a small hollow or dent, especially a natural one on the skin of the cheek or chin **dimple** v 1 to produce dimples in something 2 to show dimples

dim sum n a Chinese dish of small steamed or fried savoury dumplings containing various fillings

din n a loud and annoying noise **din** v **dinned**, **dinning to din something into** to force a person to learn something by continually repeating it

dine v 1 to eat dinner 2 to give someone dinner ♦ We were wined and dined. **diner** n **dining room** n

ding-dong adj, adv informal 1 with the sound of alternate chimes of a bell 2 (said about a contest) fiercely fought

dinghy (say **ding**-gi) n pl **dinghies** 1 a small open boat driven by oars or sails 2 a small inflatable rubber boat

dingo n pl **dingoes** an Australian wild dog

dingy (say **din**-ji) adj **dingier**, **dingiest** gloomy and drab, dirty-looking **dingily** adv **dinginess** n

dinky adj informal **dinkier**, **dinkiest** attractively small and neat

dinner n 1 the main meal of the day, either at midday or in the evening 2 a formal evening meal in honour of a person or event

dinosaur (say **diy**-nə-sor) n a prehistoric reptile of the Mesozoic era, often of enormous size

diocese (say **diy**-ə-sis) n a district under the care of a bishop in the Christian Church **diocesan** adj

dioxide (say diy-**ok**-siyd) n an oxide with two atoms of oxygen to one of a metal or other element ♦ carbon dioxide

dip v **dipped**, **dipping** 1 to put or lower something into liquid 2 to go under water and emerge quickly 3 to go down ♦ The sun dipped below the horizon. 4 to lower something for a time, especially the beam of a vehicle's headlights 5 to slope or extend downwards ♦ The road dips after the bend. 6 to become lower or smaller ♦ Attendances have dipped this month. 7 to put a hand, spoon, etc. into something in order to take something out 8 to wash sheep in a vermin-killing liquid **dip** n 1 dipping or being dipped 2 a brief swim ♦ He went for a dip in the sea. 3 a downward slope 4 a brief drop in an amount or level 5 a creamy mixture into which pieces of food are dipped before eating 6 a liquid into which something is dipped ♦ sheep dip **dipper** n **to dip into** 1 to read short passages here and there in a book ♦ I've dipped into 'War and Peace'. 2 to draw money from your financial resources and spend it ♦ She had to dip into her savings.

diphtheria (say dif-**theer**-iə) n an acute infectious disease that causes severe inflammation of a mucous membrane, especially in the throat

diploma n a certificate awarded by a college, etc. to a person on completion of a course of study

diplomacy (say dip-**loh**-mə-si) n 1 the work or skill of making agreements with other countries 2 skill in dealing with people and gently persuading them to agree to things; tact **diplomat** n 1 a person who represents their country officially abroad 2 a tactful person **diplomatic** adj 1 to do with diplomats or diplomacy ♦ the diplomatic service 2 tactful ♦ a diplomatic reply **diplomatically** adv

dipstick *n* a rod for measuring the depth of a liquid, especially oil in an engine

diptych (say **dip**-tik) *n* a painting on two hinged wooden panels that can be closed like a book

dire *adj* **1** extremely serious or urgent ♦ *The refugees are in dire need.* **2** ominous, predicting trouble ♦ *dire warnings* **3** *informal* of poor quality ♦ *a dire performance*

direct *adj* **1** going from one place to another without changing direction or stopping ♦ *the direct route* **2** with nothing or no one coming in between ♦ *Are you in direct contact with them?* **3** going straight to the point, frank ♦ *a direct way of speaking* **4** exact, complete ♦ *the direct opposite* **direct** *adv* by a direct route ♦ *We travelled to Rome direct.* ◊ Note that *directly* is not used with this meaning. **direct** *v* **1** to tell or show someone the way ♦ *Can you direct me to the station?* **2** to guide or aim something in a certain direction or to a target **3** to supervise the acting, filming, etc. of a play, film, or opera **4** to control or manage someone or something ♦ *There was no one to direct the workmen.* **5** to command or order something ♦ *The general directed his men to advance.* **direction** *n* **1** the line along which something moves or faces ♦ *They are heading in the direction of London.* **2** directing or managing people **directions** *pl n* instructions on how to use or do something or how to get somewhere **directional** *adj* **directive** *n* an official instruction or command **directly** *adv* **1** in a direct line, in a direct manner **2** without delay **3** very soon **directly** *conjunction informal* as soon as ♦ *I went directly I knew.* **directness** *n* **director** *n* **1** a person who supervises or manages things, especially a member of the board managing a business company on behalf of shareholders **2** a person who directs a film or play **directorate** *n* **1** a part of a government department in charge of some activity **2** a board of directors **directorial** *adj* **directorship** *n* **direct debit** *n* an arrangement that allows bills to be paid directly from your bank account **direct speech** *n* words quoted in the form in which

they were actually spoken (e.g. *Has he come?*), not altered by being reported (e.g. *She asked whether he had come*) **direct tax** *n* a tax, such as income tax, which is levied on the money that people earn rather than on the money that they spend

directory *n pl* **directories 1** a book containing a list of telephone subscribers, inhabitants of a district, members of a profession, business firms, etc. **2** *ICT* a file containing a group of other files

dirge (say derj) *n* **1** a slow mournful song **2** a lament for the dead

dirt *n* **1** any unclean substance such as dust, soil, or mud **2** loose earth or soil **3** unpleasant or unkind words or talk **dirtily** *adv* **dirtiness** *n* **dirty** *adj* **dirtier**, **dirtiest**, **dirt track** *n* a course made of earth or rolled cinders, for flat racing or motorcycle racing

dis- *prefix* (changing to **dif-** before *f*, **di-** before some consonants). **1** not; the reverse of (as in *dishonest*) **2** apart or separated (as in *disarm*, *disperse*)

disable *v* **1** to limit a person's movements, senses, or activities **2** to put something out of action **disability** *n pl* **disabilities 1** a physical or mental condition that limits a person's movements, senses, or activities **2** a lack of something that prevents someone doing something **disabled** *adj* unable to use part of your body properly because of illness or injury ◊ This term should be used instead of older words such as *crippled*, which can now cause offence. **disablement** *n*

disabuse (say dis-ə-bewz) *v* to free someone from a false idea ♦ *He was soon disabused of this notion.*

disadvantage *n* something that hinders or is unfavourable **disadvantage** *v* to put someone at a disadvantage **disadvantaged** *adj* suffering from socially or economically unfavourable circumstances **disadvantageous** *adj*

disaffected *adj* no longer willing to support someone or believe in something **disaffection** *n*

disagree *v* **disagrees**, **disagreed**, **disagreeing 1** to have or express a different opinion **2** to fail to correspond or be consistent **3** to quarrel **disagreeable** adj **disagreeably** adv **disagreement** n **to disagree with 1** to differ in opinion from someone **2** (said about food or climate) to have a bad effect on someone ♦ *Rich food disagrees with me.*

disallow v to refuse to allow or accept something as valid ♦ *The referee disallowed the goal.*

disappear v **1** to stop being visible, to pass from sight **2** to stop existing **disappearance** n

disappoint v to fail to do what someone hoped for or desired or expected **disappointed** adj **disappointment** n

disapprobation (say dis-ap-rə-**bay**-shən) n strong disapproval

disapprove v to have or express an unfavourable opinion of something **disapproval** n

disarm v **1** to take away someone's weapons **2** to reduce the size of the armed forces **3** to remove the fuse from a bomb **4** to make it difficult for a person to feel angry or hostile ♦ *We were completely disarmed by his honesty.* **disarmament** n **disarming** adj **disarmingly** adv

disarrange v to make something disordered or untidy **disarrangement** n

disarray n a state of disorder or untidiness

disassemble v to take something to pieces **disassembly** n

disassociate v another word for *dissociate*

disaster n **1** an accident or natural event that causes great damage, injury, or loss of life **2** a complete failure **disastrous** adj **disastrously** adv

disavow v to deny any knowledge of or responsibility for something **disavowal** n

disband v (said about a group or organization) to break up, or cause it to break up ♦ *We decided to disband the choir.*

disbelief n refusal or unwillingness to believe something **disbelieve** v **disbeliever** n

disburse v to pay out money **disbursal** n **disbursement** n

disc n **1** a flat thin circular object **2** something shaped or looking like this

♦ *the sun's disc* **3** (**disk**) a computer storage device consisting of a rotatable disc on which data is stored either magnetically or optically ♦ *a floppy disk* ♦ *a compact disk* **4** a layer of cartilage between vertebrae in the spine **5** a CD or record

discard[1] (say dis-**kard**) v to get rid of something because it is no longer wanted or useful

discard[2] (say **dis**-kard) n something discarded

discern (say di-**sern**) v **1** to recognize or perceive something clearly ♦ *Can you discern what her intentions are?* **2** to be able to see or notice something, to make something out ♦ *I could just discern a figure in the shadows.* **discernible** adj **discerning** adj **discernment** n

discharge (say dis-**charj**) v **1** to allow someone to leave ♦ *My mother was discharged from hospital last week.* **2** to dismiss someone from employment ♦ *He was discharged from the army.* **3** to send something out; to pour out ♦ *The engine was discharging smoke.* **4** to give out an electric charge, or to cause something to do this **5** to carry out a duty or responsibility **6** to fire a missile or gun **discharge** (say dis-**charj** or **dis**-charj) n **1** discharging or being discharged **2** something that has been discharged ♦ *the discharge from the wound* **3** the release of an electric charge, especially with a spark

disciple (say di-**siy**-pəl) n **1** a follower or pupil of a leader, teacher, or philosophy **2** any of the original followers of Jesus Christ during his life

discipline (say **dis**-i-plin) n **1** training that produces obedience, self-control, or a particular skill **2** controlled behaviour produced by such training **3** a subject for study **discipline** v **1** to train someone to be obedient and self-controlled **2** to punish someone ♦ *Anyone who breaks the rules will be disciplined.* **disciplinarian** n **disciplinary** adj

disc jockey n a person who introduces and plays records on radio or at a disco

disclaim v to say that you do not have responsibility for or knowledge of something ♦ *They disclaim all responsibility for the accident.* **disclaimer** *n*

disclose *v* to reveal something or make it known **disclosure** *n*

disco *n* *pl* **discos** *informal* a party or club where people dance to pop music

discolour *v* **1** to spoil or change the colour of something **2** to become changed in colour or stained **discoloration** *n*

discomfit (say dis-**kum**-fit) *v* **discomfited**, **discomfiting** to make someone feel uneasy or embarrassed **discomfiture** *n*

discomfort *n* **1** slight pain **2** a feeling of uneasiness or embarrassment

discompose *v* to disturb or agitate someone **discomposure** *n*

disconcert (say dis-kən-**sert**) *v* to make a person feel uneasy **disconcerting** *adj*

disconnect *v* **1** to break a connection **2** to put a piece of equipment out of action by detaching it from a power supply ♦ *The phone has been disconnected.* **disconnected** *adj* **disconnection** *n*

disconsolate (say dis-**kon**-sə-lət) *adj* unhappy at the loss of something **disconsolately** *adv*

discontent *n* lack of contentment or satisfaction **discontentment** *n*

discontented *adj* not contented, feeling discontent

discontinue *v* to stop doing or providing something **discontinuance** *n* **discontinuity** *n* **discontinuous** *adj*

discord (say **dis**-kord) *n* **1** disagreement or quarrelling **2** *Mus* a combination of notes producing a harsh or unpleasant sound **discordance** *n* **discordant** *adj* **discordantly** *adv*

discotheque (say **dis**-kə-tek) *n* a disco

discount[1] (say **dis**-kownt) *n* an amount of money taken off the usual price or cost of something **discount store** *n* a shop selling goods regularly at less than the standard price

discount[2] (say dis-**kownt**) *v* **1** to ignore or disregard a factor or possibility **2** to reduce something in price

discourage *v* **1** to take away someone's enthusiasm or confidence **2** to try to persuade someone not to do something

3 to show disapproval of something **discouragement** *n* **discouraging** *adj*

discourse[1] (say **dis**-korss) *n* a formal speech or piece of writing on a subject

discourse[2] (say dis-**korss**) *v* to speak or write at length about something

discourteous (say dis-**ker**-ti-əs) *adj* lacking courtesy, rude **discourteously** *adv* **discourtesy** *n*

discover *v* **1** to find or become aware of something, especially by searching or other effort **2** to be the first person to find something ♦ *Herschel discovered the planet Uranus.* **discoverer** *n* **discovery** *n* *pl* **discoveries 1** discovering or being discovered **2** something that is discovered

discredit *v* **discredited**, **discrediting 1** to damage a person's reputation **2** to cause an idea, piece of evidence, etc. to be disbelieved or doubted ♦ *This theory has since been discredited.* **discredit** *n* damage to a person's reputation **discreditable** *adj* **discreditably** *adv*

discreet *adj* **1** showing caution and good judgement in what you say or do; not giving away secrets ♦ *I'll make a few discreet inquiries.* **2** not showy or obtrusive **discreetly** *adv* **discretion** *n* **discretionary** *adj* ◊ Do not confuse this word with *discrete*, which has a different meaning.

discrepancy (say dis-**krep**-ənsi) *n* *pl* **discrepancies** lack of agreement between things which should be the same

discrete (say dis-**kreet**) *adj* individually separate and distinct ♦ *a series of discrete scenes* **discretely** *adv* ◊ Do not confuse this word with *discreet*, which has a different meaning.

discriminate *v* **1** to notice and understand the differences between things **2** to treat people differently or unfairly, usually because of their race, sex, age, or religion **discriminating** *adj* **discrimination** *n* **discriminatory** *adj*

discursive *adj* wandering from one subject to another

discus *n* *pl* **discuses** a heavy thick-centred disc, thrown in athletic contests

discuss *v* **1** to examine a subject in speech

or writing **2** to have a conversation in order to decide something **discussion** n

disdain n the feeling that someone or something is not worthy of your consideration or respect **disdain** v **1** to regard something with disdain **2** to refuse to do something because of disdain ♦ *She disdained to reply.* **disdainful** adj **disdainfully** adv

disease n an unhealthy condition of the body or mind **diseased** adj

disembark v to get off a ship or aircraft **disembarkation** n

disembodied adj **1** (said about the soul or spirit) separated or freed from the body **2** (said about a voice) lacking any obvious source

disembowel v **disembowelled**, **disembowelling** to take out the bowels or internal organs of a person or animal

disenchanted adj no longer believing that something is worthwhile ♦ *She's become disenchanted with her job.* **disenchantment** n

disenfranchise (say dis-in-**fran**-chiyz) v to take away someone's right to vote **disenfranchisement** n

disengage v **1** to disconnect or detach something **2** (said about an army, etc.) to stop fighting and leave a battle area **disengagement** n

disentangle v **1** to take the knots or tangles out of something **2** to free something from difficulty or confusion, to extricate something **disentanglement** n

disestablish v to deprive a national Church of its official connection with the State **disestablishment** n

disfavour n dislike or disapproval

disfigure v to spoil the appearance of a person or thing **disfigurement** n

disgorge v **1** to pour or send something out ♦ *The pipe disgorged its contents.* **2** to throw something out from the stomach or throat ♦ *The whale swallowed Jonah and then disgorged him.*

disgrace n **1** shame, loss of approval or respect **2** something that is shameful or unacceptable ♦ *The bus service is a disgrace.* **disgrace** v to bring disgrace on someone

disgraceful adj **disgracefully** adv

disgruntled adj discontented or resentful

disguise v **1** to make a person or thing look or seem different so that they cannot be recognized **2** to conceal something ♦ *She could not disguise her amazement.* **disguise** n **1** something worn or used for disguising your identity **2** the state of being disguised ♦ *in disguise*

disgust n a strong feeling of dislike or revulsion ♦ *He turned away in disgust.* **disgust** v to cause disgust in someone **disgusted** adj **disgusting** adj

dish n **1** a shallow flat-bottomed container for cooking or serving food **2** a particular kind of food ♦ *We specialize in vegetarian dishes.* **3** a shallow concave object ♦ *a soap dish* **4** a concave dish-shaped aerial used for receiving satellite communications and in radio astronomy **5** *informal* an attractive person **dish** v

disharmony n lack of harmony **disharmonious** adj

dishcloth n a cloth for washing dishes

dishearten v to cause someone to lose hope or confidence **disheartening** adj

dishevelled (say dish-**ev**-əld) adj ruffled and untidy ♦ *his usual dishevelled appearance* **dishevelment** n

dishonest adj not honest **dishonestly** adv **dishonesty** n

dishonour n **1** loss of honour or respect, disgrace **2** something that causes this **dishonour** v **1** to bring dishonour to someone, to disgrace someone **2** to refuse to honour a cheque, agreement, etc. **dishonourable** adj **dishonourably** adv

dishwasher n a machine for washing dishes automatically

disillusion v to get rid of someone's pleasant but mistaken beliefs **disillusion** n the state of being disillusioned **disillusionment** n

disincentive n something that discourages an action or effort

disincline v to make a person feel reluctant or unwilling to do something **disinclination** n

disinfect v to make something clean by destroying bacteria that may cause disease **disinfectant** n **disinfection** n

disinformation n deliberately false information

disingenuous (say dis-in-jen-yoo-əs) adj not frank or sincere **disingenuously** adv

disinherit v to deprive a person of the right to inherit something, especially by making a will naming another person as your heir

disintegrate v 1 to break up into small parts or pieces 2 to become weakened and come to an end **disintegration** n

disinterest n 1 impartiality 2 lack of interest **disinterested** adj **disinterestedly** adv

disjointed adj (said about talk or writing) not having parts logically fitting together and so difficult to understand

disk n another spelling of *disc*, used in computing and in American English **disk drive** n an apparatus that turns the disk on a computer while data is recorded or retrieved

dislike n 1 a feeling of not liking someone or something 2 something that you do not like ♦ *She listed her likes and dislikes.* **dislike** v to feel dislike for someone or something

dislocate v 1 to move or force a bone from its proper position in a joint 2 to put something out of order, to disrupt something ♦ *Fog has dislocated the traffic.* **dislocation** n

dislodge v to move or force something from its place **dislodgement** n

disloyal adj not loyal **disloyally** adv **disloyalty** n

dismal adj 1 gloomy or dreary 2 *informal* of poor quality, feeble ♦ *a dismal attempt at humour* **dismally** adv

dismantle v to take something to pieces

dismay n a feeling of alarm and discouragement **dismay** v to fill someone with dismay

dismember v 1 to tear or cut the limbs from a body 2 to divide something into parts **dismemberment** n

dismiss v 1 to send someone away from your presence 2 to tell someone that you will no longer employ them ♦ *She claims she was unfairly dismissed.* 3 to put something out of your thoughts because it is not worth thinking about 4 to mention or discuss something only briefly 5 to reject a legal case without further hearing ♦ *The court dismissed his appeal.* **dismissal** n **dismissive** adj **dismissively** adv

dismount v 1 to get off a horse or bicycle 2 to remove something from its support

disobey v to fail to obey someone, to refuse to follow rules or orders **disobedience** n **disobedient** adj **disobediently** adv

disorder n 1 lack of order; untidiness or confusion 2 a disturbance of public order, a riot 3 disturbance of the normal working of the body or mind, an illness ♦ *a nervous disorder* **disorder** v to throw something into disorder **disordered** adj **disorderly** adj

disorganized adj 1 not properly planned or controlled 2 (said about a person) not organized or efficient **disorganization** n

disorientate (say dis-or -i-ən-tayt), **disorient** (say dis-or -i-ənt) v to confuse someone and make them lose their sense of direction **disorientated** adj **disorientation** n **disoriented** adj

disown v to refuse to acknowledge that someone or something has any connection with you

disparage (say dis-pa-rij) v to speak of someone or something in a slighting way **disparagement** n **disparagingly** adv

disparate (say dis-per-ət) adj different in kind **disparity** n pl **disparities**

dispassionate adj free from emotion, calm and impartial **dispassionately** adv

dispatch v 1 to send someone off to a destination or for a purpose ♦ *Warships were dispatched to the region.* 2 to complete or dispose of a task or problem quickly 3 to kill a person or animal **dispatch** n 1 dispatching or being dispatched 2 an official message or report sent quickly 3 a news report sent in from abroad by a journalist 4 promptness and efficiency ♦ *He acted with dispatch.*

dispel v **dispelled**, **dispelling** to drive away doubts, fears, etc. ♦ *We need to dispel these rumours of a takeover.*

dispensable adj able to be done without, not essential

dispensary n pl **dispensaries** a place where medicines are dispensed ♦ *the hospital dispensary*

dispensation n 1 dispensing or distributing

something ♦ *the dispensation of justice*
2 exemption from a penalty, rule, or duty

dispense *v* **1** to distribute something to a number of people, to give something out ♦ *a ruler who sought to dispense justice fairly* **2** (said about a machine) to supply a quantity of a product or money **3** to prepare and give out medicines according to prescriptions **dispenser** *n*

disperse *v* **1** to scatter something over a wide area **2** (said about people) to leave and go in different directions, or to make them do this **dispersal** *n* **dispersant** *n* **dispersion** *n*

dispiriting *adj* making you feel depressed and discouraged **dispirited** *adj*

displace *v* **1** to shift something from its usual place **2** to take the place of a person or thing **displacement** *n*

display *v* **1** to show or arrange something so that it can be seen **2** to reveal something ♦ *Don't display your ignorance.* **3** (said about birds and animals) to make a display **display** *n* **1** displaying or being displayed **2** a collection of goods, etc. displayed conspicuously **3** an electronic device for visually presenting data **4** a special pattern of behaviour used by birds and animals as a means of visual communication, especially when attracting a mate

displease *v* to annoy or offend someone **displeasure** *n*

disport *v* to play about in a lively way ♦ *children disporting themselves on the beach*

dispose *v* **1** to make someone willing or ready to do something ♦ *Their friendliness disposed us to accept the invitation.* **2** to place or arrange something in position **disposable** *adj* **disposal** *n* **disposition** *n* **disposability** *n*

dispossess *v* to deprive a person of the possession of something **dispossession** *n*

disproportionate *adj* out of proportion, relatively too large or too small **disproportion** *n* **disproportionately** *adv*

disprove *v* to prove that something is false or wrong

dispute¹ (say dis-**pewt**) *v* **1** to argue or debate **2** to quarrel **3** to question whether something is true or valid ♦ *We dispute*

their claim. **disputable** *adj* **disputant** *n* **disputation** *n*

dispute² (say dis-**pewt** or **dis**-pewt) *n* **1** an argument or debate **2** a quarrel **3** a disagreement between management and employees that leads to industrial action

disqualify *v* **disqualifies**, **disqualified**, **disqualifying 1** to bar someone from a competition because he or she has broken the rules or is not properly qualified to take part **2** to make someone or something unsuitable or ineligible **disqualification** *n*

disquiet *n* anxiety or uneasiness **disquiet** *v* to make someone anxious **disquieting** *adj* **disquietude** *n*

disregard *v* to pay no attention to something, to treat it as of no importance **disregard** *n* lack of attention to something, treating it as of no importance ♦ *She shows a complete disregard for her own safety.*

disrepair *n* a poor condition caused by not doing repairs ♦ *The old cottage is in a state of disrepair.*

disrepute (say dis-ri-**pewt**) *n* the state of having a bad reputation or being discredited ♦ *He has been charged with bringing the game into disrepute.* **disreputable** *adj* **disreputably** *adv*

disrespect *n* lack of respect, rudeness **disrespectful** *adj* **disrespectfully** *adv*

disrobe *v* **1** to take off official or ceremonial robes **2** to undress

disrupt *v* to throw something into disorder, to interrupt the flow or continuity of something ♦ *Floods disrupted traffic.* **disruption** *n* **disruptive** *adj*

dissatisfaction *n* lack of satisfaction or of contentment

dissatisfied *adj* not satisfied or pleased

dissect (say dis-**sekt**) *v* **1** to cut something up in order to examine its internal structure **2** to examine a theory, etc. carefully in great detail **dissection** *n* **dissector** *n*

dissemble *v* to conceal your true feelings

disseminate (say dis-**sem**-in-ayt) *v* to spread ideas, etc. widely **dissemination** *n*

dissent *v* to have or express a different opinion **dissent** *n* a difference in opinion **dissension** *n* **dissenter** *n*

dissertation *n* a long essay on an academic

subject

disservice n a harmful action

dissident (say **dis**-i-dənt) n someone who disagrees, especially someone who opposes the government **dissident** adj disagreeing **dissidence** n

dissimilar adj not similar, unlike **dissimilarity** n

dissipate (say **dis**-i-payt) v 1 to disappear, or to make something disappear 2 to squander something or fritter it away **dissipated** adj **dissipation** n

dissociate (say dis-**soh**-si-ayt) v to separate something in your thoughts **dissociation** n **to dissociate yourself from** to declare that you do not support or agree with something

dissoluble adj able to be dissolved

dissolute (say **dis**-ə-loot) adj having an immoral way of life **dissolution** n 1 putting an end to a marriage or partnership 2 formally ending a parliament or assembly

dissolve v 1 to mix something with a liquid so that it becomes part of the liquid; to become mixed in this way ♦ Wait for the tablet to dissolve. 2 to formally end an assembly or a parliament 3 to annul or put an end to a marriage or partnership 4 to disappear gradually ♦ As she walked home, her anger dissolved. 5 to give way to emotion ♦ He dissolved into tears.

dissonant (say **dis**-ən-ənt) adj lacking harmony, discordant **dissonance** n

dissuade v to discourage someone from doing something ♦ I tried to dissuade her from going. **dissuasion** n **dissuasive** adj

distance n 1 the length of space between one point and another 2 a distant point or place ♦ I could see a ship in the distance. 3 being far away in space or time **distant** adj **distantly** adv **distance learning** n a method of studying at home in which you take lessons by correspondence

distaste n dislike or aversion **distasteful** adj **distastefully** adv

distemper n 1 a disease of dogs 2 a kind of paint made from powdered pigment mixed with glue or size, used on walls **distemper** v to paint a wall, etc. with distemper

distend v to swell something or become swollen because of pressure from inside **distension** n

distil v **distilled**, **distilling** 1 to purify a liquid by boiling it and condensing the vapour; to treat something by distillation 2 to make spirits in this way 3 to extract the essential meaning of something **distillate** n **distillation** n **distiller** n **distillery** n pl **distilleries**

distinct adj 1 able to be perceived clearly by the senses ♦ the distinct outline of a building 2 clearly different or separate **distinction** n **distinctive** adj **distinctly** adv **distinctness** n

distinguish v 1 to see or point out a difference between two or more things ♦ We must distinguish facts from rumours. 2 to make one thing different from another, to be a characteristic mark or property of something 3 to make something out by listening or looking 4 to bring honour to yourself ♦ She distinguished herself by her bravery. **distinguishable** adj **distinguished** adj

distort v 1 to pull or twist something out of its usual shape 2 to give a false account or impression of something ♦ This film deliberately distorts the truth. 3 to change the quality of a sound that is being transmitted or amplified **distortion** n

distract v to take someone's attention away from something **distracted** adj **distraction** n

distraught (say dis-**trawt**) adj very worried and upset

distress n 1 suffering caused by pain, worry, illness, or exhaustion 2 the condition of being damaged or in danger and requiring help ♦ a ship in distress **distress** v 1 to cause distress to someone 2 to give artificial marks of wear to leather, furniture, etc. **distressing** adj

distributary n pl **distributaries** a branch of a river that does not return to it after leaving the main stream, e.g. in a delta

distribute v 1 to divide something and give a share to each of a number of people 2 to hand something out ♦ During the election he distributed leaflets. 3 to place things at different points over an area **distribution** n

distributive adj **distributor** n **1** someone who distributes things, especially an agent who supplies goods to retailers **2** a device in an engine for passing electric current to each of the spark plugs in turn

district n part of a country, city, or county having a particular feature or regarded as a unit for a special purpose

distrust n lack of trust, suspicion **distrust** v to have little trust in someone or something **distrustful** adj

disturb v **1** to spoil someone's peace, rest, or privacy **2** to cause someone to worry **3** to cause something to move from a settled position **disturbance** n **disturbed** adj **disturbing** adj

disunion n separation, lack of union

disunited adj lacking unity or agreement **disunity** n

disuse n the state of being no longer used **disused** adj

ditch n a trench dug to hold water or carry it away **ditch** v **1** to bring an aircraft down in a forced landing on the sea **2** informal to get rid of something

dither v to hesitate indecisively **dither** n a state of hesitation or agitation ♦ in a dither

ditto n (used in lists to avoid repeating something) the same thing again

ditty n pl **ditties** a short simple song

diuretic (say diy-yu-ret-ik) adj causing an increase in the flow of urine

Divali another spelling of Diwali

divan (say div-an) n a low couch or bed without a raised back or ends

dive v **1** to plunge head first into water **2** (said about an aircraft or bird) to plunge steeply downwards **3** (said about a submarine) to go to a deeper level in water **4** to swim under water using breathing equipment **5** to go down or out of sight suddenly **dive** n **1** an act of diving **2** a sharp downward movement or fall **diver** n **dive-bomb** v to drop bombs from a diving aircraft **diving bell** n an open-bottomed container supplied with air, in which a person can be lowered into deep water **diving board** n a high board used for diving from **diving suit** n a watertight suit, usually with a helmet, worn for working deep under water

diverge (say diy-verj) v **1** to go in different directions from a common point or from each other ♦ The path diverges here. **2** to depart from something ♦ This account diverges from the truth. **3** to differ ♦ Our views diverge on this matter. **divergence** n **divergent** adj

diverse (say diy-verss) adj of several different kinds **diversify** v **diversifies**, **diversified**, **diversifying** **diversification** n **diversity** n

divert v **1** to make something change course or go by a different route ♦ The stream has been diverted. **2** to distract someone's attention **3** to entertain or amuse someone **diversion** n **diversionary** adj **diverting** adj

divest (say diy-vest) v to take something away from someone, to deprive someone ♦ They divested him of his power.

divide v **1** to separate something into parts, to split or break up ♦ The river divides here into two. **2** to form a boundary between two things or places ♦ The Pyrenees divide France from Spain. **3** to distribute something or share it out ♦ Divide the prize money between you. **4** to arrange things in separate groups, to classify **5** to cause people to disagree ♦ This controversy divided the party. **6** (said about a legislative assembly) to separate into two groups to vote **7** Mathematics to find how many times one number contains another ♦ Divide 12 by 3. **divide** n a dividing line ♦ the divide between rich and poor **divided** adj **divider** n **divisible** adj **divisibility** n **division** n **divisional** adj **divisive** adj **divisor** n **division sign** n the sign $\div$ (as in $12 \div 4$) indicating that one number is to be divided by another

dividend n **1** a share of profits paid to shareholders or winners in a football pool **2** a benefit from an action ♦ This policy will pay dividends in the future.

divine adj **1** belonging to, coming from, or like God or a god **2** informal excellent, very beautiful ♦ this divine weather **divine** v **1** to discover something by guessing **2** to discover or learn about future events by supernatural or magical means **divination** n **divinely** adv **diviner** n

divinity *n pl* **divinities**

divorce *n* the legal ending of a marriage **divorce** *v* **1** to end a marriage by divorce **2** to think of two things as being separate and not connected **divorcee** *n*

divot (say div-ət) *n* a piece of turf

divulge (say diy-**vulj**) *v* to reveal information

divvy *n pl* **divvies** *informal* a dividend or share **divvy** *v* **divvies**, **divvied**, **divvying** to share something out

Diwali (say di-**wah**-li) *n* a Hindu religious festival at which lamps are lit, held in October or November

DIY *abbr* the activity of doing house repairs and decorations yourself

dizzy *adj* **dizzier**, **dizziest 1** having the feeling that everything is spinning round **2** causing giddiness **dizzily** *adv* **dizziness** *n* **dizzying** *adj*

DJ *abbr* **1** disc jockey **2** dinner jacket

DNA *abbr* deoxyribonucleic acid, a substance in chromosomes that stores genetic information

do *v* **does**, **did**, **done**, **doing 1** to perform or carry out an action, work, a duty or obligation, etc. ♦ *They did a lot to help us.* **2** to act or proceed ♦ *Do as you like.* **3** to fare or manage ♦ *How did you do in the exam?* **4** to deal with or solve something ♦ *I usually do the crossword.* **5** to produce or make something ♦ *She's done some lovely drawings.* **6** to cover a distance in travelling ♦ *We did 400 miles today.* **7** to be suitable or acceptable, to serve a purpose ♦ *It doesn't do to worry.* **8** *informal* to visit somewhere as a tourist ♦ *We did Rome last year.* **9** *informal* to undergo ♦ *He did two years for fraud.* **10** *informal* to swindle someone **11** *informal* to regularly take a drug **do** *auxiliary verb* **1** used to indicate present or past tense ♦ *What does he think?* ♦ *What did he think?* **2** used for emphasis ♦ *I do like chocolate.* **3** used to avoid repetition of a verb you have just used ♦ *We work as hard as they do.* **do** *n pl* **dos** or **do's** *informal* a party or other social event

docile (say **doh**-siyl) *adj* willing to obey or accept control **docilely** *adv* **docility** *n*

dock[1] *n* an enclosed area of water in a

port where ships are loaded, unloaded, or repaired **dock** *v* (said about a ship) to come into or bring it into a dock **docker** *n* **docks** *pl n* a dockyard **dockland** *n* the district near a dockyard **dockyard** *n* an area with docks and equipment for building and repairing ships

dock[2] *n* an enclosure in a criminal court for a defendant on trial

dock[3] *n* a weed with broad leaves

dock[4] *v* **1** to take away part of someone's wages or a number of points from someone's score **2** to cut short an animal's tail

docket *n* a document or label listing goods delivered or the contents of a package, or recording payment of duty, etc.

doctor *n* **1** a person who is qualified to practise medicine **2** a person who holds a doctorate (the highest university degree) ♦ *Doctor of Music.* **doctor** *v* to tamper with or falsify something ♦ *Somebody has doctored the evidence.* **doctorate** *n* the highest degree at a university, entitling the holder to the title of 'doctor' **doctoral** *adj* to do with a doctorate ♦ *a doctoral thesis*

doctrine (say **dok**-trin) *n* a set of principles and beliefs held by a religious or political or other group **doctrinal** *adj*

document *n* **1** a paper giving information or evidence about something **2** *ICT* a file of text or graphics stored in a computer **document** *v* **1** to provide written evidence to support or prove something **2** to record something in detail **documentary** *adj* **1** consisting of documents ♦ *documentary evidence* **2** giving a factual filmed report of a subject or activity **documentary** *n pl* **documentaries** a film giving information about real events **documentation** *n*

dodder *v* to walk unsteadily **dodderer** *n* **doddery** *adj*

doddle *n informal* a very easy task

dodecagon (say doh-**dek**-ə-gən) *n* a geometric figure with twelve sides

dodecahedron (say doh-dekə-**hee**-drən) *n pl* **dodecahedra** or **dodecahedrons** a solid body with twelve faces

dodge *v* **1** to avoid something by changing position or direction **2** to evade something by cunning or trickery ♦ *He tried to dodge military service.* **dodge** *n* **1** a quick movement to avoid something **2** *informal* a clever trick, an ingenious way of doing something **dodger** *n* **dodgy** *adj* **dodgier, dodgiest 1** not working properly **2** dishonest **3** risky or dangerous

dodo (say doh-doh) *n pl* **dodos** or **dodoes** a large non-flying bird that has been extinct since the 18th century

doe *n* the female of the fallow deer, reindeer, hare, or rabbit

doesn't *informal v* does not

doff *v* to take something off ♦ *He doffed his hat.*

dog *n* **1** a four-legged carnivorous animal, commonly kept as a pet or trained for use in hunting, etc. **2** the male of this or of the wolf or fox **dog** *v* **dogged, dogging** to follow someone closely or persistently ♦ *Reporters dogged his footsteps.* **dogged** *adj* determined, not giving up easily **doggedly** *adv* **doggedness** *n* **dog collar** *n* **1** a collar for a dog **2** *informal* a clerical collar **dog-eared** *adj* (said about a book) having the corners of the pages turned down through constant use **dogfight** *n* **1** a close fight between fighter aircraft **2** a fierce struggle or fight **dogsbody** *n pl* **dogsbodies** a person who is given boring, unimportant jobs to do

dogma *n* a belief or principle that a Church or other authority puts forward to be accepted as true without question **dogmatic** *adj* firmly and arrogantly expressing personal opinions as if there is no question that they are true **dogmatically** *adv* **dogmatism** *n*

doing *n* **1** performing a deed ♦ *It was my doing.* **2** effort ♦ *It will take some doing.*

doldrums *pl n* **1** a period of inactivity **2** the ocean regions near the equator where there is little or no wind

dole *v* to distribute something ♦ *Can you dole out the pizza?* **dole** *n informal* money paid by the state to unemployed people ♦ *He's been on the dole for six months.*

doleful *adj* mournful or sad **dolefully** *adv*

doll *n* a small model of a human figure, especially as a child's toy **doll** *v* (**to doll**

yourself up) *informal* to dress smartly **dolly** *n pl* **dollies**

dollar *n* the unit of money in the USA and some other countries

dollop *n informal* a shapeless lump of something soft ♦ *a dollop of cream*

dolomite (say dol-ə-miyt) *n* a mineral or rock of calcium magnesium carbonate

dolphin *n* a sea animal with a beak-like snout

dolt (say dohlt) *n* a stupid person **doltish** *adj*

domain (say dəm-ayn) *n* **1** an area under someone's control **2** a field of knowledge or activity ♦ *the domain of science* **3** *ICT* a distinct group of Internet addresses with the same suffix

dome *n* **1** a rounded roof with a circular base **2** something shaped like this **domed** *adj*

domestic *adj* **1** to do with the home or household or family affairs **2** to do with your own country, not foreign or international ♦ *domestic air services* **3** (said about animals) kept by humans, not wild **domestic** *n* a household servant **domestically** *adv* **domesticated** *adj* **domesticity** *n*

domicile (say dom-i-siyl) *n formal* the place where someone lives, residence **domicile** *v* **domiciliary** *adj* **to be domiciled** to have a particular country as your permanent home

dominate *v* **1** to control someone or something by being stronger or more powerful than them **2** to be the most influential or conspicuous person or thing **3** (said about a high place) to tower over something ♦ *The mountain dominates the whole valley.* **dominance** *n* **dominant** *adj* **domination** *n* **domineer** *v* **domineering** *adj*

dominion *n* **1** authority to rule others, control **2** an area controlled by a ruler or government

domino *n pl* **dominoes** each of the small oblong wooden or plastic pieces marked with up to 6 dots on each half, used in games **dominoes** *n* a game played with these

don[1] *v* **donned, donning** to put on a piece of clothing

don[2] *n* a university teacher, especially a

senior member of a college at Oxford or Cambridge **donnish** *adj*

donate *v* **1** to give money, etc. for a good cause **2** to give blood for transfusion or an organ for a transplant **donation** *n*

done past participle of *do* **done** *adj* **1** *informal* socially acceptable ♦ *the done thing* **2** cooked thoroughly **done** *interjection* (in reply to an offer) I accept **done in** *informal* tired out **done with** finished with, completed **to be done for** *informal* to be in serious trouble

doner kebab (say **don**-er kə-**bab**) *n* layers of lamb or mutton cooked on a spit and sliced downwards

donkey *n pl* **donkeys** an animal of the horse family, with long ears and a braying call **donkey's years** *informal* a very long time

donor *n* **1** someone who gives or donates something, especially to a charity **2** someone who provides blood for transfusion or semen for insemination or tissue for transplantation

don't *contraction* do not

doodle *v* to scribble or draw while thinking about something else **doodle** *n* a drawing or marks made by doodling

doom *n* a terrible fate that you cannot avoid, especially death or destruction ♦ *a sense of impending doom* **doom** *v* to destine or condemn someone to a terrible fate **doomed** *adj* **doomsday** *n* the day of the Last Judgement, the end of the world

door *n* **1** a hinged, sliding, or revolving barrier used to open or close an entrance to a building, room, vehicle, or cupboard **2** a doorway or entrance **doorbell** *n* a bell inside a house, rung from outside by visitors as a signal **doorkeeper** *n* a person on duty at the entrance to a building **doorknob** *n* a knob for turning to release the latch of a door **doorman** *n pl* **doormen** a man on duty at the entrance to a large building **doorstep** *n* **1** a step leading up to the door of a house **2** *informal* a thick slice of bread **doorstop** *n* a device for keeping a door open or preventing it from striking a wall when it opens **door-to-door** *adj* (said about selling, etc.) done at each house in turn **doorway** *n* an opening into which a

door fits

doormat *n* **1** a mat placed at a door, for wiping dirt from shoes **2** *informal* a person who meekly allows himself or herself to be bullied

dope *n informal* **1** an illegal drug **2** a drug given to an athlete, horse, or greyhound to affect performance **3** a stupid person **4** information **dope** *v* **1** to give dope to an athlete, horse, or greyhound **2** to take addictive drugs **3** *Electronics* to add an impurity to a semiconductor to achieve a specific electrical property **dopey** *adj* **dopier, dopiest, dopiness** *n*

doppelgänger (say **dop**-əl-geng-er) *n* **1** a ghost that looks exactly like a living person **2** someone who looks exactly like someone else, a double

dormant *adj* **1** temporarily inactive ♦ *a dormant volcano* **2** sleeping, lying inactive as if in sleep **3** (said about plants) alive but not actively growing **dormancy** *n*

dormer window *n* an upright window under a small gable built out from a sloping roof

dormitory *n pl* **dormitories** a room with a number of beds, especially in a school or institution

dormitory town *n* a town from which people travel to work elsewhere because there are few or no industries locally

dormouse *n pl* **dormice** a mouse-like rodent that hibernates in winter

dorsal *adj* to do with or on the back of an animal or plant ♦ *a dorsal fin* **dorsally** *adv*

dose *n* **1** an amount of medicine taken at one time **2** *informal* an amount of something, especially something that you do not want ♦ *a dose of punishment* **dose** *v* to give someone a dose of medicine **dosage** *n*

dossier (say **dos**-i-er) *n* a set of documents containing information about a person or event

dot *n* **1** a small round mark or spot **2** the shorter of the two signals used in Morse code **dot** *v* **dotted, dotting 1** to mark something with a dot or dots **2** to scatter things or be scattered here and there ♦ *Just dot a few cushions about.*

dotage (say **doh**-tij) *n* the period of time in

which someone is old and weak ♦ *He is in his dotage.*

dotard (say **doh**-terd) *n* a person who is weak or senile

dot-com *n Economics* a company that operates on the Internet

dote *v* **to dote on** to be very, perhaps foolishly, fond of someone **doting** *adj*

dotty *adj* **dottier, dottiest** *informal* slightly mad or eccentric **dottiness** *n*

double *adj* **1** twice as much or twice as many ♦ *a double whisky* **2** consisting of two things or parts that form a pair **3** suitable for two people ♦ *a double bed* **4** combining two things or qualities ♦ *The title has a double meaning.* **5** (said about flowers) having more than one circle of petals **double** *adv* twice the amount or quantity ♦ *It costs double what it cost last year.* **double** *n* **1** a double quantity or thing **2** a person or thing that looks exactly like another ♦ *You're the double of my cousin.* **doubles** *pl n* a game between two pairs of players **double** *v* **1** to make something, or become, twice as much or as many **2** to bend or fold something in two **3** to turn sharply back from a course ♦ *The fox doubled back on its tracks.* **doubly** *adv* **double agent** *n* a spy who spies for two rival countries at the same time **double-barrelled** *adj* **1** (said about a gun) having two barrels **2** (said about a surname) having two parts joined by a hyphen **double bass** *n* the largest and lowest-pitched instrument of the violin family **double bluff** *n* an action or statement that is intended to appear as a bluff, but in fact is genuine **double-breasted** *adj* (said about a jacket or coat) having two fronts that overlap to fasten across the body **double-check** *v* to verify something twice or in two ways **double chin** *n* a chin with a fold of loose flesh below it **double-click** *v ICT* to press a mouse button twice in quick succession to make a selection or perform a function **double-cross** *v* to deceive or cheat someone who thinks you are working with them **double-cross** *n* an act of double-crossing **double-dealing** *n* deceit, especially in business **double-decker** *n* a bus with two decks

double Dutch *n* talk that makes no sense at all **double entendre** *n* a word or phrase with two meanings, one of which is sexual or rude **double figures** *pl n* any of the numbers from 10 to 99, as a total **double take** *n* a delayed reaction to something unexpected, coming immediately after your first reaction

double entry *n* a system of bookkeeping in which each transaction is entered as a debit in one account and a credit in another

doublet (say **dub**-lit) *n* a man's close-fitting jacket, with or without sleeves

doubloon (say dub-**loon**) *n* a former Spanish gold coin

doubt *n* **1** a feeling of uncertainty about something, an undecided state of mind **2** a feeling of disbelief **doubt** *v* **1** to feel uncertain or undecided about something **2** to hesitate to believe something **doubter** *n* **doubtful** *adj* **doubtfully** *adv* **doubtless** *adv*

douche (say doosh) *n* a jet of liquid applied to a part of the body to clean it or for medical purposes

dough (say doh) *n* **1** a thick mixture of flour and water, used for making bread, cake, or pastry **2** *informal* money **doughy** *adj* **doughnut** *n* a small fried cake or ring of sweetened dough

dour (say door) *adj* stern and gloomy-looking **dourly** *adv* **dourness** *n*

douse (say dows) *v* **1** to put something into water, to throw water over something **2** to extinguish a fire or light ◊ Do not confuse this word with *dowse*, which has a different meaning.

dove *n* **1** a kind of bird that resembles a pigeon **2** a person who favours a policy of peace and negotiation **dovecote** *n* a shelter for domesticated pigeons **dovetail** *n* a wedge-shaped joint used to join two pieces of wood **dovetail** *v* **1** to join pieces of wood with a dovetail **2** to fit closely together, to combine neatly ♦ *My plans dovetailed with hers.*

dowager (say **dow**-ə-jer) *n* a woman who holds a title or property after her husband has died ♦ *the dowager duchess*

dowdy *adj* **dowdier, dowdiest 1** (said about

clothes) unattractively dull, not stylish **2** dressed in dowdy clothes **dowdily** adv **dowdiness** n

dowel (say dowl) n a headless wooden or metal pin for holding two pieces of wood or stone together **dowel** v **dowelled**, **dowelling** to fasten something with a dowel

dower n a widow's share of her husband's estate **dower house** n

Dow Jones index n an index of figures indicating the relative price of shares on the New York Stock Exchange

down[1] adv **1** into or towards a lower place; from an upright position to a horizontal one ♦ It fell down. **2** to or at a lower place; further south **3** to or at a lower level or value; to a smaller size **4** so as to be less active ♦ Settle down! **5** (said about a computer) out of action **6** away from a central place or a university ♦ She is down from headquarters. **7** from an earlier to a later time ♦ down to the present day **8** in writing ♦ Take down these instructions. **9** to the source or the place where something is ♦ See if you can track it down. **10** as a payment at the time of purchase ♦ We will pay £50 down and the rest later. **down** prep **1** downwards along or through or into, along, from top to bottom of ♦ Pour it down the drain. **2** at a lower part of ♦ Oxford is further down the river. **down** adj **1** directed downwards ♦ a down draught **2** travelling away from a central place ♦ a down train **down** v informal **1** to knock or bring something to the ground **2** to swallow a drink **down** n **1** a misfortune ♦ ups and downs **2** informal a dislike, a grudge against someone ♦ She has a real down on him. **downer** n **1** a depressant or tranquillizing drug **2** something depressing **downward** adj moving, leading, or pointing towards a lower point or level ♦ a downward glance **downwards** or **downward** adv towards a lower point or level ♦ The lawn slopes downwards towards the stream. **downbeat** n Mus an accented beat, for which the conductor's baton moves downwards **downbeat** adj pessimistic or gloomy **downcast** adj **1** looking downwards ♦ downcast eyes

2 (said about a person) dejected **downfall** n **1** a fall from prosperity or power **2** something that causes this **downgrade** v to reduce something to a lower grade or rank **downhearted** adj in low spirits **downhill** adv in a downward direction; further down a slope **downhill** adj going or sloping downwards **download** v to transfer data from one computer system or from the Internet to another system or to a disk **download** n the process of downloading, or a file or program that has been downloaded **downmarket** adj, adv of or towards the cheaper end of the market **down payment** n an initial payment made when buying something on credit **downplay** v to make something seem less important than it really is **downpour** n a heavy fall of rain **downright** adj **1** thorough, complete ♦ a downright lie **2** frank, straightforward **downright** adv thoroughly ♦ He was downright rude. **downsize** v (said about a company or organization) to reduce the size of its workforce **downstairs** adv down the stairs; to or on a lower floor **downstairs** adj situated downstairs **down time** n the time when a computer system is out of action **down-to-earth** adj sensible and practical **downtrodden** adj oppressed or badly treated by people in power **downturn** n a decline in something, especially economic activity **down under** adv in Australia or New Zealand **downwind** adj, adv in the direction towards which the wind is blowing **down and out** adj completely destitute **down at heel** adj shabby

down[2] n very fine soft furry feathers or short hairs **downy** adj **downier**, **downiest** like or covered with soft down

down[3], **downland** n an area of open rolling land **the Downs** n the chalk uplands of south England

Down's syndrome n an abnormal congenital condition

dowry n pl **dowries** property or money brought by a bride to her husband when she marries him

dowse v to search for underground water or minerals by using a Y-shaped stick or rod **dowser** n ◊ Do not confuse this word with *douse*, which has a different meaning.

doyen (say **doy**-ən), **doyenne** (say doy-**en**) *n* the most respected person in a particular field or profession ◊ The masculine form is **doyen** and the feminine form is **doyenne**.

doze *v* to sleep lightly **doze** *n* a short light sleep **dozy** *adj* **dozier, doziest 1** drowsy **2** *informal* stupid or lazy

dozen *n* a group or set of twelve ◊ Correct use is *ten dozen*, not *ten dozens*.

DPI *abbr ICT* dots per inch; a measurement used to describe the resolution of a computer screen, scanner, or printer

Dr *abbr* Doctor

drab *adj* **1** dull or uninteresting ♦ *a drab life* **2** of dull brownish colour **drab** *n* a dull brownish colour **drably** *adv* **drabness** *n*

draconian (say drə-**koh**-niən) *adj* very harsh or severe ♦ *draconian laws*

draft *n* **1** a rough preliminary written version ♦ *a draft of an essay* **2** a written order for a bank to pay out money **3** *N. Am* conscription **draft** *v* **1** to prepare a written draft of something ♦ *I've drafted the speech.* **2** to select someone for a special duty ♦ *He was drafted to the Paris branch.* ◊ This is also the American spelling of *draught*.

drag *v* **dragged, dragging 1** to pull something along with effort or difficulty **2** to take someone somewhere, especially against their will **3** to trail or allow something to trail along the ground **4** to move an image across a computer screen using a mouse **5** to search the bottom of a river or lake with nets and hooks ♦ *The police dragged the river for a body.* **6** to continue slowly in a boring manner ♦ *The speeches dragged on.* **drag** *n* **1** *informal* something that is tedious or a nuisance **2** women's clothes worn by men

dragon *n* **1** a mythical monster resembling a reptile, usually with wings and able to breathe out fire **2** a fierce person **dragonfly** *n pl* **dragonflies** an insect with a long thin body and two pairs of transparent wings that spread out while it is resting

dragoon *n* a member of certain cavalry regiments, originally a mounted infantryman **dragoon** *v* to force someone into doing something

drain *n* **1** a channel or pipe through which liquid or sewage is carried away **2** something that takes away your strength or resources **drain** *v* **1** to draw off liquid by means of channels or pipes, etc. **2** to flow or trickle away **3** to dry or become dried as liquid flows away **4** (said about a river) to carry off the superfluous water from an area **5** to gradually take away strength or resources **6** to drink the contents of a glass, etc. **drainage** *n* **drainpipe** *n* a pipe used for carrying rainwater or sewage from a building

drake *n* a male duck

dram *n* a small drink of spirits

drama (say **drah**-mə) *n* **1** a play **2** the art of writing and performing plays **3** an exciting or emotional series of events **4** dramatic quality ♦ *the drama of the situation* **dramatic** *adj* **dramatically** *adv* **dramatist** *n* **dramatize** *v* **dramatization** *n*

drape *v* **1** to arrange cloth or clothing loosely on or round something **2** to cover something loosely with folds of cloth **drapes** *pl n N. Am* long curtains **draper** *n* **drapery** *n pl* **draperies**

drastic *adj* having a strong or violent effect **drastically** *adv*

drat *interjection* used to express anger or annoyance **dratted** *adj*

draught (say drahft) *n* **1** a current of usually cold air indoors **2** the depth of water needed to float a ship **3** one continuous process of swallowing liquid **draughts** *pl n* a game for two players using 24 round pieces, played on a chequered board of 64 squares **draughty** *adj* **draughtier, draughtiest, draughtiness** *n* **draughtboard** *n* a chequered board used for playing draughts, identical to a chessboard **draughtsman** *n pl* **draughtsmen 1** someone who makes detailed technical drawings or plans **2** someone who is good at drawing **3** a piece used in the game of draughts **draughtsmanship** *n*

draw *v* **drew, drawn 1** to produce a picture or diagram by making marks on a surface **2** to pull something ♦ *The horse drew a cart behind it.* **3** to pull curtains shut or open

4 to attract something ♦ *The singer always draws large crowds.* **5** to take something in ♦ *He hardly had time to draw breath.* **6** to take something out ♦ *People were drawing water from the well.* **7** to obtain something in a raffle or lottery ♦ *You've drawn the winning ticket.* **8** to get information from someone ♦ *He refused to be drawn about his plans.* **9** to end a game or contest with the same score on both sides **10** to move or come ♦ *The boat drew nearer.* **11** to reach a certain point in time ♦ *The concert drew to a close.* **draw** n **1** a game or match that ends with the scores even **2** a person or thing that draws custom or attention **3** the drawing of lots, e.g. to decide the winner of a raffle or lottery **4** the drawing out of a gun in order to shoot ♦ *He was quick on the draw.* **drawing** n **drawback** n a disadvantage **drawbridge** n a bridge over a moat, hinged at one end so that it can be raised or lowered **drawing board** n a flat board on which paper is stretched while a drawing is made **drawing pin** n a flat-headed pin for fastening paper to a surface **drawstring** n a string that can be pulled to tighten or close an opening

drawer n **1** a sliding box-like compartment in a piece of furniture **2** a person who draws something **3** the person who writes out a cheque

drawl v to speak lazily or with drawn-out vowel sounds **drawl** n a drawling manner of speaking

dread n great fear or apprehension **dreads** pl n informal dreadlocks **dread** v to feel worried or apprehensive about something **dread** adj greatly feared **dreadful** adj very bad or unpleasant ♦ *dreadful weather* **dreadfully** adv

dreadlocks pl n hair worn in many ringlets or plaits, especially by Rastafarians

dream n **1** a series of pictures or events in a sleeping person's mind **2** the state of mind in which someone is daydreaming ♦ *He goes around in a dream.* **3** an ambition or ideal **4** informal a beautiful person or thing **dream** v past tense and past participle **dreamt** (say dremt) or **dreamed** (say dreemd) **1** to have a dream or dreams

while sleeping **2** to have an ambition ♦ *He had always dreamt of being champion.* **3** to think of something as a possibility ♦ *I never dreamt it would happen.* **dreamer** n **dreamless** adj n **dreamy** adj **dreamier**, **dreamiest**, **dreamily** adv **dreaminess** n

dreary adj **drearier**, **dreariest** dull, boring, or gloomy **drearily** adv **dreariness** n

dredge[1] n an apparatus for scooping things from the bottom of a river or the sea **dredge** v to bring something up or clean something out with a dredge **dredger** n

dredge[2] v to sprinkle food with sugar or flour **dredger** n

dregs pl n **1** the last drops of a liquid at the bottom of a glass, barrel, etc., together with any sediment **2** the worst and most useless part ♦ *the dregs of society*

drench v to make someone wet through ♦ *We got drenched in the rain.*

dress n **1** a woman's or girl's piece of clothing with a bodice and skirt **2** clothing, especially the visible part of it **dress** v **1** to put on your clothes or put clothes on someone else **2** to wear clothes in a particular way or of a particular type ♦ *She always dresses well.* ♦ *The children were dressed in rags.* **3** to put on formal or evening clothes ♦ *They dress for dinner.* **4** to arrange a display in a window, etc.; to decorate something **5** to put a dressing on a wound **6** to prepare poultry, crab, etc. for cooking or eating; to coat salad with dressing **dressage** n the training of a horse to perform various manoeuvres in order to show its obedience **dresser** n **dressing** n **1** a bandage, plaster, ointment, etc. for a wound **2** a sauce of oil, vinegar, herbs, etc. for a salad **dressy** adj **dressier**, **dressiest** (said about clothes) elegant or elaborate, suitable for special occasions **dress circle** n the first level of seats above the ground floor in a theatre **dressing gown** n a loose robe worn when you are not fully dressed **dressmaker** n **dressmaking** n **dress rehearsal** n the final rehearsal of a play in full costume

dresser n a kitchen sideboard with shelves above for displaying plates

dressing room n a room for dressing or

changing your clothes

dribble v 1 (said about a liquid) to flow or allow it to flow in drops 2 to let saliva trickle out of your mouth 3 to move the ball forward in football or hockey with slight touches of your feet or stick **dribble** n 1 a thin stream of liquid 2 an act of dribbling

drift v 1 to be carried gently along by or as if by a current of water or air 2 to walk along casually or aimlessly 3 to move into a situation without meaning or planning to ♦ He drifted into teaching. 4 to be piled into drifts by wind ♦ The snow had drifted. **drift** n 1 a drifting movement from one place to another 2 a mass of snow or sand piled up by wind 3 deviation from a set course 4 the general intention or meaning of what someone says ♦ I didn't understand it all, but I think I got the drift of it. 5 fragments of rock carried and deposited by wind, water, or a glacier 6 (in South Africa) a ford **drifter** n **drift net** n a large net for catching herring, etc., allowed to drift with the tide **driftwood** n wood floating on the sea or washed ashore

drill¹ n 1 a pointed tool or a machine used for boring holes or sinking wells 2 training in military exercises 3 thorough training or instruction by practical exercises, usually with much repetition 4 informal the correct or recognized procedure ♦ I expect you know the drill by now. **drill** v 1 to use a drill; to make a hole with a drill 2 to teach someone to do something by making them do repeated exercises

drill² n 1 a machine for making small furrows and sowing seed in them 2 a small furrow for sowing seeds in **drill** v to sow seed with a drill

drill³ n strong twilled linen or cotton cloth

drink v drank, drunk 1 to swallow liquid 2 (said about plants, the soil, etc.) to take in or absorb liquid 3 to drink alcohol 4 to express good wishes to someone or something by drinking, to toast someone ♦ Let's drink to your success. **drink** n 1 liquid for drinking 2 a portion of liquid for drinking ♦ Would you like a drink of water? 3 an alcoholic drink **drinker** n

drip v dripped, dripping (said about liquid)

to fall or let it fall in drops **drip** n 1 a small drop of liquid ♦ a drip of paint 2 the act or sound of liquid dripping 3 a device that drips liquid, drugs, etc. into a patient's vein 4 informal a weak or ineffectual person **dripping** n fat melted from roasted meat and allowed to set **dripping** adj extremely wet **drip-feed** v past tense and past participle **drip-fed** to feed someone with a drip

drive v drove, driven 1 to operate a motor vehicle or train and direct its course 2 to travel or carry someone in a car 3 to urge or force someone to go in some direction by blows, threats, etc. ♦ Their bickering drove me into the kitchen. 4 to push, send, or carry something along 5 to hit or kick a ball hard 6 to force a nail, etc. into something ♦ He drove the stake into the ground. 7 (said about steam or other power) to keep an engine or machine going 8 to force or compel someone to do something ♦ Hunger drove them to steal. 9 to force someone into a state ♦ Her attitude was driving him mad. **drive** n 1 a trip or journey in a car 2 a hard stroke made in cricket or golf, etc. 3 the transmission of power to machinery or to the wheels of a vehicle ♦ front-wheel drive 4 a psychological urge ♦ the sex drive 5 determination and ambition 6 an organized effort to achieve something ♦ a sales drive 7 ICT a disk drive 8 a road or track leading to a house **driver** n 1 a person or thing that drives something 2 a golf club used for driving from a tee **driving** adj 1 having a strong influence ♦ the driving force 2 (said about rain) blown by the wind with great force **drove** n 1 a herd or flock being driven or moving together 2 a large number of people moving or doing something together **drover** n a person who herds cattle or sheep to market or pasture **drive-in** adj (said about a cinema, restaurant, etc.) able to be used without getting out of your car **driveway** n a road or track leading to a house **what someone is driving at** the point that someone is trying to make

drivel n silly talk, nonsense **drivel** v **drivelled**, **drivelling** to talk or write drivel

drizzle n very fine rain **drizzle** v 1 to rain in very fine drops 2 to trickle oil or some other liquid over food in a thin stream **drizzly** adj

droll (say drohl) adj amusing in an odd way **drolly** adv

drone n 1 a male bee which does not work in a colony but can fertilize a queen 2 an idler 3 a continuous deep humming sound 4 the bass pipe of a bagpipe, or its continuous deep note **drone** v to make a deep humming sound

drool v 1 to water at the mouth, to dribble 2 to show excessive admiration or desire for something

droop v to bend or hang downwards through tiredness or weakness **droop** n an act of drooping **droopy** adj

drop v **dropped**, **dropping** 1 to allow something to fall ♦ dropping stones into the water 2 to fall by force of gravity through not being held 3 to sink from exhaustion 4 to put down a passenger or parcel, etc. ♦ Drop me at the station. 5 to become or make something lower, weaker, or less ♦ The wind dropped. 6 to form a steep or vertical descent ♦ The cliff drops sharply to the sea. 7 to abandon or stop dealing with something ♦ The charges against him were dropped. 8 to allow yourself to move to a position further back ♦ She dropped behind the others. 9 to mention or send something casually ♦ He dropped a few hints. 10 to leave someone out of a team or group **drop** n 1 a small rounded or pear-shaped portion of liquid 2 a very small quantity, especially of a drink ♦ There's just a drop left. 3 a steep or vertical descent, or the distance of this ♦ It's a long drop to the ground. 4 the act of dropping 5 a fall or decrease ♦ a drop in prices 6 a sweet or lozenge ♦ a chocolate drop 7 an earring that hangs down 8 the length of a hanging curtain **drops** pl n liquid medicine to be measured by drops

dross n 1 rubbish 2 scum on the surface of molten metal

drought (say drowt) n a long period of dry weather

drown v 1 to kill someone or be killed by suffocation under water 2 to submerge or flood an area 3 to make so much noise that another sound cannot be heard

drowse v to be half asleep **drowsy** adj **drowsier**, **drowsiest**, **drowsily** adv **drowsiness** n

drudge n a person who does hard, boring or menial work **drudgery** n

drug n 1 a substance used in medicine 2 a substance that acts on the nervous system e.g. a narcotic or stimulant, especially one causing addiction **drug** v **drugged**, **drugging** 1 to add a drug to food or drink 2 to give a drug to someone, especially to make them unconscious **druggist** n **drugstore** n

Druid (say droo-id) n a priest of an ancient Celtic religion in Britain and France **Druidic** adj **Druidism** n

drum n 1 a percussion instrument consisting of a skin stretched tightly across a round frame 2 the sound of a drum being struck, or a similar sound 3 a cylindrical object or container ♦ an oil drum **drum** v **drummed**, **drumming** 1 to play a drum or drums 2 to make a drumming sound, especially by tapping continuously or rhythmically on something ♦ She was drumming her fingers on the table. 3 to drive a lesson, facts, etc. into a person's mind by constant repetition **drummer** n a person who plays a drum or drums **drumbeat** n a pattern of strokes on a drum **drum major** n a leader of a marching band **drumstick** n 1 a stick for beating a drum 2 the lower part of a cooked fowl's leg

drunk past participle of drink **drunk** adj not able to control your behaviour through drinking too much alcohol **drunk** n a person who is drunk or often drunk **drunkard** n a person who is often drunk **drunken** adj **drunkenly** adv **drunkenness** n

dry adj **drier**, **driest** 1 containing no water or moisture ♦ Are the towels dry yet? 2 not producing water, oil, or milk ♦ a dry well 3 without rain ♦ a dry spell 4 eaten without butter, etc. ♦ dry bread 5 thirsty ♦ I'm feeling dry. 6 (said about wine) not sweet 7 boring or dull ♦ a dry book 8 (said about remarks or humour) said in a matter-of-fact or ironical way ♦ her dry wit 9 not allowing the sale of alcohol ♦ a dry state **dry** v **dries**,

dried, **drying** 1 to make something dry, or to become dry 2 to preserve food, etc. by removing its moisture ♦ *dried fruit* **drier** *n*

drily *adv* **dryness** *n* **dry-clean** *v* to clean clothes, etc. by a solvent which evaporates very quickly, not by water **dry-cleaning** *n* **dry dock** *n* a dock that can be emptied of water, used for repairing ships **dry-eyed** *adj* not crying **dry land** *n* land in contrast to the sea, a river, etc. ♦ *I couldn't wait to reach dry land.* **dry run** *n* a rehearsal or practice

DTI *abbr* Department of Trade and Industry

DTP *abbr* desktop publishing

dual *adj* having two parts or aspects, double ♦ *She has dual nationality.* **duality** *n* **dual carriageway** *n* a road with a dividing strip between lanes of traffic in opposite directions **dual-control** *adj* (said about a vehicle or aircraft) having two sets of controls, one of which is used by an instructor

dub¹ *v* **dubbed**, **dubbing** 1 to make a man a knight 2 to give a person or thing a nickname or title

dub² *v* **dubbed**, **dubbing** 1 to replace the original soundtrack of a film with one in a different language ♦ *It is a Spanish film dubbed into English.* 2 to add sound effects or music to a film or recording 3 to add additional sounds to a recording **dub** *n* an instance of dubbing sound effects or music

dubious (say dew-bi-əs) *adj* 1 doubtful or suspicious about something ♦ *I'm dubious about their motives.* 2 not to be relied on, questionable ♦ *a rather dubious character* **dubiously** *adv*

duchess *n* 1 a duke's wife or widow 2 a woman whose rank is equal to that of a duke

duchy *n pl* **duchies** the territory of a duke or duchess ♦ *the duchy of Cornwall* **ducal** *adj*

duck *n* 1 a swimming bird of various kinds 2 the female of this 3 the flesh of a duck as food 4 a ducking movement **duck** *v* 1 to bend down quickly, especially to avoid being seen or hit 2 to dip the head under water and emerge 3 to avoid a task or duty ♦ *You shouldn't duck your responsibilities.* **duckling** *n* a young duck **duckbill** *n* a platypus **duckweed** *n* a plant that grows

on the surface of ponds, etc.

duct *n* 1 a tube or channel through which liquid, gas, air, cable, etc. can pass 2 a vessel in the body through which fluid passes ♦ *tear ducts* **duct** *v* to convey something through a duct **ducting** *n* **ductless** *adj*

dud *n informal* something that is useless or a fake or that fails to work properly **dud** *adj informal* useless or defective

dude (say dewd) *n N. Am informal* 1 a man ♦ *a cool dude* 2 a dandy

dudgeon (say duj-ən) *n* deep resentment or indignation ♦ *He stormed out of the room in high dudgeon.*

due *adj* 1 expected; scheduled to do something or to arrive ♦ *The train is due in ten minutes.* 2 owing; needing to be paid ♦ *The rent was due on Monday.* 3 deserving something ♦ *You're due a bit of luck.* 4 that ought to be given to a person; proper or appropriate ♦ *with due respect* **due** *adv* exactly or directly ♦ *We sailed due east.* **due** *n* something you deserve or have a right to ♦ *A fair hearing is my due.* **dues** *pl n* a fee ♦ *harbour dues*

duel *n* 1 a fight between two people, especially with swords or pistols 2 a contest between two people or sides **duel** *v* **duelled**, **duelling** to fight a duel **duellist** *n*

duet *n* a piece of music for or performance by two players or singers

duff *adj informal* worthless or false

duffel *n* heavy woollen cloth with a thick nap **duffel bag** *n* a cylindrical canvas bag closed by a drawstring **duffel coat** *n* a hooded overcoat made of duffel, fastened with toggles

dug past tense and past participle of **dig**

dugout *n* 1 an underground shelter 2 a shelter at the side of a sports field for a team's coaches and substitutes 3 a canoe made by hollowing out a tree trunk

duke *n* a nobleman of the highest hereditary rank **dukedom** *n* the position or lands of a duke

dulcet (say dul-sit) *adj* sweet-sounding

dull *adj* 1 not interesting or exciting, boring ♦ *a dull match* 2 not bright or clear ♦ *a dull sky* 3 slow in understanding, stupid 4 not sharp; weak and indistinct ♦ *a dull* *ache* **dull** v to make something dull, or to become dull **dullness** n **dully** adv

dullard n a stupid person

duly (say dew-li) adv **1** in the correct or suitable way **2** as might be expected

dumb adj **1** without the ability to speak **2** temporarily unable or unwilling to speak ♦ *We were struck dumb by this news.* **3** *informal* stupid **dumb** v **dumbly** adv **dumbness** n **dumb-bell** n a short bar with a weight at each end, lifted to exercise the muscles **dumbfound** v to astonish someone, to strike someone dumb with surprise **dumbstruck** adj so shocked or surprised that you are unable to speak

dummy n pl **dummies 1** a model of a human figure, especially one used to display clothes **2** a rubber teat for a baby to suck **3** an imitation or counterfeit article **dummy** adj imitation **dummy** v **dummies, dummied, dummying** to make a pretended pass or swerve

dump v **1** to deposit something as rubbish **2** to get rid of something or someone that you do not want **3** to put something down carelessly **4** *ICT* to copy stored data to a different location **dump** n **1** a place where rubbish may be left **2** a temporary store **3** *informal* a dull or unattractive place **dumps** pl n **dumpy** adj **dumpier, dumpiest** short and fat **dumpiness** n

dumpling n a ball of dough cooked in a stew, etc. or baked with fruit inside it

dun adj, n dull greyish-brown

dunce n a person who is slow at learning

dune (say dewn) n a mound of loose sand shaped by the wind

dung n animal excrement **dunghill** n

dungarees pl n trousers with a bib held up by straps over the shoulders, made of coarse cotton cloth

dungeon (say dun-jən) n an underground prison cell, especially in a castle

dunk v **1** to dip a biscuit, etc. into a drink before eating it **2** to immerse someone or something in water

duo (say dew-oh) n pl **duos 1** a pair of performers ♦ *a comedy duo* **2** a piece of music for two performers

duodecimal (say dew-ə-dess-iməl) adj to do with a system of numerical notation that has twelve as a base

dupe v to deceive or trick someone **dupe** n a person who is deceived or tricked

duplex (say dew-pleks) adj **1** having two parts **2** (said about a flat) on two floors

duplicate[1] (say dew-plik-ət) n **1** something that is exactly the same as something else **2** an exact copy **duplicate** adj exactly like another thing; being a duplicate

duplicate[2] (say dew-plik-ayt) v **1** to make or be an exact copy of something **2** to multiply something by two **3** to repeat something, especially unnecessarily **duplication** n **duplicator** n

duplicity (say dew-pliss-iti) n double-dealing, deceitfulness **duplicitous** adj

durable adj **1** hard-wearing, likely to last **2** (said about goods) not for immediate consumption, able to be kept **durability** n **durably** adv

duration n the length of time that something lasts

duress (say dewr-ess) n the use of force or threats to make someone do something against their will

during prep **1** throughout the course or duration of something ♦ *She slept during the film.* **2** at some point in the duration of something ♦ *He heard a scream during the night.*

dusk n the darker stage of twilight **dusky** adj **duskier, duskiest, duskiness** n

dust n **1** fine particles of earth or other solid material **2** an act of dusting ♦ *These shelves need a dust.* **dust** v **1** to wipe away dust from the surface of something **2** to sprinkle something with dust or powder **duster** n **dustiness** n **dusty** adj **dustier, dustiest, dustbin** n a bin for household rubbish **dust bowl** n an area that has lost its vegetation because of drought or erosion **dustpan** n a pan into which dust is brushed from a floor **dust-up** n a noisy argument, a fight

Dutch adj to do with or coming from the Netherlands **Dutch** n the language of the Netherlands **the Dutch** Dutch people

duty n pl **duties 1** a moral or legal obligation **2** a task that must be done, especially as part of someone's job **3** a tax charged on

certain goods or on imports **dutiable** adj
dutiful adj **dutifully** adv **duty-bound** adj
obliged by duty **duty-free** adj (said about
goods) on which duty is not charged

duvet (say doo-vay) n a thick soft quilt used
instead of other bedclothes

DVD abbr digital videodisc

dwarf n pl **dwarfs 1** a person, animal,
or plant much below the usual size **2** (in
fairy tales) a small human-like being,
often with magic powers **dwarf** adj of a
kind that is very small in size **dwarf** v **1** to
make something seem small by contrast
or distance **2** to stunt the growth of
something

dwell v past tense and past participle **dwelt**
or **dwelled** formal to live somewhere
dweller n **dwelling** n

dwindle v to become gradually less or
smaller

dye n **1** a natural or synthetic substance
used for changing the colour of cloth,
hair, etc. **2** a colour produced by this **dye** v
dyes, dyed, dyeing to make something
a particular colour with dye ♦ *She dyed her
hair green.* **dyer** n

dying present participle of *die*[1]

dyke n **1** a long wall or embankment to hold
back water and prevent flooding **2** a ditch
for draining water from land

dynamic adj **1** (said about force) producing
motion (as opposed to *static*) **2** (said
about a person) energetic, having force
of character **dynamics** n a branch of
physics that deals with matter in motion
dynamically adv

dynamite n **1** a powerful explosive made of
nitroglycerine **2** something likely to cause
violent or dangerous reactions **3** a very
impressive person or thing **dynamite** v to
blow something up with dynamite

dynamo n pl **dynamos** a machine for
converting mechanical energy into
electrical energy

dynasty (say din-ə-sti) n pl **dynasties** a line
of rulers or powerful people all from the
same family **dynastic** adj

dysfunctional (say dis-**funk**-shə-nəl) adj
not able to act or function normally
dysfunction n

dyslexia (say dis-**leks**-iə) n abnormal
difficulty in reading and spelling, caused by
a brain condition **dyslexic** adj, n

Ee

E[1] **1** the fifth letter of the English alphabet
2 Mus the third note of the diatonic scale of
C major **3** used with a number to indicate
a product (especially a food additive) that
conforms with the regulations of the EU

E[2] abbr east or eastern

each adj every one of two or more people
or things ♦ *Each house has a garden.*
each pronoun each person or thing ♦ *Each
of them has one.*

eager adj wanting to have or do something
very strongly **eagerly** adv **eagerness** n

eagle n a large bird of prey **eaglet** n a young
eagle **eagle eye** n a close watch **eagle-
eyed** adj

ear[1] n **1** the organ of hearing and balance in
humans and some animals, especially the
external part of this **2** the ability to hear
and appreciate sounds ♦ *She has a good ear
for music.* **3** willingness to listen; attention
earache n a pain in the eardrum **eardrum** n
a membrane inside the ear that vibrates
when sounds strike it **ear lobe** n the soft
fleshy part at the lower end of the ear
earmark n a distinguishing mark, originally
one put on the ear of an animal **earmark** v
1 to set something aside for a particular
purpose **2** to put a distinguishing mark on
an animal **earphone** n an electrical device
worn on the ear to listen to radio or audio
sounds **earplug** n a piece of wax or cotton
wool inserted in the ear to keep out noise
or water **earring** n a piece of jewellery worn
on the ear, usually on the lobe **earshot** n
range of hearing ♦ *The dogs were now out
of earshot.* **ear-splitting** adj unpleasantly
loud **earwig** n a small crawling insect with
pincers at the end of its body

ear[2] n the seed-bearing part of a cereal plant

earl n a British nobleman ranking below a

marquis and above a viscount **earldom** n

early adj, adv **earlier**, **earliest** 1 before the usual or expected time ♦ We all arrived early for the film. 2 near the beginning of a period of time ♦ in the early years of this century **earliness** n **early bird** n a person who gets up early in the morning or who arrives early

earn v to get or deserve something, especially money, as a reward for work or achievement **earnings** pl n **earned income** n income you get from paid employment

earnest adj showing serious feeling or intentions **earnestly** adv **earnestness** n **in earnest 1** more seriously or with more determination ♦ They now began to shovel the snow in earnest. 2 sincere in intention

earth n 1 (also **Earth**) the planet that we live on, or the world we live in 2 the surface of the planet, the ground or dry land ♦ The rocket fell to earth in the desert. 3 the substance of the surface of the earth; soil 4 the underground home of a fox or badger 5 connection to the ground in order to complete an electrical circuit **earth** v to connect an electrical circuit to earth **earthen** adj 1 made of earth 2 (said about a pot) made of baked clay **earthly** adj **earthy** adj **earthier**, **earthiest**, **earthiness** n **earthenware** n pottery made of coarse baked clay **earthquake** n a violent shaking of the ground caused by a movement of part of the earth's crust **earth sciences** pl n the branches of science to do with the composition of the earth and its atmosphere **earthwork** n a large artificial bank of earth **earthworm** n a burrowing worm that lives in the soil

ease n 1 absence of trouble or difficulty ♦ She climbed the tree with ease. 2 freedom from anxiety or problems **ease** v 1 to relieve someone from pain or anxiety 2 to make something less difficult or severe 3 to move something gently or gradually ♦ The crane was slowly eased into position. 4 to become less severe or troublesome **easily** adv **easy** adj **easier**, **easiest**, **easiness** n **easy-going** adj pleasant and tolerant, not strict **easel** n a wooden frame used to support a painting or a blackboard

east n 1 the point on the horizon where the sun rises, or the direction in which this point lies 2 the part of a place or building that is towards the east **east** adj, adv 1 towards or in the east 2 (said about a wind) blowing from the east **the East** the part of the world lying to the east of Europe, especially India, Japan, and China **easterly** adj **eastern** adj **easterner** n **easternmost** adj **easting** n **eastward** adj, adv **East End** n the eastern part of a city, especially of London

Easter n 1 a Christian festival celebrated on a Sunday in March or April, commemorating Christ's resurrection 2 the period just before and after this **Easter egg** n a chocolate artificial egg given as a gift at Easter

eat v **ate**, **eaten** 1 to take food into the mouth and swallow it for nourishment; to chew and swallow something as food 2 to have a meal ♦ When shall we eat? 3 to destroy something gradually ♦ Unexpected expenses ate up our savings. **eatable** adj **eater** n **eats** pl n informal food

eau de cologne (say oh-də-kə-**lohn**) n a delicate perfume

eavesdrop v **eavesdropped**, **eavesdropping** to listen secretly to a private conversation **eavesdropper** n

ebb n 1 the movement of the tide when it is going out away from the land 2 a low point or condition ♦ Our courage was at a low ebb. **ebb** v 1 (said about a tide) to flow away from the land 2 to weaken or become lower ♦ Their strength was ebbing.

ebony n the hard black wood of a tropical tree **ebony** adj black like ebony

e-book n a book published in electronic form, e.g. on the Internet or as a CD-ROM

ebullient (say i-**bul**-iənt) adj cheerful, full of high spirits **ebullience** n **ebulliently** adv

eccentric adj 1 slightly strange or unconventional in appearance or behaviour 2 (said about circles) not having the same centre 3 (said about an orbit) not circular **eccentric** n a person who is slightly strange or unconventional **eccentrically** adv **eccentricity** n

ecclesiastical (say i-kleez-i-**ast**-ikəl) adj to

do with the Church or the clergy

ECG *abbr* electrocardiogram

echelon (say **esh**-ə-lən) *n* a level of rank or authority in an organization or profession ♦ *the upper echelons of the Civil Service*

echo *n pl* **echoes** **1** a repetition of a sound caused by the reflection of sound waves from a surface **2** a reflected radio or radar beam **3** something that closely imitates or resembles something else **echo** *v* **echoes**, **echoed**, **echoing 1** to repeat a sound by an echo **2** to repeat or imitate something or someone

eclair (say ay-**klair**) *n* a finger-shaped cake of choux pastry with icing and a cream filling

eclectic (say i-**klek**-tik) *adj* choosing or accepting ideas from a wide range of sources **eclectically** *adv* **eclecticism** *n*

eclipse *n* **1** the blocking of light from or to one heavenly body by another, especially of the sun by the moon or of the moon by the earth **2** a loss of power or reputation **eclipse** *v* **1** to cause an eclipse of a heavenly body **2** to make someone or something lose power or reputation

ecliptic (say i-**klip**-tik) *n* a circle representing the sun's apparent path during the year

eco- *prefix* to do with ecology or the environment ♦ *eco-friendly*

E. coli *n* a bacterium found in the intestines of some animals, certain strains of which cause food poisoning

ecology (say ee-**kol**-əji) *n* the study of living things in relation to each other and to their surroundings **ecological** *adj* **ecologically** *adv* **ecologist** *n*

e-commerce *n* commerce and business conducted electronically on the Internet

economy *n pl* **economies 1** careful use of resources; being economical **2** a saving ♦ *to make economies* **3** the resources of a country or region and the way it uses these to produce wealth **economic** *adj* **economical** *adj* **economically** *adv* **economics** *n* the study of how money is used and how goods and services are provided and used **economics** *pl n* the financial aspects of something

♦ *the economics of farming* **economist** *n* **economize** *v*

ecosystem (say **ee**-koh-sis-təm) *n* a group of plants and animals that interact with each other and form an ecological unit

ecstasy *n pl* **ecstasies** a feeling of intense delight **ecstatic** *adj* **ecstatically** *adv*

ecumenical (say ee-kew-**men**-ikəl) *adj* to do with or including all the Christian Churches

eczema (say **ek**-zim-ə) *n* a skin disease causing rough itching patches

Eden *n* (also **the Garden of Eden**) the place where Adam and Eve lived, in the biblical account of the creation **Eden** *n* a place of great happiness and beauty

edge *n* **1** the outside limit or boundary of an area or surface **2** an area or strip next to a steep drop **3** the sharpened side of a blade **4** the sharpness of a blade or tool ♦ *The knife has lost its edge.* **5** the line where two surfaces meet at an angle **edge** *v* **1** to form the border of an area or surface **2** to move gradually ♦ *As she spoke she was edging towards the door.* **edging** *n* something placed round an edge to mark it or to strengthen or decorate it **edgeways** *adv* with the edge forwards or outwards **edgy** *adj* **edgier**, **edgiest** tense and irritable **edginess** *n*

edible *adj* of a kind that can be eaten **edibility** *n*

edict (say **ee**-dikt) *n* an official order or command

edifice (say **ed**-i-fis) *n formal* a large or grand building

edify (say **ed**-i-fiy) *v* **edifies**, **edified**, **edifying** to be an improving influence on a person's mind **edification** *n*

edit *v* **edited**, **editing 1** to act as editor of a newspaper or other publication **2** to prepare written material for publication **3** to reword writing for a special purpose **4** to prepare a film or recording by choosing individual sections and putting them into a correct order **5** to prepare data for processing by computer **editor** *n* **1** a person who is responsible for the content and writing of a newspaper or magazine or a section of one **2** someone who edits written material for publication **3** someone who edits cinema film or recording tape **4** *ICT* a program that allows the user to edit text at a computer terminal **editorial** *adj* to do with editing or the work of an editor **editorial** *n* a newspaper article giving an opinion on current affairs

edition *n* **1** the form in which something is published ♦ *a paperback edition* **2** all the copies of a book or newspaper issued at the same time ♦ *the first edition* **3** a particular version or broadcast of a regular radio or television programme

educate *v* to train a person's mind and abilities; to provide education for someone **educable** *adj* **education** *n* **educational** *adj* **educationally** *adv* **educationist** *n* **educative** *adj* **educator** *n*

Edwardian (say ed-wor-diən) *adj* during or to do with the reign of King Edward VII (1901-10) **Edwardian** *n* a person living at this time

eel *n* a long fish that looks like a snake

eerie *adj* **eerier, eeriest** mysterious and frightening **eerily** *adv* **eeriness** *n*

efface *v* to rub something out or obliterate it **effacement** *n*

effect *n* **1** a change that is produced by an action or cause, a result **2** an impression produced on a spectator or hearer, etc. ♦ *The news had a cheering effect on us.* **effect** *v* to accomplish something or bring it about ♦ *None of the doctors could effect a cure.* **effects** *pl n* **1** property ♦ *personal effects* **2** sounds and lighting, etc. provided to accompany a broadcast or film **effective** *adj* **effectively** *adv* **effectiveness** *n* **effectual** *adj* **effectually** *adv* ◊ See the note at *affect*.

effeminate (say i-fem-in-ət) *adj* (said about a man) having qualities that are usually thought of as feminine **effeminacy** *n* **effeminately** *adv*

effervesce (say ef-er-vess) *v* to give off small bubbles of gas, to fizz **effervescence** *n* **effervescent** *adj*

effete (say ef-eet) *adj* having lost vitality or effectiveness **effeteness** *n*

efficient (say i-fish-ənt) *adj* acting or working effectively, with little waste of

effort **efficiency** *n* **efficiently** *adv*

effigy (say ef-iji) *n pl* **effigies** a sculpture or model of a person

effluent (say ef-loo-ənt) *n* liquid sewage or other waste that flows into the sea or a river **effluence** *n*

effort *n* **1** the use of physical or mental energy to do something **2** the energy used in this way **3** something produced by using energy ♦ *The essay was a good effort.* **effortless** *adj* **effortlessly** *adv* **effortlessness** *n*

effrontery (say i-frunt-er-i) *n* arrogant insolence

effusion (say i-few-zhən) *n* **1** a pouring forth **2** an unrestrained outpouring of thought or feeling **effusive** *adj* **effusively** *adv* **effusiveness** *n*

e.g. *abbr* for example

egalitarian (say i-gal-it-air-iən) *adj* believing that all people are equal and deserve the same rights **egalitarian** *n* someone who holds this principle **egalitarianism** *n*

egg[1] *n* **1** a more or less round object produced by a female bird, fish, reptile, or insect, which can develop into a new individual if fertilized **2** the hard-shelled egg of a hen or duck, used as food **3** a reproductive cell produced by a female being or animal; an ovum **egg cup** *n* a small cup without a handle, for holding a boiled egg **egghead** *n* an intellectual person **eggshell** *n* the shell of an egg **eggshell** *adj* **1** (said about china) very fragile **2** (said about paint) having a slight sheen when it dries

egg[2] *v* to urge someone to do something ♦ *He keeps egging us on.*

ego (say ee-goh or eg-oh) *n pl* **egos** a person's sense of importance or self-respect ♦ *The criticism has hurt their egos.* **egocentric** *adj* self-centred **egocentricity** *n* **egoism** *n* **egoist** *n* **egoistic** *adj* **egoistically** *adv* **egotism** *n* **egotist** *n* **egotistic** *adj* **egotistical** *adj* **egotistically** *adv*

egress (say ee-gress) *n* an exit or way out

Egyptian *adj* to do with or coming from Egypt in NE Africa **Egyptian** *n* **1** a person born in Egypt or descended from people born there **2** the language of ancient Egypt **Egyptology** *n* the study of the language and antiquities of ancient Egypt **Egyptologist** *n*

eh (say ay) *exclamation informal* expressing enquiry or surprise

Eid (say eed) *n* a Muslim festival marking the end of the fast of Ramadan

eiderdown *n* a quilt stuffed with soft material

eight *adj, n* **1** the number 8, one more than seven **2** an eight-oared rowing boat or its crew **eightfold** *adj, adv* **1** eight times as much or as many **2** consisting of eight parts **eighth** *adj, n* **1** next after seventh **2** one of eight equal parts of a thing **eighthly** *adv*

eighteen *adj, n* the number 18, one more than seventeen **eighteenth** *adj, n*

eighty *adj, n pl* **eighties** the number 80, equal to eight times ten **eighties** *pl n* the numbers from 80 to 89, especially representing years of age or degrees of temperature **eightieth** *adj, n*

either (say **iy**-ther or **ee**-ther) *adj, pronoun* **1** one or the other of two ♦ *Either of you can do it.* **2** each of two ♦ *There are tall buildings on either side of the road.* **either** *adv, conjunction* **1** as one alternative, the other being expressed by or ♦ *He is either ill or drunk.* **2** in the same way, what is more ♦ *I don't like it either.*

ejaculate (say i-**jak**-yoo-layt) *v formal* **1** to say something suddenly and sharply **2** (said about a man or male animal) to eject semen from the penis at a sexual climax **ejaculation** *n*

eject *v* **1** to force or throw something out ♦ *The gun ejects spent cartridges.* **2** to expel someone or force them to leave **ejection** *n* **ejector** *n*

eke (say eek) *v* **to eke out** to make something last ♦ *They managed to eke out the meat with lots of vegetables.*

elaborate[1] (say i-**lab**-er-ət) *adj* having many parts or details, complicated ♦ *The carpet has an elaborate pattern.* **elaborately** *adv*

elaborate[2] (say i-**lab**-er-ayt) *v* to work something out or describe it in detail **elaboration** *n*

elan (say ay-**lahn**) *n* stylish or dashing vitality

elapse *v* (said about time) to pass

elastic *adj* **1** able to return to its original length or shape after being stretched or squeezed **2** able to be used or understood flexibly ♦ *The rules are somewhat elastic.* **elastic** *n* cord or material that is woven with strands of rubber or plastic so that it can stretch **elastically** *adv* **elasticated** *adj* **elasticity** *n*

elate *v* to make someone feel very happy or proud **elated** *adj* **elation** *n*

elbow *n* **1** the joint between the forearm and upper arm **2** the part of a sleeve covering this **3** a sharp bend in a pipe **elbow** *v* to poke or thrust someone with the elbow **elbow grease** *n* hard physical work

elder[1] *adj* older ♦ *Meet my elder sister.* **elder** *n* **1** an older person ♦ *You must respect your elders.* **2** an official in certain Christian Churches **elderly** *adj*

elder[2] *n* a tree or shrub with white flowers and dark berries **elderberry** *n pl* **elderberries** the berry of the elder, used to make wine and jam

eldest *adj* oldest or first-born ♦ *Peter is their eldest son.*

elect *v* **1** to choose someone by a vote ♦ *The committee must elect a chairman.* **2** to choose to do something ♦ *We elected to stay on for another week.* **elect** *adj* chosen by a vote but not yet in office ♦ *the president elect* **election** *n* **electioneer** *v* **electioneering** *n* **elective** *adj* **elector** *n* **electoral** *adj* **electorate** *n*

electricity *n* **1** a form of energy carried by certain particles of matter (electrons and protons) **2** a supply of electric current for lighting, heating, etc. **electric** *adj* **1** to do with or worked by electricity **2** causing great or sudden excitement ♦ *The news had an electric effect.* **electrical** *adj* **electrically** *adv* **electrician** *n* a person whose job is to deal with electricity and electrical equipment **electrify** *v* **electrifies**, **electrified**, **electrifying**, **electrification** *n* **electrical engineer** *n* an engineer who designs and builds electrical devices

electrical engineering n **electric shock** n the sudden discharge of electricity through the body of a person or animal, stimulating the nerves and contracting the muscles

electro- prefix to do with or using electricity **electrode** n a solid conductor through which electricity enters or leaves a vacuum tube **electrolysis** n **1** Chem chemical decomposition caused by an electric current **2** the removal of blemishes, hair roots, etc. by means of an electric current **electrolyte** n a liquid or other solution that conducts an electric current **electrolytic** adj **electromotive** adj producing an electric current **electrotherapy** n the use of electricity to treat paralysis and other medical disorders

electrocute v to kill or injure someone by an electric shock **electrocution** n

electromagnet n a metal core that is magnetized by a coil carrying electric current and wound round it **electromagnetic** adj having both electrical and magnetic properties **electromagnetically** adv

electronic (say i-lek-**tron**-ik) adj **1** making use of transistors and microchips and other components that control electric currents **2** relating to or making use of electronics ♦ electronic engineering **3** done by means of a computer network ♦ electronic banking **electronically** adv **electronics** n **electronic mail** n another term for email

electrostatic adj to do with static electric charges **electrostatics** n

elegant adj graceful and dignified in appearance or style **elegance** n **elegantly** adv

elegy (say **el**-i-ji) n pl **elegies** a sorrowful or serious poem **elegiac** adj

element n **1** each of the parts that make up the whole of something **2** a trace or aspect ♦ There is an element of truth in their story. **3** each of about 100 substances composed of atoms with the same atomic number **4** each of the four substances (earth, water, air, and fire) that were regarded as the basic ingredients of matter in ancient and medieval philosophy **5** a wire that becomes red and gives out heat in an electric heater

or cooker **elements** pl n **1** (**the elements**) the forces of the weather or atmosphere **2** the basic or elementary principles of a subject ♦ the elements of geometry to do with or dealing with the simplest facts of a subject; basic or easy **elementary** adj **elementarily** adv **elementariness** n

elephant n a very large land animal with a trunk, large ears, and long curved ivory tusks **elephantine** adj **1** to do with elephants, or like elephants **2** clumsy and slow-moving

elevate v **1** to lift or raise something to a higher place or position **2** to make a discussion, conversation, etc. more serious or intellectual **elevation** n **elevator** n **1** something that lifts or raises things **2** N. Am a lift in a building

eleven adj, n the number 11, one more than ten **elevenfold** adj, adv **elevenses** pl n a break for a snack or drink in the middle of the morning **eleventh** adj, n

elf n pl **elves** in fairy tales, a small being with magic powers **elfin** adj **elfish** adj

elicit (say i-**lis**-it) v to draw out a response or information by argument or questioning

elide v to omit part of a word by the process called elision

eligible (say **el**-i-ji-bəl) adj **1** qualified or suitable for a position or privilege **2** (said about a person) regarded as suitable for marriage **eligibility** n

eliminate (say i-**lim**-in-ayt) v **1** to get rid of something that is not wanted **2** to exclude a competitor or team from the next stage of a competition when they are defeated **elimination** n **eliminator** n

elite (say ay-**leet**) n a group of people who enjoy special privileges or are regarded as superior in some way **elitism** n **elitist** n, adj

elixir (say i-**liks**-er) n a magical or medicinal liquid thought of as having special powers

Elizabethan adj during or to do with the reign of Queen Elizabeth I (1558-1603) **Elizabethan** n a person living at this time

elk n pl **elk** or **elks** a large deer of northern Europe and Asia

ellipse (say i-**lips**) n a regular oval shape that can be divided into four identical quarters **ellipsis** n pl **ellipses** Gram the omission of a word or words from speech and writing, usually leaving the meaning still clear **elliptical** *adj* **elliptically** *adv*

elm *n* **1** a tall deciduous tree with rough serrated leaves **2** the wood of this tree

elocution (say el-ə-kew-shən) *n* the art of speaking clearly and expressively **elocutionist** *n*

elongated (say ee-long-gayt-id) *adj* made longer, prolonged **elongation** *n*

elope (say i-lohp) *v* (said about a couple) to run away secretly to get married **elopement** *n*

eloquence (say el-ə-kwəns) *n* fluent and expressive speaking or writing **eloquent** *adj* **eloquently** *adv*

else *adv* **1** besides, other ♦ *I'll ask someone else.* **2** otherwise, if not ♦ *Run or else you'll be late.* **elsewhere** *adv*

elucidate (say i-loo-sid-ayt) *v* to make something clear by explaining it **elucidation** *n* **elucidatory** *adj*

elude (say i-lood) *v* **1** to avoid being caught by someone ♦ *He managed to elude all his pursuers.* **2** to escape a person's understanding or memory ♦ *I'm afraid the answer eludes me.* **elusion** *n* **elusive** *adj* **elusiveness** *n*

emaciated (say i-may-si-ayt-id) *adj* very thin from illness or starvation **emaciation** *n*

email *n* a system of sending messages and data from one computer to another by means of a network **email** *v* to send a message or data by email

emanate (say em-ən-ayt) *v* to come or originate from a particular source **emanation** *n*

emancipate (say i-man-sip-ayt) *v* to set someone free from slavery or some form of restraint **emancipation** *n* **emancipator** *n* **emancipatory** *adj*

emasculated (say i-mas-kew-layt-id) *adj* made weaker or less effective

embalm (say im-bahm) *v* to preserve a corpse from decay by using spices or chemicals **embalmment** *n*

embankment *n* a long bank of earth or stone used to hold back water or to carry a road or railway

embargo (say im-bar-goh) *n pl* **embargoes**

an official ban, especially on trade with a country

embark *v* to go on board a ship or aircraft at the start of a journey, or to put something on board **embarkation** *n*

embarrass *v* to make someone feel awkward or ashamed **embarrassment** *n*

embassy *n pl* **embassies** **1** the building in which an ambassador's office is located **2** a deputation sent to a foreign government

embattled *adj* **1** prepared for battle or attack **2** facing many difficulties or criticisms

embed *v* **embedded**, **embedding** to fix something firmly in a surrounding mass

embellish (say im-bel-ish) *v* **1** to decorate something or add ornaments to it **2** to improve a story by adding details that are entertaining but invented **embellishment** *n*

embers *pl n* small pieces of live coal or wood in a dying fire

embezzle *v* to take dishonestly for your own use money or property that has been placed in your care **embezzlement** *n* **embezzler** *n*

embittered *adj* having bitter feelings about something

emblazon (say im-blay-zən) *v* to decorate something with bright or eye-catching designs or words

emblem *n* a symbol that represents something **emblematic** *adj*

embody *v* **embodies**, **embodied**, **embodying** **1** to express principles or ideas in a visible or tangible form ♦ *The house embodies our idea of a modern home.* **2** to incorporate or include something ♦ *Parts of the old agreement are embodied in the new one.* **embodiment** *n*

embolden *v* to make someone bold, to encourage someone

emboss *v* to decorate a flat surface with a raised design **embossment** *n*

embrace *v* **1** to hold someone closely and lovingly in your arms **2** to accept something eagerly ♦ *We will have to embrace the opportunity.* **3** to adopt a cause or belief **4** to include or contain something **embrace** *n* an act of embracing, a close hug

embroider v **1** to decorate cloth with needlework **2** to add interesting details to a story **embroidery** n pl **embroideries**

embroil v to involve someone in an argument or quarrel

embryo (say **em**-bri-oh) n pl **embryos 1** a baby or young animal in the early stage of development in the womb, especially an unborn child in the first eight weeks after conception **2** an unborn bird growing in an egg **3** a rudimentary plant contained in a seed **4** something in the early stages of its development **embryonic** adj

emend (say i-**mend**) v to alter something written in order to remove errors **emendation** n

emerald n **1** a bright green precious stone **2** the colour of an emerald

emerge (say i-**merj**) v **1** to come up or out into view **2** (said about facts or ideas) to become known or obvious **emergence** n **emergent** adj

emergency n pl **emergencies 1** a sudden and unexpected serious happening that needs urgent attention **2** a medical condition needing immediate treatment

EMF abbr electromotive force

emigrate v to leave your own country and go to settle in another **emigrant** n **emigration** n

eminence (say **em**-in-əns) n **1** being famous or distinguished ♦ a musician of great eminence **2** a title of a cardinal (in Your Eminence or His Eminence) **eminent** adj **eminently** adv

emir (say em-**eer**) n the title of a Muslim ruler **emirate** n the rank or territory of an emir

emissary (say em-**iss**-er-i) n pl **emissaries** a person sent to conduct diplomatic negotiations

emit (say i-**mit**) v **emitted, emitting 1** to send out light, heat, fumes, etc. **2** to make a sudden or loud sound ♦ When he saw her he emitted a cry of amazement. **emission** n **emitter** n

emoticon (say i-**moh**-ti-kon) n an icon used in emails and text messages

emotion n a strong mental feeling, such as anger, love, or hate **emotional** adj

emotionalism n **emotionally** adv

emotive (say i-**moh**-tiv) adj arousing emotion

empathy (say **em**-pəthi) n the ability to understand and share in someone else's feelings **empathic** adj **empathize** v

emperor n the ruler of an empire

emphasis (say **em**-fə-sis) n pl **emphases 1** special importance given to something ♦ The emphasis is on quality. **2** strength of expression or feeling ♦ She nodded her head with emphasis. **3** the extra force used in speaking a particular syllable or word, or on a sound in music **emphasize** v **emphatic** adj **emphatically** adv

empire n **1** a group of countries ruled by one person or government **2** supreme power **3** a large business organization controlled by one person or group

empirical (say im-**pi**-ri-kəl) adj (said about knowledge) based on observation or experiment, not on theory **empirically** adv

employ v **1** to give work to someone, to use the services of someone **2** to make use of something ♦ How will you employ your spare time? **employ** n **employable** adj **employee** n **employer** n **employment** n

emporium (say em-**por** -iəm) n pl **emporia** or **emporiums** a large store selling a wide range of goods

empower v to give someone the power or authority to do something

empress n **1** a woman ruler of an empire **2** the wife or widow of an emperor

empty adj **emptier, emptiest 1** not containing anything **2** not having a person or people in it ♦ an empty chair **3** without real meaning or effectiveness ♦ empty promises **empty** v **empties, emptied, emptying 1** to make something empty, or to become empty **2** to take out or transfer the contents of something ♦ I'll empty the box on to the floor. **3** (said about a river) to let its contents out into something ♦ The river empties into a lake. **empties** pl n bottles or other containers that no longer have any contents **emptily** adv **emptiness** n **empty-handed** adj bringing or taking away nothing **empty-headed** adj lacking sense or intelligence, foolish

EMS *abbr* European Monetary System

EMU *abbr* Economic and Monetary Union

emu (say **ee**-mew) *n pl* **emus** a large Australian bird with rough grey or brown feathers

emulate (say **em**-yoo-layt) *v* to try to do as well as someone else **emulation** *n* **emulator** *n*

emulsion (say i-**mul**-shən) *n* **1** a creamy liquid with particles of oil or fat evenly distributed in it **2** paint or medicine in this form **emulsify** *v* **emulsifies, emulsified, emulsifying**

en- *prefix* (changing to **em-** before *b*, *m*, or *p*) in or into; on

enable *v* **1** to give someone the means or authority to do something **2** to make something possible

enact *v* **1** to make a law by a formal process ♦ *Parliament will enact new laws.* **2** to perform or act in a play **enactment** *n*

enamel *n* **1** a shiny substance with a surface like glass, used for coating metal or pottery **2** paint that dries hard and glossy **3** the hard outer covering of teeth **enamel** *v* **enamelled, enamelling** to coat or decorate a surface with enamel

enamoured (say i-**nam**-erd) *adj* very fond of someone or something

encamp *v* to settle in a camp **encampment** *n*

encapsulate *v* **1** to enclose something in a capsule, or as if in a capsule **2** to express an idea or set of ideas concisely **encapsulation** *n*

encase *v* to enclose something in a case

encash *v* to convert a cheque, etc. into cash **encashment** *n*

enchant *v* **1** to put someone under a magic spell **2** to charm or delight someone **enchanter** *n* **enchantment** *n* **enchantress** *n*

encircle *v* to surround someone or something **encirclement** *n*

enclave (say **en**-klayv) *n* a territory belonging to one country or state but lying entirely within the boundaries of another

enclose *v* **1** to put a wall or fence round something; to shut something in on all sides **2** to put something into an envelope along with a letter or into a parcel along with the contents **enclosed** *adj* **enclosure** *n*

encode *v* **1** to put words into code **2** *ICT* to put data into a coded form for processing by computer **encoder** *n*

encompass *v* **1** to surround or encircle something **2** to contain an idea or set of ideas

encore (say **ong**-kor) *n* an extra item performed at a concert, etc. after the main items have been performed and applauded **encore** *v* to call for an extra item by applauding loudly

encounter *v* **1** to meet someone by chance or unexpectedly **2** to find oneself faced with a challenge or difficulty **encounter** **1** a sudden or unexpected meeting with someone **2** a confrontation or battle

encourage *v* **1** to give hope or confidence to someone **2** to urge someone to do something ♦ *I encourage you all to try.* **3** to stimulate or help develop an activity ♦ *The new economic measures will encourage exports.* **encouragement** *n*

encroach *v* **1** to intrude on someone's rights or property **2** to extend beyond the original or proper limits ♦ *The sea encroached gradually upon the land.* **encroachment** *n*

encrust *v* **1** to cover something with a crust of hard material **2** to decorate a surface with a layer of jewels or ornaments **encrustation** *n*

encryption (say en-**krip**-shon) *n* *ICT* the process of converting confidential data into code **encrypted** *adj*

encumber *v* to hamper or be a burden to someone **encumbrance** *n*

encyclopedia *n* a book or set of books giving information on many subjects, or on one subject in detail, usually arranged alphabetically **encyclopedic** *adj*

end *n* **1** the last part or extreme point of something **2** each half of a sports pitch or court, defended or occupied by one side or player **3** the finish or conclusion of something, the final part **4** destruction, downfall, or death **5** a purpose or aim **end** *v* **1** to bring something to an end, to finish something **2** to come to an end **3** to reach a certain place or state, often by chance

♦ *We caught the wrong train and ended up in Preston.* **endways** *adv*

endanger *v* to cause danger to someone or something **endangered species** *n* a species of animal or plant that is in danger of becoming extinct

endear *v* to cause someone to be loved ♦ *She endeared herself to us all.* **endearing** *adj* **endearment** *n*

endeavour (say in-**dev**-er) *v* to attempt or try to do something **endeavour** *n* an attempt

endemic (say en-**dem**-ik) *adj* (said about a disease) commonly found in a certain area or group of people

ending *n* the last part of something, especially a story or drama

endive (say **en**-div) *n* **1** a plant with curly leaves, used as a salad **2** chicory

endless *adj* **1** not ending or stopping ♦ *You need endless patience.* **2** having the ends joined so that it forms a continuous strip for use in machinery, etc. ♦ *an endless belt*

endorphin (say en-**dor** -fin) *n* any of a group of pain-killing hormones produced naturally

endorse *v* **1** to sign or add a comment on a document **2** to sign the back of a cheque in order to transfer the money to another person **3** to make an official entry on a driving licence recording an offence committed by the holder **4** to confirm a statement or approve of a course of action **endorsement** *n* **1** approval of or permission for a course of action **2** a note added to a driving licence to record an offence committed by the holder

endoscope *n* an instrument for viewing internal parts of the body

endow *v* **1** to provide a person or organization with a permanent income **2** to provide someone with a power or quality **endowment** *n*

end product *n* the product that is made by a manufacturing process

endue *v* **endues**, **endued**, **enduing** to provide someone with a talent or quality ♦ *Experience endues us with patience.*

endure *v* **1** to experience or withstand difficulty or pain **2** to tolerate something

3 to remain in existence, to last **endurable** *adj* **endurance** *n*

enema (say **en**-im-ə) *n pl* **enemas** the medical process of inserting liquid into the rectum

enemy *n pl* **enemies** **1** someone who is hostile towards another person and tries to harm them **2** a country that is at war with another, or its armed forces

energy *n pl* **energies** **1** the capacity or strength to undertake activity **2** the ability of matter or radiation to do work **3** power obtained from fuel and other resources and used for light and heat, the operation of machinery, etc. **energies** *pl n* a person's physical powers used for a particular activity **energetic** *adj* **energetically** *adv* **energize** *v*

enfeeble *v* to weaken someone or make someone feeble

enfold *v* to surround or be wrapped round something

enforce *v* to compel someone to obey a rule or law **enforceable** *adj* **enforcement** *n*

enfranchise *v* to give someone the right to vote in elections **enfranchisement** *n*

engage *v* **1** to arrange to employ someone ♦ *We need to engage a new secretary.* **2** to occupy the attention of someone ♦ *Douglas engaged her in conversation.* **3** to take part in an activity ♦ *She engaged in politics for many years.* **4** to begin a battle against an opponent ♦ *engaged the enemy troops* **5** to promise or pledge to do something **6** (said about a machine or engine part) to move into a position that allows it to operate or to connect with another part **engaged** *adj* **engagement** *n* **engaging** *adj*

engender (say in-**jen**-der) *v* to cause something or give rise to it

engine *n* **1** a machine consisting of several parts working together to produce power or motion **2** a vehicle that provides the power for a railway train; a locomotive

engineer *n* **1** a person who is skilled in engineering **2** a person who is in charge of machines or engines, e.g. on a ship **3** someone who cleverly plans or organizes something **engineer** *v* **1** to construct or control something as an engineer **2** to make something happen by clever planning ♦ *He engineered a meeting between them.* **engineering** n

English adj to do with England or its people or language **English** n the language of England, now used in several varieties throughout the world **the English** pl n English people **Englishman**, **Englishwoman** n pl **Englishmen**, **Englishwomen**

engrave v 1 to cut or carve words or a design into a hard surface 2 to fix an idea or memory deeply in the mind **engraver** n **engraving** n

engross (say in-**grohs**) v to absorb all of someone's attention or efforts

engulf v 1 to flow over something and cover or swamp it 2 to overwhelm something

enhance (say in-**hahns**) v to make something more attractive or of greater quality or value **enhancement** n

enigma (say in-**ig**-mə) n pl **enigmas** something that is very puzzling or difficult to understand **enigmatic** adj **enigmatically** adv

enjoin v to order or instruct someone to do something

enjoy v 1 to get pleasure from something 2 to have something as an advantage or benefit ♦ *She continues to enjoy good health.* **enjoyable** adj **enjoyably** adv **enjoyment** n

enlarge v 1 to make something larger, or to become larger 2 to reproduce a photograph on a larger scale 3 to talk or write about something in more detail **enlargement** n **enlarger** n

enlighten v to give more knowledge or understanding to someone **enlightened** adj **enlightenment** n

enlist v 1 to take someone into the armed forces, or to join the armed forces ♦ *He decided to enlist in the marines.* 2 to secure someone's help or support ♦ *They succeeded in enlisting our sympathy.* **enlistment** n

enliven v 1 to make someone more lively or cheerful 2 to make something more interesting **enlivenment** n

en masse (say ahn **mass**) adv all together

enmesh v to entangle something

enmity n pl **enmities** a state of hostility between enemies

ennoble v 1 to make a person a noble 2 to make someone or something more dignified **ennoblement** n

ennui (say on-**wee**) n a state of being weary from boredom

enormity (say in-**orm**-iti) n pl **enormities** 1 great wickedness ♦ *The country was shocked by the enormity of these crimes.* 2 a terrible crime or sin 3 enormous size

enormous adj huge, very large **enormously** adv **enormousness** n

enough adj, n, adv as much or as many as necessary

enquire v to ask for information ♦ *He enquired if I was well.* **enquiry** n pl **enquiries**

enrage v to make someone very angry

enrapture v to fill someone with intense delight

enrich v 1 to make someone rich or richer 2 to improve the quality of something by adding things to it ♦ *The food has been enriched with vitamins.* **enrichment** n

enrol v enrolled, enrolling 1 to become a member of a society or institution 2 to admit someone as a member **enrolment** n

en route (say ahn **root**) adv on the way from one place to another ♦ *We met them en route from Rome to London.*

ensconce (say in-**skons**) v to settle someone securely or comfortably

ensemble (say on-**sombl**) n 1 a collection of things regarded as a whole 2 a group of musicians who perform together 3 a matching outfit of clothes

enshrine v 1 to place something precious in a special place or receptacle (such as a shrine) 2 to preserve an idea, memory, etc. with love or respect

ensign (say **en**-siyn) n a military or naval flag, especially one showing the nationality of a ship

enslave v to make a slave of someone **enslavement** n

ensnare v to catch someone, as if in a snare

ensue (say ins-**yoo**) v ensues, ensued, ensuing to happen afterwards or as a result ♦ *A violent quarrel ensued.*

en suite (say on **sweet**) adj, adv (usually said about a bathroom) next to a bedroom, with a connecting door

ensure v to make something safe or certain ♦ *Good food will ensure good health.*

entail (say in-**tayl**) v to involve something or make it necessary ♦ *These plans entail great expense.*

entangle v **1** to make things become tangled **2** to involve someone in something complicated **entanglement** n

entente (say on-**tont**) n a friendly understanding between countries

enter v **1** to go in or come into a place **2** to put a name or other details on a list or in a book **3** to register someone as a competitor in a race or competition **4** (said about an actor) to come on stage **5** to become a member of an organization ♦ *When he was 18 he entered the Navy.* **6** to record something formally or present something for consideration ♦ *The accused entered a plea of not guilty.*

enterprise n **1** a serious or difficult undertaking **2** personal initiative or adventurousness ♦ *She showed a lot of enterprise.* **3** business activity ♦ *private enterprise* **enterprising** adj

entertain v **1** to provide someone with amusement or enjoyment **2** to treat someone to hospitality ♦ *After the meeting they entertained me to lunch.* **3** to have something in the mind ♦ *I think she is entertaining doubts.* **4** to consider something favourably ♦ *We refuse to entertain the idea.* **entertainer** n **entertainment** n

enthral (say in-**thrawl**) v **enthralled**, **enthralling** to fascinate someone or hold them spellbound

enthuse (say in-**thewz**) v **1** to show interest and enthusiasm **2** to fill someone with enthusiasm **enthusiasm** n **enthusiast** n **enthusiastic** adj **enthusiastically** adv

entice v to attract or persuade someone by offering them something pleasant **enticement** n

entire adj whole or complete **entirely** adv **entirety** n

entitle v to give someone a right to do something ♦ *This ticket entitles you to free entrance to the museum.* **entitled** adj having as a title ♦ *a poem entitled 'Spring'*

entitlement n

entity (say **en**-titi) n pl **entities** something that exists as a distinct or separate thing

entomb (say en-**toom**) v to place a body in a tomb **entombment** n

entomology (say en-tə-**mol**-əji) n the study of insects **entomological** adj **entomologist** n

entourage (say on-toor-**ahzh**) n the people accompanying or attending an important person

entrails (say **en**-traylz) pl n the intestines of a person or animal

entrance[1] (say **en**-trəns) n **1** the act of entering **2** a door or passage by which you enter a place **3** the right to enter a public place, or the charge made for this **4** *Drama* the moment when an actor comes on stage **entrant** n someone who enters for a competition or exam

entrance[2] (say in-**trahns**) v to fill someone with intense delight **entrancement** n

entrap v **entrapped**, **entrapping** to catch someone or something, as if in a trap

entreat v to request someone earnestly or emotionally for something **entreaty** n

entrée (say **on**-tray) n **1** a dish served between the fish and meat courses of a formal dinner **2** the right to enter a place

entrench (say in-**trench**) v **1** to fix or establish a thought or idea firmly in the mind **2** to establish a military force in a well-defended position **entrenchment** n

entrepreneur (say on-trə-prən-**er**) n a person who sets up a commercial undertaking, especially one involving commercial risk **entrepreneurial** adj

entrust v **1** to give something as a responsibility **2** to place a person or thing in someone's care

entry n pl **entries** **1** the act of entering a place **2** a place where you enter **3** an alley between buildings **4** an item entered in a list, diary, or reference book **5** an entrant in a race or competition, or the total number of entrants

entwine v to twine one thing round another, to interweave things

enumerate (say i-**new**-mer-ayt) v to count items, or to mention them one by one

enumeration *n* **enumerator** *n*

enunciate (say i-**nun**-si-ayt) *v* **1** to pronounce words **2** to state something clearly **enunciation** *n*

envelop (say in-**vel**-əp) *v* **enveloped**, **enveloping** to wrap something up or cover it completely **envelopment** *n*

envelope (say **en**-və-lohp) *n* **1** a wrapper or covering, especially a folded cover for a letter **2** the gas container of a balloon or airship

environment *n* **1** the surroundings in which people, animals, or plants live, and which affect their lives **2** the natural world of the land, sea, and air **environmental** *adj* **environmentalist** *n*

environs (say in-**viyr**-ənz) *pl n* the surrounding districts, especially round a town ♦ *the environs of Manchester*

envisage (say in-**viz**-ij) *v* **1** to visualize or imagine something **2** to consider something or think it possible

envoy (say **en**-voi) *n* **1** an official representative **2** a diplomatic minister ranking below an ambassador

envy *n* **1** a feeling of discontent you have when someone else has something you want **2** something that causes this feeling **envy** *v* **envies**, **envied**, **envying** to have a feeling of envy towards someone or about something **enviable** *adj* **enviably** *adv* **envious** *adj* **enviously** *adv*

enzyme (say **en**-ziym) *n* a protein formed in living cells, which assists chemical processes such as digestion

ephemera (say if-**em**-er-ə) *pl n* things that are only useful or interesting for a short time **ephemeral** *adj*

epi- *prefix* on; above; in addition

epic *n* **1** a long poem or story telling of heroic deeds or history **2** a long book or film dealing with a similar subject **epic** *adj* to do with an epic or like an epic; on a grand scale

epicentre *n* the point at which an earthquake reaches the earth's surface

epicure (say **ep**-i-kewr) *n* a person who enjoys good food, drink, literature, etc. **epicurean** *adj* **epicurism** *n*

epidemic *n* an outbreak of a disease that spreads rapidly among the people of an area

epigram *n* a short witty saying or remark **epigrammatic** *adj*

epilepsy *n* a disorder of the nervous system causing convulsions **epileptic** *adj*, *n*

epilogue (say **ep**-i-log) *n* a short section at the end of a book or play, added as a conclusion to or comment on what has gone before

Epiphany (say i-**pif**-əni) *n* a Christian festival celebrated on 6 January, commemorating the showing of Christ to the Magi

episcopate (say ip-**iss**-kə-pət) *n* the office of bishop **episcopal** *adj* **Episcopalian** *adj* to do with an episcopal Church, especially the Anglican Church in Scotland and the USA **Episcopalian** *n* a member of an episcopal Church

episode *n* **1** one incident or event in a sequence of happenings, either in real life or in fiction **2** an instalment of a story or drama that is being serialized on radio or television

Epistle (say ip-**iss**-əl) *n* each of the books of the New Testament that are written in the form of letters to members of the Church

epitaph (say **ep**-i-tahf) *n* words inscribed on a tomb or in memory of a dead person

epithet (say **ep**-i-thet) *n* a word or phrase used to describe someone and often forming part of their name, e.g. 'the Great' in *Alfred the Great*

epitome (say ip-**it**-əmi) *n* a person or thing that is a perfect example of a quality or type ♦ *She is the epitome of kindness.* **epitomize** *v*

epoch (say **ee**-pok) *n* **1** a period of history marked by certain events or circumstances **2** *Geology* a division of a period

equable (say **ek**-wə-bəl) calm and constant **equably** *adv*

equal *adj* **1** the same in size, amount, value, rank, etc. **2** having the ability, strength, or courage needed ♦ *I'm not sure he's equal to the task.* **equal** *n* a person or thing that is equal to someone or something else **equal** *v* **equalled**, **equalling 1** to be equal to someone or something **2** to match or rival another achievement ♦ *No one has yet* *equalled this score.* **equality** n **equalize** v **equalization** n **equalizer** n **equally** adv

equanimity (say ek-wə-**nim**-iti) n a calm state of mind or temper

equate (say i-**kwayt**) v to consider someone or something to be equal or equivalent to another

equator (say i-**kway**-ter) n an imaginary line round the earth at an equal distance from the North and South Poles, dividing the earth into northern and southern hemispheres **equatorial** adj

equestrian (say i-**kwest**-riən) adj 1 to do with horse riding 2 (said about a portrait or statue) showing a figure on horseback **equestrian** n a person who is skilled at horse riding

equi- prefix equal; equally

equidistant (say ee-kwi-**dis**-tənt) adj at an equal distance

equilateral (say ee-kwi-**lat**-er-əl) adj (said about a triangle or other figure) having all its sides equal

equilibrium (say ee-kwi-**lib**-riəm) n pl **equilibria** 1 a state of balance between opposing forces or influences 2 a balanced or calm state of mind

equine (say **ek**-wiyn) adj to do with horses, or like a horse

equinox (say **ek**-win-oks) n a time that occurs twice each year when day and night are of equal length **equinoctial** adj

equip v **equipped**, **equipping** to supply someone or something with what is needed **equipment** n 1 the tools and other things needed for a particular job or undertaking 2 the process of providing these items

equity (say **ek**-wi-ti) n fairness, impartiality **equities** pl n stocks and shares that do not yield a fixed rate of interest **equitable** adj **equitably** adv

equivalent adj having the same value, importance, meaning, or status **equivalent** n an equivalent thing, amount, or word **equivalence** n

equivocal (say i-**kwiv**-əkəl) adj deliberately vague and open to more than one interpretation, ambiguous **equivocally** adv

ER abbr Queen Elizabeth

era (say **eer**-ə) n 1 a distinct period of history 2 Geology a major division of time, divided into periods

eradicate (say i-**rad**-ik-ayt) v to get rid of something or remove all traces of it **eradication** n

erase (say i-**rayz**) v 1 to rub out writing or other marks 2 to delete a recording from magnetic audio or video tape **eraser** n **erasure** n

erect adj 1 standing on end, upright, vertical 2 (said about a part of the body, especially the penis) enlarged and rigid from sexual excitement **erect** v to build something or set it up **erectile** adj **erection** n **erector** n

ergo adv therefore

ergonomics (say ergə-**nom**-iks) n the study of work and the most efficient ways of doing it **ergonomic** adj **ergonomically** adv

ermine n 1 an animal of the weasel family, with brown fur that turns white in winter 2 the white fur of the ermine

erode (say i-**rohd**) v to wear something away gradually, especially by rubbing or corroding **erosion** n **erosive** adj

erotic (say i-**rot**-ik) adj to do with sexual love, or arousing sexual desire **erotically** adv **eroticism** n

err v 1 to make a mistake, to be incorrect 2 to do wrong

errand n a short journey to carry a message or to deliver or collect something, usually for someone else

erratic (say i-**rat**-ik) adj irregular or uneven in movement or pattern **erratically** adv

erratum (say e-**rah**-təm) n pl **errata** an error in printing or writing

erroneous (say i-**roh**-niəs) adj incorrect or mistaken **erroneously** adv

error n 1 a mistake 2 the condition of being wrong in judgement or behaviour 3 a technical term for the amount of inaccuracy in a calculation or a measuring device ♦ an error of 2 per cent

ersatz adj substitute or imitation

erstwhile adj formal former

erudite (say **e**-rew-diyt) adj having great knowledge or learning **erudition** n

erupt v 1 to break out suddenly and violently 2 (said about a volcano) to shoot out lava 3 to form spots or patches on the skin **eruption** n **eruptive** adj

escalate (say **esk**-ə-layt) v to become greater, more serious, or more intense; to make something do this ♦ *The street fighting soon escalated into a riot.* **escalation** n **escalator** n

escalope (say **esk**-ə-lohp) n a slice of boneless meat, especially veal

escape v 1 to get yourself free from being confined or controlled 2 to succeed in avoiding something dangerous or unpleasant ♦ *The driver escaped injury by inches.* 3 to be forgotten or unnoticed by someone ♦ *Her name escapes me for the moment.* 4 (said about a liquid or gas, etc.) to get out of a container, to leak 5 (said about words or sounds) to be uttered unintentionally **escape** n 1 the act of escaping 2 a means of escaping 3 a leakage of liquid or gas 4 a temporary distraction or relief from reality or worry **escapade** n a reckless or mischievous adventure **escapement** n a mechanism that controls the movement of a watch or clock, etc. **escaper** n **escapism** n **escapist** adj, n

escapee (say ess-kay-pee) n someone who has escaped

escarpment n a steep slope at the edge of a plateau or other high level ground

eschew (say iss-**choo**) v to avoid or abstain from a choice or action

escort[1] (say **ess**-kort) n 1 one or more people, vehicles, or ships accompanying a person or thing to give protection or as an honour 2 a person who accompanies a member of the opposite sex at a social occasion

escort[2] (say i-**skort**) v to act as an escort to someone or something

Eskimo n pl **Eskimos** or **Eskimo** 1 a member of a people living near the Arctic coast of North America, Greenland, and Siberia 2 the language of this people ◊ It is now more usual, and preferred by the people themselves, to use the name *Inuit* for those who live in northern Canada and Greenland, and *Yupik* for those who live in Alaska and Asia.

esoteric (say ess-oh-**te**-rik) adj intended only for people with special knowledge or interest

ESP abbr extrasensory perception

especial adj 1 special or outstanding ♦ *of especial interest* 2 mainly suitable for one person or thing ♦ *for your especial benefit*

especially adv chiefly, more than in other cases

Esperanto (say ess-per-**an**-toh) n an artificial language

espionage (say **ess**-pi-ən-ahzh) n spying or using spies to obtain secret information

esplanade (say ess-plən-**ayd**) n a level area of ground where people may walk or ride for pleasure, especially beside the sea

espouse (say i-**spowz**) v to adopt or support an idea or cause **espousal** n

espresso n pl **espressos** strong black coffee made by forcing steam through ground coffee beans

Esq. abbr a courtesy title used in more formal correspondence, placed after a man's surname where no title is used before his name

essay[1] (say **ess**-ay) n a short piece of prose writing **essayist** n

essay[2] (say ess-**ay**) v **essays**, **essayed**, **essaying** formal to attempt to do something

essence n 1 the nature or quality that makes a thing what it is 2 a concentrated liquid taken from a plant or other substance, used for flavouring or as a perfume **essential** adj **essentially** adv **essential oil** n a natural oil obtained from a plant

establish v 1 to set up a business or government on a permanent basis 2 to settle yourself or someone else in a place or position 3 to cause people to accept a custom or belief, etc. 4 to show something to be true **established** adj **establishment** n 1 the process of establishing something 2 an organized body, especially a household or staff of servants, etc. 3 a business firm or other institution **the Establishment** people who are established in positions of power and influence

estate n 1 a property consisting of a large house with extensive grounds 2 an area of land with houses or factories built to a common plan and design 3 all that a

esteem v **1** to think highly of someone or something **2** *formal* to consider or regard something in a certain way **esteem** n respect and admiration **estimable** adj

estimate[1] (say **ess**-tim-ət) n **1** a judgement about the size or value of something **2** a written or printed statement of what a piece of work is likely to cost **3** a judgement of the character or qualities of a person or thing

estimate[2] (say **ess**-tim-ayt) v **1** to calculate the size, value, or cost of something **2** to form an estimate of a person or thing **estimation** n

estranged adj unfriendly after being friendly or loving **estrangement** n

estuary (say **ess**-tew-er-i) n pl **estuaries** the mouth of a large river where it reaches the sea and the tide flows in and out

et al. abbr and others

etc. abbr and other similar things, and the rest

etch v **1** to engrave a picture with acid on a metal plate, especially for printing **2** to affect or impress someone deeply ♦ *The scene is etched on my mind.* **etcher** n **etching** n

eternity n **1** time that goes on for ever **2** *informal* a very long time **eternal** adj **eternally** adv

ether (say **ee**-ther) n a colourless liquid produced by the action of acids on alcohol, used as an anaesthetic and as a solvent

ethereal (say i-**theer**-iəl) adj **1** light and delicate **2** to do with heaven, heavenly **ethereally** adv

Ethernet (say **ee**-ther-net) n ICT a system for connecting a number of computers to form a local area network

ethic (say **eth**-ik) n a moral principle or set of principles **ethics** pl n the study of moral rights and principles **ethical** adj **ethically** adv

ethnic adj **1** belonging to a group of people with a particular national or cultural identity **2** (said about clothes, etc.) resembling those of a non-Western

people **ethnically** adv **ethnological** adj **ethnology** n **ethnic cleansing** n the mass expulsion or killing of one ethnic group by another in an area

ethos (say **ee**-thoss) n the characteristic spirit and beliefs of a society or organization

e-ticket n an electronic authorization to travel on a train or aircraft, issued instead of a printed ticket

etiolated (say **ee**-tiə-layt-id) adj (said about a plant) pale and weak from lack of light **etiolation** n

etiquette (say **et**-i-ket) n the rules of correct behaviour in a society or profession

etymology (say et-im-**ol**-əji) n pl **etymologies** an account of the origin and development in meaning of a word **etymological** adj

EU abbr European Union

eu- (say yoo) prefix well

eucalyptus (say yoo-kə-**lip**-təs) n pl **eucalyptuses 1** a kind of evergreen tree **2** a strong-smelling oil obtained from its leaves

Eucharist (say **yoo**-kə-rist) n the Christian sacrament commemorating the Last Supper of Christ and his disciples **Eucharistic** adj

eugenics (say yoo-**jen**-iks) n the science of developing a special human or animal population by controlled breeding **eugenic** adj **eugenically** adv

eulogy (say **yoo**-lə-ji) n pl **eulogies** a speech or piece of writing in praise of a person or thing **eulogize** v **eulogistic** adj

eunuch (say **yoo**-nək) n a man who has been castrated

euphemism (say **yoo**-fim-izm) n a mild or roundabout expression or phrase used instead of a more direct or frank one, e.g. *pass away* instead of *die* **euphemistic** adj **euphemistically** adv

euphony (say **yoo**-fəni) n pleasantness of sounds, especially made by words **euphonious** adj

euphoria (say yoo-**for** -iə) n a feeling of general happiness **euphoric** adj

Eurasian (say yoor-**ay**-zhən) adj **1** of mixed European and Asian parentage **2** to do with Europe and Asia **Eurasian** n a person of mixed European and Asian parentage

eureka (say yoor-**eek**-ə) *interjection* an exclamation of triumph at a great discovery

euro *n pl* **euros** the single currency introduced in the EU in 1999

Euro- *prefix* Europe or European

European *adj* to do with or coming from Europe **European** *n* a person born in Europe or descended from people born there

Eurosceptic *n* a person who is sceptical about the benefits of the European Union and is opposed to increasing its political role

eurozone *n Economics* the group of countries of the European Union that have adopted the euro

euthanasia (say yoo-thə-**nay**-ziə) *n* the act of causing someone to die gently and without pain, especially when they are suffering from a painful incurable disease

eV *abbr* electronvolt(s)

evacuate *v* **1** to send people away from a place that has become dangerous **2** to make something empty of air, water, or other contents **evacuation** *n* **evacuee** *n*

evade (say i-**vayd**) *v* to avoid a person or thing by cleverness or trickery **evasion** *n* **evasive** *adj* **evasively** *adv* **evasiveness** *n*

evaluate *v* to find out or state the value of something **evaluation** *n*

evangelical (say ee-van-**jel**-ikəl) *adj* **1** according to the teaching of the gospel or the Christian religion **2** (in the Church of England) to do with a group that emphasizes the authority of the Bible **Evangelical** *n* an evangelical Christian **evangelicalism** *n* **evangelism** *n* **evangelist** *n* **evangelistic** *adj* **evangelize** *v*

evaporate *v* **1** to turn a liquid into vapour, or to be turned into vapour **2** to cease to exist ♦ *Their hostility soon evaporated.* **evaporation** *n*

eve *n* **1** the evening or day before an important festival ♦ *Christmas Eve.* **2** the time just before an important event ♦ *on the eve of an election* **3** *old use* evening

even *adj* **1** level and smooth, free from irregularities **2** not changing or varying, regular **3** (said about a person's temper) calm, not easily upset **4** equally balanced or matched ♦ *The match was fairly even.* **5** equal in number or amount ♦ *At half time the scores were even.* **6** (said about a number) able to be divided exactly by two **7** exact, not involving fractions ♦ *an even dozen* **even** *adv* used to emphasize a word or statement ♦ *She began to run even faster.* **even** *v* to make something even, or to become even **evenly** *adv* **evenness** *n* **even-handed** *adj* fair and impartial

evening *n* the part of the day between late afternoon and bedtime

event *n* **1** something that happens, especially something important **2** a race or competition that forms part of a sports contest **eventful** *adj*

eventual *adj* happening in the end or after a time ♦ *his eventual success* **eventuality** *n pl* **eventualities** **eventually** *adv*

ever *adv* **1** at all times, always ♦ *We are ever hopeful.* **2** at any time ♦ *It was the best thing I ever did.* **3** used for emphasis ♦ *Why ever didn't you tell me?* **evergreen** *adj* (said about a tree or shrub) having green leaves all the year round **evergreen** *n* an evergreen tree or shrub **everlasting** *adj* lasting for ever or for a long time **everlastingly** *adv* **evermore** *adv* for ever, always

every *adj* **1** each without any exception ♦ *We enjoyed every minute.* **2** each in a series of intervals ♦ *The cleaners come every third day.* **3** all that is possible ♦ *They will be given every care.* **everybody** *pronoun* every person **everyday** *adj* usual, ordinary ♦ *everyday clothes* **everyone** *pronoun* everybody **everything** *pronoun* **1** all things, all **2** the most important thing ♦ *Beauty is not everything.* **everywhere** *adv* in every place

evict (say i-**vikt**) *v* to use the law to make people leave the property they are living in **eviction** *n*

evidence *n* **1** a fact or piece of information that gives a reason for believing something **2** statements made or objects produced in a law court to prove or support a case **evidence** *v* to be evidence of something **evident** *adj* **evidential** *adj* **evidently** *adv*

evil *adj* **1** morally bad, wicked **2** harmful or tending to do harm **3** extremely unpleasant or troublesome ♦ *an evil smell*

evil n **1** extreme wickedness **2** an evil thing
evilly adv **evil-doer** n someone who does evil things
evoke (say i-vohk) v **1** to bring back special memories or feelings ♦ *The photographs evoked happy memories.* **2** to produce a particular response from someone **evocation** n **evocative** adj
evolve (say i-volv) v **1** to develop gradually, or develop something gradually ♦ *We must try to evolve a plan.* **2** (said about an organism) to develop by evolution **evolution** n **1** the process by which something evolves or changes **2** the process by which living things develop from earlier forms **evolutionary** adv **evolvement** n
ewe n a female sheep
ex prep (said about goods) as sold from a ship, factory, etc. ♦ *ex-works*
ex- prefix (changing to **ef-** before f, and to **e-** before many consonants). **1** out or away (as in *extract*) **2** thoroughly (as in *exhilarate*) **3** formerly (as in *ex-president*)
exacerbate (say eks-ass-er-bayt) v to make a pain, disease, or bad feeling worse **exacerbation** n
exact adj **1** correct in every detail **2** clearly stated, giving all details ♦ *Give me the exact instructions.* **3** capable of being precise ♦ *the exact sciences* **exact** v to insist on something and obtain it ♦ *He exacted obedience from the recruits.* **exacting** adj making great demands on your ability or stamina ♦ *an exacting task* **exactitude** n **exactly** adv **1** in an exact manner; to an exact degree **2** used to express agreement with what someone has said **exactness** n
exaggerate v to make something seem larger, better or worse, or more important than it really is **exaggeration** n
exalt (say ig-zawlt) v **1** to raise someone to a higher rank or level of power or dignity **2** to praise someone or something highly **exaltation** n
exam n a test or examination
examination n **1** the process of examining someone or something **2** a formal test of a person's knowledge or ability by means of oral or written questions **3** a formal

questioning of a witness or an accused person in a law court **examinee** n
examine v **1** to look at someone or something to check their condition or to get information about them **2** to test a person's knowledge or ability in an examination **3** to question a witness or accused person in a law court **examiner** n
example n **1** something that shows what others of the same kind are like or how they work **2** a person or thing that is good enough to imitate **for example** by way of illustrating a general rule
exasperate v to annoy someone very much **exasperation** n
excavate v **1** to make a hole or channel by digging; to dig out soil **2** to reveal or extract something by digging **3** to conduct an archaeological investigation by digging **excavation** n **excavator** n
exceed v **1** to be greater or more numerous than something **2** to go beyond the limit of what is normal or permitted **exceedingly** adv
excel v **excelled, excelling** to be better at something than someone else or other people **excellence** n very great quality or merit **Excellency** n pl **Excellencies** the title of high officials such as ambassadors or governors **excellent** adj extremely good **excellently** adv
except prep not including, apart from ♦ *The guests have all arrived except three.* **except** v to exclude someone or something from a statement or calculation, etc. **excepting** prep **exception** n **1** the process of excepting something or leaving something out **2** a person or thing that is left out or does not follow the general rule **exceptionable** adj **exceptional** adj **exceptionally** adv
excerpt[1] (say ek-serpt) n an extract from a book, film, piece of music, etc.
excerpt[2] (say ek-serpt) v to choose excerpts from something **excerption** n
excess n **1** too much of something **2** the amount by which one number or quantity, etc. is greater than another **excessive** adj **excessively** adv **in excess of** more than
exchange v to give one thing and get

another in its place **exchange** n **1** the process of exchanging things **2** the exchanging of money for its equivalent in another currency **3** a place where things (especially stocks and shares) are bought and sold ♦ *a stock exchange* **exchangeable** *adj* **exchange rate** n the value of one currency in relation to another

exchequer n a national treasury into which public money (such as taxes) is paid

excise[1] (say **ek**-siyz) n a tax charged on certain goods and licences, etc.

excise[2] (say ik-**siyz**) v to remove something by cutting it out or away **excision** n

excite v **1** to rouse a person's feelings; to make someone eager about something **2** to cause a feeling or reaction ♦ *The discovery excited great interest.* **3** to produce activity in a nerve or organ of the body, etc. **4** to cause a substance to give out radiation **excitability** n **excitable** *adj* **excited** *adj* **excitedly** *adv* **excitement** n **exciting** *adj* **excitingly** *adv*

exclaim v to shout or cry out in eagerness or surprise **exclamation** n **1** the act of exclaiming **2** a word or group of words that someone exclaims **exclamatory** *adj* **exclamation mark** n a punctuation mark (!) put at the end of an exclamation

exclude v **1** to keep someone or something out of a place, group, or privilege, etc. **2** to omit something or ignore it as irrelevant ♦ *We should not exclude this possibility.* **3** to prevent something or make it impossible **exclusion** n **exclusive** *adj* **1** not admitting or allowing other things ♦ *The two schemes are mutually exclusive.* **2** intended or available only for certain people ♦ *an exclusive department store in Mayfair* **3** (said about legal terms) excluding anything that is not specified **4** (said about a newspaper article) not published anywhere else **5** not shared by anyone else ♦ *The company has exclusive film rights to the book.* **exclusively** *adv* **exclusiveness** n **exclusivity** n **exclusive of** excluding, not counting ♦ *There are twenty people coming exclusive of the family.*

excommunicate v to deprive someone of membership of a Church

excommunication n

excrement (say **eks**-kri-mənt) n waste matter excreted from the bowels, faeces

excrete (say iks-**kreet**) v to expel waste matter from the body **excretion** n **excretory** *adj*

excruciating (say iks-**kroo**-shi-ayting) *adj* extremely painful, agonizing

excursion n a short journey made for pleasure

excuse[1] (say iks-**kewz**) v **1** to overlook or pardon someone for an offence, especially a minor one **2** to justify a fault or error ♦ *Nothing can excuse such rudeness.* **3** to free someone from an obligation or duty ♦ *Steve was excused swimming because of his flu.* **excusable** *adj* **excusably** *adv* **to excuse oneself** to ask permission to leave a room or building

excuse[2] (say iks-**kewss**) n a reason given to explain a fault or offence

execute v **1** to put someone to death as a punishment **2** to carry out an order or put a plan into effect **3** to perform an action or manoeuvre ♦ *She executed a perfect somersault.* **4** to produce a work of art **5** *Law* to make a will or other legal document valid, especially by signing it **execution** n **executioner** n

executive (say ig-**zek**-yoo-tiv) n **1** a senior person or group of people with authority to manage a business organization **2** the branch of a government with responsibility for putting laws and decisions into effect **executive** *adj* having the powers to put laws or decisions into effect

exemplary (say ig-**zem**-plər-i) *adj* **1** serving as an example to follow, very good ♦ *exemplary conduct* **2** (said about a punishment) severe so as to serve as a warning to others

exemplify (say ig-**zem**-pli-fiy) v **exemplifies**, **exemplified**, **exemplifying** to serve as an example of something **exemplification** n

exempt *adj* free from an obligation or payment that is normally required **exempt** v to make someone exempt from something **exemption** n

exercise n **1** activity involving physical

effort, done to improve your health **2** an activity or task done to test or improve an ability **3** the application of a right or process ♦ *the exercise of their authority* **exercise** *v* **1** to make use of a power or right **2** to take exercise, or train by means of exercises **3** to perplex or worry someone **exercise book** *n*

exert *v* to make use of a quality or power ♦ *We needed to exert all our strength.* **exertion** *n*

exhale *v* to breathe out **exhalation** *n*

exhaust *v* **1** to make someone extremely tired **2** to use up something completely **3** to find out or say all there is about a subject **exhaust** *n* **1** the waste gases or steam from an engine **2** the pipe or other device through which they are sent out **exhaustible** *adj* **exhaustion** *n* **exhaustive** *adj* **exhaustively** *adv*

exhibit (say ig-**zib**-it) *v* to show or display something in public **exhibit** *n* something on display in a museum or gallery **exhibition** *n* **exhibitionism** *n* **exhibitionist** *n* **exhibitor** *n*

exhilarate (say ig-**zil**-er-ayt) *v* to make someone very happy and excited **exhilaration** *n*

exhume (say ig-**zewm**) *v* to dig up a body that has been buried, especially to examine it **exhumation** *n*

exigency (say **eks**-i-jən-si) *n pl* **exigencies** an urgent need or demand, an emergency **exigent** *adj* **exigently** *adv*

exile *n* **1** being sent away from your own country as a punishment **2** an exiled person **exile** *v* to send someone away from their own country

exist *v* **1** to be present as part of what is real ♦ *Do ghosts exist?* **2** to stay alive ♦ *We cannot exist without food.* **3** to occur or be found ♦ *Various types of plant exist here.* **existence** *n* **existent** *adj* **existential** *adj* **1** to do with existence **2** *Philosophy* to do with human experience as viewed by existentialism **existentially** *adv*

exit *n* **1** the way out of a room or building **2** the act of going away or out of a room or building **3** an actor's or performer's departure from the stage **exit** *v* **exited**, **exiting 1** to leave a room or building **2** (as a

stage direction) he or she leaves the stage **exit poll** *n* a poll of people leaving a polling station after voting, to estimate the result

exo- *prefix* outside, from outside (as in *exoskeleton*)

exodus *n* a departure of many people **Exodus** the second book of the Old Testament, describing the exodus of the Jews from Egypt

exonerate (say ig-**zon**-er-ayt) *v* to declare or prove that someone is not to blame for something **exoneration** *n*

exorbitant (say ig-**zorb**-i-tənt) *adj* (said about a price or demand) much too great, excessive

exorcize (say **eks**-or-siyz) *v* to drive out a supposed evil spirit from a person or place **exorcism** *n* **exorcist** *n*

exotic (say ig-**zot**-ik) *adj* **1** from another part of the world **2** strikingly colourful or unusual ♦ *exotic clothes* **exotically** *adv*

expand *v* **1** to make something larger, or to become larger **2** to unfold something or spread it out **3** (said about a person) to become more lively or talkative **expandable** *adj* **expander** *n* **expansion** *n* **expansionism** *n* **expansionist** *n*, *adj* **expansive** *adj* **expansively** *adv* **expansiveness** *n*

expanse *n* a wide area of open land, sea, or space

expatriate[1] (say eks-**pat**-ri-ət) *n* a person living permanently abroad **expatriate** *adj* living abroad

expatriate[2] (say eks-**pat**-ri-ayt) *v* to settle abroad, or send someone to live abroad **expatriation** *n*

expect *v* **1** to think or believe that something will happen **2** to demand something or think it to be necessary ♦ *The shop expects prompt payment.* **3** to think, to suppose **expectancy** *n* **expectant** *adj* **expectantly** *adv* **expectation** *n*

expectorate *v* to cough and spit out phlegm from the throat or lungs **expectorant** *n* **expectoration** *n*

expedient (say iks-**pee**-diənt) *adj* **1** suitable or convenient **2** useful or advantageous rather than right or just **expedient** *n* a convenient means of achieving something

expediency n **expediently** adv
expedite (say **eks**-pi-diyt) v to get something done quickly or efficiently **expeditious** adj **expeditiously** adv
expedition n 1 a journey or voyage made by a group of people for a special purpose 2 the people or vehicles making such a journey 3 *formal* speed or promptness **expeditionary** adj
expel v **expelled**, **expelling** 1 to send or force something out ♦ *The fan expels stale air.* 2 to compel a person to leave a school or country, etc.
expend v to spend money or use time or care to get something done **expendable** adj **expenditure** n
expense n 1 the cost of doing something 2 something that you have to spend money on ♦ *The car has become a great expense.* **expenses** pl n the amount spent in doing something **expensive** adj **expensively** adv **expensiveness** n
experience n 1 actual practice in doing something or observation of facts or events 2 skill or knowledge gained over time 3 an event or activity that has an effect on you **experience** v 1 to have something happen to you 2 to be affected by a feeling **experienced** adj
experiment n a test or trial done to see how something works or to find out what happens **experiment** v 1 to carry out an experiment 2 to try out new things **experimental** adj **experimentalism** n **experimentally** adv **experimentation** n
expert n a person with great knowledge or skill in something **expert** adj having great knowledge or skill **expertly** adv **expertise** n
expire v 1 to stop being valid, to be no longer usable ♦ *Your ticket has expired.* 2 a technical term meaning to breathe out air 3 to breathe your last breath, to die **expiration** n **expiry** n
explain v 1 to make something plain or clear, to show the meaning of something 2 to account for something ♦ *That explains his absence.* **explanation** n **explanatory** adj
expletive (say iks-**plee**-tiv) n an oath or swear word

explicable (say eks-**plik**-əbəl) adj able to be explained
explicit (say iks-**pliss**-it) adj stating something openly and exactly. (Compare *implicit*.) **explicitly** adv **explicitness** n
explode v 1 to burst violently or suddenly release energy with a loud noise 2 (said about a person) to show sudden strong emotion, especially anger ♦ *When he heard about it he exploded with rage.* 3 (said about a population or a supply of goods, etc.) to increase suddenly or rapidly 4 to destroy an idea or theory by showing it to be false **explosion** n **explosive** adj **explosively** adv
exploit[1] (say **eks**-ploit) n a bold or exciting deed
exploit[2] (say iks-**ploit**) v 1 to develop a resource and get benefit from it 2 to make unfair use of someone or something **exploitation** n
explore v 1 to travel into or through a country or region in order to learn about it 2 to examine or investigate a subject or idea carefully ♦ *We will explore all the possibilities.* 3 to examine something by touch **exploration** n **exploratory** adj **explorer** n
exponent (say iks-**poh**-nənt) n someone who favours a particular theory or policy
export[1] (say eks **port** or **eks**-port) v to send goods to another country to be sold **exportable** adj **exportation** n **exporter** n
export[2] (say **eks**-port) n 1 the process of exporting goods 2 something exported
expose v 1 to leave someone or something uncovered or unprotected, especially from the weather 2 to subject someone or something to a risk or danger 3 to allow light to reach photographic film so as to take a picture 4 to make something visible, to reveal something 5 to reveal information about a wrongdoing or the person who has committed it
exposition n 1 an explanatory account of a plan or theory 2 a large public exhibition
exposure n 1 the process of exposing someone or something to air, cold, or harm 2 the process of exposing film to the light so as to take a picture, or a piece of film exposed in this way 3 publicity

expound v to describe or explain something in detail

express¹ adj **1** definitely and clearly stated ♦ *These were her express instructions.* **2** going or sent quickly; designed for high speed **express** adv at high speed, by an express service **express** n a fast train stopping only at a few stations **express** v to send something by express service **expressible** adj **expression** n **1** the process of expressing thoughts or ideas **2** a word or phrase that expresses an idea **3** a look on someone's face that expresses their feelings **4** speaking or playing music in a way that shows feeling **5** *Mathematics* a collection of symbols expressing a quantity **expressionless** adj **expressive** adj **expressively** adv **expressiveness** n **expressly** adv

express² v **1** to put a thought or idea into words; to make your feelings or ideas known **2** to represent something by means of symbols, e.g. in mathematics **3** to press or squeeze something out, especially liquid

expulsion n the process of expelling someone or something **expulsive** adj

exquisite (say **eks**-kwiz-it) adj **1** having great beauty and delicacy **2** highly refined or sensitive ♦ *exquisite taste* **3** acute or keenly felt ♦ *the exquisite pain of love* **exquisitely** adv

ex-serviceman, ex-servicewoman n pl **ex-servicemen** or **ex-servicewomen** a man or woman who is a former member of the armed services

extant (say eks-**tant**) adj still existing

extempore (say eks-**tem**-per-i) adv, adj spoken or done without preparation, impromptu **extemporaneous** adj **extemporary** adj **extemporize** v **extemporization** n

extend v **1** to make something longer or larger **2** to make something last longer **3** to stretch out a hand or foot or limb, etc. **4** to continue for a specified distance, to reach something ♦ *The house has land that extends to the river.* **5** to offer or grant something ♦ *We extend a warm welcome to all our friends.* **extendible** adj **extensible** adj **extended family** n a family including other

relatives who live in the same household or nearby

extension n **1** the process of extending something **2** extent or range **3** something added on, especially an extra section added to a building **4** an extra period for something to be done **5** an individual telephone connected to a main telephone line or switchboard and having its own additional number

extensive adj **1** covering a large area ♦ *extensive gardens* **2** large in scope, wide-ranging ♦ *an extensive search* **extensively** adv **extensiveness** n

extent n **1** the space or length over which a thing extends **2** the range or scope of something ♦ *We need to find out the extent of the damage.*

extenuating (say iks-ten-yoo-ayt-ing) adj making an offence or error seem less great by providing a partial excuse ♦ *There were extenuating circumstances.* **extenuation** n

exterior adj on the outside, or coming from the outside **exterior** n an exterior surface or part

exterminate v to kill or get rid of all the existing examples of something, to destroy something completely **extermination** n **exterminator** n

external adj **1** on or belonging to or forming the outside or visible part of something **2** on or for the outside of the body ♦ *The lotion is for external use only.* **3** coming or obtained from an independent or outside source ♦ *external influences* **4** belonging to the world outside a person or people, not in the mind **externally** adv

extinct adj **1** (said about an animal or species) no longer alive or existing **2** (said about a volcano) no longer active **extinction** n

extinguish v **1** to put out a light, fire, or flame **2** to end the existence of a hope or feeling, etc. **extinguisher** n

extol (say iks-**tohl**) v **extolled, extolling** to praise something or someone enthusiastically

extort v to obtain something by force or threats **extortion** n **extortionate** adj charging or demanding far too much

extortionately adv **extortioner** n

extra adj additional, more than is usual or expected ♦ Where did you find the extra money? **extra** adv more than usually ♦ The locks are extra strong. **extra** n 1 an extra person or thing 2 an item for which an extra charge is made 3 a person taken on to form part of a crowd in a film or play

extra- prefix outside or beyond (as in extraterrestrial)

extract[1] (say iks-**trakt**) v 1 to take something out or remove it, especially by force or effort 2 to obtain money, information, etc. from someone who is reluctant to give it 3 to obtain a substance or liquid by a special process 4 to take or copy passages or quotations from a book, film, piece of music, etc. **extraction** n **extractor** n

extract[2] (say **eks**-trakt) n 1 a passage taken from a book, play, film, piece of music, etc. 2 a substance separated or obtained from another

extradite (say **eks**-trə-diyt) v to hand over an accused person to the police of the country where the crime was committed **extraditable** adj **extradition** n

extraneous (say iks-**tray**-niəs) adj 1 coming from outside 2 not belonging to the matter or subject in hand **extraneously** adv

extranet (say **eks**-trə-net) n ICT part of the intranet system of an organization that can be accessed by authorized outside users

extraordinary adj 1 very unusual or remarkable 2 (said about a meeting) specially called or arranged **extraordinarily** adv

extrapolate (say iks-**trap**-ə-layt) v to draw conclusions from available data about something unknown or beyond the range of the available data **extrapolation** n

extraterrestrial adj from beyond the earth or its atmosphere **extraterrestrial** n a fictional or supposed being from outer space

extravagant adj 1 spending or using much more than is necessary 2 (said about prices) excessively high 3 (said about ideas, behaviour, etc.) going beyond what is reasonable, not properly controlled

extravagance n **extravagantly** adv

extravaganza (say iks-trav-ə-**gan**-zə) n a lavish or spectacular film or show

extreme adj 1 very great or intense ♦ extreme cold 2 furthest away, outermost ♦ the extreme edge 3 going to great lengths in actions or opinions, not moderate ♦ That is an extreme view. **extreme** n 1 either end of something 2 something extreme, either of two concepts or opinions that are as different from each other as they can be **extremely** adv **extremism** n **extremist** n **extremities** pl n the hands and feet **extremity** n pl **extremities** 1 an extreme point, the very end of something 2 an extreme feeling or need of danger, etc.

extricate (say **eks**-trik-ayt) v to free someone or something from a difficult position or state **extricable** adj **extrication** n

extrovert (say **eks**-trə-vert) n a lively sociable person, or one more interested in external things than in internal thoughts. (Compare introvert.) **extroverted** adj

exuberant (say ig-**zew**-bər-ənt) adj lively, full of high spirits **exuberance** n **exuberantly** adv

exude (say ig-**zewd**) v 1 to give off moisture or a smell, or to ooze out in this way 2 to display a feeling or quality openly ♦ She exuded confidence. **exudation** n

exult (say ig-**zult**) v to rejoice or feel triumphant **exultant** adj **exultation** n

eye n 1 the organ of seeing in humans and some animals 2 the iris of the eye ♦ She has lovely blue eyes. 3 the power of seeing, observation ♦ You'll need sharp eyes in this traffic. 4 something compared to an eye, especially a leaf bud on a potato 5 the hole in a needle through which the thread is passed **eye** v **eyes**, **eyed**, **eyeing** to watch someone or something carefully **eyeball** n the ball-shaped part of the eye inside the eyelids **eyebrow** n the fringe of hair growing on the face above the eye **eye-catching** adj striking or attractive **eyeful** n pl **eyefuls** 1 a long close look ♦ getting an eyeful 2 a striking or attractive person or thing **eyeglass** n a single lens for a defective eye, a monocle **eyelash** n each of the short hairs growing on the edge of the eyelids **eyelid** n each of the two folds of skin that can close together to cover the eyeball **eye-opener** n something very surprising or revealing **eyesight** n 1 the ability to see 2 a range of vision ♦ *within eyesight* **eyesore** n something that is ugly to look at **eyewitness** n a person who saw a crime or other incident take place and can give information about it

eyrie (say **iy**-ri) n the nest of an eagle or other bird of prey

Ff

F[1] **1** the sixth letter of the English alphabet **2** *Mus* the fourth note of the diatonic scale of C major **3** *Chem* the symbol for fluorine

F[2] *abbr* Fahrenheit

f *abbr Mus* forte (loudly)

FA *abbr* Football Association

fable n **1** a short story, usually with animals as characters, intended to convey a moral **2** these stories or legends collectively **fabled** *adj* **fabulous** *adj* **1** told of in fables ♦ *a fabulous creature* **2** incredibly great ♦ *fabulous wealth* **3** *informal* wonderful, marvellous ♦ *We all had a fabulous time.* **fabulously** *adv*

fabric n **1** material produced from woven or knitted textile fibres, cloth **2** the basic structure or framework of something, especially the walls, floors, and roof of a building **fabricate** v **1** to construct or manufacture something **2** to invent a story or excuse so as to deceive people **fabrication** n **fabricator** n

facade (say fǝ-**sahd**) n **1** the outer face of a building **2** an outward appearance, especially a deceptive one

face n **1** the front part of the head from the forehead to the chin **2** the expression on a person's face ♦ *She had a cheerful face.* **3** an aspect of something ♦ *the unacceptable face of capitalism* **4** each of the surfaces of a three-dimensional object such as a cube **5** the sloping or vertical side of a mountain or cliff **6** the front of something, or the surface that is the one normally looked at or has a distinctive function ♦ *The playing cards were on the table face up.* **face** v **1** to have or turn the face in a specified direction **2** to meet and deal with a difficulty or an opponent ♦ *She went in to face her accusers.* **3** to have the prospect of something unpleasant or difficult to deal with ♦ *The travellers faced further delays.* **4** to present itself to you ♦ *This is the problem that faces us.* **5** to cover a surface with a layer of different material **faceless** *adj* **1** not having an identity **2** (said about an authority, organization, etc.) impersonal and inaccessible **facecloth** n **face flannel** a small cloth for washing the face **facelift** n **1** surgery done to improve the appearance of a person's face **2** an alteration or renovation that improves the appearance of something, especially a building **face value** n **to take something at its face value** to assume that something is what it seems to be

facet (say **fas**-it) n **1** each of the many sides of a cut stone or jewel **2** one aspect of a situation or problem

facile (say fa-siyl) *adj* **1** done too easily, superficial ♦ *a facile solution* **2** (said about a person) able to do something easily ♦ *a facile speaker* **facilitate** v to make something easy or easier to do **facilitation** n

facility (say fǝ-**sil**-iti) n pl **facilities 1** a building or piece of equipment used for a special purpose ♦ *sports facilities* **2** ease or ability in doing something ♦ *She reads music with great facility.* **3** the quality of being easy, absence of difficulty

facsimile (say fak-**sim**-ili) n pl **facsimiles** an exact copy of something written or printed

fact n **1** something that is known to have happened or to be true **2** a thing asserted to be true as a basis for reasoning **factual** *adj* **factually** *adv*

faction (say **fak**-shǝn) n a small united group within a larger one, especially in politics **factional** *adj* **factionally** *adv*

factor n **1** a circumstance or influence that helps to bring about a result ♦ *The weather* *was a decisive factor in the army's defeat.* **2** *Mathematics* a number by which a larger number can be divided exactly ♦ *1, 2, 3, and 6 are factors of 6* **3** a business agent, or (in Scotland) a land agent or steward

factory *n pl* **factories** a building or group of buildings in which goods are manufactured

faculty (say **fak**-əl-ti) *n pl* **faculties 1** any of the powers of the body or mind ♦ *the faculty of sight* **2** a particular kind of ability ♦ *a faculty for learning languages* **3** a department teaching a particular subject in a university or college ♦ *the faculty of music*

fad *n* **1** a temporary fashion or craze **2** a person's particular like or dislike **faddish** *adj* **faddy** *adj*

fade *v* **1** to lose colour, freshness, or strength, or to make something or someone do this **2** (said about something seen or heard) to disappear gradually, to become indistinct **3** to make the sound or picture in a cinema film or a television or radio recording decrease (*fade out*) or increase (*fade in*) gradually **fade** *n* an act or sound of fading

faeces (say **fee**-seez) *pl n* solid waste matter passed out of the body **faecal** *adj*

Fahrenheit (say **fa**-rən-hiyt) *adj* relating to or using a temperature scale in which water freezes at 32° and boils at 212°

fail *v* **1** to be unsuccessful in doing something or in trying to do it **2** to become weak or useless, to stop working ♦ *The brakes failed on a steep hill.* **3** to be or become insufficient; (said about crops) to produce a poor harvest **4** to neglect or be unable to do something ♦ *They failed to warn us.* **5** to disappoint the hopes of someone **6** to become bankrupt **7** to be unable to meet the standard needed in an examination **8** to judge that a candidate has not passed an examination **fail** *n* a failure in an examination **failing** *n* **failure** *n* **1** the act of failing, a lack of success **2** a situation in which power has failed, or a machine or a part of the body has stopped working ♦ *heart failure* **3** a person or thing that has failed **fail-safe** *adj* (said about equipment or machinery) returning to a safe state in the event of a failure or breakdown

faint *adj* **1** not clear to the senses, dim or indistinct **2** pale in colour **3** weak or vague ♦ *There is a faint hope.* **4** timid or feeble **5** (said about a person) weak and giddy, and about to lose consciousness **faint** *v* to lose consciousness briefly when insufficient oxygen is supplied to the brain **faint** *n* an act or state of fainting **faintly** *adv* **faintness** *n* **faint-hearted** *adj* timid or reserved

fair[1] *n* **1** right or just, in accordance with the rules ♦ *It was a fair decision to award a penalty.* **2** treating people equally and with justice **3** (said about the hair or skin) light in colour; (said about a person) having fair hair **4** *old use* beautiful **5** (said about the weather) fine and dry **6** moderate in quality or amount ♦ *A fair number of people had come.* **fair** *adv* in a fair manner **fairly** *adv* **1** in a fair or just manner ♦ *She treated us fairly.* **2** moderately, somewhat ♦ *It seems fairly difficult.* **3** actually, really ♦ *He fairly jumped for joy.*

fair[2] *n* **1** a gathering of shows and amusements for public entertainment **2** a periodic gathering to sell goods **3** an exhibition of commercial or industrial goods ♦ *the annual book fair* **fairground** *n* an open outdoor space where a fair is held

fairy *n pl* **fairies** an imaginary small being with magic powers **fairy godmother** *n* a woman in fairy stories who brings unexpected good fortune to the hero or heroine **fairyland** *n* **1** the world of fairies **2** a very beautiful place **fairy lights** *pl n* strings of small decorative coloured lights **fairy story** or **fairy tale** *n* a story about imaginary or magical beings and places

fait accompli (say fayt ah-**kom**-pli) *n* a thing that is already done and cannot be changed

faith *n* **1** strong trust or confidence in a person or thing **2** belief in a religious doctrine **3** a system of religious beliefs ♦ *the Christian faith* **faithful** *adj* **1** loyal and trustworthy ♦ *faithful fans* **2** sexually loyal to one partner **3** true to the facts, accurate **faithfully** *adv* **faithfulness** *n* **faithless** *adj* **1** not having a religious faith **2** breaking promises, disloyal

fake n **1** something that looks genuine but is not **2** a person who makes false claims in order to deceive others **fake** adj false, not genuine **fake** v **1** to make something that looks genuine, in order to deceive people **2** to pretend something ♦ *He faked illness so as to stay at home.* **faker** n

fakir (say **fay**-keer) n a Muslim or Hindu religious beggar regarded as a holy man

falafel (say fə-**laf**-əl) n a Middle Eastern dish of spiced mashed chickpeas

falcon (say **fawl**-kən) n a kind of hawk **falconry** n the breeding and training of hawks

fall v **fell, fallen 1** to come or go freely from a higher position to a lower one **2** to hang down **3** to slope downwards **4** to become less in amount, number, or strength ♦ *House prices are falling at last.* **5** to happen or be noticed ♦ *An eerie silence fell on the crowd.* **6** to lose a position of power or authority **7** (said about a person's face) to show disappointment by appearing to droop **8** to die in battle **9** to be captured or overthrown ♦ *The city fell after a long siege.* **10** to pass into a specified state ♦ *We fell in love.* ♦ *Then she fell asleep.* **11** to occur, to have as a date ♦ *Easter falls late this year.* **fall** n **1** the act of falling **2** the amount by which something falls or becomes less **3** N. Am autumn **falls** pl n a waterfall

fallacy (say **fal**-əsi) n pl **fallacies 1** a false or mistaken belief **2** faulty reasoning **fallacious** adj containing a fallacy, faulty **fallaciously** adv **fallaciousness** n

fallible (say **fal**-ibəl) adj liable to make mistakes **fallibility** n

Fallopian tubes (say fə-**loh**-piən) pl n the two tubes in female mammals carrying eggs from the ovaries to the uterus

false adj **1** incorrect or wrong **2** (said about a person) deceitful or unfaithful **3** not genuine, artificial ♦ *false teeth* **falsehood** n **1** an untrue statement, a lie **2** telling lies **falsely** adv **falseness** n **falsify** v **falsifies, falsified, falsifying 1** to alter a document dishonestly **2** to misrepresent facts **falsification** n **falsity** n pl **falsities**

falter v **1** to move or function unsteadily **2** to become weaker, to begin to give way ♦ *His courage began to falter.* **3** to speak or utter hesitatingly, to stammer **falteringly** adv

fame n **1** being known to many people, being famous **2** a good reputation **famed** adj

familiar adj **1** well known, often seen or experienced ♦ *The old car was a familiar sight in the town.* **2** knowing something well ♦ *Are you familiar with this song?* **3** friendly and informal ♦ *She addressed him in familiar terms.* **4** too informal, over-friendly **familiar** n in stories, an animal or creature believed to be the pet of a witch or wizard **familiarity** n **familiarization** n **familiarize** v **familiarly** adv

family n pl **families 1** parents and their children, sometimes including grandchildren and other relatives **2** a person's children ♦ *They have a large family.* **3** all the descendants of a common ancestor **4** a group of things that are alike in some way **5** a group of related plants or animals ♦ *Lions belong to the cat family.* **family planning** n use of contraception to plan the size of a family **family tree** n a diagram showing how people in a family are related

famine n extreme scarcity of food in a region

famished adj informal very hungry

famous adj known to many people **famously** adv

fan¹ n a device or machine for creating a current of air in a room or building **fan** v **fanned, fanning 1** to send a current of air on someone or something **2** to stimulate flames with a current of air **3** to spread from a central point ♦ *The troops fanned out to the left.*

fan² n an enthusiastic admirer or supporter **fan club** n an organized group of supporters or admirers

fanatic (say fə-**nat**-ik) n a person filled with excessive enthusiasm for something **fanatical** adj **fanatically** adv **fanaticism** n

fancy n pl **fancies 1** the power of imagining things **2** something imagined, an unfounded idea or belief **3** a liking or desire for something **fancy** adj **fancier, fanciest** ornamental or elaborate **fancy** v

fancies, fancied, fancying 1 to imagine something **2** to be inclined to believe or suppose something ♦ *I fancy he may be in love with Mary.* **3** *informal* to feel a wish or desire for something ♦ *Do you fancy a doughnut?* **4** *informal* to find someone sexually attractive **fancier** n **fanciful** adj **fancifully** adv **fancy dress** n an unusual costume worn for a party

fanfare n a short piece of loud music played on trumpets, especially as part of a ceremony

fang n **1** a long sharp tooth **2** a tooth a snake uses to inject its venom

fantasy n pl **fantasies 1** something imaginary or fantastic **2** imagination used to produce fanciful ideas **3** a fanciful design **4** an imaginative piece of music or writing **fantasize** v **fantastic** adj **1** *informal* very remarkable, excellent **2** highly fanciful **3** designed in an imaginative way **fantastically** adv

far adv **farther** or **further**, **farthest** or **furthest** at or to a great distance ♦ *We shan't go far.* **far** adj distant or remote ♦ *They like to travel to far countries.* **farther** adv, adj at or to a greater distance, more remote **farthest** adv, adj at or to the greatest distance, most remote **faraway** adj

farce n **1** a comedy with exaggerated humour **2** this kind of drama **3** events that are absurd or useless **farcical** adj **farcically** adv

fare n **1** the price charged for a passenger to travel **2** a passenger who pays a fare **3** food and drink provided for people ♦ *There was only very simple fare.* **fare** v to have good or bad treatment, to progress ♦ *How did you fare?*

Far East n China, Japan, and other countries of east and south-east Asia

farewell interjection goodbye **farewell** n an act of leaving or parting

farm n **1** an area of land and its buildings used for raising crops or rearing animals **2** a farmhouse **farm** v **1** to grow crops or rear farm animals **2** to use land for this purpose **farmer** n a person who owns or manages a farm **farmhand** n a worker on a farm

Farsi n the modern form of the Persian language

fart v *informal* to let out wind from the anus **fart** n the act or sound of wind let out of the anus

fascinate v to be very attractive or interesting to someone **fascinating** adj **fascination** n **fascinator** n

fascism (say **fash**-izm) n a system of extreme right-wing government **fascist** n

fashion n **1** the popular style of dress or behaviour at a particular time **2** a manner of doing something ♦ *We decided to continue in the same fashion.* **fashion** v to make something into a particular form or shape **fashionable** adj **fashionably** adv

fast[1] adj **1** moving or able to move at a high speed **2** suitable for travel at high speed ♦ *a fast road* **3** done or happening quickly ♦ *We need a fast response to our appeal.* **4** (said about a clock or watch) showing a time later than the correct time **5** firmly fixed or attached **6** (said about a person or activity) involved in or involving great or shocking excitement **7** (said about colours or dyes) not likely to fade **fast** adv **1** quickly **2** firmly or tightly, securely ♦ *The window was stuck fast.* ♦ *The children are fast asleep.* **fast food** n quickly-prepared food **fast-forward** v to advance a video tape or DVD at accelerated speed **fast track** n a quick route or method

fast[2] v to go without food **fast** n an act or time of fasting

fasten v **1** to fix something firmly in place, or join things together **2** to become fastened ♦ *The door fastens with a latch.* **fastener** n

fastidious (say fas-**tid**-i-os) adj **1** fussy and hard to please **2** very careful about small details **fastidiously** adv **fastidiousness** n

fat n **1** a natural oily substance that is insoluble in water and is found in animal bodies and certain seeds **2** oil or grease for use in cooking **fat** adj **fatter**, **fattest 1** containing much fat **2** (said about a person) having a thick round body **3** (said about an animal) made plump for slaughter **4** thick ♦ *a fat book* **fatness** n **fatten** v **fatty** adj **fattier**, **fattiest**

fate n **1** an irresistible power that is thought to make things happen **2** what has happened or will happen to a person **fatal** adj **1** causing or ending in death ♦ a fatal wound **2** causing failure or disaster ♦ a fatal mistake **fatalist** n a person who accepts whatever happens and regards it as inevitable **fatalism** n **fatalistic** adj **fatality** n pl **fatalities** death caused by accident, war, or other disaster **fatally** adv **fated** adj destined by fate, doomed **fateful** adj bringing events that are important and usually unpleasant

father n **1** a male parent **2** a male ancestor ♦ land of our fathers **3** the founder or originator of something **4 the Father** (in Christian belief) God, the first person of the Trinity **5** the title of certain priests **father** v **1** to be the father of a child ♦ He fathered six children. **2** to be the founder or originator of an idea or plan **fatherhood** n **fatherless** adj without a living or known father **fatherly** adj like a father **father-in-law** n pl **fathers-in-law** the father of your wife or husband **fatherland** n a person's native country

fathom n a unit used to measure the depth of water, equal to 1.83 metres or 6 feet **fathom** v **1** to understand something difficult **2** to measure the depth of something **fathomless** adj

fatigue n **1** tiredness resulting from hard work or exercise **2** weakness in metals, caused by constant stress **3** (**fatigues**) the non-military duties of soldiers **fatigue** v **fatigues**, **fatigued**, **fatiguing** to make someone very tired

fatuous (say fat-yoo-əs) adj pointless and silly **fatuity** n **fatuously** adv **fatuousness** n

fatwa n a formal ruling on a point of Islamic law

fault n **1** a flaw or weakness **2** a mistake or error **3** an offence or wrongdoing **4** the responsibility for something wrong ♦ Whose fault is this? **5** an incorrect serve in tennis **faultless** adj not having any faults, perfect **faultlessly** adv **faultlessness** n **faulty** adj **faultier**, **faultiest**, **at fault** responsible for a mistake or failure **to find fault with** to find and comment on mistakes in someone or something

fauna n the animals of a particular area or

period of time. (Compare flora.)

faux pas (say foh **pah**) n pl **faux pas** (say foh **pahz**) an embarrassing mistake or blunder

favour n **1** a kind act done specially to help someone **2** approval or liking **3** support or preference given to one person or group but not to another **favour** v **1** to regard or treat someone with approval or liking **2** to be in favour of someone or something **3** to give someone what they want ♦ She favoured us with a song. **4** (said about events or circumstances) to make something possible or easy **5** informal to resemble a relative in facial features ♦ The boy favours his father. **favourable** adj **1** showing approval **2** pleasing or satisfactory ♦ I think we made a favourable impression. **3** helpful or advantageous ♦ favourable winds **favourably** adv **favourite** adj liked or preferred above others **favourite** n **1** a favoured person or thing **2** a competitor that is generally expected to win **favouritism** n unfairly favouring one person or group and not another

fawn[1] n **1** a young deer in its first year **2** light yellowish-brown **fawn** adj of a light yellowish brown colour

fawn[2] v **1** to get someone to like you by flattering or praising them too much **2** (said about a dog or other animal) to show extreme affection for someone

fax n **1** an exact copy of a document transmitted electronically **2** a machine used to transmit copies **fax** v to transmit a document by this process

FBI abbr (in the USA) Federal Bureau of Investigation

fear n **1** an unpleasant feeling caused by the threat of danger or pain **2** a danger or likelihood ♦ There is no fear of that happening. **fear** v to feel fear **fearful** adj **1** feeling fear **2** causing horror **3** informal extremely bad **fearfully** adv **fearless** adj **fearlessly** adv **fearlessness** n **fearsome** adj frightening, alarming

feasible (say **fee**-zi-bəl) adj **1** able to be done ♦ It will not be feasible to finish the work before tomorrow. **2** informal likely or probable ♦ It is feasible that it will snow today. **feasibility** n **feasibly** adv

feast *n* **1** a large elaborate meal **2** an annual religious festival **feast** *v* **1** to eat heartily **2** to give a feast to people

feat *n* a brave or remarkable action or achievement

feather *n* any of the flat pieces that grow from a bird's skin and cover its body **feather** *v* **1** to cover or line something with feathers **2** to turn an oar edgeways **feathery** *adj* **feather bed** *n* a mattress stuffed with feathers **featherweight** *n* in boxing, a weight (57 kg) between lightweight and bantamweight

feature *n* **1** a part of the face that helps to form its appearance **2** an important or noticeable quality that a thing has ♦ *The wooden ceiling is one of the interesting features of the old church.* **3** a special newspaper or magazine article or radio or television programme **4** the main film in a cinema programme **feature** *v* **1** to give special prominence to something **2** to be a feature or important part of something **featureless** *adj*

February *n* the second month of the year

feckless *adj* feeble and incompetent **fecklessly** *adv* **fecklessness** *n*

fecund (say feek-ənd or fek-ənd) *adj* highly fertile **fecundity** *n*

federal *adj* **1** to do with a system of government in which several states are combined under a central authority but remain independent in internal affairs **2** to do with the central government in a federal system ♦ *federal laws* **federalism** *n* **federally** *adv*

federate *v* to organize states on a federal basis, or to be organized in this way **federation** *n* a federal group of states **federative** *adj*

fee *n* **1** a payment made to an official or a professional person for advice or services **2** payment made for a right or privilege

feeble *adj* **1** weak, lacking physical strength **2** (said about a person) ineffective **feebleness** *n* **feebly** *adv* **feeble-minded** *adj* foolish or stupid

feed *v* past tense and past participle **fed 1** to give food to a person or animal **2** to give something as food to animals ♦ *We feed oats to horses.* **3** (said about animals) to take food **4** to serve as food for someone **5** to supply someone with material, water, power, etc. **6** (in ball games) to pass the ball to a player **feed** *n* **1** a meal, especially for animals or babies **2** food for animals

feeder *n* **1** a person or animal that takes in food in a particular way ♦ *a greedy feeder* **2** a container for feeding an animal or young child **3** a road or rail route that links outlying areas with a central line or service

feedback *n* **1** information about a product or service given to the supplier by its users **2** the return to its source of part of the output of an amplifier, microphone, or other device

feel *v* past tense and past participle **felt 1** to use touch to identify something or find out about it **2** to be physically or mentally aware of something ♦ *He felt a little nervous about this.* **3** to be affected by something ♦ *The old man felt the cold.* **4** to give a certain sensation or impression ♦ *The water feels warm.* **5** to have a vague conviction or impression of something **6** to have something as an opinion ♦ *We felt it was necessary to tell them.* **feel** *n* **1** the sense of touch **2** an act of feeling **3** the sensation produced by something touched ♦ *The curtains have a silky feel.*

feet plural of **foot**

feign (say fayn) *v* to pretend to have a particular feeling ♦ *When threatened, the animal feigns death.*

feint[1] (say faynt) *n* a pretended attack or blow made to deceive an opponent **feint** *v* to make a feint

feint[2] (say faynt) *adj* (said about paper) ruled with faint lines as a guide for writing

feisty (say fiy-sti) *adj informal* **feistier, feistiest** (said about a person) lively and rather aggressive

felicity *n* **1** great happiness **2** a pleasing manner or style ♦ *He expressed himself with great felicity.* **felicitations** *pl n* congratulations **felicitous** *adj* (said about words or remarks) well chosen, apt **felicitously** *adv*

feline (say fee-liyn) *adj* to do with cats **feline** *n* an animal of the cat family

fell[1] past tense of *fall*

fell[2] v 1 to strike someone down with a hard blow 2 to cut down a tree

fell[3] n a stretch of hilly country or high moorland in the north of England

fellow n 1 a man or boy 2 a person who is associated with someone else 3 a thing of the same class or kind as another 4 a member of a learned society, or of the governing body of certain colleges **fellowship** n 1 friendly association with other people 2 a society or group of friends 3 the position of a college fellow **fellow feeling** n sympathy arising from a shared experience

felon (say fel-ən) n a person guilty of a crime **felonious** adj **felony** n pl **felonies** a serious, often violent, crime

felt n a thick fabric made of fibres of wool or fur, etc. pressed together **felt** v past of **feel** to cover a surface with felt

female adj 1 to do with or belonging to the sex that can bear offspring 2 (said about plants) able to produce fruit 3 to do with a woman or women 4 (said about a fitting or machinery part) made hollow to receive a corresponding inserted part **female** n a female person, animal, or plant

feminine adj 1 to do with women 2 having qualities traditionally associated with women 3 *Grammar* belonging to the class that includes words referring to females or regarded as female **feminine** n *Gram* a feminine word or gender **femininity** n

feminist n someone who believes that women should have a status and rights equal to those of men **feminism** n

femur (say fee-mer) n pl **femurs** or **femora** the thigh bone **femoral** adj

fen n an area of low-lying marshy or flooded ground

fence n 1 a barrier made of wood or wire, etc. put round a field or garden 2 a raised structure for a horse to jump over 3 *informal* a person who deals in stolen goods **fence** v 1 to surround an area with a fence 2 to practise the sport of fencing **fencer** n **fencing** n 1 a set of fences, or a length of fence 2 the sport of fighting with long narrow swords (called *foils*)

fend v **to fend for yourself** to provide for and look after yourself **to fend off** to defend yourself against an attack

fender n 1 a low frame round a fireplace to stop coals falling into the room 2 a tyre or pad hung over the side of a ship to protect it

fennel n a fragrant herb with yellow flowers, used for flavouring

feral (say feer-əl) adj 1 wild and untamed 2 like a wild animal

ferment[1] (say fer-ment) v 1 to undergo a chemical change caused by the action of an organic substance such as yeast 2 to seethe with excitement or agitation **fermentation** n

ferment[2] (say fer-ment) n 1 a state of excitement or agitation 2 the process of fermenting

fern n a plant with feathery green leaves and no flowers **ferny** adj

ferocious adj fierce or savage **ferociously** adv **ferocity** n

ferret n a small animal of the weasel family **ferret** v **ferreted**, **ferreting** 1 to search or rummage for something 2 to hunt with ferrets **ferrety** adj

ferric adj made of or containing iron

ferry n pl **ferries** a boat or ship used for transporting people or things across a short stretch of water **ferry** v **ferries**, **ferried**, **ferrying** to transport people or things across water or for a short distance **ferryman** n pl **ferrymen**

fertile adj 1 able to produce, young crops, or vegetation 2 able to produce ideas ♦ *She has a fertile imagination* **fertility** n **fertilize** v 1 to make soil fertile or productive 2 to introduce pollen into a plant or sperm into an egg so that it develops and young **fertilization** n **fertilizer** n a natural or artificial substance added to soil to make it more fertile

fervour n warm or strong feeling **fervency** n **fervent** adj **fervently** adv

fester v 1 to become septic and filled with pus 2 to cause a long period of resentment

festive adj 1 to do with a festival 2 suitable for a festival, joyful **festival** n 1 a day or time of celebration, especially for religious reasons **2** an organized series of concerts, dramas, films, etc., especially one held annually in the same place ♦ *the Salzburg Festival* **festivity** *n pl* **festivities** a festive occasion or celebration

festoon *v* to decorate a room or place with hanging ornaments

feta (say **fet**-ə) *n* a salty white Greek cheese

fetch *v* **1** to go to get something or someone and bring them back **2** to sell for a price **fetching** *adj* attractive

fête (say fayt) *n* an outdoor entertainment with stalls and sideshows **fête** *v* to honour a person with celebrations

fetid (say **fet**-id or **fee**-tid) *adj* smelling unpleasant

fetish (say **fet**-ish) *n* **1** an object worshipped for its supposed magical powers **2** something that a person has an obsession about

fetus (say **fee**-təs) *n pl* **fetuses** a developing embryo, especially a human embryo more than eight weeks after conception **fetal** *adj*

feud (say fewd) *n* a long-lasting quarrel or hostility between people, especially between two families **feud** *v* to carry on a feud

fever *n* **1** an abnormally high body temperature, often with shivering, as a symptom of a disease **2** a state of nervous excitement or agitation **fevered** *adj* **feverish** *adj* **feverishly** *adv* **feverishness** *n*

few *adj*, *n* not many **a few** some, not none **a good few** or **quite a few** *informal* a fairly large number ◊ See the note at *less*.

fey (say fay) *adj* **1** having a strange other-worldly charm **2** having clairvoyant powers

fez *n pl* **fezzes** a high flat-topped red hat with a tassel, worn by Muslim men in some countries

fiancé, fiancée (say fee-**ahn**-say) *n* a man (**fiancé**) or woman (**fiancée**) to whom someone is engaged to be married

fiasco (say fi-**ass**-koh) *n pl* **fiascos** a humiliating or ludicrous failure

fib *n* a trivial or unimportant lie **fib** *v* **fibbed, fibbing** to tell a fib **fibber** *n*

fibre *n* **1** a thin strand from which animal and vegetable tissue or a textile is made **2** a substance made from fibres **3** indigestible

material in certain foods **4** strength of character ♦ *moral fibre* **fibroid** *adj* **fibrous** *adj* **fibreboard** *n* board made of compressed fibres **fibreglass** *n* **1** textile fabric made from glass fibres **2** plastic containing glass fibres **fibre optics** *n* the use of thin flexible transparent fibres to transmit light signals

fibula (say **fib**-yoo-lə) *n pl* **fibulae** or **fibulas** *Anatomy* the bone on the outer side of the leg between the knee and the ankle

fickle *adj* constantly changing **fickleness** *n*

fiction *n* **1** prose writing that describes imaginary people and events **2** something produced by the imagination **fictional** *adj* **fictionalize** *v* **fictionally** *adv* **fictitious** *adj* **fictitiously** *adv*

fiddle *n* **1** *informal* a violin **2** *informal* a cheat or swindle **fiddle** *v* **1** to handle or fidget with something restlessly **2** *informal* to cheat or swindle **3** *informal* to play the fiddle **fiddler** *n* **fiddling** *adj* **fiddly** *adj* **fiddlier, fiddliest, fiddlesticks** *interjection informal* nonsense

fidelity (say fid-**el**-iti) *n* **1** faithfulness or loyalty **2** accuracy or truthfulness **3** the quality or precision with which sound is recorded and reproduced

fidget *v* **fidgeted, fidgeting** to make small restless movements **fidget** *n* a person who fidgets **fidgety** *adj*

fie *interjection old use* an exclamation of disapproval

fiend (say feend) *n* **1** an evil spirit **2** a very wicked or cruel person **3** *informal* a devotee or addict ♦ *a fresh-air fiend* **fiendish** *adj* **fiendishly** *adv*

fierce *adj* **1** angry and violent or cruel **2** eager or intense ♦ *She showed a fierce loyalty to her friends.* **fiercely** *adv* **fierceness** *n*

fiesta (say fee-**est**-ə) *n* a religious festival in Spanish-speaking countries

fifteen *adj*, *n* the number 15 **fifteenth** *adj*, *n*

fifth *adj*, *n* **1** next after fourth **2** one of five equal parts of a thing **fifthly** *adv* **fifth column** *n* an organized group working for the enemy within a country at war **fifth columnist** *n*

fifty *adj*, *n pl* **fifties** the number 50, equal to five times ten **fifties** *pl n* the numbers

fig 220 **fill**

from 50 to 59, especially representing years of age or degrees of temperature **fiftieth** adj, n **fifty-fifty** adj, adv **1** shared or sharing equally between two people or groups **2** evenly balanced ♦ *a fifty-fifty chance of success*

fig n **1** a soft fruit with a sweet dark flesh and many seeds **2** the tree that produces this fruit

fig. abbr figure

fight v past tense and past participle **fought** **1** to struggle against a person or country in physical combat or in war **2** to carry on a battle **3** to struggle or strive hard to achieve or overcome something **4** to make your way by fighting or effort ♦ *We had to fight our way out of the crowd.* **fight** n **1** an act of fighting, a battle **2** a struggle or conflict **3** a boxing match **fighter** n

figment n a thing that only exists in the imagination

figure n **1** a written symbol that represents a number **2** an amount or number ♦ *There are a lot but it's hard to put a figure on it.* **3** the external form or shape of something, especially of the human body ♦ *Rose has a slim figure.* **4** a geometrical shape enclosed by lines or surfaces **5** a representation of a person or animal in drawing, painting, sculpture, etc. **6** a decorative pattern **7** a diagram or illustration in a book **8** a person as seen or studied ♦ *She is an important figure in twentieth-century history.* **figure** v **1** to appear in something or form part of it ♦ *He figures in all the books on the subject.* **2** to understand or consider something **3** to picture something mentally **4** to represent something or someone in a diagram or picture **figurative** adj (said about a word or expression) using or containing a figure of speech **figuratively** adv **figures** pl n calculation by numbers ♦ *I'm afraid I'm no good at figures.* **figurine** n a small statue of a person **figurehead** n **1** a carved figure at the prow of a sailing ship **2** a person who is at the head of a country or organization but has no real power **figure of speech** n a word or phrase used for special effect and not meant literally

filament n **1** a fine wire in an electric lamp **2** a thread-like fibre or strand

filch v informal to steal something of small value

file[1] n **1** a folder or box, etc. for keeping papers in order **2** ICT a collection of data stored under one name **3** a line of people one behind the other **file** v **1** to put something in a file **2** to submit a document or form to be put on official record **3** (said about a reporter) to send in a story or article **4** to walk in a row one behind the other ♦ *People were asked to file out slowly.*

file[2] n a metal tool with a rough surface that is rubbed on surfaces to shape them or make them smooth **file** v to shape or smooth a surface with a file

filial (say **fil-iəl**) adj to do with a son or daughter ♦ *to do your filial duty*

filibuster n an attempt to delay or prevent the passing of a law by making long speeches **filibuster** v to delay legislation in this way

filigree (say **fil-i-gree**) n ornamental lace-like work of twisted metal wire **filigreed** adj

fill v **1** to make something full; to occupy the whole of something **2** (said about a container, room, etc.) to become full **3** to block up a hole or cavity **4** to spread over or through an area ♦ *Smoke began to fill the room.* **5** to hold a position; to appoint a person to a vacant post **6** to occupy a period of time **fill** n **1** enough to fill something **2** enough to satisfy a person's appetite or desire ♦ *We ate our fill.* **filler** n something used to fill a cavity or to increase the bulk of something **filling** n **1** material used to fill a hole or cavity, for example in a tooth **2** something put in pastry to make a pie, or between layers of bread to make a sandwich **filling station** n a place where petrol is sold to motorists **to fill in** to act as a substitute for someone **to fill out** to become larger or plumper **to fill someone in** to give someone more detailed information **to fill something in** **1** to add information needed to complete a form or document **2** to complete a drawing by shading or colouring inside an outline **to fill something up** to fill something completely

fillet n 1 a piece of boneless meat or fish 2 a strip of ribbon, etc. worn round the head 3 *Architecture* a narrow flat band between mouldings **fillet** v **filleted, filleting** to remove the bones from fish or meat

fillip n something that boosts or stimulates an activity

filly n pl **fillies** a young female horse

film n 1 a motion picture shown in a cinema or on television 2 a rolled strip or sheet coated with light-sensitive material and used for taking photographs or making a motion picture 3 a thin coating or covering layer **film** v 1 to record something on film 2 to cover something, or become covered, with a thin coating or covering layer **filmy** adj **filmier, filmiest** thin and almost transparent **filminess** n **filmstrip** n a strip of transparencies for projection

filter n 1 a device for holding back dirt or other unwanted material from a liquid or gas that is passed through it 2 a screen for preventing light of certain wavelengths from passing through 3 a device for suppressing electrical and sound waves of frequencies other than the ones required 4 an arrangement for allowing traffic to pass in one direction while other traffic is stopped **filter** v 1 to pass through a filter or put something through a filter; to remove impurities in this way 2 to come or make a way in or out gradually ♦ *News began to filter out.* 3 (said about traffic) to move forward in one direction while other traffic is stopped

filth n 1 disgusting dirt 2 obscene or offensive writing, pictures, or language **filthy** adj **filthier, filthiest, filthily** adv **filthiness** n

filtrate n liquid that has passed through a filter **filtration** n

fin n 1 a thin flat part projecting from the body of a fish 2 a rubber flipper worn when swimming underwater 3 a small projection on an aircraft or rocket

final adj 1 coming at the end, last 2 putting an end to doubt or discussion or argument **final** n the last in a series of contests in sports or a competition **finals** pl n examinations held at the end of

a degree course **finale** n the final section of a piece of music or an entertainment **finalist** n **finality** n **finalize** v **finalization** n **finally** adv

finance (say fiy-**nanss**) n 1 the management and use of money 2 money used to support an undertaking **finances** pl n the money resources and organization of a country, company, or person **financier** n a person who is involved in managing financial affairs **finance** v to provide money for an undertaking **financial** adj **financially** adv **finance company** or finance **house** n a company that is mainly concerned with lending money for credit transactions **financial year** n a period of twelve months reckoned for accounting purposes

finch n any of a number of small birds with short stubby bills

find v past tense and past participle **found** 1 to discover something or someone by looking for them or by chance 2 to become aware of something, to discover a fact by experience ♦ *He soon found that digging was hard work.* 3 to arrive at a state by a natural process ♦ *Water finds its own level.* 4 to succeed in obtaining something ♦ *I haven't found time to do it yet.* 5 to decide and declare a verdict ♦ *The jury found him guilty.* **find** n 1 the finding of something useful or pleasing 2 a person or thing that proves to be useful **findings** pl n **to find out** 1 to get information about something 2 to discover someone who has done wrong ♦ *They were afraid they might be found out.*

fine¹ adj 1 of high quality, excellent 2 (said about the weather) bright and clear 3 in good health, comfortable ♦ *I'm fine, thank you.* 4 slender or thin; consisting of small particles 5 requiring very skilful workmanship 6 difficult to distinguish ♦ *making fine distinctions* **fine** adv 1 finely 2 *informal* very well ♦ *That will suit me fine.* **fine** v to become, or to make something become, finer, thinner, or less coarse **finely** adv **fineness** n **finery** n **fine arts** pl n the arts that appeal to a sense of beauty **fine-tooth comb** n a comb with narrow close-set teeth **fine-tune** v 1 to adjust something very precisely 2 to make detailed adjustments to a plan in order to improve it

fine² *n* a sum of money that has to be paid as a penalty **fine** *v* to punish someone with a fine

finesse (say fin-**ess**) *n* tact and cleverness in doing something

finger *n* **1** each of the four parts extending from each hand, or five including the thumb **2** the part of a glove that fits over a finger **3** an object having the shape of a finger **finger** *v* **1** to touch or feel something with the fingers **2** to play a musical instrument with the fingers **fingering** *n* **finger mark** *n* a mark left on a surface by a finger **fingernail** *n* the nail on a finger **fingerplate** *n* a plate fastened on a door to prevent finger marks **fingerprint** *n* a mark made by the tiny ridges on a person's fingertip, especially as a means of identification **fingertip** *n* the tip of a finger

finicky *adj* **1** fussy about details, hard to please **2** excessively detailed or elaborate

finish *v* **1** to bring something to an end, or to come to an end **2** to reach the end of an undertaking **3** to eat or drink all of something ♦ *Can you finish the pie?* **4** to complete the manufacture of something by giving it an attractive surface **finish** *n* **1** the last stage of something **2** the point at which a race ends **3** the state of being finished or perfect **4** the surface or coating on woodwork, etc.

finite (say **fiy**-niyt) *adj* limited, not infinite

Finn *n* a person born in Finland or descended from people born there **Finnish** *adj*

fiord *n* another spelling of *fjord*

fir *n* **1** an evergreen tree that produces cones and has needle-like leaves on its shoots **2** the wood of this tree

fire *n* **1** the process of burning that produces light and heat **2** burning that destroys property ♦ *They are insured against fire.* **3** something burning ♦ *They could see a fire in the distance.* **4** an amount of fuel burning in a grate or furnace **5** an angry or excited feeling, enthusiasm **6** the firing of guns ♦ *Hold your fire.* **fire** *v* **1** to shoot a gun; to send out a bullet or missile **2** to deliver or utter a rapid succession of

questions or statements **3** *informal* to dismiss an employee from a job **4** to set fire to something **5** to catch fire; (said about an engine) to become ignited **6** to supply a furnace, etc. with fuel **7** to bake pottery or bricks in a kiln **8** to excite or stimulate someone ♦ *The idea fired them with enthusiasm.* **fiery** *adj* **fierier**, **fieriest fierily** *adv* **fieriness** *n* **fire alarm** *n* a device that gives off a loud sound to warn of fire **firearm** *n* a small gun, such as a rifle, pistol or revolver **firebrand** *n* a person who stirs up trouble **firebreak** *n* an obstacle to the spread of fire in a forest, etc. **fire brigade** *n* an organized body of people trained to extinguish fires **firecracker** *n* a loud explosive firework **firedamp** *n* methane, making an explosive mixture with air in coal mines **fire drill** *n* rehearsal of the procedure that needs to be followed in case of fire **fire engine** *n* a large vehicle that carries firefighters and their equipment to the scene of a fire **fire escape** *n* a special staircase or apparatus for escaping from a burning building **firefighter** *n* a member of a fire brigade **firefly** *n* a kind of beetle that gives off a phosphorescent light **fire irons** *pl n* a set of equipment, including poker, tongs, and shovel, for tending a domestic fire **firelight** *n* the light from a fire in a fireplace **firelighter** *n* a piece of inflammable material to help start a fire in a grate **fireman** *n pl* **firemen 1** a male member of a fire brigade **2** a person who tends a furnace **fireplace** *n* an open recess for a domestic fire **firepower** *n* the destructive capacity of guns and missiles **fire-raising** *n* setting fire to buildings, arson **fire-raiser** *n* **fireside** *n* the part of a room round a fireplace, regarded as the focus of a home **fire station** *n* the headquarters of a fire brigade **firestorm** *n* a fierce fire fanned by high winds and air currents **firewood** *n* wood for use as fuel **firework** *n* a device containing chemicals that burn or explode with spectacular effects, used at celebrations **firing line** *n* **1** the front line of troops in a battle **2** a situation in which you are vulnerable to criticism or blame **firing squad** *n* a group of soldiers given the duty of shooting a condemned person

firm[1] adj 1 not giving way when pressed, hard or solid 2 steady, not shaking or moving 3 securely fixed 4 definite, and unlikely to change ♦ *This is my firm belief.* **firm** adv firmly ♦ *We must stand firm.* **firm** v to become firm or compact, or to make something firm

firm[2] n a company or business organization

first adj coming before all others in time, order, or importance **first** n 1 a person or thing that is first; the first day of a month 2 the first time something is done or occurs 3 first-class honours in a university degree 4 first gear in a motor vehicle **first** adv 1 before all others 2 before something else happens or is done ♦ *I must finish this work first.* 3 for the first time ♦ *When did you first meet her?* **firstly** adv **first aid** n emergency treatment given to an injured person **first-born** adj eldest of several brothers or sisters **first class** n 1 a category of mail that is to be delivered quickly 2 the best accommodation on a train, ship, or aircraft **first-class** adj 1 of the best quality 2 using the best class of a service **first-footing** n the practice of being the first person to cross someone's threshold in the New Year **first-hand** adj, adv obtained directly from the original source **first lady** n the wife of the US President **first minister** n the leader of the ruling political party or group in some regions **first name** n someone's personal name, which comes before the family name **first officer** n 1 the first mate on a merchant ship 2 the officer who is second in command on an aircraft **first person** n see person **first-rate** adj of the best quality, excellent

firth n an estuary or narrow inlet of the sea in Scotland

fiscal adj to do with public finances

fish n pl **fish** or **fishes** 1 an animal with gills and fins, which lives and breathes wholly in water 2 the flesh of a fish eaten as food **fish** v 1 to try to catch fish 2 to search or feel for something hidden 3 to try to get something by hinting at it ♦ *He was obviously fishing for a compliment.* **fishery** n pl **fisheries** 1 a part of the sea where fishing

is carried on 2 the business of catching fish **fishiness** n **fishing** n **fishy** adj **fishier**, **fishiest**, **fisherman** n pl **fishermen** a person who catches fish for a living or for sport **fishmonger** n a shopkeeper who sells fish **fishnet** adj (said about a fabric) made in a kind of open mesh **to fish out** to pull something out of a place where it is hidden or hard to find

fissure (say **fish**-er) n a narrow opening made when something splits or separates

fist n a tightly closed hand, with the fingers bent into the palm

fit[1] adj **fitter**, **fittest** 1 suitable or well adapted for something, good enough ♦ *We had a meal fit for a king.* 2 healthy or in good physical condition 3 feeling in a suitable condition to do something **fit** v **fitted**, **fitting** 1 to be the right shape and size for something 2 to put clothing on a person and adjust it to the right shape and size 3 to put something into place ♦ *We must fit a new catch on the window.* 4 to make someone suitable or competent for an activity ♦ *Her training fitted her for the position.* **fit** n the way something fits ♦ *The coat is a good fit.* **fitly** adv **fitment** n a piece of fixed furniture **fitness** n **fitted** adj **fitter** n **fitting** adj

fit[2] n 1 a sudden attack or convulsion 2 a sudden attack of coughing 3 an outburst of strong feeling ♦ *a fit of rage* 4 a short period of activity ♦ *a fit of energy* **fitful** adj happening in short periods **fitfully** adv

five adj, n the number 5, one more than four **fiver** n a five-pound note, or the sum of five pounds **fivefold** adj, adv 1 five times as much or as many 2 consisting of five parts

fix v 1 to fasten or place something firmly 2 to make something permanent and unable to be changed 3 to repair something or put it into working condition 4 to decide or specify an arrangement ♦ *A date has been fixed for the trial.* 5 to put facts or ideas firmly in the mind and memory 6 to direct your eyes or attention steadily 7 (in photography) to make an image permanent 8 *informal* to influence or affect the outcome of something fraudulently **fix** n 1 *informal* an awkward situation ♦ *Now* *we are in a fix.* **2** *informal* a dose of a narcotic drug taken by an addict **3** the position of a ship or aircraft determined by taking bearings **fixed assets** *pl n* the property and equipment owned by a company and used for carrying on its business activity

fizz *v* to make a hissing sound **fizz** *n* **1** a hissing sound **2** *informal* a fizzy drink **fizzle** *v* **fizzy** *adj* **fizzier, fizziest, fizziness** *n* to **fizzle out** to end feebly or unsuccessfully

fjord (say fjord or **fee**-ord) *n* a long narrow inlet of the sea between high cliffs, especially in Norway

flab *n* *informal* soft loose flesh, fat **flabby** *adj* **flabbier, flabbiest, flabbily** *adv* **flabbiness** *n*

flabbergasted *adj* extremely surprised

flaccid (say **flass**-id or **flak**-sid) *adj* soft and limp **flaccidity** *n* **flaccidly** *adv*

flag[1] *n* **1** a piece of cloth with a distinctive pattern or design on it, raised on a pole as the emblem of a country or as a sign or signal **2** a small piece of paper or plastic that looks like a flag **flag** *v* **flagged, flagging 1** to mark something out with flags **2** to signal with a flag or with the arms ♦ *A police officer flagged the vehicle down.* **3** to hang down limply, to droop **4** to lose vigour **flagship** *n* **1** a ship that carries an admiral and flies the admiral's flag **2** the best or most important part of an organization

flag[2] *n* a flagstone **flag** *v* **flagged, flagging** to pave an area with flagstones

flag[3] *n* a plant with long flat leaves, especially an iris

flagellate (say **flaj**-əl-ayt) *v* to whip someone, especially as a religious discipline **flagellation** *n*

flagpole, flagstaff *n* a pole from which a flag is flown

flagrant (say **flay**-grənt) *adj* (said about an offence or wrongdoing) very bad and noticeable **flagrancy** *n* **flagrantly** *adv*

flail *n* an old-fashioned tool for threshing grain **flail** *v* **1** to wave or swing about wildly **2** to beat or flog someone

flair *n* a natural ability or talent ◊ Do not confuse this word with *flare*, which has a different meaning.

flak *n* **1** shells fired by anti-aircraft guns

2 strong criticism

flake *n* **1** a small light flat piece of snow **2** a small thin piece of something **flake** *v* **1** to come off in flakes **2** to separate something into flakes **flaky** *adj*

flambé (say **flahm**-bay) *adj* (said about food) covered with spirit and set alight briefly before eating

flamboyant *adj* **1** highly coloured or showy **2** (said about a person) having a showy appearance or manner **flamboyance** *n* **flamboyantly** *adv*

flame *n* **1** a tongue-shaped portion of fire or burning gas **2** a bright red colour **3** an intense feeling or passion **flame** *v* **1** to burn with flames, to send out flames **2** to become bright red **flaming** *adj* **flammability** *n* **flammable** *adj* **flame-thrower** *n* a weapon that shoots out a jet of flame

flamenco (say flə-**menk**-oh) *n* a lively Spanish style of song, guitar playing, and dance

flamingo (say flə-**ming**-goh) *n* *pl* **flamingoes** a wading bird with long thin legs, a long neck, and pinkish feathers

flan *n* a dish consisting of an open pastry case filled with a sweet or a savoury filling

flank *n* **1** the side of a person's or animal's body between the ribs and the hip **2** the side of a building or mountain **3** the right or left side of a body of people, especially of an army **flank** *v* to be positioned at the side of something

flannel *n* **1** a soft loosely woven woollen or cotton fabric **2** a soft cloth used for washing yourself **flannels** *pl n* trousers made of flannel or similar fabric **flannelette** *n* cotton fabric made to look and feel like flannel

flap *v* **flapped, flapping 1** to sway loosely up and down or from side to side **2** to give a light blow with something flat **3** *informal* to fuss or panic about something **flap** *n* **1** the action or sound of flapping **2** a light blow with something flat **3** a flat or broad piece that is hinged or fixed to something else at one side **4** a hinged or sliding section of an aircraft wing **5** *informal* a state of fuss or panic ♦ *in a flap*

flapjack *n* a cake made from oats and syrup

flare *v* **1** to blaze with a sudden bright

flame **2** to become suddenly angry or violent ♦ *Tempers flared*. **3** to become gradually wider ♦ *flared trousers* **flare** *n* **1** a sudden outburst of flame or light **2** a device producing a bright flame or light **3** a gradually widening shape **to flare up 1** to burst into flame **2** to become suddenly angry ◊ Do not confuse this word with *flair*, which has a different meaning.

flash *v* **1** to give out a brief or intermittent bright light **2** to be suddenly visible or thought about ♦ *An idea flashed through my mind*. **3** to move rapidly ♦ *Several cars flashed past*. **4** to make something shine briefly **5** to signal with a light or lights **6** to send news or information by radio or telegraph **flash** *n* **1** a sudden burst of bright flame or light **2** a sudden occurrence or appearance of something ♦ *a flash of inspiration* **3** a very short time ♦ *in a flash* **4** a rush of water **5** a brief news item on radio or television **6** a camera attachment that makes a sudden bright light **7** a bright patch of colour, especially as an emblem on a uniform **flash** *adj informal* flashy **flasher** *n* **flashing** *n* **flashy** *adj* **flashier, flashiest** showy or gaudy **flashily** *adv* **flashiness** *n* **flashback** *n* a scene in a story or film that is set at an earlier time than the main part of the story **flashbulb** *n* a bulb used for flash photography **flash flood** *n* a sudden local flood caused by heavy rainfall **flashlight** *n* an electric torch with a powerful beam

flask *n* **1** a bottle with a narrow neck **2** a vacuum flask

flat *adj* **flatter, flattest 1** having a level surface **2** level, not sloping **3** spread out; lying at full length ♦ *Lie flat on the ground*. **4** having a broad level surface and little depth ♦ *a flat cap* **5** (said about a tyre) having lost all or most of its air **6** absolute or unqualified ♦ *We were given a flat refusal*. **7** dull or monotonous **8** (said about a drink) having lost its effervescence **9** (said about a battery) unable to produce any more electric current **10** *Mus* below the correct pitch ♦ *Our singing was flat*. **flat** *adv* **1** so as to be flat ♦ *Lay it down flat*. **2** *informal* completely ♦ *I am flat broke*. **3** exactly ♦ *in ten seconds flat* **4** *Mus* below the correct

pitch ♦ *He was singing flat*. **flat** *n* **1** a flat thing or part, level ground **2** a set of rooms on one floor, used for living in **3** *Mus* a note that is a semitone lower than the natural note; the sign ♭ indicating this **flatly** *adv* **flatness** *n* **flatten** *v* **flattish** *adj*

flatter *v* **1** to praise someone more than they deserve **2** to please someone with an honour ♦ *We were flattered to receive an invitation*. **3** to make a person or thing seem more attractive than they really are ♦ *She thought the photograph flattered her*. **flatterer** *n*

flatulent (say flat-yoo-lənt) *adj* affected by gas building up in the digestive tract **flatulence** *n* **flatulency** *n*

flaunt *v* to display something in a showy or over-enthusiastic way ♦ *He liked to flaunt his expensive clothes and cars*. ◊ Do not confuse this word with *flout*, which has a different meaning.

flavour *n* **1** a distinctive taste **2** a special quality or characteristic ♦ *The story has a romantic flavour*. **flavour** *v* to give something a flavour, to season something **flavouring** *n*

flaw *n* something that makes a person or thing imperfect **flaw** *v* to spoil something with a flaw **flawless** *adj* **flawlessly** *adv* **flawlessness** *n*

flax *n* **1** a blue-flowered plant from which linen is made **2** textile fibre made from this plant **flaxen** *adj*

flay *v* **1** to strip the skin from an animal **2** to whip or beat someone **3** to criticize someone fiercely

flea *n* a small jumping insect that feeds on human and animal blood

fleck *n* **1** a very small patch of colour **2** a particle or speck **flecked** *adj*

fled past tense and past participle of *flee*

fledgling *n* a young bird that has grown wing feathers and is newly able to fly

flee *v* **flees, fled, fleeing 1** to run or hurry away **2** to run away from a place ♦ *The criminals fled the country*. **3** to pass away swiftly, to vanish ♦ *All hope had fled*.

fleece *n* **1** the woolly hair of a sheep or similar animal **2** a soft fabric made from this **fleece** *v* *informal* to swindle someone or deprive them of something by trickery **fleecy** adj

fleet¹ n 1 the warships of a country 2 a number of ships, aircraft, or vehicles owned by a company or moving together

fleet² adj moving swiftly, nimble **fleeting** adj **fleetly** adv **fleetness** n

Flemish adj to do with Flanders in Belgium or its people or language **Flemish** n the Flemish language

flesh n 1 the soft substance of a human or animal body 2 the body as opposed to the mind or soul 3 the pulpy part of fruits and vegetables **fleshy** adj **fleshier**, **fleshiest**, **fleshiness** n **flesh wound** n a wound that does not reach a bone or vital organ

flew past tense of **fly**²

flex¹ v to bend or stretch a limb or muscle **flexible** adj **flexibility** n **flexibly** adv **flexor** n a muscle that bends a part of the body **flexitime** n a system allowing workers to vary their working hours

flex² n a flexible insulated electric wire or cable

flick n a quick light blow or movement **flick** v to hit or move something with a quick light blow **flick knife** n a knife with a blade that springs out when a button is pressed **to flick through** to turn over cards or pages quickly

flicker v 1 to burn or shine unsteadily 2 used to describe a feeling that occurs briefly 3 to move quickly to and fro **flicker** n 1 a flickering light or movement or light 2 a brief occurrence of a positive feeling

flier n another spelling of **flyer**

flies pl n informal a zip or set of buttons used to fasten the front of a pair of trousers

flight n 1 the process of flying 2 a journey in an aircraft 3 a flock of birds or insects 4 a number of aircraft regarded as a unit ♦ the Queen's flight 5 the action of fleeing or escaping 6 a series of stairs between two floors or levels 7 a series of hurdles in a race 8 a free exercise of the mind or thought ♦ a flight of fancy 9 the feathers or fins on a dart or arrow **flightless** adj **flighty** adj **flightier**, **flightiest** silly and frivolous **flight deck** n the cockpit of a large aircraft **flight lieutenant** n an RAF officer below squadron

leader in rank **flight path** n the plotted course of an aircraft **flight recorder** n an electronic device in an aircraft, which records technical information about its flight

flimsy adj **flimsier**, **flimsiest** 1 light and thin; fragile or loose in structure 2 weak or unconvincing ♦ a flimsy excuse **flimsily** adv **flimsiness** n

flinch v 1 to move or shrink back in fear, to wince 2 to shrink from a duty or obligation

fling v past tense and past participle **flung** 1 to throw something with great force 2 to send someone somewhere suddenly or forcefully ♦ They have flung him into prison. 3 to rush angrily or impulsively ♦ She flung out of the room. **fling** n 1 a lively dance ♦ the Highland fling 2 a short time of enjoyment ♦ a final fling before the exams

flint n 1 a very hard kind of stone 2 a piece of flint used to produce sparks **flinty** adj **flintier**, **flintiest**, **flintlock** n an old type of gun fired by a spark from a flint

flip v **flipped**, **flipping** 1 to turn over with a quick movement 2 to toss something in the air so that it turns over **flip** n the action or movement of flipping **flip** adj glib or flippant

flippant adj not showing proper seriousness **flippancy** n **flippantly** adv

flipper n 1 a limb that some sea animals use for swimming 2 a flat rubber attachment worn on the feet for underwater swimming

flirt v 1 to behave as though you are sexually attracted to someone 2 to play or experiment in your mind with an idea ♦ He flirted with the idea of moving abroad. 3 to risk danger ♦ to flirt with death **flirt** n a person who flirts **flirtation** n **flirtatious** adj

flit v **flitted**, **flitting** 1 to fly or move lightly and quickly 2 to run away secretly **flit** n informal an act of running away secretly

float v 1 to stay or move on the surface of a liquid or in the air 2 to make something do this 3 to move lightly or gently 4 to make a ball move gently in the air so that another player can reach it 5 to allow a currency to have a variable rate of exchange 6 to put forward an idea to test people's reactions to it 7 to launch a business by getting financial support from the sale of shares

float n 1 a device that is designed to float on liquid 2 a cork or other floating object used on a fishing line 3 a floating device used as part of a valve to control the flow of water or other liquid 4 a structure on an aircraft that allows it to float on water 5 a small electric vehicle or cart, especially one used for delivering milk 6 a vehicle with a platform for carrying a display in a parade or carnival 7 a small amount of money kept for minor expenses or for giving change in a shop

flock[1] n 1 a number of birds that are flying or resting together 2 a number of sheep or goats that are kept together 3 a large number of people together 4 a number of people in someone's charge **flock** v to gather together or move in a group

flock[2] n 1 wool or cotton waste used for stuffing cushions or quilts 2 a tuft of wool or cotton

flog v **flogged**, **flogging** 1 to beat a person or animal with a stick or whip as a punishment 2 informal to sell something **flogging** n

flood n 1 a large amount of water over a place that is usually dry 2 a great amount of something demanding or unwelcome ♦ We have had a flood of requests. 3 the movement of the tide when it is coming in towards the land **flood** v 1 to cover or fill with a flood 2 (said about a river, etc.) to become flooded 3 to come in large amounts ♦ The letters started to flood in.

floodgate n a gate that can be opened or closed to control the flow of water

floodlight n a lamp that gives a broad bright beam to light up a stage, stadium, or large building **floodlight** v past tense and past participle **floodlit** to light up a place with floodlights

floor n 1 the surface of a room on which people stand and walk 2 a storey of a building, all the rooms on the same level ♦ Her office is on the third floor. 3 the bottom of the sea or of a cave 4 the part of the assembly hall where members sit **floor** v 1 to put a floor into a building 2 informal to baffle someone 3 informal to knock

someone down in a fight **floorboard** n one of the boards forming the floor of a room

flop v **flopped**, **flopping** 1 to hang or sway heavily and loosely 2 to fall or sit down clumsily 3 informal to be a failure **flop** n 1 a flopping movement or sound 2 informal a failure or disappointment

floppy adj **floppier**, **floppiest**, **floppily** adv **floppiness** n **floppy disk** n a flexible removable magnetic disk for storing data for use in a computer

flora n the plants of a particular area or period of time. (Compare fauna.) **floral** adj

florid (say flo-rid) adj 1 (said about a person's complexion) red and flushed 2 elaborate and ornate

florist (say flo-rist) n a person who sells cut flowers

floss n 1 a mass of silky fibres 2 a soft medicated thread pulled between the teeth to clean them **flossy** adj

flotation n 1 the process of offering shares in a company on the stock market in order to launch it or finance it 2 the process of floating something

flotilla (say flə-til-ə) n a small fleet of ships or boats

flotsam n wreckage or cargo found floating after a shipwreck **flotsam and jetsam** odds and ends

flounce[1] v to go in an impatient or annoyed manner ♦ She flounced out of the room. **flounce** n a flouncing movement

flounce[2] n a wide frill of material sewn to a skirt or dress

flounder[1] v 1 to move clumsily and with difficulty 2 to make mistakes or become confused when trying to do something

flounder[2] n a small flatfish used for food

flour n a fine powder made from wheat or other grain **flour** v to cover or sprinkle something with flour **floury** adj

flourish v 1 to grow or develop strongly 2 to prosper or be successful 3 to be alive and working at a certain time 4 to wave something about dramatically **flourish** n 1 a dramatic sweeping gesture 2 a flowing ornamental curve in writing or drawing 3 a musical fanfare

flout v to disobey a rule or instruction openly

or defiantly ◊ Do not confuse this word with *flaunt*, which has a different meaning.

flow v **1** to move continuously and freely in a stream **2** to move steadily and continuously ♦ *It was important to keep the traffic flowing.* **3** to hang loosely ♦ *flowing hair* **4** to gush out **5** (said about the tide) to come in towards the land **6** to come from a source, to be the result of something ♦ *Several consequences flowed from their actions.* **flow** n **1** a flowing movement or mass **2** a steady continuous stream of something ♦ *the flow of traffic* **3** the movement of the tide towards the land **flow chart** n a diagram showing the successive stages of a process

flower n **1** the part of a plant from which the seed or fruit develops **2** a blossom and its stem for use for decoration **flower** v **1** to produce flowers **2** to reach a peak of development **flowered** adj **flowery** adj **flowerpot** n an earthenware pot for growing a plant in

flown past participle of *fly²*

flu n influenza or a similar infection

fluctuate v to vary irregularly ♦ *Prices have been fluctuating.* **fluctuation** n

flue n **1** a duct in a chimney for smoke and gases to escape **2** a channel for conveying heat

fluent (say **floo-ənt**) adj **1** skilful at speaking clearly and without hesitating, especially in a foreign language **2** (said about language) used with ease and clarity **fluency** n **fluently** adv

fluff n **1** a light soft substance **2** *informal* a mistake, especially in speaking **fluff** v *informal* to bungle something **fluffy** adj **fluffier, fluffiest, fluffiness** n

fluid n a substance that is able to flow freely, a liquid or gas **fluid** adj **1** able to flow freely, not solid or rigid **2** (said about a situation) likely to change **fluidity** n **fluid ounce** n a unit of capacity equal to one-twentieth of a pint (0.028 litre)

fluke n an unexpected or unlikely stroke of good luck

flummox v *informal* to baffle someone

flung past tense and past participle of *fling*

fluoresce (say **floo-er-ess**) v to become fluorescent **fluorescence** n **fluorescent** adj

fluoridate (say **floo-er-i-dayt**) v to add traces of fluoride to a water supply to reduce tooth decay **fluoridation** n **fluoride** n

flurry n pl **flurries 1** a sudden short rush of wind, rain, or snow **2** a short period of activity or excitement **3** a number of things arriving together **flurry** v **flurries, flurried, flurrying** to swirl about

flush¹ v **1** to become red in the face because of a rush of blood to the skin **2** to cause the face to redden in this way **3** to fill someone with pride ♦ *They appeared flushed with success.* **4** to cleanse something, especially a lavatory, with a fast flow of water **5** (said about water) to rush out in a flood **6** to drive a bird or animal out of its cover **flush** n **1** a reddening of the face, a blush **2** a fast flow of water **3** a feeling of excitement ♦ *in the first flush of victory* **4** a fresh growth of leaves or vegetation **5** (in card games) a hand of cards of the same suit

flush² adj **1** level with the surrounding surface ♦ *The door was flush with the wall.* **2** *informal* having plenty of money

fluster v to make someone feel nervous and confused **fluster** n a flustered state

flute n **1** a wind instrument consisting of a tube with holes stopped by fingers or keys and held horizontally across the mouth **2** *Architecture* an ornamental groove **flute** v **1** to speak in melodious tones **2** to make ornamental grooves in a surface **flautist** n a flute player **fluting** n

flutter v **1** to flap the wings rapidly in flying or trying to fly **2** to wave or flap quickly and irregularly **3** (said about the heart) to beat feebly and irregularly **flutter** n **1** a fluttering movement or beat **2** a state of nervous excitement **3** *informal* a small bet ♦ *to have a flutter*

flux n **1** constant change ♦ *in a state of flux* **2** the process of flowing

fly¹ n pl **flies 1** a small flying insect with two wings **2** a natural or artificial fly used as bait in fishing **flyleaf** n pl **flyleaves** a blank leaf at the beginning or end of a book **flyweight** n (in boxing) a weight (51 kg) below bantamweight

fly² v **flies, flew, flown, flying 1** to move

through the air by means of wings **2** to travel through the air or through space **3** to travel in an aircraft **4** to direct or control the flight of an aircraft; to transport people or cargo in an aircraft **5** to raise a flag so that it waves; (said about a flag) to wave in the air **6** to make a kite rise into the air **7** to go or move quickly **8** (said about time) to pass quickly **9** to be scattered violently ♦ *Sparks flew in all directions.* **10** to become suddenly angry ♦ *flew into a rage* **11** to flee from a place ♦ *The traitors had to fly the country.*

fly *n pl* **flies 1** the front opening of a pair of trousers, closed with a zip or buttons **2** a flap at the entrance of a tent **flyer** *n* **1** a person or thing that flies **2** a small poster advertising an event **flying doctor** *n* a doctor who visits patients by air, especially in the Australian outback **flying fish** *n* a tropical fish with wing-like fins, able to rise into the air and glide for some distance **flying fox** *n* a large fruit bat with a face resembling a fox **flying officer** *n* an RAF officer next in rank below flight lieutenant **flying saucer** *n* saucer-shaped spaceship seen in the sky **flying squad** *n* a team of police officers organized so that they can move rapidly from place to place **fly-past** *n* a ceremonial flight of aircraft past a person or place **flysheet** *n* a cover over a tent for extra protection against bad weather **flywheel** *n* a heavy wheel revolving on a shaft to regulate machinery or build up a reserve of power

fly[3] *adj* **flyer**, **flyest** *informal* clever and knowing

flyover *n* a bridge that carries one road or railway over another

foal *n* a young horse or related animal **foal** *v* to give birth to a foal

foam *n* **1** a mass of tiny bubbles formed on a liquid, froth **2** a liquid containing many small bubbles **3** a lightweight spongy form of rubber or plastic **foam** *v* to form or produce foam **foamy** *adj*

fob[1] *n* **1** a chain for a pocket watch **2** an ornament attached to a watch chain **3** a tab on a key ring

fob[2] *v* **fobbed**, **fobbing to fob off** to make someone accept something they don't

really want

focal *adj* to do with a focus

focus (say foh-kəs) *n pl* **focuses** or **foci**, (say **foh**-siy) **1** the point at which rays appear to meet or from which they appear to spread out **2** *Geometry* one of several fixed points used in drawing an ellipse, parabola, or other curve **3** the point or distance from the eye or a lens at which an object is most clearly seen **4** an adjustment on a lens for producing a clear image at different distances **5** something that is an object of activity or attention **focus** *v* **focuses**, **focused**, **focusing 1** to adjust the focus of the eye or of a lens, camera, telescope, etc. **2** to concentrate or direct attention on something

fodder *n* food for horses and farm animals

foe *n literary* an enemy

foetid (say fee-tid) *adj* another spelling of *fetid*

foetus (say fee-təs) *n* another spelling of *fetus*

fog *n* **1** thick mist that is difficult to see through **2** (in photography) cloudiness on a negative, obscuring the image **3** a state of confusion or ignorance **fog** *v* **fogged**, **fogging 1** to cover a surface with fog or condensed vapour, or to become covered in this way **2** to cause cloudiness on a negative **3** to bewilder or perplex someone **foggy** *adj* **foggier**, **foggiest**, **fogginess** *n* **foghorn** *n* a device that makes a deep booming sound as a warning to ships in fog **fog lamp** *n* a lamp for use in fog

fogey *n pl* **fogeys** a person with old-fashioned ideas ♦ *an old fogey*

fogy *n pl* **fogies** another spelling of *fogey*

foible (say foi-bəl) *n* a minor peculiarity in a person's character

foil[1] *n* **1** metal hammered or rolled into a thin sheet ♦ *tin foil* **2** a person or thing that makes another look better in contrast

foil[2] *v* to prevent someone or something from succeeding

foil[3] *n* a long narrow sword with a button on the point, used in fencing

foist *v* to make someone accept something inferior or unwelcome ♦ *They foisted the job on us.*

fold[1] v 1 to bend or turn something so that one part lies on another 2 to close or flatten something by pressing its parts together 3 to become folded, or be able to be folded 4 to embrace someone affectionately in the arms 5 to blend an ingredient by spooning one part over another 6 *informal* (said about a business or undertaking) to collapse or fail **fold** n 1 a line where something has been folded 2 a folded part, a hollow between two thicknesses 3 *Geology* a curvature of strata in the earth's crust 4 a slight hollow among hills or mountains

fold[2] n 1 an enclosure for sheep 2 a community of people with the same beliefs or aims, especially the members of a Church

folder n 1 a folding cover for loose papers 2 *ICT* a directory containing a set of files

foliage (say **foh**-li-ij) n the leaves of a tree or plant **foliaceous** *adj* **foliate** *adj* **foliated** *adj* **foliation** n

folio (say **foh**-li-oh) n pl **folios** 1 a large sheet of paper folded once to form two leaves (four pages) of a book 2 a book made of these sheets 3 the page number of a printed book

folk pl n 1 people in general 2 the people of a certain country or place ♦ *country folk* **folks** pl n a person's family or relatives **folksy** *adj* **folksier**, **folksiest** simple in style, especially in an affected or pretentious way **folk dance** n a dance in the traditional style of a country **folklore** n the traditional beliefs and tales of a community **folklorist** n **folk song** n a song in the traditional style of a country

follicle (say **fol**-i-kəl) n a small sac or cavity in the body, especially one containing the root of a hair

follow v 1 to go or come after someone or something 2 to go after someone to watch them or check on them 3 to go along a particular route ♦ *You follow the path all the way to the river.* 4 to succeed someone in a job or position ♦ *James I followed Elizabeth in 1603.* 5 to provide a sequel or continuation to something ♦ *The performers followed their act with a few jokes.* 6 to take someone or something as

a guide or model ♦ *Try to follow your sister's example.* 7 to understand something or grasp its meaning ♦ *I didn't follow what he was saying.* 8 to take an interest in an activity, or to support a sports team, etc. 9 to happen as a result of something 10 to be necessarily true because of something else **follower** n **following** n a body of believers or supporters ♦ *The local team has a large following.* **following** *adj* about to be mentioned ♦ *Answer the following questions.* **following** *prep* after or as a result of ♦ *Following the bomb attack, new security measures have been introduced.*

folly n pl **follies** 1 foolishness, or a foolish act 2 an ornamental building with no practical purpose

fond *adj* 1 loving or affectionate ♦ *We have fond memories of your visit.* 2 (said about hopes) foolishly optimistic **fondly** *adv* **fondness** n

fondant n a thick paste made with water and flavoured sugar, or a sweet made from this

fondle v to touch or stroke someone or something lovingly

fondue (say **fon**-dew) n a dish of flavoured melted cheese

font n 1 a basin in a church, to hold water for baptism 2 (in printing) a set of characters of a particular style of type

food n any substance that an animal eats or drinks, or that a plant absorbs **food chain** n a series of plants and animals each of which serves as food for the next **food poisoning** n illness caused by bacteria or other toxins in food **food processor** n an electrical device with blades for cutting or mixing food **foodstuff** n something that can be used as food

fool n 1 a person who acts unwisely or lacks good sense and judgement 2 a jester or clown in the Middle Ages 3 a creamy pudding made from fruit purée mixed with cream or custard **fool** v 1 to behave in a joking way, to play about 2 to trick or deceive someone **foolhardiness** n **foolhardy** *adj* bold but rash or foolish; reckless **foolish** *adj* **foolishly** *adv* **foolishness** n **foolproof** *adj* easy to understand or do **foolscap** n a large size of paper **fool's paradise** n a state of happiness maintained by ignoring realities

foot n pl **feet 1** the lower part of the leg below the ankle, on which a person or animal stands and moves **2** the lower end of a bed or table **3** the part of a sock or stocking covering the foot **4** a person's step or pace of movement ♦ *fleet of foot* **5** the lowest supporting part of the leg of a table or other piece of furniture **6** the part of a sewing machine that is lowered on to the material to hold it steady **7** the lowest part of something that has height or length, especially the bottom of a hill, ladder, or page **8** a measure of length, equal to 12 inches (30.48 cm) **9** a unit of rhythm in a line of poetry, usually containing a stressed syllable, e.g. each of the four divisions in ♦ *Jack/and Jill/went up/the hill.* **foot** v informal to meet the cost of something ♦ *In the end we had to foot the bill ourselves.* **footage** n **1** an amount of cinema or television film **2** a length of something measured in feet **footing** n **1** a secure placing of the feet, a foothold ♦ *He lost his footing and fell.* **2** a status, conditions ♦ *The talks were kept on a friendly footing.* **foot-and-mouth disease** n a contagious virus disease affecting cattle and sheep **football** n **1** a ball game played by two teams who try to get the ball into their opponents' net **2** a large inflated leather or plastic ball used in this game **footballer** n **footbrake** n a brake in a motor vehicle, operated by the driver's foot **footbridge** n a bridge for pedestrians **footfall** n the sound of a footstep **foothill** n one of the low hills near the bottom of a mountain or range of mountains **foothold** n **1** a place wide enough to put a foot when climbing **2** a secure position from which further progress can be made **footlights** pl n a row of lights along the front of a stage at floor level **footloose** adj independent, not having any responsibilities **footman** n pl **footmen** a male servant who opens the door to visitors, serves at table, etc. **footmark** n a footprint **footnote** n a note printed at the bottom of a page of a book **footpath** n a path for pedestrians

footprint n a mark left by a foot or shoe **footsore** adj having feet that are sore from walking **footstep** n a step taken in walking, or the sound of this **footstool** n a stool for resting the feet on when sitting **footwear** n shoes, boots, and other coverings for the feet **footwork** n the manner of moving or using the feet in dancing or sport **by foot** or **on foot** walking rather than using a car or transport

fop n a man who is preoccupied with his own appearance **foppery** n **foppish** adj **foppishly** adv **foppishness** n

for prep **1** with regard to ♦ *We're ready for anything.* **2** as an objective or intention ♦ *After lunch she went for a walk.* **3** in the direction of ♦ *After that we set out for home.* **4** intended to be given to ♦ *a cage for the hamster* **5** in place of ♦ *I need to change a five-pound note for pound coins.* **6** so as to happen at a stated time ♦ *I have an appointment for two o'clock.* **7** because of, on account of ♦ *The region is famous for its wine production.* **8** to the extent or duration of ♦ *The old man walked for several miles.* ♦ *It will last for years.* **9** as the price or penalty of ♦ *She had been fined for speeding.* **10** in defence or support of ♦ *The solicitor was acting for three clients.* **for** conjunction because ♦ *They hesitated, for they were afraid.*

for- prefix **1** away or off (as in *forgive*) **2** prohibiting (as in *forbid*) **3** neglecting or going without (as in *forgo, forsake*)

forage (say **for** -ij) v to go searching for something, especially food or fuel **forage** n **1** food for horses and cattle **2** the act of foraging **forager** n

foray (say **fo**-ray) n a sudden attack or raid **forbade** past tense of *forbid*

forbear, v **forbore, forborne** to refrain from doing something ♦ *We forbore to mention it.* **forbearance** n **forbearing** adj, n

forbid v **forbade** (say for-**bad**) **forbidden, forbidding 1** to order someone not to do something ♦ *I forbid you to go.* ♦ *His mother forbade him from saying any more.* **2** to refuse to allow something ♦ *They can hardly forbid the marriage.* **forbidding** adj

forbore past tense of *forbear*

forborne past participle of *forbear*

force *n* **1** physical strength or power **2** *Phys* a measurable influence that causes movement of a body, or the intensity of this influence **3** strong influence or coercion **4** an organized body of soldiers, police, or workers **5** effectiveness or validity ♦ *The new law has little force.* **force** *v* **1** to use force in order to get or do something, or to make someone obey **2** to break something open by using force ♦ *The intruder had forced the lock.* **3** to strain something to the utmost or too hard **4** to impose or inflict something on someone **5** to cause or produce something by effort ♦ *Despite her suffering she forced a smile.* **6** to cause plants to grow or bloom earlier than is normal **forceful** *adj* **forcefully** *adv* **forcefulness** *n* **forcible** *adj* **forcibly** *adv* **force-feed** *v* past tense and past participle **force-fed** to feed someone by force and against their will

forceps (say for -seps) *n pl* **forceps** pincers or tongs used by dentists, surgeons, etc.

ford *n* a shallow place where a river can be crossed in a vehicle or on foot **ford** *v* to cross a river at a ford **fordable** *adj*

fore *adj* positioned at or towards the front **fore** *n* the front or forward part of something **fore** *interjection* a cry warning a person in danger of being hit by a golf ball **fore and aft** *adj* (said about a ship's sails) set along the length of the boat (as opposed to *square-rigged*) **forearm** *n* the arm from the elbow to the wrist or fingertips **forearm** *v* to arm or prepare someone in advance against a possible danger or attack

fore- *prefix* **1** before (as in *forecast*) **2** in front (as in *foreleg*)

forebears *pl n* your ancestors

forebode *v* *literary* to be an advance sign or token of trouble or difficulty

forecast *v* past tense and past participle **forecast** or **forecasted** to tell in advance what is likely to happen **forecast** *n* a prediction about something likely to happen

foreclose *v* to take possession of a property when the mortgage on it is not being repaid **foreclosure** *n*

forecourt *n* an open area in front of a large building or petrol station

forefathers *pl n* your ancestors

forefinger *n* the finger next to the thumb

forefoot *n pl* **forefeet** an animal's front foot

forefront *n* the leading place or position ♦ *at the forefront of medical research*

foregoing *adj* preceding, previously mentioned ◊ Note that this word is spelt *fore-* (with an e). Do not confuse it with *forgo*, which has a different meaning.

foregone conclusion *n* a result that is predictable or bound to happen

foreground *n* **1** *Art* the part of a scene or picture that is nearest to an observer **2** the most prominent position **foreground** *v* to emphasize something or make it more prominent

forehand *n* a stroke in tennis and similar games played with the palm of the hand turned forwards **forehanded** *adj*

forehead (say fo-rid or for -hed) *n* the part of the face above the eyes

foreign *adj* **1** belonging to or coming from another country **2** dealing with or involving other countries ♦ *foreign affairs* **3** not belonging naturally to a place or to someone's character ♦ *Jealousy is foreign to her nature.* **4** coming from outside ♦ *a foreign body* **foreigner** *n*

foreknowledge *n* knowledge of something before it occurs

foreleg *n* an animal's front leg

forelock *n* a lock of hair growing just above the forehead

foreman *n pl* **foremen 1** a worker who supervises a group of other workers **2** a member of a jury who is in charge of its discussions and speaks on its behalf

foremost *adj* **1** most advanced in position or rank **2** most important **foremost** *adv* in the front or most important position

forename *n* a person's first name

forensic (say fer-en-sik) *adj* **1** to do with or used in law courts **2** involving medical knowledge or science needed in legal matters or police investigations **forensically** *adv*

forerunner *n* a person or thing that comes before another and prepares the way

foresee *v* **foresees, foresaw, foreseen,**

foreseeing to be aware of or realize something before it happens **foreseeable** adj

foreshadow v to be a sign of something that is likely to happen

foreshore n the part of a shore between high-water and low-water marks

foreshorten v 1 (in drawing) to represent an object with reduced depth or size, to give an effect of distance 2 to shorten or reduce something in time or scale

foresight n 1 the ability to foresee and prepare for future needs 2 the front sight of a gun

foreskin n the fold of skin covering the end of the penis

forest n trees and undergrowth covering a large area **forested** adj **forester** n **forestry** n

forestall v to prevent or foil a person or their plans by taking action first

foretaste n an advance experience of something that is to come

foretell v past tense and past participle **foretold** to forecast or predict something

forethought n careful thought and planning for the future

forever adv 1 (also **for ever**) for all time, or for a long time 2 continually or constantly ♦ They are forever arguing.

forewarn v to warn someone about something so they can take action about it

forewoman n pl **forewomen** 1 a woman who supervises a group of other workers 2 a woman member of a jury who is in charge of its discussions and speaks on its behalf

foreword n a short introduction at the beginning of a book

forfeit (say **for** -fit) v to have to pay something or give it up as a penalty **forfeit** n something that has to be paid or given up as a penalty **forfeit** adj paid or given up as a penalty ♦ Their house and lands were forfeit to the king. **forfeiture** n

forgave past tense of **forgive**

forge¹ v to **forge ahead** to move forward or make progress steadily

forge² n 1 a workshop where metals are heated and shaped 2 a furnace or hearth

for melting or refining metal **forge** v 1 to shape metal by heating it in a fire and hammering it 2 to make a copy or imitation of a document or banknote in order to use it fraudulently **forger** n

forgery n pl **forgeries** 1 the act of forging a document or banknote 2 a copy made by forging

forget v **forgot**, **forgotten**, **forgetting** 1 to fail to remember a fact, duty, commitment, etc. 2 to stop thinking about something

forgetful adj tending to forget things **forgetfully** adv **forgetfulness** n

forgive v **forgave**, **forgiven** to stop feeling angry with someone for something they have done **forgiveness** n **forgiving** adj

forgo v **forgoes**, **forwent**, **forgone**, **forgoing** to give something up or go without it ◊ See the note at **foregoing**.

forgot past tense of **forget**

fork n 1 a small device with prongs, used for lifting or holding food 2 a large device with prongs, used for digging or lifting things 3 something shaped like a fork 4 a place where something separates into two or more parts ♦ a fork in the road **fork** v 1 to lift or dig something with a fork 2 (said about an object or road) to form a fork by separating into two branches 3 to follow one of the branches in a road or path ♦ Fork left. **forklift truck** n a truck with two metal bars pointing forward at the front, for lifting and moving heavy loads

forlorn adj left alone and unhappy **forlornly** adv

form n 1 the shape, appearance, or structure of something 2 a person or animal as it can be seen or touched 3 the way in which something exists ♦ Ice is a form of water. 4 a document with blank spaces for writing in information 5 a class in a school 6 a customary or fixed method of doing something 7 a set order of words in a prayer or ritual 8 the condition of health and training of a person or animal ♦ in good form 9 a bench 10 a wooden framework for holding concrete in shape while it is setting **form** v 1 to shape or construct something 2 to bring something into existence ♦ We formed a committee. 3 to be the material of something **4** to come into existence; to take shape or become solid ♦ *It was so cold that icicles formed.* **5** to develop an idea or concept in the mind ♦ *The boys formed a plan.* **6** to arrange things in a certain way ♦ *They formed the bricks into a large cube.*

formal *adj* **1** strictly following the accepted rules or custom ♦ *formal dress* **2** following a set structure or form ♦ *a formal education* **3** outward or superficial ♦ *There was only a formal resemblance.* **formality** *n pl* **formalities formalization** *n* **formalize** *v* **formally** *adv*

format (say **for** -mat) *n* **1** the shape and size of something, e.g. a book **2** the way in which something is organized or presented **3** *ICT* the way in which data is organized for processing or storage by a computer **format** *v* **formatted, formatting** *ICT* to organize data in the correct format

formation *n* **1** the process of forming something **2** something that has been formed in a particular way ♦ *a rock formation* **3** a particular arrangement or order of things ♦ *flying in formation*

formative (say **form**-ətiv) *adj* forming or developing something

former *adj* belonging to an earlier time ♦ *She is a former club president.* **formerly** *adv* **the former** the first of two people or things mentioned ◊ When you are referring to the first of three or more people or things, use *the first*, not *the former*.

formidable (say **for** -mid-əbəl) *adj* **1** difficult to do or overcome ♦ *a formidable challenge* **2** inspiring fear or awe ♦ *a formidable woman* **formidably** *adv*

formless *adj* not having any distinct or regular form

formula *n pl* **formulas** or **formulae** (say **for** -mew-lee) **1** a set of chemical symbols showing what a substance is made of **2** *Mathematics* a rule or statement expressed in symbols or numbers **3** a fixed form of words **4** a list of ingredients needed for making something **5** one of the groups by which racing cars are classified, according to their engine size

formulate *v* **1** to express an idea clearly and exactly **2** to express something in a formula

formulation *n*

fornicate (say **for** -ni-kayt) *v formal* to have sexual intercourse with someone you are not married to **fornication** *n*

forsake *v* **forsook, forsaken** *literary* **1** to give up or renounce something ♦ *They were determined to forsake their former way of life.* **2** to abandon someone ♦ *He forsook his wife and children and travelled the world.*

fort *n* a fortified building or position

forte (say **for** -ti) *n* a person's strong point

forth *adv* **1** out or into view ♦ *The travellers ventured forth into the snow.* **2** onwards or forwards ♦ *from this day forth*

forthcoming *adj* **1** about to happen or appear ♦ *forthcoming events* **2** available when needed ♦ *The money was still not forthcoming.* **3** (said about a person) willing to talk or give information

forthright *adj* frank or outspoken

forthwith *adv* immediately

fortieth see *forty*

fortify *v* **fortifies, fortified, fortifying 1** to strengthen a place against attack by building strong walls and other defensive works **2** to strengthen a person mentally or morally **3** to increase the nutritional value of food by adding vitamins **4** to strengthen wine with alcohol **fortification** *n*

fortitude *n* courage in bearing pain or trouble

fortnight *n* a period of two weeks **fortnightly** *adv, adj*

fortress *n* a fortified building or town

fortuitous (say for-**tew**-it-əs) *adj* happening by chance **fortuitously** *adv* ◊ Note that this word does not mean the same as *fortunate.*

fortunate *adj* having or caused by good fortune **fortunately** *adv*

fortune *n* **1** chance as a power affecting human affairs **2** the events that chance brings to a person or undertaking **3** a person's destiny **4** prosperity or success ♦ *He went abroad to seek his fortune.* **5** a very large amount of wealth ♦ *Her uncle had left her a fortune.* **fortune-teller** *n* a person who claims to predict future events in people's lives

forty *adj, n pl* **forties** the number 40, equal to four times ten **forties** *pl n* the numbers

from 40 to 49, especially representing years of age or degrees of temperature
fortieth adj, n

forum n 1 pl **fora** the public square in an ancient Roman city 2 pl **forums** a meeting where a public discussion is held

forward adj 1 directed or moving towards the front 2 having made more than normal progress 3 too assertive or eager 4 ahead in time ♦ forward buying **forward** adv forwards or ahead; towards the future **forward** n (in football or hockey) an attacking player in the front line of a team **forward** v 1 to send on a letter or package to another address 2 to send or dispatch (goods) to a customer 3 to help someone to make progress **forwardness** n

forwards adv 1 to or towards the front 2 in the direction you are facing

forwent past tense of forgo

fossil n the remains or traces of a prehistoric animal or plant embedded and preserved in rock **fossilize** v **fossilization** n **fossil fuel** n a natural fuel such as coal or gas formed in the geological past

foster v 1 to help a person to grow or develop 2 to take care of and bring up a child who is not your own

foul adj 1 having an offensive smell or taste, disgusting 2 morally offensive, wicked 3 (said about language) disgusting, obscene 4 (said about the weather) wet and stormy 5 contaminated or polluted with something 6 colliding or entangled with something 7 against the rules of a game, unfair ♦ a foul stroke **foul** n an action that breaks the rules of a game **foul** v 1 to make something foul, or to become foul 2 to entangle or collide with something 3 to commit a foul against a player in a game or sport **foully** adv **foul-mouthed** adj using foul language **foul play** n 1 unfair play in a game or sport 2 a violent crime, especially murder

found[1] past tense and past participle of find

found[2] v 1 to establish an organization or institution, or to provide money for starting one 2 to base something ♦ The story is founded on fact.

found[3] v 1 to melt and mould metal 2 to

fuse materials for making glass 3 to make an object in this way

foundation n 1 the solid base on which a building is built up 2 the underlying principle or idea on which something is based 3 the founding of an organization or institution 4 an organization or institution that has been established 5 a fund of money established for a charitable purpose 6 a cosmetic cream or powder applied to the skin as the first layer of make-up

founder[1] n a person who founds an organization or institution

founder[2] v 1 to stumble or fall 2 (said about a ship) to fill with water and sink 3 to fail completely ♦ Their plans foundered.

foundling n a child that is found abandoned and whose parents are unknown

foundry n pl **foundries** a factory or workshop where metal or glass is made

fount n a source of something good or desirable

fountain n 1 an ornamental structure in a pool or lake, in which a jet of water is made to spring into the air 2 a structure providing a supply of drinking water in a public place **fountain pen** n a pen that can be filled with a supply of ink

four adj, n 1 the number 4, one more than three 2 a four-oared boat or its crew **fourfold** adj, adv 1 four times as much or as many 2 consisting of four parts **four-poster** n a bed with posts at each corner **foursome** n a group of four people **four-square** adj solidly based, steady

fourteen adj, n the number 14 **fourteenth** adj, n

fourth adj, n 1 next after third 2 one of four equal parts of a thing **fourthly** adv

fowl n pl **fowls** or **fowl** a kind of bird kept to supply eggs and flesh for food **fowling** n **fowler** n

fox n 1 a wild animal of the dog family with a pointed snout, reddish fur, and a bushy tail 2 the fur of a fox 3 a crafty person **fox** v to deceive or confuse someone by cunning **foxy** adj **foxglove** n a tall plant with purple or white flowers like the fingers of a glove **foxhound** n a kind of hound bred and trained to hunt foxes in packs **fox terrier** n a kind of short haired terrier **foxtrot** n a ballroom dance with slow and quick steps, or the music for this dance

foyer (say foi-ay) n the entrance hall of a large building, especially a theatre, cinema, or hotel

fracas (say frak-ah) n pl **fracas** (say frak-ahz) a noisy quarrel or disturbance

fraction n 1 a number that is not a whole number, e.g. ½, 0.5 2 a very small part or piece of something **fractional** adj 1 expressed as a fraction 2 very small ♦ The difference is only fractional. **fractionally** adv

fractious (say frak-shəs) adj irritable or peevish **fractiously** adv **fractiousness** n

fracture n the breaking of something, especially of a bone **fracture** v to break or make something break

fragile adj 1 easily damaged or broken 2 having a weak constitution or health **fragilely** adv **fragility** n

fragment[1] (say frag-mənt) n 1 a small piece broken off something 2 a small part

fragment[2] (say frag-ment) v to break something into fragments, or to be broken into fragments **fragmentary** adj **fragmentation** n

fragrance n 1 a sweet or pleasant smell 2 something fragrant, a perfume **fragrant** adj

frail adj not strong, physically weak **frailty** n pl **frailties**

frame n 1 a holder that fits round a picture or photograph 2 a rigid structure built round a door or window 3 a rigid structure supporting other parts of a building, vehicle, piece of furniture, etc. 4 a human or animal body in terms of its size ♦ a small frame 5 a single exposure on a strip of cinema film 6 a box-like structure for protecting plants from the cold 7 a triangular structure for setting up the red balls in snooker **frame** v 1 to put or form a frame round something 2 to express something in words ♦ The question was framed awkwardly. 3 informal to produce false evidence against an innocent person so that they appear guilty **framework** n 1 the supporting structure of a building or other construction 2 the structural basis of

an organization or a plan

franchise (say fran-chiyz) n 1 the right to vote in public elections, especially for MPs 2 a licence or authorization to sell a firm's goods or services in a particular area **franchise** v to grant a franchise to someone

Franco- prefix French (and) ♦ a Franco-German treaty

Frank n a member of a Germanic people that conquered Gaul (modern France) in the 6th century **Frankish** adj

frank[1] adj expressing your thoughts and feelings openly **frankly** adv **frankness** n

frank[2] v to mark letters and packages automatically in a machine to show that postage has been paid

frankfurter n a smoked sausage

frankincense n a sweet-smelling gum resin burnt as incense

frantic adj wildly excited or agitated **frantically** adv

fraternal (say frə-ter-nəl) adj to do with a brother or brothers **fraternally** adv **fraternity** n pl **fraternities**

fraternize (say frat-er-niyz) v to associate with other people in a friendly way **fraternization** n

Frau (say frow) n pl **Frauen** (say frow-ən) the title of a German-speaking married woman, equivalent to 'Mrs'

fraud n 1 criminal deception; a dishonest trick 2 a person or thing that is not what they pretend to be, an impostor **fraudulence** n **fraudulent** adj **fraudulently** adv

fraught (say frawt) adj involving something unpleasant or unwelcome ♦ an undertaking fraught with danger

fray[1] n a fight or conflict ♦ ready for the fray

fray[2] v 1 to make cloth or other material worn so that loose threads show 2 to strain or upset a person's nerves or temper 3 to become worn or frayed

frazzle n informal a completely exhausted state ♦ worn to a frazzle **frazzled** adj

freak n 1 a person or thing that is unusual or abnormal in form 2 something very unusual or irregular ♦ a freak storm 3 a person who is obsessed with a particular thing ♦ a fitness

freak **freakish** *adj*
freckle *n* a light brown spot on the skin **freckled** *adj* **freckly** *adj*
free *adj* **freer, freest 1** (said about a person) not in the power or control of someone else; able to do what you want and go where you want **2** (said about a country or its inhabitants) not controlled by a foreign or despotic government; having private rights which are respected **3** allowed to do something ♦ *You are free to leave.* **4** not fixed or held down, able to move without hindrance ♦ *Leave one end free.* **5** costing nothing, not requiring payment **6** unrestricted, not controlled by rules ♦ *a free vote* **7** open to anyone to join in ♦ *a free fight* **8** not subject to or affected by something ♦ *free from blame* ♦ *The roads were free of ice.* **9** (said about a place or time) not occupied, not being used; (said about a person) not having any commitments or things to do **10** given or giving readily ♦ *He is very free with his advice.* **free** *v* **frees, freed, freeing 1** to make someone free **2** to relieve someone of something unwelcome ♦ *The court's verdict freed him from suspicion.* **3** to disengage or disentangle something **freebie** *n* **freedom** *n* **1** the condition of being free, independence **2** being frank in what you say **3** exemption or immunity from a duty **4** unrestricted use of a facility ♦ *Students have the freedom of the library.* **Free Church** *n* a nonconformist Church **freedom fighter** *n* someone who takes part in armed resistance to a government or regime **free enterprise** *n* an economic system in which private businesses operate in competition with little or no state control **free fall** *n* **1** the downward movement of a body towards earth under the force of gravity **2** the movement of a spacecraft in space without thrust from the engines **free flight** *n* the flight of a spacecraft or rocket without thrust from its engines **free-for-all** *adj* a fight or discussion in which anyone present may join **freehand** *adj* (said about a drawing) done without a ruler or other instrument **freehold** *n* the holding of land or a house in absolute ownership **freeholder** *n* **free kick** *n* (in football) a kick

allowed to be taken without interference from the other side, awarded for a foul or other infringement **freelance** *adj* self-employed and available to do work for several companies **freelance** *n* someone who works in this way **freelance** *v* to work as a freelance **freely** *adv* **freeman** *n pl* **freemen 1** a free person, someone who is not a slave or serf **2** a person who has been given the freedom of a city, as an honour **Freemason** *n* a member of an international order set up to promote fellowship and mutual help, with elaborate secret ceremonies **Freemasonry** *n* **free port** *n* **1** a port that is open to all traders **2** a port that is free from duty on goods in transit **free-range** *adj* (said about hens or their eggs) bred and kept in natural conditions **free speech** *n* the right to express your opinions **free-standing** *adj* not supported by a framework or other structure **freestyle** *adj* (in sports) having few restrictions on the style or technique that may be used **free trade** *n* trade left to its natural course **free verse** *n Language* poetry that does not rhyme or have a regular rhythm **freeware** *n ICT* software that can be downloaded from the Internet and used free of charge **freewheel** *v* to ride a bicycle without pedalling; to act without effort **free will** *n* the power to act free of the constraints of fate **free world** *n* the non-Communist countries' name for themselves
freesia *n* a small plant with fragrant colourful flowers, growing from a bulb
freeze *v* **froze, frozen 1** to change from a liquid to a solid as a result of extreme cold, or to make something change in this way **2** to become full of ice or covered in ice **3** to be so cold that water turns to ice ♦ *It was freezing last night.* **4** to preserve food by storing it at a very low temperature **5** to become paralysed from fear or shock **6** (said about a computer screen) to become locked because of a fault **7** to prevent money or assets from being used for a period **8** to hold prices or wages at a fixed level for a period **freeze** *n* **1** a period of freezing or very cold weather **2** the freezing of prices or wages **to freeze up** to obstruct

something when ice forms over it

freight (say frayt) n **1** the large-scale transport of goods by water, air, or land **2** goods transported by freight, cargo **freight** v **1** to send or carry goods as cargo **2** to load a ship with cargo **freighter** n

French adj to do with or coming from France **French** n the language of France, also used in other countries **French bean** n a kidney bean or haricot bean used as a vegetable **French chalk** n finely powdered talc used as a dry lubricant and for marking cloth **French dressing** n a salad dressing of seasoned oil and vinegar **French fries** pl n deep-fried potato chips **French horn** n a brass wind instrument with valves and a long tube coiled in a circle and broadening into a wide opening **French polish** n a shellac polish for producing a bright shine on wood **french-polish** v to polish wood with shellac polish **French toast** n N. Am bread dipped in a mixture of egg and milk and fried **French window** n a long hinged window on an outside wall, also serving as a door to a garden or balcony **the French** French people

frenzy n pl **frenzies** wild excitement or agitation **frenzied** adj

frequent (say free-kwənt) adj happening or appearing often **frequent** (say fri-kwent) v to be in a place often or go to it often **frequency** n pl **frequencies** **frequently** adv

fresco (say fress-koh) n pl **frescoes** a picture painted in watercolours on a wall or ceiling before the plaster is dry

fresh adj **1** newly made, produced, or gathered, not stale **2** new or different, not previously known or used **3** (said about food) recently made, not preserved by being tinned, frozen, or salted **4** not salty or bitter **5** (said about the air or weather) cool, refreshing; (said about the wind) moderately strong **6** bright and pure in colour, not dull or faded **7** feeling vigorous or energetic **8** impudent or presumptuous **freshen** v n **fresher** a first-year student at a college or university ◊ The American word for this is freshman. **freshly** adv **freshness** n **freshwater** adj living in fresh water, not sea

water ♦ freshwater fish

fret[1] v **fretted, fretting 1** to become anxious and unhappy, or to make someone do this **2** to wear something away by gnawing or rubbing it **fret** n a state of worry and unhappiness **fretful** adj **fretfully** adv **fretfulness** n

fret[2] n each of a series of raised bars or wires across the fingerboard of a guitar or other stringed instrument **fretted** adj

friable (say friy-ə-bəl) adj easily crumbled **friability** n

friar n a member of certain Christian religious orders of men **friary** n pl **friaries**

fricassée (say frik-ə-see) n a dish of stewed or fried pieces of meat served in a thick sauce

friction n **1** the resistance that one surface meets when it moves over another **2** the action of one thing rubbing against another **3** conflict or disagreement between people **frictional** adj

Friday n the day of the week following Thursday

fridge n a refrigerator

friend n **1** a person you enjoy spending time with **2** a helpful thing or quality ♦ Darkness was our friend. **3** someone who helps or supports a cultural organization **Friend** n a member of the Society of Friends, a Quaker **friendless** adj **friendly** adj **friendlier, friendliest, friendliness** n **-friendly** suffix **friendship** n **friendly fire** n fire from one's own weapons in war, causing damage to one's own forces **friendly society** n a mutual society providing sickness, insurance, and pension benefits to its members

fries pl n N. Am another word for French fries

Friesian (say free-zhən) n a large black-and-white dairy cow originally from Friesland in the Netherlands

frieze n a decoration round the top of a wall or building

frigate (say frig-ət) n a small warship, smaller than a destroyer

fright n **1** sudden great fear **2** informal a person or thing that looks ridiculous **frighten** v **frightful** adj **frightfully** adv

frigid (say frij-id) adj **1** intensely cold

2 aloof and formal in manner **3** (said about a woman) unable to be aroused sexually **frigidity** n **frigidly** adv

frill n **1** a decorative gathered or pleated trimming attached at one edge to a dress, curtain, etc. **2** something extra that is pleasant but unnecessary ♦ *We are looking for simple accommodation with no frills.* **frilled** adj **frilly** adj

fringe n **1** a decorative edging with many threads or cords hanging down loosely **2** something hanging over **3** a straight line of hair hanging down over the forehead **4** the edge of something **5** not part of the main activities ♦ *fringe theatre* **fringe** v **1** to decorate something with a fringe **2** to form a fringe to something **fringe benefits** pl n extra benefits provided for an employee in addition to wages or salary

frippery n pl **fripperies** showy unnecessary finery or ornaments

frisk v **1** to play or skip about **2** to run your hands over a person to search for something hidden on them **frisky** adj **friskier**, **friskiest**, **friskiness** n

frisson (say **free**-sawn) n a thrill of excitement or fear

fritter[1] n a piece of sliced meat, fruit, or vegetable coated in batter and fried

fritter[2] v to waste time, money, or energy on unimportant things

frivolous adj lacking a serious purpose, pleasure-loving **frivolity** n **frivolously** adv

frizz v (said about hair) to form a mass of tight curls **frizz** n a mass of curled hair **frizziness** n **frizzle** v **frizzy** adj

fro adv **to and fro** see **to**

frock n a woman's or girl's dress

frog n **1** a small cold-blooded animal with long hind legs for leaping **2** a horny pad growing on the sole of a horse's foot **3** a fastener consisting of a button and an ornamentally looped cord **frogman** n pl **frogmen** a swimmer equipped with a rubber suit, flippers, and breathing apparatus for swimming and working underwater **frogmarch** v to force someone to move forward by holding their arms from behind and pushing them

frolic v **frolicked**, **frolicking** to play about in

a lively cheerful way **frolic** n lively cheerful playing or entertainment

from prep **1** indicating a starting point, either a place or a time ♦ *The group will travel from London.* ♦ *Teas will be available from three o'clock.* **2** indicating a source or origin ♦ *I'll get a glass from the cupboard.* **3** indicating separation, release, or prevention ♦ *The men had escaped from prison.* ♦ *Try to refrain from laughing.* **4** indicating difference or discrimination ♦ *I can't always tell red from green.* **5** indicating a cause or means ♦ *The children had died from starvation.* **6** indicating a material used to make something ♦ *Wine is made from grapes.*

frond n a leaf-like part of a fern, palm tree, or other plant

front n **1** the part or side of something that faces forward or is normally seen ♦ *A car was waiting at the front of the house.* **2** the most important side or surface of something **3** the place where fighting is taking place in a war **4** a particular area of activity or concern ♦ *What is happening on the job front?* **5** an outward appearance or show **6** the leading edge of an advancing mass of cold or warm air **7** a road or promenade by the sea at a seaside resort **8** the part of a piece of clothing that covers the front of the body **9** the part of a theatre where the audience sits, facing the stage **10** (in names) an organized political group ♦ *the Patriotic Front* **front** adj of the front; situated in front **front** v **1** to face or have the front towards something ♦ *a hotel fronting the sea* **2** to be the host of a television programme **frontage** n **frontal** adj **front bench** n the seats at the front on each side of the House of Commons, where members of the cabinet and shadow cabinet sit **frontbencher** n **front-runner** n the contestant who seems most likely to succeed in a race, competition, or election **in front** at the front of something **in front of** in the presence of someone

frontier n **1** the land border between two countries or regions **2** the limit of achievement or understanding in a subject

frost n **1** a weather condition with the

temperature below the freezing point of water **2** a white powdery coating of frozen vapour produced in cold weather **3** a chilling influence; great coolness of manner **frost** v **1** to cover a surface with frost, or to become covered with frost **2** to freeze **frosted** adj **frosting** n **frosty** adj **frostier, frostiest, frostily** adv **frostiness** n **frostbite** n injury to the tissue of the body caused by exposure to extreme cold **frostbitten** adj

froth n a mass of tiny bubbles formed on a liquid, foam **froth** v to make froth in a liquid, to form froth **frothy** adj

frown v to wrinkle your brow because you are concentrating or worried, or disapprove of something **frown** n a frowning movement or look

frozen past participle of freeze

frugal (say **froo**-gəl) adj **1** careful and economical with money **2** scanty or costing little ♦ a frugal meal **frugality** n **frugally** adv

fruit n **1** the juicy part of a plant that contains the seeds and can be used as food **2** any plant product used as food ♦ the fruits of the earth **3** Biol the seed-bearing structure of a plant, e.g. an acorn **4** the results or rewards of doing something **fruit** v (said about a plant) to produce fruit **fruiterer** n **fruitful** adj **fruitfully** adv **fruitfulness** n **fruitless** adj **fruitlessly** adv **fruitlessness** n **fruity** adj **fruitier, fruitiest, fruit machine** n a gambling machine worked by putting coins in a slot **fruit salad** n a mixture of chopped fruit in juice or syrup

fruition (say froo-**ish**-ən) n the achievement of what you intended or worked for

frump n an unattractive woman who wears dowdy clothes **frumpish** adj **frumpy** adj

frustrate v to prevent someone from doing what they want to do **frustration** n

fry v **fries, fried, frying** to cook food or be cooked in hot fat **fry** n pl **fries** a meal of fried food **fryer** n **frying pan** n a shallow pan used for frying food **fry-up** n a meal of fried food

ft. abbr foot or feet (as a measure)

FTSE abbr a figure indicating the relative values of shares on the London Stock Exchange

fuchsia (say **few**-shə) n an ornamental shrub with drooping flowers

fuddled adj in a confused state

fuddy-duddy n pl **fuddy-duddies** informal a person who is out of date or unable to accept new ideas

fudge n a soft sweet made of milk, sugar, and butter **fudge** v to put something together in a makeshift or inadequate way

fuel n **1** material that is burnt or lit to produce heat or power **2** something that causes or increases anger or other strong feelings **fuel** v **fuelled, fuelling** to provide something with fuel

fug n informal a stuffy atmosphere in a room **fuggy** adj

fugitive (say **few**-ji-tiv) n a person who is running away from something **fugitive** adj **1** running away or escaping **2** quick to disappear, fleeting

fulcrum (say **ful**-krəm) n pl **fulcra** or **fulcrums** the point on which a lever turns

fulfil v **fulfilled, fulfilling 1** to accomplish or carry out a task **2** to do what is required by a treaty or contract **3** to make a prophecy come true **to fulfil yourself** or **be fulfilled** to develop and use your abilities **fulfilment** n

fuller n a person who cleans and thickens freshly woven cloth

fulminate (say **ful**-min-ayt) v to protest loudly and angrily **fulmination** n **fulminator** n

fulsome (say **fuul**-səm) adj praising something or thanking someone excessively and cloyingly

fumble v **1** to hold or handle something clumsily **2** to grope about

fume n **fumes** pl n strong-smelling or dangerous smoke or gas **fume** v **1** to give off fumes **2** to be very angry **3** to darken wood with chemical fumes **fumigate** v **fumigation** n

fun n **1** light-hearted amusement or enjoyment **2** something that provides this **fun run** n a non-competitive sponsored run done for charity

function n **1** the special activity or purpose that a person or thing is meant to perform

2 an important social event or ceremony **3** any of the basic operations done by a computer *Mathematics* a variable quantity whose value depends on the value of other variable quantities ♦ *X is a function of Y and Z.* **function** *v* to perform a function; to work properly **functional** *adj* **functionalism** *n* **functionalist** *n* **functionally** *adv* **functionary** *n pl* **functionaries**

fund *n* **1** money collected or available for a particular purpose **2** a stock or supply of something ♦ *a fund of good ideas* **fund** *v* to provide someone or something with money **funds** *pl n* the money a person or organization has, financial resources

fundamental *adv* **1** forming the basis or foundation of a subject **2** very important **fundamentalism** *n* strict observation of traditional beliefs in any religion **fundamentalist** *n* **fundamentally** *adv* **fundamentals** *pl n* basic facts or principles

funeral *n* the ceremony of burying or cremating a dead person **funerary** *adj* **funereal** *adj* **funereally** *adv* **funeral director** *n* an undertaker

funfair *n* a fair consisting of amusements and sideshows

fungus *n pl* **fungi** (say **fung**-giy) a plant without leaves or flowers that grows on other plants, including mushrooms, toadstools, and moulds **fungal** *adj* **fungicide** *n* a substance that destroys fungus **fungicidal** ♦ *adj* **fungoid** *adj* **fungous** *adj*

funk[1] *n informal* a state of fear or anxiety **funk** *v informal* to avoid something from fear

funk[2] *n* a style of popular music with a strong rhythm **funky** *adj*

funnel *n* **1** a tube-shaped device that is wide at the top and narrow at the bottom **2** a metal chimney on a ship or steam engine **funnel** *v* **funnelled**, **funnelling** to move or guide something through a funnel or a narrowing space

funny *adj* **funnier**, **funniest 1** causing amusement or laughter ♦ *a funny story* **2** strange or puzzling ♦ *a funny smell* **3** *informal* slightly unwell **funnily** *adv* **funny bone** *n* part of the elbow over which a very sensitive nerve passes

fur *n* **1** short fine soft hair covering the bodies of some animals **2** animal skin with the fur on it, used for making or trimming clothes **3** a coat made from real or imitation fur **4** a coating formed on the tongue as a symptom of sickness or poor health **5** a coating formed by hard water on the inside of a kettle or pipes **fur** *v* **furred**, **furring** to cover a surface with fur, or to become covered with fur **furry** *adj* **furrier**, **furriest**

furious *adj* **1** very angry **2** violent or intense ♦ *They drove at a furious pace.* **furiously** *adv*

furl *v* to roll up and fasten a sail, flag, or umbrella

furlong *n* a measure of distance, equal to one-eighth of a mile or 220 yards

furnace *n* **1** an enclosed chamber or structure for burning fuel **2** a very hot place

furnish *v* **1** to provide a room or building with furniture **2** to provide or supply something **furnishings** *pl n* furniture, curtains, and other fittings in a room or building **furniture** *n* **1** tables, chairs, and other movable articles needed in a room or building **2** a set of accessories, especially the handles and lock fitted to a door

furore (say **fewr-or** -i) *n* an outbreak of great anger or excitement

furrier (say **fu**-ri-er) *n* a person who buys and sells furs

furrow *n* **1** a long cut in the ground made by a plough or other implement **2** a groove resembling this **3** a deep wrinkle in the skin **furrow** *v* to make furrows in a surface

further *adv, adj* **1** more distant in space or time **2** to a greater extent, more ♦ *We shall have to enquire further.* ♦ *We have made further enquiries.* **further** *v* to help someone make progress ♦ *to further someone's interests* **furtherance** *n* **furthermore** *adv* also, moreover **furthermost** *adj* most distant **furthest** *adj* **further education** *n* education for people above school age

furtive *adj* stealthy, trying not to be seen **furtively** *adv* **furtiveness** *n*

fury *n pl* **furies 1** wild anger or rage **2** extreme force or violence in nature ♦ *The storm's fury continued all night.*

fuse[1] *n* a safety device in an electric circuit,

consisting of a short piece of wire that is designed to melt and break the circuit if the current exceeds a safe level **fuse** v **1** to blend or amalgamate materials, especially by melting **2** to merge things together **3** to fit an electric circuit or appliance with a fuse **4** to stop functioning because a fuse has melted **fuse box** n a box or panel containing the fuses of an electrical system

fuse[2] n a length of material along which a flame moves to ignite an explosive or firework **fuse** v to fit a fuse to an explosive device

fuselage (say few-zəl-ahzh) n the main body of an aeroplane

fusible adj able to be fused or melted **fusibility** n

fusion (say few-zhən) n **1** the process of fusing or blending things into a whole **2** the uniting of atomic nuclei to form a heavier nucleus, usually with a release of energy

fuss n **1** unnecessary excitement or concern **2** an agitated protest or dispute **fuss** v **1** to make a fuss about something **2** to bother someone about something unimportant **fussy** adj **fussier**, **fussiest**, **fussily** adv **fussiness** n **fusspot** n a fussy person

fusty adj **fustier**, **fustiest 1** (said about a room) smelling stale, damp, or stuffy **2** (said about a person) having old-fashioned ideas **fustiness** n

futile (say few-tiyl) adj producing no useful result **futility** n

futon (say foo-tonn) n a light kind of Japanese mattress

future adj belonging or referring to the time that is still to come **future** n **1** future time or events **2** Gram the tense of a verb that expresses action or state in the future, expressed by using shall, will, or be going to **futuristic** adj **future perfect** n the tense of a verb expressed in the form 'will have done'

fuzz n **1** something fluffy or frizzy **2** informal the police **fuzzy** adj **fuzzier**, **fuzziest**, **fuzzily** adv **fuzziness** n

Gg

G the seventh letter of the English alphabet

g abbr **1** gram(s) **2** gravity

gab v informal **gabbed**, **gabbing** to chatter **gab** n chatter **gabble** v **gabbler** n

gable n the triangular upper part of an outside wall, between two sloping roofs **gabled** adj

gad v **gadded**, **gadding to gad about** or **around** informal to go about in search of pleasure

gadfly n pl **gadflies** a fly that bites horses and cattle

gadget n a small mechanical device or tool **gadgetry** n

Gael (say gayl) n a Gaelic-speaking person

Gaelic n **1** the Celtic language of the Scots **2** the Irish language **Gaelic** adj to do with Gaelic

gaffe n an embarrassing blunder

gaffer n informal **1** a boss **2** the chief electrician in a film or television production unit

gag[1] n **1** something put into a person's mouth or tied across it to prevent them from speaking or crying out **2** a device used by a dentist or surgeon for holding a patient's mouth open **3** anything that prevents free speech **gag** v **gagged**, **gagging 1** to put a gag on a person **2** to prevent someone from speaking or writing freely ♦ We should not gag the press. **3** to retch or choke

gag[2] n a joke or funny story, especially as part of a comedian's act **gag** v **gagged**, **gagging** to tell jokes

gaga (say gah-gah) adj informal senile or slightly mad

gaggle n **1** a flock of geese **2** a disorderly group of people

gain v **1** to obtain something, especially something desirable **2** to make a profit **3** to increase the amount or rate of something, to build something up ♦ He needs to gain some weight. **4** to improve or increase ♦ *Salsa dancing is gaining in popularity.* **5** (said about a clock or watch) to become ahead of the correct time **6** to reach a destination ♦ *At last we gained the shore.* **gain** *n* **1** an increase in wealth or possessions **2** an improvement, an increase in amount or power **gainful** *adj* **gainfully** *adv* **gainsay** *v* past tense and past participle **gainsaid** to deny or contradict something ♦ *There is no gainsaying it.* **to gain on** to come closer to someone or something you are chasing or racing

gait *n* **1** a person's manner of walking or running ♦ *a shuffling gait* **2** any of the forward movements of a horse, such as trotting or cantering

gala (say **gah**-lə) *n* **1** a festive entertainment or performance **2** a sports meeting ♦ *a swimming gala*

galactic (say gə-**lak**-tik) *adj* **1** to do with a galaxy or galaxies **2** to do with the Galaxy or Milky Way

galaxy (say **gal**-ək-si) *n pl* **galaxies 1** any of the large independent systems of stars existing in space **2** a large group of famous, important, or talented people **3** (**the Galaxy**) the galaxy containing the solar system, the Milky Way

gale *n* **1** very strong wind **2** a noisy outburst, especially of laughter

gall (say gawl) *n* **1** bold and impudent behaviour **2** bitterness of feeling **galling** *adj*

gallant (say **gal**-ənt, or in meaning 2 also say gə-**lant**) *adj* **1** brave or heroic ♦ *a gallant effort* **2** (said about a man) chivalrous, courteous to women **gallantly** *adv* **gallantry** *n*

gall bladder *n* a pear-shaped organ attached to the liver, in which bile is stored

galleon (say **gal**-i-ən) *n* a large Spanish sailing ship used in the 15th-17th centuries

gallery *n pl* **galleries 1** a room or building for showing works of art **2** a balcony or platform projecting from the inner wall of a church or hall **3** the highest balcony in a theatre **4** the spectators at a golf tournament **5** a long room or passage, especially one used for a special purpose ♦ *a shooting gallery* **6** a raised covered platform

or passage along the wall of a building **galleried** *adj*

galley *n pl* **galleys 1** a long low medieval ship with sails and one or more banks of oars **2** an ancient Greek or Roman warship propelled by oars **3** the kitchen in a ship or aircraft

Gallic (say **gal**-ik) *adj* **1** to do with France, typically French ♦ *a Gallic shrug* **2** to do with ancient Gaul

gallivant *v informal* to go from place to place in search of pleasure, to gad about

gallon *n* a unit of volume for measuring liquids, equal to 8 pints (4.546 litres)

gallop *n* **1** a horse's fastest pace, with all four feet off the ground together in each stride **2** a ride on a horse at this pace **gallop** *v* **galloped, galloping 1** to go or ride at a gallop **2** to go very fast, to rush

gallows *n* a framework with a suspended noose for hanging criminals **the gallows** execution by hanging

galore *adv* in great numbers or in a large amount ♦ *There will be bargains galore.*

galvanic (say gal-**van**-ik) *adj* **1** producing an electric current by chemical action ♦ *a galvanic cell* **2** sudden and dramatic **galvanize** *v* **galvanization** *n* **galvanometer** *n* an instrument for measuring small electric currents

gambit *n* an action or remark intended to gain some advantage

gamble *v* **1** to play games of chance for money **2** to bet a sum of money **3** to take a risk or chance ♦ *We gambled on its being a fine day.* **gamble** *n* **1** an act of gambling, a bet **2** a risky attempt or venture **gambler** *n*

gambol *v* **gambolled, gambolling** to jump or skip about playfully **gambol** *n* a gambolling movement

game[1] *n* **1** a form of play or sport, especially one with rules **2** a single section forming a scoring unit in games such as tennis **3** a secret plan or a trick ♦ *So that's his little game!* **4** wild animals or birds hunted for sport or food **5** their flesh as food ♦ *game pie* **games** *pl n* **1** a meeting for sporting contests ♦ *the Olympic Games* **2** athletics or sports as a subject taught at school **game** *adj* eager and willing to do something new or difficult **gamely** *adv* **gameness** *n* **gaming** *n* **gamekeeper** *n* a person employed to protect and breed game **game plan** *n* a strategy worked out in advance **game show** *n* a television programme in which people compete to win prizes **gamesmanship** *n* the art of winning contests by gaining a psychological advantage over your opponent

game² *adj* lame ♦ *a game leg*

gamelan (say gam-ə-lan) *n* a type of orchestra in Java and Bali

gamine (say gam-een) *n* a young woman with a mischievous, boyish appearance

gamma *n* the third letter of the Greek alphabet, equivalent to Roman *G*, *g* **gamma rays** *pl n* X-rays of very short wavelength emitted by radioactive substances

gammon *n* ham which has been cured like bacon

gammy *adj informal* (said about a limb) unable to function properly because of a permanent injury ♦ *a gammy leg*

gamut (say gam-ət) *n* the whole range or scope of anything ♦ *He ran the whole gamut of emotion from joy to despair.*

gander *n* a male goose

gang *n* **1** a band of people going about together or working together, especially for some criminal purpose **2** a number of labourers working together ♦ *a roadmending gang* **gang** *v* to form a gang or group ♦ *They ganged together to complain.*

gangster *n* a member of a gang of violent criminals

gangling *adj* tall, thin, and awkward-looking

gangplank *n* a movable plank used as a bridge for walking into or out of a boat

gangrene *n* death and decay of body tissue, usually caused by blockage of the blood supply to that part **gangrenous** *adj*

gangway *n* **1** a gap left for people to pass between rows of seats **2** a movable bridge that links a ship to the shore **3** a passageway, especially on a ship **gangway** *interjection* make way!

gannet (say gan-it) *n* a large seabird

gantry *n pl* **gantries 1** a light bridge-like overhead framework for supporting

equipment such as a crane, railway signals, etc. **2** a structure supporting a space rocket before it is launched

gaol (say jayl) *n* another spelling of *jail* **gaoler** *n*

gap *n* **1** a break or opening in something continuous such as a hedge or fence, or between hills **2** a space ♦ *Mind the gap between the train and the platform.* **3** an interval **4** a wide difference in ideas or understanding **gapped** *adj*

gape *v* **1** to stare with your mouth wide open, in surprise or wonder **2** to be or become wide open ♦ *a gaping chasm* **gape** *n* **1** an open-mouthed stare **2** a wide opening

garage (say ga-rahzh or ga-rij) *n* **1** a building in which to keep a motor vehicle or vehicles **2** a place which sells petrol or which repairs and services motor vehicles **garage** *v* to put or keep a motor vehicle in a garage

garb *n* clothing, especially of a distinctive kind ♦ *clerical garb* **garb** *v* to dress someone in distinctive clothes

garbage *n* rubbish, especially household rubbish

garble *v* to distort or mix up a message or story so that it is difficult to understand ♦ *I received garbled instructions.*

Garda *n* the police force of the Republic of Ireland

garden *n* a piece of ground attached to a house, used for growing flowers, fruit, or vegetables **gardens** *pl n* ornamental public grounds **garden** *v* to tend a garden **gardener** *n* **gardening** *n* **garden centre** *n* an establishment where plants and gardening equipment are sold

gardenia (say gar-deen-iə) *n* **1** a tree or shrub with large fragrant white or yellow flowers **2** its flower

gargantuan (say gar-gan-tew-ən) *adj* gigantic

gargle *v* to wash the inside of your throat by breathing out through a liquid held at the back of your mouth **gargle** *n* **1** an act of gargling **2** a liquid used for this

gargoyle *n* a grotesque carved face or figure

garish (say gair-ish) *adj* too bright or

showy, gaudy **garishly** adv

garland n a wreath of flowers and leaves worn or hung as a decoration **garland** v to put a garland or garlands on someone or something

garlic n 1 a bulb that has a strong taste and smell, used as a flavouring 2 the onion-like plant which produces this bulb **garlicky** adj

garment n a piece of clothing

garner v to gather or collect something
♦ *The film has garnered a host of awards.*

garnet n a semi-precious stone of deep transparent red

garnish v to decorate something, especially food for the table **garnish** n something used to decorate food or give it extra flavour **garnishing** n

garret n a top-floor or attic room

garrison n 1 troops who stay in a town or fort to defend it ♦ *a garrison town* 2 the building they live in **garrison** v to provide a place with a garrison

garrotte (say gǝ-rot) n a cord or wire used to strangle someone **garrotte** v to kill someone with a garrotte

garrulous (say ga-roo-lǝs) adj talkative **garrulity** n **garrulously** adv **garrulousness** n

garter n a band worn round the leg to keep a stocking or sock up

gas n pl **gases** 1 a substance with particles that can move freely, especially one that does not become liquid or solid at ordinary temperatures 2 any of the gases or mixtures of gases used for lighting, heating, or cooking ♦ *a gas cooker* 3 poisonous gas used as a weapon in war 4 nitrous oxide or another gas used as an anaesthetic 5 N. Am informal petrol **gas** v **gassed**, **gassing** 1 to expose someone to gas, especially to kill them or make them unconscious 2 informal to talk idly for a long time **gaseous** adj to do with or in the form of a gas **gassy** adj **gassier**, **gassiest** full of gas, fizzy **gassiness** n **gaslight** n light given by a jet of burning gas **gaslit** adj **gas mask** n a protective mask worn over the face to protect the wearer against poisonous gas **gasworks** n a place where gas for heating, etc. is manufactured

gash n a long deep cut or wound **gash** v to make a gash in something

gasoline n N. Am petrol

gasp v 1 to breathe in sharply when you are shocked or surprised 2 to struggle for breath with the mouth open 3 to speak in a breathless way **gasp** n a breath drawn in sharply

gastric adj to do with the stomach

gastritis n inflammation of the stomach

gastronomy n the practice or art of eating and drinking well **gastronomic** adj **gastric flu** n any stomach disorder involving sickness and diarrhoea

gate n 1 a movable barrier, usually on hinges, used as a door in a wall or fence 2 the opening it covers 3 an exit from an airport building to an aircraft 4 a barrier for controlling the flow of water in a dam or lock 5 the total number of spectators who pay to attend a football match, etc. 6 an arrangement of slots controlling the movement of a gear lever in a motor vehicle 7 an electric circuit with an output that is activated only by a combination of input signals **gatecrash** v to go to a private party without being invited **gatecrasher** n **gatehouse** n a house built at the side of or over a large gate **gateway** n 1 an opening or structure containing a gate 2 a way of entering or reaching something ♦ *the gateway to success* 3 ICT a device for connecting computer networks

gateau (say gat-oh) n pl **gateaus** or **gateaux** (say gat-ohz) a large rich cake, usually containing cream or fruit

gather v 1 to come together, to bring people or things together 2 to collect something or obtain it gradually 3 to collect something as harvest ♦ *Gather the corn when it is ripe.* 4 to increase gradually ♦ *Downhill we gathered speed.* 5 to understand or conclude something ♦ *I gather your proposal was accepted.* 6 to summon something up 7 to draw parts together in folds or wrinkles 8 to pull cloth into folds by running a thread through it ♦ *a gathered skirt* **gathering** n

gauche (say gohsh) adj lacking in ease and grace of manner, socially awkward

gaudy *adj* **gaudier, gaudiest** showy or bright in a tasteless way **gaudily** *adv* **gaudiness** *n*

gauge (say gayj) *n* **1** an instrument used for measuring **2** a standard measure of something **3** the distance between the rails of a railway track **gauge** *v* **1** to measure something exactly **2** to estimate or form a judgement of something

gaunt *adj* lean and haggard **gauntness** *n*

gauntlet *n* **1** a heavy glove with a wide cuff covering the wrist **2** a glove with metal plates worn by soldiers in the Middle Ages **to throw down the gauntlet** to challenge someone to a contest or fight

gauze (say gawz) *n* **1** thin transparent woven material of silk, cotton, etc. **2** fine wire mesh **gauzy** *adj*

gave past tense of *give*

gawky *adj* **gawkier, gawkiest** awkward and ungainly **gawkiness** *n*

gawp *v informal* to stare in a rude or stupid way

gay *adj* **1** homosexual **2** *old use* light-hearted and cheerful **3** *old use* brightly coloured; dressed or decorated in bright colours **gay** *n* a homosexual person **gaiety** *n* **gaily** *adv* **gayness** *n*

gaze *v* to look at something steadily and for a long time **gaze** *n* a long steady look

gazebo (say gə-zee-boh) *n pl* **gazebos** a small building in the garden of a house, giving a wide view of the surroundings

gazelle *n* a small graceful Asian or African antelope

gazette *n* a journal or newspaper, especially the official one of an organization or institution **gazetteer** *n* an index of place names, names of rivers and mountains, etc.

GB *abbr* **1** Great Britain **2** gigabyte(s)

GCE *abbr* General Certificate of Education

GCSE *abbr* General Certificate of Secondary Education

GDP *abbr* gross domestic product

gear *n* **1** a set of toothed wheels working together to transmit motion from an engine to the driven parts **2** a particular setting of these ♦ *in second gear* **3** equipment or apparatus ♦ *camping gear* **4** *informal* clothes ♦ *I've bought some new gear.* **gear** *v* **1** to

change machinery to a different gear **2** to fit something with gears **gearing** *n* a set or arrangement of gears **gearbox** *n* a case enclosing a gear mechanism **gear lever** *n* a lever used to engage or change gear in a motor vehicle **in gear** with a gear engaged **out of gear** with no gear engaged

gecko (say gek-oh) *n pl* **geckos** or **geckoes** a lizard of warm climates, able to climb walls by the adhesive pads on its toes

gee *v* **gees, geed, geeing gee up!** a command to a horse to go faster **to gee someone up** to encourage someone to work more quickly

geese plural of *goose*

geezer *n informal* a man

Geiger counter (say giy-ger) *n* an instrument for detecting and measuring radioactivity

gel (say jel) *n* a jelly-like substance ♦ *hair gel* **gel** *v* **gelled, gelling** **1** to set as a gel **2** to smooth your hair with gel

gelatin (say jel-ə-tin), **gelatine** (say jel-ə-teen) *n* a clear tasteless substance made by boiling the bones of animals **gelatinize** *v* **gelatinization** *n* **gelatinous** *adj*

geld *v* to castrate or spay an animal **gelding** *n*

gelignite (say jel-ig-niyt) *n* an explosive used especially for blasting rock

gem *n* **1** a precious or semi-precious stone, especially when cut and polished **2** something valued because of its excellence or beauty **gemstone** *n* a precious or semi-precious stone

Gemini (say jem-i-niy) (the Twins) the sign of the zodiac which the sun enters about 21 May **Geminian** *adj, n*

-gen *suffix* used in scientific language to form nouns meaning 'producing' or 'produced' (as in *oxygen, hydrogen*)

gender *n* **1** the class into which a noun or pronoun is placed in the grammar of some languages, e.g. masculine, feminine, or neuter **2** a person's sex

gene (say jeen) *n* a unit of heredity which is transferred from a parent to offspring **genealogy** *n pl* **genealogies** **1** an account or diagram showing how a person is descended from an ancestor

2 the study of family history and ancestors **genealogical** *adj* **genealogist** *n*
gene pool *n* the stock of genes in an interbreeding population
general *adj* **1** involving or affecting all or most people or things, not limited or particular ♦ *in general use* **2** involving various kinds, not specialized ♦ *a general education* **3** involving only the main features, not detailed or specific ♦ *I've got the general idea.* **4** chief or head ♦ *the general manager* **general** *n* **1** a commander of an army **2** a lieutenant general or major general **generality** *n pl* **generalities generalize** *v* **generally** *adv* **generalization** *n* **general anaesthetic** *n* an anaesthetic that affects the whole body and makes you lose consciousness **general election** *n* an election of Members of Parliament for the whole country **general knowledge** *n* knowledge of a wide variety of subjects **general practitioner** *n* a doctor who treats cases of all kinds in a section of the community **general strike** *n* a strike of workers in all or most industries **in general** as a general rule, usually

generate *v* to produce or create something **generator** *n*
generation *n* **1** all the people born about the same time and therefore of the same age ♦ *our parents' generation* **2** the average period in which children grow up and have children of their own, usually thought of as about 30 years **3** a single stage in a family ♦ *three generations of the Brown family* **4** a set of models of a machine at one stage of development ♦ *a new generation of computers* **5** generating or being generated **generational** *adv*

generic (say jin-**e**-rik) *adj* **1** belonging to a whole class, group, or genus **2** (said about goods) having no brand name **generically** *adv*

generous *adj* **1** giving or ready to give something freely, especially money **2** given freely, plentiful ♦ *a generous gift* **3** kind and thoughtful in your treatment of other people **generosity** *n* **generously** *adv*

genesis (say **jen**-i-sis) *n* the beginning or origin of something

genetic (say ji-**net**-ik) *adj* **1** to do with genes or heredity **2** to do with genetics **genetics** *n* the scientific study of heredity **genetically** *adv* **geneticist** *n* **genetically modified** *adj* (said about an organism) having genetic material that has been artificially altered to produce one or more different characteristics

genial (say **jee**-niəl) *adj* kindly, pleasant, and cheerful **geniality** *n* **genially** *adv*

genie (say **jee**-ni) *n* (in Arabian tales) a spirit with strange powers, especially one who can grant wishes

genital (say **jen**-i-təl) *adj* to do with human or animal reproductive organs **genitals** *pl n* the external sexual organs of people and animals **genitalia** *pl n formal* the genitals

genius *n pl* **geniuses 1** a person who has exceptional intelligence, creativity, or natural ability **2** exceptional intelligence, creativity, or natural ability

genocide (say **jen**-ə-siyd) *n* deliberate extermination of a race of people

genome (say **jeen**-ohm) *n* the complete set of an individual's chromosomes

genre (say zhahnr) *n* a particular kind or style of art or literature, e.g. epic, romance, or western

gent *n informal* a man, a gentleman **the Gents** *informal* a men's public toilet

genteel (say jen-**teel**) *adj* trying to seem polite and refined **genteelly** *adv* **gentility** *n*

gentile (say **jen**-tiyl) *n* a person who is not Jewish **gentile** *adj* not Jewish

gentle *adj* **1** mild or kind, not rough **2** moderate, not harsh or severe ♦ *a gentle breeze* **gentleness** *n* **gently** *adv* **gentlefolk** *pl n old use* people of good family or social position **gentleman** *n pl* **gentlemen 1** a man of honourable and courteous behaviour **2** a man of good social position **3** (in polite use) a man **gentlemanly** *adj*

gentry *pl n old use* people of good social position, especially those next below the nobility in position **gentrify** *v* **gentrifies**, **gentrified**, **gentrifying gentrification** *n*

genuine *adj* **1** really what it is said to be, authentic ♦ *genuine pearls* ♦ *with genuine pleasure* **2** (said about a person) sincere and honest **genuinely** adv **genuineness** n

genus (say jee-nəs) n pl **genera** (say jen-er-ə) 1 a group of animals or plants with common characteristics 2 a kind or class

geo- prefix earth

geode (say jee-ohd) n 1 a small cavity lined with crystals 2 a rock containing this

geography n 1 the scientific study of the earth's surface and its physical features, climate, products, and population 2 the physical features and arrangement of a place **geographer** n **geographic** adj **geographical** adj **geographically** adv

geology (say jee-ol-əji) n 1 the scientific study of the earth's crust and its strata 2 the geological features of an area **geological** adj **geologically** adv **geologist** n

geometry (say jee-om-itri) n the branch of mathematics dealing with the properties and relations of lines, angles, surfaces, and solids **geometric** adj **geometrical** adj **geometrically** adv

Geordie (say jor -di) n informal a person from Newcastle or Tyneside

geranium n a garden plant with red, pink, or white flowers

gerbil (say jer-bil) n a mouse-like desert rodent with long hind legs

geriatric (say je-ri-at-rik) adj to do with old people **geriatric** n an old person, especially one receiving special care **geriatrics** n the branch of medicine dealing with the diseases and care of old people

germ n 1 a micro-organism, especially one causing disease 2 a portion of a living organism capable of becoming a new organism ♦ wheat germ 3 an initial stage from which something may develop ♦ the germ of an idea **germicide** n a substance that kills germs or micro-organisms **germicidal** adj **germinal** adj 1 to do with germs 2 in the earliest stage of development 3 producing new ideas

German adj to do with Germany or its people or language **German** n 1 a native of Germany 2 the language of Germany **Germanic** adj **German measles** n another term for rubella

germane (say jer-mayn) adj relevant to the subject you are discussing

germinate v 1 (said about a seed) to begin to develop and grow, to put forth shoots 2 to cause a seed to do this **germination** n

Gestapo (say ges-tah-poh) n the German secret police of the Nazi regime

gestation (say jes-tay-shən) n 1 the process of carrying or being carried in the womb between conception and birth 2 the time this process takes 3 the development of a plan or idea over time **gestate** v

gesticulate (say jes-tik-yoo-layt) v to make expressive movements with your hands and arms **gesticulation** n

gesture (say jes-cher) n 1 a movement of any part of the body that expresses what a person feels 2 something done to convey your intentions or attitude, especially your goodwill ♦ It would be a nice gesture to send her some flowers. **gesture** v to tell a person something by making a gesture ♦ She gestured me to be quiet.

get v past tense and past participle **got**; **getting** 1 to come into possession of something, to obtain or receive something 2 to become something ♦ There's no need to get angry. ♦ I got very wet. 3 to bring or put someone or something into a certain condition ♦ I need to get my hair cut. 4 to fetch something ♦ Get your coat. 5 to travel by or catch a train, bus, taxi, etc. 6 to catch an illness or suffer a punishment ♦ I got the flu over Christmas. 7 to catch and punish someone ♦ I'll get him for that. 8 informal to understand ♦ I don't get that joke. 9 to prepare a meal ♦ I'll get supper. 10 to move or go somewhere ♦ Get off the grass. 11 to reach a place ♦ What time did you get here? 12 to succeed in bringing something or persuading someone ♦ I got a message to her. **get-out** n a means of avoiding something **get-together** n a social gathering **to be getting on** informal to be advancing in age **to get at** 1 to reach somewhere 2 informal to mean or imply something ♦ What are you getting at? 3 informal to keep criticizing someone subtly ♦ She's always getting at the way I speak. 4 informal to bribe or unfairly influence someone **to get back at** to take revenge on someone **to get by** to manage to survive **to get down to** to begin working on something **to get in** to arrive **to get off 1** to begin a journey **2** to escape with little or no punishment, to be acquitted **3** to go to sleep **to get on 1** to make progress with something **2** to be on friendly terms with someone **to get out of** to avoid something **to get over 1** to recover from an illness, shock, etc. **2** to overcome a difficulty **to get someone off** to obtain an acquittal for someone ♦ *A clever lawyer got him off.* **to get to** *informal* to annoy or upset someone **to get up 1** to stand after sitting or kneeling, etc. **2** to get out of your bed in the morning **3** (said about the wind or sea) to become strong or rough

geyser *n* **1** (say **gee**-zer or **giy**-zer) a natural spring that shoots up a tall column of hot water and steam at intervals **2** (say **gee**-zer) a kind of water heater

ghastly *adj* **ghastlier**, **ghastliest 1** causing horror or fear ♦ *a ghastly accident* **2** very unpleasant or bad ♦ *a ghastly mistake* **3** looking pale and ill **ghastliness** *n*

ghee (say gee) *n* Indian clarified butter made from the milk of a buffalo or cow

gherkin (say **ger**-kin) *n* a small cucumber used for pickling

ghetto (say **get**-oh) *n pl* **ghettos** or **ghettoes** an area of a city, often a slum area, occupied by a minority group (especially as a result of social or economic conditions)

ghost *n* **1** a person's spirit appearing after his or her death **2** a very slight trace of something ♦ *a ghost of a smile* **ghost** *v* to write a book, etc. as a ghostwriter **ghostly** *adj* **ghostliness** *n* **ghostwrite** *v* **ghostwriter** *n* a person who writes a book, article, or speech for another person, who is the named author

ghoul (say gool) *n* **1** an evil spirit, especially one said to rob graves and devour the corpses in them **2** a person who is interested in gruesome things such as death **ghoulish** *adj* **ghoulishly** *adv*

GHQ *abbr* General Headquarters

giant *n* **1** in stories and myths, a being of human form but of very great height and

size **2** a person, animal, or plant that i much larger than the usual size **3** a perso of outstanding ability or influence ♦ *a literary giant* **giant** *adj* of a kind that is very large in size **giantess** *n*

gibber (say **jib**-er) *v* to talk very quickly without making sense, especially when shocked or terrified **gibberish** *n*

gibbon *n* a small long-armed ape of SE Asia

gibbous (say **jib**-əs) *adj* (said about the moon) having the bright part greater than a semicircle and less than a circle

gibe (say jiyb) *v* to jeer **gibe** *n* a jeering remark

giblets (say **jib**-lits) *pl n* the edible parts of the inside of a chicken

giddy *adj* **giddier**, **giddiest 1** having the feeling that everything is spinning round, dizzy **2** (said especially about a superior line of work or social position) as though causing a dizzy feeling **3** frivolous and excited **giddily** *adv* **giddiness** *n*

gift *n* **1** something given without payment, a present **2** a natural ability or talent ♦ *He has a gift for languages.* **3** *informal* something that is very easy to do or cheap to buy ♦ *Their first goal was an absolute gift.* **gift** *v* to give something as a gift **gifted** *adj* **gift wrap** *n*

gig *informal* a live performance by a musician, comedian, etc.

giga- *prefix* **1** denoting a factor of 109, one thousand million **2** *ICT* denoting a factor of 230

gigabyte (say **gi**-gə-biyt or **ji**-gə-biyt) *n ICT* a unit of information equal to one thousand million bytes, or (more precisely) 230 bytes

gigantic *adj* extremely large **gigantically** *adv*

giggle *v* to laugh in a silly or nervous way **giggle** *n* **1** a silly or nervous laugh **2** *informal* something amusing, a joke ♦ *We only did it for a giggle.* **giggly** *adj*

gild *v* to cover something with a thin layer of gold or gold paint

gill (say jil) *n* a unit of liquid measure, equal to a quarter of a pint

gills *pl n* **1** the organ with which a fish breathes in water **2** the vertical plates on the underside of a mushroom cap

gilt adj covered thinly with gold or gold paint **gilt** n a thin covering of gold or gold paint **gilts** pl n gilt-edged securities

gimmick n a trick, device, or mannerism used to attract people's attention, or to make an entertainer, etc. easily recognized and remembered **gimmicky** adj

gin (say jin) n a colourless alcoholic spirit flavoured with juniper berries

ginger n 1 the hot-tasting root of a tropical plant, or a flavouring made from this root 2 this plant 3 liveliness or energy 4 a light reddish-yellow colour **ginger** v to make something more lively ♦ *This will ginger things up!* **ginger** adj ginger-coloured **gingerly** adv cautiously **gingery** adj **ginger ale** n a ginger-flavoured fizzy drink **ginger beer** n a slightly alcoholic ginger-flavoured drink **gingerbread** n a ginger-flavoured cake or biscuit

gingham (say **ging**-əm) n a cotton fabric often with a striped or checked pattern

gingivitis (say jin-ji-**viy**-tiss) n inflammation of the gums

ginormous (say jiy-**naw**-məs) adj informal enormous, very large

ginseng (say **jin**-seng) n 1 a plant found in eastern Asia and North America 2 its root, used in medicine

gipsy n another spelling of *gypsy*

giraffe n a long-necked African mammal, the tallest living animal

girder n a metal beam supporting part of a building or a bridge

girdle n 1 a belt or cord worn round the waist 2 a woman's elastic corset covering from the waist to the thigh 3 a connected ring of bones in the body ♦ *the pelvic girdle* **girdle** v to surround something

girl n 1 a female child 2 a young woman 3 a girlfriend **girlhood** n **girlish** adj **girlishly** adv **girlishness** n **girlfriend** n a person's usual female companion in a romantic relationship

giro (say **jiy**-roh) n pl **giros** 1 a system, run by a bank or post office, by which one customer can make a payment to another by transferring credit from his or her own account to the other person's 2 informal a cheque or payment by giro, especially a social security payment

girth n 1 the distance around the middle of something, especially a person's waist 2 a band passing under a horse's body to hold the saddle in place

gist (say jist) n the essential points or general sense of what someone says

give v gave, given 1 to let someone have something of yours, to provide someone with something 2 to deliver a message 3 to produce a sound ♦ *He gave a sigh.* 4 to carry out an action ♦ *She gave the door a kick.* 5 to make someone experience or suffer something ♦ *You gave me a fright.* 6 to state or offer something ♦ *Let me give my reasons.* 7 to pledge something ♦ *I've given my word.* 8 to be the host at a party or meal 9 to yield something as a product or result 10 to be the source of something 11 to allow a view of or access to a place ♦ *The window gives on to the street.* 12 (said about a referee, umpire, etc.) to deliver a judgement on whether a goal should be allowed, a player is out, etc. ♦ *The referee didn't give the goal.* 13 to be flexible, to bend or collapse when pressed or pulled **give** n springiness or elasticity **given** adj 1 specified or stated ♦ *all the people in a given area* 2 having a certain tendency ♦ *He is given to swearing.* **given** prep taking into account **giver** n **giveaway** n 1 something given without charge 2 something that reveals a secret **given name** n a person's first name, not their surname **to give in** to admit that you are defeated **to give out** 1 to become exhausted or used up 2 to stop working ♦ *The engine has given out at last.* **to give something out** 1 to emit something ♦ *The chimney was giving out smoke.* 2 to distribute something ♦ *Can you give the books out?* **to give something over to** to devote a period of time to some activity ♦ *Afternoons are given over to sport.* **to give up** 1 to stop trying 2 to admit that you are not able to do something **to give way** see *way*

gizmo (say **giz**-moh) n pl **gizmos** informal a gadget, especially one that you do not know the name of

gizzard n a bird's second stomach, in which

food is ground up

glacé (say **gla**-say) adj iced with sugar, preserved in sugar ♦ *glacé fruits*

glacier (say **glas**-i-er) n a mass of ice moving very slowly **glacial** adj **1** icy **2** to do with or from glaciers or other ice ♦ *glacial deposits* **3** (said about a person) cold and unfriendly **glacially** adv **glaciated** adj **glaciation** n

glad adj **gladder, gladdest 1** pleased or happy **2** making someone pleased or happy ♦ *We brought the glad news.* **gladden** v **gladly** adv **gladness** n

glade n an open space in a forest

gladiator (say **glad**-i-ay-ter) n a man trained to fight for public entertainment in ancient Rome **gladiatorial** adj

glamour n **1** an attractive and exciting quality that something has **2** physical attractiveness **glamorize** v **glamorous** adj **glamorously** adv

glance v **1** to look at something briefly **2** to strike something at an angle and slide off it ♦ *a glancing blow* **glance** n a brief or hurried look

gland n an organ of the body that separates substances from the blood that are to be used by the body or secreted from it **glandular** adj

glare v **1** to shine with an unpleasantly strong or dazzling light **2** to stare angrily or fiercely **glare** n **1** a strong unpleasant light **2** an angry or fierce stare **glaring** adj **glaringly** adv

glass n **1** a hard brittle substance, usually transparent, made by fusing sand with soda and lime **2** a drinking container made of glass **3** an object made of glass, such as a mirror or a covering for a watch face **4** ornaments or other objects made of glass **glasses** pl n a pair of lenses in a frame that rests on the nose and ears, used to correct or improve weak eyesight **glass** v to fit or enclose something with glass **glassful** n pl **glassfuls** the amount contained by a drinking glass **glassy** adj **glassier, glassiest, glassily** adv **glassiness** n **glasshouse** n **1** a greenhouse **2** informal a military prison

Glaswegian (say glaz-**wee**-jən) adj to do with or coming from Glasgow **Glaswegian** n a person born or living in Glasgow

glaucoma (say glaw-**koh**-mə) n a disease of the eye

glaze v **1** to fit a window or building with panes of glass **2** to coat something with a glossy surface **3** to become fixed or glassy ♦ *Her eyes glazed over with boredom.* **glaze** n a shiny surface or coating, especially on pottery **glazier** n

gleam n **1** a beam or ray of soft light, especially one that comes and goes **2** a small amount of some quality or emotion ♦ *a gleam of hope* **gleam** v to shine brightly, especially after cleaning or polishing **gleaming** adj

glean v to gather things, especially scraps of information, from various sources **gleaner** n **gleanings** pl n

glee n **1** great delight **2** a song with three or more male voice parts, often without accompaniment **gleeful** adj **gleefully** adv

glen n a narrow valley, especially in Scotland or Ireland

glib adj ready with words but insincere or superficial **glibly** adv **glibness** n

glide v **1** to move along smoothly **2** to fly in a glider or in an aeroplane without engine power **3** (said about a bird) to fly without beating its wings **glide** n a gliding movement **glider** n

glimmer n **1** a faint, flickering light **2** a faint sign or trace of something ♦ *a glimmer of hope* **glimmer** v to shine with a faint, flickering light

glimpse n a brief view **glimpse** v to see something briefly

glint n a very brief flash of light **glint** v to shine with brief flashes of light

glissade (say glis-**ayd**) v **1** to slide skilfully down a steep slope, especially in mountaineering **2** to make a gliding step in dancing **glissade** n a glissading movement or step

glisten v to shine like something wet or polished

glitch n informal a sudden malfunction or setback

glitter v to shine with tiny flashes of light, to sparkle **glitter** n **1** tiny sparkling pieces used for decoration **2** sparkling light

glittery adj

glitz n informal extravagant display **glitzy** adj

gloat v to show how pleased you are about your success or someone else's misfortune, in a smug or mean way **gloat** n an act of gloating

global adj 1 to do with the whole world, worldwide 2 involving all parts or aspects of something 3 ICT applying to the whole of a file or program ♦ a global search **globalization** n the process of making ideas and institutions affect the whole world **globalized** adj **globally** adv **global village** n the world regarded as a single community linked by telecommunications **global warming** n the gradual increase in the temperature of the earth's atmosphere

globe n 1 an object shaped like a ball, especially one with the map of the earth on it 2 the world ♦ She has travelled all over the globe. **globular** adj **globetrotter** n a person who travels all over the world

globule (say **glob**-yool) n a small rounded drop

glockenspiel (say **glok**-ən-speel) n a musical instrument consisting of tuned steel bars fixed in a frame and struck with two small hammers

gloom n 1 darkness or dimness 2 a feeling of sadness and depression **gloomy** adj **gloomier**, **gloomiest**, **gloomily** adv **gloominess** n

glory n pl **glories** 1 fame and honour won by great deeds 2 praise and worship offered to God 3 beauty or magnificence ♦ the glory of a sunset 4 a thing deserving praise and honour **glory** v **glories**, **gloried**, **glorying** to rejoice or take pride in something ♦ We are all glorying in his success. **glorify** v **glorifies**, **glorified**, **glorifying**, **glorification** n **glorified** adj **glorious** adj **gloriously** adv

gloss n 1 the shine on a smooth surface 2 an explanatory comment **gloss** v to make something glossy **glossy** adj **glossier**, **glossiest**, **glossiness** n

glossary (say **glos**-er-i) n pl **glossaries** a list of technical or special words with their definitions

glove n a covering for the hand, usually with separate parts for each finger and the thumb **gloved** adj

glow v 1 to give out light and heat without flame 2 to have a warm or flushed look or colour 3 to express or feel great pleasure ♦ She glowed with pride. **glow** n 1 brightness and warmth without flames 2 a warm or cheerful feeling ♦ We felt a glow of pride. **glowing** adj

glower (say **glow**-ə) v to scowl or stare angrily

glow-worm n a kind of beetle that can give out a greenish light at its tail

glucose (say **gloo**-kohz) n a form of sugar that is found in fruit juice and honey and is an important source of energy in living things

glue n a sticky substance used for joining things **glue** v **glues**, **glued**, **gluing** to fasten something with glue **gluey** adj

glum adj **glummer**, **glummest** sad and gloomy **glumly** adv **glumness** n

glut n an excessive supply of something, a surfeit ♦ a glut of apples **glut** v **glutted**, **glutting** to supply or fill something with much more than is needed ♦ to glut the market

gluten (say **gloo**-tən) n a sticky protein substance that remains when starch is washed out of flour **glutinous** adj

glutton n a person who eats far too much **gluttonous** adj **gluttony** n

glycerine (say **glis**-er-een) n glycerol

GM abbr genetically modified

gm abbr gram(s)

GMT abbr Greenwich Mean Time

gnarled (say narld) adj (said about a tree or a person's hands) knobbly and twisted

gnash v 1 to grind your teeth together, especially in anger 2 (said about teeth) to strike together

gnat n a small biting fly

gnaw v 1 to keep on biting at something so that it wears away 2 to keep worrying or troubling someone ♦ a gnawing doubt

gneiss (say nyiss) n a kind of coarse-grained rock

gnome n 1 a kind of dwarf in fairy tales and legends 2 a garden ornament in the form of a bearded man with a pointed hat

gnostic (say **nos**-tik) adj 1 to do with knowledge 2 having special mystical knowledge

GNP abbr gross national product

GNVQ abbr General National Vocational Qualification

go v **goes**, **went**, **gone** 1 to move from one place to another ♦ Where are you going? 2 to leave ♦ We must go at one o'clock. 3 to pass into a certain condition, to become something ♦ The milk has gone sour. 4 to spend time doing something ♦ Let's go shopping. 5 to lead or stretch from one place to another ♦ The road goes to Kent. 6 to be in a certain state ♦ They will just have to go hungry. 7 to be working properly ♦ The car won't go. 8 (said about time) to pass 9 to belong in some place or position ♦ Plates go on the shelf. 10 to match or look good with something else ♦ Those shoes don't go with that suit. 11 (said about a story, tune, etc.) to have a certain wording or content ♦ I forget how the chorus goes. 12 to make a specified sound ♦ The gun went bang. 13 to turn out in a certain way ♦ I hope the show goes well. 14 to be sold ♦ It's going cheap. 15 (said about money or supplies) to be spent or used up 16 to be given up or got rid of ♦ Some luxuries will have to go. 17 to disappear, fail, or die ♦ My eyesight is going. 18 to carry an action to a certain point ♦ I'm not prepared to go any further with my offer. 19 to be able to be put somewhere ♦ Your clothes won't go into that suitcase. 20 to be given or allotted to someone ♦ His estate went to his nephew. 21 to be allowable or acceptable ♦ Anything goes. **go** n pl **goes** 1 a turn or try ♦ Can I have a go? 2 energy or liveliness ♦ She is full of go. 3 busy activity ♦ It's all go today. **goer** n 1 a person who attends a place or event, especially regularly ♦ a cinema-goer 2 informal a person or thing that goes well **go-ahead** n permission to proceed **go-ahead** adj informal willing to try new methods, enterprising **go-between** n a person who acts as a messenger or negotiator between others **go-slow** n a deliberately slow pace of work as a form of industrial

protest **on the go** very active or busy **to go** 1 remaining ♦ just ten miles to go 2 (said about food or drink) to be eaten or drunk away from the restaurant or café where it has been bought **to go ahead** to proceed immediately **to go down** 1 to be received or accepted ♦ The suggestion went down very well. 2 to be recorded or remembered in a particular way ♦ This will go down as a classic final. 3 to catch an illness ♦ She's gone down with the flu. 4 informal to go to prison **to go over** to examine or check something **to go round** to be enough for everyone **to go slow** to work at a deliberately slow pace as a form of industrial protest **to go through** 1 to experience a difficult or painful event or time 2 to be approved or made official ♦ We are waiting for our claim to go through. **to go up** to explode or burn rapidly **to go without** to put up with the lack of something

goad n something that stimulates a person into action **goad** v to stir someone into action, especially by being annoying ♦ Don't let him goad you into retaliating.

goal n 1 a structure or area into which the ball must be sent to score a point in football, hockey, etc. 2 a point scored in this way 3 something that you are trying to reach or achieve **goalie** n a goalkeeper **goalkeeper** n a player who stands in the goal and tries to keep the ball out **goalpost** n either of the pair of posts marking the limits of the goal

goat n 1 a hardy mammal with shaggy hair, horns, and (in the male) a beard, often kept for its milk and meat 2 a related wild mammal ♦ mountain goat **goatherd** n a person who looks after a herd of goats

goatee (say goh-**tee**) n a short pointed beard

gob n informal a person's mouth

gobble v 1 to eat something quickly and greedily 2 (said about a turkeycock) to make a throaty swallowing sound

gobbledegook n informal the pompous and technical language that is often used by officials and is difficult to understand

goblet n 1 a drinking glass with a stem and a foot 2 the container of liquid in a liquidizer

goblin *n* a mischievous ugly elf

god *n* **1** a superhuman being regarded as having power over nature and human affairs ♦ *Mars was the Roman god of war.* **2** (**God**) the creator of the universe in Christian, Jewish, and Muslim belief; the supreme being **3** a person or thing that is greatly admired or adored ♦ *Money is his god.* **the gods** *informal* the gallery of a theatre **goddess** *n* **1** a female god **2** a woman who is adored for her beauty ♦ *a Hollywood goddess* **godless** *adj* **godlessly** *adv* **godlessness** *n* **godly** *adj* **godlier, godliest, godliness** *n* **godchild** *n pl* **godchildren** a person in relation to his or her godparent **god-daughter** *n* a female godchild **godfather** *n* **1** a male godparent **2** the mastermind behind an illegal organization **godforsaken** *adj* (said about a place) wretched or dismal **godlike** *adj* **godmother** *n* a female godparent **godparent** *n* a person who promises at a child's baptism to help to bring it up as a Christian **godson** *n* a male godchild

godsend *n* something very helpful that comes to you unexpectedly

goggle *v* to stare with wide open eyes **goggles** *pl n* large close-fitting spectacles for protecting your eyes from wind, water, dust, etc.

going present participle of **go** **going** *n* **1** the state of the ground for walking or riding on ♦ *rough going* **2** rate of progress ♦ *It was good going to get there by noon.* **going** *adj* **1** available or remaining ♦ *Is there any apple pie going?* **2** (said about a price, etc.) current and fair ♦ *the going rate* **going-over** *n* **1** a thorough inspection or overhaul **2** a thrashing **goings-on** *pl n* surprising or suspicious behaviour or events

gold *n* **1** a yellow metal of very high value, a chemical element (symbol Au) **2** coins or other objects made of gold **3** a deep yellow colour **4** a gold medal, usually given as first prize **5** something very good or precious **gold** *adj* made of gold; coloured like gold **golden** *adj* **gold dust** *n* **1** fine particles of gold **2** something very valuable **golden age** *n* a time of great prosperity in the past **golden rule** *n* a basic principle which

should always be followed **golden syrup** *n* a kind of pale treacle **goldfish** *n pl* **goldfish** a small reddish Chinese carp kept in a bowl or pond **goldfish bowl** *n* **1** a round glass container for goldfish **2** a place or situation with no privacy **gold leaf** *n* gold that has been beaten into a very thin sheet **gold mine** *n* **1** a place where gold is mined **2** a source of great wealth ♦ *The shop was a little gold mine.* **gold-plated** *adj* coated with a thin layer of gold **goldsmith** *n* a person who makes things in gold

golf *n* a game played by hitting a small hard ball with clubs towards and into a series of holes **golfer** *n* **golf ball** *n* a ball used in golf

golly *interjection informal* an exclamation of surprise

gonad (say **goh**-nad) *n* an animal's reproductive organ, such as a testis or ovary

gondola (say **gon**-dəl-ə) *n* **1** a boat with high pointed ends, used on the canals in Venice **2** a cabin attached to a ski lift **gondolier** *n*

gone past participle of **go** **gone** *adj* departed or dead **gone** *prep* past ♦ *It's gone six o'clock.* **goner** *n* a person or thing that is dead, ruined, or doomed

gong *n* **1** a round metal plate that makes an echoing sound when it is struck **2** *informal* a medal or other award

good *adj* **better, best 1** having the right or desirable properties, satisfactory ♦ *good food* **2** appropriate or suitable ♦ *That would be a good thing to do.* **3** morally correct, virtuous **4** strictly following the principles of a religion or cause ♦ *a good Catholic* **5** kind ♦ *It was good of you to help us.* **6** (said about a child) well-behaved **7** enjoyable or satisfying ♦ *We had a really good time.* **8** healthy, giving benefit ♦ *Exercise is good for you.* **9** skilled or talented ♦ *a good driver* **10** thorough, considerable ♦ *Give it a good clean.* **11** used in exclamations ♦ *good God!* **good** *n* benefit or advantage ♦ *It's for your own good.* **goods** *pl n* **1** movable possessions **2** things that are bought and sold ♦ *leather goods* **3** (used before a noun) freight ♦ *a goods train* **goodness** *n* **1** the quality of being good **2** the beneficial or nourishing part of food ♦ *The goodness is in the gravy.* **goodness** *interjection* used to express surprise, anger, relief, etc. ♦ *Goodness knows.* ♦ *For goodness' sake!* **goody** *n pl* **goodies** a hero in a story or film ♦ *the goodies and the baddies* **goodbye** *interjection* an expression used when you leave someone **goodbye** *n* an instance of saying goodbye **good-for-nothing** *adj* worthless **good-for-nothing** *n* a worthless person **Good Friday** *n* the Friday before Easter **good-hearted** *n* kind and well-meaning **good-looking** *adj* (said about a person) attractive **good-tempered** *adj* having or showing good temper **goodwill** *n* **1** friendly or helpful feelings towards another person **2** the established custom or reputation of a business, considered as an asset that can be sold **goody-goody** *adj* smugly virtuous **goody-goody** *n pl* **goody-goodies** a smugly virtuous person **as good as** very nearly, almost ♦ *The war was as good as over.* ◊ In standard English, *good* cannot be used as an adverb. You can say *She's a good player* but not *She played good.* The adverb that goes with *good* is *well.*

goofy *adj* **goofier**, **goofiest** *informal* stupid or silly

goon *n informal* **1** a stupid person **2** a hired thug

goose *n pl* **geese** **1** a large waterbird with a long neck and webbed feet, larger than a duck **2** *informal* a foolish person **gooseflesh** *n pl n* skin that has turned rough with small bumps on it because of cold or fear **goose step** *n* a way of marching without bending the knees **goose-step** *v*

gooseberry *n pl* **gooseberries** **1** a small green fruit with a hairy skin **2** the thorny shrub which bears this fruit **3** an unwanted extra person

gore[1] *n* blood that has been shed, especially as a result of violence

gore[2] *v* to pierce a person or animal with a horn or tusk

gorge *n* a narrow steep-sided valley **gorge** *v* to eat a large amount greedily, to stuff yourself with food

gorgeous *adj* **1** strikingly beautiful

2 *informal* very pleasant ♦ *gorgeous weather* **gorgeously** *adv* **gorgeousness** *n*

gorilla *n* a large powerful ape of central Africa

gormless *adj informal* stupid, lacking sense

gory *adj* **gorier**, **goriest** **1** involving bloodshed ♦ *a gory battle* **2** covered with blood **gorily** *adv* **goriness** *n*

gosh *interjection informal* an exclamation of surprise

gosling (say **goz**-ling) *n* a young goose

gospel *n* **1** the teachings of Jesus Christ as recorded in the first four books of the New Testament **2** (**Gospel**) each of these books, describing the life and teachings of Jesus Christ **3** something true or reliable ♦ *You can take it as gospel.* **gospel music** *n* a style of black American evangelical religious singing

gossamer *n* **1** a fine filmy piece of cobweb made by small spiders **2** any flimsy delicate material

gossip *n* **1** casual talk especially about other people's affairs **2** a person who is fond of gossiping **gossip** *v* **gossiped**, **gossiping** to engage in or spread gossip **gossipy** *adj*

got past tense and past participle of *get* **have got to do it** must do it **to have got to** possess ♦ *Have you got a car?*

gouge (say gowj) *v* **1** to make a hole in a surface with a pointed object **2** to scoop or force something out by pressing it

goulash (say **goo**-lash) *n* a stew of meat and vegetables, seasoned with paprika

gourd (say goord) *n* the hard-skinned fleshy fruit of a climbing plant

gourmand (say **goor**-mənd) *n* a lover of food, a glutton

gourmet (say **goor**-may) *n* a person who appreciates good food and drink

govern *v* **1** to rule people with authority; to conduct the affairs of a country, state, organization, etc. **2** to influence, determine, or guide something ♦ *Everything she does is governed by her religious faith.* **3** to keep something under control ♦ *You need to govern your temper better.* **governance** *n* the act or manner of governing **governess** *n* a woman employed to teach children in a private household **government** *n* **1** the group of people who are in charge of the public affairs of a country **2** the system or method of governing **governmental** *adj* **governor** *n* **1** a person who governs a province or colony **2** the head of each state in the USA **3** a member of the governing body of a school or other institution **4** the person in charge of a prison

gown *n* **1** a loose flowing piece of clothing, especially a woman's long dress **2** protective clothing worn by medical staff **3** a loose robe worn as official dress by judges, etc. **gowned** *adj*

GP *abbr* general practitioner

GPS *abbr* Global Positioning System, a satellite navigational system

grab *v* **grabbed**, **grabbing** **1** to take hold of something suddenly **2** to take advantage of something without hesitating ♦ *He grabbed the opportunity.* **3** *informal* to make a favourable impression on someone ♦ *How does this idea grab you?* **grab** *n* a sudden clutch or an attempt to seize something

grace *n* **1** beauty and elegance of movement **2** good manners or elegance of manner ♦ *At least he had the grace to apologize.* **3** a person's favour ♦ *I seem to have fallen from grace.* **4** a delay before something has to be completed or paid, allowed as a favour ♦ *Can you give me a week's grace?* **5** a short prayer of thanks said before or after a meal **6** God's loving mercy towards mankind **grace** *v* **1** to bring honour to an event by agreeing to be present ♦ *I hope you will grace us with your presence.* **2** to make something more attractive **graceful** *adj* **gracefully** *adv* **gracefulness** *n* **graceless** *adj* **gracious** *adj* **graciously** *adv* **graciousness** *n*

grade *n* **1** a level of rank, quality, or value ♦ *a salary grade* **2** the mark given to a student for his or her standard of work **3** a class of people or things of the same rank or quality, etc. **4** a gradient or slope **grade** *v* **1** to arrange people or things in grades ♦ *The eggs are next graded by size.* **2** to give a grade to a student **3** to reduce the slope of a road **gradation** *n* a process of gradual change, or a stage in such a process

gradient (say **gray**-di-ənt) *n* the steepness of a slope ♦ *The road has a gradient of 1 in*

10.

gradual *adj* **1** taking place or developing slowly and in stages ♦ *a gradual improvement* **2** (said about a slope) not steep **gradually** *adv*

graduate[1] (say **grad**-yoo-ət) *n* a person who holds a university or college degree

graduate[2] (say **grad**-yoo-ayt) *v* **1** to complete a university or college degree **2** to progress to something more advanced **3** to mark something into regular divisions or units of measurement **graduation** *n*

graffiti (say grə-**fee**-ti) *n* writing or drawings scribbled or sprayed on a wall or other public place

graft *n* **1** a shoot from one tree fixed into a cut in another to form a new growth **2** a piece of living tissue transplanted surgically to replace diseased or damaged tissue ♦ *a skin graft* **3** an operation in which tissue is transplanted **4** *informal* hard work **graft** *v* **1** to put a graft in or on something **2** to join one thing to another **3** *informal* to work hard

grain *n* **1** a cereal plant such as wheat or rice, used as food **2** a small hard seed of a cereal plant **3** a small hard particle of a substance ♦ *a grain of sand* **4** the smallest possible amount ♦ *There isn't a grain of truth in this story.* **5** the pattern of lines made by fibres in wood, paper, etc. or by layers in rock or coal, etc.; the direction of threads in woven fabric **6** a unit of weight, about 65 milligrams **grainy** *adj* **grainier**, **grainiest**, **graininess** *n*

gram *n* a metric unit of mass equal to one thousandth of a kilogram

grammar *n* **1** the study of words and of the rules for their formation and their relationships to each other in sentences **2** the rules for using the words of a language correctly **3** a book about these rules **4** speech or writing judged as good or bad according to these rules ♦ *His grammar is appalling.* **grammatical** *adj* **grammatically** *adv* **grammar school** *n* a secondary school for pupils of high academic ability

gran *n informal* grandmother

granary *n pl* **granaries** a storehouse for

grain

grand adj **1** large or impressive, splendid **2** of the highest rank, most important ♦ the Grand Duke Alexis **3** haughty and pompous ♦ She puts on a grand manner. **4** informal very enjoyable or satisfactory ♦ We had a grand time. **grand** n **1** a grand piano **2** informal a thousand pounds or dollars ♦ five grand **grandee** n a person of high rank **grandeur** n impressive beauty or splendour **grandiose** adj **1** trying to seem impressive, pompous **2** imposing, planned on a large scale **grandiosity** n **grandly** adv **grandness** n **grandad** n grandfather **grandchild** n pl **grandchildren** the child of your son or daughter **granddaughter** n the daughter of your son or daughter **grandfather** n the father of a person's father or mother **grandfather clock** n a clock in a tall wooden case **grandma** n grandmother **grandmother** n the mother of a person's father or mother **grandpa** n grandfather **grandparent** n a grandfather or grandmother **grandson** n the son of a person's son or daughter **grand total** n the final amount after everything is added up

granite (say **gran**-it) n a hard grey stone for building

granny n pl **grannies** informal grandmother

grant v **1** to give or allow someone what he or she has asked for ♦ We have decided to grant your request. **2** to admit or agree that something is true ♦ I grant that your offer is generous. **3** to give a right or property to someone formally or legally **grant** n a sum of money given by a government or public body for a particular purpose ♦ a research grant

granule (say **gran**-yool) n a small grain **granular** adj **granulate** v **granulation** n

grape n a green or purple berry growing in clusters on vines, used for making wine **grapefruit** n pl **grapefruit** a large round yellow citrus fruit with an acid juicy pulp **grapevine** n **1** the kind of vine on which grapes grow **2** a way by which news spreads unofficially

graph n a diagram consisting of a line or lines showing the relationship between corresponding values of two quantities

graph v to draw a graph of something

graphic (say **graf**-ik) adj **1** to do with drawing, lettering, or engraving ♦ the graphic arts **2** giving a vivid description ♦ a graphic account of the fight **graphics** pl n **1** the use of diagrams in calculation or in design **2** diagrams, lettering, and drawings, especially pictures that are produced by a computer ♦ a computer game with superb graphics **graphical** adj **graphically** adv **graphic design** n the art or skill of combining text and pictures in advertisements, magazines, or books

graphite n a soft black form of carbon used in lead pencils, as a lubricant, and in nuclear reactors

-graphy suffix forming nouns which are the names of descriptive sciences (as in geography) or methods of writing, drawing, or recording (as in photography)

grapple v **1** to struggle or wrestle at close quarters **2** to struggle to deal with a problem, etc. ♦ I've been grappling with this essay all day.

grasp v **1** to seize and hold something firmly, especially with your hands or arms **2** to understand something ♦ He couldn't grasp what we meant. **grasp** n **1** a firm hold or grip **2** a person's ability to obtain, achieve or understand something ♦ The title is now within his grasp. **grasping** adj

grass n **1** any of a group of common wild low-growing plants with green blades and stalks that are eaten by animals **2** any plant of the family that includes cereal plants, reeds, and bamboos **3** ground covered with grass ♦ Keep off the grass. **grass** v **1** to cover an area of ground with grass **2** informal to inform the police of some criminal activity **grassy** adj **grassier**, **grassiest**, **grasshopper** n a jumping insect that makes a shrill chirping noise **grass roots** n the ordinary people who form a group

grate¹ n **1** a metal frame that keeps fuel in a fireplace **2** the recess of a fireplace

grate² v **1** to shred food into small pieces by rubbing it against a jagged surface **2** to have an irritating effect **grater** n

grateful adj feeling or showing that you value or are thankful for something that has been done for you **gratefully** adv

gratify v **gratifies**, **gratified**, **gratifying** 1 to give pleasure to someone 2 to satisfy a feeling or desire ♦ *Please gratify our curiosity.* **gratification** n **gratifying** adj

grating¹ adj 1 sounding harsh and unpleasant ♦ *a grating laugh* 2 irritating

grating² n a screen of spaced metal or wooden bars placed across an opening

gratis (say **grah**-tiss) adv, adj free of charge

gratitude n being grateful

gratuitous (say grə-**tew**-ə-əs) adj 1 given or done without good reason, uncalled for ♦ *a gratuitous insult* 2 given or done without payment **gratuitously** adv

gratuity (say grə-**tew**-iti) n pl **gratuities** formal money given to someone who has done you a service, a tip

grave¹ n 1 a hole dug in the ground to bury a corpse 2 the place where a corpse is buried ♦ *She often visits her father's grave.* **gravestone** n a stone monument over a grave **graveyard** n a burial ground beside a church

grave² adj 1 serious, causing great anxiety ♦ *grave news* 2 solemn ♦ *a grave expression* **gravely** adv

grave accent (say grahv) n a backward-sloping mark over a vowel, as in à la carte

gravel n small stones mixed with coarse sand **gravel** v **gravelled**, **gravelling** to cover something with gravel **gravelly** adj

gravitas n dignity or solemnity of manner

gravity n 1 the force that pulls all objects in the universe towards each other 2 the force that attracts bodies towards the centre of the earth 3 seriousness ♦ *the gravity of the situation* **gravitate** v **gravitation** n **gravitational** adj

gravy n the juices that come out of meat while it is cooking and made into a sauce

graze¹ v 1 to feed on growing grass ♦ *cattle grazing in the fields* 2 to put animals into a field to eat the grass

graze² v 1 to scrape the skin from a part of your body 2 to touch something lightly in passing **graze** n a raw place where the skin has been scraped

grease n 1 any thick semi-solid oily substance, especially one used as a lubricant 2 melted animal fat **grease** v to put grease on or in something **greasy** adj **greasier**, **greasiest**, **greasily** adv **greasiness** n

great adj 1 much above average in size, amount, or intensity 2 larger than others of a similar kind ♦ *the great auk* 3 of remarkable ability or character, important ♦ *one of the great painters* 4 doing something frequently or intensively or very well ♦ *She is a great reader.* 5 informal excellent ♦ *That's a great idea.* 6 used to describe a family relationship that is older or younger by one generation, as in *great-grandfather* or *great-niece* **great** n an outstanding or distinguished person ♦ *He is one of the literary greats.* **greatly** adv **greatness** n **Great War** n the First World War

greed n an excessive desire for food or wealth **greedy** adj **greedier**, **greediest**, **greedily** adv **greediness** n

Greek adj to do with Greece, its people, or their language **Greek** n 1 a member of the people living in ancient or modern Greece 2 their language **Grecian** adj to do with ancient Greece

green adj 1 of the colour between blue and yellow, the colour of growing grass 2 covered with grass or with growing leaves 3 unripe or unseasoned ♦ *This wood is still green and will not burn well.* 4 inexperienced or naive 5 pale and sickly-looking 6 concerned with protecting the natural environment **green** n 1 green colour 2 a green substance or material 3 a green light 4 a piece of grassy land in the middle of a village 5 a grassy area specially prepared for playing a game on ♦ *the 18th green* 6 (**Green**) informal a member of an environmentalist party or movement **greens** pl n green vegetables, such as cabbage and spinach **greenery** n green foliage or growing plants **greenness** n **greeny** adj **green belt** n an area of open land round a town, where the amount of building is restricted **greenfield site** n a site for a new factory, etc. which has not previously been built on **green fingers** n skill in making plants grow **greenfly** n pl **greenflies** 1 a small green insect that sucks juices from plants **2** these insects collectively **greengrocer** n a shopkeeper selling vegetables and fruit **greenhouse** n a building with glass sides and roof, where plants are protected from cold weather **greenhouse effect** n the process by which heat from the sun is trapped in the lower atmosphere, because visible radiation from the sun passes through the atmosphere more easily than infrared radiation emitted from the earth's surface **greenhouse gas** n any of the gases, especially carbon dioxide and methane, that are found in the earth's atmosphere and contribute to the greenhouse effect **green light** n **1** a signal to proceed on a road **2** permission to go ahead with a project

Greenwich Mean Time (say **gren**-ich) n the time on the line of longitude which passes through Greenwich in London

greet v **1** to speak in a welcoming way to someone who arrives or who you meet **2** to receive something with a certain reaction ♦ *The news was greeted with dismay.* **3** (said about a sight or sound) to present itself to someone **greeting** n

gregarious (say gri-**gair**-iəs) adj **1** fond of company **2** living in flocks or communities **gregariously** adv **gregariousness** n

grenade n a small bomb thrown by hand or fired from a rifle

grew past tense of **grow**

grey adj **1** of the colour between black and white, coloured like ashes or lead **2** (said about hair) turning grey with age **3** (said about the weather) cloudy and dull, without sun **4** dull, lacking individuality ♦ *an office full of grey men* **grey** n **1** grey colour **2** a grey substance or material; grey clothes **3** a grey horse **grey** v to become or make something grey **greyish** adj **greyness** n **grey area** n an aspect of a subject that does not easily fit into any category and so is difficult to deal with **grey matter** n **1** the material of the brain and spinal cord **2** informal intelligence

grid n **1** a network of squares printed on a map, etc., numbered for reference **2** a framework of spaced parallel bars **3** an arrangement of electric-powered cables

or gas-supply lines for distributing current or supplies over a large area **gridiron** n a framework of metal bars for cooking on **gridlock** n a traffic jam that affects a large number of intersecting streets **gridlocked** adj **grid reference** n a set of numbers that allows you to describe the exact position of something on a map

griddle n a round iron plate for cooking things on

grief n **1** deep sorrow, especially at a person's death **2** something causing deep sorrow **grieve** v

grievance n a real or imagined cause for complaint

grievous (say **gree**-vəs) adj formal extremely serious ♦ *a grievous error* **grievously** adv

grill n **1** a device on a cooker that radiates heat downwards **2** a gridiron for cooking food on **3** a dish of meat or other food cooked using a grill **4** a restaurant that serves grilled food **5** another spelling of *grille* **grill** v **1** to cook food using a grill **2** informal to question someone closely and severely

grille n a grating of bars or wires covering a window, piece of machinery, etc.

grim adj **grimmer, grimmest 1** stern or severe in appearance **2** unattractive and depressing ♦ *a grim place* **3** worrying, not hopeful ♦ *The future looks grim.* **grimly** adv **grimness** n

grimace (say grim-**ayss**) n a twisted expression on the face showing pain or disgust, or intended to cause amusement **grimace** v to make a grimace

grime n dirt in a layer on a surface or on the skin **grimy** adj **griminess** n

grin v **grinned, grinning** to smile broadly, showing your teeth **grin** n a broad smile, showing your teeth

grind v past tense and past participle **ground 1** to crush something or be crushed into grains or powder **2** to sharpen or smooth something by rubbing it on a rough surface **3** to rub things harshly together **4** to work a machine by turning a handle **grind** n **1** the act of grinding **2** hard dull work ♦ *the daily grind* **grinder** n **grinding** adj

grip v **gripped**, **gripping** 1 to take a firm hold of something ♦ *He gripped my hand.* 2 to deeply affect someone ♦ *She was gripped by fear.* 3 to hold a person's attention ♦ *The opening chapter really gripped me.* **grip** n 1 a firm grasp or hold 2 the power of gripping ♦ *These shoes don't have enough grip.* 3 a way of holding something, especially a tennis racket, golf club, etc. 4 understanding ♦ *He has a good grip of his subject.* 5 control or influence ♦ *The whole country is in the grip of lottery fever.* 6 the part of a tool or machine, etc. that grips things 7 the part of a weapon or device designed to be held 8 a travelling bag 9 a hairgrip

gripe v 1 *informal* to grumble or complain 2 to cause colic **gripe** n *informal* a grumble or complaint

gristle n tough flexible tissue of animal bodies, especially in meat **gristly** adj

grit n 1 tiny pieces of stone or sand 2 a kind of coarse sandstone, used for millstones 3 courage and determination **grit** v **gritted**, **gritting** to spread grit on an icy road or path **to grit your teeth** 1 to clench your teeth 2 to summon up your courage and determination when facing a difficult situation

gritty adj **grittier**, **grittiest** 1 full of or covered with grit 2 showing courage and determination **grittiness** n

groan v 1 to make a long deep sound expressing pain, grief, or disapproval 2 to make a creaking noise under a heavy load **groan** n a groaning sound

grocer n a shopkeeper who sells food and other household goods **grocery** n pl **groceries**

grog n 1 a drink of alcoholic spirits, usually rum, mixed with water 2 *informal* alcoholic drink **groggy** adj **groggier**, **groggiest**, **groggily** adv **grogginess** n

groin n 1 the hollow between your thigh and the trunk of the body 2 *informal* the area of the body where the genitals are situated

groom n 1 a person whose job is to look after horses 2 a bridegroom **groom** v 1 to clean and brush a horse or other animal 2 to make something neat and tidy 3 to prepare

or train a person for a career or position ♦ *She was being groomed for stardom.*

groove n 1 a long narrow channel in the surface of a hard material 2 a way of living that has become a habit or routine **groove** v to make a groove or grooves in something **grooved** adj

grope v to feel about with your hands for something you cannot see

gross (say grohss) adj 1 unattractively large or bloated 2 not refined, vulgar ♦ *gross manners* 3 glaringly obvious, blatant ♦ *gross negligence* 4 total, without anything being deducted ♦ *gross income* (Compare net².) 5 *informal* repulsive, disgusting **gross** n pl **gross** twelve dozen, 144 ♦ *ten gross* **gross** v to produce or earn an amount as total profit or income

grotesque (say groh-tesk) adj 1 fantastically ugly or distorted 2 so inappropriate that it is shocking or ridiculous **grotesque** n a comically distorted figure **grotesquely** adv **grotesqueness** n

grotto (say grot-oh) n pl **grottoes** or **grottos** a small cave, especially an artificial and brightly decorated one in a garden

grotty adj **grottier**, **grottiest** *informal* 1 unpleasant and of poor quality 2 unwell

grouch n *informal* 1 a bad-tempered person who is always grumbling 2 a complaint or grumble **grouch** v *informal* to complain or grumble **grouchy** adj

ground¹ n 1 the solid surface of the earth, especially contrasted with the air surrounding it 2 earth or soil 3 land of a certain kind ♦ *marshy ground* 4 an area of land used for a certain purpose, especially a sports field ♦ *a football ground* 5 the amount of a subject that is dealt with ♦ *The course covers a lot of ground.* 6 a position, point of view, or advantage ♦ *The party needs to make up some ground in the polls.* 7 a prepared surface to be worked upon in painting or embroidery **grounds** pl n 1 an area of enclosed land belonging to a large house or an institution 2 solid particles that sink to the bottom of a liquid ♦ *coffee grounds* 3 reasons for doing or believing something ♦ *You have no grounds for complaint.* **ground** v 1 to prevent an aircraft or pilot from flying ♦ *All aircraft are grounded because of the fog.* **2** to give someone a good basic training in a subject **3** to run a ship aground **4** *informal* to keep a child indoors as a punishment **grounding** n **groundless** adj **groundlessly** adv **groundbreaking** adj innovative **ground control** n the people and machinery that control and monitor an aircraft or spacecraft from the ground **ground floor** n the floor of a building at ground level **ground rule** n a basic principle **groundsman** n pl **groundsmen** a person employed to look after a sports ground **groundswell** n **1** a build-up of opinion in a large section of the population **2** heavy slow-moving waves caused by a distant or recent storm **groundwork** n work that lays the basis for something **ground zero** n the point on the earth's surface directly above or below an exploding nuclear bomb

ground² past tense and past participle of *grind*

group n **1** a number of people or things gathered, placed, or classed together, or working together for some purpose **2** a number of musicians who play together, especially a pop group **3** a number of commercial companies under one owner **group** v **1** to form or gather into a group or groups **2** to place people or things in a group, or to organize them into groups **grouping** n

grouse n pl **grouse** a game bird with a plump body and feathered feet

grout n thin fluid mortar used to fill narrow cavities **grout** v to fill something in with grout

grove n a group of trees, a small wood

grovel v **grovelled**, **grovelling** **1** to lie or crawl on the ground in a show of humility or fear **2** to act in an excessively humble way, e.g. by apologizing a lot

grow v **grew**, **grown** **1** (said about a living thing) to develop ♦ *Tadpoles grow into frogs.* **2** (said about a plant) to be capable of developing somewhere ♦ *Rice grows in warm climates.* **3** to increase in size, degree, or quantity; to become larger or greater **4** to become something gradually ♦ *It grew dark.* **5** to arise or develop from something **6** to make or let something grow ♦ *He's growing a beard.* **7** to plant and look after flowers, crops, etc. ♦ *She grows roses.* **growable** adj **grower** n **grown-up** adj adult **grown-up** n *informal* an adult **to grow on** to become more acceptable or attractive to someone ♦ *It's a CD that grows on you.* **to grow up** to become an adult

growl v **1** (said especially about a dog) to make a low threatening sound **2** to say something in a low grating voice **growl** n a growling sound **growler** n

growth n **1** the process of growing or developing **2** something that is growing or has grown ♦ *a thick growth of weeds* **3** a tumour or other abnormal formation of tissue in the body

grub n **1** the thick worm-like larva of an insect, especially a beetle **2** *informal* food **grub** v **grubbed**, **grubbing** **1** to dig around in the surface of the soil **2** to search laboriously for something, to rummage **grubby** adj **grubbier**, **grubbiest**, **grubbily** adv **grubbiness** n

grudge n a feeling of resentment or ill will ♦ *She isn't the sort of person who bears a grudge.* **grudge** v **1** to resent having to give or allow something **2** to resent that someone has achieved something and feel that they do not deserve it ♦ *I don't grudge him his success.* **grudging** adj **grudgingly** adv

gruel (say *groo-əl*) n a thin porridge made by boiling oatmeal in milk or water **gruelling** adj extremely tiring or difficult **gruesome** adj

gruff adj **1** (said about a voice) rough and low in pitch **2** abrupt or surly in manner **gruffly** adv **gruffness** n

grumble v **1** to complain in a bad-tempered way **2** to rumble ♦ *Thunder was grumbling in the distance.* **grumble** n a complaint, especially a bad-tempered one **grumbler** n

grumpy adj **grumpier**, **grumpiest** bad-tempered and sulky **grumpily** adv **grumpiness** n

grunt v **1** (said about an animal, especially a pig) to make a short, low snorting sound **2** (said about a person) to make a sound like this ♦ *When I asked if I could go in he just grunted.* **grunt** *n* a grunting sound

guano (say **gwah**-noh) *n* dung of seabirds, used as a fertilizer

guarantee *n* **1** a formal promise that a product will be repaired or replaced free if it develops a fault within a specified period ♦ *a watch with a five-year guarantee* **2** a formal promise given by one person to another that he or she will be responsible for something to be done by a third person **3** something that makes it certain that something will happen ♦ *A good idea is no guarantee of success.* **4** a promise or assurance ♦ *She gave me a guarantee that it would not happen again.* **5** something offered or accepted as security **guarantee** *v* **guaranteed**, **guaranteeing** **1** to give or be a guarantee for something ♦ *If you are not satisfied, we guarantee to refund your money.* **2** to promise to pay another person's debts if he or she does not **3** to promise something, to state something with certainty ♦ *I guarantee that you will enjoy the show.* **4** to make it certain that something will happen ♦ *Money does not guarantee happiness.* **guarantor** *n*

guard *v* **1** to watch over and protect someone or something, to keep them safe **2** to keep watch over someone, especially to prevent them from escaping **3** to try to prevent something by taking precautions ♦ *We must guard against errors.* **guard** *n* **1** a state of watchfulness or alertness for possible danger ♦ *Keep the prisoners under close guard.* **2** someone who guards a person or place **3** a railway official in charge of a train **4** a body of soldiers or others guarding a place or a person **5** a device or part used to protect against injury ♦ *a fire guard* **6** a defensive position taken by a person in boxing, fencing, cricket, etc. **Guards** *pl n* the royal household troops of the British army **guarded** *adj* **guardsman** *n pl* **guardsmen** **1** a soldier belonging to a body of guards **2** a soldier of a regiment of Guards **off guard** or **off your guard** unprepared against attack or surprise **on guard** or **on your guard** alert for possible danger or difficulty, vigilant

guardian *n* **1** someone who guards or protects **2** a person who is legally responsible for a child whose parents have died **guardianship** *n* **guardian angel** *n* an angel thought of as watching over and protecting a person or place

guerrilla (say gə-ril-ə) *n* a member of a small unofficial army that fights a stronger official army by making surprise attacks

guess *v* **1** to form an opinion or make a statement or give an answer without enough information to be sure you are correct ♦ *I don't know the answer so I'll have to guess.* **2** to estimate or identify something correctly by guessing ♦ *It wasn't difficult to guess the reason.* **3** *informal* to suppose or believe something ♦ *I guess we ought to be going.* **guesser** *n* **guesswork** *n*

guest *n* **1** a person who is invited to visit another person's home or is being entertained to a meal **2** a person staying at a hotel **3** a person who takes part in another's show as a visiting performer ♦ *a guest artist*

guff *n informal* empty talk, nonsense

guffaw *n* a coarse noisy laugh **guffaw** *v* to laugh noisily

guide *n* **1** a person who leads others or shows them the way **2** a person employed to point out places of interest on a journey or visit **3** something that influences your behaviour or decisions ♦ *My first impressions of people are usually a good guide.* **4** a book giving information about a place or subject ♦ *Guide to Italy* **5** a thing that marks a position, guides the eye, or steers moving parts **Guide** *n* a member of a girls' organization corresponding to the Scout Association **guide** *v* **1** to show someone the way or how to do something **2** to direct the course of something **3** to advise someone or influence their behaviour or decisions ♦ *I'll be guided by you.* **guidance** *n* **guidebook** *n* a book of information about a place for visitors or tourists **guide dog** *n* a dog trained to lead a blind person **guidelines** *pl n* statements that give general advice about how something should be done

guild *n* a society of people with similar

interests and aims

guile (say giyl) n cunning or craftiness **guileful** adj **guileless** adj **guilelessly** adv **guilelessness** n

guillotine (say gil-ə-teen) n **1** a machine with a heavy blade sliding down in grooves, used for beheading people **2** a device with a long blade for cutting paper or metal **guillotine** v **1** to execute someone with a guillotine **2** to cut something with a guillotine

guilt n **1** the fact of having committed some offence or crime **2** a feeling that you are to blame for something or have failed to do something you should have done **guiltless** adj **guilty** adj **guiltier**, **guiltiest**, **guiltily** adv **guiltiness** n

guinea (say gin-ee) n a former British gold coin worth 21 shillings (£1.05)

guinea pig n **1** a small furry rodent without a tail, kept as a pet or a laboratory animal **2** a person or thing used as the subject of an experiment

guise (say giyz) n an outward manner or appearance put on in order to conceal the truth, a pretence ♦ *They exploited him under the guise of friendship.*

guitar (say gi-tar) n a stringed musical instrument, played by plucking or strumming with the fingers or a plectrum **guitarist** n

Gujarati (say goo-jer-ah-ti) n **1** a native or inhabitant of the Indian state of Gujarat **2** a language descended from Sanskrit and spoken mainly in Gujarat

gulf n **1** an area of sea, larger than a bay, that is partly surrounded by land **2** a deep chasm or ravine **3** a wide difference in opinions or outlook **the Gulf** n the Persian Gulf

gull n a large seabird with long wings

gullet n the passage by which food goes from the mouth to the stomach

gullible (say gul-i-bəl) adj easily deceived or tricked **gullibility** n

gully n pl **gullies** a narrow channel cut by water or made for carrying rainwater away from a building

gulp v **1** to swallow food or drink quickly or greedily **2** to make a loud swallowing noise, especially because of fear **gulp** n **1** the

act of gulping **2** a large mouthful of liquid drunk quickly

gum[1] n the firm flesh in which the teeth are rooted **gummy** adj **gummier**, **gummiest**, **gumminess** n

gum[2] n **1** a sticky substance produced by some trees and shrubs **2** a glue for sticking paper together, made from this **3** chewing gum **4** a hard transparent sweet made of gelatine ♦ *a fruit gum* **5** a gum tree **gum** v **gummed**, **gumming** to smear or cover something with gum; to stick things together with gum **gum tree** n a tree that produces gum, especially a eucalyptus

gumption (say gump-shən) n informal common sense and initiative

gun n **1** a weapon that fires bullets or shells from a metal tube **2** a starting pistol **3** a device that forces a substance out of a tube ♦ *a grease gun* **gun** v **gunned**, **gunning** to shoot someone with a gun ♦ *He was gunned down in broad daylight.* **gunner** n **1** a soldier in an artillery unit, the official term for a private in such a unit **2** a member of an aircraft crew who operates a gun **3** a naval warrant officer in the past who was in charge of a battery of guns **gunnery** n the construction and firing of large guns **gunfire** n the repeated firing of guns **gunman** n pl **gunmen** a man armed with a gun **gunpoint** n **at gunpoint** while being threatened by someone holding a gun **gunpowder** n an explosive made from a powdered mixture of potassium nitrate, sulphur, and charcoal **gunshot** n a shot fired from a gun **gunsmith** n a person who makes and repairs small firearms

gunge n informal a sticky or messy mass of a substance **gunge** v **gunged**, **gungeing** informal to clog something with gunge ♦ *The pipe is completely gunged up.*

gurdwara (say gerd-wah-rə) n a Sikh temple

gurgle n a low bubbling sound **gurgle** v to make a low bubbling sound

Gurkha (say ger-kə) n a member of a Hindu people in Nepal, forming regiments in the British army

guru (say goor -oo) n pl **gurus** **1** a Hindu spiritual teacher or head of a religious sect

2 an influential teacher, a mentor

gush *v* **1** to flow or pour out quickly in great quantities **2** to keep saying how much you admire or are pleased with something, especially in an exaggerated way **gush** *n* **1** a sudden or great stream of liquid **2** an outpouring of feeling, effusiveness **gushing** *adj*

gusset *n* a piece of cloth inserted in a garment to strengthen or enlarge it **gusseted** *adj*

gust *n* **1** a sudden rush of wind **2** a burst of rain or smoke or sound **gust** *v* to blow in gusts **gusty** *adj* **gustily** *adv*

gusto *n* great enjoyment or energy in doing something

gut *n* **1** the lower part of the alimentary canal, the intestine **2** the stomach or belly **3** a thread made from the intestines of animals, used especially for violin and racket strings **guts** *pl n* **1** the internal organs of the abdomen **2** *informal* courage and determination **3** the inside parts or essence of something ♦ *the guts of a problem* **gut** *v* **gutted, gutting 1** to remove the guts from a fish **2** to destroy or remove the inside of a building ♦ *The factory was gutted by fire.* **gutless** *adj* **gutsy** *adj* **gutsier, gutsiest 1** showing courage and determination **2** greedy **gutted** *adj* extremely disappointed or upset **gut feeling** *n* a feeling or reaction that you have instinctively

guttural (say **gut**-er-əl) *adj* throaty, harsh-sounding ♦ *a guttural voice* **gutturally** *adv*

guy[1] *n* **1** *informal* a man **2** *informal* a person of either sex ♦ *Hi, guys.* **3** a figure in the form of a man dressed in old clothes, representing Guy Fawkes and burnt on 5 November **guy** *v* to make fun of someone or something

guy[2] *n* a rope or line fixed to the ground to secure a tent

guzzle *v* to eat or drink something greedily **guzzler** *n*

gym (say jim) *n* *informal* **1** a gymnasium **2** gymnastics

gymkhana (say jim-**kah**-nə) *n* an event in which people, especially children, take part in horse-riding competitions

gymnasium *n pl* **gymnasiums** or **gymnasia** a hall or building equipped for physical training and exercise

gymnastics *pl n* **1** physical exercises performed to develop the muscles or demonstrate agility and coordination **2** other forms of physical or mental agility **gymnast** *n* **gymnastic** *adj*

gynaecology (say giy-ni-**kol**-əji) *n* the scientific study of the female reproductive system and its diseases **gynaecological** *adj* **gynaecologist** *n*

gypsy *n pl* **gypsies** a member of a travelling people of Europe

gyrate (say jiy-**rayt**) *v* to move round in circles or spirals **gyration** *n* **gyratory** *adj*

Hh

H[1] the eighth letter of the English alphabet

H[2] *abbr* (said about a pencil lead) hard

ha *interjection* an exclamation of triumph or surprise

ha. *abbr* hectare(s)

haberdashery *n* small articles, such as buttons, threads, and ribbons, used in sewing and dressmaking **haberdasher** *n*

habit *n* **1** something that you do often; a settled way of behaving ♦ *I got into the habit of walking home after work.* **2** something that is hard to give up ♦ *a smoking habit* **3** the long dress worn by a monk or nun **habitual** *adj* **habitually** *adv* **habituate** *v* **habituation** *n*

habitat (say **hab**-i-tat) *n* the natural environment of an animal or plant **habitable** *adj* **habitation** *n*

hack[1] *v* **1** to cut or chop something roughly **2** to kick someone hard ♦ *He hacked at my shins.* **3** to break into a computer system **hacker** *n*

hack[2] *n* **1** a person paid to do hard and uninteresting work, especially as a writer **2** a horse for ordinary riding

hacking[1] *n* riding on horseback at an ordinary pace

hacking² *adj* (said about a cough) dry and frequent

hackles *pl n* **1** the hairs along an animal's back, which rise when it is angry or alarmed **2** the long feathers on the neck of a domestic cock and other birds

hackneyed (say **hak**-nid) *adj* (said about a phrase or idea) used so often that it is no longer interesting

hacksaw *n* a saw for cutting metal, with a short blade in a frame

had past tense and past participle of *have*

haddock *n pl* **haddock** a sea fish like cod but smaller, used for food

Hades (say **hay**-deez) *n* **1** *Greek Mythology* the underworld; the place where the spirits of the dead go **2** hell

hadn't *v informal* had not

haematology (say hee-mə-**tol**-əji) *n* the scientific study of blood and its diseases

haemoglobin (say heem-ə-**gloh**-bin) *n* the red substance that carries oxygen in the blood

haemophilia (say heem-ə-**fil**-iə) *n* a disease that causes a person to bleed severely from even a slight cut, because the blood does not clot quickly **haemophiliac** *n* **haemophilic** *adj*

haemorrhage (say **hem**-er-ij) *n* bleeding, especially inside a person's body **haemorrhage** *v* to bleed heavily

haemorrhoids (say **hem**-er-oidz) *pl n* varicose veins at or near the anus

hag *n* an ugly old woman

haggard *adj* looking ill or very tired

haggis *n* a Scottish dish made from sheep's heart, lungs, and liver

haggle *v* to argue about price or terms when settling a bargain

ha-ha *n* a ditch strengthened by a wall

haiku (say **hiy**-koo) *n pl* **haiku** or **haikus** a Japanese poem of 17 syllables, in three lines of five, seven, and five

hail¹ *n* **1** pellets of frozen rain falling in a shower **2** something coming in great numbers ♦ *a hail of blows* **hail** *v* **1** to come down as hail ♦ *It is hailing.* **2** to come down or send something down like hail **hailstone** *n* a pellet of hail **hailstorm** *n* a storm of hail

hail² *v* **1** to call out to someone in order to attract your attention ♦ *I tried to hail a taxi.* **2** to acclaim someone or something **to hail from** to come from ♦ *She hails from Ireland.*

hair *n* **1** each of the fine thread-like strands that grow from the skin of people and animals or on certain plants **2** a mass of these, especially on a person's head **hairless** *adj* **hairy** *adj* **hairier, hairiest, hairiness** *n* **hairbrush** *n* a brush for smoothing your hair **haircut** *n* **1** shortening the hair by cutting it **2** the style in which someone's hair is cut **hairdo** *n pl* **hairdos** the style of a woman's hair **hairdresser** *n* a person whose job is to cut and arrange hair **hairdressing** *n* **hairdryer** *n* an electrical device for drying the hair with warm air **hairgrip** *n* a strong springy clip for holding the hair in place **hairline** *n* **1** the edge of a person's hair round the face **2** a very thin line ♦ *a hairline fracture* **hairpin** *n* a U-shaped pin for keeping the hair in place **hairpin bend** *n* a sharp U-shaped bend in a road **hair-raising** *adj* terrifying **hair-splitting** *n* making distinctions of meaning that are too small to be of any real importance **hairstyle** *n* a way in which someone's hair is cut or arranged

hajj *n* the pilgrimage to Mecca which all Muslims are expected to make at least once **haji** *n* a Muslim who has made the pilgrimage to Mecca

haka (say **hah**-ka) *n NZ* a warlike Maori dance with chanting, or an imitation of this by a New Zealand sports team before a match

hake *n pl* **hake** a sea fish of the cod family

halal (say hah-**lahl**) *adj* to do with meat prepared according to Muslim law **halal** *n* meat prepared according to Muslim law

halcyon (say **hal**-si-ən) *adj* (said about a time in the past) happy and prosperous ♦ *halcyon days*

hale *adj* strong and healthy ♦ *hale and hearty*

half *n pl* **halves 1** each of two equal or corresponding parts into which a thing is divided **2** either of the two equal periods into which a sports game or performance is divided **3** a lower-price ticket for a child on a bus or train **4** *informal* half a pint of beer

half adj amounting to a half ♦ a half share **half** adv 1 partly, not completely ♦ The meat is only half-cooked. **2** to a certain extent ♦ I half expected to find that nobody else had turned up. **3** informal half past ♦ half seven **half a dozen** n six **half-and-half** adj being half of one thing and half of another **half-baked** adj not well planned or thought out **half board** n provision of bed, breakfast, and one main meal at a hotel or guest house **half-hearted** adj not very enthusiastic **half-heartedly** adv **half-hour** n **1** a period of thirty minutes **2** a point of time 30 minutes after any hour o'clock **half-hourly** adv **half mast** n a point about halfway up a mast, to which a flag is lowered as a mark of respect for a person who has died **half measure** n a policy lacking thoroughness **halfpenny** n pl **halfpennies** for separate coins or pl **halfpence** for a sum of money a former British coin worth half a penny **half-term** n a short holiday in the middle of a school term **half-time** n the interval between the two halves of a game of football or hockey, etc. **half-truth** n a statement conveying only part of the truth **halfway** adj, adv **1** at a point between and equally distant from two others **2** to some extent ♦ halfway decent **halfwit** n a stupid person **half-witted** adj stupid

halibut n pl **halibut** a large flat fish used for food

halitosis n unpleasant-smelling breath

hall n **1** the room or space just inside the front entrance of a house **2** a large room or a building for meetings, meals, concerts, etc. **3** a large country house **hallway** n

hallelujah interjection, n another spelling of alleluia

hallmark n **1** an official mark made on gold, silver, and platinum to show its quality **2** a characteristic by which something is easily recognized **hallmarked** adj marked with a hallmark

hallo interjection, n pl **hallos** another spelling of hello

hallowed adj honoured as being holy

Hallowe'en n 31 October, traditionally a time when ghosts and witches are believed to appear

hallucinate (say ha-loo-sin-ayt) v to experience hallucinations **hallucination** n **hallucinatory** adj **hallucinogen** n **hallucinogenic** adj

halo n pl **haloes** or **halos 1** a circle of light shown round the head of a holy person in paintings, etc. **2** a circle of diffused light round a luminous body such as the sun or moon **haloed** adj

halogen (say hal-ə-jən) n any of the five chemically related elements fluorine, chlorine, bromine, iodine, and astatine

halt n **1** a temporary stop, an interruption of progress ♦ Work came to a halt. **2** a minor stopping place on a railway line **halt** v to stop or bring something to a stop **halter** n **1** a rope or strap put round a horse's head so that it can be led or fastened to something **2** a style of dress top held up by a strap passing round the back of the neck, leaving the back and shoulders bare **halting** adj **haltingly** adv

halve v **1** to divide or share something equally between two **2** to reduce something by half

ham¹ n **1** meat from the upper part of a pig's leg, dried and salted or smoked **2** the back of the thigh and buttock **ham-fisted** adj clumsy

ham² n **1** informal an actor who overacts **2** informal someone who operates a radio to send and receive messages as a hobby **ham** v **hammed**, **hamming** informal (usually **to ham it up**) to overact or exaggerate your actions

hamburger n a flat round cake of minced beef served fried, often eaten in a bread roll

hamlet n a small village, usually without a church

hammer n **1** a tool with a heavy metal head used for breaking things and driving in nails **2** something shaped or used like this, e.g. part of the firing device in a gun, or the part of a piano mechanism that strikes the string **3** an auctioneer's mallet **4** a metal ball of about 7 kg, attached to a wire for throwing in an athletic contest **hammer** v **1** to hit or beat something with a hammer **2** to strike loudly **3** to force someone to

learn something by frequently repeating it
♦ *The rules of grammar were hammered into
us at school.* **4** *informal* to defeat someone
utterly

hammock *n* a hanging bed of canvas or
rope network

hamper[1] *n* **1** a large box-shaped basket with
a lid, used for carrying food, cutlery, etc.
on a picnic **2** a hamper or box of food as a
present

hamper[2] *v* to prevent someone or
something from moving or working freely

hamster *n* a small rat-like rodent with cheek
pouches for carrying grain

hamstring *n* **1** any of the five tendons at the
back of a person's knee **2** the great tendon
at the back of an animal's hock **hamstring** *v*
past tense and past participle **hamstrung**
to cripple a person or animal by cutting the
hamstrings

hand *n* **1** the end part of the arm beyond
the wrist **2** a pointer on a clock or dial **3** a
manual worker in a factory, farm, etc.;
a member of a ship's crew ♦ *All hands on
deck!* **4** the set of cards dealt to a player in
a card game, or one round of a card game
5 either the right or left side or direction
♦ *The queen sat at his right hand.* **6** each of
two contrasted sides in an argument, etc.
♦ *on the other hand* **7** active help ♦ *Give him
a hand with these boxes.* **8** control or care ♦ *I
know my money is in safe hands.* **9** someone's
influence or role in a situation or activity
♦ *Many people had a hand in it.* **10** a pledge
of marriage ♦ *He asked for her hand.* **11** skill
or style of workmanship ♦ *My mother has a
light hand with pastry.* **12** a person's style
of handwriting **13** a unit of 4 inches (10.16
cm) used in measuring a horse's height
14 *informal* a round of applause ♦ *Please
give them all a big hand.* **hand** *v* **1** to give
or pass something to someone ♦ *Hand it
over.* **2** to help a person into a vehicle, etc.

handful *n pl* **handfuls 1** as much as can be
carried in one hand **2** a small number of
people or things **3** *informal* a person who
is difficult to control or deal with **handy** *adj*
handier, **handiest 1** convenient to handle
or use **2** conveniently placed for being
reached or used **3** good at using your hands

handily *adv* **handiness** *n* **handbag** *n* a
small bag for holding a purse and personal
items **handball** *n* **1** a game in which a ball
is hit with the hand in a walled court **2** (in
football) the foul of touching the ball
with the hand or arm **handbook** *n* a small
book giving useful facts or instructions
handbrake *n* a brake operated by hand,
used to hold a vehicle that has already
stopped **handcuff** *n* each of a pair of linked
metal rings for fastening a prisoner's wrists
together **handcuff** *v* to put handcuffs
on a prisoner **handily** *adv* in a handy way
handiwork *n* **1** something made by hand
2 something done or made by a person
handmade *adj* made by hand rather than
machine **hand-me-down** *n* a piece of
clothing that has been passed on from
another person **handout** *n* **1** money given
to a needy person **2** a sheet of information
given out in a lesson or lecture **hand-
pick** *v* to choose people or things carefully
hand-picked *adj* **handrail** *n* a narrow
rail for people to hold on to as a support
handset *n* **1** the part of a telephone that
you hold up to speak into and listen to
2 a hand-held control device for a piece
of electronic equipment **handshake** *n*
shaking hands with someone as a greeting
or to show you agree to something **hands-
on** *adj* involving practical experience of
using equipment ♦ *a hands-on computing
course* **handspring** *n* a somersault in which
a person lands first on the hands and then
on the feet **handstand** *n* balancing on
your hands with your feet in the air **hand-
to-hand** *adj* (said about fighting) at close
quarters **handwriting** *n* **1** writing done by
hand with a pen or pencil **2** a person's style
of writing **handwritten** *adj* written by hand
handyman *n pl* **handymen** a person who
is good at or is employed to do household
repairs and other odd jobs

handicap *n* **1** anything that lessens your
chance of success or makes progress
difficult **2** a physical or mental disability
3 a disadvantage imposed on a superior
competitor in golf or horse racing in
order to make the chances more equal
handicap *v* **handicapped**, **handicapping**

1 to impose a handicap on someone **2** to put someone at a disadvantage **handicapped** *adj* suffering from a physical or mental disability **handicapper** *n*

handkerchief *n pl* **handkerchiefs** or **handkerchieves** a small square of cloth, usually carried in a pocket, for wiping your nose

handle *n* **1** the part of a thing by which it is to be held, carried, or controlled **2** a means of understanding or approaching something **handle** *v* **1** to touch, feel, or move something with your hands **2** to be able to be driven or operated in a certain way ♦ *The car handles well.* **3** to manage or cope with something ♦ *Don't worry, I can handle it.* **4** to deal with someone or something ♦ *She knows how to handle people.* **5** to deal in goods **6** to discuss or write about a subject **handler** *n* **handlebar** *n* the bar, with a handle at each end, that steers a bicycle or motorcycle

handsome *adj* **1** good-looking **2** imposing and attractive ♦ *a handsome building* **3** generous ♦ *a handsome present* **4** (said about an amount) very large ♦ *a handsome profit* **handsomely** *adv* **handsomeness** *n*

hang *v* past tense and past participle **hung** or (in meaning 5) **hanged 1** to support or be supported from above so that the lower end is free **2** to attach a door or gate to hinges so that it swings freely to and fro, or to be attached in this way **3** to stick wallpaper to a wall **4** to decorate something with drapery or hanging ornaments ♦ *The tree was hung with lights.* **5** to execute or kill someone by hanging them from a rope that tightens round the neck, or to be executed in this way **6** to droop or lean ♦ *People hung over the gate.* **7** to remain in the air ♦ *Smoke hung over the area.* **8** to remain as something unpleasant ♦ *The threat is still hanging over him.* **hang** *n* the way something hangs **hanging** *n* a decorative piece of cloth hung on a wall **hangdog** *adj* having a miserable or guilty expression **hang-glider** *n* a device used for flying, consisting of a frame covered in fabric from which a person is suspended in a harness, controlling flight by their own movements **hang-glide** *v* **hang-gliding** *n* **hangnail** *n* torn skin at the root of a fingernail **hang-out** *n* a place where you live or often visit **hangover** *n* **1** a severe headache or other unpleasant after-effects from drinking too much alcohol **2** something left from an earlier time **hang-up** *n* an emotional problem or inhibition **to get the hang of** *informal* to learn how to do or use something **to hang about**, **around 1** to loiter or wait around **2** to not go away **to hang back 1** to remain behind **2** to show reluctance to act or move **to hang fire** to delay in taking action **to hang on 1** to hold tightly **2** *informal* to wait for a short time **3** to depend on something ♦ *Much hangs on this decision.* **4** to pay close attention to something ♦ *They hung on his every word.* **to hang out** *informal* to spend time relaxing or enjoying yourself **to hang up** to end a telephone conversation by replacing the receiver

hangar *n* a large shed where aircraft are kept

hanger *n* **1** a person who hangs things **2** a loop or hook by which something is hung **3** a shaped piece of wood, plastic, or metal for hanging clothes on ♦ *a coat hanger* **hanger-on** *n pl* **hangers-on** a person who attaches himself or herself to another in the hope of personal gain

hanker *v* to feel a longing for something

hanky *n pl* **hankies** *informal* a handkerchief

hanky-panky *n informal* **1** naughty behaviour, especially involving sexual activity **2** dishonest dealing

Hanukkah (say hah-nək-ə) *n* an eight-day Jewish festival of lights, beginning in December, commemorating the rededication of the Temple at Jerusalem in 165 BC

haphazard (say hap-**haz**-erd) *adj* done or chosen at random, not by planning **haphazardly** *adv*

hapless *adj* unlucky

happen *v* **1** to take place or occur **2** to do something by chance ♦ *I happened to see him.* **3** to be the fate or experience of someone or something ♦ *What happened to you?* **happening** *n*

happy adj **happier**, **happiest** 1 feeling or showing pleasure or contentment 2 fortunate ♦ *a happy coincidence* **happily** adv **happiness** n **happy-go-lucky** adj taking events cheerfully as they happen

harangue (say hə-**rang**) v to spend a long time criticizing someone aggressively **harangue** n a forceful and aggressive speech

harass (say **ha**-rəs) v to trouble and annoy someone continually

harbinger (say **har**-bin-jər) n a person or thing whose presence is a sign of the approach of something

harbour n a place where ships can shelter or unload **harbour** v 1 to keep a thought or feeling in your mind ♦ *I think she still harbours a grudge against them.* 2 to give shelter or refuge to someone ♦ *He was charged with harbouring a criminal.*

hard adj 1 firm, not yielding to pressure; not easily broken or cut 2 difficult to do or understand or answer 3 needing or using a lot of effort ♦ *a hard climb* 4 causing unhappiness, difficult to bear 5 strict, severe, and unsympathetic 6 (said about people) tough and aggressive 7 extreme and most radical ♦ *the hard left of the Labour party* 8 (said about information) not able to be disputed ♦ *I'll give you some hard facts.* 9 (said about weather) severe, frosty ♦ *a hard winter* 10 done with great force ♦ *a hard kick* 11 (said about drinks) strongly alcoholic 12 (said about drugs) strong and likely to cause addiction 13 (said about water) containing mineral salts that prevent soap from lathering freely and cause a hard coating to form inside kettles, water tanks, etc. 14 (said about currency) not likely to drop suddenly in value 15 (said about colours or sounds) harsh to the eye or ear 16 (said about consonants) sounding sharp not soft. The letter 'g' is hard in 'gun' and soft in 'gin'. **hard** adv 1 with great force or force, intensively ♦ *We worked hard.* ♦ *It's raining hard.* 2 with difficulty ♦ *hard-earned money* 3 so as to be hard ♦ *hard-baked* **harden** v **hardened** adj **hardener** n **hardship** n severe discomfort

or lack of the necessaries of life ♦ *a life of hardship* **hardy** adj **hardier**, **hardiest** 1 able to endure cold or difficult conditions 2 (said about plants) able to grow in the open air all the year round **hardiness** n **hardness** n **hardback** n a book bound in stiff covers **hardboard** n stiff board made of compressed wood pulp **hard cash** n coins and banknotes, not a cheque or a promise to pay later **hard copy** n a printed version on paper of computer data **hard core** n 1 the most committed or active members of a group 2 broken bricks and rubble used as a road foundation **hard disk** n a rigid disk fixed inside a computer, able to store large amounts of data **hard-headed** adj tough and realistic, not sentimental **hard-hearted** adj unfeeling or unsympathetic **hard labour** n heavy manual work as a punishment **hard line** n unyielding adherence to a firm policy **hardliner** n **hard-nosed** adj realistic and tough-minded **hard-pressed** adj 1 closely pursued 2 in difficulties **hard shoulder** n a strip of hardened land beside a motorway, for use by vehicles in an emergency **hard up** adj short of money **hardware** n 1 heavy military equipment such as tanks and missiles 2 the mechanical and electronic parts of a computer as opposed to the software 3 tools and household implements, etc. sold by a shop **hard-wearing** adj able to stand a lot of wear **hardwood** n the hard heavy wood obtained from deciduous trees, e.g. oak and teak

hardly adv 1 only just, scarcely 2 only with difficulty ◊ It is not acceptable in standard English to use 'not' with *hardly*, as in 'She can't hardly walk'.

hare n an animal like a rabbit but larger **hare** v to run rapidly **hare-brained** adj wild and foolish, rash ♦ *a hare-brained scheme* **harelip** n a birth defect consisting of a vertical slit in the upper lip

Hare Krishna (say **hah**-ri **krish**-nə) n a Hindu religious cult founded in the USA in 1966

harem (say **har**-eem) n 1 the women of a Muslim household, living in a separate part of the house 2 their apartments

hark v poetic to listen **to hark back** to return to an earlier subject

harlequin adj in mixed colours

harm n damage or injury **harm** v to damage or injure something or someone **harmful** adj **harmfully** adv **harmless** adj **harmlessly** adv **harmlessness** n

harmonica n n a small musical instrument played by passing it along the lips while blowing or sucking air

harmonium n a musical instrument with a keyboard, in which notes are produced by air pumped through brass reeds

harmony n pl **harmonies** 1 the combination of musical notes to produce chords which sound pleasant together 2 a sweet or melodious sound 3 being friendly to each other **harmonic** adj **harmonious** adj **harmoniously** adv **harmonize** v **harmonization** n

harness n 1 the straps and fittings put round a horse's head and neck to control it and fasten it to the cart, etc. that it pulls 2 fastenings resembling this, e.g. for attaching a parachute to a person's body **harness** v 1 to put a harness on a horse, etc. 2 to control and make use of resources ♦ Could we harness the power of the wind?

harp n a musical instrument consisting of strings stretched on a roughly triangular frame **harpist** n **harp** v **to harp on** to keep on talking about something in a tiresome way

harpoon n a spear-like missile with a rope attached **harpoon** v to spear something with a harpoon

harpsichord (say **harp**-si-kord) n a keyboard instrument with the strings sounded by a mechanism that plucks them **harpsichordist** n

harrier n 1 a hound used for hunting hares 2 a kind of falcon

harrowing adj very upsetting or distressing ♦ a harrowing film

harry v **harries**, **harried**, **harrying** 1 to harass or worry someone 2 to keep carrying out attacks on an enemy

harsh adj 1 rough and unpleasant, especially to the senses 2 severe or cruel ♦ harsh treatment **harshly** adv **harshness** n

hart n an adult male deer

harvest n 1 the time when farmers gather in the corn, fruit, or vegetables that they have grown 2 the season's yield or crop **harvest** v to gather in a crop **harvester** n

has v a form of have; used with a singular noun and with he, she, or it

has-been n pl **has-beens** informal a person who is no longer as famous or successful as he or she used to be

hash¹ n 1 a dish of cooked meat cut into small pieces and reheated with potatoes 2 a jumble or mess **hash** v to make meat into a hash

hash² n the symbol #

hashish n cannabis

Hasid n pl **Hasidim** a member of a devout mystical Jewish sect **Hasidic** adj

hasn't v informal has not

hassle n informal 1 something that is troublesome and annoying 2 harassment **hassle** v informal to harass or pester someone

haste n urgency of movement or action, great hurry **hasten** v **hasty** adj **hastier**, **hastiest**, **hastily** adv **hastiness** n

hat n 1 a covering for the head, worn out of doors 2 one of a person's positions or roles ♦ I'm wearing my managerial hat today. **hatter** n **hat-trick** n three successes in a row

hatch¹ n 1 an opening in a wall between two rooms, especially one used for serving food 2 a door in an aircraft, spacecraft, or submarine 3 an opening in a ship's deck, or the cover for this **hatchback** n a car with a sloping back, hinged at the top so that it can be opened

hatch² v 1 (said about a young bird, fish, or reptile) to emerge from its egg 2 (said about an egg) to open and produce a young animal 3 to cause eggs to produce young by incubating them 4 to plan or devise something ♦ They were hatching a plot. **hatch** n a newly hatched brood **hatchery** n pl **hatcheries**

hatchet n a light short-handled axe

hate n 1 extreme dislike 2 informal a hated person or thing **hate** v 1 to feel hatred towards someone 2 to dislike something greatly **3** *informal* to be reluctant to do something ♦ *I hate to interrupt you, but it's time to go.* **hateful** *adj* **hatred** *n*

haughty (say **haw**-ti) *adj* **haughtier**, **haughtiest** proud of yourself and looking down on other people **haughtily** *adv* **haughtiness** *n*

haul *v* **1** to pull or drag something with great effort **2** to transport something in a truck or cart **3** (said about a sailing ship) to turn course abruptly **haul** *n* **1** the amount of something gained as a result of effort ♦ *The robbers made a good haul.* **2** a number of fish caught at one time **3** a distance to be travelled ♦ *It's only a short haul from here.* **haulage** *n* **haulier** *n*

haunch *n* **1** the fleshy part of the buttock and thigh **2** the leg and loin of an animal as food

haunt *v* **1** (said about ghosts) to appear often in a place **2** to visit a place often **3** to stay in your mind ♦ *The memory haunts me.* **haunted** *adj* **haunting** *adj* **haunt** *n* a place often visited by the people named ♦ *The market is a favourite haunt of pickpockets.*

haute couture (say oht koo-**tewr**) *n* the designing and making of high-quality fashionable clothes by the leading fashion houses

haute cuisine (say oht kwee-**zeen**) *n* high-quality cooking

have *v* **has**; past tense and past participle **had 1** to possess, own, or hold something ♦ *We have two dogs.* **2** to contain something ♦ *This tin has biscuits in it.* **3** to experience or undergo something ♦ *You've had quite a shock.* **4** to do or engage in something ♦ *Will you have a talk with me later?* **5** to be obliged to do something ♦ *We have to go now.* **6** to put someone into a certain state ♦ *You had me worried.* **7** to allow or tolerate something ♦ *I won't have him bullied.* **8** to receive or accept something ♦ *We never have news of her now.* **9** to cause something to be done for you by someone else ♦ *I'm having my hair cut.* **10** to give birth to a baby **11** *informal* to cheat or deceive someone ♦ *We've been had!* **12** *informal* to have put someone at a disadvantage in an argument ♦ *Ah, you have me there.* **have** *auxiliary verb* used to form

the past tense of verbs ♦ *He has gone.* ♦ *We had expected it.* **to have it out** to settle a problem by discussing it openly and frankly

haven *n* a place of safety or refuge

haven't *v informal* have not

haversack *n* a strong bag carried on your back or over your shoulder

havoc (say **hav**-ək) *n* widespread destruction, great disorder

hawk¹ *n* **1** a bird of prey with very strong eyesight and rounded wings shorter than a falcon's **2** a person who is in favour of an aggressive foreign policy

hawk² *v* to clear the throat of phlegm noisily

hawk³ *v* to carry goods about and try to sell them **hawker** *n*

hawthorn *n* a thorny tree or shrub with small dark red berries, called haws

hay *n* grass that has been mown and dried for feeding to animals **hay fever** *n* an allergy caused by pollen or dust, in which the nose, throat, and eyes become inflamed and irritated **haystack** *n* a pile of hay firmly packed for storing, with a pointed or ridged top **haywire** *adj* badly disorganized, out of control ♦ *In the film a robot goes haywire.*

hazard (say **haz**-erd) *n* **1** a danger or risk **2** an obstacle, e.g. a pond or bunker, on a golf course **hazard** *v* to risk something **hazardous** *adj* **hazardously** *adv* **hazard lights** *pl n* flashing indicator lights on a vehicle, used especially to warn that the vehicle is stationary

haze *n* **1** thin mist **2** mental confusion or obscurity ♦ *He went to bed in an alcoholic haze.* **hazy** *adj* **hazier**, **haziest**, **hazily** *adv* **haziness** *n*

hazel *n* **1** a shrub or small tree with small edible nuts **2** a light brownish colour **hazelnut** *n*

HB *abbr* hard black, a medium grade of pencil lead

H-bomb *n* a hydrogen bomb

HE *abbr* His or Her Excellency

he *pronoun* **1** the male person or animal mentioned **2** a person, male or female ♦ *He who hesitates is lost.* **he** *n* a male animal ♦ *a he-goat*

head *n* **1** the part of the body containing the eyes, nose, mouth, and brain **2** the top or upper end or front of something ♦ *at the head of the procession* **3** the intellect, the imagination, the mind ♦ *Use your head!* **4** a mental ability, talent, or tolerance ♦ *She has a good head for heights.* **5** a person ♦ *It costs £12 a head.* **6** a number of animals ♦ *sixty head of dairy cattle* **7** the person in charge of a group or organization **8** a head teacher **9** a thing like a head in form or position, e.g. the rounded end of a pin, the cutting or striking part of a tool etc. **10** the foam on top of a glass of beer **11** (in place names) a promontory ♦ *Beachy Head* **heads** *n* the side of a coin on which a head appears, turned upwards after the coin has been tossed **head** *adj* chief or principal **head** *v* **1** to be at the head or top of something ♦ *United head the league table.* **2** to give a title or heading to something ♦ *The column is headed 'World's longest bridges'.* **3** (in football) to strike a ball with the head **4** to move in a particular direction ♦ *We headed for the coast.* **5** to force someone to turn back or aside by getting in front of them ♦ *Let's see if we can head him off.* **header** *n* (in football) a shot or pass made with the head **heading** *n* a word or words put at the top of a section of printing or writing as a title, etc. **headless** *adj* **heady** *adj* **headier, headiest, headiness** *n* **headache** *n* **1** a continuous pain in the head **2** *informal* a worrying problem **headcount** *n* a count of the number of people present **headdress** *n* an ornamental covering or band worn on the head **headgear** *n* a hat, helmet, or headdress **headlamp** *n* a headlight **headland** *n* a narrow piece of high land that sticks out into the sea **headlight** *n* **1** a powerful light at the front of a motor vehicle or railway engine **2** the beam from this **headlong** *adv, adj* **1** falling or plunging head first **2** in a hasty and rash way **headman** *n pl* **headmen** the chief or leader of a tribe **headmaster** *n* a male head teacher **headmistress** *n* a female head teacher **head of state** *n* the chief public representative of a country **head-on** *adj, adv* with the front parts colliding ♦ *a head-on collision* **headphones** *pl n* a radio or telephone receiver held over

the ears by a band fitting over the head **headquarters** *n* the place from which an organization is controlled **headroom** *n* the space between the top of a person's head and the ceiling **headset** *n* a set of headphones with a microphone attached **headship** *n* the position of head teacher in a school **headstone** *n* a stone set up on a grave **headstrong** *adj* determined to do as you want **head teacher** *n* the person in charge of a school **head-to-head** *adj, adv* involving two sides confronting each other **headwater** *n* the tributary stream that partly forms the source of a river **headway** *n* forward movement or progress **head wind** *n* a wind blowing from directly in front **a head start** an advantage you are given or get at the beginning **head over heels 1** turning your body upside-down in a circular movement **2** madly in love **in your head** in your mind, not written down **off the top of your head** without much careful thought **off your head** *informal* crazy **over your head** beyond your ability to understand **to go to a person's head 1** (said about alcohol) to make him or her slightly drunk **2** (said about success) to make him or her conceited **to keep your head** to remain calm in a crisis **to lose your head** to lose your self-control or panic **to make head or tail of** to be able to understand **to put heads together** to work together and share ideas **to turn someone's head** to make them conceited

headline *n* **1** a heading in a newspaper especially the largest one at the top of the front page **2** (**the headlines**) a summary of the main items of news

heal *v* **1** to become or make part of the body healthy again ♦ *The wound healed slowly* **2** to cure someone of a disease ♦ *He went around healing the sick.* **3** to put a situation right ♦ *How can we heal the rift between them?* **healer** *n*

health *n* **1** the condition of a person's body or mind ♦ *His health is bad.* **2** the state of being well and free from illness ♦ *She is bursting with health.* **healthful** *adj* **healthfully** *adv* **health centre** *n* an establishment where the practice of group of doctors is based **health food** n food that contains only natural substances and is thought to be good for your health **health service** n a public service providing medical care **health visitor** n a trained person visiting babies or sick or elderly people at their homes

healthy adj **healthier**, **healthiest 1** having or showing good health **2** producing good health ♦ a healthy diet **3** normal, natural, and desirable ♦ She has a healthy respect for her opponent. **4** of a satisfactory size or amount ♦ a healthy profit **healthiness** n **healthily** adv

heap n a mound or pile, especially an untidy one **heaps** pl n informal a great amount, plenty ♦ We have heaps of room. **heap** v **1** to put things in a pile **2** to put large quantities on something ♦ She heaped the plate with food.

hear v past tense and past participle **heard 1** to take in sounds through the ears **2** to listen to something ♦ I heard them on the radio. **3** to listen to and try a case in a law court **4** to receive news or information or a message or letter, etc. ♦ I hear that you have not been well. ♦ Have you heard from Maria? **hearer** n **hearing** n **1** the ability to hear ♦ My grandmother's hearing is poor. **2** the distance within which you can hear something ♦ He should not have said that in your hearing. **3** an opportunity to state your case ♦ She will be given a fair hearing. **4** a trial of a case in a law court, especially before a judge without a jury **hearing aid** n **hearsay** n

hearse (say herss) n a vehicle for carrying the coffin at a funeral

heart n **1** the hollow muscular organ that keeps blood circulating in the body by contracting rhythmically **2** the part of the body where this is **3** the centre of a person's emotions or affections or inmost thoughts ♦ She knew it in her heart. **4** the ability to feel emotion ♦ He has no heart. **5** courage or enthusiasm ♦ They may lose heart as the work gets harder. ♦ His heart isn't in it. **6** the central, innermost, or most important part of something ♦ the heart of the matter **7** the close compact head of a cabbage or lettuce

8 a symmetrical figure conventionally representing a heart **9** a playing card of the suit (called hearts) marked with red hearts **hearten** v to make a person feel cheerful or encouraged **heartening** adj **heartily** adv **1** in a hearty manner **2** very ♦ I'm heartily sick of it. **hearty** adj **heartier**, **heartiest 1** enthusiastic and sincere ♦ hearty congratulations **2** strong and healthy ♦ hale and hearty **3** (said about a meal or appetite) large **heartiness** n **heartless** adj not feeling any pity or sympathy **heartlessly** adv **heartlessness** n **heartache** n deep sorrow or grief **heart attack** n a sudden failure of the heart to work properly **heartbeat** n the pulsation of the heart **heartbreak** n overwhelming unhappiness **heartbreaking** adj causing overwhelming unhappiness **heartbroken** adj suffering from overwhelming unhappiness **heartburn** n a burning sensation in the lower part of the chest resulting from indigestion **heart failure** n gradual failure of the heart to work properly **heartfelt** adj felt deeply and sincerely ♦ my heartfelt thanks **heartland** n the central or most important part of an area or country **heart-rending** adj very distressing **heart-searching** n thinking hard about your own feelings and motives **heart-throb** n a good-looking man who women are attracted to **heart-to-heart** adj frank and personal ♦ a heart-to-heart talk **heart-to-heart** n a frank and personal conversation **heart-warming** adj making people feel happy and uplifted

hearth (say harth) n **1** the floor of a fireplace, or the area in front of it **2** the fireside as a symbol of the home

heat n **1** a form of energy produced by the movement of molecules **2** the quality of being hot **3** hot weather **4** an intense feeling of anger or excitement ♦ I tried to take the heat out of the situation. **5** the most intense part or stage of something **6** intense pressure or criticism ♦ The heat is on. **7** one of the preliminary rounds in a race or contest **heat** v to make something hot or warm, or to become hot or warm **heated** adj **heatedly** adv **heater** n **heating** n

heatstroke n illness caused by too much exposure to heat or sun **heatwave** n a long period of very hot weather

heath n 1 an area of flat uncultivated land with low shrubs 2 a small shrubby plant of the heather kind

heathen (say hee-thən) n a person who is not a believer in any of the world's chief religions, especially someone who is neither Christian, Jewish, nor Muslim **heathen** adj to do with heathens

heather n an evergreen plant or shrub with small purple, pink, or white bell-shaped flowers, growing on uplands

heave v past tense and past participle **heaved** or (in sense 3) **hove** 1 to lift or move something heavy with great effort 2 informal to throw something ♦ One of the youths heaved a brick at him. 3 to rise and fall regularly like waves at sea 4 to make an effort to vomit **heave** n 1 the act of heaving 2 Geology a sideways shift of strata at a fault in the earth's crust

heaven n 1 the place where God, angels, and good people after death are thought to live in some religions 2 informal a state of great happiness or enjoyment **heavens** pl n the sky as seen from the earth, in which the sun, moon, and stars appear **heavens** interjection an exclamation of surprise **heavenly** adj **heavenly body** n a planet, star, or other large mass in space

heavy adj **heavier, heaviest** 1 having great weight, difficult to lift or carry 2 of more than average weight, amount, or force ♦ a heavy cold ♦ heavy rain 3 (said about work) needing a lot of physical effort 4 severe or intense ♦ a heavy sleeper 5 dense ♦ a heavy mist 6 (said about ground) clinging, difficult to travel over 7 (said about food) stodgy and difficult to digest 8 (said about the sky) gloomy and full of clouds 9 clumsy or ungraceful in appearance, effect, or movement 10 full of sadness or worry ♦ with a heavy heart 11 important or serious ♦ a heavy subject to talk about 12 strict or harsh **heavily** adv **heaviness** n **heavy-duty** adj intended to withstand hard use **heavy-handed** adj clumsy or insensitive **heavy industry** n industry producing

metal, large machines, etc. **heavy metal** n a type of loud rock music with a strong beat **heavyweight** n 1 a person of more than average weight 2 the heaviest boxing weight 3 a person of great influence or importance **heavyweight** adj 1 of more than average weight 2 having great influence or importance

Hebrew n 1 a member of an ancient Semitic people living in what is now Israel and Palestine 2 the Semitic language of the Hebrews **Hebrew** adj 1 to do with the Hebrews 2 to do with Hebrew

heckle v to interrupt and harass a public speaker with awkward questions and abuse **heckler** n

hectare (say hek-tar) n a metric unit of area, equal to 10,000 square metres (2.471 acres)

hectic adj full of frantic activity ♦ a hectic day **hectically** adv

hecto- prefix one hundred (as in hectogram = 100 grams)

hector v to talk to someone in a bullying way **hectoring** adj

he'd v informal he had or he would

hedge n 1 a row of closely-planted bushes or shrubs forming a barrier or boundary 2 a means of protecting yourself against possible loss ♦ He bought diamonds as a hedge against inflation. **hedge** v 1 to surround an area with a hedge or other barrier 2 to avoid giving a direct answer or commitment 3 to reduce the possible loss on an investment by making other speculations or transactions **hedger** n **hedgerow** n

hedgehog n a small insect-eating animal with a pig-like snout and a back covered in stiff spines, able to roll itself up into a ball when attacked

hedonist (say hee-dən-ist) n someone who believes that pleasure is the main aim in life **hedonism** n **hedonistic** adj

heebie-jeebies pl n informal nervous anxiety or fear

heed v to pay attention to someone or something **heedless** adj **heedlessly** adv **heedlessness** n **to pay** or **take heed** to pay careful attention

hee-haw n a donkey's bray

heel n 1 the rounded back part of the human foot 2 the part of a sock or stocking covering this 3 the part of a boot or shoe that supports a person's heel 4 something like a heel in shape or position ♦ *the heel of a loaf* **heel** v 1 to repair the heel of a shoe or boot 2 (in rugby) to pass the ball with the heel

hefty adj **heftier**, **heftiest** 1 (said about a person) big and strong 2 (said about a thing) large, heavy, and powerful **heftily** adv **heftiness** n

hegemony (say hi-**jem**-ən-i or hi-**gem**-ən-i) n leadership, especially by one country or group over others

Hegira (say **hej**-i-rə) n the flight of Muhammad from Mecca in AD 622, from which the Muslim era is reckoned

heifer (say **hef**-er) n a young cow, especially one that has not given birth to a calf

height n 1 the measurement of someone or something from head to foot or from base to top 2 the quality of being tall or high 3 the distance of an object or position above ground level or sea level ♦ *What height are we flying at?* 4 a high place or area ♦ *I don't like heights.* 5 the highest degree of something ♦ *at the height of the holiday season* **heighten** v

heinous (say **hay**-nəs) adj very wicked ♦ *a heinous crime*

heir (say air) n a person who inherits property or rank from its former owner **heiress** n a female heir, especially to great wealth **heirloom** n a valuable possession that has been handed down in a family for several generations

held past tense and past participle of *hold*[1]

helicopter n a type of aircraft with horizontal revolving blades or rotors

helipad (say **hel**-i-pad) n a pad or landing ground for a helicopter

heliport (say **hel**-i-port) n a place equipped for helicopters to take off and land

helium (say **hee**-li-əm) n a chemical element (symbol He), a light colourless gas that does not burn

helix (say **hee**-liks) n pl **helices** (say **hee**-li-seez) a spiral, especially a three-dimensional one **helical** adj

hell n 1 in some religions, a place where wicked people are thought to be punished after they die 2 a place or state of great misery or suffering ♦ *The next few days were hell.* **hell** interjection an exclamation of anger **hellish** adj

he'll v informal he will

hello interjection, n an exclamation used in greeting or to attract someone's attention or express surprise, or to answer a telephone call

helm n the tiller or wheel for steering a ship or boat **at the helm** at the head of an organization, etc., in control

helmet n a strong covering worn to protect the head

help v 1 to make it easier for someone to do something by doing some of the work or giving them what they need ♦ *Can you help with the washing-up?* 2 to make it easier for something to happen, to improve a situation ♦ *This will help ease the pain.* 3 to prevent or avoid something ♦ *It can't be helped.* **help** n 1 the action of helping or being helped 2 a person or thing that helps ♦ *Thanks, you've been a great help.* 3 a person employed to help with housework 4 ICT (used before a noun) giving assistance in the form of displayed instructions ♦ *a help menu* **helper** n **helpful** adj **helpfully** adv **helpfulness** n **helping** n **helpless** adj **helplessly** adv **helplessness** n **helpline** n

helter-skelter adv in great haste **helter-skelter** n a tower-shaped structure at a funfair, with a spiral track outside it which people slide down **to help yourself to** 1 to serve yourself with food at a meal 2 to take something without permission

hem n the edge of a piece of cloth or clothing which has been turned under and sewn or fixed down **hem** v **hemmed**, **hemming** to turn and sew a hem on something **hemline** n

he-man n informal a strong masculine man

hemisphere n 1 a half of a sphere 2 either of the halves into which the earth is divided either by the equator (*the Northern* and *Southern hemisphere*) or by a line passing through the poles (*the Eastern hemisphere,* including Europe, Asia, and Africa; *the Western hemisphere*, the Americas) **hemispherical** *adj*

hemp *n* **1** the cannabis plant, from which coarse fibres are obtained for the manufacture of rope and cloth **2** the drug cannabis **hempen** *adj*

hen *n* a female bird, especially of the common domestic fowl **hen night** *n* a celebration for a woman who is about to get married, attended only by women

hence *adv* **1** from this time ♦ *five years hence* **2** for this reason **henceforth** *adv* from this time on, in future

henchman *n pl* **henchmen** a trusted supporter or follower, especially one who uses violence

henna *n* **1** a reddish-brown dye used especially on the hair **2** the tropical plant from which this is obtained **henna** *v* **hennaed, hennaing** to dye hair, etc. with henna

hepta- *prefix* seven

heptagon (say **hep**-tə-gən) *n* a geometric figure with seven sides

heptathlon (say hep-**tath**-lon) *n* an athletic contest for women in which each competitor takes part in seven events **heptathlete** *n*

her *pronoun* the form of *she* used as the object of a verb or after a preposition ♦ *We saw her.* **her** *adj* **1** of or belonging to her **2** used in women's titles ♦ *Her Majesty.*

herald *n* **1** an official in former times who made announcements and carried messages from a ruler **2** a person or thing that indicates the approach of something ♦ *Spring is the herald of summer.* **3** an official employed to record people's pedigrees and grant coats of arms **herald** *v* to show that something is approaching ♦ *Loud applause heralded the first runner to enter the stadium.*

heraldry *n* the study of coats of arms and the right to bear them **heraldic** *adj*

herb *n* **1** any plant whose leaves or seeds are used for flavouring or for making medicine **2** *Botany* any soft-stemmed plant that dies down to the ground after flowering **herbaceous** *adj* to do with or like herbs **herbal** *adj* to do with herbs, or made from

herbs **herbal** *n* a book that describes herbs and their uses in medicine and cooking **herbalist** *n* a dealer in medicinal herbs **herbicide** *n* a substance that is poisonous to plants, used to destroy unwanted vegetation **herbivore** *n* an animal that feeds on plants **herbivorous** *adj* feeding on plants **herby** *adj*

Herculean (say her-kew-lee-ən) *adj* needing great strength or effort ♦ *a Herculean task*

herd *n* **1** a large group of cattle or other animals feeding or staying together **2** a mass of people, a mob **herd** *v* **1** to move or gather in a large group ♦ *We all herded into the dining room.* **2** to look after a herd of animals

here *adv* **1** in or at or to this place **2** at this point in a process or a series of events **here** *interjection* used to attract someone's attention or as a reply in answer to a roll-call **hereabouts** *adv* near this place **hereafter** *adv formal* from now on or at some time in the future **the hereafter** *n* life after death **hereby** *adv formal* as a result of this, by this means **herein** *adv* in this place, document, etc. **hereinafter** *adv formal* in a later part of this document **hereof** *adv formal* of this document **herewith** *adv formal* with this letter ♦ *A cheque is enclosed herewith.*

hereditary (say hi-**red**-it-er-i) *adj* **1** inherited, able to be passed or received from one generation to another ♦ *a hereditary disease* **2** holding a position by inheriting it ♦ *a hereditary ruler*

heredity (say hi-**red**-iti) *n* inheritance of physical or mental characteristics from parents or ancestors

heresy (say **herri**-si) *n pl* **heresies** **1** a belief or opinion that disagrees with the accepted beliefs of the Christian Church, or with those on any subject **2** the holding of such an opinion

heretic (say **herri**-tik) *n* a person who holds a heresy or is guilty of heresy **heretical** *adj*

heritable *adj* able to be inherited

heritage *n* **1** the things that have been or may be inherited **2** valued things such as historic buildings and traditions that have been passed down from previous generations

hermaphrodite (say her-**maf**-rə-diyt) *n* a person or animal that has both male and female sexual organs or other sexual characteristics **hermaphroditic** *adj*

hermetic *adj* with an airtight closure ♦ *a hermetic seal* **hermetically** *adv*

hermit *n* **1** a person who has withdrawn from human society and lives in solitude for religious reasons **2** a person who lives alone away from other people **hermitage** *n*

hernia *n* an abnormal condition in which a part or organ of the body pushes through a wall of the cavity (especially the abdomen) that normally contains it

hero *n pl* **heroes 1** a man who is admired for his brave or noble deeds **2** the chief male character in a story, play, or poem **heroic** *adj* **heroically** *adv* **heroism** *n*

heroine *n* **1** a woman who is admired for her brave or noble deeds **2** the chief female character in a story, play, or poem **hero worship** *n* excessive admiration for someone **hero-worship** *v* **hero-worshipped**, **hero-worshipping** to admire someone excessively **hero-worshipper** *n*

heroin *n* a powerful sedative drug prepared from morphine, used medically and by addicts ◊ Do not confuse this word with *heroine*, which has a different meaning.

Herr (say hair) *n pl* **Herren** the title of a German man, equivalent to *Mr*

herring *n* a silvery North Atlantic fish much used for food

hers *possessive pronoun* used to refer to a thing or things belonging to a female person or animal already mentioned ♦ *This bag must be hers.* ♦ *Hers are best.* ◊ It is incorrect to write *her's*.

herself *pronoun* the form of *her* used in reflexive constructions (e.g. *She cut herself*) and for emphasis (e.g. *She herself told me* or *She told me herself*)

hertz *n pl* **hertz** a unit of frequency of electromagnetic waves, equal to one cycle per second

hesitate *v* **1** to be slow to speak, act, or move because you feel uncertain or reluctant, to pause in doubt **2** to be

reluctant to do something ♦ *He wouldn't hesitate to break the rules if it suited him.* **hesitant** *adj* **hesitancy** *n* **hesitantly** *adv* **hesitation** *n*

hetero- *prefix* other or different

heterogeneous (say het-er-ə-**jee**-niəs) *adj* made up of people or things that are unlike each other

heterosexual *adj* feeling sexually attracted to people of the opposite sex **heterosexual** *n* a heterosexual person **heterosexuality** *n*

het up *adj informal* angry and agitated ♦ *What is she so het up about?*

hew *v past participle* **hewn** or **hewed 1** to chop or cut something with an axe or sword, etc. **2** to cut a hard material into shape **hewer** *n* **hewn** *adj*

hexagon (say **heks**-ə-gən) *n* a geometric figure with six sides **hexagonal** *adj*

hexagram *n* a six-pointed star formed by two intersecting triangles

hey *interjection* an exclamation used to attract attention or to express surprise or interest

heyday *n* the period when someone or something is at its most successful or popular ♦ *He was a superb player in his heyday.*

HGV *abbr* heavy goods vehicle

hi *interjection* used as a friendly greeting

hiatus (say hiy-**ay**-təs) *n pl* **hiatuses** a pause or gap in a sequence or series

hibernate (say **hiy**-bər-nayt) *v* (said about an animal or plant) to spend the winter in a state like deep sleep **hibernation** *n*

Hibernian (say hiy-**ber**-niən) *adj* to do with Ireland

hibiscus (say hib-**isk**-əs) *n* a cultivated shrub or tree with brightly coloured trumpet-shaped flowers

hiccup, **hiccough** *n* **1** a high gulping sound made when your breath is briefly interrupted **2** a brief hitch or setback **hiccup** *v* **hiccuped**, **hiccuping** to make the sound of a hiccup **hiccups** *pl n* an attack of hiccuping

hide[1] *v* **hid**, **hidden 1** to put or keep something out of sight, to prevent something from being seen **2** to keep something secret **3** to conceal yourself ♦ *There was nowhere to hide.* **hide** *n* a camouflaged shelter used to observe wildlife at close quarters **hid hidden hiding** *n* **hidden agenda** *n* a person's secret but real motive for doing something **hide-and-seek** *n* a children's game in which one player looks for others who are hiding **hideaway** *n* a hiding place, especially somewhere quiet away from people **hideout** *n* a hiding place, especially one used by someone who has broken the law

hide² *n* an animal's skin, especially when tanned or dressed

hideous *adj* extremely ugly or unpleasant **hideously** *adv* **hideousness** *n*

hiding *n* **1** a thrashing or beating **2** *informal* a severe defeat

hierarchy (say **hiyr**-ark-i) *n pl* **hierarchies 1** an organization or system that ranks people one above another according to the power or authority that they hold **2** an arrangement according to relative importance **hierarchical** *adj*

hieroglyph (say **hiyr**-ə-glif) *n* **1** one of the pictures or symbols used in ancient Egypt and elsewhere to represent sounds, words, or ideas **2** a written symbol with a secret or cryptic meaning **hieroglyphic** *adj*

hi-fi *adj pl* **hi-fis** *informal* high fidelity **hi-fi** *n informal* equipment for reproducing recorded sound with very little distortion

high *adj* **1** reaching a long way upwards, extending above the normal or average level ♦ *high hills* **2** situated far above the ground or above sea level ♦ *high clouds* **3** measuring a specified distance from base to top ♦ *two metres high* **4** ranking above others in importance or quality ♦ *High Admiral.* ♦ *the higher animals* **5** great in amount, value, or intensity ♦ *high temperatures* ♦ *high prices* **6** (said about a period or movement) at its peak ♦ *high summer* **7** noble or virtuous ♦ *high ideals* **8** (said about a sound or voice) having rapid vibrations, not deep or low **9** *informal* under the influence of drugs or alcohol **high** *n* **1** a high point, level, or figure ♦ *Exports reached a new high.* **2** an area of high barometric pressure **3** *informal* a

state of euphoria **high** *adv* **1** in, at, or to a high level or position ♦ *They flew high above us.* **2** in or to a high degree ♦ *Feelings were running high.* **highly** *adv* **high chair** *n* a small chair with long legs used by a baby or small child at mealtimes **High Church** *n* the section of the Church of England that gives an important place to ritual and to the authority of bishops and priests **high-class** *adj* of high quality **high commission** *n* an embassy of one Commonwealth country in another **high commissioner** *n* the head of a high commission **High Court** *n* the supreme court dealing with civil law cases **Higher** *n* the advanced level of the Scottish Certificate of Education **higher education** *n* education above the level given in schools, especially to degree level **highest common factor** *n* the highest number that can be divided exactly into each of two or more numbers **high fidelity** *n* reproduction of sound with little or no distortion **high-flyer** *n* a person with the capacity to be very successful **high frequency** *n* (in radio) a frequency of 3 to 30 megahertz **high-handed** *adj* using authority in an arrogant way **high jinks** *pl n* boisterous fun or mischief **high jump** *n* an athletic competition in which competitors jump over a high horizontal bar **highland** *n* (also **highlands**) mountainous country **Highlands** *n* the mountainous northern part of Scotland **highlander** *n* **high-level** *adj* **1** involving important or high-ranking people ♦ *high-level negotiation.* **2** (said about a computer language) designed for convenience in programming, often by resembling ordinary language **high life** *n* an extravagant or luxurious way of living **highlight** *n* **1** the most interesting or outstanding feature of something ♦ *the highlight of the tour* **2** a light or bright area in a painting, etc. **3** a light-coloured streak in a person's hair **highlight** *v* **1** to draw special attention to something **2** to emphasize a section of text using a highlighter pen **highly strung** *adj* nervous and easily upset **high-minded** *adj* having strong moral principles **Highness** *n* the title used in speaking of or to a prince or princess ♦ *Your Highness.* **high-pitched** *adj* (said about a voice or sound) high **high priest** *n* the chief priest of a non-Christian religion **high-profile** *adj* involving much publicity ♦ *a high-profile court case* **high-rise** *adj* (said about a building) with many storeys **high school** *n* a secondary school **high seas** *pl n* the open seas not under any country's jurisdiction **high-speed** *adj* operating at great speed **high spirits** *pl n* cheerful and lively behaviour **high-spirited** *adj* **high street** *n* the main street of a town, with shops, etc. **high-tech** *adj* using or involved in high technology **high technology** *n* advanced technology, especially in electronics **high tide** *n* the tide at its highest level **highway** *n* 1 a public road 2 a main route by land, sea, or air **highwayman** *n pl* **highwaymen** a man, usually on horseback, who held up and robbed passing travellers

highbrow *adj* very intellectual, cultured

hijack *v* to seize control of an aircraft, ship, or vehicle while it is in transit in order to steal its goods, take its passengers hostage, or force it to a new destination **hijack** *n* a hijacking **hijacker** *n*

hike *n* 1 a long walk, especially a cross-country walk taken for pleasure 2 *informal* a sharp increase in something ♦ *a price hike* **hike** *v* 1 to go on a hike 2 *informal* to increase a price sharply **hiker** *n*

hilarious *adj* extremely funny **hilariously** *adv* **hilarity** *n*

hill *n* 1 a raised area of land, not as high as a mountain 2 a slope in a road 3 a heap or mound **hilly** *adj* **hillier**, **hilliest**, **hilliness** *n* **hillock** *n* **hillside** *n* the sloping side of a hill

hilt *n* the handle of a sword, dagger, or knife **to the hilt** completely ♦ *I support you to the hilt.*

him *pronoun* the form of *he* used as the object of a verb or after a preposition

himself *pronoun* the form of *him* used in reflexive constructions (e.g. *He cut himself*) and for emphasis (e.g. *He himself had said it, He told me himself*)

hind¹ *adj* situated at the back ♦ *hind legs* **hindmost** *adj* furthest back **hindquarters** *pl n* an animal's rear legs and

hind parts **hindsight** *n* looking back on an event with knowledge or understanding that you did not have at the time

hind² *n* a female deer

hinder (say **hin**-der) *v* to get in someone's way or make things difficult for them

Hindi (say **hin**-di) *n* one of the official languages of India

hindrance *n* something that hinders

Hindu *n* a person whose religion is Hinduism **Hindu** *adj* to do with Hindus or Hinduism

Hinduism (say **hin**-doo-izm) *n* a major religion and philosophy of the Indian subcontinent, including belief in reincarnation and the worship of a large number of gods

Hindustani (say hin-də-**stah**-ni) *n* 1 a group of languages and dialects spoken in NW India, especially Hindi and Urdu 2 the dialect of Hindi spoken in Delhi, widely used throughout India

hinge *n* 1 a joint on which a lid, door, or gate, etc. turns or swings 2 a natural joint working in the same way 3 a small piece of gummed paper for fixing stamps in an album **hinge** *v* 1 to attach or be attached by a hinge or hinges 2 to depend on something ♦ *Everything hinges on this meeting.*

hint *n* 1 a slight indication, a suggestion made indirectly 2 a very small trace of something ♦ *white with a hint of pink* 3 a small piece of practical information ♦ *household hints* **hint** *v* to make a hint

hinterland *n* a district lying inland beyond a coast or port or other centre

hip¹ *n* the bony part at the side of the body between the waist and the thigh **hips** *pl n* the measurement round the body here **hipped** *adj*

hip² *n* the fruit of the wild rose

hip³ *adj informal* aware of and understanding the latest trends

hippie *n* another spelling of *hippy*

hippo *n pl* **hippos** *informal* a hippopotamus

Hippocratic oath (say hip-ə-**krat**-ik) *n* an oath, formerly taken by people beginning medical practice, to observe the code of professional behaviour

hippodrome *n* 1 (in names) a theatre or

concert hall **2** (in ancient Greece or Rome) a course for chariot or horse races

hippopotamus n pl **hippopotamuses** or **hippopotami** a large African river animal with massive jaws, short legs, and thick dark skin

hippy n informal pl **hippies** a young person who joins with others to live in an unconventional way

hire v **1** to pay to use something temporarily **2** to pay for someone's services **3** to lend something for payment ♦ He hires out bicycles. **hire** n the act of hiring ♦ boats for hire **hireable** adj **hirer** n **hire purchase** n buying something by paying in regular instalments

hirsute (say herss-yoot) adj formal hairy

his adj **1** of or belonging to him ♦ That is his book. **2** used in men's titles ♦ His Majesty. **his** possessive pronoun the thing or things belonging to him ♦ That book is his.

Hispanic (say hiss-pan-ik) adj **1** to do with Spain or other Spanish-speaking countries **2** to do with the Spanish-speaking people of the USA

hiss v **1** to make a sound like that of s ♦ The snakes were hissing. **2** to express disapproval in this way **hiss** n a hissing sound

histamine (say hist-ə-min) n a chemical compound present in all body tissues, causing some allergic reactions

history n pl **histories 1** the study of past events, especially of human affairs **2** what happened in the past, either in general or in connection with a particular person or thing **3** a continuous methodical record of important past events **4** an interesting or eventful past ♦ The house has quite a history. **historian** n **historic** adj famous or important in history ♦ a historic town ♦ a historic meeting **historical** adj **1** that actually existed or took place in the past ♦ The novel is based on historical events. **2** to do with history or based on things that happened in the past ♦ historical research **historically** adv

histrionic (say histri-on-ik) adj dramatic or theatrical in manner **histrionics** pl n dramatic behaviour intended to attract people's attention

hit v past tense and past participle **hit**, **hitting 1** to aim a blow at someone or something **2** to strike a target ♦ The bridge was hit by a missile. **3** to come against something with force ♦ The car hit a tree. **4** to have a bad effect on someone; to cause someone to suffer ♦ Famine has hit the poor countries. **5** to be realized by someone ♦ It suddenly hit me what she was talking about. **6** to propel a ball with a bat, racket, or club; to score runs or points in this way **7** to reach or come to something ♦ I can't hit the high notes. **hit** n **1** a blow or stroke **2** a shot that hits its target **3** a success, especially by being popular ♦ You are certainly a hit with my family. **4** a successful record, show, etc.

hit-and-miss adj done or happening at random **hit-and-run** adj injuring someone in an accident and driving off without stopping ♦ a hit-and-run driver

hitch v **1** to raise or pull something with a slight jerk **2** to fasten something or be fastened with a loop or hook **3** to get a lift by hitch-hiking **hitch** n **1** a slight difficulty that causes delay **2** a type of knot or noose **hitcher** n **hitch-hike** v to travel by getting rides in passing vehicles **hitch-hiker** n

hi-tech adj another spelling of high-tech

hither adv to or towards this place **hitherto** adv until this time

HIV abbr human immunodeficiency virus, a virus which causes Aids

hive n **1** a beehive **2** the bees living in a beehive **hive** v to gather bees in a hive

hives pl n an itchy rash caused by an allergic reaction, especially nettlerash

HM abbr Her or His Majesty('s)

HMS abbr Her or His Majesty's Ship

HMSO abbr Her or His Majesty's Stationery Office

HNC abbr Higher National Certificate

HND abbr Higher National Diploma

hoard n a carefully saved store of money, food, or treasured objects **hoard** v to save and store something away **hoarder** n **hoarding** n

hoarse adj (said about a voice) sounding rough, as if from a dry throat **hoarsely** adv **hoarseness** n

hoary adj **hoarier**, **hoariest 1** white or grey

from age ♦ **hoary hair 2** with grey hair, aged

hoax v to deceive someone as a joke **hoax** n a joking deception **hoaxer** n

hob n **1** a flat heating surface on a cooker **2** a flat metal shelf at the side of a fireplace, where a kettle or pan can be heated

hobble v to walk awkwardly, especially because of pain **hobble** n a hobbling walk

hobby n pl **hobbies** something you do for pleasure in your spare time

hobgoblin n a mischievous or evil spirit

hobnail n a heavy-headed nail used for the soles of boots **hobnailed** adj

hobnob v **hobnobbed**, **hobnobbing** informal to spend time with someone socially ♦ I hear you've been hobnobbing with film stars.

hock[1] n the middle joint of an animal's hind leg

hock[2] v informal to pawn something **hock** n **in hock 1** that has been pawned **2** in debt

hockey n a game played on a field between two teams of players with curved sticks and a small hard ball

hocus-pocus n meaningless talk used to trick or deceive people

hoe n a tool with a blade on a long handle **hoe** v **hoes**, **hoed**, **hoeing** to dig up earth or plants with a hoe

hog n **1** a pig, especially a castrated male pig reared for meat **2** informal a greedy person **hog** v **hogged**, **hogging** informal to take more than your fair share of something; to hoard something selfishly **hoggish** adj

Hogmanay (say **hog**-mə-nay) n New Year's Eve in Scotland

hoick v informal to lift or pull something, especially with a jerk

hoi polloi (say hoi pə-**loi**) pl n the common people, the masses

hoist v **1** to lift or raise something with ropes and pulleys **2** to haul something up ♦ She hoisted herself up onto the wall. **hoist** n an apparatus for hoisting things

hold[1] v past tense and past participle **held 1** to take and keep something in your hands, arms, teeth, etc. **2** to keep something in a particular position or condition ♦ Hold your head up. **3** to keep someone and not allow them to leave, to detain them ♦ The police are holding three men in connection with the robbery. **4** to be able to contain a certain amount ♦ The jug holds two pints. **5** to have something that you have gained or achieved ♦ He holds the record for the high jump. **6** to support or bear the weight of something ♦ Will that branch hold your weight? **7** to remain secure or unbroken under strain ♦ I hope the shelf will hold with all these books on it. **8** to remain in force or valid, to continue or last ♦ My offer still holds. **9** to have or occupy a job or position **10** to defend a place successfully **11** to manage to achieve a draw against an opponent **12** to keep a person's attention by being interesting **13** to stay on the phone ♦ Please hold while we try to connect you. **14** to reserve something for someone ♦ Can you hold the tickets for me? **15** to arrange for something to take place ♦ The meeting will be held in the village hall. **16** to have in store ♦ I don't know what the future holds. **17** to believe or consider something ♦ We will hold you responsible. **hold** n **1** a grip on something **2** something to hold on to for support; a handhold **3** a means of exerting influence or control on a person **holder** n **holding** n **holdall** n a large bag with handles and a shoulder strap **hold-up** n **1** a stoppage or delay **2** a robbery by armed robbers **to hold off** (said about bad weather) to not begin ♦ I hope the rain will hold off. **to hold out 1** to last ♦ Our supplies will not hold out for much longer. **2** to resist difficult circumstances **to hold the fort** to cope on your own in an emergency **to hold with** informal to approve of something ♦ We don't hold with bullying here.

hold[2] n a storage space in the lower part of a ship or aircraft, where cargo is stored

hole n **1** an empty space or opening in a solid body, mass, or surface **2** an animal's burrow **3** informal a small or unpleasant place **hole** v to make a hole or holes in something ♦ The ship was holed. **holey** adj

Holi (say **hoh**-li) n a Hindu spring festival celebrated in February or March

holiday n **1** (also **holidays**) a period of recreation, especially away from home **2** a day of festivity or recreation, when no work is done **holiday** v **holidayed**, **holidaying** to spend a holiday **holidaymaker** n a person on holiday

holistic (say hol-**ist**-ik) adj (said about medical treatment) treating the whole person, not just the symptoms

holler v to shout loudly **holler** n a loud shout

hollow adj 1 having a hole or empty space inside, not solid 2 sunken or concave ♦ *hollow cheeks* 3 (said about sound) echoing, as if from something hollow 4 empty or worthless ♦ *a hollow victory* 5 insincere or cynical ♦ *a hollow promise* ♦ *a hollow laugh* **hollow** n 1 a sunken place 2 a small valley **hollow** v to make something hollow, or to form something by doing this ♦ *Now hollow out the melon.* **hollowly** adv

holly n an evergreen shrub with prickly dark green leaves and red berries

holocaust (say hol-ə-kawst) n large-scale destruction, especially by fire or nuclear explosion ♦ *a nuclear holocaust* **Holocaust** the mass murder of Jews under the German Nazi regime in World War II

hologram (say hol-ə-gram) n 1 a three-dimensional image formed by laser beams 2 an image produced on photographic film in such a way that under suitable illumination a three-dimensional representation of an object is seen **holographic** adj **holography** n

holster n a leather case for a pistol or revolver, fixed to a belt or under the arm

holy adj **holier**, **holiest** 1 to do with or belonging to God or religion ♦ *the Holy Bible* 2 devoted to the service of God ♦ *a holy man* 3 consecrated or blessed ♦ *holy water* **holiness** n being holy or sacred **His Holiness** the title of the pope **holy orders** pl n the status of being ordained as a member of the clergy **Holy Week** n the week before Easter Sunday

homage (say hom-ij) n 1 things said as a mark of respect ♦ *We paid homage to his achievements.* 2 a formal expression of loyalty to a ruler

home n 1 the place where you live, especially with your family 2 the place where you were born or where you have lived for a long time or where you feel you belong 3 a house or flat 4 an institution where those needing care may live ♦ *an old people's home* 5 the natural environment of an animal or plant 6 the finishing point in a race or in certain games **home** 1 to do with or connected with your own home or country ♦ *home industries* ♦ *home produce* 2 played on a team's own ground ♦ *a home match* **home** adv 1 to or at home ♦ *Go home.* ♦ *Is she home yet?* 2 into the intended or correct position ♦ *He drove the nail home.* **home** v 1 (said about a trained pigeon) to fly home 2 to be guided to or make for a target ♦ *The missiles homed in on the airfield.* **homeless** adj having no home **homelessness** n **homely** adj **homelier**, **homeliest** simple and informal, not pretentious ♦ *a homely meal* **homeliness** n **homeward** adj going or leading towards home **homeward**, **homewards** adv towards home **homey** adj **homier**, **homiest** like a home, cosy **homecoming** n arrival at home **Home Counties** pl n the counties nearest to London **home economics** n the study of cookery and household management **home-grown** adj grown or produced in your own garden or country **homeland** n 1 a person's native land 2 any of the areas formerly reserved for the black population in South Africa and abolished in 1993 **home-made** adj made at home, not bought from a shop **Home Office** n the British government department dealing with law and order, immigration, etc. in England and Wales **home page** n the introductory document of a website on the World Wide Web **home rule** n government of a country by its own citizens **home run** n (in baseball) a hit that allows the batter to make a complete circuit of the bases **Home Secretary** n the government minister in charge of the Home Office **homesick** adj upset because you are away from home **homesickness** n **homespun** adj 1 simple and unsophisticated ♦ *homespun wisdom* 2 made of yarn spun at home **homestead** n a farmhouse or similar building with the land and buildings round it **home straight** n the stretch of a racecourse between the last turn and the finishing line **home**

truth n an unpleasant truth about yourself that you are made to realize **homework** n 1 school work that has to be done at home 2 preparatory work that you need to do before discussing something, making a speech, etc. **homeworker** n a person who works from home

homeopathy (say hohm-i-**op**-ə-thi) n the treatment of a disease by very small doses of natural substances **homeopath** n a person who practises homeopathy **homeopathic** adj

homicide (say hom-i-siyd) n murder **homicidal** adj

homily n pl **homilies** a sermon; a moralizing lecture

homing adj 1 (said about a pigeon) trained to fly home from a great distance 2 (said about a missile) having an inbuilt guidance system

homo- prefix the same

homogeneous (say hom-ə-jee-niəs) adj formed of parts that are all of the same kind **homogeneity** n **homogenize** v 1 to treat milk so that the particles of fat are broken down and cream does not separate 2 to make something homogeneous **homogenization** n

homograph (say hom-ə-graf) n a word that is spelt like another but has a different meaning or origin, e.g. bat (a flying animal) and bat (for striking a ball)

homonym (say hom-ə-nim) n a word with the same spelling or pronunciation as another but with a different meaning, e.g. grate (meaning fireplace), grate (meaning to rub), great (meaning large)

homophobia (say hoh-mə-**foh**-bi-ə) n strong dislike of homosexuals **homophobic** adj

homophone (say hom-ə-fohn) n a word with the same pronunciation as another, e.g. son, sun **homophonic** adj

Homo sapiens (say hoh-moh **sap**-i-enz) n human beings regarded as a species

homosexual (say hoh-mə-**seks**-yoo-əl) adj sexually attracted to people of the same sex as yourself **homosexual** n a homosexual person **homosexuality** n

Hon. abbr 1 Honorary 2 Honourable

hone (say hohn) v to spend time developing and improving an argument, skill, etc.

honest adj 1 not likely to lie, cheat, or steal; able to be trusted ♦ an honest trader 2 truthful and sincere ♦ I haven't been completely honest with you. 3 earned by fair means ♦ He makes an honest living. 4 done with good intentions ♦ an honest mistake **honestly** adv **honesty** n **honest-to-goodness** adj genuine and straightforward

honey n pl **honeys** 1 a sweet sticky yellowish substance made by bees from nectar 2 a yellowish-brown colour **honeybee** n the common bee that lives in a hive **honeycomb** n 1 a bees' wax structure of six-sided cells for holding their honey and eggs 2 a pattern or arrangement of six-sided sections **honeycomb** v to fill something with holes or tunnels ♦ The rock was honeycombed with passages. **honeymoon** n 1 a holiday spent together by a newly married couple 2 an initial period of goodwill towards someone in a new job or position **honeymoon** v to spend a honeymoon

honk v 1 to sound the horn of a car 2 to make the cry of a goose **honk** n a honking sound

honour n 1 great respect or public regard 2 something given as a reward or mark of respect 3 a title or decoration awarded by a monarch for service to the country 4 a feeling of pleasure and pride from being shown respect ♦ It is a great honour to accept this position. 5 a person or thing that brings honour 6 a clear sense of what is morally right and just ♦ a man of honour 7 a title of respect given to certain judges or people of importance ♦ your Honour **honour** v 1 to feel or show honour for a person 2 to confer honour on someone ♦ You honour us with your presence. 3 to keep to the terms of an agreement or promise 4 to acknowledge and pay a cheque, etc. when it is due **honorary** adj 1 given as an honour ♦ an honorary degree 2 (said about an office or its holder) unpaid ♦ the honorary treasurer **honourable** adj **honourably** adv

hood n 1 a covering for the head and neck, usually forming part of a coat or cloak 2 a loose piece of clothing like a hood, forming part of academic dress **3** something resembling a hood in shape or use, e.g. a folding roof over a car, a canopy over a machine, etc. **hooded** *adj* **1** having or wearing a hood **2** (said about animals) having a hood-like part **hoody** *n* **1** a jacket or sweatshirt with a hood that goes over the head **2** a young person who wears this

hoodlum *n* a hooligan or gangster

hoodwink *v* to deceive or trick someone

hoof *n pl* **hoofs** or **hooves** the horny part of the foot of a horse or other animal **hoofed** *adj*

hook *n* **1** a bent or curved piece of metal, etc. for catching hold of things or for hanging things on **2** something shaped like this **3** a curved cutting tool ♦ *a reaping hook* **hook** *v* **1** to grasp or catch something with a hook; to fasten something with a hook or hooks **2** to hit a ball in a curving path, in the direction of the follow-through **hooked** *adj*

hookah *n* an oriental tobacco pipe with a long tube passing through a glass container of water that cools the smoke as it is drawn through

hook-up *n* a connection to electricity or to a communications system

hooligan *n* a violent young troublemaker **hooliganism** *n*

hoop *n* **1** a band of metal or wood, etc. forming part of a framework **2** a large ring used as a child's toy for bowling along the ground, or for circus performers to jump through **3** a small metal arch used in croquet **4** a horizontal band on a sports shirt **hoop** *v* to bind or encircle something with hoops

hoopla *n* a game in which rings are thrown to encircle a prize

hooray *interjection, n* another spelling of *hurray*

hoot *n* **1** the cry of an owl **2** the sound made by a horn, siren, etc. **3** a cry expressing scorn or disapproval **4** an outburst of laughter **5** *informal* an amusing person or thing ♦ *Your aunt really is a hoot.* **hoot** *v* **1** to make a hoot **2** to sound a horn ♦ *The cars behind us started hooting.* **hooter** *n*

Hoover *n trademark* a vacuum cleaner

hoover *v* to clean a carpet with a vacuum cleaner

hop[1] *v* **hopped, hopping 1** (said about a person) to jump on one foot **2** (said about a bird) to jump with both its feet at once **3** *informal* to jump over or on to something ♦ *We hopped on to the bus.* **4** *informal* to make a short quick trip **hop** *n* **1** a hopping movement **2** a short journey, especially by plane **3** an informal dance

hop[2] *n* a climbing plant cultivated for its cones (called *hops*) which are used for giving a bitter flavour to beer **hoppy** *adj*

hope *n* **1** a feeling of expectation and desire; a desire for certain events to happen **2** a person or thing that gives cause for hope **3** what is hoped for **hope** *v* **1** to feel hope; to expect and desire something **2** to intend if possible to do something **hopeful** *adj* **hopefully** *adv* **hopefulness** *n* **hopeless** *adj* **hopelessly** *adv* **hopelessness** *n*

hopper *n* a V-shaped container for grain, rock, etc.

hopscotch *n* a children's game of hopping and jumping over squares marked on the ground to retrieve a stone tossed into these

horde *n* a large group or crowd

horizon *n* **1** the line at which the earth and the sky appear to meet **2** the limit of a person's experience, knowledge, or interests

horizontal *adj* parallel to the horizon **horizontally** *adv*

hormone (say **hor** -mohn) *n* a substance produced within the body of an animal or plant, or made synthetically, and carried by the blood or sap to an organ which it stimulates **hormonal** *adj*

horn *n* **1** a hard pointed outgrowth on the heads of cattle, sheep, and other animals **2** the hard smooth substance of which this consists **3** a projection resembling a horn **4** any of various wind instruments with a trumpet-shaped end, originally made of horn, now usually of brass **5** a device for sounding a warning signal **horn** *v* (said about an animal) to gore a person or another animal with the horns **horned** *adj* **horny** *adj* **hornier, horniest**

ornet n a large kind of wasp inflicting a serious sting

oroscope n a forecast of a person's future based on the relative positions of the planets and stars at a particular time

orrendous adj extremely unpleasant

orrible adj **1** causing horror ◆ a horrible accident **2** informal very unpleasant **horribly** adv

orrid adj **1** causing horror **2** informal very unpleasant **horridly** adv

orror n **1** a feeling of loathing, shock, or fear **2** intense dislike or dismay **3** informal a troublesome or mischievous person, especially a child **horrific** adj causing horror **horrifically** adv **horrify** v **horrifies**, **horrified**, **horrifying** to fill someone with horror, to shock someone **horrified** adj **horrifying** adj

orse n **1** a four-legged animal with a flowing mane and tail, used for riding on or to carry loads or pull carts, etc. **2** an adult male horse, as opposed to a mare or colt **3** cavalry **4** a frame on which something is supported, e.g. a clothes horse **horse** v **to horse around** informal to fool about **horsey** adj **horsier**, **horsiest 1** to do with or like a horse **2** interested in horses **horseback** n **horse chestnut** n **1** a large tree with conical clusters of white, pink, or red flowers **2** the dark-brown nut of this tree; a conker **horse-drawn** adj (said about a vehicle) pulled by a horse **horsehair** n hair from a horse's mane or tail, used for padding furniture

horseman, horsewoman n pl **horsemen, horsewomen** a rider on horseback, especially a skilled one **horsemanship** n **horseplay** n rough boisterous play **horsepower** n a unit for measuring the power of an engine (550 foot-pounds per second, about 750 watts) **horseradish** n a plant with a hot-tasting root used to make a sauce **horseshoe** n **1** a U-shaped strip of metal nailed to a horse's hoof **2** anything shaped like this ◆ The seats were arranged in a horseshoe around the stage.

horsewhip n a whip for horses **horsewhip** v **horsewhipped**, **horsewhipping** to beat an animal or person with a horsewhip

horticulture n the art of garden cultivation **horticultural** adj **horticulturist** n

hosanna interjection, n a cry of praise or joy, especially expressing adoration to God and the Messiah

hose n **1** a flexible tube for taking water somewhere, used for watering plants and in firefighting **2** (in shops) stockings, socks, and tights **hose** v to water or spray something with a hose ◆ I'll just hose the car down. **hosepipe** n a hose

hosiery n (in shops) stockings, socks, and tights

hospice (say hos-pis) n a home providing care for sick or terminally ill people

hospital n an institution providing medical and surgical treatment and nursing care for people who are ill or injured **hospitalize** v **hospitalization** n

hospitality n the friendly and generous reception and entertainment of guests or strangers **hospitable** adj **hospitably** adv

host[1] n **1** a person who receives and entertains other people as guests **2** the presenter of a television or radio programme **host** v **1** to act as host at a meal, party, etc. **2** to present a television or radio programme **hostess** n **1** a woman who receives and entertains other people as guests **2** a stewardess on an aircraft or train

host[2] n a large number of people or things ◆ a host of golden daffodils

host[3] n the bread consecrated in the Eucharist

hostage n a person seized or held as security until the holder's demands are met

hostel n an establishment providing lodging and cheap food for young travellers, students, or other groups ◆ a youth hostel **hostelry** n pl **hostelries** an inn or pub

hostile adj **1** unfriendly ◆ a hostile glance **2** opposed ◆ They are hostile towards reform. **3** belonging to a military enemy ◆ hostile aircraft **hostility** n pl **hostilities**

hot adj **hotter**, **hottest 1** having great heat or a high temperature ◆ a hot day ◆ a hot iron **2** having an uncomfortable feeling of heat ◆ I'm too hot—let's go in. **3** producing a burning sensation in the mouth **4** passionate or excitable ♦ *a hot temper* **5** currently popular, fashionable, or interesting ♦ *They are a hot band at the moment.* **6** (said about the scent in hunting) fresh and strong **7** (said about news) fresh **8** (in children's games) very close to finding or guessing what is sought **9** *informal* knowledgeable or skilful **10** *informal* keen on or strict about something ♦ *He's hot on punctuality.* **11** *informal* good or promising ♦ *Things aren't looking too hot.* **12** *informal* radioactive **13** *informal* (said about goods) recently stolen **hot** *v* **hotted, hotting** *informal* **to hot up** *informal* to become more intense or exciting **hotly** *adv* **hotness** *n* **hot air** *n informal* empty or boastful talk **hotbed** *n* **1** a bed of earth heated by fermenting manure **2** an environment favourable to the growth of something **hot-blooded** *adj* excitable or passionate **hot cross bun** *n* a bun marked with a cross, traditionally eaten hot on Good Friday **hot dog** *n* a hot sausage served in a long soft roll of bread **hothead** *n* an impetuous person **hot-headed** *adj* **hothouse** *n* a heated building made of glass, for growing plants in a warm temperature **hot key** *n ICT* a key that provides quick access to a function within a program **hotplate** *n* a heated surface for cooking food or keeping it hot **hot seat** *n informal* the position of someone who has difficult responsibilities or is being subjected to searching questions **hot-tempered** *adj* easily becoming very angry **hot-water bottle** *n* a rubber container that is filled with hot water and is used to warm a bed

hotchpotch *n* a confused mixture

hotel *n* a building where meals and rooms are provided for travellers and tourists **hotelier** *n* a person who owns or manages a hotel

hound *n* a dog used for hunting, especially a foxhound **hound** *v* to harass or pursue someone ♦ *He was hounded out of society.*

hour *n* **1** a twenty-fourth part of a day and night, 60 minutes **2** a time of day, a point of time ♦ *Who is calling at this hour?* **3** a period set aside for a specified activity ♦ *the lunch hour* **4** an important or special

time ♦ *This was our finest hour.* **hours** *pl* **1** a fixed period for daily work ♦ *Office hour are 9 a.m. to 5 p.m.* **2** the time according t the 24-hour clock ♦ *17.00 hours* **hourly** *a* **hourglass** *n* a glass container with a ver narrow part in the middle through whic a quantity of fine sand trickles from th upper to the lower section, taking one hou **houri** (say **hoor** -i) *n pl* **houris** a young an beautiful woman of the Muslim paradise **house**[1] *n* **1** a building made for people t live in **2** a building used for a particula purpose ♦ *the opera house* **3** a busines firm ♦ *a publishing house* **4** a building use by an assembly, the assembly itself ♦ *th Houses of Parliament* **5** a family or dynast ♦ *the House of Windsor* **6** a group of pupi living in the same building at a boardin school **7** each of the divisions of a school fo sports competitions, etc. **8** the audienc in a theatre, or a performance in a theatr ♦ *a full house* **9** a style of fast popula dance music produced electronicall **houseful** *n pl* **housefuls** all that a hous can hold **house arrest** *n* being kept as prisoner in your own house, not in priso **houseboat** *n* a barge-like boat used as dwelling **housebound** *adj* unable to leav your house because of illness or old ag **housebreaking** *n* breaking into a buildin to commit a crime **housebreaker** **household** *n* all the people who liv together in the same house **householder** a person who owns or rents a hous **household name** *n* a famous person thing **housekeeper** *n* a person employe to look after a household **housekeeping** **1** management of household affai **2** money set aside for this **3** routine wor such as record-keeping and administratic **housemaster** *n* a teacher in charge c a house at a boarding school **House c Commons** *n* the assembly of electe representatives in the British Parliamer **house officer** *n* a recent medical gradua who is being trained in a hospital and actin as an assistant physician or surgeon **Hous of Lords** *n* the upper assembly in the Britis Parliament, made up of peers and bishop **house-warming** *n* a party to celebra a move to a new home **housewife** n pl **housewives** a married woman whose main occupation is looking after the household **housewifely** adj **housework** n the regular work done in housekeeping, such as cleaning and cooking **housing estate** n a set of houses planned and built together in one area

house² (say howz) v 1 to provide someone with accommodation or shelter 2 to provide space for something 3 to enclose or encase something **housing** n 1 houses and flats 2 a rigid casing enclosing a piece of machinery

hove a past tense of heave

hovel (say hov-əl) n a small, shabby or squalid house

hover v 1 (said about a bird or aircraft) to remain in one place in the air 2 to wait about near someone or something 3 to remain at or near a particular level **hovercraft** n pl **hovercraft** a vehicle that travels over land or water on a cushion of air thrust downwards from its engines

how adv 1 by what means, in what way 2 to what extent or degree 3 in what condition or health **however** adv 1 all the same, nevertheless ♦ Later, however, she decided to go. 2 in whatever way, to whatever extent ♦ You will never catch him, however hard you try.

howl v 1 (said about an animal) to make a long loud wailing cry 2 (said about a person) to weep loudly **howl** n 1 a loud cry of amusement, pain, or scorn 2 a similar noise made by a strong wind or in a loudspeaker

howler n informal a foolish mistake

hp, HP abbr 1 high pressure 2 hire purchase 3 horsepower

HQ abbr headquarters

HRH abbr His or Her Royal Highness

hub n 1 the central part of a wheel, from which spokes radiate 2 a central point of activity or interest ♦ the financial hub of the city

hubbub n a loud confused noise of voices

hubcap n a round metal cover over the hub of a motor vehicle's wheel

hubris (say hew-bris) n arrogant pride or

presumption **hubristic** adj

huddle v 1 to crowd together into a small space 2 to curl your body into a small space **huddle** n a number of people or things crowded together

hue¹ n a colour or tint

hue² n **hue and cry** a public outcry of alarm or protest

huff v to blow out noisily **huff** n a fit of annoyance ♦ in a huff **huffy** adj

hug v **hugged, hugging** 1 to squeeze or hold someone or something tightly in your arms 2 to keep close to something ♦ The ship hugged the shore. **hug** n a tight embrace

huge adj extremely large; enormous **hugely** adv very much ♦ We are hugely grateful. **hugeness** n

hulk n 1 the body or wreck of an old ship 2 a large clumsy person or thing **hulking** adj

hull n 1 the framework of a ship or other vessel 2 the outer covering of a fruit or seed, especially the pod of peas and beans **hull** v 1 to hit and pierce the hull of a ship 2 to remove the hulls from peas or beans

hullo interjection, n another spelling of hello

hum v **hummed, humming** 1 to make a low steady continuous sound like that of a bee 2 to sing a tune with your lips closed **hum** n a low steady continuous sound **hum** interjection an exclamation of hesitation or disagreement

human adj 1 to do with or consisting of human beings ♦ the human race 2 having the qualities that are characteristic of people as opposed to God, animals, or machines ♦ human error 3 showing the better qualities of humankind, such as kindness, pity, etc. **human** n a human being **humanist** n a person who is concerned with people's needs and with finding rational ways to solve human problems **humanism** n **humanistic** adj **humanity** n 1 the human race, people ♦ crimes against humanity 2 being human, human nature 3 being humane, compassion **humanities** pl n arts subjects, such as literature, history, music, and philosophy, as opposed to the sciences **humanize** v 1 to give a human character to something 2 to make someone more humane **humanization** n **humanly** adv **1** in a human way, from a human point of view **2** by human means, with human limitations ♦ *as accurate as is humanly possible* **human being** n a man, woman, or child of the species *Homo sapiens* **humanitarian** adj concerned with human welfare and the reduction of suffering **humanitarian** n a humanitarian person **humanitarianism** n **humankind** n human beings collectively **humanoid** adj having a human form or human characteristics **humanoid** n (in science fiction) a humanoid thing or being **human rights** pl n rights that are believed to belong justifiably to any living person

humane (say hew-**mayn**) adj **1** compassionate or merciful **2** inflicting as little pain as possible, especially in killing animals **humanely** adv

humble adj **humbler**, **humblest 1** having or showing a modest estimate of your own importance, not proud **2** offered with such feelings ♦ *humble apologies* **3** of low rank or importance ♦ *He came from humble origins.* **4** not large, showy, or elaborate ♦ *a humble cottage* **humble** v **1** to make someone feel humble, to lower the rank or self-importance of someone **2** to defeat an opponent thought to be superior **humbleness** n **humbly** adv

humbug n **1** insincere or misleading talk or behaviour **2** a hypocrite **3** a kind of hard boiled sweet usually flavoured with peppermint

humdrum adj dull or monotonous ♦ *a humdrum existence*

humerus (say hew-**mer**-əs) n the bone in the upper arm, from shoulder to elbow

humid (say hew-mid) adj (said about the air or climate) warm and damp **humidifier** n a device for keeping the air moist in a room or enclosed space **humidify** v **humidifies**, **humidified**, **humidifying**, **humidity** n pl **humidities**

humility n a humble opinion of your own importance **humiliate** v to make someone feel disgraced or ashamed **humiliating** adj **humiliation** n

hummingbird n a small tropical bird that vibrates its wings rapidly, producing a humming sound

hummus (say huu-məs) n a dip made from ground chickpeas and sesame oil flavoured with lemon and garlic

humour n **1** the quality of being amusing **2** the ability to enjoy comical things or situations ♦ *She has a good sense of humour.* **3** a mood or state of mind ♦ *He was in a good humour.* **humour** v to keep a person contented by giving way to his or her wishes, even if they seem unreasonable **humorist** n **humorous** adj **humorously** adv **humourless** adj

hump n **1** a rounded lump or mound ♦ *a camel's hump* **2** an abnormal outward curve at the top of a person's back **hump** v **1** informal to lift or carry something heavy with difficulty **2** to form something into a hump **humped** adj **humpback** n a hunchback **humpbacked** adj

humph interjection used to express doubt or dissatisfaction

hunch v to bend the top of your body forward and raise your shoulders and back ♦ *She hunched her shoulders against the cold.* **hunch** n a feeling or guess based on intuition **hunched** adj **hunchback** n **hunchbacked** adj

hundred adj, n the number 100, equal to ten times ten ♦ *a few hundred* **hundredth** adj, n **hundredfold** adj, adv one hundred times as much or as many **hundredweight** n pl **hundredweight** a measure of weight equal to 112 lb (about 50.8 kg) ◊ Notice that you say *three hundred* and *a few hundred*, not *hundreds*.

hung past tense and past participle of *hang* **hung-over** adj suffering from a hangover **hung parliament** n a parliament that has no political party with an overall majority

Hungarian adj to do with or coming from Hungary **Hungarian** n **1** a person born in Hungary or descended from people born there **2** the language of Hungary

hunger n **1** need for food, the feeling you have when you have not eaten for some time **2** a strong desire for something **hunger** v to have a strong desire for something

hungry adj **hungrier**, **hungriest 1** feeling

hunger 2 having a strong desire for something ♦ *hungry for power* **hungrily** *adv*

hunk *n* **1** a large piece broken or cut off something ♦ *a hunk of bread* **2** *informal* a muscular good-looking man

hunt *v* **1** to chase and kill wild animals for food or as a sport **2** to pursue someone ♦ *Police are hunting three armed robbers.* **3** to search for something ♦ *I've been hunting for this pen everywhere.* **hunt** *n* **1** hunting **2** an association of people hunting with a pack of hounds, or the district where they hunt **hunted** *adj* **hunter** *n* **hunting** *n*

hurdle *n* **1** one of a series of upright frames to be jumped over by athletes in a race **2** an obstacle or difficulty **3** a portable rectangular frame with bars, used for a temporary fence **hurdles** *pl n* a hurdle race ♦ *the 400 metre hurdles* **hurdle** *v* **1** to run in a hurdle race **2** to jump over an obstacle while running **hurdler** *n* **hurdling** *n*

hurdy-gurdy *n pl* **hurdy-gurdies** a stringed musical instrument with a droning sound

hurl *v* **1** to throw something with great force ♦ *She hurled the book across the room.* **2** to shout abuse or insults at someone ♦ *The crowd hurled insults at the prisoner.*

hurling, **hurley** *n* an Irish form of hockey played with broad sticks

hurray, **hurrah** *interjection, n* an exclamation of joy or approval

hurricane (say hurri-kən) *n* **1** a storm with a violent wind, especially a tropical cyclone in the Caribbean **2** a wind of 73 m.p.h. or more, force 12 on the Beaufort scale

hurry *v* **hurries**, **hurried**, **hurrying** **1** to move or do something with eager haste or too quickly **2** to try to make a person or thing move or proceed quickly ♦ *I'll have to hurry you for an answer.* **hurry** *n* **1** great haste **2** a need for haste ♦ *What's the hurry?* **hurried** *adj* **hurriedly** *adv*

hurt *v* past tense and past participle **hurt** **1** to cause pain or injury to someone **2** (said about a part of the body) to suffer pain ♦ *My leg hurts.* **3** to cause mental pain or distress to someone ♦ *I'm sorry if I hurt your feelings.* **4** to have a bad effect on something ♦ *A couple of late nights won't hurt.* **hurt** *n* physical or mental pain or injury **hurt** *adj*

upset and offended ♦ *a hurt look* **hurtful** *adj* **hurtfully** *adv*

hurtle *v* to move at great or dangerous speed ♦ *The train hurtled along.*

husband *n* a man to whom a woman is married **husband** *v* to use money, strength, etc. economically and try to save it ♦ *We must husband our resources.* **husbandry** *n* **1** farming **2** management of resources

hush *v* to make something quiet or silent, or to become quiet or silent **hush** *n* a silence **hush-hush** *adj* highly secret or confidential

husk *n* the dry outer covering of certain seeds and fruits **husk** *v* to remove the husk from something

husky[1] *adj* **huskier**, **huskiest** **1** (said about a person's voice) dry in the throat, hoarse **2** big and strong, burly **3** dry, like husks **huskily** *adv* **huskiness** *n*

husky[2] *n pl* **huskies** a powerful dog used in the Arctic for pulling sledges

hussy *n pl* **hussies** *old use* an immoral or cheeky woman

hustings *pl n* political speeches and campaigning just before an election

hustle *v* **1** to push or shove someone roughly, to jostle someone **2** to force someone to move hurriedly ♦ *The protestors were hustled away by the police.* **3** to make someone do something quickly and without time to consider things ♦ *I felt I had been hustled into making a hasty decision.* **4** *informal* to earn money by dishonest means or aggressive selling **hustle** *n* busy movement and activity **hustler** *n*

hut *n* a small roughly-made house or shelter ♦ *a beach hut*

hutch *n* a box or cage for keeping rabbits or other small pet animals

hybrid *n* **1** an animal or plant that is the offspring of two different species or varieties **2** something made by combining two different elements **hybrid** *adj* produced in this way, cross-bred

hydrant *n* a pipe from a water main, especially in a street, with a nozzle to which a hose can be attached for use in dealing with fires

hydrate *n* a chemical compound of water with another compound or element

hydrate v to combine chemically with water; to cause a substance to absorb water **hydration** n

hydraulic (say hiy-**draw**-lik) adj **1** (said about water, oil, etc.) conveyed through pipes or channels under pressure **2** operated by the movement of water or other fluid ♦ hydraulic brakes **3** to do with the science of hydraulics ♦ a hydraulic engineer **4** hardening under water ♦ hydraulic cement **hydraulically** adv

hydro n pl **hydros** informal **1** a hotel originally providing treatment by hydrotherapy **2** a hydroelectric power plant

hydro- prefix (changing to **hydr-** before a vowel) **1** water (as in hydroelectric, hydraulic) **2** (in chemical names) containing hydrogen (as in hydrochloric)

hydroelectric adj using water power to produce electricity **hydroelectricity** n

hydrogen n a chemical element (symbol H), a colourless odourless tasteless gas. It is the lightest substance known and combines with oxygen to form water

hydrogen bomb n an immensely powerful bomb releasing energy by fusion of hydrogen nuclei

hydrotherapy n the use of water in the treatment of disease and abnormal physical conditions, especially exercises in a swimming pool

hyena n a flesh-eating animal like a wolf, with a howl that sounds like wild laughter

hygiene (say **hiy**-jeen) n keeping things clean in order to remain healthy and prevent the spread of disease **hygienic** adj **hygienically** adv **hygienist** n

hymen n a membrane partly closing the external opening of the vagina of a girl or woman who is a virgin

hymn n a religious song, usually of praise to God **hymnal** n a book of hymns

hype n informal extravagant or misleading publicity ♦ Don't believe all the hype about this film. **hype** v informal to promote a product with extravagant publicity **hyped up** adj overexcited or overstimulated

hyper- prefix over or above; excessive

hyperbola (say hiy-**per**-bələ) n Mathematics the curve produced when a cone is cut by a plane that makes a larger angle with the base than the side of the cone does **hyperbolic** adj

hyperbole (say hiy-**per**-bəli) n a deliberately exaggerated statement that is not meant to be taken literally, e.g. a stack of work a mile high **hyperbolical** adj

hypercritical adj excessively critical, especially of small faults **hypercritically** adv

hypermarket n a very large supermarket, usually situated outside a town

hypersensitive adj excessively sensitive

hypertext n ICT a system of cross-referencing between linked sections of documents

hyphen n the sign (-) used to link two words (e.g. hot-tempered) or to divide a word into parts, e.g. at the end of a line in print **hyphenate** v **hyphenated** adj **hyphenation** n

hypnosis (say hip-**noh**-sis) n **1** a sleep-like state produced in a person who is then very susceptible to suggestion and acts only if told to do so **2** the producing of this state **hypnotic** adj **hypnotically** adv **hypnotism** n **hypnotist** n **hypnotize** v

hypnotherapy n the treatment of disease by hypnosis **hypnotherapist** n

hypo- prefix below or under

hypochondria (say hiy-pə-**kon**-driə) n a mental condition in which a person constantly imagines that he or she is ill **hypochondriac** n

hypocrisy (say hip-**ok**-risi) n falsely pretending to be virtuous **hypocrite** n **hypocritical** adj **hypocritically** adv

hypodermic adj injected beneath the skin; used for such injections **hypodermic** n a hypodermic syringe **hypodermically** adv

hypothermia n the condition of having an abnormally low body temperature

hypothesis (say hiy-**poth**-i-sis) n pl **hypotheses** (say -seez) a suggestion or possible explanation put forward to account for certain facts and used as a basis for further investigation by which it may be proved or disproved **hypothesize** v

hypothetical (say hiy-pə-**thet**-ikel) adj **1** based on or serving as a hypothesis

2 supposed but not necessarily true **hypothetically** *adv*

hysterectomy (say hiss-ter-**ek**-təmi) *n pl* **hysterectomies** the surgical removal of the womb

hysteria (say hiss-**teer**-iə) *n* wild uncontrollable emotion, panic, or excitement **hysterical** *adj* **hysterically** *adv* **hysterics** *pl n*

Hz *abbr* hertz

Ii

I¹ 1 the ninth letter of the English alphabet **2** the Roman numeral for 1

I² *pronoun* used to refer to the person who is speaking or writing

ice *n* **1** frozen water, a brittle transparent solid **2** an ice cream or water ice **ice** *v* **1** to become covered with ice ♦ *The pond has iced over.* **2** to make something very cold ♦ *iced tea* **3** to decorate a cake with icing **icy** *adj* **icier, iciest, icily** *adv* **iciness** *n* **ice age** *n* a period when much of the earth's surface was covered with glaciers **iceberg** *n* a huge mass of ice floating in the sea with the greater part under water **ice cap** *n* a permanent covering of ice and snow at the North and South Poles **ice cream** *n* a sweet creamy frozen food **ice field** *n* a large expanse of floating ice **ice hockey** *n* a form of hockey played on ice with a flat disc (called a *puck*) instead of a ball **ice lolly** *n* a piece of flavoured water ice on a stick **ice rink** *n* a place made for skating on ice

Icelandic *adj* to do with Iceland or its people or language **Icelandic** *n* the language of Iceland

icicle *n* a pointed hanging piece of ice, formed when dripping water freezes

icing *n* a sugary mixture used to decorate cakes and biscuits **icing sugar** *n*

icon (say **iy**-kon) *n* **1** a sacred painting, usually on wood, or mosaic of a holy person, especially in the Byzantine and other Eastern Churches **2** *ICT* a small symbol or picture on a computer screen **3** a famous person who is widely revered as an example or model **iconic** *adj* **iconoclast** *n* a person who attacks cherished institutions or beliefs **iconoclasm** *n* **iconoclastic** *adj* **iconography** *n* **1** the illustration of a subject by drawings or figures **2** a study of the portraits of a person

ICT *abbr* information and communication technology

I'd *v informal* **1** I had **2** I would

idea *n* **1** a plan or thought formed in the mind **2** a mental impression ♦ *I'll try to give you an idea of what is needed.* **3** an opinion or belief **4** a vague belief or fancy, a feeling that something is likely ♦ *I had an idea this would happen.*

ideal *adj* **1** satisfying an idea of what is perfect or suitable ♦ *This is an ideal time for a meeting.* **2** existing only in an idea ♦ *in an ideal world* **ideal** *n* a person or thing or idea that is regarded as perfect or as a standard to follow **idealism** *n* **idealist** *n* **idealistic** *adj* **idealize** *v* **idealization** *n* **ideally** *adv*

identical *adj* **1** one and the same ♦ *This is the identical place we visited last year.* **2** exactly alike ♦ *All the houses in the street looked identical.* **3** (said about twins) developed from a single fertilized ovum and therefore of the same sex and similar in appearance **identically** *adv*

identify *v* **identifies, identified, identifying 1** to establish who or what a particular person or thing is, to recognize them as being a specified person or thing **2** to associate someone closely in feeling or interest ♦ *The company identifies us with progress and efficiency.* **3** to think of yourself as sharing the characteristics or fortunes of another person ♦ *Anyone can identify with the hero of the play.* **identifiable** *adj* **identification** *n*

Identikit *n trademark* a picture of a person who is wanted by the police, assembled from features as described by witnesses

identity *n pl* **identities 1** who or what a person or thing is **2** the distinctive character of a person or thing **3** the state of being identical, absolute sameness **identity card** *n* a card that identifies the person who carries it for official purposes

ideology (say iy-dee-ol-əji) n pl **ideologies** a set of ideas or beliefs that form the basis of an economic or political theory ♦ *Marxist ideology.* **ideological** adj **ideologist** n

idiom (say id-i-əm) n 1 a phrase with a meaning that cannot be worked out from the individual words in it, e.g. *in hot water* and *over the moon* 2 the use of words in a way that is natural in a language 3 the language used by a particular group ♦ *in the scientific idiom* 4 a characteristic style of expression in art or music **idiomatic** adj **idiomatically** adv

idiosyncrasy (say idi-ə-sink-rəsi) n pl **idiosyncrasies** a person's particular way of thinking or behaving **idiosyncratic** adj

idiot n informal a stupid or foolish person **idiocy** n pl **idiocies**, **idiotic** adj **idiotically** adv

idle adj 1 (said about a person) avoiding work, lazy 2 (said about machinery) doing no work, not active or in use 3 (said about time) not spent in doing something 4 worthless, having no purpose or basis ♦ *idle gossip* **idle** v 1 to pass time without working, to be idle 2 (said about an engine) to run slowly in a neutral gear **idleness** n **idler** n **idly** adv

idol n 1 a statue or image of a god, used as an object of worship 2 a famous person who is widely admired **idolatrous** adj **idolatry** n **idolize** v **idolization** n

idyll (say id-il) n 1 a beautiful or peaceful scene or situation 2 a short verse or prose description of a peaceful or romantic scene or incident, especially in country life **idyllic** adj **idyllically** adv

i.e. abbr that is, that is to say ♦ *the person who wrote the play, i.e. Pinter*

if conjunction 1 on condition that, supposing that ♦ *I'll do it if you pay me.* 2 in the event that ♦ *If you are tired we can rest.* 3 supposing or granting that ♦ *Even if she said it, she didn't mean it.* 4 even though ♦ *We'll finish it, if it takes us all day.* 5 whenever ♦ *If they wanted anything, they got it.* 6 whether ♦ *See if the light works now.* 7 used in exclamations of wish or surprise ♦ *If only he would come!* **if** n a condition or

supposition ♦ *There are too many ifs about it.*

igloo n pl **igloos** a round Inuit house built of blocks of hard snow

ignite (say ig-niyt) v 1 to set fire to something 2 to catch fire **ignition** n

ignoble adj not noble in character, shameful or unworthy **ignobly** adv

ignominy (say ig-nəm-ini) n disgrace or humiliation **ignominious** adj **ignominiously** adv

ignoramus (say ig-ner-ay-məs) n pl **ignoramuses** an ignorant person

ignorant adj 1 not knowing about something or about many things 2 informal rude or impolite from not knowing how to behave **ignorance** n **ignorantly** adv

ignore v to take no notice of something or someone

iguana (say ig-wah-nə) n a large tree-climbing tropical lizard

ilk n **of that ilk** of that kind

ill adj 1 physically or mentally unwell, in bad health 2 bad or harmful ♦ *There were no ill effects.* 3 hostile or unkind ♦ *no ill feelings* **ill** adv 1 badly or wrongly ♦ *The child had been ill-treated.* 2 imperfectly or scarcely ♦ *We can ill afford to do this.* **ill** n harm or injury **ill-advised** adj unwise, not sensible **ill-bred** adj having bad manners **ill-fated** adj bound to fail, unlucky **ill-gotten** adj obtained by unlawful means **ill-mannered** adj having bad manners **ill-natured** adj bad-tempered or unkind **ill-treat** v to treat someone or something badly or cruelly **ill-use** v to ill-treat someone or something **ill will** n hostility, unkind feeling

I'll v informal I shall or I will

illegal adj against the law **illegality** n **illegally** adv

illegible (say i-lej-ibəl) adj not clear enough to read **illegibility** n **illegibly** adv

illegitimate (say ili-jit-im-ət) adj 1 (said about a child) born of parents who are not married to each other 2 not conforming to the law or to normal standards **illegitimacy** n **illegitimately** adv

illicit (say i-lis-it) adj not allowed by the law or by custom **illicitly** adj

illness n 1 the state of being ill in body or

mind **2** a particular form of ill health

illogical *adj* not logical, having no sense **illogicality** *n* **illogically** *adv*

illuminate *v* **1** to light something up or make it bright **2** to throw light on a subject or make it understandable **3** to decorate a place with lights **4** to decorate a manuscript with coloured designs **illumination** *n*

illusion (say i-loo-zhən) *n* **1** something unreal that a person supposes to exist **2** a false idea or belief **3** *Art* a special effect created by deceiving the eye in a painting or drawing **illusionist** *n* **illusory** *adj*

illustrate *v* **1** to put drawings or pictures in a book, magazine, or newspaper **2** to make something clear by giving examples or pictures, etc. **3** to serve as an example of something **illustration** *n* **illustrative** *adj* **illustratively** *adv* **illustrator** *n*

illustrious (say i-lus-triəs) *adj* famous and distinguished **illustriousness** *n*

I'm *v informal* I am

image *n* **1** something that represents the outward form of a person or thing, such as a statue or picture **2** the appearance of something as seen in a mirror or through a lens **3** a person or thing that is very much like another in appearance ♦ *She's the image of her mother.* **4** a mental picture of something **5** the general impression or reputation of a person, organization, or product as seen by the public **imagery** *n*

imagine *v* **1** to form a mental image of something, to picture something in the mind **2** to suppose or assume ♦ *Don't imagine you'll get away with this.* **3** to guess ♦ *I can't imagine what it will be like.* **imaginable** *adj* **imaginary** *adj* **imagination** *n* **imaginative** *adj* **imaginatively** *adv*

imam (say im-ahm) *n* **1** the leader of prayers in a mosque **2** the title of various Muslim religious leaders

imbalance *n* a lack of balance or proportion

imbecile (say **im**-bi-seel) *n informal* a stupid person **imbecile** *adj informal* stupid **imbecility** *n*

imbibe (say im-biyb) *v formal* **1** to drink, especially to drink an alcoholic drink **2** to absorb ideas or information into the mind

imbue (say im-bew) *v* **imbues, imbued, imbuing** to fill a person with a feeling or quality

imitate *v* **1** to copy a person or their behaviour **2** to mimic someone for amusement or entertainment **3** to copy or be like something else **imitable** *adj* **imitation** *n* **imitative** *adj* **imitator** *n*

immaculate *adj* **1** completely clean **2** without any fault or blemish, free of mistakes **immaculacy** *n* **immaculately** *adv*

immanent (say im-ə-nənt) *adj* (said about a quality) existing within a person, inherent **immanence** *n* ◊ Do not confuse this word with *imminent*, which has a different meaning.

immaterial *adj* **1** of no importance or relevance ♦ *It is largely immaterial what you think.* **2** having no physical body ♦ *our immaterial souls*

immature *adj* not mature or developed, especially emotionally **immaturity** *n*

immeasurable *adj* too large or too many to be measured **immeasurably** *adv*

immediate *adj* **1** happening or done without any delay **2** nearest, with nothing or no one between ♦ *our immediate neighbours* **3** nearest in relationship ♦ *Their immediate family lived abroad.* **4** most urgent or pressing ♦ *Our immediate concern is to pay off the debt.* **immediacy** *n* **immediately** *adv*

immemorial *adj* going far back into the past ♦ *The town had immemorial rights to the land.*

immense *adj* very large or great **immensely** *adv* **immensity** *n*

immerse *v* **1** to put something completely into a liquid **2** to absorb or involve someone deeply in thought ♦ *She was immersed in her work.* **immersion** *n*

immigrate *v* to come into a foreign country to live there permanently **immigrant** *n* **immigration** *n*

imminent *adj* (of events) about to occur, likely to occur at any moment **imminence** *n* ◊ Do not confuse this word with *immanent*, which has a different meaning.

immobile *adj* not moving, or not able to move **immobility** *n* **immobilize** *v*

immobilization n

immoderate adj excessive, lacking moderation **immoderately** adv

immodest adj **1** not modest, indecent **2** conceited **immodestly** adv **immodesty** n

immoral adj not conforming to the accepted standards of morality, morally wrong **immorality** n **immorally** adv

immortal adj **1** living for ever, not mortal **2** famous for all time **immortal** n an immortal being or person, especially an ancient deity **immortality** n **immortalize** v

immovable adj **1** unable to be moved **2** (said about a person) not willing to change an opinion or decision **3** (said about property) consisting of land, houses, and other permanent things **immovability** n **immovably** adv

immune adj **1** resistant to a disease ♦ She is not immune against infection. **2** safe from a danger or obligation ♦ They are immune from prosecution. **immunity** n pl **immunities**

immure (say im-**yoor**) v to imprison someone or shut them in

immutable (say i-**mewt**-əbəl) adj unchangeable **immutability** n **immutably** adv

imp n **1** a small devil **2** a mischievous child **impish** adj **impishly** adv **impishness** n

impact[1] (say **im**-pakt) n **1** the action or force of one object coming into collision with another **2** a significant effect or influence caused by something ♦ the impact made by computers on our lives

impact[2] (say im-**pakt**) v **1** to collide or come into violent contact with something **2** to have a significant effect on something

impair v to damage something or cause it to weaken ♦ Smoking impairs your health. **impairment** n

impale v to fix or pierce something by passing a sharp-pointed object into it or through it

impalpable (say im-**palp**-əbəl) adj **1** unable to be felt by touch **2** not easily understood **impalpability** n **impalpably** adv

impart v **1** to give information **2** to provide something with a quality ♦ Lemon imparts a sharp flavour to drinks. **impartation** n

impartial (say im-**par**-shəl) adj not favouring one person or side more than another **impartiality** n **impartially** adv

impasse (say **am**-pahss) n a situation in which no progress can be made

impassable adj **impassably** adv **impassability** n

impassioned (say im-**pash**-ənd) adj full of deep feeling

impassive adj not feeling or showing any emotion **impassively** adv **impassiveness** n **impassivity** n

impatient adj **1** unable to wait patiently, restlessly eager ♦ The boys are impatient to set off. **2** showing a lack of patience, irascible or intolerant **impatience** n **impatiently** adv

impeach v **1** to charge a person with a serious crime against the state **2** to question a practice or intention **impeachment** n

impeccable adj of the highest standard, faultless **impeccability** n **impeccably** adv

impede v to hinder someone or something **impedance** n **impediment** n

impel v **impelled**, **impelling** **1** to urge or drive someone to do something ♦ Curiosity impelled her to investigate. **2** to send or drive something forward, to propel something

impending adj soon to happen, imminent

impenetrable adj **1** impossible to enter or pass through **2** impossible to understand **impenetrability** n **impenetrably** adv

imperative (say im-**pe**-rə-tiv) adj **1** expressing a command **2** essential or unavoidable ♦ Further economies are imperative. **imperative** n **1** something essential or unavoidable ♦ Speed is an imperative in this operation. **2** Gram a form of a verb used in making commands (e.g. come in here!)

imperceptible adj so slight or gradual that it is difficult to notice it **imperceptibly** adv

imperfect adj not perfect; incomplete **imperfect** n the imperfect tense **imperfection** n **imperfectly** adv

imperial adj **1** to do with an empire or its rulers **2** majestic **3** used to denote non-metric weights and measures fixed by law in the UK ♦ an imperial gallon **imperialism** n

imperialist *n* **imperialistic** *adj* **imperially** *adv*

mperious (say im-**peer**-iəs) *adj* domineering or bossy **imperiously** *adv* **imperiousness** *n*

mpermanent *adj* not permanent **impermanence** *n* **impermanency** *n*

mpermeable (say im-**per**-mi-əbəl) *adj* not allowing liquid to pass through **impermeability** *n*

mpersonal *adj* **1** not influenced by personal feeling, showing no emotion **2** not referring to a particular person **3** having no existence as a person ♦ *nature's impersonal forces* **impersonality** *n* **impersonally** *adv*

mpersonate *v* to pretend to be another person, either for entertainment or fraudulently **impersonation** *n* **impersonator** *n*

mpertinent *adj* **1** insolent, not showing proper respect **2** *formal* not pertinent, irrelevant **impertinence** *n* **impertinently** *adv*

mpervious (say im-**per**-viəs) *adj* **1** not allowing water or heat, etc. to pass through ♦ *impervious to water* **2** not influenced by something or affected by it ♦ *impervious to criticism*

mpetigo (say imp-i-**tiy**-goh) *n* a contagious skin disease causing spots that form yellowish crusts

mpetuous (say im-**pet**-yoo-əs) *adj* **1** acting hastily without thinking **2** moving quickly or violently ♦ *He made an impetuous dash for the exit.* **impetuosity** *n* **impetuously** *adv*

mpetus (say **im**-pit-əs) *n* **1** the force or energy that makes a body move and keep moving **2** a driving force ♦ *The ceasefire gave an impetus to peace talks.*

mpiety (say im-**piy**-iti) *n pl* **impieties** a lack of piety or reverence

mpinge *v* **1** to influence something or have an important effect on it ♦ *The economic recession impinged on all aspects of our lives.* **2** to encroach on something

mplacable (say im-**plak**-əbəl) *adj* not able to be placated, relentless **implacability** *adv* **implacably** *adv*

mplant¹ (say im-**plahnt**) *v* **1** to plant or insert something **2** to put an idea in the

mind **3** *Medicine* to insert tissue or other substance in a living thing **implantation** *n*

implant² (say im-**plahnt**) *n* something that has been implanted, especially an organ or piece of tissue inserted in the body

implausible *adj* not plausible or probable **implausibility** *n* **implausibly** *adv*

implement¹ (say **im**-pli-mənt) *n* a tool or instrument for a special purpose

implement² (say **im**-pli-ment) *v* to put something into effect ♦ *We have already implemented the scheme.* **implementation** *n*

implicate *v* **1** to involve a person in a crime or act of wrongdoing, or to show that a particular person is involved **2** to imply something as a meaning or consequence **implication** *n*

implicit (say im-**pliss**-it) *adj* **1** implied but not stated openly (Compare *explicit*) **2** absolute or unquestioning ♦ *She expects implicit obedience.* **implicitly** *adv*

implode *v* to burst or cause something to burst inwards **implosion** *n*

implore *v* to beg someone to do something, to entreat someone **imploring** *adj* **imploringly** *adv*

imply *v* **implies**, **implied**, **implying 1** to suggest something without stating it directly **2** to suggest or entail something as a consequence ♦ *A creation implies a creator.*

impolite *adj* not polite **impolitely** *adv*

impolitic (say im-**pol**-i-tik) *adj* unwise, not advisable

import¹ (say im-**port**) *v* **1** to bring in goods from another country **2** *ICT* to transfer data into a file or document **importation** *n* **importer** *n*

import² (say **im**-port) *n* **1** something that has been imported from another country, or the process of importing goods **2** a meaning implied by something **3** importance ♦ *The message was of great import.*

important *adj* **1** having or able to have a great effect **2** having great authority or influence **importance** *n* **importantly** *adv*

impose *v* **1** to put a tax or obligation on someone or something ♦ *The government has imposed heavy duties on tobacco.*

2 to inflict a difficulty on someone ♦ *The expense of the trip imposed a great strain on their resources.* **3** to force something to be accepted ♦ *He was always imposing his ideas on the group.* **imposing** *adj* **imposition** *n*

impossible *adj* **1** not possible, unable to be done or to exist **2** difficult to deal with ♦ *an impossible person* **impossibility** *n* **impossibly** *adv*

impostor *n* a person who dishonestly pretends to be someone else

impotent (say im-pə-tənt) *adj* **1** powerless, unable to take action **2** (said about a man) unable to have an erection or to reach orgasm **impotence** *n* **impotently** *adv*

impound *v* **1** to seize someone's property and take it into legal custody, to confiscate something **2** to shut up cattle in a pound

impoverish *v* **1** to make someone poor **2** to make something poor in quality ♦ *impoverished soil* **impoverishment** *n*

impracticable *adj* not able to be done in practice **impracticability** *n* **impracticably** *adv*

impractical *adj* not practical, unwise **impracticality** *n*

imprecise *adj* not precise **imprecisely** *adv* **imprecision** *n*

impregnable (say im-preg-nəbəl) *adj* strong enough to be safe against attack ♦ *an impregnable fortress* **impregnability** *n* **impregnably** *adv*

impregnate (say im-preg-nayt) *v* **1** to introduce sperm into a female animal or pollen into a plant to fertilize it **2** to soak or saturate a substance ♦ *The cloth was impregnated with a cleaning liquid.* **impregnation** *n*

impresario (say impri-sar-i-oh) *n pl* **impresarios** a person who manages a theatre or music company and organizes productions

impress[1] (say im-press) *v* **1** to make a person admire or respect someone or something **2** to fix an idea firmly in the mind ♦ *We must impress on them the need for speed.* **3** to press a mark into something **impressive** *adj* **impressively** *adv*

impress[2] (say im-press) *n* a mark pressed into something

impression *n* **1** an effect produced on the mind **2** a vague or unclear idea, belief or memory **3** an imitation of a person or sound, done for entertainment **4** a mark pressed into a surface **5** a printing of a book with few or no alterations to its contents **impressionable** *adj* **impressionability** *n* **impressionably** *adv* **Impressionism** *n* **1** Art a style of painting in the late 19th century giving the general visual impression of a subject at a particular moment, rather than with accurate or elaborate detail **2** a similar style in music or literature **impressionist** *n* **impressionistic** *adj*

imprint[1] (say im-print) *n* a mark made by pressing or stamping a surface

imprint[2] (say im-print) *v* **1** to impress or stamp a mark on something **2** to establish an idea firmly in the mind

imprison *v* to confine someone, especially in a prison **imprisonment** *n*

improbable *adj* not likely to be true or to happen **improbability** *n* **improbably** *adv*

impromptu (say im-promp-tew) *adv*, *adj* without preparation or rehearsal **impromptu** *n pl* **impromptus** a short improvised musical composition, usually for piano

improper *adj* **1** unsuitable or wrong **2** not conforming to the rules of social or lawful conduct **3** indecent **improperly** *adv* **impropriety** *n pl* **improprieties**

improve *v* to make something better or to become better **improvable** *adj* **improvement** *n*

improvise (say im-prə-viyz) *v* **1** to compose or perform something without any preparation or rehearsal **2** to make or provide something quickly with whatever is available ♦ *We had to improvise a bed from cushions and rugs.* **improvisation** *n* **improviser** *n*

impudent (say im-pew-dənt) *adj* cheeky or disrespectful **impudence** *n* **impudently** *adv*

impugn (say im-pewn) *v* to express doubts about the truth or honesty of a statement or attitude ♦ *We do not impugn their motives.*

impulse *n* **1** a sudden desire to do

something ♦ *I did it on impulse.* **2** a push or impetus **impulsive** *adj* **impulsively** *adv* **impulsiveness** *n*

impulsion *n* **1** the force behind a process **2** a strong desire to do something

impunity (say im-**pewn**-iti) *n* freedom from punishment or injury ♦ *Gangs were using violence with impunity.*

impure *adj* **1** not pure, mixed with a foreign substance **2** morally wrong, indecent **impurity** *n pl* **impurities**

in *prep* **1** expressing a position or state of being enclosed or surrounded by something ♦ *in the house* **2** expressing movement into an enclosed or surrounded position ♦ *Then we went in the garden.* **3** expressing a period of time that something takes ♦ *We did it in three hours.* **4** expressing an interval of time after which something will happen ♦ *The train will arrive in half an hour.* **5** expressing a state, condition, or arrangement ♦ *The curtain hung in folds.* ♦ *She was dressed in red.* **6** expressing an activity or occupation ♦ *His father was in the army.* **7** expressing a method or means ♦ *He spoke in German.* ♦ *I paid in cash.* **8** expressing identity ♦ *Kate found a true friend in Mary.* **in** *adv* **1** expressing position or movement that involves being enclosed or surrounded ♦ *I opened the door and Charlie came in.* **2** present at home or at some other regular place ♦ *Will the manager be in this afternoon?* **3** favourable or fashionable ♦ *My luck was in that day.* **4** (in cricket and baseball) batting ♦ *Which side is in?* **5** expressing arrival or receipt ♦ *The train is already.* **in** *adj* *informal* fashionable ♦ *It's the in thing to do.*

in. *abbr* inch(es)

in- *prefix* (changing to **il-** before *l*, **im-** before *b, m, p,* **ir-** before *r*) **1** not (as in *incorrect, indirect*) **2** in, into, towards, or on (as in *include, invade*)

inability *n* being unable to do something

in absentia (say ab-**sent**-iǝ) *adv* in his, her, or their absence

inaccessible *adj* **1** (said about a place) not easy to find or reach **2** (said about a person) not easy to approach or talk to **inaccessibility** *n* **inaccessibly** *adv*

inaccurate *adj* not accurate **inaccuracy** *n*

inaccurately *adv*

inactive *adj* not active or working **inaction** *n* **inactively** *adv* **inactivity** *n*

inadequate *adj* **1** not adequate **2** (said about a person) not sufficiently able to deal with a situation or to cope generally ♦ *I felt so inadequate.* **inadequacy** *n* **inadequately** *adv*

inadmissible *adj* not allowable **inadmissibility** *n* **inadmissibly** *adv*

inadvertent (say in-ǝd-**ver**-tǝnt) *adj* unintentional, not deliberate **inadvertency** *adv* **inadvertently** *adv*

inadvisable *adj* not advisable, unwise **inadvisability** *n* **inadvisably** *adv*

inane *adj* silly, having no sense **inanely** *adv* **inanity** *n*

inanimate (say in-**an**-im-ǝt) *adj* **1** not having life in the way that animals and humans do **2** showing no sign of life

inapplicable (say in-ap-**lik**-ǝbǝl) *adj* not applicable or relevant

inappropriate (say in-ǝ-**proh**-pri-ǝt) *adj* not appropriate, unsuitable **inappropriately** *adv* **inappropriateness** *n*

inarticulate (say in-ar-**tik**-yoo-lǝt) *adj* **1** unable to speak distinctly or to express ideas clearly **2** not expressed in words ♦ *They heard an inarticulate cry from the landing.* **inarticulately** *adv*

inattentive *adj* not attentive, not paying attention **inattention** *n* **inattentively** *adv* **inattentiveness** *n*

inaudible (say in-**aw**-dibel) *adj* unable to be heard, not audible **inaudibility** *n* **inaudibly** *adv*

inaugurate (say in-awg-your-ayt) *v* **1** to admit a person formally to office **2** to begin or introduce an important project or undertaking **inaugural** *adj* **inauguration** *n* **inaugurator** *n*

inauspicious (say in-aw-**spish**-ǝs) *adj* unlikely to be successful **inauspiciously** *adv*

inborn *adj* existing in a person or animal from birth, natural ♦ *an inborn ability*

inbreeding *n* breeding from closely related individuals **inbred** *adj*

in-built *adj* built-in

Inc. *abbr* N. Am (in company names)

Incorporated

Inca n pl **Inca** or **Incas** a member of a South American Indian people living in Peru and the central Andes before the Spanish conquest

incalculable adj too great to be calculated, enormous ♦ *The damage was incalculable.* **incalculability** n **incalculably** adv

incandescent (say in-kan-dess-ənt) adj 1 giving out light when heated, shining 2 *informal* extremely angry **incandescence** n

incantation (say in-kan-tay-shən) n a set of words or sounds uttered as a magic spell or charm **incantatory** adj

incapable adj not able to do something ♦ *They seemed incapable of understanding the problem.* **incapability** n **incapably** adv

incapacitate (say in-kə-pas-i-tayt) v 1 to disable someone 2 to make someone ineligible for something **incapacitation** n

incapacity n 1 inability to do something or to manage your affairs 2 lack of sufficient strength or power

incarcerate (say in-kar-ser-ayt) v to imprison someone **incarceration** n

incarnate (say in-kar-nət) adj having a body or human form ♦ *a devil incarnate* **incarnation** n

incautious (say in-kaw-shəs) adj not cautious, rash **incautiously** adv

incendiary (say in-sen-di-er-i) adj 1 (said about a bomb or other device) designed to cause widespread fires 2 tending to stir up conflict **incendiary** n pl **incendiaries** an incendiary bomb or other device

incense[1] (say in-sens) n a substance that produces a sweet-smelling smoke when it burns

incense[2] (say in-sens) v to make someone angry

incentive (say in-sen-tiv) n something that encourages a person to do something or to work harder

inception (say in-sep-shən) n the beginning of an activity or institution

incessant (say in-sess-ənt) adj unceasing, continually repeated **incessantly** adv

incest (say in-sest) n sexual relations between people regarded as too closely

related to marry each other **incestuous** adj

inch n 1 a measure of length, equal to one twelfth of a foot (2.54 cm) 2 an amount of rainfall that would cover a surface to a depth of 1 inch 3 a very small amount ♦ *They would not yield an inch.* **inch** v to move slowly and gradually ♦ *The crows began to inch forward.*

incidence (say in-si-dəns) n the rate at which something, especially crime or disease, occurs or affects people or things ♦ *the lower incidence of heart disease in Mediterranean countries*

incident n 1 an event or happening, especially something short or relatively minor 2 public disturbance or violence ♦ *The protest went off without incident.* 3 an event that attracts general attention **incident** adj liable to happen as part of an activity ♦ *the dangers incident to mountaineering* **incidental** adj **incidentally** adv

incinerate (say in-sin-er-ayt) v to destroy something, especially waste material, by burning it completely **incineration** n **incinerator** n

incipient (say in-sip-iənt) adj in its early stages, beginning ♦ *incipient decay*

incise (say in-siyz) v to cut or engrave something into a surface **incision** n **incisive** adj clear and sharp **incisively** adv **incisiveness** n **incisor** n each of the sharp-edged front teeth in the upper and lower jaws

incite (say in-siyt) v to urge someone on to action, to stir someone up **incitement** n

incivility n pl **incivilities** rude or impolite remarks or behaviour

inclement (say in-klem-ənt) adj (said about the weather) cold, wet, or stormy **inclemency** n

incline[1] (say in-kliyn) v 1 to lean or slope 2 to bend the head or body forward 3 to cause someone to think a certain way ♦ *His behaviour inclines me to think he may be drunk.* **inclination** n

incline[2] (say in-kliyn) n a slope

include v 1 to have or treat something or someone as part of a whole 2 to put something or someone into a certain category **inclusion** n **inclusive** adj

inclusively *adv*

incognito (say in-kog-**nee**-toh) *adj*, *adv* with your name or identity kept secret ♦ *The film star was travelling incognito.* **incognito** *n pl* **incognitos** an identity assumed by someone who is incognito

incoherent (say in-koh-**heer**-ənt) *adj* not speaking or reasoning in an intelligible way **incoherence** *n* **incoherently** *adv*

income *n* money received regularly from doing work or from investments **income tax** *n*

incommensurate *adj* not in proportion, out of keeping

incommunicable *adj* unable to be communicated to other people

incommunicado (say in-kə-mew-ni-**kah**-doh) *adj* not able or allowed to communicate with other people ♦ *The prisoner was held incommunicado.*

incomparable (say in-**komp**-er-əbəl) *adj* without an equal, too good to be compared **incomparability** *n* **incomparably** *adv*

incompatible (say in-kəm-**pat**-ibəl) *adj* not able to exist or be used together **incompatibility** *n* **incompatibly** *adv*

incompetent (say in-**kom**-pi-tənt) *adj* not able or skilled enough to do something **incompetence** *n* **incompetently** *adv*

incomplete *adj* not complete **incompletely** *adv* **incompleteness** *n*

incomprehensible (say in-kom-pri-**hen**-sibəl) *adj* not able to be understood **incomprehensibility** *n* **incomprehensibly** *adv*

incomprehension (say in-kom-pri-**hen**-shən) *n* failure to understand

inconceivable *adj* **1** unable to be imagined **2** impossible to believe, most unlikely **inconceivably** *adv*

inconclusive *adj* (said about evidence or an argument) not fully convincing, not decisive **inconclusively** *adv* **inconclusiveness** *n*

incongruous (say in-**kong**-groo-əs) *adj* not in keeping with its surroundings, out of place **incongruity** *n* **incongruously** *adv*

inconsequent (say in-**kon**-si-kwənt) *adj* not following logically, irrelevant **inconsequence** *n* **inconsequential** *adj* **inconsequentially** *adv*

inconsequently *adv*

inconsiderable *adj* not worth considering, of small size or amount or value

inconsiderate *adj* not considerate towards other people **inconsiderately** *adv* **inconsiderateness** *n*

inconsistent *adj* not consistent **inconsistency** *n* **inconsistently** *adv*

inconsolable (say in-kən-**soh**-lə-bəl) *adj* too upset or distressed to be consoled **inconsolably** *adv*

inconspicuous *adj* not attracting attention or clearly visible **inconspicuously** *adv* **inconspicuousness** *n*

incontinent *adj* unable to control the bladder or bowels **incontinence** *n*

incontrovertible (say in-kon-trə-**vert**-ibəl) *adj* unable to be denied, indisputable **incontrovertibility** *n* **incontrovertibly** *adv*

inconvenient *adj* not convenient, slightly troublesome **inconvenience** *n* **inconveniently** *adv*

incorrect *adj* not correct, wrong **incorrectly** *adv* **incorrectness** *n*

incorrigible (say in-**ko**-ri-jibəl) *adj* (said about a person or behaviour) not able to be reformed or improved ♦ *an incorrigible liar* **incorrigibility** *n* **incorrigibly** *adv*

incorruptible (say in-kə-**rupt**-ibəl) *adj* **1** not able to be corrupted, especially by bribery **2** not subject to decay or death **incorruptibility** *n*

increase[1] (say in-**kreess**) *v* to make something greater in size or amount, or to become greater **increasingly** *adv*

increase[2] (say **in**-kreess) *n* **1** the process of increasing **2** an amount by which something increases ♦ *an increase of 50%*

incredible *adj* **1** unbelievable **2** hard to believe, very surprising **incredibly** *adv* **1** unbelievably **2** very

incredulous (say in-**kred**-yoo-ləs) *adj* not believing someone, showing disbelief **incredulity** *n* **incredulously** *adv*

increment (say **in**-kri-mənt) *n* an increase, an added amount, especially a regular increase in salary **incremental** *adj*

incriminate *v* to show a person to have been involved in a crime **incrimination** *n*

incrustation *n* **1** the process of forming a

crust **2** a crust or deposit that forms on a surface

incubate v **1** to hatch eggs by keeping them warm **2** to cause bacteria or a disease to develop **incubation** n **incubator** n

incumbent (say in-**kum**-bənt) adj forming an obligation or duty ♦ *It is incumbent on you to warn people of the danger.* **incumbent** n a person who holds a particular office **incumbency** n pl **incumbencies**

incur v **incurred**, **incurring** to undergo something unwelcome as a result of your own actions ♦ *We incurred great expense on our journey.*

incurable adj unable to be cured **incurable** n a person with an incurable disease **incurability** n **incurably** adv

incursion n a sudden raid or brief invasion

indebted adj owing money or gratitude to someone **indebtedness** n

indecent adj offending against generally accepted standards of decency **indecency** n **indecently** adv

indecipherable adj too difficult or untidy to be deciphered

indecision n inability to make up your mind, hesitation **indecisive** adj **indecisively** adv **indecisiveness** n

indecorous (say in-**dek**-er-əs) adj not in good taste, improper **indecorously** adv

indeed adv **1** truly, really ♦ *It is indeed a remarkable story.* **2** used to make a meaning stronger ♦ *The house is very nice indeed.* **3** admittedly ♦ *It is, indeed, their first attempt.* **4** used to express surprise or disapproval ♦ *Does she indeed!*

indefatigable (say indi-**fat**-ig-əbəl) adj not tiring easily, having a lot of stamina **indefatigably** adv

indefensible adj not able to be defended or justified **indefensibility** n **indefensibly** adv

indefinable (say indi-**fiy**-nəbəl) adj not able to be defined or described clearly **indefinably** adv

indefinite adj not clearly defined or decided, vague **indefinite article** n **indefinitely** adv

indelible adj **1** impossible to rub out or remove **2** not able to be forgotten ♦ *The incident left an indelible impression on them.* **indelibly** adv

indelicate adj **1** slightly indecent **2** tactless **indelicacy** n **indelicately** adv

indemnity n pl **indemnities 1** protection or insurance against penalties incurred by your actions **2** compensation for damage done **indemnify** v **indemnifies**, **indemnified**, **indemnifying**

indent[1] (say in-**dent**) v **1** to make notches or recesses in something **2** to start a line of print or writing further from the margin than the others **3** to place an official order for goods **indentation** n

indent[2] (say in-dent) n an official order for goods

independent adj **1** free from the control or authority of another person, country, or thing **2** not depending on someone else for an income ♦ *He has independent means.* **3** separate, not connected with anything else **4** (said about a person) wanting to avoid the influence of other people **Independent** n a politician who is not a member of any political party **independence** n **independently** adv **independent school** n a school that is not controlled by a local authority and does not receive a government grant

in-depth adj detailed and thorough

indescribable adj too unusual, extreme, or beautiful to be described **indescribably** adv

indestructible adj not able to be destroyed **indestructibility** n **indestructibly** adv

indeterminate adj not fixed or decided exactly; vague **indeterminable** adj **indeterminately** adv **indeterminately** adv

index n pl **indexes** or in technical uses pl **indices** (say **in**-di-seez) **1** an alphabetical list of names, titles, subjects, etc., especially one at the end of a book, showing where items occur in the text **2** a number indicating how prices or wages have changed from a previous level ♦ *the retail price index* **index** v **1** to make an index to a book, etc. **2** to enter an item in an index **3** to link the level of prices or wages to a price index **indexer** n **index finger** n the forefinger **index-linked** adj (said about wages or prices) adjusted according to the level of a price index

Indian *adj* to do with or coming from India in southern Asia **Indian** *n* **1** a person born in India or descended from people born there **2** a Native American **Indian summer** *n* a period of dry sunny weather in late autumn; a period of tranquil enjoyment late in life

indicate *v* **1** to point something out or make it known **2** to be a sign of something or show its presence **3** to show the need for a course of action ♦ *Immediate hospital treatment is indicated.* **4** to state something briefly ♦ *He indicated that we should follow him.* **5** (said of a driver) to use an indicator to show the intention of making a turn **indication** *n* **indicative** *adj* **1** giving an indication ♦ *The damage is indicative of an accident.* **2** *Gram* (said about the form of a verb) used to make a statement, not a command or wish, e.g. ♦ *He said.* or ♦ *She is coming.* **indicative** *n* the indicative form of a verb **indicator** *n* **1** a thing that indicates or points to something **2** a meter or gauge **3** an information board at an airport or railway station **4** a flashing light on a vehicle used to indicate a turn

indict (say in-**diyt**) *v* to formally accuse someone of a serious crime **indictable** *adj* **indictment** *n*

indifferent *adj* **1** not interested in something or not caring about it **2** not very good, fairly bad **indifference** *n* **indifferently** *adv*

indigenous (say in-**dij**-in-əs) *adj* (said about plants, animals, or inhabitants) growing or originating in a particular country, native ♦ *The koala bear is indigenous to Australia.*

indigent (say **in**-dij-ənt) *adj* poor or needy **indigence** *n*

indigestible (say indi-**jest**-ibəl) *adj* difficult or impossible to digest **indigestibility** *n* **indigestion** *n*

indignant *adj* feeling or showing anger about something unjust **indignantly** *adv* **indignation** *n*

indignity *n pl* **indignities 1** the quality of causing shame or humiliation **2** treatment that makes a person feel ashamed or humiliated

indigo *n* a deep-blue dye or colour

indirect *adj* not direct **indirectly** *adv*

indiscipline *n* lack of discipline, bad behaviour

indiscreet *adj* **1** revealing secrets or confidences too readily **2** not cautious, unwise **indiscreetly** *adv* **indiscretion** *n*

indiscriminate *adj* showing no discrimination, not making a careful choice **indiscriminately** *adv* **indiscrimination** *n*

indispensable *adj* not able to be dispensed with, essential **indispensability** *n* **indispensably** *adv*

indisposed *adj* **1** slightly unwell **2** unwilling to do something ♦ *They seem indisposed to help us.*

indisputable (say in-dis-**pewt**-əbəl) *adj* not able to be challenged or denied **indisputability** *n* **indisputably** *adv*

indissoluble (say indi-**sol**-yoo-bəl) *adj* not able to be dissolved or destroyed, firm and lasting **indissolubly** *adv*

indistinct *adj* not distinct, unclear **indistinctly** *adv* **indistinctness** *n*

indistinguishable *adj* not able to be distinguished from something else **indistinguishably** *adv*

indium *n* a soft silvery-white metallic element (symbol In) used in making semiconductors

individual *adj* **1** single or separate ♦ *Count each individual word.* **2** of or for one person ♦ *The gifts were wrapped in individual boxes.* **3** characteristic of one particular person or thing ♦ *She has a very individual style.* **individual** *n* **1** one person, plant, or animal considered separately **2** *informal* a person ♦ *He is a most selfish individual.* **individualist** *n* **individualism** *n* **individualistic** *adj* **individuality** *n* **individually** *adv*

indivisible (say indi-**viz**-ibəl) *adj* not able to be divided **indivisibility** *n* **indivisibly** *adv*

Indo- *prefix* Indian, Indian (and) (as in *Indo-Chinese*)

indoctrinate (say in-**dok**-trin-ayt) *v* to make someone believe particular ideas or doctrines by constantly instructing them **indoctrination** *n*

Indo-European *adj* to do with the family of languages spoken over most of Europe and Asia as far as north India **Indo-European** *n*

1 this family of languages **2** a speaker of any of these languages

indolent (say **in**-dəl-ənt) *adj* lazy **indolence** *n* **indolently** *adv*

indoor *adj* situated, used, or done inside a building ♦ *indoor games* ♦ *an indoor aerial* **indoors** *adv*

induce (say in-**dewss**) *v* **1** to persuade someone to do something **2** to produce or cause something **3** to bring on labour in childbirth by artificial means **inducement** *n*

induct *v* to admit someone, especially a member of the clergy, formally into an office **induction** *n*

indulge *v* **1** to allow someone to have whatever they want **2** to gratify a wish **indulgence** *n* **indulgent** *adj* **indulgently** *adv*

industry *n pl* **industries 1** the manufacture or production of goods **2** a particular branch of this, or any business activity ♦ *the motor industry* ♦ *the tourist industry* **3** the quality of working hard **industrial** *adj* **industrialist** *n* a person who owns or manages an industrial business **industrialization** *n* **industrialized** *adj* (said about a country or area) having many industries **industrially** *adv* **industrious** *adj* **industriously** *adv* **industriousness** *n* **industrial action** *n* a strike or other action taken against an employer **industrial estate** *n* an area of land developed as a site for industries **industrial relations** *pl n* relations between workers and managers in industry **Industrial Revolution** *n* the expansion of British industry by the use of machines in the late 18th and early 19th centuries

inebriated (say in-ee-bri-ayt-id) *adj* drunk; intoxicated **inebriation** *n*

inedible *adj* not suitable for eating

ineducable (say in-ed-yoo-kəbəl) *adj* incapable of being educated

ineffable (say in-ef-əbəl) *adj* too great to be described ♦ *ineffable joy* **ineffably** *adv*

ineffective *adj* **1** not effective **2** (said about a person) inefficient **ineffectively** *adv*

ineffectual *adj* not producing the result that is wanted **ineffectually** *adv*

inefficient *adj* not making the best use

of time and resources **inefficiency** *n* **inefficiently** *adv*

ineligible *adj* not eligible **ineligibility** *n*

inept *adj* lacking any skill; awkward or clumsy **ineptitude** *n* **ineptly** *adv*

inequality *n pl* **inequalities** lack of equality in size or status

inequitable (say in-ek-wit-əbəl) *adj* unfair or unjust **inequitably** *adv* **inequity** *n*

inert *adj* **1** not having the power to move or act **2** without active chemical or other properties; incapable of reacting ♦ *an inert gas* **3** slow to move or take action **inertly** *adv* **inertness** *n*

inertia (say in-er-shə) *n* slowness to take action **inertial** *adj*

inescapable *adj* unavoidable **inescapably** *adv*

inessential *adj* not essential **inessential** *n* an inessential thing

inestimable (say in-est-im-əbəl) *adj* too great or precious to be estimated **inestimably** *adv*

inevitable (say in-ev-it-əbəl) *adj* not able to be prevented; certain to happen **inevitability** *n* **inevitably** *adv*

inexact *adj* not exact **inexactitude** *n* **inexactly** *adv*

inexcusable *adj* not able to be excused or justified **inexcusably** *adv*

inexhaustible *adj* not able to be used up, never ending

inexorable (say in-eks-er-əbəl) *adj* **1** relentless **2** not able to be persuaded by requests or entreaties **inexorably** *adv*

inexpensive *adj* not expensive, offering good value for the price **inexpensively** *adv*

inexperience *n* lack of experience **inexperienced** *adj*

inexpert *adj* not expert, unskilful **inexpertly** *adv*

inexplicable (say in-eks-plik-əbəl or in-iks-plik-əbəl) *adj* unable to be explained or accounted for **inexplicably** *adv*

inexpressible *adj* not able to be expressed in words **inexpressibly** *adv*

infallible (say in-fal-ibəl) *adj* **1** incapable of making a mistake or being wrong **2** never failing, always effective ♦ *an infallible remedy* **infallibility** *n* **infallibly** *adv*

infamous (say in-fə-məs) adj well known for some bad quality or action **infamy** n

infancy n 1 early childhood, babyhood 2 an early stage of development

infant n a baby or young child **infanticide** n the act of killing an infant soon after its birth **infantile** adj

infantry n soldiers who fight on foot **infantryman** n pl **infantrymen**

infatuated adj having an intense but short-lived love for a person or thing **infatuation** n

infect v 1 to affect a person or organism with a disease or with bacteria that cause disease 2 to cause someone to share a feeling ♦ Parents are infected by their children's humour. **infection** n **infectious** adj

infer v **inferred, inferring** to reach an opinion from what someone says or does, rather than from an explicit statement ♦ I infer from all your bags that you have been shopping. **inference** n **inferential** adj

inferior adj less good or less important than someone or something else; lower in quality or ability **inferior** n a person who is lower than someone else in rank or ability **inferiority** n

inferno (say in-fer-noh) n pl **infernos** a raging fire; somewhere intensely hot **infernal** adj **infernally** adv

infertile adj 1 unable to produce young, not fertile 2 (said about land) unable to bear crops or vegetation **infertility** n

infest v (said about pests or vermin) to be numerous and troublesome in a place **infestation** n

infidelity n pl **infidelities** unfaithfulness, or an unfaithful act **infidel** n (used about people in the past) someone who did not believe in a religion

infighting n 1 hidden conflict within a group or organization 2 boxing closer to an opponent than at arm's length

infiltrate (say **in**-fil-trayt) v 1 to enter a place or organization gradually and without being noticed, usually in order to harm or change it or to spy on it 2 to pass fluid by filtration **infiltration** n **infiltrator** n

infinite (say **in**-fin-it) adj 1 having no limit, endless 2 too great or too many to

be measured or counted **infinitely** adv **infinitude** n **infinity** n

infinitesimal (say in-fini-**tess**-iməl) adj extremely small **infinitesimally** adv

infirm adj physically weak, especially from old age or illness **infirmary** n pl **infirmaries** **infirmity** n pl **infirmities**

inflame v 1 to provoke someone to strong feelings or emotion, especially anger 2 to cause a painful redness and swelling in a part of the body **inflammation** n **inflammatory** adj

inflammable adj able to be set on fire ◊ This word means the same as flammable. If you want to say that something is not able to be set on fire, use non-flammable.

inflatable (say in-**flayt**-əbəl) adj able to be inflated

inflate v 1 to fill something with air or gas so that it swells out 2 to swell out from being filled with air or gas 3 to puff someone up with pride, etc. 4 to increase prices or wages more than is necessary or justified 5 to cause inflation in a country's economy **inflation** n **inflationary** adj

inflect v to change the pitch of the voice in speaking

inflexible adj 1 not flexible; not able to be bent 2 not able to be altered ♦ an inflexible rule 3 refusing to change your mind or be persuaded **inflexibility** n **inflexibly** adv

inflict v to make a person suffer something painful or unpleasant **infliction** n

inflow n 1 an inward flow ♦ the inflow of traffic 2 an amount that flows in ♦ a large inflow of cash

influence n 1 the ability or power to affect the character or behaviour of someone or something 2 a person or thing with this ability 3 power arising from a person's position or authority **influence** v to have an influence on someone or something **influential** adj **influentially** adv

influenza n a contagious virus disease causing fever, muscular pain, and catarrh

influx n an inflow, especially of people or things into a place

inform v to give information to someone **informative** adj **informed** adj **informer** n

informal adj 1 not formal, unofficial ♦ an

informal interview **2** (said about clothes) suitable for casual or everyday wear **3** (said about words or language) used in everyday speech **informality** *n* **informally** *adv*

informant *n* a person who gives information about someone else

information *n* **1** facts or knowledge learned or provided **2** data put into a computer **information science** *n* the study or use of processes for storing and retrieving information **information superhighway** *n* the rapid availability of information, especially on the Internet **information technology** *n* the study or use of computer systems for storing, retrieving, and sending information

infra- *prefix* below

infraction (say in-frak-shən) *n* an infringement of a law or agreement

infra-red *adj* (said about radiation) having a wavelength that is slightly longer than that of visible light-rays at the red end of the spectrum

infrastructure *n* the buildings, physical communications, and organization that form the basis of an enterprise

infrequent *adj* occasional; not frequent **infrequency** *n* **infrequently** *adv*

infringe *v* **1** to break a rule or agreement **2** to encroach on a person's rights, etc. **infringement** *n*

infuriate *v* to make someone very angry **infuriating** *adj*

infuse *v* **1** to inspire someone with a feeling ♦ *She infused them all with courage.* **2** to put tea or herbs in a liquid to extract the flavour; (said about tea, etc.) to undergo this process **infuser** *n* **infusion** *n*

ingenious *adj* **1** clever at inventing things or devising methods **2** cleverly made ♦ *an ingenious machine* ◊ Do not confuse this word with *ingenuous*, which has a different meaning. **ingeniously** *adv* **ingenuity** *n*

ingenuous (say in-jen-yoo-əs) *adj* without artfulness, innocent ♦ *an ingenuous manner* ◊ Do not confuse this word with *ingenious*, which has a different meaning. **ingenuously** *adv* **ingenuousness** *n*

ingest (say in-jest) *v* to take food or drink into the body by swallowing it **ingestion** *n*

inglorious *adj* **1** not worthy of honour **2** not famous or well-known, obscure

ingrained *adj* **1** (said about habits or attitudes) firmly established **2** (said about dirt) deeply embedded in a surface

ingratiate (say in-gray-shi-ayt) *v* to **ingratiate yourself** to try to please or flatter someone

ingratitude *n* lack of gratitude when it is due

ingredient *n* any of the parts or elements used in a mixture, especially one of the foods used in a recipe

ingrowing *adj* growing abnormally into the flesh ♦ *an ingrowing toenail*

inhabit *v* **inhabited, inhabiting** to live in a place as your home or environment **inhabitable** *adj* **inhabitant** *n*

inhale *v* to breathe in; to draw air, smoke, gas, etc. into the lungs by breathing **inhalation** *n* **inhaler** *n*

inherent (say in-heer-ənt) *adj* existing in something as one of its natural or permanent characteristics or qualities **inherence** *n* **inherently** *adv*

inherit *v* **inherited, inheriting 1** to receive money, property, or a title by legal right when the previous owner or holder has died **2** to receive something from a predecessor **3** to receive a characteristic from your parents or ancestors **inheritance** *n* **inheritor** *n*

inhibit *v* **inhibited, inhibiting 1** to restrain or prevent something ♦ *a substance that inhibits the growth of weeds* **2** to prevent or discourage someone from behaving naturally **inhibition** *n*

inhospitable (say in-hoss-pit-əbəl or in-hoss-pit-əbəl) *adj* **1** not hospitable **2** (said about a place or climate) providing no shelter or favourable conditions

inhuman *adj* cruel or brutal; without pity or kindness **inhumanity** *n*

inhumane (say in-hew-mayn) *adj* without pity for suffering; not humane

inimitable (say in-im-it-əbəl) *adj* impossible to imitate, unique **inimitably** *adv*

iniquity (say in-ik-witi) *n pl* **iniquities** great injustice or wickedness **iniquitous** *adj*

initial *adj* belonging to the beginning

of something ♦ *the initial stages of the project* **initial** *n* the first letter of a word or name **initial** *v* **initialled**, **initialling** to sign or mark a document with your initials **initially** *adv*

nitiate[1] (say in-**ish**-i-ayt) *v* **1** to make a process or activity begin **2** to admit someone formally to a society or organization, often with a ceremony **3** to give someone basic instruction or information about something that is new to them **initiation** *n* **initiative** *n* **1** the action that starts something **2** the ability to start things on your own **initiator** *n* **initiatory** *adj*

nitiate[2] (say in-**ish**-i-ət) *n* a person who has been initiated

nject *v* **1** to put a medicine or drug into the body by means of a syringe **2** to put liquid into something under pressure **3** to introduce a new element or quality ♦ *We have tried to inject some energy into the project.* **injector** *n*

njection *n* **1** the process of injecting **2** a liquid or other substance that is injected

njunction *n* a command given with authority, especially an order from a law court

njure *v* **1** to harm or hurt someone **2** to do wrong to someone **injurious** *adj*

njury *n* *pl* **injuries 1** damage or harm **2** a particular form of harm ♦ *a leg injury* **3** a wrong or unjust act

njustice *n* **1** lack of justice **2** an unjust action or treatment

nk *n* a black or coloured liquid used in writing or printing **ink** *v* to mark or cover something with ink **inky** *adj* **inkier, inkiest**

nkling *n* a hint, a slight knowledge or suspicion

nland *adj*, *adv* in or towards the interior of a country, away from the coast

n-laws *pl n informal* a person's relatives by marriage

nlay[1] (say in-**lay**) *v* past tense and past participle **inlaid** to set pieces of wood or metal into a surface to form a design **inlaid** *adj*

nlay[2] (say **in**-lay) *n* **1** an inlaid design or piece of material **2** a dental filling shaped to

fit the cavity in a tooth

inlet *n* **1** a strip of water reaching into the land from a sea or lake **2** a passage or way in ♦ *an air inlet*

inmate *n* a person living in an institution such as a hospital or prison

in memoriam (say mi-**mor**-i-am) *prep* in memory of someone dead

inmost *adj* furthest inward

inn *n* a hotel or public house, especially in the country **innkeeper** *n*

innards *pl n informal* **1** the internal organs of a person or animal, the entrails **2** the inner working parts of a machine

innate (say in-**ayt**) *adj* inborn, natural **innately** *adv*

inner *adj* nearer to the inside or centre; interior, internal **innermost** *adj* furthest in; closest to the centre **inner city** *n* the central area of a city, especially where there is overcrowding and poverty **inner tube** *n* a separate inflatable tube inside the casing of a pneumatic tyre

innings *n pl* **innings** (in cricket) a side's turn at batting or a particular player's turn

innocent *adj* **1** not guilty of a particular crime or offence **2** free of wickedness or wrongdoing **3** harmless; not intended to cause offence ♦ *an innocent remark* **4** foolishly trusting **innocence** *n* **innocent** *n* **innocently** *adv*

innocuous (say in-**ok**-yoo-əs) *adj* harmless **innocuously** *adv* **innocuousness** *n*

innovate *v* to introduce a new process or way of doing things **innovation** *n* **innovator** *n* **innovatory** *adj*

innuendo (say in-yoo-**en**-doh) *n pl* **innuendoes** or **innuendos** an indirect reference to something rude or insulting

innumerable *adj* too many to be counted **innumerably** *adv*

innumerate *adj* having a poor basic knowledge of numbers and mathematics **innumeracy** *n*

inoculate *v* to treat or inject a person or animal with a vaccine or serum as a protection against a disease **inoculation** *n*

inoffensive *adj* not offensive, harmless

inoperable (say in-**op**-er-əbəl) *adj* (said about a disease) not able to be cured by surgical operation

inoperative *adj* not functioning

inopportune (say in-**op**-er-tewn) *adj* coming or happening at an unsuitable time **inopportunely** *adv*

inordinate (say in-**or**-din-ət) *adj* excessive **inordinately** *adv*

inorganic (say in-or-**gan**-ik) *adj* not made of living organisms; of mineral origin

inpatient *n* a patient who lives in hospital while receiving treatment

input *n* 1 what is put into something 2 electrical or other energy supplied to a device or system 3 *ICT* the data or programs put into a computer **input** *v* past tense and past participle **input** or **inputted**; **inputting** *ICT* to put data or programs into a computer

inquest *n* an official investigation to establish the facts about how a person died

inquire *v* to investigate something carefully or officially **inquirer** *n* **inquiry** *n pl* **inquiries**

inquisition (say inkwi-**zish**-ən) *n* a detailed questioning or investigation **inquisitor** *n* **inquisitorial** *adj* the Inquisition a council of the Roman Catholic Church in the Middle Ages

inquisitive *adj* 1 curious or prying 2 eagerly seeking knowledge **inquisitively** *adv*

inroad *n* a sudden attack made into a country

insane *adj* 1 not sane; mad 2 extremely foolish **insanely** *adv* **insanity** *n*

insanitary *adj* unclean and likely to be harmful to health

insatiable (say in-**say**-shə-bəl) *adj* impossible to satisfy ♦ *an insatiable appetite* **insatiability** *n* **insatiably** *adv*

inscribe *v* 1 to write or carve words or a design on a surface ♦ *They inscribed their names on the stone.* 2 to enter a name on a list or in a book **inscription** *n*

inscrutable (say in-**skroot**-əbəl) *adj* mysterious; impossible to understand or interpret **inscrutability** *n* **inscrutably** *adv*

insect *n* a small animal with six legs, no backbone, and a body divided into three parts (head, thorax, and abdomen) **insecticide** *n* **insectivore** *n*

insectivorous *adj*

insecure *adj* not secure or saf **insecurely** *adv* **insecurity** *n*

inseminate (say in-**sem**-in-ayt) *v* to inser semen into the womb **insemination** *n*

insensible *adj* 1 unconscious or withou feeling 2 unaware of something ♦ *The seemed insensible of the danger they wer in.* 3 too small or gradual to be notice ♦ *insensible changes* **insensibility insensibly** *adv*

insensitive *adj* showing little concer for other people's feelings, not sensitiv **insensitively** *adv* **insensitivity** *n*

insentient (say in-**sen**-shənt) *adj* incapabl of feeling, not sentient

inseparable *adj* 1 unable to be separate 2 liking to be constantly together ♦ *Th friends were inseparable.* **inseparability inseparably** *adv*

insert[1] (say in-**sert**) *v* to put somethin in, between, or among other thing **insertion** *n*

insert[2] (say **in**-sert) *n* something inserte especially a loose page or advertisement i a magazine

in-service *adj* undertaken by people i connection with their jobs while they ar employed ♦ *in-service training*

inset[1] (say in-**set**) *v* past tense and pas participle **inset** or **insetted**; **insetting** t decorate something with something se into its surface ♦ *The crown is inset wit jewels.*

inset[2] (say **in**-set) *n* 1 something set into larger thing 2 a small map printed withi the frame of a larger one

inshore *adv*, *adj* near or nearer to the shore

inside *n* 1 the inner side, surface, or part c something 2 (**insides**) *informal* the orgar in the abdomen; the stomach and bowe **inside** *adj* on or coming from the insid in or nearest to the middle **inside** *adv* 1 c or to the inside of something ♦ *Please com inside.* 2 *informal* in prison **inside** *prep* c the inner side of, within ♦ *The rabbit is insic the box.* ♦ *He arrived inside an hour.* **insider**

insight *n* 1 the ability to recognize an understand the truth about somethin 2 knowledge obtained by this ability

insignia (say in-**sig**-niə) pl n a badge or symbol that marks a military rank or a particular office or position

insignificant adj having little or no importance or influence **insignificance** n **insignificantly** adv

insincere adj not sincere **insincerely** adv **insincerity** n

insinuate (say in-**sin**-yoo-ayt) v 1 to hint something unpleasant or offensive 2 to introduce yourself gradually to a place ♦ They insinuated themselves into the group. **insinuation** n

insipid (say in-**sip**-id) adj 1 lacking flavour 2 not lively or interesting **insipidly** adv

insist v to say or ask for something firmly ♦ We insist that you stay. **insistent** adj **insistence** n **insistently** adv

in situ (say **sit**-yoo) adv, adj in its original place

insobriety (say in-sə-**briy**-iti) n lack of sobriety, drunkenness

insole n 1 the inner sole of a boot or shoe 2 a loose piece of material put in the bottom of a shoe for warmth or to improve the fit

insolent adj behaving insultingly or arrogantly **insolence** n **insolently** adv

insoluble adj 1 unable to be dissolved 2 unable to be solved ♦ an insoluble problem **insolubility** n **insolubly** adv

insolvent adj unable to pay your debts **insolvency** n

insomnia n habitual inability to sleep **insomniac** n

insomuch adv to such an extent

insouciant (say in-**soo**-si-ənt or an-**soo**-si-ahn) adj casual and unconcerned **insouciance** n

inspect v 1 to examine something carefully and critically 2 to examine a place officially **inspection** n **inspector** n

inspire v 1 to fill someone with an urge to do something or with a strong feeling about something ♦ She inspires confidence in everyone. 2 to inhale **inspiration** n

instability n lack of stability

install v 1 to put equipment or machinery in position and ready for use 2 to place someone in office, especially with ceremonies 3 to settle someone in a place

installation n **instalment** n each of the parts in which something is presented or paid for over a period of time

instance n a case or example of something **instance** v to mention something as an instance or example

instant adj 1 happening immediately ♦ instant success 2 (said about food) designed to be prepared quickly and easily ♦ instant coffee **instant** n 1 an exact point of time; the present moment ♦ Come here this instant! 2 a very short space of time, a moment **instantaneous** adj **instantaneously** adv **instantly** adv

instead adv as an alternative or substitute for something else

instep n 1 the top of the foot between the toes and the ankle 2 the part of a shoe that fits over or under this

instigate v 1 to urge or encourage someone to do something 2 to make something happen by using persuasion ♦ We shall instigate an inquiry into the affair. **instigation** n **instigator** n

instil v instilled, instilling to put ideas into someone's mind gradually **instillation** n **instilment** n

instinct n 1 an inborn impulse or tendency to perform certain acts or behave in certain ways 2 a natural ability ♦ She has an instinct for saying the right thing. **instinctive** adj **instinctively** adv **instinctual** adj **instinctually** adv

institute n a society or organization that promotes a particular scientific or educational activity **institute** v 1 to establish or found an organization or practice 2 to cause an inquiry to be started **institution** n **institutional** adj **institutionalize** v **institutionalization** n

instruct v 1 to teach a person a subject or skill 2 to inform someone officially of something 3 to tell someone what they must do 4 to authorize a solicitor or counsel to act on your behalf **instruction** n **instructional** adj **instructive** adj **instructively** adv **instructor** n

instrument n 1 a tool or implement that is designed for delicate or scientific work 2 a measuring device giving information about the operation of an engine or machine or used in navigation **3** a device designed for producing musical sounds **4** a person made use of or controlled by someone else **5** *formal* a formal or legal document ♦ *an instrument of abdication* **instrumental** *adj* **instrumentalist** *n* **instrumentation** *n*

insubordinate *adj* disobedient or rebellious **insubordination** *n*

insubstantial *adj* **1** not existing in reality, imaginary **2** lacking strength or force ♦ *The prosecution could only offer insubstantial evidence.*

insufferable *adj* **1** unbearable ♦ *The weather was insufferable.* **2** unbearably conceited or arrogant **insufferably** *adv*

insufficient *adj* not sufficient **insufficiency** *n* **insufficiently** *adv*

insular (say **ins**-yoo-ler) *adj* **1** isolated from outside influences, narrow-minded ♦ *insular prejudices* **2** like an island or forming an island **insularity** *n*

insulate (say **ins**-yoo-layt) *v* **1** to cover or protect something to prevent heat, cold, electricity, etc. from passing in or out **2** to isolate a person or place from external influences **insulation** *n* **insulator** *n*

insulin (say **ins**-yoo-lin) *n* a hormone produced in the pancreas, which controls the amount of glucose in the blood

insult[1] (say in-**sult**) *v* to speak or act in a way that offends someone or makes them angry

insult[2] (say **in**-sult) *n* an offensive or hurtful remark or action

insupportable *adj* not able to be supported or justified; intolerable **insupportably** *adv*

insure *v* to protect someone or something by a contract of insurance **insurance** *n* **insurer** *n*

insurgent (say in-**ser**-jent) *adj* rebellious, rising in revolt **insurgence** *n* **insurgent** *n* a rebel

insurmountable (say in-ser-**mount**-ebel) *adj* impossible to overcome, insuperable

insurrection (say in-ser-**ek**-shen) *n* a rebellion **insurrectionist** *n*

intact *adj* undamaged, complete

intake *n* **1** the process of taking something

in **2** the place where liquid or air is fe into something **3** the number or quantit of people or things that are received o admitted ♦ *The school's annual intake c pupils is over 100.*

intangible (say in-**tan**-jibel) *adj* not able t be touched, not material **intangibly** *adv*

integral (say **in**-ti-grel) *adj* **1** formin an essential part, necessary to mak something complete ♦ *The garage is a integral part of the building.* **2** complete forming a whole ♦ *an integral desig* **integral** *n* Mathematics a quantity c which a given function is the derivativ **integrally** *adv*

integrate (say **in**-ti-grayt) *v* **1** to make part into a whole, to combine parts **2** to join community, or to bring someone into community **integration** *n*

integrity (say in-**teg**-riti) *n* **1** being hones or incorruptible **2** wholeness

intellect (say **in**-ti-lekt) *n* power of the min to reason and absorb knowledge, as distinc from feeling and instinct **intellectual** *ad* **intellectually** *adv*

intelligent *adj* **1** able to absorb knowledg and understand things **2** (said about device in a computer system) containin a capacity to process informatio **intelligence** *n* **intelligently** *ad* **intelligentsia** *n* intelligent people

intelligible (say in-**tel**-i-jibel) *adj* abl to be understood **intelligibility** **intelligibly** *adv*

intend *v* **1** to have something in min as what you want to do or achieve **2** t plan that something should be used o understood in a particular way

intense *adj* **1** very strong or great ♦ *intens pain* **2** (said about a person) feeling thing strongly, highly emotional **intensely** *ad* **intensify** *v* **intensifies**, **intensified intensifying**, **intensification** *n* **intensity** **intensive** *adj* **intensively** *adv* **intensiv care** *n*

intent *n* intention or purpose **intent** *ad* **1** having your mind fixed on a purpos ♦ *They are intent on finishing the building th week.* **2** with the attention concentrate ♦ *an intent gaze* **intention** *n* what

...person intends to do **intentional** adj
intentionally adv **intently** adv
intentness n

...ter (say in-ter) v **interred**, **interring** to
bury a dead body in the earth or in a tomb

...ter- prefix between or among

...teract v to have an effect on each other
...teraction n **interactive** adj allowing
information to be exchanged between a
computer and its user

...tercede (say inter-seed) v to intervene
on behalf of another person or as a
peacemaker

...tercept (say inter-sept) v to stop or
catch a person or thing while it is going
from one place to another **interception** n
interceptor n

...terchange[1] (say inter-chaynj) v **1** to put
each of two things into the other's place
2 to give and receive one thing for another
3 to alternate **interchangeable** adj

...terchange[2] (say in-ter-chaynj) n **1** the
process of interchanging **2** a road junction

...tercity adj existing or travelling between
cities

...tercom (say in-ter-kom) n a system
of communication between parts of a
building, operating like a telephone

...terconnect v to connect with each other
interconnection n

...tercontinental adj relating to or
travelling between two continents

...tercourse n regular dealings or
communication between people or
countries

...terdependent adj dependent on each
other **interdependence** n

...terdict (say inter-dikt) v to prohibit or
forbid something formally **interdiction** n

...terdisciplinary adj relating to or
involving different branches of learning

...terest n **1** a feeling of wanting to know
about something or to become involved
in it **2** the quality of arousing this sort of
feeling ♦ The subject has no interest for me.
3 a subject or activity that someone likes
to follow ♦ Music is one of her interests. **4** an
advantage or benefit ♦ We need to protect
our own interests. **5** a legal right to a share in
something, or a financial stake in a business

6 money paid regularly in return for the use
of money that has been lent **interest** v **1** to
arouse the interest of someone **2** to lead
someone to take an interest in something
♦ He interested himself in welfare work.
interested adj **interesting** adj

interface n **1** a point or surface where two
thing meet and interact **2** ICT a connection
between two parts of a computer system
interface v to connect with something by
means of an interface **interfacing** n

interfere v **1** to take a part in other people's
affairs without any right to do so **2** to get in
the way of something or make something
difficult **3** Phys to produce interference

interference n **1** the process of interfering
2 disturbance to radio signals caused by
atmospherics or unwanted signals

interim (say in-ter-im) n a period of time
between two events ♦ in the interim
interim adj relating to a period of time
when there is more to come, temporary
♦ an interim report

interior adj nearer to the centre, inner
interior n **1** an inside part or region, the
central or inland part of a country **2** the
inside of a building or room

interject v to add a remark when someone
is speaking **interjection** n

interlace v to weave or lace things together

interlock v to fit into each other so that
parts engage and work together

interloper n someone who interferes in
other people's affairs

interlude n **1** an interval or pause,
especially between parts of a performance
in a theatre, etc. **2** something performed
during an interval or between other events
3 a temporary activity or diversion ♦ a
romantic interlude

intermediary (say inter-meed-i-er-i) n
pl **intermediaries** someone who tries to
settle a disagreement by negotiating with
both sides; a mediator **intermediary** adj
intermediate in position or form

intermediate adj **1** coming between two
things in time, place, or order **2** having
more than the basic knowledge of a subject
but not yet advanced

interment (say in-ter-mənt) n the burial of

a dead person

interminable (say in-**ter**-min-əbəl) *adj* seeming to be endless; long and boring **interminably** *adv*

intermission *n* 1 an interval during a play or film 2 a pause in work or action

intermittent *adj* happening at intervals; not continuous ♦ *periods of rain with intermittent sunshine* **intermittently** *adv*

intern (say in-**tern**) *v* to confine someone as a prisoner, especially during a war **internment** *n* **intern** (say **in**-tern) *n* a trainee doing work experience

internal *adj* 1 of or on the inside of something 2 to do with the domestic affairs of a country 3 used as or applying within an organization 4 to do with the mind or soul **internally** *adv*

international *adj* 1 to do with several countries or all countries 2 agreed on by all or most countries ♦ *international law* **international** *n* 1 a sports contest between players representing different countries 2 a player who has taken part in a contest of this kind **internationally** *adv*

Internet *n* an international computer network that allows users throughout the world to communicate and exchange information with one another

interpersonal *adj* to do with relations or communication between people

interplanetary *adj* travelling between planets

interplay *n* interaction between people or things

interpose *v* 1 to insert something between one thing and another 2 to add a remark during a conversation 3 to intervene **interposition** *n*

interpret (say in-**ter**-prit) *v* 1 to explain the meaning of something said or written, or of someone's actions 2 to understand something in a specified way 3 to translate the words of a speaker orally into a different language **interpretation** *n* **interpreter** *n*

interrelated *adj* related to each other **interrelation** *n*

interrogate (say in-**te**-rə-gayt) *v* 1 to question someone closely or formally 2 to get information from a computer or

database **interrogation** *n* **interrogative** *a*

interrogator *n*

interrupt *v* 1 to break the continuity of process, to prevent something continuir 2 to break in on what someone is sayir by inserting a remark 3 to obstruct a vie **interrupter** *n* **interruption** *n*

intersect *v* 1 to divide something by passir or lying across it 2 (said about lines or road etc.) to cross each other **intersection** *n*

intersperse *v* to insert things here ar there in something different

interval *n* 1 a time between two events ♦ parts of an action 2 a pause between tw parts of a theatrical or musical performanc 3 a space between two objects or points

intervene (say inter-**veen**) *v* 1 to happen the time between events ♦ *in the intervenir years* 2 to interrupt an action or proce by happening 3 to join in a discussion ♦ dispute in order to stop it or change i result **intervention** *n*

interview *n* a formal meeting ♦ conversation with a person in order obtain information about them **interview** to hold an interview with someor **interviewee** *n* **interviewer** *n*

intestine (say in-**test**-in) *n* the long tubul section of the passage in which food digested (called the *alimentary canal*), fro the stomach to the anus **intestinal** *adj*

intimate[1] (say **in**-tim-ət) *adj* 1 having a clo acquaintance or friendship with someor 2 having a sexual relationship wi someone 3 private and personal ♦ *intima thoughts* 4 (said about knowledge) detaile and obtained from long experience ♦ *intimate friel* **intimacy** *n* **intimately** *adv*

intimate[2] (say **in**-tim-ayt) *v* to mal something known, especially by hintir **intimation** *n*

intimidate (say in-**tim**-i-dayt) *v* to subdu or influence someone by frightening threatening them **intimidation** *n*

into *prep* 1 expressing movement direction to a point within somethin ♦ *We went into the house.* ♦ *The child f into the river.* 2 expressing change to ♦ certain state or condition ♦ *You will get in*

trouble. ♦ *Soon she had grown into an adult.*
3 expressing active interest or involvement
♦ *She is into rock music.* **4** Mathematics
expressing division ♦ *4 into 20 gives 5.*

intolerable *adj* not able to be tolerated,
unbearable **intolerably** *adv*

intolerant *adj* not tolerant, unwilling to
tolerate other ideas or beliefs **intolerance** *n*
intolerantly *adv*

intone *v* to say or recite words in a chanting
voice, often on one note **intonation** *n*

intoxicated *adj* (said about a person) drunk
intoxicant *n* a drink or drug that makes you
intoxicated **intoxication** *n*

intra- *prefix* within

intranet (say **in**-trə-net) *n* ICT an
organization's private communications
network using Internet technology

intrepid (say in-**trep**-id) *adj* fearless and
brave **intrepidity** *n* **intrepidly** *adv*

intricate *adj* very complicated or detailed
intricacy *n* **intricately** *adv*

intrigue (say in-**treeg**) *v* **1** to arouse a
person's interest or curiosity ♦ *The subject
intrigues me.* **2** to plot with someone in a
devious way, especially to do harm **intrigue**
(also say **in**-treeg) *n* devious or secret
plotting; a secret plot

intrinsic (say in-**trin**-sik) *adj* belonging
naturally or essentially to a person or
thing ♦ *The coin has little intrinsic value.*
intrinsically *adv*

intro- *prefix* into or inwards

introduce *v* **1** to bring an idea or practice
into use **2** to make a person known by
name to other people **3** to announce
a speaker or broadcast programme to
listeners or viewers **4** to bring a bill before
Parliament **5** to cause a person to become
acquainted with a subject **introduction** *n*
introductory *adj*

introspection *n* the process of
concentrating on your own thoughts and
feelings **introspective** *adj*

introvert (say **in**-trə-vert) *n* a quiet reticent
person **introverted** *adj*

intrude *v* to come or join in without being
invited or wanted **intruder** *n* **intrusion** *n*
intrusive *adj*

intuition (say in-tew-**ish**-ən) *n* the ability

to know or understand something
immediately without conscious
reasoning or being taught **intuitive** *adj*
intuitively *adv*

Inuit (say **in**-yoo-it) *n pl* **Inuit 1** a member
of a people of northern Canada and parts
of Greenland and Alaska **2** the language of
this people

inundate (say **in**-ən-dayt) *v* **1** to flood an
area or cover it with water **2** to overwhelm
someone with work or other matters to
be dealt with ♦ *The television company
was inundated with letters of complaint.*
inundation *n*

invade *v* **1** to attack and enter a country or
region with armed forces in order to occupy
it **2** (said about a large number of people) to
crowd into a place **3** (said about a disease)
to attack an organism or part of the body
4 to intrude on someone ♦ *Our privacy is
being invaded.* **invader** *n* **invasive** *adj*

invalid[1] (say **in**-və-leed) *n* a person who
is ill or weakened by illness or injury
invalid *v* **1** to take someone away from
active military service because of ill health
or injury ♦ *He was invalided home after the
attack.* **2** to disable someone by injury or
illness **invalidity** *n*

invalid[2] (say in-**val**-id) *adj* not valid

invalidate (say in-**val**-i-dayt) *v* to make an
argument, proposition, or rule ineffective
or not valid **invalidation** *n*

invaluable *adj* extremely useful or valuable,
having a value that is too great to be
measured **invaluably** *adv*

invariable (say in-**vair**-i-əbəl) *adj* not
variable, always the same **invariably** *adv*

invasion *n* the process of invading,
especially territory with an attacking army

invective (say in-**vek**-tiv) *n* strongly critical
or abusive language

invent *v* **1** to make or design something that
did not exist before **2** to make up a false
story ♦ *She was forced to invent an excuse.*
invention *n* **inventive** *adj* **inventor** *n*

inventory (say **in**-vən-ter-i) *n pl* **inventories**
a detailed list of goods or furniture
inventory *v* **inventories**, **inventoried**,
inventorying to list items in an inventory

inverse *adj* reversed in position, direction, or

order **inverse** n **1** a thing that is the reverse or opposite of another **2** *Mathematics* a reciprocal quantity **inversely** adv

invert v **1** to turn something upside down **2** to reverse the position or order of things **inversion** n

invest v **1** to use money to make a profit, especially by buying stock or property that you hope will increase in value **2** to spend money, time, or effort on something useful or worthwhile **3** to confer a rank, office, or power on a person **investment** n **investor** n a person who invests money

investigate v **1** to make a careful study of something in order to discover the facts about it **2** to make a search or systematic inquiry **investigation** n **investigative** adj **investigator** n **investigatory** adj

invigilate (say in-**vij**-i-layt) v to supervise candidates in an examination **invigilation** n **invigilator** n

invigorate (say in-**vig**-er-ayt) v to fill someone with vigour, to give someone strength or courage

invincible (say in-**vin**-si-bəl) adj too powerful to be defeated **invincibility** n **invincibly** adv

inviolate (say in-**viy**-ə-lət) adj not violated or harmed

invisible adj **1** not visible, unable to be seen **2** (in economics) denoting earnings that a country receives or payments that it makes for services in which no physical imports and exports are involved, e.g. in insurance **invisibility** n **invisibly** adv

invite[1] (say in-**viyt**) v **1** to ask someone to come to your house or to a social event **2** to ask someone formally to do something ♦ *The company invites applications from suitably qualified candidates.* **3** to ask for comments or suggestions **4** to act in a way that might bring a particular outcome or response ♦ *You are inviting disaster.* **invitation** n **inviting** adj attractive or tempting

invite[2] (say in-**viyt**) n *informal* an invitation

invoice n a list of goods sent or services performed, with prices and charges **invoice** v to make or send an invoice for goods or services

invoke (say in-**vohk**) v **1** to call on a deity in prayer **2** to appeal to an authority for support or protection ♦ *to invoke the law* **3** to summon up a spirit with words or charms **4** to call earnestly for vengeance, etc. **invocation** n

involuntary adj done without intention or conscious effort **involuntarily** adv

involve v **1** to have something as a part, to make something necessary as a condition or result ♦ *The job involves a lot of hard work.* **2** to let someone share in an experience or undertaking ♦ *They want to involve us in their charity work.* **3** to cause someone difficulties ♦ *The repairs will involve us in much expense.* **4** to show a person to be concerned in a crime or wrongdoing **involved** adj **involvement** n

invulnerable (say in-**vul**-ner-ə-bəl) adj impossible to harm, not vulnerable **invulnerability** n

inward adj **1** on the inside **2** going or facing towards the inside **3** in the mind or spirit ♦ *inward happiness* **inward, inwards** adv **inwardly** adv

IQ abbr intelligence quotient

IRA abbr Irish Republican Army

irascible (say i-**ras**-ibəl) adj irritable or bad-tempered **irascibility** n **irascibly** adv

irate (say iy-**rayt**) adj angry or enraged **irately** adv

ire n *literary* anger

iridescent (say i-ri-**dess**-ənt) adj showing bright colours that appear to change when looked at from different positions **iridescence** n

iris n **1** the coloured part of the eyeball, with a round opening (called the *pupil*) in the centre **2** a plant with long pointed leaves and bright, often purple, flowers with large petals

Irish adj to do with or coming from Ireland **Irish** n the Celtic language of Ireland **the Irish** Irish people

irk v to annoy someone, to be tiresome to someone **irksome** adj

iron n **1** a hard grey metal, a metallic element (symbol Fe), capable of being magnetized **2** a device with a flat base that is heated for smoothing cloth or clothes **3** a tool made of iron ♦ *a branding iron* **4** a golf club with an iron or steel head **5** a metal splint or support worn on the leg **6** great strength or firmness ♦ *a will of iron* **iron** *adj* **1** made of iron **2** strong or unyielding ♦ *an iron constitution* ♦ *an iron will* **iron** *v* to smooth cloth or clothes with an iron **irons** *pl n* shackles, fetters **Iron Age** *n* a period of history that followed the Bronze Age, when weapons and tools were mostly made of iron **ironmonger** *n* a shopkeeper who sells tools and household implements **ironmongery** *n pl* **ironmongeries** an ironmonger's shop or goods

irony (say **iy**-rən-i) *n pl* **ironies** **1** the use of words that mean the opposite of what you really intend, done either for emphasis or for humour. For example, it is irony to say 'What a lovely day' when it is raining hard **2** an oddly contradictory or perverse situation ♦ *The irony is that I had just told them to be careful when I tripped over myself.* **ironic** *adj* **ironically** *adv*

irrational (say **i-rash**-ən-əl) *adj* **1** not rational or logical ♦ *irrational fears* ♦ *irrational behaviour* **2** not capable of reasoning **irrationality** *n* **irrationally** *adv*

irreconcilable *adj* not able to be reconciled **irreconcilably** *adv*

irrecoverable *adj* unable to be recovered **irrecoverably** *adv*

irredeemable *adj* not able to be saved or redeemed **irredeemably** *adv*

irregular *adj* **1** not regular; uneven **2** contrary to the rules or to established custom **3** (said about troops) not in the regular armed forces **irregularity** *n pl* **irregularities** **irregularly** *adv*

irrelevant (say i-**rel**-i-vənt) *adj* not relevant **irrelevance** *n* **irrelevantly** *adv*

irreparable (say i-**rep**-er-əbəl) *adj* not able to be repaired or made good ♦ *The fire caused irreparable damage.* **irreparably** *adv*

irreplaceable *adj* not able to be replaced if it is lost

irreproachable *adj* blameless, faultless

irresistible *adj* too strong or attractive to be resisted **irresistibly** *adv*

irrespective *adj* not taking something into account ♦ *You can apply for a grant*

irrespective of your parents' income.

irresponsible *adj* not behaving in .. responsible way **irresponsibly** *adv*

irretrievable *adj* not able to be retrieved **irretrievably** *adv*

irreverent *adj* not reverent, not respectful **irreverence** *n* **irreverently** *adv*

irreversible *adj* not reversible, unable to be altered or revoked **irreversibly** *adv*

irrigate *v* to supply land with water so that crops can grow **irrigation** *n* **irrigator** *n*

irritable *adj* **1** easily annoyed; bad-tempered **2** *Medicine* (said about an organ) abnormally sensitive **irritability** *n* **irritably** *adv*

irritate *v* **1** to annoy someone; to make someone angry or impatient **2** to cause itching **irritant** *n* **irritation** *n*

is see **be**

-ise *suffix* see **-ize**

Islam (say **iz**-lahm) *n* **1** the Muslim religion, based on the teaching of Muhammad **2** the Muslim world **Islamic** *adj*

island (say **iy**-lənd) *n* **1** a piece of land surrounded by water **2** a thing that is compared to an island because it is detached or isolated, e.g. a paved or raised area in the middle of a road **islander** *n* someone who lives on an island

isle (say iyl) *n poetic and in place names* an island **islet** *n* a small isle

isn't *v informal* is not

iso- *prefix* equal (as in *isobar*)

isolate *v* **1** to place a person or thing apart or alone **2** to separate an infectious person from others **3** to separate a substance from a mixture or compound **isolation** *n*

isometric (say iy-sə-**met**-rik) *adj* **1** having equal size or dimensions **2** (said about muscle action) developing tension without contraction of the muscle

isotonic (say iy-sə-**ton**-ik) *adj* (said about the action of muscles) taking place with normal contraction

ISP *abbr ICT* Internet service provider, a company providing individual users with a connection to the Internet

Israelite (say **iz**-rə-liyt) *n* a member of the ancient Hebrew nation **Israelite** *adj* to do with the ancient Hebrews

issue *n* **1** an important topic for thought or discussion **2** an outgoing or outflow **3** the publication or release of things for use or for sale ♦ *The issue of passports is often delayed in the summer months.* **4** one set of publications in a series issued regularly ♦ *The May issue will be out at the end of April.* **5** offspring, children **issue** *v* **issues, issued, issuing 1** to come or go or flow out **2** to supply or distribute for use ♦ *The campers were issued with blankets.* **3** to put something out for sale; to publish something **4** to send something out or make it known ♦ *The order to attack was issued at dawn.*

IT *abbr* information technology

it *pronoun* **1** used to refer to a thing that has already been mentioned **2** used to refer to a person being identified ♦ *Who is it?* ♦ *It's only me.* **3** used as the subject of a verb making a general statement about the weather (as in *It has been raining*) or about circumstances (as in *It is 50 miles to London*) **4** used as the subject or object of a verb, when a more specific reference follows ♦ *It is seldom that they fail.* **5** exactly what is needed **6** (in children's games) the player who has to catch the others ◊ See the note at *its*.

Italian *adj* to do with or coming from Italy **Italian** *n* **1** a person born in Italy or descended from people born there **2** the language of Italy **Italianate** *adj*

italic (say i-**tal**-ik) *adj* **1** printed with sloping letters *like this* **2** (said about handwriting) compact and pointed like an early form of Italian handwriting **italics** *pl n* sloping printed letters *like these* **italicize** *v*

itch *n* **1** a tickling feeling in the skin that makes you want to scratch it **2** *informal* a restless desire or longing to do something **itch** *v* **1** to have or feel an itch **2** *informal* to feel a restless desire or longing **itchy** *adj* **itchier, itchiest, itchiness** *n*

item *n* **1** a single thing in a list or number of things **2** a single piece of news in a newspaper or bulletin **itemize** *v* **itemization** *n*

itinerant (say iy-**tin**-er-ənt) *adj* travelling from place to place ♦ *an itinerant preacher*

itinerary (say iy-**tin**-er-er-i) *n pl* **itineraries** a list of places to be visited on a journey; a route

it'll *informal v* it will

its *possessive pronoun* of or belonging to it ◊ Do not put an apostrophe in *its*, unless you mean 'it is' or 'it has'.

it's *informal v* it is or it has ♦ *It's very hot.* ♦ *It's broken all records.* ◊ Do not confuse this word, which has an apostrophe, with *its*, which has a different meaning.

itself *pronoun* **1** the reflexive form of *it*, used as the object of a verb or preposition when it is the same as the subject (normally a thing or an animal) ♦ *The cat was licking itself by the fire.* **2** used for emphasis ♦ *The town itself was hidden in fog.*

ivory *n pl* **ivories 1** the hard creamy-white substance forming the tusks of elephants **2** an object made of this **3** a creamy-white colour **ivory** *adj* creamy-white

ivy *n* a climbing evergreen shrub with shiny five-pointed leaves

-ize *suffix* forming verbs meaning 'to bring or come into a certain condition' (as in *civilize, privatize*), treat in a certain way (as in *pasteurize*), or have a certain feeling (as in *sympathize*) ◊ These verbs can also be spelled with the ending *-ise* (e.g. *privatise*). Some words ending in *-cise* and *-vise* have to be spelled with *-ise* (e.g. *exercise, supervise*).

Jj

J¹ the tenth letter of the English alphabet

J² *abbr* joule(s)

jab *v* **jabbed, jabbing** to poke something roughly with something pointed **jab** *n* **1** a sharp poke or blow, especially with something pointed **2** *informal* a hypodermic injection

jabber *v* to talk rapidly and unintelligibly **jabber** *n* jabbering talk

jack *n* **1** a portable device for raising something heavy, especially a motor vehicle, off the ground **2** a playing card with a picture of a young man, ranking below a queen in card games **3** a device using a single plug to connect an electrical circuit **4** a star-shaped piece of metal or plastic used in tossing and catching games **5** a small ship's flag that shows its nationality **6** the small white ball that players aim at in the game of bowls **jacks** n a game played by tossing and catching jacks **jack** v to lift something with a jack **jackboot** n a large military boot reaching above the knee **jack-in-the-box** n a toy figure that springs out of a box when the lid is lifted **jackknife** n pl **jackknives 1** a large knife with a folding blade **2** a dive in which the body is first bent double and then straightened **jackknife** v (said about an articulated vehicle) to bend into a V-shape in an uncontrolled skidding movement **jackpot** n a large cash prize or accumulated stake in a game or lottery **jack of all trades** someone who can do many different kinds of work **to hit the jackpot** to have sudden great success or good fortune **to jack it in** informal to give up or abandon an attempt

ackal n a wild animal of Africa and Asia, related to the dog

ackass n **1** a male ass or donkey **2** a stupid or foolish person

ackdaw n a bird like a small crow with black and grey feathers

acket n **1** a short coat, usually reaching to the hips **2** an outer covering round something **3** a paper wrapper for a book **4** the skin of a potato baked without being peeled

acobean (say jak-ə-bee-ən) adj from the reign of James I of England (1603-25)

acobite (say **jak**-ə-biyt) n a supporter of the deposed James II of England after the revolution of 1688, or of the exiled Stuarts

acuzzi (say ja-**koo**-zi) n trademark a large bath in which underwater jets of water massage the body

ade n **1** a hard green stone that is carved to make ornaments and jewellery **2** a light bluish-green colour

aded adj tired and no longer interested or enthusiastic

agged (say **jag**-id) adj having an uneven

edge or outline with sharp points

jaguar n a large animal of the cat family that has a yellowish-brown coat with black spots, found in tropical America

jail n a prison **jail** v to put someone into prison **jailer** n

jalopy (say jə-**lop**-i) n pl **jalopies** informal a battered old car

jam¹ v **jammed, jamming 1** to squeeze or pack something tightly into a space **2** to make part of a machine become stuck so that the machine will not work; to become stuck in this way **3** to crowd or block a road or area with people or things **4** to block a telephone line **5** to cause interference to a radio transmission **6** to push or apply something forcibly ♦ *He jammed on the brakes.* **7** (said about musicians) to improvise together **jam** n **1** a crowded mass making movement difficult ♦ *a traffic jam* **2** informal a difficult situation

jam² n a sweet substance made by boiling fruit with sugar until it is thick

jamb (say jam) n the vertical side post of a doorway or window frame

jamboree (say jam-ber-**ee**) n a large party or celebration

jangle v **1** to make or cause something to make a harsh ringing sound **2** (said about your nerves) to be set on edge **jangle** n a harsh ringing sound

janitor n the caretaker of a building

January n the first month of the year

Japanese adj to do with or coming from Japan **Japanese** n **1** pl **Japanese** a person born in Japan or descended from people born there **2** the language of Japan

jar¹ n a cylindrical container made of glass or pottery

jar² v **jarred, jarring 1** to make a harsh discordant sound **2** to have a harsh or disagreeable effect on someone ♦ *Her voice really jars on my nerves.* **3** to cause an unpleasant jolt or vibration ♦ *He jarred his neck in the fall.* **4** to clash or conflict with something **jar** n a sudden jolt or vibration

jargon n words or expressions used by a particular profession or group that are difficult for other people to understand

jasmine n a shrub with fragrant yellow or

white flowers

jasper n an opaque variety of quartz, usually red, yellow, or brown

jaundice (say **jawn**-dis) n a condition in which the skin becomes abnormally yellow **jaundiced** adj **1** discoloured by jaundice **2** filled with resentment or bitterness

jaunt n a short trip, especially one taken for pleasure

jaunty adj **jauntier**, **jauntiest 1** cheerful and self-confident in manner **2** (said about clothes) stylish and cheerful **jauntily** adv

javelin (say **jav**-ə-lin) n a long light spear thrown in an athletics competition or as a weapon

jaw n either of the two bones that form the framework of the mouth and in which the teeth are set **jaws** pl n the gripping parts of a wrench or vice **jaw** v informal to talk long and boringly; to gossip **jawbone** n

jay n a bird of the crow family, with pinkish-brown plumage and a small blue patch on each wing

jaywalking n walking carelessly in a road **jaywalker** n

jazz n a type of music with strong rhythm, often improvised **jazz** v **to jazz something up** to make something more lively or interesting **jazzy** adj **jazzier**, **jazziest 1** of or like jazz **2** bright and showy ♦ a jazzy sports car

jealous (say **jel**-əs) adj **1** feeling resentful or suspicious of a person who you feel is your rival or is better or luckier than you **2** careful in keeping something ♦ He is very jealous of his reputation. **jealously** adv **jealousy** n

jeans pl n trousers made of denim or another strong cotton fabric

Jeep n trademark a small sturdy motor vehicle with four-wheel drive

jeer v to laugh or shout at someone rudely and scornfully **jeer** n

Jehovah (say ji-**hoh**-və) n the traditional English form of one of the Hebrew names for God

jejune (say ji-**joon**) adj formal **1** naive and simplistic **2** dull and lacking imagination

jell v variant of **gel**

jelly n pl **jellies 1** a clear fruit-flavoured

dessert set with gelatin **2** a substance o similar consistency **jellied** adj set in jell **jellyfish** n pl **jellyfish** or **jellyfishes** a se animal with a jelly-like body and stingin tentacles

jemmy n pl **jemmies** a short crowbar use by burglars to force doors, windows, an drawers

jenny n pl **jennies** a female donkey

jeopardy (say **jep**-er-di) n dange **jeopardize** v to put someone in danger, t put something at risk

jerboa (say jer-**boh**-ə) n a small rat-lik animal with long hind legs

jerk n **1** a sudden sharp movement; a abrupt pull or push **2** informal a stupid o insignificant person **jerk** v to pull or mov something with a jerk **jerky** adj **jerkie jerkiest**, **jerkily** adv **jerkiness** n

jerkin n a sleeveless jacket

jerry-built adj built badly and with poo materials

jerrycan n a large flat-sided can for petrol o water

jersey n pl **jerseys 1** a close-fitting woolle pullover with sleeves **2** a shirt worn by player in certain sports **3** a soft knitte fabric **4** (**Jersey**) a breed of light-brow dairy cattle

jest n a joke **jest** v to make jokes **jester** n professional entertainer employed at royal court in the Middle Ages

jet[1] n **1** a stream of water, gas, flame, etc shot out from a small opening **2** a spou or opening from which a jet comes **3** a je engine **4** an aircraft powered by jet engine **jet** v **jetted**, **jetting 1** to spurt out in jet **2** to travel by jet aircraft **jet engine** an engine using jet propulsion **jet lag** extreme tiredness that a person fee after a long flight between different tim zones **jet-propelled** adj **jet propulsion** propulsion by engines that give forwar thrust by sending out a high-speed jet o gases, etc. at the back **jet set** n wealth people who travel widely and frequentl for pleasure **jet ski** n a small jet-propelle vehicle like a scooter, which skims acro the surface of water

jet[2] n a hard black mineral that can b

polished, used as a gem

etsam n goods thrown overboard from a ship in distress and washed ashore

ettison v 1 to throw goods overboard from a ship; to drop goods or fuel from an aircraft or spacecraft 2 to get rid of something that is no longer wanted

etty n pl **jetties** a landing stage or small pier

ew n a person of Hebrew descent, or one whose religion is Judaism **Jewish** adj **Jewry** n the Jewish people **Jew's harp** n a musical instrument consisting of a small U-shaped metal frame held in the teeth while a metal strip is twanged with a finger

ewel n 1 a precious stone 2 a person or thing that is highly valued **jewelled** adj **jeweller** n a person or company that makes or sells jewels or jewellery **jewellery** n ornaments that people wear made of jewels and precious metal

ezebel (say jez-ə-bəl) n a shameless or immoral woman

b¹ n 1 a triangular sail stretching forward from the mast 2 the arm of a crane

b² v **jibbed**, **jibbing** (said about a horse) to stop suddenly and refuse to go on **to jib at** to be unwilling to do or accept something

be v, n another spelling of gibe

ffy, **jiff** n informal a moment ♦ I'll be with you in a jiffy.

g n 1 a lively jumping dance, or the music for this 2 a device that holds a piece of work in place and guides the tools working on it **jig** v **jigged**, **jigging** to move or make something move up and down rapidly and jerkily **jiggle** v to rock or jerk something lightly

ggery-pokery n informal trickery, underhand dealing

gsaw n 1 a puzzle consisting of a picture printed on board or wood and cut into irregular pieces which have to be fitted together 2 a mechanically operated saw used to cut curved lines

had (say ji-hahd) n a war or struggle undertaken by Muslims

lt v to abandon a boyfriend or girlfriend

ngle v to make or cause something to make a metallic ringing or clinking sound

jingle n 1 a jingling sound 2 a short catchy tune used in advertising

jingoism (say jing-goh-izm) n an aggressive attitude of excessive patriotism **jingoistic** adj

jinx n a person or thing that is thought to bring bad luck **jinx** v to bring bad luck to someone

jitters pl n informal a feeling of extreme nervousness **jittery** adj

jive n a style of lively dance performed to fast jazz music or rock and roll **jive** v to dance the jive

job n 1 work that someone does regularly to earn a living 2 a piece of work to be done ♦ Can you do a couple of jobs for me? 3 a responsibility or duty ♦ It's your job to lock the gates. 4 work done to improve or repair something ♦ a nose job ♦ They've done a nice job on the car. 5 informal a crime, especially a robbery **jobbing** adj doing casual or occasional work for payment **jobless** adj **jobcentre** n a government office in a local area, providing information about available jobs **job lot** n a collection of miscellaneous articles bought together

jockey n pl **jockeys** a person who rides horses in horse races **jockey** v **jockeyed**, **jockeying** to manoeuvre in order to gain an advantage ♦ On the final bend the runners were jockeying for position.

jocular (say jok-yoo-ler) adj joking, avoiding seriousness **jocularity** n **jocularly** adv

jodhpurs (say jod-perz) pl n trousers for horse riding, fitting closely below the knee and loose above it

jog v **jogged**, **jogging** 1 to run at a steady leisurely pace 2 to give something a slight knock or push **jog** n a slow run or trot **to jog someone's memory** to help them to remember something **jogger** n **joggle** v to shake something slightly; to move by slight jerks

joie de vivre (say zhwah də veevr) n a feeling of great enjoyment of life

join v 1 to put things together; to link or connect things 2 to come together; to become united with something ♦ The Cherwell joins the Thames at Oxford. 3 to become a member or employee of a group or organization 4 to take part with others in doing something ♦ *We all joined in the chorus.* **5** to come into the company of other people ♦ *Will you join us for lunch?* **6** to become part of something ♦ *We joined the queue.* **join** *n* a place where two or more things are joined **joiner** *n* a person who makes doors, window frames, etc. and furniture out of wood **joinery** *n* **joint** *n* **1** a place where two things are joined **2** a structure in a body by which two bones are fitted together **3** a place or device at which two parts of a structure are joined **4** a large piece of meat cut ready for cooking ♦ *a joint of lamb* **5** *informal* a cannabis cigarette **joint** *adj* shared, held, or done by two or more people together ♦ *a joint account* ♦ *joint authors* **joint** *v* **1** to connect things by a joint or joints **2** to divide the body of an animal into joints **jointly** *adv* **out of joint 1** dislocated **2** in disorder **to join up** to become a member of the armed forces

joist *n* any of the parallel beams on which floorboards or ceiling laths are fixed

jojoba (say hə-**hoh**-bə) *n* an oil obtained from the seeds of a North American shrub, used in cosmetics

joke *n* **1** something said or done to make people laugh **2** a ridiculous person or thing **joke** *v* **1** to make jokes **2** to tease someone or not be serious ♦ *It's all right, I'm only joking.* **joker** *n* **1** a person who likes making jokes **2** an extra playing card with a jester on it, used as a wild card in certain card games **jokey** *adj* **jokingly** *adv*

jolly *adj* **jollier, jolliest** full of high spirits, cheerful **jolly** *adv informal* very ♦ *jolly good* **jolly** *v* **jollies, jollied, jollying, to jolly someone along** or **up** to try to keep someone cheerful **jollification** *n* merrymaking or festivity **jollity** *n pl* **jollities**

jolt *v* **1** to shake or dislodge something with a sudden sharp movement **2** to give someone a shock **jolt** *n* **1** a jolting movement or effect **2** a surprise or shock

jonquil (say **jon**-kwil) *n* a kind of narcissus with clusters of fragrant flowers

josh *v informal* to tease someone in a good-natured way

joss stick *n* a thin stick that burns to give off a smell of incense

jostle *v* to push or bump roughly against people, especially in a crowd

jot *v* **jotted, jotting** to write something quickly ♦ *Let me jot down your phon number.* **jot** *n* a very small amount ♦ *Sh doesn't care a jot about it.* **jotter** *n* a smal notepad or notebook **jottings** *pl n* brie notes

joule (say jool) *n* an SI unit of work or energy

journal (say **jer**-nəl) *n* **1** a newspaper o magazine dealing with a particular subjec **2** a diary or daily record **journalist** *n* person who writes for newspapers o magazines **journalism** *n*

journey *n pl* **journeys 1** going from one place to another **2** the distance travelled o the time taken to travel somewhere ♦ *Th river is two days' journey from here.* **journey** *v* **journeys, journeyed, journeying** to mak a journey

journeyman *n pl* **journeymen** a skille workman who works for an employer

joust (say jowst) *v* to fight on horsebac with lances **joust** *n* a jousting contes **jousting** *n*

jovial (say **joh**-viəl) *adj* cheerful and good humoured **joviality** *n* **jovially** *adv*

jowl *n* the lower part of a cheek

joy *n* **1** a feeling of great pleasure o happiness **2** a thing that causes jo **joyful** *adj* **joyfully** *adv* **joyless** ad **joyous** *adj* **joyride** *n* a fast ride in a stole car for amusement **joyrider** *n* **joyriding** **joystick** *n* **1** the control lever of an aircra **2** a device for moving a cursor or image o a computer screen

JP *abbr* Justice of the Peace

jubilant *adj* happy and triumphan **jubilation** *n*

jubilee *n* a special anniversary, especiall one celebrating 25, 50, or 60 years

Judaism (say **joo**-day-izm) *n* the religion o the Jewish people, based on the teaching of the Old Testament and the Talmu **Judaic** *adj*

Judas *n* a person who betrays a friend

judder *v* to shake noisily or violently

judge *n* **1** a public officer appointed to hea and try cases in a law court **2** a perso appointed to decide who has won a contest **3** a person who is able to give an authoritative opinion on something ♦ *She is a good judge of character.* **judge** *v* **1** to try a case in a law court **2** to act as judge of a contest **3** to form and give an opinion about something **4** to estimate something ♦ *She judged the distance accurately.*

judgement or **judgement** *n* **1** the ability to judge wisely, good sense **2** an opinion or conclusion **3** the decision of a judge or law court **judgemental** *adj* **1** involving judgement **2** inclined to make moral judgements

judicial (say joo-**dish**-əl) *adj* **1** to do with law courts or the administration of justice ♦ *the British judicial system* **2** to do with a judge or judgement **judicially** *adv*

judiciary (say joo-**dish**-er-i) *n pl* **judiciaries** all the judges in a country

judicious (say joo-**dish**-əs) *adj* judging wisely, showing good sense ♦ *a judicious choice* **judiciously** *adv*

judo *n* a Japanese system of unarmed combat

jug *n* a container for holding and pouring liquids, with a handle and a shaped lip

juggernaut *n* **1** a very large long-distance transport vehicle **2** a large overwhelmingly powerful institution or other force

juggle *v* **1** to toss and catch a number of objects skilfully for entertainment, keeping one or more in the air at any time **2** to cope with all the things you have to do by skilfully balancing the time you spend on each of them **3** to rearrange facts or figures in order to achieve something or to deceive people **juggler** *n*

jugular vein *n* either of the two great veins of the neck carrying blood from the head

juice *n* **1** the liquid from fruit or vegetables **2** liquid coming from meat or other food during cooking **3** liquid secreted by an organ of the body ♦ *the digestive juices* **juicy** *adj* **juicier**, **juiciest** **1** full of juice **2** *informal* interesting, especially because of its scandalous nature ♦ *juicy stories*

ju-jitsu (say joo-**jit**-soo) *n* a Japanese method of self-defence

jukebox *n* a machine that automatically plays a selected disc when a coin is inserted

July *n* the seventh month of the year

jumble *v* to mix things up in a confused way **jumble** *n* **1** a confused mixture of things, a muddle **2** articles collected for a jumble sale **jumble sale** *n* a sale of miscellaneous second-hand goods

jumbo *n pl* **jumbos** a jumbo jet **jumbo** *adj* very large **jumbo jet** *n* a very large airliner

jump *v* **1** to push yourself off the ground suddenly by bending and then extending the legs **2** to move somewhere suddenly and quickly ♦ *I jumped up to answer the door.* ♦ *We jumped on the next train.* **3** to pass over something to a point beyond it; to skip part of a book, etc. in reading or studying **4** to move suddenly in shock or excitement ♦ *You made me jump!* **5** to rise suddenly in amount or in price or value **6** to pass abruptly from one subject or state to another ♦ *Your essay jumps from idea to idea too much.* **7** to pounce on someone, to attack someone without warning **jump** *n* **1** a jumping movement **2** a startled movement **3** a sudden rise in amount, price, or value **4** an abrupt change to a different subject or state; a gap in a series of things **5** a step taken or a move made by someone ♦ *He always seemed to be one jump ahead.* **jumpy** *adj* **jumpier**, **jumpiest** anxious or nervous **jumped-up** *adj* thinking you are more important than you really are **jump jet** *n* a jet aircraft that can take off and land vertically **jump lead** *n* a cable for conveying current from the battery of a motor vehicle to recharge the battery of another **jump-start** *v* to start a car with a flat battery by pushing it or by using jump leads **jumpsuit** *n* a piece of clothing for the whole body, combining trousers and a top with sleeves **to jump at** to accept an opportunity eagerly **to jump the gun** to start something before you should **to jump the queue** to obtain something without waiting for your proper turn

jumper *n* a pullover or sweater

junction *n* **1** a point where two or more things join or meet **2** a place where roads or railway lines meet

juncture (say **junk**-cher) *n* **1** a particular

point in time, especially an important one **2** a place where things join

June *n* the sixth month of the year

jungle *n* **1** an area of land with dense forest and tangled vegetation, especially in the tropics **2** a wild tangled mass **3** a scene of bewildering complexity or confusion ♦ *The city is a concrete jungle.*

junior *adj* **1** younger in age ♦ *Tom Brown junior* **2** lower in rank or importance ♦ *a junior minister* **3** for schoolchildren aged 7 to 11 ♦ *a junior school* **junior** *n* **1** a person younger in age ♦ *He is six years her junior.* **2** a person employed to work in a junior capacity ♦ *the office junior*

juniper (say **joo**-nip-er) *n* an evergreen shrub with prickly leaves and dark purplish berries

junk[1] *n informal* rubbish or worthless stuff **junkie** *n* a drug addict **junk food** *n* food that is not nutritious **junk mail** *n* unwanted advertising material sent by post

junk[2] *n* a kind of Chinese flat-bottomed ship with sails

junket *n* **1** a sweet food made of milk curdled with rennet and flavoured **2** an extravagant trip or party, especially at public expense

junta (say **jun**-tə or **hun**-tə) *n* a military or political group of people who combine to rule a country, especially after seizing power by force

jurisdiction (say joor-iss-**dik**-shən) *n* **1** authority to make legal decisions and judgements **2** the extent or territory over which legal or other power extends

jurisprudence (say joor-iss-**proo**-dəns) *n* the study of law

jurist (say **joor** -ist) *n* a person who is skilled in the law

jury *n pl* **juries 1** a group of people appointed to give a verdict on a case presented to them in a court of law **2** a group of people appointed to judge a competition **juror** *n* a member of a jury

just *adj* **1** giving proper consideration to the claims of everyone concerned **2** deserved or appropriate ♦ *a just reward* **just** *adv* **1** exactly ♦ *It's just what I wanted.* **2** barely ♦ *I just managed it.* ♦ *just below the knee* **3** at

this moment ♦ *She has just left.* **4** simply, only ♦ *We are just good friends.* **5** really, certainly ♦ *That idea is just ridiculous.*

justly *adv* **justness** *n*

justice *n* **1** just treatment; fairness **2** legal proceedings **3** a judge or magistrate; the title of a judge ♦ *Mr Justice Humphreys* **Justice of the Peace** *n* a magistrate

justify *v* **justifies, justified, justifying 1** to show or prove that something is fair, just, or reasonable **2** to be a good reason for something ♦ *Increased production justifies an increase in wages.* **3** to adjust a line of type in printing so that the print forms a straight edge **justifiable** *adj* **justifiably** *adv* **justification** *n*

jut *v* **jutted, jutting** to stick out

jute *n* rough fibre from the bark of certain tropical plants, used for making sacks, etc.

juvenile (say **joo**-və-niyl) *adj* **1** youthful, childish **2** to do with or for young people or animals **juvenile** *n* a young person or animal **juvenile delinquent** *n* a juvenile who has repeatedly broken the law

juxtapose (say juks-tə-**pohz**) *v* to put things side by side or close together **juxtaposition** *n*

Kk

K[1] the eleventh letter of the English alphabet

K[2] *abbr* **1** kilometre(s) **2** *informal* one thousand

kaftan (say **kaf**-tən) *n* **1** a long coat-like garment worn by men in the Middle East **2** a woman's long loose dress

kaiser (say **kiy**-zer) *n* the title of the German and Austrian emperors until 1918

kale *n* a kind of cabbage with curly leaves

kaleidoscope (say kəl-**iy**-də-skohp) *n* **1** a toy consisting of a tube containing mirrors and small brightly-coloured pieces of glass or paper which are reflected to form changing patterns as you turn the end of the tube **2** a constantly changing pattern **kaleidoscopic** *adj*

kamikaze (say kam-i-**kah**-zi) *n* (in the Second World War) a Japanese aircraft loaded with explosives and suicidally crashed on an enemy target by its pilot **kamikaze** *adj* recklessly self-destructive

kangaroo *n* an Australian marsupial that jumps along on its strong hind legs **kangaroo court** *n* an unofficial court formed by a group of people to settle disputes among themselves

kaolin (say **kay**-ə-lin) *n* a fine white clay used in porcelain and some medicines

kapok (say **kay**-pok) *n* a substance resembling cotton wool which grows around the seeds of a tropical tree, used for stuffing pillows and cushions

kaput (say kə-**puut**) *adj informal* broken or useless; out of order

karaoke (say ka-ri-**oh**-ki) *n* a form of entertainment in which people sing well-known songs over a pre-recorded backing track

karate (say kə-**rah**-ti) *n* a Japanese system of unarmed combat in which the hands and feet are used as weapons

karma *n* (in Buddhism and Hinduism) the sum of a person's actions in successive existences, thought to decide their destiny

kart *n* a kind of miniature racing car **karting** *n*

kasbah (say **kaz**-bah) *n* the citadel of an Arab city in North Africa, or the crowded area near this

kayak (say **kiy**-ak) *n* 1 an Inuit canoe with a sealskin covering that fits round the canoeist's waist 2 a small covered canoe resembling this

kazoo *n* a simple musical instrument which produces a buzzing sound when you hum into it

KB, **Kb** *abbr* kilobyte(s)

KBE *abbr* Knight Commander of the Order of the British Empire

kebab (say ki-**bab**) *n* small pieces of meat, fish, or vegetables cooked on a skewer or spit

kedgeree (say **kej**-er-ee) *n* a cooked dish of smoked fish, rice, and hard-boiled eggs

keel *n* the timber or steel structure along the base of a ship, on which the ship's framework is built up **on an even keel** steady **to keel over 1** (said about a boat or ship) to turn over on its side **2** to fall over or collapse

keen[1] *adj* **1** enthusiastic, very interested in or eager to do something ♦ *a keen swimmer* ♦ *I am keen to go.* **2** sharp **3** quick and acute ♦ *keen wit* **4** (said about senses) perceiving things very distinctly **5** intense or strong ♦ *a keen rivalry* **6** cold and biting ♦ *a keen wind* **7** (said about prices) low because of competition **keenly** *adv* **keenness** *n*

keen[2] *v* to wail in grief for a dead person

keep *v* past tense and past participle **kept** **1** to stay or cause something to stay in a specified state, position, or condition ♦ *She kept quiet about it.* ♦ *I'll keep it hot for you.* **2** to have possession of something and not give or throw it away ♦ *She's kept the letter all these years.* **3** to continue doing something, to do something frequently or repeatedly ♦ *The strap keeps breaking.* **4** to make someone late, to hold someone back from doing something ♦ *What kept you?* **5** to put or store something in its usual place ♦ *Where do you keep your mugs?* **6** to respect and not break something ♦ *I always keep a promise.* **7** to provide someone with the necessities of life **8** to manage something ♦ *My grandparents keep a shop.* **9** (said about food) to remain in good condition **keep** *n* **1** food, clothes, and the other essential things you need to live ♦ *She earns her keep.* **2** the central tower of a castle **keeping** *n* care or protection **keeper** *n* **1** a person who keeps or looks after something **2** a goalkeeper or wicketkeeper **3** a gamekeeper **4** a person in charge of animals in a zoo **keep-fit** *n* regular exercising done to improve your fitness and health **keepsake** *n* a gift to be kept in memory of the person who gave it **in keeping with** suiting or appropriate for something **to keep something up** to continue something **to keep up** to progress at the same pace as others

keg *n* a small barrel

kelp *n* a large brown seaweed

kelvin *n* the SI base unit of temperature, equivalent to the degree Celsius **Kelvin**

scale n a scale of temperature with absolute zero as zero (-273.15°C)

ken n the range of a person's knowledge ♦ *How the stock market works is beyond my ken.* **ken** v Scottish to know something or someone

kennel n a small shelter for a dog **kennels** pl n an establishment where dogs are bred or where they can be looked after while their owners are away

keratin (say ke-rə-tin) n a strong protein substance forming the basis of horns, claws, nails, feathers, and hair

kerb n a stone edging to a pavement or raised path **kerbstone** n

kerchief n a square scarf worn on the head

kerfuffle n informal fuss or commotion

kernel n 1 the softer part inside the shell of a nut, seed, or fruit stone 2 the central or most important part of something

kerosene (say ke-rə-seen) n a fuel oil distilled from petroleum; paraffin oil

kestrel n a type of small falcon

ketch n a small sailing boat with two masts

ketchup n a thick sauce made from tomatoes and vinegar

kettle n a container with a spout and handle, for boiling water in **kettledrum** n a large bowl-shaped drum **a different kettle of fish** something altogether different

key[1] n 1 a small piece of metal shaped so that it will open or close a lock 2 a similar instrument used for turning something, e.g. for winding a clock or tightening a spring, etc. 3 each of a set of small levers pressed by the fingers in playing a musical instrument or operating a computer, etc. 4 a thing that helps you to achieve, understand, or solve something ♦ *a key to success* 5 a list of answers, symbols used in a map or code, etc. 6 Mus a system of related notes based on a particular note **key** adj very important or essential ♦ *a key figure in the affair* **key** v **keyed**, **keying** to enter data into a computer using a keyboard ♦ *Now key in your password.* **keyboard** n 1 the set of keys on a piano, computer, typewriter, etc. 2 an electronic musical instrument with keys arranged like a piano **keyboard** v to key data into a computer system

keyhole n the hole through which a key is put into a lock **keyhole surgery** n surgery carried out through a very small incision, using fibre optics and special instruments **keynote** n 1 Mus the note on which a key is based 2 the main tone or theme of a speech or conference **keypad** n a miniature keyboard or set of buttons used to operate a portable electronic device **key ring** n a metal ring for holding keys together in a bunch **keystone** n 1 the central wedge-shaped stone at the top of an arch, locking the others in position 2 the central principle or part of a policy or system **keystroke** n pressing down an individual key on a keyboard **keyword** n 1 the key to a cipher or code 2 a significant word or heading in an index or reference book **to be keyed up** to be nervously tense or excited

key[2] n a reef or a low island, especially in the Caribbean

kg abbr kilogram(s)

khaki (say kah-ki) n 1 cotton or wool fabric of a dull brownish-yellow colour, used for military uniforms 2 a dull brownish-yellow colour

khan (say kahn) n a title given to rulers and officials in central Asia

kHz abbr kilohertz

kibbutz (say kib-uuts) n pl **kibbutzim** (say kib-uuts-eem) a communal farming settlement in Israel

kibosh (say kie-bosh) n **to put the kibosh on** informal to put an end to something

kick v 1 to strike or move a person or thing with your foot 2 to move your legs about vigorously 3 informal to succeed in giving something up 4 (said about a gun) to recoil when fired **kick** n 1 an act of kicking; a blow from being kicked 2 informal a sharp stimulant effect ♦ *a drink with a real kick to it* 3 informal a thrill; a pleasurable effect ♦ *They just did it for kicks.* **kicker** n **kickback** n 1 a recoil 2 informal a payment made to someone for help they have given, especially in doing something dishonest **kick-off** n the time a football match starts **kick-start** v 1 to start the engine of a motorcycle by pushing down a lever with your foot 2 to help something to get started or become active again

kid n 1 informal a child 2 a young goat 3 fine leather made from a young goat's skin

kid v kidded, kidding informal to deceive or lie to someone in fun **to handle** or **treat someone with kid gloves** to deal with someone gently or carefully

kidnap v kidnapped, kidnapping to take someone away by force, usually in order to obtain a ransom **kidnapper** n

kidney n pl kidneys 1 either of a pair of glandular organs that remove waste products from the blood and secrete urine 2 the kidney of a sheep, ox, or pig eaten as food **kidney bean** n a dark red bean with a curved shape like a kidney **kidney machine** n an apparatus that performs the functions of a kidney

kill v 1 to cause the death of a person, animal, or plant 2 to destroy or put an end to something 3 to pass time while waiting for something ♦ We played cards to kill a few hours. 4 informal to cause someone severe pain or mental suffering ♦ My feet are killing me. **kill** n 1 the act of killing an animal 2 the animal or animals killed by a hunter or another animal **killer** n **killing** n an act causing death **killer whale** n a large-toothed whale with distinctive black-and-white markings **killjoy** n a person who deliberately spoils or questions the enjoyment of others **to make a killing** to make a lot of money

kiln n an oven or furnace for hardening or drying things such as pottery, bricks, or hops, or for burning lime

kilo (say kee-loh) n pl kilos a kilogram

kilo- prefix one thousand, as in kilolitre

kilobyte n ICT a unit of memory or data equal to 1,024 bytes

kilogram n a unit of mass equal to 1,000 grams (2.205 lb)

kilohertz n a unit of frequency of electromagnetic waves, equal to 1,000 cycles per second

kilojoule n 1,000 joules, especially as a measure of the energy value of foods

kilolitre n 1,000 litres

kilometre (say kil-ə-meet-er or kil-om-it-er) n a unit of length equal to 1,000 metres (0.62 miles)

kilovolt n 1,000 volts

kilowatt n a unit of electrical power equal to 1,000 watts **kilowatt-hour** n an amount of energy equal to one kilowatt operating for one hour

kilt n a knee-length skirt of pleated tartan wool, traditionally worn by men as part of Scottish Highland dress

kimono (say kim-oh-noh) n pl kimonos 1 a long loose Japanese robe with wide sleeves, worn with a sash 2 a dressing gown resembling this

kin n a person's family and relatives **kindred** n a person's family and relatives **kindred** adj 1 related 2 of a similar kind **kinship** n 1 a family relationship 2 a close feeling between people who have similar attitudes or origins **kindred spirit** n a person whose tastes or attitudes are similar to your own **kinsfolk** pl n a person's relatives **kinsman, kinswoman** n pl **kinsmen, kinswomen** one of a person's relatives

kind¹ n 1 a class or type of similar people, animals, or things 2 character or nature **in kind 1** in the same way ♦ She repaid his insults in kind. 2 (describing payment) in goods or services, not in money **kind of** informal slightly ♦ I felt kind of sorry for him.

kind² adj friendly, helpful, and considerate in your manner or conduct towards others **kindly** adj kindlier, kindliest kind in character, manner, or appearance **kindly** adv 1 in a kind way 2 please ♦ Kindly, shut the door. **kindliness** n **kindness** n

kindergarten n a school for very young children

kindle v 1 to set light to something, to start a fire burning 2 to arouse or stimulate something **kindling** n small pieces of dry wood used for lighting fires

kinetic (say kin-et-ik or kiy-net-ik) adj to do with or produced by movement; characterized by movement ♦ kinetic energy

king n 1 the male ruler of an independent country or state, especially one who inherits the position by right of birth 2 a person or thing regarded as supreme in some way ♦ The lion is the king of beasts. 3 a large species of animal ♦ *king penguins* **4** the most important chess piece, which has to be protected from checkmate **5** a playing card with a picture of a king on it, ranking next below an ace **kingship** *n* being a king; a king's position or reign **kingdom** *n* **1** a country or state ruled by a king or queen **2** a division of the natural world ♦ *the animal kingdom* **kingfisher** *n* a bird with bright bluish plumage, that dives to catch fish **kingpin** *n* **1** a vertical bolt used as a pivot **2** an indispensable person or thing **king-size** *adj* extra large

kink *n* **1** a short twist or curve in a wire, rope, piece of hair, etc. **2** an unusual characteristic in a person's mind or personality **kinky** *adj* **kinkier, kinkiest** **1** full of kinks **2** *informal* involving unusual sexual behaviour

kiosk (say kee-osk) *n* **1** a small hut or stall where newspapers, tickets, refreshments, etc. are sold **2** a public telephone booth

kip *n informal* a sleep **kip** *v* **kipped, kipping** *informal* to sleep

kipper *n* a herring that has been split open, salted, and dried or smoked

kirk *n Scottish* a church

kirsch (say keersh) *n* a colourless brandy made from the juice of wild cherries

kismet (say kiz-met) *n* destiny, fate

kiss *n* touching someone with your lips as a sign of affection or as a greeting **kiss** *v* **1** to give someone a kiss **2** to touch something lightly **kissogram** *n* a greetings message delivered with a kiss **kiss of life** *n* mouth-to-mouth resuscitation

kit *n* **1** the equipment needed for a particular activity or situation **2** a set of parts sold ready to be fitted together **kit** *v* **kitted, kitting** to provide someone with the clothing or equipment they need ♦ *We were all kitted out for a day's skiing.* **kitbag** *n* a long canvas bag for holding a soldier's kit

kitchen *n* a room in which meals are prepared **kitchenette** *n* a small room or part of a room used as a kitchen **kitchen garden** *n* a garden for growing your own fruit and vegetables

kite *n* **1** a toy consisting of a light frame with thin material stretched over it, flown in a

strong wind on the end of a long string **2** a large bird of prey of the hawk family

kith and kin *n* friends and relatives

kitsch (say kich) *n* sentimentality and lack of good taste in art; art of this type

kitten *n* a young cat **kittenish** *adj*

kitty[1] *n pl* **kitties 1** a fund of money for use by several people **2** the pool of stakes to be played for in some card games

kitty[2] *n pl* **kitties** a pet name for a cat

kiwi (say kee-wee) *n* a New Zealand bird that does not fly, with a long bill and no tail **Kiwi** *n pl* **Kiwis** *informal* a New Zealander **kiwi fruit** *n* a fruit with thin hairy skin, green flesh, and black seeds

kJ *abbr* kilojoule(s)

kl *abbr* kilolitre(s)

Klaxon *n trademark* a powerful electric horn

kleptomania (say kleptə-**may**-niə) *n* an uncontrollable urge to steal things **kleptomaniac** *n, adj*

km *abbr* kilometre(s)

knack *n* **1** a skilful or effective way of doing something **2** a talent for doing something

knacker *n* a person who buys and slaughters useless horses **knackered** *adj informal* exhausted, worn out

knapsack *n* a bag with shoulder straps, carried on the back by soldiers, hikers, etc.

knead *v* **1** to work dough or clay by pressing and stretching it with your hands **2** to massage something with kneading movements

knee *n* **1** the joint between the thigh and the lower part of the leg **2** a person's lap **knee** *v* **knees, kneed, kneeing** to strike someone with the knee **kneecap** *n* the small bone covering the front of the knee joint **kneecap** *v* **kneecapped, kneecapping** to shoot someone in the knee or leg as a punishment **knee-jerk** *adj* automatic and unthinking ♦ *a knee-jerk reaction*

kneel *v* past tense and past participle **knelt** to take or be in a position where the body is supported on the knees

knell *n* the sound of a bell rung solemnly after a death or at a funeral

knickerbockers *pl n* loose-fitting breeches gathered in at the knee

knickers *pl n* underpants worn by women

and girls

knick-knack n a small ornament

knife n pl **knives** a cutting instrument or weapon consisting of a sharp blade with a handle **knife** v to stab someone with a knife **on a knife-edge** in a situation involving extreme tension or anxiety

knight n 1 a man who has been awarded a rank as an honour by the monarch and is entitled to use the title 'Sir' 2 a chess piece with the form of a horse's head **knight** v to make someone a knight **knighthood** n **knightly** adv

knit v past tense and past participle **knitted** or **knit**; **knitting** 1 to make something by looping together wool or other yarn, using long needles or a machine 2 to unite or grow together ♦ The broken bones had knit well. **knitter** n **knitting** n **knitwear** n **to knit your brow** to frown ◊ The past tense of the verb in sense 1 is knitted. The past tense in sense 2 is usually knit.

knob n 1 a round handle on a door or drawer 2 a round button on a dial or machine 3 a round lump on something 4 a small round piece of something ♦ a knob of butter **knobbly** adj **knobblier**, **knobbliest** with many small lumps on it

knock v 1 to make a noise striking a surface with your hand or a hard object 2 to strike or bump into something with a sharp blow 3 (said about an engine) to make a thumping or rattling noise while running 4 to make something by knocking ♦ The builders knocked a hole in the wall. 5 informal to say critical or insulting things about something **knock** n 1 an act or sound of knocking 2 a sharp blow or collision **knocker** n a hinged metal flap for knocking against a door **knockabout** adj rough, boisterous ♦ knockabout comedy **knock-down** adj (said about prices) very low **knock knees** pl n an abnormal inward curving of the legs at the knees **knock-kneed** adj **knock-on effect** n an indirect result of some action **knockout** n 1 a blow that knocks a boxer out 2 a competition in which the loser in each successive round has to drop out 3 informal an extremely attractive or outstanding person or thing

knock-up n a practice or casual game of tennis, etc. **to knock about** informal to wander around casually **to knock it off** informal to stop doing something **to knock off** informal to stop work **to knock someone out** 1 to make someone unconscious 2 to defeat someone in a knockout competition 3 to greatly impress or astonish someone **to knock someone up** 1 informal to make someone pregnant 2 to wake someone by knocking at their door **to knock something down** to reduce the price of something **to knock something off** 1 informal to produce a piece of work quickly 2 to deduct an amount from a price 3 informal to steal something **to knock something up** to make something hastily

knoll (say nohl) n a small round hill, mound

knot n 1 a fastening made by intertwining one or more pieces of string or rope, etc. and pulling the ends tight 2 a tangle 3 a round cross-grained spot in timber where a branch joined 4 a cluster of people or things 5 a unit of speed used by ships and aircraft, equal to one nautical mile (1,852 metres or 2,025 yards) per hour **knot** v **knotted**, **knotting** 1 to tie or fasten something with a knot 2 to become tangled up 3 (said about a muscle) to become tense and hard **knotty** adj **knottier**, **knottiest** 1 full of knots 2 difficult or puzzling ♦ a knotty problem

know v **knew**, **known** 1 to have something in your mind or memory as a result of experience, learning, or information 2 to be absolutely sure about something ♦ I know I left it here! 3 to recognize or have met a person; to be familiar with a place ♦ I've known him for years. ♦ How well do you know Glasgow? 4 to understand and be able to use a subject, language, or skill **knowable** adj **knowing** adj showing that you know or are aware of something ♦ a knowing look **knowingly** adv **knowledge** n 1 information and skills you have through experience or education 2 awareness or familiarity gained by experience ♦ I have no knowledge of that. 3 all that is known ♦ every branch of knowledge **knowledgeable** adj well-informed **knowledgeably** *adv* **know-all** *n* a person who behaves as if they know everything **know-how** *n* practical knowledge or skill in a particular activity **in the know** *informal* having inside information

knuckle *n* **1** a finger joint **2** the knee joint of an animal **knuckleduster** *n* a metal guard worn over the knuckles in fighting to increase the injury done by a blow **to knuckle under** to yield or submit

knurl (say nerl) *n* a small ridge or knob **knurled** *adj*

KO *n* a knockout in a boxing match

koala (say koh-ah-lə) *n* an Australian tree-climbing animal with thick grey fur and large ears, feeding on eucalyptus leaves

kohl *n* a black powder used as eye make-up

kookaburra *n* a very large Australian kingfisher that has a loud cackling call

Koran (say kor-ahn) *n* the sacred book of Islam

kosher (say koh-sher) *adj* **1** conforming to the requirements of Jewish law concerning the preparation of food **2** *informal* genuine and legitimate

kowtow *v* to behave in an extremely submissive and respectful way towards a person

kph *abbr* kilometres per hour

krill *n* the mass of tiny crustaceans that forms the principal food of certain whales

krypton (say krip-ton) *n* a chemical element (symbol Kr); a colourless odourless gas used in various types of lamps and bulbs

kudos (say kew-doss) *n* honour and glory

Ku Klux Klan *n* a secret society in the USA that is hostile to and uses violence against black people, originally formed in the southern States after the Civil War

kung fu (say kuung foo) *n* a Chinese form of unarmed combat, similar to karate

Kurd *n* a member of a pastoral Islamic people of Kurdistan, a mountainous region of eastern Turkey, northern Iraq, and NW Iran **Kurdish** *adj, n*

kV *abbr* kilovolt(s)

kW *abbr* kilowatt(s)

Ll

L 1 the twelfth letter of the English alphabet **2** the Roman numeral for 50

l *abbr* **1** length **2** litre(s)

lab *n informal* a laboratory

label *n* **1** a slip of paper, cloth, etc. fixed on or beside something to show what it is or what it costs, or its owner or destination, etc. **2** a descriptive word or phrase classifying people or things **label** *v* **labelled**, **labelling** **1** to attach a label to something **2** to describe or classify something ♦ *He was labelled as a troublemaker.*

labia (say lay-bi-ə) *pl n* the lips of the female genitals **labial** *adj*

laboratory (say lə-bo-rə-ter-i) *n pl* **laboratories** a room or building equipped for scientific experiments or research

labour *n* **1** work, especially hard physical work **2** a difficult task **3** the process of childbirth from the start of contractions of the womb to delivery **4** workers, working people distinguished from management or considered as a political force **Labour** *n* the Labour Party **labour** *v* **1** to work hard **2** to have to make a great effort **3** (said about an engine) to work noisily and with difficulty **4** to explain or discuss something at great length or in excessive detail ♦ *I will not labour the point.* **laborious** *adj* **laboriously** *adv* **laboured** *adj* **labourer** *n* **Labour Party** *n* a British political party, formed to represent the interests of working people

labyrinth (say lab-er-inth) *n* **1** a complicated network of paths or passages through which it is difficult to find your way **2** a complex and confusing arrangement **labyrinthine** *adj*

lace *n* **1** a delicate net-like material with decorative patterns of holes in it **2** a cord or narrow leather strip threaded through holes or hooks to fasten a shoe or piece of clothing **lace** *v* **1** to fasten something with a lace or laces **2** to thread a lace through something **3** to add alcohol to food or drink to flavour it

lacerate (say **las**-er-ayt) *v* to injure flesh by cutting or tearing it **laceration** *n*

lack *n* the state of being without or not having enough of something **lack** *v* to be without something ♦ *He lacks courage.* ♦ *They lack for nothing.* **lacking** *adj*

lacklustre *adj* **1** showing little energy or vitality **2** not bright or shining, dull

lackadaisical (say lak-ə-**day**-zikəl) *adj* **1** lacking energy or determination **2** lazy and careless

lackey *n pl* **lackeys 1** a footman or servant **2** a person's servile follower

laconic (say lə-**kon**-ik) *adj* using very few words, terse ♦ *a laconic reply* **laconically** *adv*

lacquer (say **lak**-er) *n* **1** a hard glossy varnish **2** a chemical substance sprayed on hair to keep it in place **lacquer** *v* to coat something with lacquer

lacrosse (say lə-**kross**) *n* a game resembling hockey but with players using a stick with a net

lactic *adj* to do with or obtained from milk **lactation** *n* **lactose** *n* a sugar present in milk

lacy *adj* **lacier, laciest** made of or like lace

lad *n* **1** *informal* a boy or young man **2** *informal* a man who enjoys boisterous or rowdy behaviour ♦ *He's a bit of a lad.* **laddish** *adj* **laddishness** *n*

ladder *n* **1** a set of crossbars (called *rungs*) between two upright pieces of wood, metal, etc., used for climbing up or down something **2** a vertical ladder-like flaw in a pair of stockings or tights **3** a series of stages by which a person may advance in his or her career ♦ *the political ladder* **ladder** *v* to get a ladder in a pair of stockings or tights

laden *adj* heavily loaded or weighed down

ladle *n* a large deep spoon with a long handle, used for serving soup or sauce **ladle** *v* to serve out soup or sauce with a ladle

lady *n pl* **ladies 1** (in polite or formal use) a woman **2** a woman of good social position **3** a well-mannered or kindly woman

Lady *n* a title used by peeresses, female relatives of peers, the wives and widows of knights, etc. **the Ladies** a women's public toilet **ladylike** *adj* suitable for a lady; well-mannered and refined **Her** or **Your Ladyship** a title used in speaking about or to a woman of the rank of Lady **ladybird** *n* a small flying beetle, usually red with black spots

lag[1] *v* **lagged, lagging** to go too slowly, to fail to keep up with others **lag** *n* a delay **laggard** *n* **lagger** *n* a person who lags behind

lag[2] *v* **lagged, lagging** to wrap pipes, a boiler, etc. in a layer of insulating material to prevent loss of heat **lagger** *n* **lagging** *n*

lager (say **lah**-ger) *n* a kind of light beer

lagoon *n* **1** a salt-water lake separated from the sea by a sandbank or coral reef, etc. **2** a small freshwater lake near a larger lake or river

laid past tense and past participle of *lay*[1] **laid-back** *adj informal* relaxed and easygoing

lair *n* **1** a sheltered place where a wild animal lives **2** a person's hiding place

laird *n Scottish* a person who owns a large estate

laissez-faire (say lay-say-**fair**) *n* a government's policy of not interfering

lake *n* a large area of water entirely surrounded by land **the Lakes** *pl n* the Lake District **Lake District** *n* a region of lakes and mountains in Cumbria

lakh (say lak) *n* (in India) a hundred thousand ♦ *a lakh of rupees*

lama (say **lah**-mə) *n* a Buddhist priest or monk in Tibet and Mongolia **Lamaism** *n* **lamasery** *n pl* **lamaseries**

lamb *n* **1** a young sheep **2** meat from a lamb **3** a gentle or endearing person ♦ *You poor lamb!* **lamb** *v* **1** (said about a ewe) to give birth to a lamb **2** to tend lambing ewes **lambing** *n* **lambskin** *n* **lambswool** *n*

lambaste (say lam-**bayst**), **lambast** (say lam-**bast**) *v* to criticize someone severely

lame *adj* **1** unable to walk normally because of an injury or disability in a foot or leg **2** (said about an excuse or explanation) weak or unconvincing **lame** *v* to make a person or animal lame **lamely** adv **lameness** n

lament n 1 a passionate expression of grief 2 a song or poem expressing grief or regret **lament** v 1 to mourn a person's death 2 to feel or express regret or disappointment about something **lamentable** adj **lamentably** adv **lamentation** n **lamented** adj

lamina (say **lam**-in-ə) n pl **laminae** (say lam-i-nee) a technical term for a thin plate, scale, or layer of rock or tissue

laminated (say **lam**-in-ət) adj made of layers joined one upon the other **laminate** n a laminated material

lamp n 1 a device for giving light, either by the use of electricity or gas or by burning oil or spirit 2 a glass container enclosing a filament that is made to glow by electricity 3 an electrical device producing radiation ♦ an infra-red lamp **lamplight** n **lamp post** n a tall post supporting a street lamp **lampshade** n a shade placed over a lamp to soften or screen its light

lampoon (say lam-**poon**) n a piece of writing that attacks a person by ridiculing him or her **lampoon** v to ridicule someone in a lampoon

Lancastrian adj to do with Lancashire **Lancastrian** n a Lancastrian person

lance n 1 a weapon consisting of a long wooden shaft with a pointed metal head 2 a device resembling this, used for spearing fish, etc. **lance** v 1 to prick or cut open a boil, etc. with a surgical lancet 2 to pierce someone or something with a lance **lancer** n

lance corporal n a soldier ranking above a private and below a corporal

lancet (say **lahn**-sit) n 1 a pointed two-edged knife used by surgeons 2 a tall narrow pointed arch or window

land n 1 the solid part of the earth's surface, the part not covered by water 2 an area of ground owned by someone or used for a particular purpose 3 the ground or soil used for farming ♦ a lifetime spent working the land 4 an expanse of country ♦ forest land 5 a country, state, or region ♦ her native land 6 property consisting

of land **land** v 1 to bring an aircraft or its passengers, etc. down to the ground or other surface; to come down in this way 2 to arrive or put people, goods, etc. on land from a ship 3 to come to rest after a jump, fall, or throw ♦ One parachutist landed in a tree. 4 to succeed in getting or winning something ♦ She landed an excellent job. 5 to bring a fish out of the water 6 to arrive or cause someone to arrive at a certain place, stage, or position ♦ They landed up in jail. 7 to strike someone with a blow ♦ He didn't land a single punch. 8 to present someone with something difficult or unpleasant to deal with ♦ They landed me with the job of sorting it out. **landed** adj 1 owning land ♦ landed gentry 2 consisting of land ♦ landed estates **landing** n 1 the process of coming to or bringing something to land or of alighting after a jump 2 a place where people and goods can get on and off a boat 3 a level area at the top of a flight of stairs **landward** adj facing towards the land **landward, landwards** adv towards the land **landfall** n approach to land after a journey by sea or air **landform** n a natural feature of the earth's surface **landing stage** n a platform on which people and goods are taken on and off a boat **landing strip** n an airstrip **landlady** n pl **landladies** 1 a woman who lets out rooms, etc. to tenants 2 a woman who runs a public house **landlocked** adj almost or entirely surrounded by land **landlord** n 1 a person who lets land or a house or room, etc. to tenants 2 a person who runs a public house **landlubber** n a person who is not accustomed to the sea or sailing **landmark** n 1 a conspicuous and easily recognized object in or feature of a landscape 2 an event that marks an important stage or development in the history of something **land mass** n a continent or other large body of land **landmine** n an explosive mine laid on or just under the surface of the ground **landowner** n a person who owns land **landscape** n 1 the scenery of a land area 2 a picture of an area of countryside **landscape** v to lay out a piece of land

attractively, with natural features
landslide n 1 a landslip 2 an overwhelming majority of votes for one side in an election
landslip n a huge mass of soil and rocks sliding down a slope or mountain
lane n 1 a narrow road or track, especially in the country 2 (in names) a street ♦ *Drury Lane* 3 a strip of road for a single line of traffic 4 a strip of track or water for a runner, rower, or swimmer in a race 5 a route prescribed for or regularly followed by ships or aircraft ♦ *shipping lanes*
language n 1 communication by the use of words 2 a system of words used by a particular nation or people ♦ *the German language* 3 any method of expressing or communicating meaning ♦ *body language* ♦ *the language of algebra* 4 a system of symbols and rules used to write computer programs 5 a particular style of wording 6 the vocabulary of a particular group of people ♦ *medical language*
languid (say lang-gwid) adj 1 without energy or vitality 2 weak or faint because of tiredness or illness **languidly** adv **languish** v 1 to grow weak 2 to be neglected
languor (say lang-ger) n 1 a feeling of tiredness or laziness; lack of energy 2 oppressive stillness of the air **languorous** adj
lank adj 1 (said about hair) long, straight, and limp 2 tall and lean **lanky** adj **lankier**, **lankiest**, **lankiness** n
lanolin (say lan-ə-lin) n fat extracted from sheep's wool and used as a base for ointments
lantern n a lamp with a transparent case for holding the light and shielding it against the wind
lap[1] n the flat area formed by the upper part of the thighs when a person is sitting down **lapdog** n a small pampered pet dog **laptop** n a portable computer
lap[2] n 1 a single circuit of something, e.g. of a racetrack 2 one section of a journey ♦ *the last lap* 3 an overlapping part, or the amount of overlap **lap** v **lapped**, **lapping** 1 to overtake another competitor who is one or more laps behind 2 to overlap something or fold it round

lap[3] v **lapped**, **lapping** 1 (said about an animal) to take up liquid by movements of the tongue 2 (said about water) to wash against something with a gentle rippling sound ♦ *Waves lapped against the shore.*
lapel (say lə-pel) n each of the two flaps folded back against the front opening of a coat or jacket, below the collar
Laplander n a native or inhabitant of Lapland
Lapp n 1 a Laplander 2 the language of Lapland **Lappish** adj
lapse n 1 a slight error or failure, especially one caused by forgetfulness, weakness, or inattention ♦ *a lapse of memory* 2 a decline to a lower state or standard 3 a passing of time 4 the loss of a privilege or legal right through disuse **lapse** v 1 to pass or slip gradually into a state or condition ♦ *He lapsed into unconsciousness.* 2 to fail to maintain your position or standard 3 (said about rights and privileges) to be lost or no longer valid through not being used, claimed, or renewed ♦ *My insurance policy has lapsed.* 4 to no longer follow the rules and practices of a religion ♦ *a lapsed Catholic*
larceny (say lar-sən-i) n theft of personal property **larcenous** adj
lard n a white greasy substance prepared from pig fat and used in cooking
larder n a cupboard or small room for storing food
large adj greater than normal in size or extent **largely** adv **largeness** n **largesse** n 1 money or gifts given generously 2 generosity **largish** adj **large-scale** adj
lark n informal 1 a joke or piece of fun ♦ *We did it for a lark.* 2 an amusing incident 3 a type of activity ♦ *I'm fed up with this queueing lark.* **lark** v informal to have fun ♦ *We were just larking about.*
larva n pl **larvae** (say lar-vee) an insect or other creature in the first stage of its life after coming out of the egg **larval** adj
larynx (say la-rinks) n the part of the throat that contains the vocal cords **laryngitis** n inflammation of the larynx, causing hoarseness
lasagne (say lə-san-yeh) n pasta in the form

of sheets; a dish made with this

lascivious (say lə-siv-i-əs) adj lustful **lasciviously** adv **lasciviousness** n

laser (say lay-zer) n a device that generates an intense and highly concentrated beam of light or other electromagnetic radiation **laser printer** n

lash v 1 to flick something violently in a whip-like movement ♦ The crocodile lashed its tail. 2 to strike a person or animal with a whip or stick 3 to beat violently against something ♦ Rain lashed against the panes. 4 to fasten or secure something with a cord or rope ♦ Lash the sticks together. **lash** n 1 a stroke with a whip or stick 2 the flexible leather part of a whip 3 an eyelash **to lash out 1** to attack someone with blows or words 2 to spend money extravagantly

lass, **lassie** n Scottish and N. English a girl or young woman

lasso (say la-soo) n pl **lassoes** a rope with a sliding noose at one end, used for catching cattle **lasso** v lassoes, lassoed, lassoing to catch an animal with a lasso

last[1] adj 1 coming after all others in position or time, final 2 latest, most recent ♦ last night 3 only remaining ♦ our last hope 4 least likely or suitable ♦ She is the last person I'd have chosen. **last** adv 1 after all others, at the end ♦ I'm afraid we came last. 2 previously, most recently ♦ A lot has happened since we last met. 3 lastly ♦ And last but not least this is Jake. **last** n 1 the last person or thing 2 the only remaining part ♦ That's the last of the bread. 3 the last mention or sight of something ♦ We shall never hear the last of it. **lasting** adj **last-ditch** adj final; desperate **last minute** n the latest possible time before an event **last-minute** adj **Last Supper** n the meal eaten by Christ and his disciples on the night before the Crucifixion **last word** n 1 a final or definitive statement on a subject 2 the most modern or advanced example of something ♦ the last word in mobile phones

last[2] v 1 to continue for a period of time ♦ The rain lasted all day. 2 to be enough for your needs ♦ The food will last us for three days. 3 to keep fresh or in good health or condition ♦ I don't think I'll be able to last long in this heat.

latch n 1 a small bar fastening a door or gate, lifted from its catch by a lever 2 a spring lock that catches when the door is closed and can only be opened from the outside by a key **latch** v to fasten something or be fastened with a latch

late adj, adv 1 after the usual or expected time ♦ Sorry I'm late. 2 far on in the day or night, a period of time, or a series, etc. ♦ We arrived late in the afternoon. ♦ in the late 1920s 3 of recent date or time ♦ the latest news 4 no longer alive ♦ the late president **lately** adv recently **lateness** n **later** adj, adv

latent (say lay-tənt) adj existing but not yet active or developed or visible ♦ her latent talent **latency** n

lateral (say lat-er-əl) adj 1 to do with the side or sides 2 sideways ♦ lateral movement **laterally** adv **lateral thinking** n the solving of problems by thinking about them in an indirect and creative way

latex (say lay-teks) n 1 a milky fluid produced by certain plants, e.g. the rubber tree 2 a synthetic product resembling this, used to make paints and coatings

lather n 1 a frothy white mass of bubbles produced by soap or detergent mixed with water 2 frothy sweat, especially on horses 3 informal a state of agitation **lather** v 1 to form a lather 2 to cover something with lather 3 to cover or spread something with a substance

Latin n 1 the language of the ancient Romans 2 a native or inhabitant of a country whose language developed from Latin **Latin** adj 1 to do with or in Latin 2 to do with the countries or peoples using languages developed from Latin **Latin American** adj to do with the parts of Central and South America where Spanish or Portuguese is the main language **Latin American** n a native or inhabitant of this region

latitude n 1 the distance of a place from the equator, measured in degrees 2 freedom from restrictions on what people can do or believe **latitudes** pl n regions with reference to their temperature and distance from the equator ♦ northern latitudes ♦ low latitudes

latitudinal *adj*

latrine (say lə-**treen**) *n* a toilet in a camp or barracks

latte (say **lat**-ay) *n* a drink made by adding espresso coffee to frothy steamed milk

latter *adj* **1** being the second of two people or things mentioned ♦ *He decided to take the latter course of action.* **2** nearer to the end than to the beginning ♦ *the latter half of the year* **3** recent ♦ *in latter years* **the latter** *n* the second of two people or things just mentioned **latterly** *adv* **latter-day** *adj* modern or recent ♦ *He is a latter-day Robin Hood.*

lattice (say **lat**-iss) *n* **1** a framework of crossed strips or bars with spaces between, used as a screen or fence, etc. **2** a structure or pattern resembling this **latticework** *n*

laud (say lawd) *v formal* to praise someone or something highly **laudable** *adj* **laudably** *adv* **laudatory** *adj* praising

laugh *v* to make the sounds and movements of the face and body that express lively amusement and sometimes also scorn **laugh** *n* **1** an act, sound, or manner of laughing **2** *informal* an amusing incident or person **laughable** *adj* **laughter** *n* **laughing stock** *n* a person or thing that is the object of ridicule and scorn

launch[1] *v* **1** to cause a boat or ship to move from land into the water **2** to send a rocket or missile upwards into space or into the air **3** to send something on its course **4** to bring a new product on to the market ♦ *The company has recently launched a new soft drink.* **5** to start something off ♦ *They launched an attack at dawn.* **6** to begin something with enthusiasm and energy ♦ *She launched into her speech.* **launch** *n* **1** the process of launching a ship, rocket, etc. **2** the start of something **launch pad** *n* a platform from which a rocket is launched

launch[2] *n* a large motor boat

laundry *n pl* **laundries 1** a batch of clothes and linen that needs to be washed or that has just been washed **2** a place where clothes and linen are washed and ironed for customers **launder** *v* **launderette** *n* an establishment fitted with washing machines that customers pay to use

laureate (say **lorri**-ət) *n* **1** a person given an award for outstanding creative or intellectual achievement ♦ *a Nobel laureate* **2** the Poet Laureate **laureate** *adj* wreathed with laurel as a mark of honour **laureateship** *n*

laurel (say **lo**-rəl) *n* **1** an evergreen shrub with smooth glossy leaves **2** (also **laurels**) a crown of laurel leaves worn as an emblem of victory or mark of honour in classical times

lava (say **lah**-və) *n* flowing molten rock that flows or erupts from a volcano, or the solid rock formed when this cools

lavatory *n pl* **lavatories 1** a toilet **2** a room or compartment containing a toilet

lavender *n* **1** a shrub with fragrant purple flowers that are dried and used to scent linen, etc. **2** light purple

lavish (say **lav**-ish) *adj* **1** giving or producing something in large quantities **2** plentiful or luxurious ♦ *a lavish display* **lavish** *v* to give something in generous or plentiful quantities ♦ *Her latest novel has been lavished with praise.* **lavishly** *adv* **lavishness** *n*

law *n* **1** a rule or set of rules that everyone in a country or community must obey **2** the use of these rules to provide a remedy against wrongs ♦ *law and order* **3** the subject or study of these rules **4** *informal* the police **5** something that must be obeyed ♦ *His word was law.* **6** a rule of a sport or game ♦ *the laws of cricket* **7** a factual statement of what always happens in certain circumstances, e.g. of regular natural occurrences ♦ *the laws of nature* ♦ *the law of gravity* **lawful** *adj* **lawfully** *adv* **lawless** *adj* **1** (said about a place) where laws do not exist or are not applied **2** not obeying the law ♦ *a lawless mob* **lawlessly** *adv* **lawlessness** *n* **lawyer** *n* a person who is trained in and qualified to practise law **law-abiding** *adj* **lawbreaker** *n* **law court** *n* **law lord** *n* a member of the House of Lords who is qualified to perform its legal work **lawsuit** *n* a dispute or claim that is brought to a law court to be settled

lawn *n* an area of mown grass in a garden or park **lawnmower** *n* a machine with revolving blades for cutting the grass on a lawn

lax adj slack, not strict or severe enough ♦ *Discipline was lax.* **laxity** n **laxly** adv

laxative (say **laks-ə-tiv**) n a drug or medicine that stimulates the bowels to empty **laxative** adj having this effect

lay[1] v past tense and past participle **laid** **1** to put something down on a surface, especially in a horizontal position ♦ *He laid the letter on the table.* **2** to put something in a particular position or place ♦ *She laid a hand on his shoulder.* **3** to arrange things, especially for a meal ♦ *Can you lay the table?* **4** to place or assign something ♦ *He lays great emphasis on neatness.* **5** to formulate or prepare something ♦ *We laid our plans.* **6** to present something or put it forward for consideration ♦ *He laid his proposal before us.* **7** (said about a female bird or reptile) to produce an egg from inside its body **8** to stake an amount of money in a wager or bet **lay** n the way or position in which something is lying **layabout** n a person who lazily avoids doing any work **lay-by** n pl **lay-bys** an area at the side of a main road, where vehicles may stop without obstructing the flow of traffic **lay-off** n **1** a temporary or permanent discharge of a worker or workers **2** a period during which someone cannot take part in a sport, etc. because of injury or illness **layout** n **1** the arrangement or plan of something ♦ *I like the layout of the gallery.* **2** the arrangement of text, illustrations, etc. on a page **3** something displayed or set out ♦ *a model railway layout*

lay[2] adj **1** not ordained into the clergy ♦ *a lay preacher* **2** not professionally qualified, especially in law or medicine **layman, laywoman, layperson** n pl **laymen, laywomen, laypeople 1** a person who does not have specialized knowledge or training, e.g. as a doctor or lawyer **2** a person who is not ordained as a member of the clergy

layer n **1** a single thickness or coating of something, often one of several, laid over a surface **2** a person or thing that lays something **3** a shoot fastened down to take root while still attached to the parent plant **layer** v **layering, layered 1** to arrange or cut something in layers **2** to propagate a plant as a layer

laze v to spend time in a relaxed lazy manner **laze** n a time spent lazing **lazy** adj **lazier, laziest, lazily** adv **laziness** n **lazybones** n a lazy person

lb abbr pound(s) in weight

LCD abbr liquid crystal display

leach v to make liquid, especially rainwater, percolate through soil or ore, etc. in order to remove a soluble substance

lead[1] (say **leed**) v past tense and past participle **led 1** to show someone the way by going in front or accompanying them **2** to make a person or animal go with you by pulling them along **3** to be in first place or position in a race or contest, to be ahead ♦ *Rangers are leading by two goals to nil.* **4** to be in charge of a group of people, to be the leader **5** to be a route or means of access ♦ *This path leads to the beach.* **6** to have something as its result ♦ *This led to confusion.* **7** to be someone's reason or motive for something ♦ *What led you to become a journalist?* **8** to live or pass your life ♦ *He leads a dull life.* **9** (in boxing) to make your first punch in a series **10** to play the first card in a round of a card game **lead** n **1** a leading place or position, first place; the amount by which one competitor is in front ♦ *She took the lead on the final bend.* **2** guidance or leadership given by being the first to do something ♦ *Britain should be taking a lead on this issue.* **3** a clue to be followed ♦ *The police have few leads.* **4** the chief part in a play or film, or the person who takes this part ♦ *He played the lead in 'Hamlet'.* **5** (used before a noun) playing the main part in a musical group ♦ *the lead singer* **6** a strap or cord for leading a dog or other animal **7** a wire carrying electric current from a source to a place of use **8** the act or right of playing your card first in a round of a card game; the card played ♦ *Whose lead is it?* **leader** n **leadership** n **leading** adj **lead-in** n an introduction to or the opening of something **leading lady/ man** n the actor taking the chief part in a play or film **leading light** n a prominent or influential member of a group **leading**

question n a question that is worded so that it prompts a person to give the answer that is wanted **lead-up** n the sequence of events leading up to something

lead² (say led) n 1 a heavy metal of dull greyish colour, a chemical element (symbol Pb) 2 a thin stick of graphite forming the writing substance in a pencil 3 a lump of lead suspended on a line to determine the depth of water **leaded** adj 1 covered or framed with lead; mixed with lead 2 (said about petrol) containing a lead compound **leaden** adj 1 heavy 2 dull grey 3 made from lead **leads** pl n strips of lead used to cover a roof

leaf n pl **leaves** 1 a flat, usually green, part of a plant growing from its stem or branch or directly from the root 2 the state of having leaves out ♦ The trees are now in leaf. 3 a single thickness of the paper in a book 4 a very thin sheet of metal ♦ gold leaf 5 a hinged flap of a table, or an extra section that may be inserted to extend a table **leafy** adj **leafier**, **leafiest**, **leafiness** n **leafless** adj

leaflet n 1 a printed sheet of paper giving information, especially one given out free 2 a small leaf or leaf-like part of a plant

league n 1 a group of people or countries who combine formally for some common purpose 2 a group of sports teams which compete against each other for a championship 3 a class or level of quality or ability ♦ As artists they are not remotely in the same league. **league table** n 1 a table of competitors in a league ranked according to their performances 2 a list in which things are ranked according to achievement or merit ♦ school league tables

leak n 1 a hole or crack through which liquid or gas may accidentally escape 2 an escape of liquid or gas 3 a similar escape of an electric charge, or the charge itself 4 a deliberate disclosure of secret information **leak** v 1 (said about liquid or gas) to escape accidentally through a hole or crack 2 (said about a container) to let out liquid or gas in this way 3 to deliberately reveal secret information ♦ Someone leaked the report's findings to the press. **leakage** n **leaky** adj

leakier, leakiest

lean¹ v past tense and past participle **leaned** or **leant** 1 to bend your body towards or over something 2 to be or put something in a sloping position 3 to rest against or on something for support 4 to rely or depend on someone for help **lean** n a sloping position **leaning** n a tendency

lean² adj 1 (said about a person or animal) thin, without much flesh 2 (said about meat) containing little or no fat 3 efficient and with no wastage ♦ a lean company 4 meagre or scanty ♦ a lean harvest **lean** n the lean part of meat **leanness** n

leap v past tense and past participle **leaped** (say leept or lept) or **leapt** (say lept) 1 to jump vigorously, to jump across something 2 to move somewhere suddenly and quickly ♦ He leapt out of his chair. 3 to rise suddenly in amount or in price or value **leap** n 1 a vigorous jump 2 an abrupt change or increase **leap year** n a year, occurring once every four years, with an extra day (29 February)

learn v past tense and past participle **learned** (say lernt or lernd) or **learnt** (say lernt) 1 to gain knowledge of or skill in something by study or experience or by being taught 2 to memorize something ♦ I'll try to learn all your names. 3 to become aware of something by information or from observation **learned** (say lern-id) adj 1 having much knwledge acquired by study 2 to do with or for learned people **learnedly** adv **learner** n **learning** n **learning difficulties** pl n difficulties in learning, especially because of mental handicap

lease n a contract by which the owner of land or a building, etc. allows another person to use it for a fixed period **lease** v 1 to allow the use of a property by lease 2 to obtain or take a property by lease **leasehold** n the holding of land or a house or flat, etc. by means of a lease **leaseholder** n

leash n a dog's lead **leash** v to put a leash on a dog

least adj 1 smallest in amount or degree 2 lowest in rank or importance **least** n the least amount or degree ♦ The least you could *do is apologize.* **least** *adv* in the least degree

leather *n* **1** material made from animal skins by tanning or a similar process **2** a piece of leather for polishing with **leathers** *pl n* leather clothes worn by a motorcyclist **leather** *v* to cover something with leather **leathery** *adj*

leave[1] *v* past tense and past participle **left 1** to go away from a person or place ♦ *What time did you leave the party?* **2** to stop belonging to a group or organization; to stop working somewhere **3** to cause or allow something to stay where it is or as it is ♦ *Only a few crumbs were left.* ♦ *You left the door open.* **4** to go away without taking something ♦ *I left my gloves on the bus.* **5** to let someone deal with something without interfering or offering help ♦ *We left him to get on with it.* ♦ *I was left with the bill.* **6** to refrain from eating or dealing with something ♦ *Let's leave the washing-up.* **7** to entrust or commit something to another person ♦ *Leave the shopping to me.* **8** to have an amount as a remainder ♦ *11 from 43 leaves 32.* **9** to give something as a legacy **10** to deposit something to be collected or passed on ♦ *You can leave your coat in the hall.* ♦ *Would you like to leave a message?* **11** to abandon or desert someone or something ♦ *His wife has left him.* ♦ *A captain should never leave a sinking ship.* **leave-taking** *n* an act of saying goodbye **to leave someone** or **something out** to fail to include someone or something

leave[2] *n* **1** time when you have official permission to be away from work ♦ *three days' leave* **2** *formal* permission

leaven (say lev-ən) *n* a substance such as yeast that is added to dough to make it ferment and rise **leaven** *v* to add leaven to dough

lechery *n* excessive sexual desire **lecher** *n* **lecherous** *adj*

lectern *n* a tall stand with a sloping top to hold a book or notes for someone to read from

lecture *n* **1** a speech or talk giving information about a subject to an audience or class **2** a long serious speech, especially

one giving a reprimand or warning **lecture** *v* **1** to give a lecture or series of lectures **2** to talk to someone seriously or reprovingly **lecturer** *n*

LED *abbr* light-emitting diode

led past tense and past participle of *lead*[1]

ledge *n* a narrow horizontal projection, a narrow shelf ♦ *a mountain ledge*

ledger *n* a book of financial accounts

leech *n* **1** a small blood-sucking worm usually living in water **2** a person who drains the resources of another

leek *n* a vegetable

leer *v* to look at someone in a lustful or unpleasant way **leer** *n* a leering look **leering** *adj* **leery** *adj* **leerier, leeriest**

leeway *n* the amount of freedom to move or act that is available ♦ *These instructions give us plenty of leeway.*

left[1] *adj* **1** on or towards the side which is to the west when you are facing north **2** to do with left-wing politics **left** *adv* on or to the left side **left** *n* **1** the left-hand side or direction **2** a person's left fist, or a blow with this **3** (often **the Left**) a political party or other group in favour of radical, reforming, or socialist views **lefty** *n pl* **lefties 1** a left-wing person **2** a left-handed person **leftie** *n* a supporter of left-wing politics **leftist** *adj* to do with the left wing in politics **leftism** *n* **leftovers** *pl n* food not finished at a meal **leftover** *adj* remaining after the rest has been used or finished **left-hand** *adj* of or towards the left side **left-handed** *adj* **1** using the left hand usually **2** operated by the left hand **left-handedness** *n* **left-hander** *n* a left-handed person **left wing** *n* the radical, reforming, or socialist section of a political party or system **left-wing** *adj* **left-winger** *n*

left[2] past tense and past participle of *leave*[1]

leg *n* **1** each of the limbs on which a person or animal stands or walks **2** the leg of an animal or bird as food **3** the part of a piece of clothing covering the leg **4** each of the long thin supports beneath a chair or other piece of furniture **5** any branch of a forked object **6** a section of a journey **7** each of a pair of matches between the same opponents in a round of a competition

leggings pl n **1** a woman's tight-fitting stretchy trousers **2** protective outer coverings for each leg from knee to ankle

leggy adj **leggier**, **leggiest**, **legless** adj **1** without legs **2** informal very drunk

legroom n space for someone sitting down to put their legs

legacy (say **leg**-əsi) n pl **legacies 1** something left to a person in a will **2** something received from a predecessor or because of earlier events ♦ a legacy of distrust **legatee** n

legal adj **1** in accordance with the law; authorized or required by law **2** to do with or based on the law ♦ my legal adviser **legality** n pl **legalities** the quality or state of being legal **2** something you have to do by law **legalize** v to make something legal **legalization** n **legally** adv **legal aid** n payment from public funds towards the cost of legal advice or proceedings

legate (say **leg**-ət) n an official representative, especially of the Pope

legend (say **lej**-ənd) n **1** an old story, which may or may not be true, handed down from the past **2** such stories collectively **3** an extremely famous person ♦ a screen legend **4** an inscription, caption, or key **legendary** adj

legible (say **lej**-i-bəl) adj (said about print or handwriting) clear enough to read **legibility** n **legibly** adv

legion (say **lee**-jən) n **1** a division of the ancient Roman army **2** a national association of former servicemen and servicewomen ♦ the British Legion **3** a vast number of people or things **the Legion** n the Foreign Legion **legion** adj great in number ♦ Her fans are legion. **legionary** adj, n **legionnaire** n a member of a legion

legislate (say **lej**-iss-layt) v **1** to make or pass laws **2** to bring something into effect by making laws **legislation** n **legislative** adj **legislator** n **legislature** n

legitimate[1] (say **li-jit**-i-mət) adj **1** in accordance with the law or rules **2** logical; justifiable ♦ a legitimate reason for absence **3** (said about a child) born of parents who are married to each other **legitimacy** n

legitimately adv **legitimize** v

legitimate[2] (say **li-jit**-i-mayt) v to make something legitimate

leisure (say **lezh**-er) n time that is free from work; time in which you can do what you like **leisured** adj **leisurely** adj, adv **at leisure 1** not occupied **2** in an unhurried way **at your leisure** when you have time **leisureliness** n **leisure centre** n

lemon n **1** an oval yellow citrus fruit with a sour taste **2** the tree that bears this fruit **3** a pale yellow colour **4** informal a useless or disappointing person or thing **lemony** adj **lemonade** n a lemon-flavoured drink **lemon curd** n a lemon-flavoured creamy jam

lemur (say **lee**-mer) n a monkey-like animal with a pointed snout and long tail, found only in Madagascar

lend v past tense and past participle **lent 1** to allow someone to use something of yours temporarily on the understanding that it will be returned **2** to provide a sum of money under an agreement to pay it back later, often with interest **3** to contribute or add a quality to something ♦ She lent dignity to the occasion. **lender** n

length n **1** how long something is; measurement or extent from end to end **2** the quality of being long **3** the amount of time occupied by something ♦ the length of our holiday **4** the length of a horse or boat as a measure of the lead in a race **5** the degree of thoroughness in taking a course of action ♦ They went to great lengths to make us comfortable. **6** a piece of cloth, rope, wire, etc. cut from a larger piece **lengthen** v to make longer **lengthy** adj **lengthier**, **lengthiest**, **lengthily** adv **lengthiness** n **lengthways** adv **lengthwise** adv, adj

lenient (say **lee**-ni-ənt) adj merciful, not severe **lenience** n **leniently** adv

lens n pl **lenses 1** a piece of glass or other transparent substance with one or both sides curved, for use in optical instruments **2** the transparent part of the eye, behind the pupil **3** a contact lens **4** a combination of lenses used in a camera

Lent n the period from Ash Wednesday to Easter Saturday, of which the 40 weekdays are observed as a time of fasting and penitence **Lenten** adj

lent past tense and past participle of lend

lentil n 1 a kind of bean plant 2 the edible seed of this plant ♦ lentil soup

Leo (say lee-oh) n (the Lion) the sign of the zodiac which the sun enters about 21 July

leopard (say lep-erd) n a large mammal of the cat family (also called a panther), having a yellowish coat with dark spots, found in Africa and southern Asia **leopardess** n

leotard (say lee-a-tard) n a close-fitting piece of clothing covering the body to the top of the thighs, worn for dance, exercise, and gymnastics

leprechaun (say lep-ra-kawn) n (in Irish folklore) an elf who looks like a little old man

leprosy n an infectious disease affecting the skin and nerves, resulting in mutilations and deformities **leper** n **leprous** adj

lesbian n a homosexual woman **lesbian** adj **lesbianism** n

lesion (say lee-zhan) n a harmful change in the tissue of an organ of the body, caused by injury or disease

less adj 1 not as much, a smaller quantity of ♦ Make less noise. 2 smaller in amount or degree ♦ It is less important. **less** adv to a smaller extent **less** n a smaller amount or quantity ♦ He is paid less than he deserves. **less** prep minus, deducting ♦ She earned £2000, less tax. ◊ It is better not to use less when you are referring to a number of individual things, in which case use fewer: If we use less batter we will make fewer pancakes. **lessen** v to reduce **lesser** adj

-less suffix forming adjectives meaning 'without' (as in colourless) or 'unable to be' (as in countless)

lesson n 1 an amount of teaching given at one time 2 something to be learnt by a pupil or student 3 an example or experience from which you should learn ♦ Let this be a lesson to you! 4 a passage from the Bible read aloud during a church service

lest conjunction formal 1 in order to prevent, to avoid the risk that ♦ Lest we forget, let me remind you of her achievements. 2 because of the possibility that ♦ We were afraid lest

we should be late.

let v past tense and past participle **let; letting** 1 to allow someone or something to do something, to not prevent or forbid someone from doing something ♦ Let me see. ♦ You shouldn't let him speak to you like that. 2 to cause something to happen ♦ I'll let you know what happens. 3 to allow or cause someone or something to come, go, or pass ♦ Can you let the dog in? 4 used to express an intention, proposal, or instruction ♦ Let's have a drink. 5 used to express an assumption ♦ Let AB equal CD. 6 to allow someone to use a room or property in return for payment **let** n the letting of a room or property ♦ a long let **let-down** n a disappointment **let-off** n a situation in which someone unexpectedly escapes or avoids something **let-out** n a way of escaping an obligation **let-up** n a pause or reduction in the intensity of something **to let on** informal to reveal a secret **to let someone** or **something be** to stop interfering with someone or something **to let someone down** 1 to fail to support or help someone 2 to disappoint someone **to let something down** 1 to deflate a balloon or tyre 2 to lengthen a piece of clothing by adjusting the hem **to let something out** 1 to make a sound or cry 2 to make a piece of clothing looser by adjusting the seams 3 to let rooms or property to tenants **to let up** informal 1 to become less intense 2 to relax your efforts

lethal (say lee-thal) adj deadly, causing or able to cause death **lethally** adv

lethargy (say leth-er-ji) n extreme lack of energy or vitality **lethargic** adj, **lethargically** adv

let's v informal let us

letter n 1 a symbol representing a sound used in speech 2 a written message usually sent by post **letters** n literature ♦ the world of letters **letter** v to inscribe or provide something with letters **lettering** n **letter bomb** n an explosive device hidden in a package sent by post **letter box** n 1 a slit in a door, with a movable flap through which letters are delivered 2 a postbox **letterhead** n a printed heading on

lettuce *n* stationery, showing the sender's name and address

lettuce *n* a salad plant with broad crisp leaves

leukaemia (say lew-**kee**-miə) *n* a disease in which the white corpuscles multiply uncontrollably in the body tissues and usually in the blood

Levant (say li-**vant**) *n* old use the countries and islands in the eastern part of the Mediterranean Sea **Levantine** *adj, n*

levee (say **lev**-i) *n* an embankment built up naturally along a river, or made artificially as a protection against floods

level *n* **1** an imaginary line or plane joining points of equal height **2** a measured height or value, etc., a position or stage on a scale ♦ *the level of alcohol in the blood* **3** relative position in rank, class, or status ♦ *decisions at Cabinet level* **4** a more or less flat surface or area **5** an instrument for testing a horizontal line **level** *adj* **1** having a flat horizontal surface **2** (said about ground) flat, without hills or hollows **3** at the same height as something else **4** having the same relative position; not in front or behind **5** calm and steady ♦ *a level voice* **level** *v* **levelled**, **levelling 1** to make something level, or to become level **2** to knock down buildings to the ground **3** to aim a gun or missile **4** to direct an accusation or criticism at a person **leveller** *n* **1** a person or thing that levels something **2** a member of a group of radicals in the English Civil War **levelly** *adv* **level crossing** *n* a place where a railway and a road cross each other at the same level **level-headed** *adj* (said about a person) sensible

lever (say **lee**-ver) *n* **1** a bar or other device pivoted on a fixed point (called the *fulcrum*) in order to lift something or force something open **2** a projecting handle used to operate or control a piece of machinery ♦ *a gear lever* **lever** *v* **1** to lift or move something by means of a lever **2** to move yourself with an effort ♦ *She levered herself up onto the wall.* **leverage** *n*

leveret (say **lev**-er-it) *n* a young hare

leviathan (say li-**viy**-əth-ən) *n* something of enormous size and power

levitate *v* to rise or cause something to rise and float in the air in defiance of gravity **levitation** *n*

levity (say **lev**-iti) *n* a humorous attitude towards serious matters

levy *v* **levies**, **levied**, **levying** to impose or collect a tax, fine, or other payment **levy** *n pl* **levies 1** levying a tax, fine, etc. **2** an amount of money paid in tax

lewd *adj* indecent or crude, treating sexual matters in a vulgar way **lewdly** *adv* **lewdness** *n*

lexical *adj* **1** to do with the words of a language **2** to do with a lexicon or dictionary

liable (say **liy**-əbəl) *adj* **1** able or likely to do or suffer something ♦ *The cliff is liable to crumble.* ♦ *She is liable to colds.* **2** held responsible by law **liability** *n pl* **liabilities**

liaise (say lee-**ayz**) *v* to act as a go-between **liaison** *n*

liar *n* a person who tells lies

Lib Dem *n informal* Liberal Democrat

libel (say **liy**-bəl) *n* **1** an untrue written, printed, or broadcast statement that damages a person's reputation **2** the act of publishing or broadcasting a libel ♦ *The newspaper was charged with libel.* **libel** *v* **libelled**, **libelling** to publish or broadcast a libel against someone **libellous** *adj*

liberal *adj* **1** tolerant or open-minded **2** (in politics) in favour of individual freedom and moderate political and social reform **3** giving generously **4** ample, given in large amounts **5** not strict or literal ♦ *a liberal interpretation of the rules* **6** (said about education) broadening the mind in a general way, not only training it in technical subjects **Liberal** *adj* to do with the Liberal Democrat party **Liberal** *n* a Liberal Democrat **liberal** *n* a person of liberal views **liberalism** *n* **liberality** *n* **liberally** *adv* **Liberal Democrat** *n* a member of the Liberal Democrat political party **liberalize** *v* to make something less strict **liberalization** *n*

liberate *v* to set someone free, especially from control by an authority that is considered to be oppressive **liberated** *adj* **liberation** *n* **liberator** *n*

liberty n pl **liberties** 1 freedom from imprisonment or oppression 2 the right or power to do as you choose 3 a right or privilege granted by authority 4 informal a presumptuous remark or action **libertarian** n a person who believes in freedom of thought and action **libertine** n a person who lives an irresponsible and immoral life **at liberty** 1 (said about a person) not imprisoned, free 2 allowed or entitled to do something ♦ You are at liberty to leave. **to take liberties** 1 to behave too familiarly towards a person 2 to treat or interpret facts, etc. too freely

libido (say lib-**ee**-doh) n pl **libidos** sexual desire **libidinal** adj **libidinous** adj

Libra (say **leeb**-rə) n (the Scales or Balance) the sign of the zodiac which the sun enters about 22 September **Libran** adj, n

library (say **liy**-brə-ri) n pl **libraries** 1 a building or room where books, CDs, etc. are kept for people to use or borrow 2 a private collection of books 3 a series of books issued in similar bindings as a set **librarian** n **librarianship** n

lice plural of louse

licence n 1 an official permit to own or do something or to carry on a certain trade ♦ a driving licence 2 permission 3 freedom to disregard the usual rules or customs, etc., or to behave without restraint 4 a writer's or artist's exaggeration, or deliberate disregard of rules, etc., to achieve a certain effect ♦ poetic licence **licensee** n **licentiate** n

license v 1 to grant a licence to someone ♦ We are licensed to sell alcohol. 2 to authorize someone to do something

licentious (say liy-**sen**-shəs) adj promiscuous and lacking principles in sexual matters **licentiousness** n

lichen (say **liy**-kən or **lich**-ən) n a dry-looking plant that grows on rocks, walls, and tree trunks, usually green or yellow or grey

lick v 1 to move the tongue over something in order to eat or clean it or make it wet 2 (said about waves or flames) to move over something lightly and quickly like a tongue 3 informal to defeat someone **lick** n 1 an act

of licking with the tongue 2 informal a small amount or quick application of something ♦ The walls could do with a lick of paint. 3 informal a short phrase or solo in jazz or rock music **licking** n a defeat

lid n 1 a hinged or removable cover for the top of a container 2 an eyelid **lidded** adj

lido (say lee-doh) n pl **lidos** a public open-air swimming pool or bathing beach

lie[1] n 1 a statement that the person making it knows is untrue 2 something that deceives ♦ She has been living a lie. **lie** v **lies, lied, lying** 1 to tell a lie or lies 2 to give a false impression ♦ The camera does not lie.

lie[2] v **lay, lain, lying** 1 to have or put your body in a flat or resting position horizontal to the ground ♦ He lay on the grass. 2 (said about a thing) to rest on a surface ♦ A book lay open on the table. 3 to be buried somewhere ♦ Here lies Anne Spencer. 4 to be or remain in a particular state ♦ These machines have lain idle for months. 5 to be situated ♦ The island lies to the north of here. 6 to extend in front of you or behind you ♦ A green valley lay before us. 7 to exist or be found ♦ The remedy lies in education and training. 8 Law to be admissible or able to be upheld ♦ Their appeal will not lie. **lie** n the way or position in which something lies **lie-down** n a brief rest on a bed or sofa **lie-in** n staying in bed late in the morning **to lie down** to have a brief rest on a bed or sofa **to lie in** to stay in bed late in the morning

lieu (say lew) n **in lieu** instead; in place ♦ He accepted a cheque in lieu of cash.

lieutenant (say lef-**ten**-ənt) n 1 an army officer next below a captain 2 a navy officer next below a lieutenant commander 3 a deputy or chief assistant

life n pl **lives** 1 being alive; the ability to function and grow 2 living things in general ♦ plant life ♦ Is there life on Mars. 3 the period between birth and death or between birth and the present time 4 a living person ♦ Many lives were lost in the earthquake. 5 an aspect of someone's life or a type or manner of existence ♦ in private life ♦ village life 6 a biography 7 the length of time that something exists or continues to function ♦ The battery has a life of two years. **8** liveliness or energy ♦ *His music is full of life.* **9** human activities in general, especially the exciting or enjoyable aspects of human existence **10** *informal* a life sentence **lifeless** *adj* **lifelessly** *adv* **lifelessness** *n* **lifelike** *adj* **lifebelt** *n* a ring of buoyant or inflatable material used to support the body of a person who has fallen into the water **lifeboat** *n* **1** a boat specially constructed for going to the help of people in danger at sea along a coast **2** a small boat carried on a ship for use if the ship has to be abandoned at sea **life cycle** *n* the series of changes in the life of a living thing **life expectancy** *n* the average length of time that a person of a specified age may be expected to live **life form** *n* any living thing **lifeguard** *n* a person whose job is to rescue swimmers who are in difficulty at a beach or swimming pool **life imprisonment** *n* a long term of imprisonment, in theory (though rarely in practice) for the rest of the offender's life **life jacket** *n* a sleeveless jacket of buoyant or inflatable material used to support a person's body in the water **lifeline** *n* **1** a rope or line used in rescuing people, e.g. one attached to a lifebelt **2** a diver's signalling line **3** a vital means of communication or support on which someone relies **lifelong** *adj* continuing for the whole of someone's life **life raft** *n* an inflatable raft used in an emergency at sea **lifesaver** *n* something that saves you from serious difficulty **life sciences** *pl n* the sciences that deal with the study of living things **life sentence** *n* a punishment of life imprisonment **life-size** *adj* of the same size as the person or thing represented **lifespan** *n* the length of a person's or animal's life **lifestyle** *n* a person's way of life **life support** *n* equipment and procedures that allow the body to continue functioning **life-threatening** *adj* potentially fatal ♦ *a life-threatening disease* **lifetime** *n* **1** the duration of a person's life or of a thing's existence **2** *informal* a very long time

lift *v* **1** to raise something to a higher level or position **2** to pick something up and move it to a different position **3** to dig something up **4** to rise or go upwards **5** (said about fog, etc.) to disperse **6** to remove or end something ♦ *The ban has been lifted.* **7** *informal* to steal or copy something **lift** *n* **1** an apparatus for taking people or goods from one floor of a building to another **2** a device for carrying people up or down a mountain ♦ *a ski lift* **3** a free ride in someone else's car ♦ *Can you give me a lift to the station?* **4** lifting, or being lifted **5** the upward pressure that air exerts on an aircraft in flight **6** a feeling of increased confidence or cheerfulness ♦ *Her words of encouragement gave me a real lift.* **lift-off** *n* the vertical take-off of a rocket or spacecraft

ligament *n* a short band of tough flexible tissue that holds bones together or keeps organs in place in the body

ligature (say lig-ə-cher) *n* **1** a thing used in tying something tightly, especially in surgical operations **2** a tie in music **3** joined printed letters such as æ **ligature** *v* to tie something with a ligature

light[1] *n* **1** the radiation that stimulates the sense of sight and makes things visible **2** the presence, amount, or effect of this ♦ *Have you got enough light to read in?* ♦ *The light is beautiful at this time of year.* **3** something that provides light, especially an electric lamp ♦ *Please leave the light on.* **4** a flame or spark; something used to produce this ♦ *Do you have a light?* **5** brightness; the bright parts of a picture, etc. **6** enlightenment ♦ *Light dawned in her eyes.* **7** the way something appears to your mind ♦ *I see the matter in a completely different light now.* **8** a window or opening to let light in **lights** *pl n* **1** traffic lights **2** a person's mental ability, attitudes, or knowledge ♦ *He did his best according to his lights.* **light** *v* past tense **lit**; past participle **lit** or **lighted** **1** to start something burning; to begin to burn **2** to provide light for something ♦ *A single spotlight lit the stage.* **3** to guide someone with a light **4** to brighten something **lighten** *v* **lighter** *n* a device for lighting cigarettes **lighting** *n* **lightning** *n* a flash of bright light produced by natural electricity during a thunderstorm **lightning** *adv* very quick

♦ with lightning speed **light bulb** n a glass bulb which provides light when an electric current is passed through it **lighthouse** n a tower or other structure containing a beacon light to warn or guide ships **light year** n a unit of distance equivalent to the distance that light travels in one year, 9.4607 x 10^{12} km (nearly 6 million million miles) **in the light of** taking something into consideration **to come to light** to become widely known or noticeable **to light up 1** to put lights on at dusk **2** to become brightly lit **3** to suddenly become animated with liveliness or happiness ♦ When she opened the box her whole face lit up. **4** to begin to smoke a pipe or cigarette **to see the light** to realize or understand something **to throw** or **shed** or **cast light on** to help to explain something ◊ The usual form for the past tense and past participle is lit: She lit a candle. She had lit a candle. When the past participle is used as an adjective before a noun or pronoun, lighted is more usual: She came in with a lighted candle.

light^2 adj **1** having little weight, easy to lift or carry **2** of less than average weight, amount, or force ♦ light rain ♦ a light punishment **3** (said about work) needing little physical effort **4** not intense ♦ a light sleeper **5** not dense ♦ light mist **6** (said about food) small in quantity and easy to digest ♦ a light snack **7** moving easily and quickly **8** not serious or profound, intended as entertainment ♦ light music **9** cheerful, free from worry ♦ I left with a light heart. **lightly** adv **lightness** n **light-fingered** adj apt to steal **light-headed** adj dizzy and slightly faint **light-hearted** adj **1** amusing and entertaining, not serious **2** cheerful and free from worry **light industry** n an industry producing small or light articles **lightweight** adj **1** of thin material or build **2** having little influence **lightweight** n **1** a boxing weight between welterweight and featherweight **2** informal a person of little influence

light^3 v past tense and past participle **lit** or **lighted to light on** or **upon** to come upon something by chance

like^1 prep **1** similar to or resembling ♦ Those curtains are just like ours. **2** used when asking for or giving a description of someone or something ♦ What was the film like? **3** in the manner of; to the same degree as ♦ He swims like a fish. **4** in a suitable state for ♦ It looks like rain. ♦ I feel like a cup of tea. **5** such as ♦ He's good at subjects like music and art. **6** characteristic of ♦ It was like him to do that. **like** conjunction informal **1** in the same way that; to the same degree as ♦ You don't know her like I do. **2** as if ♦ She doesn't act like she belongs here. **like** adj similar ♦ We have like minds. **like** n a similar person or thing ♦ We shall not see his like again. **likely** adj **likelier**, **likeliest**, **likelihood** n **liken** v **likeness** n **likewise** adv being likely, probability **like-minded** adj having similar tastes or opinions

like^2 v **1** to think a person or thing is pleasant or satisfactory **2** to wish for something ♦ I would like to think about it. **likes** pl n the things you like or prefer **likeable** adj, **liking** n

lilo (say **liy**-loh) n pl **lilos** an inflatable mattress used as a bed or for floating on water

lilt n **1** a pleasant gentle accent **2** a light pleasant rhythm in a tune **lilting** adj

lily n pl **lilies** a garden plant growing from a bulb, with large white or reddish trumpet-shaped flowers

limb n **1** a leg, arm, or wing **2** a large branch of a tree **3** an arm of a cross

limber adj flexible or supple

limbo^1 n **in limbo** in an uncertain situation where you are waiting for something to happen or be decided ♦ Lack of money has left our plans in limbo.

limbo^2 n pl **limbos** a West Indian dance in which the dancer bends back and passes repeatedly under a horizontal bar which is gradually lowered

lime^1 n quicklime; a white substance (calcium oxide) used in making cement and mortar and as a fertilizer **lime** v to treat something with lime **limestone** n a kind of hard rock composed mainly of calcium carbonate, used as building material and in cement

lime^2 n **1** a green citrus fruit like a lemon but

smaller and more acid **2** a drink made from lime juice **3** a bright light green colour

imelight n great publicity and attention

imerick n a type of humorous poem with five lines

Limey n pl **Limeys** N. Am Austral. informal a British person

imit n **1** the point, line, or level beyond which something does not continue **2** the greatest amount allowed ♦ *the speed limit* ♦ *an age limit* **3** Mathematics a quantity which a function or the sum of a series can be made to approach as closely as desired **limit** v **limited**, **limiting 1** to keep something within certain limits **2** to be a limit to something **limitation** n **limited** adj

imousine (say lim-oo-zeen) n a large luxurious car

imp¹ v to walk or proceed with difficulty because of injury or damage **limp** n a limping walk

imp² adj **1** not stiff or firm **2** without strength or energy **limply** adv **limpness** n

impet n a small shellfish that attaches itself firmly to rocks

inchpin n **1** a pin passed through the end of an axle to keep a wheel in position **2** a person or thing that is vital to the success of an organization or plan, etc.

ine¹ n **1** a long narrow mark or band on a surface **2** a wrinkle or crease in the skin **3** Mathematics a straight or curved continuous extent of length without breadth **4** an outline or edge of a shape **5** a limit or boundary ♦ *the county line* ♦ *There's a thin line between genius and madness.* **6** a row or series of people or things **7** a series of people coming one after the other or several generations of a family ♦ *a line of kings* **8** each of a set of military defences facing an enemy force **9** a row of written or printed words **10** the words of an actor's part ♦ *That's my favourite line in the film.* ♦ *She is busy learning her lines.* **11** a brief letter ♦ *I wanted to drop you a line to say good luck.* **12** a direction, course, or track **13** a railway track or route ♦ *the main line north* **14** a series of ships, buses, or aircraft, etc. regularly travelling between certain places, or a company running these **15** a

course or way of procedure, thought, or conduct ♦ *We've been thinking along quite different lines.* **16** a field of activity or type of business **17** a range of goods **18** something that a person is skilled at or interested in ♦ *Cooking is not really my line.* **19** a length of rope, string, wire, etc. used for a particular purpose ♦ *a washing line* **20** the starting or finishing point in a race **21** a wire or cable used to connect electricity or telephones **22** a telephone connection **line** v **1** to stand at intervals along something ♦ *Trees lined the pavement.* **2** to arrange things into a line or lines ♦ *Line them up.* **3** to mark something with lines ♦ *Use lined paper.* **lineage** n ancestry, the line of descendants from an ancestor **line dancing** n a type of country and western dancing in which people dance in a line **line drawing** n a drawing consisting only of lines **linesman** n pl **linesmen 1** an official in football or tennis, etc. who decides whether or where a ball has crossed a line **2** a person who repairs electrical or telephone wires **line-up** n **1** a group of people or things assembled for a particular purpose **2** an identity parade

line² v to cover the inside surface of something with a layer of different material **lining** n **1** a layer of material used to cover the inside of something **2** the tissue covering the inner surface of an organ of the body

lineal (say lin-i-əl) adj in a direct line of descent or ancestry **lineally** adv

linear (say lin-i-er) adj **1** arranged in a line **2** to do with a line or length **3** Mathematics (said about an equation, function, etc.) in which only the first power of any variable occurs; able to be represented by a straight line on a graph **linearity** n

linen n **1** cloth made of flax **2** sheets or clothes that were originally made of linen **linen basket** n a basket for clothes that need to be washed

liner¹ n a large passenger ship

liner² n a removable lining ♦ *nappy liners*

ling¹ n a kind of heather

ling² n a sea fish of northern Europe, usually eaten salted

-ling suffix forming nouns meaning 'having

a certain quality' (as in *weakling*) or diminutives meaning 'little' (as in *duckling*)

linger v 1 to stay for a long time, especially as if reluctant to leave 2 to take a long time to disappear ♦ *The smell lingered in the kitchen for days.* ♦ *a few lingering doubts* 3 to spend a long time over something ♦ *We lingered over our meal.* 4 to remain alive although becoming weaker **lingering** adj

lingerie (say **lan**-zher-ee) n women's underwear and night clothes

lingo n pl **lingos** or **lingoes** informal 1 a foreign language 2 jargon ♦ *I don't understand all this legal lingo.*

lingua franca (say ling-gwə **frank**-ə) n a language used as a common language between the people of an area where several languages are spoken

linguistic (say ling-**gwist**-ik) adj to do with language or linguistics **linguist** n **linguistics** n the study of language and its structure

link n 1 one ring or loop of a chain 2 a relationship or connection between people or things 3 a means of communication or travel between people or places ♦ *a rail link* **link** v 1 to connect or join things together 2 to be or become connected **linkage** n **links** n, or pl n a golf course, especially near the sea

link-up n a connection between two or more machines, systems, etc.

linnet (say **lin**-it) n a kind of finch

lino (say **liy**-noh) n informal linoleum

linoleum (say lin-**oh**-liəm) n a stiff shiny floor covering

lint n 1 a soft material for dressing wounds 2 fluff

lion n a large powerful flesh-eating animal of the cat family found in Africa and India **lioness** n **lionize** v treat as a celebrity

lip n 1 either of the two fleshy edges of the mouth opening; a similar edge 2 the edge of a cup, crater, or other hollow container or opening 3 a pointed part at the top of a jug, etc. from which you pour things 4 informal impudence **lipped** adj **lip-read** v past tense and past participle **lip-read** to understand what a person is saying by watching the movements of their lips, not by hearing **lip-**reader n **lipstick** n a cosmetic for colouring the lips in the form of a stick

liposuction n a technique in cosmetic surgery for removing excess fat from under the skin by suction

liqueur (say lik-**yoor**) n a strong sweet alcoholic spirit with fragrant flavouring

liquid n a substance like water or oil that flows freely but (unlike a gas) has a constant volume **liquid** adj 1 in the form of a liquid 2 having the clearness of water 3 (said about a sound) flowing clearly and pleasantly 4 (said about assets) easily converted into cash **liquefy** v **liquefies**, **liquefied**, **liquefying** to make something liquid or become liquid **liquefaction** n

liquidate v 1 to close down a business and divide its assets between its creditors 2 to convert assets into cash 3 to pay off a debt **liquidation** n the process of liquidating a business **liquidator** n **liquidity** n 1 being liquid 2 availability of liquid assets **liquidize** v to make solid food into a liquid or pulp **liquidizer** n a machine for liquidizing food

liquor (say **lik**-er) n 1 alcoholic drink especially spirits 2 liquid produced in cooking or in which food has been cooked

liquorice (say **lik**-er-ish) n 1 a chewy black substance used in medicine and as a sweet 2 the plant from whose root it is obtained

lisp n a speech defect in which s is pronounced like th in thin and z like th in they **lisp** v to speak with a lisp

list[1] n a number of names, items, figures, etc. written or printed one after another **list** v 1 to make a list of people or things 2 to enter a name, etc. in a list

list[2] v (said about a ship) to lean over to one side **list** n a listing position, a tilt

listed adj (said about a building) protected from being demolished or altered because of its historical importance

listen v 1 to pay attention in order to hear something 2 to make an effort to hear something 3 to follow a piece of advice, suggestion, or request **listen** n an act of listening ♦ *Have a listen to this.* **listener** n

listless adj without energy or enthusiasm **listlessly** adv **listlessness** n

lit past tense and past participle of *light*[1] and *light*[3]

litany *n pl* **litanies 1** a series of prayers and petitions to God, recited by a priest and with set responses by the congregation **2** a long tedious list or recital ♦ *a litany of complaints*

literal *adj* **1** meaning exactly what is said, not metaphorical or exaggerated **2** keeping strictly to the words of the original ♦ *a literal translation* **3** (said about a person) tending to interpret things in a literal way, unimaginative **literally** *adv* really; exactly as stated ♦ *The old car was literally falling to pieces.* **literalness** *n*

literary (say **lit**-er-er-i) *adj* **1** to do with literature **2** knowing about or interested in literature

literate (say **lit**-er-ət) *adj* able to read and write **literati** *n pl* literate people **literacy** *n* the ability to read and write

literature *n* **1** written works such as novels, poetry, and plays, especially those considered to have been written well **2** writings on a particular subject **3** printed pamphlets, brochures, or leaflets, etc.

lithe *adj* flexible and supple

litho (say **liyth**-oh) *n pl* **lithos** *informal* lithography, or a lithograph

lithography (say lith-**og**-rəfi) *n* a process of printing from a smooth surface, e.g. a metal plate, treated so that ink will stick to the design to be printed and not to the rest of the surface **lithograph** *n* a lithographic print **lithographic** *adj*

litigation (say lit-i-**gay**-shən) *n* a lawsuit; the process of going to law **litigant** *n* **litigious** *adj*

litre (say **lee**-ter) *n* a unit of capacity in the metric system (about 1¾ pints), used for measuring liquids

litter *n* **1** rubbish or untidy things left lying about, especially in the street **2** the young animals born to a mother at one time **3** (also **cat litter**) absorbent material put down on a tray for a cat to urinate and defecate on indoors **4** straw, etc. put down as bedding for animals **5** a kind of stretcher **litter** *v* **1** to be scattered around a place making it untidy ♦ *Paper cups littered the*

pavement. **2** to leave rubbish or objects lying around untidily ♦ *Her room was littered with magazines.*

little *adj* **1** small in size, amount, or degree **2** smaller than others of the same kind ♦ *the little finger* **3** young or younger ♦ *his little sister* **4** unimportant or trivial **little** *n* **1** only a small amount, some but not much **2** a short time or distance **little** *adv* **1** to a small extent only ♦ *little-known authors* **2** not at all ♦ *He little knew what really happened.*

live[1] (say liv) *v* **1** to have life, to be or remain alive **2** to have somewhere as your home ♦ *She lives in Dublin.* **3** to pass your life in a certain way ♦ *He lived as a hermit.* **4** to get a livelihood from something ♦ *They lived off her earnings.* **5** to last or survive in someone's mind ♦ *His name lives on.* **to live in** (said about an employee) to live on the premises **to live something down** to succeed in making people forget a past mistake or embarrassment **to live with** to accept or endure the effects of something

live[2] (say liyv) *adj* **1** alive **2** (said about yogurt) containing living micro-organisms **3** (said about a performance) actually taking place in front of an audience, not recorded **4** (said about a broadcast) transmitted while it is actually happening or being performed, not recorded or edited **5** actual or authentic ♦ *a real live princess* **6** glowing or burning ♦ *live coals* **7** (said about a shell or bomb) not yet exploded **8** (said about a wire or cable) connected to a source of electric current **9** of interest or importance at the present time ♦ *Pollution is a live issue.* **live** *adv* as or at a live performance ♦ *Have you seen them play live on stage?* **liveable** *adj* **live action** *n* action in films involving real people or animals, as opposed to animation or computer-generated effects **lived-in** *adj* **1** (said about a room or building) showing comforting signs of being used or occupied **2** *informal* (said about a face) marked by life's experiences **live-in** *adj* **1** living where you work ♦ *a live-in nanny* **2** sharing a home ♦ *a live-in lover* **livelihood** *n* a way of earning money or providing enough food to support yourself **lively** *adj* **livelier**, **liveliest** full of life, energy, or activity **liveliness** *n*

liven v to make something lively, or to become lively ♦ *I'll put some music on to liven things up.* **livestock** n animals kept for use or profit, e.g. cattle, sheep, etc. on a farm **living** adj 1 alive 2 (said about a language) still spoken and used 3 (said about rock) not detached from the earth **living** n 1 being alive 2 a way of earning money or providing enough food to support yourself 3 the way that a person lives ♦ *a good standard of living* 4 a position held by a member of the clergy and providing them with an income or property **living room** n a room for general use during the day

liver n 1 a large organ in the abdomen that processes digested food, purifies the blood, and secretes bile 2 an animal's liver, used as food **liverish** adj 1 suffering from a disorder of the liver 2 irritable; bad-tempered

Liverpudlian adj to do with Liverpool, a city in NW England **Liverpudlian** n a native or inhabitant of Liverpool

livery n pl **liveries** 1 a distinctive uniform worn by a servant, an official, or a member of the London trade guilds (called *Livery Companies*) 2 the distinctive colour scheme used by a railway, bus company, etc.

lives plural of *life*

livid adj 1 informal furiously angry 2 of the colour of lead, bluish-grey ♦ *a livid bruise*

lizard n a reptile with a rough or scaly skin, four legs, and a long body and tail

llama (say **lah-mə**) n a South American animal with woolly fur, related to the camel but with no hump

load n 1 something that is carried or transported 2 the quantity that can be carried 3 the weight carried by a wall or structure 4 the amount of work to be done by a person or machine ♦ *a heavy teaching load* 5 a burden of responsibility, worry, or grief ♦ *That's a load off my mind.* 6 informal a large amount ♦ *It's a load of nonsense.* 7 the amount of electric current supplied by a dynamo or generating station **loads** pl n informal plenty ♦ *We've got loads of time.* **load** v 1 to put a load in or on something; to fill something with goods or cargo, etc. ♦ *Help me load the dishwasher.* 2 (said about a ship or vehicle) to receive a load 3 to make

someone or something carry a lot of heavy things ♦ *A woman came out, loaded with parcels.* 4 to weight a thing with something heavy ♦ *loaded dice* 5 to put ammunition into a gun or film into a camera ready for use 6 to enter a program or data into a computer **loaded** adj 1 (said about a gun) containing bullets 2 informal very rich **loader** n

loaf¹ n pl **loaves** a mass of bread shaped and baked in one piece **to use your loaf** informal to use your common sense

loaf² v to spend time idly, to loiter or stand about **loafer** n

loan n 1 something lent, especially a sum of money 2 lending, being lent ♦ *These books are on loan from the library.* **loan** v to lend

loath (say lohth) adj unwilling, reluctant ♦ *I was loath to go.*

loathe (say lohth) v to feel great hatred and disgust for something **loathing** n **loathsome** adj

loaves plural of *loaf*¹

lob v **lobbed**, **lobbing** 1 to hit or kick a ball in a high arc in tennis, football, etc. 2 to throw something, especially in a high arc **lob** n 1 a lobbed ball in tennis, etc. 2 a slow underarm delivery in cricket

lobby n pl **lobbies** 1 a porch or entrance hall leading to other rooms 2 (in the Houses of Parliament) a large hall where members of the public can meet MPs 3 either of two corridors in the Houses of Parliament to which MPs retire to vote ♦ *division lobby* 4 a group of people lobbying an MP, etc. or seeking to influence legislation ♦ *the anti-hunting lobby* **lobby** v **lobbies**, **lobbied**, **lobbying** to try to persuade an MP or other person to support your cause, by speaking to them in person or writing letters **lobbyist** n

lobe n 1 a rounded flattish part or projection, especially of an organ of the body 2 the lower soft part of the ear **lobed** adj

lobster n 1 a large shellfish with eight legs and two long claws that turns scarlet after being boiled 2 its flesh as food

local adj 1 belonging to a particular place or a small area ♦ *local politics* 2 affecting a particular place or part, not general

♦ *a local infection* **local** *n* **1** someone who lives in a particular district **2** *informal* the pub near to a person's home **locale** *n* the scene or locality of operations or events **locality** *n* *pl* **localities 1** the position or site of something **2** a district or neighbourhood **localize** *v* to restrict something to a particular area ♦ *a localized infection* **locally** *adv* **local anaesthetic** *n* an anaesthetic affecting only the part of the body where it is applied **local area network** *n* ICT a computer network that links devices in a building or group of buildings **local authority** *n* the body of people given responsibility for administration in local government **local government** *n* the system of administration of a town or county, etc. by the elected representatives of people who live there **local time** *n* the time in a particular place in the world, depending on which time zone it is in

locate *v* to discover exactly where something is ♦ *We need to locate the electrical fault.* **location** *n* **1** the place where something is situated **2** the actual place where a film or broadcast is made **3** finding a thing's location; being found

loch *n Scottish* **1** a lake **2** (also **sea loch**) an arm of the sea, especially when narrow or partially landlocked

lock[1] *n* **1** a device for keeping a door, lid, or container fastened, usually needing a key to work it **2** a section of a canal or river where the water level changes, **3** the turning of a vehicle's front wheels by use of the steering wheel **lock** *v* **1** to fasten something or be able to be fastened with a lock **2** to shut something into a place that is fastened by a lock **3** to store something away securely or inaccessibly ♦ *His capital is locked up in land.* **4** to make something fixed, or to become fixed in one position ♦ *The wheels have locked.* **5** to hold or engage someone in something ♦ *She locked me in a warm embrace.* **6** to go through a lock on a canal **lockable** *adj* **locker** *n* a small lockable cupboard or compartment, especially for an individual's use in a public place **lock-up** *n* **1** a temporary jail **2** premises that can be locked up, especially a garage

lock[2] *n* a portion of hair that hangs together **locks** *pl n* a person's hair

locket *n* a small ornamental case holding a portrait or lock of hair, etc., worn on a chain round the neck

locksmith *n* a person who makes and repairs locks

locomotion *n* movement, the ability to move from place to place **locomotive** *n* a railway engine used for pulling trains **locomotive** *adj* to do with locomotion ♦ *locomotive power*

locum (say loh-kəm) *n* a deputy acting for a doctor or clergyman in his or her absence

locust (say loh-kəst) *n* a kind of grasshopper that migrates in vast swarms and eats all the vegetation in an area

lodge *n* **1** a small house at the gates of a park or in the grounds of a large house **2** a porter's room at the main entrance to a college or other large building **3** a country house for use in certain seasons ♦ *a hunting lodge* **4** a beaver's den **5** the members or meeting place of a branch of a society such as the Freemasons **lodge** *v* **1** to stay somewhere as a lodger **2** to provide someone with somewhere to live temporarily **3** to become or make something firmly fixed or embedded somewhere ♦ *The bullet lodged in his brain.* **4** to present something formally for attention ♦ *I wish to lodge a complaint.* **lodger** *n* **lodgings** *pl n* a room or rooms, not in a hotel, rented for living in **lodging house** *n* a private house in which rooms can be rented

loft *n* **1** a space or room under the roof of a house **2** a space under the roof of a stable or barn, used for storing hay, etc. **3** a gallery or upper level in a church or hall ♦ *the organ loft* **4** a backward slope in the face of a golf club **5** a lofted stroke **loft** *v* to send a ball in a high arc **lofty** *adj* **loftier, loftiest 1** very tall **2** noble **3** haughty **loftily** *adv* **loftiness** *n*

log[1] *n* **1** a length of tree trunk that has fallen or been cut down **2** a short piece of this, especially as firewood **3** a detailed record of a ship's voyage or an aircraft's flight

4 any detailed record ♦ *You need to keep a log of phone calls.* **5** a device for gauging a ship's speed **log** v **logged, logging 1** to enter facts in a logbook **2** to achieve a certain speed, distance, or number of hours worked, etc. ♦ *The pilot had logged 200 hours on jets.* **3** *ICT* to key in a command to become connected to a computer **4** to cut down forest trees for timber **logger** n **logging** n **logbook** n a book in which details of a voyage, etc. or the registration details of a motor vehicle are recorded **log cabin** n a hut built of logs

log² n a logarithm ♦ *log tables*

logarithm (say **log-er-ithəm**) n a quantity representing the power to which a fixed number (called the *base*) must be raised to produce a given number **logarithmic** adj

logic (say **loj-ik**) n **1** the science of reasoning **2** a particular system or method of reasoning **3** a chain of reasoning regarded as good or bad ♦ *I don't really understand your logic there.* **4** the ability to reason correctly **5** the principles used in designing a computer or electronic device; the circuits involved in this **logical** adj **logicality** n **logically** adv **logician** n

logistics (say **ləj-ist-iks**) pl n the organizing and coordinating of everything involved in a large complex operation **logistic** adj **logistical** adj **logistically** adv

logo (say **loh-goh** or **log-oh**) n pl **logos** a printed symbol or design used by an organization as its emblem

loin n **1** the side and back of the body between the ribs and the hip bone **2** a joint of meat that includes the vertebrae of this part **loins** pl n the region of the sexual organs

loincloth n a piece of cloth wrapped round the hips

loiter v to linger or stand around idly **loiterer** n

loll v **1** to stand, sit, or rest lazily; to lean lazily against something **2** to hang loosely ♦ *The dog's tongue was lolling out.*

lollipop n **1** a large round usually flat boiled sweet on a small stick **2** an ice lolly **lollipop lady** n *informal* an official using a circular sign on a stick to signal traffic to stop so that children can cross a road safely near a school

lolly n pl **lollies** *informal* **1** a lollipop **2** *informal* money

Londoner n a native or inhabitant of London

lone adj solitary; without companions ♦ *a lone horseman* **lonely** adj **lonelier, loneliest 1** sad because you are on your own or have no friends **2** solitary, without companions **3** (said about places) far from inhabited places, not often visited or used ♦ *a lonely road* **loneliness** n **loner** n **lonesome** adj

long¹ adj **1** having great length, measuring a lot from one end to the other **2** taking a lot of time ♦ *a long holiday* **3** having a certain length or duration ♦ *The river is twenty miles long.* **4** seeming to be longer than it really is ♦ *He was in prison ten long years.* **5** lasting, going far into the past or future ♦ *a long memory* **6** (said about odds in betting) reflecting a low level of probability **7** (said about vowel sounds) having a pronunciation that is considered to last longer than that of a corresponding 'short' vowel (e.g. *oo* is long in *moon* but short in *book*) **long** adv **1** for a long time, by a long time ♦ *Have you been waiting long?* **2** at a distant time ♦ *They left long ago.* **3** throughout a period of time ♦ *all night long* **longevity** n long life **longish** adj **longboat** n **1** the largest boat carried by a sailing ship **2** a longship **long-distance** adj travelling or operating between distant places **long division** n the process of dividing one number by another with all the calculations written down **long life long jump** n an athletic contest in which competitors jump as far as possible along the ground in one leap **long jumper** n **long-life** adj (said about perishable goods) remaining fresh or usable for a long time **long-lived** adj having a long life **long-range** adj **1** having a long range ♦ *a long-range missile* **2** relating to a period far into the future ♦ *a long-range weather forecast* **longship** n a long narrow warship, with oars and a sail, used by the Vikings **long shot** n a guess or venture that is unlikely to be correct or successful **long sight** n the ability to see clearly only what is at a distance **long-sighted** adj having long sight **long-standing** adj having existed for a long time ♦ a long-standing grievance **long-suffering** adj putting up with things patiently **long-term** adj of or for a long period **long-winded** adj talking or writing at tedious length

long[2] v to feel a strong desire for something **longing** n a strong desire or intense wish

longitude (say lonj-i-tewd) n the distance east or west, measured in degrees, from the Greenwich meridian **longitudinal** adj **longitudinally** adv

loo n informal a toilet

loofah (say loo-fə) n a rough sponge made from the dried pod of a kind of gourd

look v 1 to use your eyes, to turn your eyes in a particular direction 2 to face in a certain direction 3 to have a certain appearance, to seem to be something ♦ The fruit looks ripe. ♦ These clothes make me look an idiot. 4 to try to find something ♦ I've been looking everywhere for those keys. ♦ Keep looking. **look** n 1 the act of looking, a gaze or glance 2 an expression on someone's face 3 a search or inspection ♦ I'll have a look for it. 4 appearance ♦ I don't like the look of this place. ♦ He is blessed with good looks. **look** interjection used to call attention to what you are going to say **lookalike** n a person or thing closely resembling another **look-in** n a chance of participation or success **looking glass** n a mirror **lookout** n 1 a place from which you can keep watch 2 a person whose job is to keep watch 3 looking out or watching for something ♦ Be on the lookout for pickpockets. 4 informal a future prospect ♦ It's a poor lookout for us. 5 informal a person's own concern ♦ If he wastes his money, that's his lookout. **to look after** 1 to protect or take care of someone 2 to be in charge of something **to look at** 1 to examine a matter ♦ She promised to look at my application. 2 to regard something in a certain way ♦ It all depends how you look at it. **to look like** informal to be likely to be something ♦ It looks like rain. **to look on** to watch something without getting involved **to look out** to be careful or vigilant **to look to** 1 to rely on someone to do something 2 to hope to do something **to look up** to improve ♦ Things are looking up. **to look up to** to admire and respect someone

loom[1] n an apparatus for weaving cloth

loom[2] v 1 to come into view suddenly; to appear close at hand or with threatening appearance ♦ An iceberg loomed up through the fog. 2 to seem about to happen

loony n pl **loonies** informal a mad or silly person **loony** adj **loonier, looniest** informal mad or silly

loop n 1 the shape made by a curve that bends round and crosses itself 2 a piece of thread, ribbon, wire, etc. in this shape, used as a fastening or handle 3 any path or pattern roughly in this shape 4 a series or process in which the end is connected to the beginning 5 an endless strip of tape or film that continually repeats itself 6 a complete circuit for an electrical current 7 ICT a set of instructions that is carried out repeatedly until some specified condition is satisfied **loop** v 1 to form something into a loop or loops 2 to follow a course that forms a loop or loops 3 to fasten or join something with a loop or loops **loophole** n 1 a way of avoiding a law, rule, or contract, especially because of something missing, or not precise enough in its wording 2 a narrow opening in the wall of a fort, etc., for shooting arrows through

loose adj 1 not firmly fixed in place ♦ a loose tooth 2 not fastened or tied together; not packed in a box or packet 3 not fitting tightly or closely ♦ loose clothing ♦ a loose lid 4 not tied up or shut in 5 (said about a ball in football, etc.) not in any player's possession 6 relaxed or slack, not tense or tight 7 not strict or exact ♦ a loose translation 8 careless and indiscreet ♦ loose talk 9 not compact or dense, arranged at wide intervals ♦ a loose weave 10 not organized strictly ♦ a loose confederation **loose** adv loosely ♦ loose-fitting **loose** v 1 to untie or release someone or something 2 to loosen something **loosely** adv **looseness** n

loosen v to make something looser, or to become loose or looser

loot n **1** goods stolen by thieves or taken from an enemy in war **2** informal money

loot v **1** to steal from shops or houses left unprotected after a riot, battle, or other violent event **2** to take something as loot **looter** n

lop v **lopped**, **lopping 1** to cut off branches or twigs **2** to remove or cut something

lope v to run with a long bounding stride **lope** n a long bounding stride

lop-eared adj having drooping ears

lopsided adj with one side lower or smaller than the other

loquacious (say lə-kway-shəs) adj talkative **loquaciously** adv **loquacity** n

lord n **1** a master or ruler **2** a male member of the nobility, especially one who is allowed to use the title 'Lord' in front of his name **Lord** n **1** the title or form of address to certain peers or high officials ♦ the Lord Bishop of Oxford ♦ the Lord Chief Justice **2** a title for God or Christ **the Lords** n the House of Lords **lordly** adj **lordlier**, **lordliest 1** haughty **2** suitable for a lord **lordship** n **Lord Chancellor** n the highest officer of the Crown, presiding over the House of Lords **Lord Mayor** n the mayor of certain large cities **Lord's Prayer** n the prayer taught by Christ to his disciples, beginning 'Our Father'

lore n a body of traditions and knowledge on a subject or possessed by a group of people ♦ farming lore ♦ gypsy lore

lorry n pl **lorries** a large heavy motor vehicle for carrying goods or troops

lose v past tense and past participle **lost 1** to become unable to find something ♦ I've lost my keys. **2** to be deprived of something ♦ He lost a leg in a climbing accident. **3** to no longer have or maintain something ♦ She began to lose confidence. **4** to fail to keep something in sight or to follow a piece of reasoning mentally ♦ We lost him in the crowd. **5** to fail to obtain or catch something ♦ They lost the contract. **6** to get rid of something ♦ He's trying to lose weight. **7** to elude someone who is following you ♦ We managed to lose our pursuers. **8** to be defeated in a contest or argument **9** to waste time or an opportunity ♦ You may

have lost your chance. **10** to earn less than you spend, to be worse off ♦ We lost on the deal. **11** (said about a clock or watch) to become slow ♦ It loses two minutes a day. **loser** n **losing battle** n a struggle in which failure seems certain

loss n **1** losing something or someone **2** a defeat in sport **3** a disadvantage caused by losing something **4** the suffering felt when a close relative or friend dies **5** a person or thing lost **6** money lost in a business transaction; the excess of spending over income

lost past tense and past participle of lose **lost** adj **1** not knowing where you are or not able to find your way ♦ I think we're lost. **2** missing, not able to be found ♦ I want to report a lost wallet. **3** strayed or separated from its owner ♦ a lost dog **4** engrossed ♦ She was lost in thought. **lost cause** n an undertaking that can no longer be successful

lot¹ n **1** informal a large number or amount ♦ She has a lot of friends. **2** much, a great deal ♦ I'm feeling a lot better today. **3** a number of people or things of the same kind ♦ Come on, you lot!

lot² n **1** one of a set of objects used in choosing or deciding something by chance ♦ We drew lots to see who would go first. **2** this method of choosing or deciding ♦ A leader was chosen by lot. **3** a person's fate or condition in life **4** an item or set of items put up for sale at an auction **5** a piece of land, especially an area used for a particular purpose ♦ a parking lot

lotion n a thick liquid for putting on the skin as a medicine or cosmetic

lottery n pl **lotteries 1** a system of raising money by selling numbered tickets and giving prizes to the holders of numbers drawn at random **2** something where the outcome depends on luck

lotto n a game resembling bingo but with numbers drawn instead of called out

louche (say loosh) adj appealingly dubious or disreputable

loud adj **1** easily heard, producing much noise **2** strongly expressed ♦ loud protests **3** (said about colours, etc.) unpleasantly bright, gaudy **loud** adv **loudly** adv **loudness** n **loudhailer** n a megaphone **loudspeaker** n a device that converts electrical signals into audible sound

lough (say lok) n Irish a lake or an arm of the sea

lounge n 1 a sitting room 2 a public sitting room in a hotel or theatre 3 a waiting room at an airport, etc., with seats for waiting passengers ♦ the departure lounge **lounge** v to sit or stand in a lazy and relaxed way **lounger** n **lounge bar** n a more comfortable bar in a pub or hotel

louse n 1 pl **lice** a small insect that lives as a parasite on animals or plants 2 pl **louses** informal a contemptible person **lousy** adj **lousier**, **lousiest** 1 infested with lice 2 informal very poor, bad, or ill

lout n a bad-mannered or aggressive man **loutish** adj

love n 1 an intense feeling of deep affection for a person 2 sexual affection or passion 3 strong liking for something ♦ a love of music 4 affectionate greetings ♦ Send my love to your parents. 5 a person or thing that you love 6 informal a friendly form of address 7 (in tennis or squash, etc.) no score, nil **love** v 1 to feel love for someone 2 to like something very much **lovable** adj **lovably** adv **loveless** adj **lovely** adj **lovelier**, **loveliest** beautiful or pleasant **loveliness** n **lover** n a person who loves someone or something **loving** adj **lovingly** adv **love affair** n a romantic or sexual relationship between two people **love life** n the part of a person's life concerning romantic relationships **lovelorn** adj pining with love, especially when abandoned **love match** n a marriage based on love **lovesick** adj longing for someone you love, especially someone who does not love you **love song** n a song expressing love **love story** n a novel or film, etc. of which the main theme is romantic love

low[1] adj 1 not high or tall, not extending far upwards 2 situated not far above the ground or above sea level ♦ low clouds 3 ranking below others in importance or quality ♦ Music seems to be given a low priority at the school. 4 less than what is

normal in amount, value, or intensity ♦ low prices 5 not noble, dishonest ♦ low cunning 6 (said about a sound or voice) deep not shrill, having slow vibrations ♦ low notes 7 not loud ♦ She spoke in a low voice. 8 lacking in energy, depressed **low** n 1 a low point, level, or figure ♦ Share prices reached a new low. 2 an area of low barometric pressure **low** adv 1 in, at, or to a low level or position ♦ The plane was flying low. 2 in or to a low degree 3 in a low tone; at a low pitch **lower** adj 1 less high in place or position 2 on less high land 3 ranking below others 4 (said about a geological or archaeological period) earlier v 1 to make something move downward; to let something down ♦ The crew lowered the lifeboats. 2 to make something lower, or to become lower ♦ She lowered her voice. 3 to reduce something in amount or quantity, etc. **lowly** adj **lowlier**, **lowliest** of humble rank or condition **lowliness** n **lowbrow** adj not intellectual or cultured **Low Church** n that section of the Church of England that gives only a low place to ritual **low-class** adj of low quality or social class **low-down** n the true facts or relevant information **low-down** adj informal mean and dishonourable **lower case** n small letters, not capitals **Lower Chamber** n the House of Commons as an assembly **lower class** n the working class **lowest common denominator** n the least desirable common feature of members of a group **low frequency** n (in radio) a frequency of 30 to 300 kilohertz **low-key** adj restrained, not intense or emotional **lowland** n (also **lowlands**) low-lying country **Lowlands** n the part of Scotland lying south and east of the Highlands **lowlander** n **low-level** adj 1 involving people of low rank or little importance ♦ low-level negotiations 2 (said about a computer language) close to machine code in form **low-lying** adj at a low height above sea level **Low Mass** n (in the Catholic Church) a mass with no music and the minimum of ceremony **low-pitched** adj (said about a voice or sound) low **low-rise** adj (said about a building) with few storeys **low season** n the least popular time of year for a holiday, when prices are lowest **low spirits** *pl n* sadness and disappointment **low-spirited** *adj* **low tide** *n* the tide at its lowest level

low² *v* to make the deep sound of cattle **low** *n* a lowing sound

loyal *adj* showing firm and constant support or allegiance to a person, cause, institution, etc. **loyalist** *n* **loyalism** *n* **loyally** *adv* **loyalty** *n*

lozenge *n* **1** a small flavoured tablet, especially one containing medicine, for dissolving in the mouth **2** a diamond shape

L-plate *n* a sign bearing the letter 'L', fixed to a motor vehicle that is being driven by a learner driver

LSD *n* a powerful synthetic drug that produces hallucinations

Ltd *abbr* (after a company name) Limited

lubricate (say loo-brik-ayt) *v* to oil or grease machinery, etc. so that it moves smoothly **lubricant** *n* **lubrication** *n* **lubricator** *n*

lucid (say loo-sid) *adj* **1** clear and easy to understand **2** showing an ability to think clearly **lucidity** *n* **lucidly** *adv*

luck *n* **1** chance thought of as a force that brings either good or bad fortune ♦ *This is a game of luck rather than skill.* **2** good or bad fortune in your life ♦ *It is about time she had a change of luck.* **3** success or good fortune ♦ *This locket will bring you luck.* **lucky** *adj* **luckier, luckiest, luckily** *adv* **luckless** *adj* **lucky dip** *n* a game in which small prizes are hidden in a container and taken out at random by people playing

lucrative (say loo-krə-tiv) *adj* profitable, earning you a lot of money **lucrativeness** *n*

Luddite (say lud-diyt) *n* a person who opposes the introduction of new technology or methods

ludicrous (say loo-dik-rəs) *adj* ridiculous or laughable **ludicrously** *adv*

lug¹ *v* **lugged, lugging** to drag or carry something heavy with great effort

lug² *n* **1** an ear-like part on an object, by which it may be carried or fixed in place **2** *informal* an ear

luge (say loozh) *n* a light toboggan ridden sitting or lying down

luggage *n* suitcases and bags containing a person's belongings when travelling

lugubrious (say lə-goo-briəs) *adj* gloomy or mournful **lugubriously** *adv*

lukewarm *adj* **1** only slightly warm **2** not very enthusiastic ♦ *His latest book got a lukewarm reception.*

lull *v* **1** to soothe someone or send them to sleep **2** to make someone feel safer or in a better position than they actually are ♦ *We were lulled into a false sense of security.* **3** to calm suspicions, fears, or doubts **4** (said about a storm or noise) to lessen, to become quiet **lull** *n* a temporary period of quiet or inactivity **lullaby** *n* *pl* **lullabies** a soothing song sung to send a young child to sleep

lumber¹ *n* *N. Am* timber sawn into planks **lumber** *v* **1** *informal* to leave someone with an unwanted or unpleasant task **2** to move in a heavy clumsy way ♦ *I could hear him lumbering around upstairs.* **lumberjack** *n* a person whose job is cutting down trees

luminescent (say loo-min-**ess**-ənt) *adj* giving out light without being hot **luminescence** *n*

luminous (say loo-min-əs) *adj* giving out light; glowing in the dark **luminosity** *n*

lump¹ *n* **1** a solid piece of something **2** a swelling **3** *informal* a heavy clumsy person **lump** *v* to put or treat things together in a group because you think of them as alike in some way ♦ *For convenience I will lump these last few points together.* **lumpiness** *n* **lumpish** *adj* **lumpy** *adj* **lumpier, lumpiest** full of lumps **lump sum** *n* a single payment covering a number of items or paid all at once rather than in instalments

lump² *v* **to lump it** *informal* to put up with something you dislike

lunacy *n* *pl* **lunacies** great foolishness

lunar *adj* to do with the moon **lunar month** *n* the interval between new moons (about 29½ days); four weeks

lunatic *n* **1** someone who is extremely foolish or reckless **2** an insane person **lunatic** *adj* extremely foolish or reckless

lunch *n* a meal eaten in the middle of the day **lunch** *v* to eat lunch

luncheon *n* *formal* lunch

lung *n* either of the two breathing organs in

the chest that draw in air when you breathe and bring it into contact with the blood

lunge *n* **1** a sudden forward movement of the body towards something **2** a sudden thrust with a sword **3** a long rein on which a horse is held by its trainer while it is made to canter in a circle **lunge** *v* **lunged**, **lunging 1** to make a lunge **2** to exercise a horse on a lunge

lupine (say **loo**-piyn) *adj* to do with or like wolves

lurch[1] *n* an unsteady swaying movement to one side **lurch** *v* to lean suddenly to one side, to stagger

lurch[2] *n* **to leave someone in the lurch** to abandon someone so that they are left in an awkward situation without help

lure *v* to tempt someone to do something or to go somewhere **lure** *n* **1** something that tempts or entices a person or animal to do something has ♦ *the lure of adventure*

lurid (say **lewr**-id) *adj* **1** in glaring colours **2** sensationally and shockingly vivid ♦ *the lurid details of the murder* **luridly** *adv* **luridness** *n*

lurk *v* **1** to lie hidden while waiting to attack someone **2** to wait where you cannot be seen **3** to be present in a latent state ♦ *a lurking sympathy for the rebels*

luscious (say **lush**-əs) *adj* **1** having a delicious rich taste **2** (said about a woman) sexually attractive **lusciously** *adv* **lusciousness** *n*

lush *adj* **1** growing thickly and strongly ♦ *lush vegetation* **2** luxurious ♦ *lush furnishings* **3** (said about music) beautifully rich ♦ *a lush orchestration* **lushly** *adv* **lushness** *n*

lust *n* **1** strong sexual desire **2** an intense desire for something ♦ *a lust for power* **lust** *v* to have an intense desire for a person or thing ♦ *She lusted for adventure.* **lustful** *adj* **lustfully** *adv* **lusty** *adj* **lustier**, **lustiest** strong and vigorous, full of vitality **lustily** *adv* **lustiness** *n*

lustre (say **lus**-ter) *n* **1** the soft brightness of a smooth or shining surface **2** glory or distinction ♦ *His presence added lustre to the assembly.* **3** a kind of metallic glaze on pottery and porcelain **lustrous** *adj*

lute (say **loot**) *n* a stringed musical instrument with a pear-shaped body, popular in the 14th-17th centuries

luxury *n pl* **luxuries 1** something expensive that is enjoyable but not essential **2** expensive and comfortable surroundings and food, dress, etc. ♦ *a life of luxury* **luxuriant** *adj* **1** growing profusely **2** (said about hair) thick and healthy **luxuriance** *n* **luxuriate** *v* **luxurious** *adj* supplied with luxuries, very comfortable **luxuriously** *adv* **luxuriousness** *n*

-ly *suffix* **1** forming adjectives, as in *friendly, heavenly, sickly* **2** forming adverbs from adjectives, as in *boldly, sweetly, thoroughly*

lychee (say **liy**-chi) *n* a small fruit with a sweet white scented pulp and a large stone in a thin brown shell

Lycra *n trademark* a kind of fabric containing elasticated threads, used especially for close-fitting sports clothing

lying present participle of *lie*[1] and *lie*[2]

lying-in-state *n* the display of the corpse of an eminent person in a public place of honour before burial or cremation

lynch (say **linch**) *v* (said about a group of people) to execute someone without a proper trial, especially by hanging them

lynx (say **links**) *n* a wild animal of the cat family with spotted fur, noted for its very sharp sight

lyre *n* a musical instrument with strings fixed in a U-shaped frame, used especially in ancient Greece

lyric (say **li**-rik) *adj* to do with poetry that expresses the poet's emotions **lyric** *n* **1** (also **lyrics**) the words of a song **2** a short poem that expresses emotions **lyrical** *adj* **lyrically** *adv* **lyricist** *n*

Mm

M[1] **1** the thirteenth letter of the English alphabet **2** the Roman numeral for 1,000
M[2] *abbr* **1** mega- **2** (in British road identifications) motorway ♦ *M25*

m *abbr* **1** metre(s) **2** mile(s) **3** million

M. *abbr* **1** Master **2** Monsieur

MA *abbr* Master of Arts

ma *n informal* mother

ma'am *n* madam (used in addressing the Queen or a royal lady)

mac *n informal* a mackintosh

macabre (say mə-**kahbr**) *adj* gruesome, strange, and horrible

macadam (say mə-**kad**-əm) *n* broken stone used in layers in road-making, each layer being rolled hard before the next is put down

macaroni *n* a kind of pasta formed into narrow tubes

macaroon *n* a small sweet cake or biscuit made with sugar, egg white, and ground almonds or coconut

macaw (say mə-**kaw**) *n* a brightly coloured parrot with a long tail, from Central and South America

mace[1] *n* a ceremonial staff carried or placed before an official

mace[2] *n* a spice made from the dried outer covering of nutmeg

Mach *n* **Mach number** the ratio of the speed of a moving object to the speed of sound in the same medium

machete (say mə-**shet**-i) *n* a broad heavy knife used as a tool or weapon

Machiavellian (say maki-ə-**vel**-iən) *adj* cunning or deceitful in politics or business

machinations (say mash-in-**ay**-shənz) *pl n* clever scheming or plotting

machine *n* **1** an apparatus having several parts, each with a definite function, to perform a particular task **2** something operated by such apparatus, such as a bicycle or aircraft **3** a complex or well-organized group of powerful people ♦ *the publicity machine* **machine** *v* to make something or work on something with a machine **machinery** *n* **1** machines, or the parts of machines **2** an organized system for doing something **machinist** *n* a person who operates machine tools, or who makes machinery **machine code** or **machine language** *n* a computer programming language that a computer can respond to directly without further translation

machine gun *n* an automatic gun that fires a rapid continuous series of bullets

machismo (say mə-**kiz**-moh) *n* strong or aggressive male pride or exhibitionism

macho (say **mach**-oh) *adj* showing aggressive male pride

mackerel *n pl* **mackerel** a sea fish used for food

mackintosh *n* a waterproof raincoat

macramé (say mə-**krah**-mi) *n* the art of knotting thread or cord in decorative patterns

macrocosm (say **mak**-rə-kozm) *n* **1** the universe **2** the whole of a complex organization or structure

mad *adj* **madder**, **maddest** **1** having something wrong with the mind, not sane **2** extremely foolish or odd ♦ *It was a mad idea.* **3** wildly enthusiastic ♦ *The girls are all mad about sport.* **4** *informal* very annoyed **5** frenzied **like mad** *informal* with great energy or enthusiasm **madden** *v* to make someone mad, angry, or annoyed **madly** *adv* **madness** *n* **madhouse** *n* **1** a scene of great confusion or uproar **2** a former name for an institution for care of the mentally ill

madam *n* a word used in speaking politely to a woman

Madame (say mə-**dahm**) *n pl* **Mesdames** (say may-**dahm**) the title of a French-speaking woman, equivalent to 'Mrs' or 'madam'

madder *n* **1** a plant with yellowish flowers **2** a red dye obtained from the root of this plant

made past tense and past participle of *make*

Mademoiselle (say mad-mwə-**zel**) *n pl* **Mesdemoiselles** (say mayd-mwə-**zel**) the title of a French-speaking girl or unmarried woman, equivalent to 'Miss' or 'madam'

madonna *n* a picture or statue of the Virgin Mary

madrigal (say **mad**-ri-gəl) *n* an old form of part song for several voices

maelstrom (say **mayl**-strəm) *n* **1** a great whirlpool **2** a state of great confusion

maestro (say **miy**-stroh) *n pl* **maestros** a master of any art, especially music

Mafia (say **ma**-fiə) *n* an international

criminal organization that originated in Sicily **mafia** n any network of people who exert a hidden and sinister influence

magazine n 1 an illustrated paper that is published regularly and contains articles, stories, or features by several writers 2 a store for weapons and ammunition or for explosives 3 a part of a gun that holds the cartridges

magenta (say mə-jen-tə) n, adj bright purplish red

maggot n the larva of a bluebottle or other fly **maggoty** adj

Magi (say may-jiy) pl n the wise men from the East who brought offerings to the infant Jesus at Bethlehem

magic n 1 the art of supposedly influencing events or producing effects by a mysterious or supernatural power 2 mysterious tricks performed for entertainment 3 a mysterious and enchanting quality **magic** adj 1 to do with magic, or using magic 2 informal very enjoyable or exciting **magical** adj 1 to do with magic, or using magic 2 wonderful to see or hear **magically** adv **magician** n 1 a person who can do magic, a wizard 2 a conjuror

magistrate n a legal official who hears and judges minor cases in a local law court **magisterial** adj 1 to do with a magistrate 2 having or showing authority, masterful

magma n hot fluid material under the earth's crust, from which lava is formed

magnanimous (say mag-nan-imǝs) adj generous and forgiving in behaviour, not petty-minded **magnanimity** n **magnanimously** adv

magnate (say mag-nayt) n a wealthy and influential person, especially in business

magnesia (say mag-nee-zhǝ) n a white powder that is a compound of magnesium, used in medicine

magnesium (say mag-nee-ziǝm) n a chemical element (symbol Mg), a silvery-white metal that burns with an intensely bright flame

magnet n 1 a piece of iron or steel that can attract iron and that points north and south when suspended 2 a person or thing that has a powerful attraction **magnetism** n

1 the properties and effects of magnetic substances 2 great personal charm and attraction **magnetize** v 1 to give magnetic properties to a substance 2 to attract things as a magnet does 3 to exert charm or attraction on someone

magnetic adj 1 having the properties of a magnet 2 produced or acting by magnetism 3 having the power to attract people ♦ a magnetic personality **magnetic field** n the area around a magnetic substance in which the force of magnetism acts **magnetic north** n the direction in which a magnetic needle points, at a slight angle to true north **magnetic tape** n a plastic strip coated with a magnetic substance for recording sound or pictures or storing computer data

magneto (say mag-nee-toh) n pl **magnetos** a small electric generator using magnets

magnificent adj 1 grand or splendid in appearance 2 excellent in quality **magnificence** n **magnificently** adv

magnify v **magnifies**, **magnified**, **magnifying** 1 to make an object appear larger than it really is, as a lens or microscope does 2 to exaggerate something **magnifying glass** n a lens that magnifies things **magnification** n 1 the process of magnifying 2 the amount by which a lens or microscope magnifies things **magnifier** n

magnitude n largeness or importance

magnolia (say mag-noh-liǝ) n a tree with large waxy white or pale pink flowers

magnum n a wine bottle of about twice the standard size (about 1.5 litres)

magpie n 1 a large bird with a long tail, black and white feathers, and a loud cry 2 someone who chatters constantly 3 someone who collects things obsessively, as a magpie is supposed to do

maharaja (say mah-hǝ-rah-jǝ) n hist the title of certain Indian princes

maharani (say mah-hǝ-rah-ni) n hist the title of a maharaja's wife or widow

Maharishi (say mah-hǝ-rish-i) n a Hindu wise man or leader

mahatma (say mǝ-hat-mǝ) n (in the Indian subcontinent) a title of respect for a distinguished person

mah-jong n a Chinese game for four people, played with pieces called tiles

mahogany (say mə-**hog**-əni) n 1 a hard reddish-brown wood used to make furniture 2 the tropical tree that produces this wood 3 a rich reddish-brown colour

mahout (say mə-**howt**) n (in the Indian subcontinent) a person who rides and works with an elephant

maid n 1 a female servant in a house 2 old use a girl or young woman **maidservant** n a female servant

maiden n old use a girl or young unmarried woman **maiden** adj 1 (said about a woman, especially an older one) unmarried ♦ a maiden aunt 2 (said about a horse) that has not yet won a race 3 first of its kind or in a series ♦ a maiden voyage **maidenhair** n a fern with fine hair-like stalks and delicate foliage **maiden name** n a woman's family name before she marries **maiden over** n a cricket over in which no runs are scored

mail[1] n letters and packets sent by post **mail** v to send a letter or packet by post **mailbag** n 1 a large bag for carrying mail 2 the letters received by a public figure **mailbox** n 1 a box into which mail is delivered 2 ICT a computer file in which email messages are stored **mailing list** n a list of addresses for sending mail to regularly, especially advertising material **mail order** n a system of ordering goods by post

mail[2] n armour made of metal rings or plates ♦ a suit of chain mail

maim v to wound or injure someone so that part of the body is made useless

main adj principal or most important; greatest in size or extent **main** n 1 the main pipe or cable in a public system carrying water, gas, or electricity 2 old use the high seas **mainly** adv for the most part, chiefly **mainframe** n ICT a large high-speed computer, as distinct from a PC **mainland** n the main part of a country or continent, without the neighbouring islands **mainmast** n the tallest part of a sailing ship **mainspring** n 1 the principal spring of a watch or clock 2 the chief force motivating or supporting the actions of a person or group **mainstay** n 1 a strong cable that secures the mainmast of a sailing ship 2 the chief support or main part **mainstream** n the most widely held ideas or opinions about something **in the main** for the most part; on the whole

maintain v 1 to cause a state or condition to continue, to keep something in existence 2 to keep a building, vehicle, etc. in a good state of repair 3 to support or provide for someone financially 4 to state that something is true ♦ She still maintained that she had never been to the place. **maintenance** n 1 the process of maintaining something 2 provision of the means to support life 3 money to be paid by a husband or wife to the other partner after a divorce

maisonette (say may-zən-**et**) n 1 a small house 2 part of a house, often on more than one floor, used as a separate dwelling

maize n 1 a tall cereal plant bearing grain on large cobs 2 the grain of this plant

majesty n pl **majesties** 1 impressive dignity or stateliness 2 royal power 3 **His** or **Her Majesty** the title of a king or queen or of a king's wife or widow **majestic** adj stately and dignified, imposing **majestically** adv

major adj 1 greater, very important ♦ The journey is quicker if you stick to the major roads. 2 Mus based on a scale which has a semitone above the third and seventh notes and a whole tone elsewhere **major** n an army officer ranking below a lieutenant colonel and above a captain **major** v N. Am to specialize in a certain subject at college or university **major general** n an army officer ranking below a lieutenant general

majority n pl **majorities** 1 the greatest part of a group of people or things 2 the number of votes by which a candidate or party in an election wins ♦ She had a majority of over 5,000. 3 the age at which a person gains full legal rights, usually 18 or 21

make v past tense and past participle **made** 1 to construct or create something, especially by putting parts together 2 to cause something to exist ♦ They seem to be making difficulties. 3 to result in or amount to a total ♦ Three and eight make eleven.

4 to cause someone to be in a certain state ♦ *The news made me happy.* **5** to succeed in arriving at a place or achieving a position ♦ *We only just made the shore by dark.* ♦ *She has finally made the team.* **6** to gain or earn something ♦ *The company will make a profit this year.* **7** to reckon something ♦ *What do you make the time?* **8** to cause or compel someone to do something ♦ *I'd better make them stay.* **9** to perform an action ♦ *to make an attempt* ♦ *to make war* **make** *n* **1** the way a thing is made **2** the manufacturer or place where a thing is made ♦ *What make is your car?* **maker** *n* **make-believe** *n* pretending or imagining **makeshift** *adj* improvised or used because there is nothing better ♦ *We had to use an old box as a makeshift table.*

make-up *n* **1** cosmetics used on the face **2** the way something is made up or built **3** a person's character and temperament **makeweight** *n* a person or thing added to make something complete **on the make** *informal* wanting to make money **to have the makings of** to have the essential qualities for a role or activity ♦ *She had all the makings of a good teacher.* **to make do** to manage with something that is not what you really want or need **to make for** to go towards a place or try to reach it **to make it** to achieve what you want, to be successful **to make off with** to carry something away, to steal something **to make out** **1** to manage to see, hear, or understand something **2** to claim or pretend that something is true ♦ *They made out that they'd arrived early.* **to make up 1** to build something or put the parts together **2** to invent a story or excuse **3** to compensate for something ♦ *This good news makes up for all our worries.* **4** to become reconciled after a quarrel **5** to use cosmetics, to put on make-up

mal- *prefix* bad; badly (as in *malnourished*)
malachite (say mal-ə-kiyt) *n* a bright green mineral that can be polished
maladjusted *adj* (said about a person) not able to cope with the normal demands of social life **maladjustment** *n*
maladministration *n* bad or dishonest management of business or public affairs

maladroit (say mal-ə-droit) *adj* inept or clumsy
malady (say mal-ə-di) *n pl* **maladies** a disease or ailment
malaise (say mal-ayz) *n* a feeling of illness or discomfort
malapropism (say mal-ə-prop-izm) *n* a comical confusion of words, e.g. using *hooligan* instead of *hurricane*
malaria (say mə-lair-iə) *n* a disease causing fever, transmitted by mosquitoes **malarial** *adj*
Malay (say mə-lay), **Malayan** *n* **1** a member of a people living in Malaysia and Indonesia in SE Asia **2** the language of the Malays **Malay**, **Malayan** *adj* to do with or coming from Malaysia and Indonesia
malcontent (say mal-kən-tent) *n* a discontented person who is likely to cause trouble
male *adj* to do with or belonging to the sex that reproduces by fertilizing cells produced by the female **male** *n* a male person, animal, or plant
malediction (say mali-dik-shən) *n* a curse
malefactor (say mal-i-fak-ter) *n* a criminal or wrongdoer
malevolent (say mə-lev-ə-lənt) *adj* wishing harm to others **malevolence** *n* **malevolently** *adv*
malformation *n* an abnormal or faulty formation **malformed** *adj*
malfunction *v* (said about equipment or machinery) to fail to work normally **malfunction** *n* a failure to work properly
malice *n* a vicious desire to harm other people **malicious** *adj* **maliciously** *adv*
malign (say mə-liyn) *adj* **1** harmful ♦ *a malign influence* **2** showing malice **malign** *v* to say unpleasant and untrue things about someone **malignity** *n*
malignant (say mə-lig-nənt) *adj* **1** (said about a tumour) growing into areas of normal tissue **2** wanting to harm other people, malevolent **malignancy** *n* **malignantly** *adv*
malinger (say mə-ling-ger) *v* to pretend to be ill or unwell in order to avoid work **malingerer** *n*
mall (say mal or mawl) *n* **1** a sheltered walk

or promenade **2** a shopping area closed to traffic

mallard (say **mal**-erd) *n pl* **mallard** a wild duck, the male of which has a glossy green head

malleable (say **mal**-i-əbəl) *adj* **1** able to be pressed or hammered into shape **2** (said about a person) easy to influence, adaptable **malleability** *n*

mallet *n* a hammer with a large wooden head

malnutrition *n* bad health from not having enough to eat or not enough of the right kind of food

malodorous (say mal-**oh**-der-əs) *adj* stinking

malpractice *n* wrong or negligent advice or treatment given by a professional person such as a doctor or lawyer

malt *n* **1** barley or other grain that has been allowed to sprout and then dried, used for brewing, distilling, or vinegar-making **2** malt liquors **malt** *v* to make grain into malt **malted milk** *n* a drink made from dried milk and malt **malt whisky** *n* whisky made entirely from malted barley

maltreat *v* to treat a person or animal badly or cruelly **maltreatment** *n*

mama, mamma (say mə-**mah**) *n old use* mother

mamba *n* a poisonous black or green African snake

mammal *n* a member of the class of animals that give birth to live young which are fed from the mother's body **mammalian** *adj*

mammary (say **mam**-er-i) *adj* to do with the breasts **mammary gland** *n* a milk-secreting gland of female mammals

Mammon *n* wealth regarded as a bad influence

mammoth *n* a large extinct elephant with a hairy skin and curved tusks **mammoth** *adj* huge

man *n pl* **men 1** an adult male human being **2** a human being, an individual person **3** human beings in general **4** a male member of a team, workforce, or army **5** a playing piece used in a board game **man** *v* **manned, manning** to provide a place, piece of machinery, etc. with the people

needed to run or work it **manful** *adj* brave or resolute **manfully** *adv* **manhole** *n* an opening, usually with a cover, through which a person can enter a sewer or a boiler, etc. to inspect or repair it **manhood** *n* **manliness** *n* **manly** *adj* **1** having the qualities traditionally associated with men, such as strength and courage **2** suitable for a man **manned** *adj* (said about a spacecraft or other equipment) containing a human crew **mannish** *adj* (said about a woman) having masculine characteristics, suitable for a man **manhunt** *n* an organized search for a person, especially a criminal **mankind** *n* human beings in general, the human race **man-made** *n* made by humans and not by nature **manpower** *n* the number of people working or available for work **manservant** *n* a male servant **manslaughter** *n* the act of killing a person unlawfully but not intentionally **the man in the street** a typical person

manacle (say **man**-ə-kəl) *n* each of a pair of shackles for the hands **manacle** *v* to tie someone's hands with manacles

manage *v* **1** to have resources under your control **2** to be in charge of a business or group of people **3** to succeed in doing or producing something in spite of difficulties ♦ *Can you manage without help?* **manageable** *adj* **management** *n* **1** the process of managing a business or group of people **2** the people who manage a business, managers **manager** *n* **1** a person who is in charge of a business or group of people **2** a person who directs the activity or performance of a sports team or entertainer **manageress** *n* a woman manager, especially of a shop or hotel **managerial** *adj*

mandarin (say **man**-der-in) *n* **1** an important or high-ranking official **2** a kind of small flattened orange grown in China and North Africa **Mandarin** *n* the standard literary and official form of Chinese

mandate *n* authority given to someone to perform a task or carry out decisions **mandate** *v* to give a person authority to perform a task **mandatory** *adj* obligatory

mandolin (say **man**-dəl-in) *n* a music

instrument of the lute family

mane n 1 the long hair on a horse's or lion's neck 2 a person's long hair

mange (say **maynj**) n a skin disease of dogs and other hairy animals **mangy** adj **mangier, mangiest 1** affected by mange 2 squalid or shabby

manger n a long open trough in a stable for horses or cattle to eat from

mangetout n a kind of pea eaten together with the pod

mangle[1] n a machine with rollers for drying and pressing wet laundry

mangle[2] v to damage something badly by cutting or crushing it

mango n pl **mangoes** or **mangos 1** a tropical fruit with yellow flesh 2 the tree that bears this fruit

mangrove n a tropical tree or shrub which grows in muddy coastal swamps

manhandle v to handle someone or something roughly

mania (say **may**-niə) n 1 a mental illness marked by periods of excitement and over-activity 2 an extreme enthusiasm for something **maniac** n a person who is behaving wildly or violently **maniacal** adj like a mania or a maniac

manic (say **man**-ik) adj affected with mania **manic-depression** n a manic disorder with alternating bouts of excitement and depression

manicure n care and treatment of the hands and nails **manicure** v to apply treatment to the hands and nails **manicurist** n

manifest adj clear and obvious to see or understand **manifest** v 1 to show a thing clearly ♦ The crowd manifested its approval by cheering. 2 (said about a ghost) to appear **manifestation** n **manifestly** adv

manifesto n pl **manifestos** a public statement of the policies and principles of a group or party

manifold adj of many kinds, very varied

manikin n 1 a very small person 2 a model of the human body, with limbs that can be moved

Manila n brown paper used for wrapping and for envelopes

manipulate v 1 to handle or arrange

something skilfully 2 to control or influence someone cleverly **manipulable** adj able to be manipulated **manipulation** n **manipulator** n

manna n 1 a substance miraculously supplied as food to the Israelites in the wilderness after the Exodus from Egypt, according to the account in the Bible 2 an unexpected or delightful benefit

mannequin (say **man**-i-kin) n a dummy for displaying clothes in a shop window

manner n 1 the way a thing is done or happens 2 a person's way of behaving 3 a kind or sort **mannered** adj 1 behaving in a certain way ♦ well-mannered 2 (said about an artistic style) full of mannerisms **mannerism** n a person's distinctive habit or way of doing something **manners** pl n how a person behaves towards other people; polite behaviour

manoeuvre (say mə-**noo**-ver) n 1 a planned and controlled movement of a vehicle or a body of troops 2 a skilful or crafty action or scheme **manoeuvre** v **manoeuvred, manoeuvring 1** to move a thing's position or course, etc. carefully 2 to perform military exercises 3 to guide someone or something skilfully or craftily to get what you want ♦ He gradually manoeuvred the conversation towards money. **manoeuvres** pl n large-scale exercises of troops or ships

manor n a large country house or the landed estate belonging to it **manorial** adj

mansard (say **man**-sard) n a type of roof that has a steep lower part and a less steep upper part on all four sides of a building

manse n a church minister's house, especially in Scotland

mansion (say **man**-shən) n a large stately house

mantel n a structure of wood or marble above and around a fireplace **mantelpiece** n a shelf above a fireplace

mantilla (say man-**til**-ə) n a lace veil worn by Spanish women over the hair and shoulders

mantis n (also **praying mantis**) an insect like a grasshopper, with a triangular head and forelegs that it folds as if in prayer

mantle n 1 a loose sleeveless cloak 2 a covering ♦ *a mantle of snow* 3 a mesh cover fitted round the flame of a gas lamp, producing a strong light when heated 4 the region of very dense rock between the earth's crust and its core

mantra n a word or sound chanted repeatedly as an aid to concentration in meditating

manual adj 1 to do with the hands 2 done or worked with the hands **manual** n a book giving information or instructions; a handbook **manually** adv

manufacture v 1 to make or produce goods on a large scale by machinery 2 to invent something ♦ *I tried to manufacture an excuse.* **manufacture** n the process of manufacturing **manufacturer** n

manure n animal dung used as a fertilizer

manuscript (say **man**-yoo-skript) n 1 something written by hand, not printed 2 a written or typed version of an author's work, before it is printed

Manx adj to do with or coming from the Isle of Man **Manx** n the Celtic language of the Manx people **Manx cat** n a kind of domestic cat with no tail or only a short one

many adj **more**, **most** great in number; numerous **many** n many people or things

Maori (say **mow**-ri) n pl **Maoris** 1 a member of the aboriginal people of New Zealand 2 the language of this people

map n 1 a diagram of an area of land or of the earth's surface, showing the principal physical features 2 a diagram of the sky or of another planet **map** v **mapped**, **mapping** 1 to make a map of an area 2 to make each element of a set correspond to one of another set **to map out** to plan something in detail

maple n a tree with broad leaves, grown for its wood or sugar

mar v **marred**, **marring** to damage or spoil something

marabou (say ma-rə-boo) n a large African stork

maracas (say mə-**rak**-əz) pl n a pair of gourds or other club-like containers filled with beads or beans and shaken as a musical instrument

marathon n 1 a long-distance running race, especially that of 26 miles 385 yards (42.195 km) in the modern Olympic Games 2 any long race or test of endurance

marauding (say mə-**raw**-ding) adj going about in search of plunder or prey **marauder** n

marble n 1 a kind of limestone polished and used in sculpture and building 2 a piece of sculpture in marble ♦ *the Elgin Marbles* 3 a small glass ball used in games **marbled** adj having a veined or mottled appearance

marcasite (say **mark**-ə-siyt) n crystallized iron pyrites, or a piece of this used as an ornament

March n the third month of the year

march v 1 to walk with regular steps 2 to walk purposefully 3 to make someone march or walk ♦ *He marched them up the hill.* 4 to progress steadily ♦ *Time marches on.* **march** n 1 marching; the distance covered in marching 2 a piece of music for marching to 3 progress **marcher** n

Marches pl n border regions

marchioness (say mar-shən-ess) n 1 the wife or widow of a marquess 2 a woman holding the rank of marquess in her own right

mare n a female horse or donkey **mare's nest** n a discovery that is thought to be interesting but turns out to be false or worthless

margarine (say mar-jer-**een**) n a substance used like butter, made from animal or vegetable fats

margin n 1 an edge or border 2 a blank space between the edge of a page and the writing or pictures printed on it 3 an amount over and above the necessary minimum ♦ *Keep your speed down to allow a good safety margin.* 4 (in commerce) the difference between the cost price and the selling price **marginal** adj 1 written in a margin 2 of or at an edge 3 very slight in amount ♦ *The difference is only marginal.* 4 (said about a parliamentary seat) having very small majority in the previous election **marginally** adv

marguerite (say marg-er-**eet**) n a large daisy

marigold n a garden plant with golden or bright yellow flowers

marijuana (say ma-ri-**hwah**-nə) n a form of the drug cannabis, especially in the form of cigarettes

marina (say mə-**ree**-nə) n a harbour for yachts and pleasure boats

marinade (say ma-rin-**ayd**) n a flavoured liquid in which meat or fish is soaked before being cooked **marinade** v to soak meat or fish in a marinade

marine (say mə-**reen**) adj 1 to do with the sea, or living in the sea 2 to do with ships or shipping 3 for use at sea **marine** n a member of a body of troops trained to serve on land or sea **mariner** n a sailor

marionette (say ma-ri-ən-**et**) n a puppet worked by strings or wires

marital (say **ma**-ritəl) adj to do with marriage or the relations between husband and wife **maritally** adv

maritime (say **ma**-ri-tiym) adj 1 to do with the sea or ships 2 living or found near the sea

marjoram (say **mar**-jər-əm) n a herb with a mild flavour, used in cooking

mark n 1 a small area on a surface that differs in appearance from the rest of the surface, especially a spot or stain that spoils it 2 a distinguishing feature or characteristic 3 a sign or symbol of a quality or feeling ♦ They all stood as a mark of respect. 4 a line or object serving to indicate a position 5 a written or printed symbol ♦ punctuation marks 6 a point awarded for the quality of a piece of work, or the total points awarded 7 a target or standard to be aimed at **mark** v 1 to make a mark on something 2 to distinguish or characterize something 3 to assign points or a grade to a piece of work 4 to notice or watch something carefully ♦ Just you mark my words! 5 (in ball games) to keep close to an opposing player so as to prevent them getting or passing the ball

marked adj clearly noticeable ♦ a marked improvement **markedly** adv

marker n 1 something that serves to mark a position 2 a pen with a broad felt tip 3 a person who records the score in games

market n 1 a regular gathering of people to buy and sell goods or livestock 2 a building or open space used for this 3 a demand for a particular product or service 4 a place or group of people where goods may be sold ♦ foreign markets 5 the stock market **market** v **marketed**, **marketing** to offer goods or services for sale **marketable** adj able or fit to be sold **market garden** n a place where vegetables and fruit are grown for sale **marketplace** n 1 an open space in a town, where a market is held 2 the world of commercial buying and selling **market research** n the study of what people want to buy and what type of products and services they prefer **on the market** offered for sale

marking n 1 a mark that identifies something 2 the colouring and pattern of marks on an animal's skin, feathers, or fur

marksman n pl **marksmen** a person who is skilled in shooting at a target **marksmanship** n

mark-up n 1 ICT a set of codes given to parts of a text to identify or classify them in some way 2 (in commerce) the amount a seller adds to the cost price of an article to determine its selling price

marl n a soil consisting of clay and lime, formerly used as a fertilizer

marmalade n a kind of jam made from oranges or other citrus fruit

marmoset (say **mar**-mə-zet) n a small bushy-tailed monkey of tropical America

marmot (say **mar**-mət) n a small burrowing animal of the squirrel family

maroon[1] n a dark brownish-red colour

maroon[2] v to abandon or isolate someone in a deserted place

marquee (say mar-**kee**) n a large tent used for a party or exhibition

marquess (say **mar**-kwis) n a British nobleman ranking between a duke and an earl

marquetry (say **mar**-kit-ri) n inlaid work using small pieces of coloured wood or ivory

marquis (say **mar**-kwis) n a nobleman ranking between a duke and an earl

marquise (say mar-**keez**) n 1 the wife or widow of a marquis 2 a woman holding the rank of marquis in her own right

marram (say **ma**-rəm) n a coarse grass that grows in sand by the shore

marriage n **1** the state in which a man and a woman are formally united as husband and wife **2** the act or ceremony of being married

marriageable adj old enough or suitable to be married

marrow n **1** a large gourd eaten as a vegetable **2** the soft fatty substance inside bones **marrowbone** n a bone containing edible marrow

marry v **marries**, **married**, **marrying 1** to join two people in marriage **2** to become a person's husband or wife **3** to put things together as a pair

marsh n an area of wet low-lying ground **marshland** n an area of marsh **marshy** adj

marshal n **1** an officer of the highest rank in the armed forces **2** an official with responsibility for arranging public events or ceremonies **3** an official accompanying a judge on circuit, with secretarial duties **4** a federal law officer in the USA **5** an official at a race **marshal** v **marshalled**, **marshalling 1** to arrange things in their proper order **2** to make people assemble **3** to usher people

marshmallow n a soft spongy sweet, that is usually pink or white and is made from sugar, egg white, and gelatine

marsupial (say mar-**soo**-piəl) n an animal, such as the kangaroo or wallaby, the female of which carries its young in a pouch

mart n a market or place for trading

marten n an animal like a weasel, with thick soft fur

martial (say **mar**-shəl) adj to do with war, or suitable for war **martial arts** pl n fighting systems such as judo and karate **martial law** n government of a country by the armed forces in a time of crisis

Martian (say **mar**-shən) adj to do with the planet Mars **Martian** n (in fiction) an inhabitant of Mars

martin n a bird of the swallow family

martinet (say mar-tin-**et**) n a person who enforces obedience strictly

martyr n **1** a person who is killed because

of their religious beliefs **2** a person who puts up with great suffering in support of a cause or principle **martyr** v to kill someone or make them suffer for their beliefs **martyrdom** n

marvel n a wonderful thing **marvel** v **marvelled**, **marvelling** to be filled with wonder

marvellous adj excellent, extremely good **marvellously** adv

Marxism n the theories of the German political philosopher and economist Karl Marx (1818-83), on which Communism is based **Marxist** adj, n

marzipan (say **mar**-zi-pan) n a soft sweet food made of ground almonds, eggs, and sugar, often used as a covering on large cakes

mascara n a cosmetic for darkening the eyelashes

mascot n a person or thing that is believed to bring good luck

masculine adj **1** to do with men or suitable for men **2** having qualities traditionally associated with men **3** Gram (in some languages) belonging to the class that includes words referring to males or regarded as male **masculine** n Gram a masculine word or gender **masculinity** n

maser (say **may**-zer) n a device for amplifying microwaves

mash v to beat or crush something (especially food) into a soft mixture **mash** n **1** a soft mixture of cooked grain or bran, used as animal food **2** informal mashed potatoes

mask n **1** a covering worn over the face to disguise or protect it **2** a likeness of a person's face made in wax or clay **3** a respirator worn over the face to filter air for breathing or to supply gas for inhaling **mask** v **1** to cover the face with a mask **2** to disguise or conceal something

masochist (say **mas**-ə-kist) n a person who gets sexual excitement from experiencing pain or humiliation **masochism** n **masochistic** adj

Mason n a Freemason **Masonic** adj **Masonry** n

mason n a person who builds or works with

stone **masonry** n the work of a mason, stonework

masquerade (say mas-ker-**ayd**) n a false show or pretence **masquerade** v to pretend to be what you are not

Mass n (especially in the Roman Catholic Church) a celebration of the Eucharist

mass n **1** a coherent unit of matter with no specific shape **2** a large quantity or heap of something **3** Phys the quantity of matter a body contains **mass** adj involving a large number of people ♦ mass murder **mass** v to gather into a mass, or assemble people or things into a mass **mass media** pl n the main media of news information, especially newspapers and broadcasting **mass-produce** v to manufacture products in large numbers by standardized processes **mass-production** n **the masses** the common people

massacre (say mass-ə-ker) n the killing of a large number of people **massacre** v to slaughter people in large numbers

massage (say mas-ahzh) n the rubbing and kneading of the body to lessen tension or pain **massage** v to give someone a massage **masseur** n a person who provides massage professionally **masseuse** n a female masseur

massif (say **ma**-seef or ma-**seef**) n a group of mountains forming a compact group

massive adj **1** large and heavy or solid **2** unusually large or severe **massively** adv

mast n **1** a long upright pole that supports a ship's sails **2** a tall pole from which a flag is flown **3** a tall steel structure holding the aerials of a radio or television transmitter

master n **1** a man who has charge of people or things **2** a male teacher **3** a person with great skill, a great artist **4** an original document, film, or recording from which copies can be made **master** v **1** to overcome someone or something, to bring someone or something under control **2** to learn a subject or skill thoroughly **masterful** adj **1** (said about a person) powerful or domineering **2** very skilful **masterfully** adv **masterly** adj worthy of a master, very skilful **mastery** n **1** thorough knowledge or skill **2** complete control over

someone or something **master key** n a key that opens several locks **mastermind** n **1** a person with outstanding mental ability **2** the person who is planning or directing a complex enterprise **masterpiece** n an outstanding piece of work **master of ceremonies** n a person who introduces the speakers at a formal event, or the entertainers at a variety show

mastic n **1** a gum or resin exuded from certain trees **2** a filler or sealant used in building

masticate v to chew food **mastication** n

mastiff n a large strong dog with drooping ears

mastoid n part of a bone behind the ear

masturbate v to get sexual pleasure by stimulating the genitals with the hand **masturbation** n

mat n **1** a piece of material used as a floor covering or placed on a surface to prevent damage to it **2** a small piece of material for resting a computer mouse on **mat** v **matted, matting** to become entangled or form a thick mass ♦ matted hair **matting** n rough material for covering floors

matador (say **mat**-ə-dor) n a performer who challenges and kills the bull in a bullfight

match¹ n a short thin piece of wood with a head made of material that bursts into flame when rubbed on a rough or specially prepared surface **matchbox** n **matchstick** n **matchwood** wood that splinters easily, or that has been reduced to splinters

match² n **1** a contest between people or teams in a game or sport **2** a person or thing equal to, exactly like, or corresponding to another **3** a marriage **match** v **1** to be the equal of someone else in quality or skill **2** to place a competitor or team in a competition ♦ Once again England and Scotland are matched against each other. **3** to be like or harmonize with something else in colour or quality ♦ His new hat matches his coat. **4** to find something similar to another thing ♦ I want to match this wool. **matchmaker** n a person who arranges marriages between other people **matchmaking** adj, n **matchless** adv having no equal, incomparable

mate[1] n **1** *informal* a companion or friend **2** each of a mated pair of birds or animals **3** a fellow member or sharer of something ♦ *a team-mate* **4** an officer on a merchant ship **5** an assistant or deputy in some trades **mate** v **1** (said about birds or animals) to come together or bring two together in order to breed **2** to put things together as a pair or because they correspond **matey** *adj* **matier**, **matiest** *informal* sociable or friendly

mate[2] n a position in chess in which the king is in check and cannot escape, checkmate

material n **1** the substance or things from which something is or can be made **2** cloth or fabric **3** facts, information, or ideas that can be used in writing or composing something **material** *adj* **1** made of physical matter, as distinct from things of the mind or spirit **2** to do with bodily comfort ♦ *our material well-being* **3** important or relevant ♦ *Your objection is not material to the issue we are discussing.* **materialism** n **1** a tendency to regard material possessions as more important than spiritual or intellectual values **2** a belief that only the material world exists **materialist** n **materialistic** *adj* **materialization** n **materialize** v **1** to appear or become visible **2** to become a fact, to happen ♦ *The threatened strike did not materialize.* **materially** *adv* significantly, considerably

maternal (say mə-**ter**-nəl) *adj* **1** to do with a mother or with motherhood **2** motherly **3** related through your mother ♦ *my maternal uncle* **maternity** n **1** motherhood **2** suitable for women in pregnancy or childbirth

mathematics n the science of numbers, measurements, and shapes **mathematical** *adj* **mathematically** *adv* **mathematician** n a person who is skilled in mathematics

maths n *informal* mathematics

matinee (say **mat**-in-ay) n an afternoon performance at a theatre or cinema

matins n (in the Church of England) a service of morning prayer

matriarch (say **may**-tri-ark) n a woman

who is the head of a family or tribe **matriarchal** *adj*

matricide (say **may**-tri-siyd) n **1** the act of killing one's mother **2** a person who is guilty of this **matricidal** *adj*

matriculate (say mə-**trik**-yoo-layt) v to be admitted as a member of a university **matriculation** n

matrimony (say **mat**-ri-məni) n marriage **matrimonial** *adj*

matrix (say **may**-triks) n *pl* **matrices** **1** a mould or framework in which something is made or develops **2** *Mathematics* an array of quantities or expressions in rows or columns

matron n **1** a woman in charge of the domestic and medical arrangements at a boarding school **2** a woman in charge of the nursing in a hospital or other institution, now officially called **senior nursing officer** **3** a married woman, especially one who is dignified or elderly **matronly** *adj* like or suitable for a dignified married woman

matt *adj* (said about a colour or surface) having a dull finish, not shiny

matter n **1** a substance or material that you can touch and see **2** a particular substance or material ♦ *solid matter* **3** things of a specified kind ♦ *reading matter* **4** a situation or subject ♦ *a serious matter* **matter** v to be of importance ♦ *It doesn't matter.* **as a matter of fact** in fact, indeed **for that matter** as well, as an important factor **matter-of-fact** *adj* keeping to facts, not imaginative or emotional **the matter** the thing that is causing a problem or difficulty ♦ *I can't think what the matter could be.*

mattock n an agricultural tool with the blade set at right angles to the handle, used for loosening soil and digging out roots

mattress n a fabric covering filled with soft or springy material, used on or as a bed

mature *adj* **1** fully grown or developed **2** having or showing fully developed mental powers, capable of reasoning and acting sensibly **3** (said about wine) having reached a good stage of development **4** (said about a bill) due for payment **mature** v to become mature, or to make something mature **maturation** n the process of becoming mature **maturely** adv **maturity** n

maudlin adj sentimental in a silly or tearful way

maul v to injure a person or animal badly by treating them very roughly

maunder v to act or talk in a rambling way

mausoleum (say maw-sə-**lee**-əm) n a large or magnificent tomb

mauve (say mohv) n a pale purple colour

maverick (say **mav**-er-ik) n a person who belongs to a group but often disagrees with its beliefs or acts independently

maw n the jaws or throat of an animal

mawkish adj sentimental in a feeble or sickly way

maxim n a short saying giving a general truth or rule of behaviour, e.g. 'Waste not, want not'

maximum n pl **maxima** the greatest possible number or amount **maximum** adj greatest, greatest possible **maximal** adj greatest or largest possible, being a maximum **maximize** v 1 to make something as great or as large as possible 2 to make the best use of something ♦ *The aim is to maximize our limited resources.* **maximization** n

May n the fifth month of the year **mayfly** n an insect that lives for only a short time in the spring **maypole** n a tall pole for dancing round on the first of May, with ribbons attached at the top

may auxiliary verb 1 expressing possibility ♦ *It may or may not be true.* 2 expressing permission ♦ *You may go if you like.* 3 expressing a wish ♦ *Long may she reign.*

maybe adv perhaps; possibly

Mayday n an international radio signal of distress

mayhem n violent or damaging chaos or confusion

mayonnaise (say may-ən-**ayz**) n a creamy sauce made with egg yolks, oil, and vinegar

mayor n the head of the municipal corporation of a city or borough **mayoral** adj

mayoress n the wife of a mayor, or a woman holding the office of mayor

maze n 1 a confusing or disorganized amount of information 2 a network of

paths and hedges designed as a puzzle in which you try to find your way

MB, Mb abbr ICT megabyte(s)

MBE abbr Member of the Order of the British Empire

MC abbr 1 Master of Ceremonies 2 Military Cross

MD abbr Doctor of Medicine

ME abbr myalgic encephalomyelitis, a medical condition of unknown cause with fever, fatigue, and muscular pain

me pronoun the form of *I* used as the object of a verb or after a preposition

mead n an alcoholic drink made from fermented honey and water

meadow n a field of grass

meagre (say **meeg**-er) adj scanty in amount, barely enough ♦ *a meagre diet*

meal[1] n 1 each of the regular occasions when food is eaten 2 food eaten at this time **to make a meal of** informal to carry out a task with unnecessary effort

meal[2] n coarsely ground grain or pulse **mealy** adj **mealy-mouthed** adj reluctant or too timid to speak honestly and frankly

meal ticket n a person or thing that provides you with a livelihood

mean[1] v past tense and past participle **meant** 1 to intend ♦ *They clearly mean to win.* 2 to signify or refer to ♦ *The sign means no entrance.* ♦ *'Maybe' means 'perhaps'.* 3 to have something as a consequence ♦ *It means catching the early train.* 4 to be of a specified importance ♦ *The honour meant a lot to her.*

mean[2] adj 1 not generous; miserly 2 unkind or spiteful **meanly** adv **meanness** n

mean[3] n 1 a point or number midway between two extremes 2 the average of two or more quantities **mean** adj midway between two points; average

meander (say mee-an-der) v 1 (said about a river or road) to take a winding course 2 to wander about aimlessly

meaning n what you mean, or what something means **meaningful** adj full of meaning; significant **meaningfully** adv **meaningless** adj having no meaning **meaninglessly** adv

means pl n 1 a way of achieving something

or producing a result **2** money or other wealth as a means of supporting someone **by all means** certainly **by no means** not nearly ♦ *It is by no means certain.* **means test** *n* an inquiry to see how much money or income a person has, in order to determine the level of state assistance they need

meantime *adv* (also **in the meantime**) meanwhile

meanwhile *adv* in the time between two events or while something else is happening

measles *n* an infectious disease producing small red spots on the skin

measly *adj informal* miserably small or inadequate

measure *v* **1** to find the size, amount, or extent of something **2** to be of a certain size ♦ *The room measures four metres by three.* **measure** *n* **1** action taken ♦ *The government will take measures to stop tax evasion.* **2** the size or quantity of something **3** an extent or amount ♦ *They have had a measure of success.* **4** a unit or standard used in measuring **5** a device used in measuring **6** the rhythm or metre of poetry or music **measurable** *adj* **measured** *adj* **1** rhythmical or regular in movement ♦ *He walked with a measured tread.* **2** carefully considered ♦ *She spoke in measured language.* **measurement** *n* **1** the process of measuring something **2** a size or amount found by measuring **to measure up to** to reach the standard required by someone or something

meat *n* the flesh of an animal (especially a mammal) used as food **meaty** *adj* **meatier, meatiest 1** like meat **2** full of meat, fleshy **3** full of information or substance ♦ *a meaty book*

Mecca *n* a city in western Saudi Arabia considered by Muslims to be the holiest city of Islam

mechanic *n* a person who maintains and repairs machinery **mechanical** *adj* **1** to do with or produced by machinery **2** done or doing things without much thought or effort **3** to do with forces and motion **mechanically** *adv* **mechanics** *n* **1** the scientific study of forces and motion **2** the

science of machinery **mechanism** *n* **1** the moving parts of a machine **2** the way a machine works **3** the process by which something is done ♦ *There is no mechanism for making complaints.* **mechanize** *v* to equip a place or organization with machines **mechanization** *n*

medal *n* a small flat piece of metal commemorating an event or given as an award for an achievement **medallion** *n* a large medal, usually worn round the neck as an ornament **medallist** *n* a competitor who wins a medal as a prize

meddle *v* **1** to interfere in people's affairs **2** to tinker with something **meddler** *n* **meddlesome** *adj*

media (say **meed**-iə) *pl n* plural of *medium* **the media** newspapers, radio, television, and the Internet which convey information to the public

mediaeval *adj* another spelling of *medieval*

medial (say **mee**-di-əl) *adj* situated in the middle **medially** *adv*

median (say **mee**-di-ən) *adj* situated in or passing through the middle **median** *n* **1** a middle point or line **2** a medial number or point in a series

mediate (say **mee**-di-ayt) *v* **1** to negotiate between the opposing sides in a dispute **2** to bring about a settlement by negotiation **mediation** *n* **mediator** *n*

medic *n informal* a doctor or medical student

medical *adj* to do with medicine or the treatment of disease **medical** *n* an examination to see how healthy and fit a person is **medically** *adv* **medicated** *adj* treated or impregnated with a medicinal substance ♦ *medicated shampoo* **medication** *n* **1** a medicine **2** treatment using medicine

medicine (say **med**-sən) *n* **1** a substance, usually swallowed, used to treat a disease or ailment **2** the study and treatment of diseases and disorders of the body **medicinal** *adj* having healing properties **medicinally** *adv* **medicine man** *n* (among some peoples) a shaman; a person who treats illness by calling on good and evil spirits in others

medieval (say med-i-**ee**-vəl) *adj* belonging to or to do with the Middle Ages

mediocre (say meed-i-**oh**-ker) *adj* only of medium quality; not very good **mediocrity** *n*

meditate *v* 1 to think deeply and quietly 2 to plan something in the mind **meditation** *n* **meditative** *adj*

Mediterranean *adj* to do with the Mediterranean Sea, the sea which lies between Europe and Africa, or the countries round it

medium *n pl* **media** or **mediums** 1 a middle quality or degree between two extremes 2 a substance or surroundings in which something exists or moves or is transmitted ♦ *Air is the medium through which sound travels.* 3 a means for doing something ♦ *Television is a powerful medium for advertising.* 4 the material or form used by an artist or composer ♦ *Sculpture is his medium.* 5 *pl* **mediums** a person who claims to be able to communicate with the spirits of the dead **medium** *adj* between two extremes or amounts; average, moderate **medium wave** *n* a radio wave of a frequency between 300 kilohertz and 3 megahertz

medley *n pl* **medleys** 1 an assortment of things 2 a collection of musical items or songs played as a continuous piece

meek *adj* quiet and obedient **meekly** *adv* **meekness** *n*

meerkat *n* a small mongoose of southern Africa

meerschaum (say **meer**-shəm) *n* a tobacco pipe with a bowl made from a white clay-like substance that darkens in use

meet¹ *v* past tense and past participle **met** 1 to come face to face with a person or people 2 to make the acquaintance of a person ♦ *We met at a party.* 3 to come together, usually for a purpose 4 to come into contact 5 to go or to a place to receive someone when they arrive ♦ *I will try to meet your train.* 6 to experience or receive something ♦ *They have met with difficulties.* 7 to satisfy or fulfil a demand or requirement **meet** *n* a gathering for a sports competition **meeting** *n* 1 coming

together 2 a number of people who have come together for a discussion, contest, etc.

meet² *adj old use* proper or suitable

mega- (say **meg**-ə) *prefix* 1 large or great (as in *megaphone*) 2 one million (as in *megavolts, megawatts*)

megabyte *n pl* **megabytes** *ICT* a unit of information roughly equal to one million bytes

megahertz *n* a unit of frequency of electromagnetic waves, equal to one million hertz

megalomania (say meg-əl-ə-**may**-niə) *n* 1 an exaggerated idea of your own importance 2 an obsessive desire to do things on a grand scale **megalomaniac** *n*

megaphone *n* a funnel-shaped device for amplifying the voice

megaton (say **meg**-ə-tun) *n* a unit of explosive power equal to that of one million tons of TNT

megavolt *n* a unit of electromotive force equal to one million volts

megawatt *n* a unit of electrical power equal to one million watts

melamine (say **mel**-ə-meen) *n* a tough kind of plastic

melancholy *n* 1 depression or deep sadness 2 an atmosphere of gloom **melancholy** *adj* sad or gloomy **melancholia** *n* mental depression **melancholic** *adj*

melange (say may-**lahnzh**) *n* a mixture

melanin (say **mel**-ən-in) *n* a dark pigment found in skin and hair

melanoma (say melə-**noh**-mə) *n* a form of skin cancer that develops in melanin-forming cells

melee (say **mel**-ay) *n* 1 a confused fight 2 a muddle

mellifluous (say mel-**if**-loo-əs) *adj* soft and pleasant to hear

mellow *adj* 1 sweet and rich in flavour 2 (said about a sound or colour) soft and rich, free from harshness or sharp contrast 3 (said about a person) made kindly and sympathetic by age or experience **mellow** *v* to make something or someone mellow, or to become mellow **mellowness** *n*

melodrama (say **mel**-ə-drah-mə) *n*

1 a play full of dramatic excitement and strong emotion **2** plays of this kind **3** language or behaviour resembling this **melodramatic** adj **melodramatically** adv

melody n pl **melodies 1** sweet music or tunefulness **2** a song or tune **3** the main part in a piece of harmonized music **melodic** adj **1** to do with melody **2** pleasant-sounding **melodious** adj tuneful or pleasant-sounding

melon n a large sweet fruit with a yellow or green skin, a sweet flesh, and many pips

melt v **1** to become liquid, or to make something liquid, by heating **2** (said about food) to be softened or dissolved easily **3** to fade or disappear gradually **4** to make someone gentler through pity or love **meltdown** n **1** the overheating of the core of a nuclear reactor **2** a disastrous collapse or failure **melting point** n the temperature at which a solid melts

member n **1** a person or thing that belongs to a particular group or society **2** a part of the body **membership** n **1** being a member **2** the total number of members

Member of Parliament n a person elected to represent a constituency and take part in the proceedings of Parliament

membrane (say **mem**-brayn) n a thin skin or similar covering **membranous** adj

memento (say mim-**ent**-oh) n pl **mementos** or **mementoes** a souvenir

memo (say **mem**-oh) n pl **memos** a memorandum

memoir (say **mem**-wahr) n a short personal biography written by the subject or someone who knew the subject

memorandum (say mem-er-**an**-dəm) n pl **memoranda** or **memorandums 1** a note or record of events written as a reminder, for future use **2** a note or message from one person to another in an organization

memory n pl **memories 1** the ability to keep things in your mind **2** something that you remember ♦ happy memories of childhood **3** the length of time that people remember things ♦ within living memory **4** the part of a computer in which data is stored for retrieval to operate programs **memorable** adj **1** worth remembering ♦ a

memorable experience **2** easy to remember ♦ a memorable tune **memorably** adv

memorial n a structure or object put up in memory of a person or event **memorial** adj serving as a memorial **memorize** v to learn a thing so as to know it from memory

men plural of man **menfolk** pl n men in general; the men of one's family

menace n **1** something that seems likely to bring harm or danger; a threat **2** an annoying or troublesome person or thing **menace** v to threaten someone with harm or danger **menacingly** adv

ménage (say may-**nahzh**) n the members of a household

menagerie (say min-**aj**-er-i) n a collection of wild or strange animals kept in captivity for exhibition

mend v **1** to repair something that is damaged or make it whole again **2** to make something better, or to become better ♦ He said we should mend our manners. **mend** n a repair or mended place in something **on the mend** improving in health or condition

mendacious (say men-**day**-shəs) adj untruthful, telling lies **mendacity** n

mendicant (say **men**-dik-ənt) adj begging **mendicant** n a beggar

menial (say **meen**-iəl) adj lowly, not needing any skill

meningitis (say men-in-**jiy**-tiss) n inflammation of the membranes that enclose the brain

menopause (say **men**-ə-pawz) n the time of life (usually between 45 and 55) when a woman stops menstruating **menopausal** adj

menorah (say mən-**or**-ə) n a branched candelabrum

menstruate (say **men**-stroo-ayt) v to bleed from the womb about once a month, as girls and women do between puberty and the menopause **menstrual** adj **menstruation** n

mensuration (say men-sewr-**ay**-shən) n the process of measuring

mental adj to do with the mind, existing in or performed by the mind **mentality** n pl **mentalities** a person's mental ability or attitude of mind **mentally** adv

menthol *n* a solid white substance found in peppermint and other natural oils

mention *v* to refer to someone or something briefly **mention** *n* an example of mentioning someone or something

mentor (say **men**-tor) *n* a trusted adviser

menu (say **men**-yoo) *n pl* **menus 1** a list of dishes available in a restaurant **2** *ICT* a list of options or commands displayed on a screen, from which the user makes a choice

MEP *abbr* Member of the European Parliament

mercantile (say **mer**-kən-tiyl) *adj* to do with trade or commerce

mercenary (say **mer**-sin-er-i) *adj* working mainly for money or other gain **mercenary** *n pl* **mercenaries** a soldier hired to serve in a foreign country

merchandise *n* goods or commodities bought and sold, goods for sale **merchandise** *v* **1** to buy and sell goods **2** to advertise an idea or person

merchant *n* **1** a person involved in trade **2** *informal* a person who is fond of an activity ♦ *a speed merchant* **merchant bank** *n* a bank that gives loans and advice to businesses **merchant navy** *n* shipping used in commerce

mercurial (say mer-**kewr**-iəl) *adj* having sudden changes of mood

mercury *n* a heavy silvery metal that is usually liquid, a chemical element (symbol Hg), used in some thermometers and barometers

mercy *n pl* **mercies 1** kindness or compassion shown by not inflicting punishment or pain on an offender or enemy who is in your power **2** something to be thankful for ♦ *It's a mercy no one was killed.* **merciful** *adj* **1** showing mercy **2** giving relief from pain or suffering **mercifully** *adv* **merciless** *adj* showing no mercy, cruel **mercilessly** *adv*

mere *adj* nothing more than ♦ *He's a mere child.* **merely** *adv* **merest** *adj* even very small or insignificant ♦ *The merest movement caused her pain.*

meretricious (say merri-**trish**-əs) *adj* showily attractive but cheap or false

merge *v* **1** to unite or combine into a whole, or to make something do this **2** to pass slowly into something else, to blend or become blended **merger** *n* the combining of two business companies into one

meridian (say mer-**rid**-iən) *n* a line on a map or globe passing from the North Pole to the South Pole and having a constant longitude

meringue (say mer-**rang**) *n* a crisp cake made from egg white and sugar

merino (say mer-**ree**-noh) *n pl* **merinos 1** a kind of sheep with fine soft wool **2** a kind of fine soft woollen material

merit *n* **1** the quality of deserving praise, excellence **2** a feature or quality that deserves praise **merit** *v* **merited**, **meriting** to deserve something **meritocracy** *n* government by people of high ability **meritorious** *adj* having merit, deserving praise

mermaid *n* a mythical sea creature having the body of a woman and the tail of a fish **merman** *n*

merry *adj* **merrier**, **merriest 1** cheerful and lively, joyous **2** *informal* slightly drunk **merry-go-round** *n* a revolving machine with models of horses or cars for riding on for amusement **merrymaking** *n* a lively time, fun or enjoyment **merrily** *adv* **merriment** *n*

mescaline, **mescalin** (say **mesk**-ə-leen or **mesk**-ə-lin) *n* a drug that produces hallucinations, made from the dried disc-shaped tops of a Mexican cactus called mescal

Mesdames plural of *Madame*

Mesdemoiselles plural of *Mademoiselle*

mesh *pl n* **1** the spaces between threads in a net, sieve, or wire screen, etc. **2** network fabric **mesh** *v* (said about a toothed wheel, etc.) to engage with one or more others

mesmerize *v* to fascinate someone, to hold their attention completely

mesosphere (say **mess**-ə-sfeer) *n* the region of the earth's atmosphere above the stratosphere, between 50 and 80 km in altitude

mess *n* **1** a dirty or untidy condition, or an untidy collection of things **2** a difficult or confused situation, trouble **3** a place where members of the armed forces have meals

mess v **1** to make something untidy or dirty **2** (in the armed forces) to take meals with a group **messy** adj **messier, messiest 1** untidy or dirty **2** complicated and difficult to deal with **messily** adv **messiness** n to **mess about** or **around** to behave in a silly or playful way **to mess up** to bungle or mishandle something **to mess with** to meddle or interfere with something

message n **1** a spoken or written communication sent by one person to another **2** the central theme or moral of a book, film, etc. **message** v to send a message to someone **messenger** n someone who delivers a message **to get the message** informal to understand what someone means

Messiah (say mi-**siy**-ə) n **1** the expected deliverer and ruler of the Jewish people **2** Jesus Christ **Messianic** adj

Messieurs plural of Monsieur

Messrs (say **mess**-erz) abbr used as a plural of Mr to denote several people ♦ Messrs Smith and Jones

Met abbr informal **1** the Meteorological Office **2** the Metropolitan Police

metabolism (say mi-**tab**-əl-izm) n the process by which food is built up into living material in a plant or animal, or used to supply it with energy **metabolic** adj **metabolize** v to process food in metabolism

metal n a solid and usually hard mineral substance such as gold, silver, copper, iron, and uranium, or an alloy of any of these **metal** adj made of metal **metallurgy** n the study of the properties of metals and alloys **metallurgical** adj **metallurgist** n **metalwork** n **1** the art of making things from metal **2** a shaped metal object **metallic** adj

metamorphic (say met-ə-**mor**-fik) adj (said about rock) that has had its structure or other properties changed by natural agencies such as heat and pressure, as in the transformation of limestone into marble

metamorphose (say met-ə-**mor**-fohs) v to change, or to change something, in form

or character

metaphor (say **met**-ə-fer) n the use of a word or phrase in a special meaning that provides an image, as in a blanket of fog and to take the rough with the smooth **metaphorical** adj **metaphorically** adv

metaphysics (say met-ə-**fiz**-iks) n a branch of philosophy that deals with the nature of existence and of truth and knowledge **metaphysical** adj

mete v to mete out to give out punishment

meteor (say **meet**-i-er) n a small body of matter from outer space that becomes luminous from compression of air as it enters the earth's atmosphere, and appears as a streak of light in the sky **meteoric** adj **1** to do with meteors **2** like a meteor in brilliance or sudden appearance ♦ a meteoric career **meteorite** n a piece of rock or metal that has fallen to earth as a meteor

meteorology (say meet-i-er-**ol**-əji) n the study of the conditions of the atmosphere, especially in order to forecast the weather **meteorological** adj **meteorologist** n

meter n a device that measures and indicates the quantity or rate of something, such as the amount of electricity used or the distance travelled **meter** v to measure the use of something by means of a meter ◊ Do not confuse this word with metre, which has a different meaning.

methinks v **methought** old use I think

method n **1** a procedure or way of doing something **2** orderliness of thought or behaviour **methodical** adj orderly or systematic **methodically** adv **methodology** n a system or set of methods used in a particular activity

Methodist n a member of a Christian denomination originating in the 18th century and based on the teachings of John and Charles Wesley and their followers **Methodism** n

meths n informal methylated spirit

methyl (say **meth**-il) n a chemical unit present in methane and in many organic compounds **methylated spirit** n a form of alcohol used as a solvent and for heating, and made unpleasant for drinking by the addition of methyl and a violet dye

meticulous (say mi-**tik**-yoo-ləs) adj very careful and precise **meticulously** adv **meticulousness** n

métier (say **met**-yay) n **1** a trade, profession, or field of activity **2** what a person does best

metonymy (say mi-**ton**-imi) n a means of referring to an important or well-known person or institution by something it is closely associated with, such as the Crown for 'the Queen' or 'the King'

metre n **1** a unit of length in the metric system (about 39.4 inches) **2** rhythm in poetry, or a particular form of it ◊ Do not confuse metre with meter, which has a different meaning.

metric adj **1** of or using the metre or the metric system **2** to do with metre in poetry **metrically** adv **metrication** n change to a metric system of measurement **metric system** n a decimal system of weights and measures, using the metre, litre, and gram as units **metric ton** n a unit of weight equal to 1,000 kilograms

metro n pl **metros** an underground railway in a city, especially Paris

metronome (say **met**-rə-nohm) n a device that makes a regular tick to indicate a tempo in music

metropolis (say mi-**trop**-əlis) n the chief city of a country or region **metropolitan** adj

mettle n a person's ability to deal with difficulties and challenges **to be on your mettle** to be ready to show courage or ability

mew v to make the cry of a cat **mew** n this cry

mews n a row of houses in a small street or square, converted from former stables

Mexican adj to do with or coming from Mexico **Mexican** n a person born in Mexico or descended from people born there

mezzanine (say **mets**-ə-neen) n an extra storey between the ground floor and first floor of a building, often in the form of a wide balcony

MHz abbr megahertz

miaow n to make the cry of a cat **miaow** n this cry

miasma (say mi-**az**-mə) n unpleasant or unhealthy air

mica (say **miy**-kə) n a mineral substance structured in layers, used to make electrical insulators

mice plural of mouse

Michaelmas (say **mik**-əl-məs) n a Christian festival in honour of St Michael (29 September) **Michaelmas daisy** n an aster that flowers in autumn, with purple, dark-red, pink, or white blooms

micro- prefix **1** very small **2** one-millionth of a unit (as in microgram)

microbe n a micro-organism, especially one that causes disease or is used for fermentation

microbiology n the study of micro-organisms **microbiologist** n

microchip n a very small piece of silicon or similar material made to work like a complex wired electric circuit

microclimate n the climate of a very small area, such as part of a garden

microcomputer n a small computer with a microprocessor as its central processor

microcosm (say **miy**-krə-kozm) n something regarded as resembling on a very small scale something much larger

microdot n a photograph of a printed document reduced to the size of a dot

microelectronics n the design, manufacture, and use of microchips and microcircuits **microelectronic** adj

microfiche (say **miy**-krə-feesh) n a piece of film on which written or printed material is photographed in greatly reduced size

microfilm n a length of film on which written or printed material is photographed in greatly reduced size

microlight n a very small aircraft for one person, like a hang-glider with a motor

micrometer (say miy-**krom**-it-er) n an instrument for measuring small lengths or thicknesses

micron (say **miy**-kron) n a unit of measurement equal to one-millionth of a metre

micro-organism n an organism that cannot be seen by the naked eye, e.g. a bacterium or virus

microphone n an instrument that picks up sound waves for amplifying, recording, or broadcasting

microprocessor n an integrated circuit functioning as the processor of a computer

microscope n an instrument with lenses that magnify objects or details too small to be seen by the naked eye **microscopic** adj 1 to do with a microscope 2 too small to be visible without the aid of a microscope **microscopically** adv

microscopy (say miy-**kros**-kə-pi) n the use of a microscope

microsecond n one-millionth of a second

microsurgery n intricate surgery done with miniature instruments and the use of a microscope

microwave n 1 an electromagnetic wave of length between about 30 cm and 1 mm 2 a microwave oven **microwave oven** n an oven that uses microwaves to heat or cook food quickly

mid adj 1 in the middle of ♦ in mid-air 2 middle ♦ He is in his mid thirties.

mid-air n the area above ground level; the open sky

midday n the middle of the day, noon

midden n a heap of dung, a rubbish heap

middle adj 1 at an equal distance from the extremes or outer limits of something 2 occurring halfway between the beginning and end of a process or period of time 3 intermediate in rank or quality, moderate in size or importance **middle** n a middle point or position **middle age** n the period between youth and old age **middle-aged** adj **Middle Ages** pl n the period between youth and old age **middle class** n the class of society between the upper and working classes, including business and professional people **Middle East** n an area of SW Asia and northern Africa extending from the eastern Mediterranean to Iran **middleman** n 1 a person who buys from producers of goods and sells to consumers 2 a go-between or intermediary **middle-of-the-road** adj favouring a moderate policy, avoiding extremes **middle school** n a school for children aged from about 9 to

13 years **middleweight** n a boxing weight between light heavyweight and welterweight

middling adj moderate or average in size or quality **middlingly** adv fairly or moderately

midfield n the central part of a football pitch away from the goals

midge n a small biting insect like a gnat

midget n an extremely small person or thing

midland adj 1 to do with the middle part of a country 2 to do with the Midlands **Midlands** pl n the inland counties of central England

midnight n twelve o'clock at night, or the time near this

midriff n the part of the body just above the waist

midshipman n pl **midshipmen** a rank in the navy between cadet and sub lieutenant

midst n in the midst of in the middle of or surrounded by

midsummer n the middle part of summer, or the summer solstice

midway adv halfway

midwife n pl **midwives** a person trained to look after a woman who is giving birth **midwifery** n

midwinter n the middle of winter, or the winter solstice

mien (say meen) n a person's manner or bearing

might[1] n great strength or power **mighty** adj very strong or powerful **mighty** adv informal very ♦ That was mighty good of them. **mightily** adv **mightiness** n **with all your might** using all your strength and determination

might[2] auxiliary verb 1 used as the past tense of may ♦ We told her she might go. 2 used to express possibility ♦ It might be true.

migraine (say **mee**-grayn) n a severe kind of headache often affecting one side of the head

migrate (say miy-**grayt**) v 1 to leave one place or country and settle in another 2 (said about birds or animals) to go from one habitat to another according to the time of year **migrant** n a person or animal that migrates or has migrated **migrant** adj migration *n* migratory *n*

mikado (say mi-kah-doh) *n pl* **mikados** *hist* a title of the emperor of Japan

mike *n informal* a microphone

milch cow *n* a cow that is kept for its milk

mild *adj* **1** moderate in intensity, not severe or harsh **2** (said about a person) gentle in manner **3** (said about food or drink) not strongly flavoured **4** (said about weather) moderately warm and pleasant **mildly** *adv* **mildness** *n*

mildew *n* a white coating formed by a minute fungus on things kept in damp conditions **mildewed** *adj*

mile *n* a measure of length equal to 1,760 yards (about 1.609 kilometres)

milestone *n* **1** a stone set beside a road to mark the distance between places **2** an important event or stage in life or history

mileage *n* **1** a distance measured in miles **2** the number of miles a vehicle travels on one gallon of fuel **3** *informal* benefit or advantage **milometer** *n* an instrument for measuring the number of miles travelled by a vehicle

milieu (say **meel**-yer) *n pl* **milieux** (say **meel**-yer) environment or surroundings

militant *adj* prepared to take strong or aggressive action in support of a cause **militant** *n* a militant person **militancy** *n*

military *adj* to do with soldiers or armed forces **the military** *n* the armed forces of a country **militarism** *n* belief in the use of military strength and methods **militarist** *n* **militaristic** *adj* **militarize** *v* **1** to equip a country or people with military resources **2** to give a place or organization a military character

militate (say **mil**-i-tayt) *v* to be a strong influence ♦ *Several factors militated against the success of our plan.*

militia (say **mil-ish**-ə) *n* a military force, especially one raised from civilians

milk *n* **1** a white liquid that female mammals produce in their bodies as food for their young **2** the milk of cows, used as food by human beings **3** a milk-like liquid, e.g. that in a coconut **milk** *v* **1** to draw milk from a cow or other animal **2** to exploit a person or organization by illegally or unfairly taking money from them **milky** *adj* **milkiness** *n*

milk float *n* a light low vehicle with open sides, used in delivering milk **milkmaid** *n* a woman who milks cows or works in a dairy **milkman** *n* a man who sells and delivers milk **milkshake** *n* a cold drink made from milk whisked with ice cream and a flavouring **milksop** *n* a timid or indecisive person **milk tooth** *n* each of the first set of teeth that a child or young animal has, later replaced by adult teeth **Milky Way** *n* the broad band of stars formed by our galaxy

mill *n* **1** a machine for grinding or crushing **2** a factory or building for processing materials ♦ *a cotton mill* **mill** *v* **1** to grind or crush something in a mill **2** to produce regular markings on the edge of a coin **miller** *n* a person who owns or runs a grain mill **millstone** *n* **1** each of a pair of circular stones used for grinding corn between them **2** a great burden of responsibility **to mill about** or **around** (said about people or animals) to move round in a confused crowd

millennium (say mil-**en**-iəm) *n pl* **millennia** or **millenniums** **1** a period of 1,000 years **2** a period of great happiness and prosperity **millennium bug** *n* a fault in some older computer systems that prevented them from dealing with dates from 1 January 2000

millet *n* a cereal plant that produces a large crop of small seeds

milli- *prefix* **1** one thousandth (as in *milligram*) **2** one thousand (as in *millipede*)

milliard *n* one thousand million

milligram *n* one thousandth of a gram

millilitre *n* one thousandth of a litre

millimetre *n* one thousandth of a metre (0.04 inch)

milliner *n* a person who makes or sells women's hats **millinery** *n*

million *adj, n* one thousand thousand (1,000,000) **millionaire** *n* a person who owns a million pounds or dollars, or one who is extremely rich **millionth** *adj, n*

millipede (say **mil**-i-peed) *n* a small crawling creature like a centipede, with two pairs of legs on each segment of its body

milt *n* the sperm or roe of a male fish

mime *n* acting with movements of the body and without words **mime** *v* to act with mime

mimic *v* mimicked, mimicking **1** to copy the appearance or ways of a person playfully or for entertainment **2** to imitate someone or pretend to be someone **mimic** *n* a person who mimics others, especially for entertainment **mimicry** *n*

mimosa (say mim-oh-zə) *n* a tropical tree or shrub with clusters of small ball-shaped flowers

minaret (say min-er-et) *n* a tall slender tower on or beside a mosque

minatory (say min-ə-ter-i) *adj formal* threatening

mince *v* **1** to cut food, especially meat, into small pieces in a machine with revolving blades **2** to walk in an affected way with short quick steps and swinging hips **mince** *n* minced meat **mincer** *n* **mincemeat** *n* a mixture of currants, raisons, apples, sugar, candied peel, spices, and suet, used in pies **mince pie** *n* a small pie containing mincemeat **to mince words** to criticize someone gently or discreetly

mind *n* **1** the ability to be aware of things and to think **2** a person's thoughts and attention ♦ *Try to keep your mind on the job.* **3** a way of thinking and feeling ♦ *What was his state of mind?* **mind** *v* **1** to take care of someone or something ♦ *Who is minding the children?* **2** to be careful about something ♦ *Please mind the step.* **3** to feel annoyed or discomforted by something ♦ *She doesn't seem to mind the cold.* **4** to concern yourself about something ♦ *Never mind the expense.* **minded** *adj* **1** having a mind of a certain kind ♦ *independent-minded* **2** having certain interests ♦ *politically minded* **minder** *n* a person who attends to or takes care of a person or thing **mindless** *adj* **mindlessly** *adv* **to be in two minds** to be unable to decide about something **to change your mind** to have a different opinion about something **to have a good mind** or **half a mind to** to feel tempted or inclined to do something **to mind your Ps and Qs** to be careful to be polite

mine[1] *possessive pronoun* belonging to me

mine[2] *n* **1** a place where metal, coal, or precious stones are dug out of the ground **2** an abundant source of something ♦ *a mine of information* **3** an explosive device placed in the ground or in water and detonated when anything passes over it **mine** *v* **1** to dig coal or minerals from the ground **2** to lay explosive mines in an area **miner** *n* a person who works in a mine **minefield** *n* **1** an area where explosive mines have been laid **2** a subject or situation that has hidden dangers or problems **minesweeper** *n* a ship equipped for clearing away explosive mines laid in the sea

mineral *n* **1** an inorganic substance that occurs naturally in the ground **2** a cold fizzy non-alcoholic drink **mineral** *adj* of or containing minerals **mineralogy** *n* the study of minerals **mineralogist** *n* **mineral water** *n* water that has dissolved mineral salts naturally present

minestrone (say mini-stroh-ni) *n* an Italian soup containing vegetables and pasta

mingle *v* **1** to mix or blend **2** to go about among people

mingy *adj* mingier, mingiest *informal* mean or stingy

mini- *prefix* miniature

miniature (say min-i-cher) *adj* **1** very small **2** imitating something on a small scale ♦ *a miniature railway* **miniature** *n* **1** a small and detailed portrait **2** a small-scale copy or model of something **miniaturist** *n* a person who paints miniature portraits **miniaturization** *n* **miniaturize** *v* to produce something in a small-scale version

minibus *n* a small bus, seating about ten people

minicab *n* a car used as a taxi that must be booked in advance

minimum *n pl* minima the lowest or the lowest possible number or amount **minimum** *adj* smallest; least possible **minimal** *adj* very small; the least possible **minimally** *adv* **minimize** *v* **1** to reduce something to a minimum **2** to estimate or represent something at less than its true value or importance

minion (say min-yən) *n* a subordinate assistant

miniskirt n a short skirt

minister n 1 a member of the government who is in charge of a department 2 a diplomatic representative 3 a member of the clergy **minister** v to attend to people's needs **ministerial** adj **ministry** n 1 a government department headed by a minister 2 a period of government under one Prime Minister 3 the work or office of the clergy

mink n 1 a small animal of the weasel family 2 the highly valued fur of this animal, or a coat made from it

minnow (say min-oh) n a small freshwater fish of the carp family

minor adj 1 lesser or less important ♦ The accident had only been a minor one. 2 Mus based on a scale which has a semitone above the second note **minor** n a person under the age of legal responsibility **minority** n 1 the smallest part of a group of people or things 2 a small group that is different from others 3 (in law) the state of being under the age of legal responsibility

minster n a name given to certain large or important churches

minstrel n a travelling singer and musician in the Middle Ages

mint¹ n 1 a plant with fragrant leaves that are used for flavouring 2 peppermint, or a sweet flavoured with peppermint **minty** adj

mint² n 1 a place where a country's coins are made 2 informal a huge amount of money **mint** v 1 to make coins by stamping metal 2 to invent or coin a word or expression

minuet (say min-yoo-et) n a slow stately dance in triple time, or a piece of music suitable for this

minus (say miy-nəs) prep reduced by the subtraction of ♦ Seven minus three equals four. **minus** adj 1 (used before a number) less than zero ♦ temperatures of minus 20 degrees 2 (used after a grade) slightly less than ♦ B minus **minus** n 1 the sign - 2 a disadvantage ♦ There are pluses and minuses.

minuscule (say min-əs-kewl) adj extremely small

minute¹ (say min-it) n 1 one sixtieth of an hour 2 a very short time, a moment 3 one sixtieth of a degree (used in measuring angles)

minute² (say miy-newt) adj 1 extremely small 2 very detailed and precise **minutely** adv **minutiae** pl n the small or precise details of something

minute³ (say min-it) n an official memorandum **minutes** pl n a summary of points discussed at a meeting **minute** v to record a point in a set of minutes

minx n a cheeky or mischievous girl

miracle n something wonderful that happens, especially when believed to have a supernatural cause **miraculous** adj **miraculously** adv

mirage (say mi-rahzh) n an optical illusion caused by atmospheric conditions

mire n 1 swampy ground or bog 2 mud or sticky dirt **mire** v 1 to plunge something in mud 2 to involve someone or something in difficulties

mirror n a piece of coated glass that reflections can be seen in **mirror** v to show a reflection of something **mirror image** n a reflection or copy in which the right and left sides of the original are reversed

mirth n merriment or laughter **mirthful** adj **mirthless** adj

mis- prefix badly, wrongly

misadventure n a piece of bad luck

misanthrope (say mis-ən-throhp), **misanthropist** (say mis-an-thrəp-ist) n a person who dislikes people **misanthropic** adj **misanthropy** n

misapprehend (say mis-apri-hend) v to misunderstand something **misapprehension** n

misappropriate (say mis-ə-proh-pri-ayt) v to take something dishonestly for your own use **misappropriation** n

misbehave v to behave badly **misbehaviour** n

miscalculate v to calculate something incorrectly **miscalculation** n

miscarriage (say mis-ka-rij) n 1 the spontaneous birth of a fetus before it has developed enough to survive outside the womb 2 a mistake or failure to achieve the correct result ♦ a miscarriage of justice

miscast adj (said about an actor) cast in an unsuitable role

miscellaneous (say mis-əl-**ay**-niəs) adj of various kinds; mixed ♦ miscellaneous items

miscellany n a collection of various items

mischance n misfortune; bad luck

mischief n 1 bad behaviour that causes trouble without being malicious 2 harm or damage **mischievous** adj **mischievously** adv

miscible (say **mis**-ibəl) adj (said about liquids) able to be mixed **miscibility** n

misconceive (say mis-kən-**seev**) v to misunderstand something, or to interpret something wrongly **misconception** n a mistaken idea

misconduct (say mis-**kon**-dukt) n bad behaviour by someone in a responsible position

misconstrue (say mis-kən-**stroo**) v **misconstrues**, **misconstrued**, **misconstruing** to understand or interpret something wrongly **misconstruction** n

miscreant (say **mis**-kri-ənt) n a wrongdoer or criminal

misdeed n a wrong or illegal act

misdemeanour (say mis-dim-**een**-er) n a minor misdeed or wrongdoing

misdirect v to direct someone wrongly **misdirection** n

miser n a person who hoards money and spends as little as possible **miserly** adj **miserliness** n

miserable adj 1 wretchedly unhappy or uncomfortable 2 disagreeable or unpleasant ♦ miserable weather 3 wretchedly poor or inadequate ♦ a miserable attempt **miserably** adv **misery** n 1 a feeling of great unhappiness or discomfort 2 informal a person who is constantly unhappy or disagreeable

misfire v 1 (said about a gun) to fail to fire correctly 2 (said about an engine) to fail to start or function correctly 3 to fail to have the intended effect ♦ The joke misfired.

misfit n a person who does not fit in well with other people or with their surroundings

misfortune n 1 bad luck 2 an unfortunate event

misgiving n a feeling of doubt or slight fear or mistrust

misguided adj showing bad judgement or reasoning

mishandle v to deal with something badly or inefficiently

mishap (say **mis**-hap) n an unlucky accident

mishear v past tense and past participle **misheard** to hear something incorrectly

mishit v mishit, **mishitting** to hit a ball faultily or badly

mishmash n a confused mixture

misinform v to give wrong information to someone

misinterpret v to interpret something wrongly **misinterpretation** n

misjudge v 1 to form a wrong opinion of someone or something 2 to estimate an amount or distance incorrectly **misjudgement** n

mislay v past tense and past participle **mislaid** to lose something temporarily

mislead v past tense and past participle **misled** to give someone a wrong impression about something

mismanage v to manage affairs badly or wrongly **mismanagement** n

mismatch v to match something unsuitably or incorrectly **mismatch** n a bad match

misnomer (say mis-**noh**-mer) n an unsuitable name or description for something

misogynist (say mis-**oj**-in-ist) n a person who hates women **misogyny** n

misplace v to put something in the wrong place **misplaced** adj unsuitable or inappropriate ♦ misplaced humour **misplacement** n

misprint n an error in printing

misquote v to quote something or someone incorrectly **misquote** n

misread v past tense and past participle **misread** (say mis-**red**) to read or interpret something incorrectly

misrepresent v to represent someone or something in a false or misleading way **misrepresentation** n

misrule n bad government

miss[1] v 1 to fail to hit, reach, or catch

something **2** to fail to see, hear, or understand someone or something ♦ *I missed what you said.* ♦ *Did you miss the signpost?* **3** to fail to catch a train, bus, etc., or to keep an appointment with someone **4** to notice the absence or loss of something **5** to avoid something ♦ *Go this way and you'll miss the traffic.* **6** (said about an engine) to misfire **miss** *n* failure to hit or reach what is aimed at **missing** *adj* **1** lost; not in the proper place ♦ *Two chairs are missing.* **2** absent ♦ *He's always missing when we need him.* **to miss out** to omit something **to miss out on** to fail to get any benefit or enjoyment from something that others have enjoyed

miss² *n* **1** a girl or unmarried woman **2** (**Miss**) a title used to refer to a girl or unmarried woman

missal *n* a book containing the prayers used in the Mass in the Roman Catholic Church

misshapen *adj* distorted or badly shaped

missile *n* **1** a weapon that is guided remotely to its target **2** an object that is thrown at a target

mission *n* **1** an important task or assignment **2** a group of people sent on a mission **3** an organization for spreading a religious belief, or the place where it is based **missionary** *n* a person who is sent to another country to spread a religious faith

missive *n* a letter or written message

misspell *v* past tense and past participle **misspelt** or **misspelled** to spell a word incorrectly

misspend *v* past tense and past participle **misspent** to spend time or money badly or unwisely

mist *n* **1** a cloud of water vapour in tiny drops **2** something resembling mist in its form or effect **mist** *v* to become covered with mist ♦ *The windscreen has misted up.* ♦ *My glasses misted over.* **misty** *adj* **1** full of mist **2** not clear or distinct **mistiness** *n*

mistake *n* **1** something done incorrectly ♦ *I've made some mistakes in the accounts.* **2** an incorrect idea or opinion ♦ *It would be a mistake to think they don't care.* **mistake** *v* **mistook, mistaken 1** to be wrong about something ♦ *Don't mistake my meaning.*

2 to choose or identify a person or thing wrongly ♦ *She is often mistaken for her sister.* **mistakable** *adj* able to be mistaken for another person or thing **mistaken** *adj* **1** having a wrong opinion ♦ *You are mistaken if you think that.* **2** badly judged or used ♦ *Their kindness seems to have been mistaken.* **mistakenly** *adv*

mister *n informal* a form of address to a man

mistime *v* to say or do something at an inappropriate time

mistletoe *n* a plant with white berries that grows as a parasite on trees

mistral (say **mis**-trəl or mis-**trahl**) *n* a strong cold north-west wind in southern France

mistreat *v* to treat someone or something badly **mistreatment** *n*

mistress *n* **1** a woman who has charge of people or things **2** a female teacher **3** a woman who is a married man's female lover but is not his wife

mistrial *n* a trial made invalid by an error in procedure

mistrust *v* to feel no trust in someone or something **mistrust** *n* a lack of trust **mistrustful** *adj*

misunderstand *v* past tense and past participle **misunderstood** to understand someone or something incorrectly

misuse (say mis-**yooz**) *v* **1** to use something wrongly or incorrectly **2** to treat a person or thing badly **misuse** (say mis-**yooss**) *n* wrong or incorrect use of something

mite *n* **1** a tiny spider-like animal, many of which are parasites **2** a small child or animal **3** a very small amount

mitigate (say **mit**-i-gayt) *v* to make something less serious or severe **mitigation** *n*

mitre (say **miy**-ter) *n* **1** a tall headdress worn by bishops **2** a joint of two pieces of wood or cloth with their ends evenly tapered so that together they form a right angle **mitre** *v* **mitred, mitring** to join pieces of wood or cloth with a mitre

mitt *n* a mitten

mitten *n* a glove that has no partition between the fingers

mix *v* **1** to combine things or put things

together ♦ *to mix business with pleasure* **2** (said about a person) to get on well with other people **mix** *n* **1** a mixture of people or things **2** a mixture prepared for making something ♦ *a cake mix* ♦ *a concrete mix* **mixer** *n* **1** a person who gets on in a certain way with others ♦ *He is a good mixer.* **2** a soft drink for mixing with an alcoholic drink **3** a machine or device for mixing or blending things **mixture** *n* **1** something made by mixing different things together **2** a combination of different things **to mix up 1** to mix things thoroughly **2** to confuse things in the mind **mixed-up** *adj* **mix-up** *n*

mixed blessing *n* something that has advantages and disadvantages

mixed *adj* **1** consisting of different kinds of things or people **2** involving people from different races or social classes

mizzen, mizzenmast *n* the mast nearest to and behind the main mast of a ship

ml *abbr* millilitre(s)

mm *abbr* millimetre(s)

mnemonic (say nim-**on**-ik) *n* a verse or saying that helps you to remember something

MO *abbr* Medical Officer

mo *n informal* a moment ♦ *I'll be there in half a mo.*

moan *n* **1** a long low sound of pain or suffering **2** *informal* a grumble **moan** *v* **1** to make a moan **2** *informal* to complain or grumble

moat *n* a deep wide ditch round a castle or large house, usually filled with water

mob *n* **1** a large disorderly crowd of people **2** *informal* a group of people **mob** *v* **mobbed, mobbing** to crowd round a person or place

mobile (say **moh**-biyl) *adj* able to move or be moved easily and quickly **mobile** *n* **1** a decoration for hanging from a ceiling so that its parts move freely in currents of air **2** a mobile phone **mobile phone** *n* a portable phone that uses a cellular radio system **mobility** *n* **mobilize** *v* **1** to organize troops for active service in war **2** to bring people or resources together for a particular purpose **mobilization** *n*

moccasin (say **mok**-ə-sin) *n* a soft leather shoe

mocha (say **moh**-kə) *n* a kind of coffee, or a flavouring made with this

mock *v* **1** to make fun of someone or something by imitating them **2** to taunt or defy someone with scorn **mock** *adj* imitation; not real ♦ *mock exams* **mockery** *n*

mockingbird *n* a long-tailed American bird that mimics the notes of other birds **mock-up** *n* a model of something, made to test or study it

MOD *abbr* Ministry of Defence

mod *n* (in the 1960s) a young person belonging to a group noted for its smart style of clothes

mod cons *pl n informal* modern conveniences, especially in houses and buildings

mode *n* **1** the way in which a thing is done **2** the current fashion **modish** *adj* fashionable

model *n* **1** a copy or reproduction of something, usually on a smaller scale **2** a particular design or version of a product, especially a car **3** a person or thing that is worth imitating **4** a person who poses for an artist **5** a person who displays clothes to buyers by wearing them **6** a description of a system or process **model** *adj* excellent of its kind, worth imitating ♦ *a model patient* **model** *v* **modelled, modelling 1** to make a model of something **2** to use a material to make a model **3** to design something using another thing as an example ♦ *The new system is modelled on the old one.* **4** to display clothes as a model

modem (say **moh**-dəm) *n* a device that links a computer system to a telephone line for transmitting data

moderate (say **mod**-er-ət) *adj* **1** average or medium in amount or quality **2** not extreme or excessive ♦ *a moderate climate* **3** not extreme or unreasonable ♦ *moderate political views* **moderate** *n* a person with moderate views, especially in politics **moderate** (say **mod**-er-ayt) *v* to make or become moderate or less intense **moderately** *adv* **moderation** *n* **moderator** *n* **1** a Presbyterian minister presiding over a church court or assembly

2 an arbitrator or mediator

modern adj **1** belonging to the present or recent times ♦ modern history **2** in current fashion, using methods or materials that are new or recent **modernism** n modern views or methods **modernist** n **modernity** n **modernize** v **1** to make something more modern **2** to adapt to modern ideas or tastes **modernization** n

modest adj **1** not vain or boastful **2** moderate in size or amount ♦ a modest pay rise **3** not showy or pretentious **4** behaving or dressing decently or decorously **modestly** adv **modesty** n

modicum (say mod-i-kəm) n a small amount

modify v modifies, modified, modifying **1** to change something in small ways **2** to make something less severe or harsh **3** to qualify a word or phrase by describing it ♦ Adjectives modify nouns. **modification** n

modulate v **1** to adjust or regulate something **2** to vary the tone or pitch of your voice **3** Mus to change from one key to another **4** to alter the amplitude, frequency, or phase of a carrier wave so as to convey a particular signal **modulation** n

module (say mod-yool) n **1** each of a set of standardized parts or units used to make something more complex **2** a section of a course of study **3** a self-contained unit attached to a spacecraft **modular** adj

modus operandi (say moh-dəs op-er-an-di) n a particular way of doing something

mogul (say **moh**-gəl) n informal an important or powerful person

mohair n **1** the silky hair of the angora goat **2** a yarn or fabric made from this

Mohican n a hairstyle in which the head is shaved except for a strip of hair along the top, which is worn upright and often brightly coloured

moire (say mwah) n a fabric that looks like watered silk

moist adj slightly wet; damp **moisten** v **moistness** n **moisture** n water or other liquid in a substance or present in the air as vapour or condensed on a surface **moisturize** v to make the skin less dry by using cosmetics **moisturizer** n

molar (say moh-ler) n any of the wide teeth at the back of the mouth used for grinding

molasses (say mə-las-iz) n dark syrup made from raw sugar

mole[1] n **1** a small burrowing animal **2** a spy working within an organization and passing information to another organization or country **molehill** n a small mound of earth thrown up by a burrowing mole

mole[2] n a small dark spot on the skin

mole[3] n a structure built out into the sea as a breakwater or causeway

molecule (say mol-i-kewl) n **1** the smallest unit, usually a group of atoms, into which a substance can be divided without changing its chemical qualities **2** a small particle of something **molecular** adj

molest (say mə-lest) v **1** to annoy or pester someone in a hostile way **2** to assault or abuse someone sexually **molestation** n

mollify v mollifies, mollified, mollifying to make someone less angry

mollusc (say mol-əsk) n any of a group of animals including snails, slugs, and mussels, with soft bodies and (in some cases) external shells

mollycoddle v to pamper someone

molten (say mohl-tən) adj melted; made liquid by great heat

moment n **1** a very short period of time **2** a particular point in time **momentary** adj lasting only a moment **momentarily** adv

momentous (say mə-ment-əs) adj very important or significant

momentum (say mə-ment-əm) n impetus gained by movement

monarch (say mon-erk) n a ruler with the title of king, queen, emperor, or empress **monarchic** adj **monarchical** adj **monarchist** n a person who favours government by a monarch **monarchy** n **1** government by a monarch **2** a country ruled by a monarch

monastery (say mon-ə-ster-i) n pl monasteries a building occupied by monks living in a secluded community, or the community itself **monastic** adj to do with monks or monasteries **monasticism** n

Monday n the day of the week following Sunday

money n 1 coins and banknotes used as a medium of exchange for goods and services 2 wealth **monetarism** n control of the supply of money as a means of stabilizing the economy of a country **monetarist** n, adj **monetary** adj to do with money or currency **moneyed** adj wealthy or affluent **moneylender** n a person who lends money to be repaid with interest

mongolism (say **mong**-gǝl-izm) n Down's syndrome ◊ This term is now considered to be offensive. Use Down's syndrome instead.

mongoose (say **mon**-gooss) n pl **mongooses** a small tropical animal like a stoat, which can attack and kill snakes

mongrel (say **mung**-grǝl) n a dog of no identifiable type or breed, or of mixed breeds

monitor n 1 a device used for observing or testing the operation of something 2 a television screen used in a studio to check and control transmissions 3 a screen that displays data and images produced by a computer 4 a pupil who is given special duties in a school **monitor** v to record or test or control the working of something

monk n a member of a community of men who live apart from the world under the rules of a religious order

monkey n pl **monkeys** 1 an animal of a group closely related to humans, having long arms and hands with thumbs, and often a tail 2 a mischievous person, especially a child **monkey** v **monkeys**, **monkeyed**, **monkeying** to tamper with something ♦ Please don't monkey with the switches.

monkey nut n a peanut

monkey puzzle n an evergreen tree with sharp stiff leaves and intertwining branches

monkey wrench n a large spanner with adjustable jaws

mono adj monophonic **mono** n pl **monos** monophonic sound or recording

mono- prefix one; single

monochrome (say **mon**-ǝ-krohm) adj done in one colour or in black and white **monochromatic** adj

monocle (say **mon**-ǝ-kǝl) n a lens worn over one eye and held in place by th muscles round the eye

monogamy (say mǝn-**og**-ǝmi) n th practice of being married to only on person at a time (Compare polygamy. **monogamous** adj

monogram (say **mon**-ǝ-gram) n a desig made up of a letter or letters, especially person's initials **monogrammed** adj

monograph (say **mon**-ǝ-grahf) n scholarly book or article on a single subject

monolith (say **mon**-ǝ-lith) n a large singl upright block of stone **monolithic** a 1 formed from a single block of ston 2 (said about an organization) large an difficult to change

monologue (say **mon**-ǝ-log) n 1 a speec by one actor in a play 2 a long tediou speech by one person in a group

monomania (say monǝ-**may**-niǝ) an obsession with one idea or interes **monomaniac** n

monophonic (say mon-ǝ-**fon**-ik) adj (sai about sound reproduction) using only on transmission channel

monoplane n a type of aeroplane with onl one set of wings

monopoly (say mǝn-**op**-ǝli) n p **monopolies** the exclusive right to se a commodity or service **monopolist** **monopolize** v to control or use somethin so that other people are excluded ♦ M uncle always seems to monopolize th conversation.

monorail n a railway in which the trac consists of a single rail, usually built abov ground level

monosyllable (say **mon**-ǝ-sil-ǝbǝl) n word of only one syllable **monosyllabic** ad

monotheism (say **mon**-ǝth-ee-izm) the belief that there is only one Go **monotheist** n **monotheistic** adj

monotone (say **mon**-ǝ-tohn) n a leve unchanging sound or tone of voice i speaking or singing **monotonous** adj 1 du or tedious because it does not chang much 2 lacking in variation of tone or pitc **monotonously** adv **monotony** n a dull o tedious situation

Monseigneur (say mawn-sen-**yer**) n

title or form of address for an eminent Frenchman, such as a prince or bishop

Monsieur (say mes-**yer**) *n pl* **Messieurs** (say mes-**yer**) the title of a Frenchman, equivalent to 'Mr' or 'sir'

Monsignor (say mon-**seen**-yor) *n* the title of certain Roman Catholic priests and officials

monsoon *n* **1** a strong seasonal wind that blows in the region of the Indian subcontinent and South Asia **2** the rainy season accompanying this

monster *n* **1** a large ugly or frightening creature **2** a huge thing **3** an extremely cruel or wicked person **monstrosity** *n* a huge and ugly thing **monstrous** *adj* **1** huge and ugly **2** outrageously wrong or unjust **monstrously** *adv*

montage (say mon-**tahz**h) *n* **1** the process of making a composite work of art, music, or film by putting together separate pieces **2** a work produced in this way

month *n* **1** any of the twelve named periods into which a year is divided **2** a period between the same dates in successive months **monthly** *adj* happening or produced once a month **monthly** *adv* once a month, every month

monument *n* **1** a statue or building intended to celebrate or commemorate an important person or event **2** a building or site that is preserved because of its historical importance **monumental** *adj* **1** belonging to or serving as a monument **2** extremely great or important

moo *v* **moos**, **mooed**, **mooing** to make the low deep sound of a cow **moo** *n pl* **moos** a mooing sound

mooch *v informal* to loiter in a bored or listless manner

mood *n* **1** a temporary state of mind or spirits ♦ *She seemed to be in a subdued mood.* **2** a fit of bad temper or depression ♦ *He's in one of his moods.* **3** *Gram* a form of a verb that shows whether it is a statement, command, question, or wish **moody** *adj* **1** gloomy or sullen **2** having sudden changes of mood for no apparent reason **moodily** *adv* **moodiness** *n*

moon *n* **1** the natural satellite of the earth,

visible from light reflected from the sun **2** a natural satellite of another planet **moon** *v* to move or pass time in a dreamy or listless manner **moonlight** *n* light from the moon **moonlight** *v* past tense and past participle **moonlighted** *informal* to have a second job, especially in the evening when your main job is during the day **moonlit** *adj* **moonshine** *n* **1** foolish talk or ideas **2** *N. Am* illicit liquor **moonstone** *n* a pearly-white semi-precious stone, especially of feldspar **moonstruck** *adj* unable to act sensibly

moony *adj* **moonier**, **mooniest** dreamy or listless

Moor *n* a member of a Muslim people of north-west Africa **Moorish** *adj*

moor[1] *n* a stretch of open uncultivated land with heather and other low shrubs **moorhen** *n* a small waterbird

moor[2] *v* to secure a boat to the shore or to a fixed object by means of a cable **mooring** *n* **moorings** *pl n* **1** a place where a boat is moored **2** cables and ropes for mooring a boat

moose *n pl* **moose** a North American elk

moot *adj* debatable or undecided ♦ *That's a moot point.* **moot** *v* to raise a question for discussion

mop *n* **1** a bunch or pad of soft material fastened to the end of a long handle, used for cleaning floors **2** a thick mass of hair **mop** *v* **mopped**, **mopping** to clean or wipe a floor or other surface with a mop

mope *v* to be listless and in low spirits

moped (say **moh**-ped) *n* a kind of small motorcycle that can be pedalled

moral *adj* **1** to do with what is right and wrong in human behaviour ♦ *moral philosophy* **2** good or virtuous **3** psychological or mental, not practical or physical ♦ *moral courage* **moral** *n* a lesson in right behaviour taught by an event or story **moralist** *n* a person who expresses or teaches moral principles **moralistic** *adj* **morality** *n* **1** conforming to moral principles; goodness or rightness **2** moral principles or rules **moralize** *v* to talk or write about the principles of right and wrong in human behaviour **morally** *adv* **morals** *pl n* standards of behaviour

morale (say mə-**rahl**) n the spirits and confidence of a person or group at a particular time

morass (say mo-**rass**) n 1 a marsh or bog 2 a confused mass

moratorium (say mo-rə-**tor** -iəm) n pl **moratoriums** or **moratoria** 1 a temporary ban imposed on an activity 2 legal authorization to debtors to delay payment

morbid adj concerned with or interested in gloomy or unpleasant things **morbidity** n **morbidly** adv

mordant (say mor -dənt) adj (said about humour) sharp or critical

more adj greater in amount or degree **more** n a greater amount or number **more** adv 1 to a greater extent ♦ more beautiful 2 again ♦ once more **moreover** adv besides, in addition to what has already been said

morganatic (say mor-gən-**at**-ik) adj (said about a marriage) concluded between people of different social rank, in which the spouse of lower rank has no claim to the other spouse's possessions or title

morgue (say morg) n a mortuary

moribund (say mo-ri-bund) adj lacking energy or vigour

Mormon (say mor -mən) n a member of a religious organization, the Church of Jesus Christ of Latter-Day Saints

morn n poetic morning

morning n the early part of the day, up to noon or lunchtime **morning dress** n formal dress for a man consisting of a tailcoat, striped trousers, and a top hat **morning star** n a planet, especially Venus, seen in the east before sunrise

morocco n a fine flexible leather made from goatskins

moron (say mor -on) n informal a very stupid person **moronic** adj

morose (say mə-**rohss**) adj bad-tempered and gloomy **morosely** adv **moroseness** n

morphine (say mor -feen) n a drug made from opium, used for relieving pain

morris dance n a traditional English folk dance performed by dancers in costume with ribbons and bells

morrow n poetic the following day

Morse code n a system of signalling in which letters of the alphabet ar represented by combinations of short an long sounds or flashes of light (dots an dashes)

morsel n a small piece of food

mortal adj 1 not living for ever; boun to die ♦ All humans are mortal. 2 causin death; fatal ♦ He suffered a mortal woun 3 lasting until death ♦ mortal enemies 4 (i Christian teaching, said about a sin) seriou enough to deprive the soul of divin grace **mortal** n an ordinary human being especially contrasted with a god or spir **mortality** n 1 the state of being mortal an bound to die 2 loss of life on a large scal **mortally** adv

mortar n 1 a mixture of lime or cement wit sand and water, for joining bricks or stone 2 a hard bowl in which substances ar pounded with a pestle 3 a short cannon fo firing shells at a high angle **mortar board** n an academic cap with a stiff square top

mortgage (say mor -gij) n a loan from bank or building society to buy a hous or other property, with the property a security for the loan **mortgage** v to offer property as security for a loan

mortify v mortifies, mortified, mortifyin 1 to humiliate someone 2 to subdu physical desires by discipline or self-deni 3 (said about flesh) to be affected b gangrene **mortification** n

mortise (say mor -tiss) n a hole o slot made in a piece of wood so that projecting part on the end of another piec can be inserted in it to hold the two piec together **mortise lock** n a lock that is s into the framework of a door

mortuary (say mor -tew-er-i) n mortuaries a place where dead bodies a kept until they are buried

mosaic (say mə-**zay**-ik) n a picture or desi made by putting together small pieces glass or stone of different colours

Moslem (say **moz**-ləm) adj, n anoth spelling of Muslim

mosque (say mosk) n a building in whi Muslims worship

mosquito (say mos-**kee**-toh) n

mosquitoes a small insect which bites and sucks blood

moss n a small plant with no flowers, which forms a dense growth on moist surfaces or in bogs **mossy** adj

most adj greatest in amount or degree **most** n the greatest amount or number **most** adv 1 to the greatest extent 2 very ♦ It is a most interesting story. **mostly** adv for the most part

MOT abbr (in Britain) a compulsory annual test of motor vehicles of more than a specified age

mote n a speck

motel (say moh-**tel**) n a hotel near a major road, providing accommodation for motorists

motet (say moh-**tet**) n a short piece of sacred choral music

moth n an insect resembling a butterfly, which usually flies at night **mothball** n a small ball of naphthalene, etc. placed near clothes to keep away moths **in mothballs** stored out of use for a considerable time

mother n 1 a female parent 2 a woman who is head of a female religious community ♦ Mother Superior **mother** v to look after someone in a motherly way **motherhood** n **motherless** adj **motherly** adj like a mother, especially in being caring and protective **mother-in-law** n the mother of your wife or husband **motherland** n a person's native country **mother-of-pearl** n a pearly substance lining the shells of oysters, mussels, and some other molluscs **mother tongue** n the language a person speaks as their first or only language

motif (say moh-**teef**) n 1 a repeated image or feature 2 a decorative design on a piece of clothing

motion n 1 the action of moving or changing position 2 a particular movement or gesture 3 a formal proposal put before a meeting for discussion 4 an emptying of the bowels; excrement **motion** v to make a gesture directing someone to do something ♦ She motioned him to sit beside her. **motionless** adj not moving **motion picture** n a film shown in a cinema

motive n what makes a person do something or act in a certain way **motive** adj producing movement or action **motivate** v to give a motive or incentive to someone **motivated** adj **motivation** n

motley adj 1 varied in colour or appearance 2 made up of various sorts ♦ a motley group of people

motocross n a motorcycle race over rough ground

motor n 1 a machine that supplies power for a vehicle or machinery; an engine 2 informal a motor car **motor** v to travel in a motor car **motorist** n the driver of a car **motorized** adj 1 equipped with a motor 2 equipped with motor vehicles **motorbike** n a motorcycle **motorcade** n a procession or parade of motor vehicles **motor car** n a car **motorcycle** n a two-wheeled road vehicle with an engine **motorcyclist** n **motorway** n a road designed for fast motor traffic

mottled adj marked with spots or patches of colour

motto n pl **mottoes** or **mottos** a short phrase or saying adopted as a guide for behaviour

mould[1] n 1 a hollow container of a particular shape, into which a substance is poured to set 2 a distinctive style or character ♦ a cricketer in the mould of Botham **mould** v 1 to make something in a particular shape 2 to influence or guide the development of something ♦ The experience helped to mould his character.

mould[2] n a fine growth of fungi that forms in moist warm conditions **moulder** v to decay or rot slowly **mouldy** adj 1 covered with mould 2 stale and smelling of mould 3 dull or tedious

mould[3] n soft loose earth ♦ leaf mould

moult (say mohlt) v (said about an animal) to shed its skin, hair, or feathers to make way for a new growth **moult** n the process of moulting

mound n 1 a built-up pile of earth or stones 2 a small hill

mount[1] n a mountain or hill

mount[2] v 1 to go upwards; to rise to a higher level 2 to get on to a horse or bicycle so as to ride it 3 to increase in amount or intensity 4 to fix something in position for use or display ♦ *You can mount your photographs in an album.* **5** to take action to achieve something ♦ *The enemy mounted a strong offensive.* **mount** *n* **1** a horse for riding **2** something on which a thing is mounted for support or display **mounted** *adj* serving on horseback ♦ *mounted police*

mountain *n* **1** a mass of land that rises to a large height **2** a large heap or pile ♦ *a mountain of work* **mountaineer** *n* a person who climbs mountains **mountaineering** *n* **mountainous** *adj* **1** having many mountains **2** huge

mountebank (say **mownt**-i-bank) *n* a swindler or charlatan

mourn *v* to feel or show sorrow for someone who has died or something that has been lost **mourner** *n* **mournful** *adj* feeling or showing sorrow or grief **mourning** *n* **1** the process of showing sorrow for someone who has died **2** black or dark clothes worn in mourning

mouse *n pl* **mice 1** a small rodent with a long thin tail and a pointed nose **2** a quiet or timid person **3** *pl* **mice** or **mouses** *ICT* a small hand-held device which is dragged across a flat surface to control the position of a cursor on a screen **mousing** *n* hunting mice, especially by a cat **mousy** *adj* **1** (said about hair) dull or light brown in colour **2** (said about a person) quiet and timid

moussaka (say moo-**sah**-kə) *n* a Greek dish consisting of layers of minced meat and aubergine with a cheese sauce

mousse (say mooss) *n* **1** a creamy light whipped pudding **2** a frothy creamy substance used for styling the hair

moustache (say məs-**tahsh**) *n* a strip of hair growing on a man's upper lip

mouth *n* **1** the opening in the face through which food is taken into the body and from which sounds are made **2** the place where a river enters the sea **3** the opening of something hollow or enclosed, such as a cave, horn, etc. **mouth** (say mowth) *v* **1** to say words pompously or with exaggerated distinctness **2** to form words with the lips, usually without saying them aloud **mouthful** *n* **1** a quantity of food or drink

that fills the mouth **2** a long or awkward word or phrase that is difficult to say **mouth organ** *n* a small musical instrument played by passing it along the lips while blowing or sucking air; a harmonica **mouthpiece** *n* **1** the part of a musical instrument or other device (such as a telephone) that is placed between or near the lips **2** someone who speaks on behalf of another person or an organization **mouthwash** *n* a liquid for cleansing the mouth or for gargling

move *v* **1** to change in position or posture **2** to go in a certain direction **3** to change the place where you live **4** to provoke a strong feeling in someone, especially sorrow or sympathy ♦ *They were deeply moved by the story.* **5** to prompt or motivate someone to do something ♦ *What moved them to invite us?* **6** to propose an item for discussion and decision at a meeting **7** to take prompt action ♦ *We need to move quickly.* **move** *n* **1** the act or process of moving **2** an action done to achieve a purpose ♦ *The union has made a move towards settling the dispute.* **moveable** *adj* **movement** *n* **1** an act of moving **2** *Mus* each of the principal divisions in a long work **3** a a group of people working together to advance a cause **4** the moving parts in a mechanism, especially a clock or watch **mover** *n* **moving** *adj* arousing strong emotions, especially of sorrow or sympathy ♦ *It was a very moving story.*

movie *n chiefly North Amer.* a cinema film

mow *v* past participle **mowed** or **mown** to cut down grass or a cereal crop with a machine or a scythe **mower** *n* **to mow down** to kill or destroy people at random or in great numbers

mozzarella (say mot-sə-**rel**-lə) *n* a soft white Italian cheese

MP *abbr* Member of Parliament

MP3 *n* a method of compressing sound into a very small file, used to download audio files from the Internet

mph *abbr* miles per hour

Mr *n pl* **Messrs 1** a title put before a man's name **2** a title put before the name of an office when addressing the holder ♦ *Mr President.*

Mrs *n* a title put before a married woman's name

MS *abbr* **1** manuscript **2** multiple sclerosis

Ms (say miz) *n* a title put before a woman's name regardless of her married or unmarried status

MSP *abbr* Member of the Scottish Parliament

Mt. *abbr* Mount

much *adj* existing in a large amount ♦ *much noise* **much** *n* a large quantity **much** *adv* **1** to a great extent ♦ *much to my surprise* **2** approximately ♦ *They are much the same.* **much of a muchness** hardly different, nearly the same

muck *n* **1** farmyard manure **2** dirt or filth **muck** *v* to make something dirty **mucky** *adj* **muckraking** *n informal* seeking for and exposing scandal **to muck in** *informal* to contribute to tasks or expenses **to muck out** to remove muck or dirt from a place

mucus (say **mew**-kəs) *n* a moist sticky substance secreted by a mucous membrane and forming a protective covering inside hollow organs of the body **mucous membrane** *n* a moist skin lining the nose, mouth, throat, and other hollow organs of the body **mucous** *adj*

mud *n* wet soft earth **mudflat** *n* a stretch of muddy land left uncovered at low tide **muddy** *adj* **1** like mud, or full of mud **2** (said about a colour) dull; not clear or bright **muddiness** *n* **muddy** *v* to make something muddy or unclear **mudguard** *n* a curved cover over the wheel of a bicycle, to protect the rider from mud thrown up

muddle *v* **1** to make someone or something confused or disorganized **2** to confuse or mistake one person or thing for another **muddle** *n* a muddled state or condition; confusion or disorder

muesli (say **myooz**-li) *n* a breakfast food of mixed cereals, dried fruit, and nuts

muezzin (say moo-**ez**-in) *n* a Muslim crier who proclaims the hours of prayer from a minaret

muff¹ *n* a short tube-shaped piece of warm material into which the hands are placed for warmth, one at each end

muff² *v informal* to bungle something

muffin *n* **1** a flat round bun, eaten toasted and buttered **2** a small round sponge cake

muffle *v* **1** to wrap or cover something to protect it or keep it warm **2** to wrap or pad a source of sound in order to deaden its sound **3** to deaden or reduce a sound **muffler** *n* **1** a scarf worn round the neck for warmth **2** a device for muffling sound

mufti *n* ordinary clothes worn by someone who usually wears a uniform

mug¹ *n* **1** a large drinking vessel with a handle, used without a saucer **2** *informal* a person's face or mouth **3** *informal* a person who is easily deceived **mug** *v informal* **mugged, mugging** to rob someone with violence in a public place **mugger** *n*

mug² *v* **mugged, mugging** to mug up *informal* to learn a subject by studying hard

muggins *n informal* a person, especially the person speaking or writing, who is easily deceived or victimized

muggy *adj* **muggier, muggiest** (said about the weather) oppressively damp and warm **mugginess** *n*

mulberry *n pl* **mulberries 1** a purple or white fruit rather like a blackberry **2** the tree that bears this fruit

mulch *n* a mixture of leaves, grass, or compost spread on the ground to protect plants or to enrich the soil **mulch** *v* to cover the ground with a mulch

mule¹ *n* an animal that is the offspring of a mare and a donkey, used for carrying loads **mulish** *adj* stubborn, as a mule is supposed to be

mule² *n* a light shoe or slipper without a back

mull¹ *v* to heat wine or beer and add sugar and spices to it

mull² *v* **to mull over** to think carefully about something

mullah (say **mul**-ə) *n* a Muslim who has studied Islamic theology and sacred law

mullet (say **mul**-it) *n* a kind of fish used for food

mulligatawny (say mul-ig-ə-**taw**-ni) *n* a spicy hot soup originally made in India

mullion (say **mul**-iən) *n* an upright bar between the panes of a tall window

multi- *prefix* many (as in *multicultural*)

multicoloured *adj* having many colours

multicultural *adj* made up of people of different races and cultures

multifarious (say multi-**fair**-iəs) *adj* of many kinds; very varied **multifariously** *adv*

multilateral (say multi-**lat**-er-əl) *adj* (said about an agreement or treaty) made between three or more people, organizations, or countries

multimedia *adj* using more than one medium of communication ♦ *a multimedia show with pictures, lights, and music*

multimillionaire *n* a person with a fortune of several million pounds or dollars

multinational *adj* (said about a business company) operating in several countries **multinational** *n* a multinational company

multiple *adj* having several parts or elements **multiple** *n* a number that contains another number (called a *factor*) an exact amount of times without a remainder ♦ *8 and 12 are multiples of 4.*

multiple sclerosis *n* a chronic disease of the nervous system causing partial or complete paralysis

multiplex *adj* having many parts or forms, or consisting of many elements **multiplex** *n* a large cinema complex with many screens

multiplicity (say multi-**plis**-iti) *n* a great variety or large number

multiply *v* **multiplies, multiplied, multiplying 1** to take a number and obtain another number which contains the first number a specified number of times ♦ *Multiply 8 by 4 and get 32.* **2** to increase in number **3** to increase by breeding **multiplicand** *n* a number that is to be multiplied by another number **multiplication** *n* **multiplier** *n* a number by which another number is multiplied

multitude *n* a large number of things or people **multitudinous** *adj*

mum[1] *n informal* mother

mum[2] *adj informal* silent ♦ *Try to keep mum.*

mumble *v* to speak indistinctly so you cannot easily be heard **mumble** *n* indistinct speech **mumbler** *n*

mumbo-jumbo *n informal* meaningless talk or ritual

mummy[1] *n informal pl* **mummies** mother

mummy[2] *n pl* **mummies** (especially in ancient Egypt) a corpse treated with oils and wrapped in cloth to preserve it for burial **mummify** *v* to preserve a corpse as a mummy by embalming it

mumps *n* a virus that causes painful swellings in the neck

munch *v* to chew food steadily and vigorously

mundane (say mun-**dayn**) *adj* **1** dull or routine **2** concerned with practical matters, not ideals

municipal (say mew-**nis**-i-pəl) *adj* to do with a town or city or its local government **municipality** *n* a town or district that has local government

munificent (say mew-**nif**-i-sənt) *adj* extremely generous **munificence** *n*

munitions (say mew-**nish**-ənz) *pl n* military weapons, ammunition, and equipment

mural (say **mewr**-əl) *n* a wall painting **mural** *adj* on or to do with a wall

murder *n* the intentional and unlawful killing of one person by another **murder** *v* to kill a person unlawfully and intentionally **murderer** *n* **murderous** *adj*

murk *n* darkness or poor visibility **murky** *adj* **1** dark and gloomy **2** (said about water) muddy or full of sediment **3** scandalous or immoral in an obscure way ♦ *a family with a murky past* **murkiness** *n*

murmur *n* **1** a low continuous background sound **2** softly spoken words **3** a subdued expression of feeling ♦ *murmurs of discontent* **4** a low abnormal sound made by the heart **murmur** *v* to make a murmur; to speak or utter something in a low voice

muscle *n* **1** a band or bundle of fibrous tissue able to contract and so produce movement in parts of the body **2** power or strength **muscle** *v* **to muscle in** *informal* to force your way into someone else's affairs **muscular** *adj* **1** of or affecting the muscles **2** having well-developed muscles **muscularity** *n*

muse *v* to ponder deeply about something

museum *n* a building in which objects of historical, cultural, or scientific interest are collected and exhibited

mush *n* **1** soft pulp **2** feeble sentimentality

mushy *adj*

mushroom *n* an edible fungus with a stem and domed cap **mushroom** *v* to grow or appear rapidly in large numbers

music *n* 1 the art of arranging the sounds of voices or instruments in a harmonious and pleasing sequence or combination 2 the sounds or compositions produced in this way, or a set of written or printed symbols showing these sounds **musical** *adj* 1 to do with music 2 producing music ♦ *a musical instrument* 3 (said about a person) fond of or skilled in music **musical** *n* a play or film containing a large number of songs **musically** *adv* **musician** *n* a person who plays a musical instrument or is musically accomplished

musk *n* a strong-smelling substance secreted by male deer, used as an ingredient in perfumes **musky** *adj*

musket *n* a gun with a long barrel, formerly used by infantry soldiers **musketeer** *n* a soldier armed with a musket

muskrat a large North American water animal with a musky smell, valued for its fur

Muslim *n* a person who follows the Islamic faith **Muslim** *adj* to do with Muslims or their faith

muslin *n* a thin cotton cloth

mussel *n* a black shellfish, some forms of which can be eaten

must[1] *auxiliary verb* 1 used to express necessity or obligation ♦ *We must try to find them.* 2 used to express certainty or probability ♦ *The train must be late.* 3 used to express insistence ♦ *I must emphasize that I did everything possible.* **must** *n informal* a thing that should not be overlooked or missed

must[2] *n* grape juice before or during fermentation

mustang *n* a wild horse of Mexico and the south-west USA

mustard *n* 1 a hot-tasting yellow or brownish paste used to flavour food 2 a plant with sharp-tasting seeds, from which mustard paste is made 3 a darkish-yellow colour **mustard gas** *n* a poisonous gas that burns the skin

muster *v* 1 to come together, or bring people or things together 2 to summon something you need ♦ *to muster up your strength* **muster** *n* an assembly or gathering of people or things **to pass muster** to be up to the required standard

musty *adj* **mustier**, **mustiest** 1 smelling or tasting mouldy or stale 2 antiquated or outdated **mustiness** *n*

mutation *n* a change or alteration in form **mutable** *adj* able or likely to change **mutate** *v* to undergo mutation

mute *adj* 1 silent; not speaking 2 unable to speak or make sounds **mute** *n* 1 *old use* a person who is unable to speak 2 a device fitted to a musical instrument to deaden its sound **mute** *v* 1 to deaden or muffle the sound of a musical instrument 2 to make something quieter or less intense **mutely** *adv*

mutilate *v* to injure or damage something by breaking or cutting off part of it **mutilation** *n*

mutiny (say *mew*-tin-i) *n pl* **mutinies** an open rebellion against authority, especially by members of the armed forces against their officers **mutiny** *v* **mutinies**, **mutinied**, **mutinying** to engage in mutiny **mutineer** *adj* **mutinous** *adj*

mutter *v* 1 to speak or utter something in a low unclear voice 2 to grumble quietly or in private **mutter** *n* muttered words

mutton *n* the flesh of sheep eaten as food

mutual (say *mew*-tew-əl) *adj* 1 (said about a feeling or action) felt or done by each of two or more people towards or to the other ♦ *mutual affection* 2 shared by two or more people ♦ *a mutual friend* **mutually** *adv*

Muzak (say *mew*-zak) *n trademark* recorded light music played through speakers in public places

muzzle *n* 1 the projecting nose and mouth of dogs and some other animals 2 the open end of a gun 3 a cover put over an animal's head to prevent it from biting or feeding **muzzle** *v* 1 to put a muzzle on an animal 2 to prevent a person or organization from expressing opinions openly

muzzy *adj* **muzzier**, **muzziest** confused or blurred

my *adj* belonging to me

mycology (say miy-**kol**-əji) *n* the study of fungi **mycologist** *n*

mynah (say **miy**-nə) *n* a southern Asian bird, some kinds of which can mimic human speech

myopia (say miy-**oh**-piə) *n* short-sightedness **myopic** *adj* **myopically** *n*

myriad (say **mi**-ri-əd) *n* a vast number

myrrh (say mir) *n* a fragrant gum resin used in perfumes, incense, and medicine

myrtle (say **mer**-təl) *n* an evergreen shrub with dark leaves and scented white flowers

myself *pronoun* used to refer to the person speaking when that person is also the subject of the sentence ♦ *I have hurt myself.*

mysterious *adj* full of mystery, puzzling **mysteriously** *adv*

mystery *n pl* **mysteries** 1 something that cannot be explained or understood 2 the quality of being unexplained or obscure ♦ *Its origins are wrapped in mystery.* 3 a religious truth that the human mind is incapable of understanding 4 a story or play that deals with a puzzling crime

mystic (say **mis**-tik) *adj* having hidden or symbolic meaning, especially in religion **mystic** *n* a person who seeks to obtain union with God by deep religious meditation **mystical** *adj* **mysticism** *n* 1 a spiritual quality 2 the beliefs or practices of mystics

mystify *v* **mystifies, mystified, mystifying** to cause a person to feel puzzled **mystification** *n*

mystique (say mis-**teek**) *n* an air of mystery or mystical power

myth *n* 1 a traditional story containing ideas or beliefs about ancient times or about supernatural beings 2 these stories collectively 3 an imaginary person or thing 4 an idea that forms part of the beliefs of a group or class but is not founded on fact **mythical** *adj* **mythological** *adj* **mythology** *n* 1 a body of myths ♦ *Greek mythology.* 2 the study of myths

myxomatosis (say miksə-mə-**toh**-sis) *n* a fatal disease of rabbits

Nn

N[1] the fourteenth letter of the English alphabet

N[2] *abbr* north or northern

nab *v* **nabbed, nabbing** *informal* 1 to catch someone doing wrong 2 to seize or grab something

nabob (say **nay**-bob) *n* a wealthy person

nacre (say **nay**-ker) *n* mother-of-pearl **nacreous** *adj*

nadir (say **nay**-deer) *n* 1 (in astronomy) the part of the sky that is directly below the observer 2 the lowest or most unsuccessful point

naff *adj* *informal* lacking taste; unfashionable

nag[1] *v* **nagged, nagging** 1 to bother someone by constantly criticizing, complaining, or asking for things 2 (said about pain or worry) to keep on hurting or bothering you

nag[2] *n* *informal* a horse

nail *n* 1 a hard covering on the upper surface of the tip of a finger or toe 2 a small metal spike, often with a flattened head, driven into wood or other materials with a hammer to hold pieces together **nail** *v* 1 to fasten wood or other materials with a nail or nails 2 to catch or arrest someone in the act of doing wrong **on the nail** (said about payment) made immediately **to hit the nail on the head** to state the truth exactly

naive (say niy-**eev**) *adj* 1 showing a lack of experience or judgement; innocent and trusting 2 simple and unsophisticated in style **naively** *adv* **naivety** *n*

naked *adj* 1 without any clothes on; nude 2 without the usual coverings or protection ♦ *a naked sword* 3 obvious or undisguised ♦ *the naked truth* **naked eye** the eye unassisted by a telescope or microscope, etc. **nakedly** *adv* **nakedness** *n*

namby-pamby *adj* lacking character; feeble or sentimental

name *n* 1 the word or words by which a

person, animal, place, or thing is known **2** a reputation ♦ *This place has got a bad name.* **3** a famous person ♦ *The film has some big names in it.* **name** v **1** to give a name to a person, place, or thing ♦ *They named their cat Albert.* **2** to state the name of a person, place, or thing ♦ *Can you name the people in the photograph?* **3** to mention or specify a piece of information ♦ *Name your price.*

nameless *adj* **1** having no name or no known name **2** not mentioned by name ♦ *There are others who shall be nameless.* **3** difficult or too bad to describe ♦ *Nameless misfortunes hit the village.* **namely** *adv* that is to say; specifically ♦ *my two best subjects, namely French and German* **namesake** *n* a person or thing with the same name as another **to call a person names** to speak abusively to or about someone

nan[1] *n informal* a person's grandmother

nan[2] *n* a type of flat leavened Indian bread

nanny *n pl* **nannies 1** a person employed to look after a child in its own home **2** *informal* a person's grandmother **nanny goat** *n* a female goat

nano- *prefix* **1** one thousand millionth ♦ *nanosecond* **2** extremely small

nanotechnology *n* chemical and biological engineering concerned with the manipulation of molecules

nap[1] *n* a short sleep, especially during the day **nap** v **napped, napping** to have a nap

nap[2] *n* short raised fibres on the surface of cloth or leather

nap[3] *n* a card game in which players have five cards and declare how many tricks they expect to take

napalm (say **nay**-pahm) *n* a sticky jelly-like petrol substance used in incendiary bombs

nape *n* the back part of the neck

napkin *n* a piece of cloth or paper used at meals to protect your clothes or for wiping your lips or fingers

nappy *n pl* **nappies** a piece of towelling or other absorbent material put round a baby's bottom and legs to absorb or hold its urine and faeces

narcissism (say nar-**sis**-izm) *n* abnormal interest in or admiration for yourself **narcissistic** *adj*

narcissus (say nar-**sis**-əs) *n pl* **narcissi** a daffodil with white or pale outer petals and an orange or yellow centre

narcotic (say nar-**kot**-ik) *n* a drug that causes sleep or drowsiness, and relieves pain **narcotic** *adj* causing sleep or drowsiness

nark *n informal* a police informer **nark** v *informal* to annoy someone

narrate (say nə-**rayt**) v to tell a story or give an account of events in the order in which they happened **narration** *n* **narrative** *n* a spoken or written account of something **narrative** *adj* in the form of a narrative **narrator** *n*

narrow *adj* **1** small in width compared to length **2** with little scope or variety; small ♦ *a narrow circle of friends* **3** uncomfortably close; only just achieved ♦ *We had a narrow escape.* **narrow** v to make something narrower, or to become narrower **narrowly** *adv* **narrowness** *n* **narrowboat** *n* a long narrow boat used on canals **narrow-minded** *adj* not willing to consider other people's opinions; prejudiced

narwhal (say **nar**-wəl) *n* a small Arctic whale, the male of which has a long spiral tusk

nasal (say **nay**-zəl) *adj* **1** to do with the nose **2** (said about a voice or speech) sounding as if the breath comes out through the nose **nasally** *adv*

nasturtium (say nə-**ster**-shəm) *n pl* **nasturtiums** a garden plant with bright orange, yellow, or red flowers

nasty *adj* **nastier, nastiest 1** very unpleasant or repulsive **2** unkind or spiteful **3** difficult to deal with ♦ *a nasty problem* **nastily** *adv* **nastiness** *n*

natal (say **nay**-təl) *adj* **1** to do with birth **2** from or since birth

nation *n* a large community of people who live in the same part of the world under one government **nationwide** *adj, adv* extending over the whole of a nation

national *adj* to do with a nation, or belonging to a whole nation **national** *n* a citizen or subject of a particular country **nationalism** *n* **1** patriotic feeling, principles, or efforts **2** a movement favouring independence for a country that is controlled by another or forms part of another **nationalist** n **nationalistic** adj **nationality** n pl **nationalities** the condition of belonging to a particular nation **nationalize** v to put an industry or business under state ownership or control **nationalization** n **nationally** adv **national anthem** n the official song of a nation **national debt** n the total amount of money borrowed by a government **national grid** n a network of high-voltage electric power lines between major power stations **National Insurance** n a system of compulsory payments made by employees and employers to provide state assistance for people who are ill, unemployed, or retired **national park** n an area of countryside which is protected by the state for the public to visit **national service** n a period of compulsory service in the armed forces in peacetime

native adj **1** to do with a place of birth ♦ a native language **2** belonging to a particular place by birth **3** originating in a specified place ♦ a plant native to China **4** inborn or natural ♦ a native ability **native** n **1** a person who was born in a particular place **2** a local inhabitant of a place **3** an animal or plant grown or originating in a particular place **Native American** n one of the original inhabitants of North and South America and the Caribbean Islands

Nativity n the birth of Jesus Christ

natter v informal to chat informally **natter** n informal a chat

natty adj **nattier**, **nattiest** informal neat and trim; dapper **nattily** adv

natural adj **1** produced or done by nature, not by people or machines **2** in accordance with nature; normal ♦ He died a natural death. **3** having certain inborn qualities or abilities ♦ She seemed to be a natural leader. **4** not looking artificial; not affected in manner ♦ Their behaviour was very natural. **5** not surprising; to be expected ♦ Anger was a natural reaction to the news. **6** Mus neither sharp nor flat ♦ B natural **natural** n **1** a person or thing that seems to be naturally suited for something **2** Mus

a natural note; the sign ♮ indicating this **naturalist** n someone who studies natural history **naturalism** n (in art and literature) the theory or practice of drawing, painting, or describing things as they are in nature **naturalistic** adj **naturalize** v **1** to give a person of foreign birth the right of citizenship of a country **2** to adopt a foreign word or custom **naturalization** n **naturally** adv **naturalness** n **natural gas** gas found naturally underground, not manufactured **natural history** n the study of plants and animals **natural selection** n the theory that organisms that are best adapted to their environment will survive, while the less well adapted ones will die out

nature n **1** the world with all its features and living things, as distinct from things made by humans **2** the physical force regarded as producing living things **3** a kind or sort of thing **4** the qualities and characteristics of a person or thing

naturist n a nudist **naturism** n

naught n old use nothing

naughty adj **naughtier**, **naughtiest** **1** behaving badly; disobedient **2** mildly shocking or indecent **naughtily** adv **naughtiness** n

nausea (say naw-ziə) n a feeling of sickness or disgust **nauseate** v to make someone feel nausea **nauseous** adj **1** feeling nausea **2** causing a feeling of nausea

nautical adj to do with ships or sailors **nautical mile** n a measure of distance at sea, equal to 2,025 yards or 1.852 kilometres

nautilus (say naw-til-əs) n pl **nautiluses** a mollusc with a spiral shell divided into compartments

nave n the main part of a church apart from the chancel, aisles, and transepts

navel (say nay-vəl) n the small hollow in the centre of the abdomen where the umbilical cord was attached

navigate v **1** to direct the course of a ship, aircraft, or vehicle **2** to travel in, through, or over **navigable** adj **1** suitable for ships to sail in **2** (said about a boat or ship) able to be steered and sailed **navigation** n **navigator** n

navvy *n pl* **navvies** a labourer digging a road, railway, or canal

navy *n pl* **navies 1** a country's warships and the crews trained to use them **2** (also **navy blue**) a dark blue colour like that of the navy uniform **naval** *adj*

nay *adv old use* no

Nazi (say **nah**-tsi) *n pl* **Nazis** a member of the National Socialist party in Germany under Hitler, having Fascist beliefs **Nazism** *n*

NB *abbr* take note of something

NCO *abbr* non-commissioned officer

NE *abbr* north-east or north-eastern

Neanderthal (say ni-an-der-təl) *n* an extinct type of human who lived in Europe during the early Stone Age

neap *n* **neap tide** the tide when there is the least rise and fall of water

near *adv* **1** at or to a short distance **2** a short time away in the future **near** *prep* not far away from ♦ *The house is near the station.* **near** *adj* **1** with only a short distance or interval between ♦ *in the near future* **2** with little margin ♦ *a near escape* **near** *v* to come near to something **nearby** *adj* near in position ♦ *a nearby house* **nearby** *adv* not far off ♦ *They live nearby.* **nearly** *adv* almost ♦ *We have nearly finished.* **nearness** *n* **Near East** *n* an area of SW Asia extending from the eastern Mediterranean to Iran and including the Middle East **near miss** *n* a bomb or shot that narrowly misses its target **nearside** *n* the side of a vehicle that is by the kerb **near-sighted** *adj* short-sighted

neat *adj* **1** simple and clean and tidy **2** done or doing things in a precise and skilful way **3** undiluted ♦ *neat whisky* **neaten** *v* **neatly** *adv* **neatness** *n*

nebula (say **neb**-yoo-lə) *n pl* **nebulae** (say **neb**-yoo-lee) a bright or dark patch in the sky caused by a distant galaxy or a cloud of dust or gas **nebular** *adj* **nebulous** *adj* indistinct or vague

necessary *adj* **1** essential in order to achieve something **2** unavoidable; happening as an inevitable result ♦ *Suffering is the necessary consequence of their actions.* **necessaries** *pl n* food, warmth, and other basic needs of life **necessarily** *adv* **necessitate** *v* to make

something necessary **needy necessity** *n pl* **necessities 1** the state or fact of being necessary ♦ *the necessity for complete discretion* **2** something that is necessary

neck *n* **1** the part of the body connecting the head to the rest of the body **2** the part of a piece of clothing that covers the neck **3** a narrow opening or connecting part of anything, especially of a bottle near its mouth **4** the length of a horse's head and neck as a measure of its lead in a race **neckerchief** *n* a square of cloth worn round the neck **necklace** *n* an ornamental string of beads or precious stones worn round the neck **neckline** *n* the edge of a woman's piece of clothing at or below the neck **neck and neck** running level in a race or contest

necromancy (say **nek**-rə-man-si) *n* **1** the supposed practice of communicating with the dead in order to predict future events **2** witchcraft or sorcery **necromancer** *n*

nectar *n* **1** a sugary sweet fluid produced by plants and collected by bees for making honey **2** the drink of the gods

nectarine (say **nek**-ter-in) *n* a kind of peach with a thin smooth skin

née (say nay) *adj* born (used in giving a married woman's maiden name) ♦ *Mrs Jane Smith, née Jones*

need *v* **1** to be without something you should have ♦ *We need two more chairs.* **2** to be obliged to do something ♦ *You do not need to answer.* **need** *n* **1** circumstances in which something is needed ♦ *There was no need for them to stay.* **2** lack of the basic necessities of life, poverty **3** something you need or want ♦ *My needs are few.* **needful** *adj* necessary **needy** *adj* **needier, neediest** lacking things necessary for life, extremely poor **neediness** *n* **needless** *adj* not needed, unnecessary **needlessly** *adv* **needs must** it is necessary or unavoidable

needle *n* **1** a small thin piece of metal with a point at one end and a hole for thread at the other, used in sewing **2** a long thin piece of metal or plastic with one or both ends pointed, used in knitting **3** something that is long, thin, and sharp ♦ *The ground was covered in pine needles.* **4** the pointer of a compass or gauge **needle** *v* to annoy or provoke someone **needlecord** n a fine corduroy fabric **needlepoint** n a kind of fine embroidery on canvas **needlework** n sewing or embroidery

ne'er adv poetic never

nefarious (say ni-**fair**-iəs) adj wicked or criminal **nefariously** adv

negate (say ni-**gayt**) v 1 to make something ineffective 2 to disprove or deny something **negation** n **negative** adj 1 denying or disagreeing; giving the answer 'no' 2 involving the absence of something sought or in question ♦ Her pregnancy test was negative. 3 (said about a quantity) less than zero; minus 4 containing or producing the kind of electric charge carried by electrons **negative** n 1 a negative word or statement 2 a photographic image with reversed tones, from which positive prints can be made **negatively** adv

neglect v 1 to fail to take proper care of someone or something 2 to pay no attention to something 3 to omit or fail to do something **neglect** n neglecting or being neglected; failure to do something **neglectful** adj

negligee (say **neg**-li-zhay) n a woman's light flimsy dressing gown

negligence (say **neg**-li-jəns) n failure to take care or pay attention; carelessness **negligent** adj **negligently** adv

negligible (say **neg**-lij-ibəl) adj so small or insignificant as to be not worth taking into account

negotiate (say nig-**oh**-shi-ayt) v 1 to discuss a matter with others in order to reach an agreement or arrangement about it 2 to get over an obstacle or difficulty successfully **negotiable** adj able to be changed after being discussed ♦ The salary is negotiable. **negotiation** n **negotiator** n

Negro n pl **Negroes** a member of a dark-skinned people originating in Africa ◊ Negro and Negress are usually considered to be old-fashioned and offensive.

neigh (say nay) v (said about a horse) to make a long high-pitched cry **neigh** n this cry

neighbour n 1 a person who lives next to or near to another 2 a person or thing situated near or next to another **neighbourhood** n 1 the surrounding district or area 2 a part of a town where people live **neighbouring** adj **neighbourly** adj kind and friendly to the people living near you

neither (say **niy**-ther or **nee**-ther) adj, pronoun not either ♦ Neither road is the right one. ♦ Neither of them likes it. **neither** adv, conjunction 1 not either ♦ We neither know nor care. 2 also not ♦ They don't know and neither do I. ◊ Note that neither is followed by a singular verb (Neither road is the right one. Neither of them likes it.); but when one of its subjects is plural you use a plural verb: Neither he nor his children like it.

nelson n a kind of hold in wrestling, with the arm placed under the opponent's arm and the hand round the back of the opponent's neck

nemesis (say **nem**-i-sis) n deserved punishment that comes to someone who hoped to escape it

neo- prefix new, or a new form of something (as in neoclassical)

neoclassical adj to do with a style of art, literature, or music that is based on a classical style **neoclassicism** n

neologism (say ni-**ol**-ə-jizm) n a newly coined word or expression

neon (say **nee**-on) n a chemical element (symbol Ne), a kind of gas that glows orange-red when electricity is passed through it

nephew (say **nef**-yoo) n the son of your brother or sister

nepotism (say **nep**-ə-tizm) n showing favouritism to relatives in appointing them to jobs

nerve n 1 any of the fibres in the body that carry impulses of sensation or movement between the brain or spinal cord and parts of the body 2 courage or calmness in the face of danger ♦ It took a lot of nerve to walk through the wood in the dark. 3 impudence ♦ They had the nerve to ask for more money. **nerve** v to give strength or courage to someone **nerveless** adj 1 lacking strength or feeling 2 not nervous, confident **nerves** pl n a state of being nervous and easily upset **nervy** adj **nervier**, **nerviest**

easily agitated or nervous **nerve centre** n
1 a cluster of neurons **2** the place from
which a system or organization is controlled
nerve gas n a poison gas that affects the
nervous system **nerve-racking** adj causing
great stress or anxiety **to get on a person's
nerves** to be irritating to someone

nervous adj **1** easily agitated or excited
2 to do with the nerves or the nervous
system ♦ a nervous disorder **nervously** adv
nervousness n **nervous breakdown** n
a mental illness resulting from severe
depression and anxiety **nervous system** n
the system that sends electrical messages
from one part of the body to another,
consisting of the brain, spinal cord, and
nerves

-ness suffix forming nouns from adjectives
(as in kindness, happiness)

nest n **1** a structure or place in which a bird
lays its eggs and feeds its young **2** a place
where certain creatures live, such as mice
or wasps **3** a snug place **4** a set of similar
things that fit inside each other ♦ a nest
of tables **nest** v to make or have a nest
nestling n a bird that is too young to leave
the nest **nest egg** n a sum of money saved
up for the future

nestle v **1** to curl up comfortably **2** (said
about a place) to lie in a sheltered position

net[1] n **1** material of thread, cord, wire, etc.
woven or joined in an open mesh **2** a piece
of this used to cover or hold something **3** a
structure with a net used in various games,
e.g. as a goal in football or to divide a tennis
court **net** v **netted, netting 1** to make
netting **2** to cover something with a net
netting n a piece of net fabric **netball** n a
team game in which players try to throw a
ball into a net hanging from a ring on a high
post

net[2] adj **1** (said about an amount or value)
after tax, expenses, etc. have been
deducted **2** (said about a weight) excluding
the packing **3** (said about an effect or
result) overall, excluding incidental factors
net v **netted, netting** to earn or acquire
money as a net profit

nether (say **neth**-er) adj lower in position
♦ the nether regions **nethermost** adj

nettle n a wild plant with leaves that sting
and redden the skin when they are touched
nettle v to irritate or provoke someone
nettle rash n a rash of red patches on the
skin, caused by an allergy

network n **1** an arrangement or pattern
of intersecting lines or parts ♦ a railway
network **2** a chain of interconnected people
or operations ♦ a spy network **3** a group of
radio or television stations which broadcast
the same programmes **4** ICT a set of
computers which are linked to one another
neural (say **new**-rəl) adj to do with a nerve
or the nervous system

neurology (say new-**rol**-əji) n the study
of nerve systems and their diseases
neurological adj **neurologist** n

neuron (say **new**-ron), **neurone** (say **new**-
rohn) n a cell that is part of the nervous
system and sends impulses to and from the
brain

neurosis (say new-**roh**-sis) n pl **neuroses**
a mental disorder producing depression or
abnormal behaviour **neurotic** adj

neurosurgery n surgery performed on the
nervous system

neuter (say **new**-ter) adj **1** Gram belonging
to a class that is neither masculine nor
feminine **2** (said about an animal) sexually
undeveloped, sterile **neuter** v to remove
an animal's sexual organs so that it cannot
breed

neutral adj **1** not supporting either side in
a war or dispute **2** (said about colours) not
strong or positive; grey or fawn **neutral** n
1 a neutral person or country **2** a position
of a set of gears in which the engine
is disconnected from the driven parts
neutrality n

neutralize v to make something ineffective
or neutral **neutralization** n

neutron (say **new**-tron) n a particle with no
electric charge **neutron bomb** n a nuclear
bomb that kills people by intense radiation
but does little damage to property

never adv at no time, on no occasion
never interjection informal surely
not **nevermore** adj at no future
time **never-never** n hire purchase
nevertheless adv, conjunction in spite of

this, although this is a fact

new adj 1 not existing before; recently made, invented, discovered, or experienced 2 unfamiliar or unaccustomed ♦ I was new to the work. 3 recently changed or renewed, different ♦ His mother has got a new house. **new** adv newly, recently ♦ a new-born baby **newly** adv 1 recently 2 again, afresh **newness** n **New Age** n a modern cultural movement that promotes interest in spiritual and environmental concerns **newcomer** n a person who has recently arrived in a place **newfangled** adj new and unfamiliar, used especially about something you do not like **newly-wed** n someone who is recently married **New Testament** n the second part of the Christian Bible, including the four gospels recording the life and teaching of Jesus Christ and other writing of the early Church **new town** n a town established as a new settlement **New World** n North and South America, as distinct from Europe, Asia, and Africa **new year** n 1 the calendar year that is about to begin or has just begun 2 1 January and the days immediately following

newel (say **new**-əl) n an upright post to which the handrail of a staircase is fixed at each end

news n 1 information about recent events, or a broadcast report of this 2 new information ♦ That's news to me. **newsagent** n a shopkeeper who sells newspapers **newsflash** n a single item of important news that is broadcast to interrupt normal programmes **newsletter** n a short informal report giving information to members of an organization **newspaper** n a daily or weekly publication printed on large sheets of paper, containing news reports, articles and features, advertisements, etc. **newsprint** n the type of paper on which a newspaper is printed **newsreel** n a short cinema film of news and current affairs **newsworthy** adj important or interesting enough to be reported as news

newt n a small animal like a lizard, which can live in water or on land

newton n a unit for measuring force

next adj 1 being nearest to something ♦ The house is next to a playing field. 2 coming immediately after ♦ It happened on the next day. **next** adv in the next place; on the next occasion ♦ Shall I tell you what happened next? **next** n the next person or thing **next door** adv in the next house or room **next of kin** n a person's closest living relative

nexus n pl **nexus** or **nexuses** a connected group or series

NHS abbr National Health Service

nib n the metal tip of a pen

nibble v to take small quick or gentle bites of something **nibble** n 1 a small quick bite 2 a small piece of food

nibs n **his nibs** informal a humorous title used to refer to a self-important man

nice adj 1 pleasant or satisfactory 2 kind and considerate 3 precise or subtle ♦ a nice distinction **nicely** adv **niceness** n **nicety** n pl **niceties** 1 precision or accuracy 2 a small or precise distinction or detail

niche (say nich or neesh) n 1 a shallow recess, especially in a wall 2 a suitable job or position in life ♦ He has found his niche. 3 a specialized part of the market for selling goods or services

nick n 1 a small cut or notch 2 **the nick** informal a police station or prison **nick** v 1 to make a nick in something 2 informal to steal something 3 informal to catch or arrest a criminal **in good nick** informal in good condition **in the nick of time** only just in time

nickel n 1 a chemical element (symbol Ni), a hard silvery-white metal used in alloys 2 N. Am a five-cent piece

nickname n a familiar or humorous name for a person **nickname** v to give a nickname to someone

nicotine (say nik-ə-teen) n a poisonous oily liquid found in tobacco

niece n the daughter of your brother or sister

nifty adj informal **niftier**, **niftiest** particularly good or stylish

niggard n a mean or stingy person **niggardly** adj

niggle v to fuss over details or small faults **niggling** adj

nigh (say niy) adv, prep old use near

night n 1 the hours between sunset and sunrise, when it is dark 2 a particular night or evening ♦ Tonight is the first night of the play. **nightly** adj, adv every night **nightcap** n 1 a soft cap for wearing in bed 2 an alcoholic or hot drink taken at bedtime **nightclub** n a club that is open at night where people go to drink and dance **nightdress** n a light loose dress worn by a woman or girl in bed **nightfall** n the beginning of darkness at the end of the day **nightgown** n a nightdress or nightshirt **nightie** n informal a nightdress **nightingale** n a small reddish-brown bird that sings sweetly, often at night **nightmare** n 1 a frightening dream 2 an unpleasant or terrifying experience **nightmarish** adj **night school** n an educational institution providing evening classes **nightshade** n any of several wild plants with poisonous berries **nightshirt** n a long shirt worn in bed **night-time** n

nihilism (say niy-il-izm) n the rejection of all religious and moral principles **nihilist** n **nihilistic** adj

nil nothing or nought

nimble adj 1 able to move quickly, agile 2 able to think quickly **nimbleness** n **nimbly** adv

nincompoop n a foolish person

nine adj, n the number 9, one more than eight **ninth** adj, n 1 next after eighth 2 one of nine equal parts of a thing **ninepins** n the game of skittles played with nine pins

nineteen adj, n the number 19, one more than eighteen **nineteenth** adj, n **talk nineteen to the dozen** to talk a great deal

ninety adj, n pl **nineties** the number 90, equal to nine times ten **ninetieth** adj, n

nip¹ v nipped, nipping 1 to pinch or squeeze something sharply 2 informal to go quickly somewhere 3 to bite something with the front teeth 4 (said about the wind or cold) to cause pain or harm **nip** n 1 a sharp pinch or bite 2 sharp coldness ♦ a nip in the air **nipper** n informal a young child **nippy** adj 1 nimble or quick 2 sharply cold **nippiness** n

nip² n a small drink of spirits

nipple n a small projecting part at the centre of a mammal's breasts

nirvana (say ner-vah-nə) n (in Buddhism and Hinduism) the state of perfect happiness from spiritual enlightenment

nit n informal 1 the egg or young form of a louse or other parasite, found in the hair 2 a stupid or foolish person **nit-picking** n petty criticism or fault-finding **nitwit** n a stupid or foolish person

nitrogen (say niy-trə-jən) n a chemical element (symbol N), a colourless odourless gas forming about four-fifths of the Earth's atmosphere **nitrogenous** adj **nitrous** adj made of or containing nitrogen **nitroglycerine** n a powerful explosive **nitrous oxide** n a colourless gas used as an anaesthetic

nitty-gritty n informal the basic facts or aspects of a matter

no adj 1 not any ♦ We have no money left. 2 not a ♦ It was no easy task. **no** adv 1 used to deny or refuse something ♦ Will you come? No. 2 not at all ♦ The result is no better than before. **no** n pl **noes** a negative reply or decision, especially in voting **no-go area** n an area that certain people or groups may not enter **no man's land** n an area of territory between two opposing armies in war **no one** n no person, nobody

No., no. abbr number

nobble v informal 1 to tamper with a racehorse to prevent it from winning 2 to thwart or influence a process by underhand means 3 informal to accost someone

noble adj 1 belonging to the aristocracy by birth or rank 2 having fine qualities or character 3 grand or impressive in appearance **noble** n a person of noble birth or rank **nobility** n 1 the quality of being noble 2 people of aristocratic birth or rank, titled people **nobly** adv **noble gas** n any of a group of gases that rarely or never combine with other elements to form compounds **nobleman, noblewoman** n pl **noblemen, noblewomen** a person of noble birth or rank

nobody pronoun no person **nobody** n pl **nobodies** a person of no importance or authority

nocturnal (say nok-ter-nəl) adj

1 happening at night **2** active at night ♦ *nocturnal animals* **nocturnally** *adv*

nocturne (say **nok**-tern) *n* a short romantic piece of music

nod *v* **nodded, nodding 1** to lower and raise the head quickly as a sign of agreement or casual greeting **2** to let the head fall forward in drowsiness; to be drowsy **nod** *n* a nodding movement used to express agreement or as a casual greeting **to nod off** *informal* to fall asleep

node *n* a swelling like a small knob

nodule *n* a small rounded lump or node **nodular** *adj*

noggin *n* **1** *informal* the head **2** a small measure of alcohol, usually a quarter of a pint

noise *n* **1** a sound, especially one that is loud or unpleasant **2** disturbances or fluctuations which interfere with the sound or picture or data being processed **noiseless** *adj* **noisily** *adv* **noisy** *adj* **noisier, noisiest** making a lot of noise

noisome (say **noi**-səm) *adj* smelling unpleasant; harmful

nomad (say **noh**-mad) *n* **1** a member of a tribe that moves from place to place looking for pasture for its animals **2** a wanderer **nomadic** *adj* **nomadism** *n*

nom de plume (say nom də **ploom**) *n* a writer's pseudonym

nomenclature (say nə-**men**-klə-cher) *n* a system of names, especially those used in a science such as botany or zoology

nominal (say **nom**-in-əl) *adj* **1** in name only **2** (said about a sum of money) small but charged or paid as a token that payment is required ♦ *a nominal fee* **nominally** *adv*

nominate (say **nom**-in-ayt) *v* **1** to propose someone as a candidate for an office or honour **2** to appoint someone to a job **nomination** *n* **nominee** *n* a person who is nominated for an office or honour

non- *prefix* not

nonagenarian (say noh-nə-jin-**air**-iən) *n* a person aged between 90 and 99

nonchalant (say **non**-shə-lənt) *adj* not feeling or showing anxiety or excitement **nonchalance** *n* **nonchalantly** *adv*

non-commissioned *adj* not holding a commission ♦ *non-commissioned officers*

non-committal (say non-kə-**mi**-təl) *adj* not committing yourself to a particular policy or decision

nonconformist *n* a person who does not conform to established principles **Nonconformist** *n* a member of a Protestant Church that does not conform to the teaching of the Church of England

non-contributory *adj* not involving payment of contributions ♦ *a non-contributory pension scheme*

nondescript (say non-dis-kript) *adj* having no distinctive characteristics

none *pronoun* **1** not any **2** no one ♦ *What the truth is, none can tell.* ◊ Note that *none* can be followed by a singular or plural verb. A singular verb emphasizes each individual (*None of them has come yet.*), whereas a plural verb emphasizes the group collectively (*None of them want to go.*). **nonetheless** *adv* in spite of that; nevertheless

nonentity (say non-**en**-titi) *n pl* **nonentities** an unimportant person or thing

non-event *n* an event that was meant to be important but proves to be disappointing

non-existent *adj* not existing or real

nonpareil (say non-pə-**rayl**) *n* an unrivalled person or thing

nonplus (say non-**plus**) *v* **nonplussed, nonplussing** to perplex someone

nonsense *n* **1** words that do not make any sense **2** absurd or foolish talk, ideas, or behaviour **nonsensical** *adj* **nonsensically** *adv*

non sequitur (say non **sek**-wit-er) *n* a conclusion that does not follow from the evidence given

non-starter *n* **1** a horse which is entered for a race but does not run in it **2** *informal* a person or an idea that has no chance of succeeding

non-stick *adj* (said about a pan or surface) coated with a substance that food will not stick to during cooking

non-stop *adj, adv* not stopping or pausing

noodles *pl n* pasta made in narrow strips and used in soups or Chinese dishes

nook *n* a secluded corner or recess

noon n twelve o'clock in the day, midday

noose n a loop of rope with a knot that tightens when pulled

nor conjunction and not ♦ She didn't say anything; nor did I. ♦ They neither care nor understand.

Nordic adj belonging to a racial type that is tall and blond with blue eyes, found especially in Scandinavia

norm n a standard or type considered to be typical or acceptable

normal adj 1 conforming to what is standard or typical 2 free from mental or emotional disorders **normal** n the normal state or condition ♦ His temperature is well above normal. **normality** n **normalize** v to make something normal, or to become normal **normalization** n **normally** adv

Norman n a member of the people of Normandy in northern France, who conquered England in 1066 **Norman** adj to do with the Normans or Normandy

Norse adj to do with ancient Norway or Scandinavia **Norse** n the Norwegian language or the Scandinavian group of languages **Norseman** n pl **Norsemen** a Viking

north n 1 the point on the horizon that a compass needle normally indicates, or the direction in which this point lies, to the left of a person facing east 2 the part of a place or building that is towards the north **north** adj, adv 1 towards or in the north 2 (said about a wind) blowing from the north **northerly** adj **northern** adj **northerner** n someone who lives in the north of a country or region **northward** adj, adv **northwards** adv **north-east** n, adj, adv in, to, or from the point or direction midway between north and east **North Pole** n the northernmost point of the earth **north-west** n, adj, adv in, to, or from the point or direction midway between north and west

Norwegian adj to do with or coming from Norway **Norwegian** n 1 a person born in Norway, or descended from people born there 2 the language of Norway

Nos., nos. abbr numbers

nose n 1 the organ above the mouth in humans and animals, used for breathing and smelling 2 a sense of smell 3 an ability or instinct for detecting things of a particular kind ♦ She has a nose for scandal. 4 the front end of a vehicle or aircraft 5 the aroma of wine or other substance **nose** v 1 to rub something with the nose 2 to push your way cautiously ahead ♦ The car nosed slowly through the crowd. **nosy** adj **nosier, nosiest** inquisitive **nosily** adv **nosiness** n **nosebag** n a bag containing fodder, for hanging on a horse's head **nosebleed** n a spell of bleeding from the nose **nosedive** n a sudden drop or worsening **nosegay** n a small bunch of flowers

nosh n informal food **nosh** v informal to eat something

nostalgia (say noss-**tal**-jə) n a sentimental memory of or longing for things of the past **nostalgic** adj

nostril n each of the two openings in the nose through which air is admitted

nostrum (say **noss**-trəm) n a quack or bogus remedy

not adv expressing a negative or opposite

notary (say **noh**-ter-i) n pl **notaries** a person officially authorized to witness the signing of documents

notation n a system of signs or symbols representing numbers, quantities, or musical notes **notate** v to write something in notation

notch n 1 a small cut or indentation in a surface 2 a point or level in a graded system or scale **notch** v 1 to make a notch or notches in something 2 to score something ♦ The team notched up a win.

note n 1 a brief written record or comment 2 a short or informal letter or message 3 a banknote 4 a single tone of definite pitch 5 a significant sound or indication of feeling ♦ a note of optimism 6 eminence or distinction ♦ a family of note 7 notice or attention ♦ Take note of what they say. **note** v 1 to notice or pay attention to something 2 to write something down **notable** adj worth noticing, remarkable or famous **notable** n a famous or eminent person **notably** adv **noted** adj famous or well-known **notebook** n a book with blank pages on which to write notes **notelet** n a small sheet of folded paper, often with a design on the front, used for short informal letters **noteworthy** adj worth noting, remarkable

nothing n **1** no thing, not anything **2** no amount, nought **3** a person or thing of no importance

notice n **1** a publicly displayed sign with information or instructions **2** attention or observation ♦ It escaped my notice. **3** information about something that is about to happen **4** a formal announcement that you are about to end an agreement or leave a job ♦ You will need to give a month's notice. **5** an account or review in a newspaper **notice** v **1** to become aware of something or take notice of it **2** to remark on something or speak of it **noticeable** adj easily seen or noticed **noticeably** adv **noticeboard** n a board for displaying notices

notify v **notifies, notified, notifying** to inform someone officially or formally **notifiable** adj that must be reported officially ♦ a notifiable disease **notification** n

notion n a vague idea or opinion **notional** adj imaginary or hypothetical; assumed to be correct or valid **notionally** adv

notorious (say noh-**tor**-ies) adj well-known for a bad quality or deed **notoriety** n **notoriously** adv

notwithstanding prep in spite of **notwithstanding** adv nevertheless

nougat (say **noo**-gah) n a chewy sweet made from nuts, sugar or honey, and egg white

nought (say nawt) n **1** the figure 0 **2** nothing

noun n a word or phrase used as the name of a person, place, or thing

nourish (say **nu**-rish) v **1** to feed a person, animal, or plant **2** to foster or cherish a feeling **nourishment** n

nous (say nows) n informal common sense

nova (say **noh**-və) n pl **novae** (say **noh**-vee) or pl **novas** a star that suddenly becomes much brighter for a short time

novel n a fictional story that fills an entire book **novel** adj of a new kind, original

novelette n a short novel **novelist** n a person who writes novels **novelty** n pl **novelties 1** the quality of being new or original **2** a novel thing or occurrence **3** a small unusual object

November n the eleventh month of the year

novice (say **nov**-iss) n **1** a beginner or inexperienced person **2** a person who belongs to a religious order but has not yet taken final vows

now adv **1** at the present time, or at the time being spoken or written of **2** immediately **now** conjunction as a result of or at the same time as ♦ Now that you have come, we'll start. **now** n the present time ♦ They ought to be here by now. **nowadays** adv at the present time, as contrasted with the past **now and again** or **now and then** occasionally

nowhere adv not anywhere **nowhere** pronoun no place

noxious (say **nok**-shəs) adj unpleasant and harmful

nozzle n the spout at the end of a pipe, hose, or tube

nuance (say new-ahns) n a slight difference or shade of meaning

nub n **1** a small knob or lump **2** the central point of a matter or problem

nubile (say **new**-biyl) adj (said about a girl or woman) young but sexually mature and attractive

nuclear adj **1** to do with a nucleus or nuclei **2** using energy that is released or absorbed during reactions taking place in the nuclei of atoms ♦ nuclear weapons ♦ nuclear power **nuclear family** n a father, mother, and their child or children **nuclear reactor** n an apparatus that produces nuclear energy

nucleus (say **new**-kli-əs) n pl **nuclei** (say **new**-kli-iy) **1** the central positively charged portion of an atom **2** the central part of a seed or of a plant or animal cell **3** the part in the centre of something, round which other things are grouped

nude adj not wearing any clothes **nude** n a naked human figure as a subject in painting or photography **nudist** n a person who believes that going naked is enjoyable and good for the health **nudism** n **nudity** n

nudge v to push someone or something gently, especially with the elbow **nudge** n a light touch or push

nugatory (say **new**-gə-ter-i) adj **1** trivial or futile **2** useless or invalid

nugget (say **nug**-it) n **1** a rough lump of gold or platinum as found in the earth **2** a small but valuable fact

nuisance n a person or thing that causes annoyance or inconvenience

null adj not having any legal force **nullify** v **nullifies, nullified, nullifying 1** to make something legally invalid **2** to cancel or neutralize the effect of something **nullity** n

numb adj temporarily unable to feel or move ♦ numb with cold ♦ numb with shock **numb** v to make someone or a part of the body numb **numbly** adv **numbness** n **numbskull** n a stupid person

number n **1** a symbol or word indicating a quantity or amount, a numeral or figure **2** a numeral or set of numerals assigned to a person or thing to identify it ♦ a telephone number **3** a single issue of a magazine **4** a song or piece of music **5** a quantity or amount ♦ We could see a number of new houses. **number** v **1** to count things **2** to amount to a certain number ♦ The crowd numbered 10,000. **3** to assign a number to each in a series **4** to include someone or something in a category ♦ I number him among my dearest friends. **numberless** adj too many to count **number one** n yourself ♦ You must take care of number one. **number plate** n a plate on a motor vehicle, bearing its registration number

numeral (say **new**-mər-əl) n a symbol that represents a certain number, a figure **numerate** adj having a good basic knowledge of numbers and mathematics **numeracy** n **numeration** n numbering **numerator** n the number written above the line in a fraction, e.g. 3 in ¾ **numerical** adj of a number or series of numbers ♦ in numerical order **numerically** adv **numerous** adj many, consisting of many items

numinous (say **new**-min-əs) adj having a strong religious quality

numismatics (say new-miz-**mat**-iks) n the study of coins and medals **numismatist** n

nun n a member of a community of women who live apart from the world under the rules of a religious order

nunnery n pl **nunneries** a religious house for nuns

nuptial (say **nup**-shəl) adj to do with marriage or a wedding **nuptials** pl n a wedding

nurse n **1** a person trained to look after people who are ill or injured **2** a woman employed to look after young children **nurse** v **1** to work as a nurse **2** to look after people as a nurse **3** to feed a baby at the breast **4** to hold something carefully or protectively **nursing home** n a privately run hospital or home for invalids

nursery n pl **nurseries 1** a room or place where young children are looked after or play **2** a place where young plants are grown for sale **nurseryman** n pl **nurserymen** a person who owns or works in a plant nursery **nursery rhyme** n a simple traditional song or poem for children **nursery school** n a school for children below normal school age

nurture (say **ner**-cher) v **1** to bring up a child **2** to cherish an idea or hope **nurture** n upbringing and education

nut n **1** a fruit consisting of a hard shell round an edible kernel **2** informal the head **3** informal a crazy or eccentric person **4** a small piece of metal with a hole in its centre, for screwing on a bolt **nuts** adj crazy or eccentric **nutty** adj **nuttier, nuttiest 1** full of nuts **2** tasting like nuts **3** informal crazy or eccentric **nutcrackers** pl n a pair of pincers for cracking nuts **nutmeg** n the hard seed of a tropical tree, grated as a spice in cooking **nutshell** n **in a nutshell** stated or explained very briefly **nuts and bolts** the basic practical details of a scheme or plan

nutrient (say **new**-tri-ənt) n a substance that nourishes people

nutriment (say **new**-trim-ənt) n nourishing food

nutrition (say new-**trish**-ən) n **1** nourishment **2** the study of what nourishes people **nutritional** *adj* **nutritionally** *adv* **nutritious** *adj* nourishing

nuzzle *v* to press or rub someone or something gently with the nose

NW *abbr* north-west, north-western

nylon *n* a strong light synthetic fibre or fabric

nymph (say nimf) *n Mythology* a spirit in the form of a beautiful maiden, representing nature

NZ *abbr* New Zealand

Oo

O 1 the fifteenth letter of the English alphabet **2** the number zero, especially when spoken in a sequence of numbers

oaf *n pl* **oafs** a stupid badly-behaved or clumsy man **oafish** *adj*

oak *n* **1** a deciduous forest tree with irregularly shaped leaves, bearing seeds called acorns **2** the hard wood of this tree **oaken** *adj*

oakum *n* loose fibre obtained by picking old rope to pieces

OAP *abbr* old-age pensioner

oar *n* a pole with a flat blade at one end, used to row or steer a boat through the water **oarsman, oarswoman** *n* **oarsmen, oarswomen** *n* a rower

oasis (say oh-ay-sis) *n pl* **oases** (say oh-ay-seez) a fertile spot in a desert

oast *n* a kiln for drying hops **oast house** *n* a building containing an oast

oath *n* **1** a solemn promise to do something or that something is true, sometimes appealing to God as witness **2** a swear word, especially one using the name of God or Jesus

oats *pl n* **1** a hardy cereal plant grown in cool climates for food **2** the grain of this plant **oatcake** *n* a thin biscuit made of oatmeal **oatmeal** *n* **1** ground oats, used to make porridge, etc. **2** a greyish-fawn colour **to sow your wild oats** to lead a wild life while young, before settling down

ob- *prefix* (changing to **oc-** before *c*, **of-** before *f*, **op-** before *p*) **1** to or towards (as in *observe*) **2** against (as in *opponent*) **3** in the way, blocking (as in *obstruct*)

obbligato (say obli-**gah**-toh) *n pl* **obbligatos** or **obbligati** an important accompanying part in a musical composition

obdurate (say **ob**-dewr-ət) *adj* stubbornly refusing to change your mind **obduracy** *n*

OBE *abbr* Order of the British Empire

obeisance (say ə-**bay**-səns) *n* **1** an attitude of great respect or deference **2** a deep bow or curtsy showing respect

obelisk (say **ob**-əl-isk) *n* a tall pillar set up as a monument or landmark

obese (say ə-**beess**) *adj* very fat **obesity** *n*

obey *v* **obeyed, obeying 1** to do what you are told to do **2** to behave in accordance with a rule ♦ *Even pole vaulters must eventually obey the law of gravity.* **obedient** *adj* willing to obey **obedience** *n* **obediently** *adv*

obituary (say ə-**bit**-yoo-eri) *n pl* **obituaries** a notice of a person's death, especially in a newspaper, often with a short account of his or her life

object[1] (say **ob**-jikt) *n* **1** something solid that can be seen or touched **2** a person or thing to which some action or feeling is directed ♦ *She has become an object of pity.* **3** a purpose or intention **4** *Gram* a noun or its equivalent acted upon by a transitive verb or by a preposition ('him' is the object in *the dog bit him* and *against him*) **objective** *adj* **1** not influenced by personal feelings ♦ *an objective account of the problem* **2** having real existence outside a person's mind ♦ *Dreams have no objective existence.* **objective** *n* what you are trying to achieve or reach **objectively** *adv* **no object** not an obstacle or problem ♦ *Money is no object.*

object[2] (say əb-**jekt**) *v* to say that you are not in favour of something ♦ *Many residents objected to the plans for a new supermarket.* **objection** *n* **objectionable** *adj* causing objections, unpleasant **objectionably** *adv* **objector** *n*

objet d'art (say ob-zhay **dar**) *n pl* **objets d'art** (say ob-zhay **dar**) a small artistic or decorative object

oblation (say əb-**lay**-shən) *n* an offering to God or a god

oblige *v* 1 to force or compel someone by law, agreement, custom, or necessity ♦ *You are not obliged to answer our questions.* 2 to help someone by performing a favour ♦ *Can you oblige me with a loan?* **obligation** *n* 1 a duty 2 a debt to another person for some favour **obligatory** *adj* required; compulsory **obliging** *adj* willing to be helpful or do a favour **obligingly** *adv*

oblique (say ə-**bleek**) *adj* 1 slanting 2 expressed indirectly, not going straight to the point ♦ *an oblique reply* **obliquely** *adv* **oblique angle** *n* an acute or obtuse angle

obliterate (say ə-**blit**-er-ayt) *v* 1 to destroy something completely, leaving no traces 2 to blot something out **obliteration** *n*

oblivious (say ə-**bliv**-iəs) *adj* completely unaware ♦ *She seemed oblivious to the danger.* ♦ *I was oblivious of my surroundings.* **oblivion** *n* 1 the state of being unconscious or unaware of what is happening around you 2 the state of being forgotten

oblong *n* a rectangular shape that is longer than it is wide **oblong** *adj* having this shape

obnoxious (say əb-**nok**-shəs) *adj* extremely unpleasant **obnoxiously** *adv*

oboe (say **oh**-boh) *n* a woodwind instrument of treble pitch **oboist** *n*

obscene (say əb-**seen**) *adj* indecent in a very offensive way **obscenely** *adv* **obscenity** *n pl* **obscenities** 1 being obscene 2 an obscene action or expression ♦ *Some members of the crowd shouted obscenities at him.*

obscure *adj* 1 hard to see properly 2 not easy to understand 3 not well known ♦ *an obscure poet of the eighteenth century* **obscure** *v* 1 to keep something from being seen ♦ *Clouds obscured the sun.* 2 to make something unclear **obscurity** *n*

obsequies (say **ob**-si-kwiz) *pl n* funeral rites

obsequious (say əb-**see**-kwi-əs) *adj* too willing to obey or serve someone **obsequiously** *adv* **obsequiousness** *n*

observance *n* the keeping of a law, rule, or custom, etc.

observe *v* 1 to see and notice something; to watch something carefully 2 to pay attention to a rule or law 3 to make a remark **observable** *adj* **observant** *adj* quick at noticing things **observation** *n* 1 watching something carefully ♦ *This will test your powers of observation.* 2 a comment or remark **observatory** *n pl* **observatories** a room or building equipped for observation of the stars or weather **observer** *n*

obsess (say əb-**sess**) *v* to occupy a person's thoughts continually ♦ *My sister is obsessed with clothes.* **obsession** *n* **obsessional** *adj* **obsessive** *adj* **obsessively** *adv*

obsidian (say əb-**sid**-i-ən) *n* a dark glassy kind of hardened lava or volcanic rock

obsolete (say **ob**-sə-leet) *adj* no longer used, out of date **obsolescent** *adj* becoming obsolete ♦ *an obsolescent missile system* **obsolescence** *n*

obstacle *n* something that stands in the way or hinders progress

obstetrics (say əb-**stet**-riks) *n* the branch of medicine and surgery that deals with childbirth **obstetric** *adj* **obstetrician** *n*

obstinate *adj* 1 stubbornly refusing to change your mind, not easily persuaded 2 not easily overcome ♦ *an obstinate problem* **obstinacy** *n* **obstinately** *adv*

obstreperous (say əb-**strep**-er-əs) *adj* noisy and unruly **obstreperously** *adv*

obstruct *v* 1 to be or get in the way of something ♦ *A parked car was obstructing the entrance to their house.* 2 to prevent something from making progress ♦ *The Opposition have said they intend to obstruct the immigration bill.* **obstruction** *n*

obtain *v* to get or come into possession of something **obtainable** *adj*

obtrude (say əb-**trood**) *v* 1 to become obtrusive 2 to force yourself or your opinions on someone **obtrusion** *n* **obtrusive** *adj* unpleasantly noticeable ♦ *Didn't you find the music obtrusive?* **obtrusively** *adv*

obtuse (say əb-**tewss**) *adj* 1 slow to understand something 2 of blunt shape, not sharp or pointed **obtusely** *adv* **obtuseness** *n* **obtuse angle** *n* an angle of more than 90° but less than 180°

obverse (say **ob**-verss) *n* the side of a

coin or medal that bears the head or the principal design

obviate (say **ob**-vi-ayt) v to make something unnecessary ♦ *The bypass obviates the need to drive through the town.*

obvious adj easy to see or recognize or to understand **obviously** adv

occasion n **1** the time at which a particular event takes place **2** a special event or celebration ♦ *The wedding was a very happy occasion.* **3** a suitable time for doing something, an opportunity **4** formal a need, reason, or cause ♦ *I have little occasion to visit them these days.* **occasion** v formal to cause something **occasional** adj **1** happening from time to time ♦ *occasional showers* **2** produced, used, or meant for a special event ♦ *an occasional table* **occasionally** adv

Occident (say **oks**-i-dənt) n the countries of the West, as opposed to the Orient **Occidental** adj

occlude v to obstruct something or stop it up **occlusion** n

occult (say ə-**kult**) adj to do with the supernatural or magic **the occult** n supernatural beliefs or events

occupation n **1** a person's profession **2** something you do to keep yourself busy or pass the time **3** capturing a country or region by military force **occupational** adj to do with or caused by your occupation ♦ *an occupational disease* **occupational therapy** n creative activities designed to help people recover from certain illnesses

occupy v **occupies, occupied, occupying** **1** to live or work in a place **2** to take up or fill space or time ♦ *Looking after the baby seems to occupy most of her time.* **3** to keep someone busy ♦ *She has plenty to occupy herself with in her retirement.* **4** to enter and stay in a place by force **5** to hold a position or job ♦ *He occupies the post of finance director.* **occupant** n a person who occupies a place or position **occupancy** n **occupier** n

occur v **occurred, occurring 1** to happen or take place **2** to exist ♦ *These plants occur in marshy areas.* **occurrence** n **to occur to** to come into your mind ♦ *An idea has just occurred to me.*

ocean n the expanse of sea surrounding the continents of the earth ♦ *the Pacific Ocean* **oceanic** adj **oceanography** n the scientific study of the sea **oceanographer** n **ocean-going** adj (said about ships) made for crossing the sea

ochre (say **oh**-kər) n **1** a yellow, red, or brownish mineral **2** pale brownish yellow

o'clock adv used to specify the hour when telling the time ♦ *six o'clock*

octa-, octo- prefix eight

octagon (say **ok**-tə-gən) n a geometric figure with eight sides **octagonal** (say ok-**tag**-ən-əl) adj

octahedron (say oktə-**hee**-drən) n pl **octahedra** (say oktə-**hee**-drə) or pl **octahedrons** a solid geometric shape with eight faces

octave (say **ok**-tiv) n Mus the series of eight notes filling the interval between one note and the next note of the same name above or below it

octet (say ok-**tet**) n a group of eight musicians, or a musical composition for eight voices or instruments

October n the tenth month of the year

octogenarian (say ok-toh-jin-**air**-iən) n a person who is between 80 and 89 years old

octopus n pl **octopuses** a sea creature with eight long tentacles and a soft body

ocular (say **ok**-yoo-lər) adj to do with the eyes or vision

odd adj **1** strange or unusual ♦ *This is all very odd.* ♦ *an odd sort of person* **2** occasional ♦ *do the crossword at odd moments.* **3** (said about a number) not even, not exactly divisible by two **4** being part of a pair or set ♦ *an odd glove* ♦ *several odd volumes of an encyclopedia* **oddity** n pl **oddities** a strange person or thing **oddly** adv **oddment** n something left over from a larger piece or set **oddness** n **odds** pl n **1** the chances that a certain thing will happen; this expressed as a ratio ♦ *The odds are 5 to 1 against throwing a six.* **2** the balance of advantage or strength ♦ *She somehow won against all the odds.* **oddball** n a strange or eccentric person **odds and ends** pl n miscellaneous items or pieces left over

ode n a poem expressing noble feelings

often addressed to a person or thing

odious (say **oh**-di-əs) *adj* extremely unpleasant; detestable **odiousness** *n* **odium** *n* widespread hatred or disgust felt towards a person or actions

odour (say **oh**-dər) *n* a smell, especially an unpleasant one **odorous** *adj* **odourless** *adj*

odyssey (say **od**-iss-i) *n pl* **odysseys** a long adventurous journey

o'er *prep, adv* old use, poetic over

oesophagus (say ee-**sof**-ə-gəs) *n pl* **oesophagi** (say ee-**sof**-ə-jiy) or *pl* **oesophaguses** the tube from the throat to the stomach

oestrogen (say **ees**-trə-jən) *n* a hormone capable of developing and maintaining female bodily characteristics

of *prep* **1** belonging to ♦ *a friend of mine* ♦ *the poems of Ted Hughes* **2** concerning or showing ♦ *news of the disaster* ♦ *a map of France* **3** composed or made from ♦ *a house built of brick* ♦ *a farm of 100 acres* **4** with reference or regard to ♦ *I've never heard of it.* **5** for, involving, or directed towards ♦ *the love of your country*

off *adv* **1** away, at, or to a distance ♦ *The bandits rode off.* ♦ *My exams are six months off.* **2** out of position, not touching or attached, separate ♦ *Can you take the lid off?* **3** disconnected, not working, no longer obtainable, cancelled ♦ *Turn the gas off.* ♦ *The match is off because of snow.* ♦ *You had better take the day off.* **off** *prep* not on; away or down from ♦ *She fell off a ladder.* **off** *adj* **1** (said about food) no longer fresh **2** not satisfactory **offbeat** *adj* unconventional or unusual **off chance** *n* a slight possibility **off-colour** *adj* slightly unwell **offcut** *n* a piece of wood, hardboard, etc. that is left behind after cutting a larger piece **offhand** *adj* rather casual and without thought or consideration, often in a way that seems rude **offhand** *adv* without previous thought or preparation ♦ *Offhand I can't think of anyone who would be suitable.* **offhanded** *adj* **offhandedly** *adv* **off-licence** *n* a shop with a licence to sell alcoholic drinks to be drunk away from the shop **off-limits** *adj* out of bounds **off-line** *adj* not directly controlled by or

connected to a computer **offload** *v* to get rid of something **offset** *v* past tense and past participle **offset**; **offsetting** to counterbalance or compensate for something **offshoot** *n* **1** a side shoot on a plant **2** something that develops from something else **offside** *adj, adv* (said about a player in football, etc.) in a position where the rules do not allow him or her to play the ball **offspring** *n pl* **offspring** a person's child or children **off-white** *n* white with a grey or yellowish tinge **in the offing** likely to happen soon

offal *n* the organs of an animal (e.g. heart, kidneys, liver) used as food

offend *v* **1** to cause offence or displeasure to someone **2** to do wrong or commit a crime ♦ *criminals who persistently offend* **offence** *n* **1** breaking of the law, an illegal act **2** a feeling of annoyance or resentment ♦ *I didn't think anyone would take offence.* **offender** *n* **offensive** *adj* **1** causing offence ♦ *offensive remarks* **2** disgusting or repulsive ♦ *an offensive smell* **3** used in attacking ♦ *offensive weapons* **offensive** *n* a forceful attack or campaign **offensively** *adv* **offensiveness** *n*

offer *v* **1** to present something so that people can accept it if they want **2** to state what you are willing to do, pay, or give **offer** *n* **1** an expression of willingness to give, do, or pay something **2** an amount offered ♦ *offers above £500* **3** a specially reduced price **offering** *n* something that is offered **offertory** *n pl* **offertories** **1** in the Christian Church, the offering of bread and wine for consecration at the Eucharist **2** a collection of money made at a religious service

office *n* **1** a room or building used as a place of business, especially for clerical work ♦ *the enquiry office* ♦ *an office job* **2** a government department ♦ *the Foreign and Commonwealth Office* **3** an important position of authority or trust ♦ *He has announced that he seeks office as president.* ♦ *She holds the office of Attorney-General.* **4** an authorized form of Christian worship ♦ *the Office for the Dead* **officer** *n* **1** a person holding a position of authority or trust

♦ *customs officers* **2** a person who holds authority in any of the armed forces **3** a member of the police force

official *adj* **1** to do with an authority or public body ♦ *in his official capacity* **2** done or said by someone with authority ♦ *The news is official.* **official** *n* a person holding a position of authority **officially** *adv*

officiate *v* to be in charge of a meeting, ceremony, etc. ◊ Do not confuse this word with *officious*, which has a different meaning.

officious (say ə-**fish**-əs) *adj* too ready to give orders, bossy ◊ Do not confuse this word with *official*, which has a different meaning.

oft *adv old use* often

often *adv* frequently, many times

ogle (say **oh**-gəl) *v* to stare at someone in a lustful way

ogre *n* **1** a man-eating giant in fairy tales and legends **2** a terrifying person

oh *interjection* an exclamation of surprise, delight, disappointment, etc.

ohm (say ohm) *n* a unit of electrical resistance

OHMS *abbr* On Her (or His) Majesty's Service

oil *n* **1** a thick slippery liquid that will not dissolve in water **2** a form of petroleum used as fuel or lubricant **3** petroleum **4** oil paint **oil** *v* to put oil on something, especially to make it work smoothly **oily** *adj* **oilier, oiliest, oilcloth** *n* strong fabric treated with oil to make it waterproof **oilfield** *n* an area where oil is found in the ground or beneath the sea **oil paint** *n* paint made by mixing powdered pigment in oil **oil rig** *n* a structure with equipment for drilling for oil **oilskin** *n* cloth made waterproof by treatment with oil

oink *n* the grunting sound that a pig makes **oink** *v* to make this sound

ointment *n* a thick slippery paste rubbed on the skin to heal sore skin and cuts

OK, okay *adv, adj informal* all right, satisfactory **OK** *n informal* approval, agreement to a plan, etc. **OK** *v* **OK's, OK'ed, OK'ing** *informal* to give your approval or agreement to something

okapi (say ə-**kah**-pi) *n pl* **okapis** an animal of Central Africa, like a giraffe but with a shorter neck

okra (say **oh**-krə or **ok**-rə) *n* a tropical plant with edible seed pods

old *adj* **1** having lived or existed for a long time **2** from long ago **3** of a particular age ♦ *He is ten years old.* ♦ *a ten-year-old* **4** former or original ♦ *in its old place* **olden** *adj* of former times ♦ *the olden days* **oldie** *n informal* an old person or thing **old age** *n* the period of a person's life from about 65 or 70 onwards **old-age pension** *n* a state pension paid to people above a certain age **old-age pensioner** *n* **old boy, old girl** *n* a former pupil of a school **Old English** *n* the English language from about 700 to 1150, also called *Anglo-Saxon* **old-fashioned** *adj* having the styles, views, or tastes current a long time ago **old hand** *n* a person with a lot of experience **old maid** *n* a single woman thought of as too old to get married **old master** *n* **1** a great painter of former times, especially the 13th-17th centuries in Europe **2** a painting by such a painter **Old Nick** *n* a name for the Devil **Old Testament** *n* the first part of the Christian Bible, telling of the history of the Jews **Old World** *n* Europe, Asia, and Africa, as distinct from the Americas

oleaginous (say oh-li-**aj**-in-əs) *adj* oily or greasy

oleander (say oh-li-**an**-der) *n* a poisonous evergreen shrub of Mediterranean regions with red, white, or pink flowers

olfactory (say ol-**fak**-ter-i) *adj* to do with the sense of smell ♦ *olfactory organs*

oligarchy (say **ol**-i-gar-ki) *n pl* **oligarchies 1** government by a small group of people **2** a country governed in this way **oligarch** *n*

olive *n* **1** a small oval fruit with a hard stone and bitter flesh from which oil is obtained **2** the evergreen tree that bears it **olive** *adj* **1** greyish-green like an unripe olive **2** (said about the complexion) yellowish-brown **olive branch** *n* something done or offered to show that you want to make peace

Olympiad (say ə-**limp**-i-ad) *n* a celebration of the Olympic Games

Olympian (say ə-**limp**-i-ən) *adj* **1** to do with Mount Olympus in Greece, traditiona home of the Greek gods **2** fit for or like a god; majestic, imposing, or aloof **Olympian** n a competitor in the Olympic Games

Olympic Games pl n an international sports festival held every four years in a different part of the world **Olympic** adj to do with the Olympic Games **Olympics** pl n the Olympic Games

ombudsman (say **om**-buudz-mən) n pl **ombudsmen** an official appointed to investigate individuals' complaints against government organizations, etc.

omega (say **oh**-mig-ə) n the last letter of the Greek alphabet

omelette (say **om**-lit) n a dish made of beaten eggs cooked in a frying pan

omen (say **oh**-men) n an event regarded as a sign of what is going to happen in the future **ominous** adj making you think that something bad is going to happen ♦ an ominous silence **ominously** adv

omit v omitted, omitting **1** to leave or miss something out **2** to fail to do something **omission** n

omni- prefix all

omnibus n **1** a single edition of two or more books or radio or television programmes **2** old use a bus

omnipotent (say əm-**nip**-ə-tənt) adj having unlimited power **omnipotence** n

omnipresent adj present everywhere

omniscient (say om-**niss**-iənt) adj knowing everything **omniscience** n

omnivorous (say om-**niv**-er-əs) adj **1** feeding on both plants and animal flesh **2** reading or taking in whatever comes your way **omnivore** n an omnivorous animal

on prep **1** supported by, attached to, or covering something ♦ We sat on the floor. ♦ Have you got any money on you? **2** in the area or direction of ♦ They live on the coast. ♦ The army advanced on Paris. **3** (said about time) exactly at, during ♦ on the next day ♦ on my birthday **4** in a certain manner or state ♦ The house was on fire. ♦ Be on your best behaviour. **5** about or concerning ♦ a book on grammar **on** adv **1** so as to be supported by, attached to, or covering something ♦ Make sure you put the lid on

tightly. **2** further forward ♦ Let's move on to another subject. ♦ from that day on **3** with continued movement or action ♦ She slept on all morning. **4** in operation or activity ♦ Someone left the light on all night. **5** taking place ♦ Where is the film on? **on** n (in cricket) the part of the field opposite the off side and in front of the batsman **oncoming** adj approaching, coming towards you ♦ oncoming traffic **ongoing** adj continuing, still in progress **online** adj, adv connected to a computer, the Internet, etc. **onlooker** n a spectator **onset** n the beginning of something ♦ the onset of winter **onslaught** n a fierce attack **onto** prep to a position on ◊ Note that onto cannot be used where on is an adverb, e.g. We walked on to the river (continued walking until we reached it). Compare this with We walked onto the escalator. **onward** adv, adj going or moving forward, further on **onwards** adv **to be on** to be acceptable or practical ♦ This plan just isn't on. **to be on about** informal to keep talking about something in a boring way ♦ He's always on about his pigeons. **to be on to something** to have a good idea or realize the importance of something

once adv **1** for one time or on one occasion only ♦ They came only once. **2** formerly ♦ people who once lived here **once** conjunction as soon as ♦ You can go once I have taken your names. **once** n one time or occurrence ♦ Once is enough. **once-over** n a rapid inspection or search ♦ I'd better give the tyres the once-over. **at once 1** immediately **2** at the same time

one adj single **one** n **1** the smallest whole number, **1 2** a single thing or person **one** pronoun **1** a person or thing previously mentioned ♦ The town is full of restaurants but I've yet to find one I like. **2** a person ♦ loved ones **3** any person; the speaker or writer as representing people in general ♦ One doesn't want to seem mean. **one-armed bandit** n a fruit machine operated by pulling down a long handle at the side **one-sided** adj **1** with one side or person in a contest, conversation, etc. being much stronger or doing it more than the other ♦ a one-sided match **2** showing only one

point of view in an unfair way ♦ *This is a very one-sided account of what happened.*
one-upmanship n the art of gaining a psychological advantage over someone else **one-way** adj where traffic is allowed to travel in one direction only **one by one** separately and in succession
onerous (say **ohn**-ər-əs) adj difficult to bear or do; burdensome
oneself pronoun the form of the pronoun *one* used in reflexive constructions
onion n a vegetable with an edible rounded bulb that has a strong smell and flavour
only adj being the one specimen or all the specimens of a class ♦ *my only wish* **only** adv 1 no more than, without anything or anyone else ♦ *There are only three cakes left.* 2 no longer ago than ♦ *I saw her only yesterday.* **only** conjunction except that, but then ♦ *He often makes promises, only he never keeps them.*
o.n.o. abbr or nearest offer
onomatopoeia (say on-ə-mat-ə-**pee**-ə) n the formation of words that imitate or suggest what they stand for, e.g. *cuckoo, plop, sizzle* **onomatopoeic** adj
ontology (say on-**tol**-əji) n a branch of philosophy dealing with the nature of being **ontological** adj
onus (say **oh**-nəs) n a duty or responsibility ♦ *The onus is on the prosecution to prove he did it.*
onyx (say **on**-iks) n a stone like marble with different colours in layers
oodles n informal a great quantity
ooze v 1 (said about liquid) to trickle or flow out slowly 2 to show a quality freely ♦ *She oozes confidence on the tennis court.* **ooze** n mud at the bottom of a river or sea
opal n a quartz-like stone with a rainbow sheen **opalescent** adj having a rainbow sheen like an opal **opalescence** n
opaque (say ə-**payk**) adj 1 not able to be seen through; not transparent 2 not clear, difficult to understand **opacity** n
OPEC (say **oh**-pek) abbr Organization of Petroleum Exporting Countries
open adj 1 not closed; not sealed or locked 2 not covered or blocked up 3 not limited or restricted ♦ *an open championship*

4 letting in visitors or customers 5 spread out, unfolded 6 honest and frank ♦ *with open hostility* 7 not yet settled or decided ♦ *an open mind* v 1 to make something open ♦ *Open your books on page 72.* 2 to begin something ♦ *Who would like to open the discussion?* ♦ *The play opens next month* ♦ *Open fire!* **open** n 1 (**the open**) open space or open air 2 (**Open**) a championship or competition with no restriction on who can take part **opener** n **opening** n **openly** adv
openness n **open-and-shut** adj perfectly straightforward ♦ *an open-and-shut case*
opencast adj (said about a mine or mining) with layers of earth removed from the surface and worked from above, not from underground shafts **open day** n a day when the public may visit a place that is not normally open to them **open-ended** adj with no fixed limit ♦ *an open-ended ticket* **open-handed** adj generous in giving **open-hearted** adj warm and kindly **open-heart surgery** n surgery with the heart exposed and with blood circulating temporarily through a bypass **open house** n a place where all visitors are welcome **open letter** n a letter of comment or protest addressed to a person by name but printed in a newspaper **open-minded** adj willing to consider new ideas **open-plan** adj (said about a room or building) having no or few dividing walls between areas ♦ *an open-plan office* **open prison** n a prison with few physical restraints on the prisoners
opera n 1 a play in which the words are sung to a musical accompaniment 2 dramatic works of this kind **operatic** adj **opera glasses** pl n small binoculars used at the opera or theatre
operate v 1 to make a machine, process, etc work or function ♦ *He operates the lift.* 2 to be in action; to produce an effect ♦ *The new tax operates to our advantage.* 3 to perform a surgical or other operation **operable** adj 1 able to be treated by a surgical operation 2 able to be operated **operation** n 1 operating or being operated 2 the way a thing works 3 a piece of work, something to be done ♦ *begin operations* 4 a business organization 5 an act performed by a

surgeon on part of the body to take away or repair a diseased, injured, or deformed part **operational** adj 1 in or ready for use ♦ *Is the system operational yet?* 2 to do with the operation of an organization **operative** adj 1 working or functioning 2 (said about a word) having most significance in a phrase **operative** n a worker, especially a skilled one **operator** n

operetta n a short or light opera

ophthalmic (say off-**thal**-mik) adj to do with or for the eyes **ophthalmia** n inflammation of the eye, especially conjunctivitis **ophthalmology** n the scientific study of the eye and its diseases **ophthalmologist** n **ophthalmic optician** n a person who is qualified to examine a person's eyes and to prescribe glasses and contact lenses as well as to sell them

opinion n 1 what you think of something 2 a judgement or comments given by an expert who is consulted ♦ *a medical opinion* **opine** v to express an opinion **opinionated** adj having strong opinions

opium n an addictive drug made from the juice of certain poppies, smoked or chewed as a narcotic, and occasionally used in medicine as a sedative **opiate** n 1 a sedative drug containing opium 2 something that soothes the feelings or dulls activity

opossum (say ə-**poss**-əm) n a small furry American or Australian marsupial

opponent n a person or group opposing another in a contest or war

opportunity n pl **opportunities** a suitable time or set of circumstances for doing something **opportune** adj at a favourable time **opportunist** n a person who is quick to take advantage of opportunities, often in an unprincipled way **opportunism** n **opportunistic** adj taking advantage of opportunities

oppose v 1 to argue or fight against someone or something 2 to place something or be in opposition to something else **opposition** n 1 resistance, being hostile or in conflict or disagreement 2 the people who oppose something; your competitors or rivals 3 a contrast **the Opposition** the chief parliamentary party opposing the one that is in power **as opposed to** in contrast with

opposite adj 1 having a position on the other or further side, facing ♦ *on the opposite side of the road* 2 moving away from or towards each other ♦ *The trains were travelling in opposite directions.* 3 as different as possible from ♦ *opposite characters* ♦ *the opposite end of the price range* **opposite** n an opposite person or thing **opposite** adv, prep in an opposite place, position, or direction to a person or thing ♦ *I'll sit opposite.* ♦ *They live opposite the school.*

oppress v 1 to govern or treat someone harshly, cruelly, or unjustly 2 to weigh someone down with worry or unhappiness **oppression** n **oppressive** adj 1 cruel or harsh ♦ *an oppressive regime* 2 worrying and difficult to bear 3 (said about weather) unpleasantly hot and humid **oppressively** adv **oppressor** n

opprobrium (say ə-**proh**-briəm) n harsh criticism or scorn **opprobrious** adj

opt v to make a choice **option** n 1 a thing that is or may be chosen ♦ *None of the options is satisfactory.* 2 the freedom or right to choose ♦ *He had no option but to go.* 3 the right to buy or sell something at a certain price within a set time ♦ *We have 10 days' option on the house.* **optional** adj available to be chosen but not compulsory **to opt out** to choose not to take part in something

optic adj to do with the eye or the sense of sight **optic** n a device for measuring out spirits from a bottle **optics** n the scientific study of sight and the behaviour of light **optical** adj **optician** n a person qualified to prescribe and dispense glasses and contact lenses, and to detect eye diseases **optical fibre** n thin glass fibre used in fibre optics **optical illusion** n a mental misinterpretation of something you see, caused by its deceptive appearance

optimism n a tendency to take a hopeful view of things, or to expect that results will be good **optimist** n **optimistic** adj **optimistically** adv

optimum adj best or most favourable

optimum *n* the best or most favourable conditions or amount, etc. **optimal** *adj*

optimize *v* to make something as effective or favourable as possible **optimization** *n*

opulent (say op-yoo-lənt) *adj* 1 wealthy or luxurious 2 plentiful or abundant **opulence** *n*

opus (say oh-pəs) *n pl* **opuses** or **opera** (say op-er-ə) an artistic work

or *conjunction* used to join choices or alternatives ♦ *Do you want rice or chips?*

-or *suffix* forming nouns meaning 'a person or thing that does something' (as in *tailor, refrigerator*)

oracle *n* 1 a place where the ancient Greeks consulted one of their gods for advice or a prophecy 2 the reply given 3 a person or thing thought of as able to give wise guidance **oracular** *adj*

oral (say or -əl) *adj* 1 spoken, not written ♦ *oral evidence* 2 to do with the mouth; done or taken by the mouth **oral** *n* a spoken examination or test **orally** *adv* ◊ Do not confuse this word with *aural*, which has a different meaning.

orange *n* 1 a round juicy citrus fruit with reddish-yellow peel 2 a reddish-yellow colour **orangeade** *n* a fizzy orange-flavoured soft drink **Orangeman** *n pl* **Orangemen** a member of the Orange Order, a Protestant political society

orang-utan (say or-ang-oo-tan) *n* a large long-armed ape with long red hair

oration (say ə-ray-shən) *n* a long formal speech, especially one given on a ceremonial occasion

oratorio (say o-rə-tor -i-oh) *n pl* **oratorios** a musical composition for solo voices, chorus, and orchestra, usually with a religious theme

oratory[1] (say o-rə-ter-i) *n* 1 the art of public speaking 2 eloquent speech **orator** *n* a person who is good at making speeches in public **oratorical** *adj*

oratory[2] (say o-rə-ter-i) *n pl* **oratories** a small private chapel

orb *n* 1 a sphere or globe 2 an ornamental globe with a cross on top, held on ceremonial occasions by a monarch

orbit *n* 1 the curved path of a planet, satellite, or spacecraft, etc. around a star or planet ♦ *The spacecraft was now in orbit around the moon.* 2 the range of someone's influence or control **orbit** *v* **orbited** **orbiting** to move in an orbit around a star or planet ♦ *The satellite has been orbiting the earth since 1986.* **orbital** *adj* **orbiter** *n*

orchard *n* a piece of land planted with fruit trees

orchestra *n* 1 a large group of people playing various musical instruments including stringed and wind instruments 2 (also **orchestra pit**) the part of a theatre where the orchestra plays, in front of the stalls and lower than the stage **orchestral** *adj* **orchestrate** **orchestration** *n*

orchid (say or -kid) *n* a plant of a family with showy often irregularly-shaped flowers

ordain *v* 1 to make a person a member of the clergy in the Christian Church 2 to declare or order something **ordinance** *n* an order or rule made by authority, a decree **ordination** *n* ordaining or being ordained as a member of the clergy

ordeal (say or-**deel**) *n* a difficult or horrific experience

order *n* 1 a state in which everything is in its proper place or state 2 the way in which things are arranged ♦ *in alphabetical order* ♦ *Are these pages in the right order.* 3 a command, an instruction given with authority 4 a request for goods to be supplied or food to be served; the goods themselves 5 a kind, sort, or quality ♦ *She showed courage of the highest order.* 6 a rank or class in society ♦ *the lower orders* 7 a group of monks or nuns who live by certain religious rules 8 a company of people to which distinguished people are admitted as an honour or reward ♦ *the Order of the Garter* 9 a group of plants or animals classified as similar **order** *v* 1 to issue a command 2 to give an order for goods, etc. to be supplied 3 to arrange things methodically **orders** *pl n* the status of being ordained as a member of the clergy **orderly** *adj* 1 well arranged, tidy 2 methodical 3 well-behaved and obedient ♦ *an orderly crowd* **orderly** *n pl* **orderlies** 1 an attendant in a hospital 2 a soldier whose job is to assist an officer or carry orders **orderliness** n **in order 1** in the correct condition **2** appropriate ♦ *I think congratulations are in order.* **in order to** or **that** with the intention that, for the purpose of **out of order 1** not working properly or at all **2** *informal* not acceptable or wrong

ordinal number n a number that denotes a position in a series (*first, fifth, twentieth,* etc.)

ordinary *adj* usual or normal, not special **ordinarily** *adv* **ordinary seaman** n a sailor in the Royal Navy ranking lower than an able seaman

ordnance n weapons and other military equipment **Ordnance Survey** n an official survey organization that prepares accurate and detailed maps of the British Isles

ordure (say or -dewr) n dung or excrement

ore n solid rock or mineral from which metal can be extracted ♦ *iron ore*

oregano (say o-ri-**gah**-noh) n the dried leaves of wild marjoram used as a herb in cooking

organ n **1** a musical keyboard instrument consisting of pipes that sound notes when air is forced through them **2** a part of an animal or plant body with a particular function ♦ *digestive organs* ♦ *organs of speech* **3** a newspaper or journal that puts forward the views of a particular group **organist** n a person who plays the organ

organdie n a kind of thin stiff cotton fabric

organic (say or-**gan**-ik) *adj* **1** to do with or formed from living things ♦ *organic matter* **2** (said about food, etc.) produced without the use of artificial fertilizers or pesticides ♦ *organic farming* **3** organized or arranged as a system of related parts ♦ *The business forms an organic whole.* **4** developing or growing naturally **organically** *adv* **organism** n a living being, an individual animal or plant **organic chemistry** n chemistry of carbon compounds

organize v **1** to make arrangements or preparations for something ♦ *He helped to organize a fund-raising concert.* **2** to arrange things in an orderly or systematic way **organization** n **1** an organized body

of people **2** the organizing of something **organizational** *adj* **organizer** n

orgasm (say or -gazm) n the climax of sexual excitement **orgasmic** *adj*

orgy n pl **orgies 1** a wild party that involves a lot of drinking and sex **2** an extravagant activity ♦ *an orgy of spending*

oriel window (say or -i-əl) n a kind of projecting window in an upper storey

Orient (say or -i-ənt) n the countries of the East, especially east Asia **Oriental** *adj* to do with the countries east of the Mediterranean Sea, especially China and Japan

orient (say or -i-ənt), **orientate** v **1** to place or determine the position of a thing with regard to the points of the compass ♦ *orient a map* **2** to face or direct something towards a certain direction **orientation** n **orienteering** n the sport of finding your way on foot across rough country with a map and compass **to orient yourself 1** to get your bearings **2** to become accustomed to a new situation

orifice (say o-ri-fiss) n an opening

origami (say o-ri-**gah**-mi) n the Japanese art of folding paper into attractive shapes and figures

origin n **1** the point, source, or cause from which a thing begins **2** a person's ancestry or background ♦ *a man of humble origins* **originate** v **1** to cause something to begin **2** to begin ♦ *This feud seems to have originated in a childhood rivalry.* **origination** n **originator** n

original *adj* **1** existing from the start, earliest **2** new, not copying something else **3** thinking or acting for yourself, inventive, creative ♦ *an original mind* **original** n a document, painting, etc. which was the first one made and from which another is copied **originality** n **originally** *adv* **original sin** n (in Christianity) the condition of wickedness thought to be common to all human beings since Adam's sin

oriole (say or -i-ohl) n a kind of bird of which the male has black and yellow plumage

ornament n **1** an object displayed or worn as a decoration **2** decoration ♦ *This candlestick is for use, not for ornament.* **ornament** v to decorate something with beautiful things **ornamental** *adj* **ornamentation** *n*

ornate (say or-**nayt**) *adj* elaborate, decorated

ornithology (say orni-**thol**-əji) *n* the scientific study of birds **ornithological** *adj* **ornithologist** *n*

orphan *n* a child whose parents are dead **orphan** *v* to make a child an orphan **orphanage** *n* a home for orphans

orris (say o-riss), **orris root** *n* the fragrant root of a kind of iris which is dried for use in perfumery and medicine

orthodontics (say orthə-**don**-tiks) *n* the treatment of irregularities in the teeth and jaws **orthodontic** *adj* **orthodontist** *n*

orthodox *adj* **1** holding beliefs that are traditional or generally accepted, especially in religion **2** conventional or normal **orthodoxy** *n* **Orthodox Church** *n* the Christian Churches of eastern Europe, recognizing the Greek patriarch of Constantinople as their head **Orthodox Judaism** *n* a major branch within Judaism that follows traditional observances strictly

orthography (say or-**thog**-rə-fi) *n pl* **orthographies** the spelling system of a language **orthographic** *adj*

orthopaedics (say orthə-**pee**-diks) *n* the branch of surgery dealing with deformities of bones or muscles **orthopaedic** *adj*

OS *abbr* **1** *ICT* operating system **2** Ordnance Survey

Oscar *n* a gold statuette awarded for excellence in the acting or directing of films

oscillate (say **oss**-i-layt) *v* **1** to move to and fro like a pendulum **2** to vary between extremes **3** (said about an electric current) to reverse its direction with high frequency **oscillation** *n* **oscillator** *n* **oscilloscope** *n* a device for showing oscillations on the screen of a cathode ray tube

osier (say **oh**-zi-er) *n* a kind of willow with flexible twigs used in making baskets

-osis *suffix* **1** a diseased condition (as in *tuberculosis*) **2** an action or process (as in *metamorphosis*)

osmosis (say oz-**moh**-sis) *n* **1** diffusion of fluid through a porous partition into another more concentrated fluid **2** the process of gradually or unconsciously acquiring knowledge or ideas **osmotic** *adj*

osprey (say **oss**-pri) *n pl* **ospreys** a large bird preying on fish

ossify *v* **ossifies, ossified, ossifying 1** to change into bone; to become hard like bone **2** to stop developing **ossification** *n*

ostensible (say oss-**ten**-sibəl) *adj* apparently true, but actually concealing the true reason **ostensibly** *adv*

ostentation *n* a showy display **ostentatious** *adj* **ostentatiously** *adv*

osteopath (say **oss**-ti-əp-ath) *n* a person who treats certain medical conditions by manipulating a patient's bones and muscles **osteopathic** *adj* **osteopathy** *n*

ostler (say **oss**-ler) *n* a person who looked after the horses of people staying at an inn

ostracize (say **oss**-trə-siyz) *v* to exclude someone from a group **ostracism** *n*

ostrich *n* a large long-legged African bird that can run very fast but cannot fly

other *adj* **1** additional or remaining ♦ *one of my other friends* ♦ *She has no other income.* **2** different, not the same ♦ *Can you phone some other time?* ♦ *We wouldn't want her to be other than she is.* **other** *n, pronoun* the other person or thing ♦ *Where are the others?* **otherwise** *adv* **1** if things happen differently; or else ♦ *Write it down, otherwise you'll forget.* **2** in a different way ♦ *We could not do otherwise.* **3** in other respects ♦ *There's a small mistake in the first line but your answer is otherwise correct.*

otter *n* a fish-eating animal with webbed feet, a flat tail, and thick brown fur, living near water

Ottoman *adj* of the Turkish empire in the late 13th-early 20th century **ottoman** *n* a storage box with a padded top

oubliette (say oo-bli-et) *n* a secret dungeon to which entrance is through a trapdoor

ouch *interjection* an exclamation of sudden pain

ought *auxiliary verb* expressing duty, rightness, advisability, or strong probability ♦ *We ought to feed them.* ♦ *You ought to take more exercise.* ♦ *At this speed, we ought to be there by noon.*

Ouija board (say **wee**-jə) n trademark a board marked with the alphabet, used in spiritualistic seances

ounce n a unit of weight equal to one-sixteenth of a pound (about 28 grams)

our adj to do with or belonging to us **ours** possessive pronoun belonging to us; the things belonging to us ♦ These seats are ours. ◊ It is incorrect to write our's.

ourselves pronoun the form of we and us used in reflexive constructions and for emphasis

oust (say owst) v to drive a person out from a position

out adv **1** away from or not in a place or position; not in its normal or usual state **2** outdoors **3** not in action or use; no longer in fashion; no longer available **4** into the open; into existence or hearing or view, etc. ♦ The sun came out. ♦ Our secret is out.

outer adj outside or external; further from the centre or from the inside **outermost** adj furthest from the centre, most remote **outing** n a short trip taken for pleasure

out of 1 without a supply of something **2** beyond the range of ♦ out of hearing **out of the way** remote

out- prefix **1** away from, out of (as in outcast) **2** more than, so as to exceed (as in outbid, outgrow) **outback** n the remote inland districts of Australia **outbid** v outbid, **outbidding** to bid more for something than another person does **outboard** adj (said about a motor) fitted to the outside of the stern of a boat **outbreak** n a sudden or violent breaking out of war, disease, etc. **outbuilding** n a small building in the grounds of a main building **outburst** n a sudden bursting out of anger, laughter, etc. **outcast** n a person who has been driven out of a group **outclass** v to be far superior to someone **outcome** n the result of something **outcrop** n part of an underlying layer of rock that sticks out on the surface of the ground **outcry** n pl **outcries** a strong protest **outdated** adj out of date, obsolete **outdo** v outdid, **outdone** to do better than another person **outdoor** adj in the open air **outdoors** adv in or into the open air **outdoors** n anywhere outside **outface** v

to disconcert someone by your defiant or confident manner **outfall** n an outlet where water falls or flows out **outfield** n the outer part of a cricket or baseball field **outfit** n **1** a set of clothes to be worn together **2** a complete set of equipment needed for a particular purpose **3** informal an organization, a group of people regarded as a unit **outfitter** n a shop selling equipment or men's clothing **outflank** v to move round the side of an enemy in order to outmanoeuvre them **outgrow** v outgrew, **outgrown** to grow out of clothes or habits **outgrowth** n **1** something that grows out of another thing **2** a natural development or result **outhouse** n a small building belonging to but separate from a house **outlandish** adj looking or sounding strange or unfamiliar **outlast** v to last longer than something else **outlaw** n **1** a fugitive from the law **2** (in the Middle Ages) a person who was placed outside the protection of the law **outlaw** v **3** to declare something to be illegal; to ban something **4** to make a person an outlaw **outlay** n what is spent on something **outlet** n **1** a way out for water or gas, etc. **2** a means of expressing your feelings **3** a place from which goods are sold or distributed **outline** n **1** a line round the outside of something, showing its shape **2** a statement of the main features of something **outline** v **3** to make an outline of something **4** to give a summary of something **outlook** n **1** a person's attitude **2** a view you look out on ♦ a pleasant outlook over the lake **3** future prospects ♦ The outlook is bleak. **outlying** adj situated far from the centre, remote ♦ the outlying districts **outmanoeuvre** v to use skill to gain an advantage over someone **outmoded** adj old-fashioned **outnumber** v to be more numerous than another group **out of date** adj **1** old-fashioned **2** no longer valid ♦ This rail card is out of date. ♦ an out-of-date passport **outpatient** n a person who visits a hospital for treatment but does not stay there overnight **outpost** n a remote branch or settlement **output** n **1** the amount produced **2** the data produced by a computer **output** v past tense and past participle **output** or **outputted**; **outputting** (said about a computer) to produce or supply data **outrider** *n* a person riding on a motorcycle as an escort or guard **outrigger** *n* a beam, spar, or structure sticking out from a boat **outright** *adv* 1 completely 2 openly, frankly ♦ *I told him outright he was a fool.* **outright** *adj* thorough, complete ♦ *an outright fraud* **outset** *n* the beginning of something ♦ *from the outset of his career* **outshine** *v* past tense and past participle **outshone** to be much better than something else **outsize** *adj* much larger than average **outskirts** *pl n* the outer parts of a town or city **outspoken** *adj* frank in giving your opinions **outstanding** *adj* 1 exceptionally good 2 not yet paid or dealt with ♦ *Some of his debts are still outstanding.* **outstay** *v* to stay longer than you are expected to **outstrip** *v* **outstripped**, **outstripping** 1 to go faster than someone else 2 to surpass someone **out-take** *n* a scene cut from the final version of a film **outward** *adj* 1 situated on the outside 2 going out or away from a place 3 to do with the external appearance of something rather than its true nature **outward** *adv* outwards **outwardly** *adv* **outwards** *adv* towards the outside **outweigh** *v* to be greater in weight, importance, or significance than something else **outwit** *v* **outwitted**, **outwitting** to get the better of a person by cleverness

outrage *n* 1 an act that shocks and angers people 2 great anger or indignation **outrage** *v* to shock and anger people greatly **outrageous** *adj* greatly exceeding what is moderate or reasonable, shocking **outrageously** *adv*

outré (say **oo**-tray) *adj* unusual and rather shocking

outside *n* the outer side, surface, or part of something **outside** *adj, adv, prep* on or at or to the outside; outdoors **outsider** *n* 1 a person who does not belong to a certain group 2 a horse or person thought to have no chance of winning a race or competition **an outside chance** a remote possibility

ouzel (say **oo**-zəl) *n* a kind of diving bird

oval *n* a rounded symmetrical shape longer than it is broad **oval** *adj* having this shape

ovary (say **oh**-ver-i) *n pl* **ovaries** 1 either of the two organs in which egg cells are produced in a woman's or female animal's body 2 part of a plant, from which fruit is formed **ovarian** *adj*

ovation (say ə-**vay**-shən) *n* enthusiastic applause

oven *n* 1 an enclosed compartment in which things are cooked 2 a small kiln or furnace

over *adv* 1 with movement outwards and downwards ♦ *He fell over.* 2 from one side to the other ♦ *Turn it over.* ♦ *Let's cross over at the lights.* 3 remaining, more than is needed ♦ *There are a few bits of wood left over.* **over** *adj* at an end, finished **over** *prep* 1 in or to a position higher than 2 across the top of something and covering it; on or to the other side of ♦ *a hat over his eyes* ♦ *We flew over the Alps.* 3 out and down from; down from the edge of ♦ *The car must have driven straight over the cliff.* 4 throughout the length or extent of, during ♦ *over the years* ♦ *You can stay over the weekend.* 5 on the subject of ♦ *They are always quarrelling over money.* 6 more than ♦ *It's over a mile away.* **over** *n* (in cricket) a series of six balls bowled in succession **overly** *adv* excessively **to be over something** to be no longer affected or upset by something

over- *prefix* 1 over, above (as in *overturn, overlay*) 2 too much, excessively (as in *overanxious*) **overact** *v* to act your part in an exaggerated manner **overall** *adj, adv* including everything, total **overall** *n* a type of coat worn over other clothes to protect them when working **overalls** *pl n* a combined piece of clothing covering the body and legs, worn over other clothes to protect them **overarm** *adj, adv* (in cricket, etc.) bowling or bowled with the hand brought forward and down from above shoulder level **overawe** *v* to overcome or inhibit a person with awe **overbalance** *v* to lose balance and fall over **overbearing** *adj* domineering or overpowering **overblown** *adj* exaggerated or pretentious **overcast** *adj* (said about the sky or weather) covered with cloud

overcharge v to charge too high a price
overcome v **overcame**, **overcome 1** to defeat someone **2** to have a strong physical or emotional effect on someone ♦ *One of the firefighters was overcome by gas fumes.* ♦ *She was overcome with grief.* **3** to find a way of dealing with a problem **overcrowd** v to crowd too many people into a place **overcrowded** *adj* **overcrowding** n
overdose n too large a dose of a drug **overdose** v to take an overdose **overdraft** n a debt in a bank account **overdue** *adj* not paid or arrived, etc. by the due or expected time **overestimate** v to form too high an estimate of something **overflow** v **1** to flow over the edge, limits, or banks, etc. **2** (said about a crowd) to spread beyond the limits of a room, etc. **overflow** n **1** what overflows **2** an outlet for excess liquid **overgrown** *adj* **1** covered with weeds or unwanted plants **2** grown too large **overhang** v past tense and past participle **overhung** to jut out over something **overhang** n an overhanging part **overhaul** v **1** to examine and repair something **2** to overtake someone or something **overhaul** n an examination and repair of something **overhead** *adv, adj* **1** above the level of your head **2** in the sky **overheads** *pl* n the expenses involved in running a business **overhear** v past tense and past participle **overheard** to hear something accidentally or without the speaker intending you to hear it **overjoyed** *adj* extremely happy **overkill** n excessive use or treatment of something **overland** *adv, adj* by land, not by sea or air **overlap** v **overlapped**, **overlapping 1** to partly cover something **2** to partly coincide ♦ *Our holidays overlap.* **overlap** n an overlapping part or amount **overlay** v **overlaid** to cover something with a surface layer **overleaf** *adv* on the other side of the page **overlook** v **1** to fail to notice or consider something **2** to deliberately ignore something **3** to view from above **overlord** n a supreme lord **overman** v **overmanned**, **overmanning** to provide a ship, factory, etc. with too many workers **overmuch** *adv* too much **overnight** *adj, adv* for or during a night **overplay** v to give too much

importance to something **overpower** v to defeat someone by greater strength or numbers **overpowering** *adj* extremely intense **overrate** v to have a higher opinion of something than it deserves **overreact** v to respond more emotionally or strongly than is justified **overreaction** n **override** v **overrode**, **overridden 1** to set aside an order by having superior authority **2** to be more important than something else ♦ *Safety overrides all other considerations.* **3** to interrupt the operation of an automatic mechanism **overrule** v to reject or disallow a suggestion, decision, etc. by using your authority **overrun** v **overran**, **overrun**, **overrunning 1** to spread over and occupy a place in large numbers ♦ *The place is overrun with mice.* **2** to go on for longer than it should **overseas** *adv, adj* across or beyond the sea, abroad **oversee** v **oversaw**, **overseen** to watch over or supervise people working **overseer** n **overshadow** v **1** to tower above something and cast a shadow over it **2** to cast a gloom over something **3** to make a person or thing seem unimportant or unsuccessful in comparison **overshoe** n a protective shoe worn over an ordinary one **overshoot** v past tense and past participle **overshot** to pass beyond a target or limit, etc. ♦ *The plane overshot the runway when landing.* **oversight** n a failure to notice or do something **oversleep** v past tense and past participle **overslept** to sleep longer or later than you intended **overspill** n the surplus population of a town, etc. who seek accommodation in other districts **overstate** v to exaggerate something **overstatement** n **overstay** v to stay longer than the duration or limits of something **overstep** v **overstepped**, **overstepping** to go beyond a limit **overtake** v **overtook**, **overtaken 1** to pass a person or vehicle by moving faster **2** to exceed a compared value or amount **overtax** v to tax someone too heavily **2** to put too heavy a burden or strain on someone **overthrow** v **overthrew**, **overthrown** to remove someone from power by force ♦ *The rebel forces overthrew the government.*

overthrow *n* a downfall or defeat
overtime *adv* in addition to normal working hours **overtime** *n* time spent working outside the normal hours **overtone** *n* an additional quality or implication ♦ *There were overtones of malice in his comments.*
overture *n* a piece of music written as an introduction to an opera or ballet, etc.
overtures *pl n* a friendly approach showing willingness to begin negotiations or start a relationship **overturn** *v* 1 to turn over or upside down, or to make something do this 2 to reverse a legal decision
overview *n* a general review or summary
overweight *adj* weighing more than is normal, required, or allowed **overwhelm** *v* 1 to defeat someone completely, especially by force of numbers 2 to have a strong emotional effect on someone ♦ *I was overwhelmed by their generosity.*
overwhelming *adj* **overwork** *v* 1 to work or make someone work too hard 2 to use something too often or too much ♦ *an overworked phrase* **overwork** *n* excessive work causing exhaustion **overwrought** *adj* in a state of nervous excitement or anxiety
overdraw *v* **overdrew, overdrawn** to draw more money from a bank account than the amount you have in it **to be overdrawn** to have taken more money from your bank account than you have in it **overdrive** *n* a mechanism providing an extra gear above the normal top gear in a vehicle **to go into overdrive** to become highly active **overboard** *adv* from a ship into the water ♦ *She jumped overboard.* **to go overboard** 1 to be very enthusiastic 2 to go too far **overdo** *v* **overdid, overdone** 1 to do something too much or use too much of something 2 to cook food too long **to overdo it** or **things** to exhaust yourself, to work too hard **overreach** *v* to **overreach yourself** to fail through being too ambitious
overt (say oh-**vert**) *adj* done or shown openly ♦ *overt hostility* **overtly** *adv*
ovoid (say **oh**-void) *adj* egg-shaped
ovulate (say **ov**-yoo-layt) *v* to produce or discharge an egg from an ovary **ovulation** *n*

owe *v* 1 to have an obligation to pay or repay money, etc. in return for what you have received 2 to be under an obligation to show or offer something to someone ♦ *I think I owe you an apology.* 3 to have something because of the work or action of another person or cause ♦ *We owe the discovery to Newton.* ♦ *He owes his success to luck.* **owing** *adj* owed and not yet paid **owing to** because of or on account of
owl *n* a bird of prey with a large head, large eyes, and a hooked beak, usually flying at night
own[1] *adj* to do with or belonging to the person or thing specified **on your own** alone; independently **to get your own back** *informal* to have your revenge **to hold your own** to succeed in holding your position against competition or attack
own[2] *v* 1 to have something as your property, to possess something 2 to acknowledge or admit to something ♦ *She owns to having said it.* **to own up** to admit that you have done something wrong or embarrassing **owner** *n*
ox *n pl* **oxen** a fully grown bullock, used as a draught animal or as food
Oxbridge *n* the universities of Oxford and Cambridge
oxidize *v* 1 to combine or cause a substance to combine with oxygen 2 to form or make something form a layer of metal oxide, as when something becomes rusty **oxidization** *n* **oxidant** *n* an oxidizing agent
oxygen *n* a colourless odourless tasteless gas existing in air and combining with hydrogen to form water **oxygenate** to supply, treat, or mix something with oxygen
oxymoron (say oksi-**mor** -ən) *n* putting together words which seem to contradict one another, e.g. *bitter-sweet, living death*
oyez (say oh-**yez**) *interjection* a cry uttered usually three times, by a public crier to call for attention
oyster *n* a kind of shellfish used as food
oz. *abbr* ounce(s)
ozone (say **oh**-zohn) *n* 1 a form of oxygen with a sharp smell 2 *informal* invigorating air at the seaside **ozone layer** a layer in

the stratosphere where ozone is generated, serving to protect the earth from harmful ultraviolet rays from the sun

Pp

P[1] the sixteenth letter of the English alphabet

P[2] *abbr* (on road signs) parking

p *abbr* **1** page **2** penny or pence

p. & p. *abbr* postage and packing

PA *abbr* **1** personal assistant **2** public address

pace[1] *n* **1** a single step taken in walking or running **2** the distance covered by this ♦ *We measured out twenty paces.* **3** the rate of progress or change in an activity **pace** *v* **1** to walk at a steady speed, especially up and down a room **2** to measure a distance in paces **pacemaker** *n* **1** a competitor who sets the pace in a race **2** an electrical device placed on the heart to stimulate contractions **to keep pace with** to advance at the same speed as something else **to pace yourself** to do something at a restrained rate

pace[2] (say **pay**-si or **pah**-chay) *prep* with due respect to a named person who disagrees

pacify (say **pas**-i-fiy) *v* **pacifies**, **pacified**, **pacifying 1** to calm a person down **2** to bring peace to a country or warring sides **pacific** *adj* peaceful; making or loving peace **pacification** *n* **pacifist** *n* a person who totally opposes war, believing that disputes should be settled by peaceful means **pacifism** *n*

pack *n* **1** a set of things wrapped or tied together for carrying or selling ♦ *a pack of envelopes* ♦ *an information pack* **2** a set of 52 playing cards **3** a bag carried on your back **4** a number of people or things ♦ *a pack of lies* **5** a group of wolves, etc. that live and hunt together **pack** *v* **1** to put things into a suitcase, bag, box, etc. **2** to put food or goods into a box, wrapper, etc. ready to be sold **3** to fill something with a large number

of things **packhorse** *n* a horse for carrying loads **pack ice** *n* large crowded floating pieces of ice in the sea **to pack someone off** *informal* to send someone away **to pack something in** *informal* to stop doing something **to pack up 1** to put your things together to get ready for leaving or stopping work **2** *informal* (said about a machine) to break down

package *n* **1** something wrapped up, a parcel **2** a number of separate items or proposals offered together as a whole **package** *v* **1** to put things together in a box or wrapping **2** to present something in a particular way **packaging** *n* wrappings or containers for goods

packet *n* **1** a paper or cardboard container **2** *informal* a large sum of money **3** *old use* a mail boat

pact *n* an agreement or treaty

pad *n* **1** a thick piece of soft material used to protect against jarring, to add bulk, to hold or absorb fluid, etc. **2** the soft fleshy part under an animal's foot or at the end of a finger or toe **3** a set of sheets of blank paper fastened together at one edge **4** a flat surface from which rockets and spacecraft are launched or where helicopters take off and land **5** *informal* a person's home **pad** *v* **padded**, **padding 1** to cover or stuff something with a pad or pads **2** to walk with soft steady steps **3** to fill a book or speech, etc. with unnecessary material in order to lengthen it **padding** *n* material used to pad things

paddle[1] *n* a short oar with a broad blade **paddle** *v* to move a boat along by using a paddle or paddles **paddle steamer** *n* a boat powered by steam and moved along by paddle wheels **paddle wheel** *n* a large wheel with boards round its rim that drives a paddle steamer

paddle[2] *v* to walk about with bare feet in shallow water

paddock *n* a small field where horses are kept

paddy[1] *n pl* **paddies** a field where rice is grown

paddy[2] *n pl* **paddies** *informal* a fit of temper

padlock *n* a detachable lock with a U-shaped

bar or a chain, etc. that fastens through the loop of a staple or ring **padlock** v to fasten something with a padlock

padre (say **pah**-dray) n informal a chaplain in the armed forces

paean (say **pee**-ən) n a song of praise or triumph

paediatrics (say peed-i-**at**-triks) n the branch of medicine dealing with children and their diseases **paediatric** adj **paediatrician** n

paella (say piy-**el**-ə) n a Spanish dish of rice, chicken, seafood, etc. cooked and served in a large shallow pan

pagan (say **pay**-gən) n a person whose religion is not one of the main world religions **pagan** adj not believing in one of the main world religions **paganism** n

page[1] n 1 a piece of paper that is part of a book or newspaper, etc. 2 one side of this, or what is written or printed on it 3 a screenful of information on a computer **paginate** v to number the pages of a book, etc. **pagination** n

page[2] n 1 (also **pageboy**) a boy or man employed in a hotel or club to go on errands, open doors, etc. 2 (also **pageboy**) a young boy attending a bride at a wedding 3 hist a boy training to be a knight and acting as a servant to a knight **page** v 1 to summon a person over a public address system or by calling their name 2 to contact a person by means of a pager **pager** n a small radio device which bleeps or vibrates to tell you that someone wants to contact you or that it has received a short message

pageant (say **paj**-ənt) n a public show consisting of a procession of people in elaborate costumes, or an outdoor performance of a historical play **pageantry** n

pagoda (say pə-**goh**-də) n a Hindu temple or Buddhist tower shaped like a pyramid

paid past tense and past participle of *pay* **paid** adj receiving payment or a salary **to put paid to** informal to put an end to someone's hopes, prospects, or activities

pail n a bucket

pain n 1 an unpleasant feeling caused by injury or illness 2 mental suffering or distress 3 informal an annoying or tediou person or thing **pains** pl n careful effor trouble taken **pain** v to cause sufferin or distress to someone **painful** ad **painfully** adv **painless** adj **painlessly** ad **painkiller** n a medicine or drug tha relieves pain **painstaking** adj very carefu and thorough **on** or **under pain of** with th threat of

paint n a substance spread over a surface i liquid form to colour it **paint** v 1 to coat c decorate something with paint 2 to mak a picture with paints **painter** n **painting** **paintwork** n a painted surface in a buildin or on a vehicle

painter n a rope attached to the bow of boat for tying it up

pair n 1 a set of two things used or though of together 2 something made of tw joined corresponding parts ♦ *a pair* scissors 3 two people or animals groupe together **pair** v to put two things togethe as a pair; to arrange things in groups of tw

paisley n a pattern of tapering petal-shape figures with much detail

pal n informal a friend **pally** adj **pallie palliest** friendly

palace n 1 the official residence of sovereign, president, archbishop, etc. 2 large splendid house or other buildin **palatial** adj like a palace, spacious an grand

palaeontology (say pal-i-on-**tol**-əji) n th scientific study of fossil animals and plant **palaeontologist** n

palate (say **pal**-ət) n 1 the roof of the mout 2 a person's sense of taste **palatable** ad 1 pleasant to taste 2 acceptable

palaver (say pə-**lah**-ver) n informal a fuss c time-consuming procedure

pale[1] adj 1 (said about colour or light) fain not bright 2 (said about a person's face having little colour **pale** v 1 to turn pale 2 t seem less important ♦ *Their other problem* paled into insignificance in the light of th news. **paleness** n

pale[2] n 1 a wooden stake forming part c a fence 2 a boundary **paling** n 1 a fenc made from wooden posts 2 one of its post **beyond the pale** outside the bounds o acceptable behaviour

palette (say **pal**-it) n a thin board on which an artist mixes colours when painting ◊ Do not confuse this word with **palate** or **pallet**, which have different meanings. **palette knife** n **1** an artist's knife for mixing or spreading paint **2** a knife with a long blunt flexible blade used in painting and cookery

palindrome (say **pal**-in-drohm) n a word or phrase that reads the same backwards as forwards, e.g. *radar* or *Madam, I'm Adam*

palisade n a fence of pointed stakes

pall[1] (say **pawl**) n **1** a cloth spread over a coffin **2** a dark cloud or covering of something ♦ *a pall of smoke* **pall-bearer** n a person helping to carry the coffin at a funeral

pall[2] (say **pawl**) v to become less interesting or enjoyable

pallet[1] n **1** a mattress stuffed with straw **2** a simple or makeshift bed

pallet[2] n a large tray or platform for carrying or storing goods

palliate (say **pal**-i-ayt) v to make something less serious or less severe **palliative** adj reducing the bad effects of something

pallor (say **pal**-er) n paleness in a person's face, especially from illness **pallid** adj

palm n **1** the inner surface of the hand between the wrist and the fingers **2** (also **palm tree**) a kind of tree growing in warm or tropical climates, with large leaves growing in a mass at the top **palm** v to pick up something secretly and hide it in the palm of your hand **palmist** n **palmistry** n the supposed art of telling someone's future by examining the palm of their hand **Palm Sunday** n the Sunday before Easter **palmtop** n a small light computer that can be held in one hand **to palm something off** to deceive a person into accepting something

palpable (say **pal**-pə-bəl) adj **1** easily perceived, obvious ♦ *a palpable sense of loss* **2** able to be touched or felt **palpably** adv

palpate (say pal-**payt**) v to examine a part of the body by feeling with the hands

palpitate (say **pal**-pit-ayt) v **1** (said about the heart) to beat rapidly **2** (said about a person) to quiver with fear or excitement

palpitation n

palsy (say **pawl**-zi) n old use paralysis **palsied** adj affected with palsy

paltry (say **pol**-tri) adj **paltrier**, **paltriest** very small and almost worthless ♦ *a paltry amount*

pampas (say **pam**-pəs) n vast grassy plains in South America **pampas grass** n a kind of tall grass with feathery plumes

pamper v to treat someone very indulgently

pamphlet (say **pamf**-lit) n a leaflet or booklet containing information or arguments on a subject

pan[1] n **1** a metal container with a flat base, sometimes with a lid, used for cooking **2** the bowl of a toilet **pan** v **panned**, **panning 1** to wash gravel in a pan in search of gold **2** informal to criticize something severely **to pan out** (said about events) to turn out in a particular way, especially successfully

pan[2] v **panned**, **panning** to turn a camera horizontally to give a panoramic effect or follow a moving object

pan- prefix all (as in panorama)

panacea (say pan-ə-**see**-ə) n a remedy or solution for all kinds of diseases or troubles

panache (say pən-**ash**) n a confident stylish manner

panama (say pan-ə-**mah**) n a wide-brimmed hat made of fine straw-like material

pancake n a thin round cake of batter fried on both sides

pancreas (say **pank**-ri-əs) n a gland near the stomach producing a digestive secretion into the duodenum and insulin into the blood **pancreatic** adj

panda n a large rare bear-like black-and-white animal living in the mountains of south-west China **panda car** n a police patrol car

pandemic (say pan-**dem**-ik) adj (said about a disease) occurring over a whole country or the whole world **pandemic** n an outbreak of such a disease

pandemonium (say pandi-**moh**-niəm) n uproar and complete confusion

pander v **to pander to** to indulge someone

by giving them whatever they want or satisfying a weakness

Pandora's box n a process that once begun will generate many unmanageable problems

pane n a single sheet of glass in a window or door

panegyric (say pan-i-**ji**-rik) n a speech or piece of writing praising a person or thing

panel n 1 a flat piece of wood, metal, material, etc. that forms a section of a wall, door, vehicle, item of clothing, etc. 2 a flat board with controls or instruments on it 3 a group of people brought together to discuss or decide something, or to form a team in a quiz 4 a list of jurors, or a jury **panel** v **panelled**, **panelling** to cover or decorate something with panels **panelling** n **panellist** n

pang n a sudden sharp feeling of pain or a painful emotion ♦ *pangs of jealousy*

panic n sudden uncontrollable fear or anxiety, especially when this affects a large group of people **panic** v **panicked**, **panicking** to feel panic or to make someone feel panic **panicky** adj **panic-stricken** adj affected with panic

pannier n 1 a large basket carried on either side of a pack animal 2 a bag or container on a motorcycle or bicycle

panoply (say pan-ə-pli) n a splendid display or collection of things

panorama n 1 a view or picture of a wide area 2 a view of a constantly changing scene or series of events **panoramic** adj

pan pipes pl n a musical instrument consisting of a row of short pipes fixed together side by side

pansy n pl **pansies** a small brightly coloured garden flower of the violet family, with velvety petals

pant v to breathe with short quick breaths, usually after running or working hard **pant** n a short quick breath

pantaloons pl n baggy trousers gathered at the ankle

pantheism (say **pan**-thi-izm) n the belief that God is everything and everything is God **pantheist** n **pantheistic** adj

pantheon (say **pan**-thi-ən) n 1 all the gods of a people or religion collectively 2 a temple dedicated to all the gods

panther n a leopard, especially a black one

panties pl n informal short knickers

pantomime n 1 a type of theatrical entertainment, usually based on a fairy tale and produced around Christmas 2 acting with movements of the body and without words

pantry n pl **pantries** a small room for storing food; a larder

pants pl n 1 N. Am trousers 2 underpants or knickers

pap n 1 soft or semi-liquid food suitable for babies or invalids 2 worthless or trivial reading matter or entertainment

papa n old use father

papacy (say **pay**-pə-si) n pl **papacies** the office or authority of the pope **papal** adj to do with the pope or the papacy **papist** n a derogatory term for a Roman Catholic

paparazzi (say pap-ə-**rat**-si) pl n photographers who chase famous people to get photographs of them

papaya (say pə-**piy**-ə) n 1 an oblong orange-coloured edible fruit 2 the palm-like tropical American tree bearing this fruit

paper n 1 a substance manufactured in thin sheets from wood fibre, rags, etc., used for writing or printing or drawing on or for wrapping things 2 a newspaper 3 a set of examination questions ♦ *the biology paper* 4 a document ♦ *Can I see your papers?* 5 an essay or dissertation, especially one read to an academic society **paper** v to cover a wall or room with wallpaper **paperback** n a book bound in a flexible paper binding, not in a stiff cover **paperweight** n a small heavy object placed on loose papers to keep them in place **paperwork** n all the writing of reports, keeping of records, etc. that someone has to do as part of their job **on paper** in theory, though not necessarily in practice ♦ *The scheme looked fine on paper.*

papier mâché n moulded paper pulp used for making models, ornaments, etc.

papoose (say pə-**pooss**) n a bag for carrying a baby, worn on the back

paprika (say **pap**-rik-ə or pə-**pree**-kə) n a

powdered spice made from red pepper

papyrus (say pə-**piy**-rəs) n 1 a reed-like water plant with thick fibrous stems from which a kind of paper was made by the ancient Egyptians 2 this paper 3 pl **papyri** a manuscript written on this paper

par n 1 the usual or expected amount, condition, or degree ♦ *I was feeling well below par that morning.* 2 (in golf) the number of strokes that a good player should normally take for a particular hole or course 3 the face value of stocks and shares, etc., not their market value **parity** n equality in status, pay, or value **on a par with** equal to in amount or quality

para n *informal* 1 a parachutist or paratrooper 2 a paragraph

para- *prefix* 1 beside (as in *parallel*) 2 beyond (as in *paradox*)

parable n a simple story told to illustrate a moral or spiritual truth

parabola (say pə-**rab**-ə-lə) n a curve like the path of an object thrown into the air and falling back to earth **parabolic** adj

paracetamol (say pa-rə-**see**-tə-mol) n a medicinal drug used to relieve pain and reduce fever

parachute n a rectangular or umbrella-shaped device used to slow the descent of a person or heavy object falling from a great height, especially from an aircraft **parachute** v 1 to descend by parachute 2 to drop supplies, etc. by parachute **parachutist** n

parade n 1 a public procession 2 a formal assembly of troops for inspection or display 3 a row of shops or a promenade **parade** v 1 to march or walk in a parade 2 to make a display of something

paradigm (say **pa**-rə-diym) n something serving as an example or model of how things should be done

paradise n heaven or a heavenly place

paradox (say **pa**-rə-doks) n a statement that seems to contradict itself but which contains a truth (e.g. 'more haste, less speed') **paradoxical** adj **paradoxically** adv

paraffin n an oil obtained from petroleum or shale, used as a fuel and solvent

paragliding n the sport of gliding through the air while being supported by a wide parachute after jumping from or being hauled to a height **paraglider** n

paragon (say **pa**-rə-gən) n a person or thing that seems to be a model of excellence or perfection

paragraph n one or more sentences on a single theme, forming a distinct section of a piece of writing and beginning on a new line

parakeet (say **pa**-rə-keet) n a kind of small parrot, often with a long tail

parallax (say **pa**-rə-laks) n an apparent difference in the position or direction of an object when you look at it from different points **parallactic** adj

parallel adj 1 (said about lines, planes, etc.) side by side and the same distance apart from each other at every point ♦ *The road runs parallel to the railway.* 2 occurring or existing at the same time or in a similar way; corresponding ♦ *When petrol prices rise there is a parallel rise in bus fares.* **parallel** n 1 something similar or corresponding ♦ *There are interesting parallels between the two cases.* 2 a comparison ♦ *You can draw a parallel between the two situations.* 3 a line showing latitude **parallel** v **paralleled**, **paralleling** 1 to run or lie parallel to something 2 to be similar or corresponding to something **parallelogram** n a plane four-sided figure with its opposite sides parallel to each other

paralysis n 1 loss of the power of movement, caused by disease or an injury to nerves 2 inability to move or act normally **paralyse** v 1 to affect a person or part of the body with paralysis, to make someone unable to act or move normally 2 to bring something to a standstill **paralytic** adj 1 affected by paralysis 2 *informal* very drunk

paramedic n a person who is trained to do medical work, especially emergency first aid, but is not a fully qualified doctor **paramedical** adj

parameter (say pə-**ram**-it-er) n a limiting factor that defines the scope of something ♦ *We are working within the parameters of time and money.*

paramilitary adj organized like a military force but not part of the armed services **paramilitary** n pl **paramilitaries** a member of a paramilitary organization

paramount adj more important than anything else

paramour (say pa-rə-moor) n old use a lover, especially a married person's lover

paranoia (say pa-rə-noi-ə) n 1 a mental disorder in which a person has delusions of being persecuted or of self-importance 2 an unjustified suspicion and mistrust of others **paranoiac** adj, n **paranoid** adj

paranormal (say pa-rə-nor -məl) adj beyond what is normal and can be rationally explained; supernatural

parapet (say pa-rə-pit) n a low protective wall along the edge of a balcony, roof, or bridge

paraphernalia (say pa-rə-fer-nay-liə) n numerous small pieces of equipment or other belongings

paraphrase (say pa-rə-frayz) v to give the meaning of a passage by using different words **paraphrase** n a rewording of a passage in this way

paraplegia (say pa-rə-plee-jiə) n paralysis of the legs and lower body **paraplegic** adj, n

parapsychology (say pa-rə-siy-kol-əji) n the scientific study of mental phenomena such as clairvoyance and telepathy

paraquat (say pa-rə-kwot) n trademark an extremely poisonous weedkiller

parasite n 1 an animal or plant that lives on or in another from which it draws its nourishment 2 a person who lives off others and gives nothing in return **parasitic** adj **parasitically** adv

parasol n a light umbrella used to shade yourself from the sun

paratroops pl n troops trained to be dropped from aircraft by parachute **paratrooper** n

parboil v to boil food until it is partly cooked

parcel n a thing or things wrapped up for carrying or for sending by post **parcel** v **parcelled, parcelling 1** to wrap something up as a parcel **2** to divide something into portions ♦ I've decided to parcel out the work

between you.

parch v to make something dry because o great heat **parched** adj very thirsty

parchment n a heavy paper-like materia made from animal skins

pardon n 1 forgiveness for a mistake o offence 2 cancellation of the punishment for an offence ♦ a free pardon **pardon** v to forgive or excuse someone for something **pardon** interjection (also **I beg your pardon** or **pardon me**) used to mean 'I didn't hear or understand what you said' or ' apologize' **pardonable** adj

pare (say pair) v 1 to trim something by cutting away the edges 2 to reduce something little by little **parings** pl n

parent n a father or mother **parent** v to be a parent of a child, etc. **parentage** n who your parents are **parental** adj **parenthood** n

parenthesis (say pə-ren-thi-sis) n p **parentheses 1** an additional word, phrase, or sentence inserted in a passage and usually marked off by brackets, dashes, or commas **2** either of the pair of round brackets (like these) used to mark off words from the rest of a sentence

par excellence (say par-eks-el-ahns) adj more than all others, to the highest degree

pariah (say pə-riy-ə) n an outcast

parish n an area within a Christian diocese, having its own church and clergy **parishioner** n an inhabitant of a parish

park n 1 a large public garden or recreation ground for public use in a town 2 an enclosed area of grassland or woodland attached to a country house 3 a parking area for vehicles ♦ a coach park 4 an area of land for a particular activity ♦ a wildlife park ♦ a science park **park** v to leave a vehicle somewhere for a time **parking meter** n a coin-operated machine in which fees are inserted for parking a vehicle beside it in the street **parking ticket** n a notice of a fine imposed for parking a vehicle illegally

parka n a windproof jacket with a hood, worn in cold weather

Parkinson's disease n a disease of the nervous system that makes a person's arms and legs shake and the muscles become stiff

parky adj **parkier**, **parkiest** informal chilly

parlance (say par-ləns) n a way of using words, phraseology ♦ medical parlance ♦ a word in common parlance

parley n pl **parleys** a discussion between enemies or opponents to settle points in dispute **parley** v **parleyed**, **parleying** to hold a parley

parliament (say par-lə-mənt) n an assembly that makes the laws of a country **parliamentarian** n a person who is skilled at debating in parliament and has a good knowledge of its procedures **parliamentary** adj

parlour n 1 old use a sitting room in a private house 2 a shop or business ♦ an ice-cream parlour

parlous (say par-ləs) adj old use precarious, hard to deal with ♦ the parlous state of the economy

Parmesan (say par-mi-zan) n a kind of hard dry Italian cheese, usually grated before use

parochial (say pə-roh-kiəl) adj 1 to do with a church parish 2 showing interest in your own area only **parochialism** n

parody (say pa-rə-di) n pl **parodies** 1 an amusing imitation of the style of a writer, composer, literary work, etc. 2 a poor or grotesque imitation of something **parody** v **parodies**, **parodied**, **parodying** to produce a parody of something

parole (say pə-rohl) n the release of a convicted person from a prison before the end of his or her sentence, on condition of good behaviour **parole** v to release a prisoner on parole

paroxysm (say pa-rək-sizm) n a sudden attack or outburst of pain, rage, or laughter, etc.

parquet (say par-kay) n flooring of wooden blocks arranged in a pattern

parrot n a tropical bird with a short hooked bill and often with brightly coloured plumage **parrot** v **parroted**, **parroting** to repeat another person's words, especially without understanding what you are saying

parry v **parries**, **parried**, **parrying** 1 to turn aside an opponent's weapon or blow by using your own weapon, etc. to block the thrust 2 to avoid an awkward question skilfully **parry** n pl **parries** an act of parrying

parse (say parz) v to identify the grammatical form and function of words in a sentence

parsimonious (say par-si-moh-niəs) adj stingy, very sparing in the use of resources **parsimony** n

parsley n a garden plant with crinkled green leaves used for seasoning and decorating food and in sauces

parsnip n a large yellowish tapering root with a sweet flavour that is used as a vegetable

parson n a member of the clergy, especially a rector or vicar **parsonage** n a rectory or vicarage **parson's nose** n the rump of a cooked fowl

part n 1 some but not all of a thing or number of things; anything that belongs to something bigger 2 each of several equal portions of a whole ♦ Add three parts oil to one part vinegar. 3 a component of a machine ♦ spare parts 4 a region ♦ What brings you to these parts? 5 the character played by an actor or actress; the words spoken by this character 6 how much someone is involved in something ♦ She played a huge part in her daughter's success. 7 a side in an agreement or in a dispute **part** v 1 to separate or divide 2 (said about two people) to leave each other **partiality** n **partial** adj 1 in part but not complete or total 2 favouring one side more than the other; biased **to be partial to** to have a strong liking for something **partially** adv **parting** n 1 leaving or separation 2 a line where hair is combed away in different directions **partly** adv to some extent but not completely or wholly **part of speech** n one of the classes into which words are divided in grammar, e.g. noun, adjective, pronoun, verb, adverb, preposition, conjunction, and interjection **part-time** adj, adv for only part of the usual working day or week ♦ a part-time job **in part** partly **part and parcel of** an essential part of **to take part** to join in or be involved in an activity **to take something in good part** to not take offence at something

partake v **partook**, **partaken 1** to join in something **2** to eat or drink something

participate (say par-**tiss**-i-payt) v to take part in something **participant** n **participation** n

particle n a very small portion of matter

particular adj **1** relating to one person or thing as distinct from others, individual ♦ *This particular stamp is very rare.* **2** especially great ♦ *Take particular care when handling these substances.* **3** selecting carefully, insisting on certain standards ♦ *He is very particular about what he eats.* **particular** n a detail, a piece of information ♦ *Here are the particulars of the case.* **particularize** v to treat something individually or in detail **particularly** adv

partisan (say parti-**zan**) n **1** a strong supporter of a person, group, or cause **2** a member of an armed group resisting the authorities in a conquered country **partisan** adj strongly supporting a particular cause **partisanship** n

partition (say par-**tish**-ən) n **1** a thin wall that divides a room or space **2** dividing something, especially a country, into separate parts **3** a part formed in this way **partition** v to divide something into separate parts

partner n **1** a person who shares in some activity with one or more other people, especially in a business firm **2** either of two people doing something as a pair **3** a person that someone is married to or is having a sexual relationship with **partner** v to be the partner of someone **partnership** n

partridge n pl **partridge** or **partridges** a game bird with brown feathers and a plump body

parturition (say par-tewr-**ish**-ən) n a technical term for giving birth; childbirth

party n pl **parties 1** a social gathering, usually of invited guests **2** a political group **3** a number of people travelling or working together as a unit ♦ *a search party* **4** a person or group forming one side in an agreement or dispute **party line** n the set policy of a political party **party wall** n a wall

that is common to two rooms or buildings which it divides

pascal (say pas-kəl) n a unit of pressure

paschal (say pas-kəl) adj formal **1** to do with the Jewish Passover **2** to do with Easter

pashmina (say pash-**mee**-nə) n a shawl made from fine goat's wool

pass v **1** to go or move past something or to the other side of something ♦ *An old man passed me on the stairs.* **2** to go or move in a certain direction ♦ *The road passes through the centre of town.* **3** to hand or transfer something to another person; (in ball games) to kick or throw the ball to another player of your own side **4** to go away **5** (said about time) to go by **6** to occupy time **7** to be accepted or currently known in a certain way ♦ *You could easily pass for 18.* **8** to be successful in a test or examination; to be accepted as satisfactory **9** to approve a law or measure, especially by voting on it **10** to go beyond something **11** to utter remarks; to pronounce a judgement or sentence ♦ *I don't like to pass criticism.* **12** to discharge urine, etc. from the body **13** (in a card game or a quiz) to let your turn go by or choose not to answer **pass** n **1** a success in an examination **2** a permit to go into or out of a place or travel on a bus, etc. **3** (in ball games) kicking or throwing the ball to another player of your own side **4** a gap in a mountain range, allowing access to the other side **passable** adj **1** satisfactory, fairly good but not outstanding **2** able to be travelled along or over **passing** adj not lasting long, casual ♦ *a passing glance* **passbook** n a book recording a customer's deposits and withdrawals from a bank or building society account **passer-by** n pl **passers-by** a person who happens to be going past something **Passover** n a Jewish festival commemorating the liberation of the Jews from slavery in Egypt **passport** n an official document entitling a person to travel abroad **password** n a secret word used to gain access to something **to make a pass at** informal to try to attract someone sexually **to pass away** to die **to pass out** to faint **to pass something off** to offer or sell something under false pretences

♦ *He passed it off as his own work.* **to pass something over** to disregard something **to pass something up** to refuse to accept an opportunity

passage *n* **1** a way through something, especially with walls on either side **2** the process of passing ♦ *the passage of time* **3** a particular section of a piece of writing or music **4** a journey by sea or air **5** the right to pass through somewhere **passageway** *n* a corridor or other passage between buildings or rooms

passé (say **pas**-ay) *adj* no longer fashionable

passenger *n* **1** a person who travels in a vehicle or ship or aircraft, other than the driver, pilot, or members of the crew **2** a member of a team who does no effective work

passim (say **pas**-im) *adv* at various places throughout a book or article, etc.

passion *n* **1** strong emotion **2** sexual love **3** great enthusiasm for something, or the object of this ♦ *Chess is his passion.* **Passion** *n* the suffering and death of Jesus Christ **passionate** *adj* **passionately** *adv* **passion flower** *n* a tropical flowering plant **passion fruit** *n* the edible fruit of some kinds of passion flower

passive *adj* **1** acted upon by an external force; not active **2** not resisting or opposing what happens or what others do **3** *Gram* denoting the form of a verb used when the subject of the sentence receives the action, e.g. *they were killed* as opposed to *he killed them* **passively** *adv* **passivity** *n* **passive resistance** *n* non-violent resistance to authority by a refusal to cooperate **passive smoking** *n* breathing in smoke from cigarettes, etc. smoked by others

past *adj* **1** belonging or referring to the time before the present ♦ *in past centuries* ♦ *his past achievements* **2** just gone by ♦ *the past twelve months* **3** *Gram* (said about a tense) denoting an action or state that went on before the time of speaking or writing (e.g. *he came, he had come*) **past** *n* **1** time that is gone by ♦ *I've been there in the past.* **2** a person's earlier life or career, especially when this is disreputable ♦ *a man with a past*

past *prep* **1** up to and beyond ♦ *She hurried past me.* **2** beyond ♦ *It is past midnight.* **past** *adv* beyond in time or place, up to and further ♦ *I looked into the window as I walked past.* **past master** *n* a person who is experienced in and skilled at a subject or activity **past it** *informal* too old to be able to do something

pasta (say **pas**-tə) *n* an Italian food consisting of a dried paste made with flour and produced in various shapes (e.g. spaghetti, lasagne)

paste *n* **1** a moist fairly stiff mixture **2** an adhesive **3** a hard glass-like substance used to make imitation jewellery **paste** *v* **1** to stick something onto a surface with paste **2** to coat something with paste **pasteboard** *n* thin board made of layers of paper or wood fibres pasted together

pastel (say **pas**-təl) *n* **1** a chalk-like crayon **2** a drawing made with this **3** a light delicate shade of a colour

pasteurize (say **pahs**-chəriyz) *v* to sterilize milk, etc. by partially heating and then chilling it **pasteurization** *n*

pastiche (say pas-**teesh**) *n* a piece of music or writing, etc. in a style that imitates another work, artist, or period

pastille (say **pas**-təl) *n* a small sweet or lozenge

pastime *n* something you do regularly for enjoyment

pastor (say **pah**-stər) *n* a member of the Christian clergy in charge of a church or congregation **pastoral** *adj* **1** to do with shepherds or country life **2** to do with the giving of spiritual guidance

pastry *n pl* **pastries** **1** a dough made of flour, fat, and water, used for covering pies or holding a filling **2** a cake of sweet pastry with a cream, jam, or fruit filling

pasture *n* land covered mainly with grass, suitable for grazing cattle or sheep

pasty[1] (say **pas**-ti) *n pl* **pasties** pastry with a filling of meat and vegetables

pasty[2] (say **pay**-sti) *adj* **pastier, pastiest** unhealthily pale

pat *v* **patted, patting** to tap something gently **pat** *n* **1** a patting movement or sound **2** a small mass of butter or other soft substance **pat** *adj, adv* readily given or prepared in advance ♦ *a pat answer* ♦ *He had his excuses off pat.*

patch *n* **1** a piece of material or metal, etc. put over a hole or damaged place to mend it **2** a shield worn over the eye, to protect it **3** a large or irregular area on a surface, differing in colour or texture, etc. from the rest **4** a piece of ground, especially for growing vegetables **5** a small area or piece of something ♦ *patches of fog* **6** a short period ♦ *Their marriage was going through a bad patch.* **patch** *v* **1** to sew a patch on something **2** to piece things together **patchy** *adj* **patchier, patchiest 1** existing in small isolated areas ♦ *patchy fog* **2** uneven in quality **patchwork** *n* needlework in which assorted small pieces of cloth are joined edge to edge **to patch something up 1** to repair something roughly **2** to settle a quarrel or dispute

pate (say payt) *n old use* the top of a person's head

pâté (say **pa**-tay) *n* a rich paste made of meat or fish

patent (say **pat**-ənt or **pay**-tənt) *n* the official right given to an inventor to make or sell his or her invention exclusively **patent** (say **pay**-tənt) *adj* **1** obvious, unconcealed **2** protected by a patent **patent** *v* to obtain a patent for an invention **patently** *adv* **patent leather** *n* leather with a glossy varnished surface

paternal (say pə-**ter**-nəl) *adj* **1** to do with a father or fatherhood **2** fatherly **3** related through your father ♦ *my paternal grandmother* **paternalism** *n* the policy of providing for people's needs but giving them no responsibility **paternalistic** *adj* **paternally** *adv* **paternity** *n* **1** being the father of a particular child **2** descent from a father

path *n* **1** a way by which people or animals can walk, a track **2** a line along which a person or thing moves **3** a course of action

pathetic (say pə-**thet**-ik) *adj* **1** making you feel pity or sadness **2** *informal* miserably inadequate or useless **pathetically** *adv* **pathos** *n* a quality of making people feel pity or sadness

pathology (say pə-**thol**-əji) *n* **1** the scientific study of diseases of the body **2** abnormal changes in body tissue, caused by disease **pathological** *adj* **1** to do with pathology **2** to do with or caused by disease **3** *informal* compulsive ♦ *a pathological liar* **pathologist** *n*

-pathy *suffix* forming nouns meaning 'feeling or suffering something' (as in *sympathy, telepathy*)

patience *n* **1** the ability to put up calmly with delay, inconvenience, or annoyance **2** a card game for one player in which cards have to be brought into a particular arrangement

patient *n* a person receiving or registered to receive medical treatment by a doctor or dentist, etc. **patient** *adj* **patiently** *adv*

patina (say **pat**-in-ə) *n* **1** an attractive green film on the surface of old bronze **2** a gloss on the surface of wooden furniture produced by age and from polishing

patio (say **pat**-i-oh) *n pl* **patios** a paved area beside a house

patois (say **pat**-wah) *n* a dialect

patriarch (say **pay**-tri-ark) *n* **1** the male head of a family or tribe **2** a bishop of high rank in the Orthodox Christian Churches **patriarchal** *adj*

patrician (say pə-**trish**-ən) *n* an aristocrat or nobleman **patrician** *adj* aristocratic

patricide (say **pat**-ri-siyd) *n* **1** the crime of killing your own father **2** a person who kills their own father

patrimony (say **pat**-rim-əni) *n pl* **patrimonies** property inherited from your father or ancestors

patriot (say **pay**-tri-ət or **pat**-ri-ət) *n* a person who loves their country and supports it loyally **patriotic** *adj* **patriotically** *adv* **patriotism** *n*

patrol *v* **patrolled, patrolling** to walk or travel regularly over an area in order to guard it and see that all is well **patrol** *n* the people, ships, or aircraft whose job is to patrol an area

patron (say **pay**-trən) *n* **1** a person who supports a person or cause with money or encouragement **2** a regular customer of a restaurant, hotel, shop, etc. **patronage** *n* support given by a patron **patronize** v 1 to talk to someone in a way that shows you think they are stupid or inferior to you 2 to be a regular customer at a restaurant, shop, etc. **patron saint** n a saint who is thought to give special protection to a person, place, or activity

atronymic (say pat-rə-**nim**-ik) n a person's name that is taken from the name of the father or a male ancestor

atter[1] v 1 to make a series of light quick tapping sounds ♦ *Rain pattered on the window panes.* 2 to run with short quick steps **patter** n a series of light quick tapping sounds

atter[2] n the rapid continuous talk of a comedian, conjuror, salesperson, etc.

pattern n 1 a repeated arrangement of lines, shapes, or colours; a decorative design 2 the regular way in which something happens ♦ *behaviour patterns* 3 a model, design, or instructions according to which something is to be made **pattern** v 1 to decorate something with a pattern 2 to model something according to a pattern

patty n pl **patties** 1 a small pie or pasty 2 a small flat cake of minced meat, etc.

paucity (say **paw**-siti) n smallness of supply or quantity

paunch n a large stomach that sticks out

pauper n a very poor person

pause n a temporary stop in speaking or doing something **pause** v to stop speaking or doing something for a short time

pave v to cover a road or path, etc. with stones or concrete, etc. **pavement** n a paved path for pedestrians at the side of a road

pavilion n 1 a building on a sports ground for use by players and spectators, especially at a cricket ground 2 an ornamental building or shelter used for dances, concerts, exhibitions, etc.

pavlova (say pav-**loh**-və) n an open meringue case filled with cream and fruit

paw n the foot of an animal that has claws **paw** v 1 to feel or scrape something with a paw or hoof 2 *informal* to touch something awkwardly or rudely with the hands

pawn[1] n 1 the least valuable chess piece

2 a person used by others for their own purposes

pawn[2] v to leave something with a pawnbroker as security for money borrowed **pawnbroker** n a shopkeeper who lends money at interest to people in return for objects that they leave as security

pawpaw n 1 another word for *papaya* 2 a North American tree with edible yellow fruit with sweet pulp 3 the fruit of this tree

pay v past tense and past participle **paid** 1 to give someone money in return for work, goods, or services 2 to give what is owed ♦ *Have you paid the rent?* 3 to be profitable or worthwhile ♦ *It pays to advertise.* 4 to suffer a penalty or misfortune 5 to give or express something ♦ *Now pay attention.* ♦ *She was not used to people paying her compliments.* **pay** n money paid for work **payable** adj needing to be paid **payee** n a person to whom money is paid or is to be paid **payer** n **payment** n 1 paying or being paid 2 money given in return for work, goods, or services **payload** n 1 the part of an aircraft's load from which revenue is derived, i.e. passengers or cargo 2 an explosive warhead carried by an aircraft or missile **payroll** n a list of a firm's employees receiving regular pay **to pay off** *informal* to yield good results ♦ *The risk paid off.* **to pay someone off** to dismiss an employee with a final payment **to pay something off** to pay a debt in full

PAYE abbr pay-as-you-earn: a method of collecting income tax by deducting it at source from an employee's wages

PC abbr 1 personal computer 2 police constable 3 politically correct

p.c. abbr 1 per cent 2 postcard

PE abbr physical education

pea n 1 a small round green seed eaten as a vegetable 2 the climbing plant bearing these seeds in pods

peace n 1 freedom from or the ending of war 2 a treaty ending a war ♦ *After three years of conflict, the peace was signed.* 3 freedom from civil disorder ♦ *a breach of the peace* 4 undisturbed quietness and calm ♦ *peace of mind* 5 a state of harmony between people

peaceable adj 1 not quarrelsome, wanting to be at peace with others 2 peaceful, without strife **peaceably** adv **peaceful** adj 1 quiet and calm 2 not involving war or violence **peacefully** adv **peacefulness** n

peach n a round juicy fruit with downy yellowish or reddish skin and a large rough stone **peach** adj yellowish-pink **peachy** adj

peacock n a male bird with a long brightly-coloured tail that it can spread upright like a fan **peahen** n the female of a peacock

peak n 1 a pointed top of a mountain 2 the part of a cap that sticks out in front 3 the point of highest value, achievement, or activity ♦ the peak of her career **peak** v to reach its highest point or value **peak** adj 1 maximum 2 when use or demand is at its highest ♦ peak viewing hours **peaked** adj **peaky** adj **peakier**, **peakiest** looking pale from illness or fatigue

peal n 1 the loud ringing of a bell or set of bells 2 a loud burst of thunder or laughter **peal** v (said about bells) to ring loudly

peanut n 1 a plant bearing pods that ripen underground, containing two edible seeds 2 this seed, eaten as a snack or used to make oil **peanuts** n informal a small or trivial amount of money

pear n a rounded fleshy fruit that tapers towards the stalk

pearl n 1 a round usually white mass of a shiny substance formed inside the shells of some oysters and valued as a gem 2 something resembling a pearl ♦ pearls of dew **pearly** adj **pearlier**, **pearliest**

peasant (say **pez**-ənt) n a member of a class of farm labourers and small farmers **peasantry** n

peat n decomposed vegetable matter found in bogs, used in gardening or cut in pieces as fuel **peaty** adj

pebble n a small stone worn round and smooth by the action of water **pebble-dash** n mortar with pebbles in it, used as a coating for an outside wall

pecan n a smooth pinkish-brown nut like a walnut

peccadillo (say pek-ə-**dil**-oh) n pl **peccadilloes** or **peccadillos** a small and unimportant fault or offence

peck[1] v 1 to bite or strike something with the beak 2 to kiss someone lightly on the cheek **peck** n 1 a quick bite or stroke made with the beak 2 a light kiss on the cheek **peckish** adj hungry **pecking order** n a series of ranks of status or authority in a group

peck[2] n a measure of capacity for dry goods, equivalent to 2 gallons (9.092 litres)

pectin n a jelly-like substance found in ripe fruits, used to make jams and jellies set

pectoral (say **pek**-ter-əl) adj to do with, in, or on the chest or breast **pectoral** n a pectoral muscle or fin

peculiar adj 1 strange or odd 2 belonging exclusively to a particular person, place, or thing ♦ customs peculiar to the 18th century 3 formal particular or special ♦ a point of peculiar interest **peculiarity** n pl **peculiarities** 1 an unusual or distinctive characteristic or habit 2 being peculiar **peculiarly** adv

pecuniary (say pi-**kew**-ni-er-i) adj formal to do with money

pedagogue (say **ped**-ə-gog) n formal a teacher, especially one who teaches in a pedantic way **pedagogic** adj **pedagogical** adj

pedal n a lever pressed by the foot to operate a bicycle, car, or other machine, or in certain musical instruments **pedal** v **pedalled**, **pedalling** to move or operate something by means of pedals; to ride a bicycle

pedant (say **ped**-ənt) n a person who is too concerned with minor detail or with the strict observance of formal rules **pedantic** adj **pedantry** n

peddle v 1 to go from house to house selling goods 2 to sell illegal drugs **peddler** n someone who sells illegal drugs

pederast (say **peed**-er-ast) n a man who has sexual intercourse with a boy **pederasty** n

pedestal n the raised base on which a column, statue, etc. stands

pedestrian n a person who is walking, especially in a street **pedestrian** adj dull and unimaginative **pedestrianize** v to make a street or area accessible only to pedestrians

pedlar *n* a person who goes from house to house selling small goods

pedometer (say pid-**om**-it-er) *n* an instrument that calculates the distance a person walks by counting the number of steps taken

peek *v* to have a quick or sly look at something **peek** *n* a quick or sly look

peel *n* the skin or rind of certain fruits and vegetables **peell** *v* 1 to remove the peel from a fruit or vegetable 2 to pull off an outer layer or covering 3 (said of a surface) to lose its outer layer in small strips or pieces **peeler** *n* **peelings** *pl n*

peep¹ *v* to look quickly or surreptitiously **peep** *n* a brief or surreptitious look

peep² *n* a brief high-pitched sound **peep** *v* to make a peep

peer¹ *v* 1 to look at something closely or with difficulty 2 to be just visible

peer² *n* 1 a member of the nobility in Britain 2 a person of the same age, status, or ability as someone else **peerage** *n* 1 peers as a group 2 the rank of peer or peeress **peerless** *adj* without an equal; better than the others **peer group** *n* a group of people of roughly the same age or status

peeve *v* *informal* to annoy or irritate someone **peevish** *adj* irritable

peewit *n* a lapwing

peg *n* a short pin or bolt for hanging things on, fastening things together, holding a tent rope taut, or marking a position **peg** *v* **pegged**, **pegging** 1 to fix or mark something by means of a peg or pegs 2 to keep wages or prices at a fixed level **off the peg** (describing clothes) ready-made

pejorative (say pij-**o**-rə-tiv) *adj* showing disapproval or contempt **pejoratively** *adv*

Pekinese, **Pekingese** *n pl* **Pekinese**, **Pekingese** a small dog with short legs, a flat face, and long silky hair

pelican *n* a large waterbird with a pouch in its long bill for scooping up and storing fish **pelican crossing** *n* a pedestrian crossing controlled by lights that signal traffic to stop

pellagra (say pil-**ag**-rə) *n* a deficiency disease causing cracking of the skin and mental disorders

pellet *n* a small ball of something

pell-mell *adv*, *adj* in a confused rush; headlong

pellucid (say pil-**oo**-sid) *adj* very clear

pelmet (say **pel**-mit) *n* an ornamental strip of cloth or wood used to conceal a curtain rail

pelt¹ *v* 1 to throw a lot of things at someone 2 (said about rain, etc.) to fall heavily 3 to run fast **at full pelt** as fast as possible

pelt² *n* an animal skin, especially with the fur or hair still on it

pelvis *n* the basin-shaped framework of bones at the lower end of the body **pelvic** *adj*

pen¹ *n* an instrument for writing with ink **pen** *v* **penned**, **penning** to write or compose something **penknife** *n pl* **penknives** a small folding knife **pen name** *n* a name used by an author instead of his or her real name

pen² *n* a small fenced enclosure, especially for sheep, pigs, hens, etc. **pen** *v* **penned**, **penning** 1 to shut animals in a pen 2 to force someone to stay in a restricted space ♦ *Once the scandal broke, reporters kept him penned up at home.*

pen³ *n* a female swan

penal (say **pee**-nəl) *adj* to do with punishment **penalize** *v* 1 to inflict a penalty on someone 2 to place someone at a serious disadvantage **penalty** *n pl* **penalties** 1 a punishment for breaking a law, rule, or contract 2 a disadvantage imposed on a sports player or team for breaking a rule

penance (say **pen**-əns) *n* a punishment that you willingly suffer to express your regret for something wrong that you have done

pence a plural of *penny*

penchant (say **pahn**-shahn) *n* a liking or inclination ♦ *He has a penchant for old films.*

pencil *n* an thin cylindrical instrument for drawing or writing, consisting of a stick of graphite or coloured chalk, etc. **pencil** *v* **pencilled**, **pencilling** to write, draw, or mark something with a pencil

pendant *n* a piece of jewellery that hangs from a chain worn round the neck

pendent *adj* hanging down

pending adj **1** waiting to be decided or settled **2** about to happen **pending** prep while waiting for, until ♦ *in custody pending trial*

pendulous (say pen-dew-ləs) adj hanging downwards

pendulum (say pen-dew-ləm) n a weight hung from a cord so that it can swing to and fro

penetrate v **1** to make a way into or through something **2** to discover or understand something **penetrating** adj **1** having or showing great insight ♦ *a penetrating mind* **2** (said about a voice or sound) clearly heard above or through other sounds **penetration** n **penetrative** adj able to penetrate, penetrating

penguin n a black and white seabird of the Antarctic, with wings developed into flippers used for swimming

penicillin (say pen-i-sil-in) n an antibiotic obtained from mould fungi

peninsula (say pən-ins-yoo-lə) n a long narrow piece of land sticking out into the sea or a lake **peninsular** adj

penis (say pee-nis) n the part of the body with which a male animal has sexual intercourse and, in mammals, urinates

penitent adj feeling or showing regret that you have done wrong **penitent** n a penitent person **penitence** n **penitential** adj **penitentiary** n pl **penitentiaries** a prison for people convicted of a serious crime

pennant (say pen-ənt) n a long narrow triangular flag

pennon n a long narrow flag

penny n pl **pennies** or **pence 1** a British bronze coin worth ¹⁄₁₀₀ of £1 **2** a former British coin worth ¹⁄₁₂ of a shilling **penniless** adj having no money, very poor **penny-farthing** n an early type of bicycle with a very large front wheel and a small rear one **penny-pinching** adj unwilling to spend money; miserly

pension¹ (say pen-shən) n regular payments made to someone who is retired, widowed, or disabled **pensionable** adj **1** entitled to receive a pension **2** (said about a job) entitling a person to receive a pension **pensioner** n a person who receives

a retirement or other pension

pension² (say pahn-si-awn or pen-shən) n a small hotel or boarding house in France and other European countries

pensive adj deep in thought; thoughtful and gloomy

penta- prefix five

pentagon (say pen-tə-gən) n a geometric figure with five sides **pentagonal** adj

pentagram (say pen-tə-gram) n a five-pointed star

pentameter (say pen-tam-it-er) n a line of verse with five rhythmic beats

pentathlon (say pen-tath-lən) n an athletic contest in which each competitor takes part in five events **pentathlete** n

Pentecost (say pen-ti-kost) n **1** a Christian festival commemorating the descent of the Holy Spirit on the apostles **2** the Jewish harvest festival of Shavuoth, fifty days after the second day of Passover **Pentecostal** adj to do with any of the Christian groups characterized by an emphasis on the gifts of the Holy Spirit and a fundamental interpretation of the Bible

penthouse n a flat on the top floor of a tall building

pent-up adj shut in; kept from being expressed ♦ *pent-up anger*

penultimate (say pən-ul-tim-ət) adj last but one

penumbra (say pin-um-brə) n an outer area of shadow that is partly but not fully shaded, e.g. during a partial eclipse **penumbral** adj

penury (say pen-yoor-i) n great poverty **penurious** adj

peony (say pee-əni) n pl **peonies** a garden plant with large round red, pink, or white flowers

people pl n **1** human beings in general **2** the men, women, and children belonging to a place or forming a group or social class; the mass of citizens in a country **people** n a community, tribe, race, or nation **people** v to fill a place with people, to populate a place

pep n informal vigour or energy **pep** v **pepped**, **pepping** informal **to pep someone or something up** to make

someone or something more lively
pep talk n a talk given to someone to encourage them

pepper n 1 a hot-tasting powder made from the dried berries of certain plants, used to season food 2 a kind of capsicum grown as a vegetable **pepper** v 1 to sprinkle food with pepper 2 to sprinkle or scatter things here and there 3 to pelt someone or something with small objects **peppery** adj 1 like pepper, containing much pepper 2 hot-tempered **peppercorn** n the dried black berry from which pepper is made **pepper mill** n a mill for grinding peppercorns by hand

peppermint n 1 a kind of mint grown for its strong fragrant oil, used in medicine and in sweets, etc. 2 a sweet flavoured with this mint

pepperoni n beef and pork sausage seasoned with pepper

peptic adj to do with digestion **peptic ulcer** n an ulcer in the stomach or duodenum

per prep 1 for each ♦ The charge is £12 per person. 2 in accordance with ♦ I have signed and returned the contract, as per instructions.

per- prefix 1 through (as in perforate) 2 thoroughly (as in perturb) 3 away entirely; towards badness (as in pervert)

perambulate (say per-am-bew-layt) v formal 1 to walk about 2 to walk round an area in order to inspect it **perambulation** n **perambulator** n a baby's pram

per annum adv for each year; yearly

per capita (say **kap**-it-ə) adv, adj for each person

perceive v 1 to see, notice, or become aware of something 2 to regard or understand something in a particular way ♦ I perceived the situation quite differently. **perceptible** adj able to be seen or noticed **perceptibly** adv **perception** n 1 the process of receiving information through the senses and making sense of it 2 the ability to notice or understand something **perceptive** adj quick to notice or understand things **perceptively** adv **percipient** adj quick to notice or understand things

per cent adv in or for every hundred ♦ three per cent (3%) **percentage** n 1 an amount or rate expressed as a proportion of 100 2 a proportion or share of something

perch[1] n 1 a place where a bird sits or rests; a bar or rod provided for this purpose 2 a high seat or place on which a person sits **perch** v 1 to rest on a perch 2 to position something on the edge or at the very top of something

perch[2] n pl **perch** an edible freshwater fish with spiny fins

perchance adv old use perhaps

percolate (say **per**-kəl-ayt) v 1 to filter or cause something to filter, especially through small holes 2 to prepare coffee in a percolator 3 to spread gradually through a group of people **percolation** n **percolator** n a machine for making coffee, in which boiling water is made to circulate through ground coffee held in a perforated drum

percussion (say per-**kush**-ən) n 1 the percussion instruments in an orchestra 2 the striking of one object against another **percussive** adj **percussion instrument** n a musical instrument, such as a drum or cymbals, played by being struck or shaken

perdition (say per-**dish**-ən) n (in Christian belief) eternal damnation

peregrine (say **pe**-ri-grin) n a kind of falcon that can be trained to hunt and catch small animals and birds

peremptory (say per-**emp**-ter-i) adj giving an urgent command and expecting to be obeyed at once

perennial (say per-**en**-yəl) adj 1 lasting a long time; continually recurring ♦ a perennial problem 2 (said about a plant) living for several years **perennial** n a perennial plant **perennially** adv

perfect (say **per**-fikt) adj 1 having all its essential qualities or characteristics ♦ in perfect health 2 so good that it cannot be made any better ♦ a perfect score 3 exact or precise ♦ a perfect circle 4 complete, total ♦ It made perfect sense to me. 5 excellent or satisfactory in every respect ♦ It's been a perfect day. 6 Gram (said about a verb) in the tense used to denote a completed past action, as in ♦ *He has returned.* **perfect** *n* *Gram* the perfect tense **perfect** (say per-**fekt**) *v* to make something perfect **perfection** *n* **perfectionist** *n* a person who is only satisfied if something is perfect **perfectionism** *n* **perfectly** *adv*

perfidious (say per-**fid**-i-əs) *adj* treacherous or disloyal **perfidiously** *adv* **perfidy** *n*

perforate *v* to pierce something and make a hole or holes in it **perforation** *n*

perforce *adv* *formal* by force of circumstances, necessarily

perform *v* 1 to do or carry out something ♦ *to perform a ceremony* 2 to function or work ♦ *The car performs well at low speeds.* 3 to do something in front of an audience **performance** *n* **performer** *n*

perfume *n* 1 a fragrant liquid for giving a pleasant smell, especially to the body 2 a pleasant smell **perfume** *v* to give a pleasant smell to something; to apply perfume to something **perfumery** *n* *pl* **perfumeries**

perfunctory (say per-**funk**-ter-i) *adj* done as a duty or routine but without much care or interest ♦ *a perfunctory glance* **perfunctorily** *adv*

pergola (say **per**-gələ) *n* an arched structure forming a framework for climbing or trailing plants

perhaps *adv* it may be, possibly

peri- *prefix* around (as in *perimeter*)

perigee (say **pe**-ri-jee) *n* the point in the orbit of the moon or of a satellite when it is nearest to the earth. (Compare apogee.)

peril *n* serious danger **perilous** *adj* full of risk, dangerous **perilously** *adv*

perimeter (say per-**im**-it-er) *n* 1 the outer edge or boundary of something 2 the distance round the edge

period *n* 1 a length of time 2 a time with particular characteristics ♦ *the colonial period* 3 the time allocated for a lesson in school 4 the time when a woman menstruates 5 a full stop in punctuation **period** *adj* (said about furniture, dress, drama, etc.) belonging to a past historical time **periodic** *adj* occurring or appearing at intervals **periodical** *adj* occurring or appearing at intervals **periodical** *n* a magazine, etc. published at regular intervals **periodically** *adv* **periodic table** *n* a table of the chemical elements

peripatetic (say pe-ri-pə-**tet**-ik) *adj* going from place to place

periphery (say per-**if**-er-i) *n* *pl* **peripheries** 1 the boundary of a surface or area; the region immediately inside or beyond this 2 the fringes of a subject, group, etc. **peripheral** *adj* 1 of minor but not central importance to something 2 to do with or on the periphery **peripheral** *n* *ICT* any device that can be attached to and used with a computer but is not an integral part of it

periscope *n* a device with a tube and mirrors by which a person in a submerged submarine or behind a high obstacle can see things that are otherwise out of sight

perish *v* 1 to die or be destroyed 2 to rot or decay **perishable** *adj* likely to rot or go bad in a short time **perishing** *adj* freezing cold

peritoneum (say pe-ri-tə-**nee**-əm) *n* the membrane lining the abdomen **peritonitis** *n* inflammation of the peritoneum

periwinkle[1] *n* an evergreen trailing plant with blue or white flowers

periwinkle[2] *n* a winkle

perjury (say **per**-jer-i) *n* *pl* **perjuries** the deliberate giving of false evidence while on oath; the evidence itself **perjure** *v* **to perjure yourself** to commit perjury

perk[1] *v* **perky** *adj* **perkier**, **perkiest** lively and cheerful **to perk up** to become or cause a person or thing to become more cheerful or lively

perk[2] *n* *informal* a benefit given to an employee in addition to normal pay, such as health insurance or the use of a company car

perm *n* treatment of the hair with chemicals to give it long-lasting waves or curls **perm** *v* to give a perm to someone's hair

permafrost *n* the permanently frozen subsoil in polar regions

permanent *adj* lasting for always; meant to last indefinitely **permanence** *n* **permanently** *adv*

permeate (say **per**-mi-ayt) *v* to pass or spread into every part of something

permeable *adj* allowing liquids or gases to pass through

permit (say per-**mit**) *v* **permitted**, **permitting** 1 to give someone permission or consent to do something 2 to make something possible or give someone the opportunity to do something ♦ *We're having a barbecue tomorrow, weather permitting.*

permit *n* an official document giving someone permission to do something or go somewhere **permissible** *adj* permitted or allowable **permission** *n* the right to do something, given by someone in authority **permissive** *adj* allowing a lot of freedom in behaviour, especially in sexual matters

permutation (say per-mew-**tay**-shən) *n* 1 variation of the order or arrangement of a set of things 2 any one of these arrangements ♦ *3, 1, 2 is a permutation of 1, 2, 3* 3 a selection of specified items from a larger group, to be arranged in a number of combinations, e.g. in a football pool **permutate** *v* to change the order or arrangement of a set of things

pernicious (say per-**nish**-əs) *adj* having a harmful effect, especially in a subtle way

pernickety *adj informal* fussy about small details

peroration (say pe-rer-**ay**-shən) *n* the concluding part of a speech

peroxide *n* hydrogen peroxide, used for bleaching hair

perpendicular *adj* 1 at an angle of 90° to another line or surface 2 at an angle of 90° to the horizontal; upright or vertical 3 (said about a cliff, etc.) having a vertical face **perpendicular** *n* a perpendicular line or direction

perpetrate (say **per**-pit-rayt) *v* to commit or be guilty of something wrong, such as a crime or error **perpetration** *n* **perpetrator** *n*

perpetuate *v* to cause something to last or continue ♦ *The statue will perpetuate his memory.* **perpetual** *adj* 1 never ending 2 frequent, often repeated **perpetually** *adv* **perpetuation** *n* **perpetuity** *n* the state or quality of lasting forever

perplex *v* to bewilder or puzzle someone **perplexity** *n* bewilderment

perquisite (say **per**-kwiz-it) *n formal* a benefit or perk

perry *n pl* **perries** a drink made from the fermented juice of pears

per se (say per **say**) *adv* by or in itself ♦ *I don't object to violence in films per se, but there just seems to be too much of it these days.*

persecute *v* 1 to be continually hostile and cruel to someone, especially because you disagree with their beliefs 2 to keep harassing someone **persecution** *n* **persecutor** *n*

persevere *v* to go on doing something even though it is difficult or tedious **perseverance** *n*

Persian *adj* to do with Persia, a country in the Middle East now called Iran, or its people or language **Persian** *n* 1 a native or inhabitant of Persia 2 the language of Persia 3 a cat with long silky fur

persist *v* 1 to continue doing something firmly or obstinately in spite of opposition or failure ♦ *She persists in breaking the rules.* 2 to continue to exist ♦ *The custom persists in some countries.* **persistence** *n* **persistent** *adj* **persistently** *adv*

person *n pl* **people** or **persons** 1 an individual human being 2 an individual's body ♦ *She had a microphone concealed in her person.* 3 *Gram* any of the three classes of personal pronouns and verb forms that shows if a person is speaking, spoken to, or spoken about **persona** *n pl* **personas** or **personae** 1 a role or character taken by a writer or actor 2 the aspect of a person's character that other people are aware of **personable** *adj* pleasant in appearance and manner **personage** *n* an important or distinguished person **personal** *adj* 1 to do with or belonging to a particular person ♦ *The story is written from personal experience.* 2 done, dealt with, or made in person ♦ *I will give it my personal attention.* ♦ *several personal appearances* 3 to do with a person's private life ♦ *This is a personal matter.* 4 making remarks about a person's appearance, character, or private affairs, especially in an offensive way 5 to do with a person's body ♦ *personal hygiene*

personality n pl **personalities** 1 a person's own distinctive character ♦ *She has a cheerful personality.* 2 the qualities that make someone interesting or popular 3 a celebrity **personalize** v to make something personal, especially by marking it with your initials, name, etc. or by making it fit your own requirements **personally** adv 1 in person, not through someone else ♦ *The chairman showed us round personally.* 2 as a person, in a personal capacity ♦ *We don't know him personally.* 3 in a personal manner ♦ *Don't take it personally.* 4 as regards yourself ♦ *Personally, I like it.* **personify** v **personifies, personified, personifying** 1 to represent an idea in human form or a thing as having human characteristics ♦ *Justice is personified as a blindfolded woman holding a pair of scales.* 2 to embody a quality in your life or behaviour ♦ *He was vanity personified.* **personification** n **personal column** n the part of a newspaper that includes private messages or advertisements **personal pronoun** n each of the pronouns (*I, me, we, us, you, he, him, she, her, it, they, them*) that indicate person, gender, number, and case **in person** physically present

personnel (say per-sən-**el**) n the body of people employed by a firm or other large organization

perspective n 1 the art of drawing solid objects on a flat surface so as to give the impression of depth and space and relative distance 2 the apparent relationship between visible objects as to position, distance, etc. 3 a balanced understanding of the relative importance of things ♦ *Try to keep a sense of perspective.* 4 a particular way of thinking about something

Perspex n trademark a tough transparent plastic material

perspicacious (say per-spi-**kay**-shəs) adj having or showing great insight **perspicacity** n

perspire v to sweat **perspiration** n

persuade v 1 to make someone believe or agree to do something by reasoning with him or her 2 to be a good reason for someone to do something **persuasion** n

1 persuading, or being persuaded 2 belief, especially religious belief **persuasive** adj 1 good at persuading someone to do or believe something 2 providing sound reasoning or argument **persuasively** adv

pert adj 1 lively or cheeky 2 neat and jaunty

pertain (say per-**tayn**) v to be relevant to or belong to something ♦ *evidence pertaining to the case*

pertinacious (say per-tin-**ay**-shəs) adj formal stubbornly persistent and determined

pertinent adj relevant to what you are talking about **pertinence** n

perturb v to make someone anxious or uneasy **perturbation** n

peruse (say per-**ooz**) v formal to read something carefully **perusal** n

pervade v to spread or be present throughout something **pervasion** n **pervasive** adj widespread

perverse (say per-**verss**) adj deliberately or obstinately doing something different from what is reasonable or normal **perversely** adv **perverseness** n **perversion** n 1 perverting, or being perverted 2 a perverted form of something 3 abnormal sexual behaviour **perversity** n

pervert v 1 to turn something from its proper course or use ♦ *perverting the course of justice* 2 to cause someone to behave wickedly or abnormally **pervert** n a person whose sexual behaviour is thought to be abnormal or disgusting

pervious (say per-vi-əs) adj allowing liquids to pass through, permeable

pesky adj **peskier, peskiest** informal annoying

pessimism n a tendency to take a gloomy view of things, or to expect that results will be bad **pessimist** n **pessimistic** adj **pessimistically** adv

pest n 1 an insect or animal that is destructive to crops or to stored food, etc. 2 a troublesome or annoying person or thing **pester** v to keep annoying someone with frequent requests or questions **pesticide** n a substance for killing harmful insects and other pests **pestilence** n a deadly epidemic disease

pestle n a tool with a heavy rounded end for pounding substances in a mortar

pet n 1 an animal that is tamed and treated with affection, kept for companionship and pleasure 2 a person treated as a favourite **pet** adj 1 kept or treated as a pet 2 favourite or particular ♦ *Sport is his pet subject.* **pet** v **petted, petting** 1 to stroke or pat an animal 2 to stroke or fondle someone sexually

petal n each of the coloured outer parts of a flower head

peter v **to peter out** to become gradually less and cease to exist

petite (say pə-**teet**) adj (said about a woman) of small dainty build

petition n 1 a formal written request appealing to an authority for some action to be taken, especially one signed by a large number of people 2 an earnest request 3 a formal application made to a court of law for a writ or order, etc. **petition** v to make or address a petition to someone **petitioner** n

petrel n a kind of seabird that flies far from land

petrify v **petrifies, petrified, petrifying** 1 to make someone so terrified that he or she cannot move 2 to turn something into stone **petrification** n

petrochemical n a chemical substance obtained from petroleum or natural gas

petrol n an inflammable liquid made from petroleum, used as fuel in engines **petrol station** n a place selling petrol for motor vehicles

petroleum (say pi-**troh**-liəm) n a mineral oil found underground, refined for use as fuel (e.g. petrol, paraffin) or in the manufacture of plastics, solvents, etc.

petticoat n a woman's or girl's piece of underwear worn hanging from the waist beneath a dress or skirt

pettifogging adj paying too much attention to unimportant details

petty adj **pettier, pettiest** 1 unimportant or trivial ♦ *petty regulations* 2 minor, on a small scale ♦ *petty crime* 3 small-minded ♦ *petty spite* **pettily** adv **pettiness** n **petty cash** n a small amount of money kept by an office for small payments **petty officer** n an NCO in the navy

petulant (say pet-yoo-lənt) adj irritable or bad-tempered, especially in a childish way **petulance** n **petulantly** adv

petunia n a garden plant with funnel-shaped flowers in bright colours

pew n 1 a long bench with a back and sides, one of a number fixed in rows for the congregation in a church 2 informal a seat

pewter n a grey alloy that used to be made of tin and lead and is nowadays made of tin, copper, and antimony

PG abbr (in film classification) parental guidance

phalanx n a number of people or soldiers forming a compact mass or banded together for a common purpose

phallic (say fal-ik) adj to do with or resembling an erect penis, often symbolizing male reproductive power

phantasm (say fan-tazm) n an illusion or apparition **phantasmagoria** n a shifting scene of real or imagined images, as if in a dream **phantasmal** adj

phantom n 1 a ghost or apparition 2 something that does not really exist, a figment of the imagination **phantom** adj imaginary, not really existing

Pharaoh (say fair-oh) n the title of the king of ancient Egypt

Pharisee n 1 a member of an ancient Jewish sect represented in the New Testament as making a show of sanctity and piety 2 a hypocritical self-righteous person

pharmacology (say farm-ə-kol-əji) n the scientific study of medicinal drugs and their effects on the body **pharmacological** adj **pharmacologist** n

pharmacy (say farm-əsi) n pl **pharmacies** 1 a place where medicinal drugs are prepared and sold 2 the preparation and dispensing of medicinal drugs **pharmaceutical** adj to do with medicinal drugs or with pharmacy **pharmacist** n a person who is trained to prepare and sell medicinal drugs

pharynx (say fa-rinks) n pl **pharynges** the cavity at the back of the nose and throat

phase n a stage in a process of change or

development **phase** v to carry something out in stages, not all at once ♦ *a phased withdrawal*

PhD *abbr* Doctor of Philosophy; a university degree awarded to someone who has done advanced research in their subject

pheasant (say **fez**-ənt) n a long-tailed game bird with bright feathers

phenomenon (say fin-**om**-inən) n pl **phenomena 1** a fact or occurrence that can be observed ♦ *Snow is a common phenomenon in winter.* **2** a remarkable or extraordinary person or thing ◊ Note that *phenomena* is a plural noun. It is not correct to say *this phenomena* or *these phenomenas*. **phenomenal** adj extraordinary or remarkable **phenomenally** adv

phew *interjection informal* an exclamation of relief, wonder, discomfort, etc.

phial (say **fiy**-əl) n a small glass bottle, especially for perfume or liquid medicine

philander (say fil-**and**-er) v (said about a man) to have casual affairs with women **philanderer** n

philanthropy (say fil-**an**-thrəp-i) n concern for your fellow human beings, especially as shown by kind and generous acts that benefit large numbers of people **philanthropic** adj **philanthropist** n

philately (say fil-**at**-əl-i) n stamp-collecting **philatelist** n

philharmonic (say fil-ar-**mon**-ik) adj (in the names of orchestras) devoted to music

philistine (say **fil**-i-stiyn) n a person who dislikes culture and the arts

philology (say fil-**ol**-əji) n the study of the structure and development of a language **philological** adj **philologist** n

philosophy n pl **philosophies 1** the study by logical reasoning of the fundamental nature of knowledge, reality, and existence **2** a system of ideas of a particular philosopher **3** a system of principles for the conduct of life or behaviour **philosopher** n someone who studies or is an expert in philosophy **philosophical** adj **1** to do with philosophy **2** calm in the face of disappointment or misfortune **philosophically** adv **philosophize** v to reason like a philosopher **philtre** (say **fil**-ter) n a love potion

phlegm (say flem) n thick mucus in the throat and bronchial passages

phlegmatic (say fleg-**mat**-ik) adj not easily excited or agitated

phobia (say **foh**-biə) n an extreme or irrational fear or great dislike of something **phobic** adj

-phobia *suffix* forming nouns meaning 'fear or great dislike of something' (as in *hydrophobia*)

phoenix (say **fee**-niks) n a mythical bird said to live for hundreds of years and then burn itself on a funeral pyre, rising from its ashes young again to live for another cycle

phone n a telephone **phone** v to telephone someone **phonecard** n a plastic card that you can use to make calls from some public telephones

phonetic (say fə-**net**-ik) adj **1** representing each speech sound by a particular symbol which is always used for that sound ♦ *the phonetic alphabet* **2** (said about spelling) corresponding to pronunciation **3** to do with phonetics **phonetics** n the study of speech sounds

phoney adj **phonier, phoniest** *informal* not genuine **phoney** n pl **phonies** *informal* a phoney person or thing

phonograph (say **fohn**-ə-grahf) n old use a record player

phonology (say fə-**nol**-oji) n the study of the speech sounds in a language **phonic** adj to do with speech sounds

phosphorescent (say foss-fer-**ess**-ənt) adj glowing with a faint light without burning or perceptible heat **phosphorescence** n

phosphorus (say **foss**-fer-əs) n a chemical element (symbol P) that appears luminous in the dark and is highly inflammable

photo n pl **photos** a photograph **photo finish** n a very close finish of a race, where the winner can only be identified from a photograph of competitors crossing the line

photo- *prefix* **1** light (as in *photograph*) **2** photography (as in *photofit*) **photocopier** n a machine for making photocopies **photocopy** n pl **photocopies** a photographic copy of something **photocopy** v **photocopies, photocopied,**

photocopying to make a photocopy of something **photofit** n a likeness of a person that is put together by assembling photographs of separate features **photogenic** adj coming out well in photographs **photosensitive** adj reacting to light **photoshop** v to alter or edit a photographic image digitally **photosynthesis** n the process by which green plants use sunlight to turn carbon dioxide (taken from the air) and water into complex substances, giving off oxygen

photograph n a picture formed by means of the chemical action of light or other radiation on a sensitive surface **photograph** v 1 to take a photograph of someone or something 2 to come out in a certain way when photographed ♦ *I don't photograph well.* **photographer** n a person who takes photographs **photographic** adj **photographically** adv **photography** n the taking and processing of photographs

phrase n 1 a group of words without a finite verb, forming a unit within a sentence or clause 2 an expression someone uses, especially an idiom or a striking or clever way of saying something 3 *Mus* a short distinct passage forming a unit in a melody **phrase** v 1 to put something into words 2 to divide music into phrases **phraseology** n pl **phraseologies** the words someone chooses to express things **phrase book** n a book listing useful expressions and their equivalents in a foreign language, for use by travellers

physical adj 1 to do with the body rather than the mind or feelings ♦ *physical fitness* ♦ *a physical examination* 2 to do with things that you can touch or see, as opposed to moral, spiritual, or imaginary things ♦ *the physical world* **physical** n a physical examination **physically** adv **physical education** n instruction in physical exercise and games done at school

physician (say fiz-ish-ən) n a doctor

physics (say fiz-iks) n the scientific study of the properties and interactions of matter and energy, e.g. heat, light, sound, movement **physicist** n an expert in physics

physio n pl **physios** informal physiotherapy or a physiotherapist

physiognomy (say fiz-i-on-əmi) n pl **physiognomies** the features of a person's face

physiology (say fiz-i-ol-əji) n 1 the scientific study of the bodily functions of living organisms and their parts 2 the way in which a living organism or bodily part functions **physiological** adj **physiologist** n

physiotherapy (say fiz-i-oh-**the**-rə-pi) n the treatment of a disease, injury, deformity, or weakness by massaging, exercises, heat, etc., not by drugs or surgery **physiotherapist** n

physique (say fiz-**eek**) n a person's physical build and muscular development

pi (pie) n the value of the ratio of the circumference of a circle to its diameter (approximately 3.14159)

piano (say pee-**an**-oh) n pl **pianos** a large keyboard musical instrument in which metal strings are struck by hammers operated by pressing the keys **pianist** n a person who plays the piano

piazza (say pee-**ats**-ə) n a public square in an Italian town

picador (say **pik**-ə-dor) n (in bullfighting) a person on horseback with a lance

picaresque (say pik-er-**esk**) adj (said about a style of fiction) dealing with the adventures of a likeable rogue in a series of episodes

piccalilli n a pickle of chopped vegetables, mustard, and hot spices

piccolo n pl **piccolos** a small flute

pick v 1 to choose or select something 2 to separate a flower or fruit from the plant bearing it 3 to take hold of something and lift or move it ♦ *She bent down to pick up the milk bottle.* 4 to use a finger or pointed instrument in order to remove bits from something **pick** n 1 choice ♦ *Take your pick.* 2 the best of a group ♦ *The last song on the CD is the pick of the bunch.* **picker** n **pickings** pl n 1 scraps of food, etc. remaining 2 profits or gains ♦ *There were rich pickings for thieves that day.* **picky** adj **pickier**, **pickiest** fussy or choosy, especially excessively so **pick-me-up** n something that makes you feel more energetic or cheerful **pickpocket** n a thief who steals from people's pockets or bags **pickup** n a small open truck or van **to pick a fight** to provoke a quarrel or fight deliberately **to pick a lock** to use a piece of wire or a pointed tool to open a lock without using a key **to pick on** to single someone out as a target for criticism or unkind treatment **to pick someone** or **something off** to select and shoot or destroy members of a group one by one, especially from a distance **to pick someone's pocket** to steal from it **to pick someone up 1** to call for someone and take them with you, especially in a vehicle **2** informal to meet someone casually and become acquainted with them, especially in the hope of sexual relations **to pick something out 1** to distinguish something from surrounding objects or areas **2** to recognize something **to pick something up 1** to collect something that has been left somewhere **2** to get, acquire, or learn something **to pick up** to get better or recover ♦ The game picked up in the second half.

pickaxe, **pick** n a tool consisting of a curved iron bar with one or both ends pointed, mounted on a long handle, used for breaking up hard ground or rock

picket n **1** a person or group of people standing outside their place of work and trying to persuade other people not to enter during a strike **2** a pointed wooden stake set into the ground as part of a fence **picket** v **picketed**, **picketing** to act as a picket during a strike

pickle n **1** a food consisting of vegetables or fruit preserved in vinegar or brine **2** informal a difficult situation **pickle** v to preserve food in vinegar or brine **pickled** adj drunk

picnic n an informal meal eaten in the open air away from home **picnic** v **picnicked**, **picnicking** to have a picnic **to be no picnic** informal to be difficult or unpleasant

pico- (say **pee-koh**) prefix one million millionth of a unit ♦ picosecond

Pict n a member of an ancient people of northern Britain **Pictish** adj

pictograph, **pictogram** n a pictorial symbol used as a form of writing

picture n **1** a painting, drawing, or photograph **2** an image on a television screen **3** how something seems; the impression formed about something ♦ A full picture of the incident is yet to emerge. **4** a cinema film ♦ Let's go to the pictures. **5** a perfect example of something ♦ She looked a picture of health. **picture** v **1** to represent something in a picture **2** to form a mental image of something ♦ Can you picture the flat we used to live in? **pictorial** adj with or using pictures **pictorial** n a newspaper or magazine in which pictures are the main feature **picturesque** adj **1** forming a striking and pleasant scene ♦ a picturesque village **2** (said about words or a description) very expressive, vivid ♦ picturesque language **picture window** n a large window made from a single sheet of glass **in the picture** informal fully informed

piddling adj informal trivial, unimportant

pidgin (say **pij-in**) n a simplified form of a language containing elements of other languages ♦ pidgin English

pie n a baked dish of meat, fish, or fruit, etc. enclosed in or covered with pastry **pie chart** n a type of graph in which a circle is divided into sectors to represent the way in which a quantity is divided up

piebald adj (said about a horse, etc.) having irregular patches of white and black or other dark colour

piece n **1** one of the distinct portions of which a thing is composed or into which it is divided or broken **2** one of a set of things ♦ a three-piece suite **3** an instance of something ♦ a fine piece of work ♦ a crucial piece of evidence **4** a musical, literary, or artistic composition ♦ a piece of music **5** a coin ♦ a 50p piece **6** one of the set of objects used to make moves in a game on a board ♦ a chess piece **piece** v **to piece something together 1** to discover what happened by putting together several different pieces of information **2** to make something by joining or adding pieces together **piecemeal** adj, adv done or made a bit at a time **piecework** n work paid according to the quantity done, not by the time spent on it

pièce de résistance (say pee-ess də ray-**zee**-stahns) *n* the most important or remarkable item

pied *adj* having two or more different colours ♦ *a pied wagtail*

pier (say peer) *n* **1** a long structure built out into the sea for people to walk on or as a landing stage for boats **2** a pillar supporting an arch or bridge

pierce *v* **1** to make a hole in or through something with a sharp pointed object **2** to force or cut a way through something ♦ *A shrill voice pierced the air.* **piercing** *adj* **1** (said about a voice or sound) very loud and shrill **2** (said about cold or wind, etc.) penetrating sharply

piffle *n informal* nonsense, worthless talk

pig *n* **1** a domestic or wild animal with short legs, cloven hooves, and a broad blunt snout **2** *informal* a greedy, dirty, or unpleasant person **pig** *v* **pigged**, **pigging**, **to pig out** *informal* to gorge yourself with food **piggery** *n pl* **piggeries** a place where pigs are bred or kept **piggy** *adj* like a pig ♦ *piggy eyes* **piglet** *n* a young pig **piggyback** *n* a ride on a person's shoulders and back **piggy bank** *n* a money box made in the shape of a hollow pig **pig-headed** *adj* obstinate or stubborn **pig iron** *n* crude iron that has been processed in a smelting furnace **pigsty** *n pl* **pigsties 1** a pen for pigs **2** a filthy room or house **pigtail** *n* long hair worn hanging in a plait at the back of the head

pigeon[1] *n* a plump bird of the dove family **pigeonhole** *n* one of a set of small compartments in a desk, on a wall, etc., used for holding papers, letters, or messages **pigeonhole** *v* to decide that a person belongs only to a particular category or group ♦ *He doesn't want to be pigeonholed simply as a stand-up comedian.* **pigeon-toed** *adj* having the toes or feet turned inwards

pigeon[2] *n informal* a person's responsibility or business ♦ *That's not really my pigeon.*

pigment *n* **1** a substance that colours skin or other tissue in animals and plants **2** a substance that gives colour to paint, inks, dyes, etc. **pigmentation** *n*

pike[1] *n pl* **pike** a large voracious freshwater fish with a long narrow snout

pike[2] *n hist* a long wooden shaft with a pointed metal head, used as a weapon

pilaf (say pi-**laf**), **pilau** (say pi-**low**) *n* an Indian or Middle Eastern dish of spiced rice with meat and vegetables

pilchard *n* a small sea fish related to the herring

pile[1] *n* **1** a number of things lying on top of one another **2** *informal* a large quantity ♦ *I've a pile of work to do.* **3** a large imposing building **pile** *v* **1** to put things into a pile **2** to crowd somewhere ♦ *They all piled into one car.* **pile-up** *n* a road accident that involves a number of vehicles

pile[2] *n* a heavy beam driven vertically into the ground as a foundation or support for a building or bridge

pile[3] *n* a raised surface on a carpet or fabric, consisting of many small upright threads

piles *pl n* haemorrhoids

pilfer *v* to steal small items or in small quantities

pilgrim *n* a person who travels to a sacred or revered place as an act of religious devotion **pilgrimage** *n* a pilgrim's journey

pill *n* a small ball or flat round piece of medicine for swallowing whole **the pill** *informal* a contraceptive pill **pill** *v* (said about fabric) to form tiny balls of fluff on the surface

pillage *v* to carry off goods using violence, especially in a war **pillage** *n* the act of pillaging

pillar *n* **1** a tall vertical structure, usually made of stone, used as a support or ornament **2** a person who is one of the chief supporters of something ♦ *He is a pillar of the local community.* **pillar box** *n* a large red cylindrical postbox standing in the street

pillion *n* a seat for a passenger behind the driver of a motorcycle

pillory *n pl* **pillories** a wooden framework with holes for a person's head and hands, into which offenders were formerly locked and exposed to public ridicule as a punishment **pillory** *v* **pillories**, **pilloried**, **pillorying** to ridicule, attack, or abuse someone publicly

pillow n a cushion for a person's head to rest on, especially in bed **pillow** v to rest the head on something soft ♦ *She pillowed her head on her arms.* **pillowcase** n a cloth cover for a pillow

pilot n 1 a person who operates the flying controls of an aircraft 2 a person qualified to take charge of ships entering or leaving a harbour or travelling through a difficult stretch of water **pilot** adj testing on a small scale how something will work before it is introduced ♦ *a pilot scheme* **pilot** v **piloted, piloting** 1 to be the pilot of an aircraft or ship 2 to guide or steer something 3 to test a scheme, etc. before introducing it more widely **pilot light** n a small jet of gas kept alight and lighting a larger burner when this is turned on **pilot officer** n an officer of the lowest commissioned rank in the RAF

pimento (say pim-**ent**-oh) n pl **pimentos** 1 another word for *allspice* 2 another spelling of *pimiento*

pimiento (say pim-**yent**-oh) n pl **pimientos** a red sweet pepper

pimp n a man who gets clients for prostitutes and lives off their earnings

pimpernel (say pimp-er-nel) n a wild plant with small scarlet, blue, or white flowers

pimple n a small hard inflamed spot on the skin **pimply** adj

PIN abbr personal identification number, a number allocated by a bank, etc. to a customer, e.g. for use with a card for obtaining cash from an automatic device

pin n 1 a short thin piece of metal with a sharp point and a rounded head, used for fastening pieces of fabric or paper, etc. together 2 a peg of wood or metal used for various purposes **pin** v **pinned, pinning** 1 to fasten something with a pin or pins 2 to hold someone firmly so that they are unable to move ♦ *He was pinned under the wreckage.*

pinball n a game played on a sloping board across which you shoot small metal balls so that they strike various targets in order to score points **pin money** n a small sum of money someone earns for spending on personal expenses **pinpoint** adj absolutely precise ♦ *with pinpoint accuracy* **pinpoint** v to locate or identify something precisely

pins and needles n a tingling sensation in a limb **pinstripe** n 1 one of the very narrow stripes that form a pattern on cloth 2 cloth with parallel stripes of this kind **pin-tuck** n a very narrow ornamental tuck **pin-up** n a picture of an attractive or famous person, for pinning on a wall **to pin someone down** to force someone to make a definite arrangement or to state clearly their intentions **to pin something down** to establish something clearly

pinafore n 1 an apron 2 a dress with a bib and no collar or sleeves

pince-nez (say **panss**-nay) n pl **pince-nez** a pair of glasses with a spring that clips on the nose and no side pieces

pincer n a front claw of a lobster, crab, etc. **pincers** pl n a tool for gripping and pulling things, consisting of a pair of pivoted jaws with handles that are pressed together to close them

pinch v 1 to squeeze something tightly or painfully between two surfaces, especially between the finger and thumb 2 informal to steal something 3 informal to arrest someone **pinch** n 1 a pinching movement 2 the amount that can be held between the tips of the thumb and forefinger ♦ *a pinch of salt* **pinched** adj having a drawn appearance from feeling tense or cold **at a pinch** if absolutely necessary **to feel the pinch** to suffer from lack of money

pine¹ n 1 an evergreen tree with needle-shaped leaves growing in clusters 2 the soft wood of this tree

pine² v 1 to feel an intense longing for someone or something ♦ *She pined for the mountains of her homeland.* 2 to suffer and become ill through grief or a broken heart

pineapple n a large juicy tropical fruit with a tough prickly skin and yellow flesh

ping v to make a short sharp ringing sound **ping** n a pinging sound

ping-pong n informal table tennis

pinion¹ (say **pin**-yən) n a bird's wing, especially the outer part **pinion** v to hold or fasten someone's arms or legs in order to prevent them from moving

pinion² (say **pin**-yən) n a small cogwheel that fits into a larger one or into a rod

(called a *rack*)

pink *n* **1** pale red **2** a garden plant with fragrant flowers **pink** *adj* of pale red colour **in the pink** *informal* in good health

pinking shears *pl n* dressmaker's scissors with serrated blades for cutting a zigzag edge

pinnacle *n* **1** a pointed ornament on a roof **2** a high pointed piece of rock **3** the highest or most successful point ♦ *It was the pinnacle of her career.*

pinny *n pl* **pinnies** *informal* a pinafore

pint *n* **1** a measure for liquids, equal to one eighth of a gallon (in Britain 0.568 litres, in the USA 0.473 litres) **2** a pint of beer

pioneer (say piy-ǝn-eer) *n* **1** someone who is the first to explore or settle a new region **2** someone who is the first to investigate a new subject or develop new methods **pioneer** *v* to be the first person to develop new methods, etc.

pious *adj* **1** devoutly religious **2** ostentatiously virtuous **piety** *n pl* **pieties** being very religious and devout **piously** *adv*

pip¹ *n* a small hard seed of an apple, pear, orange, etc.

pip² *n* a short high-pitched sound, especially one used to give a time signal on the radio

pip³ *n* **1** a star, indicating rank, on the shoulder of an army officer's uniform **2** a spot on a domino, dice, or playing card

pipe *n* **1** a tube through which something can flow **2** a narrow tube with a bowl at one end in which tobacco burns for smoking **3** a wind instrument consisting of a single tube **the pipes** *pl n* bagpipes **pipe** *v* **1** to convey water, etc. through pipes **2** to transmit music or other sound by wire or cable **3** to play music on a pipe or the bagpipes **4** to say or sing something in a shrill voice **5** to decorate a dress, etc. with piping **piper** *n* a person who plays a pipe or bagpipes **pipette** *n* a slender glass tube used for transferring or measuring small quantities of liquids **piping** *n* **1** lengths of pipe **2** a decorative line of icing or cream piped on a cake or dessert **3** a long narrow pipe-like fold decorating edges or seams of clothing or upholstery **pipeline** *n* **1** a pipe for carrying oil, gas, water, etc. over long distances **2** a channel of supply or information **pipe cleaner** *n* a piece of wire covered with fibre, used to clean a tobacco pipe **pipe dream** *n* an impractical hope or scheme **to pipe down** *informal* to be quiet **in the pipeline** in the process of being prepared or developed **to pipe up** to begin to say something **piping hot** (describing water or food) very hot

pippin *n* a kind of apple

piquant (say pee-kǝnt) *adj* **1** pleasantly sharp in its taste or smell **2** pleasantly stimulating or exciting to the mind **piquancy** *n*

pique (say peek) *n* a feeling of hurt pride ♦ *She left in a fit of pique.* **pique** *v* **piques**, **piqued**, **piquing 1** to hurt the pride or self-respect of someone **2** to stimulate something ♦ *Their curiosity was piqued.*

piqué (say pee-kay) *n* a firm fabric woven in a ribbed or raised pattern

piranha (say pi-rahn-ǝ) *n* a tropical South American freshwater fish that has sharp teeth and eats flesh

pirate *n* **1** a person on a ship who attacks and robs other ships at sea **2** someone who reproduces or uses another person's work without legal permission ♦ *pirate videos* **3** someone who broadcasts illegally ♦ *a pirate radio station* **pirate** *v* to reproduce or use another person's work without legal permission **piracy** *n* **piratical** *adj*

pirouette (say pi-roo-et) *n* a spinning movement of the body made while balanced on the point of the toe or the ball of the foot **pirouette** *v* to perform a pirouette

Pisces (say piy-seez) *n* (the Fishes) the sign of the zodiac which the sun enters about 20 February **Piscean** *adj, n*

pistachio (say pis-tash-i-oh) *n pl* **pistachios** a kind of nut with an edible green kernel

piste (say peest) *n* a ski track of compacted snow

pistol *n* a small gun held in one hand

piston *n* a sliding disc or cylinder fitting closely inside a tube in which it moves up and down as part of an engine or pump

pit *n* **1** a large hole in the ground, especially

one from which material is dug out ♦ *a chalk pit* **2** a coal mine **3** a depression or hollow in the skin or in any surface **4** an area at the side of a track where racing cars are serviced and refuelled during a race **pit** *v* **pitted, pitting 1** to make holes or hollows in something ♦ *The runway was pitted with craters.* **2** to set someone in competition with someone else ♦ *He found himself pitted against the champion.* **pit bull terrier** *n* a small strong and fierce dog **pitfall** *n* an unsuspected danger or difficulty **pithead** *n* the top of a mineshaft and the area around it

pitch¹ *n* **1** a piece of ground marked out for football, cricket, or another game **2** the degree of highness or lowness of a musical note or a voice **3** a level of intensity or strength ♦ *Excitement was at fever pitch.* **4** the steepness of a slope ♦ *the pitch of the roof* **5** a place at which a street performer or trader, etc. is stationed **6** persuasive talk, especially when selling something **pitch** *v* **1** to throw or fling something **2** to erect and fix a tent or camp **3** to fall heavily ♦ *She pitched forward into the blackness.* **4** (said about a ship or vehicle) to plunge forward and backward alternately **5** to set a piece of music at a particular pitch **6** to set or aim something at a particular degree or level ♦ *I hope I've pitched this talk at the right level.* **pitched battle** *n* a fierce battle fought by troops in prepared positions **pitchfork** *n* a long-handled fork with two prongs, used for lifting hay **to pitch in** *informal* to join in an activity with enthusiasm

pitch² *n* a dark resinous tarry substance that sets hard, used for caulking seams of ships, etc. **pitch-black** *adj* completely dark

pitcher¹ *n* a large jug

pitcher² *n* (in baseball) the player who delivers the ball to the batter

pith *n* **1** the spongy substance in the stems of certain plants or lining the rind of citrus fruits **2** the essential part of something ♦ *the pith of the argument* **pithy** *adj* **pithier, pithiest** brief and full of meaning ♦ *pithy comments*

pitta *n* a kind of flat bread with a hollow inside, originally from Greece and the Middle East

pittance *n* a very small or inadequate amount of money

pitter-patter *n* a sound of quick light taps or steps

pituitary, pituitary gland (say pit-**yoo**-it-eri) *n pl* **pituitaries** a small ductless gland at the base of the brain, with important influence on growth and bodily functions

pity *n pl* **pities 1** the feeling of being sorry because someone is in pain or trouble **2** a cause for regret or disappointment ♦ *What a pity you can't come.* **pity** *v* **pities, pitied, pitying** to feel pity for someone **piteous** *adj* making you feel pity **piteously** *adv* **pitiable** *adj* making you feel pity; pitiful **pitiably** *adv* **pitiful** *adj* **1** making you feel pity **2** miserably inadequate or useless ♦ *a pitiful attempt* **pitifully** *adv* **pitiless** *adj* showing no pity **pitilessly** *adv*

pivot *n* **1** a central point or shaft, etc. on which something turns or swings **2** a person or thing that plays a central part in an activity or organization **pivot** *v* **pivoted, pivoting 1** to turn or fix something on a pivot **2** to depend on something **pivotal** *adj* of crucial importance ♦ *a pivotal moment in the match*

pixel (say **piks**-əl) *n* one of the tiny illuminated dots on a computer display screen from which the image is composed

pixie *n* a small supernatural being in fairy tales, with pointed ears and a pointed hat

pizza (say **peets**-ə) *n* an Italian dish consisting of a layer of dough baked with a savoury topping

placard *n* a poster or other notice for displaying, especially one carried at a demonstration

placate (say plə-**kayt**) *v* to make someone feel calmer and less angry **placatory** *adj*

place *n* **1** a particular part of space, especially where something belongs, an area or position **2** a particular town, district, or building ♦ *This is one of the places we want to visit.* **3** the part of a book a reader has reached ♦ *I've lost my place.* **4** proper position for a thing, or a position in a series ♦ *Put each piece in its place.* **5** space or seat or other accommodation

for a person ♦ *Save me a place on the train.*
6 a person's rank or position **7** a duty or
responsibility associated with a person's
rank or position ♦ *It is not my place to argue.*
place *v* **1** to put something in a particular
place or position ♦ *Place the vase on the
table.* **2** to identify someone or something
in relation to circumstances or memory ♦ *I
know her face but can't quite place her.* **3** to
arrange for an instruction or request to be
carried out ♦ *We have placed an order with a
German company.* **placement** *n* the action
of placing something **place setting** *n* a set
of dishes and cutlery for one person at table
to be placed to be among the first three (or
sometimes four) winners in a race
placebo (say plə-**see**-boh) *n pl* **placebos**
a harmless substance given as if it were
medicine, to reassure a patient or as part of
an experiment
placenta (say plə-**sent**-ə) *n* an organ that
develops in the womb during pregnancy
and supplies the developing fetus with
nourishment through the umbilical cord
placid *adj* calm and peaceful, not easily
made anxious or upset **placidity** *n*
placidly *adv*
plagiarize (say **play**-ji-ə-riyz) *v* to take
another person's ideas or writings and use
them as your own **plagiarism** *n* **plagiarist** *n*
plague (say playg) *n* **1** a deadly contagious
disease that spreads very quickly **2** a
large number of pests infesting a place or
causing damage to it ♦ *a plague of greenfly*
plague *v* **plagues**, **plagued**, **plaguing** to
annoy or pester someone
plaice *n pl* **plaice** a flat sea fish used for food
plaid (say plad) *n* **1** a piece of cloth with a
chequered or tartan pattern **2** a long piece
of this worn over the shoulder as part of
Highland dress
plain *adj* **1** easy to see or hear or understand
2 simple, not elaborate or intricate ♦ *a
plain design* ♦ *plain cooking* **3** frank and
straightforward ♦ *We could do with some
plain speaking.* **4** ordinary in manner,
without affectation **5** not pretty or
beautiful, ordinary looking **plain** *n* a large
area of flat country **plainly** *adv* **plainness** *n*
plain clothes *pl n* civilian clothes worn

instead of a uniform **plain sailing** *n* a
course of action that is free from difficulties
plainsong *n* medieval unaccompanied
church music for voices singing in unison
in free rhythm **plain-spoken** *adj* frank and
direct in what you say ◊ Do not confuse
this word with *plane*, which has a different
meaning.
plaintiff *n* the person that brings an action
in a court of law
plaintive *adj* sounding sad **plaintively** *adv*
plait (say plat) *v* to weave or twist three or
more strands of hair or rope to form one
thick length **plait** *n* a length of hair or rope
that has been plaited
plan *n* **1** a detailed scheme or method for
doing something **2** a drawing showing the
layout and parts of something, especially
a building **plan** *v* **planned**, **planning 1** to
make detailed arrangements for doing
something ♦ *Have you planned your holiday?*
2 to intend or propose to do something
♦ *We are planning to stay for longer this year.*
3 to make a plan or design of something
planner *n*
plane[1] *n* **1** a flat or level surface **2** a level of
thought or existence ♦ *on a spiritual plane*
plane *adj* lying in a plane, level ♦ *a plane
figure* ◊ Do not confuse this word with *plain*,
which has a different meaning. **planar** *adj*
plane[2] *n* an aeroplane
plane[3] *n* a tool with a blade projecting from
the base, used for smoothing the surface of
wood or metal **plane** *v* to smooth or pare a
surface with a plane
plane[4] *n* a tall spreading tree with broad
leaves
planet *n* any of the bodies that move in
an orbit round the sun **planetarium** *n*
a room with a domed ceiling on which
images of stars and planets are projected
planetary *adj*
plangent (say **plan**-jənt) *adj* (said about a
sound) loud and resonant, with a mournful
tone
plank *n* a long flat piece of wood used in
building
plankton *n* microscopic organisms (plants
and animals) that float in the sea or in fresh
water

plant *n* **1** a living organism that grows in the ground and lacks the power of movement that animals have **2** a factory or its machinery and equipment **plant** *v* **1** to place a seed, bulb, or plant in the ground or in soil for growing **2** to fix something firmly in position **3** to station a person as a lookout or spy **4** to put something in a place where other people will discover it, especially to trick or incriminate someone

plantation *n* **1** a large area of land on which crops such as cotton, sugar, tobacco, or tea are grown **2** an area where trees have been planted, especially for commercial uses

planter *n* **1** a person who owns or manages a plantation **2** a machine for planting seeds or bulbs **3** a container for decorative plants

plantain[1] (say **plan**-tin) *n* a wild plant with broad flat leaves

plantain[2] (say **plan**-tin) *n* a tropical tree and fruit resembling the banana

plaque (say plak) *n* **1** a flat piece of metal or porcelain fixed on a wall as an ornament or memorial **2** a filmy substance that forms on teeth, where bacteria can live

plasma (say **plaz**-mə) *n* the colourless liquid part of blood, which carries the corpuscles

plaster *n* **1** a soft mixture of lime, sand, and water, used for covering walls and ceilings **2** plaster of Paris, or a cast made of this to hold broken bones in place **3** a piece of sticking plaster **plaster** *v* **1** to cover a wall or ceiling with plaster or a similar substance **2** to cover a surface with something thick **plasterer** *n* **plasterboard** *n* board made of paper sheets with a core of plaster between, used for lining walls and making partitions **plaster of Paris** *n* white paste made from gypsum, used for making moulds or casts

plastic *n* a strong light synthetic substance that can be moulded into any permanent shape **plastic** *adj* **1** made of plastic **2** able to be shaped or moulded ♦ *Clay is a plastic substance.* **plasticine** *n* a soft modelling material used especially by children **plasticity** *n* **plastic surgery** *n* surgery done by transferring tissue to repair deformed or injured parts of the body **plastic surgeon** *n*

plate *n* **1** an almost flat dish, usually circular in shape, from which food is eaten or served **2** dishes and other domestic utensils made of gold, silver, or other metal **3** a flat thin sheet of metal, glass, or other rigid material **4** an illustration on special paper in a book **5** a piece of plastic material moulded to the shape of the gums or roof of the mouth for holding artificial teeth **plate** *v* **1** to cover a surface with plates of metal **2** to coat metal with a thin layer of silver, gold, or tin

plateful *n pl* **platefuls** as much as a plate will hold **platelet** *n* a small colourless disc found in the blood and involved in clotting

plate glass *n* thick glass of fine quality for windows and doors

plateau (say **plat**-oh) *n pl* **plateaux** (say **plat**-oh) **1** an area of high level ground **2** a state or period of inactivity or no change, following a period of progress or change

platform *n* **1** a flat surface that is above the rest of the ground or floor **2** a raised area along the side of the line at a railway station, where passengers wait for and get on and off trains **3** the declared policy or programme of a political party or group **4** *ICT* a standard for the hardware of a computer system

platinum *n* a silver-white metal, a chemical element (symbol Pt), that does not tarnish

platitude (say **plat**-i-tewd) *n* a trite or insincere remark that is commonly used **platitudinous** *adj*

platonic (say plə-**tonn**-ik) *adj* (said about love or friendship) close and affectionate but not sexual

platoon *n* a small group of soldiers, a subdivision of a military company

platter *n* **1** a large flat dish or plate **2** a selection of food served on a platter

platypus (say **plat**-i-pəs) *n pl* **platypuses** an Australian animal with a beak like a duck's and a flat tail

plaudits (say **plaw**-dits) *pl n* applause or strong approval

plausible (say **plaw**-zib-əl) *adj* **1** (said about a statement) seeming to be reasonable or probable but perhaps deceptive **2** (said about a person) persuasive but perhaps not trustworthy **plausibility** *n* **plausibly** *adv*

play *v* **1** to take part in a game or sport or

other activity ♦ *On Saturdays we play hockey.* ♦ *The children were playing in the garden.* **2** to compete against a player or team in a game ♦ *France play Italy in the final.* **3** to move a piece or put a card on the table in a game **4** to perform a part in a drama or film **5** to perform a part in a process or undertaking ♦ *She played an important role in reaching an agreement.* **6** to perform music on a musical instrument **7** to make a radio or other piece of equipment produce sounds **8** to move lightly or quickly ♦ *A smile played on her lips.*

play *n* **1** games and other activities done for enjoyment, especially by children **2** a dramatic work written for performance on the stage or for broadcasting **3** activity or operation ♦ *Other factors come into play.* **4** free movement ♦ *The bolts should have a small amount of play.* **player** *n* **playful** *adj* **1** fond of fun and amusement **2** done in fun, not meant seriously **playfully** *adv* **playfulness** *n* **play-act** *v* **1** to act in a play **2** to pretend in a dramatic way **playboy** *n* a wealthy man who spends his time seeking pleasure **playground** *n* a piece of ground for children to play on **playgroup** *n* a group of young children who play together regularly under supervision **playhouse** *n* a theatre **playing card** *n* each of a set of oblong pieces of card (usually 52 divided into four suits) marked on one side with numbers and symbols to show their rank, used to play various games **playing field** *n* a field used for outdoor games **play-off** *n* an extra match played to decide a draw or tie in previous matches **playpen** *n* a portable enclosure for a young child to play in **plaything** *n* **1** a toy **2** a person exploited for amusement and not taken seriously **playwright** *n* a person who writes plays **to play along** to pretend to cooperate with. **play on** to make use of a person's sympathy or weakness **to play someone off** to make one person oppose another in order to serve your own interests **to play something down** to minimize the importance of something **to play up 1** (said about a person) to cause trouble **2** (said about a machine) to fail to work properly

plaza (say **plah**-zə) *n* a public square or open space in a town

PLC *abbr* Public Limited Company

plea *n* **1** an appeal or entreaty ♦ *The villagers made a plea for help after the floods.* **2** an excuse ♦ *He stayed at home on the plea of a headache.* **3** a formal statement of 'guilty' or 'not guilty' made in a law court by a person accused of a crime **plead** *v* **1** to put forward a plea of 'guilty' or 'not guilty' in a law court **2** to make an appeal or entreaty **3** to offer an excuse ♦ *She stayed at home, pleading her work.*

pleasant *adj* **1** pleasing, giving pleasure or enjoyment **2** (said about a person) having a friendly manner **pleasantly** *adv* **pleasantness** *n* **pleasantry** *n* *pl* **pleasantries** a humorous remark

please *v* to give pleasure to someone or make them feel satisfied or glad **please** *adv* used to make a polite request or order ♦ *Please close the door.* **pleased** *adj* feeling or showing pleasure or satisfaction **to please yourself** to do as you choose

pleasure *n* **1** a feeling of satisfaction or enjoyment **2** something that causes pleasure or enjoyment **pleasurable** *adj* causing pleasure, enjoyable **pleasurably** *adv*

pleat *n* a flat fold made by doubling cloth on itself **pleat** *v* to make a pleat or pleats in cloth

plebeian (say pli-**bee**-ən) *adj* **1** belonging to the ordinary people as distinct from the upper classes **2** lacking in refinement, uncultured **plebeian** *n* a member of the ordinary people **plebs** *pl n* the ordinary people

plebiscite (say **pleb**-i-sit) *n* a referendum

plectrum *n* *pl* **plectrums** or **plectra** a small piece of metal or bone or plastic for plucking the strings of a guitar or other stringed instrument

pledge *n* **1** a formal or solemn promise ♦ *They gave a pledge that they would return.* **2** a thing that is given as security for payment of a debt or fulfilment of a contract **pledge** *v* **1** to deposit an article as a pledge **2** to promise solemnly to do something

plenary (say **pleen**-er-i) *adj* attended by all

members ♦ *a plenary session of the council*

plenty *n* quite enough, as much as is needed or wanted **plenteous** *adj* plentiful **plentiful** *adj* producing or existing in large quantities, abundant **plentifully** *adv*

plethora (say pleth-er-ə) *n* an excess

pleurisy (say **ploor** -i-si) *n* inflammation of the membranes surrounding the lungs

pliable *adj* 1 bending easily, flexible 2 (said about a person) easily influenced or persuaded **pliability** *n* **pliant** *adj* pliable **pliantly** *adv*

pliers *pl n* pincers having jaws with flat surfaces, used for gripping small objects or bending wire

plight[1] *n* a dangerous or difficult situation for someone

plight[2] *v old use* to pledge devotion or loyalty

plimsoll *n* a canvas sports shoe with a rubber sole

plinth *n* a block or slab forming the base of a column or a support for a statue or vase

plod *v* **plodded, plodding** 1 to walk slowly and heavily 2 to work at a slow but steady rate **plod** *n* a slow heavy walk **plodder** *n*

plonk[1] *v informal* to put something down heavily or clumsily

plonk[2] *n informal* cheap inferior wine

plop *v* **plopped, plopping** to make a sound like something dropping into water without a splash **plop** *n* a plopping sound

plot *n* 1 a small measured piece of land ♦ *a building plot* 2 the story in a play, novel, or film 3 a secret plan or conspiracy **plot** *v* **plotted, plotting** 1 to make a plan or map of a place 2 to mark a point on a chart or diagram 3 to plan something secretly **plotter** *n*

plough (say plow) *n* a farming implement pulled by horses or a tractor for cutting furrows in the soil and turning it over **plough** *v* 1 to turn over the soil with a plough 2 to go through something with great effort or difficulty ♦ *He had to plough through a pile of work.* 3 (said about a vehicle) to move in a fast and uncontrolled manner ♦ *The train ploughed into the buffers.*

ploughman *n pl* **ploughmen** a man who guides a plough **ploughman's lunch** *n* a meal of bread and cheese with pickle and salad **ploughshare** *n* the main cutting blade of a plough

plover (say pluv-er) *n* a kind of wading bird

ploy *n* a cunning action or plan designed to gain an advantage

pluck *v* 1 to take hold of something and quickly pull or remove it from its place 2 to strip a bird of its feathers 3 to sound the string of a musical instrument by pulling it with the fingers or a plectrum and then releasing it **pluck** *n* 1 courage or spirit 2 an action of plucking, a pull **plucky** *adj* **pluckier, pluckiest** showing pluck; brave or spirited **pluckily** *adv* **to pluck up courage** to summon up courage and overcome fear

plug *n* 1 a piece of solid material fitting into a hole to stop or fill it 2 a device with metal pins that fit into a socket to make an electrical connection 3 *informal* a piece of unofficial or spontaneous publicity promoting a commercial product **plug** *v* **plugged, plugging** 1 to put a plug into a hole or cavity to stop or fill it 2 *informal* to promote an event or commercial product by mentioning it favourably **to plug away** *informal* to work steadily or persistently **to plug something in** to connect a device to an electrical supply by putting its plug into a socket

plum *n* 1 a soft fleshy fruit with a flattish pointed stone 2 the tree that bears this fruit 3 a reddish-purple colour 4 (usually used before a noun) the best of its kind ♦ *a plum job*

plumb[1] (say plum) *v* 1 to measure the depth of water 2 to explore or experience something fully ♦ *She plumbed the depths of misery.* **plumb** *n* a piece of lead tied to the end of a cord, used for finding the depth of water or testing whether an upright surface is vertical **plumb** *adv informal* exactly ♦ *It landed plumb in the middle.* **plumb line** *n* a line with a plumb weight on the end of it

plumb[2] (say plum) *v* to fit a room or building with a plumbing system **plumber** *n* a person who fits and repairs plumbing **plumbing** *n* the water pipes, water tanks, and drainage pipes in a building **to plumb something in** to install a washing machine or dishwasher so that it is connected directly to the water supply

plume (say ploom) n a large feather or set of feathers used by a bird for display or worn as a decoration **plumage** n a bird's feathers

plummet v plummeted, plummeting 1 to fall or plunge suddenly and without control 2 to decrease rapidly in value ♦ Share prices plummeted.

plump¹ adj having a full rounded shape; slightly fat **plump** v to make something full and rounded ♦ to plump a cushion **plumpness** n

plump² v to drop or plunge abruptly ♦ He plumped down in a chair. **to plump for** to choose or decide on something or someone

plunder v to rob a place or person by force, especially in a time of war **plunder** n 1 the action of plundering 2 property taken by plundering

plunge v 1 to push or thrust a thing forcefully into something 2 to fall or drop steeply 3 to jump or dive into water 4 to embark suddenly or impetuously on a course of action **plunge** n the action of plunging, a dive **plunger** n a rubber cup on a handle used for clearing blocked pipes by alternate thrusting and suction **to take the plunge** informal to take a bold decisive step

plural (say ploor -əl) adj 1 more than one 2 Gram (said about a form of a noun or verb) used when it refers to more than one person or thing ♦ The plural form of 'child' is 'children'. **plural** n a plural word or form

plus prep 1 with the addition of ♦ 15 plus 6 equals 21 2 informal together with ♦ The family arrived plus dog and parrot. **plus** adj 1 denoting a grade slightly higher ♦ B plus. 2 denoting a number above zero ♦ a temperature between minus ten and plus ten degrees **plus** n 1 the sign + 2 an advantage

plush n a thick velvety cloth used in furnishings **plush, plushy** adj luxurious

plutocrat (say ploo-tə-krat) n a person who is powerful because of their wealth **plutocratic** adj

plutonium (say ploo-toh-niəm) n a radioactive element used in nuclear weapons and reactors

ply¹ n pl plies 1 a thickness or layer of wood or cloth, etc. 2 a strand in yarn ♦ 4-ply wool **plywood** n strong thin board made of layers of wood glued and pressed together

ply² v plies, plied, plying 1 to use or wield a tool or weapon 2 to work steadily at something ♦ Weavers plied their trade. 3 to keep offering or supplying something ♦ They plied her with food. 4 to go regularly along a route ♦ The boat plies between the two ports.

PM abbr Prime Minister

p.m. abbr after noon

pneumatic (say new-mat-ik) adj filled with or worked by compressed air ♦ a pneumatic drill

pneumonia (say new-moh-niə) n a serious illness caused by inflammation of one or both lungs

PO abbr 1 postal order 2 Post Office

poach¹ v to cook food by simmering it in liquid

poach² v 1 to steal game or fish from private land or water 2 to take something unfairly from someone else ♦ The company has been poaching staff from its rivals. **poacher** n

pocket n 1 a small bag-shaped part sewn into or on a piece of clothing, for holding small articles 2 a pouch-like compartment in a suitcase or on a car door, etc. 3 each of the pouches at the corners or sides of a billiard table, into which balls are driven 4 an isolated group or area ♦ The army met small pockets of resistance. **pocket** adj small enough to carry in a pocket ♦ a pocket calculator **pocket** v pocketed, pocketing 1 to put something into your pocket 2 to take something for yourself, especially dishonestly **pocket money** n 1 money regularly given to a child by its parents 2 money for minor expenses **out of pocket** having lost money in a transaction

pockmark n a scar or mark left on the skin by a spot or pustule **pockmarked** adj

pod n a long seed container of the kind found on a pea or bean plant

podcast n a digital recording of a radio broadcast that can be downloaded over the Internet

podgy adj podgier, podgiest short and fat

podium (say poh-di-əm) *n pl* **podiums** or **podia** a pedestal or platform

poem *n* a piece of writing in verse, usually arranged in short lines with a particular rhythm or set of rhythms, and expressing deep feeling or noble thought in an imaginative way **poet** *n* someone who writes poems **poetic** *adj* to do with poetry, like poetry **poetical** *adj* written in verse ♦ *poetical works* **poetically** *adv* **poetry** *n* writing in verse, poems collectively **poetic justice** *n* suitable and well-deserved punishment or reward, as found in literature **poetic licence** *n* departing from the normal rules and conventions of writing in order to create an artistic effect **Poet Laureate** *n* an eminent poet appointed to write poems for important state occasions

pogrom (say pog-rəm) *n* an organized massacre of an ethnic group of people

poignant (say poin-yənt) *adj* arousing sympathy, deeply moving to the feelings **poignancy** *n* **poignantly** *adv*

point *n* **1** the tapered or sharp end of a tool, weapon, pencil, or other object **2** a dot used as a punctuation mark; a decimal point **3** a particular place or time, or a particular stage in a process ♦ *At this point in the game the home team was winning.* **4** each of the directions marked on the compass, or a corresponding direction towards the horizon **5** a unit of measurement, value, or scoring **6** a separate item or detail ♦ *The two sides differed on several points.* **7** a distinctive feature or characteristic ♦ *The plan has some good points.* **8** the thing that matters or is under discussion ♦ *I'll try to come to the point.* **9** the important feature of a story, joke, or remark **10** aim or purpose ♦ *The point of the game is to get rid of all your cards.* **11** an electrical socket ♦ *a power point* **12** a place where two railway lines meet, with rails which can be moved to allow a train to pass from one line to the other **13** a narrow piece of land jutting out into the sea **point** *v* **1** to direct or aim something ♦ *The man was pointing a gun at her.* **2** to show where something is, especially by holding out a finger towards it ♦ *He pointed to the post office across the road.* **3** to fill in the joints of brickwork or stonework with mortar or cement **pointed** *adj* **1** tapering or sharpened to a point **2** (said about a remark or look) clearly aimed at a particular person or thing **pointer** *n* **1** a stick, rod, or mark used to point at something **2** a long thin piece of metal that points to figures or other marks on a dial or scale **3** a hint or indication **4** a dog that scents game and then stands rigidly with its muzzle pointing towards it **pointless** *adj* having no purpose or meaning **pointlessly** *adv* **point-blank** *adj* **1** (said about a shot) aimed at or fired at very close range **2** (said about a remark) direct or straightforward ♦ *We got a point-blank refusal.* **point-blank** *adv* directly, in a point-blank manner ♦ *They refused point-blank.* **on the point of** about to do something **point of view** a way of thinking about something, an opinion **to point something out** to indicate something or draw attention to it **to point something up** to emphasize something

poise *v* to balance something, or to be balanced **poise** *n* **1** a dignified self-confident manner **2** balance, the way something is poised **poised** *adj* (said about a person) dignified and self-confident

poison *n* **1** a substance that can harm or destroy a living thing **2** a harmful influence **poison** *v* **1** to kill someone with poison **2** to put poison on or in something **3** to corrupt someone or make them prejudiced ♦ *He poisoned their minds with his ideas.* **poisoner** *n* **poisonous** *adj*

poke *v* **1** to prod or jab something with the end of a finger or a long thin object **2** to thrust something forward, or to be thrust forward **poke** *n* a poking movement, a thrust or nudge **poker** *n* a stiff metal rod for poking a fire **poky** *adj* **pokier**, **pokiest** small and cramped ♦ *The family lived in one poky little room.*

poker *n* a card game in which players bet on the value of their cards, often using bluff

Polaroid *n trademark* **1** a material that changes the light passing through it, used in the lenses of sunglasses to protect the eyes from glare **2** a type of camera that develops and prints a photograph rapidly when each exposure is made

pole[1] *n* a long slender rounded piece of wood or metal, especially one used as a support **pole position** *n* the most favourable position on the starting grid in a motor race **pole vault** *n* an athletic event in which competitors vault over a high crossbar with the help of a long flexible pole held in the hands

pole[2] *n* **1** either of the two points on the earth's surface which are at the ends of its axis of rotation, the North Pole or South Pole **2** each of the two opposite points in a magnet which most strongly attract or repel magnetic bodies **polar** *adj* **1** to do with or near the North Pole or South Pole **2** to do with one of the poles of a magnet **polarity** *n* the property of possessing negative and positive poles **polarize** *v* to separate into two extremes of opinion ♦ *The debate has become polarized.* **polarization** *n* **polar bear** *n* a white bear living in Arctic regions **Pole Star** *n* a star above the North Pole

poleaxe *v* to strike someone down with a blow

polecat *n* a small dark brown animal of the weasel family with an unpleasant smell

polemic (say pəl-**em**-ik) *n* a verbal attack on a belief or opinion **polemic, polemical** *adj* **1** controversial **2** argumentative

police *n* **1** a civil force responsible for keeping public order and detecting crime **2** a force responsible for enforcing the regulations of an organization ♦ *military police* **police** *v* to keep order in a place by means of a police force **policeman** *n pl* **policemen** a male police officer **police officer** *n* a member of a police force **police state** *n* a country (usually a totalitarian state) in which political police supervise and control citizens' activities **police station** *n* the office of a local police force **policewoman** *n pl* **policewomen** a female police officer

policy[1] *n pl* **policies** a course or general plan of action adopted by a government, party, or person

policy[2] *n pl* **policies** a contract of insurance

polio (say **poh**-li-oh) *n* short for *poliomyelitis*

poliomyelitis (say poh-li-oh-miy-ə-**liy**-tiss) *n* an infectious disease caused by a virus, producing temporary or permanent paralysis

Polish *adj* to do with or coming from Poland **Polish** *n* the language of Poland **Pole** *n* a person born in Poland or descended from people born there

polish *v* **1** to make something smooth and shiny by rubbing **2** to improve or perfect a piece of work **polish** *n* **1** smoothness and glossiness **2** the process of polishing **3** a substance for polishing a surface **4** elegance or refinement of manner **polished** *adj* **1** elegant or refined ♦ *polished manners* **2** done with great ability and distinction ♦ *The singers gave a polished performance.* **polisher** *n*

polite *adj* **1** respectful and well-mannered towards other people **2** refined ♦ *polite society* **politely** *adv* **politeness** *n*

politics *n* **1** the activities and principles involved in governing a country or region **2** political affairs or life **politic** *adj* prudent and wise **political** *adj* **1** to do with the government or public affairs of a country or region **2** to do with status and power within an organization **politically** *adv* **politician** *n* a person who is professionally involved in politics, especially a holder of an elected political office **political asylum** *n* refuge and safety offered by one country to political refugees from another **political correctness** *n* the use of language and behaviour that avoid discrimination affecting certain groups of people **politically correct** *adj* **political prisoner** *n* a person imprisoned for political beliefs or activities

polka *n* a lively dance of Bohemian origin **polka dot** *n* each of a number of round dots evenly spaced to form a pattern on fabric

poll (say pohl) *n* **1** the process of voting at an election ♦ *to go to the polls* **2** the number of votes cast in an election ♦ *a heavy poll* **3** a questioning of a sample of people to ascertain general opinion **poll** *v* **1** to vote at an election **2** (said about a candidate) to receive a specified number of votes ♦ *The winner polled over 20,000 votes.* **polling**

booth n a booth or cubicle in which a vote is made **polling station** n a place used for people to vote in an election **poll tax** n a tax that every adult has to pay regardless of income

pollard (say **pol**-erd) n a tree that is cut off at the top to produce a close head of young branches **pollard** v to cut the top off a tree

pollen n a fine powdery substance produced by the anthers of flowers, containing male cells for fertilizing other flowers **pollinate** v to fertilize a flower or plant with pollen **pollination** n **pollen count** n an index of the amount of pollen in the air, published as information for people who are allergic to pollen

pollute v 1 to make the air, water, etc. dirty or impure, especially by adding harmful or offensive substances 2 to corrupt someone or someone's mind **pollutant** n a substance that causes pollution **pollution** n

polo n a game like hockey, played by teams on horseback with long-handled mallets **polo neck** n a high close-fitting collar turned over at the top **polo shirt** n a casual shirt with short sleeves and a collar and buttons at the neck

poltergeist (say **pol**-ter-giyst) n a ghost or spirit that supposedly causes a disturbance by throwing things about

poly- prefix many (as in polymath)

polychrome (say **pol**-i-krohm) adj painted, printed, or decorated in several colours

polyester n a synthetic resin or fibre used to make clothing

polygamy (say pə-**lig**-əmi) n the custom or practice of having more than one wife at a time (Compare monogamy.) **polygamist** n **polygamous** adj

polyglot (say **pol**-i-glot) n a person who knows several languages

polymath (say **pol**-i-math) n a person who has knowledge of a large number of subjects

polyp (say **pol**-ip) n 1 a simple organism with a tube-shaped body 2 an abnormal growth projecting from a mucous membrane

polyphonic (say pol-i-**fon**-ik) adj Mus (said about music, especially vocal music) written in counterpoint

polystyrene (say poli-**stiyr**-een) n a kind of plastic used for insulation and in packaging

polysyllabic (say poli-sil-**ab**-ik) adj (said about a word) having several syllables

polytechnic (say poli-**tek**-nik) n formerly, an institution of higher education giving courses to degree level

polytheism (say **pol**-ith-ee-ism) n the belief in or worship of more than one god **polytheist** n **polytheistic** adj

polythene n a kind of tough light plastic material used mainly in packaging

polyurethane (say poli-**yoor** -i-thayn) n a kind of synthetic resin or plastic

pomander (say pəm-**an**-der) n a ball or container of mixed sweet-smelling substances

pomegranate (say **pom**-i-gran-it) n a tropical fruit with a tough rind and reddish pulp enclosing many seeds

Pomeranian (say pom-er-**ayn**-iən) n a small dog with a silky coat and a pointed nose

pommel (say **pum**-əl) n 1 a part that projects upward at the front of a saddle 2 a knob on the handle of a sword or dagger

Pommy n pl **Pommies** Austral. and NZ informal a British person, especially a recent immigrant

pomp n the splendour and ceremony that is associated with important state occasions

pompom n a ball of coloured threads used as a decoration

pompous adj affectedly solemn and self-important in manner **pomposity** n **pompously** adv

poncho n pl **ponchos** a short cloak with a slit in the centre for the head

pond n a small area of still water, especially in a town or village or on a common

ponder v to think long and carefully about something **ponderous** adj 1 heavy and clumsy 2 dull and laborious in style **ponderously** adv

pong n informal an unpleasant smell **pong** v informal to smell unpleasantly

pontiff n the Pope **pontificate** v to express opinions in a pompous or self-important way **pontificate** n the office of pope

pontoon¹ n 1 each of a number of boats or

hollow metal cylinders used to support a temporary bridge over a river **2** a kind of flat-bottomed boat

pontoon[2] *n* a card game in which players try to get cards with a face value totalling 21

pony *n pl* **ponies** a small horse **ponytail** *n* long hair drawn back and tied at the crown of the head so that it hangs down **pony-trekking** *n* travelling across country on ponies for pleasure

poodle *n* a dog with thick curly hair that is often clipped and partly shaved

pooh *interjection informal* **1** an exclamation of disgust at an unpleasant smell **2** an exclamation of impatience or contempt **pooh-pooh** *v* to dismiss an idea or suggestion scornfully

pool[1] *n* **1** a small area of still water, especially one that is naturally formed **2** a puddle or shallow patch of water or other liquid lying on a surface **3** a swimming pool

pool[2] *n* **1** a common fund of money that several contributors pay into **2** a shared supply of vehicles, personnel, or resources that can be drawn on when needed **3** a game resembling billiards **the pools** a form of gambling on the results of several football matches **pool** *v* to put money or other resources into a common fund or supply, for sharing

poop *n* the raised deck at the stern of a ship

poor *adj* **1** having too little money or other resources to live a normal or comfortable life **2** lacking in something ◆ *soil poor in minerals* **3** of a low quality or standard ◆ *The work was poor.* **4** deserving pity or sympathy ◆ *The poor man could hardly speak.* **poorly** *adv* in a poor way, badly **poorly** *adj* unwell ◆ *She is feeling poorly.* **poorness** *n*

pop[1] *n* **1** a small sharp explosive sound **2** a fizzy drink **pop** *v* **popped**, **popping 1** to make a pop, or to cause something to make a pop **2** to put something quickly somewhere ◆ *I'll pop it in the microwave.* **3** to come or go quickly or suddenly or unexpectedly ◆ *He's just popped out for a newspaper.* **popcorn** *n* maize heated so that it bursts to form fluffy balls

pop[2] *n* (also **pop music**) popular music of a kind promoted commercially since the 1950s **pop** *adj* to do with pop music **pop art** *n* art that uses themes drawn from popular culture

pope *n* the Bishop of Rome as head of the Roman Catholic Church **popish** *adj* Roman Catholic

popinjay *n old use* a vain or conceited person

poplar *n* a kind of tall slender tree with leaves that quiver easily

poplin *n* a plain woven fabric usually of cotton

poppadom (say pop-ə-dəm) *n* (in Indian cookery) a thin crisp biscuit made of lentil flour

poppet *n informal* a small and lovable person, especially a child

poppy *n pl* **poppies** a plant with showy flowers and milky juice

poppycock *n informal* nonsense

populace (say pop-yoo-ləs) *n* the general public

popular *adj* **1** liked or enjoyed by many people **2** intended for the general public **3** (said about a belief or attitude) held by many people ◆ *popular superstitions* **popularity** *n* **popularize** v **1** to make something popular or suitable for the general public **2** to present a subject, especially a technical one in a way that can be understood by ordinary people **popularly** *adv*

populate *v* to supply a place with a population; to inhabit a place **population** *n* all the inhabitants of a place, or the total number of these **populous** *adj* having a large population

porcelain (say por -sǝl-in) *n* the finest kind of china

porch *n* a covered shelter outside the entrance of a building

porcupine *n* a small animal with a body and tail covered with protective spines

pore[1] *n* each of many tiny openings on the skin or other surface, through which moisture can pass **porous** *adj* having pores, allowing liquid or air to pass through **porosity** *n*

pore[2] *v* **pore over** to study something

closely and with great interest ◊ Do not confuse this word with *pour*, which has a different meaning.

pork *n* meat from a pig **porker** *n* a young pig raised for its meat

porn *n informal* short for *pornography*

pornography *n* pictures or descriptions that are intended to stimulate sexual excitement **pornographic** *adj*

porpoise (say **por**-pəs) *n* a sea animal resembling a dolphin or small whale

porridge *n* a food of oatmeal or other cereal boiled in water or milk

port¹ *n* 1 a town or city with a harbour 2 the left-hand side of a ship or aircraft when facing forward, the opposite to *starboard*

port² *n* 1 an opening in the side of a ship for boarding or loading 2 a porthole 3 a socket in a computer or computer network into which a device can be plugged **porthole** *n* a small window in the side of a ship or aircraft

port³ *n* a sweet fortified red wine

portable *adj* suitable or light enough to be carried ♦ *a portable television* **portability** *n*

portal *n* a doorway or gateway, especially a large imposing one

portcullis *n* a strong heavy grating that can be lowered in grooves to block a gateway

portend (say por-**tend**) *v* to be a sign that something important or calamitous will happen **portent** *n* a sign that something important or calamitous will happen **portentous** *adj*

porter¹ *n* a person employed to look after the entrance to a large building and help people coming in

porter² *n* a person employed to carry luggage or other goods

portfolio *n pl* **portfolios** 1 a case for holding loose documents or drawings 2 a set of investments held by one investor 3 the position of a Minister or Secretary of State

portico (say **port**-i-koh) *n pl* **porticoes** or **porticos** a structure consisting of a roof supported by columns, usually forming a porch to a building

portion *n* 1 a part or share of something 2 an amount of food given to one person **portion** *v* to divide something into portions and share it out

portly *adj* **portlier**, **portliest** large and rather fat

portmanteau (say port-**man**-toh) *n pl* **portmanteaus** or **portmanteaux** a large travelling bag made of stout material that opens into two equal parts **portmanteau word** *n* an invented word that combines the sounds and meanings of two other words, e.g. *brunch* for *breakfast* and *lunch*

portrait *n* 1 a picture of a person or animal 2 a description in words

portray (say por-**tray**) *v* 1 to make a picture of a person or animal 2 to describe someone or something in words or represent them in a play or film ♦ *The queen is portrayed as a lonely and pathetic character.* **portrayal** *n*

Portuguese *adj* to do with or coming from Portugal **Portuguese** *n* 1 *pl* **Portuguese** a person born in Portugal or descended from people born there 2 the language of Portugal, also spoken in Brazil **Portuguese man-of-war** *n* a sea animal with stinging tentacles

pose *v* 1 to take a position for being painted or photographed for a portrait, or to put someone in this position 2 to take a particular attitude for effect 3 to pretend to be someone ♦ *The man was posing as a police officer.* 4 to put forward or present something that needs attention ♦ *The increasing costs pose a major problem.* **pose** *n* 1 a position or attitude that a person takes for a portrait 2 a way of behaving that someone adopts to give a particular impression **poser** *n* 1 a puzzling question or problem 2 a poseur **poseur** *n* a person who behaves in an affected way to impress others

posh *adj informal* 1 smart or luxurious ♦ *a posh restaurant* 2 upper-class ♦ *a posh accent*

posit (say **poz**-it) *v* **posited**, **positing** to propose something as a fact or a basis for argument

position *n* 1 the place occupied by a person or thing 2 the correct or usual place for something ♦ *The chair is out of position.* 3 the way in which a person or thing is placed or arranged ♦ *She was in a sitting position.* ♦ *Make a note of our chess positions.*

4 a policy or point of view ♦ *What is the Bank's position about loans?* **5** rank or status, high social standing ♦ *a family of position* **6** a job or paid employment **position** *v* to place something or someone in a certain position

positive *adj* **1** agreeing, giving the answer 'yes' ♦ *Their reply was a positive one.* **2** definite, leaving no room for doubt ♦ *There is positive proof of their guilt.* **3** holding an opinion confidently ♦ *I am positive that was George.* **4** constructive and helpful ♦ *She made some positive suggestions.* **5** involving the presence of something sought or in question ♦ *The result of her pregnancy test was positive.* **6** (said about a quantity) greater than zero **7** containing or producing the kind of electric charge opposite to that carried by electrons **positive** *n* a positive quality or character **positively** *adv* **positiveness** *n*

posse (say **poss**-i) *n hist* a body of men summoned by a sheriff to enforce the law

possess *v* **1** to have something as belonging to you, to own something **2** to control or dominate the thoughts or actions of someone ♦ *What possessed you to do such a thing?* **possession** *n* **1** something you possess or own **2** the state of possessing something or of being possessed **possessive** *adj* **1** wanting to keep what you possess for yourself and not to share it **2** demanding someone's total attention and love **3** *Gram* denoting a form of a word that indicates possession, such as *hers* and *Jack's* **possessively** *adv* **possessiveness** *n* **possessor** *n*

possible *adj* able to exist or happen or to be done or used **possible** *n* a candidate who may be successful for a job or membership of a team **possibility** *n pl* **possibilities** **1** something that is possible or might happen **2** the fact or condition of being possible **possibly** *adv* **1** in terms of what is possible ♦ *I could not possibly do it.* **2** perhaps ♦ *They are possibly right about that.*

possum *n* a small Australian marsupial **to play possum** to pretend to be unconscious or dead (as an opossum does when threatened)

post[1] *n* a piece of wood, concrete, or metal, etc. set upright in the ground to support something or to mark a position **post** *v* to announce something by putting up a notice or placard about it

post[2] *n* **1** the place where a soldier is on watch, a place of duty ♦ *The sentries are at their posts.* **2** a place occupied by soldiers, especially a frontier fort **3** a place occupied for purposes of trade ♦ *trading posts* **4** a position of paid employment, a job **post** *v* **1** to place or station people somewhere ♦ *Sentries are posted at the gates.* **2** to appoint someone to a post or command ♦ *Her husband was posted to Washington.*

post[3] *n* **1** the collection and delivery of letters, parcels, etc. **2** the letters and parcels sent in this way **3** a single collection or delivery of letters and parcels ♦ *Is there an afternoon post on Saturdays?* **post** *v* to take a letter or parcel into a post office or put it into a postbox for delivery to an address **postage** *n* the charge for sending something by post **postal** *adj* **postally** *adv* **postal order** *n* a money order bought from a post office for sending to a named recipient **postbox** *n* a large container with a slot into which letters are put for posting **postcard** *n* a card for sending a message by post without an envelope **postcode** *n* a group of letters and figures included in a postal address to assist sorting **postman** *n pl* **postmen** a person who delivers or collects letters and parcels **postmark** *n* an official mark stamped on something sent by post, giving the place and date and cancelling the stamp **postmaster** *n* an official in charge of a post office **post office** *n* **1** a public department or corporation responsible for postal services **2** a building in which postal business is conducted **to keep someone posted** to keep someone informed about something

post- *prefix* after (as in *post-war*)

postage stamp *n* a small adhesive stamp for sticking on things to be posted, showing the amount paid

post-date *v* to put a date on a document or cheque, etc. that is later than the actual one

poster *n* a large printed notice or picture put up to announce something or as decoration

poste restante (say pohst ress-**tahnt**) *n* a department in a post office where letters are kept until called for

posterior *adj* situated behind or at the back **posterior** *n* the buttocks

posterity (say poss-**te**-riti) *n* future generations of people ♦ *We need to preserve these documents for posterity.*

postern (say **poss**-tern) *n* a small entrance at the back or side of a fortress or other large building

postgraduate *adj* to do with studies carried on after taking a first degree **postgraduate** *n* a student engaged in these studies

post-haste *adv* with great speed or haste

posthumous (say **poss**-tew-məs) *adj* coming or happening after a person's death ♦ *a posthumous award for bravery* **posthumously** *adv*

postilion *n* a rider on a nearside horse pulling a coach or carriage, when there is no coachman

post-mortem *n* **1** an examination of a dead body to determine the cause of death **2** a detailed discussion of something, especially a failure, after it is over

post-natal *adj* occurring in or to do with the period after childbirth

postpone *v* to arrange for an event to take place at a later time than originally planned ♦ *The match has been postponed until next week.* **postponement** *n*

postscript *n* a remark or paragraph added at the end of a letter, after the signature

postulant (say **poss**-tew-lənt) *n* someone who has applied to join a religious order

postulate (say **poss**-tew-layt) *v* to assume something to be true, especially as a basis for reasoning or argument **postulation** *n*

posture (say **poss**-cher) *n* a particular position of the body, or the way in which a person stands, sits, or walks

posy *n pl* **posies** a small bunch of flowers

pot[1] *n* a deep rounded container **pot** *v* **potted, potting** **1** to plant something in a pot **2** (in billiards and snooker) to put a ball into a pocket **potted** *adj* **1** shortened or abridged **2** (said about food) preserved in a pot ♦ *potted shrimps* **potty** *n pl* **potties** a chamber pot for a child **pot belly** *n* a fat rounded stomach **pothole** *n* **1** a deep underground cave formed in rock by the action of water **2** a hole in the surface of a road **pothole** *v* to explore underground potholes **potholer** *n* **pot luck** *n* a chance taken with whatever happens to be available **pot shot** *n* a shot aimed casually at something **potting shed** *n* a shed used for potting plants and keeping garden tools

pot[2] *n informal* cannabis

potable (say **poh**-tə-bəl) *adj formal* drinkable

potash *n* a potassium compound, especially potassium carbonate

potassium (say pə-**tas**-iəm) *n* a soft silvery-white metallic element

potato *n pl* **potatoes** **1** a plant with starchy tubers that are used as food **2** one of these tubers

potent (say **poh**-tənt) *adj* having a powerful effect ♦ *a potent drug* **potency** *n*

potential *adj* capable of coming into being or of being developed or used ♦ *a potential source of energy* **potential** *n* **1** an ability or resources available for development or use **2** *Electricity* the voltage between two points **potentiality** *n* **potentially** *adv*

potentate (say **poh**-tən-tayt) *n* a monarch or ruler

potion (say **poh**-shən) *n* a liquid for drinking as a medicine or drug

potpourri (say poh-**poor** -ee) *n pl* **potpourris** **1** a mixture of dried petals and spices put in a bowl to perfume a room **2** a mixture of things, a medley

potter *v* to work or move about in a leisurely relaxed way **potterer** *n*

pottery *n pl* **potteries** **1** vessels and other objects made of baked clay **2** the work of making pottery, or the place where it is made **potter** *n* a person who makes pottery

potty *adj* **pottier, pottiest** *informal* **1** crazy or foolish ♦ *a potty idea* **2** extremely keen on something ♦ *potty about football*

pouch *n* a small bag, or something shaped

like a bag

pouffe (say poof) n a padded stool

poultice (say **pohl**-tiss) n a soft heated dressing applied to an inflamed or sore area of skin

poultry (say **pohl**-tri) n domestic fowls such as ducks, geese, chickens, and turkeys, kept for their eggs and meat

pounce v to jump or swoop down quickly on something **pounce** n a pouncing movement

pound[1] n 1 a measure of weight equal to 16 oz. avoirdupois (0.4536 kg) or 12 oz. troy (0.3732 kg) 2 the unit of currency of Britain and some other countries

pound[2] n 1 a place where stray dogs are taken and kept until claimed 2 an enclosure for motor vehicles impounded by the police

pound[3] v 1 to crush or beat something with heavy repeated strokes 2 to walk or run with heavy steps ♦ *He pounded down the stairs.* 3 to beat or throb with a heavy rhythm

pour v 1 to flow or cause liquid to flow in a stream or shower 2 to prepare and serve a drink 3 to rain heavily 4 to come or go in large amounts ♦ *Letters of complaint poured in.* **pourer** n

pout v to push out your lips when you are annoyed or sulking **pout** n a pouting expression

poverty n 1 the state of being poor, a lack of money or resources 2 a scarcity or lack of something **poverty trap** n a situation in which there is no advantage in an increased income because this would be offset by the loss of state benefits that a lower income brings

POW abbr prisoner of war

powder n 1 a mass of fine dry particles produced by grinding or crushing a solid substance 2 a medicine or cosmetic made as a powder **powder** v 1 to apply powder to something; to cover a surface with powder 2 to reduce a substance to powder **powdered** adj **powdery** adj **powder puff** n a soft pad for putting powder on the skin **powder room** n a woman's toilet in a public building

power n 1 strength or energy 2 the ability to do something ♦ *the power of speech* 3 political control or authority ♦ *the party in power* 4 legal right or authority ♦ *the power to levy taxes* 5 an influential person, country, or organization 6 *Mathematics* the product of a number multiplied by itself a given number of times ♦ *the third power of $2 = 2 \times 2 \times 2 = 8$* 7 mechanical or electrical energy as opposed to hand labour ♦ *power tools* 8 electricity supply ♦ *a power failure* **power** v 1 to equip a place with mechanical or electrical power 2 to travel with great speed or strength **powerful** adj having great power, strength, or influence **powerfully** adj **powerless** adj having no power to take action, wholly unable **power cut** n a temporary failure of an electricity supply **power station** n a building where electrical power is generated for distribution

powwow n informal a meeting for discussion

pp abbr pages (as in pp. 25-6)

PR abbr 1 proportional representation 2 public relations

practicable adj able to be done **practicability** n

practical adj 1 involving activity as distinct from study or theory ♦ *She has had practical experience.* 2 likely to be useful ♦ *a clever invention but not very practical* 3 (said about a person) adept at making things and doing useful things 4 virtual, very nearly so ♦ *He now has practical control of the business.* **practicality** n **practically** adv 1 in a practical way 2 virtually, almost ♦ *I have practically finished.* **practical joke** n a trick played on someone to make them appear foolish

practice n 1 actual use of a plan or method as opposed to theory ♦ *It works well in practice.* 2 a habitual action or custom ♦ *It is her practice to work until midnight.* 3 repeated exercise to improve a skill ♦ *You need to do more piano practice.* 4 the business or professional work done by a doctor, lawyer, etc., or the building where this is done ♦ *There is a doctors' practice near the bank.* ◊ Note that the noun is spelt *practice* and the verb is spelt *practise*.

practise *v* **1** to do something repeatedly in order to become more skilful at it **2** to do something actively or habitually ♦ *Practise what you preach.* **3** to follow the teaching and rules of a religion **4** (said about a doctor or lawyer, etc.) to be actively doing professional work ◊ See the note at **practice**. **practised** *adj* experienced or expert **practitioner** *n* a professional or practical worker, especially a doctor

pragmatic (say prag-**mat**-ik) *adj* treating things in a practical way ♦ *Take a pragmatic approach to the problem.* **pragmatically** *adv* **pragmatism** *n* **pragmatist** *n*

prairie *n* a large area of flat grassland, especially in North America

praise *v* **1** to express approval or admiration of someone or what they have done **2** to express honour or reverence for a deity **praise** *n* words that praise someone or something **praiseworthy** *adj* deserving praise

praline (say **prah**-leen) *n* a sweet made by boiling nuts in sugar

pram *n* a four-wheeled carriage for a baby, pushed by a person walking

prance *v* to move about in a lively or eager way

prang *v informal* to crash or damage a vehicle **prang** *n informal* a crash or damage to a vehicle

prank *n* a practical joke or piece of mischief

prattle *v* to chatter foolishly **prattle** *n* foolish chatter

prawn *n* an edible shellfish like a large shrimp

pray *v* **1** to say prayers **2** to wish or hope earnestly for something

prayer *n* **1** a solemn request or thanksgiving to God or to another deity **2** a set form of words used in this ♦ *the Lord's Prayer* **3** an earnest wish or hope

pre- *prefix* before or beforehand (as in *prehistoric*)

preach *v* **1** to give a sermon or a religious or moral talk **2** to urge people to adopt a certain practice or principle ♦ *They preached economy.* **3** to give moral advice ostentatiously or self-righteously ♦ *What right have they to preach to us?* **preacher** *n*

preamble (say pree-**am**-bəl) *n* the introductory part of a document or law, etc.

precarious (say pri-**kair**-ies) *adj* not very safe or secure **precariously** *adv*

precaution *n* something done in advance to prevent trouble or danger **precautionary** *adj*

precede (say pri-**seed**) *v* to come or go before someone or something else ◊ Do not confuse this word with *proceed*, which has a different meaning. **precedence** *n* the right of something to be put first, or of someone to go first **precedent** *n* a previous action or decision that is taken as an example to be followed in other cases of the same kind **to take precedence** to have priority

precentor (say pri-**sent**-er) *n* a person who leads a congregation in singing or prayers

precept (say **pree**-sept) *n* a rule or principle about how people should act or behave

precinct (say **pree**-sinkt) *n* **1** an area round a place, especially round a cathedral or college **2** an area in a town set aside for some purpose, especially one closed to traffic ♦ *a pedestrian precinct*

precious *adj* **1** having great value or worth **2** greatly loved by someone **3** affectedly refined or elegant **preciousness** *n* **precious stone** *n* a valuable and attractive piece of mineral used in jewellery

precipice (say **press**-i-piss) *n* a very steep or vertical rock face or cliff **precipitous** (say pri-**sip**-ites) *adj* steep

precipitate (say pri-**sip**-i-tayt) *v* **1** to throw something down headlong ♦ *The shove precipitated him through the window.* **2** to cause something to happen suddenly or without warning ♦ *The remarks precipitated an argument.* **3** to condense vapour into drops which fall as rain or dew, etc. **precipitate** (say pri-**sip**-i-tət) *adj* **1** headlong or sudden ♦ *a precipitate fall in popularity* **2** (said about a person or action) hasty or rash

precis (say **pray**-see) *n pl* **precis** (say **pray**-seez) a written or spoken summary of a text or speech **precis** *v* **precised**, **precising** to make a summary of a text or speech

precise adj 1 exact, correctly and clearly stated 2 (said about a person) taking care to be exact **precisely** adv **precision** n

preclude (say pri-**klood**) v to prevent something or exclude the possibility of its happening

precocious (say pri-**koh**-shəs) adj having developed certain abilities at an earlier age than usual **precociously** adv **precocity** n

preconceived adj (said about an idea or opinion) formed before full knowledge or information is available **preconception** n

precondition n a condition that must be fulfilled before something else can happen or be done

precursor (say pri-**ker**-ser) n a person or thing that comes before another of the same kind, a forerunner

predator (say **pred**-ə-ter) n 1 an animal that hunts or preys on others 2 a person or organization that exploits or threatens others **predatory** adj

predecease (say pree-di-**seess**) v to die earlier than another person

predecessor (say **pree**-di-sess-er) n 1 someone who held an office or position before the present holder 2 a thing that has been followed or replaced by another

predestine v to destine something beforehand, to determine an outcome in advance **predestination** n the doctrine that God has foreordained all that happens

predetermine v to determine an outcome in advance

predicament (say pri-**dik**-ə-mənt) n a difficult or unpleasant situation

predict v to say what will happen in the future, to foretell something **predictable** adj 1 able to be predicted 2 tediously or boringly behaving in the same way always **predictability** n **predictably** adv **prediction** n

predilection (say pree-di-**lek**-shən) n a special liking or preference

predispose v 1 to influence someone in advance so that they are likely to take a particular attitude ♦ *We were predisposed to help them.* 2 to make someone liable to a disease **predisposition** n

predominate v to be the largest or most important or powerful element **predominant** adj being the main force or element **predominantly** adv **predominance** n

pre-eminent adj excelling all others, outstanding **pre-eminence** n

pre-empt v to take action to prevent an attack or other expected event from happening **pre-emption** n **pre-emptive** adj

preen v (said about a bird) to smooth its feathers with its beak **to preen yourself** 1 to make yourself look attractive 2 to congratulate yourself ostentatiously

prefabricate v to manufacture a building or piece of furniture in sections ready for assembly when they are delivered to a site **prefab** n a prefabricated building

preface (say **pref**-əs) n an introduction to a book, outlining its contents and aims **preface** v 1 to begin a speech with some introductory words ♦ *She prefaced her remarks with a round of thanks.* 2 to introduce or lead up to an event ♦ *The ceremony was prefaced by grand music.* **prefatory** adj

prefect n 1 a senior pupil in a school, given authority to help maintain discipline 2 a regional official in France, Japan, and some other countries

prefer v **preferred, preferring** 1 to choose or like one person or thing more than another 2 formal to put forward an accusation for consideration by an authority ♦ *They have preferred charges of fraud against him.* **preferable** adj more desirable or suitable **preferably** adv **preference** n 1 a choice or greater liking for one person or thing over another 2 a person or thing preferred **preferential** adj showing or based on a preference ♦ *preferential treatment* **preferment** n appointment or promotion to an office or job

prefigure v to be an early version of something

prefix n 1 a word or syllable placed in front of a word to add to or change its meaning (as in *dis*order, *non*-existent, *out*stretched, *un*happy) 2 a title placed before a name (e.g. *Dr*) **prefix** v to add something as a prefix or introduction

pregnant *adj* **1** (said about a woman or female animal) having a child or young animal developing in the womb **2** full of meaning or significance ♦ *There was a pregnant silence.* **pregnancy** *n*

prehensile (say pri-**hen**-siyl) *adj* (said about an animal's limb or tail) able to grasp things

prehistoric *adj* to do with the ancient period of time before written records of events were made **prehistory** *n* prehistoric times

prejudge *v* to form a judgement about a person or action before all the information is available

prejudice *n* **1** an unfavourable opinion or dislike formed on the basis of preconceived ideas and without regard to the actual facts or circumstances **2** *Law* harm done to a person's rights **prejudice** *v* **1** to cause a person to have a prejudice **2** *Law* to cause harm to a person's rights **prejudiced** *adj* having a prejudice **prejudicial** *adj* harmful to a person's rights or claims

prelate (say **prel**-ət) *n formal* a bishop or other clergyman of high rank

preliminary *adj* coming before an important action or event and preparing for it **preliminary** *n pl* **preliminaries** a preliminary action or event

prelude (say **prel**-yood) *n* **1** an action or event that precedes another and leads up to it **2** *Mus* an introductory movement

premarital (say pree-**ma**-ritəl) *adj* to do with or happening in the time before marriage

premature (say **prem**-ə-tewr) *adj* **1** occurring or done before the usual or proper time, too early **2** (said about a baby) born three or more weeks before the full term of gestation **prematurely** *adv*

premeditated (say pree-**med**-i-tayt-id) *adj* (said about an action, especially a crime) planned beforehand **premeditation** *n*

premenstrual (say pree-**men**-stroo-əl) *adj* to do with or experienced in the time immediately before menstruation

premier (say **prem**-i-er) *adj* first in importance, order, or time **premier** *n* a prime minister or other head of government **premiership** *n*

premiere (say **prem**-yair) *n* the first public performance or showing of a play or film **premiere** *v* to give a premiere of a play or film

premise, **premiss** (say **prem**-iss) *n* a statement used as a basis for reasoning

premises (say **prem**-i-siz) *pl n* a house or other building with its grounds and outbuildings

premium (say **pree**-mi-əm) *n* **1** an amount or instalment paid for an insurance policy **2** an extra charge or payment **Premium Bond** *n* a government security that pays no interest but is entered in a regular draw for cash prizes **at a premium** in demand but scarce

premonition (say prem-ə-**nish**-ən) *n* a strong feeling that a particular thing is going to happen

preoccupy *v* **preoccupies**, **preoccupied**, **preoccupying** to occupy someone's thoughts completely, excluding other thoughts **preoccupation** *n* **preoccupied** *adj*

preordain *v* to decide or determine something beforehand

prepare *v* to get ready, or to make something ready **prep** *n* school work or homework done outside lessons **preparation** *n* **1** the process of preparing something **2** something done to make ready for an event or activity **3** a substance or mixture prepared for use, especially a food or medicine **preparatory** *adj* preparing for an event or activity ♦ *preparatory training* **preparatory school** *n* a school for pupils between the ages of seven and thirteen **to be prepared to** to be ready and willing to do something

prepay *v* to pay for something in advance, especially to pay the postage on a letter or parcel by fixing a stamp on it **prepaid** *adj*

preponderate (say pri-**pond**-er-ayt) *v* to be greater than others in number or importance **preponderance** *n* **preponderant** *adj* **preponderantly** *adv*

prepossessing *adj* attractive, making a good impression ♦ *The front of the house is not very prepossessing.*

preposterous (say pri-**poss**-ter-əs) *adj* utterly absurd or ridiculous **preposterously** *adv*

prerequisite (say pree-**rek**-wiz-it) *n* something that is required as a condition or in preparation for something else ♦ *Knowledge of a foreign language is normally a prerequisite for working abroad.*

prerogative (say pri-**rog**-ətiv) *n* a right or privilege that belongs to a particular person or group

presage (say pri-**sayj**) *v* to be an advance sign or warning of something about to happen

presbyter (say **prez**-bit-er) *n* a priest or elder in certain Christian Churches **Presbyterian** *adj* denoting a Christian Church governed by elders who are all of equal rank **Presbyterianism** *n* **presbytery** *n pl* **presbyteries** 1 the house of a Roman Catholic parish priest 2 a body of presbyters

prescribe *v* 1 to advise and authorize the use of a medicine 2 to recommend or lay down a procedure or rule to be followed ◊ Do not confuse this word with *proscribe*, which has a different meaning. **prescription** *n* 1 a doctor's written instruction for a medicine or treatment to be provided to a patient 2 an authorization or recommendation **prescriptive** *adj* stating or laying down rules

present¹ (say **prez**-ənt) *adj* 1 being in a particular place ♦ *Three people were present when the alarm went off.* 2 existing or occurring now ♦ *The estate then passed to the present Duke.* 3 *Gram* (said about a tense) denoting an action or state that is going on at the time of speaking or writing, or occurs habitually **present** *n* present time, the time now passing **presence** *n* 1 the state or fact of being present in a place ♦ *The bird seemed unaware of our presence.* 2 the impressive bearing or manner of a person ♦ *She has a fine presence.* **presently** *adv* 1 after a short time, soon 2 at the present time, now **presence of mind** the ability to act quickly and sensibly in a difficult situation

present² (say pri-**zent**) *v* 1 to give something as a gift or award, to offer something for acceptance 2 to introduce someone to another person or to others, or to an audience 3 to put a performance or exhibition before the public 4 to show or reveal ♦ *They presented a brave front to the world.* **present** (say **prez**-ənt) *n* something given or received as a gift **presentable** *adj* fit to be presented to other people, of good appearance **presentation** *n* **presenter** *n*

presentiment (say pri-**zent**-i-mənt) *n* a feeling or foreboding about the future

preserve *v* 1 to keep something safe or in an unchanged condition 2 to treat food to prevent it from decaying **preserve** *n* 1 jam made with preserved fruit 2 an area where game or fish are protected for private hunting or fishing 3 an activity or interest that is regarded as belonging to a particular person or group **preservation** *n* the process of preserving something **preservative** *n* a substance that preserves food, wood, or other perishable substances

preset *v* past tense and past participle **preset**; **presetting** to set a function of a device to operate at a certain time or in a certain way

president *n* 1 the elected head of a state that is a republic 2 the head of a club, society, or other organization **preside** *v* to have the position of authority or control at a meeting, in a law court, etc. **presidency** *n* **presidential** *adj*

press *v* 1 to apply weight or force steadily to something 2 to flatten or smooth clothes by ironing them 3 to exert pressure on an enemy or opponent 4 to urge or force someone to accept something 5 to throng closely 6 to push your way **press** *n* 1 a device or machine for pressing, flattening, or shaping something 2 a printing press 3 newspapers and periodicals, and the people involved in producing them ♦ *a press photographer* **pressing** *adj* needing quick action, urgent ♦ *a pressing need* **press conference** *n* a meeting with journalists to make an announcement or answer questions **press stud** *n* a small fastener with two parts that engage when pressed together **press-up** *n* an exercise in which a person lies face downwards and presses down on the hands so that the shoulders and trunk are raised **to be pressed for** to have barely enough of ♦ *We are a little pressed for time.*

press gang *n hist* a group of men employed to force people to enlist in the army or navy

pressure *n* **1** the exertion of a continuous physical force on something **2** the force exerted by the atmosphere ♦ *Pressure is high in eastern areas.* **3** a strong influence that persuades you to do something ♦ *The government is under pressure to reduce taxes.* **pressure** *v* to influence or persuade someone to take a certain action **pressurize** *v* **1** to keep a closed compartment, e.g. an aircraft cabin, at a constant atmospheric pressure **2** to influence or persuade someone to take a certain action **pressure cooker** *n* an airtight pan in which things can be cooked quickly by steam under high pressure **pressure group** *n* an organized group that tries to influence public policy by concerted action

prestige (say press-teezh) *n* respect and admiration for a person or organization resulting from a widespread high opinion of their achievements or quality **prestigious** *adj*

presume *v* **1** to take something for granted, or suppose it to be true **2** to take the liberty of doing something, to venture ♦ *May I presume to advise you?* **presumably** *adv* as you may presume **presumption** *n* **1** the act of presuming something to be true **2** an idea that is presumed to be true **3** presumptuous behaviour **presumptive** *adj* presumed when no further information is available **presumptuous** *adj* behaving too boldly, or acting without authority

presuppose *v* **1** to assume something to be the case before having all the information **2** to require something as a prior condition ♦ *Exceptions presuppose the existence of a rule.* **presupposition** *n*

pretend *v* **1** to act or talk in a way that falsely suggests something to be the case, either in play or so as to deceive other people **2** to put forward a claim ♦ *The son*

of James II pretended to the British throne. **pretence** *n* **1** the act of pretending **2** a false or over-ambitious claim **3** pretentious behaviour **pretender** *n* a person who claims a throne or title **pretension** *n* **1** a claim or aspiration, especially a false one **2** pretentious behaviour **pretentious** *adj* trying to impress by claiming greater importance or merit than is actually the case **pretentiously** *adv* **pretentiousness** *n*

preternatural (say pree-ter-nach-er-əl) *adj* outside what is normal or natural

pretext (say pree-tekst) *n* a reason put forward to conceal the true reason

pretty *adj* **prettier**, **prettiest** attractive in a delicate way **pretty** *adv* fairly, moderately ♦ *The food was pretty good.* **prettily** *adv* **prettiness** *n*

pretzel (say pret-zəl) *n* a crisp biscuit flavoured with salt

prevail *v* **1** to be victorious, to be more powerful or successful **2** to be the most usual or most frequently occurring **prevalent** *adj* most usual or most frequently occurring **prevalence** *n*

prevaricate (say pri-va-ri-kayt) *v* to speak evasively or misleadingly **prevarication** *n*

prevent *v* **1** to keep something from happening, or make it impossible **2** to keep someone from doing something **preventable** *adj* **preventative** *adj* designed or serving to prevent something **prevention** *n*

preview *n* an advance showing or viewing of a film or play, etc. before it is shown to the general public

previous *adj* coming before in time or order **previously** *adv*

prey (say pray) *n* **1** an animal that is hunted or killed by another animal **2** victim **prey** *v* **preys**, **preyed**, **preying**, **to prey on 1** (said about an animal) to hunt and kill other animals for food **2** to cause anxiety or worry to someone ♦ *The problem was preying on his mind.*

price *n* **1** the amount of money for which something is bought or sold **2** something that must be given or done in order to achieve something ♦ *Loss of freedom is a high price to pay in defence of one's principles.*

price *v* to fix or estimate the price of something **priceless** *adj* 1 so valuable that its price cannot be determined 2 *informal* very amusing or absurd **pricey** *adj* **pricier**, **priciest** *informal* expensive

prick *v* 1 to pierce something slightly or make a tiny hole in it 2 to make someone feel anxious or guilty ♦ *My conscience has been pricking me.* **prick** *n* 1 an act of pricking 2 a mark or puncture made by pricking **to prick up your ears** 1 (said about a dog) to raise its ears erect when on the alert 2 (said about a person) to become suddenly attentive

prickle *n* 1 a small thorn 2 one of the hard pointed spines on a hedgehog, cactus, etc. 3 a pricking sensation **prickle** *v* to feel or cause someone to feel a sensation of pricking **prickly** *adj* **pricklier**, **prickliest** 1 covered in prickles 2 causing a prickling feeling 3 (said about a person) irritable or touchy

pride *n* 1 a feeling of deep pleasure or satisfaction derived from your actions, qualities, or possessions, etc. 2 a person or thing that causes you pride 3 a proper sense of what is fitting for your position or character, self-respect 4 an unduly high opinion of your qualities or merits 5 a group of lions **pride** *v* **to pride oneself on** to be proud of an achievement or quality **pride of place** the most prominent or important position

priest *n* 1 an ordained member of the clergy in certain Christian Churches 2 a person who performs rites in a non-Christian religion **priestess** *n* a female priest of a non-Christian religion **priesthood** *n* **priestly** *adj* like a priest, or suitable for a priest

prig *n* a person who self-righteously displays or demands moral correctness **priggish** *adj* **priggishness** *n*

prim *adj* **primmer**, **primmest** stiffly formal and precise in manner or behaviour, disliking what is rough or improper **primly** *adv* **primness** *n*

prima ballerina (say **pree-mə**) *n* the chief female dancer in a ballet

primacy (say **priy-mə-si**) *n* pre-eminence

prima donna (say **pree-mə don-ə**) *n* 1 the chief female singer in an opera 2 a self-important and demanding person

prima facie (say **priy-mə fay-shee**) *adj, adv* at first sight, based on a first impression

primal (say **priy-məl**) *adj* primitive or primeval

primary (say **priy-mə-ri**) *adj* 1 of the first importance, chief ♦ *Safety is our primary concern.* 2 earliest in time or order, first in a series ♦ *the primary stage in a process* **primarily** *adv* **primary colour** *n* any of the colours from which all others can be made by mixing, (of paint) red, yellow, and blue, (of light) red, green, and violet **primary school** *n* a school for children between the ages of five and eleven

primate (say **priy-mət**) *n* 1 a chief bishop or archbishop 2 a member of the highly developed order of animals that includes humans, apes, and monkeys

prime[1] *adj* 1 chief or most important ♦ *the prime cause* 2 excellent or first-rate ♦ *prime quality* **prime** *n* the best or most fully developed part or stage of something ♦ *in the prime of life* **primer** *n* an elementary textbook **prime minister** *n* the chief minister in a government **prime number** *n* a number that can be divided exactly only by itself and one (e.g. 2, 3, 5, 7, 11)

prime[2] *v* 1 to prepare something, especially a weapon or bomb, for use or action 2 to prepare a surface for painting 3 to prepare someone for an undertaking or situation by providing information **primer** *n* a substance used to prime a surface for painting

primeval (say **priy-mee-vəl**) *adj* to do with the earliest time in history

primitive *adj* 1 at an early stage of history or civilization ♦ *primitive peoples* 2 simple or crude, not developed or advanced ♦ *primitive tools*

primogeniture (say **priy-mə-jen-i-cher**) *n* the system by which an eldest son inherits all his parents' property

primordial (say **priy-mor -di-əl**) *adj* to do with the earliest time in history, primeval

primrose *n* a plant bearing pale yellow flowers in spring

primula *n* a perennial plant with clusters of

flowers in various colours

prince n **1** a male member of a royal family, especially a son or grandson of the reigning queen or king **2** a ruler of a small state **princely** adj **1** relating to or suitable for a prince **2** splendid, generous **princess** n **1** the wife of a prince **2** a female member of a royal family; especially a daughter or granddaughter of the reigning queen or king **principality** n pl **principalities** a country ruled by a prince **prince consort** n the husband of a reigning queen **princess royal** n a title that may be conferred on the eldest daughter of the British sovereign

principal adj chief or most important **principal** n **1** the most important or senior person in an organization **2** the head of certain schools or colleges **3** a person who takes a leading part in an activity or in a play or musical performance **4** a capital sum as distinguished from the interest or income earned on it ◊ Do not confuse this word with principle, which has a different meaning. **principally** adv for the most part, chiefly **principal boy** n a woman who plays the leading male part in a pantomime

principle n **1** a basic truth or general rule used as a basis of reasoning or behaviour **2** a personal code of moral conduct ♦ a person of principle **3** a scientific rule or natural law shown in the way a thing works ◊ Do not confuse this word with principal, which has a different meaning. **in principle** in theory, as regards the main elements but not necessarily the details **on principle** because of the principles of conduct someone believes in ♦ We refused their offer on principle.

print v **1** to produce lettering on a book or newspaper, etc. by transferring text or designs to paper by various mechanical or electronic processes **2** to publish books or newspapers in this way **3** to impress or stamp a surface or fabric, etc. with a mark or design **4** to write letters clearly without joining them up **5** (in photography) to produce a picture from a negative, transparency, or digital file **print** n **1** printed lettering or writing, the text of a book or newspaper, etc. **2** a printed

picture or design **3** a piece of printed cotton fabric **4** a mark made by something pressing on a surface **printer** n **1** a person whose job or business is the printing of books, newspapers, etc. **2** a machine for printing text or pictures **printout** n material produced in printed form from a computer or teleprinter **printed circuit** an electronic circuit made with thin strips of a conducting material on an insulating board **printing press** n a machine for printing from raised type **out of print** no longer available from a publisher

prior¹ adj earlier ♦ a prior engagement **prior** adv prior to before ♦ prior to our meeting **priority** n pl **priorities** **1** the fact or state of being earlier or more important, the right to be first **2** something that is considered more important than other items or considerations

prior² n a monk who is the head of a religious house or order **prioress** n a nun who is the head of a religious house or order **priory** n pl **priories** a community of monks governed by a prior, or of nuns governed by a prioress

prise v to force something open or apart by leverage ◊ Do not confuse this word with prize, which has a different meaning.

prism n **1** Geometry a solid geometric shape with ends that are similar, equal, and parallel **2** a transparent object having this form and usually with triangular ends, which breaks up light into a spectrum **prismatic** adj **1** of or having the form of a prism **2** (said about colours) formed or distributed as if by a prism, like a rainbow

prison n a building used to confine criminals or people accused of crimes **prisoner** n **1** a person kept in prison as a legal punishment for a crime **2** a person who has been captured and confined **prisoner of war** n a person captured and imprisoned by the enemy in a war

prissy adj **prissier**, **prissiest** fussily respectable or prim

pristine (say pris-teen) adj **1** in its original condition, unspoilt **2** fresh as if new ♦ a pristine layer of snow

private adj **1** of or belonging to a particular

person or group, not public ♦ *private property* **2** confidential **3** (said about a place) quiet and secluded **4** (said about a service or industry) run as a commercial operation and not by the state **private** *n* a soldier of the lowest rank **privacy** *n* a state of being private and not disturbed by other people **privately** *adv* **privatize** *v* to transfer a business or industry from state ownership to private enterprise **privatization** *n* **private member** *n* an MP who does not hold a government appointment **private school** *n* a school supported wholly by the payment of fees or endowments **private sector** *n* businesses and industries run by private enterprise as distinct from the state

privation (say priy-**vay**-shən) *n* the loss or lack of essentials, such as food and warmth

privet (say **priv**-it) *n* a bushy evergreen shrub with small leaves, used to make hedges

privilege *n* a special right or advantage given to one person or group **privileged** *adj* having privileges or advantages over other people

privy *adj old use* hidden or secret **privy** *n pl* **privies** *old use* a lavatory **Privy Council** *n* a body of distinguished people who advise the sovereign on matters of state **to be privy to** to be sharing in the knowledge of something secret

prize *n* an award given as a reward to a winner or to acknowledge an outstanding achievement **prize** *adj* winning or likely to win a prize; excellent of its kind **prize** *v* to value something highly **prizefighter** *n* a professional boxer

pro[1] *n pl* **pros** *informal* a professional

pro[2] *adj, prep* for, in favour of **pro** *n pl* **pros** a reason for or in favour of something, an advantage **pros and cons** reasons for and against something, advantages and disadvantages

pro- *prefix* **1** favouring or supporting (as in *pro-choice*) **2** deputizing or substituted for (as in *pronoun*) **3** onwards or forwards (as in *proceed*)

probable *adj* likely to happen or be true **probably** *adv* **probability** *n pl* **probabilities** **1** the state of being probable **2** something

that is probable; the most probable event **3** a ratio expressing the chances that a certain event will occur

probate (say proh-**bayt**) *n* **1** the official process of proving that a will is valid **2** a copy of a will with a certificate that it is valid, handed to executors

probation *n* **1** the process of testing a person's character and abilities in a certain role **2** a system whereby certain offenders are not sent to prison but have to complete a period of good behaviour under supervision **probationary** *adj* **probationer** *n* an person who is on probation

probe *n* **1** a device for exploring an otherwise inaccessible place or object **2** a blunt-ended surgical instrument for exploring a wound or part of the body **3** a thorough investigation **probe** *v* to make a thorough investigation of something

probity (say **proh**-biti) *n* honesty or integrity

problem *n* **1** something difficult to deal with or understand **2** something that has to be done or answered **problematic** *adj* **problematically** *adv*

proboscis (say prə-**boss**-iss) *n pl* **probosces** (say prə-**boss**-eez) **1** a long flexible snout, such as an elephant's trunk **2** an elongated mouthpart in certain insects, used for sucking things

procedure *n* an established series of actions for doing something **procedural** *adj*

proceed (say prə-**seed**) *v* **1** to go forward or onward **2** to go on to do something ♦ *She proceeded to tell us the latest news.* **3** to carry on an activity ♦ *We told the builders to proceed with the work.* **4** *Law* to start a lawsuit against someone **5** to originate with or be caused by something ♦ *the evils that proceed from war* ◊ Do not confuse this word with *precede*, which has a different meaning. **proceedings** *pl n* **1** an event or series of activities that follows a set procedure **2** a lawsuit ♦ *His wife has started proceedings for divorce.* **3** the activities and discussions that take place at a conference **proceeds** *pl n* the money raised by a sale or activity

process (say **proh**-sess) n 1 a series of actions or operations used in making or doing something 2 a natural operation or series of changes ◆ *the digestive process*
process v 1 to put something through a process or course of treatment 2 *ICT* to perform operations on data **processor** n 1 a machine that processes things 2 *ICT* a central processing unit

procession n a line of people or vehicles moving steadily forward

proclaim v to announce something officially or publicly **proclamation** n

proclivity (say prə-**kliv**-iti) n pl **proclivities** a tendency or inclination

procrastinate (say prə-**kras**-tin-ayt) v to keep delaying or postponing action **procrastination** n

procreate (say proh-kri-**ayt**) v to produce young by the natural process of reproduction **procreation** n

procurator fiscal (say **prok**-yoor-ayt-er) n (in Scotland) the public prosecutor and coroner of a district

procure v to obtain or acquire something, often by special effort **procurement** n

prod v **prodded**, **prodding** 1 to poke something or someone 2 to urge or stimulate someone into action **prod** n 1 a poke 2 a stimulus to action

prodigal adj wasteful or extravagant **prodigal** n a wastefully extravagant person

prodigy (say **prod**-iji) n pl **prodigies** 1 a person with exceptional abilities or talents 2 a marvellous or unusual thing **prodigious** adj remarkably large or impressive

produce (say prə-**dewss**) v 1 to make or manufacture something ◆ *The factory produces washing machines.* 2 to bring something forward for consideration or use 3 to organize the performance of a play, making of a film, etc. 4 to cause something to exist or occur ◆ *The remarks produced a round of applause.* **produce** (say **prod**-yewss) n things that have been produced, especially things grown or farmed for food **producer** n 1 a person who produces goods or produce 2 a person who directs the performance of a play or controls the business of a film or broadcast programme

product n 1 something manufactured or produced by agriculture 2 a substance produced during a natural process 3 the result obtained by multiplying two amounts together (e.g. 12 in 3 x 4 = 12)

production n 1 the process of producing things 2 something produced, especially a play or film 3 the amount produced ◆ *Production has increased this year.*
productive adj 1 able to produce things in large quantities 2 useful, producing good results **productivity** n

profane (say prə-**fayn**) adj 1 secular and not religious 2 irreverent or blasphemous **profane** v to treat something with irreverence or lack of due respect **profanity** n pl **profanities**

profess v 1 to claim that you have a quality or feeling ◆ *She professed ignorance.* 2 to affirm your faith in a religion

profession n 1 an occupation that involves special knowledge and training, such as medicine and law 2 the people engaged in a profession 3 a declaration or avowal ◆ *They made many professions of loyalty.*

professional adj 1 to do with or belonging to a profession 2 having or showing the skill of a professional 3 doing work or an activity for payment or as a livelihood and not as an amateur ◆ *a professional writer* **professional** n 1 a person working or performing for payment 2 someone who is highly skilled **professionalism** n the qualities or skills expected of professional people **professionally** adv

professor n a university teacher of the highest rank **professorship** n

proffer (say **prof**-er) v to offer something

proficient (say prə-**fish**-ənt) adj doing something correctly and competently through training or practice, skilled **proficiency** n

profile (say **proh**-fiyl) n 1 a side view of a person's face 2 an outline 3 a short description of a person's character or career **profile** v to describe someone in a profile

profit n 1 an advantage or benefit obtained from doing something 2 the money

gained in a business transaction **profit** v
profited, **profiting** to obtain an advantage
or benefit **profitable** adj providing a profit
or benefits **profitability** n **profitably** adv
profiteering n making large profits unfairly
profiterole (say prə-**fit**-er-ohl) n a small
hollow ball of choux pastry filled with
cream

profligate (say **prof**-lig-ət) adj 1 recklessly
wasteful or extravagant 2 indulging too
much in pleasure **profligate** n a profligate
person **profligacy** n

profound adj 1 very deep or intense ♦ We
have made some profound changes. 2 having
or showing great knowledge or insight
profoundly adv **profundity** n

profusion (say prə-**few**-zhən) n an
abundance or plentiful supply ♦ a profusion
of ideas **profuse** adj lavish or plentiful ♦ The
guests made profuse apologies for being so
late. **profusely** adv

progeny (say **proj**-ini) n offspring or
descendants **progenitor** n an ancestor

progesterone (say prə-**jest**-er-ohn) n a
hormone that stimulates the uterus to
prepare for pregnancy

prognosis (say prog-**noh**-sis) n pl
prognoses a forecast or advance
indication, especially about the way a
disease will develop

program n a series of coded instructions
for a computer **program** v **programmed**,
programming to input instructions
in a computer by means of a program
programmable adj **programmer** n

programme n 1 a planned series of events
2 a sheet or booklet giving details of the
items and performers at an event 3 a radio
or television broadcast **programme** v to
plan events according to a programme

progress (say **proh**-gress) n 1 forward or
onward movement 2 a development or
improvement **progress** (say prə-**gress**) v
1 to develop or improve, or to make
something develop 2 to move forward or
onward **progression** n **progressive** adj
1 making continuous forward movement
2 proceeding steadily or in regular degrees
♦ a progressive reduction in pollution levels
3 in favour of political or social change or

reform **progressively** adv **in progress**
taking place, in the course of occurring

prohibit v **prohibited**, **prohibiting** to forbid
something **prohibition** n **prohibitive** adj
1 serving to prevent or prohibit
something 2 (said about a charge or price)
unacceptably high **prohibitively** adv

project (say prə-**jekt**) v 1 to extend outward
♦ a projecting balcony 2 to cause an image
or shadow to fall on a surface 3 to cause a
sound to be heard further away 4 to present
or promote an idea ♦ The advertisements
were meant to project a strong brand image.
5 to estimate or forecast future trends on
the basis of the present situation **project**
(say **proj**-ekt) n 1 an undertaking aimed
at achieving a particular objective; a
plan or scheme 2 an educational task
of conducting research into a topic and
writing up the results **projectile** n a missile
that can be fired or thrown at a target
projection n **projectionist** n a person who
works a projector **projector** n a device
for projecting photographs or film on to a
screen

prolapse (say **proh**-laps) n a movement
of an organ of the body, in which it
slips forward or down out of its place
prolapsed adj

proletariat (say proh-li-**tair**-iət) n the
working class **proletarian** adj

proliferate (say prə-**lif**-er-ayt) v 1 to
produce new growth or offspring
rapidly 2 to increase rapidly in number
proliferation n

prolific (say prə-**lif**-ik) adj 1 producing
much fruit or many flowers or offspring
2 producing many works ♦ a prolific writer

prolix (say **proh**-liks) adj formal (said about
speech or writing) tediously wordy or
lengthy **prolixity** n

prologue (say **proh**-log) n an introduction
to a poem or play, etc.

prolong (say prə-**long**) v to make
something last longer **prolonged** adj

promenade (say prom-ən-**ahd**) n 1 a
paved public walk, especially along a sea
front 2 a leisurely walk in a public place
promenade v to go for a promenade
prom n 1 a promenade along a sea front

2 a promenade concert **promenade concert** *n* a concert at which all or part of the audience stands or walks about

prominent *adj* 1 important or well-known ♦ *prominent politicians* 2 conspicuous or noticeable ♦ *The house stood in a prominent position.* **prominence** *n* **prominently** *adv*

promiscuous (say prə-**miss**-kew-əs) *adj* having casual sexual relations with many people **promiscuity** *n*

promise *n* 1 an assurance that you will do or not do a certain thing 2 an indication that something is likely to occur ♦ *the promise of thunderstorms* 3 an indication of future success or excellence ♦ *The work shows promise.* **promise** *v* 1 to make a promise to someone, to declare that you will do or not do a certain thing 2 to make something seem likely **promising** *adj* likely to succeed or produce good results **promisingly** *adv* **promissory note** *n* a signed promise to pay a sum of money on a certain date

promontory (say prom-ən-ter-i) *n pl* **promontories** a piece of high land jutting out into the sea or a lake

promote *v* 1 to give someone a higher rank or more senior office 2 to help the progress of something, to support or encourage something ♦ *promoting friendship between nations* 3 to publicize a product in order to sell it **promoter** *n* **promotion** *n* **promotional** *adj*

prompt *adj* made or done without delay ♦ *We would like a prompt reply.* **prompt** *adv* in good time, punctually **prompt** *v* 1 to urge or encourage someone to do something 2 to cause a certain feeling, thought, or action 3 to help an actor or speaker by reminding them of words they have forgotten **prompter** *n* a person out of sight of the audience who prompts actors during the performance of a play **promptly** *adv* **promptness** *n*

promulgate (say prom-əl-gayt) *v* to make something known to the public, to proclaim something **promulgation** *n* **promulgator** *n*

prone *adj* 1 likely to do or suffer something ♦ *He is prone to sudden changes of mood.* ♦ *Some of the players seemed injury-prone.*

2 lying face downwards

prong *n* each of the pointed parts of a fork **pronged** *adj*

pronoun (say proh-nown) *n* a word used in place of a noun, such as *I, she, us, this, which*

pronounce *v* 1 to utter a speech sound in a particular way ♦ *'Two' and 'too' are pronounced the same* 2 to declare something formally ♦ *I now pronounce you man and wife.* **pronunciation** *n*

pronto *adv informal* immediately

proof *n* 1 a fact or piece of evidence that shows something to be true 2 a standard of strength for distilled alcoholic liquors ♦ *80% proof* 3 a trial impression of the pages of a book or other printed work, produced so that corrections can be made before it is finally printed 4 a trial print of a photograph **proof** *adj* able to resist or withstand penetration or damage ♦ *a bulletproof jacket* **proof-read** *v* past tense and past participle **proof-read** to read a proof of printed matter and mark corrections **proof-reader** *n*

prop[1] *n* a support, especially one made of a long piece of wood or metal, used to keep something from falling or sagging **prop** *v* **propped, propping** 1 to support something with or as if with a prop 2 to lean something against an upright surface ♦ *Prop your bicycle against the wall.*

prop[2] *n* a movable object or piece of furniture used on the set of a play or film

propaganda *n* biased or misleading publicity that is intended to promote a political point of view **propagandist** *n*

propagate *v* 1 to breed or reproduce animals or plants from a parent stock 2 to spread information or ideas widely **propagation** *n*

propel *v* **propelled, propelling** to drive or push something forward **propellant** *n* a substance that propels things **propeller** *n* a device consisting of a shaft with blades that spin round to propel a ship or aircraft **propulsion** *n* the process of propelling or driving something forward

propensity (say prə-**pen**-siti) *n pl* **propensities** a tendency or inclination ♦ *a propensity for violence*

proper adj **1** genuinely or fully what something is called ♦ It will be good to sleep in a proper bed again. **2** correct or suitable ♦ You need to make your application at the proper time. ♦ What is the proper way to address a bishop? **3** according to social conventions, respectable ♦ Their behaviour did not seem quite proper. **properly** adv
proper name n the name of an individual person or thing, e.g. Mary, London, Spain
property n pl **properties 1** a thing or things that someone owns **2** a building and the land belonging to it ♦ Their property borders on ours. **3** a quality or characteristic ♦ It has the property of becoming soft when heated.
prophet n **1** a person who predicts the future **2** a religious teacher inspired by God
prophecy n pl **prophecies 1** the power of foreseeing the future **2** a statement that predicts what will happen **prophesy** v **prophesies, prophesied, prophesying** to predict what will happen **prophetic** adj **1** predicting the future **2** to do with a prophet or prophecy **prophetically** adv
prophylactic (say proh-fil-**ak**-tik) adj tending to prevent a disease **prophylactic** n a prophylactic medicine or course of treatment
propitiate (say prə-**pish**-i-ayt) v to win the favour or forgiveness of someone, to placate someone **propitiation** n **propitious** adj favourable, providing a suitable opportunity
proponent (say prə-**poh**-nənt) n a person who puts forward a theory or proposal
proportion n **1** a part or share of something considered in relation to the whole **2** the ratio of one thing to another ♦ the proportion of skilled workers to unskilled **3** the correct relation in size or amount between one thing and another or between parts of a thing **proportions** pl n size or dimensions ♦ a palace of vast proportions **proportion** v to give the correct proportions to things, to make one thing proportionate to another **proportional** adj corresponding in size or amount to something **proportionally** adv **proportionate** adj in proportion, corresponding ♦ Penalties are proportionate to the seriousness of the

offence. **proportional representation** n
propose v **1** to put forward an idea or plan for consideration **2** to plan or intend to do something ♦ We propose to wait here. **3** to nominate someone as a candidate **4** to make an offer of marriage **proposal** n **1** the process of proposing something **2** something proposed, a plan or suggestion **3** an offer of marriage **proposer** n **proposition** n **1** a statement or assertion **2** a suggestion or proposal **3** something to be considered or dealt with ♦ The work was not an attractive proposition. **proposition** v informal to make an offer to someone, especially of sexual intercourse
propound v to put forward an idea or suggestions for consideration
proprietor (say prə-**priy**-ət-er) n the owner of a shop or business **proprietary** adj **1** manufactured and sold by one firm as a registered trademark ♦ proprietary medicines **2** to do with an owner or ownership **proprietorial** adj of or indicating ownership
propriety (say prə-**priy**-əti) n **1** being proper or suitable **2** correct behaviour or morals
pro rata (say proh **rah**-tə) adj, adv in proportion
prosaic (say prə-**zay**-ik) adj **1** in the style of prose writing **2** unimaginative, plain and ordinary
proscenium (say prə-**seen**-iəm) n pl **prosceniums** or **proscenia** the part of a theatre stage in front of the curtain
proscribe v to forbid something by law **proscription** n **proscriptive** adj ◊ Do not confuse this word with prescribe, which has a different meaning.
prose n ordinary written or spoken language that is not in verse
prosecute v **1** to start legal proceedings against someone **2** to continue an activity so as to complete it ♦ The state prosecuted the war with determination. **prosecution** n **1** the process of starting legal proceedings against someone **2** the party prosecuting someone in a lawsuit **prosecutor** n
proselyte (say **pross**-i-liyt) n a person who has been converted to a religion or opinion

proselytize v to convert people to your own beliefs or opinions

prosody (say **pross**-ə-di) n **1** the patterns of sound and rhythm used in poetry **2** the study of these patterns

prospect (say **pross**-pekt) n **1** a possibility or expectation of something ♦ *The prospects of success are quite good.* **2** a person regarded as likely to succeed **3** a wide or extensive view **prospect** (say prə-**spekt**) v to search for something, especially mineral deposits **prospective** adj expected to happen or exist ♦ *prospective customers* **prospector** n **prospectus** n pl **prospectuses** a booklet describing and advertising a school, university, or business

prosper v to be successful, especially financially **prosperous** adj financially successful **prosperity** n

prostate (say **pross**-tayt) n a gland round the neck of the bladder in males, which releases semen

prostitute n a person who takes part in sexual activity for payment **prostitute** v to put something worthwhile to an unworthy use ♦ *They were accused of prostituting their artistic abilities.* **prostitution** n

prostrate (say **pross**-trayt) adj **1** lying on the ground face downwards **2** overcome with emotion or exhaustion ♦ *prostrate with grief* **prostrate** (say pross-**trayt**) v **to prostrate yourself** to throw yourself flat on the ground as an act of reverence or submission

protagonist (say proh-**tag**-ən-ist) n **1** the chief character, or one of the leading characters, in a drama or narrative **2** an important figure in a real situation **3** someone who supports a cause or idea

protean (say **proh**-tiən or proh-**tee**-ən) adj able to adapt or take many forms

protect v to keep someone or something from harm or injury **protection** n **protectionism** n a policy of protecting domestic industries from foreign competition, e.g. by controlling imports **protectionist** n **protective** adj serving to protect something or someone **protectively** adv **protector** n **protectorate** n a country that is under the official protection and partial control of a stronger country

protégé, **protégée** (say prot-**ezh**-ay) n someone who is being helped and supported by an older or more experienced person ◊ The masculine form is *protégé* and the feminine form is *protégée*.

protest (say **proh**-test) n a statement or action showing disapproval of something **protest** (say prə-**test**) v **1** to express disapproval of something **2** to declare something firmly or solemnly ♦ *All the accused men protested their innocence.* **protestation** n a firm declaration about something ♦ *He was full of protestations of goodwill towards us.* **protester** n

Protestant n a member of any of the western Christian Churches that separated from the Roman Catholic Church at the Reformation **Protestantism** n

proto- prefix first or original (as in *prototype*)

protocol (say **proh**-tə-kol) n **1** the correct or official procedure for dealing with certain situations, especially affairs of state or diplomacy **2** the first or original draft of a diplomatic agreement

prototype (say **proh**-tə-tiyp) n a first or original example of something from which others are developed

protozoon (say proh-tə-**zoh**-ən) n pl **protozoa** a microscopic animal such as an amoeba **protozoan** adj, n

protract (say prə-**trakt**) v to prolong something or make it last longer **protraction** n **protractor** n an instrument for measuring angles

protrude v to stick out or project from a surface **protrusion** n

protuberance n a part that bulges out from a surface **protuberant** adj

proud adj **1** feeling or showing pride or satisfaction in what you have done or in what someone else has done **2** full of self-respect and independence ♦ *They were too proud to ask for help.* **3** having an unduly high opinion of yourself **proudly** adv

prove v **1** to show that something is true, to give or be a proof of something **2** to be seen or found to be something ♦ *The forecast proved to be correct.* **proven** adj proved or established ♦ *a person of proven ability*

provenance (say **prov**-in-əns) *n* a place of origin

provender (say **prov**-in-der) *n* animal fodder

proverb *n* a short well-known saying stating a general truth or piece of advice, such as *many hands make light work* **proverbial** *adj* **1** of or like a proverb, or mentioned in a proverb or idiom ♦ *She was up in the morning like the proverbial early bird.* **2** well-known ♦ *His generosity is proverbial.*

provide *v* **1** to make something available for someone to use **2** to supply the necessities of life ♦ *She has to provide for a large family.* **3** to make suitable preparation or arrangements for something ♦ *Try to provide for emergencies.* **provided** *conjunction* on the condition that ♦ *They can stay provided that they help.* **provider** *n* **provision** *n* **1** the act of providing something **2** preparation of resources for future needs ♦ *They made good provision for their old age.* **3** a statement or requirement in a legal document **provision** *v* to supply someone with provisions **provisions** *pl n* supplies of food and drink **provisional** *adj* arranged or agreed upon for the time being but possibly to be altered later **provisionally** *adj*

providence *n* **1** being provident **2** care and protection seen as being provided by God or nature **provident** *adj* taking care to be ready for future needs or events, thrifty **providential** *adj* happening at a fortunate time, opportune

province *n* **1** one of the principal administrative divisions of a country or empire **2** a person's special area of knowledge or responsibility ♦ *I'm afraid chemistry is not my province.* **the provinces** the parts of a country outside its capital city **provincial** *adj* **1** to do with a province or provinces ♦ *provincial government* **2** culturally limited or narrow-minded ♦ *provincial attitudes* **provincial** *n* a person born or living in a province or the provinces

proviso (say prə-**viy**-zoh) *n pl* **provisos** a condition that is insisted on in advance

provoke *v* **1** to make someone angry **2** to produce a reaction or effect **provocation** *n*

1 the process of provoking **2** something said or done that provokes anger or retaliation **provocative** *adj* **provocatively** *adv*

provost (say **prov**-əst) *n* **1** a Scottish official with authority comparable to that of mayor in England and Wales **2** the head of certain colleges

prow *n* the pointed front part of a ship

prowess (say prow-**ess**) *n* great ability or daring

prowl *v* **1** to go about stealthily in search of prey or plunder or to catch other people unawares **2** to pace or wander restlessly **prowl** *n* an act of prowling ♦ *on the prowl* **prowler** *n*

proximity (say proks-**im**-iti) *n* being near in space or time **proximate** *adj* closest or nearest, next before or after

proxy *n pl* **proxies** **1** the authority to act for another person **2** a person authorized to represent or act for another person

prude (say prood) *n* a person who is easily shocked by matters relating to sex or nudity **prudery** *n* **prudish** *adj*

prudent *adj* acting with or showing care and foresight, not rash or reckless **prudence** *n* **prudential** *adj* **prudently** *adv*

prune¹ *n* a dried plum

prune² *v* **1** to trim a tree or shrub by cutting away dead or overgrown branches or shoots **2** to shorten and improve a speech or book, etc. by removing unnecessary parts

pry *v* **pries**, **pried**, **prying** to look or enquire intrusively

PS *abbr* postscript

psalm (say sahm) *n* a sacred song, especially one of those in the Book of Psalms in the Old Testament **psalmist** *n* **psalter** *n* a copy of the Book of Psalms

pseudo- *prefix* false

pseudonym (say **syoo**-dən-im) *n* a false name used by an author

psyche (say **siy**-ki) *n* the human soul or mind

psychedelic (say siy-ki-**del**-ik) *adj* **1** producing hallucinations **2** having vivid or luminous colours

psychiatry (say siy-**kiy**-ə-tri) *n* the study and treatment of mental illnesses

psychiatric adj **psychiatrist** n a doctor who treats people with mental illnesses

psychic (say **siy**-kik) adj **1** to do with the mind or the soul **2** to do with processes that seem to be outside normal physical laws, especially those involving extrasensory perception or clairvoyance

psycho- prefix to do with the mind

psychoanalysis n a method of examining or treating mental illnesses by bringing certain memories that are in a person's unconscious mind into their consciousness **psychoanalyse** v **psychoanalyst** n

psychology n **1** the study of the human mind and its workings, especially as these affect behaviour **2** mental characteristics **psychological** adj **1** to do with or affecting the mind and its working **2** to do with psychology **psychologically** adv **psychologist** n

psychopath (say **siy**-kə-path) n a person suffering from a severe mental disorder with aggressive or violent antisocial behaviour **psychopathic** adj

psychosis (say siy-**koh**-sis) n a severe mental disorder involving a person's whole personality **psychotic** adj

psychosomatic (say siy-kə-sə-**mat**-ik) adj (said about an illness) caused or made worse by psychological factors such as stress

psychotherapy (say siy-kə-**the**-rəpi) n treatment of mental illness by psychological methods **psychotherapist** n

PT abbr physical training

pt. abbr pint

PTA abbr parent-teacher association

ptarmigan (say **tar**-mig-ən) n a bird of the grouse family with plumage that turns white in winter

pterodactyl (say te-rə-**dak**-til) n an extinct flying reptile with a long neck, thin head, and large wings

PTO abbr please turn over

pub n a building licensed to sell beer and other alcoholic drinks to the general public for drinking on the premises

puberty (say **pew**-ber-ti) n the stage at which a young person becomes sexually mature and is capable of producing offspring

pubic (say **pew**-bik) adj to do with the lower part of the abdomen at the front of the pelvis ♦ pubic hair

public adj belonging to or known to people in general, not private **public** n (**the public**) people in general or a particular group of people ♦ the British public **publican** n the keeper of a public house **publicly** adv **public house** n a pub **public limited company** n a business company whose shares may be bought and sold on the open market **public relations** pl n the promotion of goodwill between an organization and the general public **public school** n a secondary school that charges fees **public sector** n all the businesses and industries that are owned or controlled by the state and not by private enterprise **public servant** n a person who works for the state or for local government **public-spirited** adj willing to do things for the benefit of people in general

publicity n **1** public attention directed upon a person or thing **2** the process of drawing public attention to a person or thing; the spoken, written, or other material by which this is done **publicize** v to bring something to the attention of the public

publish v **1** to issue copies of a book, newspaper, magazine, or piece of music to the public **2** to make something generally known **3** to announce something formally ♦ They will publish the results of the competition next month. **publication** n **1** the process of publishing or being published **2** something published, e.g. a book or newspaper **publisher** n

puce (say pewss) n a brownish purple colour

puck n a hard rubber disc used in ice hockey

pucker v to come together in small wrinkles or folds, or to cause something to do this **pucker** n a wrinkle or fold

pudding n **1** a cooked sweet dish, or the sweet course of a meal **2** a sweet or savoury cooked food made with a mixture of flour and other ingredients **3** a kind of sausage ♦ black pudding

puddle n a shallow patch of liquid on a surface, especially of water on a road

pudenda (say pew-**den**-də) *pl n* a person's genitals, especially a woman's

puerile (say **pyoo**-riyl) *adj* immature or childish ♦ *asking puerile questions* **puerility** *n*

puff *n* **1** a short blowing of breath, wind, etc. **2** a small amount of smoke or vapour sent out by this **3** a soft pad for putting powder on the skin **4** a cake of light pastry filled with cream or a sweet filling **puff** *v* **1** to breathe with short hard gasps **2** to blow smoke or dust in puffs **3** to smoke a cigarette, cigar, or pipe **4** to swell or become inflated, or to make something do this **puffy** *adj* **puffier, puffiest** swollen or puffed out **puffiness** *n* **puff pastry** *n* very light flaky pastry

puffin *n* a seabird with a large brightly coloured bill

pug *n* a small dog like a bulldog, with a flat nose and a wrinkled face

pugilist (say **pew**-jil-ist) *n* a boxer **pugilism** *n* **pugilistic** *adj*

pugnacious (say pug-**nay**-shəs) *adj* eager or quick to fight, aggressive

puke *v informal* to vomit

pukka (say puk-ə) *adj informal* **1** real or genuine **2** excellent

pull *v* **1** to exert force on something or someone so as to move them towards you or towards the source of the force **2** to remove something by pulling it **3** to attract people ♦ *The new exhibition is pulling the crowds.* **pull** *n* **1** the act of pulling, or the force exerted by it **2** a means of exerting influence **3** a deep draught of a drink, or a draw at a cigarette, cigar, or pipe **pullover** *n* a knitted garment put on over the head and covering the top part of the body **to pull back** to retreat or withdraw, or to cause someone to do this **to pull in 1** (said about a train) to enter and stop at a station **2** (said about a vehicle) to move to the side of the road **to pull out 1** to withdraw from an activity or commitment **2** (said about a train) to move out of a station **3** (said about a vehicle) to move away from the side of a road, or from behind another vehicle to overtake it **to pull someone in** *informal* to take someone into custody **to pull someone's leg** to tease someone **to**

pull someone up to scold or reprimand someone **to pull something off** *informal* to succeed in achieving or winning something **to pull strings** to use your influence to get what you want **to pull through** to recover from an illness or difficulty **to pull up** (said about a vehicle) to stop abruptly **to pull yourself together** to regain your self-control

pullet *n* a young hen less than one year old

pulley *n pl* **pulleys** a wheel with a grooved rim over which a rope, chain, or belt passes, used to lift heavy objects

Pullman *n pl* **Pullmans** a type of railway carriage providing passengers with a high level of comfort

pulmonary (say **pul**-mən-er-i) *adj* to do with or affecting the lungs

pulp *n* **1** a soft moist mass of material, especially of wood fibre as used for making paper **2** the soft moist part of fruit **3** the soft tissue inside a tooth **4** (used before a noun) indicating cheap popular publications of a kind originally printed on rough paper made from wood pulp ♦ *pulp magazines* **pulp** *v* to become pulp, or to make something into pulp

pulpit *n* a raised enclosed platform for a preacher in a church or chapel

pulse[1] *n* **1** the rhythmical throbbing of the arteries as blood is propelled along them **2** a steady throb **pulse** *v* to pulsate **pulsar** *n* an object in space that gives out radio signals that pulsate in a rapid regular rhythm **pulsate** *v* to expand and contract rhythmically

pulse[2] *n* the edible seed of peas, beans, lentils, etc.

pulverize *v* **1** to become powder, or to crush something into powder **2** to defeat someone thoroughly

puma (say **pew**-mə) *n* a large brown American animal of the cat family

pumice (say **pum**-iss) *n* a light porous kind of lava used for rubbing stains from the skin or as powder for polishing

pummel *v* **pummelled, pummelling** to strike something or someone repeatedly with the fists

pump[1] *n* a machine or device that forces

liquid, air, or gas into or out of something, or along pipes **pump** v 1 to move liquid, air, or gas with a pump 2 (also **pump up**) to fill something with air, especially to inflate it 3 to move something vigorously up and down like the handle of a pump 4 informal to question someone persistently to get information

pump[2] n a light shoe

pumpkin n a large round fruit with a hard orange skin and flesh that is used as a vegetable

pun n a humorous use of a word to suggest another that sounds the same, as in 'Deciding where to bury him was a grave decision.' **pun** v **punned**, **punning** to make a pun

punch[1] v to strike someone or something with the fist **punch** n 1 a blow with the fist 2 informal force or vigour ♦ a speech with plenty of punch **punchy** adj **punchier**, **punchiest** forceful or effective **punch-drunk** adj stupefied through being severely punched **punchline** n words that give the climax of a joke or story

punch[2] n 1 a device for making holes in paper or metal 2 a tool or machine for stamping a design on material **punch** v to make a hole in something with a punch

punch[3] n a drink made of wine or spirits mixed with fruit juices, spices, etc.

punctilious (say punk-til-iəs) adj very careful about correct behaviour and detail

punctual adj arriving or doing things at the correct time **punctuality** n **punctually** adv

punctuate v 1 to put punctuation marks in a piece of writing 2 to put something in at intervals ♦ His speech was punctuated with cheers. **punctuation** n 1 the use of marks such as comma, full stop, and question mark to clarify the structure and meaning of a piece of writing 2 the set of marks used in this

puncture n a small hole made by something sharp, especially one made accidentally in a tyre **puncture** v to make a puncture in something, or to receive a puncture

pundit n a person who is an authority on a subject

pungent (say pun-jənt) adj having a strong sharp taste or smell **pungency** n

punish v 1 to cause someone to suffer a penalty for doing wrong 2 to treat or test someone severely ♦ The race was run at a punishing pace. **punishable** adj **punishment** n **punitive** adj inflicting or intended as a punishment

punk n 1 (also **punk rock**) a loud aggressive form of rock music 2 a person who enjoys this music

punnet (say pun-it) n a small container for fruit or vegetables

punt[1] n a flat-bottomed boat with square ends, usually moved along by pushing a pole **punt** v to travel in a punt

punt[2] v to kick a ball after it has dropped from the hands and before it touches the ground **punt** n a kick of this kind

punt[3] v informal to bet or gamble **punter** n 1 informal a customer or client 2 a person who bets, a gambler

puny (say pew-ni) adj **punier**, **puniest** 1 small or undersized 2 weak or feeble

pup n 1 a young dog 2 a young wolf, rat, seal, or other mammal

pupa (say pew-pə) n pl **pupae** (say pew-pee) a chrysalis **pupal** adj

pupil n 1 a person who is taught by a teacher, especially at a school 2 an opening in the centre of the iris of the eye, through which light passes to the retina

puppet n 1 a kind of doll that can be made to move by pulling strings attached to it or by putting a hand inside it 2 a person or group whose actions are controlled by someone else **puppetry** n

puppy n pl **puppies** a young dog **puppy fat** n temporary fat on the body of a child or young adolescent

purchase v to buy something **purchase** n 1 the process of buying something 2 something bought 3 a firm hold to pull or raise something or prevent it from slipping **purchaser** n

purdah (say per-də) n the custom in certain Muslim and Hindu communities of keeping women from the sight of men or strangers by means of a curtain or of clothes that cover the entire body except for the eyes

pure adj 1 not mixed with any other

substance, free from impurities **2** mere, nothing but ♦ *What they said was pure nonsense.* **3** morally good, free from evil or sin **4** (said about a subject) dealing with the theory only and not with its practical applications ♦ *pure mathematics* **purely** *adv* **pureness** *n* **purify** *v* **purifies, purified, purifying** to make something pure or cleanse it of impurities **purification** *n* **purist** *n* someone who insists on correctness **purity** *n*

purée (say **pewr**-ay) *n* fruit or vegetables made into pulp **purée** *v* **purées, puréed, puréeing** to make fruit or vegetables into a purée

purge (say perj) *v* to rid a place or organization of people or things considered to be undesirable or harmful **purge** *n* an act of purging or ridding a place of undesirable people or things **purgative** *n* a strong laxative **purgatory** *n* **1** (in Roman Catholic belief) a place or condition in which souls undergo purification by temporary punishment before they can enter heaven **2** a place or condition of suffering

Puritan *n* an English Protestant of the 16th and 17th centuries who wanted simpler forms of church ceremony **puritan** *n* a person who is extremely strict in morals **puritanical** *adj*

purl *n* a knitting stitch that makes a ridge towards the person knitting

purlieus (say **perl**-yooz) *pl n formal* the outskirts of a place

purloin (say per-**loin**) *v formal* to steal something

purple *adj* of a deep reddish blue colour

purport (say **per**-port) *n* the general meaning or intention of something said or written **purport** (say per-**port**) *v* to pretend or be intended to seem, especially falsely ♦ *The letter purports to come from you.*

purpose *n* **1** something that you intend to do or achieve, an intended result ♦ *This will serve our purpose.* **2** wanting to get something done, determination ♦ *They acted with a real sense of purpose.* **purposeful** *adj* **1** having a particular purpose **2** determined, resolute

purposefully *adv* **purposely** *adv* deliberately, on purpose **on purpose** deliberately, not by chance

purr *v* (said about a cat) to make a low murmuring sound expressing contentment **purr** *n* a purring sound

purse *n* **1** a small leather or plastic pouch for carrying money **2** an amount of money available for a purpose **3** a sum of money given as a prize in a sporting competition **purse** *v* to pucker the lips, especially in indignation **purser** *n* an officer on a ship who is in charge of the accounts, especially the chief steward on a passenger ship

pursue *v* **pursues, pursued, pursuing 1** to chase someone or something in order to catch or attack them **2** to continue or proceed along a course or route **3** to be occupied in an activity ♦ *She would like to pursue a career as a journalist.* **pursuer** *n* **pursuit** *n* **1** the act of pursuing someone or something **2** an activity to which you devote time

purvey (say per-**vay**) *v* to supply articles of food as a trader **purveyor** *n*

pus *n* thick yellowish matter produced in inflamed or infected tissue, e.g. in an abscess or boil **pustule** *n* a small pimple or blister containing pus **pustular** *adj*

push *v* **1** to exert force on something or someone so as to move them away from you or away from the source of the force **2** to grip something and apply force to it so that it moves along in front of you **3** to move oneself forcibly into a position ♦ *Several people pushed to the front.* **4** to make a vigorous effort in order to succeed or to surpass others **5** to urge someone to do something ♦ *We must push you for prompt payment.* **6** *informal* to sell illegal drugs **push** *n* **1** the act of pushing, or the force used in this **2** a vigorous effort, especially a military attack made in order to advance **3** determination or enterprise **pusher** *n* **pushy** *adj* **pushier, pushiest** too assertive or ambitious **pushchair** *n* a folding chair on wheels, for pushing a baby or young child along **pushover** *n* something that is easily done; a person who is easily convinced or charmed, etc.

to give or **get the push** *informal* to dismiss someone or be dismissed from a job

pusillanimous (say pew-zi-**lan**-iməs) *adj* timid or cowardly

puss, **pussy** *n pl* **pussies** *informal* a cat **pussyfoot** *v* **1** to move stealthily **2** to act cautiously and avoid committing yourself

put *v* past tense and past participle **put**; **putting 1** to move something to a specified place or position ♦ *Put the bag on the table.* **2** to cause something or someone to be in a certain state ♦ *Put the light on.* ♦ *Try to put them at their ease.* **3** to express or state something in a certain way ♦ *I will put it as tactfully as I can.* **4** to estimate an amount ♦ *I put the cost at £1000.* **put** *n* a throw of the shot or weight **to put someone down 1** to snub someone or make them look foolish **2** to enter someone's name in a list or register **to put someone off 1** to postpone or cancel an appointment with someone **2** to make someone less enthusiastic about something **3** to distract someone **to put someone out** to annoy or inconvenience someone **to put someone up** to provide someone with accommodation for a short period **to put something across** to succeed in communicating an idea or making it seem acceptable **to put something down 1** to write something down or make a note of it **2** to have an animal destroyed **3** to suppress a revolt or rebellion **to put something off** to postpone an arrangement, meeting, etc. **to put something on 1** to stage a performance of a play **2** to switch on a device **3** to display a certain feeling or emotion **to put something out** to extinguish a fire, light, etc. **to put something over** to succeed in communicating an idea or making it seem acceptable **to put something up 1** to construct or build something **2** to raise the price of something **3** to provide or contribute the necessary resources ♦ *The company will put up the money.* **4** to attempt or offer something ♦ *The enemy put up no resistance.* **to put up with** to endure or tolerate something unpleasant or unwelcome

putative (say **pew**-tə-tiv) *adj* supposed or considered to be ♦ *his putative father*

putrid (say **pew**-trid) *adj* **1** decomposed or rotting **2** smelling bad **putrefy** *v* **putrefies**, **putrefied**, **putrefying** to decay or make something decay **putrefaction** *n*

putsch (say puuch) *n* a violent attempt to overthrow a government

putt *v* to strike a golf ball gently to make it roll along the ground **putt** *n* a stroke of this kind **putter** *n* a golf club used in putting **putting green** *n* (in golf) an area of smooth cut grass round a hole

putty *n* a soft paste that sets hard, used for fitting glass in a window frame

puzzle *n* **1** a difficult question or problem **2** a game or toy that sets a problem to solve or a difficult task to complete **puzzle** *v* to confuse someone or cause them uncertainty

PVC *abbr* polyvinyl chloride

pygmy (say **pig**-mi) *n pl* **pygmies 1** a person or thing of unusually small size **2** a member of certain unusually short peoples of equatorial Africa and SE Asia **pygmy** *adj* very small

pyjamas *pl n* a suit of loose-fitting jacket and trousers for sleeping in

pylon *n* a tall framework made of steel strips, used for carrying overhead electricity cables

pyramid *n* **1** a structure with a square base and sloping sides that meet at the top **2** a stone structure shaped like this, especially an ancient Egyptian tomb **pyramidal** *adj*

pyre *n* a pile of wood or other material for burning a corpse as part of a funeral ceremony

Pyrex *n trademark* a hard heat-resistant glass

pyrites (say piy-**riy**-teez) *n* a shiny yellow mineral that is a sulphide of iron (**iron pyrites**) or copper and iron (**copper pyrites**)

pyromania (say piyr-ə-**may**-niə) *n* an obsessive desire to set things on fire **pyromaniac** *n*

pyrotechnics (say piy-rə-**tek**-niks) *n* **1** a firework display **2** the art of making or staging fireworks

pyrrhic victory (say **pi**-rik) *n* a victory

gained at so great a cost that it cannot be exploited

python *n* a large snake that squeezes its prey so as to suffocate it

Q the seventeenth letter of the English alphabet

QC *abbr* Queen's Counsel

QED *abbr* quod erat demonstrandum, put at the end of a formal proof to show that the proposition has been proved

qt. *abbr* quart(s)

quack[1] *v* to make the harsh cry of a duck **quack** *n* this cry

quack[2] *n* a person who falsely claims to have medical skill or to have remedies for curing diseases

quad (say kwod) *n* **1** a quadrangle **2** a quadruplet

quadrangle (say **kwod**-rang-gəl) *n* a rectangular court with buildings on each side

quadrant (say **kwod**-rənt) *n* a quarter of a circle

quadri- *prefix* four

quadrilateral (say kwod-ri-**lat**-er-əl) *n* a flat figure with four sides **quadrilateral** *adj* having four sides

quadrille (say kwod-**ril**) *n* a square dance for four couples, or the music for this

quadruped (say **kwod**-ruu-ped) *n* an animal with four feet

quadruple *adj* **1** consisting of four parts, or involving four people or groups **2** four times as much **quadruple** *v* to multiply by four **quadruplet** *n* each of four children born at one birth

quaff (say kwof) *v* to drink something heartily

quagmire (say **kwag**-miyr) *n* a bog or marsh

quail[1] *n pl* quail or quails a game bird with a short tail, related to the partridge

quail[2] *v* to show fear or apprehension

quaint *adj* pleasingly or attractively odd or old-fashioned **quaintly** *adv* **quaintness** *n*

quake *v* to shake or tremble **quake** *n* **1** a quaking movement **2** *informal* an earthquake

Quaker *n* a member of the Religious Society of Friends, a Christian movement which emphasizes peaceful principles

qualify *v* **qualifies**, **qualified**, **qualifying 1** to give someone the right or competence to do something **2** to have the right or competence to do something; to have fulfilled the conditions for something **3** to limit or restrict a statement or make it less general or extreme **4** to describe someone or something in a certain way **5** *Gram* (said of a word or phrase) to describe or add meaning to another word, especially a noun **qualification** *n* **1** the process of qualifying or being qualified **2** something that qualifies a person to do something or to have a certain right ♦ *She wants to get a good teaching qualification.* **3** a statement that limits or restricts another statement ♦ *We welcome the report without any qualifications.* **qualifier** *n*

quality *n pl* **qualities 1** how good something is in relation to others of the same kind ♦ *The quality of English wine has improved in the last decade.* **2** general excellence ♦ *They are producing work of quality.* **3** a special characteristic or ability ♦ *The paper has a shiny quality.* **qualitative** *adj* to do with the presence or quality of a substance and not its quantity ♦ *qualitative analysis*

qualm (say kwahm) *n* a doubt or misgiving about what you have done or might do

quandary (say **kwon**-der-i) *n pl* **quandaries** a state of uncertainty about what to do for the best

quango *n pl* **quangos** an administrative body with financial support from and senior appointments made by the government but acting independently

quantity *n pl* **quantities 1** how much of something there is, or how many of a certain thing there are **2** a large number or amount **3** the property of something that can be measured **quantify** *v* **quantifies**, **quantified**, **quantifying** to express

something as a quantity **quantifiable** *adj*
quantitative *adj* to do with quantity
♦ *quantitative analysis*

quantum (say kwon-təm) *n pl* **quanta** *Phys*
a minimum amount of a physical quantity
(such as energy) which can exist in a given
situation

quantum leap, **quantum jump** *n* a sudden
great advance or increase

quarantine (say kwo-rən-teen) *n* isolation
imposed on people or animals who may
have been exposed to a disease which
could spread to others **quarantine** *v* to put
a person or animal into quarantine

quarrel *n* **1** an angry argument or
disagreement **2** a cause for complaint
against someone ♦ *We have no quarrel with
them.* **quarrel** *v* **quarrelled**, **quarrelling**
to have a disagreement **quarrelsome** *adj*
likely to quarrel often with people

quarry[1] *n pl* **quarries** a person or animal
being hunted

quarry[2] *n pl* **quarries** a pit or other open
place from which stone or other materials
are obtained **quarry** *v* **quarries**, **quarried**,
quarrying to dig stone, etc. from a quarry

quart *n* a unit of volume for measuring
liquids, equal to 2 pints or a quarter of a
gallon

quarter *n* **1** each of the four equal parts into
which a thing is or can be divided **2** *N. Am*
a quarter of a dollar, 25 cents **3** a period
of three months, one fourth of a year **4** a
fourth part of a lunar month **5** a district or
division of a town ♦ *the artists' quarter* **6** a
person or group, especially regarded as a
possible source of help or information, etc.
♦ *We got no sympathy at all from that quarter.*
7 mercy towards an enemy or opponent
♦ *The enemy gave no quarter.* **quarters** *pl n*
lodgings or accommodation **quarter** *v* **1** to
divide something into quarters **2** to put
soldiers, etc. into lodgings **quarterly** *adj*
happening or produced once every three
months **quarterly** *adv* once every three
months **quarterly** *n pl* **quarterlies** a
quarterly magazine **quarterdeck** *n* the
part of the upper deck of a ship nearest
the stern **quarter-final** *n* each of the
matches or rounds preceding a semi-final,

in which there are eight contestants or
teams **quartermaster** *n* a military officer in
charge of stores and allocating quarters

quartet *n* **1** a group of four musicians or
singers **2** a musical composition for four
performers **3** a set of four people or things

quarto *n pl* **quartos 1** a size of paper made
by folding a sheet of standard size twice to
form four leaves **2** a book of this size

quartz (say kwortz) *n* a hard mineral
occurring in various forms

quasar (say kway-zar) *n* a distant object
with the appearance of a star, a source of
intense electromagnetic radiation

quash *v* **1** to reject something as invalid by
legal authority **2** to suppress something,
such as a rebellion or hostile rumour

quasi- (say kway-ziy) *prefix* seeming to
be something but not really so ♦ *a quasi-
scientific explanation*

quaver *v* to tremble or vibrate **quaver** *n* a
quavering sound

quay (say kee) *n* a landing place where ships
can be tied up for loading and unloading

queasy *adj* **queasier**, **queasiest 1** feeling
slightly sick **2** slightly nervous or anxious
queasiness *n*

queen *n* **1** the female ruler of an
independent country or state, especially
one who inherits the position by right of
birth **2** the wife of a king **3** a female person
or thing regarded as supreme in some way
4 the most powerful piece in chess, able
to move in any direction **5** a female bee,
wasp, or ant that is capable of reproduction
queenly *adj* **queen mother** *n* the widow of
a king who is the mother of a reigning king
or queen

queer *adj* **1** strange or eccentric **2** *offensive*
homosexual **3** slightly ill or faint **to queer
someone's pitch** to spoil someone's
chances beforehand

quell *v* to suppress something, especially a
rebellion, by force

quench *v* **1** to satisfy your thirst by drinking
2 to put out a fire or flame

querulous (say kwe-rew-ləs) *adj*
complaining in a peevish or petulant
manner

query *n pl* **queries** a question, especially

one that expresses a doubt or uncertainty **query** v queries, queried, querying to ask a question or express a doubt about something

quest n the act of seeking something, a search

question n **1** a sentence that asks for information or an answer **2** something being discussed or for discussion; a problem requiring a solution **3** doubt or uncertainty ♦ *There is some question about whether he is fit.* **question** v **1** to ask questions of someone **2** to express doubt about something ♦ *He seemed to be questioning her competence.* **questioner** n **questionable** adj open to doubt or suspicion **questionnaire** n a list of questions seeking information from people for use in a survey or statistical study **question mark** n the punctuation mark (?) placed after a question under discussion or in dispute ♦ *Their honesty is not in question.* **out of the question** not possible or practicable

queue n a line or series of people, vehicles, etc. waiting to move forward or for their turn for something **queue** v queues, queued, queuing to wait in a queue

quibble n a minor or petty objection or complaint **quibble** v to make petty objections

quiche (say keesh) n an open tart with a savoury filling

quick adj **1** moving fast or taking only a short time to do something **2** done in a short time **3** (said about a person) able to think well, alert and intelligent **4** (said about a person's temper) easily roused **quick** n (**the quick**) the sensitive flesh below the nails **quick** adv quickly **quicken** v **1** to make something quicker, or to become quicker **2** to stimulate a feeling, or to become stimulated ♦ *Our interest began to quicken.* **quickly** adv **quickness** n **quicklime** n a white substance (calcium oxide) used in making cement and mortar and as a fertilizer **quicksand** n an area of loose wet deep sand that sucks in anything resting or falling on top of it **quicksilver** n liquid mercury **quickstep** n a ballroom

dance with quick steps **to be cut to the quick** to be deeply offended or insulted

quid[1] n pl quid *informal* one pound sterling

quid[2] n a lump of tobacco for chewing

quid pro quo n something given in return for something else

quiescent (say kwi-**ess**-ənt) adj quiet or inactive **quiescence** n

quiet adj **1** making little or no sound, not loud or noisy **2** with little or no movement **3** free from disturbance or vigorous activity, peaceful **quiet** n quietness **quiet** v **quieted**, **quieting** to make someone or something quiet, or to become quiet **on the quiet** discreetly or secretly **quieten** v **quietly** adv **quietness** n **quietude** n a state of quiet or calm

quiff n an upright tuft of hair above a man's forehead

quill n **1** each of the large feathers on the wing or tail of a bird **2** an old type of pen made from a bird's feather **3** each of the spines on a porcupine or hedgehog

quilt n a padded cover for a bed **quilt** v to line material with padding and fix it with lines of stitching

quin n *informal* a quintuplet

quince n a hard yellowish pear-shaped fruit used for making jam

quinine (say kwin-**een**) n a bitter-tasting medicinal drug used to treat malaria and as a tonic

quinsy (say **kwin**-zi) n inflammation of the throat, especially an abscess on one of the tonsils

quintessence (say kwin-**tess**-əns) n a perfect example of a quality

quintet n **1** a group of five musicians or singers **2** a musical composition for five performers **3** a set of five people or things

quintuple adj **1** consisting of five parts, or involving five people or groups **2** five times as much **quintuple** v **1** to multiply something by five **2** to increase fivefold **quintuplet** n each of five children born at one birth

quip n a witty remark **quip** v quipped, quipping to make a quip

quire n 25 (formerly 24) sheets of writing paper

quirk n **1** a peculiarity of a person's behaviour **2** a strange occurrence or trick of fate

quisling (say **kwiz**-ling) n a traitor who collaborates with an invading enemy

quit v past tense and past participle **quitted** or **quit**; **quitting 1** to leave or go away from a place **2** informal to resign from a job **3** informal to stop doing something ♦ He wants to quit smoking. **quits** adj on equal terms after a retaliation or repayment **quitter** n a person who gives up too easily

quite adv **1** completely or utterly ♦ I haven't quite finished. ♦ We are all quite exhausted. **2** fairly, somewhat ♦ The news was quite bad, though not as bad as we feared. **3** really or actually ♦ It's quite a change. **4** used as an expression of agreement

quiver¹ v to shake or tremble with a slight rapid motion **quiver** n a quivering movement or sound

quiver² n a case for holding arrows

quixotic (say kwik-**sot**-ik) adj formal chivalrous and unselfish, often to an extravagant or impractical extent

quiz n pl **quizzes** a series of questions testing general knowledge, especially as a form of entertainment **quiz** v **quizzed, quizzing** to question someone **quizzical** adj showing mild curiosity or amusement

quoit (say koit) n a ring of metal or rubber or rope thrown round an upright peg in the game called **quoits**

quorum (say **kwor**-əm) n pl **quorums** the minimum number of people that must be present at a meeting for its proceedings to be valid

quota n pl **quotas 1** a fixed share that must be done, given, or received **2** the maximum number of people or things that can be allowed or admitted, e.g. imported goods into a country

quote v **1** to repeat words that were first used by someone else, e.g. in a book or speech **2** to state the price of goods or services, to give a quotation or estimate **quote** n a quotation **quotable** adj worth quoting **quotation** n **1** a passage or group of words from a book or speech that is repeated by someone other than the

original writer or speaker **2** the process of quoting or being quoted **3** a statement or estimate of a price **quotation marks** pl n punctuation marks (either single '' or double "") put round words that are being quoted or have some special significance ◊ These are also called inverted commas.

quoth (say kwohth) v old use said

q.v. abbr used to direct a reader to another part of a book or text for further information

Rr

R¹ the eighteenth letter of the English alphabet

R² abbr **1** Regina (Queen) ♦ Elizabeth R. **2** Rex (King) ♦ George R. **3** (in names) river

r abbr radius

RA abbr **1** Royal Academy **2** Royal Artillery

rabbi (say **rab**-iy) n pl **rabbis** a Jewish religious leader **rabbinic** adj

rabbit n a burrowing animal with long ears and a short furry tail **rabbit** v **rabbited, rabbiting 1** to hunt rabbits **2** informal to chatter or talk lengthily

rabble n a disorderly crowd or mob **rabble-rouser** n a person who stirs up a crowd

rabies (say **ray**-beez or **ray**-biz) n a dangerous contagious virus disease affecting dogs and other mammals, transmitted to humans usually by the bite of an infected animal **rabid** adj **1** suffering from rabies **2** extreme or fanatical

raccoon n a North American animal with a bushy striped tail, sharp snout, and greyish-brown fur

race¹ n **1** a contest of speed in reaching a certain point or in doing something **2** a situation in which people compete to be the first to achieve or get something **3** a strong fast current of water **race** v **1** to take part in a race; to have a race with someone **2** to move or go quickly **3** to operate or cause an engine, etc. to operate at full speed **racer** n **racing** n **racecourse** n a

racehorse n a horse bred or kept for racing

racetrack n a track for horse or vehicle races

race² n each of the major divisions of humankind with certain inherited physical characteristics in common, e.g. colour of skin, type of hair, shape of eyes and nose **racial** adj **racially** adv **racism** n **1** the belief that there are characteristics, abilities, or qualities specific to each race **2** discrimination against or hostility towards people of other races **racist** n, adj

rack¹ n **1** a framework, usually with bars or pegs, for holding things or for hanging things on **2** a bar or rail with teeth or cogs into which those of a wheel or gear, etc. fit **3** an instrument of torture on which people were tied and stretched **rack** v to inflict great physical or mental pain on someone **to rack your brains** to think hard, especially when you are trying to remember something

rack² n **to go to rack and ruin** to gradually become worse in condition due to neglect

racket¹, **racquet** n a bat with strings stretched across a frame, used in tennis, badminton, and squash **rackets** n a ball game for two or four people played with rackets in a four-walled court

racket² n **1** a loud noise **2** informal a business or other activity in which dishonest methods are used **racketeer** n a person who runs or works in a racket or dishonest business **racketeering** n

raconteur (say rak-on-**ter**) n a person who tells anecdotes well

racoon n another spelling of raccoon

racy adj **racier**, **raciest 1** slightly shocking or indecent **2** lively or spirited

radar n a device for detecting the presence, position, or movement, etc. of objects by sending out short radio waves which are reflected back off the object

raddled adj worn out

radial (say **ray**-di-əl) adj **1** to do with rays or radii **2** having spokes or lines radiating from a central point **3** (also **radial-ply**) (said about a tyre) having fabric layers with cords lying radial to the hub of the wheel,

not crossing each other

radian (say **ray**-di-ən) n a unit of measurement of angles equal to about 57.3°

radiant adj **1** shining or glowing brightly **2** looking very happy and healthy **3** transmitting heat by radiation **4** (said about heat) transmitted in this way **radiance** n **radiantly** adv

radiate v **1** to send out light, heat, or other energy in the form of rays or waves; to be sent out in this way **2** to give out a strong feeling or quality ♦ She radiated confidence. **3** to spread outwards from a central point like the spokes of a wheel; to cause something to do this **radiation** n **1** the sending out of the rays and atomic particles characteristic of radioactive substances; these rays and particles **2** the action or process of radiating **radiator** n **1** a device that radiates heat, especially a metal case through which steam or hot water circulates, or one heated electrically **2** a device that cools the engine of a motor vehicle or an aircraft

radical adj **1** going to the root or foundation of something, fundamental **2** drastic, thorough **3** wanting to make great reforms; holding extremist views **radical** n **1** a person who wants to make great reforms or holds extremist views **2** a quantity forming or expressed as the root of another **radicalism** n **radically** adv

radio n pl **radios 1** the process of sending and receiving messages, etc. by electromagnetic waves **2** sound broadcasting; a sound-broadcasting station ♦ She works in radio. ♦ Radio Oxford. **3** an apparatus for receiving radio programmes or for sending or receiving radio messages; a transmitter or receiver **radio** adj to do with or operated by radio **radio** v **radioes**, **radioed**, **radioing** to send a message or communicate with someone by radio **radio telescope** n an instrument used to detect radio waves emitted from space

radio- prefix **1** to do with radio **2** to do with rays or radiation **radiologist** n **radiology** n the scientific study of X-rays and similar radiation, especially in treating diseases

radioactive *adj* **radioactivity** *n* **1** the property of having atoms that break up spontaneously and send out radiation capable of penetrating opaque bodies and producing electrical and chemical effects **2** radioactive particles **radiocarbon** *n* a radioactive form of carbon that is present in organic materials and is used in carbon dating **radiographer** *n* **radiography** *n* the production of X-ray photographs **radiotherapy** *n* the treatment of cancer or other disease by X-rays or similar forms of radiation

radish *n* **1** a crisp hot-tasting red-skinned root that is eaten raw in salads **2** the plant that produces this root

radium *n* a radioactive metallic element often used in radiotherapy

radius (say **ray**-di-əs) *n pl* **radii** (say **ray**-di-iy) or *pl* **radiuses 1** a straight line from the centre of a circle or sphere to its circumference **2** the length of this line; the distance from a centre **3** the thicker of the two long bones in the forearm

radon *n* a radioactive gas and chemical element (symbol Rn)

RAF *abbr* Royal Air Force

raffia *n* soft fibre from the leaves of a kind of palm tree, used for making mats, baskets, etc.

raffish *adj* slightly disreputable, but attractively so

raffle *n* a lottery with an object as the prize, especially as a method of raising money for a charity **raffle** *v* to offer something as a prize in a raffle

raft *n* a flat floating structure made of timber or other materials, used especially as a boat **rafting** *n*

rafter *n* any of the sloping beams forming the framework of a roof

rag[1] *n* **1** a piece of old cloth, especially one torn from a larger piece **2** *informal* a newspaper of low quality **rags** *pl n* old and torn clothes **ragged** *adj* **1** torn or frayed **2** dressed in torn clothes **3** uneven or irregular **raggedness** *n* **ragbag** *n* a miscellaneous collection **ragtag** *adj* consisting of an odd and varied mixture

rag[2] *n* a series of entertainments and activities held by students to collect money for charity **rag** *v* **ragged**, **ragging** to tease or play jokes on someone

ragamuffin *n* a person in ragged dirty clothes

rage *n* violent anger that is difficult to control, or a fit of this **rage** *v* **1** to show violent anger **2** (said about a storm or battle, etc.) to continue violently or with great force **to be all the rage** to be temporarily very popular or fashionable

raglan *adj* (said about a sleeve) continuing to the neck and joined to the body of the coat, jumper, etc. by sloping seams

ragout (say ra-**goo**) *n* a stew of meat and vegetables

ragtime *n* a form of jazz music played especially on the piano

raid *n* a sudden surprise attack or search **raid** *v* to make a raid on a place **raider** *n*

rail[1] *n* **1** a horizontal or sloping bar forming part of a fence or barrier or the top of banisters, or for hanging things on **2** any of the lines of metal bars on which trains or trams run **3** railways as a means of transport ♦ *We sent the parcel by rail.* **railing** *n* a fence of rails supported on upright metal bars **railroad** *n* a railway **railroad** *v* to rush or force someone into hasty action ♦ *He felt he had been railroaded into accepting.* **railway** *n* **1** a set of rails on which trains run **2** a system of transport using these; the organization and people required for its working **to go off the rails** *informal* to start behaving oddly or out of control

rail[2] *v* to complain strongly about a person or thing **raillery** *n* good-humoured joking or teasing

raiment *n old use* clothing

rain *n* **1** condensed moisture of the atmosphere falling in separate drops **2** a large quantity of things coming down ♦ *rain of blows* **the rains** *pl n* the rainy season in tropical countries **rain** *v* **1** to fall as rain **2** to come down or send something down like rain ♦ *They rained blows on him.* **rainy** *adj* **rainier**, **rainiest** having a lot of rainfall **rainbow** *n* an arch of all the colours of the spectrum formed in the sky when the sun's rays are reflected and refracted through rain or spray **raincoat** *n* a waterproof or water-resistant coat **rainfall** *n* the total amount of rain falling within a given area in a given time **rainforest** *n* a thick forest in tropical areas where there is heavy rainfall **to save something for a rainy day** to save money for a time when you may need it

raise *v* **1** to move or lift something to a higher or upright position **2** to increase the amount, level, or strength of something ♦ *We may need to raise prices.* **3** to collect, assemble, or manage to obtain something ♦ *an auction to raise money for charity* **4** to bring up a child **5** to breed or grow animals or plants **6** to put something forward ♦ *Does anyone have questions they would like to raise?* **7** to bring a siege, blockade, or embargo to an end **raise** *n N. Am* an increase in salary

raisin *n* a partially dried grape

raison d'être (say ray-zawn **detr**) *n pl* **raisons d'être** the reason or purpose for a thing's existence

Raj (say rahj) *n* the period of Indian history when the country was ruled by Britain

raja, rajah (say **rah**-jə) *n hist* an Indian king or prince

rake[1] *n* a tool with prongs used for drawing together leaves, cut grass, etc. or for smoothing loose soil or gravel **rake** *v* **1** to gather or smooth something with a rake **2** to search through something **3** to direct gunfire or your eyes along a line from end to end **to rake it in** *informal* to make a lot of money **to rake something up** to remind people of an old quarrel, scandal, or other incident that is best forgotten

rake[2] *n* the angle at which something slopes, such as a stage or seating **rake** *v* to set something at a sloping angle

rake[3] *n* a man who lives an irresponsible and immoral life **rakish** *adj* jaunty and dashing in appearance

rally *v* **rallies, rallied, rallying** **1** to bring people together, or come together, for a united effort or after being scattered ♦ *She's been trying to rally support for the election campaign.* ♦ *All his family rallied round.* **2** to summon up or revive something ♦ *It's time to rally our courage.* **3** to recover

your strength after illness **rally** *n pl* **rallies** **1** a mass meeting of people to support a cause, protest about something, or share an interest **2** a driving competition for cars or motorcycles over public roads or rough country **3** (in tennis, etc.) a series of strokes between players before a point is won **4** a recovery of energy or spirits, etc.

ram *n* **1** an uncastrated male sheep **2** a striking or plunging device in various machines **ram** *v* **rammed, ramming** **1** to force something into place by pressure **2** to crash against or drive into something with great force **ramrod** *n* an iron rod formerly used for ramming an explosive charge into muzzle-loading guns

Ramadan (say ram-ə-**dan**) *n* the ninth month of the Muslim year, when Muslims fast between sunrise and sunset

ramble *n* a walk in the countryside taken for pleasure **ramble** *v* **1** to take a ramble **2** to talk or write in a confused or disorganized way, to wander from the subject **rambler** *n* **rambling** *adj* **1** (said about speech or writing) confused or disorganized, wandering from one subject to another **2** extending in various directions irregularly

ramekin (say **ram**-i-kin) *n* a small dish for baking and serving an individual portion of food

ramification *n* one of the complicated consequences of something

ramp *n* **1** a slope joining two different levels of floor or road, etc. **2** a movable set of steps put beside an aircraft so that people can enter or leave **3** a ridge built across a road to control the speed of traffic

rampage (say ram-**payj**) *v* to rush about wildly or destructively **on the rampage** rushing about wildly or destructively

rampant *adj* **1** unrestrained, flourishing or spreading excessively **2** *Heraldry* (said about an animal on a coat of arms) standing upright on one hind leg with the other legs raised ♦ *a lion rampant*

rampart *n* a defensive wall of a castle or walled city

ramshackle *adj* in a state of severe disrepair

ranch *n* a large farm in North America where cattle or other animals are bred **rancher** *n*

rancid (say **ran**-sid) *adj* smelling or tasting unpleasant like stale fat

rancour (say **rank**-er) *n* bitter feeling or ill will **rancorous** *adj*

R & B *abbr* rhythm and blues

R & D *abbr* research and development

random *adj* done or made or taken, etc. without any method or conscious decision ♦ *a random choice* **randomly** *adv* **randomness** *n* **at random** using no particular method or conscious decision ♦ *numbers chosen at random*

randy *adj* **randier, randiest** *informal* sexually aroused or excited; lustful

range *n* **1** the limits between which something varies ♦ *the age range 15 to 18* **2** a set of different things of the same type ♦ *a lovely range of colours* **3** the scope or extent of something ♦ *Such questions fall outside the range of this enquiry.* **4** the extent of pitch which a particular singing voice or musical instrument is capable of **5** the distance over which you can see or hear, or to which a sound, signal, or missile can travel; the distance that a ship or aircraft, etc. can travel without refuelling **6** the distance to a thing being aimed at or looked at ♦ *at close range* **7** a line or series of mountains or hills **8** a place with targets for shooting practice **9** a kitchen fireplace with ovens, etc. for cooking in **range** *v* **1** to vary between certain limits ♦ *Prices range from £20 to £50.* **2** to cover a number of different subjects ♦ *Our discussion ranged over several key topics.* **3** to wander or travel about a wide area

ranger *n* a keeper of a park or forest **Ranger** *n* a senior Guide

rangy (say **rayn**-ji) *adj* (said about a person) tall and thin

rank¹ *n* **1** a position or grade in a hierarchy ♦ *the rank of colonel* **2** high social position ♦ *people of rank* **3** a line or row of people or things **4** a place where taxis stand to wait for passengers **the ranks** *pl n* ordinary soldiers, not officers **rank** *v* **1** to have a certain rank ♦ *He ranks among the great statesmen.* **2** to arrange things in a row or sequence **rank and file** *n* the ordinary people of an organization, not the leaders

rank² *adj* **1** growing too thickly ♦ *rank vegetation* **2** smelling very unpleasant **3** unmistakably bad, out-and-out ♦ *rank injustice*

rankle *v* to cause lasting and bitter annoyance or resentment

ransack *v* **1** to rob a place, causing damage **2** to search somewhere thoroughly or roughly

ransom *n* money that has to be paid for a captive to be set free **ransom** *v* **1** to free someone by paying a ransom **2** to get a ransom for someone

rant *v* to speak or shout loudly and wildly **rant** *n* a spell of ranting

rap *v* **rapped, rapping 1** to strike something quickly and sharply **2** to speak words rapidly and rhythmically to a backing of rock music **rap** *n* **1** a quick sharp knock or blow **2** words recited rapidly and rhythmically to a backing of rock music; a type of popular music in which this is done **rapper** *n* **to take the rap** *informal* to be punished or blamed for something

rapacious (say rə-**pay**-shəs) *adj* greedy and grasping, especially for money **rapacity** *n*

rape¹ *n* **1** the act or crime of having sexual intercourse with a person without their consent, usually by using force **2** spoiling or destroying a place **rape** *v* to commit rape on a person **rapist** *n* a person who commits rape

rape² *n* a plant with bright yellow flowers grown as food for sheep and for its seed from which oil is obtained

rapid *adj* happening in a short time or at great speed **rapids** *pl n* a fast-flowing part of a river, caused by a steep downward slope in the river bed **rapidity** *n* **rapidly** *adv*

rapier (say **rayp**-i-er) *n* a thin light sharp pointed sword

rapport (say rap-**or**) *n* a harmonious and understanding relationship between people

rapt *adj* very intent and absorbed, enraptured

rapture *n* intense pleasure or joy **rapturous** *adj*

rare¹ *adj* **1** not often found or happening **2** exceptionally good, remarkable ♦ *a player* of rare skill **rarefied** adj 1 (said about air) of lower pressure than usual; thin 2 remote from everyday life **rarely** adv **rareness** n **rarity** n pl **rarities** 1 rareness 2 something uncommon; a thing valued because it is rare

rare² adj (said about meat) lightly cooked so that the inside is still red

rarebit n a dish of melted cheese on toast

raring (say **rair**-ing) adj informal very eager to do something ♦ We're all raring to go.

rascal n a mischievous or cheeky person **rascally** adj

rash¹ n 1 an outbreak of spots or patches on a person's skin 2 a number of unwelcome events happening in a short time ♦ a rash of accidents

rash² adj acting or done without careful consideration of the possible effects or risks **rashly** adv **rashness** n

rasher n a slice of bacon

rasp n 1 a coarse file with raised sharp points on its surface 2 a rough grating sound **rasp** v 1 to scrape or rub something roughly, especially with a rasp 2 to make a rough grating sound

raspberry n pl **raspberries** 1 an edible sweet red conical berry 2 informal a rude sound made with the tongue and lips to express disapproval or contempt

Rastafarian (say ras-tə-**fair**-iən) n a member of a religious group that originated in Jamaica and reveres Haile Selassie, the former emperor of Ethiopia, as God

rat n 1 a rodent resembling a mouse but larger 2 informal a treacherous or despicable person **rat** v **ratted**, **ratting** to hunt or kill rats **ratty** adj **rattier**, **rattiest** bad-tempered and irritable **rat race** n a fiercely competitive struggle to maintain your position in work or life **to rat on someone** informal to betray, desert, or inform on someone

ratatouille (say rat-ə-**too**-i) n a vegetable dish consisting of onions, courgettes, tomatoes, and peppers, stewed in oil

ratchet (say **rach**-it) n a series of notches on a bar or wheel in which a device catches to allow movement in one direction only

rate n 1 a measure obtained by expressing the quantity or amount of one thing with respect to another ♦ walking at a rate of four miles per hour 2 a fixed charge, cost, or value ♦ Postal rates have gone up. 3 speed of movement or change ♦ Our rate of progress has been good. **rates** pl n a local tax assessed on the value of commercial land and buildings and formerly also levied on private property **rate** v 1 to estimate the worth or value of a person or thing; to give a value or rank to a person or thing ♦ She is highly rated as a musician. 2 to deserve or be worthy of something ♦ That joke didn't even rate a smile. 3 informal to have a high opinion of someone or something **rateable** adj liable to payment of rates **rating** n 1 a classification assigned to a person or thing based on quality, standard, etc. 2 a sailor who is not an officer **ratings** pl n the estimated audience size of a particular television or radio programme **at any rate** no matter what happens; at least

rather adv 1 slightly or somewhat ♦ It's rather dark. 2 preferably, sooner ♦ I would rather have tea than coffee. 3 more accurately ♦ I crashed my car, or rather my mother's car. 4 instead of; as opposed to ♦ He is lazy rather than incompetent.

ratify v **ratifies**, **ratified**, **ratifying** to give formal consent to something or make something officially valid **ratification** n

ratio (say **ray**-shi-oh) n pl **ratios** the relationship between two amounts expressed as the number of times one contains the other

ration n a fixed quantity of something, especially food, allowed to one person **ration** v 1 to limit the supply of food, etc. to a fixed ration 2 to allow someone only a certain amount of something

rational adj 1 capable of reasoning or thinking sensibly 2 based on reason or logic ♦ a rational explanation **rationale** n a fundamental reason, the logical basis of something **rationalism** n basing opinions and actions on reason rather than on religious belief or emotions **rationalist** n **rationality** (say rash-ən-**al**-iti) n **rationalize** v 1 to try to justify something with a rational explanation ♦ *I think you are just rationalizing your fears.* **2** to make something more efficient or consistent ♦ *Attempts to rationalize English spelling have failed.* **rationalization** *n* **rationally** *adv*

rattle *v* **1** to make or cause something to make a rapid series of short sharp hard sounds; to make such sounds by shaking something **2** *informal* to make someone feel nervous, flustered, or irritated **rattle** *n* **1** a rattling sound **2** a device or baby's toy for making a rattling sound **rattlesnake** *n* a poisonous American snake with a rattling structure in its tail

raucous (say **raw**-kəs) *adj* loud and harsh-sounding

raunchy *adj* **raunchier**, **raunchiest** *informal* earthy and sexually explicit

ravage *v* to do great damage to something, to devastate something **ravages** *pl n* damaging effects

rave *v* **1** to talk wildly or incoherently **2** to speak with great enthusiasm or admiration about something **rave** *n informal* **1** a very enthusiastic review **2** a large party or event with dancing to loud fast electronic music **raving** *adj*, *adv* **1** completely mad **2** complete, absolute ♦ *a raving beauty*

ravel *v* **ravelled**, **ravelling** to untangle something or separate it into threads

raven *n* a large bird with glossy black feathers and a hoarse cry

ravening (say **rav**-ən-ing) *adj* hungrily seeking prey ♦ *a ravening beast*

ravenous (say **rav**-ən-əs) *adj* very hungry

ravine (say rə-**veen**) *n* a deep narrow gorge with steep sides

ravioli (say rav-i-**oh**-li) *n* an Italian dish consisting of small pasta cases containing meat or vegetables

ravish *v old use* **1** to rape someone **2** to fill someone with delight, to enrapture someone **ravishing** *adj* very beautiful

raw *adj* **1** not cooked **2** in its natural state, not processed or treated ♦ *raw hides* **3** (said about data) not organized or analysed **4** inexperienced, fresh to something ♦ *raw recruits* **5** stripped of skin and with the underlying flesh exposed **6** (said about weather) damp and chilly **rawness** *n* **a raw**

deal unfair treatment

ray^1 *n* **1** a single line or narrow beam of light or other radiation **2** a trace of something good ♦ *a ray of hope* **3** each of a set of lines or parts extending from a centre

ray^2 *n* any of several large sea fish with a flattened body and a long tail

rayon *n* a synthetic fibre or fabric made from cellulose

raze *v* to destroy a building or town completely

razor *n* an instrument with a sharp blade or cutters, used to shave hair from the face or body

razzmatazz, **razzle-dazzle** *n informal* showy publicity or display

RC *abbr* Roman Catholic

Rd *abbr* (used in street names) Road

RE *abbr* religious education

re (say ree) *prep* in the matter of, about, concerning

re- *prefix* again (as in *redecorate*, *revisit*)

reach *v* **1** to arrive at or go as far as a place or thing **2** to stretch out your hand or arm in order to touch, grasp, or take something ♦ *He reached for his gun.* ♦ *Can you reach the ceiling?* **3** to stretch out or extend to a place or point ♦ *The carpet does not quite reach to the door.* **4** to make contact with someone ♦ *You can reach me on this number.* **5** to achieve or attain something ♦ *The committee has yet to reach a conclusion.* **reach** *n* **1** the distance a person or thing can reach **2** the extent or range of a thing's effect or influence **reachable** *adj*

react *v* **1** to act in response to something **2** to undergo a chemical change **reaction** *n* **1** what someone feels, does, etc. as a result of or response to something ♦ *My immediate reaction was one of shock.* **2** a chemical change produced by two or more substances acting upon each other **reactionary** *adj* opposed to progress or reform **reactor** *n* an apparatus for the controlled production of nuclear energy

read (say reed) *v* past tense and past participle **read** (say red) **1** to be able to understand the meaning of something written or printed **2** to speak written or printed words, etc. aloud ♦ *She reads to the* *children every night.* **3** to carry out a course of study ♦ *She is reading Chemistry at Oxford.* **4** to have a certain wording ♦ *The sign reads 'Keep Left'.* **5** (said about a computer) to copy, search, or transfer data; to enter or extract data in an electronic storage device **6** (said about a measuring instrument) to indicate or register a value ♦ *The thermometer reads 20° Celsius.* **7** to interpret something, especially by looking at it ♦ *Do you know how to read a map?* **read** *n* **1** a time spent reading **2** a book thought of in terms of how readable it is ♦ *Her latest novel is an exciting read.* **readable** *adj* **1** pleasant and interesting to read **2** legible **reader** *n* **1** a person who reads **2** a book containing passages for practice in reading by students of a language **readership** *n* the readers of a newspaper or magazine; the number of these **reading** *n*

readjust *v* to adapt yourself to a new situation or environment **readjustment** *n*

ready *adj* **readier, readiest 1** fully prepared to do something ♦ *Are you ready to go?* **2** completed and available to be used ♦ *The meal's ready.* **3** willing to do something ♦ *She's always ready to help a friend.* **4** about or likely to do something ♦ *The woman looked ready to collapse.* **readily** *adv* **1** without reluctance, willingly **2** without any difficulty **readiness** *n* being ready

reagent (say ree-ay-jənt) *n* a substance used to produce a chemical reaction, especially to detect another substance

real *adj* **1** actually existing, not imaginary **2** actual or true ♦ *That's not the real reason.* **3** genuine, not imitation ♦ *real pearls* **realism** *n* **1** accepting a situation as it really is; the attitude of a realist **2** (in art and literature) representing things in a way that is accurate and true to life **realist** *n* **realistic** *adj* representing things in a way that is accurate and true to life **2** facing facts, having a sensible and practical idea of what can be achieved or expected **realistically** *adv* **reality** *n* *pl* **realities** all that is real; the state of things as they actually exist as distinct from imagination or fantasy **realize** *v* **1** to be fully aware of something, to accept something as a fact

♦ *Almost at once he realized his mistake.* **2** to achieve something or make it happen ♦ *She realized her ambition to become an astronomer.* **realization** *n* **really** *adv* **1** truly or in fact **2** very, indeed ♦ *a really nice girl* **real estate** *n* property consisting of land and buildings

realign *v* **1** to change something to a different or former position **2** to change your position or attitude with regard to something **realignment** *n*

realm (say relm) *n* **1** a kingdom **2** a field of knowledge, activity, or interest

ream *n* a quantity of paper (about 500 sheets) of the same size **reams** *pl n* a great quantity of written matter

reap *v* **1** to cut or gather a crop or harvest **2** to receive something as the result of something done ♦ *reap a reward* **reaper** *n*

rear[1] *n* the back part of something **rear** *adj* situated at the back **rearmost** *adj* **rearward** *adj, adv* **rear admiral** *n* a rank of naval officer, above commodore **rearguard** *n* a body of troops whose job is to protect the rear of the main force **to bring up the rear** to come last in a line or race

rear[2] *v* **1** to bring up and educate children **2** to breed and look after animals; to cultivate crops **3** (said about a horse, etc.) to raise itself upright on its hind legs

rearm *v* to get or supply someone with a new supply of weapons **rearmament** *n*

rearrange *v* to arrange something in a different way or order **rearrangement** *n*

reason *n* **1** a cause, explanation, or justification of something **2** the ability to think, understand, and draw conclusions **3** a person's sanity ♦ *Later in the play Lear loses his reason.* **4** good sense or judgement; common sense ♦ *She won't listen to reason.* **reason** *v* **1** to use your ability to think, understand, and draw conclusions **2** to try to persuade someone by giving reasons ♦ *We tried reasoning with the protestors.* ◊ The phrase *the reason is* should not be followed by *because* (which means the same thing). Correct usage is *We are unable to come; the reason is that we both have flu* (not 'the reason is because we both have flu'). **reasonable** adj **1** fair and sensible ♦ a reasonable person **2** in accordance with reason, not absurd ♦ a reasonable argument **3** not too expensive ♦ reasonable prices **4** acceptable or fairly good ♦ a reasonable standard of living **reasonableness** n **reasonably** adv

reassure (say ree-ə-**shoor**) v to restore someone's confidence by removing fears and doubts **reassurance** n

rebate (say ree-bayt) n a reduction in the amount to be paid, a partial refund

rebel (say reb-əl) n a person who rebels, especially against the government or against accepted standards of behaviour **rebel** (say ri-bel) v **rebelled, rebelling 1** to resist an established government or ruler; to take up arms against it **2** to resist authority, control, or convention **rebellion** n open resistance to authority, especially organized armed resistance to an established government **rebellious** adj rebelling, not easily controlled

rebirth n a return to life or activity, a revival

reboot v to boot a computer system again

rebound (say ri-bownd) v **1** to bounce back after hitting something **2** to have an unexpected adverse effect on the person doing something **rebound** (say ree-bownd) an act or instance of rebounding

rebuff n an unkind or contemptuous refusal **rebuff** v to give someone a rebuff

rebuke v to speak severely to someone who has done something wrong **rebuke** n a sharp or severe criticism

rebus (say ree-bəs) n pl **rebuses** a puzzle in which a name or word is represented by means of a picture or pictures suggesting its syllables

rebut (say ri-but) v **rebutted, rebutting** to claim or prove that a criticism or accusation is not true **rebuttal** n

recalcitrant (say ri-kal-si-trənt) adj disobedient, resisting authority or discipline **recalcitrance** n

recall v **1** to remember or cause someone to remember something **2** to ask or order a person to return **3** to ask for something to be returned **recall** n **1** the ability to remember; remembering **2** an order to return

recant (say ri-kant) v to state formally and publicly that you no longer hold an opinion or belief

recap (say ree-kap) v **recapped, recapping** informal to recapitulate **recap** n informal recapitulation

recapitulate (say ree-kə-pit-yoo-layt) v to state again the main points of what has been said or discussed **recapitulation** n

recapture v **1** to capture a person or animal that has escaped or something that has been lost to an enemy **2** to succeed in experiencing a former state, mood, or emotion again

recast v past tense and past participle **recast** to cast something again, to put something into a different form

recce (say rek-i) n informal a reconnaissance

recede v **1** to move back or further away **2** (said about a man's hair) to stop growing at the temples and above the forehead

recess n **1** a part or space set back from the line of a wall, etc.; a small hollow place inside something **2** a time when work or business is stopped for a while **recess** v to set something back into a wall or surface **recession** n a decline in economic activity **recessive** adj

receive v **1** to get, accept, or take something offered, sent, or given **2** to be awarded something ♦ She received the OBE in 1998. **3** to experience or be treated with something ♦ One man received injuries to his face and hands. **4** to pick up broadcast signals **5** to support or take the weight of something **6** to allow someone to enter as a member or guest **7** to greet someone on arrival **receipt** n **1** a written statement that money has been paid or something has been received **2** receiving, or being received ♦ on receipt of your letter **receiver** n **1** a person or thing that receives something **2** a radio or television set that receives broadcast signals and converts them into sound or a picture **3** the part of a telephone that receives the incoming sound and is held to the ear **4** (also **official receiver**) an official who takes charge of the financial affairs of a bankrupt business

receivership n the state of being managed by an official receiver **recipient** n a person who receives something

recent adj not long ago, happening or begun in a time shortly before the present **recently** adv

reception n 1 receiving, or being received 2 the way a person or thing is received ♦ The speech got a cool reception. 3 a formal party or gathering held to welcome someone or celebrate an event 4 a place in a hotel, office, etc. where visitors are greeted 5 the quality with which broadcast signals are received **receptacle** n something for holding or containing what is put into it **receptionist** n a person employed to greet and deal with visitors, clients, patients, etc. **receptive** adj able or willing to receive knowledge, ideas, or suggestions, etc. **receptiveness** n **receptivity** n

recherché (say rə-**shair**-shay) adj rare, exotic, or obscure

recidivist (say ri-**sid**-i-vist) n a person who constantly commits crimes and seems unable to be cured of criminal tendencies **recidivism** n

recipe n 1 instructions for preparing or cooking a dish 2 a course of action likely to lead to something ♦ a recipe for disaster

reciprocal (say ri-**sip**-rə-kəl) adj 1 given or felt by each towards the other, mutual ♦ reciprocal affection 2 given or done in return ♦ a reciprocal favour **reciprocally** adv **reciprocate** v 1 to return a feeling, gesture, etc. to someone who gives it to you; to do the same thing in return 2 (said about a machine part) to move backwards and forwards alternately **reciprocation** n **reciprocity** n

recite v 1 to repeat a passage aloud from memory, especially before an audience 2 to state facts in order **recital** n 1 a musical performance given by a soloist or small group 2 reciting **recitation** n

reckless adj ignoring risk or danger **recklessly** adv **recklessness** n

reckon v 1 to calculate or count up something ♦ Let's just reckon up the cost. 2 to regard something in a particular way ♦ She is reckoned an expert on the subject.

3 informal to have something as your opinion ♦ I reckon we shall win. 4 to rely or base your plans on something ♦ We reckoned on your support. **reckoning** n **to reckon with** to take something into account ♦ We didn't reckon with the train strike when we planned the journey.

reclaim v 1 to take action in order to get something back 2 to make flooded or waste land able to be used again, e.g. by draining or irrigating it 3 to recycle something **reclamation** n

recline v to lean or lie back

recluse (say ri-**klooss**) n a person who lives alone and avoids mixing with people **reclusive** adj

recognize v 1 to know who someone is or what something is because you have seen that person or thing before 2 to realize or admit the nature of something ♦ She recognized the hopelessness of the situation. 3 to acknowledge or accept something formally as genuine, valid, or lawful 4 to show appreciation of ability or service, etc. by giving an honour or reward **recognition** n recognizing, or being recognized ♦ a presentation in recognition of his services **recognizable** adj **recognizably** adv

recoil v 1 to draw yourself back in fear or disgust 2 (said about a gun) to jerk backwards when it is fired 3 (said about an action) to have an adverse effect on the person who did it **recoil** n the act or sensation of recoiling

recollect v to remember something **recollection** n

recommend v 1 to praise someone or something as suitable for something 2 to advise a course of action 3 (said about qualities or conduct) to make something acceptable or desirable ♦ This plan has much to recommend it. **recommendation** n

recompense (say **rek**-əm-penss) v 1 to repay or reward someone 2 to compensate someone for a loss or injury **recompense** n compensation or reward for something

reconcile (say **rek**-ən-siyl) v 1 to make people who have quarrelled become friendly again 2 to get someone to accept an unwelcome fact or situation ♦ *It took him a while to reconcile himself to wearing glasses.* **3** to make facts or statements, etc. compatible ♦ *I cannot reconcile what you say with what you do.* **reconciliation** *n*

recondite (say rek-ən-diyt) *adj formal* (said about a subject) obscure

recondition *v* to overhaul and make any necessary repairs to something

reconnaissance (say ri-kon-i-səns) *n* an exploration or examination of an area in order to gather information about it, especially for military purposes

reconnoitre *v* to make a reconnaissance of an area; to make a preliminary survey

reconsider *v* to consider something again and perhaps change your earlier decision

reconstitute *v* **1** to form something again, especially in a different way **2** to make dried food edible again by adding water **reconstitution** *n*

reconstruct *v* **1** to construct or build something again **2** to create or enact past events again, e.g. in investigating the circumstances of a crime **reconstruction** *n*

record (say rek-ord) *n* **1** information kept in a permanent form, especially in writing **2** a disc on which sound has been recorded; a piece of music recorded on a disc **3** facts known about a person's past life, performance, or career ♦ *He has a superb record at Wimbledon.* **4** the best performance or most remarkable event, etc. of its kind that is known ♦ *She holds the world record for the 100 metres.* **record** (say ri-kord) *v* **1** to put something down in writing or other permanent form **2** to store sound or visual scenes, especially television pictures, on a disc or magnetic tape, etc. so that they can be played or shown later **3** (said about a measuring instrument) to show or register a figure **record** *adj* best, highest, or most extreme recorded up to now **recorder** *n* **1** a kind of flute held forward and downwards from the mouth as it is played **2** a machine for recording sound, pictures, or data **3** a person who keeps records **recording** *n* **off the record** stated unofficially or not for publication or broadcast

recount[1] (say ri-kownt) *v* to give an account of something

recount[2] (say ree-kownt) *v* to count something again **recount** *n* a second counting, especially of election votes to check the totals

recoup (say ri-koop) *v* to recover what you have lost or its equivalent

recourse (say ri-korss) *n* a source of help **to have recourse to** to turn to a person or thing for help

recover *v* **1** to get something back again after losing it **2** to get well again after being ill or weak **3** to obtain something as compensation ♦ *We sought to recover damages from the company.* **recoverable** *adj* **recovery** *n pl* **recoveries**

recreation (say rek-ri-ay-shən) *n* **1** the process of refreshing or entertaining yourself after work by some enjoyable activity **2** a game or hobby, etc. that is an enjoyable activity **recreational** *adj*

recrimination *n* an accusation made against a person who has criticized or blamed you

recruit *n* **1** a person who has just joined the armed forces and is not yet trained **2** a new member or employee of a society, company, or other group **recruit** *v* **1** to enlist someone in the armed forces **2** to find new people to join a society, company, or other group **recruitment** *n*

rectangle *n* a four-sided geometric figure with four right angles, especially one with adjacent sides unequal in length **rectangular** *adj*

rectify *v* **rectifies**, **rectified**, **rectifying** to correct or put something right **rectifiable** *adj* **rectification** *n*

rectilinear (say rek-ti-lin-i-er) *adj* bounded by straight lines ♦ *a rectilinear figure*

rectitude *n formal* morally correct behaviour

recto *n pl* **rectos** the right-hand page of an open book, or the front of a sheet of paper

rector *n* **1** a member of the clergy in charge of a parish; (in the Church of England) one formerly entitled to receive all the tithes of the parish **2** the head of certain universities, colleges, schools, and religious institutions

rectory n pl **rectories** a rector's house

rectum n the last section of the large intestine, ending at the anus **rectal** adj

recumbent adj lying down, reclining

recuperate (say ri-koo-per-ayt) v 1 to get better after an illness or exhaustion 2 to recover losses **recuperation** n **recuperative** adj

recur v **recurred**, **recurring** to happen again, to keep on happening **recurrent** adj happening often or repeatedly **recurrence** n

recycle v 1 to convert waste material into a form in which it can be reused 2 to use something again **recyclable** adj

red adj **redder**, **reddest** 1 of the colour of blood 2 (said about hair or fur) of a reddish-brown colour 3 (said about the face) flushed with embarrassment or anger **red** n 1 red colour 2 informal a communist or socialist **redden** v **redness** n **red-blooded** adj vigorous or virile **red card** n a red card shown by the referee in a football match to a player being sent off the field **Red Crescent** n the equivalent of the Red Cross in Muslim countries **Red Cross** n an international organization for the treatment of the sick and wounded in war and for helping those affected by large-scale natural disasters **redhead** n a person with reddish hair **red herring** n a misleading clue; something that draws attention away from the main subject **red-hot** adj 1 so hot that it glows red 2 extremely exciting or popular **red-letter day** n a special or memorable day **red-light district** n an area in a city where there are many prostitutes, strip clubs, etc. **red tape** n use of too many rules and forms in official business **redwood** n a very tall evergreen coniferous tree of California **red-handed** adj **in the red** having spent more than is in your bank account, in debt **to catch someone red-handed** to catch someone while they are actually committing a crime or doing something wrong **to see red** informal to become very angry suddenly

redeem v 1 to make up for faults or deficiencies ♦ His one redeeming feature is his generosity. 2 to buy something back, to recover a thing in exchange for payment 3 to clear a debt by paying it off 4 to exchange a coupon or token for goods or cash 5 to save a person from damnation or from the consequences of sin **redeemable** adj **redeemer** n **redemption** n **redemptive** adj

redeploy v to deploy someone or something differently **redeployment** n

redevelop v **redeveloped**, **redeveloping** to develop land, etc. in a different way **redevelopment** n

redirect v to send or direct someone or something to a different place **redirection** n

redolent (say red-ə-lənt) adj 1 strongly suggesting or reminding you of something ♦ a castle redolent of history and romance 2 smelling strongly ♦ redolent of onions **redolence** n

redouble v to make something greater, or to become greater or more intense ♦ We must redouble our efforts in the second half.

redoubt (say ri-dowt) n a temporary fortification with no defences flanking it

redoubtable adj formidable, especially as an opponent

redound v formal to cause someone credit or honour

redress (say ri-dress) v to remedy or set something right **redress** n compensation or amends for a wrong done

reduce v 1 to make something less 2 to become less 3 to boil a sauce or other liquid so that it becomes thicker and more concentrated 4 to force someone into an undesirable state or condition ♦ This news reduced her to despair. 5 to change something into a simpler or more basic form ♦ The problem may be reduced to two main elements. **reducible** adj **reduction** n

redundant adj 1 no longer needed or useful; superfluous 2 (said about workers) no longer needed for any available job and therefore **redundancy** n

reduplicate v to double a letter or syllable, e.g. bye-bye, goody-goody

reed n 1 a water or marsh plant with tall straight hollow stems 2 the stem of this plant 3 a thin strip that vibrates to produce

the sound in certain wind instruments
reedy adj **reedier, reediest 1** (said about a
voice) having a thin high tone **2** full of reeds
reef[1] n a ridge of rock, coral, or sand that
reaches to or close to the surface of the sea
reef[2] n each of several strips at the top or
bottom of a sail that can be drawn in to
reduce the area of sail exposed to the wind
reef v to shorten a sail by drawing in a reef
or reefs **reef knot** n a symmetrical double
knot that is very secure
reek v **1** to have a foul smell **2** to strongly
suggest something ♦ *The whole thing reeks
of corruption.* **reek** n a foul smell
reel n **1** a cylinder or similar device on which
film, cotton, wire, etc. is wound **2** a length
of something wound on a reel **3** a lively
Scottish or Irish folk dance, or the music for
this **reel** v **1** to pull a thing in by using a reel
2 to stagger or lurch **to reel something
off** to say something quickly and without
effort
re-enter v to enter something again
re-entry n pl **re-entries 1** re-entering
something **2** the return of a spacecraft or
missile into the earth's atmosphere
ref n informal a referee
refectory (say ri-**fek**-teri) n pl **refectories**
the dining room of a college, monastery, or
similar establishment
refer v **referred, referring 1** to mention
or speak about someone or something ♦ *I
wasn't referring to you.* **2** to send or direct
a person to some authority, specialist,
or source of information **3** to describe or
denote something ♦ *Who does the phrase
'the Bard of Avon' refer to?* **reference** n **1** the
act of mentioning something ♦ *The report
made no reference to recent events.* **2** a
direction to a book, page, file, etc. where
information can be found; the book or
passage, etc. to which the reader is directed
3 a source of facts or information **4** a letter
from a previous employer testifying to
someone's ability or reliability **referable**
(say ri-**fer**-əbəl) adj **referee** n **1** an official
who closely watches a game or match and
makes sure that people keep to the rules
2 a person to whom disputes are referred
for decision **3** a person willing to testify

about the character or ability of someone
applying for a job **referee** v **referees,
refereed, refereeing** to act as referee in
a football match, etc. **referral** n **in** or **with
reference to** in connection with, about
referendum n pl **referendums** or
referenda the referring of a single political
question to the people of a country, etc.
for direct decision by a general vote; a vote
taken in this way
refill (say ree-**fil**) v to fill something again
refill (say **ree**-fil) n a second or later filling,
or a glass that is refilled
refine v **1** to remove impurities or defects
from something **2** to improve something
by making small changes to it **refined** adj
1 purified or processed **2** having good taste
or good manners **refinement** n **1** refining,
or being refined **2** elegance of behaviour
or manners **3** an improvement added to
something **refinery** n pl **refineries** a factory
where crude substances are refined
refit (say ree-**fit**) v **refitted, refitting**
to replace or repair the machinery,
equipment, and fittings in a ship, building,
etc. **refit** (say **ree**-fit) n the refitting of a
ship, building, etc.
reflect v **1** to throw back light, heat, or
sound **2** (said about a mirror, etc.) to show
an image of something **3** to be a sign of
something or make it apparent ♦ *Her hard
work was reflected in her exam results.* **4** to
think deeply or carefully about something
5 to bring about a good or bad impression
of something ♦ *This failure reflects badly
upon the whole industry.* **reflection** n
1 reflecting, or being reflected **2** reflected
light or heat, etc.; a reflected image
3 something that brings discredit **4** a
serious thought or consideration; an idea or
statement produced by this **reflective** adj
1 reflecting **2** thoughtful ♦ *in a reflective
mood* **reflector** n a thing that reflects light,
heat, sound, etc.
reflex (say **ree**-fleks) n an involuntary or
instinctive movement in response to a
stimulus **reflex** adj **1** (said about an action)
done as a reflex **2** (said about an angle)
more than 180° **reflexology** n a system of
massage used to treat illness and relieve

tension **reflexive pronoun** n any of the pronouns *myself, himself, itself, themselves,* etc., which refer back to the subject of the verb

reform v **1** to make changes in something in order to improve it **2** to give up a criminal or immoral lifestyle, or to make someone do this **reform** n **1** reforming, or being reformed **2** a change made in order to improve something **reformation** n the action or process of reforming **reformer** n **reformist** adj supporting gradual reform rather than abolition or revolution **the Reformation** n a religious movement in Europe in the 16th century that resulted in the establishment of the Reformed and Protestant Churches

refract (say ri-**frakt**) v to bend a ray of light at the point where it enters water or glass, etc. at an angle **refraction** n **refractive** adj

refractory adj formal **1** resisting control or discipline, stubborn **2** (said about a disease, etc.) not yielding to treatment **3** (said about a substance) resistant to heat; hard to fuse or melt

refrain[1] v to keep yourself from doing something

refrain[2] a repeated line or number of lines in a poem or song

refresh v to give new strength or energy to a tired person, etc. by food, drink, or rest **refresher** n **refreshing** adj **1** restoring strength and energy ♦ *a refreshing sleep* **2** welcome and interesting because it is new or different ♦ *refreshing honesty* **refreshment** n the giving of fresh strength or energy **refreshments** pl n drinks and snacks

refrigerate v to make food or drink extremely cold, especially in order to preserve it and keep it fresh **refrigeration** n **refrigerator** n a cabinet or room in which food is stored at a very low temperature

refuel v **refuelled, refuelling** to supply a ship or aircraft with more fuel

refuge n a place or state of safety from pursuit, danger, or trouble **refugee** n a person who has had to leave their country and seek refuge elsewhere

refund (say ri-**fund**) v to pay back money

received or expenses that a person has paid out **refund** (say **ree**-fund) n money paid back

refurbish v to make something clean or bright again; to redecorate and repair something

refuse[1] (say ri-**fewz**) v (said about a person) to say or show that you are unwilling to accept or give or do something ♦ *I refused to go.* ♦ *Your request has been refused.* **refusal** n

refuse[2] (say **ref**-yooss) n what is rejected as worthless, waste material

refute v to prove that a statement, opinion, or person is false or wrong **refutation** n

regain v **1** to get something back again after losing it **2** to reach a place again

regal (say **ree**-gəl) adj like or fit for a king or queen, especially in being magnificent or dignified **regalia** pl n clothing or emblems worn as a sign of high office **regally** adv

regale (say ri-**gayl**) v to entertain someone with conversation

regard v **1** to consider or think of something in a certain way ♦ *We regard the matter as serious.* **2** to look steadily at someone or something **regard** n **1** heed or consideration ♦ *You acted without regard to the safety of others.* **2** high opinion, respect ♦ *We have a great regard for her.* **3** a steady gaze **regards** pl n kindly greetings or wishes sent in a message **regardful** adj mindful **regarding** prep about or concerning ♦ *There are laws regarding picketing.* **regardless** adv paying no attention to something ♦ *Do it, regardless of the cost.* **as regards** concerning

regatta n a series of boat or yacht races organized as a sporting event

regenerate (say ri-**jen**-er-ayt) v **1** to give new life or strength to something **2** to reform someone spiritually or morally **3** to grow new tissues or organs to replace damaged ones **regeneration** n

regent n a person appointed to rule a country while the monarch is too young or unable to rule, or is absent **regency** n pl **regencies 1** being a regent **2** a period when a country is ruled by a regent

reggae (say **reg**-ay) n a West Indian style

of popular music with a strongly accented subsidiary beat

regicide (say **rej**-i-siyd) n 1 the killing of a king 2 a person who does this

regime (say ray-zheem) n a system of government or administration

regiment n 1 a permanent unit of an army, usually divided into companies or troops or battalions 2 a large number of people or things **regiment** v to organize people, work, data, etc. rigidly into groups or into a pattern **regimental** adj **regimentation** n

region n 1 an area of a country or of the world 2 an administrative division of a city or country 3 an area of the body ♦ the abdominal region **regional** adj **in the region of** approximately ♦ The cost will be in the region of £100.

register n 1 an official list recording names or items, etc., or a book containing this list 2 the range of a human voice or musical instrument **register** v 1 to put a name, etc. on a register 2 (said about an instrument) to indicate or show something ♦ The thermometer registered 100°. 3 to make an impression on someone ♦ His name did not register with me. 4 to express an emotion on your face or by gesture ♦ Her face registered disappointment. **registrar** n 1 an official with responsibility for keeping written records or registers 2 a judicial and administrative officer of the High Court 3 a doctor undergoing hospital training to be a specialist **registration** n 1 registering, or being registered 2 (also **registration number**) a series of letters and figures identifying a motor vehicle **registry** n pl **registries** a place where written records or registers are kept

regress (say ri-**gress**) v to go back to an earlier or less advanced form, state, or way of behaving **regression** n **regressive** adj

regret n 1 a feeling of sorrow, disappointment, or repentance 2 a polite expression of sorrow or apology, especially when refusing an invitation ♦ My mother is unable to come to your wedding and sends her regrets. **regret** v **regretted**, **regretting** to feel regret about something ♦ He regrets what he has done. **regretful** adj

regretfully adv **regrettable** adj **regrettably** adv it is regrettable that ♦ Regrettably I will not be able to meet you at the airport.

regular adj 1 happening or repeated in a uniform manner, or constantly at a fixed time or interval ♦ Her pulse is regular. ♦ Plant the seeds at regular intervals. 2 even or symmetrical ♦ a regular pentagon 3 usual or normal ♦ regular customers 4 belonging to a country's permanent armed forces 5 of medium size ♦ a regular coffee **regular** n 1 a member of the permanent armed forces of a country 2 a frequent customer or client **regularity** n **regularly** adv

regulate v 1 to control or direct something by means of rules and restrictions 2 to adjust or control a machine or the amount or rate of something so that it works correctly or according to your requirements **regulation** n 1 a rule, law, or restriction 2 regulating, or being regulated **regulator** n

regurgitate (say ri-**gerj**-it-ayt) v 1 to bring swallowed food up again to the mouth 2 to repeat information without really thinking about or understanding it **regurgitation** n

rehabilitate v 1 to restore a person to health or normal life by training and treatment after a period of imprisonment, addiction, or illness 2 to restore the reputation of a person or thing **rehabilitation** n

rehash (say ree-**hash**) v to use old ideas or material again with no great change or improvement **rehash** (say **ree**-hash) n something made of rehashed material

rehearse v 1 to practise something before performing to an audience 2 to train a person by doing this 3 to recite a list of points, especially ones that have been made many times before ♦ You will be given an opportunity to rehearse your grievances. **rehearsal** n

reign (say rayn) n 1 the period during which a king or queen rules 2 the period during which someone or something is dominant or in control ♦ a reign of terror **reign** v 1 to rule a country as king or queen 2 to prevail or dominate ♦ Confusion reigned. ◊ Do not confuse this word with rein, which has a different meaning.

reimburse v to repay money that has been spent or lost ♦ *Your travelling expenses will be reimbursed.* **reimbursement** n

rein n **1** a long narrow strap fastened to the bit of a bridle and used to guide or check a horse being ridden or driven **2** a similar device to restrain a young child **reins** pl n the power to control something ♦ *The company has prospered since she took over the reins.* **rein** v to check or control a horse by pulling on its reins **to give free rein to** to allow freedom to something ♦ *Give your imagination free rein.* **to rein someone** or **something in** or **back** to restrain someone or something ◊ Do not confuse this word with *reign*, which has a different meaning.

reincarnate (say ree-in-**kar**-nayt) v to cause someone to be born again in another body **reincarnate** (say ree-in-**kar**-nət) adj born again in another body **reincarnation** n **1** the belief that after death the soul is born again in another body **2** a person or animal in whom a soul is believed to have been reborn

reindeer n pl **reindeer** or **reindeers** a kind of deer with large antlers, living in Arctic regions

reinforce v **1** to strengthen or support something by additional people or material **2** to emphasize or increase something ♦ *These setbacks only served to reinforce my determination.* **reinforcement** n

reinstate v to restore a person or thing to a previous position **reinstatement** n

reiterate (say ree-**it**-er-ayt) v to say something again or repeatedly **reiteration** n

reject (say ri-**jekt**) v **1** to refuse to accept, believe, or agree to something ♦ *The committee has rejected the latest proposals.* **2** to discard or not use something, especially because it is below standard **3** (said about the body) to fail to accept tissue or an organ that has been transplanted **4** to fail to give due affection to someone ♦ *The child was rejected by both his parents.* **reject** (say **ree**-jekt) n a person or thing that is rejected, especially as being below standard **rejection** n

rejig v **rejigged**, **rejigging 1** *informal* to rearrange something **2** to re-equip a factory, etc. for a new type of work

rejoice v to feel or show great joy

rejoin[1] (say ree-**join**) v **1** to join something together again **2** to return to something ♦ *What time did you rejoin the party?*

rejoin[2] (say ri-**join**) v to say something in reply; to retort **rejoinder** n a sharp or witty reply

rejuvenate (say ri-**joo**-vən-ayt) v to make a person seem young again **rejuvenation** n

rekindle v **1** to relight a fire **2** to revive something that has been lost

relapse v **1** (said about a sick or injured person) to get worse after a period of improvement **2** to return to a worse or less active state **relapse** n relapsing, especially after partial recovery from illness

relate v **1** to tell a story or give an account of something **2** to establish a link between one thing and another **related** adj **relation** n **1** the way in which two or more people or things are connected or related to one another **2** being connected by birth or marriage **3** a relative **4** telling a story or giving an account **relations** pl n **1** dealings with others ♦ *the country's foreign relations* **2** *formal* sexual intercourse ♦ *She had relations with him.* **relationship** n **1** the way in which two or more people or things are connected or related to one another **2** the way in which two or more people or groups think of and behave towards each other **3** an emotional or sexual association between two people **relative** adj **1** considered in relation or proportion to something else ♦ *the relative merits of the two plans* ♦ *They lived in relative comfort.* **2** having a connection with something ♦ *Let's review the facts relative to the matter in hand.* **3** *Gram* referring or attached to an earlier noun, clause, or sentence **relative** n a person who is related to another by birth or marriage **relatively** adv **relativity** n **1** the state or quality of being relative **2** *Phys* a description of matter, energy, space, and time according to Einstein's theory of the universe **relative pronoun** n any of the pronouns *who*, *whom*, *whose*, *which*, and *that*, which refer back to an earlier noun or phrase as in *the people who know us* **to relate to 1** to concern or have a link with something ♦ *He notices only what relates to himself.* **2** to understand and get on well with someone ♦ *She relates to children extremely well.*

relax v **1** to stop working and rest or enjoy yourself **2** to become or cause someone to become less tense or anxious **3** to make a limb or muscle become less rigid **4** to make a rule, etc. less strict or severe **5** to let something become less intense ♦ *We can't relax our vigilance for a second.* **relaxation** n **relaxed** adj

relay (say ree-lay) n **1** a fresh set of people or animals taking the place of others who have completed a spell of work **2** a race between teams in which each person in turn covers a part of the total distance **3** an electronic device that receives and passes on a signal, often strengthening it **4** an electronic device activated by a current in one circuit to open or close another circuit **relay** (say ree-lay) v past tense and past participle **relayed** to receive and pass on or retransmit a message or broadcast, etc.

release v **1** to set someone or something free **2** to make a film, record, information, etc. available to the public **3** to let a thing fall or fly or go out ♦ *One of the archers released an arrow.* **release** n **1** releasing, or being released **2** something released **3** information or a film or record, etc. released to the public ♦ *a press release* **4** a handle or catch, etc. that unfastens a device or machine part

relegate (say rel-i-gayt) v **1** to put or send someone or something to a less important position or rank **2** to transfer a sports team to a lower division of a league **relegation** n

relent v **1** to abandon your harsh intentions and become more lenient **2** to become less intense **relentless** adj **1** (said about people) not relenting **2** not becoming less severe ♦ *relentless pressure* **relentlessly** adv

relevant (say rel-i-vənt) adj related to what is being discussed or dealt with **relevance** n

relic (say rel-ik) n **1** something that has survived from an earlier time **2** part of a

holy person's body or belongings kept after their death as an object of reverence **relics** pl n the remnants or residue of something

relief n **1** ease given by the ending or lessening of pain, anxiety, or difficulty **2** a feeling or cause of relief **3** help or assistance given to people in need **4** a person or group taking over another's turn of duty **5** the raising of the siege of a besieged town **6** a method of carving or moulding in which the design stands out from the surface **relieve** v to provide relief **relief map** n a map showing hills and valleys either by shading or by their being moulded in relief **to relieve yourself** to urinate or defecate

religion n a system of belief in the existence of a superhuman controlling power, especially of God or gods, usually expressed in worship **religious** adj **1** to do with religion **2** believing firmly in a religion and paying great attention to its practices **3** very conscientious or scrupulous ♦ *with religious attention to detail* **religiously** adv

relinquish v **1** to give up a plan, belief, struggle, etc. **2** to surrender possession or control of something ♦ *She has relinquished control of the company.* **relinquishment** n

reliquary (say rel-i-kwer-i) n pl **reliquaries** a container for holy relics

relish n **1** great enjoyment of food or other things **2** anticipating something with pleasure **3** a strong-tasting sauce or pickle eaten with plainer food to add flavour **relish** v **1** to enjoy something greatly **2** to look forward to something with pleasure ♦ *I don't relish the prospect of driving home in this weather.*

relive v to remember an experience or feeling very vividly, as though it was happening again

relocate (say ree-lə-kayt) v to move your home or business from one place to another **relocation** n

reluctant adj unwilling and slow to do something **reluctance** n **reluctantly** adv

rely v **relies, relied, relying to rely on** or **upon 1** to trust a person or thing to help or support you ♦ *You can rely on me not to tell anyone.* **2** to be dependent on something

♦ *Many people rely on this local bus service.*
reliable *adj* able to be relied on **reliability** *n*
reliably *adv* **reliance** *n* depending on
something; trust or confidence felt about
something ♦ *Don't place too much reliance
on his promises.* **reliant** *adj*

remain *v* **1** to be in the same place or
condition during further time, to continue
to be ♦ *We remained in London for another
two years.* ♦ *You must remain alert.* **2** to
be left over after other parts have been
removed, used, or dealt with **remainder** *n*
1 the remaining people or things or part
2 the number left after dividing one
quantity into another **remainder** *v* to
dispose of unsold copies of a book at a
reduced price **remains** *pl n* **1** what remains
after other parts or things have been
removed, used, or destroyed **2** ancient
buildings or objects that have survived
when others are destroyed **3** a person's
body after death

remand *v Law* to send a person accused of
a crime back into custody while further
evidence is being gathered **on remand** in
custody or on bail while waiting for a trial

remark *n* a written or spoken comment,
anything that is said **remark** *v* **1** to
make a remark **2** to notice something
remarkable *adj* extraordinary or striking
remarkably *adv*

remarry *v* **remarries**, **remarried**,
remarrying to marry again

rematch *n* a second game or match
between two teams or players

remedy *n pl* **remedies** something that
cures or relieves a disease, etc. or that
puts a matter right **remedy** *v* **remedies**,
remedied, **remedying** to be a remedy
for something, to put something right
remedial *adj* helping to cure an illness or
deficiency

remember *v* **1** to bring something back
into your mind **2** to keep something in
your mind ♦ *Remember to lock the door.*
3 to make a present to someone ♦ *My
Uncle Paul remembered me in his will.* **4** to
mention someone as sending greetings
♦ *Please remember me to your mother.*
remembrance **1** remembering, or

being remembered **2** something that is
remembered **3** something kept or given
as a reminder or in commemoration of
someone

remind *v* to cause someone to remember
or think of something ♦ *Remind me to
phone Jack.* ♦ *She reminds me of my history
teacher.* **reminder** *n* **1** a thing that reminds
someone of something **2** a letter sent to
remind someone to pay a bill

reminisce (say rem-in-**iss**) *v* to think or
talk about past events and experiences
reminiscence *n* **1** thinking or talking about
past events and experiences **2** a spoken or
written account of what you remember
♦ *He wrote his reminiscences of his life as
a diplomat.* **reminiscent** *adj* tending to
remind you of something ♦ *His style is
reminiscent of Picasso's.*

remiss (say ri-**miss**) *adj* negligent, careless
about doing what you ought to do

remission *n* **1** the shortening of a prison
sentence, especially for good behaviour
while in prison **2** a temporary lessening of
the intensity of an illness or pain **3** *formal*
forgiveness of sins

remit (say ri-**mit**) *v* **remitted**, **remitting**
1 to cancel a debt or refrain from inflicting a
punishment **2** to send money in payment to
a person or place ♦ *Please remit the interest
to my home address.* **3** to send a matter
for decision to some authority **remit**
(say **ree**-mit) *n* the task or area of activity
officially given to a person or organization
♦ *Staff training is outside the remit of this
committee.*

remix (say ree-**miks**) *v* to produce a
different version of a musical recording by
changing the balance of the separate tracks
remix (say **ree**-mix) *n* a remixed recording

remnant *n* **1** a part or piece left over from
something **2** a surviving trace of something

remonstrate (say **rem**-ən-strayt) *v* to make
a forceful protest ♦ *We remonstrated with
him about his behaviour.* **remonstrance** *n* a
forceful protest

remorse *n* deep regret for your wrongdoing
remorseful *adj* **remorseless** *adv* relentless

remote *adj* **remoter**, **remotest** **1** far away
in place or time ♦ *the remote past* **2** far from

the main centres of population; isolated ♦ *a remote village* **3** slight ♦ *I haven't the remotest idea.* **4** aloof and unfriendly ♦ *I find him a rather remote individual.* **remotely** *adv* **remoteness** *n* **remote control** *n* **1** controlling something from a distance, usually by means of electricity or radio **2** a device used to do this

remould (say ree-**mohld**) *v* **1** to mould something again **2** to put a new tread on a worn tyre **remould** (say ree-mohld) *n* a worn tyre that has been given a new tread

remove *v* **1** to take something off or away from where it was **2** to get rid of something **3** to dismiss someone from office **remove** *n* a stage or degree away from something **removable** *adj* **removal** *n* **1** removing, or being removed **2** the transfer of furniture, etc. when moving house **removed** *adj* **1** separated or distant ♦ *a dialect not far removed from Cockney* **2** (said about cousins) separated by a particular number of steps of descent ♦ *his first cousin once removed*

remunerate (say ri-**mewn**-er-ayt) *v* to pay or reward a person for work done or services rendered **remuneration** *n* **remunerative** *adj*

renaissance (say rə-**nay**-səns) *n* a revival of something **Renaissance** *n* the revival of art and literature in Europe in the 14th-16th centuries

renal (say **ree**-nəl) *adj* to do with the kidneys

rend *v* past tense and past participle **rent** **1** to tear something apart with force **2** to pierce the silence with a loud noise

render *v* **1** to cause a person or thing to become something ♦ *The shock rendered us all speechless.* **2** to give something, especially in return or exchange or as something due ♦ *a reward for services rendered* **3** to represent or perform something ♦ *The artist has rendered her features with great delicacy.* **4** to melt down fat **5** to cover stone or brick with a first coat of plaster **rendition** *n* the way a dramatic role or musical piece, etc. is rendered or performed

rendezvous (say **ron**-day-voo) *n pl*

rendezvous (say **ron**-day-vooz) **1** a meeting with someone at an agreed time and place **2** a place arranged for this **rendezvous** *v* **rendezvoused**, **rendezvousing** to meet at an agreed time and place

renegade (say **ren**-i-gayd) *n* **1** someone who deserts a group, cause, or faith, etc. for another **2** an outlaw **renege** *v* **to renege on** to break your word or an agreement

renew *v* **1** to begin or make or give something again ♦ *They renewed their requests for help.* **2** to arrange for something to be valid for a further period of time ♦ *I'd like to renew my passport.* **3** to give new strength to something ♦ *We ran out for the second half with renewed enthusiasm.* **4** to replace something with a fresh supply ♦ *The tyres need renewing.* **renewable** *adj* **renewal** *n*

rennet (say **ren**-it) *n* a substance used to curdle milk in making cheese

renounce *v* **1** to give up a claim or right, etc. formally ♦ *He decided to renounce his title.* **2** to reject or abandon a belief, way of life, etc. ♦ *This former terrorist has renounced violence completely.* **renunciation** *n*

renovate (say **ren**-ə-vayt) *v* to repair something and make it look new **renovation** *n* **renovator** *n*

renown *n* fame **renowned** *adj*

rent *n* a regular payment made for the use of land, accommodation, equipment, etc. **rent** *v* **1** to pay rent for temporary use of something **2** to allow something to be used in return for payment **rental** *n* **1** the amount paid or received as rent **2** renting something

reorganize *v* to change the way in which something is organized **reorganization** *n*

rep[1] *n informal* a business firm's travelling representative

rep[2] *adj informal* repertory ♦ *a rep theatre* **rep** *n* a repertory theatre or company

repair[1] *v* **1** to put something into good condition after damage or the effects of wear and tear **2** to put something right ♦ *Attempts to repair their marriage failed.* **repair** *n* **1** the act or process of repairing something **2** a part that has been repaired ♦ *Look, the repair is hardly visible.* **repairable** *adj* **reparation** *n* making amends; paying for damage or loss **in good repair** in good condition; well maintained

repair² *v formal* to go ♦ *The guests repaired to the dining room.*

repartee (say rep-ar-tee) *n* witty replies and remarks

repast (say ri-**pahst**) *n formal* a meal

repatriate (say ree-**pat**-ri-ayt) *v* to send a person back to their own country **repatriation** *n*

repay *v past tense and past participle* **repaid** 1 to pay back money borrowed or owed 2 to do or make or give something in return ♦ *How can we ever repay you for your kindness?* **repayment** *n*

repeal *v* to cancel a law officially **repeal** *n* the repealing of a law

repeat *v* to say or do something again **repeat** *n* 1 repeating 2 something that is repeated ♦ *There are too many repeats on television.* **repeatedly** *adv* again and again **repetition** *n* 1 repeating, or being repeated 2 something repeated **repetitive** *adj* characterized by repetition

repel *v* **repelled, repelling** 1 to drive someone or something away 2 to produce a feeling of disgust in someone **repellent** *adj* 1 causing disgust or distaste 2 not able to be penetrated by a specified substance ♦ *The fabric is water-repellent.* **repellent** *n* a substance that repels something ♦ *insect repellents*

repent *v* to feel regret about what you have done or failed to do **repentance** *n* **repentant** *adj*

repercussion (say ree-per-**kush**-ən) *n* a consequence of an event or action

repertoire (say rep-er-twar) *n* a stock of songs, plays, or acts, etc. that a person or company knows and is able to perform

repertory (say rep-er-ter-i) *n pl* **repertories** 1 theatrical performances of various plays for short periods, not for long runs 2 a repertoire **repertory company** *n* a theatrical company that gives performances of various plays for short periods

rephrase *v* to express something in an alternative way

replace *v* 1 to take the place of another person or thing 2 to find or provide a substitute for something 3 to put something back in its place **replaceable** *adj* **replacement** *n*

replay (say ree-play) *n* 1 a playback of a piece of action in the broadcast of a sports event, often in slow motion 2 the playing of a match again **replay** (say ree-**play**) *v* 1 to play a match again 2 to play back a recording

replenish *v* 1 to fill something up again 2 to add a new supply of something **replenishment** *n*

replete (say ri-**pleet**) *adj* 1 well stocked or supplied 2 feeling full after eating

replica (say rep-lik-ə) *n* an exact copy or reproduction of something **replicate** *v* to make or be an exact copy of something

reply *v* **replies, replied, replying** to say, write, or do something in answer or response **reply** *n pl* **replies** a spoken or written response

report *v* 1 to give an account of something you have seen, done, or studied 2 to give information about something or make something known ♦ *Do you have much progress to report?* 3 to make a formal complaint or accusation ♦ *I wish to report a break-in.* 4 to present yourself as having arrived or as ready to do something ♦ *Visitors are asked to report to reception.* 5 to be responsible to a certain person as your manager or supervisor **report** *n* 1 a spoken or written account of something you have seen, done, or studied 2 a regular statement about a pupil's or employee's work and conduct 3 a rumour or piece of gossip 4 an explosive sound like that made by a gun **reportage** *n* the reporting of news by journalists **reportedly** *adv* according to reports **reporter** *n* a person whose job is to report news for publication or broadcasting **reported speech** *n* a speaker's words as reported by another person, as in *She said I was not looking well*

repose¹ *n* 1 rest or sleep 2 a peaceful state or effect, tranquillity **repose** *v* to rest or lie somewhere

repose[2] v to place your trust or confidence in a person or thing

repository n pl **repositories** a place where things are stored

repossess v to take back possession of property or goods on which payments have not been kept up **repossession** n

reprehend (say **rep-ri-hend**) v to reprimand someone **reprehensible** adj extremely bad and deserving blame or rebuke

represent v 1 to act or speak on someone's behalf 2 to be an example or expression of something ♦ The election results represent the views of the electorate. 3 to symbolize or stand for something 4 to show a person, thing, or scene in a picture or play, etc. 5 to describe or declare someone or something to be something ♦ He has been falsely representing himself as an expert. **representation** n **representative** adj typical of a group or class **representative** n 1 a person chosen or appointed to act or speak on behalf of others 2 a firm's agent who travels to potential clients to sell its products

repress v 1 to keep your feelings or desires under control 2 to subdue people by force **repression** n **repressive** adj

reprieve (say **ri-preev**) n 1 postponement or cancellation of a punishment, especially of the death sentence 2 temporary relief from danger; postponement of trouble **reprieve** v to give a reprieve to someone

reprimand (say **rep**-ri-mahnd) n an expression of disapproval, especially a formal or official one **reprimand** v to give someone a reprimand

reprint (say **ree-print**) v to print something again in the same or a new form **reprint** n a reprinted copy

reprisal (say ri-**priy**-zǝl) n an act of retaliation

reprise (say ri-**preez**) n a repeated passage of music or performance of something **reprise** v to repeat a piece of music or a performance

reproach v to express disapproval to a person for a fault or offence **reproach** n an expression of disapproval or disappointment **reproachful** adj

reprobate (say **rep**-rǝ-bayt) n an immoral or unprincipled person

reproduce v 1 to produce a copy of something 2 to produce further members of the same species by natural means; to produce offspring 3 to cause something to be seen or heard again or to happen again ♦ Scientists are trying to reproduce these conditions in a laboratory. **reproducible** adj **reproduction** n 1 reproducing, or being reproduced 2 a copy of something, especially a work of art 3 the process of producing offspring **reproduction** adj (said about furniture) made in imitation of an earlier style **reproductive** adj

reprove v to rebuke or reprimand someone **reproof** n an expression of condemnation for a fault or offence

reptile n a member of the class of cold-blooded egg-laying animals, e.g. snakes, lizards, crocodiles, tortoises **reptilian** adj, n

republic n a country in which the supreme power is held by the people and their elected representatives **republican** adj, n

repudiate (say ri-**pew**-di-ayt) v 1 to refuse to deal with or be associated with someone or something 2 to deny or reject something **repudiation** n

repugnant (say ri-**pug**-nǝnt) adj distasteful or objectionable **repugnance** n

repulse v 1 to drive back an attacking force 2 to reject an offer or help, etc. firmly 3 to make someone feel strong distaste or disgust **repulsion** n **repulsive** adj 1 disgusting 2 repelling things ♦ a repulsive force **repulsiveness** n

reputation n the opinion that is generally held about a person or thing **reputable** adj having a good reputation **repute** n reputation **reputed** adj said or thought to have done or to be something ♦ This is reputed to be the best hotel in the area. **reputedly** adv

request n 1 asking or being asked for a thing or to do something 2 a thing asked for **request** v to make a request for something

requiem (say **rek**-wi-em) n a special Mass for someone who has died; a musical setting for this

require v 1 to need or depend on something

♦ *Cars require regular servicing.* **2** to demand that someone does something ♦ *These measures are required by law.* **requirement** *n* a thing required; a need

requisite (say **rek**-wiz-it) *adj* required by circumstances, necessary to success **requisite** *n* a thing needed for some purpose **requisition** *n* a formal written demand for something that is needed **requisition** *v* to take something over for official use

requite (say ri-**kwiyt**) *v formal* **1** to make a return for a service or to a person **2** to avenge a wrong or injury, etc. **requital** *n*

rerun *v* **reran**, **rerun**, **rerunning** **1** to run a race again **2** to broadcast a programme, film, etc. again **rerun** *n* **1** a race that is run again **2** a repeat of a programme, film, etc.

resale *n* sale to another person of something you have bought

rescind (say ri-**sind**) *v* to repeal or cancel a law or rule, etc.

rescue *v* to save a person or thing from danger, harm, etc.; to free someone from captivity **rescue** *n* rescuing, or being rescued **rescuer** *n*

research (say ri-**serch** or **ree**-serch) *n* careful study and investigation, especially in order to discover new facts or information **research** *v* to carry out research into something **researcher** *n*

resemble *v* to look like or have features in common with another person or thing **resemblance** *n*

resent (say ri-**zent**) *v* to feel bitter and indignant about something **resentful** *adj* **resentment** *n*

reserve *v* **1** to put something aside for a later occasion or for special use **2** to order or set aside seats, tickets, accommodation, etc. for a particular person to use at a future date **3** to retain or hold something ♦ *The company reserves the right to offer a substitute.* **reserve** *n* **1** something kept back for future use; an extra amount or stock kept available for use when needed ♦ *dwindling oil reserves* **2** (also **reserves**) forces outside the regular armed services and liable to be called out in an emergency **3** an extra player chosen in case a substitute

should be needed in a team **4** an area of land set aside for some special purpose ♦ *a nature reserve* **5** a tendency to avoid showing your feelings and to lack warmth towards other people **reservation** *n* **1** reserving, or being reserved **2** a reserved seat, table, room, etc. **3** an area of land set aside for the exclusive use of Native Americans or Australian Aboriginals **4** a limit on how far you agree with or accept an idea, etc. ♦ *I can recommend her for the job without reservation.* **5** a strip of land between the carriageways of a road **reserved** *adj* (said about a person) restrained in your behaviour, unwilling to show your feelings **reservist** *n* a member of a country's reserve forces **reservoir** *n* **1** a natural or artificial lake that is a source of water supply for a town, etc. **2** a supply or collection of information, etc.

reshuffle *v* to rearrange the posts or responsibilities of a group of people, especially government ministers **reshuffle** *n* reshuffling

reside *v* to have your permanent home in a certain place **residence** *n* **1** the place where a person lives **2** the fact of living in a place ♦ *When can I take up residence in college?* **residency** *n pl* **residencies** the fact of living in a place **resident** *n* a person living somewhere, not a visitor **resident** *adj* residing, in residence **residential** *adj* **1** containing or suitable for private houses ♦ *a residential area* **2** providing accommodation ♦ *a residential course* **in residence** (said about an artist, writer, etc.) working in a specified place for a period of time ♦ *The local museum has appointed a writer in residence.*

residue (say **rez**-i-dew) *n* the remainder, what is left over **residual** *adj* left over as a residue, remaining

resign *v* to give up your job or position **resignation** *n* **1** resigning **2** a resigned attitude or expression **resigned** *adj* having or showing patient acceptance of something unwelcome that cannot be avoided **to resign yourself to** to accept that something cannot be avoided and you must put up with it

resilient (say ri-**zil**-iənt) adj **1** able to spring back into shape after being bent or stretched **2** (said about a person) able to recover quickly from difficult circumstances **resilience** n

resin (say **rez**-in) n **1** a sticky substance that oozes from fir and pine trees and from many other plants **2** a similar substance made synthetically, used in making plastics, paints, varnishes, etc. **resinous** adj

resist v **1** to oppose or refuse to accept something ♦ I would definitely resist any plans to close the school down. **2** to be undamaged or unaffected by something ♦ pans that resist heat **3** to refrain from yielding to something although you are tempted by it ♦ I find it difficult to resist chocolate. **resistance** n **1** resisting; the power to resist something **2** an influence that hinders or stops something **3** the ability of a substance to resist the passage of heat or electricity; the measure of this **4** (also **Resistance**) a secret organization resisting the authorities, especially in a conquered or enemy-occupied country **resistant** adj offering resistance, capable of resisting ♦ heat-resistant plastics **resistor** n a device having resistance to the passage of electric current

resit v past tense and past participle **resat**; **resitting** to sit an examination again after a previous failure **resit** n an examination that you sit again

resolute (say **rez**-ə-loot) adj showing great determination **resolutely** adv **resoluteness** n **resolution** n **1** the quality of being resolute, great determination **2** a formal decision or statement of opinion agreed on by a committee or assembly **3** a mental pledge, something you intend to do ♦ New Year resolutions **4** the solving of a problem or question **5** the degree to which a photographic or television image can reproduce fine detail

resolve v **1** to solve or settle a problem or doubts, etc. **2** to decide something firmly **3** (said about a committee or assembly) to pass a resolution **resolve** n a firm decision or determination **resolved** adj (said about a person) determined, resolute

resonant (say **rez**-ən-ənt) adj **1** (said about a sound, room, etc.) resounding or echoing **2** suggesting or bringing to mind a feeling, memory, etc. **resonance** n **resonate** v

resort (say ri-**zort**) v to turn to and make use of a course of action to help you deal with a situation **resort** n **1** a place where people go for relaxation or holidays **2** a course of action resorted to; resorting to something ♦ I'm sure you can persuade him without resort to threats.

resound (say ri-**zownd**) v **1** (said about a voice or sound, etc.) to fill a place with sound; to produce echoes **2** (said about a place) to be filled with sound; to echo **resounding** adj **1** loud and echoing **2** (said about a success, victory, etc.) clear and emphatic

resource n something that can be used to achieve a purpose **resources** pl n **1** a source of wealth to a country ♦ The country's natural resources include coal and oil. **2** available assets, especially money **resource** v to provide money or other resources for something **resourceful** adj clever at finding ways of dealing with difficulties **resourcefulness** n

respect n **1** admiration felt towards a person or thing that has good qualities or achievements **2** consideration or attention ♦ You should show more respect for other people's feelings. **3** a particular detail or aspect ♦ In this respect he is like his sister. **respects** pl n polite greetings **respect** v **1** to feel or show respect for a person or thing **2** to agree to abide by a rule, agreement, etc. **respectable** adj **1** honest and decent; of good social standing **2** fairly good; adequate or acceptable ♦ a respectable score **respectability** n **respectably** adv **respecter** n **respectful** adj **respectfully** adv **respecting** prep concerning, with respect to **with respect to** or **in respect of** as regards; with reference to

respective adj belonging separately to each one mentioned ♦ We went off to our respective rooms. **respectively** adv for each separately in the order mentioned

respiration n **1** breathing **2** a process in living organisms involving the production of energy, especially a plant's taking in of oxygen and release of carbon dioxide

respirator n 1 a device worn over the nose and mouth to filter or purify the air before it is inhaled 2 an apparatus for giving artificial respiration **respiratory** adj **respire** v to breathe

respite (say ress-pyt) n a short period of rest or relief from something difficult or unpleasant

resplendent adj impressively bright and colourful

respond v 1 to speak or write in reply 2 to act or behave in answer to or because of something ♦ The public have responded marvellously to our appeal. 3 to show a favourable reaction to something ♦ The disease did not respond to treatment. **respondent** n the defendant in a lawsuit, especially in a divorce case **response** n 1 an answer 2 a reaction to something ♦ The appeal for help met with an enthusiastic response. **responsive** adj responding well or quickly to something **responsiveness** n

responsible adj 1 legally or morally obliged to take care of something or to carry out a duty 2 being the main cause of something ♦ This faulty piece of equipment was responsible for many deaths. 3 reporting to someone; having to account for your actions ♦ You will be responsible to the president himself. 4 involving important duties or decisions ♦ a responsible position 5 reliable and trustworthy ♦ a responsible person **responsibility** n pl **responsibilities** 1 being responsible 2 something for which a person is responsible **responsibly** adv

respray v to spray something with a new coat of paint **respray** n the act or process of respraying

rest[1] v 1 to be still, to stop moving or working, especially in order to relax or recover your strength 2 to allow something to be inactive in order to recover or save strength or energy ♦ Sit down and rest your feet. 3 to place something or be placed somewhere for support ♦ Rest the ladder against the wall. 4 to depend or be based on something ♦ The entire case rests on evidence of identification. 5 (said about a

look) to be directed in a particular direction ♦ His gaze rested on his son. 6 (said about a matter under discussion) to be left without further discussion or investigation **rest** n 1 a time of sleep or inactivity as a way of recovering your strength 2 an interval of silence between notes in music; a sign indicating this 3 an object used to hold or support something **restful** adj **restless** adj **restlessness** n

rest[2] v to remain in a specified state ♦ Rest assured, we will do everything we can. **the rest** n the remaining part of something; the others

restaurant n a place where people pay to sit and eat meals that are cooked there **restaurateur** n a person who owns and manages a restaurant

restitution n 1 restoring something to its proper owner or its original state 2 compensation for injury or damage

restive adj restless or impatient because of delay, boredom, or restraint

restore v 1 to bring something back to its original state, e.g. by repairing or rebuilding it 2 to bring someone back to good health or full strength 3 to return something that was lost or stolen to its original owner 4 to establish something again ♦ The new head's priority was to restore discipline. **restoration** n **restorative** adj tending to restore health or strength **restorative** n a restorative food, drink, or medicine **restorer** n

restrain v 1 to hold someone back, to stop them moving or doing something 2 to keep something under control **restrained** adj showing restraint **restraint** n 1 restraining, or being restrained 2 something that restrains, a limiting influence 3 the ability to keep calm and control your emotions

restrict v to put a limit on something, to subject something to limitations **restriction** n **restrictive** adj

restructure v to organize something differently

result n 1 what is produced by an activity or operation, an effect or consequence 2 a statement of the score or marks or the name of the winner in a sporting event, competition, or examination **3** a satisfactory outcome, such as a victory **4** an answer or formula, etc. obtained by calculation **result** v **1** to happen as a result ◆ *All sorts of troubles resulted from the merger.* **2** to have a specified result ◆ *The match resulted in a draw.* **resultant** adj happening as a result

resume v **1** to begin again or continue after stopping for a while **2** to get or take or occupy something again **resumption** n

résumé (say **rez**-yoom-ay) n a summary

resurgence (say ri-**ser**-jəns) n a rise or revival after a period of decline or inactivity **resurgent** adj

resurrect v to bring something back into use or existence **resurrection** n **1** coming back to life after being dead **2** the revival of something after disuse

resuscitate (say ri-**sus**-i-tayt) v to revive a person from unconsciousness or apparent death **resuscitation** n

retail n the selling of goods to the general public **retail** adv being sold in such a way **retail** v **1** to sell something or be sold to the general public **2** to recount or relate the details of something **retailer** n

retain v **1** to keep something in your possession or use **2** to continue to have something and not lose it ◆ *The fire had retained its heat.* **3** to book the services of someone **retainer** n **1** a thing that holds something in place **2** a sum of money regularly paid to someone so that they will work for you when needed **3** a servant who has worked for a person or family for a long time **retention** n retaining or keeping something **retentive** adj able to retain things ◆ *a retentive memory*

retake v retook, retaken to take a test or examination again **retake** n **1** a test or examination taken again **2** a scene filmed again

retaliate (say ri-**tal**-i-ayt) v to repay an injury or insult, etc. with a similar one; to attack someone in return for a similar attack **retaliation** n **retaliatory** adj

retard (say ri-**tard**) v to slow down or delay the progress or development of something **retardation** n **retarded** adj **1** slowed down

or delayed **2** (said about a person) mentally less developed than is usual for their age

retch v to strain your throat as if vomiting

rethink v past tense and past participle **rethought** to think about something again; to plan something again and differently **rethink** n an instance of rethinking

reticent (say **ret**-i-sənt) adj not revealing your thoughts and feelings readily **reticence** n

retina (say **ret**-in-ə) n pl **retinas** a layer of membrane at the back of the eyeball, sensitive to light

retinue (say **ret**-in-yoo) n a number of attendants accompanying an important person

retire v **1** to give up your regular work because you are getting old **2** to withdraw from a race, match, etc. because of injury **3** to go to bed or to a private room **retired** adj **retirement** n **retiring** adj shy, avoiding company

retort v to make a sharp, witty, or angry reply **retort** n a sharp, witty, or angry reply

retouch v to improve or alter a picture or photograph by making minor alterations or removing flaws, etc.

retrace v to go back over the route that you have just taken

retract v **1** to pull something or be pulled back or in ◆ *The snail retracts its horns.* **2** to withdraw a statement or accusation **retractable** adj **retraction** n

retread (say ree-**tred**) v to put a fresh tread on a worn tyre by moulding rubber to a used foundation **retread** (say **ree**-tred) n a retreaded tyre

retreat v **1** to go back after being defeated or to avoid danger or difficulty **2** to go away to a quiet or secluded place **retreat** n **1** retreating; the military signal for this **2** a quiet or secluded place **3** a period of withdrawal from worldly activities for prayer and meditation

retrench v to reduce your costs or spending **retrenchment** n

retrial n a second or further trial

retribution (say ret-ri-**bew**-shən) n a deserved punishment **retributive** adj

retrieve v **1** to bring or get something back

2 to find or extract information stored in a computer **3** to rescue or save something; to restore something to a flourishing state ♦ *His quick thinking retrieved the situation.* **retrievable** *adj* **retrieval** *n* **retriever** *n* a dog that can be trained to retrieve game

retro (say **ret**-roh) *adj informal* (said about a design) based on the style of an earlier period

retro- *prefix* back; backwards (as in *retrograde*)

retrograde *adj* **1** going backwards **2** reverting to an earlier and less good condition

retrospect *n* a survey of past time or events **retrospective** *adj* **1** looking back on the past **2** taking effect from a date in the past ♦ *The law could not be made retrospective.* **in retrospect** when you look back on a past event or situation

retroussé (say rə-**troo**-say) *adj* (said about a person's nose) turned up at the tip

return *v* **1** to come or go back **2** to bring, give, put, or send something back **3** to say something in reply **4** (in tennis, etc.) to hit the ball back to an opponent **5** to state or present something officially ♦ *The jury returned a verdict of not guilty.* **6** to elect someone as an MP ♦ *She was returned as MP for Finchley.* **return** *n* **1** coming or going back **2** bringing, giving, putting, or sending back **3** the proceeds or profits of a transaction **4** something that has been returned, such as an unwanted theatre ticket **5** a return ticket **6** a formal report or statement, e.g. of a set of transactions ♦ *an income-tax return* **returnable** *adj* **returning officer** *n* an official who conducts an election in a parliamentary constituency **return ticket** *n* a ticket for a journey to a place and back again

reunify *v* **reunifies, reunified, reunifying** to make a divided country into one again **reunification** *n*

reunion *n* **1** reuniting, or being reunited **2** a meeting of people who were formerly associated and have not seen each other for some time **reunite** *v* to come together or bring people together after a period of separation

reuse (say ree-**yooz**) *v* to use something again **reusable** *adj*

rev *n informal* a revolution of an engine **rev** *v* **revved, revving** to make an engine run quickly, especially when starting

Rev., Revd *abbr* Reverend ♦ *the Rev. John Smith*

revalue *v* **revalues, revalued, revaluing** **1** to make a new valuation of something **2** to give a new value to a currency in relation to other currencies **revaluation** *n*

revamp *v* to improve the appearance of or give a new structure to something

reveal *v* **1** to make something known **2** to uncover and allow something to be seen **revealing** *adj* **1** giving interesting or significant information ♦ *a revealing slip of the tongue* **2** (said about a piece of clothing) allowing a lot of someone's body to be seen **revelation** *n* **revelatory** *adj*

reveille (say ri-**val**-i) *n* a military waking signal sounded on a bugle or drums

revel *v* **revelled, revelling** **1** to take great delight in something ♦ *Some people revel in gossip.* **2** to engage in lively and noisy festivities **revels** *pl n* lively and noisy festivities **reveller** *n* **revelry** *n pl* **revelries**

revenge *n* harming or punishing someone in return for what they have made you suffer **revenge** *v* to get satisfaction by inflicting revenge; to avenge **revengeful** *adj*

revenue (say **rev**-ən-yoo) *n* a country's or company's income

reverberate (say ri-**verb**-er-ayt) *v* **1** (said about a loud noise) to be repeated as an echo **2** to have continuing serious effects **reverberation** *n*

revere (say ri-**veer**) *v* to feel deep respect or admiration for someone **reverence** *n* **Reverend** *adj* a title or form of address to members of the clergy **reverent** *adj* **reverential** *adj*

reverie (say **rev**-er-i) *n* a daydream, a state of daydreaming

revers (say ri-**veer**) *n pl* **revers** (say ri-**veerz**) a turned-back edge of a piece of clothing, especially at the lapel

reversal *n* **1** a change to an opposite direction, position, or course of action **2** a piece of bad luck

reverse *v* **1** to put or turn something the other way round or up, or inside out **2** to move or make something move backwards or in an opposite direction ♦ *He reversed the car out of the drive.* **3** to change something to the opposite of what it was **reverse** *adj* **1** facing or moving in the opposite direction **2** opposite in character or order **reverse** *n* **1** the opposite or contrary of something **2** a complete change of direction or action **3** the reverse side or face of something **4** a setback or defeat **5** reverse gear **reversal** *adj* **1** a change to an opposite direction, position, or course of action **2** a piece of bad luck **reversible** *adj* **reverse gear** *n* a gear that allows a vehicle to be driven backwards

revert *v* **1** to return to a previous state, practice, or belief **2** to return to a subject in talk or thought **3** *Law* (said about property, etc.) to return or pass to another owner by reversion **reversion** *n* **1** reverting to a previous state, practice, or belief **2** the legal right to possess something when its present holder relinquishes it; the returning of a right or property in this way

review *n* **1** a re-examination or reconsideration of something ♦ *The salary scale is under review.* **2** a published report assessing the merits of a book, film, play, etc. **3** a general survey of past events or of a subject **review** *v* **1** to re-examine or reconsider something **2** to write a review of a book, film, play, etc. **reviewer** *n*

revile *v* to criticize someone angrily in abusive language

revise *v* **1** to go over work that you have already learnt in preparation for an examination **2** to change or amend something ♦ *I have revised my opinion about her.* **3** to examine something again and correct any faults in it **4** to prepare a new edition of a book **revision** *n*

revitalize *v* to put new strength or vitality into something

revive *v* **1** to come or bring something back to life, consciousness, or strength **2** to restore interest in or the popularity of something **revival** *n* **1** an improvement in the condition or strength of something

2 something brought back into use, popularity, or fashion **3** a reawakening of interest in religion, especially by means of evangelistic meetings **revivalist** *n*

revoke (say ri-**vohk**) *v* to withdraw or cancel a decree or licence, etc.

revolt *v* **1** to take part in a rebellion **2** to be in a mood of protest or defiance **3** to cause someone to feel strong disgust **revolt** *n* an attempt to end the authority of someone by rebelling **revolting** *adj* causing disgust **revulsion** *n* a feeling of strong disgust

revolution *n* **1** substitution of a new system of government, especially by force **2** a complete or drastic change ♦ *a revolution in the treatment of burns* **3** turning or moving around an axis; a single complete turn of a wheel, engine, etc. **revolutionary** *adj* **1** involving a great change ♦ *revolutionary new ideas* **2** to do with political revolution **revolutionary** *n pl* **revolutionaries** a person who begins or supports a political revolution **revolutionize** *v* to alter a thing completely

revolve *v* **1** to turn or cause something to turn round **2** to move in a circular orbit **revolver** *n* a pistol with a revolving mechanism that makes it possible to fire it a number of times without reloading

revue *n* an entertainment consisting of songs, sketches, etc., often about current events

reward *n* **1** something given or received in return for what is done or for a service or merit **2** a sum of money offered for the detection of a criminal or return of lost property, etc. **reward** *v* to give a reward to someone **rewarding** *adj* giving satisfaction and a feeling of achievement ♦ *a rewarding job*

rewind *v* past tense and past participle **rewound** to wind a film or tape back to or towards the beginning

rewire *v* to renew the electrical wiring of something

rewrite *v* **rewrote**, **rewritten** to write something again in a different form or style

Rh *abbr* rhesus

rhapsody *n pl* **rhapsodies 1** an extremely enthusiastic and emotional written or spoken statement **2** *Mus* a romantic and emotional composition written in an irregular form **rhapsodize** *v* to talk or write about something in an extremely enthusiastic way

rhesus factor (say **ree**-səs) *n* a substance present in the blood of most people and some animals

rhetoric (say **ret**-er-ik) *n* **1** the art of using words impressively, especially in public speaking **2** language used for its impressive effect, but often lacking sincerity or meaningful content **rhetorical** *adj* **1** expressed in a way that is designed to be impressive **2** to do with rhetoric **rhetorically** *adv* **rhetorical question** *n* a question asked for dramatic effect and not intended to get an answer, e.g. ♦ *Who cares?* (i.e. nobody cares)

rheumatism (say **room**-ə-tizm) *n* any of several diseases causing pain in the joints, muscles, or fibrous tissue, especially a form of arthritis **rheumatic** *adj* to do with or affected with rheumatism **rheumatics** *pl n* rheumatism **rheumatoid** *adj*

rhinestone *n* an imitation diamond

rhino *n pl* **rhino** or **rhinos** *informal* a rhinoceros

rhinoceros *n pl* **rhinoceros** or **rhinoceroses** a large thick-skinned animal of Africa and south Asia, with a horn or two horns on its nose

rhododendron (say roh-də-**den**-drən) *n* an evergreen shrub with large clusters of trumpet-shaped flowers

rhombus (say **rom**-bəs) *n* a geometric figure shaped like the diamond on playing cards, a parallelogram with all sides equal **rhomboid** *n* a parallelogram with adjacent sides not equal

rhubarb *n* a garden plant with fleshy reddish leaf stalks that are used like fruit

rhyme *n* **1** identity of sound between words or syllables or the endings of lines of verse (e.g. *line/mine/pine, visit/is it*) **2** a poem with rhymes **3** a word that rhymes with another **rhyme** *v* to form a rhyme; to have rhymes

rhythm (say **rith**-əm) *n* **1** the pattern produced by emphasis and duration of notes in music or by long and short or stressed syllables in words **2** a movement with a regular succession of strong and weak elements ♦ *the rhythm of the heart beating* **rhythmic** *adj* **rhythmical** *adj* **rhythmically** *adv* **rhythm and blues** *n* a kind of popular music with elements of blues and jazz

rib *n* **1** each of the curved bones round the chest **2** a cut of meat from this part of an animal **3** a curved structural part resembling a rib, e.g. a curved timber forming part of a ship's hull **4** a raised pattern of lines in knitting **rib** *v* **ribbed**, **ribbing 1** to support a structure with ribs **2** *informal* to tease someone **ribcage** *n* the framework of ribs round the chest

ribald (say **rib**-əld) *adj* humorous in a cheerful but vulgar or disrespectful way **ribaldry** *n*

riband (say **rib**-ənd) *n* a ribbon

ribbon *n* **1** a narrow band of silk, nylon, etc. used for decoration or for tying something **2** a ribbon of special colour or pattern worn to indicate the award of a medal or order, etc. **3** a long narrow strip of material, e.g. an inked strip used in a typewriter or printer

rice *n* **1** a cereal plant grown in flooded fields in hot countries, producing seeds that are used as food **2** the seeds of this plant used as food **ricepaper** *n* thin edible paper

rich *adj* **1** having a lot of wealth **2** having a large supply of something ♦ *The country is rich in natural resources.* **3** splendid or elaborate, made of costly materials ♦ *rich furnishings* **4** producing or produced abundantly ♦ *rich soil* ♦ *a rich harvest* **5** (said about food) containing a large proportion of fat, butter, eggs, or spices, etc. **6** (said about colour, sound, or smell) pleasantly deep or strong **7** varied or complex in an interesting way **riches** *pl n* a great quantity of money, property, or valuable possessions **richly** *adj* **1** in a rich way **2** fully or thoroughly ♦ *Her success is richly deserved.* **richness** *n*

Richter scale (say **rik**-ter) *n* a scale for measuring the magnitude of earthquakes

rick¹ *n* a built stack of hay, corn, or straw

rick² *n* a slight sprain or strain **rick** *v* to sprain or strain your neck or back slightly

rickets n a children's disease caused by deficiency of vitamin D, resulting in softening and deformity of the bones

rickety adj poorly made and likely to fall down

rickshaw n a light two-wheeled hooded vehicle used in countries of the Far East, pulled by one or more people

ricochet (say rik-ə-shay) v **ricocheted** (say rik-ə-shayd) **ricocheting** (say rik-ə-shay-ing) (said about a bullet, etc.) to rebound off a surface **ricochet** n a shot or hit that ricochets

rid v past tense and past participle **rid**; **ridding** to free a person or place from something unpleasant or unwanted ♦ First we had to rid the house of mice. **good riddance** used to express relief that you are free of a person or thing **to get rid of** to cause someone or something to go away, to dispose of something

ridden adj full of or dominated by something ♦ rat-ridden cellars ♦ guilt-ridden

riddle[1] n 1 a question or statement designed to test ingenuity or give amusement in finding its answer or meaning 2 something puzzling or mysterious

riddle[2] n a coarse sieve for gravel or cinders, etc. **riddle** v to pierce something with many holes

ride v **rode**, **ridden** 1 to sit on a horse, bicycle, or motorcycle and control it as it carries you along 2 to travel in a car, bus, train, etc. 3 to be carried over or supported on something; to float or seem to float ♦ The ship rode the waves. ♦ The moon was riding high. **ride** n 1 a spell of riding 2 a journey or lift in a vehicle 3 a roundabout, roller coaster, etc. on which people ride at a fair or amusement park **rider** n 1 a person who rides a horse, bicycle, or motorcycle 2 an extra clause added to a document or statement; an expression of opinion added to a verdict **to ride something out** to come safely through something **to ride up** (said about a piece of clothing) to work upwards when worn

ridge n 1 a long narrow hilltop or mountain range 2 a narrow raised strip, a line where

two upward-sloping surfaces meet 3 Meteorology an elongated region of high atmospheric pressure **ridged** adj

ridicule n words or behaviour intended to make a person or thing appear ridiculous; mockery or derision **ridicule** v to make fun of a person or thing **ridiculous** adj so silly or foolish that it makes people laugh or despise it

rife adj 1 happening frequently, widespread ♦ Crime was rife in the city. 2 full of something ♦ The country was rife with rumours of war.

riff n a short repeated phrase in popular music or jazz

riffle v to flick through pages or papers quickly and casually

riff-raff n disreputable or undesirable people

rifle[1] n a gun with a long barrel

rifle[2] v to search and rob a place

rift n 1 a crack, split, or break in something 2 a serious break in friendly relations between people or in the unity of a group

rift valley n a steep-sided valley formed by subsidence of the earth's crust

rig[1] v **rigged, rigging** 1 to provide someone or something with clothes or equipment ♦ Everyone was rigged out in waterproofs. 2 to set up a structure quickly or with makeshift materials ♦ We've managed to rig up a shelter for the night. **rig** n 1 the way a ship's masts and sails, etc. are arranged 2 equipment for a special purpose, e.g. for drilling an oil well 3 informal (also **rig-out**) an outfit of clothes **rigging** n the ropes, etc. used to support masts and to set or work the sails on a ship

rig[2] v **rigged, rigging** to manage or control something fraudulently

right adj 1 on or towards the side which is to the east when you are facing north 2 proper, correct, or true ♦ the right answer ♦ Is this paint the right colour? 3 (said about conduct or actions, etc.) morally good, in accordance with justice 4 in a good or normal condition ♦ All's right with the world. **right** adv 1 on or to the right side ♦ Turn right here. 2 correctly or appropriately ♦ Did I do that right? 3 straight ♦ Go right on. **4** *informal* immediately ♦ *I'll be right back.* **5** all the way, completely ♦ *We went right round the town centre.* **6** exactly ♦ *right in the middle* **right** *n* **1** the right-hand side or direction **2** what is morally right or just **3** something that people are entitled to ♦ *the right to vote in elections* **4** (often **the Right**) the right wing of a political party or other group **right** *v* **1** to restore something to a proper or correct or upright position **2** to set something right, to make amends or take vengeance for something ♦ *This wrong must be righted.* **3** to correct something ♦ *The fault should right itself.* **right** *interjection* all right, that is correct, I agree **righteous** *adj* **1** doing what is morally right, making a show of this **2** morally justifiable ♦ *full of righteous indignation* **righteousness** *n* **rightful** *adj* in accordance with what is deserved, just, or proper ♦ *in her rightful place* **rightfully** *adv* **rightist** *n* a member of the right wing of a political party **rightly** *adv* justly, correctly, properly, or justifiably **right angle** *n* an angle of 90° **right-hand** *adj* of or towards the right side **right-handed** *adj* **1** using the right hand usually **2** operated by the right hand **right-hand man** *n* a person's trusted, indispensable, or chief assistant **right-minded** *adj* having ideas and opinions which are sensible and morally good **right of way** *n* **1** the right to pass over someone else's land, a path that is subject to such a right **2** the right of one vehicle to pass or cross a junction, etc. before another **right wing** *n* the section of a political party or system supporting more conservative or traditional policies **right-wing** *adj* **right-winger** *n* **in the right** having justice or truth on your side **in your own right** as a result of your own claims, qualifications, or efforts **right away** immediately

rigid *adj* **1** not able to bend or be forced out of shape **2** strict and inflexible ♦ *rigid rules* **rigidity** *n* **rigidly** *adv*

rigmarole (say **rig**-mə-rohl) *n* **1** a complicated formal procedure **2** a long rambling statement

rigor mortis (say **rig**-ə **mor** -tiss) *n* stiffening of the body after death

rigour (say **rig**-er) *n* **1** severity or strictness **2** harshness of weather or conditions **rigorous** *adj* **1** strictly accurate or detailed ♦ *a rigorous search* **2** strict or severe ♦ *rigorous discipline* **3** harsh or unpleasant ♦ *a rigorous climate* **rigorously** *adv*

rile *v informal* to annoy or irritate someone

rill *n* a small stream

rim *n* **1** the upper or outer edge of something more or less circular **2** the outer edge of a wheel, on which a tyre is fitted **rimmed** *adj* edged or bordered

rime *n* frost

rind *n* a tough outer layer or skin on fruit, cheese, bacon, etc.

ring[1] *n* **1** a small circular band, often made of precious metal, worn on the finger **2** the outline of a circle **3** something shaped like this, a circular band **4** a flat circular device forming part of a gas or electric hob **5** a circular or other enclosure for a circus, sports event, cattle show, etc. **6** a square area in which a boxing match or wrestling match takes place **7** a group of people acting together, especially in some illegal activity ♦ *a drugs ring* **ring** *v* **1** to put or draw a ring round something **2** to surround or encircle something **3** to put a ring on the leg of a bird to identify it **ringlet** *n* a long spiral-shaped curl of hair **ring finger** *n* the finger next to the little finger, especially of the left hand, on which a wedding ring is worn **ringleader** *n* a person who leads others in doing something illegal or mischievous **ringmaster** *n* the person in charge of a circus performance **ring road** *n* a bypass encircling a town **ringworm** *n* a skin disease producing round scaly patches on the skin, caused by a fungus

ring[2] *v* **rang**, **rung** **1** to make a loud clear resonant sound, like that of a bell when struck **2** to make a bell to do this **3** to be filled with sound ♦ *The stadium rang with cheers.* **4** to telephone someone ♦ *I'll ring you tomorrow.* **ring** *n* **1** the act of ringing a bell **2** a ringing sound or tone **3** a quality given by something you have heard ♦ *This story does have the ring of truth.* **ringing** *adj* clear and forceful ♦ *a ringing endorsement* **ringtone** *n* the special sounds a mobile phone makes when it receives a call **to ring off** to end a telephone call **to ring someone up** to make a telephone call to someone **to ring something up** to record an amount on a cash register

rink n (also **ice rink**) a place made for skating on ice

rinse v 1 to wash something in clean water to remove soap or dirt 2 to wash something lightly with water **rinse** n 1 rinsing 2 a solution washed through hair to tint or condition it

riot n 1 a wild and violent disturbance by a crowd of people 2 a profuse display of something ♦ *a riot of colour* 3 *informal* a very amusing thing or person **riot** v to take part in a riot **rioter** n **riotous** adj 1 disorderly or unruly 2 boisterous or unrestrained ♦ *riotous laughter* **to read the Riot Act** to give someone a severe reprimand or warning **to run riot** 1 to behave in an unruly way 2 to grow or spread in an uncontrolled way

RIP abbr (used on graves) rest in peace

rip v **ripped**, **ripping** 1 to tear something apart roughly, to remove something by pulling it roughly 2 to become torn 3 to rush along **rip** n a rough tear or split **ripcord** n a cord that is pulled to release a parachute from its pack **rip-off** n 1 something that is greatly overpriced 2 an inferior imitation **rip-roaring** adj full of energy, wildly noisy **to let rip** *informal* 1 to do something without restraint 2 to express yourself vehemently **to rip someone off** *informal* to cheat or defraud someone **to rip something off** *informal* to steal or copy something, especially someone else's idea

ripe adj 1 (said about fruit or grain) ready to be gathered and eaten 2 fully matured ♦ *ripe cheese* 3 ready, prepared or able to undergo something ♦ *The time is ripe for revolution.* **ripen** v to make something ripe or to become ripe

riposte (say ri-**posst**) n 1 a quick clever reply 2 a quick return thrust in fencing **riposte** v to deliver a riposte

ripple n 1 a small wave or series of waves 2 a gentle sound that rises and falls ♦ *a ripple of*

laughter **ripple** v to form or cause ripples

rise v **rose**, **risen** 1 to come or go upwards; to grow or extend upwards 2 to get up from lying, sitting, or kneeling 3 to get out of bed 4 (said about a meeting or court) to finish sitting for business, to adjourn 5 to increase in amount, number, or intensity ♦ *Her spirits rose.* 6 to reach a higher position or status ♦ *He rose to the rank of colonel.* 7 to rebel ♦ *Eventually the people rose in revolt against the tyrant.* 8 (said about the sun, etc.) to become visible above the horizon 9 (said about a river) to begin its course **rise** n 1 rising, an upward movement 2 an upward slope; a small hill 3 an increase in salary or wages 4 an increase in amount, number, or intensity **riser** n 1 a person or thing that rises ♦ *an early riser* 2 a vertical piece between treads of a staircase **rising** n a revolt **to get** or **take a rise out of** *informal* to draw a person into a display of annoyance or into making a retort **to give rise to** to cause something

risible adj so ridiculous that it provokes laughter

risk n 1 the possibility that something unpleasant will happen ♦ *There is a small risk of rain.* 2 a person or thing insured or similarly representing a source of risk ♦ *a fire risk* **risk** v 1 to expose someone or something to the chance of injury or loss ♦ *She risked her life to save the children.* 2 to accept the risk of something unpleasant happening ♦ *He risks injury each time he climbs.* **risky** adj **riskier**, **riskiest** involving risk

risotto (say ri-**zot**-oh) n pl **risottos** an Italian dish of rice cooked with vegetables and meat or seafood

risqué (say **risk**-ay) adj (said about a story, etc.) slightly indecent

rissole n a cake of minced meat coated with breadcrumbs and fried

rite n a religious or other solemn ceremony **ritual** n 1 the series of actions used in a religious or other ceremony; a particular form of this 2 a procedure that is regularly followed **ritual** adj to do with or done as a ritual **ritualistic** adj **ritually** adv **rite of passage** n a ceremony or event marking an important stage in someone's life

rival n 1 a person or thing competing with another 2 a person or thing that can equal another in quality **rival** adj being a rival or rivals **rival** v **rivalled**, **rivalling** to be comparable to something else, to seem or be as good as something else ♦ scenery that cannot be rivalled anywhere in the world **rivalry** n

riven (say riv-ən) adj torn apart

river n 1 a large natural stream of water flowing in a channel 2 a great flow of something

rivet (say riv-it) n a short metal pin or bolt for holding two pieces of metal together **rivet** v **riveted**, **riveting** 1 to fasten something with rivets 2 to fix something or hold it firmly ♦ We stood riveted to the spot. 3 to attract and hold someone's complete attention **riveter** n

riviera (say rivi-air-ə) n a coastal region with a subtropical climate and vegetation

rivulet (say riv-yoo-lit) n a small stream

RN abbr Royal Navy

roach n pl **roach** a small freshwater fish related to the carp

road n 1 a level way with a hard surface made for traffic to travel on 2 a way of achieving something ♦ the road to success **roadblock** n a barrier set up across a road by the police or army to stop and check vehicles **road hog** n a reckless or inconsiderate driver **road rage** n violent or aggressive behaviour by a driver towards other drivers **roadworks** pl n construction or repair of roads **roadworthy** adj (said about a vehicle) fit to be used on the road **on the road** on a long journey or series of journeys

roam v to wander over a wide area

roan adj (said about an animal) having a coat that is thickly sprinkled with white or grey hairs **roan** n a roan horse or other animal

roar n 1 a long deep loud sound, like that made by a lion 2 loud laughter **roar** v 1 to give a roar 2 to express something in this way, to laugh loudly **roaring** adj great, emphatic ♦ a roaring success

roast v 1 to cook meat, etc. in an oven or by exposing it to heat 2 to undergo roasting

3 to make something very hot, or to become very hot **roast** adj roasted ♦ roast beef **roast** n roast meat; a joint of meat for roasting **roasting** adj very hot and dry **roasting** n informal a severe reprimand

rob v **robbed**, **robbing** 1 to steal from a person or place; to commit robbery 2 to deprive someone of something they need or deserve ♦ Our noisy neighbours robbed us of a good night's sleep again. **robber** n **robbery** n pl **robberies**

robe n a long loose piece of clothing **robe** v to dress someone or yourself in a robe

robin n a small brown red-breasted European bird

robot (say roh-bot) n 1 (in science fiction) a machine that resembles and can act like a person 2 an automatic machine programmed to perform specific tasks 3 a person who seems to work or act like a machine **robotic** adj **robotics** n the study of the design, construction, and use of robots

robust (say rə-bust) adj 1 strong and vigorous 2 sturdily built **robustly** adv **robustness** n

rock[1] n 1 the hard part of the earth's crust, under the soil 2 a mass of this; a large stone or boulder 3 a hard sugar sweet made in cylindrical sticks, usually flavoured with peppermint **rockery** n pl **rockeries** a mound or bank in a garden, where plants are made to grow between large rocks **rocky** adj **rockier**, **rockiest**, **rock bottom** n the lowest possible level **rock pool** n a pool of water among rocks on a shoreline **rock salt** n common salt (sodium chloride) as it is found naturally in the earth **on the rocks** informal 1 (said about a drink) served neat with ice cubes 2 experiencing difficulties and likely to fail

rock[2] v 1 to move or be moved gently backwards and forwards or from side to side 2 to shake something violently ♦ The earthquake rocked the city. 3 to disturb or shock someone greatly ♦ The scandal rocked the financial world. **rock** n (also **rock music**) a kind of popular modern music usually with a strong beat **rocker** n 1 a fan or performer of rock music 2 a rocking chair **3** each of the curved bars on which a rocking chair, etc. is mounted **off your rocker** *informal* mad **rocky** *adj* **rockier**, **rockiest** unsteady or unstable **rock and roll** *n* a kind of popular dance music with a strong beat, originating in the 1950s **rocking chair** *n* a chair mounted on rockers or with springs so that it can be rocked by the person sitting on it **rocking horse** *n* a wooden horse mounted on rockers or springs so that it can be rocked by a child sitting on it

rocket¹ *n* **1** a firework or similar device that shoots high into the air when ignited and then explodes **2** a structure that flies by sending out a backward jet of gases that are the products of combustion, used to send up a warhead or a spacecraft; a bomb or shell propelled by this **3** *informal* a severe reprimand **rocket** *v* **rocketed**, **rocketing** to move rapidly upwards or away

rocket² *n* a Mediterranean plant of the cabbage family, eaten in salads

rococo (say rə-**koh**-koh) *n* an ornate style of decoration common in Europe in the 18th century

rod *n* a thin straight round stick or metal bar

rodent *n* an animal, e.g. rat, mouse, or squirrel, with strong front teeth used for gnawing things

rodeo (say roh-**day**-oh) *n pl* **rodeos** a display of cowboys' skill in riding and handling horses, roping calves, etc.

roe¹ *n* a mass of eggs in a fish

roe² *n pl* **roe** or **roes** a kind of small deer of Europe and Asia **roebuck** *n* a male roe deer

roentgen (say **runt**-yən or **ront**-yən) *n* a unit of ionizing radiation

roger *interjection* (in radio communication) your message has been received and understood

rogue *n* **1** a dishonest or unprincipled person **2** a mischievous but likeable person **3** a wild animal driven away from the herd or living apart from it ♦ *a rogue elephant* **4** something that is defective or found in an unexpected place **roguery** *n* **roguish** *adj*

roister *v* to enjoy yourself in a noisy or boisterous way

role *n* **1** an actor's part **2** a person's or thing's purpose or function ♦ *the role of computers in education* **role model** *n* a person looked to by others as an example of how to behave

roll *v* **1** to move or cause something to move along in contact with a surface, either on wheels or by turning over and over **2** to turn on an axis or over and over; to cause something to revolve **3** to turn something over and over on itself to form it into a cylindrical or spherical shape **4** to rock or sway from side to side **5** to flatten something by pushing a roller over it **6** to move forward or stretch out with undulations ♦ *The hills rolled down to the sea.* **7** to make a long continuous vibrating sound ♦ *Thunder rolled overhead.* **roll** *n* **1** a cylinder formed by turning flexible material over and over on itself **2** something having this shape, an undulation ♦ *rolls of fat* **3** a small individual portion of bread baked in a rounded shape; one of these split and containing a filling **4** an official list or register of names **5** a rolling movement **6** a long steady vibrating sound ♦ *a drum roll* **roller** *n* **1** a cylinder used for flattening or spreading things, or on which something is wound **2** a small cylinder on which hair is rolled in order to produce curls **3** a long swelling wave **rolling** *adj* **1** steady and continuous ♦ *a rolling programme of reforms* **2** (said about land) stretching out in gentle undulations **roll-call** *n* the calling out of a list of names to check who is present **rolled gold** *n* a thin coating of gold applied to another metal **Rollerblade** *n trademark* a boot like an ice-skating boot, with a line of wheels in place of the skate **rollerblading** *n* **roller coaster** *n* a type of railway used for amusement at fairgrounds, etc. with a series of alternate steep descents and ascents **roller skate** *n* a boot or metal frame fitted under a shoe, with small wheels on it so that the wearer can roll smoothly over the ground **roller skating** *n* **rolling pin** *n* a cylindrical device for rolling out dough **rolling stock** *n* the railway engines, carriages, wagons, etc. used on a railway **roll-on roll-off** *adj* (said about a ferry, etc.) that vehicles can be driven on

to and off **rollover** *n* (in a lottery) a jackpot prize which has not been won and is carried over to be added to the prize money for the following draw **to roll up** *informal* to arrive
rollicking *adj* full of boisterous high spirits
roly-poly *adj* round and plump
Roman *adj* **1** to do with ancient or modern Rome **2** to do with the ancient Roman republic or empire **Roman** *n* an inhabitant of ancient or modern Rome **roman** *n* plain upright type (not italic) used in printing **Roman alphabet** *n* the alphabet in which most European languages are written **Roman candle** *n* a tubular firework that sends out coloured sparks **Roman Catholic** *adj* belonging to or to do with the Christian Church that acknowledges the Pope as its head **Roman Catholic** *n* a member of this Church **Roman nose** *n* a nose with a high bridge **Roman numeral** *n* any of the letters representing numbers in the Roman system: I = 1, V = 5, X = 10, L = 50, C = 100, D = 500, M = 1,000
romance (say rə-**manss**) *n* **1** a feeling of excitement and wonder associated with love **2** a love affair **3** a love story **4** a quality or feeling of mystery, excitement, and remoteness from everyday life ♦ *the romance of ocean cruises* **5** a medieval story about the adventures of heroes **romantic** *adj* **1** to do with or characterized by romance **2** idealistic, not at all realistic or practical **3** (also **Romantic**) (said about music or literature) richly imaginative, not conforming to classical conventions **romantic** *n* a person with romantic beliefs or attitudes **romantically** *adv* **romanticize** *v* to describe or think about something in an idealized or unrealistic way
Romanian (say roh-**may**-niən) *adj* to do with or coming from Romania **Romanian** *n* **1** a person born in Romania, or descended from people born there **2** the language of Romania
Romany (say **rom**-ə-ni) *n pl* **Romanies** a gypsy **Romany** *adj* to do with Romanies or their language
romp *v* to play about together in a rough and lively way, as children do **romp** *n* a spell

of romping **rompers** *pl n* a piece of clothing for a baby or young child, covering the body and legs **to romp home** or **in** to win a race or competition easily
rondo *n pl* **rondos** a piece of music with a theme that recurs several times
rood *n* a crucifix
roof *n pl* **roofs 1** a structure covering the top of a house or building **2** the top of a car or tent, etc. **3** the top inside surface of something ♦ *the roof of the mouth* **roof** *v* to cover something with a roof; to be the roof of something
rook[1] *n* a black crow that nests in colonies **rook** *v informal* to swindle or overcharge someone **rookery** *n pl* **rookeries 1** a colony of rooks; a place where rooks nest **2** a colony or breeding place of penguins or seals
rook[2] *n* a chess piece with a top shaped like battlements
rookie *n informal* a new recruit or novice
room *n* **1** space that is or could be occupied by something ♦ *Do you have enough room?* **2** a part of a building enclosed by walls, floor, and ceiling **3** opportunity or scope for something ♦ *There is definitely room for improvement.* **rooms** *pl n* a set of rooms rented out to a person or family **roomy** *adj* **roomier, roomiest** having plenty of room to contain things
roost *n* a place where birds settle to rest at night **roost** *v* (said about birds) to settle for rest **rooster** *n* a male domestic fowl
root[1] *n* **1** the part of a plant that attaches it to the earth and absorbs water and nourishment from the soil **2** a vegetable which grows as a root, such as a carrot or turnip ♦ *root crops* **3** the part of a bodily organ or structure that is embedded in tissue ♦ *the root of a tooth* **4** a source or basis ♦ *We need to get to the root of the matter.* **5** a number that when multiplied by itself one or more times produces a given number ♦ *3 is the square root of 9.* ♦ *2 is the cube root of 8.* **6** *Language* a word from which other forms are made by adding prefixes and suffixes, e.g. *happy* is the root of *unhappy* and *happiness* **roots** *pl n* a person's family origins, or their sense of belonging

to a place **root** v **1** to take root, or to cause something to take root **2** to cause someone to stand fixed and unmoving ♦ *He was rooted to the spot by fear.* **3** to establish something deeply and firmly ♦ *The feeling is deeply rooted in our society.* **rootless** adj **1** having no root or roots **2** (said about a person) having no roots in a community **to root something out** or **up** to find and get rid of something

root² v **1** (said about an animal) to turn up the ground with its snout in search of food **2** to rummage; to find or extract something by doing this ♦ *I've managed to root out some facts and figures.* **to root for** informal to support someone enthusiastically

rope n **1** a length of strong thick cord made of twisted strands of fibre **2** a quantity of similar things strung together ♦ *a rope of pearls* **rope** v **1** to fasten, catch, or secure something with rope **2** to fence something off with rope **ropy** adj **ropier, ropiest** informal poor in quality or health **the ropes** informal the procedure for doing things in an organization, activity, etc. ♦ *I'll show you the ropes.* **to rope someone in** to persuade someone to take part in an activity

Roquefort (say **rok**-for) n trademark a kind of soft blue cheese, made from ewes' milk

rosary n pl **rosaries 1** a set series of prayers **2** a string of beads for keeping count of these prayers

rose n **1** a prickly bush or shrub bearing ornamental usually fragrant flowers **2** a flower from this bush or shrub **3** the perforated sprinkling nozzle of a watering can, hosepipe, or shower **4** a deep pink colour **roseate** adj deep pink, rosy **rosette** n **1** a rose-shaped badge or decoration made of ribbon **2** a rose-shaped carving **rosy** adj **rosier, rosiest 1** rose-coloured, deep pink **2** promising or hopeful ♦ *a rosy future* **rose-coloured** adj (also **rose-tinted**) involving an unduly cheerful or favourable view of things ♦ *You tend to see things through rose-coloured spectacles.*

rosé (say **roh**-zay) n a light pink wine

rosemary (say **rohz**-mer-i) n an evergreen shrub with fragrant leaves used as a herb

Rosh Hashana, Rosh Hashanah n the Jewish New Year festival

rosin (say **roz**-in) n a kind of resin

roster (say **ros**-ter) n a list showing people's turns to be on duty

rostrum (say **ros**-trəm) n pl **rostra** or **rostrums** a raised platform for one person, especially for public speaking or conducting an orchestra

rot v **rotted, rotting 1** to decompose or decay by chemical action caused by bacteria or fungi; to make something do this **2** to gradually become worse in condition through lack of use or activity ♦ *The two men were left to rot in jail.* **rot** n **1** rotting or decay **2** informal nonsense or rubbish **rotter** n a mean or unkind person

rota (say **roh**-tə) n a list of duties to be done and the order in which people are to take their turn in doing them

rotate v **1** to go round like a wheel, to move in a circle around an axis; to make something do this **2** to arrange or deal with something in a set sequence **3** to take turns at doing something, to be used in turn ♦ *The crews rotate every three weeks.* **rotary** adj rotating; acting by rotating **rotation** n **1** the action of rotating **2** the practice of growing a different crop each year on a plot of land in a regular order, to avoid exhausting the soil **rotational** adj

rote n **by rote** by memory or routine without fully understanding the meaning

rotisserie (say rə-**tiss**-er-i) n a cooking device for roasting food on a revolving spit

rotor n **1** a rotating part of a machine **2** a horizontally rotating vane of a helicopter

rotten adj **1** suffering from decay; breaking easily or falling to pieces from age or use **2** morally corrupt **3** informal very bad or unpleasant **rottenness** n

Rottweiler (say **rot**-viy-ler) n a large black German dog

rotund (say rə-**tund**) adj **1** (said about a person) plump **2** rounded in shape **rotundity** n

rotunda (say rə-**tun**-də) n a circular domed building or hall

rouble (say **roo**-bəl) n the unit of money in Russia and some other countries

roué (say **roo**-ay) n a debauched elderly

man

rouge (say roozh) n a reddish cosmetic for colouring the cheeks **rouge** v to colour the cheeks with rouge

rough adj 1 having an uneven or irregular surface; not level or smooth 2 not gentle, restrained, or careful; violent ♦ a rough push 3 (said about weather or the sea) wild and stormy 4 (said about a person) coarse or rude 5 informal difficult and unpleasant ♦ She's had a rough time recently. 6 not finished in detail ♦ a rough draft 7 approximate, not exact ♦ a rough estimate **rough** n 1 (on a golf course) the area of longer grass around the fairway and the green 2 a rough drawing or design, etc. **rough** v to make something rough **roughage** n indigestible material in plants which are used as food that stimulates the action of the intestines **roughen** v **roughly** adv **roughness** n **rough and ready** adj crude or hastily put together, but effective or adequate **rough and tumble** n disorderly fighting or rough play **roughcast** n plaster of lime, cement, and gravel, used for covering the outsides of buildings **rough house** n a disturbance with violent behaviour or fighting **roughshod** adj **to ride roughshod over** to treat someone inconsiderately or arrogantly **to sleep rough** to sleep out of doors, not in a proper bed

roulette (say roo-let) n a gambling game in which players bet on where the ball on a revolving wheel will come to rest

round adj 1 having a curved shape or outline; shaped like a circle, ball, or cylinder 2 (said about a number) expressed to the nearest whole number or the nearest ten, hundred, etc. 3 full or complete ♦ a round dozen **round** prep 1 on all sides of; circling or enclosing 2 at points on or near the circumference of ♦ We sat round the table. 3 in a curve or circle at an even distance from a central point ♦ The earth moves round the sun. 4 from place to place in, to all parts of ♦ Let me show you round the house. **round** adv 1 in a circle or curve; surrounding something ♦ Go round to the back of the house. ♦ Gather round, everyone.

2 so as to face in a different direction ♦ Turn your chair round. 3 to all people present; in every direction ♦ Hand the biscuits round. 4 from place to place ♦ We wandered round for a while. 5 to a person's house or office, etc. ♦ I'll be round in an hour. **round** n 1 a round object 2 a series of visits made by a doctor, postman, etc., especially in a fixed order as part of their duties 3 a recurring course or series, or one event in a series ♦ another round of negotiations 4 one stage in a competition or struggle; one section of a boxing match 5 the playing of all the holes on a golf course once 6 a single shot or volley of shots from a gun; ammunition for this 7 a slice of bread; a sandwich made with two slices of bread 8 a song for two or more voices in which each sings the same melody but starts at a different time 9 a set of drinks bought for all the members of a group **round** v 1 to make something round in shape, or to become round 2 to make an amount into a round figure or number ♦ Let's round the distance up to the nearest kilometre. 3 to travel or go round something **rounded** adj 1 round or curved 2 well developed, complete ♦ a rounded character **roundel** n a circular identifying mark on an aircraft, etc. **rounders** n a team game played with bat and ball, in which players have to run round a circuit of bases **roundly** adv thoroughly or severely ♦ She was roundly scolded. **roundabout** n 1 a road junction with a circular structure round which traffic has to pass in the same direction 2 a circular revolving ride in a playground or a merry-go-round at a funfair **roundabout** adj indirect, not using the shortest or most direct route or phrasing, etc. ♦ I heard the news in a roundabout way. **Roundhead** n a supporter of the Parliamentary party in the English Civil War **round robin** n 1 a statement or petition signed by a number of people, often with signatures written in a circle to conceal who signed first 2 a competition in which each player or team plays in turn against every other one **round-table** adj involving people meeting on equal terms to discuss something ♦ round-table talks

round-the-clock adj lasting or happening all day and all night **round trip** n a journey to a place and back to where you started **round-up** n 1 a gathering together of people or things ♦ a police round-up of suspects 2 a summary ♦ a round-up of the news **to come round** to become conscious again **to round on** to make a verbal attack on someone, especially unexpectedly **to round something off** 1 to complete something in a pleasant way ♦ Let's round the evening off with a nightcap. 2 to make the edges of something smooth **to round something up** to gather animals, people, or things into one place

rouse v 1 to cause someone to wake up 2 (said about a person or animal) to wake up 3 to cause someone to become active or excited **rousing** adj loud or stirring

roustabout n a labourer, especially one on an oil rig

rout n utter defeat; a disorderly retreat of defeated troops **rout** v to defeat an enemy completely and force them to retreat

route (say root) n the course or way taken to get from a starting point to a destination **route** v present participle **routeing** or **routing** to send someone by a certain route **router** n ICT a device which sends data to different parts of a computer network **route march** n a long training march for soldiers

routine (say roo-teen) n 1 a standard way of doing things; a series of acts performed regularly in the same way 2 a set sequence in a performance, especially in a comedy act 3 a sequence of instructions to a computer **routine** adj performed as part of a regular procedure **routinely** adv

roux (say roo) n a mixture of heated fat and flour used as a basis for a sauce

rove v to roam or wander **rover** n

row[1] (say roh) n a number of people or things in a line **in a row** in succession

row[2] (say roh) v to make a boat move by using oars **row** n a spell of rowing

row[3] (say row) n informal 1 a noisy quarrel or argument 2 a loud noise or uproar **row** v informal to quarrel or argue noisily

rowan (say roh-ən) n a tree that bears

hanging clusters of scarlet berries

rowdy adj **rowdier**, **rowdiest** noisy and disorderly **rowdy** n pl **rowdies** a rowdy person

royal adj 1 to do with, suitable for, or worthy of a king or queen 2 splendid **royal** n informal a member of the royal family **royalist** n a person who favours the idea of a monarchy **Royalist** n a supporter of the monarchy in the English Civil War **royally** adv **royalty** n pl **royalties** 1 a royal person or royal people 2 being royal 3 a payment made to an author or composer for each copy of a book sold or for each public performance of a work **royal blue** n a deep vivid blue

rpm abbr revolutions per minute

RSVP abbr (in an invitation) please reply

Rt Hon. abbr Right Honourable

rub v **rubbed**, **rubbing** 1 to press something against a surface and move it back and forth ♦ He rubbed his eyes. 2 to polish or clean something by rubbing; to make something dry or smooth in this way 3 to keep moving against a surface and make it sore or worn **rub** n 1 the act or process of rubbing 2 the chief difficulty or problem ♦ There's the rub. **to rub it in** informal to emphasize or remind a person constantly of an unpleasant or embarrassing fact **to rub off** to be transferred through close contact ♦ I hope some of your good luck rubs off on me. **to rub something out** to remove pencil marks by using a rubber

rubber[1] n 1 a tough elastic substance made from the latex of certain tropical plants or synthetically, used for making tyres, balls, hoses, etc. 2 a piece of rubber used for rubbing out pencil or ink marks **rubberize** v to treat or coat something with rubber **rubbery** adj **rubberneck** v to stare inquisitively **rubber plant** n a tall evergreen plant with tough shiny leaves, often grown as a house plant **rubber stamp** n a device with lettering or a design on it, which is inked and used to mark paper, etc. **rubber-stamp** v to give official approval to a decision without thinking properly about it

rubber[2] n 1 a contest consisting of a series of matches between the same sides in cricket, tennis, etc. **2** (in bridge) a match of three successive games

rubbish n **1** waste material to be thrown away **2** something that is worthless **3** nonsense **rubbish** v informal to criticize something severely or dismiss it as being worthless **rubbish** adj informal very poor in quality **rubbishy** adj

rubble n broken pieces of stone, brick, or concrete, especially those left after a building has been demolished

rubella n an infectious disease which causes a red rash

rubicund (say **roo**-bik-ənd) adj having a ruddy complexion

rubric (say **roo**-brik) n words put as a heading or a note of explanation or instructions of how something must be done

ruby n pl **rubies 1** a red gem **2** a deep red colour **ruby wedding** n the 40th anniversary of a wedding

ruche (say roosh) n a frill or pleat of fabric

ruck¹ n **1** (in rugby) a loose scrum with the ball on the ground **2** a tightly packed crowd of people

ruck² v to form creases or wrinkles **ruck** n a crease or wrinkle

rucksack n a bag worn slung by straps from both shoulders and resting on the back

ructions pl n informal angry protests or arguments; trouble

rudder n a vertical piece of metal or wood hinged to the stern of a boat or rear of an aircraft and used for steering

ruddy adj **ruddier, ruddiest 1** having a healthy reddish colour ♦ a ruddy complexion **2** informal bloody

rude adj **1** impolite, bad-mannered **2** indecent or vulgar **3** roughly made, not sophisticated ♦ rude stone implements **4** vigorous or hearty ♦ rude health **5** abrupt or startling ♦ a rude awakening **rudely** adv **rudeness** n

rudiments (say **roo**-dim-ənts) pl n the basic or elementary principles of a subject **rudimentary** adj **1** involving or limited to basic principles; elementary **2** not fully developed ♦ Penguins have rudimentary wings.

rue v **rues, rued, ruing** to regret something and wish it had not happened **rueful** adj **ruefully** adv

ruff n **1** a deep starched pleated frill worn around the neck in the 16th century **2** a collar-like ring of feathers or fur round the neck of a bird or animal

ruffian n a violent or lawless person

ruffle v **1** to disturb the smoothness or evenness of something **2** (said about a bird) to make its feathers stand up in anger or display **3** to upset the calmness or even temper of someone **ruffle** n a gathered ornamental frill **ruffled** adj

rug n **1** a small carpet or thick mat for the floor **2** a thick woollen blanket

rugby, rugby football n a kind of football played with an oval ball which may be kicked or carried

rugged adj **1** having a rocky and uneven surface **2** (said about a man's face) having strong masculine features **3** needing or showing toughness and determination **ruggedly** adv **ruggedness** n

rugger n informal rugby

ruin n **1** severe damage or destruction **2** complete loss of your fortune, resources, or prospects **3** a building, or the remains of a building, that has fallen down or been badly damaged **ruin** v **1** to damage something so severely that it is useless; to bring something into a ruined condition **2** to make someone bankrupt **ruination** n **ruinous** adj **1** bringing or likely to bring ruin **2** falling to pieces, in a state of disrepair

rule n **1** a statement of what can, must, or should be done in a certain set of circumstances or in playing a game **2** control or government **3** the customary or normal state of things or course of action ♦ Seaside holidays became the rule. **4** a straight often jointed measuring device used by carpenters, etc. **5** a thin printed line or dash **rule** v **1** to have control or power over people or a country, to govern **2** to have a powerful influence over something ♦ Don't let your heart rule your head. **3** to give a decision as judge or other authority **4** to draw a straight line using a ruler or other straight edge **ruler** n **1** a person who governs **2** a straight strip of wood or metal, etc. used for measuring or for drawing straight lines **ruling** *n* an authoritative decision or judgement **rule of thumb** *n* a rough practical method of procedure **as a rule** usually, more often than not **to rule something out** to exclude something as a possibility

rum[1] *n* a strong alcoholic drink distilled from sugar-cane residues or molasses

rum[2] *adj* **rummer**, **rummest** *informal* strange or odd

rumba *n* a lively ballroom dance of Cuban origin, or music for this

rumble *v* **1** to make a deep heavy continuous sound like thunder **2** *informal* to detect the true character of a person or thing, to see through a deception **rumble** *n* a rumbling sound

rumbustious *adj informal* boisterous or unruly

ruminate (say **roo**-min-ayt) *v* **1** to chew the cud **2** to think deeply about something **ruminant** *n* an animal that chews the cud, such as cattle, sheep, deer, etc. **rumination** *n*

rummage *v* to search for something by turning things over or moving them about in an untidy way **rummage** *n* a search of this kind

rummy *n* a card game in which players try to form sets or sequences of cards

rumour *n* a story or report that spreads to a lot of people by word of mouth but may not be true **rumour** *v* **to be rumoured** to be spread as a rumour

rump *n* **1** the hind part of an animal's or bird's body **2** a person's buttocks

rumple *v* to make something look untidy or dishevelled

rumpus *n informal* an uproar or an angry dispute

run *v* **ran**, **run**, **running 1** to move with quick steps, never having both or all feet on the ground at the same time **2** to go or travel smoothly or swiftly **3** to pass over or through something, or to make something do this ♦ *His eyes ran over the names on the list.* **4** to flow, to produce mucus or other liquid **5** to compete in a race or contest; to

seek election **6** (said about dye, ink, etc.) to spread when it is wet ♦ *Wash this separately in case the colours run.* **7** to work, function, or operate, or make something do this ♦ *Have you left the engine running?* **8** to continue or proceed ♦ *Everything's running according to plan.* **9** to manage or organize something ♦ *She runs a coffee shop.* **10** to publish a story in a newspaper or magazine, or to be published **11** to make a regular journey on a particular route ♦ *The bus runs every hour.* **12** to travel or take someone in a vehicle ♦ *We'll run you to the station.* **13** to smuggle goods **run** *n* **1** an act or spell or course of running **2** a journey, especially in a car **3** a point scored in cricket or baseball **4** a continuous stretch, sequence, or spell ♦ *He's had a run of bad luck.* **5** a general demand for goods ♦ *There has been a run on bread.* **6** an enclosed area where domestic animals can run freely in the open ♦ *a chicken run* **7** a track for some purpose ♦ *a ski run* **8** permission to make unrestricted use of something ♦ *You can have the run of the house.* **9** a ladder in a pair of stockings or tights **10** a large number of salmon going up river from the sea **running** *adj* **1** following each other without interval ♦ *It rained for four days running.* **2** continuous ♦ *a running joke* **runner** *n* **1** a person or animal that runs, especially in a race **2** a messenger **3** a creeping stem that grows away from the main stem and takes root **4** a groove, rod, or roller for something to move on; each of the long strips on which a sledge slides **5** a long narrow rug or strip of carpet **runny** *adj* **runnier**, **runniest 1** liquid or watery **2** (said about a person's nose) producing a flow of liquid **runaway** *n* a person who has run away **rundown** *n* a brief analysis or summary **run-down** *adj* **1** tired and in bad health, especially from working too hard **2** in bad condition; dilapidated **run-in** *adj* a quarrel or argument **runner bean** *n* a kind of climbing bean with long green pods which are eaten **runner-up** *n* a person or team finishing second in a contest **run-of-the-mill** *adj* ordinary, nothing special **run-up** *n* the period leading to an event **runway** *n* a strip of hard ground along which aircraft take off and land **in** or **out of the running** with a good chance, or no chance, of winning **to run across** to happen to meet or find a person or thing **to run away** to leave a place quickly or secretly **to run down 1** to stop working gradually because of loss of power **2** to deteriorate gradually **to run into 1** to meet someone by chance **2** to experience a problem or difficulty **to run out 1** (said about time or a stock of something) to become used up **2** (said about a person) to have used up your stock of something **to run someone down** to criticize someone unkindly or unfairly **to run someone in** *informal* to arrest someone and take them into custody **to run someone or something over** to knock down or crush someone or something with a vehicle **to run something down** to reduce the numbers or supply of something **to run something up** to allow a bill or score to mount up

rune (say roon) *n* any of the letters in an alphabet used by early Germanic peoples **runic** *adj*

rung *n* one of the crosspieces of a ladder

runt *n* an undersized animal, especially the smallest in a litter

rupee (say roo-pee) *n* the unit of money in India, Pakistan, and certain other countries

rupture *v* to break or burst suddenly, or cause something to do this **rupture** *n* **1** breaking; a breach **2** an abdominal hernia

rural *adj* to do with, in, or like the countryside rather than the town

ruse (say rooz) *n* a deception or trick

rush[1] *v* **1** to go, come, or take something with great speed **2** to do something with urgent, perhaps excessive, haste, or make someone do this ♦ *Don't rush me - I need to think about it.* **3** to dash towards a person or place in an attempt to attack or capture them or it **rush** *n* **1** rushing; an instance of this **2** a period of great activity **3** a sudden great demand for goods **rushes** *pl n* the first prints of a cinema film before it is cut and edited **rush hour** *n* the time each day when traffic is busiest

rush[2] *n* a marsh plant with slender pithy stems used for making mats, chair seats, baskets, etc.

rusk *n* a kind of dry biscuit, especially one used for feeding babies

russet *adj* soft reddish brown **russet** *n* **1** a reddish-brown colour **2** an apple with a rough skin of this colour

Russian *adj* to do with or coming from Russia **Russian** *n* **1** a person born in Russia or descended from people born there **2** the language of Russia **Russian roulette** *n* a dangerous game of chance in which a revolver is loaded with a single bullet and the people taking part spin the cylinder in turn and fire the gun at their head

rust *n* **1** a reddish-brown or yellowish-brown coating of iron oxide that forms on iron or steel by the effect of moisture, and gradually corrodes it **2** a reddish-brown colour **3** a plant disease with rust-coloured spots; the fungus causing this **rust** *v* **1** to be affected with rust **2** to lose quality or efficiency by lack of use **rusty** *adj* **rustier**, **rustiest 1** affected with rust **2** rust-coloured **3** weakened by lack of use or practice ♦ *My French is a bit rusty.*

rustic *adj* **1** having the qualities that country people or peasants are thought to have; simple and unsophisticated, or rough and unrefined **2** to do with living in the country **3** made of rough branches or timber ♦ *a rustic bridge* **rustic** *n* a country person, a peasant

rustle *v* **1** to make a soft crackling sound like that of paper being crumpled **2** to steal horses or cattle **rustle** *n* a rustling sound **to rustle something up** *informal* to prepare or produce something quickly **rustler** *n*

rut[1] *n* **1** a deep track made by the wheels of vehicles **2** a course of life that has become dull but is hard to change

rut[2] *n* a period of sexual excitement in male deer and other mammals during which they fight each other for females **rut** *v* **rutted**, **rutting** to be affected with this

ruthless *adj* having no pity or compassion **ruthlessly** *adv* **ruthlessness** *n*

rye *n* **1** a kind of cereal used for making flour or as food for cattle **2** a kind of whisky made from rye

Ss

S¹ the nineteenth letter of the English alphabet

S² *abbr* **1** Saint **2** south or southern

SA *abbr* South Africa

sabbath *n* a weekly religious day of rest, observed on Saturday by Jews and on Sunday by Christians **sabbatical** *n* a period of paid leave granted to a university teacher for study or travel **sabbatical** *adj*

sable *n* **1** a small weasel-like animal native to Japan and Siberia **2** its dark brown fur **sable** *adj poetic* black

sabotage (say **sab**-ə-tahzh) *n* deliberate damage done to machinery or materials for political or military purposes **sabotage** *v* **1** to commit sabotage on something **2** to make something useless or impossible ♦ *Their arrival sabotaged all my plans.* **saboteur** *n* a person who commits sabotage

sabre (say **say**-ber) *n* **1** a heavy sword with a curved blade **2** a light fencing sword with a tapering blade

sac *n* a bag-shaped part in an animal or plant

saccharin (say **sak**-er-in) *n* a sweet substance used as a substitute for sugar **saccharine** *adj* unpleasantly sweet or sentimental

sachet (say **sash**-ay) *n* a small sealed packet or bag containing a small amount of something

sack¹ *n* **1** a large bag of strong material for storing and carrying goods **2** (**the sack**) *informal* dismissal from a job or position ♦ *They gave him the sack.* **sack** *v informal* to dismiss someone from a job

sack² *v* to plunder a captured town in a violent destructive way **sack** *n* the act of sacking a place

sacrament *n* **1** an important Christian religious ceremony, such as baptism and the Eucharist **2** the consecrated elements in the Eucharist, especially the bread **sacramental** *adj*

sacred *adj* **1** associated with or dedicated to God or a god, and so deserving to be worshipped or venerated **2** dedicated to some person or purpose ♦ *sacred to the memory of those who fell in battle* **3** used in connection with religion, not secular ♦ *sacred music* **sacred cow** *n* an idea or institution which its supporters will not allow to be criticized

sacrifice *n* **1** the slaughter of a victim or the presenting of a gift or doing of an act in order to win the favour of a god **2** giving up something you value for the sake of something that is more important or more valuable **3** something offered or given up **sacrifice** *v* **1** to offer something or give something up as a sacrifice **2** to give up something in order to achieve something else ♦ *Their description of the events sacrificed brevity to accuracy.* **sacrificial** *adj*

sacrilege (say **sak**-ri-lij) *n* disrespect or damage to something regarded as sacred **sacrilegious** *adj*

sacristy (say **sak**-rist-i) *n pl* **sacristies** the place in a church where the sacred vessels are kept **sacristan** *n* a person in charge of the sacred vessels and other contents of a church

sacrosanct (say **sak**-roh-sankt) *adj* sacred and respected and therefore not to be violated or damaged

sad *adj* **sadder**, **saddest 1** feeling sorrow, unhappy **2** causing sorrow ♦ *a sad story in the newspaper about an abandoned baby* **3** *informal* inadequate or unfashionable **sadden** *v* to make someone sad **sadly** *adv* **sadness** *n*

saddle *n* **1** a seat placed on a horse or other animal **2** the seat of a bicycle **3** a joint of meat consisting of the two loins **saddle** *v* **1** to put a saddle on an animal **2** to burden someone with a task or responsibility **saddler** *n* someone who makes or deals in saddles and other equipment for horses

sadism (say **say**-dizm) *n* sexual or general pleasure derived from inflicting or watching pain **sadist** *n* **sadistic** *adj* **sadistically** *adv*

sae *abbr* stamped addressed envelope

safari (say sə-**far**-i) *n pl* **safaris** an expedition to hunt or observe wild animals in their environment, especially in East Africa **safari park** *n* a park where wild animals are kept in the open for observation by visitors driving through

safe *adj* **1** free or protected from risk or danger **2** not causing or resulting in harm or injury **safe** *n* a strong, locked cupboard or cabinet for keeping valuables **safely** *adv* **safeness** *n* **safety** *n* a state of being safe, freedom from risk or danger **safeguard** *n* a measure taken to prevent a danger or mishap **safeguard** *v* to protect something by means of a safeguard **safety net** *n* a net placed to catch an acrobat in case of a fall **safety pin** *n* a U-shaped pin with a guard covering the point when it is closed **safety valve** *n* **1** a valve that opens automatically to relieve excessive pressure **2** a harmless way of releasing feelings of anger or excitement

saffron *n* an orange-coloured spice used for colouring and flavouring food, made from the stigmas of a kind of crocus

sag *v* **sagged**, **sagging 1** to sink or curve down in the middle under weight or pressure **2** to hang down loosely and unevenly **sag** *n* an instance of sagging

saga (say **sah**-gə) *n* a long story with many episodes

sage[1] *n* a herb with fragrant greyish green leaves

sage[2] *n* a wise and respected person **sage** *adj* wise **sagacious** *adj* showing wisdom in your judgement and behaviour **sagacity** *n* **sagely** *adv*

Sagittarius (say saj-i-**tair**-iəs) (the Archer) the sign of the zodiac which the sun enters about 22 November **Sagittarian** *adj*, *n*

sago *n* a starchy food in the form of hard white grains obtained from a palm and used in puddings

sahib (say **sah**-ib) *n* (in India) a title or form of address for a man

sail *n* **1** a piece of canvas or other material spread on rigging to catch the wind and make a ship or boat move **2** a journey by ship or boat, used especially in indications of distance ♦ *Portsmouth is four hours' sail from St Malo.* **3** an arm on a windmill for catching the wind **sail** *v* **1** to travel on water

in a ship or boat **2** to start on a voyage ♦ *We sail at noon.* **3** to control the navigation of a ship or boat **4** to move swiftly and smoothly, or in a stately manner **sailor** *n* **1** a member of a ship's crew, or of a country's navy, especially one below the rank of officer **2** a traveller considered as prone or not prone to seasickness ♦ *a poor sailor* **sailboard** *n* a board with a mast and a sail fitted to it, used in windsurfing

saint *n* **1** in Christian belief, a holy person worthy of veneration **2** *informal* an exceptionally virtuous or unselfish person **sainthood** *n* **saintly** *adj* **saintlier**, **saintliest** like a saint, very virtuous **saintliness** *n*

sake *n* **for the sake of 1** in order to please or honour someone ♦ *They organized a holiday for their children's sake.* **2** in order to achieve or obtain something ♦ *For the sake of clarity, each question has a number.*

salaam (say sə-**lahm**) *n* a gesture of greeting in Arabic and Muslim countries, made by lowering the head and body and touching the forehead with the fingers **salaam** *v* to make a salaam

salacious (say sə-**lay**-shəs) *adj* sexually indecent

salad *n* a dish consisting of raw vegetables and other cold ingredients **salad days** *pl n* a time of youth and inexperience

salamander (say **sal**-ə-mand-er) *n* a lizard-like amphibian animal related to the newts

salami (say sə-**lah**-mi) *n* a strongly flavoured sausage, originally from Italy

salary *n* *pl* **salaries** a fixed payment made by an employer at regular intervals (usually monthly) to an employee, calculated on an annual basis

sale *n* **1** the process of selling or being sold **2** a transaction in which something is sold **3** the amount sold, or the profit from being sold ♦ *Sales were up last year.* **4** an event at which goods are sold, especially by public auction or for charity **5** a time when goods are sold at a reduced price **saleable** *adj* **saleroom** *n* a room in which auctions are held **salesman**, **saleswoman** *n* *pl* **salesmen**, **saleswomen** a person who sells goods commercially **salesmanship** *n* skill in selling goods commercially **salesperson** *n*

salient (say **say**-li-ənt) *adj* **1** most noticeable ♦ *the salient features of the plan* **2** projecting or prominent **salient** *n* a projecting piece of land or part of a fortification

saline (say **say**-liyn) *adj* containing salt or salts **salinity** *n*

saliva (say sə-**liy**-və) *n* a natural liquid secreted into the mouth by various glands, used to help chewing and swallowing **salivate** *v* to produce saliva

sallow *adj* (said about the skin or complexion) slightly yellow

sally *n pl* **sallies 1** a sudden rush forward **2** a lively or witty remark **sally** *v* **sallies**, **sallied**, **sallying sally out** or **forth** to make a sally, to set forth

salmon (say **sam**-ən) *n* **1** *pl* **salmon** a large fish with light pink flesh, used for food **2** a salmon pink colour

salmonella (say sal-mə-**nel**-lə) *n* a bacterium that causes food poisoning

salon *n* **1** a room or establishment where a hairdresser, beauty specialist, or couturier, etc. receives clients **2** a large elegant room used for receiving guests

saloon *n* **1** a public room on a ship **2** *N. Am* a place where alcoholic drinks may be bought and drunk **3** a passenger car with a closed body **saloon bar** *n* a comfortable bar in a pub

saloon car *n* a passenger car with a closed body

salsa *n* **1** a hot spicy tomato sauce **2** a type of Latin American dance music with jazz and rock elements, or a dance to this music

salt *n* **1** sodium chloride, a crystalline substance that gives seawater its taste and is used to flavour and preserve food **2** (usually **old salt**) *informal* an experienced sailor **salt** *adj* **1** impregnated with or preserved in salt **2** tasting of salt **salts** *pl n* a substance resembling salt in form, especially a laxative **salty** *adj* **saltier**, **saltiest**, **saltiness** *n* **salt cellar** *n* a small dish or perforated pot holding salt for use at meals **to salt something away** to put money aside for the future **to take something with a grain** or **pinch of salt** be cautious about believing a statement

saltpetre (say solt-**peet**-er) *n* a salty white powder (potassium nitrate) used in making gunpowder

salubrious (say sə-**loo**-bri-əs) *adj* good for people's health

salutary (say **sal**-yoo-ter-i) *adj* (said about something unpleasant) having a beneficial effect

salute *n* **1** a gesture of respect or recognition **2** a formal movement to denote respect, especially the raising of the hand to the head by a soldier acknowledging a superior or in reply to this **3** a firing of guns in a ceremony to show respect or as a celebration **salute** *v* **1** to perform a formal military salute, or to greet someone with this **2** to greet someone with a polite gesture **3** to express respect or admiration for someone or something **salutation** *n* a statement or gesture of greeting or respect

salvage *v* **1** to rescue a wrecked or damaged ship or its cargo at sea **2** to rescue goods from a building destroyed by fire **salvage** *n* **1** the rescue of property, especially of a ship or its cargo, or of the contents of a building destroyed by fire **2** the goods or property saved

salvation *n* **1** (in some religious beliefs) the saving of the soul from sin and its consequences **2** preservation from loss or calamity **3** a source or means of being saved ♦ *The loan was our salvation.*

salve *n* a soothing ointment **salve** *v* to soothe a person's conscience or feelings

salver *n* a metal tray on which letters, cards, or refreshments are placed for handing to people on formal occasions

salvo *n pl* **salvos** or **salvoes 1** the firing of a number of guns together as a salute **2** a volley of applause

Samaritan *n* someone who readily gives help to a person in need

same *adj* **1** of one kind, not changed or changing or different ♦ *We hear the same story every time.* **2** identical, the very one ♦ *Is that the same man you saw yesterday?* **3** used to refer to something or someone previously mentioned **same** *pronoun* (**the same**) the same person, thing, manner, etc. **sameness** *n*

samovar (say **sam-ə-var**) n a metal tea urn with an interior heating tube to keep water at boiling point, used in Russia and elsewhere

sampan n a small flat-bottomed boat used along coasts and rivers in China

samphire (say **sam-fiyr**) n a plant with fragrant fleshy leaves, growing near the sea

sample n a small part or amount of something that shows what the whole is like **sample** v to take a sample of something

sampler n 1 a piece of embroidery worked in various stitches to show skill in needlework 2 a typical sample or part of something

samurai (say **sam-oor-iy**) n pl **samurai** a member of a powerful military caste in feudal Japan

sanatorium n pl **sanatoriums** or **sanatoria** a hospital for treating chronic diseases or convalescents

sanctify v **sanctifies**, **sanctified**, **sanctifying** to make something or someone holy or sacred **sanctification** n

sanctimonious (say sənk-ti-moh-niəs) adj making a show of being righteous or pious **sanctimoniously** adv **sanctimoniousness** n

sanction n 1 action taken by one country or several countries against a country or organization to force it to conform to a law or principle of behaviour that it is considered to have violated 2 a threatened penalty for disobeying a law 3 formal permission or approval for an action **sanction** v to give official permission for an action

sanctity n being sacred, holiness

sanctuary n pl **sanctuaries** 1 a sacred place 2 the holiest part of a temple 3 the part of the chancel of a church containing the main altar 4 an area where birds or wild animals are protected and encouraged to breed 5 refuge, or a place of refuge

sanctum n 1 a person's private room 2 a holy place

sand n 1 a substance consisting of fine loose particles resulting from the wearing down of rock and covering the ground in deserts and on beaches, the seabed, and river beds 2 (**sands**) an expanse of sand **sand** v 1 to sprinkle or cover a surface with sand 2 to smooth or polish a surface with sandpaper or another abrasive **sander** n a device for sanding surfaces **sandy** adj **sandier**, **sandiest**, **sandbag** n a bag filled with sand, used to build defences, e.g. to protect a wall or building against floods **sandblast** v to clean a surface with a jet of sand under pressure **sandcastle** n a model of a castle made in sand on the seashore **sandpaper** n paper with a coating of sand or another abrasive, used for smoothing or polishing surfaces **sandpit** n a shallow box or hollow partly filled with sand for children to play in **sandstone** n rock formed of compressed sand **sandstorm** n a storm of wind in the desert, carrying huge clouds of sand

sandal n a light shoe consisting of a sole with straps or thongs over the foot

sandalwood n a kind of scented wood from a tropical tree

sandwich n a food consisting of two or more slices of bread with a filling such as meat, jam, cheese, etc. between them **sandwich** v to insert something tightly between two other things **sandwich board** n a linked pair of boards bearing advertisements, hung over a person's shoulders **sandwich course** n a training course with alternating periods of instruction and practical experience

sane adj 1 having a sound mind, not mad 2 sensible and practical **sanely** adv **sanity** n the state of being sane

sangfroid (say **sahn-frwah**) n calmness at a time of danger or difficulty

sanguinary (say **sang-gwin-er-i**) adj 1 full of bloodshed 2 bloodthirsty

sanguine (say **sang-gwin**) adj hopeful or optimistic

sanitary (say **san-it-er-i**) n 1 to do with hygiene or health, hygienic 2 to do with sanitation **sanitation** n arrangements for drainage and the disposal of sewage **sanitize** v to make something hygienic **sanitary towel** n an absorbent pad worn by a woman to absorb blood during menstruation

sank past tense of **sink**

Sanskrit n the ancient and sacred language of the Hindus in India

Santa Claus n Father Christmas

sap¹ n **1** the liquid that circulates in plants, carrying food to all parts **2** informal a foolish person **sap** v **sapped, sapping** to take away a person's strength gradually

sap² n a trench or tunnel made in order to get closer to an enemy **sapper** n a soldier who lays or detects mines

sapient (say **say**-pi-ənt) adj formal wise

sapling n a young tree

sapphire n **1** a transparent blue precious stone **2** a bright blue colour

Saracen (say **sa**-rə-sən) n an Arab or Muslim of the time of the Crusades

sarcasm (say **sar**-kazm) n the use of wit and irony to mock or criticize someone **sarcastic** adj **sarcastically** adv

sarcophagus (say **sar-kof**-ə-gəs) n pl **sarcophagi** an ancient stone coffin

sardine n a young pilchard or other small fish, tinned as food tightly packed in oil

sardonic (say sar-**don**-ik) adj humorous in a grim or sarcastic way **sardonically** adv

sari (say **sar**-i) n pl **saris** a length of cloth worn draped round the body as a traditional item of dress by Indian women

sarong (say sə-**rong**) n a skirt-like piece of clothing worn by men and women in SE Asia, consisting of a strip of cloth worn tucked round the waist or under the armpits

sartorial (say sar-**tor** -iəl) adj to do with tailoring or clothes

sash¹ n a long strip of cloth worn round the waist or over one shoulder and across the body for ornament or as part of a uniform

sash² n each of a pair of frames holding the glass panes of a window and sliding up and down in grooves

sashay v to walk in a showy way, with exaggerated hip and shoulder movements.

SAT abbr standard assessment task

Satan n a name for the Devil **satanic** adj **satanism** n the worship of Satan, involving parodies of Christian symbols and worship **satanist** n

satchel n a small bag with a strap, used especially for school books and hung over the shoulder or carried on the back

sate v to satisfy someone fully

satellite n **1** a spacecraft or other artificial body put in orbit round a planet to collect information or transmit communications signals **2** a heavenly body revolving round a planet **3** a small country that is dependent on a larger and more powerful neighbouring country **satellite dish** n a bowl-shaped aerial for receiving broadcasting signals transmitted by satellite

satiate (say **say**-shi-ayt) v to satisfy someone fully **satiety** n

satin n a silky material woven in such a way that it is glossy on one side only **satiny** adj

satire n **1** the use of ridicule, irony, or sarcasm to show up apparent weaknesses of people and institutions **2** a novel, play, etc. that uses satire **satirical** adj **satirically** adv **satirist** n **satirize** v to attack or criticize someone by using satire

satisfy v **satisfies, satisfied, satisfying 1** to give someone what they want or demand, to make someone pleased or contented **2** to put an end to a demand or craving by giving what is required ♦ to satisfy your hunger **3** to provide someone with sufficient evidence of something, to convince someone ♦ The police are satisfied that the death was accidental. **4** to pay a creditor **satisfaction** n **satisfactory** adj satisfying expectations or needs, adequate **satisfactorily** adv

satnav n a system of electronic road navigation using information from satellites

satsuma (say sat-**soo**-mə) n a kind of tangerine with a loose skin

saturate v **1** to soak something with liquid, to make something thoroughly wet **2** to cause something to absorb as much as possible until no more can be absorbed ♦ The market for used cars is saturated. **saturation** n the state of being saturated, maximum absorption

Saturday n the day of the week following Friday

saturnine (say **sat**-er-niyn) adj (said about a person) having a gloomy and forbidding appearance

satyr (say **sat**-er) *n Mythology* a woodland god with a man's body and a goat's ears, tail, and legs

sauce *n* **1** a thick liquid served with food to add flavour or richness **2** *informal* cheek, impudence **saucy** *adj* **saucier**, **sauciest** **1** sexually suggestive **2** cheeky or impudent **saucily** *adv* **sauciness** *n* **saucepan** *n* a round metal cooking pan with a long handle at the side

saucer *n* **1** a small shallow curved dish on which a cup is placed **2** something having a similar shape

sauna (say **saw**-nə) *n* a steam bath, or a building or room for this

saunter *v* to walk in a slow relaxed manner **saunter** *n* a leisurely walk

saurian (say **sor** -iən) *adj* of or like a lizard

sausage *n* a tube of minced seasoned meat enclosed in a skin **sausage roll** *n* a piece of sausage meat cooked in a roll of pastry

sauté (say **soh**-tay) *v* **sautés**, **sautéd**, **sautéing** to fry food quickly in a small amount of fat

savage *adj* **1** wild and brutal ♦ *a savage attack* **2** fiercely hostile ♦ *savage criticism* **3** (said about a people) primitive or uncivilized **savage** *n* a member of a people regarded as primitive or uncivilized **savage** *v* to attack someone fiercely, to maul someone **savagely** *adv* **savageness** *n* **savagery** *n*

savannah (say sə-**van**-ə) *n* a grassy plain in hot regions, with few or no trees

savant (say **sav**-ənt) *n* a learned person

save *v* **1** to rescue someone or something or keep them from danger or harm **2** to keep something (especially money) so that it can be used later **3** to avoid wasting something **4** to make something unnecessary ♦ *Sending it by post will save you a journey.* **5** (in football or other sports) to prevent an opponent from scoring **save** *n* the act of saving in football or other sports **save** *prep* except **saver** *n* **saving** *n* a reduction or economy in time, money, or other resource **savings** *pl n* money put aside for future use

saviour *n* a person who rescues or delivers people from harm or danger

savoir faire (say sav-wahr-**fair**) *n*

knowledge of how to behave in any social situation

savour *v* **1** to enjoy the taste or smell of something **2** to suggest or show a trace of something ♦ *The reply savoured of arrogance.* **savour** *n* the taste or smell of something **savoury** *adj* **1** (said about food) salty or piquant rather than sweet **2** having an appetizing taste or smell **savoury** *n pl* **savouries** a savoury dish or snack

savoy *n* a hardy cabbage with dense wrinkled leaves

savvy *n informal* common sense or good understanding

saw[1] *n* a tool with a toothed edge for cutting wood, etc. with a backwards and forwards movement **saw** *v* past tense **sawed**; past participle **sawn** **1** to cut something with a saw **2** to make a backwards and forwards movement as in sawing **sawdust** *n* powdery fragments of wood produced when sawing **sawmill** *n* a factory with power-operated saws for cutting timber

saw[2] *n* a proverb or saying

sax *n informal* a saxophone

Saxon *n* **1** a member of a Germanic people who occupied parts of England in the 5th-6th centuries **2** the language of this people **Saxon** *adj* to do with the Saxons or their language

saxophone *n* a brass wind instrument with a reed in the mouthpiece and keys like those of a clarinet, used especially for jazz and dance music **saxophonist** *n*

say *v* past tense and past participle **said** **1** to speak words to make a statement ♦ *I said we ought to be leaving.* **2** to express a fact, feeling, etc. ♦ *Colin tried to say what he really thought.* **3** to utter something ♦ *She was too angry to say his name.* **4** (said about something written or printed) to have a specified wording ♦ *The notice said 'no parking'.* **5** to give something as an opinion or decision ♦ *It's hard to say which of them is better.* **say** *n* the power to decide something ♦ *He has no say in the matter.* **saying** *n* a well-known phrase or proverb **say-so** *n* the power to decide something; a command

scab *n* **1** a hard crust that forms over a

wound or sore as it heals **2** a skin disease or plant disease that causes rough scab-like patches **3** *informal* a term of contempt for a person, especially a blackleg **scab** *v* **scabbed, scabbing** to become covered by a scab **scabby** *adj*

scabbard *n* a sheath for the blade of a sword or dagger

scabies (say **skay**-beez) *n* a contagious skin disease causing severe itching

scaffold *n* **1** a wooden platform formerly used for public executions **2** a structure of scaffolding **scaffolding** *n* **1** a temporary structure made of metal poles and planks to provide a platform or series of platforms for working on the outside of a building **2** the poles and planks used to make this

scald *v* **1** to injure someone with hot liquid or steam **2** to heat milk to near boiling point **scald** *n* a burn or other injury caused by scalding

scale¹ *n* **1** each of the thin overlapping hard or horny plates protecting the skin of fishes and reptiles **2** a dry flake of skin **3** a flaky deposit inside a boiler or kettle, etc., resulting from use of hard water **4** a flaky deposit on the teeth **scale** *v* **1** to remove scales or scale from something **2** to come off in scales or flakes **scaly** *adj* **scalier, scaliest**

scale² *n* each of the pans of a balance **scales** *pl n* an instrument for weighing things

scale³ *n* **1** a regular series of units, degrees, or qualities, etc. for measuring or grading something **2** *Mus* an arrangement of notes ascending or descending by fixed intervals **3** the ratio of the actual measurements of something and those of a drawing, map, or model of it **4** the relative size or extent of something ♦ *bribery on a grand scale* **scale** *v* to climb something tall and precipitous, such as a cliff face **to scale up** or **down** to make something larger or smaller in proportion

scallop (say **skol**-əp) *n* **1** a shellfish with two hinged fan-shaped shells **2** each of a series of curves forming an ornamental edging

scallywag *n informal* a rascal

scalp *n* the skin covering the top and back

of the head **2** the scalp with the hair cut away from an enemy's head as a trophy **scalp** *v* to take the scalp of an enemy

scalpel (say **skal**-pəl) *n* a knife with a small sharp blade, used by a surgeon

scamp *n* a mischievous child

scamper *v* to run hastily; to run about playfully as a child does **scamper** *n* a scampering run

scampi (say **skamp**-i) *pl n* large prawns

scan *v* **scanned, scanning** **1** to glance at different parts of something quickly in order to check for something ♦ *He scanned the newspaper for a report of the incident.* **2** to sweep a radar or electronic beam over an area in search of something **3** (said about verse) to be correct in rhythm ♦ *This line doesn't scan.* **4** *ICT* to use a scanner to read data from printed text or graphics into a computer **scan** *n* an act of scanning **scanner** *n* **1** a machine for examining the body by radiation, ultrasound, or other means, as an aid in diagnosis **2** *ICT* a device for converting printed text and images into machine-readable data **scansion** *n* the scanning of lines of verse

scandal *n* **1** an act that is regarded as morally wrong and causes widespread public disapproval **2** gossip or disapproval about people's behaviour **scandalize** *v* to shock someone by doing something considered to be shameful or disgraceful **scandalous** *adj* **scandalously** *adv*

Scandinavian *adj* to do with or coming from Scandinavia (Norway, Sweden, and Denmark, and sometimes also Finland, Iceland, and the Faroe Islands) **Scandinavian** *n* a person born in Scandinavia or descended from people born there

scant *adj* barely enough or adequate ♦ *We were treated with scant courtesy.* **scanty** *adj* **scantier, scantiest** **1** small in amount or extent **2** barely enough **scantily** *adv*

scapegoat *n* a person who is made to take the blame or punishment for what others have done

scar¹ *n* **1** a mark left where an injury or sore has healed **2** a lasting effect left by an unpleasant experience **scar** *v* **scarred,**

scarring to mark something with a scar, or to form a scar

scar² n a steep mountainside or high cliff

scarab (say ska-rəb) n an ancient Egyptian carving of a beetle

scarce adj not enough to supply a demand or need, rare **scarcely** adv **1** only just, almost not ♦ *She is scarcely 10 years old.* ♦ *I scarcely know him.* **2** surely not ♦ *You can scarcely expect me to believe that.* **scarcity** n pl **scarcities**, **to make yourself scarce** informal to leave or keep out of the way

scare v to frighten a person or animal, or to become frightened suddenly **scare** n **1** a sudden fright **2** a sudden widespread sense of alarm about something ♦ *a bomb scare* **scary** adj **scarier**, **scariest** frightening, causing alarm **scarily** adv **scarecrow** n an object made to resemble a human figure dressed in old clothes, set up in a field to scare birds away from crops

scarf¹ n pl **scarves** a length of material worn round the neck or head for warmth or decoration

scarf² n a joint made by thinning the ends of two pieces of timber or metal, so that they overlap without an increase of thickness

scarify (say ska-ri-fiy or skair-i-fiy) v **scarifies**, **scarified**, **scarifying 1** to loosen the surface of soil, etc. **2** to make light surgical cuts in the skin or tissue

scarlatina (say skar-lə-teen-ə) n scarlet fever

scarlet adj of a brilliant red colour **scarlet** n scarlet colour **scarlet fever** n an infectious fever caused by bacteria, producing a scarlet rash

scarp n a steep slope on a hillside

scarper v informal to run away

scathing (say skay-thing) adj severely scornful or critical

scatter v **1** to throw or move something in different directions **2** to leave in different directions after being in a group **scatter** n an amount of something scattered about **scatterbrain** n a person who is disorganized and absent-minded **scatterbrained** adj

scatty adj **scattier**, **scattiest** informal scatterbrained, absent-minded

scavenge v **1** (said about an animal) to search for decaying flesh as food **2** to search for useful objects or material among rubbish or discarded things **scavenger** n

scenario (say sin-ar-i-oh) n pl **scenarios 1** an outline of a story **2** an imagined sequence of events

scene n **1** the place at which something happened ♦ *Police were at the scene of the crime.* **2** a piece of continuous action in a play or film, or an incident thought of as resembling this **3** a dramatic or public outburst of temper or emotion ♦ *Try not to make a scene.* **4** pieces of scenery used on a stage **5** a landscape or view as seen by a spectator **6** informal an area of activity ♦ *the music scene* **scenery** n **1** the natural features of a landscape regarded in terms of their visual effect **2** painted background and other equipment used on a theatre stage to represent features in the scene of the action **scenic** adj having fine natural scenery

scent n **1** a distinctive pleasant smell **2** a sweet-smelling liquid made from essence of flowers or aromatic chemicals; perfume **3** the trail left by an animal and perceptible to other animals, especially to hounds in pursuit **scent** v **1** to discover something by a sense of smell ♦ *The dog had scented a rat.* **2** to begin to suspect the presence or existence of something ♦ *She scented trouble.* **3** to put scent on something to make it fragrant

sceptic (say skep-tik) n someone who doubts the truth of beliefs and claims ◊ Note the difference between *sceptic* and *cynic*. A sceptic tends by nature to doubt the things that people say, whereas a cynic doubts the integrity and worth of the people saying them. **sceptical** adj **sceptically** adv **scepticism** n

sceptre (say sep-ter) n a staff or rod carried by a king or queen as a symbol of their power

schedule (say shed-yool) n a plan for carrying out work or completing a sequence of events, with times for the completion of each stage **schedule** v **1** to include an item or event in a schedule **2** to organize or arrange something for a

scheme 522 scoop

certain time ♦ *We are scheduled to arrive at ten o'clock.*

scheme (say skeem) *n* **1** a systematic or detailed plan of action or work **2** a secret or underhand plan, a plot **3** a planned arrangement of something ♦ *a colour scheme* **scheme** *v* to make plans, especially in a secret or underhand way **schematic** *adj* having the form of a diagram or chart **schemer** *n*

schism (say sizm) *n* the division of a group or organization into opposing sections because of an important difference in belief or opinion **schismatic** *adj*

schizophrenia (say skitz-ə-freen-iə) *n* a mental illness in which a person becomes unable to relate their thoughts and feelings to reality, often leading to a withdrawal into fantasy and delusion **schizophrenic** *adj*

schmaltz (say shmawlts) *n* cloying sentimentality, especially in music or literature **schmaltzy** *adj*

schnapps (say shnaps) *n* a strong alcoholic drink like gin

scholar *n* **1** a person with great knowledge of a particular subject **2** a university student who holds a scholarship **scholarly** *adj* **scholarship** *n* **1** a grant of money to pay for a person's education, usually awarded on the basis of academic achievement **2** the work of scholars, advanced academic work **scholastic** *adj* to do with schools or education, academic

school[1] *n* **1** an institution for educating children **2** an institution for teaching a particular subject or activity ♦ *a driving school* **3** the pupils of a school **4** a department of a university ♦ *the School of Medicine* **5** a group of people following the same teachings or principles **school** *v* to train or educate someone **schooling** *n* education received at a school **schoolchild** *n pl* **schoolchildren** a child at school **schoolboy** *n* **schoolgirl** *n*

school[2] *n* a large group of sea mammals or fish

schooner (say skoo-ner) *n* **1** a sailing ship with two or more masts **2** a tall glass

sciatic (say siy-at-ik) *adj* **1** to do with the hip **2** to do with a nerve (called the *sciatic nerve*) which runs from the lower end of the spinal cord to the thigh **sciatica** *n* a pain in the sciatic nerve, affecting the back, hip, and outer side of the leg

science *n* **1** a branch of knowledge concerned with the physical world, studied by means of observation and experiment, e.g. physics, chemistry, and biology **2** any study involving experiment and observation of data, as distinct from creative or imaginative study **scientific** *adj* **1** to do with science or scientists **2** using careful and systematic study and methods **scientifically** *adv* **scientist** *n* someone who studies or is an expert in one or more of the natural or physical sciences **science fiction** *n* stories about imaginary scientific discoveries or about space travel and life on other planets

sci-fi (say siy-fiy) *n informal* science fiction

scimitar (say sim-it-er) *n* a short sword with a curved blade, originally used in oriental countries

scintillate (say sin-til-ayt) *v* **1** to give off sparks or flashes of light **2** to be lively and witty **scintillation** *n*

scion (say siy-ən) *n* a descendant of a noble family or one with a long lineage

scissors *pl n* a cutting instrument made of two blades with handles for the thumb and fingers of one hand, pivoted in the middle

scoff[1] *v* to speak with scorn or contempt about something

scoff[2] *v informal* to eat food quickly or greedily

scold *v* to rebuke someone angrily **scold** *n old use* a woman who constantly nags or grumbles

sconce *n* an ornamental wall bracket for holding a candle or electric light

scone (say skon or skohn) *n* a soft flat unsweetened or slightly sweetened cake

scoop *n* **1** a tool like a spoon with a deep bowl, used for taking liquids or other substances out of a container **2** a scooping movement **3** an important piece of news published by one newspaper ahead of its rivals **scoop** *v* **1** to lift something out with a scoop **2** to be ahead of a rival newspaper with a news story

scoot v to go away or leave somewhere hurriedly **scooter** n 1 a child's toy for riding on, with a footboard on wheels and a long handle for steering 2 a kind of lightweight motorcycle with small wheels and a protective shield below the handlebars

scope n 1 the range or limit of an activity or task ♦ *This topic is outside the scope of the inquiry.* 2 an opportunity or possibility for doing something ♦ *She is looking for work that gives her scope for her abilities.*

scorch v to make something go brown by burning it slightly, or to become brown in this way **scorch** n a mark made by scorching **scorcher** n 1 a very hot day 2 something remarkable

score n 1 the number of points or goals achieved by each player or side in a game or competition 2 a reason or motive ♦ *He was rejected on the score of being too young.* 3 old use a set of twenty 4 a large amount or number ♦ *I have written scores of letters.* 5 a line or mark cut into a surface 6 Mus a written version of a composition showing the notes on sets of staves ◊ The plural in meaning 3 is **score**: *three score and ten = 70.* **score** v 1 to gain a point or goal in a game 2 to keep a record of the score 3 to achieve something ♦ *She scored a great success with her first novel.* 4 to cut a line or mark into a surface 5 Mus to write out a composition as a musical score, or to arrange a piece of music for particular instruments **scorer** n

scorn n strong contempt openly expressed **scorn** v 1 to show strong contempt for something or someone 2 to reject or refuse something with scorn **scornful** adj **scornfully** adv

Scorpio n (the Scorpion) the sign of the zodiac which the sun enters about 23 October **Scorpian** adj, n

scorpion n a small animal of the spider family with claws like a lobster and a long jointed tail that bends over and has a sting at the end

Scot n a native of Scotland **Scotch** adj old use to do with Scotland or Scottish people **Scotch** n whisky distilled in Scotland, especially from malted barley **Scots** adj Scottish **Scots** n the form of English used

in Scotland **Scottish** adj to do with or coming from Scotland **Scotch egg** n a hard-boiled egg enclosed in sausage meat and breadcrumbs and fried

scotch v to put an end to something ♦ *The rumour had to be scotched without delay.*

scot-free adj without being punished or harmed

scoundrel n a dishonest or wicked person

scour[1] v 1 to cleanse or brighten something by rubbing it 2 to clear out a pipe or channel by the force of water flowing through it **scour** n the action of scouring **scourer** n

scour[2] v to search an area thoroughly

scourge (say skerj) n 1 a whip for flogging people 2 a person or thing that causes great trouble or difficulty **scourge** v 1 to whip someone with a scourge 2 to cause someone great trouble or difficulty

Scouse (say skowss) n informal 1 (also **Scouser**) a person born or living in Liverpool 2 the dialect of Liverpool **Scouse** adj informal to do with or coming from Liverpool

scout n 1 a person sent out to collect information, e.g. about an enemy's movements or strength 2 a ship or aircraft used for reconnaissance 3 (**Scout**) a member of the Scout Association **scout** v 1 to act as scout 2 to make a search

scowl n a severe or angry frown **scowl** v to make a scowl

scrabble v 1 to grope or struggle to find or obtain something 2 to make a scratching movement or sound with the hands or feet

scrag v **scragged**, **scragging** informal to seize or handle someone roughly **scraggy** adj **scraggier**, **scraggiest** thin and bony

scram v **scrammed**, **scramming** informal to go away

scramble v 1 to move hurriedly and with difficulty over rough ground, often using the hands and feet 2 to struggle to do or obtain something ♦ *Everyone scrambled for the ball.* 3 (said about an aircraft or the crew) to hurry and take off quickly, especially to attack an invading enemy 4 to mix things together indiscriminately 5 to cook eggs by mixing them and heating the mixture in a pan until it thickens **6** to alter the frequency of a radio or telephone signal so that the information transmitted is unintelligible except to a person with a decoding device **scramble** n **1** a climb or walk over rough ground, using the hands and feet **2** an eager struggle to do or obtain something **3** a motorcycle race over rough ground **scrambler** n

scrap[1] n **1** a small piece of something, especially when it is left after the rest has been used **2** rubbish or waste material, especially discarded metal suitable for reprocessing **scrap** v **scrapped, scrapping** to discard something that is useless or unwanted **scrappy** adj **scrappier, scrappiest** made up of an odd or untidy assortment of things **scrapbook** n a book of blank pages for sticking in newspaper cuttings, drawings, etc.

scrap[2] n informal a fight or quarrel **scrap** v **scrapped, scrapping** informal to fight or quarrel

scrape v **1** to pass a hard or sharp object across a surface **2** to make something clean, smooth, or level by doing this **3** to make the sound of scraping **4** to obtain or accumulate something with difficulty or by careful saving ♦ *They managed to scrape a living.* **5** to be very economical **scrape** n **1** a scraping movement or sound **2** a mark or injury made by scraping **3** an awkward situation resulting from mischief or foolishness **scraper** n **to scrape through** to get through a difficult situation or pass an examination by only a small margin

scratch v **1** to make a shallow mark or wound on a surface with something sharp **2** to scrape the skin with the fingernails to relieve itching **3** to obtain something with difficulty ♦ *They managed to scratch a living.* **4** to cancel something by drawing a line through it **5** to withdraw from a race or competition **scratch** n **1** a mark or wound made by scratching **2** the action or a spell of scratching **scratch** adj collected from whatever is available ♦ *a scratch team* **scratchy** adj **scratchier, scratchiest, to start from scratch** to begin at the very beginning or with nothing prepared **up to**

scratch up to the required standard

scrawl n hurried or careless handwriting that is difficult to read **scrawl** v to write in a scrawl

scrawny adj **scrawnier, scrawniest** thin and bony **scrawniness** n

scream v **1** to make a long piercing cry of pain, fear, anger, or excitement **2** to utter something in a screaming tone **scream** n **1** a screaming cry or sound **2** informal an extremely amusing person or thing

scree n a mass of loose stones on a mountainside

screech n a harsh, high-pitched scream or sound **screech** v **1** to make a screech **2** to utter something with a screech

screed n a long and tedious piece of writing

screen n **1** an upright partition used to divide an area or to conceal or protect something **2** a blank surface on which pictures, cinema films, television transmissions, or computer data are projected or displayed **screen** v **1** to shelter, conceal, or protect someone or something **2** to show a film or television pictures on a screen **3** to examine or test people for the presence or absence of a disease **4** to examine an applicant for a post or position of authority to ensure they are suitable **screenplay** n the script of a film, with directions for the movement and behaviour of the actors **screen printing** n a printing process like stencilling with ink or dye forced through a prepared sheet of fine fabric **screen test** n a trial to see if a person is suitable for a part in a film

screw n **1** a metal pin with a spiral ridge (called a *thread*) round its length, used for holding things together by being twisted in, or secured by a nut **2** informal a prison officer **screw** v **1** to fasten or tighten something with a screw **2** to turn a screw **3** to turn something with a twisting movement **4** informal to swindle someone **screwy** adj **screwier, screwiest** crazy or eccentric **screwdriver** n a tool with a narrow end that fits into the slot on the head of a screw to turn it **to screw something up 1** to crush a piece of paper or material into a tight mass **2** to tense the muscles of the face or eyes **3** to summon up courage **4** *informal* to bungle or mismanage something

scribble *v* **1** to write hurriedly or untidily **2** to make meaningless marks **scribble** *n* something written or drawn hurriedly or untidily

scribe *n* **1** a person who made copies of writings before the development of printing **2** a professional religious scholar in New Testament times

scrimmage *n* a confused struggle or fight

scrimp *v* to skimp

script *n* **1** handwriting, especially as distinct from print **2** the text of a play, film, or broadcast **3** a candidate's written answers in an examination **script** *v* to write a script for a film or broadcast

scripture *n* **1** the sacred writings of a religion **2** the biblical writings of the Christians (the Old and New Testaments) or the Jews (the Old Testament) **scriptural** *adj*

scrofula (say **skrof**-yoo-lə) *n* a disease causing glandular swellings

scroll *n* **1** a roll of paper or parchment for writing on **2** an ornamental design resembling a partly unrolled scroll **scroll** *v* to move the display on a computer screen up or down in order to view different parts of it

Scrooge *n* a person who is mean with money

scrotum (say **skroh**-təm) *n* a pouch of skin that contains the testicles

scrounge *v informal* to get something you are not really entitled to, especially by stealth **scrounger** *n*

scrub[1] *v* **scrubbed, scrubbing 1** to rub a surface hard with something coarse or bristly, especially in order to clean it **2** *informal* to cancel or scrap an arrangement **scrub** *n* the action of scrubbing

scrub[2] *n* vegetation consisting of stunted trees or shrubs, or land covered with this **scrubby** *adj* **scrubbier, scrubbiest** small and shabby

scruff *n* the back of the neck as used to grasp, lift, or drag a person or animal

scruffy *adj* **scruffier, scruffiest** shabby and untidy **scruffily** *adv*

scrum, scrummage *n* **1** (in rugby) a formation in which the forwards on each side push against each other and try to get possession of the ball when this is thrown on the ground between them **2** a milling or disorderly crowd

scrumping *n informal* stealing fruit from an orchard or garden

scrumptious *adj informal* (said about food) delicious

scrumpy *n informal* rough strong cider

scrunch *v* **1** to make a loud crunching noise **2** to crush or crumple something

scruple *n* a feeling of doubt or hesitation about doing or allowing something because you think it may be wrong **scruple** *v* to hesitate to do something you think may be wrong **scrupulous** *adj* **1** very careful and conscientious **2** very concerned not to do wrong **scrupulously** *adv* **scrupulousness** *n*

scrutiny *n pl* **scrutinies** a careful look at or examination of something **scrutinize** *v* to look at or examine something carefully

scuba diving *n* swimming underwater using a breathing apparatus strapped to the back

scud *v* **scudded, scudding** to move quickly and lightly

scuff *v* **1** to scrape or drag your feet in walking **2** to mark or damage a shoe or boot by doing this **scuff** *n* a mark made by scuffing

scuffle *n* a brief confused struggle or fight at close quarters **scuffle** *v* to take part in a scuffle

scull *n* each of a pair of small oars used by a single rower **scull** *v* to row with sculls

scullery *n pl* **sculleries** a small room where dishes, etc. are washed up

sculpture *n* **1** the art of making three-dimensional shapes and figures in wood, stone, or metal **2** a work made in this way **sculpture** *v* to make a sculpture to represent a person or thing **sculpt** *v* to make sculptures **sculptor** *n* **sculptural** *adj*

scum *n* **1** a layer of dirt or froth on the surface of a liquid **2** *informal* a worthless or contemptible person or group of people **scummy** *adj*

scupper *n* an opening in a ship's side to let

water drain from the deck **scupper** v **1** to sink a ship deliberately **2** *informal* to wreck or thwart a plan or intention

scurf n flakes of dry skin, especially from the scalp **scurfy** adj

scurrilous (say **sku-ril-əs**) adj abusive and insulting ♦ *scurrilous attacks in the newspapers*

scurry v **scurries**, **scurried**, **scurrying** to run hurriedly with quick short steps **scurry** n pl **scurries** the act of scurrying, a rush

scurvy n a disease caused by lack of vitamin C in the diet

scut n the short tail of a rabbit, hare, or deer

scuttle[1] n a container for coal in a room of a house

scuttle[2] v to let water into a ship in order to sink it

scuttle[3] v to scurry or hurry away **scuttle** n the act or sound of someone scuttling

scythe (say **siyth**) n a tool with a long curved blade for cutting long grass or crops **scythe** v to cut grass or crops with a scythe

SE abbr south-east or south-eastern

sea n **1** the expanse of salt water that covers most of the earth's surface and surrounds the continents **2** a particular named part of this ♦ *the Black Sea* **3** a large expanse of something ♦ *a sea of faces* **sea anemone** n a tube-shaped sea animal with short tentacles round its mouth **seabed** n the ground under the sea **seabird** n a bird that frequents the sea or coastal areas **seaboard** n the coastline or the region near it **seafaring** adj, n working or travelling by sea, especially as an occupation **seafood** n fish or shellfish from the sea eaten as food **seagoing** adj (said about a ship) suitable for travelling on the sea **seagull** n a gull **sea horse** n a small fish that swims in an upright position, with a head and neck like that of a horse **sea level** n the level corresponding to that of the surface of the sea halfway between high and low water **sea lion** n a kind of large seal **seaman** n pl **seamen** a sailor, especially one below the rank of officer in the navy **seaplane** n an aeroplane with floats instead of wheels, designed to land on and take off from water **seascape** n a picture or view of the

sea **seashell** n the shell of a mollusc living in salt water **seasick** adj sick or unwell from the motion of a ship **seasickness** n **sea urchin** n a sea animal with a round shell covered in sharp spikes **seaweed** n a plant that grows in the sea or on rocks washed by the sea **seaworthy** adj (said about a ship) in a fit condition for a sea voyage **at sea 1** in a ship on the sea **2** confused, not knowing what to do **to get your sea legs** to become used to the motion of a ship at sea

seal[1] n a sea mammal that breeds on land, with thick fur or bristles and short limbs that serve as flippers

seal[2] n **1** a device or substance used to close an opening or joint and prevent air or liquid, etc. from passing through it **2** a gem or piece of metal with an engraved design that is pressed on wax or other soft material to leave an impression **3** a piece of wax bearing this impression, attached to a document as a guarantee of its authenticity **seal** v **1** to fasten or close something securely **2** to attach a seal to something **3** to stamp or certify a document as authentic by attaching a seal **4** to settle or decide something ♦ *His fate was sealed.* **sealant** n a substance used for coating a surface to make it watertight **to seal something off** to prevent access to an area

seam n **1** a line where two pieces of fabric are joined together **2** a line where two pieces of wood or other material meet each other **3** a layer of a mineral such as coal or gold in the ground **seam** v **1** to join pieces of fabric by means of a seam **2** to mark something with a wrinkle or scar **seamstress** n a woman who sews, especially for a living

seamy adj **seamier**, **seamiest** disreputable or sordid

seance (say **say-ahns**) n a meeting at which people try to make contact with the dead

sear v to burn or scorch something with a strong heat **searing** adj (said about a pain) felt as a sudden burning sensation

search v **1** to look carefully and thoroughly in a place in order to find something **2** to examine the clothes and body of a person to see if something is concealed there **search** *n* the action of searching **searcher** *n* **searching** *adj* thorough or probing **searchlight** *n* an outdoor electric light with a powerful beam that can be turned in any direction

season *n* 1 each of the four main parts of the year (spring, summer, autumn, and winter) marked by particular characteristics of weather and daylight 2 the time of year when a particular fruit, vegetable, etc. is plentiful, or when a particular activity takes place ♦ *the football season* **season** *v* 1 to give extra flavour to food by adding salt, pepper, or other sharp-tasting substances 2 to dry and treat timber to make it fit for use **seasonable** *adj* 1 suitable for a particular season ♦ *Hot weather is seasonable in summer.* 2 timely or opportune **seasonal** *adj* done in or associated with a particular season of the year ♦ *the seasonal migration of birds* **seasoned** *adj* experienced and competent because of training and practice ♦ *a seasoned soldier* **seasoning** *n* a substance used to season food **season ticket** *n* a ticket that can be used repeatedly over a given period

seat *n* 1 a piece of furniture or other object made or used for sitting on 2 the level part of a chair on which a sitter's body rests 3 a place where someone can sit, especially a place for one person to sit in a theatre or vehicle 4 a place as a member of a council or committee 5 a parliamentary constituency as offering a right to sit in parliament ♦ *She won the seat at the last election.* 6 the buttocks, or the part of a skirt or trousers covering them 7 a place where something is based or located ♦ *a seat of learning* 8 a country estate belonging to an aristocratic family **seat** *v* 1 to give someone a place to sit 2 to provide sitting accommodation for a particular number of people ♦ *The hall seats 1,000.* **seat belt** *n* a belt for securing a person to a seat in a motor vehicle or aircraft

sebum (say **see**-bəm) *n* a natural oil produced by glands (called *sebacious glands*) in the skin to lubricate the skin and hair

secateurs (say sek-ə-**terz** or **sek**-ə-terz) *pl n* clippers used with one hand for pruning plants

secede (say si-**seed**) *v* to withdraw formally from membership of an organization **secession** *n*

seclude *v* to keep someone away from other people **secluded** *adj* (said about a place) sheltered from view, private **seclusion** *n*

second¹ (say **sek**-ənd) *adj* 1 next after first 2 another after the first ♦ *We deserve a second chance.* 3 inferior or less good **second** *n* 1 a person or thing that is second 2 an attendant of a person taking part in a boxing match or duel 3 a sixtieth part of a minute of time or of a degree in measuring angles **second** *adv* in second place or position **second** *v* to support a motion formally in a debate **seconds** *pl n* 1 goods of second-class quality, sold at a reduced price 2 *informal* a second helping of food at a meal **secondary** *adj* 1 coming after something that is primary 2 of lesser importance or rank than the first 3 derived from what is primary or original ♦ *secondary sources* **seconder** *n* **secondly** *adv* second, as a second consideration **secondary school** *n* a school for children over the age of about eleven **second class** *n* 1 a set of people or things grouped together as second-best 2 the second-best accommodation on a train, ship, or aircraft 3 a category of mail that is less urgent than first class **second-hand** *adj* 1 (said about goods) bought after use by a previous owner 2 obtained or experienced at second hand **second nature** *n* a habit or characteristic that has become automatic **second person** *n* see *person* **second-rate** *adj* of inferior or poor quality **second sight** *n* the supposed power to foresee future events **to get your second wind** to recover normal breathing after being out of breath **to have second thoughts** to have doubts or change your mind about a previous decision

second² (say si-**kond**) *v* to transfer a person temporarily to another job or department **secondment** *n*

secret *adj* not known or seen by other people, or not meant to be known or seen by them **secret** n **1** a fact or piece of information that is kept or meant to be kept secret **2** something no one fully understands ♦ *the secrets of nature* **3** a method for achieving something that is not known to everyone ♦ *the secret of good health* **in secret** without other people knowing **secrecy** n **secretive** adj wanting to keep things secret and not make information known **secretly** adv **secret agent** n a spy acting for a country **secret service** n a government department responsible for conducting espionage

secretariat (say sek-ri-**tair**-i-at) n an administrative office or department of a government or international body

secretary (say **sek**-rə-tri) n pl **secretaries 1** a person employed in an office to help deal with correspondence and filing, make business arrangements for people, and similar work **2** an official of a society or organization in charge of the correspondence and keeping records **3** the principal assistant of a government minister or ambassador **secretarial** adj to do with the work a secretary does

secrete (say si-**kreet**) v (said about an organ or cell) to produce a substance for use in the body (such as bile) or for excretion from the body (such as urine) **secretion** n **secretory** adj

sect n a group of people whose religious or other beliefs differ from those more generally accepted **sectarian** adj **1** to do with or belonging to a sect or sects **2** putting the beliefs or interests of a sect before more general interests

section n **1** a distinct part or portion of something **2** a division of an organization **3** a cross section **4** *Medicine* the process of cutting or separating a part of the body by surgery **section** v to divide something into sections **sectional** adj

sector n **1** a division of an area of military operations **2** a distinct division of an activity ♦ *the private sector of industry*

secular (say **sek**-yoo-ler) adj **1** to do with worldly affairs rather than spiritual or religious ones **2** not involving or belonging to religion

secure adj **1** safe, especially against attack **2** well fixed or fitted, certain not to slip or fall **3** certain or reliable **secure** v **1** to make something secure **2** to fasten something securely **3** to obtain something **4** to guarantee a loan by pledging something as security ♦ *The loan is secured on the house.* **securely** adv **security** n pl **securities 1** a state or feeling of being secure **2** something that gives this feeling **3** precautions taken to protect a country or organization from dangers such as espionage or theft **4** a thing that serves as a guarantee or pledge for a loan **5** a certificate showing ownership of financial stocks or shares

sedan (say si-**dan**) n N. Am a saloon car **sedan chair** an enclosed chair for one person, mounted on two poles and carried by two bearers

sedate[1] (say si-**dayt**) adj calm and dignified **sedately** adv **sedateness** n

sedate[2] (say si-**dayt**) v to treat someone with sedatives **sedation** n **sedative** n a medicine that makes a person calm or sends them to sleep **sedative** adj having a calming or soothing effect

sedentary (say **sed**-ən-ter-i) adj involving a lot of sitting down and not much physical exercise

sedge n a grass-like plant growing in marshes or near water

sediment n **1** fine particles of solid matter that float in a liquid or settle at the bottom of it **2** solid matter such as sand and gravel that is carried by water or wind and settles on the surface of land

sedition (say si-**dish**-ən) n actions or speech that make people rebel against the authority of the state **seditious** adj

seduce (say si-**dewss**) v **1** to persuade someone to do wrong by offering temptations **2** to persuade someone to have sexual intercourse **seducer** n **seduction** n **seductive** adj tending to seduce someone, temptingly attractive or alluring **seductively** adj **seductiveness** n

sedulous (say **sed**-yoo-ləs) adj diligent and persevering

see[1] v saw, seen **1** to perceive something or someone with the eyes **2** to have or use the power of perceiving with the eyes **3** to perceive something with the mind, to understand something ♦ *Do you see what I mean?* **4** to have a certain opinion about something ♦ *This is the way I see it.* **5** to consider or think about something ♦ *We must see what we can do.* **6** to find out about something ♦ *I'll go and see who is at the door.* **7** to watch an entertainment or be a spectator at an event ♦ *They went to see a film.* **8** to experience or undergo something ♦ *He saw active service in the war.* **9** to visit or meet someone ♦ *I am going to see my aunt tomorrow.* **10** to escort or conduct someone ♦ *I'll see you to the door.* **11** to make sure of something ♦ *See that the windows are shut.* **seeing** conjunction because, since ♦ *I'll have to do it, seeing you won't be here.* **to see about** to attend to something **to see red** to be suddenly angry **to see someone off** to go to the station, airport, etc. with someone who is leaving **to see something through** to complete a task despite difficulties **to see the light 1** to understand something after failing to do so **2** to realize your mistakes **to see through** to understand the true nature of something

see² *n* the district of which a bishop or archbishop has charge

seed *n pl* **seeds** or **seed 1** a fertilized part of a plant, capable of developing into a new plant **2** a quantity of seeds for sowing **3** something that can give rise to a feeling or tendency ♦ *The remarks sowed the seeds of hope in their minds.* **4** each of several players in a tournament who are identified as especially strong so as not to be matched against each other in early rounds **seed** *v* **1** to plant seeds in something **2** to remove seeds from fruit **3** to identify the strong players in a tournament and arrange for them not to be matched against each other in early rounds **seedling** *n* a very young plant growing from a seed **seedy** *adj* **seedier, seediest** *informal* shabby and disreputable **to go** or **run to seed 1** to stop flowering as the seed develops **2** to deteriorate in appearance or ability

seek *v* past tense and past participle **sought**

1 to try to find something or someone **2** to try to obtain or do something

seem *v* to give the appearance or impression of being something ♦ *She seems worried about her work.* **seeming** *adj* giving the impression of being something but not necessarily being this in fact **seemly** *adj* proper or suitable, in accordance with accepted standards of good taste

seep *v* (said about a liquid) to ooze slowly out or through something **seepage** *n*

seer *n* a prophet, a person who sees visions

seersucker *n* a fabric woven with a puckered surface

see-saw *n* a long board balanced on a central support so that a person (especially a child) can sit on each end and make it go up and down by pushing the ground alternately with their feet **see-saw** *v* **1** to ride on a see-saw **2** to change rapidly from one state to another and back again

seethe *v* **1** to bubble or surge like water when it boils **2** to be very angry or excited

segment (say seg-mənt) *n* a part that is cut off or separates naturally from other parts ♦ *a segment of an orange* **segmentation** *n* division into segments

segregate (say seg-ri-gayt) *v* **1** to put something apart from the rest, to isolate something **2** to separate people of different races, sexes, religions, etc. **segregation** *n*

seismic (say siy-zmik) *adj* **1** to do with earthquakes or other vibrations of the earth **2** having an enormous importance or effect **seismically** *adv* **seismograph** *n* an instrument that detects, records, and measures earthquakes **seismology** *n* the study and recording of earthquakes and other vibrations of the earth **seismological** *adj* **seismologist** *n*

seize *v* **1** to take hold of a person or thing suddenly or forcibly **2** to take possession of something by force or by legal authority **seizure** *n* **1** the process of seizing something **2** a sudden fit or attack, such as a stroke or a heart attack **to seize on** to make use of an opportunity eagerly **to seize up** (said about machinery) to become stuck or jammed because of friction or undue heat

seldom adv rarely, not often

select v to choose something or someone carefully as being the best or most suitable **select** adj **1** carefully chosen ♦ *a select group of pupils* **2** (said about a club, society, etc.) admitting only certain people as members, exclusive **selection** n **1** the process of selecting, or of being selected **2** a person or thing that has been selected **3** a group selected from a larger group **4** a range of things from which to make a choice **selective** adj **1** chosen or choosing carefully **2** involving or allowing a choice **selectively** adv **selectivity** n **selector** n

self n pl **selves 1** a person as an individual ♦ *one's own self* **2** a person's special nature ♦ *She has fully recovered and is her old self again.* **3** a person's own interests or advantage ♦ *He always puts self first.* **selfish** adj concerned with your own wishes and needs and ignoring those of other people **selfishly** adv **selfishness** n **selfless** adj thinking of other people, unselfish

self- prefix of or to or done by yourself or itself **self-assured** adj confident in yourself **self-assurance** n **self-catering** adj catering for yourself, instead of having meals provided **self-centred** adj thinking chiefly of yourself or your own affairs, selfish **self-confessed** adj openly admitting oneself to be something ♦ *a self-confessed traitor* **self-confident** adj confident of your own abilities **self-confidence** n **self-conscious** adj embarrassed or awkward in manner because you know that people are watching you **self-consciously** adv **self-consciousness** n **self-contained** adj **1** complete in itself **2** (said about accommodation) having all the necessary facilities without having to share **self-destruct** v (said about a device) to destroy itself automatically **self-determination** n a country's right to rule itself and choose its own government **self-effacing** adj keeping yourself in the background **self-employed** adj working independently and not for an employer **self-esteem** n confidence in your own worth and abilities **self-evident** adj clear without

needing to be explained or proved **self-explanatory** adj understandable without needing explanation **self-important** adj having a high opinion of your own importance, pompous **self-importance** n **self-indulgent** adj indulging your own pleasures and comforts **self-interest** n your own personal advantage **self-made** adj rich or successful from your own efforts **self-possessed** adj calm and dignified **self-raising** adj (said about flour) containing its own raising agent, without the need for baking powder **self-respect** n proper regard for yourself and your own principles and standing **self-righteous** adj smugly sure that you are thinking or behaving rightly **selfsame** adj the very same **self-satisfied** adj ostentatiously pleased with yourself and your own achievements, conceited **self-seeking** adj selfishly seeking to promote your own interests and welfare **self-service** adj (said about a restaurant, shop, etc.) at which customers help themselves and pay at a checkout **self-styled** adj using a name or description that you may not be entitled to ♦ *self-styled experts* **self-sufficient** adj able to produce or provide what you need without help from other people **self-willed** adj obstinately doing what you want, stubborn

sell v past tense and past participle **sold 1** to transfer the ownership of goods, or to provide a service, in exchange for money **2** to keep a stock of goods for sale, to be a dealer in a commodity **3** to promote the sales of something ♦ *The author's name alone will sell many copies.* **4** (said about goods) to be bought ♦ *The book is selling well.* **5** to be on sale at a certain price ♦ *It sells for £3.99.* **6** to convince someone of the merits of something ♦ *We tried to sell him the idea of merging the two departments.* **sell** n informal an act of selling something, or the manner of selling something **seller** n **1** a person who sells something **2** a thing that sells well or badly ♦ *The new models are proving to be good sellers.* **to sell out 1** to sell all the stock of a commodity **2** to abandon your principles to gain an advantage **to sell someone out** to betray someone for your own advantage **to sell something off** to dispose of something by selling it at a reduced price **to sell up** to sell a house or business and change location or line of work

Sellotape n trademark a transparent adhesive tape **sellotape** v to fix or seal something with this tape

selvedge, **selvage** n an edge of cloth woven so that it does not unravel

semantic (say sim-**an**-tik) adj to do with meaning in language **semantics** n the study of language concerned with meaning

semaphore (say **sem**-ə-for) n a system of signalling by holding the arms in positions that indicate letters of the alphabet

semblance (say **sem**-bləns) n an outward appearance or show

semen (say **see**-men) n a white fluid containing sperm, produced by male animals

semester (say sim-**est**-er) n a half-year term or course of study at a school or university, especially in America

semi n pl **semis** informal a semi-detached house

semi- prefix half or partly **semicircle** n half of a circle **semicircular** adj **semicolon** n the punctuation-mark (;), used to separate parts of a sentence where there is a more distinct break than that marked by a comma **semiconductor** n a substance that can conduct electricity but not as well as most metals do **semiconducting** adj **semi-detached** adj (said about a house) joined to another house on one side by a common wall, but not joined on the other side **semi-final** n each of the matches or rounds preceding a final, in which there are four contestants or teams **semi-finalist** n **semi-precious** adj (said about a mineral or gem) considered to be less valuable than those called precious

seminal (say **sem**-in-əl) adj 1 to do with seed or semen 2 giving rise to new ideas or developments ♦ seminal ideas

seminar (say **sem**-in-ar) n a small class or meeting for advanced discussion and research

seminary (say **sem**-in-er-i) n pl **seminaries**

a training college for priests or rabbis

Semite (say **see**-miyt) n a member of the group of people speaking a Semitic language, including the Jews and Arabs and formerly the Phoenicians and Assyrians **Semitic** adj to do with the Semites or their languages

semolina n hard round grains left when flour has been milled, used to make puddings and pasta

senate (say **sen**-ət) n 1 the state council of the ancient Roman Republic and Roman Empire 2 the upper house of the parliamentary assemblies of the USA, France, and certain other countries 3 the governing body of a university or college **senator** n a member of a senate **senatorial** adj

send v past tense and past participle **sent** 1 to cause someone or something to go or be taken to a place 2 to make someone or something move, especially violently ♦ The blow sent him flying. 3 to put a person or animal into a certain state ♦ The lecture sent everyone to sleep. **sender** n **send-off** n a friendly demonstration at a person's departure **send-up** n a humorous parody or imitation **send for 1** to order someone to come to you 2 to order goods to be brought or delivered **send someone down** 1 to expel a student from a university 2 to send a convicted person to prison **to send something up** informal to make fun of something by imitating it

senile (say **see**-niyl) adj suffering from the physical or mental weaknesses of old age **senility** n

senior adj 1 older than someone else 2 higher in rank or authority 3 to do with children above a certain age ♦ senior school **senior** n a senior person **senior citizen** n an elderly person, especially a pensioner **seniority** n

senna n the dried pods or leaves of a tropical tree, used as a laxative

sensation n 1 a physical feeling or awareness resulting from stimulation of a sense organ or of the mind 2 the ability to feel this stimulation ♦ loss of sensation in the fingers 3 a condition of great public interest or excitement ♦ *The news caused a sensation.*

sensationalism n the use of sensational subjects or language to produce public interest or excitement **sensationalist** n, adj

sensational adj **1** producing great public interest or excitement **2** informal wonderful, amazing **sensationally** adv

sense n **1** the ability to see, hear, touch, taste, or smell things **2** ability to perceive or feel or be conscious of a thing ♦ *He has no sense of shame.* **3** the power to make good decisions; a sound practical judgement ♦ *They had the sense to keep out of the way.* **4** the meaning, or one of the meanings, of a word, phrase, or passage **sense** v to perceive something **senseless** adj **1** not showing good sense, foolish **2** unconscious, having no sensation **sensor** n a device that measures or reacts to a physical property **sensory** adj to do with the senses or sensation ♦ *sensory nerves* **sensual** adj **1** to do with the physical senses, especially as a source of pleasure **2** liking physical or sexual pleasures, or suggesting these **sensually** adv **sensuality** n **sensuous** adj affecting or giving pleasure to the senses, especially on account of beauty or delicacy **sensuously** adv

sensible adj **1** having or showing good sense **2** formal aware ♦ *We are sensible of the fact that maths is not a popular subject generally.* **3** (said about clothing) practical rather than fashionable **sensibility** n pl **sensibilities** sensitiveness, delicacy of feeling **sensibly** adv

sensitive adj **1** affected by or responsive to a physical stimulus ♦ *Plants are sensitive to light.* **2** receiving impressions quickly and easily ♦ *She has sensitive fingers.* **3** easily hurt or damaged ♦ *sensitive skin* **4** alert and considerate about other people's feelings **5** (said about a person) easily hurt or offended **6** (said about a subject) requiring tactful treatment **7** (said about an instrument, etc.) readily responding to or recording slight changes of condition **sensitively** adv **sensitivity** n **sensitize** v to make something sensitive or abnormally sensitive

sentence n **1** a group of words, usually containing a verb, that expresses a complete thought and forms a statement, question, exclamation, or command **2** the punishment given by a law court to a person convicted of a crime **sentence** v to give a convicted person a sentence in a law court

sententious (say sen-ten-shos) adj giving moral advice in an affected or self-satisfied way **sententiousness** n

sentient (say sen-shont) adj capable of perceiving and feeling things

sentiment n **1** an opinion or mental attitude produced by your feeling about something **2** emotion as opposed to reason, sentimentality **sentimental** adj **1** showing or affected by feelings of tenderness, sadness, or nostalgia **2** having these feelings in an exaggerated or self-indulgent way **sentimentality** n **sentimentally** adv

sentinel n a guard or sentry

sentry n pl **sentries** a soldier posted to keep watch and guard something

separate (say sep-er-ot) adj forming a unit by itself, not joined or united with others **separate** (say sep-er-ayt) v **1** to divide something or make or keep it separate **2** to be between two places ♦ *The Channel separates England from France.* **3** to become separate, to go different ways **4** to stop living together as a couple **separable** adj **separately** adv **separation** n **1** the process of separating, or of being separated **2** a legal arrangement by which a couple live apart while remaining married

separatism n a policy of separation from a larger unit, especially in order to achieve political independence **separatist** n

sepia (say seep-io) n **1** a brown colouring matter used in inks and water colours **2** a rich reddish-brown colour of a kind found in early photographic prints

sepoy (say see-poi) n hist a native Indian soldier serving under British or other European orders

September n the ninth month of the year

septet n a group of seven musicians, or a musical composition for seven voices or instruments

septicaemia (say septi-seem-io) n blood

poisoning caused by bacteria

septuagenarian (say sep-tew-ə-jin-**air**-iən) *n* a person who is between 70 and 79 years old

septum *n pl* **septa** the partition in the nose between the nostrils

sepulchre (say **sep**-əl-ker) *n* a tomb **sepulchral** *adj*

sequel *n* **1** a book or film, etc. that continues the story of an earlier one **2** something that happens after an earlier event or as a result of it

sequence *n* **1** the following of one thing after another in a regular or continuous way **2** the order in which things occur **3** a series or set of things that belong next to each other in a particular order **4** a section dealing with one scene or topic in a film or broadcast **sequential** *adj* **sequentially** *adv*

sequester (say si-**kwest**-er) *v* **1** to isolate or seclude someone or something **2** to confiscate something **sequestration** *n*

sequin (say **see**-kwin) *n* a small bright disc, one of several sewn on clothing for decoration

sequoia (say si-**kwoi**-ə) *n* a coniferous tree of California, growing to a great height

Serb *n* a person born in Serbia or descended from people born there **Serbian** *n* **1** another word for *Serb* **2** the language of Serbia **Serbian** *adj* to do with or coming from Serbia **Serbo-Croat** *n* the language spoken in Serbia, Croatia, and elsewhere in the former republics of Yugoslavia

serenade *n* a song or tune of a kind played by a man under his lover's window **serenade** *v* to sing or play a serenade to someone

serendipity (say se-rən-**dip**-iti) *n* the ability or habit of making pleasant or interesting discoveries by accident

serene *adj* calm and peaceful **serenely** *adv* **serenity** *n*

serf *n* in the Middle Ages, a farm labourer who worked for a landowner and was not allowed to leave the place where he worked **serfdom** *n*

serge *n* a strong woven fabric used for making clothes

sergeant (say **sar**-jənt) *n* **1** a soldier ranking

below a sergeant major and above a corporal **2** a police officer ranking below an inspector **sergeant major** *n* a warrant officer in the British army who assists the adjutant of a regiment or battalion

serial *n* a story or film, etc. that is shown in separate instalments **serial** *adj* to do with or forming a series **serialize** *v* to produce a story or film, etc. as a serial **serially** *adv*

series *n pl* **series** **1** a number of similar things that are related to each other or come one after another **2** a number of separate television or radio programmes on the same theme

serious *adj* **1** solemn and thoughtful, not smiling **2** sincere and earnest, not casual or light-hearted ♦ *He made a serious attempt to improve.* **3** needing serious thought, important ♦ *a serious matter* **4** causing great concern, not slight ♦ *a serious illness* **seriously** *adv* **seriousness** *n*

sermon *n* **1** a talk on a religious or moral subject, especially one given by a member of the clergy during a religious service **2** a long or tedious talk admonishing or rebuking someone **sermonize** *v* to give a long moralizing talk

serpent *n* a large snake, especially in stories **serpentine** *adj* twisting and curving like a snake

serrated (say ser-**ay**-tid) *adj* having a jagged or notched edge like the teeth of a saw

serried *adj* (said about rows of people or things) arranged or standing close together

serum (say **seer**-əm) *n pl* **sera** or **serums** **1** a thin pale yellow fluid that remains from blood when the rest has clotted **2** this fluid taken from an animal and used in inoculations to provide immunity

servant *n* **1** a person employed to work in a household or as a personal attendant **2** an employee regarded as performing services for an employer

serve *v* **1** to perform duties or services for a person, organization, country, etc. **2** to be employed as a member of the armed forces ♦ *He served in the Navy for many years.* **3** to be suitable for something ♦ *This will serve our purpose very well.* **4** to provide a facility for people, a community, etc. ♦ *The area is served by a number of buses.* **5** to spend time in something, to undergo something ♦ *He had served a long prison sentence.* **6** to attend to customers in a shop **7** to set out or present food or drink for people **8** (in tennis and other games) to hit the ball to your opponent to start play **9** to deliver a legal writ, etc. to the person named **serve** *n* a service in tennis, etc. **server** *n* **1** a person or thing that serves **2** a computer or program that controls or supplies information to several computers connected to a network **serving** *n* a portion of food at a meal **it serves you right** it is what you deserve

service *n* **1** the status or process of working for a person or organization **2** a department of people employed by the state or by a public organization ♦ *the Secret Service* **3** a system or arrangement that supplies people with their needs ♦ *a train service* **4** a religious ceremony following a prescribed form **5** the process of serving food or drink in a restaurant, etc. **6** the process of attending to customers in a shop, etc. **7** a regular process of maintaining and repairing a motor vehicle or piece of machinery **8** a set of dishes, plates, etc. for serving a meal ♦ *a dinner service* **9** (in tennis and other games) the act or manner of serving, or the game in which a particular player serves **service** *v* **1** to maintain or repair a motor vehicle or piece of machinery **2** to supply someone with a service or services **serviceable** *adj* **1** serving its purpose well, practical **2** suitable for ordinary use or wear, hard-wearing **serviceman**, **servicewoman** *n pl* **servicemen**, **servicewomen** a man or woman serving in the armed services **service station** *n* a place beside a road, where petrol and other services are available

serviette *n* a table napkin

servile (say **ser**-viyl) *adj* **1** to do with slaves or slavery **2** excessively submissive or willing to serve others **servility** *n*

servitude *n* the condition of having to work for others and having no freedom or independence

sesame (say sess-ə-mi) *n* a plant of tropical Asia with seeds that are used as food or as a source of oil

session *n* **1** a meeting or series of meetings for discussion ♦ *The Queen will open the new session of Parliament.* **2** a period spent in an activity ♦ *a recording session* **3** the academic year in certain universities

set *v* past tense and past participle **set**; **setting** **1** to put or place something in position ♦ *Set the vase on the table.* **2** to adjust a clock or other mechanism **3** to represent a story or film, etc. as happening in a certain place or at a certain time ♦ *The story is set in Russia at the time of the Revolution.* **4** to provide music for words ♦ *The composer also set several poems by Blake.* **5** to fix or decide on something ♦ *Have they set a date for the wedding?* **6** to arrange and protect a broken bone so that it will heal **7** to establish something ♦ *She has set a new record for the high jump.* **8** to offer or assign something as a task to be done ♦ *She set them an essay to write over the weekend.* **9** to become firm or hard, or to make something do this ♦ *Leave the jelly to set.* **10** to put someone or something into a specified state ♦ *The soldiers set them free.* **11** (said about the sun) to appear to move towards or below the horizon by the earth's movement **set** *n* **1** a number of people or things that belong together or are used together **2** *Mathematics* a collection of things having a common property **3** a radio or television receiver **4** (in tennis and other games) a group of games forming a unit or part of a match **5** the way something sets or is set, placed, or arranged ♦ *the set of his jaw* **6** the scenery used for a play or film, or the stage or location where this is being performed **set** *adj* **1** fixed or arranged in advance ♦ *a set time* **2** (said about a substance) having become solid **3** ready or prepared to do something **4** (said about a statement, etc.) having a fixed wording **setting** *n* **1** the way or place in which something is set **2** music for the words of a song, etc. **3** a set of cutlery or crockery for one person at a meal **setback** *n* something that stops or slows progress **set square** *n* an instrument in the shape of a right-angled triangle, used for drawing lines in a certain relation to each other **set-to** n a fight or argument **set-up** n the structure of an organization **to set off** to start on a journey **to set someone up 1** *informal* to lead someone on in order to cheat or incriminate them **2** to establish someone in a role **to set something** or **someone back** to halt or slow the progress of something or someone **to set something off 1** to make it begin working or cause it to happen **2** to cause a bomb, firework, etc. to explode **3** to improve the appearance of something by providing a contrast **to set something up** to arrange or organize something **to set to** to begin doing something with energy

sett n a badger's burrow

settee n a long soft seat with a back and arms, for two or more people; a sofa

setter n a long-haired dog that is trained to stand rigid when it scents game

settle[1] v **1** to arrange or deal with something, especially to end a disagreement or dispute **2** to agree or decide on something ♦ *We still have to settle where we are going for our holiday.* **3** to become calm and able to concentrate, especially after being restless, or to make someone do this ♦ *I'm finding it hard to settle to work.* **4** to establish someone or something more or less permanently, or to become established in this way **5** to come to rest in a certain position, or to become compact by doing this ♦ *The snow has settled on minor roads.* **6** to pay a debt or claim **7** to bestow something legally on someone ♦ *He settled all his property on his wife.* **settlement** n **1** the process of settling something **2** an amount or property settled legally on a person **3** a place where people establish a community or colony **settler** n a person who goes to live in a place, especially one that was previously uninhabited **to settle down 1** to become settled after movement or restlessness **2** to follow a steady lifestyle, especially by establishing a home or family

settle[2] n a wooden seat for two or more people, with a high back and arms and often a box-like compartment under the seat

seven adj, n the number 7, one more than six **seventh** adj, n **1** next after sixth **2** one of seven equal parts of a thing

seventeen adj, n the number 17, one more than sixteen **seventeenth** adj, n

seventy adj, n pl **seventies** the number 70, equal to seven times ten **seventieth** adj, n

sever (say sev-er) v **1** to separate or divide something by cutting **2** to end a connection or relationship **severance** n

several adj, n **1** more than two but not many **2** separate or individual ♦ *They all went their several ways.* **severally** adv separately

severe (say si-veer) adj **1** strict or harsh **2** (said about something bad, unwelcome, or demanding) great or intense ♦ *Severe gales are expected.* **3** plain and without decoration **severely** adv **severity** n

sew (say soh) v past participle **sewn** or **sewed 1** to join or repair material by passing thread many times through it, using a needle or sewing machine **2** to make or fasten something by sewing

sewage (say soo-ij) n waste water and excrement carried away from buildings in drains **sewer** n an underground pipe for carrying away sewage and drainage water **sewerage** n a system of sewers

sex n **1** each of the two main groups (*male* and *female*) into which human beings and other living things are placed according to their reproductive functions **2** the attraction between members of the two sexes, sexual feelings or impulses **3** sexual activity, especially sexual intercourse **sex** v to judge the sex of a living thing ♦ *to sex chickens* **sexism** n discrimination against members of one sex, especially women **sexist** n, adj **sexuality** n **1** the fact of belonging to one of the sexes **2** sexual characteristics or impulses, or the capacity for having these **sexual** adj **1** to do with sex or the sexes, or with the attraction between the sexes **2** (said about reproduction) involving the fusion of male and female cells **sexually** adv **sexy** adj **sexier**, **sexiest** sexually attractive or stimulating **sexual intercourse** n a sexual act between two people, in which a man puts his erect penis into a woman's vagina

sexagenarian (say seks-ə-jin-**air**-iən) n a person who is between 60 and 69 years old

sextant n an instrument for finding your position by measuring the altitude of the sun and stars, used in navigating and surveying

sextet n a group of six musicians, or a musical composition for six voices or instruments

sexton n a person who looks after a church and churchyard

sextuplet (say seks-tew-plit) n each of six children born at one birth

shabby adj **shabbier**, **shabbiest** 1 worn and threadbare, not kept in good condition 2 (said about a person) poorly dressed 3 unfair or dishonourable **shabbily** adv **shabbiness** n

shack n a roughly built hut or shed **to shack up with** informal to live with someone, especially as their lover

shackle n each of a pair of iron rings joined by a chain, for fastening a prisoner's wrist s or ankles **shackle** v 1 to put shackles on a person, especially a prisoner 2 to restrict or limit someone

shade n 1 slight darkness or coolness produced when something blocks rays of light or heat 2 shelter from the light and heat of the sun, or a place providing this shelter 3 a colour, or the degree or depth of a colour 4 a slight difference ♦ The word has many shades of meaning. 5 a small amount ♦ It's a shade warmer today. 6 literary a ghost 7 a screen or cover used to block or reduce light or heat **shade** v 1 to block the rays of a source of light or heat, or to protect something from these 2 to give shade to something, to make something dark 3 to darken parts of a drawing or painting so as to give effects of light and shade or differences of colour 4 to pass gradually from colour or variety to another ♦ The blue here shades into green. **shady** adj **shadier**, **shadiest** 1 giving shade ♦ a shady tree 2 situated in the shade ♦ a shady corner 3 informal disreputable, not completely honest ♦ shady dealings

shadow n 1 a dark area or shape produced when an object comes between a source of light and a surface 2 partial darkness, shade 3 someone who attends or accompanies a person closely 4 a slight trace 5 (used before a noun) a member of the Opposition in Parliament who has responsibility for a particular area of politics ♦ the shadow chancellor **shadow** v 1 to cast a shadow over a surface 2 to follow and watch someone secretly 3 to accompany and observe a person doing their work, so as to learn about it **shadowy** adj **shadow boxing** n boxing against an imaginary opponent as a form of training

shaft n 1 a long narrow straight part of something ♦ the shaft of an arrow 2 a ray of light 3 a forceful or provocative remark ♦ shafts of wit 4 a large rotating rod transmitting power in a machine 5 each of a pair of long bars between which a horse is harnessed to a vehicle 6 a deep passage or opening giving access to a mine or giving an outlet for air or smoke

shag n 1 a rough mass of hair or fibre 2 a carpet with a rough pile 3 a strong coarse kind of tobacco 4 a kind of cormorant with a long curly crest **shaggy** adj **shaggier**, **shaggiest** 1 having long rough hair or fibre 2 thick and untidy ♦ shaggy hair

shake v **shook**, **shaken** 1 to move quickly up and down or from side to side, or to make something do this 2 to shock or disturb someone, or to upset their calmness 3 to make something less firm 4 (said about a voice) to tremble or sound weak or faltering 5 to shake hands **shake** n an act of shaking, or a shaking movement **shaker** n a container in which ingredients are mixed by being shaken **shaky** adj **shakier**, **shakiest** 1 shaking or unsteady 2 unsafe or unreliable **shakily** adv **to shake someone up** to rouse someone from sluggishness or apathy **to shake something up** 1 to mix something by shaking it 2 to make radical changes to an organization or procedure

shale n a kind of stone that splits easily into fine layers, like slate

shall auxiliary verb 1 used with I and we to express the ordinary future tense in statements and questions ♦ I shall arrive tomorrow. ♦ *Shall I close the door?* **2** used with words other than *I* and *we* to express a promise or obligation ♦ *You shall have a party.* ◊ Note that in meaning 1 *will* is used with words other than *I* and *we*: *They will arrive tomorrow. Will you close the door? Will*, as well as *shall*, can be used with *I* and *we* in statements: *I will arrive tomorrow.*

shallot (say she-**lot**) *n* a plant producing an onion-like bulb that is used in cookery

shallow *adj* **1** not deep **2** not showing or needing deep thought or feeling **shallow** *n* a shallow place **shallowness** *n*

shalt *v* a form of *shall*; used with *thou* ♦ *Thou shalt not steal.*

sham *n* a person or thing that is not what they claim to be, a pretence **sham** *adj* pretended, not genuine **sham** *v* **shammed**, **shamming** to pretend to be something

shaman (say **sham**-ən) *n* a person regarded as being able to contact and influence the world of good and evil spirits

shamble *v* to walk or run in a slow or awkward way

shambles *n informal* a scene or state of great confusion or disorder **shambolic** *adj*

shame *n* **1** a feeling of sorrow and guilt caused by having done something wrong or foolish **2** the ability to feel this ♦ *They have no shame.* **3** a person or thing that causes shame **4** something regrettable, a pity ♦ *It's a shame the weather's not better.* **shame** *v* to cause someone shame ♦ *They were shamed into contributing more.* **shameful** *adj* causing shame, disgraceful **shamefully** *adv* **shameless** *adj* having or showing no feeling of shame **shamelessly** *adv* **shamefaced** *adj* looking ashamed

shammy *n pl* **shammies** *informal* a chamois leather

shampoo *n pl* **shampoos** **1** a liquid or cream used to lather and wash the hair **2** a liquid or chemical for cleaning a carpet or upholstery, or for washing a car **3** the act of washing with a shampoo **shampoo** *v* **shampoos**, **shampooed**, **shampooing** to wash or clean something with a shampoo

shamrock *n* a clover-like plant with three leaves on each stem, the national emblem of Ireland

shandy *n pl* **shandies** a drink of beer mixed with lemonade or another soft drink

shanghai (say shang-**hiy**) *v* **shanghais**, **shanghaied**, **shanghaiing** to take someone by force or trickery and force them to do something

shank *n* **1** a person's leg, especially the part below the knee **2** the lower part of an animal's leg, especially as a cut of meat **3** a long narrow part of something, a shaft

shan't *v* shall not

shantung *n* a kind of soft Chinese silk, or a fabric resembling this

shanty[1] *n pl* **shanties** a roughly built shack **shanty town** *n* a settlement of shanty dwellings

shanty[2] *n pl* **shanties** a traditional song sung by sailors

shape *n* **1** an area or form with a definite outline, or the appearance produced by this **2** the form or condition in which something appears ♦ *a monster in human shape* **3** the general form or condition of something ♦ *the shape of British industry* **shape** *v* **1** to give something a certain shape **2** to develop into a certain shape or condition ♦ *The plan is shaping well.* **3** to adapt or modify plans or ideas, etc. **shapeless** *adj* not having a distinct or an attractive shape **shapely** *adj* **shapelier**, **shapeliest** having an attractive shape, well formed or proportioned

shard *n* a broken piece of pottery or glass

share[1] *n* **1** a part given to one person or thing out of a larger amount which is being divided or allocated, or a part that an individual is entitled to **2** each of the equal parts that a company's capital is divided into and that gives the person who holds it the right to receive a proportion (called a *dividend*) of the profits **share** *v* **1** (also **share out**) to give portions of something to two or more people **2** to have a share of something, to possess or use something jointly with others ♦ *The sisters shared a room.* **shareholder** *n* a person who owns shares in a business company

share[2] *n* a ploughshare

sharia (say she-**ree**-ə) *n* the sacred law of Islam based on the teachings of the Koran

shark[1] n a large sea fish with sharp teeth and a prominent fin on its back

shark[2] n informal a person who extorts money from others

sharp adj 1 having a fine edge or point that is able to cut or pierce things 2 steep or angular, not gradual ♦ a sharp bend 3 distinct or well-defined ♦ in sharp focus 4 forceful or severe ♦ a sharp frost 5 (said about a sound) sudden and loud ♦ We heard a sharp cry. 6 (said about a taste or smell) strong and slightly sour 7 (said about a person) quick to perceive things, intelligent 8 unscrupulous 9 Mus above the correct pitch **sharp** adv 1 exactly, punctually ♦ at six o'clock sharp 2 suddenly ♦ The man stopped sharp. 3 Mus above the correct pitch **sharp** n Mus a note that is a semitone higher than the natural note; the sign # indicating this **sharpen** v **sharpener** n **sharper** n a swindler, especially at cards **sharpish** adv quickly or briskly **sharply** adv **sharpness** n **sharpshooter** n a person skilled in shooting

shatter v 1 to break something into small pieces, or to be broken in this way 2 to destroy something completely 3 to disturb or upset someone greatly

shave v 1 to cut growing hair off the skin with a razor 2 to cut or scrape thin slices from the surface of wood, metal, etc. 3 to graze something gently in passing 4 to reduce something by a small amount **shave** n the process of shaving hair from the face **shaven** adj shaved **shaver** n 1 a person or thing that shaves 2 an electric razor **shavings** pl n a **close shave** informal a narrow escape from injury or danger

shawl n a large piece of material worn round the shoulders or head or wrapped round a baby

she pronoun 1 the female person or animal mentioned 2 a vehicle, ship, or aircraft regarded as female

sheaf n pl **sheaves** 1 a bundle of corn stalks tied together after reaping 2 a bundle of arrows, papers, or other things laid lengthways together

shear v past participle **shorn** or **sheared** 1 to cut or trim something with shears or another sharp device 2 to cut the wool off a sheep or other animal 3 to break off, or cause something to break off, because of structural stress ♦ The wing bolts have sheared off. **shearer** n **shears** pl n a clipping or cutting instrument shaped like a large pair of scissors and worked with both hands

sheath n 1 a close-fitting covering 2 a cover for a blade or tool 3 a condom **sheathe** v 1 to put a knife or sword into a sheath 2 to enclose something, e.g. machinery, in a casing

shed[1] n a simply-made building, usually made of wood, used for storing things, sheltering animals, or as a workshop

shed[2] v past tense and past participle **shed**; **shedding** 1 to allow something to fall off ♦ Trees shed their leaves in autumn. 2 to take something off ♦ to shed your clothes 3 to allow a liquid to pour ♦ to shed tears 4 to give off light or heat

sheen n a shine or gloss

sheep n pl **sheep** a grass-eating animal with a thick fleecy coat, kept in flocks for its wool and its meat **sheepish** adj shy or embarrassed, especially from shame **sheepishly** adv **sheep dip** n a liquid for cleansing sheep of vermin or preserving their wool **sheepdog** n a dog trained to guard and herd sheep **sheepskin** n

sheer[1] adj 1 complete or pure, not mixed or qualified ♦ sheer joy 2 vertical or nearly vertical, with almost no slope ♦ a sheer drop 3 (said about fabric) very thin or transparent **sheer** adv directly, straight up or down ♦ The cliff rises sheer from the sea.

sheer[2] v to swerve from a course, to move sharply away

sheet[1] n 1 a large rectangular piece of cotton or similar fabric, used in pairs on a bed for a person to sleep between 2 a large thin piece of paper, glass, metal, or other material 3 a wide expanse of water, snow, or flame, etc.

sheet[2] n a rope or chain attached to the lower corner of a sail, to secure or adjust it

sheikh (say shayk) n an Arab leader, especially the head of an Arab tribe or village **sheikhdom** n

shekel (say shek-əl) n the unit of money in

Israel **shekels** pl n informal money or riches

shelf n pl **shelves 1** a flat length of wood or other rigid material fixed horizontally to a wall or in a cupboard or bookcase for books or other objects to be placed on **2** something resembling this, a ledge or step-like projection of land **shelve** v **1** to arrange something on a shelf or shelves **2** to fit a wall or cupboard, etc. with shelves **3** to put an idea or plan aside until a later time **4** to slope ♦ *The river bed shelves steeply here.* **shelving** n shelves, or material for making them **shelf life** n the length of time for which something remains usable **on the shelf** (said about a person) past an age when they are likely to get married

shell n **1** the hard outer covering of an egg, nut, etc., or of an animal such as a snail, crab, or tortoise **2** any structure that forms a framework or covering **3** a light boat for rowing races **4** a metal case filled with explosive, for firing from a large gun **shell** v **1** to take something out of its shell **2** to fire explosive shells at a target **shellfish** n pl **shellfish** a sea animal that has a shell, especially an edible kind such as an oyster, crab, or shrimp **shell shock** n a nervous disorder caused by prolonged exposure to battle conditions **to shell out** informal to pay out money

shellac (say shəl-**ak**) n thin flakes of a resinous substance used in making varnish

shelter n **1** something that offers protection against bad weather or danger **2** a place providing food and accommodation for homeless people **3** protection ♦ *Seek shelter from the storm.* **shelter** v **1** to provide someone with shelter **2** to protect someone from blame or difficulty **3** to find a shelter

shenanigans (say shin-an-i-gənz) pl n informal mischief or trickery

shepherd n a person who looks after a flock of sheep **shepherd** v to guide or direct people **shepherdess** n a woman who looks after a flock of sheep **shepherd's pie** n a pie of minced meat under a layer of mashed potato

sherbet n **1** a cooling drink of weak sweetened fruit juice **2** a fizzy sweet drink or the powder from which this is made

sheriff n **1** (in England and Wales) the chief executive officer of the Crown in a county, with certain legal and ceremonial duties **2** (in Scotland) the chief judge of a district **3** (in the USA) the chief law-enforcing officer of a county

Sherpa n pl **Sherpa** or **Sherpas** a member of a Himalayan people living on the borders of Nepal and Tibet

sherry n pl **sherries** a strong white sweet or dry wine originally from southern Spain

Shetland pony n a small strong shaggy pony

shibboleth (say shib-ə-ləth) n a custom or principle that distinguishes a particular class or group of people

shield n **1** a broad piece of armour carried on the arm to protect the body against missiles or blows in combat **2** a representation of a shield used for displaying a coat of arms, or as a trophy **3** an object, structure, or layer of material that protects something **shield** v to protect someone or something from harm or discovery

shift v **1** to change or move from one position to another, or to cause something to do this **2** (said about a situation, opinion, etc.) to change slightly **3** to transfer blame or responsibility to someone else **shift** n **1** a change of place, form, or condition **2** a group of workers who start work as another group finishes, or the time when they work ♦ *the night shift* **3** a straight dress with no waist **4** ICT a key that switches between two sets of characters or functions on a keyboard **shifty** adj **shiftier, shiftiest** deceitful or evasive, untrustworthy **shiftiness** n **shiftless** adj lazy, lacking resourcefulness and ambition

shilling n a former British coin, equal to 5p

shilly-shally v **shilly-shallies, shilly-shallied, shilly-shallying** to keep hesitating or changing your mind

shimmer v to shine with a soft light that appears to quiver **shimmer** n a shimmering effect

shin n **1** the front of the leg below the knee **2** a cut of meat from the lower part of a cow's leg **shin** v **shinned, shinning** to climb a steep surface by gripping with the arms and legs

shindig *n informal* **1** a noisy or lively party **2** a noisy disturbance

shine *v past tense and past participle* **shone** or (in meaning 4) **shined 1** to give out or reflect light, to glow or be bright **2** to excel in some way ♦ *He does not shine in maths.* **3** to direct a light ♦ *Shine the torch in the corner.* **4** *informal* to polish something to produce a shine **shine** *n* **1** brightness **2** a high polish **shiner** *n* a black eye **shiny** *adj* **shinier, shiniest, to take a shine to** *informal* to begin to like someone

shingle[1] *n* small rounded pebbles on a beach

shingle[2] *n* a rectangular piece of wood used as a roof tile

shingles *n* a painful disease caused by the chicken pox virus, with blisters forming along the path of a nerve or nerves

shinty *n* a Scottish game resembling hockey

ship *n* a large seagoing boat **ship** *v* **shipped, shipping** to transport goods, especially by sea **shipment** *n* **1** the process of shipping goods **2** a consignment of goods shipped **shipping** *n* **1** a country's ships **2** the process of transporting goods by ship **shipmate** *n* a person travelling or working on the same ship as another **shipshape** *adv, adj* tidy and in good order **shipwreck** *n* **1** the wrecking of a ship by a storm or accident at sea **2** a wrecked ship **shipwrecked** *adj* **shipyard** *n* a place where ships are built or repaired

-ship *suffix* forming nouns (as in *friendship, hardship, citizenship, membership*)

shire *n* a county **shire horse** *n* a heavy powerful breed of horse used for pulling loads

shirk *v* to avoid or neglect work or a duty **shirker** *n*

shirt *n* **1** a piece of men's clothing for the upper part of the body, made of a light material with a collar and sleeves and buttons down the front **2** a piece of clothing worn on the upper part of the body in certain sports **in your shirtsleeves** wearing a shirt without a jacket over it

shirty *adj* **shirtier, shirtiest** *informal* bad-tempered or annoyed

shiver[1] *v* to tremble with cold or fear **shiver** *n* a shivering movement **shivery** *adj*

shiver[2] *n* a splinter **shiver** *v* to break into splinters

shoal[1] *n* a large number of fish swimming together

shoal[2] *n* **1** an area of shallow water **2** an underwater sandbank visible at low tide

shock[1] *n* **1** a sudden unpleasant surprise, or the feeling that follows **2** an acute state of weakness caused by physical injury or pain or by mental shock **3** (also **electric shock**) a sudden discharge of electricity through part of the body **4** the effect of a violent shaking or impact **5** a violent shake of the earth's crust in an earthquake **shock** *v* **1** to make someone surprised and upset, to give someone a shock **2** to give someone an electric shock **shocker** *n* a person or thing that shocks **shocking** *adj* **1** causing great shock or disgust **2** *informal* very bad **shock absorber** *n* a device for absorbing jolts and vibrations in a vehicle

shock[2] *n* a bushy mass of hair

shoddy *adj* **shoddier, shoddiest** of poor quality, badly or cheaply made

shoe *n* **1** an outer covering for the foot, with a fairly stiff sole **2** a horseshoe **shoe** *v* **shoes, shod, shoeing** to fit a horse with a shoe or shoes **shoestring** *n* **on a shoestring** with only a small amount of money or other resources **shoehorn** *n* a curved piece of stiff material for easing your heel into the back of a shoe

shogun (say **shoh**-gən) *n* a hereditary commander in feudal Japan

shoo *interjection* a word used to frighten animals away **shoo** *v* **shoos, shooed, shooing** to drive away an animal by saying this

shoot *v past tense and past participle* **shot 1** to fire a gun or other weapon, or a missile **2** to kill or wound a person or animal with a bullet or arrow **3** to hunt animals with a gun for sport **4** to move or send something out swiftly or violently ♦ *He shot the rubbish into the bin.* **5** to move very fast ♦ *A police car shot past us.* **6** (said about a plant) to put forth buds or shoots **7** to take a shot at goal **8** to film or photograph something

♦ *The film was shot in Africa.* **shoot** *n* **1** a young branch of new growth of a plant **2** an expedition for shooting animals **shooter** *n* **shooting star** *n* a small rapidly moving meteor appearing like a star and then disappearing **shooting stick** *n* a walking stick with a small folding seat at the handle end and a spike at the other **shoot-out** *n* a battle or fight with guns

shop *n* **1** a building or room where goods or services are sold to the public **2** a workshop **shop** *v* **shopped**, **shopping 1** to go to a shop or shops to buy goods **2** *informal* to inform on someone, especially to the police **shopper** *n* **shopping** *n* **1** the process of buying goods in shops **2** the goods bought in shops **shop floor** *n* the part of a factory or workshop where production of goods is carried on, as distinct from administration **shoplifter** *n* a person who steals goods in a shop **shoplifting** *n* **shop-soiled** *adj* dirty, faded, or slightly damaged from being displayed or handled in a shop **shop steward** *n* a trade-union official elected by workers in a factory to represent them in dealings with the management **to shop around** to look for the best bargain **to talk shop** to talk at length or tediously about your own work

shore[1] *n* the land beside the sea or beside a lake **shoreline** *n* the line where the land meets the edge of the sea or a lake

shore[2] *v* to support a building or other structure with a beam or prop set at a slant **shore** *n* a support of this kind

short *adj* **1** small in length, measuring little from one end to the other **2** taking a small amount of time **3** (said about a person) small in height, not tall **4** not lasting, not going far into the past or future ♦ *a short memory* **5** not enough, or not having enough ♦ *Water is short.* ♦ *We are short of water.* **6** (said about a person or their manner) impolite or curt **7** (said about an alcoholic drink) small and concentrated, made with spirits **8** (said about pastry) rich and crumbly because it contains a lot of fat **9** (said about odds in betting) nearly even, reflecting a high level of probability **short** *adv* suddenly or abruptly **short** *n*

informal **1** a short drink **2** a short circuit **short** *v informal* to short-circuit, or to cause something to short-circuit **shortage** *n* a lack or scarcity of something that is needed **shorten** *v* **shortly** *adv* **1** in a short time, soon **2** in an impolite or curt manner **shorts** *pl n* short trousers that do not reach to the knee **shortbread** *n* a rich sweet biscuit made with butter **short-change** *v* **1** to give someone too little money as change, especially deliberately **2** to cheat someone **short circuit** *n* a fault in an electrical circuit in which current flows by a shorter route than the normal one **short-circuit** *v* **1** to have a short circuit, or to cause something to do this **2** to shorten or get round a process or procedure **shortcoming** *n* a fault or failure to reach the right standard **short cut** *n* a route or method that is quicker than the usual one **shortfall** *n* a shortage, or an amount by which something is less than it should be **shorthand** *n* a method of quick writing using special abbreviations and symbols **short-handed** *adj* having an insufficient number of workers or helpers **shortlist** *n* a list of selected candidates from whom the final choice is made **shortlist** *v* to put a candidate on a shortlist **short-lived** *adj* lasting a short time **short shrift** *n* impolite or curt treatment **short-sighted** *adj* **1** able to see things clearly only when they are close **2** lacking foresight or imagination **short-tempered** *adj* easily made angry **short-term** *adj* affecting only the immediate future, temporary **short wave** *n* a radio wave of a wavelength between 10 and 100 metres and a frequency of about 3 to 30 megahertz

shot[1] past tense and past participle of *shoot* **shot** *adj* (said about cloth) woven or dyed so that different colours show at different angles

shot[2] *n* **1** the firing of a gun or cannon, or the sound of this **2** a person judged by their skill in shooting ♦ *He's a good shot.* **3** *pl* **shot** a single missile for a cannon or gun, a non-explosive projectile **4** *pl* **shot** lead pellets for firing from small guns **5** a stroke in tennis, cricket, or billiards, etc. **6** an attempt to hit something or reach a target **7** *informal* an attempt to do something ♦ *Let's have a shot at the quiz.* **8** *informal* an injection **9** *informal* a small drink of spirits **10** a photograph, or a scene photographed or filmed **shotgun** *n* a gun for firing small shot at close range

should *auxiliary verb* used to express **1** an obligation or duty (= ought to) ♦ *You should have told me.* **2** something expected to happen ♦ *They should be here by ten o'clock.* **3** a possible event ♦ *If you should happen to see them.*

shoulder *n* **1** the part of the body at which an arm, or in animals a foreleg or wing, is attached **2** the part of the human body between this and the neck **3** the upper foreleg and adjacent parts of an animal as a cut of meat **4** a part that levels out below a slope or vertical surface ♦ *the shoulder of a bottle* **shoulder** *v* **1** to push someone or something with your shoulder **2** to carry something on your shoulder or shoulders **3** to take the blame or responsibility for something **shoulder blade** *n* each of the two large flat bones at the top of the back

shouldn't *v informal* should not

shout *n* a loud cry or call **shout** *v* to give a shout, to call out loudly **to shout someone down** to prevent someone from speaking by speaking loudly yourself

shove (say shuv) *n* a rough push **shove** *v* **1** to push someone or something roughly **2** *informal* to put something somewhere ♦ *Just shove it in the drawer.*

shovel *n* a tool like a spade with the sides turned up, used for lifting earth, coal, snow, etc. **shovel** *v* **shovelled, shovelling** **1** to move or clear something with a shovel **2** to scoop or push something roughly ♦ *He sat shovelling food into his mouth.*

show *v past participle* **shown** or **showed** **1** to allow or cause something to be seen ♦ *Show me your new car.* **2** to explain something or make someone understand it ♦ *Show us how to do it.* **3** to demonstrate or prove something ♦ *The evidence shows that he was speaking the truth.* **4** to guide or escort someone ♦ *I will show you out.* **5** to give an image of something ♦ *The picture*

shows the hotel. **6** to exhibit something in a show **7** to present a film or television programme for viewing **8** to display a certain feeling or quality ♦ *They showed genuine concern.* **9** to be able to be seen ♦ *The lining is showing.* **show** *n* **1** a display or exhibition **2** a public entertainment or performance **3** *informal* a business or undertaking ♦ *She runs the whole show now.* **4** an outward appearance or display ♦ *a show of friendship* **showy** *adj* **showier**, **showiest** likely to attract attention, bright and colourful **showily** *adv* **showiness** *n* **showing** *n* **1** the presentation of a cinema film or television programme **2** the evidence or quality that someone shows ♦ *On today's showing, he will succeed.* **show business** *n* the entertainment industry; the theatre, cinema, and broadcasting as a profession **showcase** *n* **1** a glass case for displaying articles in a shop, museum, etc. **2** an opportunity for presenting something publicly ♦ *The programme is a showcase for new talent.* **showdown** *n* a final test or confrontation **showjumping** *n* the sport of riding horses over fences and other obstacles, with penalty points for errors **showman** *n pl* **showmen** **1** a person who manages or organizes a circus, fair, or similar entertainment **2** a person who is good at entertaining **showmanship** *n* **show-off** *n* a person who tries to impress people boastfully **showpiece** *n* a fine example of something displayed for people to admire **showroom** *n* a large room where goods are displayed for people to look at **to show off** to try to impress people boastfully **to show something off** to display something well or conspicuously **to show up** **1** to be clearly visible **2** *informal* to appear, to come when expected

shower *n* **1** a brief fall of rain or snow **2** a lot of small things falling or arriving like rain ♦ *a shower of stones* **3** a device or cubicle in which a person stands under a spray of water to wash, or a wash in this **shower** *v* **1** to fall or arrive in a shower **2** to send or give a large number of letters or gifts to someone **3** to wash yourself in a shower **showery** *adj*

shrapnel *n* **1** pieces of metal scattered from an exploding bomb **2** a bomb designed to scatter pieces in this way

shred *n* **1** a small piece torn or cut off something **2** a small amount **shred** *v* **shredded, shredding** to tear or cut something into shreds **shredder** *n*

shrew *n* **1** a small mouse-like animal **2** *old use* a bad-tempered or nagging woman **shrewish** *adj*

shrewd *adj* having good sense or judgement, clever or astute **shrewdly** *adv* **shrewdness** *n*

shriek *n* a shrill cry or scream **shriek** *v* to give a shriek

shrike *n* a bird with a strong hooked beak that impales its prey on thorns

shrill *adj* (said about a voice or sound) piercing and high-pitched **shrill** *v* to make a shrill sound **shrillness** *n* **shrilly** *adv*

shrimp *n* **1** a small shellfish that turns pink when boiled **2** *informal* a very small person

shrine *n* an altar or chapel or other place that is considered to be holy because of its special associations

shrink *v* **shrank, shrunk 1** to make something smaller, or to become smaller; to contract **2** to move back or away from something out of fear or disgust **shrinkage** *n* the process of shrinking, or the amount by which something has shrunk **shrunken** *adj*

shrivel *v* **shrivelled, shrivelling** to become wrinkled and contract, or to make something do this, through lack of moisture

shroud *n* **1** a sheet in which a dead body is wrapped for burial **2** a thing that conceals or obscures something ♦ *a shroud of secrecy* **shroud** *v* **1** to wrap a body in a shroud **2** to protect or conceal something

shrub *n* a woody plant smaller than a tree and usually having separate stems starting at or near the ground **shrubbery** *n* *pl* **shrubberies** an area planted with shrubs **shrubby** *adj*

shrug *v* **shrugged, shrugging** to raise the shoulders slightly to show indifference, doubt, or helplessness **shrug** *n* an act of shrugging the shoulders **to shrug**

something off to dismiss something as unimportant

shudder *v* **1** to shiver violently with horror, fear, or cold **2** to make a strong shaking movement **shudder** *n* a shuddering movement

shuffle *v* **1** to walk without lifting the feet clear of the ground **2** to rearrange or jumble things **shuffle** *n* **1** a shuffling movement or walk **2** a rearrangement of people or things

shun *v* **shunned, shunning** to avoid or keep away from someone or something

shunt *v* **1** to move a train or wagons to another track **2** to divert someone or something to a less important place or position **shunt** *n* the process of shunting

shut *v* past tense and past participle **shut; shutting 1** to move something so as to cover or block an opening, to close something **2** to move or be moved into this position ♦ *The door shut with a bang.* **shutter** *n* **1** a panel or screen that can be closed over a window **2** a device in a camera that opens and closes to allow light to fall on the film **to shut down** to stop working or doing business, either for the day or permanently **to shut someone up** *informal* to make someone stop talking **to shut something up** to shut a place securely **to shut up** *informal* to stop talking

shuttle *n* **1** a form of public transport that travels regularly between two places **2** a holder carrying the weft thread to and fro across the loom in weaving, or the lower thread in a sewing machine **shuttle** *v* to move, travel, or send something backwards and forwards **shuttlecock** *n* a small, rounded piece of cork with a crown of feathers or similar materials, struck to and fro by players in badminton

shy[1] *adj* **shyer, shyest 1** (said about a person) timid and reserved in the presence of other people **2** showing shyness ♦ *a shy smile* **shy** *v* **shies, shied, shying** to jump or move suddenly in alarm **shyly** *adv* **shyness** *n*

shy[2] *v* **shies, shied, shying** to fling or throw something at a target **shy** *n* *pl* **shies** a throw

SI *abbr* an internationally recognized system of metric units and measurements, including the metre, kilogram, ampere, and kelvin

Siamese *adj* to do with or coming from Siam (now called Thailand) or its people or language **Siamese cat** *n* a cat with short pale fur and a darker face, ears, tail, and feet **Siamese twins** *pl n* twins born with their bodies partially joined

sibilant *adj* having a hissing sound **sibilant** *n* a speech sound that sounds like hissing, e.g. *s* and *sh*

sibling *n* a brother or sister

sibyl (say **sib**-il) *n* an ancient Greek or Roman prophetess

sic *adv* used or spelt in the way given ◊ This word is placed in brackets after a word that seems odd or is wrongly spelt, to show that it is being quoted exactly as in the original.

sick *adj* **1** ill; physically or mentally unwell **2** likely to vomit ♦ *He said he felt sick.* **3** distressed or disgusted ♦ *Their attitude makes me sick.* **4** (said about humour) making fun of something unpleasant or upsetting **sick** *v informal* to bring soething up by vomiting **sick** *n informal* vomit **sickly** *adj* **sicklier**, **sickliest 1** often ill or in poor health **2** causing sickness or nausea ♦ *a sickly smell* **sickness** *n* **sicken** *v* to make someone disgusted or appalled, or to become disgusted or appalled **to be sickening for** to show the first symptoms of a disease **sickbay** *n* a room or building for people who are sick, especially in a ship or school **sick of** tired of something or someone because you have had too much of them

sickle *n* a tool with a curved blade and a short handle, used for cutting corn, etc.

side *n* **1** a surface of something, especially one joining the top and bottom, front and back, or ends **2** each of the surfaces of a flat object, e.g. a piece of paper **3** each of the bounding lines of a plane figure such as a triangle or square **4** each of the two halves into which something can be divided by a line down its centre **5** the part near the edge and away from the centre of something **6** a slope of a hill or ridge **7** the place or region next to a person or thing ♦ *Her husband stood at her side.* **8** one aspect or view of something ♦ *We have to study all sides of the problem.* **9** each of two groups or teams who oppose each other **10** a person's line of descent traced through their father or mother ♦ *He was of German origin on his mother's side.* **side** *adj* at or on the side **side** *v* to support someone in a dispute or disagreement ♦ *She sided with her son.* **siding** *n* a short track at the side of a railway line and linked to it with points **sideline** *n* **1** something done in addition to your main work or activity **2** each of the lines on the two long sides of a sports pitch **on the sidelines** in a position of watching events rather than taking part in them **sideboard** *n* a long piece of furniture with a flat top and drawers and cupboards for cutlery and other things for a dining table **sideburns** *pl n* a strip of hair growing on the side of a man's face in front of his ears **sidecar** *n* a small low vehicle attached to the side of a motorcycle, for carrying a passenger **side effect** *n* a secondary and usually unwanted effect that a drug or action has as well as the main effect **sidekick** *n* a close associate or subordinate **sidelong** *adv, adj* to one side, sideways **side saddle** *n* a saddle for a rider to sit with both legs on the same side of the horse, used by women wearing skirts **side-saddle** *adv* sitting in this position on a horse **sideshow** *n* **1** a small show or display at a fair or exhibition **2** a minor but interesting or diverting incident or activity **sidestep** *v* **sidestepped**, **sidestepping 1** to avoid something by stepping sideways **2** to evade a question or responsibility **sidetrack** *v* to divert someone's attention to the main subject or issue **sideways** *adv, adj* **1** to or from one side ♦ *Move it sideways.* **2** with one side facing forward ♦ *She sat sideways.* **on the side** as a separate activity or sideline, especially a secret or illicit one

sidereal (say siy-**deer**-iəl) *adj* to do with the stars, or measured by the stars

sidle *v* to walk in a shy or nervous manner

siege *n* **1** a military operation in which a force surrounds and blockades an enemy town or fortified position to force its surrender **2** an operation by a police team to force an armed person occupying a building to surrender

sienna (say si-**en**-ə) n a kind of clay used in making brownish paints, either reddish-brown (**burnt sienna**) or yellowish-brown (**raw sienna**)

sierra (say si-**e**-rə) n a long mountain chain with sharp slopes and a jagged outline, in Spain or parts of America

siesta (say si-**est**-ə) n pl **siestas** a short afternoon rest, especially in hot countries

sieve (say siv) n a utensil consisting of wire or plastic mesh in a frame, used for sorting solid or coarse matter from liquid or fine matter **sieve** v to put something through a sieve

sift v **1** to put something dry through a sieve in order to remove lumps and large particles **2** to examine and analyse facts or evidence, etc. carefully

sigh n a long sound made by breathing out heavily when you are sad, tired, relieved, etc. **sigh** v to give a sigh, or to express something with a sigh

sight n **1** the faculty or power of seeing with the eyes **2** the action or fact of seeing or being seen ♦ We lost sight of it. **3** the range over which a person can see or an object can be seen ♦ The group were now within sight of the castle. **4** a thing that is seen or worth seeing, an attractive display ♦ The garden is a wonderful sight in the spring. **5** informal a person or thing that looks unsightly or ridiculous **6** a device you look through to observe with a telescope or take aim with a weapon, or an aim or observation you make using this device **sight** v **1** to see or observe something **2** to aim or observe something with the sight of a gun or telescope **sighted** adj able to see, not blind **sightless** adj unable to see, blind **sightseeing** n visiting interesting places in a town, etc. ◊ Do not confuse this word with **site**, which has a different meaning.

sign n **1** an object, event, or thing said that shows the existence of something ♦ There are signs of corrosion in the bodywork. **2** a mark, device, or symbol that has a special meaning **3** a board or notice that gives information or an instruction ♦ a road

sign **4** an action or movement that gives information or a command, etc. **sign** v **1** to write your name on a document as an identification or authorization **2** to engage someone, or to be engaged, as an employee by signing a contract of employment **3** to make a sign ♦ She signed to me to come. **4** to use sign language **signatory** n pl **signatories** a person, organization, or country that signs a treaty or agreement **sign language** n a system of communication by gestures with the face and hands, used by and to deaf people **signpost** n a sign on a post at a road junction, etc. showing the names of places along each road **to sign on** to register as unemployed and claim state benefit

signal n **1** an action, sound, or gesture giving information or an instruction **2** a semaphore or set of lights on a road or railway, giving instructions to drivers as to whether they can continue **3** a sequence of electrical impulses or radio waves **signal** v **signalled**, **signalling 1** to make a signal or signals **2** to give someone information or an instruction in this way **signal** adj very good or bad ♦ a signal success **signaller** n **signally** adv **signal box** n a building from which railway signals, points, etc. are controlled **signalman** n pl **signalmen** a person who controls railway signals

signature n **1** a person's name or initials written when signing something **2** Mus a sign showing the key in which a piece of music is written, or the number of beats in the bar **signature tune** n a special tune used to announce a particular programme or performer

signet (say **sig**-nit) n a small seal used with or instead of a signature **signet ring** n a ring with an engraved design, formerly used as a seal

signify v **signifies**, **signified**, **signifying 1** to be a sign or symbol of something **2** to indicate something or make it known ♦ She signified her approval. **3** to be important, to matter ♦ It doesn't signify. **significance** n **1** what something means ♦ What is the significance of this symbol? **2** importance **significant** adj **1** having a meaning, indicating something **2** important or noteworthy **significantly** adv

Sikh (say **seek**) n a member of an Indian religion founded in northern India, believing in one God **Sikhism** n

silage (say **siy-lij**) n fodder made from green crops stored and fermented in a silo

silence n **1** absence of sound **2** avoidance or absence of speaking or of making a sound **3** not mentioning something or revealing information **silence** v to make a person or thing silent **silencer** n a device for reducing the sound made by something, especially a gun or a vehicle's exhaust system **silent** adj **1** not making or accompanied by a sound **2** not speaking **silently** adv

silhouette (say **sil-oo-et**) n **1** a dark shadow or outline seen against a light background **2** a portrait of a person in profile, showing the shape and outline only in solid black **silhouette** v to show a person or thing as a silhouette

silica (say **sil-i-kə**) n a hard white compound of silicon which occurs as quartz or flint and in sandstone and other rocks

silicon (say **sil-i-kən**) n a chemical element (symbol Si) found widely in the earth's crust and used to make transistors and electrical circuits **silicone** n a compound of silicon used in paints, varnish, and lubricants **silicon chip** n a microchip made of silicon

silk n **1** a fine strong soft fibre produced by silkworms in making cocoons **2** thread or cloth made from this fibre **silken** adj **silky** adj **silkier**, **silkiest**, **silkworm** n the caterpillar of a kind of moth, which feeds on mulberry leaves and spins a cocoon of silk

sill n a strip of stone, wood, or metal at the foot of a window or door

silly adj **sillier**, **silliest** lacking good sense, foolish or unwise **silliness** n

silo (say **siy-loh**) n pl **silos 1** a pit or tower for storing grain, cement, or radioactive waste **2** an underground place where a missile is kept ready for firing

silt n sediment deposited by running water in a channel or harbour, etc. **silt** v to fill or block a place with silt, or to become blocked with silt

silver n **1** a shiny white precious metal, a chemical element (symbol Ag) **2** coins made of this or of a silver-coloured metal **3** silver dishes or ornaments, or household cutlery of any metal **4** a silver medal, usually given as second prize **silver** adj made of silver; coloured like silver **silver** v **1** to coat or plate something with silver **2** to become silvery or grey **silvery** adj **1** like silver in colour or appearance **2** having a clear gentle ringing sound **silver birch** n a birch tree with a silver-coloured bark **silverfish** n pl **silverfish** or **silverfishes** a small insect with a fish-like body found in books and damp places **silver plate** n a thin layer of silver applied as a coating to another metal **silverside** n a joint of beef cut from the upper part of the leg **silver wedding** n the 25th anniversary of a wedding

SIM card n a card in a mobile phone, which holds a record of its number and stores other information

simian (say **sim-iən**) adj like a monkey

similar adj **1** like or resembling another person or thing but not identical **2** of the same kind, nature, or amount **similarity** n **similarly** adv

simile (say **sim-i-li**) n a figure of speech in which one thing is compared to another, as in He's as fit as a fiddle and They went through it like a hot knife through butter

similitude (say **sim-il-i-tewd**) n being similar, similarity

simmer v **1** to boil something gently **2** to be in a state of excitement or anger which is only just kept under control **to simmer down** to become less excited or agitated

simper v to smile in a coy or affected way **simper** n an affected smile

simple adj **1** not complicated or difficult, easy to understand or do **2** not elaborate or luxurious, plain **3** consisting of one element or kind, not compound or complex **4** feeble-minded **simpleton** n a foolish or gullible person **simplicity** n **simplify** v **simplifies**, **simplified**, **simplifying** to make something simple or more simple **simplification** n **simplistic** adj treating complicated things as being more simple than they are **simply** adv **1** in a simple manner **2** absolutely, without doubt ♦ The food was simply delicious. **3** merely ♦ It is simply the truth.

simulate v **1** to reproduce the appearance or conditions of something **2** to pretend to have or feel something ♦ They simulated indignation. **simulation** n **simulator** n

simultaneous (say sim-əl-**tayn**-iəs) adj occurring or done at the same time **simultaneity** n **simultaneously** adv

sin n **1** the breaking of a religious or moral law, or an act which does this **2** a serious fault or offence **sin** v **sinned**, **sinning** to commit a sin **sinful** adj **1** guilty of sin **2** wicked **sinfully** adv **sinless** adj **sinner** n

since conjunction **1** from the time when ♦ Where have you been since we last met? **2** because ♦ Since we've missed the bus we'll have to walk home. **since** prep from a certain time ♦ She has been here since Sunday. **since** adv **1** between then and now ♦ He ran away and hasn't been seen since. **2** ago ♦ It all happened long since.

sincere adj having or arising from genuine feelings, free from pretence **sincerely** adv **sincerity** n

sinecure (say **siy**-ni-kewr) n a position that gives payment or honour without the need for any work

sinew (say **sin**-yoo) n **1** tough fibrous tissue that connects muscle to bone **2** a tendon **sinewy** adj

sing v **sang**, **sung 1** to make musical sounds with the voice, especially in a set tune **2** to perform a song **3** to make an attractive whistling or humming sound **singer** n **sing-song** adj having a tone of voice or rhythm that falls and rises **sing-song** n informal an informal gathering for singing

singe (say sinj) v **singed**, **singeing** to burn something slightly, or to become burnt, especially at the edges **singe** n a slight burn

single adj **1** one only, not double or multiple **2** designed for one person or thing ♦ a single bed **3** taken separately ♦ every single thing **4** (said about a person) unmarried **5** (said about a ticket) valid for a journey to a place but not to return **single** n **1** a single person or thing **2** a short record with one piece of music on each side **3** a room, etc. for one person **4** a single ticket

single v to choose or distinguish one from others ♦ They singled him out for comment.

singles pl n a game of tennis or badminton with one player on each side **singly** adv

singular adj **1** Gram (said about a form of a noun or verb) used when it refers to one person or thing ♦ The singular form is 'child' and the plural form is 'children'. **2** unusual or exceptional ♦ A person of singular courage. **singularity** n **singularly** adv

single-breasted adj (said about a jacket or coat) fastening at the front with a single row of buttons down the centre and not overlapping across the breast **single file** n a line of people one behind the other **single-handed** adj without help from anyone else **single-minded** adj with your mind set on a single purpose

singlet n a vest or similar sleeveless piece of clothing worn by a man

sinister adj suggestive of harm or evil

sink v **sank**, **sunk 1** to go down below the surface of a liquid or (said about a ship) to the bottom of the sea; to cause something to do this **2** to fall slowly downwards; to come gradually to a lower level or pitch **3** to decline in amount or strength gradually **4** to cause something sharp to penetrate a surface **5** to dig a well or bore a shaft **6** to send a ball into a pocket or hole in billiards, golf, etc. **7** to invest money **sink** n a fixed basin with a water supply and drainage pipe **sinker** n a weight used to sink a fishing line or a line used in taking soundings **to sink in 1** to penetrate a surface **2** to become understood

sinuous (say **sin**-yoo-əs) adj having many curves or bends **sinuously** adv

sinus (say **siy**-nəs) n a cavity in bone or tissue, especially that in the skull connecting with the nostrils **sinusitis** n inflammation of a sinus

sip v **sipped**, **sipping** to take a small mouthful of liquid; to drink liquid in small mouthfuls **sip** n **1** the act of sipping **2** a small mouthful of liquid

siphon (say **siy**-fən) n a pipe or tube in the form of an upside-down U, used for forcing liquid to flow from one container to another at a lower level by means of atmospheric pressure **siphon** v **1** to flow through a siphon, or to draw liquid through a siphon **2** to take small amounts of something, especially illicitly

sir n a polite form of address to a man **Sir** n a title used before the name of a knight or baronet

sire n **1** the male parent of an animal **2** old use a title used to address a king **sire** v (said about an animal) to be the sire of young

siren n **1** a device that makes a long loud sound as a signal **2** a dangerously attractive woman

sirloin n the best part of a loin of beef

sirocco (say si-rok-oh) n pl **siroccos** a hot, dry wind that reaches southern Europe from Africa

sisal (say siy-səl) n fibre made from the leaves of a tropical plant, used for making ropes

sissy n pl **sissies** informal a timid or cowardly person

sister n **1** a daughter of the same parents as another person **2** a woman who is a fellow member of a group or organization **3** a member of a religious order of women **4** a female hospital nurse in charge of other nurses **5** (used before a noun) denoting an organization that is of the same kind as another or under the same ownership ♦ a sister company **sisterhood** n **1** the relationship of sisters **2** friendliness and companionship between women **3** a society or association of women, or its members **sisterly** adj **sister-in-law** n pl **sisters-in-law** the sister of a married person's husband or wife, or the wife of a person's brother

sit v past tense and past participle **sat**; **sitting 1** to take a position or be in a position in which the body rests more or less upright on the buttocks **2** to put someone in a sitting position ♦ She sat him down on a stool. **3** to pose for a portrait **4** (said about an animal) to rest with its legs bent and its body close to the ground **5** (said about a bird) to stay on its nest to hatch eggs **6** to be situated, to lie **7** to be a candidate for an examination ♦ She wants to sit for a scholarship. **8** to occupy a seat as a

member of a committee, etc. **9** (said about Parliament or a law court or committee) to be assembled for business **10** (said about clothes) to fit in a certain way ♦ The coat sits badly on the shoulders. **sitter** n **1** a person who is sitting, especially for a portrait **2** a person who looks after children, pets, or a house while the owners are away **3** informal something very easy, especially in sport

sitting n **1** the time when people are served a meal **2** the time when a parliament or committee is conducting business **sit-in** n the occupation of a building by protesters or demonstrators **sitting duck** n a person or thing that is a helpless victim of attack **sitting room** n a room used for sitting in comfortably **to sit on the fence** to avoid taking sides in a dispute **to sit something out 1** to take no part in a dance, etc. **2** to stay till the end of something unpleasant or not enjoyable **to sit tight** informal **1** to remain firmly where you are **2** to take no action and not give way

sitar (say **sit**-ar or si-**tar**) n an Indian stringed musical instrument with a long neck, played by plucking

sitcom n informal a situation comedy

site n **1** an area of ground on which a town or building stood or stands or is going to be built **2** the place where a certain activity or event takes place or took place ♦ a camping site ♦ the site of the battle **site** v to locate or build something in a certain place ◊ Do not confuse this word with sight, which has a different meaning.

situate v to place or put something in a certain position **situation** n **1** a place, together with its surroundings, that is occupied by something **2** a set of circumstances **3** a job **situation comedy** n a radio or television comedy in which the humour comes from the characters' misunderstandings and embarrassments

six adj, n the number 6, one more than five **sixth** adj, n **1** next after fifth **2** one of six equal parts of a thing **sixpence** n a former British coin worth six pennies **sixth sense** n a supposed extra power of perception other than the five physical ones, intuition

sixteen adj, n the number 16, one more

than fifteen **sixteenth** adj, n

sixty adj, n pl **sixties** the number 60, six times ten **sixtieth** adj, n

size[1] n **1** the measurements or extent of something **2** any of a series of standard measurements in which some things are made ♦ a size eight shoe **size** v to group or sort things according to their size **sizeable** adj large or fairly large in size **to size something** or **someone up 1** to estimate the size of a person or thing **2** informal to form a judgement of a person or situation, etc.

size[2] n a gluey substance used to glaze paper or stiffen cloth, etc. **size** v to treat something with size

sizzle v (said about food) to make a hissing sound when frying or roasting

skate[1] n **1** a shoe or boot with a steel blade attached to the sole, used for sliding smoothly on ice a roller skate **skate** v to move on skates **skater** n **skateboard** n a short narrow board with wheels like rollerskates, for riding on while standing or crouching **skateboarding** n **to skate over** to ignore a subject or refer to it only briefly

skate[2] n pl **skate** a large flat sea fish used for food

skedaddle v informal to go away quickly

skein (say skayn) n **1** a loosely coiled bundle of yarn or thread **2** a number of wild geese or swans in flight

skeleton n **1** the framework of bones that support a human or animal body **2** a framework, e.g. of a building **3** an outline of a literary work, etc. **4** (used before a noun) reduced to the minimum needed ♦ a skeleton crew **skeletal** adj **skeleton key** n a key designed to fit several locks

sketch n **1** a rough drawing or painting **2** a brief account or description of something **3** a short humorous play **sketch** v to make a sketch of something **sketchy** adj **sketchier**, **sketchiest** rough and lacking detail

skew adj slanting or askew **skew** v to make something skew, to turn or twist something round

skewbald adj (said about a horse) having irregular patches of white and another colour

skewer n a long pin for holding pieces of food together during cooking **skewer** v to pierce or hold something in place with a skewer or other pointed object

ski n pl **skis** each of a pair of long narrow strips of wood, metal, or plastic fitted under the feet for travelling over snow **ski** v **skis**, **skied**, **skiing** to travel over snow on skis **skier** n

skid v **skidded**, **skidding** (said about a vehicle) to slide on slippery ground, usually after severe braking or sharp turning **skid** n an act of skidding, a skidding movement

skid row n a slum area where vagrants live

skiff n a small light boat for one person, used for rowing or sculling

skill n ability to do something well, expertise **skilful** adj **skilfully** adv **skilled** adj

skillet n a metal cooking pot with a long handle and usually legs

skim v **skimmed**, **skimming 1** to remove something from the surface of a liquid, or to clear a liquid in this way **2** to move lightly and quickly over a surface or through the air **3** to read something quickly to get the main points **skimmed milk** n milk from which the cream has been removed

skimp v to supply or use less than is needed, to scrimp ♦ Don't skimp on food. **skimpy** adj **skimpier**, **skimpiest** scanty or too small

skin n **1** the thin layer of tissue covering the body of a human or animal **2** the skin removed from a dead animal, used as a material for clothing or other covering **3** a vessel for wine or water, made from an animal's whole skin **4** a person's complexion **5** an outer layer or covering, e.g. of a fruit **6** a thin film that forms on the surface of a liquid **skin** v **skinned**, **skinning** to strip or scrape the skin from something **skinny** adj **skinnier**, **skinniest** (said about a person or animal) very thin **2** (said about clothing) tight-fitting **skin-deep** adj not substantial or lasting, superficial **skin diving** n the sport of swimming underwater without a diving suit, using flippers and a breathing apparatus **skinflint** n a miserly person **skinhead** n a young person with closely cropped hair **skintight** adj (said about clothing) very close-fitting

skint *adj informal* having no money left

skip[1] *v* **skipped**, **skipping 1** to move along lightly, especially by hopping on each foot in turn **2** to jump with a skipping rope **3** to pass quickly from one subject or point to another **4** to omit something ♦ *You can skip chapter six.* **skip** *n* a skipping movement **skipping rope** *n* a length of rope with a handle at each end, that you turn over your head and under your feet as you jump, for exercise or play

skip[2] *n* **1** a large open-topped metal container for carrying away builders' rubbish or other bulky refuse **2** a cage or bucket in which people or materials are raised and lowered in mines and quarries

skipper *n* a captain **skipper** *v* to captain a crew or team

skirl *n* a shrill sound like that made by bagpipes

skirmish *n* a small fight or conflict **skirmish** *v* to take part in a skirmish

skirt *n* **1** a woman's piece of clothing hanging from the waist **2** the part of a dress or coat below the waist **3** a covering that protects the wheels or underside of a vehicle or aircraft **4** a cut of beef from the lower flank **skirt** *v* **1** to go or be situated along the edge of something **2** to avoid dealing directly with a difficult question, controversial topic, etc. **skirting** *n* a wooden board running round the wall of a room, close to the floor

skit *n* a short comedy sketch or parody

skittish *adj* playful or frisky

skittle *n* each of the bottle-shaped objects that players try to knock down in a game of **skittles**

skive *v informal* to avoid work or a duty **skiver** *n*

skivvy *n pl* **skivvies** *informal* **1** a lowly female servant **2** a person doing menial work

skua (say **skew**-ə) *n* a seabird like a large gull

skulduggery *n* dishonest behaviour or trickery

skulk *v* to loiter or move about stealthily

skull *n* **1** a framework of bones in the head, or the part of this protecting the brain **2** a representation of a skull **skullcap** *n* a small close-fitting cap with no peak, worn on top of the head

skunk *n* a North American animal with black and white fur that can spray a bad-smelling liquid from glands near its tail

sky *n pl* **skies** the region of the atmosphere seen from the earth, appearing blue in fine weather **sky** *v* **skies**, **skied**, **skying** to hit a ball high in the air **skydiving** *n* the sport of jumping from an aircraft and floating down or performing acrobatics in the air under free fall, opening a parachute at the last safe moment **skylark** *n* a lark that sings while it hovers high in the air **skylight** *n* a window in a roof or ceiling **skyline** *n* the outline of land or buildings seen against the sky **skyrocket** *v* **skyrocketed**, **skyrocketing** to increase sharply **skyscraper** *n* a very tall building of many storeys

slab *n* a thick flat piece of something solid

slack[1] *adj* **1** loose, not held tight **2** careless or negligent **3** (said about trade or business) with little happening, not busy **slack** *n* the slack part of a rope, etc. **slack** *v* **1** to become slack **2** to avoid work or be lazy **slacken** *v* **slacker** *n* **slackness** *n* **slacks** *pl n* trousers for casual or sports wear

slack[2] *n* coal dust or small pieces of coal

slag *n* waste matter separated from metal in smelting

slain past participle of *slay*

slake *v* **1** to quench your thirst **2** to combine quicklime chemically with water to produce calcium hydroxide

slalom (say **slah**-ləm) *n* **1** a ski race down a winding course marked by poles **2** an obstacle race in canoes

slam *v* **slammed**, **slamming 1** to shut something forcefully with a loud noise **2** to put or hit something forcefully **3** *informal* to criticize someone severely **slam** *n* a slamming noise

slander *n* the act or crime of making a false spoken statement that damages a person's reputation **slander** *v* to utter a slander about someone **slanderous** *adj*

slang *n* informal language used mostly in speech and often restricted to a particular social group **slangy** *adj* **slanging match** *n* a long noisy argument in which people exchange insults

slant v 1 to slope 2 to present news or information from a particular point of view **slant** n 1 a slope 2 the way something is presented, an attitude or bias

slap v **slapped**, **slapping** to strike someone with the open hand or with something flat **slap** n a blow with the open hand or with something flat **slap** adv suddenly or directly ♦ *Then I ran slap into him.* **slapdash** adj hasty and careless **slapstick** n comedy with contrived mishaps and playful fighting **slap-up** adj large and lavish

slash v 1 to cut or strike something with a long, sweeping stroke or strokes 2 *informal* to reduce a price or total by a large amount **slash** n 1 a cut made with a long sweeping stroke 2 an oblique stroke (/) used in writing and printing

slat n each of a series of thin, narrow strips of wood, metal, or plastic arranged so as to overlap

slate n 1 a kind of grey rock that is easily split into flat, smooth plates 2 a piece of this used for covering a roof or (formerly) for writing on **slate** v 1 to cover a roof or surface with slates 2 *informal* to criticize someone severely

slattern n *old use* a dirty, untidy woman **slatternly** adj

slaughter n 1 the killing of animals for food 2 the ruthless killing of a great number of people or animals, a massacre **slaughter** v 1 to kill animals for food 2 to kill people or animals ruthlessly or in great numbers **slaughterhouse** n a place where animals are killed for food

Slav n a member of a group of peoples of central and eastern Europe who speak a Slavonic language **Slavic** adj to do with the group of languages that includes Russian, Czech, Polish, and Serbo-Croat

slave n 1 a person who is the legal property of another person and obliged to work for that person 2 someone who is dominated or greatly influenced by another person or thing ♦ *a slave to fashion* **slave** v to work very hard **slavery** n 1 the condition of a slave 2 the practice of owning or using

slaves 3 hard work or drudgery **slavish** adj 1 like a slave, excessively submissive 2 showing no independence or originality **slavishly** adv

slaver (say slav-er or slay-ver) v to have saliva running from the mouth **slaver** n saliva running from the mouth

slay v **slew**, **slain** to kill a person or animal violently

sleaze n *informal* immoral or corrupt behaviour, especially in public life **sleazy** adj **sleazier**, **sleaziest** 1 corrupt or immoral 2 (said about a place) dirty and squalid

sledge, **sledge** n a vehicle with runners instead of wheels, used for travelling over snow **sledging** n

sledgehammer n a large, heavy hammer swung with both hands

sleek adj 1 (often said about hair or fur) smooth and glossy 2 looking prosperous **sleekness** n

sleep n 1 the natural condition of rest in animals, in which the eyes are closed, the muscles are relaxed, and the mind is unconscious 2 a period of this condition ♦ *a long sleep* **sleep** v past tense and past participle **slept** 1 to rest in a state of sleep 2 to provide people with sleeping accommodation ♦ *The cottage sleeps four.* **sleeper** n 1 someone who is sleeping 2 each of the wooden or concrete beams on which the rails of a railway rest 3 a sleeping car, or a train including sleeping cars 4 a ring worn in a pierced ear to keep the hole from closing **sleepy** adj **sleepier**, **sleepiest** 1 feeling a need or wish to sleep 2 quiet and lacking activity ♦ *a sleepy little town* **sleepily** adv **sleepiness** n **sleepless** adj **sleeping bag** n a padded bag for sleeping in, especially while camping **sleeping partner** n a partner in a business firm who does not take part in its actual work **sleepover** n a night spent away from home, especially after a party **sleepwalk** v to walk around while asleep **sleepwalker** n **to sleep in** to remain asleep later in the morning than usual

sleet n a mixture of rain and snow or hail falling at the same time **sleet** v to fall as sleet **sleety** adj

sleeve n **1** the part of a piece of clothing that covers the arm or part of it **2** a paper or cardboard cover for a record **3** a protective tube fitting over a rod or another tube **sleeveless** adj **up your sleeve** kept hidden or put aside for use when needed

sleigh (say slay) n a large sledge drawn by horses

sleight (say slyt) n **sleight of hand** skill in using the hands to do conjuring tricks, etc.

slender adj **1** slim and graceful **2** barely enough ♦ people of slender means **slenderness** n

sleuth (say slooth) n a detective

slew¹ v to turn or swing round

slew² past tense of slay

slice n **1** a thin, broad piece cut from something, especially a piece of food **2** a portion or share **3** a utensil with a thin, broad blade for lifting or serving fish or cake **4** (in sports) a stroke or shot that veers off to the right or left **slice** v **1** to cut something into slices **2** to cut cleanly or easily ♦ The knife sliced through the apple. **3** (in other sports) to hit the ball with a slice **slicer** n

slick adj **1** done or doing things in a noticeably smooth and efficient way **2** glibly smooth in manner or speech **3** smooth and slippery ♦ The roads were slick with mud. **slick** n a thick patch of oil floating on the sea **slick** v to make something sleek

slide v past tense and past participle **slid 1** to move along a smooth surface keeping continuous contact with it, or to cause something to do this **2** to move quietly or discreetly, or to cause something to do this ♦ She slid a note into his hand. **3** to change gradually into a worse condition or habit ♦ The country slid into anarchy. **slide** n **1** the act of sliding **2** a smooth surface for sliding on **3** a structure with a smooth, sloping surface for children to slide down, or a similar device for sending goods from one part of a building to another **4** a sliding part of a machine or instrument **5** a small glass plate on which an object is mounted to be looked at under a microscope **6** a mounted picture or transparency for showing on a screen with a projector **7** a hairslide **slide**

rule n a ruler with a sliding central strip, marked with logarithmic scales and used for making calculations rapidly **sliding scale** n a scale of fees, taxes, or payments that varies in accordance with the variation of some standards

slight adj **1** not much or great; not serious or important **2** slender, not heavily built **slight** v to offend someone by not treating them with proper respect or courtesy **slight** n an act of slighting someone, a minor insult **slightly** adv

slim adj **slimmer**, **slimmest 1** attractively or gracefully thin or small in thickness **2** slight or inadequate ♦ There is only a slim chance of rescuing any survivors. **slim** v **slimmed**, **slimming 1** to make yourself slimmer, especially by dieting or exercise **2** to reduce the size or scale of an organization to make it more efficient **slimmer** n **slimness** n **slimline** adj slender in build or design

slime n an unpleasantly wet and thick substance **slimy** adj **slimier**, **slimiest 1** unpleasantly wet and thick like slime **2** covered or smeared with slime **3** informal revoltingly servile or obsequious

sling n **1** a belt or strap looped round an object to support or lift it **2** a bandage looped round the neck to form a support for an injured arm **3** a looped strap used to throw a stone or other small missile **sling** v past tense and past participle **slung 1** to suspend or lift something with a sling **2** informal to throw something forcefully or carelessly

slink v past tense and past participle **slunk** to move quietly in a stealthy or shamefaced way **slinky** adj **slinkier**, **slinkiest** smooth and sinuous in movement or form

slip¹ v **slipped**, **slipping 1** to slide accidentally, or to lose your balance in this way **2** to go quickly and discreetly, or to cause something to do this ♦ She slipped slowly through the crowd. ♦ John slipped a note under the door. **3** to escape hold or capture by being slippery or not grasped firmly **4** to escape or become detached from a restraint ♦ The dog slipped its leash. ♦ I'm afraid it slipped my memory. **slip** n **1** an act of slipping **2** an accidental or casual mistake **3** a loose covering or piece of clothing **slippery** adj **1** smooth and difficult to hold **2** causing slipping by being wet or smooth **3** (said about a person) untrustworthy **slippy** adj **slip knot** n a knot that can slide along the rope, etc. on which it is tied, or one that can be undone by pulling **slipped disc** n a displaced layer of cartilage between vertebrae in the spine, pressing on nerves and causing pain **slip road** n a road entering or leaving a motorway or other main road **slipshod** adj **1** not doing things carefully **2** not done or arranged carefully **slipstream** n a current of air driven backward as something is propelled forward **slipway** n a slope into water, used as a landing stage or for building or repairing ships **to give someone the slip** to escape from someone or succeed in avoiding them **to slip up** informal to make an accidental or casual mistake

slip[2] n **1** a small piece of paper for writing on **2** a cutting taken from a plant for grafting or planting **a slip of a girl** a small, slim girl

slipper n a soft, light comfortable shoe for wearing indoors

slit n a long, narrow cut or opening **slit** v past tense and past participle **slit**; **slitting** to cut a slit in something

slither v informal to slip or slide unsteadily or with an irregular movement **slithery** adj

sliver (say sliv-er) n a thin strip cut or split off a larger piece of wood or glass, etc.

slob n informal an untidy or lazy person

slobber v to dribble a lot from the mouth

sloe n the small dark plum-like fruit of the blackthorn

slog v **slogged**, **slogging 1** to hit something hard **2** to work hard for a long period **3** to walk with great effort over a long distance **slog** n **1** a hard hit **2** a spell of hard tiring work or walking

slogan n a word or phrase used to advertise something or to represent the aims of a campaign, political party, etc.

sloop n a kind of sailing ship with one mast

slop v **slopped**, **slopping 1** (said about a liquid) to spill over the edge of its container **2** to make liquid spill over, to splash liquid on a surface **slop** n **1** weak unappetizing drink or liquid food **2** an amount of slopped liquid **slops** pl n liquid refuse in a kitchen **sloppy** adj **sloppier**, **sloppiest 1** having a liquid consistency and splashing easily **2** careless or slipshod **3** weakly sentimental **sloppiness** n

slope v **1** to lie or turn at an angle from the horizontal or vertical **2** to place something in this position **slope** n **1** a sloping surface **2** a stretch of rising or falling ground **3** the amount by which something slopes **to slope off** informal to go away

slosh v **1** informal to hit someone **2** to pour liquid clumsily **3** to splash or slop about **slosh** n **1** informal a blow **2** a splashing sound

slot n **1** a narrow opening to put something through **2** a groove, channel, or slit into which something fits **3** a regular position in a scheme or schedule **slot** v **slotted**, **slotting 1** to make a slot or slots in something **2** to put something into a slot **slot machine** n a machine worked by putting a coin in a slot

sloth (say slohth) n **1** reluctance to make an effort, laziness **2** a South American animal that lives in trees and can only move very slowly **slothful** adj

slouch v to stand, sit, or move in a lazy awkward way, not with an upright posture **slouch** n a slouching movement or posture

slough[1] (say slow) n a swamp or marshy place

slough[2] (say sluf) v (said about an animal) to shed its skin **slough** n dead tissue that has dropped away

slovenly (say sluv-ən-li) adj **1** dirty and untidy **2** unmethodical in work

slow adj **1** not quick or fast, taking more time than is usual **2** (said about a clock or watch) showing a time earlier than the correct time **3** not able to understand things quickly or easily **4** sluggish, not lively ◆ Business is slow today. **slow** adv slowly **slow** v (usually **slow down** or **slow up**) to go more slowly, or to make something go more slowly **slowly** adv **slowness** n **slowcoach** n a person who is slow in actions or work **slow motion** n the process of showing cinema or video film at a lower speed than the recording speed, so that movements appear to be slower than in real life

sludge n thick greasy mud, or something like this

slug¹ n 1 a small slimy animal like a snail without a shell 2 a roundish lump of metal, especially a pellet for firing from a gun 3 an amount of alcoholic drink **sluggard** n a slow or lazy person **sluggish** adj slow-moving or inactive

slug² v **slugged**, **slugging** informal to strike someone or something with a hard heavy blow **slug** n a blow of this kind

sluice (say slooss) n 1 (also **sluice gate**) a sliding gate for controlling the volume or flow of water 2 the water controlled by this 3 a channel carrying off water **sluice** v 1 to let out water by means of a sluice 2 to flood or wash something with a flow of water

slum n an area of poor, run-down, and overcrowded houses

slumber v literary to sleep **slumber** n a period of sleep

slump v 1 to sit or fall down heavily and limply 2 to suffer a sudden great decline **slump** n a sudden or great fall in prices, business activity, the demand for goods, etc.

slur v **slurred**, **slurring** 1 to pronounce words indistinctly with each sound running into the next 2 Mus to mark notes with a slur; to perform a group of notes in the way indicated by this **slur** n 1 an insinuation or allegation ♦ a slur on his reputation 2 a slurred sound

slurp v to eat or drink with a loud sucking sound **slurp** n this sound

slurry n pl **slurries** a semi-liquid mixture, especially of cement or manure

slush n 1 partly melted snow or ice on the ground 2 informal excessively sentimental talk or writing **slushy** adj **slush fund** n a fund of money used for illegal purposes such as bribery

slut n a slovenly or promiscuous woman **sluttish** adj

sly adj **slyer**, **slyest** 1 done or doing things in an unpleasantly cunning and secretive way 2 mischievous and knowing ♦ a sly smile **slyly**, **slily** adv **slyness** n **on the sly** in a secretive way

smack¹ n 1 a sharp blow or slap, especially one given with the palm of the hand 2 a loud sharp sound 3 a loud kiss **smack** v to slap someone **smack** adv informal directly and forcefully ♦ The ball went smack through the window.

smack² n a slight flavour or trace of something **smack** v to have a slight flavour or trace of something

smack³ n a sailing boat with a single mast used for coasting or fishing

small adj 1 less than normal in size, not large or big 2 not great in number, strength, etc. 3 not important or significant ♦ a small complaint **small** adv into small pieces; in a small size or way **smalls** pl n informal underwear **the small of the back** the part of a person's back at the waist **smallness** n **smallholding** n a small area of land sold or let for farming **small hours** n the early hours of the morning, after midnight **small-minded** adj having a narrow or selfish outlook **smallpox** n a highly contagious disease caused by a virus, with fever and pustules that leave permanent scars **small talk** n social conversation about unimportant subjects

smarmy adj **smarmier**, **smarmiest** informal trying to win favour by flattery or excessive politeness

smart adj 1 neat, elegant, and well-dressed 2 fashionable and upmarket 3 clever, shrewd, or witty 4 (said about a device) controlled or guided by a computer and capable of some independent and seemingly intelligent action ♦ a smart bomb 5 forceful, brisk ♦ a smart pace **smart** v to feel a stinging pain **smarten** v **smartly** adv **smartness** n **smart alec** informal a know-all **smart card** n a plastic card with a microprocessor built in, which stores information or enables you to draw or spend money from your bank account

smash v 1 to break something or become broken suddenly and noisily into pieces 2 to hit or move something with great force 3 (in tennis, etc.) to strike a ball forcefully downwards **4** to crash a vehicle **5** to destroy something or defeat someone completely **smash** n **1** the act or sound of smashing **2** a collision **3** (also **smash hit**) informal a very successful song, show, etc. **smash** adv with a sudden smash **smasher** n an excellent or very attractive person or thing **smashing** adj excellent

smattering n a slight knowledge of a language or subject

smear v **1** to spread something with a greasy or sticky substance **2** to try to damage someone's reputation by making false allegations **smear** n **1** a greasy or sticky mark **2** a false accusation intended to damage a person's reputation **3** a smear test **smear test** n the taking and examination of a sample of the cervix lining, to check for faulty cells which may cause cancer

smell n **1** the faculty of perceiving odours by their action on the sense organs of the nose **2** the quality that is perceived in this way **3** an unpleasant quality of this kind **4** an act of smelling something **smell** v past tense and past participle **smelt** or **smelled** **1** to perceive the smell of something; to detect or test something by your sense of smell **2** to give off a smell **3** to give off an unpleasant smell **4** to detect or suspect something by intuition or instinct ♦ I was sure I could smell a cover-up. **smelly** adj **smellier**, **smelliest** having a strong or unpleasant smell **smelling salts** pl n a solid preparation of ammonia used for smelling as a stimulant to relieve faintness

smelt v to heat and melt ore to obtain the metal it contains; to obtain metal in this way

smile n a facial expression showing pleasure, friendliness, or amusement, with the corners of the mouth turned up **smile** v **1** to give a smile **2** to look favourably on something ♦ Fortune smiled on us.

smirch v **1** to make something dirty **2** to disgrace or dishonour a reputation **smirch** n **1** a dirty mark or stain **2** a flaw

smirk n a self-satisfied or silly smile **smirk** v to give a smirk

smite v **smote**, **smitten 1** old use to hit

something hard **2** old use to defeat or conquer someone **3** to afflict someone **smitten to be smitten (with) 1** to be affected by love for someone, especially suddenly and powerfully **2** to be deeply affected by an emotion

smith n **1** a person who makes things in metal **2** a blacksmith **smithy** n pl **smithies** a blacksmith's workshop

smithereens pl n informal small fragments

smock n **1** an overall shaped like a long loose shirt ♦ an artist's smock **2** a woman's long loose top **smock** v to decorate a piece of clothing with smocking **smocking** n a decoration made by gathering a section of material into tight pleats and stitching them together into a honeycomb pattern

smog n fog polluted by smoke

smoke n **1** the mixture of gas and solid particles that forms a visible vapour given off by a burning substance **2** an act of smoking tobacco **3** informal a cigarette or cigar **smoke** v **1** to give off smoke **2** to have a lighted cigarette, cigar, or pipe between your lips, and draw its smoke into your mouth; to do this as a habit **3** to preserve meat or fish by treating it with smoke **smoker** n a person who smokes tobacco as a habit **smoky** adj **smokier**, **smokiest**, **smokescreen** n something intended to conceal or disguise what someone is really doing **smokestack** n a chimney or funnel on a locomotive, ship, factory building, etc. **to smoke someone** or **something out** to drive a person or animal out of a place by using smoke

smooth adj **1** having an even surface without any lumps, wrinkles, roughness, etc. **2** moving evenly without bumps or jolts **3** without problems or difficulties **4** not harsh in sound or taste **5** pleasantly polite but perhaps insincere **smooth** v to make something smooth **smoothly** adv **smoothness** n

smorgasbord (say **smor** -gəs-bord) n a variety of open sandwiches and savoury dishes served as hors d'oeuvres or a buffet

smother v **1** to suffocate someone by covering their nose and mouth **2** to put out a fire by covering it **3** to cover something thickly ♦ *chips smothered in ketchup* **4** to restrain or suppress something

smoulder *v* **1** to burn slowly with smoke but no flame **2** to feel strong but concealed hostile feelings, especially anger or hatred

smudge *v* **1** to make something blurred or smeared **2** to become blurred or smeared **smudge** *n* a smudged mark **smudgy** *adj*

smug *adj* **smugger**, **smuggest** self-satisfied; too pleased with your own good fortune or abilities **smugly** *adv* **smugness** *n*

smuggle *v* **1** to bring goods into or out of a country illegally, especially without paying customs duties **2** to bring something into or out of a place secretly **smuggler** *n*

smut *n* **1** a small flake of soot or dirt **2** indecent or obscene talk, pictures, or writing **smutty** *adj* **smuttier**, **smuttiest**

snack *n* a small meal **snack** *v* to eat a snack

snaffle *n* a simple bit on a bridle, used with a single set of reins **snaffle** *v informal* to take something for yourself hastily, before anyone else has a chance to

snag *n* **1** an unexpected difficulty **2** a sharp or jagged part sticking out from something **3** a tear in fabric that has caught on something sharp **snag** *v* **snagged**, **snagging** to catch or tear or be caught on a snag

snail *n* a soft-bodied animal with a spiral shell that can enclose its whole body

snake *n* **1** a reptile with a long, narrow body and no legs **2** (also **snake in the grass**) a treacherous person **snake** *v* to move or stretch out with the twisting motion of a snake **snaky** *adj*

snap *v* **snapped**, **snapping** **1** to break or make something break with a sharp cracking sound **2** to bite or try to bite something with a snatching movement **3** to open or close with a sharp sound, or to make something do this **4** to speak with sudden irritation; to suddenly lose your self-control **5** to take or accept something eagerly, especially something in short supply ♦ *shoppers snapping up bargains* **6** to move suddenly or abruptly **7** to take a snapshot of something **snap** *n* **1** the act or sound of snapping **2** a snapshot **3** a sudden brief spell of cold weather **4** a card game in

which players call 'Snap!' when two similar cards are exposed **5** a crisp brittle biscuit **snap** *adj* done or arranged on the spur of the moment ♦ *a snap decision* **snap** *adv* with a snapping sound **snappy** *adj* **snappier**, **snappiest** **1** neat and stylish ♦ *a snappy dresser* **2** clever and concise ♦ *a snappy catchphrase* **snapper** *n* any of several sea fish used as food **snappish** *adj* bad-tempered and inclined to snap at people **snapdragon** *n* a garden plant with flowers that have a mouth-like opening **snapshot** *n* a photograph taken informally or casually **make it snappy** *informal* hurry up

snare *n* **1** a trap for catching birds or animals, consisting of a loop of wire or cord that pulls tight **2** something that is likely to trap someone or to expose them to danger or failure **3** each of the strings of gut or coiled metal stretched across a side drum to produce a rattling effect **snare** *v* to catch or trap someone or something in a snare, or as if in a snare ♦ *How did she manage to snare that job?* **snare drum** *n* a drum with snares

snarl[1] *v* **1** to growl angrily with the teeth bared **2** to say something aggressively **snarl** *n* the act or sound of snarling

snarl[2] *n* a tangle or knot **snarl-up** *n* **1** a muddle **2** a traffic jam **to snarl something up** to make something jammed, blocked, or tangled ♦ *We got snarled up in traffic.*

snatch *v* **1** to seize something quickly or eagerly **2** to take something quickly or when a chance occurs ♦ *We snatched a few hours' sleep on the plane.* **snatch** *n* **1** the act of snatching **2** a short and incomplete part of a song, piece of music, or conversation

snazzy *adj* **snazzier**, **snazziest** *informal* smart, stylish

sneak *v* **1** to move quietly and secretly ♦ *Her brother had sneaked up behind her.* **2** *informal* to take something secretly ♦ *He sneaked a look at the answers.* **3** *informal* to tell tales **sneak** *n informal* a telltale **sneakers** *pl n* soft-soled shoes **sneaking** *adj* persistent but not openly acknowledged ♦ *I had a sneaking affection for him.* **sneaky** *adj* **sneakier**, **sneakiest**

sneer *n* a scornful expression or remark **sneer** *v* to show contempt by a sneer

sneeze n a sudden, audible, involuntary expulsion of air through the nose and mouth, to get rid of something irritating the nostrils **sneeze** v to give a sneeze **not to be sneezed at** informal not to be disregarded; worth having or thinking about

snick v to make a small cut or notch in something **snick** n a small cut or notch

snicker v to snigger **snicker** n a snigger

snide adj sneering in a sly or indirect way

sniff v 1 to make a sound by drawing in air through the nose 2 to smell something **sniff** n the act or sound of sniffing **sniffle** v to sniff slightly or repeatedly **sniffle** n 1 the act or sound of sniffling 2 a slight cold **sniffy** adj **sniffier**, **sniffiest** contemptuous **sniffer dog** n a dog trained to find drugs or explosives by smell **to sniff at** informal to show contempt for something

snigger n a sly or mocking giggle **snigger** v to give a snigger

snip v **snipped**, **snipping** to cut something with scissors or shears, with small quick strokes **snip** n 1 the act or sound of snipping 2 a piece snipped off 3 informal a bargain **snippet** n 1 a small piece of information or news; a brief extract 2 a small piece cut off

snipe n pl **snipe** a wading bird with a long straight bill, living in marshes **snipe** v 1 to shoot at people from a hiding place 2 to make sly critical remarks attacking a person or thing **sniper** n

snitch v informal 1 to inform on someone 2 to steal something **snitch** n an informer

snivel v **snivelled**, **snivelling** 1 to cry or complain in a whining way 2 to have a runny nose

snob n a person who has an exaggerated respect for social position or wealth or for certain tastes, and who looks down on people whom he or she considers inferior ♦ a wine snob **snobbery** n **snobbish** adj **snobbishly** adv **snobbishness** n

snog v **snogged**, **snogging** informal to kiss and caress someone **snog** n an act of snogging

snood n a loose bag-like ornamental net in which a woman's hair is held at the back

snook n informal **to cock a snook 1** to make a contemptuous gesture with your thumb touching your nose and the fingers spread out **2** to show cheeky contempt or lack of respect for someone or something

snooker n 1 a game played on a billiard table with cues and 15 red and 6 other coloured balls 2 a position in snooker in which a player cannot make a direct shot at a ball they are allowed to hit **snooker** v 1 to subject an opponent to a snooker 2 informal to thwart someone or put them in an impossible position

snoop v informal to investigate or look around secretly in order to find something out **snoop** n 1 the act of snooping 2 a person who snoops **snooper** n

snooty adj **snootier**, **snootiest** informal haughty and contemptuous **snootily** adv

snooze n informal a nap **snooze** v informal to take a snooze

snore v to make snorting or grunting sounds while sleeping **snore** n one of these sounds **snorer** n

snorkel n 1 a breathing tube to enable a person to swim under water 2 a device by which a submerged submarine can take in and expel air **snorkel** v **snorkelled**, **snorkelling** to swim using a snorkel **snorkelling** n

snort n a rough sound made by forcing breath suddenly through the nose, usually expressing annoyance or disgust **snort** v to make a snort

snot n informal mucus from the nose **snotty** adj

snout n 1 an animal's long projecting nose and jaws 2 the projecting front part of something

snow n 1 crystals of ice that form from atmospheric vapour and fall to earth in light white flakes 2 a fall or layer of snow **snow** v 1 to come down as snow ♦ It is snowing. 2 to scatter or fall like snow **snowy** adj **snowier**, **snowiest**, **snowball** n snow pressed into a small, compact ball for throwing in play **snowball** v to grow quickly in size, intensity, or importance, as a snowball does when rolled in more snow **snow-blindness** n temporary blindness caused by the glare of light reflected by snow **snowboard** n a board like a wide ski, used for sliding downhill on snow **snowboarding** n **snowbound** adj **1** prevented by snow from going out or travelling **2** (said about a place) cut off or blocked by snow **snowdrift** n a bank of deep snow piled up by the wind **snowdrop** n a small flower with hanging white flowers blooming in early spring **snowflake** n a flake of snow **snowman** n pl **snowmen** a shape of a human figure made of snow **snowplough** n a vehicle or device for clearing a road or railway track by pushing snow aside **snowshoe** n a frame rather like a tennis racket, attached to the sole of a boot and used for walking on snow **to be snowed under** to be overwhelmed with a large amount of work

snub v **snubbed**, **snubbing** to insult someone by deliberately ignoring them or treating them scornfully **snub** n an act of snubbing someone **snub** adj (said about a nose) short and turned up at the end

snuff¹ v to put out a candle by covering or pinching the flame **to snuff it** informal to die

snuff² n powdered tobacco for sniffing into the nostrils

snuffle v to sniff in a noisy way, to breathe noisily through a partly blocked nose **snuffle** n a snuffling sound

snug adj **snugger**, **snuggest 1** warm and cosy **2** very tight or close-fitting **snug** n a small cosy room in a pub or hotel **snugly** adv

snuggle v to settle into a warm and comfortable position

so adv **1** to such an extent ♦ It was so dark that we could not see. **2** very ♦ We are so pleased to see you. **3** also ♦ I was wrong, but then so were you. **so** conjunction for that reason; therefore ♦ No one was in, so I left the keys next door. **so** pronoun that, the same thing ♦ Do you think so? **so-and-so** n pl **so-and-sos 1** a person or thing that need not be named **2** informal an unpleasant or objectionable person ♦ a nosy so-and-so **so-called** adj called by that name or description but perhaps not deserving it **or so** approximately ♦ two hundred or so **so long!** informal goodbye **so that** in order

that; with the result that

soak v **1** to place something or lie in a liquid so as to become thoroughly wet **2** to make something or someone extremely wet; to drench someone or something **soak** n the act or process of soaking **to soak something up** to absorb something

soap n **1** a substance used with water for washing and cleaning things, made of fat or oil combined with an alkali **2** informal a soap opera **soap** v to put soap on something **soapy** adj **soapier**, **soapiest**, **soapbox** n a box or crate used as a platform for someone making a speech in a public place **soap opera** n a television serial about the everyday lives of a group of people

soar v **1** to fly or rise high in the air **2** to rise very high

sob v **sobbed**, **sobbing** to make a loud gasping sound when crying **sob** n an act or sound of sobbing **sob story** n an account of someone's experiences, told in order to get sympathy or help

sober adj **1** not drunk **2** serious and self-controlled, not frivolous **3** (said about colour) not bright or conspicuous **sober** v to make someone sober, or to become sober **soberly** adv **sobriety** n

sobriquet (say **soh**-brik-ay) n a person's nickname

soccer n Association Football

sociable (say **soh**-shə-bəl) adj **1** liking to be with other people **2** characterized by friendliness ♦ a sociable occasion **sociability** n **sociably** adv

social adj **1** to do with human society or its organization; to do with the relationships between people or classes living in a society ♦ social problems **2** helping people to meet each other ♦ a social club **3** living in an organized community, not solitary ♦ Bees are social insects. **4** sociable **social** n a social gathering **socialism** n a political and economic theory advocating that land, transport, natural resources, and the chief industries should be owned and managed by the government **socialist** n, adj **socialite** n a person who is well known in fashionable society and often takes part in social activities **socialize** v **1** to mix socially

with other people, to take part in social activities **2** to make someone behave in a way acceptable to society **socially** *adv*
social science *n* the scientific study of human society and human relationships
social security *n* money and other assistance provided by the government for those in need through being unemployed, ill, or disabled **social services** *pl n* welfare services provided by local or national government, including education, medical care, and housing **social work** *n* work done by people trained to help people with social problems

society *n pl* **societies 1** an organized community of people in a particular country or region ♦ *We live in a multiracial society.* **2** people in general ♦ *The judge said he was a danger to society.* **3** a group of people organized for some common purpose ♦ *the school debating society* **4** being in the company of other people ♦ *She shunned the society of others.* **5** people of the higher social classes ♦ *a society wedding*

sociology (say soh-si-**ol**-əji) *n* the scientific study of human society and its development and institutions, or of social problems **sociological** *adj* **sociologist** *n*

sock *n* **1** a knitted piece of clothing for the foot and lower part of the leg **2** *informal* a forceful blow **sock** *v informal* to hit someone hard

socket *n* **1** a hollow into which something fits **2** a device into which an electric plug or bulb is put in order to make a connection

sod *n* a piece of turf

soda *n* **1** a compound of sodium in common use, especially sodium carbonate (*washing soda*), sodium bicarbonate (*baking soda*), or sodium hydroxide (*caustic soda*) **2** soda water **soda water** *n* water made fizzy by being charged with carbon dioxide under pressure

sodden *adj* soaked through

sodium (say **soh**-di-əm) *n* a chemical element (symbol Na), a soft silver-white metal **sodium bicarbonate** *n* a soluble white powder used in fire extinguishers and fizzy drinks, and to make cakes rise; baking

soda

sofa *n* a long upholstered seat with a back and arms

soft *adj* **1** not hard or firm **2** smooth in texture, not rough or stiff **3** not loud **4** gentle or delicate ♦ *a soft breeze* **5** lenient or tender-hearted **6** not physically robust, feeble **7** *informal* easy, not needing much effort ♦ *a soft option* **8** (said about drinks) not alcoholic **9** (said about drugs) not likely to cause addiction **10** (said about water) free from mineral salts that prevent soap from lathering **11** (said about colour or light) not bright or dazzling **soft** *adv* softly **soften** *v* **1** to make something soft, or to become soft **2** to make something, or become, less severe ♦ *His attitude has softened over the years.* **softener** *n* **softly** *adv* **softness** *n* **soft-pedal** *v* **soft-pedalled**, **soft-pedalling** to play down the unpleasant aspects of something

software *n* programs for databases, word processing, and other tasks a computer performs, as distinct from the machinery in which these are loaded (called *hardware*)

softwood *n* wood from coniferous trees

soggy *adj* **soggier**, **soggiest** very wet and soft **sogginess** *n*

soil[1] *n* **1** the loose upper layer of earth in which plants grow **2** the territory of a particular nation ♦ *on British soil*

soil[2] *v* to make something dirty

soirée (say **swah**-ray) *n* a social gathering in the evening for music or conversation

sojourn (say **soj**-ern) *n formal* a temporary stay **sojourn** *v formal* to stay at a place temporarily

solace (say **sol**-əs) *n* comfort given to someone in distress **solace** *v* to give solace to someone

solar (say **soh**-lər) *adj* **1** to do with or derived from the sun ♦ *solar energy* **2** reckoned by the sun ♦ *solar time* **solar plexus** *n* the network of nerves at the pit of the stomach; this area **solar system** *n* the sun together with the planets, asteroids, etc. that revolve around it

solarium (say səl-**air**-iəm) *n pl* **solariums** or **solaria 1** a room equipped with sunlamps or sunbeds **2** a room enclosed with glass to let in a lot of sunlight

solder (say **sohl**-der) *n* a soft alloy that is melted to join metal parts together **solder** *v* to join metal parts with solder

soldier *n* a member of an army, especially one who is not an officer **soldier** *v* to serve as a soldier **to soldier on** *informal* to persevere with something despite difficulties

sole[1] *n* **1** the underside of a person's foot **2** the part of a shoe or stocking, etc. that covers this **sole** *v* to put a sole on a shoe

sole[2] *n* a flat sea fish used as food

sole[3] *adj* **1** one and only ♦ *She was the sole survivor.* **2** belonging or restricted to one person or group ♦ *We have the sole right to sell these cars.* **solely** *adv*

solecism (say **sol**-i-sizm) *n* **1** a mistake in the use of language **2** a piece of bad manners or incorrect behaviour

solemn *adj* **1** formal and dignified **2** (said about a person) not smiling or cheerful **solemnity** *n* **solemnize** *v* **1** to mark something with a formal ceremony **2** to perform a marriage ceremony with formal rites **solemnly** *adv*

solicit (say səl-**iss**-it) *v* **1** to ask for or try to obtain something ♦ *She's been soliciting opinions from rail users.* **2** to approach someone as a prostitute **solicitation** *n*

solicitor *n* a lawyer who advises on legal matters, prepares legal documents, and represents clients in lower courts

solicitous (say səl-**iss**-it-əs) *adj* anxious and concerned about a person's welfare or comfort

solid *adj* **1** keeping its shape, firm; not liquid or gas **2** not hollow **3** of the same substance throughout ♦ *solid silver* **4** continuous, without a break ♦ *for two solid hours* **5** strongly built or made, not flimsy ♦ *a solid foundation* **6** having three dimensions; concerned with three-dimensional objects ♦ *solid geometry* **7** sound and reliable ♦ *There are solid arguments against it.* **solid** *n* **1** a solid substance or object **2** a body or shape with three dimensions **solids** *pl n* food that is not liquid **solidarity** *n* unity resulting from common interests, feelings, or sympathies **solidify** *v* **solidifies**, **solidified**,

solidifying to make something hard or solid, or to become hard or solid **solidity** *n* **solidly** *adv*

soliloquy (say səl-**il**-ə-kwi) *n pl* **soliloquies** a speech in which a person expresses thoughts aloud when alone or without addressing anyone

solitaire (say sol-i-**tair**) *n* **1** a game for one person, in which marbles or pegs are removed from their places on a special board after jumping others over them **2** the card game patience **3** a diamond or other gem set by itself

solitary *adj* **1** alone, without companions **2** single, only ♦ *a solitary example* **3** secluded or isolated ♦ *a solitary valley* **solitary** *n pl* **solitaries 1** a recluse **2** *informal* solitary confinement **solitude** *n* being alone

solitary confinement *n* isolation of a prisoner in a separate cell as a punishment

solo *n pl* **solos 1** a piece of music, song, or dance for one performer **2** a pilot's flight in an aircraft without an instructor or companion **solo** *adj, adv* for or done by one person ♦ *for solo flute* ♦ *flying solo* **soloist** *n* a person who performs a solo

solstice (say **sol**-stis) *n* each of the two times in the year when the sun is furthest from the equator

solution *n* **1** the answer to a problem or puzzle **2** a liquid in which something is dissolved **3** dissolving or being dissolved into liquid form **soluble** *adj* **1** able to be dissolved in liquid **2** able to be solved **solubility** *n* **solute** *n* a substance that is dissolved in another substance

solve *v* to find the answer to a problem or puzzle or the way out of a difficulty **solvable** *adj* **solver** *n*

solvent *adj* **1** having enough money to pay your debts and liabilities **2** able to dissolve another substance **solvent** *n* a substance, especially a liquid, used for dissolving something **solvency** *n*

somatic (say sə-**mat**-ik) *adj* to do with the body

sombre (say **som**-ber) *adj* **1** dark or dull **2** solemn or gloomy

sombrero (say som-**brair**-oh) *n pl* **sombreros** a felt or straw hat with a very wide brim, worn especially in Mexico

some *adj* **1** an unspecified amount or number ♦ *some apples* ♦ *some sugar* **2** an unspecified person or thing ♦ *Some fool locked the door.* **3** approximately ♦ *We waited some 20 minutes.* **4** a considerable amount or number ♦ *That was some years ago.* **5** *informal* used to express admiration ♦ *That was some storm!* **some** *pronoun* an amount that is less than the whole ♦ *Some of them were late.* **somebody** *n, pronoun* someone **somehow** *adv* **1** in some unspecified or unexplained manner ♦ *I never liked her, somehow.* **2** by one means or another ♦ *We must get it finished somehow.* **someone** *n, pronoun* **1** an unspecified person **2** a person of importance **something** *n, pronoun* **1** an unspecified thing **2** an impressive or praiseworthy thing ♦ *Winning a gold medal would be quite something.* **sometime** *adv* (also **some time**) at some unspecified time **sometime** *adj* former ♦ *her sometime friend* **sometimes** *adv* at some times but not all the time ♦ *We sometimes go there by bus.* **somewhat** *adv* to some extent ♦ *It is somewhat difficult.* **somewhere** *adv* **1** at, in, or to an unspecified place or position **2** at an approximate point ♦ *It was somewhere between 5 and 6 o'clock.*

-some *suffix* **1** forms adjectives denoting a quality or manner (as in *handsome, quarrelsome*) **2** forms nouns from numbers, denoting a group of this many (as in *foursome*)

somersault (say **sum**-er-solt) *n* an acrobatic movement in which a person rolls head over heels on the ground or in the air **somersault** *v* to do a somersault

somnambulist (say som-**nam**-bew-list) *n* a sleepwalker **somnambulism** *n*

somnolent (say **som**-nəl-ənt) *adj* sleepy or drowsy **somnolence** *n*

son *n* **1** a male child in relation to his parents **2** a male descendant **3** a form of address to a boy or young man **son-in-law** *n pl* **sons-in-law** a daughter's husband

sonar (say **soh**-ner) *n* a system or device for detecting objects under water by the reflection of sound waves

sonata (say sən-**ah**-tə) *n* a musical composition for one instrument, often with a piano accompaniment, usually with three or four movements

song *n* **1** a musical composition for singing **2** singing ♦ *He burst into song.* **3** the musical call of some birds, whales, and insects **songbird** *n* a bird that sings sweetly **for a song** *informal* very cheaply

sonic *adj* to do with or involving sound waves **sonic boom** *n* a loud noise heard when the shock wave caused by an aircraft travelling faster than the speed of sound reaches the hearer

sonnet *n* a poem of 14 lines with rhymes following any of several patterns

sonorous (say **sonn**-er-əs) *adj* resonant, giving a deep powerful sound

soon *adv* **1** in a short time from now **2** not long after something **as soon as** at the moment that, as early as; as readily or willingly as **sooner or later** at some time, eventually

soot *n* the black powdery substance that rises in the smoke of coal or wood, etc. **sooty** *adj* **sootier, sootiest**

soothe *v* **1** to calm or comfort someone **2** to ease pain or distress **soothing** *adj*

soothsayer *n* a person who foretells the future

sop *n* **1** a concession that is made in order to pacify or bribe someone **2** a piece of bread dipped in gravy, soup, or sauce **sop** *v* **sopped, sopping** to soak up liquid with something absorbent **sopping** *adj* wet through **soppy** *adj* **soppier, soppiest** sentimental in a silly way

sophisticate (say səf-**ist**-i-kayt) *v* **1** to make someone become more discerning or worldy-wise through education or experience **2** to develop something into a more complex form **sophisticated** *adj* **1** having refined or cultured tastes or experienced about the world **2** complex or elaborate ♦ *sophisticated devices* **sophistication** *n*

sophistry (say **sof**-ist-ri) *n pl* **sophistries** reasoning that is clever and subtle but unsound or misleading

soporific (say sop-er-**if**-ik) *adj* causing sleep

or drowsiness **soporific** n a drug or other substance that causes sleep

soprano (say sə-**prah**-noh) n pl **sopranos** **1** the highest female or boy's singing voice, or a singer with such a voice **2** a musical instrument of the highest pitch in its family

sorbet (say **sor** -bay) n a flavoured water ice

sorcery n the art or use of magic, especially involving evil spirits **sorcerer** n a person believed to have magic powers **sorceress** n a female sorcerer

sordid adj **1** dirty or squalid **2** dishonourable and shameful ♦ sordid dealings **sordidness** n

sore adj **1** suffering pain **2** annoyed or upset **3** serious or urgent ♦ in sore need of attention **sore** n a sore place, especially where the skin is raw **sorely** adv seriously, very ♦ I was sorely tempted. **soreness** n

sorghum (say **sor** -gəm) n a kind of tropical cereal grass

sorrel n a herb with sharp-tasting leaves used in salads

sorrow n **1** mental suffering caused by loss or disappointment **2** something that causes this **sorrow** v to feel sorrow **sorrowful** adj **sorrowfully** adv

sorry adj **sorrier**, **sorriest** **1** feeling regret or shame for something you have done **2** feeling sadness, pity, or sympathy about something **3** pitiful or regrettable ♦ His clothes were in a sorry state. ♦ a sorry episode **sorry** interjection used to express apology

sort n **1** a particular kind or variety **2** informal a person of a particular nature ♦ She's quite a good sort. **sort** v to arrange things in groups according to their kind, size, destination, etc. **out of sorts** slightly unwell or unhappy **to sort someone out** informal to deal with or punish someone **to sort something out** to resolve a problem or difficulty

sortie (say **sor** -tee) n **1** an attack by troops coming out from a besieged place **2** a flight of an aircraft on a military operation **3** a short trip

SOS n an urgent appeal for help or response

so-so adj neither very good nor very bad

sot n a drunkard

soubriquet (say **soo**-bri-kay) n another spelling of sobriquet

soufflé (say **soo**-flay) n a light spongy dish made with beaten egg white

sough (say sow or suf) v to make a moaning or whispering sound as the wind does in trees

souk (say sook) n an open-air market place in countries of the Middle East and North Africa

soul n **1** the spiritual or immortal element in a person **2** a person's mental, moral, or emotional nature **3** a personification or embodiment of some quality ♦ She is the soul of discretion. **4** a person **5** soul music **soulful** adj having or showing deep and often sorrowful feeling **soulless** adj **1** lacking human feelings **2** dull, uninteresting **soul-destroying** adj unbearably monotonous or depressing **soulmate** n a person ideally suited to another **soul music** n a kind of music combining elements of rhythm and blues and gospel music

sound[1] n **1** vibrations that travel through the air and can be detected by the ear **2** something that can be heard ♦ the sound of drums **3** the mental impression produced by a statement or description, etc. ♦ I don't like the sound of the new scheme. **sound** v **1** to produce or cause something to produce a sound ♦ Sound the trumpet! **2** to utter or pronounce something ♦ The 'h' in 'hour' is not sounded. **3** to give an impression when heard ♦ It sounds like an owl. ♦ The news sounds good. **4** to give an audible signal for something ♦ Sound the retreat! **5** to test something by noting the sound produced ♦ The doctor sounds a patient's lungs with a stethoscope. **sound barrier** n the high resistance of air to aircraft moving at speeds close to that of sound **sound bite** n a very short part of a speech, interview, or statement broadcast on radio or television because it seems to sum up the person's opinion in a few words **soundproof** adj not able to be penetrated by sound **soundproof** v to make a room, etc. soundproof **soundtrack** n the sound that goes with a cinema film

sound[2] adj **1** in good condition, not damaged **2** healthy, not diseased **3** logical and well-founded ♦ sound reasoning

4 showing good judgement, sensible ♦ *sound advice* **5** financially secure ♦ *a sound investment* **6** thorough or severe ♦ *a sound thrashing* **7** (said about sleep) deep and unbroken **soundly** *adv* **soundness** *n*

sound³ *v* **1** to test the depth or quality of the bottom of the sea or a river, etc., using a weighted line (called a *sounding line*) or sound echoes **2** to examine part of the body with a surgical probe **sounding** *n* measurement of the depth of water **sounding board** *n* a person whose reactions to ideas are used to test how good the ideas are **to sound someone out** to question someone cautiously to find out what they think or feel about something

sound⁴ *n* a strait of water

soup *n* liquid food made of stock from stewed meat, fish, or vegetables, etc. **soup** *v* **to soup something up** *informal* to increase the power of an engine **soup kitchen** *n* a place where free food is supplied to the homeless or needy

soupçon (say **soop**-sawn) *n* a very small quantity

sour *adj* **1** tasting sharp like lemon or vinegar **2** not fresh, tasting or smelling sharp or unpleasant from fermentation or staleness **3** showing resentment or anger ♦ *He gave me a sour look.* **sour** *v* to make something sour, or to become sour **sourly** *adv* **sourness** *n* **sour grapes** *n* pretending to despise something you want because you know you cannot have it yourself

source *n* **1** the place from which something comes or is obtained **2** the starting point of a river **3** a person, book, etc. providing information

souse (say sows) *v* **1** to soak something in liquid; to drench something with liquid **2** to soak fish, etc. in pickle or a marinade ♦ *soused herrings*

south *n* **1** the point or direction opposite north **2** the part of a place or building that is towards the south **south** *adj*, *adv* **1** towards or in the south **2** (said about a wind) blowing from the south **southerly** *adj* **southern** *adj* **southerner** *n* someone who lives in the south of a country or region **southward** *adj*, *adv*

southwards *adv* **south-east** *n* the point or direction midway between south and east **south-east** *adj*, *adv* in, to, or from the south-east **South Pole** *n* the southernmost point of the earth **south-west** *n* the point or direction midway between south and west **south-west** *adj*, *adv* in, to, or from the south-west

souvenir (say soo-vən-**eer**) *n* something bought or kept as a reminder of an incident or a place visited

sou'wester *n* a waterproof hat, usually of oilskin, with a broad flap at the back

sovereign (say **sov**-rin) *n* **1** a king or queen who is the supreme ruler of a country **2** an old British gold coin, originally worth £1 **sovereign** *adj* **1** possessing supreme power or authority **2** (said about a nation) independent ♦ *sovereign states* **sovereignty** *n pl* **sovereignties** **1** supreme power or authority **2** the authority of a state to govern itself or another state **3** an independent state

soviet (say **soh**-vi-ət or **sov**-i-ət) *n* an elected council in the former USSR **Soviet** *adj* to do with the former Soviet Union

sow¹ (say soh) *v* past participle **sown** or **sowed 1** to plant seed by scattering it on or in the ground **2** to spread or introduce feelings or ideas ♦ *Her words sowed doubt in my mind.*

sow² (say sow) *n* an adult female pig

soya bean *n* a kind of bean, originally from SE Asia, from which an edible oil and flour are obtained **soy sauce** *n* a salty brown sauce made by fermenting soya beans in brine, used in Chinese and Japanese cooking

sozzled *adj informal* very drunk

spa (say spah) *n* a health resort where there is a spring of water containing mineral salts

space *n* **1** the limitless expanse in which all objects exist and move **2** an area or volume that is available to be used ♦ *storage space* **3** an interval between points or objects, an empty area ♦ *There's a space here for your signature.* **4** the universe beyond the earth's atmosphere **5** an interval of time ♦ *within the space of an hour* **space** *v* to arrange things with spaces between ♦ *Space the chairs out.* **spacious** *adj* providing a lot of space **spaciousness** *n* **spacecraft** *n pl* **spacecraft** a vehicle for travelling in outer space **spaceman** *n pl* **spacemen** an astronaut **space shuttle** *n* a spacecraft designed for repeated use **space station** *n* an artificial satellite which orbits the earth and is used as a base for operations and experiments in space **spacesuit** *n* a sealed pressurized suit allowing an astronaut to survive in space

spade¹ *n* **1** a tool for digging ground, with a broad metal blade and a wooden handle **2** a tool of similar shape for other purposes **spadework** *n* hard or dull work done in preparation for something

spade² *n* a playing card of the suit (called *spades*) marked with black figures shaped like an inverted heart with a short stem

spaghetti (say spǝ-**get**-i) *n* pasta made in long thin solid sticks

spam *n* **1** *trademark* tinned pork luncheon meat **2** unwanted messages sent on the Internet to a large number of users

span *n* **1** the extent from end to end or across something **2** the length of time that something lasts **3** the distance between the tips of a person's thumb and little finger when these are stretched apart **span** *v* **spanned**, **spanning** to reach or extend across something

spangle *n* a small piece of glittering material, especially one of many decorating a dress, etc. **spangle** *v* to cover something with spangles or sparkling objects **spangly** *adj* **spanglier**, **spangliest**

Spaniard *n* a person born in Spain or descended from people born there

spaniel *n* a dog with long drooping ears and a silky coat

Spanish *adj* to do with or coming from Spain **Spanish** *n* the language of Spain, also spoken in much of Central and South America

spank *v* to smack a person on the bottom as a punishment

spanking *adj informal* brisk and lively ♦ *a spanking pace*

spanner *n* a tool for gripping and turning a

nut or bolt

spar¹ *n* a strong pole used for a mast, yard, or boom on a ship

spar² *v* **sparred**, **sparring** **1** to practise boxing **2** to argue with someone, especially in a friendly way

spare *v* **1** to part with or afford to give something ♦ *I can only spare a couple of hours.* **2** to be merciful towards someone, to refrain from hurting or harming a person or thing **3** to choose not to inflict something on someone ♦ *Spare me the gory details.* **spare** *adj* **1** additional to what is usually needed or used; kept for use when needed ♦ *a spare wheel* **2** thin or lean **3** elegantly simple ♦ *a spare style of writing* **spare** *n* a spare part or thing kept in reserve for use when needed **sparing** *adj* economical, not generous or wasteful **sparingly** *adv* **spare rib** *n* a cut of pork from the lower ribs **spare tyre** *n informal* a roll of fat round a person's waist **to spare** left over

spark *n* **1** a small fiery particle, e.g. one thrown off by something burning or caused by friction **2** a flash of light produced by an electrical discharge **3** liveliness and excitement **spark** *v* to give off a spark or sparks **a bright spark** a lively person **to spark something off** to trigger something off

sparkle *v* **1** to shine brightly with tiny flashes of light **2** to be witty and lively **sparkle** *n* **1** a glittering flash of light **2** liveliness and wit **sparkler** *n* a hand-held firework that gives off sparks **spark plug** *n* a device producing an electrical spark to ignite the fuel in an internal-combustion engine

sparrow *n* a small brownish-grey bird **sparrowhawk** *n* a small hawk that preys on small birds

sparse *adj* thinly scattered, not dense ♦ *a sparse population* **sparsely** *adv* **sparseness** *n* **sparsity** *n*

spartan *adj* (said about conditions) simple and sometimes harsh, without comfort or luxuries

spasm *n* **1** a sudden involuntary contraction of a muscle **2** a sudden brief spell of activity or emotion ♦ *a spasm of coughing* **spasmodic** *adj* **1** happening or done at irregular intervals **2** to do with or caused by a spasm or spasms **spasmodically** adv

spat[1] n a short gaiter covering the instep and ankle

spat[2] n a petty quarrel

spate (say spayt) n a sudden flood or rush

spatial (say **spay**-shəl) adj to do with or relating to space; existing in space **spatially** adv

spatter v to scatter drops of liquid over something; to be splashed in this way ♦ *The side of the car was spattered with mud.* **spatter** n a splash or splashes; the sound of spattering

spatula (say **spat**-yoo-lə) n a tool like a knife with a broad blunt flexible blade, used for spreading or mixing things

spawn n the eggs of fish, frogs, or shellfish **spawn** v **1** to release or deposit spawn **2** to produce something ♦ *The film has spawned a series of imitations.*

spay v to sterilize a female animal by removing the ovaries

speak v **spoke**, **spoken 1** to say something, to talk **2** to make a speech ♦ *He spoke for an hour.* **3** to use or be able to use a foreign language ♦ *Do you speak French?* **4** to express something or make it known ♦ *She spoke the truth.* **speaker** n **the Speaker** the person who controls the debates in the House of Commons or a similar assembly **spokesman** n pl **spokesmen** a spokesperson, especially a man **spokesperson** n pl **spokespersons**, **spokespeople** a person who speaks on behalf of a group **spokeswoman** n pl **spokeswomen**, **to speak out** to give your opinion frankly **to speak up 1** to speak more loudly **2** to give your opinion frankly

spear n **1** a weapon for throwing or stabbing, with a long shaft and a pointed tip **2** a pointed stem, e.g. of asparagus or broccoli **spear** v to pierce something with a spear or with something pointed **spearhead** n the person or group that leads an attacking or advancing force **spearhead** v to be the spearhead of something

spearmint n a common garden mint used in cookery and to flavour chewing gum

spec n **on spec** informal in the hope of being successful but without any preparation or plan ♦ *We thought we'd call round on spec to see if you were in.*

special adj **1** of a particular kind, different from the usual or normal kind ♦ *special training* ♦ *a special occasion* **2** designed for a particular purpose ♦ *You need a special key to open it.* **3** exceptional in amount, quality, or intensity ♦ *Take special care of it.* **special** n a special thing; a special train or edition, etc.

specialist n a person who is an expert in a particular branch of a subject **speciality** n pl **specialities 1** a product for which a person or region is famous **2** something in which a person specializes **specialize** v **1** to study a subject with special intensity; to become a specialist **2** to have a product, etc. to which you devote special attention ♦ *The shop specializes in sports goods.*

species (say **spee**-shiz) n pl **species** a group of animals or plants within a genus, differing only in minor details from the others

specific (say spi-**sif**-ik) adj **1** particular, clearly distinguished from others ♦ *The money was given for a specific purpose.* **2** expressing yourself in precise and clear terms, not vague **specific** n a precise detail **specifically** adv **specification** n **1** specifying, or being specified **2** a detailed description of how to make or do something **specify** v **specifies**, **specified**, **specifying 1** to mention details, ingredients, etc. clearly and definitely ♦ *The recipe specified cream, not milk.* **2** to include something in a list of specifications

specimen n **1** a part or individual taken as an example of a whole or of a class, especially for investigation or scientific examination ♦ *a specimen signature* **2** a quantity of a person's urine, etc. taken for testing **3** informal a person of a special sort ♦ *He seems a peculiar specimen.*

specious (say **spee**-shəs) adj seeming to be true or plausible at first sight but actually wrong or false ♦ *specious reasoning*

speck n a tiny spot or particle **speckle** n a small spot or patch, especially as a natural marking

specs pl n informal spectacles

spectacle n 1 a striking or impressive sight 2 a lavish public show or performance

spectacles pl n formal a pair of glasses

spectacular adj striking or impressive

spectacular n a performance or event produced on a large scale and with striking effects **spectacularly** adv

spectate v to be a spectator **spectator** n a person who watches a show, game, or other event

spectre (say **spek**-ter) n 1 a ghost 2 a haunting fear of future trouble ♦ The spectre of defeat loomed over them. **spectral** adj

spectrum n pl **spectra** 1 the bands of colour as seen in a rainbow, forming a series according to their wavelengths 2 an entire range of related qualities or ideas ♦ the political spectrum

speculate v 1 to form a theory or opinion about something without having definite knowledge or evidence 2 to invest in stocks, property, etc. in the hope of making a profit but with the risk of loss **speculation** n **speculative** adj **speculator** n

speech n 1 the act, power, or manner of speaking 2 a formal talk given to an audience 3 a sequence of lines spoken by a character in a play **speechless** adj unable to speak because of great emotion or shock **speech therapy** n treatment to improve a stammer or other defect of speech **speech therapist** n

speed n 1 the rate in time at which something moves or happens 2 rapidity of movement or action 3 the sensitivity of photographic film to light, the power of a lens to let in light **speed** v past tense and past participle **sped** or (in meanings 2 and 3) **speeded** 1 to move or pass quickly ♦ The years sped by. 2 to travel at a speed greater than the legal limit **speedy** adj **speedier**, **speediest** 1 moving quickly 2 done or coming without delay **speedily** adv **speediness** n **speedometer** n a device in a motor vehicle, showing its speed **speedboat** n a fast motor boat **speedway** n a form of motorcycle racing in which the riders travel round an oval dirt track **to speed up** to move or work at greater speed

spell[1] v past tense and past participle **spelt** or **spelled** 1 to write or name the letters that form a word in their correct sequence 2 (said about letters) to form a word **to spell something out** to explain something simply and in detail **speller** n **spelling** n

spell[2] n 1 words supposed to have magic power 2 the state of being influenced by this ♦ The wizard put them all under a spell. **spellbound** adj with the attention held as if by a spell, entranced

spell[3] n 1 a period of time during which something lasts ♦ during the cold spell 2 a period of a certain activity ♦ We each did a spell of driving.

spelt n a kind of wheat

spend v past tense and past participle **spent** 1 to pay out money in buying something 2 to use something for a certain purpose, to use something up ♦ Don't spend too much time on it. 3 to pass time ♦ We spent a holiday in Greece. **spender** n **spendthrift** n a person who spends money extravagantly and wastefully

sperm n pl **sperms** or **sperm** semen

sperm whale n a large whale from which a waxy oil can be obtained

spew v 1 to vomit 2 to cast something out in a stream

sphere (say **sfeer**) n 1 a perfectly round solid geometric figure 2 something shaped like this 3 a field of activity, influence, or interest **spherical** adj

sphincter (say **sfink**-ter) n a ring of muscle surrounding an opening in the body and able to close it by contracting

sphinx n 1 any of the ancient stone statues in Egypt with a lion's body and a human or animal's head 2 a person who does not reveal their thoughts and feelings

spice n 1 a substance, often obtained from dried parts of plants, with a strong taste or smell, used for flavouring food 2 something that adds interest or excitement **spice** v to flavour something with spice **spicy** adj **spicier**, **spiciest** 1 flavoured with spice 2 (said about stories) slightly scandalous or indecent **to spice something up** to make something more interesting or exciting

spick and span adj neat and clean

spider n an insect-like animal with eight

legs, which spins webs to trap insects on which it feeds **spidery** adj having thin, angular lines like a spider's legs ♦ spidery handwriting

spiel (say shpeel or speel) n informal a glib or lengthy speech, usually when trying to persuade someone or sell them something

spigot (say spig-ət) n a peg or plug used to stop up the vent hole of a cask or to control the flow of a tap

spike n a sharp point sticking out; a pointed piece of metal **spike** v 1 to put spikes on something 2 to pierce or fasten something with a spike 3 informal to secretly add alcohol or a drug to a drink or food **spiky** adj **spikier**, **spikiest** 1 like a spike or having many spikes 2 informal easily offended or annoyed **to spike someone's guns** to spoil someone's plans

spill[1] v past tense and past participle **spilt** or **spilled** 1 to allow or cause a liquid, etc. to run over the edge of its container 2 to become spilt 3 to go somewhere in large numbers and quickly ♦ The fans started to spill onto the pitch. **spill** n 1 a quantity of liquid that has spilt; an instance of spilling ♦ an acid spill 2 a fall from a horse, bicycle, etc. **spillage** n **to spill the beans** informal to let out information, especially without meaning to

spill[2] n a thin strip of wood or of twisted paper used for lighting a fire or pipe

spin v past tense and past participle **spun**; **spinning** 1 to turn or make something turn round quickly on its axis 2 (said about a ball) to revolve in the air and change direction when it bounces; to bowl or hit a ball so that it does this 3 to make raw cotton or wool, etc. into threads by pulling and twisting its fibres; to make thread in this way 4 (said about a spider or silkworm) to make a web or cocoon from a fine thread-like material it produces from its body 5 (said about a person's head) to give a feeling of dizziness **spin** n 1 a spinning movement 2 informal a short drive in a vehicle 3 informal a bias or slant given to a piece of news or information intended to be favourable to a particular person or group, usually a politician or political party

spinner n **spin doctor** n a person whose job is to present information or events in a way that is favourable to their employer, usually a politician or political party **spin dryer** n a machine in which moisture is removed from wet clothes by spinning them in a rapidly rotating drum **spinning wheel** n a household device for spinning fibre into yarn, with a spindle driven by a wheel **spin-off** n 1 a benefit or product produced incidentally from a larger process or while developing this; a by-product 2 a book, film, television series, etc. that is derived from an earlier successful one **to spin something out** to make something last as long as possible

spina bifida (say spiy-nə bif-id-ə) n a congenital condition in which certain bones of the spine are not properly developed and allow part of the spinal cord to stick out, sometimes causing paralysis and mental handicap

spinach n a vegetable with dark green leaves

spindle n 1 a thin rod on which thread is twisted or wound in spinning 2 a pin or axis that revolves or on which something revolves **spindly** adj long or tall and thin

spine n 1 the backbone 2 any of the sharp needle-like parts on certain plants (e.g. cacti) and animals (e.g. hedgehogs) 3 the part of a book where the pages are joined together; this section of the jacket or cover **spinal** adj **spineless** adj 1 without a backbone 2 lacking determination or strength of character **spiny** adj **spinier**, **spiniest** covered with spines, prickly **spinal cord** n the rope-like bundle of nerve fibres enclosed within the spinal column, that carries impulses to and from the brain **spine-chilling** adj causing a thrill of terror

spinnaker (say spin-ə-ker) n a large triangular extra sail on a racing yacht

spinney n pl **spinneys** a small area of trees and bushes; a thicket

spinster n an unmarried woman

spiral adj 1 going round and round a central point or axis and becoming gradually closer to it or further from it 2 winding in a continuous curve round a central line or cylinder **spiral** n 1 a spiral curve or shape; a thing of spiral form 2 a continuous increase or decrease in two or more quantities alternately because of their dependence on each other ♦ *the spiral of rising wages and prices* **spiral** v **spiralled, spiralling 1** to move in a spiral 2 to increase or decrease continuously and quickly

spire n a pointed structure in the form of a tall cone or pyramid, especially on a church tower

spirit n 1 a person's mind, feelings, or character as distinct from the body 2 the soul, believed by some people to remain after death 3 a ghost or supernatural being 4 a person's nature 5 the characteristic quality or mood of something ♦ *the spirit of the times* 6 the real meaning or intention of something as distinct from a strict interpretation of the words used to express it ♦ *the spirit of the law* 7 liveliness or courage, readiness to assert yourself 8 a distilled extract; purified alcohol **spirits** pl n 1 a person's mood ♦ *He was in good spirits.* 2 strong distilled alcoholic drink, e.g. whisky or gin **spirit** v **spirited, spiriting** to carry a person or thing off swiftly and secretly ♦ *The airport staff spirited him away before anyone noticed.* **spirited** adj 1 full of liveliness and courage 2 having a character or mood of a specified kind ♦ *a generous-spirited person* **spiritualism** n the belief that spirits of the dead can and do communicate with the living; practices based on this **spiritualist** n **spiritual** adj 1 to do with the human spirit or soul, not physical or worldly 2 to do with religion or religious belief **spiritual** n a religious folk song associated with black Christians of the southern USA **spirituality** n **spiritually** adv **spirit level** n a glass tube nearly filled with alcohol or other liquid and containing an air bubble, used to test whether a surface is perfectly level by means of the position of this bubble

spit[1] v past tense and past participle **spat** or **spit; spitting 1** to send out saliva, food, or liquid forcibly from the mouth 2 (said about fire, hot fat, etc.) to throw out sparks, fat, etc. with a series of explosive noises 3 to utter something violently 4 to fall lightly ♦ *It's spitting with rain.* **spit** n 1 saliva or spittle 2 the act of spitting **spittle** n saliva, especially when it is spat out **spittoon** n a container for spitting into **spitfire** n a person with a fierce temper **spitting image** n an exact likeness **to be the spit** or **dead spit of** informal to look exactly like someone ♦ *He's the dead spit of his father.*

spit[2] n 1 a long thin metal spike put through meat to hold and turn it while it is being roasted 2 a long narrow strip of land sticking out into the sea

spite n a malicious desire to hurt, annoy, or humiliate another person **spite** v to hurt, annoy, or humiliate someone from spite **spiteful** adj **spitefully** adv **spitefulness** n **in spite of** not being prevented by ♦ *We enjoyed ourselves in spite of the weather.*

spiv n informal a smartly-dressed man who makes money by shady dealings or by selling goods on the black market

splash v 1 to make liquid fly about or fall on something in drops 2 (said about liquid) to fall or be scattered in drops 3 to display a story or photograph in a prominent place in a newspaper or magazine 4 to decorate something with irregular patches of colour, etc. **splash** n 1 splashing, or the sound made by this 2 a quantity of liquid splashed on to a surface 3 a small quantity of liquid added to a drink 4 a bright patch of colour or light **splashdown** n the landing of a spacecraft on the sea **to make a splash** informal to attract a lot of attention **to splash out** informal to spend money freely

splatter v to splash or make something splash with large drops

splay v to spread something apart or be spread apart **splay** adj turned outward or widened

spleen n 1 an organ of the body situated at the left of the stomach and involved in keeping the blood in good condition 2 bad temper, spite ♦ *He vented his spleen on us.* **splenetic** adj bad-tempered or spiteful

splendid adj 1 magnificent, very impressive 2 excellent ♦ *a splendid achievement* **splendidly** adv **splendour** n

splice v 1 to join two ends of rope by

untwisting and interweaving the strands of each **2** to join pieces of film, tape, or timber by overlapping the ends **to get spliced** *informal* to get married

splint *n* **1** a strip of wood or metal tied to an injured part of the body to prevent movement, e.g. while a broken bone heals **2** a thin strip of wood used to light a fire **splinter** *n* a small, thin, sharp piece of wood, stone, glass, etc. broken off from a larger piece **splinter** *v* to break something or become broken into splinters **splinter group** *n* a small group of people that has broken away from a larger one, e.g. in a political party

split *v* past tense and past participle **split**; **splitting 1** to break something or become broken into parts, especially lengthways or along the grain of wood, etc. **2** to divide something or become divided into parts **3** to divide and share something **4** to come apart, to tear **5** to divide or become divided into disagreeing or hostile groups **6** *informal* to leave somewhere suddenly **split** *n* **1** a division or separation, especially one resulting from a disagreement **2** a crack or tear made by splitting **3** the splitting or dividing of something **splits** *n* an acrobatic position in which the legs are stretched in opposite directions and at right angles to the trunk **splitting** *adj* (said about a headache) very severe **split infinitive** *n* an infinitive with a word or words placed between *to* and the verb, e.g. *to thoroughly understand* ◊ Although a split infinitive is not strictly speaking a grammatical error, many people dislike this construction. For this reason it is probably best to avoid it in formal writing, e.g. by putting *to understand thoroughly*. **split-level** *adj* **1** (said about a building) having adjoining rooms at a level midway between successive storeys in other parts **2** (said about a cooker) having the oven and the hob as separate units **split second** *n* a very brief moment of time **to split on** *informal* to inform on someone or betray their secrets **to split up** to end a marriage or other relationship

splotch, splodge *n* a splash or blotch on something

splurge *v* *informal* to spend a lot of money on something, especially as a luxury **splurge** *n* *informal* a sudden burst of extravagance

splutter *v* **1** to make a rapid series of spitting or choking sounds **2** to speak rapidly but not clearly, e.g. in rage **splutter** *n* a spluttering sound

spoil *v* past tense and past participle **spoilt** or **spoiled 1** to damage something and make it useless or unsatisfactory **2** to become unfit for eating or use **3** to make a child selfish by always letting them have what they want **4** to treat someone with great or too much kindness or generosity **spoils** *pl n* **1** plunder or other benefits taken by force ♦ *the spoils of war* **2** benefits or rewards of an official position **spoiler** *n* a device on an aircraft to slow it down by interrupting the airflow **spoilsport** *n* a person who spoils the enjoyment of other people **to be spoiling for** to desire something eagerly ♦ *He is spoiling for a fight.*

spoke *n* each of the bars or wire rods that connect the centre or hub of a wheel to its rim

spoliation (say spoh-li-**ay**-shən) *n* **1** pillaging **2** spoiling

sponge *n* **1** a sea creature with a soft, porous body **2** the skeleton of this, or a substance of similar texture, used for washing, cleaning, or padding **3** (also **sponge cake**) a soft, light cake made with little or no fat **4** a wipe or wash with a sponge **sponge** *v* **1** to wipe or wash something with a sponge **2** *informal* to get money or food off other people without giving anything in return **sponger** *n* a person who lives at other people's expense **spongy** *adj* **spongier, spongiest, sponge bag** *n* a bag for holding soap and other items for washing

sponsor *n* **1** a person or organization that provides funds for a musical, artistic, or sporting event or for a broadcast in return for advertising **2** a person who promises to give money to a charity in return for something achieved by another person **3** a person who puts forward a proposal, e.g.

for a new law **4** a godparent **sponsor** v to act as sponsor for someone or something **sponsorship** n

spontaneous (say spon-**tay**-niəs) adj **1** occurring or developing naturally, without an external cause **2** done on impulse without planning ♦ a spontaneous gesture **spontaneity** n **spontaneously** adv

spoof n informal **1** a parody, especially of a type of film **2** a hoax

spook n informal **1** a ghost **2** a spy **spook** v to frighten someone, or to become frightened **spooky** adj **spookier**, **spookiest** ghostly or eerie

spool n a rod or cylinder on which something is wound, e.g. thread, film, or magnetic tape **spool** v to wind something or become wound on a spool

spoon n a utensil consisting of an oval or round bowl and a handle, used for lifting food to the mouth or for stirring or measuring things **spoon** v to take or lift something with a spoon **spoonful** n pl **spoonfuls** **spoon-feed** v past tense and past participle **spoon-fed 1** to feed a baby or invalid with liquid food from a spoon **2** to give so much help or information to someone that they do not need to think for themselves

spoonerism n an accidental exchange of the initial sounds of two words, usually as a slip of the tongue, e.g. saying a boiled sprat instead of a spoiled brat

spoor n the track or scent left by an animal

sporadic (say sper-**ad**-ik) adj occurring here and there, scattered **sporadically** adv

sporran (say **spo**-rən) n a pouch worn hanging in front of the kilt as part of Scottish Highland dress

sport n **1** a competitive activity involving physical activity and skill, especially one outdoors **2** such activities collectively **3** amusement or fun ♦ We said it in sport. **4** informal a person who behaves well in response to teasing or defeat **sport** v to wear or display something **sporting** adj **1** interested in or connected with sport **2** behaving fairly and generously **sportive** adj playful **sporty** adj **sportier**, **sportiest**, **sporting chance** n a reasonable

chance of success **sports car** n an open, low-built, fast car **sports jacket** n a man's jacket for informal wear, not part of a suit **sportsman**, **sportswoman** n pl **sportsmen**, **sportswomen 1** a person who takes part in a sport, especially professionally **2** a person who shows sportsmanship **sportsmanship** n sporting behaviour; behaving fairly and generously to rivals

spot n **1** a round area different in colour from the rest of a surface **2** a pimple or other red mark on the skin **3** a particular place or locality **4** informal a small amount of something **spot** v **spotted**, **spotting 1** to mark something with spots **2** to notice or recognize someone or something **3** to watch for and take note of something, especially as a hobby ♦ train-spotting **in a spot** informal in difficulties **on the spot 1** without delay or change of place **2** at the scene of an incident **spot on** informal exactly right or accurate **spotless** adj free from stains or marks, perfectly clean **spotted** adj **spotter** n **spotty** adj **spottier**, **spottiest**, **spot check** n a check made without warning on something chosen at random **spotlight** n **1** a beam of light directed on to a small area, or a lamp giving this **2** public attention ♦ She is not used to being in the spotlight. **to put someone on the spot** to force someone into a situation in which they must respond or take action

spouse n a person's husband or wife

spout n **1** a projecting tube through which liquid can be poured **2** a jet of liquid **spout** v **1** to come or send something out forcefully as a jet of liquid **2** to speak for a long time, expressing your views **up the spout** informal broken, ruined, or useless

sprain v to injure a joint or its muscles or ligaments by twisting it violently **sprain** n an injury caused in this way

sprat n a small, herring-like fish used for food

sprawl v **1** to sit, lie, or fall with the arms and legs spread out loosely **2** to spread out over a large area in an irregular way **sprawl** n **1** a sprawling attitude, movement, or arrangement **2** an irregular or disorganized expansion of something ♦ *an urban sprawl*

spray[1] *n* **1** liquid sent through the air in very small drops **2** a device for spraying liquid **spray** *v* **1** to put liquid on something in a spray **2** (said about a liquid) to be sent through the air in very small drops **3** to scatter something over an area with force **spray gun** *n* a gun-like device for spraying a liquid such as paint

spray[2] *n* **1** a single shoot or branch with its leaves, twigs, and flowers **2** a small bunch of cut flowers arranged decoratively

spread *v* past tense and past participle **spread** **1** to open or stretch something out, to unroll or unfold something ♦ *The peacock spread its tail.* ♦ *Spread the map out.* **2** to become longer or wider ♦ *The stain began to spread.* **3** to make something cover a surface, to apply something as a layer ♦ *He spread the bread with jam.* **4** to make something or to become more widely known, felt, or suffered ♦ *Rats spread disease.* **5** to distribute something or become distributed over a large area ♦ *Settlers soon spread inland.* **6** to distribute something over a period ♦ *You can spread the payments over 12 months.* **spread** *n* **1** spreading, or being spread **2** the extent, expanse, or breadth of something **3** the range of something **4** *informal* a lavish meal **5** a sweet or savoury paste for spreading on bread **6** an article or feature covering several columns or pages of a newspaper or magazine **spreadeagled** *adj* with arms and legs stretched out ♦ *He lay spreadeagled on the bed.* **spreadsheet** *n* a computer program that allows numerical, especially financial, data to be displayed in a table and manipulated

spree *n* a period in which you do something freely ♦ *a shopping spree*

sprig *n* **1** a small stem with leaves or flowers on it **2** an ornament or decoration in this form

sprightly *adj* **sprightlier**, **sprightliest** lively and full of energy **sprightliness** *n*

spring *v* **sprang**, **sprung** **1** to move rapidly or suddenly upwards or forwards **2** to grow, originate, or arise ♦ *Weeds had started to spring up.* ♦ *Their discontent springs from*

distrust of their leaders. **3** *informal* to help a prisoner escape **4** to cause something to operate suddenly ♦ *Just then they sprang their trap.* **spring** *n* **1** the season in which most plants begin to grow, from March to May in the northern hemisphere **2** a device, usually of bent or coiled metal, that returns to its original position after being compressed or tightened or stretched **3** elasticity **4** a sudden jump upwards or forwards **5** a place where water comes up naturally from the ground **springy** *adj* **springier**, **springiest** able to spring back easily after being squeezed or stretched **springboard** *n* **1** a flexible board that a gymnast or diver jumps on to gain height or impetus **2** something that is used to get an activity started **spring clean** *n* a thorough cleaning of your home, especially in spring **spring onion** *n* a young onion with a long green stem, eaten raw in salads **springtime** *n* the season of spring

sprinkle *v* **1** to scatter or fall in small drops or pieces **2** to scatter small drops or pieces on a surface **3** to distribute something randomly throughout a thing **sprinkler** *n* a device for sprinkling water **sprinkling** *n*

sprint *v* to run very fast over a short distance **sprint** *n* **1** a run or race of this kind **2** a short fast race in swimming, cycling, etc. **sprinter** *n*

sprite *n* an elf or fairy

sprocket *n* each of the row of teeth round a wheel, fitting into links on a chain or holes in film, tape, or paper

sprout *v* **1** to put out new leaves or shoots **2** to begin to grow or develop **sprout** *n* **1** a new shoot or bud **2** a Brussels sprout

spruce[1] *adj* neat and smart **spruce** *v* to make a person or place smarter ♦ *Spruce yourself up a bit.* **spruceness** *n*

spruce[2] *n* a kind of fir tree with dense foliage, or its wood

spry *adj* **spryer**, **spryest** active, nimble, and lively

spud *n* *informal* a potato

spume *n* froth or foam, especially on waves

spunk *n* *informal* courage and determination **spunky** *adj*

spur *n* **1** a pricking device with a small spike

or toothed wheel, worn on the heel of a rider's boot to urge a horse to go faster **2** a stimulus or incentive **3** something shaped like a spur **4** a ridge sticking out from a mountain **spur** v **spurred**, **spurring 1** to urge a horse on by pricking it with spurs **2** to encourage someone or urge them on **on the spur of the moment** on an impulse, without previous planning

spurge n a kind of plant or bush with a bitter, milky juice

spurious (say **spewr**-iəs) adj not genuine or authentic

spurn v to reject something with disdain or contempt

spurt v to gush out, to send out a liquid suddenly **spurt** n **1** a sudden gush **2** a short burst of speed or activity

sputnik (say **sput**-nik or **spoot**-nik) n a Soviet artificial satellite orbiting the earth

sputter v to splutter; to make a series of quick, explosive sounds **sputter** n a sputtering sound

sputum (say **spew**-təm) n saliva or phlegm

spy n pl **spies 1** a person employed by a government or organization to gather and report secret information about the activities of an enemy or competitor **2** someone who watches other people secretly **spy** v **spies**, **spied**, **spying 1** to be a spy **2** to keep watch secretly ♦ *Have you been spying on me?* **3** to see or notice something **spyglass** n a small telescope

sq abbr square

squab (say skwob) n a young pigeon

squabble v to quarrel in a petty or noisy way, as children do **squabble** n a quarrel of this kind

squad n **1** a small group of soldiers or police officers working together **2** a group of sports players from which a team is chosen

squadron n **1** a unit of an air force, consisting of between 10 and 18 aircraft **2** a division of an armoured or cavalry regiment, consisting of two troops **3** a detachment of warships

squalid adj **1** dirty and unpleasant, especially because of neglect or poverty **2** showing a lack of moral standards **squalor** n

squall n **1** a sudden storm of wind, especially with rain, snow, or sleet **2** a baby's loud cry **squally** adj

squander v to spend money or time, etc. wastefully

square n **1** a geometric figure with four equal sides and four right angles **2** an area or object shaped like this **3** a four-sided area surrounded by buildings ♦ *Leicester Square.* **4** the product obtained when a number is multiplied by itself ♦ *9 is the square of 3 (9 = 3 x 3)* **square** adj **1** having the shape of a square **2** of or using units that express the measurement of an area ♦ *one square metre* **3** level or parallel **4** properly arranged or organized **5** (also **all square**) equal or even, with no balance of advantage or debt, etc. on either side ♦ *The teams are all square with six points each.* **6** informal old-fashioned or boringly conventional **square** adv straight, directly **square** v **1** to make something right-angled or square **2** to multiply a number by itself **3** to settle or pay something **4** to make the score of a match even **5** to be or make something consistent ♦ *His story doesn't square with yours.* **squarely** adv **1** directly centred, not to one side **2** directly or unequivocally ♦ *Responsibility rests squarely with the local authority.* **square dance** n a country dance in which four couples face inwards from four sides **square deal** n a deal that is honest and fair **square meal** n a large satisfying meal **square root** n a number that produces a given number when it is multiplied by itself ♦ *3 is the square root of 9 (3 x 3 = 9)* **to square up to** to face and tackle a person or difficulty

squash¹ v **1** to crush or squeeze something so that it becomes flat, soft, or out of shape **2** to squeeze or force something into a small space **3** to suppress or overcome a rebellion, etc. **4** to silence someone with a crushing reply **squash** n **1** a crowd of people squashed together; a state of being squashed **2** a fruit-flavoured soft drink **3** (also **squash rackets**) a game played with rackets and a small rubber ball in a closed court **squashy** adj **squashier**, **squashiest**

squash² n a kind of gourd used as a

vegetable, or the plant that bears it

squat v **squatted**, **squatting 1** to sit on your heels or crouch with your knees drawn up closely **2** to live in an unoccupied building without authority **squat** n **1** a squatting posture **2** a building occupied by squatters; occupying a building as a squatter **squat** adj short and fat **squatter** n a person who is living in an unoccupied building without authority

squaw n an Native American woman or wife ◊ This word is now considered to be offensive.

squawk n a loud harsh cry **squawk** v **1** to make a loud harsh cry **2** informal to complain

squeak n a short high-pitched cry or sound **squeak** v to make a squeak **squeaky** adj **squeakier**, **squeakiest**, **a narrow squeak** informal a narrow escape from danger or failure

squeal n a long shrill cry or sound **squeal** v **1** to make this cry or sound **2** informal to protest sharply **3** informal to inform on someone

squeamish adj **1** easily sickened or disgusted **2** excessively scrupulous about moral principles **squeamishness** n

squeegee (say skwee-jee) n a tool with a rubber blade or roller on a handle, used for scraping away water, especially when cleaning windows

squeeze v **1** to press something firmly from opposite or all sides **2** to get moisture or juice out of something by squeezing **3** to force something into or through a place; to manage to get into or through a small or narrow place ♦ We squeezed six people into the car. ♦ She squeezed through the gap in the hedge. **4** to press a person's hand, etc. gently as a sign of affection or reassurance **5** to obtain something from someone with difficulty ♦ We managed to squeeze a promise out of him. **squeeze** n **1** squeezing, or being squeezed **2** an affectionate clasp or hug **3** a small amount of liquid squeezed out ♦ Add a squeeze of lemon. **4** a crowd or crush, the pressure of this ♦ We all got in, but it was a tight squeeze. **5** restrictions on borrowing or spending imposed during a

financial crisis

squelch v to make a sound like someone treading in thick mud **squelch** n this sound

squib n a small firework that hisses and then explodes

squid n a sea creature related to the cuttlefish, with eight arms and two long tentacles

squiffy adj **squiffier**, **squiffiest** informal slightly drunk

squiggle n a short curly line, especially in handwriting **squiggly** adv

squint v **1** to look at something with partly closed eyes **2** to have a squint affecting one eye **squint** n **1** a condition in which one eye is permanently turned from the line of gaze of the other **2** informal a quick or casual look **squint** adj informal not straight or level

squire n **1** a country gentleman, especially the chief landowner in a district **2** a young nobleman in the Middle Ages who served a knight before becoming a knight himself

squirm v **1** to wriggle or twist your body from side to side **2** to feel embarrassed or ashamed **squirm** n a wriggling movement

squirrel n a tree-climbing rodent with a bushy tail and red or grey fur

squirt v **1** to send out liquid or be sent out in a thin jet **2** to wet something with a jet of liquid **squirt** n **1** a thin jet of liquid **2** informal a small or insignificant person

squish v to make a soft squelching sound **squish** n a soft squelching sound **squishy** adj **squishier**, **squishiest**

SS abbr **1** saints **2** steamship **3** the Nazi special police force (German Schutzstaffel)

St abbr **1** Saint **2** Street

stab v **stabbed**, **stabbing 1** to wound or pierce someone or something with a pointed tool or weapon **2** to aim a blow with or as if with a pointed weapon **stab** n **1** an act of stabbing; a wound made by stabbing **2** a sudden sharp pain **3** informal an attempt **to stab someone in the back** to betray someone

stable[1] adj **stabler**, **stablest 1** steady and firmly fixed or balanced **2** strong and lasting; not likely to change or collapse ♦ a stable government **3** sensible and dependable **stability** n **stabilize** v

stabilization n **stabilizer** n **1** a device to prevent a ship from rolling **2** the horizontal tailplane of an aircraft **3** a substance to prevent the breakdown of emulsions in food or paint **stabilizers** pl n a pair of small wheels fitted to a child's bicycle to help keep it upright

stable² n **1** a building in which horses are kept **2** an establishment for training racehorses; the horses from a particular establishment **3** an establishment managing, training, or producing a group of people or things ♦ *two snooker players from the same stable* **stable** v to put or keep a horse in a stable

staccato (say stə-*kah*-toh) adj, adv **1** *Mus* with each note sounded in a sharp disconnected manner, not running on smoothly **2** with short sharp sounds ♦ *a staccato voice*

stack n **1** an orderly pile or heap **2** *informal* a large quantity **3** a tall factory chimney; a chimney or funnel for smoke on a steamer, etc. **stack** v **1** to pile things up; to arrange things in a stack **2** to instruct aircraft to fly round the same point at different altitudes while waiting to land

stadium n pl **stadiums** or **stadia** a sports ground surrounded by tiers of seats for spectators

staff n **1** the people who work in a particular organization, shop, etc. **2** a stick or pole used as a weapon, support, or measuring stick, or as a symbol of authority **staff** v to provide an organization with a staff of employees or assistants ♦ *The centre is staffed by volunteers.* **staff nurse** n a qualified nurse less senior than a sister

stag n a fully-grown male deer **stag night** n a celebration for a man who is about to get married, attended only by men

stage n **1** a point, period, or step in the course or development of something ♦ *The talks have reached a critical stage.* **2** a section of a journey or race **3** a platform on which plays, etc. are performed before an audience **4** theatrical work, the profession of actors and actresses **stage** v **1** to present a play or other performance on a stage **2** to arrange something and carry it out ♦ *The*

students decided to stage a sit-in. **stagy** adj **stagier**, **stagiest** theatrical in style or manner. **stagecoach** n a horse-drawn coach that formerly ran regularly along the same route, carrying passengers and often mail **stage fright** n nervousness before or while performing to an audience **stage-manage** v **1** to be the stage manager of a play **2** to organize and control an event in order to create a particular effect **stage manager** n the person responsible for the scenery, props, and other practical arrangements in the production of a play **stage whisper** n a loud whisper that is meant to be overheard

stagger v **1** to walk unsteadily, as if you are about to fall **2** to astonish or shock someone **3** to place things in an alternating or overlapping arrangement, not in a line ♦ *a staggered junction* **4** to arrange people's holidays or hours of work, etc. so that their times do not coincide exactly **stagger** n **1** an unsteady staggering movement **2** the staggered arrangement of the runners on a track at the start of a race **staggering** adj astonishing

stagnate (say stag-*nayt*) v **1** to become stagnant **2** (said about a person) to become dull through lack of activity, variety, or opportunity **stagnant** adj **1** (said about water) not flowing, still and stale **2** showing no activity ♦ *Business was stagnant.* **stagnation** n

staid (say stayd) adj steady and serious in manner, tastes, etc.

stain v **1** to make a dirty or coloured mark on something; to become discoloured by a substance **2** to colour something with a dye or pigment that penetrates **stain** n **1** a mark caused by staining **2** something that damages someone's reputation or past record **3** a liquid used for staining things **stainless** adj **stainless steel** n steel containing chromium and not liable to rust or tarnish under ordinary conditions

stair n each of a set of fixed indoor steps **stairs** pl n a set of these **staircase** n a set of stairs, often with banisters, and its supporting structure **stairwell** n the space going up through a building, which contains the staircase

stake n 1 a stick or post with a point at one end, driven into the ground as a support or marker 2 an amount of money bet on the result of a race or other event 3 a share or interest in a business or situation **stake** v 1 to fasten or support something with stakes 2 to mark an area with stakes 3 to bet or risk money, etc. on an event **at stake** being risked, depending on the outcome of an event **to stake a claim** to claim or obtain a right to something **to stake something out** informal to keep a place under surveillance

stalactite (say **stal**-ək-tiyt) n a deposit of calcium carbonate hanging like an icicle from the roof of a cave, etc.

stalagmite (say **stal**-əg-miyt) n a deposit like a stalactite but standing like a pillar on the floor of a cave, etc.

stale adj **staler**, **stalest** 1 (said about food) no longer fresh or pleasant to eat 2 (said about air) not fresh; musty 3 no longer new and interesting ♦ stale jokes 4 no longer able to perform well or have new ideas because you have been doing something for too long **staleness** n

stalemate n 1 a drawn position in chess, in which a player cannot make a move without putting their own king in check 2 a situation on which neither side in an argument will give way and progress seems impossible

stalk[1] n the stem of a plant

stalk[2] v 1 to track or hunt an animal or person stealthily 2 to harass someone, especially a celebrity, with unwanted and obsessive attention 3 to walk in a stiff, dignified, or angry manner **stalker** n

stall n 1 a stand, table, or counter from which things are sold, especially in a market 2 an individual compartment for an animal in a stable or cowshed 3 a compartment for one person **stalls** pl n the set of seats on the ground floor of a theatre **stall** v 1 (said about an engine or vehicle) to stop suddenly because of an overload or insufficient fuel 2 to cause an engine to stall 3 to stop making progress, or to prevent something from making progress

4 to avoid acting or giving a definite answer in order to gain time

stallion (say **stal**-yən) n an uncastrated male horse, especially one kept for breeding

stalwart (say **stawl**-wert) adj 1 strong and faithful ♦ stalwart supporters 2 sturdy **stalwart** n a stalwart supporter or member of an organization

stamina (say **stam**-in-ə) n staying power, the ability to withstand prolonged physical or mental effort

stammer v to speak with involuntary pauses or rapid repetitions of the same syllable **stammer** n a tendency to stammer **stammerer** n

stamp v 1 to bring your foot down heavily on the ground 2 to walk with loud heavy steps 3 to stick a postage stamp on something 4 to strike or press something with a device that leaves a mark or pattern, etc.; to cut or shape something in this way 5 to give a certain character to something ♦ This achievement stamps him as a genius. **stamp** n 1 a postage stamp 2 a device for stamping a pattern or mark; the mark itself 3 a distinguishing mark, a clear indication ♦ His story bears the stamp of truth. 4 the act or sound of stamping **stamping ground** n a person's or animal's usual haunt or place of action **to stamp something out 1** to put out a fire by stamping on it 2 to put an end to something

stampede n 1 a sudden rush of a herd of frightened animals 2 a rush of people under a sudden common impulse **stampede** v to take part or cause animals or people to take part in a stampede

stance n 1 the position in which a person stands 2 a person's attitude to something

stanch v another spelling of staunch[2]

stanchion (say **stan**-shən) n an upright bar or post forming a support

stand v past tense and past participle **stood**; 1 to be in or rise to an upright position ♦ We were standing at the back of the hall. 2 to place something or be situated in a particular position ♦ Stand the vase on the table. 3 to stay the same, to remain valid ♦ My offer still stands. 4 to be in a particular condition or at a particular value ♦ *The thermometer stood at 90°.* **5** to be a candidate in an election ♦ *She stood for Parliament.* **6** to put up with or endure something ♦ *I can't stand that noise.* **7** to withstand being damaged **8** to provide and pay for something ♦ *I'll stand you a drink.* **stand** *n* **1** a rack or pedestal, etc. on which something may be held or displayed **2** a stall, booth, or other structure where things are sold or displayed **3** a raised structure with seats at a sports ground, etc. **4** an attitude towards a particular issue **5** a determined effort to resist an attack, or the period of this ♦ *The time has come to make a stand.* **6** a witness box **standing** *n* **1** a person's status or reputation **2** the period for which something has existed ♦ *a friendship of long standing* **standing** *adj* permanent or regularly repeated ♦ *a standing invitation* **standby** *n pl* **standbys 1** a person or thing available to be used as a substitute or in an emergency **2** a system by which seats for a play, on an aircraft, etc. that have not yet been reserved can be bought at the last minute **standing order** *n* an instruction to a bank to make regular payments to someone, or to a trader to supply something regularly **stand-off** *n* a deadlock between two equally matched opponents **stand-offish** *adj* aloof, distant, and unfriendly in manner **standpipe** *n* a vertical pipe connected directly to a water supply, especially one set up in the street to provide water in an emergency **standpoint** *n* a point of view **standstill** *n* a complete stop ♦ *Traffic has come to a virtual standstill.* **stand-up** *adj* **1** (said about a comedian or comedy) performing or performed solo in front of a live audience **2** (said about a fight or argument) vigorous, involving direct confrontation **to stand by 1** to look on without interfering **2** to support or side with a person in a difficulty or dispute **3** to keep to a promise or agreement **4** to be ready to take action if needed **to stand down** or **stand aside** to resign from a position or office **to stand for 1** to represent or be an abbreviation for something ♦ *'US' stands for 'United States'*

2 *informal* to tolerate something **to stand in** to deputize **to stand out 1** to stick out or be conspicuous **2** to be clearly better than others **to stand someone up** *informal* to fail to keep a date or appointment with someone **to stand up** to be valid ♦ *That argument won't stand up in court.* **to stand up for** to defend or support a person or opinion **to stand up to 1** to resist someone bravely **2** to stay in good condition despite the harmful effects of something

standard *n* **1** how good something is ♦ *The standard of her work is high.* **2** a specified level of quality, attainment, or proficiency ♦ *Your work does not reach the required standard.* **3** a thing, quality, or specification by which something may be tested or measured **4** a special flag ♦ *the royal standard* **5** an upright support **standards** *pl n* principles of decent honourable behaviour **standard** *adj* **1** as or conforming to a standard ♦ *standard measures of length* **2** of average or usual quality or type ♦ *the standard model of this car* **3** accepted as being authoritative and so widely used ♦ *the standard book on spiders* **4** widely accepted as the usual form ♦ *standard English* **standardize** *v* to make things conform to a standard size, quality, etc. **standardization** *n* **standard lamp** *n* a household lamp set on a tall pillar on a base

stanza *n* a verse of poetry

staple¹ *n* **1** a U-shaped piece of metal or wire pushed through papers and clenched to fasten them together **2** a U-shaped metal nail for holding wires, etc. in place **staple** *v* to fix something with a staple or staples **stapler** *n*

staple² *adj* main or important ♦ *Rice is their staple food.* **staple** *n* a staple food or product, etc.

star *n* **1** a large mass of burning gas that is seen as a point of light in the night sky **2** a figure, object, or ornament with rays or radiating points; an asterisk **3** a star-shaped symbol indicating a category of excellence ♦ *a five-star hotel* **4** a famous or brilliant actor, singer, sports player, etc. **stars** *pl n* a horoscope **star** *v* **starred, starring 1** to perform or have someone as one of the main actors ♦ *She is to star in a new production of Cabaret.* **2** to put an asterisk or star symbol beside a name or item in a list, etc. **stardom** *n* being a star actor or performer **starry** *adj* **starrier, starriest** **1** full of stars **2** shining like stars **starfish** *n pl* **starfishes** or **starfish** a sea creature shaped like a star with five or more points **starry-eyed** *adj* naively optimistic or idealistic **star sign** *n* a sign of the zodiac

starboard *n* the right-hand side of a ship or aircraft when facing forward, the opposite to *port*

starch *n* **1** a white carbohydrate that is an important element in human food. It is found in bread, potatoes, etc. **2** a preparation of this or a similar substance used for stiffening fabric **3** stiffness of manner **starchy** *adj* **starchier, starchiest**

stare *v* to look fixedly at someone or something with the eyes wide open, especially in astonishment **stare** *n* a staring gaze

stark *adj* **1** severe or bare in appearance; desolate ♦ *a stark moorland* **2** sharply evident ♦ *in stark contrast* **3** downright, complete ♦ *stark madness* **stark naked** completely naked

starling *n* a noisy bird with glossy blackish speckled feathers, that forms large flocks

start *v* **1** to begin or cause something to begin a process or course of action **2** to make an engine or machine begin running; to begin running **3** to establish or found something; to be established or founded **4** to make a sudden movement because of pain or surprise **start** *n* **1** the beginning of a journey, activity, or race **2** the place where a race starts **3** an advantage given in starting a race ♦ *We gave the young ones 10 seconds start.* **4** a sudden movement of surprise or pain **starter** *n* **1** a person or thing that starts something **2** a person who gives the signal for a race to start **3** a horse or competitor at the start of a race **4** the first course of a meal

startle *v* to surprise or alarm someone **startling** *adj*

starve *v* **1** to die or suffer acutely from lack of food; to cause someone to do this **2** to deprive someone of something they need ♦ *starved of affection* **starvation** *n*

stash *v informal* to store something safely in a secret place **stash** *n informal* a secret store

state *n* **1** the condition of someone or something ♦ *a poor state of health* **2** the physical structure or form of a substance ♦ *a liquid state* **3** (often **State**) an organized community under one government (e.g. *the State of Israel*) or forming part of a federal republic (e.g. *the state of Texas*) **4** (often **State**) a country's civil government **5** pomp and ceremony associated with monarchy or government **6** an excited or agitated condition of mind **7** a dirty or disorderly condition **state** *adj* **1** to do with or for the State **2** involving ceremony, used or done on ceremonial occasions ♦ *the state apartments* **state** *v* to express something in spoken or written words **stateless** *adj* (said about a person) not a citizen or subject of any country **stately** *adj* **statelier, stateliest** dignified, imposing, or grand **statement** *n* **1** something expressed in spoken or written words **2** a formal account of facts or events **3** a written report of a financial account ♦ *a bank statement* **state-of-the-art** *adj* using the newest ideas and most up-to-date features **statesman, stateswoman** *n pl* **statesmen, stateswomen** an experienced or respected politician, especially a leader **statesmanlike** *adj* **statesmanship** *n* **the States** the USA

static *adj* **1** not moving, stationary **2** not changing **static** *n* **1** static electricity **2** atmospherics **static electricity** *n* electricity that is present in something and not flowing as current

station *n* **1** a regular stopping place for trains, buses, etc. with platforms and buildings for passengers and goods **2** an establishment or building where a public service is based or which is equipped for certain activities ♦ *the fire station* **3** a broadcasting company with its own frequency **4** a place where a person or thing stands or is stationed **5** a person's social rank or position ♦ *She's getting ideas above her station.* **station** *v* to put someone

at or in a certain place for a purpose
stationmaster n the official in charge of a railway station

stationary adj 1 not moving 2 not changing in condition or quantity

stationery n writing paper, envelopes, and other materials used for writing **stationer** n someone who sells stationery

statistic (say stə-**tist**-ik) n a piece of information expressed as a number **statistical** adj **statistically** adv **statistician** n an expert in statistics **statistics** n the science of collecting and interpreting information based on numerical data **stats** n statistics

statue n a carved, cast, or moulded figure of a person or animal, usually of life size or larger **statuary** n statues **statuesque** adj looking like a statue in size, dignity, or stillness **statuette** n a small statue

stature (say **stat**-yer) n 1 a person's natural height 2 greatness gained by ability or achievement

status (say **stay**-təs) n 1 a person's position or rank in relation to others 2 a person's or thing's legal position or official classification 3 the state of affairs at a particular time 4 high rank or prestige **status quo** the existing state of affairs **status symbol** n something you own or have that shows off your wealth or position in society

statute (say **stat**-yoot) n 1 a law passed by a parliament 2 a rule of an organization or institution **statutory** adj fixed, done, or required by statute ♦ statutory rights

staunch[1] adj firm in attitude or loyalty ♦ staunch supporters **staunchly** adv

staunch[2] v to stop the flow of blood from a wound

stave n 1 one of the curved strips of wood forming the side of a cask or tub 2 (also **staff**) Mus a set of five horizontal lines on which music is written **stave** v **to stave something in** to dent or break a hole in something **to stave something off** to ward something off permanently or temporarily ♦ We staved off disaster. ◊ The past tense and past participle for stave something in can be either staved or stove. For stave something off the past tense and past participle is

staved.

stay[1] v 1 to remain in the same place or state ♦ Stay here. ♦ I can hardly stay awake. 2 to spend time in a place as a guest or visitor 3 to satisfy something temporarily ♦ We stayed our hunger with a sandwich. **stay** n 1 a time spent somewhere 2 a postponement, e.g. of carrying out a judgement ♦ He was granted a stay of execution. **staying power** n endurance or stamina

stay[2] n 1 a rope or wire supporting or bracing a mast, spar, pole, etc. 2 any prop or support

STD abbr 1 subscriber trunk dialling 2 sexually transmitted disease

stead (say sted) n **in a person's** or **thing's stead** instead of this person or thing **to stand someone in good stead** to be of advantage to someone over time

steadfast (say **sted**-fahst) adj firm and not changing or yielding **steadfastly** adv

steady adj **steadier, steadiest** 1 firmly supported or balanced, not shaking or tottering ♦ Hold the camera steady. 2 constant and regular, not changing ♦ a steady pace 3 behaving in a serious and dependable manner, not frivolous or excitable **steady** v **steadies, steadied, steadying** to make something steady, or to become steady **steadily** adv **steadiness** n

steak n a thick slice of meat or fish

steal v **stole, stolen** 1 to take another person's property without right or permission 2 to move somewhere secretly or without being noticed

stealth (say stelth) n stealthiness **stealth** adj (said about aircraft, missiles, etc.) designed using advanced technology that makes detection by radar or sonar difficult ♦ a stealth bomber **stealthy** adj **stealthier, stealthiest** acting or done in a quiet or secret way so as to avoid being noticed **stealthily** adv **stealthiness** n

steam n 1 invisible gas into which water is changed by boiling, used to drive machinery 2 the mist that forms when steam condenses in the air 3 energy or momentum **steam** v 1 to give off steam or vapour 2 to cook or treat something by steam 3 to move by the power of steam

steamer n **1** a ship or boat driven by steam **2** a container in which things are cooked or treated by steam **steamy** adj **steam engine** n an engine or locomotive driven by steam **steamroller** n a heavy slow-moving engine with a large roller, used to flatten surfaces when making roads **steamroller**, **steamroll** v to force something to be accepted, or someone to do something, by being too powerful for any opposition **steamship** n a ship driven by steam

steed n literary a horse

steel n **1** a very strong alloy of iron and carbon much used for making vehicles, tools, weapons, etc. **2** a tapered usually roughened steel rod for sharpening knives **3** strength and determination **steel** v to mentally prepare yourself to face something difficult ♦ You'd better steel yourself for some bad news. **steely** adj **steelier**, **steeliest 1** like steel in colour or strength **2** cold, determined, and severe **steel drum** n a percussion instrument made out of an oil drum, with the top beaten into sections that produce different notes

steep[1] adj **1** sloping sharply not gradually **2** (said about a rise or fall) very large or rapid **3** informal (said about a price) unreasonably high **steeply** adv **steepness** n

steep[2] v to soak something or be soaked in liquid **to be steeped in** to be filled with or heavily involved in something ♦ The story is steeped in mystery.

steeple n a tall tower with a spire on top, rising above the roof of a church **steeplejack** n a person who climbs tall chimneys or steeples to do repairs

steeplechase n **1** a horse race on a course with hedges and ditches to jump **2** a long running race in which runners must jump over hurdles and water jumps

steer[1] v **1** to make a vehicle or ship, etc. go in the direction you want **2** to direct the course of something **steerage** n the cheapest section of accommodation for passengers in a ship, situated below decks **steering wheel** n a wheel turned in order to steer a vehicle

steer[2] n a young castrated bull raised for its beef

stegosaurus (say ste-gə-sor-əs) n a large dinosaur with bony plates along its back, which fed on plants

stellar adj to do with a star or stars

stem[1] n **1** the main central part of a plant or shrub **2** a slender part supporting a fruit, flower, or leaf **3** any slender part of something, e.g. the thin part of a wine glass between the bowl and the foot **4** Gram the main part of a noun or verb, from which other parts or words are made, e.g. by altering the endings **stem** v **stemmed**, **stemming** to remove the stems from something **to stem from** to arise from something

stem[2] v **stemmed**, **stemming** to stop or restrict the flow of something

stench n a strong and unpleasant smell

stencil n **1** a sheet of metal or card, etc. with a design cut out, which can be painted or inked over to produce a corresponding design on the surface below **2** the decoration or lettering, etc. produced by a stencil **stencil** v **stencilled**, **stencilling** to produce or decorate something by means of a stencil

stenography (say sten-og-rəfi) n the process or technique of writing in shorthand **stenographer** n

stentorian (say sten-tor -iən) adj (said about a voice) loud and powerful

step n **1** a movement made by lifting the foot and setting it down **2** the distance covered by this **3** the sound of a step **4** a series of steps forming a particular pattern in dancing **5** a level surface for placing the foot on in climbing up or down **6** each of a series of things done in some process or course of action ♦ The first step is to find somewhere to rehearse. **7** a stage in a scale or hierarchy **step** v **stepped**, **stepping 1** to lift and set down the foot or alternate feet as you do when you walk **2** to move a short distance in this way **stepladder** n a short folding ladder with flat steps and a small platform **stepping stone** n **1** a raised stone providing a place to step on in crossing a stream or muddy area **2** a means or stage of progress towards achieving a goal **to step in 1** to intervene **2** to act as a substitute for someone **to step something up** to increase the level of something ♦ *It's time we stepped up the campaign.*

step- *prefix* related by remarriage of one parent (as in *stepbrother*)

steppe (say step) *n* a level grassy plain with few trees

stereophonic (say ste-ri-ə-**fon**-ik) *adj* (said about sound reproduction) using two or more transmission channels so that the reproduced sound seems to surround the listener and to come from more than one source **stereo** *n pl* **stereos 1** stereophonic sound or recording **2** a stereophonic CD player, record player, etc. **stereo** *adj* stereophonic

stereoscopic (say ste-ri-ə-**skop**-ik) *adj* giving a three-dimensional effect, e.g. in photographs

stereotype (say ste-ri-ə-tiyp or steer-ri-ə-tiyp) *n* an over-simplified image or idea of a type of person or thing that has become fixed through being widely held **stereotype** *v* to represent or view something as a stereotype

sterile (say ste-riyl) *adj* **1** not able to produce children, young, fruit, or seeds **2** free from bacteria or other living micro-organisms **3** unproductive, lacking new ideas **sterility** *n* **sterilize** *v* **1** to make something sterile or free from micro-organisms, e.g. by heating it **2** to make a person or animal unable to produce offspring by removing or blocking the reproductive organs **sterilization** *n*

sterling *n* British money **sterling** *adj* excellent, of great value ♦ *her sterling qualities* **sterling silver** *n* silver of a level of purity of at least 92.25%

stern[1] *adj* strict and severe **sternly** *adv* **sternness** *n*

stern[2] *n* the rear end of a ship or boat

sternum *n* the breastbone

stertorous (say ster-ter-əs) *adj* (said about breathing) noisy and laboured

stethoscope (say steth-ə-skohp) *n* a medical instrument for listening to sounds within the body, e.g. breathing and heartbeats

stetson *n* a hat with a very wide brim and a high crown, of the type traditionally worn by cowboys

stevedore (say stee-və-dor) *n* a person employed at a dock to load and unload ships

stew *n* a dish of food, especially meat and vegetables, cooked slowly in liquid in a closed dish or pan **stew** *v* to cook something or be cooked slowly in liquid in a closed dish or pan **in a stew** *informal* very worried or agitated

steward *n* **1** a person who looks after the passengers on a ship or aircraft **2** an official who keeps order or supervises the arrangements at a large public event **3** a person employed to manage someone else's property, especially a large house or estate **stewardess** *n* **stewardship** *n*

stick[1] *n* **1** a small thin branch from a tree **2** a thin piece of wood for use as a support or weapon, etc. **3** a walking stick **4** a long implement used to hit the ball in hockey, polo, etc. **5** a long thin object or piece of a substance ♦ *a stick of celery* **the sticks** *pl n informal* rural areas **stick insect** *n* an insect with a twig-like body **to give someone stick** *informal* to criticize someone

stick[2] *v* past tense and past participle **stuck 1** to push a thing or its point into something ♦ *Stick a pin in it.* **2** to something by means of a pointed object ♦ *A sign was stuck to the door with pins.* **3** to extend upwards or outwards ♦ *His hair was sticking up at the back.* **4** *informal* to put something somewhere ♦ *Just stick the parcel on the table.* **5** to fix something or be fixed by glue or suction, etc. or as if by these **6** to become fixed in one place and unable to move ♦ *This drawer keeps sticking.* **7** to remain in the same place or for a long time ♦ *His name sticks in my mind.* **8** *informal* to endure or tolerate something **sticker** *n* an adhesive label or sign for sticking to something **sticky** *adj* **stickier**, **stickiest 1** able or tending to stick to things **2** (said about weather) hot and humid, causing perspiration **3** *informal* difficult or awkward **sticking plaster** *n* a strip of fabric with an adhesive on one side, used for covering small cuts **stick-in-the-mud** n a person who does not like doing anything new **stick-up** n an armed robbery in which a gun is used to threaten people **to stick around** informal to remain in an area **to stick out** 1 to stand out from the surrounding surface 2 to be very noticeable **to stick up for** to support or defend a person or opinion

stickleback n a small fish with sharp spines along its back

stickler n a person who insists on something

stiff adj 1 not bending or moving or changing its shape easily 2 not fluid, thick and hard to stir ♦ a stiff dough 3 difficult to do or beat ♦ a stiff examination ♦ stiff opposition 4 formal in manner, not relaxed or friendly 5 (said about a price or penalty) high, severe 6 (said about a breeze) blowing strongly 7 (said about a drink or dose) strong **stiff** n informal a corpse **stiffen** v **stiffly** adv **stiffness** n

stifle v 1 to prevent someone from breathing freely; to suffocate someone 2 to restrain or suppress something ♦ She stifled a yawn. **stifling** adj

stigma n pl **stigmas** a mark of disgrace associated with something **stigmata** pl n marks on the body corresponding to those left on Christ's body by the nails and spear at his crucifixion **stigmatize** v to brand a person or thing as something disgraceful ♦ He was stigmatized as a coward.

stile n an arrangement of steps or bars for people to climb in order to get over a fence or wall

stiletto n pl **stilettos** 1 a high pointed heel on a woman's shoe 2 a dagger with a narrow blade

still[1] adj 1 not moving 2 not disturbed by motion, wind, or sound ♦ a still evening 3 (said about drinks) not sparkling or fizzy **still** adv 1 without or almost without moving ♦ Stand still. 2 continuing then, now, or in the future as before ♦ It's still raining. 3 nevertheless ♦ They've lost. Still, they tried. 4 in a greater amount or degree ♦ I'm sure you could do better still. **still** v to make something still, or to become still ♦ a god with the power to still the waves

still n 1 silence and calm 2 a photograph of a scene from a cinema film **stillness** n **stillborn** adj (said about an infant) born dead **still life** n pl **still lifes** a painting or drawing of an arrangement of objects such as flowers, fruit, or ornaments

still[2] n an apparatus for distilling alcoholic drinks such as whisky

stilt n 1 either of a pair of poles with a rest for the foot some way up it, enabling the user to walk with their feet at a distance above the ground 2 each of a set of posts supporting a building, often above marshy ground

stilted adj stiffly or artificially formal ♦ written in stilted language

stimulus n pl **stimuli** (say stim-yool-iy) 1 something that produces a reaction in an organ or tissue of the body 2 something that rouses a person or thing to activity or energy **stimulant** n 1 a drug or drink that increases physiological or nervous activity in the body 2 something that makes people more enthusiastic, interested, or active **stimulate** v 1 to make something more lively or active ♦ The programme has stimulated a lot of interest in her work. 2 to make someone interested or excited **stimulation** n

sting n 1 a sharp-pointed part or organ of an insect, plant, etc. that can cause a wound or inflammation by injecting poison 2 a wound from a sting 3 a sharp tingling sensation or hurtful effect **sting** v past tense and past participle **stung** 1 to wound or affect a person or animal with a sting; to be able to do this 2 to make someone feel a sharp bodily or mental pain 3 to goad someone into doing something 4 informal to swindle or overcharge someone **stingray** n a tropical fish with a flat body, fins like wings, and a long tail with sharp spines that can cause severe wounds

stingy (say stin-ji) adj **stingier**, **stingiest** informal mean, not generous **stinginess** n

stink n 1 a strong unpleasant smell 2 informal an unpleasant fuss or protest **stink** v past tense **stank** or **stunk**; past participle **stunk** 1 to give off a strong unpleasant smell 2 informal to seem very unpleasant or unsavoury ♦ *This idea of yours stinks.* **stinker** *n* **1** a person or thing that stinks **2** *informal* something offensive or severe or difficult to do **stinking** *adj* **1** foul-smelling **2** *informal* very unpleasant **stinking** *adv informal* extremely ♦ *stinking rich*

stint *n* a fixed or allotted amount of work to be done ♦ *Could you do a stint of delivering leaflets?* **stint** *v* to be sparing with something ♦ *You didn't stint on the cream, did you?*

stipend (say **stiy**-pend) *n* a salary or allowance, especially the official income of a member of the clergy **stipendiary** *adj* receiving a stipend

stipple *v* **1** to paint, draw, or engrave something with small dots instead of lines or strokes **2** to roughen the surface of cement, plaster, etc.

stipulate *v* to demand or insist on something as part of an agreement **stipulation** *n*

stir *v* **stirred**, **stirring 1** to mix or move a liquid or soft mixture by moving a spoon, etc. round and round in it **2** to move slightly or cause something to move slightly ♦ *Wind stirred the sand.* **3** to wake up or begin to be active **4** to arouse, stimulate, or excite someone or something ♦ *They are always stirring up trouble.* **stir** *n* **1** the act or process of stirring **2** a commotion or disturbance ♦ *The news caused a stir.* **stirring** *adj*

stirrup *n* a metal or leather support for a rider's foot, hanging from the saddle

stitch *n* **1** a single movement of a threaded needle in and out of fabric in sewing or tissue in surgery **2** a single complete movement of a needle or hook in knitting or crochet **3** the loop of thread, wool, etc. made in this way **4** a sudden sharp pain in the muscles at the side of the body, caused by running **stitch** *v* to sew, join, or close something with stitches **in stitches** *informal* laughing uncontrollably

stoat *n* an animal of the weasel family, with brown fur that turns white in winter (when the animal is known as an *ermine*)

stock *n* **1** all the goods or raw materials kept on the premises of a shop, business,

etc. **2** an amount of something kept ready for use ♦ *a stock of jokes* **3** livestock **4** a line of ancestry ♦ *a woman of Irish stock* **5** the capital raised by a company by selling shares **6** a portion of this held in the form of shares by an individual shareholder **7** a person's standing in the opinion of others ♦ *His stock is high.* **8** liquid made by stewing bones, meat, fish, or vegetables, used as a basis for making soup, sauce, etc. **9** a garden plant with fragrant single or double flowers **10** the wooden or metal part of a rifle to which the barrel is attached **stock** *adj* **1** kept in stock and regularly available ♦ *one of our stock items* **2** commonly used, constantly recurring ♦ *a stock phrase* **stock** *v* **1** to keep goods in stock **2** to provide a place with goods, livestock, or a supply of something ♦ *He stocked his farm with Jersey cows.* **stockist** *n* a shop or business that stocks goods of a certain type for sale **stocks** *pl n* **1** *hist* a wooden framework with holes for the legs of a seated person, used like the pillory **2** a framework on which a ship rests during construction **stocky** *adj* **stockier**, **stockiest** short and solidly built **stockbroker** *n* a broker who deals in stocks and shares **stock car** *n* an ordinary car strengthened for use in racing where deliberate bumping is allowed **stock exchange** *n* a place where stocks and shares are publicly bought and sold **stock-in-trade** *n* **1** the typical subject or commodity someone uses or deals in **2** the type of stock kept regularly by a shop **stock market** *n* **1** a stock exchange **2** the buying and selling of stocks and shares **stockpile** *n* a large stock of goods or materials, etc. built up and kept in reserve **stockpile** *v* to build up a stockpile of something **stock-still** *adv* completely still, motionless **stocktaking** *n* the counting, listing, and checking of the amount of stock held by a shop or business

stockade *n* a protective fence made of upright stakes

stocking *n* a close-fitting covering for the foot and part or all of the leg

stodge *n* stodgy food **stodgy** *adj* **stodgier**, **stodgiest 1** (said about food) heavy and filling, indigestible **2** (said about a book, etc.) written in a heavy uninteresting way **3** (said about a person) dull, not lively

stoical, **stoic** (say stoh-ikəl) *adj* bearing difficulties, pain, or discomfort calmly or without complaining **stoic** *n* a stoical person **stoically** *adv* **stoicism** *n*

stoke *v* **1** to tend and add fuel to a furnace or fire, etc. **2** to encourage a strong emotion **stoker** *n*

stole *n* a scarf or shawl worn loosely round the shoulders

stolid *adj* not showing much emotion or interest

stomach *n* **1** the internal organ in which the first part of digestion takes place **2** the abdomen **3** an appetite or desire for something ♦ *Frankly I had no stomach for the fight.* **stomach** *v* to endure or tolerate something

stomp *v* to tread heavily and noisily

stone *n* **1** a piece of rock, usually detached from the earth's crust and of fairly small size **2** stones or rock as a substance or material, e.g. for building **3** a piece of stone shaped for a particular purpose, e.g. a tombstone or millstone **4** a jewel or gem **5** a gallstone or kidney stone **6** the hard seed in a plum, peach, cherry, etc. **7** *pl* **stone** a unit of weight equal to 14 lb (6.35 kg) **stone** *adv* extremely or totally ♦ *stone cold* **stone** *v* **1** to pelt someone with stones **2** to remove the stone from a fruit **stoned** *adj* under the influence of drugs or alcohol **stony** *adj* **stonier**, **stoniest 1** full of stones **2** like stone, especially in being hard **3** unfeeling or unresponsive ♦ *a stony gaze* **Stone Age** *n* the very early period of human history, when tools and weapons were made of stone not metal **stonewall** *v* to delay or obstruct something by refusing to answer questions or by giving non-committal replies

stooge *n* **1** a comedian's assistant, used as a target for jokes **2** *informal* a person who is given dull or routine work to do by someone more powerful

stool *n* **1** a seat without arms or a back **2** a lump of faeces **stool pigeon** *n* a police informer

stoop *v* **1** to bend your head or body forwards and down **2** to do something that is below your dignity or moral standards ♦ *He would never stoop to cheating.* **stoop** *n* a posture of the body with shoulders bent forwards ♦ *He walks with a stoop.*

stop *v* **stopped**, **stopping 1** to put an end to something; to cause something to halt or pause **2** to no longer continue doing something ♦ *I'm trying to stop smoking.* **3** to come to an end; to not continue moving or working **4** to prevent or obstruct something **5** to stay somewhere for a short time ♦ *Are you stopping for tea?* **6** (said about a bus or train) to call at a place to pick up or put down passengers **7** to block or close up a hole or leak **stop** *n* **1** an act of stopping **2** a place where a bus or train regularly stops **3** a full stop **4** an obstruction or device that stops or regulates movement or operation **5** a row of organ pipes providing a particular tone and range of pitch; the knob or lever controlling these **stoppage** *n* **stopper** *n* a plug for closing a bottle, etc.

stopcock *n* a valve controlling the flow of liquid or gas through a pipe **stopgap** *n* a temporary substitute **stopover** *n* a break in your journey, especially for a night **stop press** *n* late news put into a newspaper just before printing or after printing has begun **stopwatch** *n* a watch with a mechanism for starting and stopping it when you wish, used to time races, etc.

store *n* **1** a quantity or supply of something available for use when needed **2** a place where things are stored **3** a shop **4** a computer memory **store** *v* **1** to collect and keep things until they are needed **2** to put something into a store **storage** *n* **1** the storing of goods, etc. or of information **2** space available for storing **in store** about to happen ♦ *There's a surprise in store.* **to set store by** to value something greatly

storey *n pl* **storeys** one horizontal section of a building, all the rooms at the same level ◊ Do not confuse this word with *story*, which has a different meaning.

stork *n* a large long-legged wading bird with a long straight bill

storm *n* **1** a violent disturbance of the

atmosphere with strong winds and usually rain, thunder, lightning, or snow **2** a great outbreak of strong feeling **3** a violent military attack on a place **storm** v **1** to move violently or angrily **2** to shout angrily **3** to suddenly attack and capture a place **stormy** adj **stormier**, **stormiest**

story n pl **stories 1** an account of an incident or of a series of incidents, either true or invented **2** the plot of a novel, play, film, etc. **3** a report of an item of news **4** informal a lie ♦ Don't tell stories! ◊ Do not confuse this word with storey, which has a different meaning. **storyline** n the plot of a novel, play, film, etc.

stoup (say stoop) n a stone basin for holy water, especially in the wall of a church

stout adj **1** (said about a person) solidly built and rather fat **2** sturdy and thick ♦ a stout stick **3** brave and determined ♦ a stout defender of human rights **stout** n a strong dark beer brewed with roasted malt or barley **stoutly** adv **stoutness** n

stove n **1** a device containing one or more ovens **2** a closed device used for heating rooms, etc.

stow v to pack or store something tidily away **stowaway** n a person who stows away **to stow away** to conceal yourself on a ship or aircraft, etc. so as to travel without paying or unseen

straddle v **1** to sit or stand across something with one leg on either side **2** to extend across both sides of something ♦ A long bridge straddles the river.

strafe (say strahf or strayf) v to attack people or a place with gunfire or bombs from a low-flying aircraft

straggle v **1** to move along slowly and drop behind the people in front **2** to grow or spread out in an irregular or untidy manner **straggler** n **straggly** adj

straight adj **1** extending or moving continuously in one direction, not curved or bent **2** level, horizontal, or upright ♦ Is the picture straight? **3** correctly arranged, in proper order **4** in unbroken succession ♦ ten straight wins **5** not evasive; honest and frank ♦ Just give me a straight answer. **6** (said about an alcoholic drink) not diluted **7** to do

with serious drama, not comedy ♦ a straight role **8** informal conventional or respectable **9** informal heterosexual **straight** adv **1** in a straight line ♦ It's a good thing you can't shoot straight. **2** directly, without delay ♦ Go straight home. **3** straightforwardly ♦ I told him straight. **straight** n the straight part of something, especially the last section of a racecourse **straighten** v **straightaway** adv without delay, immediately **straightforward** adj **1** honest and frank **2** easy to do or understand **a straight face** a blank or serious expression on your face, especially when you are trying not to laugh **to go straight** to live an honest life after being a criminal ◊ Do not confuse this word with strait, which has a different meaning.

strain[1] v **1** to injure or weaken part of your body by excessive stretching or by too much effort ♦ Don't strain your eyes. **2** to make an intense effort ♦ People were straining to hear what she was saying. **3** to pull or push forcefully at something **4** to stretch something tightly **5** to apply a meaning or rule, etc. beyond its true application **6** to put something through a sieve or filter in order to separate solids from the liquid containing them **strain** n **1** straining, or being strained; the force of straining **2** an injury caused by straining a muscle or limb **3** a severe demand on your mental or physical strength or on your resources; exhaustion caused by this **4** a passage from a tune **strained** adj **1** (said about behaviour or manner) produced by effort, not natural or genuine **2** unpleasantly tense, showing signs of strain ♦ strained relations **strainer** n a device for straining liquids

strain[2] n **1** a line of descent of animals, plants, or micro-organisms; a variety or breed of these ♦ a new strain of flu virus **2** a slight or inherited characteristic ♦ There's a strain of insanity in the family.

strait n (also **straits**) a narrow stretch of water connecting two seas **straits** pl n a difficult state of affairs ♦ in dire straits ◊ Do not confuse this word with straight, which has a different meaning. **straitened** adj made narrow, restricted **straitjacket** n **1** a strong jacket-like piece of clothing with long sleeves that can be tied together to restrain the arms of a violent person **2** a severe restriction **strait-laced** *adj* very prim and proper **in straitened circumstances** with barely enough money to live on

strand[1] *n* **1** a single length of thread, wire, etc., twisted together to form a rope, yarn, or cable **2** an element that forms part of a whole

strand[2] *n literary* a shore **strand** *v* **1** to run or cause a ship to run onto sand or rocks in shallow water **2** to leave someone in a difficult or helpless position

strange *adj* **1** unusual or surprising ♦ *It's strange that you haven't heard.* **2** not known, seen, or encountered before ♦ *the problems of adapting to a strange culture* **strangely** *adv* **strangeness** *n* **stranger** *n* **1** a person you do not know **2** a person who does not know or is not known in a particular place

strangle *v* **1** to squeeze a person's throat, especially in order to kill them **2** to restrict or suppress something so that it does not develop **strangler** *n* **strangulation** *n* **stranglehold** *n* **1** a strangling grip **2** complete control over something

strap *n* a strip of leather, cloth, or other flexible material, often with a buckle, for holding things together or in place **strap** *v* **strapped**, **strapping 1** to fasten something with a strap or straps **2** to bind an injury **strapping** *adj* big and strong

stratagem (say **strat-ə-jəm**) *n* a cunning method of achieving something; a plan or trick

strategy (say **strat-i-ji**) *n pl* **strategies 1** a broad plan or policy for achieving something **2** the planning and directing of the whole operation of a campaign or war **strategic** *adj* **1** to do with strategy **2** giving an advantage ♦ *a strategic position* **3** (said about weapons) used against an enemy's home territory **strategically** *adv* **strategist** *n* an expert in strategy

stratosphere (say **strat-ə-sfeer**) *n* a layer of the earth's atmosphere between about 10 and 60 km above the earth's surface

stratum (say **strah-təm** or **stray-təm**) *n pl* **strata 1** one of a series of layers, especially

of rock in the earth's crust **2** a social level or class **stratified** *adj* formed or arranged into strata **stratification** *n*

straw *n* **1** dry cut stalks of grain used as material for thatching, fodder, packing, etc. **2** a single stalk or piece of this **3** a thin tube of paper or plastic for sucking up a drink **straw poll** *n* an unofficial poll taken as a rough test of general opinion

strawberry *n pl* **strawberries** a soft, juicy edible red fruit with yellow seeds on the surface

stray *v* **1** to wander away from the proper path or place **2** to go aside from a direct course; to depart from a subject **stray** *adj* **1** having strayed ♦ *a stray cat* **2** separated from a group, isolated ♦ *a stray taxi* **stray** *n* a person or domestic animal that has strayed; a stray thing

streak *n* **1** a thin line or band of a different colour or substance from its surroundings **2** an element in a person's character ♦ *a ruthless streak* **3** a spell of success, luck, etc. ♦ *a winning streak* **streak** *v* **1** to mark something with streaks **2** to move very rapidly **3** *informal* to run naked in a public place for fun or to get attention **streaker** *n* **streaky** *adj* **streakier**, **streakiest**

stream *n* **1** a small narrow river **2** a flow of liquid or of a mass of things or people **3** (in certain schools) a section into which children with the same level of ability are placed **stream** *v* **1** to run or move in a continuous flow **2** to produce a stream of liquid, to run with liquid ♦ *My eyes were streaming.* **3** to float or wave at full length ♦ *Flags were streaming in the wind.* **4** to arrange schoolchildren in streams according to their ability **streamer** *n* a long narrow strip of paper or material used as a decoration or flag **streamline** *v* **1** to give something a streamlined shape **2** to make an organization or system more efficient by using simpler or faster methods **streamlined** *adj* having a smooth even shape that offers very little resistance to movement through air or water

street *n* a public road in a town or village with buildings on one or both sides **streetcar** *n* a tram **streetwise** *adj* having the skills and knowledge needed to deal with modern city life

strenuous *adj* **1** energetic and wholehearted **2** needing great effort ♦ *a strenuous task* **strenuously** *adv*

stress *n* **1** a force that acts on or within a thing and tends to distort it, e.g. by pressing, pulling, or twisting it **2** mental distress caused by having too many problems or too much to do **3** emphasis, especially the extra force with which you pronounce part of a word or phrase **stress** *v* **1** to give emphasis to something **2** to put stress on part of a word or phrase **3** to cause stress to someone **stressful** *adj* causing stress to someone

stretch *v* **1** to pull something or be pulled so that it becomes longer or wider **2** to be able to be stretched without tearing or breaking; to tend to become stretched **3** to straighten out your body or part of it to its full length and tighten the muscles after being relaxed **4** to extend in area, length, or time ♦ *The wall stretches right round the estate.* **5** to make great demands on a person's abilities **stretch** *n* **1** stretching, or being stretched **2** a continuous expanse or period of time **stretch** *adj* able to be stretched ♦ *stretch fabrics* **stretcher** *n* a framework of poles, canvas, etc. for carrying a sick or injured person in a lying position

strew *v* past participle **strewn** or **strewed** to scatter things over a surface; to cover something with scattered things ♦ *The floor was strewn with paper cups.*

striation (say striy-ay-shən) *n* any of a series of ridges, furrows, or lines **striated** *adj*

stricken *adj* affected or overcome by an illness, shock, or grief

strict *adj* **1** demanding that rules concerning behaviour are obeyed ♦ *a strict teacher* **2** following rules or beliefs exactly **3** precisely limited or defined, exact or complete ♦ *the strict truth* **strictly** *adv* **strictness** *n*

stricture *n* **1** severe criticism or condemnation **2** a rule restricting behaviour or action

stride *v* **strode**, **stridden 1** to walk with long steps **2** to cross something with one long step **stride** *n* **1** a single long step, or the length of this **2** a person's manner of striding **3** a step in progress

strident (say striy-dənt) *adj* loud and harsh **stridently** *adv*

strife *n* conflict; fighting or quarrelling

strike *v* past tense and past participle **struck 1** to hit something, deliberately or accidentally **2** (said about a disease, disaster, etc.) to afflict someone **3** to attack suddenly **4** to bring someone into a specified state suddenly ♦ *He was struck blind.* **5** to fill someone with a sudden strong emotion ♦ *It was a sound that struck fear into me.* **6** to occur to someone, to make an impression on someone's mind ♦ *She strikes me as being efficient.* **7** to refuse to work as a form of protest **8** to reach an agreement, balance, or compromise ♦ *We finally struck a bargain.* **9** to light a match by rubbing it against a rough surface **10** to indicate the time by making a sound ♦ *The clock struck ten.* **11** to produce sparks or a sound, etc. by striking something; to produce a musical note by pressing a key **12** to make a coin or medal by stamping metal **13** to reach gold or oil, etc. by digging or drilling **strike** *n* **1** a workers' refusal to work, as a form of protest **2** a sudden attack ♦ *an air strike* **3** an act or instance of striking, a hit **4** a sudden discovery of gold or oil, etc. **striker** *n* **1** a worker who is on strike **2** a football player whose main function is to try to score goals **striking** *adj* **1** noticeable or conspicuous **2** very good-looking or impressive **to strike an attitude** or **pose** to hold your body in a certain position to create an impression **to strike out** to start out on a new or independent course **to strike someone off** to officially remove a person from membership of a professional group, usually because of misconduct **to strike something off** or **out** to cross something off or out **to strike something up** to start a friendship or conversation with someone **to strike up** to begin to play a piece of music

string *n* **1** thin cord made of twisted threads **2** a length of this or some other material used to fasten, lace, or pull something **3** a piece of catgut or wire stretched and vibrated to produce tones in a musical instrument **4** a piece of catgut, nylon, etc. interwoven with others in a frame to form the head of a racket **5** a set of objects threaded or tied together on a cord ♦ *a string of pearls* **6** a series of things coming after one another ♦ *a string of coincidences* **7** a condition that is insisted upon ♦ *The offer has no strings attached.* **string** *v* past tense and past participle **strung 1** to fit a string or strings to something **2** to thread beads, etc. on a string **strings** *pl n* the stringed instruments in an orchestra **stringed** *adj* (said about musical instruments) having strings that are played by being touched, or with a bow or a plectrum **stringy** *adj* **stringier, stringiest, string bean** *n* a bean eaten in its pod, such as a runner bean or French bean **to pull strings** see *pull* **to string along** *informal* to stay with someone while it is convenient **to string someone along** *informal* to mislead someone over a length of time **to string someone up** to kill someone by hanging **to string something out** to cause something to last a long time

stringent (say **strin**-jənt) *adj* (said about rules or conditions) strictly enforced **stringency** *n* **stringently** *adv*

strip[1] *v* **stripped, stripping 1** to take a covering or layer off something **2** to take off your clothes or another person's clothes **3** to deprive someone of something, especially a title or position **4** to take a machine to pieces in order to inspect it **strip** *n* **1** an act of undressing, especially in a striptease **2** the distinctive clothes worn by a sports team while playing **stripper** *n* **1** a device or solvent for removing paint, etc. **2** a person who performs striptease **striptease** *n* an entertainment in which a person slowly undresses to music

strip[2] *n* a long narrow piece or area **stripling** *n* a young man

stripe *n* **1** a long narrow band on a surface, having a different colour or texture from its surroundings **2** a band or chevron of cloth worn on the sleeve of a uniform to show the wearer's rank **striped** *adj*

strive *v* **strove, striven** to make great efforts to do something

strobe *n informal* a stroboscope

stroboscope (say **stroh**-bə-skohp) *n* an apparatus for producing a rapidly flashing light

stroke *n* **1** the act or process of striking something **2** a single successful or effective action or effort ♦ *a stroke of luck* ♦ *a stroke of genius* ♦ *He hasn't done a stroke of work all day.* **3** each of a series of repeated movements **4** a style of swimming **5** one hit at the ball in various games ♦ *a forehand stroke* **6** an act or spell of stroking **7** a mark made by a movement of a pen, pencil, or paintbrush **8** the sound made by a striking clock ♦ *on the stroke of ten* **9** an attack of apoplexy or paralysis, caused by an interruption in the flow of blood to the brain **stroke** *v* to move your hand gently along the surface of something

stroll *v* to walk in a leisurely way **stroll** *n* a leisurely walk

strong *adj* **1** physically powerful or healthy; done with great power ♦ *strong muscles* ♦ *a strong kick* **2** able to withstand rough treatment or great force **3** great in degree or intensity ♦ *strong colours* **4** felt, held, or expressed with intensity ♦ *strong beliefs* **5** having a lot of power or influence ♦ *a strong country* **6** having a specified number of members ♦ *an army 5,000 strong* **7** (said about a drink) concentrated, not weak or diluted **strength** *n* **1** the quality of being strong; the intensity of this **2** an ability or good quality **3** the number of people present or available, the full complement ♦ *The department is below strength.* **strengthen** *v* to make something stronger, or to become stronger **strongly** *adv* **stronghold** *n* **1** a fortified place **2** a place of strong support for a cause or political party ♦ *a Labour stronghold* **strongroom** *n* a room designed to protect valuables from fire or theft **going strong** *informal* continuing to be effective or successful **on the strength of** on the basis of, using a fact, etc. as your support

strontium (say **stron**-ti-əm) *n* a chemical element (symbol Sr), a soft silver-white metal, with a radioactive isotope

strop *n* a strip of leather or other device for sharpening razors

stroppy *adj informal* **stroppier**, **stroppiest** bad-tempered, awkward to deal with

structure *n* **1** a building or other thing that has been constructed or built **2** the way in which something is constructed or organized **structural** *adj* **structurally** *adv*

strudel (say **stroo**-dəl) *n* thin pastry filled with fruit, especially apple

struggle *v* **1** to move your limbs or body in a strong effort to get free **2** to make a strong effort under difficult circumstances **3** to make your way or a living, etc. with difficulty **4** to try to overcome an opponent or problem, etc. **struggle** *n* **1** a spell of struggling **2** a hard fight or difficult task

strum *v* **strummed**, **strumming** to sound a guitar by running your fingers up and down its strings

strumpet *n old use* a prostitute

strut *n* **1** a bar of wood or metal put into a framework to strengthen and brace it **2** a strutting walk **strut** *v* **strutted**, **strutting** to walk in a pompous self-satisfied way

strychnine (say **strik**-neen) *n* a bitter and highly poisonous substance, used in very small doses as a stimulant

stub *n* **1** a short stump left when the rest has been used or worn down **2** the counterfoil of a cheque, receipt, ticket, etc. **stub** *v* **stubbed**, **stubbing** to accidentally hurt your toe against something **stubby** *adj* **stubbier**, **stubbiest** short and thick **to stub something out** to put out a cigarette by pressing it against something hard

stubble *n* **1** the lower ends of the stalks of cereal plants left in the ground after the harvest is cut **2** short stiff hairs growing on a man's face when he has not shaved for a while **stubbly** *adj*

stubborn *adj* **1** determined not to give in or change your opinion **2** difficult to remove or deal with **stubbornly** *adv* **stubbornness** *n*

stucco *n* plaster or cement used for coating surfaces of walls or moulding to form architectural decorations **stuccoed** *adj*

stuck past tense and past participle of *stick²* **stuck** *adj* unable to move or make progress

stuck-up *adj* conceited or snobbish

stud¹ *n* **1** a short large-headed nail or other short piece of metal sticking out from a surface **2** one of a number of small knobs on the base of a shoe or boot to give better grip **3** a device like a button on a stalk, used e.g. to fasten a detachable shirt collar **stud** *v* **studded**, **studding** to decorate something with studs or precious stones set into a surface

stud² *n* **1** the place where a number of horses are kept for breeding **2** a stallion

studio *n pl* **studios** **1** the room where a painter, sculptor, photographer, etc. works **2** a room from which radio or television programmes are regularly broadcast or in which recordings are made **3** a place where cinema films are made

study *v* **studies**, **studied**, **studying** **1** to spend time learning about a subject **2** to look at or consider something carefully ♦ *We studied the map.* **study** *n pl* **studies** **1** the process of studying; the pursuit of some branch of knowledge ♦ *a course in business studies* **2** a detailed investigation into a particular subject **3** a room used by a person for writing or academic work **4** a musical composition designed to develop a player's skill **5** a drawing done for practice or in preparation for another work ♦ *a study of a woman's head* **student** *n* a person who studies a subject, especially at a college or university **studied** *adj* done with deliberate and careful effort ♦ *She answered with studied indifference.* **studious** *adj* **1** spending a lot of time studying or reading **2** deliberate or painstaking ♦ *studious politeness*

stuff *n* **1** a substance or material **2** *informal* unnamed things, belongings, subject matter, activities, etc. ♦ *Leave your stuff in the hall.* **stuff** *v* **1** to fill something tightly; to cram something in **2** to push a thing hastily into something ♦ *He stuffed his hands into his pockets.* **3** to fill poultry or other food with savoury stuffing **4** to fill the empty skin, etc. of a bird or animal with material to restore its original shape **5** *informal* to eat greedily ♦ *The kids stuffed themselves with chips.* **stuffy** *adj* **stuffier**, **stuffiest** **1** lacking fresh air or enough ventilation **2** formal and boring **3** old-fashioned and narrow-minded **4** (said about a person's nose) with blocked breathing passages **stuffiness** n **stuffing** n **1** padding used to stuff cushions, furniture, or soft toys **2** a savoury mixture put as a filling into poultry, meat, vegetables, etc. before cooking

stultify v **stultifies**, **stultified**, **stultifying 1** to prevent something from being effective ♦ *Their uncooperative approach has stultified the discussions.* **2** to make someone feel bored

stumble v **1** to strike your foot on something and lose your balance **2** to walk unsteadily **3** to make a mistake or frequent mistakes in speaking or playing music, etc. ♦ *She stumbled through her speech.* **stumble** n an act of stumbling **stumbling block** n an obstacle, something that causes difficulty or hesitation **to stumble across** or **on** to find something by chance

stump n **1** the base of a tree trunk left in the ground when the rest has fallen or been cut down **2** something left when the main part has worn down or been cut off **3** (in cricket) each of the three upright sticks of a wicket **stump** v **1** to baffle or be too difficult for someone ♦ *The last question stumped me completely.* **2** to walk stiffly or noisily **stumpy** adj **stumpier**, **stumpiest** short and thick **to stump something up** *informal* to produce the money to pay for something

stun v **stunned**, **stunning 1** to knock a person unconscious or into a dazed state **2** to astonish or shock someone so much that they cannot think clearly ♦ *She was stunned by the news.* **stunner** n an extremely attractive person or thing **stunning** adj extremely attractive **stunningly** adv

stunt[1] v to prevent something from growing or developing normally

stunt[2] n **1** something difficult and daring done as a performance or as part of the action of a film **2** something unusual done to attract attention ♦ *a publicity stunt* **stuntman**, **stuntwoman** n pl **stuntmen**, **stuntwomen** a person employed to take an actor's place in performing dangerous stunts

stupefy v **stupefies**, **stupefied**, **stupefying 1** to make someone unable to think or feel properly **2** to astonish and shock someone **stupefaction** n

stupendous (say stew-**pend**-əs) adj extremely impressive **stupendously** adv

stupid adj **1** not intelligent or clever, slow at learning or understanding things **2** without reason or common sense **3** dazed and unable to think clearly ♦ *He was knocked stupid.* **stupidity** n **stupidly** adv

stupor (say **stew**-per) n a dazed or almost unconscious condition brought on by shock, drugs, drink, etc.

sturdy adj **sturdier**, **sturdiest** strongly built or made **sturdily** adv **sturdiness** n

sturgeon n pl **sturgeon** a large shark-like fish with flesh that is valued as food and roe that is made into caviare

stutter v to speak with rapid repetitions of the same sound, especially the first consonants of words **stutter** n a tendency to stutter when speaking

sty[1] n pl **sties** a pigsty

sty[2] **stye** n pl **sties** or **styes** an inflamed swelling on the edge of the eyelid

style n **1** the way in which something is written, said, or done **2** a distinctive design or arrangement ♦ *a new style of coat* **3** elegance and confidence in doing things **style** v to design, shape, or arrange something, especially in a fashionable style **stylish** adj in a fashionable style **stylishly** adv **stylist** n **1** a person who does something with style **2** a person who cuts hair or designs fashionable clothes **stylistic** adj to do with literary or artistic style **stylized** adj represented in a way that is deliberately not realistic

stylus n pl **styli** or **styluses** a needle-like device, usually a polished jewel, used to follow a groove in a gramophone record and transmit the recorded sound for reproduction

stymie v *informal* to prevent a person or thing from progressing

suave (say swahv) adj (said about a man) confident and smooth-mannered

sub n *informal* **1** a submarine **2** a subscription **3** a substitute **4** a small loan or advance payment

sub- *prefix* (changing to **suc-**, **suf-**, **sum-**, **sup-**, **sur-**, **sus-** before certain consonants) **1** under (as in *submarine*) **2** subordinate, secondary (as in *subsection*)

subaltern (say **sub**-əl-tern) *n* an army officer ranking below a captain, especially a second lieutenant

subatomic *adj* smaller than or forming part of an atom

subconscious *adj* to do with mental processes of which we are not fully aware but which influence our actions **subconscious** *n* the part of the mind in which these processes take place **subconsciously** *adv*

subcontinent *n* a large land mass that forms part of a continent

subcontract (say sub-kən-**trakt**) *v* to hire a company or person outside your company to do a particular part of your work **subcontractor** *n*

subculture *n* a social culture within a larger culture

subdivide *v* to divide something into smaller parts after a first division **subdivision** *n*

subdue *v* **1** to overcome someone or bring them under control **2** to make something quieter or less intense **subdued** *adj*

subeditor *n* a person who checks and corrects material before it is printed in a newspaper, magazine, or book

subhuman *adj* less than human; not fully human

subject (say **sub**-jikt) *n* **1** the thing that is being discussed or dealt with **2** a branch of knowledge that is studied or taught **3** *Gram* the word or words in a sentence that name who or what does the action or undergoes what is stated by the verb, e.g. *'the book' in the book fell off the table* **4** someone who is ruled by a monarch or government **subject** *adj* not politically independent ♦ *subject peoples* **subject** (say səb-**jekt**) *v* **1** to make a person or thing undergo something ♦ *He was subjected to torture.* **2** to bring a country under your control **subject to 1** likely to be affected by something ♦ *Trains are subject to delay because of flooding.* **2** having to obey

something ♦ *We are all subject to the laws of the land.* **3** depending upon something as a condition ♦ *Our decision is subject to your approval.* **subjection** *n*

subjective *adj* **1** influenced by personal feelings or opinions **2** existing in a person's mind and not produced by things outside it **subjectively** *adv*

subjugate (say **sub**-jə-gayt) *v* to bring a country or group of people under your control, especially by conquest **subjugation** *n*

subjunctive *adj* (said about the form of a verb) used to express what is imagined, wished, or possible **subjunctive** *n* the subjunctive form of a verb

sublet *v* past tense and past participle **sublet**; **subletting** to let to another person accommodation that is let to you by a landlord

sublimate (say **sub**-lim-ayt) *v* (in psychoanalytic theory) to direct your instincts, urges, or energies into other activities, especially more socially acceptable ones **sublimation** *n*

sublime *adj* **1** of the most noble or impressive kind **2** extreme ♦ *with sublime indifference*

sub-machine gun *n* a lightweight machine gun held in the hands for firing

submarine *n* a ship that can operate under the sea for long periods **submarine** *adj* under the surface of the sea

submerge *v* **1** to cause something to be under water **2** (said about a submarine) to go below the surface **submersible** *n* **submersion** *n*

submit *v* **submitted**, **submitting 1** to surrender or yield to someone stronger than you **2** to subject a person or thing to a process **3** to present something for consideration or decision ♦ *Submit your plans to the committee.* **submission** *n* **1** submitting, or being submitted **2** something submitted for consideration **3** a theory or argument submitted by counsel to a judge or jury **submissive** *adj* meekly obedient, willing to submit to others **submissively** *adv* **submissiveness** *n*

subordinate (say səb-**or** -din-ət) *adj* of

lesser importance or rank **subordinate** n a person in a subordinate position **subordinate** v to treat something as of lesser importance than something else **subordination** n

sub-plot n a secondary plot in a play, novel, etc.

subscribe v 1 to pay in advance or at regular intervals in order to receive a periodical, be a member of a society, have the use of a telephone, etc. 2 to apply to take part in something ♦ *The course is already fully subscribed.* 3 to contribute money to a project or cause 4 to express your agreement ♦ *I do not myself subscribe to this theory.* **subscriber** n **subscription** n 1 subscribing 2 a payment to subscribe to something 3 a fee for membership of a society, etc.

subscript adj written or printed below the level of a letter, etc. (e.g. 2 in H_2O)

subsection n a division of a section

subsequent adj coming after something in time **subsequently** adv

subservient adj prepared to obey others without question **subservience** n

subset n a part of a larger group of related things

subside v 1 to become less active or intense 2 to go down to a lower or to the normal level **subsidence** n the gradual sinking or caving in of an area of land

subsidiary adj 1 of secondary importance 2 (said about a company) controlled by another company **subsidiary** n pl **subsidiaries** a subsidiary company

subsidy n pl **subsidies** a grant of money paid to an industry or other cause needing help, or to keep down the price of a commodity or service **subsidize** v 1 to pay part of the cost of producing something to reduce its price 2 to support something financially

subsist v to exist or continue to exist; to keep yourself alive ♦ *They managed to subsist on a diet of vegetables.* **subsistence** n subsisting; a means of doing this

subsonic adj (said about speed) less than the speed of sound

substance n 1 matter of a particular kind 2 the essence of something spoken or written ♦ *We agree with the substance of your report but not with its details.* 3 solid basis in reality or fact ♦ *The claim has no substance.* **substantial** adj 1 of considerable importance, amount, or worth ♦ *a substantial fee* 2 solidly built or made 3 in essentials, virtual ♦ *We are in substantial agreement.* **substantially** adv

substantiate v to produce evidence to support or prove a statement or claim

substantive adj having a firm basis in reality; substantial, important, or meaningful

substitute n a person or thing that acts or is used in place of another **substitute** v 1 to put or use something as a substitute 2 to serve as a substitute **substitution** n

subsume v to include or absorb something in something else

subterfuge (say **sub**-ter-fewj) n a trick or deception used in order to achieve something

subterranean (say sub-ter-**ayn**-iən) adj underground

subtitle n a secondary or additional title **subtitles** pl n words shown at the bottom of the screen during a film, e.g. to translate the dialogue from a foreign language **subtitle** v to provide something with a subtitle or subtitles

subtle (say **sut**əl) adj 1 not immediately obvious or understandable ♦ *a subtle argument* 2 slight and difficult to detect or describe ♦ *a subtle distinction* 3 (said about a smell, flavour, shade, etc.) delicate or faint ♦ *a subtle perfume* 4 able to perceive and make fine distinctions ♦ *a subtle mind* **subtlety** n **subtly** adv

subtotal n the total of part of a group of figures

subtract v to take away a quantity or number from another to calculate the difference **subtraction** n

subtropical adj to do with regions bordering on the tropics

suburb n a residential district lying outside the central part of a town **suburban** adj **suburbia** n the suburbs

subvert (say səb-**vert**) v to undermine the authority of an established idea, system, or institution **subversion** n **subversive** adj

subway n **1** an underground passage, e.g. for pedestrians to cross below a road **2** an underground railway

succeed v **1** to achieve an aim or purpose; to be successful ♦ *Our plan succeeded brilliantly.* **2** to come after and take the place of another person or thing **3** to become the next holder of an office, especially the monarchy ♦ *Who succeeded to the throne?*

success n **1** doing or getting what you wanted or intended **2** the attainment of wealth, fame, or position **3** a person or thing that is successful **successful** adj **successfully** adv **succession** n **1** a series of people or things following one after the other **2** succeeding to the throne or to another position or title; the right of doing this; the sequence of people with this right **successive** adj following one after another, in an unbroken series **successor** n a person or thing that succeeds another

succinct (say sək-**sinkt**) adj expressed briefly and clearly **succinctly** adv

succour (say **suk**-er) n help and support given in time of need

succulent (say **suk**-yoo-lənt) adj **1** juicy and tasty **2** (said about plants) having thick fleshy leaves or stems **succulent** n a succulent plant **succulence** n

succumb (say sə-**kum**) v to give way to something overpowering ♦ *he succumbed to temptation*

such adj **1** of the same kind ♦ *I love weddings, christenings, and all such occasions.* **2** of the kind or degree described ♦ *There's no such person.* **3** so great or intense ♦ *It gave her such a fright.* **such** pronoun the action or thing just mentioned ♦ *Such being the case, we can do nothing.* **such-and-such** adj particular but not now specified ♦ *He says he will arrive at such-and-such a time but is always late.* **suchlike** n things of the type mentioned **as such** in the exact sense of the word ♦ *He's not an artist as such, but he does paint now and again.* **such as 1** for example **2** of a similar kind as ♦ *people such as our neighbours*

suck v **1** to draw liquid or air, etc. into the mouth by using the lip muscles **2** to squeeze something in the mouth by using the tongue ♦ *She was sucking a toffee.* **3** to draw something in ♦ *Plants suck moisture from the soil.* **suck** n the act or process of sucking **sucker** n **1** an organ of certain animals, or a device of rubber, etc., that can stick to a surface by suction **2** a shoot coming up from the roots or underground stem of a tree or shrub **3** *informal* a person who is easily deceived **suction** n **1** sucking **2** producing a partial or complete vacuum so that external atmospheric pressure forces fluid, etc. into the empty space or causes adhesion of surfaces **to suck up to** *informal* to flatter someone in the hope of winning their favour

suckle v **1** to feed a baby or young animal at the breast or udder **2** (said about young) to take milk in this way **suckling** n a child or animal that is not yet weaned

sudden adj happening or done quickly and unexpectedly **all of a sudden** suddenly **suddenly** adv **suddenness** n

suds pl n froth on soapy water

sue v **sues**, **sued**, **suing** to begin legal proceedings against someone to claim money from them

suede (say swayd) n leather with the flesh side rubbed to make it velvety

suet n the hard fat from round the kidneys of cattle and sheep, used in cooking

suffer v **1** to undergo or be subjected to pain, loss, grief, damage, etc. **2** to allow or tolerate something **sufferance** n **on sufferance** tolerated but only grudgingly or because there is no positive objection **sufferer** n **suffering** n

suffice (say sə-**fiys**) v to be enough for someone's needs **sufficient** adj enough **sufficiency** n **sufficiently** adv

suffix n a letter or set of letters added at the end of a word to make another word (e.g. *y* added to *rust* to make *rusty*) or as an inflexion (e.g. *ing* added to *suck* to make *sucking*)

suffocate v **1** to kill someone by stopping them breathing; to be killed in this way **2** to have difficulty in breathing because of heat and lack of air **suffocation** n

suffrage (say **suf**-rij) n the right to vote in

political elections **suffragette** n a woman who, in the early 20th century, campaigned for women to have the right to vote

suffuse (say sə-fewz) v to spread throughout or over something gradually **suffusion** n

sugar n a sweet crystalline substance obtained from the juices of various plants **sugar** v to sweeten or coat something with sugar **sugary** adj **sugar beet** n the kind of beet from which sugar is extracted **sugar cane** n a tropical grass with tall jointed stems from which sugar is obtained

suggest v 1 to put forward an idea or plan for someone to consider 2 to cause an idea or possibility to come into the mind **suggestible** adj easily influenced by people's suggestions **suggestion** n 1 suggesting, or being suggested 2 something suggested 3 a slight trace ♦ a suggestion of a French accent **suggestive** adj 1 conveying a suggestion 2 tending to convey an indecent or improper meaning **suggestively** adv

suicide n 1 the intentional killing of yourself; an instance of this 2 a person who commits suicide 3 a course of action that is destructive to your own interests ♦ The announcement of tax increases was political suicide. **suicidal** adj 1 to do with suicide 2 (said about a person) liable to commit suicide 3 destructive to your own interests **suicidally** adv

suit n 1 a set of clothing to be worn together, especially a jacket and trousers or a jacket and skirt 2 clothing for use in a particular activity ♦ a diving suit 3 any of the four sets (spades, hearts, diamonds, and clubs) into which a pack of cards is divided 4 a lawsuit **suit** v 1 to look attractive on someone; to go well with something ♦ Red doesn't suit her. 2 to be acceptable to or convenient for a person or thing ♦ 7 o'clock suits me fine. **suitable** adj satisfactory or right for a particular person, purpose, or occasion **suitability** n **suitably** adv **suitor** n a man who is courting a woman **suitcase** n a rectangular case for carrying clothes, usually with a hinged lid and a handle

suite n 1 a set of connected rooms 2 a set of matching furniture 3 a set of musical pieces or extracts

sulky adj **sulkier**, **sulkiest** bad-tempered and silent because of resentment **sulk** v to be sulky

sullen adj silent, bad-tempered, and gloomy **sullenness** n

sully v **sullies**, **sullied**, **sullying** to stain, blemish, or spoil the purity of something

sulphur n a chemical element (symbol S), a pale-yellow substance that burns with a blue flame and a stifling smell, used in industry and medicine **sulphuric** adj containing a proportion of sulphur **sulphurous** adj 1 to do with or like sulphur 2 containing a proportion of sulphur

sultan n the ruler of certain Muslim countries **sultana** n 1 a light brown seedless raisin 2 the wife, mother, sister, or daughter of a sultan **sultanate** n the territory of a sultan

sultry adj **sultrier**, **sultriest** 1 hot and humid 2 passionate and sensual

sum n 1 a total 2 a particular amount of money 3 a problem in arithmetic **summation** n 1 finding of a total or sum 2 summing up **to sum someone** or **something up** to concisely describe or form a quick opinion of someone or something **to sum up** to summarize, especially at the end of a talk, etc.

summary n pl **summaries** a statement giving the main points of something briefly **summary** adj 1 giving the main points only, not the details ♦ a summary account 2 done or given without delay or attention to the formal procedures ♦ summary punishment **summarily** adv **summarize** v to make or be a summary of something

summer n the season between spring and autumn, when the weather is warmest **summery** adj **summer house** n a small building providing shade in a garden or park **summertime** n

summit n 1 the top of a mountain or hill 2 the highest level of achievement 3 (also **summit conference**) a meeting between heads of two or more governments

summon v to order someone to come or appear **summons** n pl **summonses**

1 an order to appear in a law court, or a document containing this **2** a command to do something or appear somewhere **summons** v to serve someone with a summons **to summon something up** to gather together your strength or courage in order to do something

sumo (say **soo**-moh) n a form of Japanese heavyweight wrestling

sump n **1** an inner casing holding lubricating oil in a petrol engine **2** a hole or pit into which waste liquid drains

sumptuous adj splendid and expensive-looking **sumptuously** adv **sumptuousness** n

sun n **1** the star round which the earth travels and from which it receives light and warmth **2** the light and warmth from the sun **3** any star in the universe, with or without planets **sun** v **sunned**, **sunning** to expose yourself to the sun **sunless** adj **sunny** adj **sunnier**, **sunniest 1** bright with sunlight, full of sunshine **2** (said about a person or mood) cheerful **sunnily** adv **sunbathe** v to sit or lie in the sun, especially to get a suntan **sunbeam** n a ray of sunlight **sunbed** n **1** a bench that you lie on under sunlamps **2** a lounger used for sunbathing **sunblock** n a cream or lotion that you put on your skin to protect it from sunburn **sunburn** n redness and inflammation of the skin caused by exposure to the sun **sundial** n an instrument that shows the time by means of the shadow of a rod or plate on a scaled dial **sundown** n sunset **sunflower** n a tall garden plant bearing large flowers with golden petals round a dark centre, producing seeds that yield an edible oil **sunglasses** pl n glasses with tinted lenses to protect the eyes from sunlight or glare **sunlamp** n a lamp producing ultraviolet rays, used to give people an artificial suntan **sunlight** n light from the sun **sunlit** adj **sunrise** n **1** the rising of the sun, or the time of this **2** the sky full of colour at sunrise **sunroof** n a panel in the roof of a car that can be opened to let in fresh air and sunlight **sunscreen** n a cream or lotion that you put on your skin to protect it from the sun **sunset** n **1** the

setting of the sun, or the time of this **2** the sky full of colour at sunset **sunshine** n **1** direct sunlight with no cloud between the sun and the earth **2** cheerfulness or happiness **sunspot** n one of the dark patches sometimes observed on the sun's surface, associated with the sun's magnetic field **sunstroke** n illness caused by being in the sun too long **suntan** n a brown colour in skin that has been exposed to the sun **suntanned** adj

sundae (say **sun**-day) n a dish of ice cream and crushed fruit, nuts, syrup, etc.

Sunday n the first day of the week, observed by Christians as a day of rest and worship **Sunday school** n a class held on Sundays to teach children about Christianity

sundry adj of various kinds **sundries** pl n various small items not named individually **all and sundry** everyone

sunken adj **1** lying below the level of the surrounding area ♦ a sunken bath **2** submerged in water **3** (said about a person's eyes or cheeks) hollow or recessed

sup v **supped**, **supping** to drink liquid by sips or spoonfuls

super adj informal excellent or superb

super- prefix **1** over or beyond (as in superimpose, superhuman) **2** of greater size or quality, etc. (as in supermarket) **3** extremely (as in superabundant) **4** beyond (as in supernatural)

superannuation n **1** regular payments made by an employee towards a pension **2** a pension of this type

superb adj **1** excellent **2** splendid or magnificent **superbly** adv

supercharge v to increase the efficiency and power of an engine by using a device that supplies air or fuel at above the normal pressure **supercharger** n

supercilious (say soo-per-**sil**-iəs) adj with an air of superiority; haughty and scornful **superciliously** adv **superciliousness** n

superficial adj **1** existing or happening on the surface ♦ a superficial wound **2** not deep or thorough ♦ superficial knowledge **3** (said about a person) having no depth of character or feeling **superficiality** n **superficially** adv

superfluous (say soo-per-floo-əs) *adj* unnecessary, more than is needed **superfluity** *n pl* **superfluities**

superhuman *adj* beyond ordinary human ability or power

superimpose *v* to place or lay one thing on top of something else

superintend *v* to supervise or be in charge of something or someone **superintendent** *n* **1** a person who superintends something or someone **2** a police officer ranking above chief inspector

superior *adj* **1** higher in position or rank **2** better or more important than another; higher in quality or ability **3** showing that you feel yourself to be above or better than others **superior** *n* a person who is higher than another in rank or ability **superiority** *n*

superlative (say soo-per-lə-tiv) *adj* **1** of the highest degree or quality ♦ *with superlative skill* **2** describing a form of an adjective or adverb that means 'most', such as *dearest*, *shyest*, *best* **superlative** *n* a superlative form of an adjective or adverb

supermarket *n* a large self-service shop selling groceries and household goods

supernatural *adj* to do with events that are apparently caused by forces beyond the laws of nature or science **the supernatural** *n* the world of supernatural events and forces

supernova *n pl* **supernovae** a star that suddenly increases very greatly in brightness because of an explosion disrupting its structure

supernumerary (say soo-per-**new**-mer-er-i) *adj* in excess of the normal number, extra

superpower *n* one of the most powerful nations of the world

superscript *adj* written or printed just above and to the right of a word, figure, or symbol (e.g. 2 in 3^2 meaning 9)

supersede (say soo-per-**seed**) *v* to take the place of another person or thing

supersonic *adj* (said about speed) greater than the speed of sound

superstar *n* an extremely successful performer in entertainment or sport

superstition *n* **1** belief that events can be influenced by certain acts, objects, or circumstances, although the connection has no rational basis **2** an idea or practice based on such belief **superstitious** *adj* based on or influenced by superstition **superstitiously** *adv*

supervene (say soo-per-**veen**) *v* to happen and interrupt or change something ♦ *The country was prosperous until an earthquake supervened.*

supervise *v* to be in charge of a person or task and inspect the work that is done **supervision** *n* **supervisor** *n* **supervisory** *adj*

supine (say **soo**-piyn) *adj* lying face upwards

supper *n* a light or informal evening meal

supplant *v* to oust and take the place of a person or thing

supple *adj* **suppler**, **supplest** bending easily; flexible, not stiff **suppleness** *n*

supplement (say **sup**-li-mənt) *n* **1** a thing added to something as an extra or to make up for a deficiency **2** a separate section, especially a colour magazine, added to a newspaper **3** an additional charge paid for an extra service **supplement** (say **sup**-li-ment) *v* to provide or be a supplement to something ♦ *She supplements her pocket money by working on Saturdays.* **supplementary** *adj*

supplicate *v* to ask or beg humbly for something **supplicant** *n* **supplication** *n*

supply *v* **supplies**, **supplied**, **supplying** to give someone or provide them with what is needed; to make something available for use **supply** *n pl* **supplies** **1** the providing of what is needed **2** a stock or amount of something provided or available ♦ *the water supply* **supply** *adj* (said about a schoolteacher, etc.) acting as a temporary substitute for another **supplier** *n* someone who supplies something

support *v* **1** to keep something from falling or sinking; to bear the weight of something **2** to give strength, help, or encouragement to someone or something **3** to supply someone with the necessities of life ♦ *She has a family to support.* **4** to be a fan of a particular sports team **5** to take a secondary part ♦ *The play has a strong supporting cast.* **6** to bring facts to confirm a statement, claim, theory, etc. ♦ *All the available evidence supports this view.* **support** *n* **1** assistance, encouragement, or approval ♦ *Thank you for your support.* **2** supporting, or being supported **3** a person or thing that supports someone or something **supporter** *n* **supportive** *adj*

suppose *v* **1** to think that something is likely to happen or be true, though without proof ♦ *I don't suppose they will come.* **2** to assume something as true for the purpose of argument ♦ *Suppose the world were flat.* **3** to consider something as a proposal or suggestion ♦ *Suppose we try another firm.* **supposed** *adj* **supposedly** *adv* according to what is generally believed or supposed **supposition** *n* an assumption or hypothesis **to be supposed to** to be expected or required to do something ♦ *You were supposed to be here an hour ago.*

suppress *v* **1** to put an end to something, especially by force or authority ♦ *Troops suppressed the rebellion.* **2** to prevent something from being known, published, or seen ♦ *The police were accused of suppressing evidence.* **3** to prevent your feelings from being expressed ♦ *She managed to suppress her anger.* **suppression** *n*

suppurate (say **sup**-yoor-ayt) *v* to form or produce pus

supreme *adj* **1** highest in authority or rank ♦ *the supreme commander* **2** highest in importance, intensity, or quality ♦ *supreme courage* **supremacy** *n* **supremely** *adv* **supremo** *n pl* **supremos** a person in overall charge

sur- *prefix* equivalent to *super-*; (as in *surcharge, surface*)

surcharge *n* payment demanded in addition to the usual charge

sure *adj* **1** completely confident that you are right, free from doubt **2** certain to do something or to happen ♦ *The book is sure to be a success.* **3** undoubtedly true ♦ *One thing is sure.* **4** completely reliable ♦ *There's only one sure way to do it.* **sure** *adv informal* certainly ♦ *It sure was cold.* **surely** *adv*

1 without doubt, certainly **2** used for emphasis ♦ *Surely you don't mean that?* **3** (as an answer) certainly, of course ♦ *'Will you help?' 'Surely.'* **sureness** *n* **surety** *n pl* **sureties 1** a person who promises to pay a debt or fulfil a contract, etc. if another person fails to do so **2** money given as a guarantee that someone will do something **sure-fire** *adj* certain to succeed

surf *n* the white foam of waves breaking on a rock or shore **surf** *v* **1** to stand or lie on a surfboard while being carried on waves to the shore **2** to spend time moving from site to site on the Internet **surfer** *n* **surfing** *n* **surfboard** *n* a long narrow board used in surfing

surface *n* **1** the outside of something **2** the uppermost area, the top of a table or desk, etc. **3** the top of a body of water or other liquid **4** the outward appearance of something ♦ *On the surface he was a charming man.* **surface** *v* **1** to rise or come up to the surface, especially from under water **2** to become apparent **3** to put a surface on a road or path

surfeit (say **ser**-fit) *n* too much of something

surge *n* **1** a sudden powerful movement forwards or upwards ♦ *tidal surges* **2** a sudden increase in something or rush of feeling **surge** *v* **1** to move forwards or upwards like waves **2** to increase suddenly and powerfully

surgery *n pl* **surgeries 1** the treatment of injuries, disorders, and disease by cutting or manipulating the affected parts **2** the place where a doctor or dentist, etc. treats or advises patients **3** the hours during which a doctor or dentist, etc. is available to patients at a surgery **4** the place where an MP, lawyer, etc. is regularly available for consultation **surgeon** *n* a medical practitioner who performs surgical operations **surgical** *adj* **surgically** *adv* **surgical spirit** *n* methylated spirits used for cleansing the skin before injections or surgery

surly *adj* **surlier**, **surliest** bad-tempered and unfriendly **surliness** *n*

surmise (say ser-**miyz**) *v* to conclude

something without much evidence, to guess something **surmise** *n* a guess or conjecture

surmount *v* to overcome a difficulty or obstacle **be surmounted by** to have something on or over the top **surmountable** *adj*

surname *n* the name held by all members of a family

surpass *v* to do or be better than all others

surplice (say **ser**-plis) *n* a loose white vestment, worn over the cassock by clergy and choir at a Christian church service

surplus (say **ser**-pləs) *n* an amount left over after spending or using all that was needed **surplus** *adj* excess or extra

surprise *n* **1** the feeling caused by something unexpected happening **2** something unexpected **3** the process of catching a person, etc. unprepared ♦ *a surprise visit* **surprise** *v* **1** to cause someone to feel surprise, to be a surprise to someone **2** to come upon or attack someone suddenly and without warning **surprising** *adj* **surprisingly** *adv* **to take someone by surprise** to happen unexpectedly to someone

surreal *adj* bizarre

surrender *v* **1** to stop fighting and give yourself up to an enemy or agree that they have won **2** to hand something over or give something up, especially on demand or under compulsion **3** to let a powerful emotion take control of you ♦ *She surrendered herself to grief.* **surrender** *n* surrendering, or being surrendered

surreptitious (say su-rəp-**tish**-əs) *adj* acting or done stealthily **surreptitiously** *adv*

surrogate (say **su**-rə-gət) *n* a deputy or substitute **surrogacy** *n* **surrogate mother** *n* a woman who carries and gives birth to a baby for a woman who cannot do so herself, using a fertilized egg from the other woman or sperm from the other woman's partner

surround *v* **1** to be all round something **2** to move into position all round something ♦ *Police quickly surrounded the building.* **3** to place something all round something

♦ *The new president surrounded himself with trusted advisors.* **surround** *n* a border or edging **surroundings** *pl n* the conditions or area around a person or thing

surtax *n* an additional tax, especially on income above a certain level

surveillance (say ser-**vayl**-əns) *n* a close watch kept on a person or thing, especially on a suspected person

survey (say **ser**-vay) *n* **1** a general look at something **2** an investigation of the opinions or experience of a group of people, in which they are asked a series of questions **3** the surveying of land or property; a map, plan, or report produced by this **survey** (say ser-**vay**) *v* **1** to conduct a survey among a group of people **2** to measure and map out the size, shape, position, and elevation, etc. of an area of land **3** to look carefully and thoroughly at something **4** to examine and report on the condition of a building, etc. **surveyor** *n* a person whose job is to survey land or buildings

survive *v* **1** to continue to live or exist **2** to remain alive or in existence after something ♦ *Few flowers survived the frost.* **3** to remain alive after someone's death ♦ *He is survived by his wife and two children.* **survival** *n* **survivor** *n*

susceptible (say sə-**sep**-ti-bəl) *adj* **1** likely to be affected or harmed by something ♦ *She is susceptible to colds.* **2** easily affected by feelings or emotions **susceptibility** *n*

suspect (say sə-**spekt**) *v* **1** to have a feeling that something is likely or possible ♦ *We suspected a trap.* **2** to feel that a person is guilty of something but have little or no proof **3** to doubt that something is genuine or true ♦ *I can't help but suspect their motives.* **suspect** (say **sus**-pekt) *n* a person who is suspected of a crime or other offence **suspect** (say **sus**-pekt) *adj* possibly dangerous or false; open to suspicion

suspend *v* **1** to hang something from somewhere **2** to put a temporary stop to something **3** to postpone or delay something ♦ *The committee has decided to suspend judgement.* **4** to remove a person temporarily from a job **5** to keep something from falling or sinking in air or liquid, etc. ♦ *Particles are suspended in the fluid.* **suspender** *n* an elastic strap fastened to the top of a stocking to hold it up **suspense** *n* a state or feeling of anxious uncertainty while waiting for something to happen or become known **suspension** *n* **1** suspending, or being suspended **2** the system of springs and shock absorbers by which a vehicle is supported on its axles **3** a mixture consisting of a fluid containing small pieces of solid material which do not dissolve **suspended sentence** *n* a sentence of imprisonment that is not to be enforced as long as no further offence is committed within a specified period **suspension bridge** *n* a bridge suspended from cables that pass over supporting towers near each end

suspicion *n* **1** the feeling that someone is guilty of something or that something is wrong ♦ *He was arrested on suspicion of fraud.* **2** a feeling that something is likely or possible ♦ *I have a suspicion that she hasn't told me everything.* **3** a slight trace ♦ *a suspicion of a smile* **suspicious** *adj* **1** feeling suspicion **2** causing suspicion **suspiciously** *adv*

suss *v informal* to understand or realize something

sustain *v* **1** to support or strengthen someone, physically or mentally **2** to keep something going continuously **3** to undergo or suffer something ♦ *We sustained a heavy defeat.* **4** to confirm or uphold the validity of something ♦ *The objection was sustained.* **sustainable** *adj* **sustenance** *n* food and drink that sustains life

suture (say soo-cher) *n* a stitch or thread, etc. used to hold together the edges of a wound

suzerain (say soo-zer-ayn) *n* **1** a country or ruler that has some control over another country which is self-governing in its internal affairs **2** an overlord in feudal times

svelte (say svelt) *adj* (said about a person) slim and elegant

SW *abbr* south-west or south-western

swab (say swob) *n* a mop or absorbent pad for cleaning, drying, or mopping things up

swab *v* **swabbed**, **swabbing** to clean or wipe something with a swab

swaddle (say swod-el) *v* to wrap someone or something in cloth or warm clothes

swag *n informal* money or goods taken by a thief or burglar

swagger *v* to walk or behave in a self-important or arrogant way, to strut **swagger** *n* a swaggering walk or manner

swain *n literary* a young lover or suitor

swallow¹ *v* **1** to make food, drink, etc. go down your throat **2** to work the muscles of the throat in the same way, because of fear or nervousness **3** to accept or believe something meekly or unquestioningly **4** to repress or resist expressing something ♦ *She will have to swallow her pride.* **swallow** *n* an act of swallowing something, or the amount swallowed **to swallow something up** to take something in so as to engulf or absorb it ♦ *She was swallowed up in the crowd.*

swallow² *n* a small migratory insect-eating bird with a forked tail

swamp *n* a bog or marsh **swamp** *v* **1** to flood a place; to submerge something in water **2** to overwhelm someone or something with too much of something **swampy** *adj*

swan *n* a large usually white water bird with a long slender neck **swan** *v* **swanned**, **swanning** *informal* to go around in a casual or showy way **swansong** *n* a person's last performance, achievement, or composition

swank *v informal* to show off your possessions or achievements in order to impress others **swank** *n informal* boastful behaviour, talk, or display **swanky** *adj*

swap *v* **swapped**, **swapping** *informal* to exchange one thing for another **swap** *n informal* an act of exchanging one thing for another

sward (say swawd) *n* an expanse of short grass

swarm¹ *n* **1** a large number of insects, birds, small animals, or people flying or moving about together **2** a cluster of honeybees leaving the hive with a queen bee to establish a new home **swarm** *v* **1** to move in a swarm, to come together in large numbers **2** (said about a place) to be crowded or overrun with insects, people, etc.

swarm² v **to swarm up** to climb by gripping with your hands and legs

swarthy (say **swor**-thi) adj **swarthier**, **swarthiest** having a dark complexion **swarthiness** n

swashbuckling adj **1** daring; loving adventure and fighting **2** (said about a film, etc.) showing daring adventures set in the past **swashbuckler** n

swastika (say **swos**-tik-ə) n an ancient symbol formed by a cross with the ends bent at right angles, adopted (in clockwise form) by the German Nazi party as its emblem

swat v **swatted**, **swatting** to hit or crush a fly, etc. with something flat **swat** n a sharp blow with a flat object **swatter** n

swathe¹ (say swawth) n **1** a line of grass, corn, etc. as it falls after being cut **2** a broad strip or area

swathe² (say swayth) v to wrap a person or thing in layers of bandage, wrappings, or warm clothes

sway v **1** to move or swing gently from side to side **2** to influence the opinions, sympathy, or actions of someone **sway** n a swaying movement **to hold sway** to have great power or influence

swear v **swore**, **sworn 1** to use offensive language, especially because you are angry **2** to promise something solemnly or on oath ♦ *She swore to tell the truth.* **3** informal to state something emphatically ♦ *He swore he hadn't touched it.* **swear word** n a word considered offensive or obscene **to swear by** informal to have or express great confidence in a person or thing **to swear someone in** to admit someone to an office or position by getting them to take a formal oath

sweat n **1** moisture given off by the body through the pores of the skin **2** a state of sweating or being covered by sweat **3** informal a state of great anxiety **4** informal a laborious task **sweat** v **1** to give off sweat; to cause a person or animal to do this **2** to be in a state of great anxiety **sweaty** adj

sweatier, **sweatiest**, **sweatband** n a band of absorbent material worn to soak up sweat **sweatshirt** n a loose cotton sweater worn for sports or casual wear **sweatshop** n a place where people work in poor conditions for low pay

sweater n a jumper or pullover

Swede n a person born in Sweden or descended from people born there **Swedish** adj to do with or coming from Sweden **Swedish** n the language of Sweden

swede n a large variety of turnip with purple skin and yellow flesh

sweep v past tense and past participle **swept 1** to clear something away with a broom or brush **2** to clean or clear a surface or area by doing this **3** to remove something swiftly and suddenly ♦ *All objections were swept aside.* **4** to go smoothly and swiftly ♦ *She swept out of the room.* **5** to move or travel quickly over or along an area ♦ *A new fashion is sweeping America.* **6** to extend in a continuous line or slope ♦ *The mountains sweep down to the sea.* **sweep** n **1** a sweeping movement **2** a sweeping line or slope **3** the act of sweeping with a broom, etc. **4** a chimney sweep **5** a sweepstake **sweeper** n **1** a person or device that sweeps **2** (in football) a player positioned just in front of the goalkeeper and free to defend at any point across the field **sweeping** adj **1** wide-ranging ♦ *The new manager made sweeping changes.* **2** (said about a statement) making no exceptions or limitations; too general ♦ *sweeping generalizations* **sweepstake** n **1** a form of gambling on sporting events in which all the money staked is divided among the winners **2** a horse race with betting of this kind

sweet adj **1** tasting as if it contains sugar, not sour or bitter **2** smelling pleasant; fragrant **3** pleasant to listen to **4** attractive and charming ♦ *a sweet face* **5** having a pleasant and kind nature **sweet** n **1** a small shaped piece of sweet food, usually made with sugar or chocolate **2** a sweet dish forming a course of a meal **sweeten** v **sweetener** n **1** a substance used to sweeten food or drink **2** informal something given to induce someone to do something; a bribe **sweetly** adv **sweetness** n **sweetbread** n an animal's thymus gland or pancreas used as food **sweetcorn** n a type of maize with juicy yellow kernels **sweetheart** n **1** a person you are in love with, one of a pair of people in love with each other **2** used as a term of endearment **sweetmeat** n a sweet or a very small fancy cake **sweet pea** n a climbing garden plant with fragrant flowers in many colours **sweet potato** n a root vegetable with reddish skin and sweet yellow flesh **sweet-talk** v to persuade someone to do something by flattering them **sweet tooth** n a liking for sweet things

swell v past participle **swollen** or **swelled** **1** to make something larger, or to become larger, because of pressure from within; to curve outwards ♦ My ankle was starting to swell. **2** to make something or become larger in amount, volume, numbers, or intensity **swell** n **1** the act or state of swelling **2** the rise and fall of the sea's surface in waves that do not break **3** a gradual increase in sound, amount, or intensity **4** informal old use a stylish person of high social position **swell** adj N. Am informal very good **swelling** n a swollen place on the body

swelter v to feel uncomfortably hot **sweltering** adj

swerve v to turn or make something turn to one side suddenly **swerve** n a swerving movement or direction

swift adj **1** happening quickly or promptly ♦ a swift response **2** able to move fast ♦ a swift runner **swift** n a swiftly-flying, insect-eating bird with long narrow wings **swiftly** adv **swiftness** n

swig v **swigged**, **swigging** informal to drink something quickly, taking large mouthfuls **swig** n informal a large mouthful of a drink

swill v **1** to wash or rinse something by pouring water over or through it **2** to drink something in large quantities **swill** n a sloppy mixture of waste food fed to pigs

swim v **swam**, **swum**, **swimming 1** to move the body through water by movements of the limbs, fins, or tail, etc. **2** to float **3** to be covered with or full of liquid ♦ The floor was swimming in water. **4** to seem to be whirling or waving, to feel dizzy ♦ My head is swimming. **swim** n a period of swimming **swimmer** n **swimmingly** adv with smooth progress **swimsuit** n a woman's one-piece swimming costume

swindle v **1** to cheat someone in a business transaction **2** to obtain something by fraud **swindle** n a piece of swindling **swindler** n

swine pl n pigs **swine** n pl **swine** or **swines** informal a very unpleasant person **swineherd** n a person taking care of a number of pigs

swing v past tense and past participle **swung 1** to move to and fro while hanging or supported; to make something do this **2** to move or make something move in a curve ♦ The car swung into the drive. **3** to try to hit or punch someone with a wide curving movement ♦ He swung at me but I managed to duck. **4** to change from one opinion or mood, etc. to another **5** to have a decisive influence on an election, a deal, etc. ♦ That speech last night may have swung it for us. **6** informal to be executed by hanging **swing** n **1** a seat hung on ropes or chains so that it can be moved backwards and forwards **2** a swinging movement, action, or rhythm **3** the amount by which votes, opinions, or points scored, etc. change from one side to the other **4** a kind of jazz music with a flowing but vigorous rhythm **swinger** n **swinging** adj lively and fashionable

swingeing (say **swinj**-ing) adj severe or drastic

swipe v informal **1** to hit or try to hit something with a swinging blow **2** to steal something, especially by snatching **3** to slide a credit card through an electronic device **swipe** n informal **1** a swinging blow **2** an attack or criticism

swirl v to move round quickly in circles; to make something do this **swirl** n a swirling movement or pattern

swish v to move something with a hissing sound **swish** n a swishing sound **swish** adj informal smart and fashionable

Swiss adj to do with or coming from Switzerland **Swiss** n pl **Swiss** a person born in Switzerland or descended from people born there

switch n 1 a device that is pressed or turned to start or stop something working, usually by opening or closing an electric circuit 2 a shift or change in something 3 the replacing of one thing with something else, especially in order to deceive people 4 a flexible shoot cut from a tree **switch** v 1 to turn an electrical or other device on or off by means of a switch 2 to change over to a different side, method, system, etc. 3 to replace something with something else; to exchange places ♦ *The blackmailer must have switched the bags somehow.* **switchback** n 1 a road with alternate sharp ascents and descents 2 a roller coaster **switchboard** n a panel with a set of switches for making telephone connections or operating electric circuits

swivel n a link or pivot between two parts enabling one of them to revolve without turning the other **swivel** v **swivelled, swivelling** to turn round or make something turn round, as if on a swivel

swizz, swizzle n *informal* an instance of being cheated or disappointed

swoon v to faint **swoon** n a faint

swoop v 1 to come down with a rushing movement like a bird upon its prey 2 to make a sudden attack **swoop** n a swooping movement or attack

swop v **swopped, swopping** n another spelling of *swap*

sword (say sord) n a weapon with a long metal blade and a hilt **swordfish** n pl **swordfish** or **swordfishes** a large sea fish with a long sword-like upper jaw **swordsman** n pl **swordsmen** a person who fights or is skilful with a sword **swordsmanship** n

sworn adj 1 given under oath ♦ *sworn testimony* 2 determined to remain so ♦ *They are sworn enemies.*

swot v **swotted, swotting** *informal* to study hard **swot** n *informal* a person who spends a lot of time studying

sybarite (say **sib**-er-riyt) n a person who is excessively fond of comfort and luxury **sybaritic** adj

sycamore (say **sik**-e-mor) n a tall tree with winged seeds, often grown for its timber

sycophant (say **sik**-e-fant) n a person who tries to win people's favour by flattering them **sycophancy** n **sycophantic** adj

syllable (say **sil**-e-bel) n a word or part of a word that has one vowel sound when you say it **syllabic** adj

syllabus (say **sil**-e-bes) n pl **syllabuses** a summary of the subjects that are included in a course of study

syllogism (say **sil**-e-jizm) n a form of reasoning in which a conclusion is reached from two statements, as in *'All men must die; I am a man; therefore I must die.'*

sylph (say silf) n a slender girl or woman **sylphlike** adj

symbiosis (say sim-bi-**oh**-sis) n 1 an association of two different organisms living together, usually to the advantage of both 2 a similar relationship between people or groups **symbiotic** adj

symbol n 1 a thing thought of as representing or standing for something else ♦ *The lion is the symbol of courage.* 2 a mark or sign with a special meaning, such as mathematical signs (e.g. + and - for addition and subtraction), letters representing chemical elements, or written forms of notes in music **symbolic** adj **symbolically** adv **symbolism** n the use of symbols to represent things **symbolist** n, adj **symbolize** v 1 to be a symbol of something 2 to represent something by means of a symbol

symmetrical (say sim-**et**-rik-el) adj able to be divided into parts that are the same in size and shape and similar in position on either side of a dividing line (**line symmetry**) or a central point (**radial symmetry** or **rotational symmetry**) **symmetrically** adv **symmetry** n 1 being symmetrical 2 pleasing proportion between parts of a whole 3 similarity or exact correspondence

sympathy n pl **sympathies** 1 a feeling of pity or tenderness towards someone suffering pain, grief, or trouble 2 the sharing or understanding of another person's feelings or sensations **sympathetic** adj

1 feeling, expressing, or resulting from sympathy **2** likeable ♦ *He's not a sympathetic character.* **3** showing approval or support ♦ *He is sympathetic to our plan.* **sympathetically** *adv* **sympathize** *v* **1** to feel or show sympathy **2** to agree with an opinion or sentiment **sympathizer** *n*

symphony (say **sim**-fən-i) *n pl* **symphonies** a long elaborate musical composition (usually in several movements) for a full orchestra **symphonic** *adj* **symphonically** *adv*

symposium (say sim-**poh**-ziəm) *n pl* **symposia** or **symposiums** a meeting or conference to discuss a particular subject

symptom *n* **1** a perceptible change from what is normal in the body or its functioning, indicating the existence of a condition or disease ♦ *Red spots are a symptom of measles.* **2** an indication of something undesirable **symptomatic** *adj*

synagogue (say **sin**-ə-gog) *n* a building for public Jewish worship

sync, synch (say sink) *n informal* synchronization

synchromesh (say **sink**-roh-mesh) *n* a device that makes parts of a gear revolve at the same speed while they are being brought into contact

synchronize (say **sink**-rə-niyz) *v* **1** to make things happen or operate at the same time or rate **2** to make watches or clocks show the same time **synchronization** *n* **synchronous** *adj* **1** existing or happening at the same time **2** operating at the same rate and simultaneously

syncopate (say **sink**-ə-payt) *v* to change the beats or accents in a passage of music by making the strong beats weak ones, and vice versa **syncopation** *n*

syndicate (say **sin**-dik-ət) *n* **1** a group of people or firms who work together in business **2** a group of people who gamble together, sharing the cost and any gains **syndicate** (say **sin**-dik-ayt) *v* **1** to sell a story, photograph, cartoon strip, etc. to several newspapers and periodicals for simultaneous publication **2** to manage something by a syndicate **syndication** *n*

syndrome (say **sin**-drohm) *n* **1** a group

of symptoms that together indicate the presence of a disease or abnormal condition **2** a combination of opinions, behaviour, etc. that are characteristic of a particular condition

synergy (say **sin**-ə-jee) *n* the cooperation of two or more organizations, etc. to produce a combined effect that is greater than the sum of their separate effects

synod (say **sin**-əd) *n* a council of senior members of the clergy to discuss questions of policy, teaching, etc.

synonym (say **sin**-ə-nim) *n* a word or phrase that means the same or almost the same as another word or phrase in the same language. 'Large' and 'great' are synonyms of 'big'. **synonymous** *adj*

synopsis (say sin-**op**-sis) *n pl* **synopses** a brief summary of something

syntax (say **sin**-taks) *n* the way in which words are arranged to form phrases and sentences **syntactic** *adj*

synthesis (say **sin**-thi-sis) *n pl* **syntheses** **1** the combining of separate parts or elements to form a complex whole **2** the combining of substances to form a compound; artificial production of a substance that occurs naturally in plants or animals **synthesize** *v* **1** to make something by synthesis **2** to produce sound electronically **synthesizer** *n* an electronic musical instrument operated by a keyboard and able to reproduce the musical tones of conventional instruments or produce a variety of artificial ones **synthetic** *adj* **1** made by chemical synthesis; artificially made, not natural **2** not genuine

syphilis (say **sif**-i-lis) *n* a serious venereal disease that if untreated can affect the bones, muscles, and brain

syphon *n, v* another spelling of *siphon*

syringe (say sə-**rinj**) *n* **1** a device for drawing in liquid and forcing it out again in a fine stream **2** a hypodermic syringe **syringe** *v* to spray liquid into or over something with a syringe

syrup *n* a thick sweet liquid; water in which sugar is dissolved **syrupy** *adj*

system *n* **1** a set of connected things or parts that form a whole or work together

♦ *a railway system* ♦ *the nervous system* **2** an organized scheme or method **3** a method of classification or notation or measurement, etc. ♦ *the metric system* **4** orderliness, being systematic ♦ *She works without system.* **5** a set of rules, principles, or practices forming a particular philosophy or form of government, etc. **systematic** *adj* methodical, according to a plan or system and not casually or at random **systematically** *adv* **systematize** *v* to arrange something according to a system **systematization** *n* **systemic** *adj* to do with or affecting the body or a system as a whole

Tt

T the twentieth letter of the English alphabet

TA *abbr* Territorial Army

ta *interjection informal* thank you

tab *n* a small flap or strip that sticks out, especially for getting hold of something or for putting information about it or identifying it **keep a tab** or **tabs on** *informal* to keep account of something or keep it under observation

tabard (say **tab**-ard) *n* **1** a short kind of tunic open at the sides, worn by a herald and decorated with the sovereign's coat of arms **2** a jerkin shaped like this

tabby *n pl* **tabbies** a cat with grey or dark brown fur and dark stripes

tabernacle *n* **1** (in the Bible) the portable shrine used by the Israelites during their wanderings **2** (in the Roman Catholic Church) an ornamental receptacle or cabinet containing the consecrated elements of the Eucharist **3** a meeting place for worship used by Nonconformists (e.g. Baptists) or Mormons

table *n* **1** a piece of furniture with a flat top supported on one or more legs **2** a list of facts or figures systematically arranged, especially in columns **table** *v* to put forward a proposal for discussion at a meeting **tabular** *adj* arranged or displayed in a table or in columns **tabulate** *v* to arrange figures or other information in a table or in columns **tabulation** *n* **tablecloth** *n* a cloth for covering a table, especially at meals **tablespoon** *n* a large spoon for serving food **tablespoonful** *n* **tablespoonfuls table tennis** *n* a game played with bats and a light hollow ball on a table with a net across it

tableau (say **tab**-loh) *n pl* **tableaux** (say **tab**-lohz) a dramatic or picturesque scene, especially a group of still figures representing a scene on a stage

tablet *n* **1** a slab or panel bearing an inscription or picture, especially one fixed to a wall as a memorial **2** a small measured amount of a medicine or drug compressed into a solid form, a pill **3** a small flattish piece of a solid substance such as soap

tabloid *n* a newspaper having pages that are half the size of broadsheet newspapers, usually popular in style with many photographs and large headlines

taboo *n* a ban or prohibition on something that is regarded by religion or custom as not to be done, used, spoken about, etc. **taboo** *adj* prohibited by a taboo ♦ *taboo words*

tachometer (say tə-kom-it-er) *n* an instrument for measuring the speed of a vehicle's engine

tacit (say **tas**-it) *adj* implied or understood without being put into words **tacitly** *adv* **taciturn** *adj* saying very little, reserved and uncommunicative

tack[1] *n* **1** a small nail with a broad flat head **2** a long stitch used to hold fabric in position lightly or temporarily **3** a course of action or policy ♦ *We seem to be on the wrong tack.* **tack** *v* **1** to nail something with a tack or tacks **2** to stitch fabric temporarily with long stitches **3** to add something as an extra ♦ *A service charge had been tacked on to the bill.* **tacky** *adj* **tackier, tackiest** (said about paint, glue, etc.) slightly sticky, not quite dry **tackiness** *n*

tack[2] *n* riding equipment including harness, saddles, etc.

tackle n 1 a set of ropes and pulleys for lifting weights or working a ship's sails 2 equipment for a task or sport, especially fishing 3 the act of tackling in football or hockey **tackle** v 1 to intercept another player and try to get the ball in football or hockey 2 to open a discussion with someone on a difficult or awkward matter 3 to try to deal with or overcome something difficult or awkward **tackler** n

tacky adj tackier, tackiest informal cheaply made, in poor taste

tact n skill and care in dealing with people sensitively and not offending them **tactful** adj **tactfully** adv **tactless** adj having or showing a lack of tact **tactlessly** adv

tactics pl n 1 the organization and deployment of military forces in battle 2 the methods used to achieve something **tactic** n a piece of tactics **tactical** adj 1 to do with tactics, especially as distinct from strategy 2 (said about weapons) intended to support the immediate needs of a military operation 3 (said about voting in elections) intended to prevent a strong candidate from winning rather than to support a candidate for reasons based on principle **tactically** adv **tactician** n an expert in tactics

tactile (say **tak**-tiyl) adj to do with or involving the sense of touch

tadpole n the larva of a frog or toad at the stage when it lives in water and has gills and a tail

taffeta n a shiny silk-like dress fabric

tag[1] n 1 a label attached to or stuck to something to identify it or give information about it 2 a metal or plastic point fixed to the end of a shoelace 3 a stock phrase or often repeated quotation **tag** v tagged, tagging 1 to label something with a tag 2 to attach something or add it as an extra thing ♦ A postscript was tagged on to her letter. **to tag along** informal to go along with another person or group, especially without being asked

tag[2] n a children's game in which one chases the rest, and anyone who is caught becomes the next chaser

tail n 1 the hindmost part of an animal, especially when this extends beyond the rest of the body 2 something resembling an animal's tail in shape or position; the rear part of something, or a part that hangs down or behind 3 informal a person who is following or shadowing another **tail** v informal to follow someone closely **tailless** adj **tails** pl n 1 a tailcoat, or a set of evening dress including a tailcoat 2 the side of a coin without the head on it, turned upwards after being tossed **tailback** n a long line of traffic stretching back from an obstruction **tailboard** n hinged doors at the rear of a lorry **tailcoat** n a man's coat with a long skirt cut away at the front and tapering and divided at the back **tailgate** n 1 a door at the back of an estate car or hatchback, hinged at the top 2 a tailboard **tailplane** n the horizontal surface of the tail of an aircraft **tailspin** n a spiral dive made by an aircraft with the tail making wider circles than the front **tailwind** n a wind blowing from behind a vehicle or aircraft, in the direction of its travel **to tail away** or **off** to become fewer, smaller, or slighter; to fall behind in a straggling line; (said about remarks, etc.) to end inconclusively

tailor n a person who makes men's clothes **tailor** v 1 to make or fit clothes as a tailor 2 to make or adapt something for a special purpose **tailor-made** adj 1 made by a tailor for a particular person 2 specially made or suited for a purpose

taint n a trace of a bad quality or condition **taint** v to affect something with a taint

take v took, taken 1 to remove something, to steal something ♦ Who has taken my pen? 2 to get possession of something, to capture or win something or someone ♦ The soldiers took many prisoners. 3 to be successful or effective ♦ The inoculation did not take. 4 to subtract one number from another 5 to make use of something ♦ to take a seat ♦ to take an opportunity 6 to use something habitually ♦ I don't take sugar in tea. 7 to have something as a requirement ♦ It takes a strong man to lift that. 8 to carry or remove something to a place ♦ Please take these letters to the post. 9 to accompany someone, or make them go with you ♦ I'll *take you to the station.* **10** to find out and record information ♦ *The police officer took his name.* **11** to interpret something in a certain way ♦ *I take it that you are satisfied.* **12** to accept or deal with something ♦ *We will just have to take the consequences.* **13** to perform or deal with something ♦ *to take an exam* ♦ *He took the corner too fast.* **take** *n* a scene or sequence of actions photographed at one time, in making a cinema or television film **takings** *pl n* money taken for goods or services, receipts **takeaway** *n* **1** a place that sells cooked meals for customers to take away **2** a meal from a takeaway **take-off** *n* **1** the process by which an aircraft becomes airborne **2** an act of mimicking **takeover** *n* the act of taking control of something, especially of one business company by another **to take after** to resemble a parent, etc. **to take against** to begin to dislike someone or something **to take off 1** (said about an aircraft) to leave the ground and become airborne **2** *informal* to leave abruptly **3** *informal* to become successful **to take place** to happen or occur **to take someone in** to deceive or cheat someone **to take someone off** to mimic someone **to take something in 1** to understand something **2** to make a piece of clothing tighter **to take something over** to take control of a business or activity **to take something up 1** to begin to pursue an interest or activity **2** to accept an offer **3** to occupy time or space **4** to investigate or pursue a matter further

talc *n* **1** a soft smooth mineral that is powdered for use as a lubricant **2** talcum powder **talcum powder** *n* powdered and scented talc for use on the skin to make it feel smooth and dry

tale *n* a narrative or story, especially one imaginatively told

talent *n* **1** a great or special natural ability **2** a unit of money used in certain ancient countries **talented** *adj*

talisman (say **tal**-iz-mən) *n pl* **talismans** an object supposed to bring good luck **talismanic** *adj*

talk *v* **1** to use spoken words to convey ideas, to hold a conversation **2** to express or utter something in words ♦ *You are talking nonsense.* **3** to speak in a particular language ♦ *I think they are talking Urdu.* **4** to influence or persuade someone by talking ♦ *She talked him into marrying her.* **5** to give away information ♦ *Do you think he'll talk?* **6** *informal* to be specifically concerned with something ♦ *We are talking big money here.* **talk** *n* **1** talking or conversation **2** an informal lecture **talkative** *adj* talking very much **talker** *n* **talking-to** *n* a scolding or reprimand

tall *adj* **1** of more than average height **2** having a certain height ♦ *He is six feet tall.* **a tall story** *informal* a story that is difficult to believe and probably untrue **tall order** *informal* a difficult thing to do

tallow *n* animal fat used to make candles, soap, lubricants, etc.

tally *n pl* **tallies** the total amount of a debt or score **tally** *v* **tallies**, **tallied**, **tallying** to agree or correspond ♦ *The two witnesses' stories do not tally.*

tally-ho *interjection* a huntsman's cry to the hounds on sighting a fox

Talmud (say **tal**-məd) *n* a collection of ancient writings on Jewish civil and religious law and tradition

talon (say **tal**-ən) *n* a claw, especially of a bird of prey

tamarind (say **tam**-er-ind) *n* **1** the fruit of a tropical tree, with a sour pulp **2** this tree

tambourine (say tam-ber-**een**) *n* a percussion instrument like a shallow drum, with metal discs in slots round the edge, played by being shaken or hit with the hand

tame *adj* **1** (said about an animal) gentle and not afraid of human beings, not wild or dangerous **2** docile **3** not exciting or interesting **tame** *v* to make an animal or person tame or manageable **tamely** *adv* **tameness** *n*

tamp *v* to pack something or ram it down tightly

tamper *v* to meddle or interfere with something

tampon *n* a plug of absorbent material that a woman inserts into her vagina to absorb blood during her menstrual period

tan *v* **tanned, tanning 1** to make the skin brown, or to become brown, by exposure to the sun **2** to convert an animal hide into leather by treating it with tannic acid **tan** *n* **1** yellowish brown **2** a brown colour in skin that has been exposed to the sun **tannery** *n* *pl* **tanneries** a place where hides are tanned into leather

tandem *n* a bicycle for two riders, sitting one behind another **in tandem** one behind another

tandoori *n* a style of Indian cooking in which food is cooked in a clay oven (called a *tandoor*)

tang *n* a strong flavour or smell **tangy** *adj* **tangier, tangiest** having a strong flavour or smell

tangent (say tan-jənt) *n* a straight line that touches the outside of a curve but does not cross it **tangential** *adj* **1** of or along a tangent **2** not relevant or only slightly relevant to a subject being considered **to go off at a tangent** to diverge suddenly from a subject or line of thought being considered

tangerine (say tan-jer-een) *n* **1** a kind of small flattened orange with a loose skin **2** a deep orange-red colour

tangible (say tan-ji-bəl) *adj* **1** able to be perceived by touch **2** clear and definite, real ♦ *The scheme has tangible advantages.* **tangibility** *n* **tangibly** *adv*

tangle *v* **1** to twist strands, or to become twisted, into a confused mass **2** *informal* to come into conflict with someone **tangle** *n* a tangled mass or condition

tango *n* *pl* **tangos** a ballroom dance with gliding steps, or the music for this

tank *n* **1** a large container for holding liquid or gas **2** a heavy armoured fighting vehicle carrying guns and moving on a continuous metal track round its wheels **tanker** *n* a ship, aircraft, or road vehicle for carrying oil or other liquid in bulk

tankard *n* a tall drinking mug with no handle, usually of silver or pewter and often with a lid

tannin *n* a compound obtained from various tree barks and also found in tea, used chiefly in tanning and dyeing

Tannoy *n trademark* a type of public address system

tantalize *v* to tease or torment someone by showing them something they want but cannot reach

tantamount (say tant-ə-mownt) *adj* equivalent, virtually the same ♦ *The Queen's request was tantamount to a command.*

tantrum *n* *pl* **tantrums** a wild outburst of bad temper or frustration, especially in a young child

Taoiseach (say tee-shək) *n* the title of the prime minister of the Republic of Ireland

tap[1] *n* **1** a device for letting out liquid or gas in a controllable flow **2** a device for listening secretly to a telephone conversation **tap** *v* **tapped, tapping 1** to draw off liquid by means of a tap or through an incision **2** to extract or obtain supplies or information from a source **3** to connect a device to a telephone in order to listen secretly to conversations **on tap 1** (said about a liquid or gas) ready to be drawn off by a tap **2** *informal* readily available

tap[2] *v* **tapped, tapping** to hit something or someone with a quick light blow **tap** *n* a quick light blow, or the sound of this **tap dance** *n* a dance performed wearing shoes with metal caps, in which an elaborate rhythm is tapped with the toes and heels

tapas (say tap-əs) *n* Spanish savoury snacks served with drinks at a bar

tape *n* **1** a narrow strip of cloth, paper, plastic, etc., used especially for tying or fastening **2** a plastic strip coated with a magnetic substance for recording sound or pictures or storing computer data **3** a cassette or reel of magnetic tape **tape** *v* **1** to tie or fasten something with tape **2** to record something on magnetic tape **tape measure** *n* a length of tape or flexible metal marked in inches or centimetres for measuring length **tape recorder** *n* an apparatus for recording and reproducing sounds on magnetic tape **tapeworm** *n* a long flat worm that can live as a parasite in the intestines of humans and animals

taper *n* a thin candle, burnt to give a light or to light other candles **taper** *v* to become gradually narrower, or to make something narrower **to taper off** to become less in amount or cease gradually, or to make something do this

tapestry (say **tap-i-stri**) *n pl* **tapestries** a piece of strong cloth with a picture or design woven into it or embroidered on it

tapioca (say tap-i-**oh**-kə) *n* a starchy substance in hard white grains obtained from cassava, used for making puddings

tapir (say **tay**-per) *n* an animal like a pig, with a long flexible snout

tappet *n* a projecting part in a piece of machinery, which makes intermittent contact with another part and causes a movement

taproot *n* the chief root of a plant, growing straight downwards

tar *n* a thick dark inflammable liquid obtained by distilling wood or coal, used in making roads and for preserving timber **tar** *v* **tarred, tarring** to coat something with tar

taramasalata (say ta-rə-mə-sə-**lah**-tə) *n* a soft paste made from the roe of certain fish

tarantula (say tə-**ran**-tew-lə) *n* **1** a large black spider of southern Europe **2** a large hairy tropical spider

tardy *adj* **tardier, tardiest 1** slow to act or move **2** not happening quickly or on time **tardily** *adv* **tardiness** *n*

tare *n* an allowance made for the weight of the container in which goods are packed or for the vehicle transporting them, when the goods are weighed together with them

target *n* **1** the object or mark that someone tries to hit in shooting, especially a disc painted with concentric circles used in archery **2** a person, place, or object that is aimed at in an attack **3** a person or thing that is being criticized **4** an aim or objective **target** *v* **targeted, targeting 1** to select something or someone as an object of attack or attention **2** to aim a weapon, etc. at a target

tariff *n* **1** a list of fixed charges made by a business, hotel, etc. **2** a tax or duty to be paid on imports or exports

tarmac *n* an area surfaced with tarmacadam, especially on an airfield **tarmac** *v* **tarmacked, tarmacking** to surface an area

with tarmacadam **tarmacadam** *n* a mixture of tar and broken stone, used as a material for surfacing roads

tarn *n* a small mountain lake

tarnish *v* **1** to lose lustre, or to cause metal to lose its lustre, by exposure to the air or to damp **2** to stain or blemish a reputation, etc. **tarnish** *n* loss of lustre, a stain or blemish

tarot cards (say ta-roh) *pl n* a pack of 78 special cards used for fortune telling

tarpaulin (say tar-**paw**-lin) *n* a large sheet of waterproof canvas

tarragon (say **ta**-rə-gən) *n* a plant with leaves that are used for flavouring salads and in cooking

tarry (say **ta**-ri) *v* **tarries, tarried, tarrying** *old use* to delay leaving, to stay longer

tart[1] *n* an open pastry case with a sweet or savoury filling **tart v to tart oneself up** *informal* to dress smartly or attractively **to tart something up** *informal* to decorate or smarten something

tart[2] *adj* **1** sharp or acid in taste **2** sharp in manner, sarcastic **tartly** *adv*

tart[3] *n informal* a prostitute

tartan *n* a woollen cloth woven in a pattern of coloured stripes crossing at right angles

tartar *n* **1** a hard chalky deposit that forms on the teeth and causes decay **2** a reddish deposit that forms on the side of a cask in which wine is fermented

tartar *n* a person who is fierce or difficult to deal with

tartar sauce (say **tar**-ter) *n* a sauce made from mayonnaise with pieces of chopped gherkin, etc.

task *n* a piece of work that has to be done **task** *v* to assign a task to someone **task force** *n* a group and resources specially organized for a particular task **taskmaster** *n* a person who imposes difficult tasks on people ♦ *a hard taskmaster* **to take someone to task** to scold or rebuke someone

tassel *n* a bunch of threads tied together at the top and hanging loosely as an ornament

taste *n* **1** the sensation caused in the tongue by things placed on it, or the particular sensation something has **2** the ability to perceive this sensation **3** a small quantity of food or drink taken as a sample **4** a slight experience of something ♦ *a taste of success* **5** a liking for something ♦ *I have developed a taste for jazz.* **6** the ability to enjoy beautiful things or to know what is suitable for an occasion ♦ *She shows good taste in her choice of clothes.* **taste** *v* **1** to discover or test the flavour of a thing by putting it in the mouth **2** to be able to perceive flavours **3** to have a certain flavour ♦ *That tastes sour.* **4** to experience something ♦ *to taste freedom* **tasteful** *adj* showing good taste **tastefully** *adv* **tasteless** *adj* **1** having no flavour **2** showing poor taste ♦ *The decor was tasteless.* **tastelessly** *adv* **taster** *n* **tasty** *adj* **tastier, tastiest** having a pleasant strong flavour **taste bud** *n* any of the small projections on the tongue which provide the sense of flavour

tat *n* tawdry or tasteless things **tatty** *adj* **tattier, tattiest** shabby and worn

tatters *pl n* torn pieces of cloth, paper, etc. **tattered** *adj* old and ragged, torn into tatters

tattle *n* idle chatter or gossip **tattle** *v* to chatter or gossip idly

tattoo[1] *n pl* **tattoos 1** an evening drum or bugle signal calling soldiers back to their quarters **2** a military display with music and marching, as an entertainment **3** a drumming or tapping sound

tattoo[2] *v* **tattoos, tattooed, tattooing** to mark the skin with indelible patterns by puncturing it and inserting a dye **tattoo** *n pl* **tattoos** a pattern made by tattooing

taunt *v* to provoke someone with scornful remarks or criticism **taunt** *n* a taunting remark

Taurus (say **tor** -əs) *n* (the Bull) the sign of the zodiac which the sun enters about 21 April

taut *adv* stretched tightly, not slack **tauten** *v* to make something taut, or to become taut

tautology (say taw-**tol**-əji) *n pl* **tautologies** saying the same thing over again in different words, as in 'free, gratis, and for nothing' **tautological** *adj* **tautologous** *adj*

tavern *n old use* an inn or public house

tawdry (say **taw**-dri) *adj* **tawdrier, tawdriest** showy or gaudy but cheap **tawdriness** *n*

tawny *adj* brownish-yellow or brownish-orange

tax *n* **1** money that people or business firms are required to pay to a government, to be used for public purposes **2** something that makes a heavy demand ♦ *a tax on one's strength* **tax** *v* **1** to impose a tax on someone **2** to make heavy demands on someone **taxation** *n* the imposition or payment of tax **taxable** *adj*

taxi *n pl* **taxis** a car that carries passengers for payment, usually with a meter to record the fare payable **taxi** *v* **taxies, taxied, taxiing 1** to go in a taxi **2** (said about an aircraft) to move slowly along the ground under its own power, especially before take-off or after landing **taxicab** *n* a taxi

taxidermy (say **tak**-si-derm-i) *n* the art of preparing, stuffing, and mounting the skins of animals so as to look lifelike **taxidermist** *n*

taxonomy (say taks-**on**-əmi) *n* the scientific process of classifying living things

TB *abbr informal* tuberculosis

tea *n* **1** a hot drink made by pouring boiling water over the dried leaves of an evergreen shrub grown in parts of south and east Asia (called *tea plant*) **2** these dried leaves **3** a similar drink made with the leaves of other plants ♦ *camomile tea* **4** a meal at which tea is served, especially a light meal in the afternoon or early evening **tea bag** *n* a small porous sachet containing tea leaves for making tea **tea cosy** *n* a cover placed over a teapot to keep the tea hot **teapot** *n* a pot with a handle, lid, and spout, for making and pouring out tea **teaspoon** *n* a small spoon for stirring tea **teaspoonful** *n pl* **teaspoonfuls tea towel** *n* a towel for drying washed dishes, cutlery, etc.

teach *v* past tense and past participle **taught 1** to give someone knowledge or skill about a subject, especially in a school or college as part of a programme of study **2** to cause someone to learn a principle or way of behaving by example or experience **teacher** *n* **teaching** *n*

teak *n* the hard strong wood of a tall evergreen Asian tree

teal *n pl* **teal** a small freshwater duck

team *n* **1** a group of players forming one side in certain games and sports **2** a group of people working together **3** two or more animals harnessed together to pull a vehicle or farm implement **team** *v* to combine into a team or set or for a common purpose **team spirit** *n* willingness to act for the good of the group you belong to **teamwork** *n* organized cooperation between members of a team

tear¹ (say tair) *v* **tore**, **torn 1** to pull something forcibly apart or to pieces **2** to make a hole or a split in this way **3** to become torn, or be able to be easily torn ♦ *This kind of paper tends to tear.* **4** to run or travel hurriedly **tear** *n* a hole or split caused by tearing **tearaway** *n* someone who behaves wildly or recklessly

tear² (say teer) *n* a drop of clear salty water that comes to the surface of the eyes when they are sore or when someone is crying **tearful** *adj* upset and starting to cry **tearfully** *adv* **teardrop** *n* **tear gas** *n* a gas that causes severe irritation of the eyes, used especially for riot control **in tears** crying

tease *v* **1** to provoke someone in a playful or unkind way **2** to pick tangled wool or hair, etc. into separate strands **tease** *n* a person who likes teasing others **teaser** *n* a tricky problem

teasel (say tee-zəl) *n* a plant with bristly heads

teat *n* **1** a nipple on the milk-secreting organ of an animal **2** a rubber or plastic bulb on a feeding bottle, pierced with a hole for sucking the contents

tech (say tek) *n informal* a technical college

technical *adj* **1** to do with the mechanical arts and applied sciences **2** to do with a particular subject or its techniques ♦ *the technical terms of chemistry* **3** in a strict legal sense ♦ *technical assault* **technicality** *n pl* **technicalities** a technical word, phrase, or point ♦ *He was acquitted on a technicality.* **technically** *adv* **technician** *n* an expert in the techniques of a particular subject

technical college *n* a college of further education providing courses in technical and practical subjects

Technicolor *n trademark* a process of producing cinema films in colour

technique (say tek-**neek**) *n* **1** a method of doing or performing something, especially in an art or science **2** skill in doing something

technology *n pl* **technologies 1** the practical application of scientific knowledge, e.g. in industry **2** the scientific study of mechanical arts and applied sciences, such as engineering **technological** *adj* **technologist** *n* an expert in technology

tectonics (say tek-**tonn**-iks) *n* the scientific study of the earth's crust and structural features

teddy bear *n* a soft furry toy bear

tedious (say **tee**-di-əs) *adj* tiresome because of its length or dullness, boring **tediously** *adv* **tedium** *n* tediousness

tee *n* **1** a cleared space on a golf course, from which each player strikes the ball at the beginning of play for each hole **2** a small peg with a shallow dip on its head, on which a golf ball is placed for being struck **tee** *v* **tees**, **teed**, **teeing** to place a ball on a tee in golf **to tee off** to begin a hole of golf by playing the ball from a tee

teem¹ *v* to be full of something ♦ *The river was teeming with fish.*

teem² *v* (said about water or rain, etc.) to flow in large quantities, to pour

teenager *n* a person aged between 13 and 19 years **teenage** *adj* **teens** *pl n* the years of a person's age from 13 to 19

teeny *adj* **teenier**, **teeniest** *informal* tiny

tee-shirt *n* another spelling of *T-shirt*

teeter *v* to stand or move unsteadily

teeth plural of *tooth*

teethe *v* (said about a baby) to have its first teeth beginning to grow through the gums **teething troubles** *pl n* short-term problems that arise in the early stages of an enterprise

teetotal *adj* abstaining completely from alcoholic drink **teetotaller** *n*

telecommunications *pl n* communications

over long distances, such as telephone, radio, or television

telegraph n a system or apparatus for sending messages over a distance, especially by transmitting electrical impulses along wires **telegraph** v to send a message by telegraph **telegram** n a message sent by telegraph **telegraph pole** n a pole for carrying overhead telegraph and telephone wires

telepathy (say til-ep-ə-thi) n supposed communication of thoughts and ideas other than by the normal senses **telepathic** adj

telephone n 1 a system of transmitting voices over a distance by wire or radio, converting sound to electrical signals and back again 2 a device used in this, with a receiver and mouthpiece and a set of numbered buttons for making a connection **telephone** v to speak to someone by telephone **telephonist** n an operator of a telephone switchboard **telephony** n

telephoto lens n a lens used to produce a large image of a distant object

teleprinter (say tel-i-print-er) n a device for transmitting messages by telegraph as they are keyed, and for printing messages received

telescope n an optical instrument using lenses and mirrors to make distant objects appear larger when viewed through it **telescope** v 1 to make something shorter, or to become shorter, by sliding overlapping sections one inside another 2 to compress something, or to become compressed 3 to condense something so as to occupy less space or time **telescopic** adj

teletext n a system for displaying news and information on a television screen

television n 1 a system for transmitting visual images and sound by means of radio waves so that they can be reproduced on a screen 2 (also **television set**) an apparatus with a screen for receiving television pictures 3 television as a medium of communication, or material seen by means of television **televise** v to broadcast a programme by television

telex n a system of international telegraphy

in which printed messages are transmitted and received by teleprinters using public transmission lines **telex** v to send a message by telex

tell v past tense and past participle **told** 1 to make something known to someone, especially in spoken or written words ♦ I told them we would be late. 2 to give someone a command or order ♦ Tell them to wait. 3 to relate a story or narrative 4 to reveal a secret ♦ Promise me you won't tell. 5 to decide or determine something ♦ How do you tell which button to press? ♦ I can't tell him from his brother. 6 to produce a noticeable effect ♦ The strain was beginning to tell on them. **teller** n 1 a person who deals with customers' routine transactions in a bank 2 a person appointed to count votes 3 a person who tells or gives an account of something **telling** adj having a noticeable effect, significant or noteworthy ♦ a telling argument **telltale** n a person who tells tales **telltale** adj revealing or indicating something ♦ a telltale blush **to tell someone off** informal to scold or reprimand someone

telly n pl **tellies** informal television, or a television set

temerity (say tim-e-riti) n boldness or rashness

temp n informal a secretary or other worker who works for short periods in different companies **temp** v informal to work as a temp

temper n 1 the state of a person's mind in terms of being calm or angry ♦ in a good temper 2 a fit of anger ♦ in a temper 3 a tendency to have fits of anger ♦ He has a temper. **temper** v 1 to harden or strengthen metal by heating and then cooling it 2 to moderate or soften the effects of something ♦ to temper justice with mercy **to lose your temper** to lose your calmness and become openly angry

temperament n a person's nature as it affects their behaviour and attitudes ♦ a nervous temperament **temperamental** adj having unpredictable changes of mood or behaviour **temperamentally** adv

temperate adj 1 (said about climate) having a mild temperature without extremes of heat and cold **2** self-restrained or moderate in behaviour **temperance** n drinking little or no alcohol

temperature n **1** the degree or intensity of heat or cold in a substance or place **2** an abnormally high body temperature

tempest n a violent storm **tempestuous** adj **1** very stormy **2** full of commotion or strong emotion

template n a piece of specially prepared rigid material used as a guide for cutting or shaping things

temple¹ n a building for the worship of a god or gods

temple² n the flat part at each side of the head between the forehead and the ear

tempo n pl **tempos** or **tempi 1** the speed at which a piece of music is played **2** the pace of any movement or activity

temporal (say **temp**-er-əl) adj **1** to do with worldly affairs, secular **2** to do with time **3** to do with the temples of the head

temporary adj lasting or meant to last for a limited time only, not permanent **temporarily** adv

temporize v to avoid giving a definite answer or decision, in order to gain time

tempt v to try to persuade or entice someone, especially into doing something wrong or unwise **temptation** n **tempter** n **tempting** adj **temptress** n **to tempt fate** or **providence** to do something rash or reckless

ten adj, n the number 10, one more than nine **tenner** n a ten-pound note, or the sum of ten pounds **tenth** adj, n **1** next after ninth **2** one of ten equal parts of a thing **tenpin bowling** n a game in which players try to knock over ten pins set up at the end of a track by rolling hard balls down it

tenable (say **ten**-əbəl) adj **1** able to be maintained or defended against attack or objection ♦ a tenable argument **2** (said about a job or office) able to be held for a certain time or by a certain type of person, etc.

tenacious (say tin-**ay**-shəs) adj holding or clinging firmly to something, especially to rights or principles **tenaciously** adv **tenacity** n

tenant n a person who rents land or buildings from a landlord **tenancy** n pl **tenancies**

tend¹ v to take care of or look after a person or thing

tend² v **1** to behave frequently in a certain way or to have a certain characteristic ♦ He tends to be rude. **2** to take a certain direction ♦ The track tends upwards. **tendency** n pl **tendencies** the way a person or thing tends to be or behave **tendentious** adj meant to promote a particular cause or point of view, not impartial

tender¹ adj **1** gentle and loving **2** (said about food, especially meat) not tough or hard, easy to chew **3** delicate or easily damaged ♦ tender plants **4** (said about a part of the body) sensitive, painful when touched **tenderize** v to make meat more tender by beating it or by slow cooking **tenderly** adv **tenderness** n

tender² v **1** to offer something formally **2** to make a tender for goods or work **tender** n a formal offer to supply goods or carry out work at a stated price

tender³ n **1** a truck attached to a steam locomotive, carrying its fuel and water **2** a small boat carrying stores or passengers to and from a ship

tendon n a strong band or cord of tissue that connects a muscle to a bone

tendril n **1** a thread-like part by which a climbing plant clings to a support **2** a thin curl of hair, etc.

tenement (say **ten**-i-mənt) n a large house or building divided into apartments or rooms that are let to a number of tenants

tenet (say **ten**-it) n a firm belief or principle held by a person or group

tennis n either of two ball games for two or four players, played with rackets over a net with a ball on an open court

tenon (say **ten**-ən) n a piece of wood or other material shaped to fit into a mortise

tenor (say **ten**-er) n **1** the general meaning or drift ♦ What was the tenor of her speech? **2** the highest ordinary adult male singing voice, or a singer with such a voice **3** a musical instrument with approximately the range of a tenor voice

tense[1] n a form of a verb that indicates the time of action or state as being past, present, or future, e.g *they came* (**past tense**), *they come* or *they are coming* (**present tense**), *they will come* (**future tense**)

tense[2] adj 1 stretched tightly 2 with muscles tight, ready for what might happen 3 anxious and unable to relax 4 causing tenseness ♦ *a tense moment* **tense** v to make something tense, or to become tense **tensely** adv **tenseness** n

tension n 1 the process of stretching or being stretched 2 tenseness, the condition when feelings are tense 3 the effect produced by forces pulling against each other **tensile** adj 1 to do with tension 2 able to be stretched

tent n a portable shelter made of canvas or cloth, supported by poles and fixed to the ground with pegs, used in camping

tentacle n a thin flexible part extending from the body of certain animals (e.g. snails and octopuses), used for feeling or grasping things or for moving

tentative (say **tent**-ə-tiv) adj hesitant or provisional ♦ *a tentative suggestion* **tentatively** adv

tenterhook n **on tenterhooks** in a state of anxious suspense or strain

tenuous (say **ten**-yoo-əs) adj having little substance or validity, very slight ♦ *a tenuous connection* **tenuously** adv **tenuousness** n

tenure (say **ten**-yer) n the holding of a position of employment, or of land, property, etc.

tepee (say **tee**-pee) n a kind of tent formerly used by Native Americans, made by fastening skins over masts or poles

tepid adj only slightly warm, lukewarm

tercentenary (say ter-sen-**teen**-er-i) n pl **tercentenaries** a 300th anniversary

term n 1 a word or expression that names or identifies something ♦ *'Larceny' is a legal term for 'theft'* 2 each of the periods of several weeks in which teaching is done in a school, college, or university 3 the time for which something lasts, a fixed or limited time ♦ *The President is seeking re-election for a second term.* ♦ *She narrowly escaped*

a term of imprisonment. 4 each of the periods in which a law court holds sessions **term** v to call something by a certain term or expression ♦ *This music is termed plainsong.* **terms** pl n 1 agreed stipulations or conditions ♦ *peace terms* 2 a relation between people ♦ *They ended up on friendly terms.* **terminology** n pl **terminologies** a set of technical terms relating to a subject

termagant (say **ter**-mə-gənt) n a bad-tempered bullying woman

terminal adj 1 to do with or situated at the end or boundary of something 2 in the last stage of a fatal disease ♦ *terminal cancer* **terminal** n 1 the end of a railway line or long-distance bus route 2 a building at an airport or in a town where air passengers arrive and depart 3 a point of connection in an electric circuit or device 4 a device by which a user enters data into a computer and which displays the output on a screen **terminally** adv **terminus** n pl **termini** or **terminuses** the last station at the end of a railway line or bus route

terminate v to end something, or to come to an end **termination** n

termite n a small insect that is very destructive to timber

tern n a seabird with long pointed wings and a forked tail

ternary adj involving sets of three; consisting of three parts

terrace n 1 a raised level place, especially each of a series of these into which a slope or hillside is formed for cultivation 2 a flight of wide shallow steps for spectators to stand on at a sports ground 3 a paved area beside a house 4 a row of houses forming a continuous block **terrace** v to form sloping land into a terrace or terraces

terracotta n 1 a kind of brownish-red unglazed pottery 2 this colour

terra firma n dry land, the ground

terrain (say tə-**rayn**) n a stretch of land with regard to its natural features ♦ *rugged terrain*

terrapin (say **te**-rə-pin) n an edible freshwater tortoise of North America

terrestrial (say tə-**rest**-riəl) adj 1 to do with the earth 2 of or living on land

terrible *adj* **1** very bad or distressing **2** extreme, hard to bear ♦ *The heat was terrible.* **3** *informal* very bad ♦ *I'm terrible at tennis.* **terribly** *adv*

terrier *n* a kind of small lively dog

terrific *adj informal* **1** very great or powerful ♦ *a terrific storm* **2** excellent ♦ *You did a terrific job.*

terrine (say tə-reen) *n* **1** pâté or a similar food cooked or prepared in its dish **2** an earthenware or other dish holding this

territory *n pl* **territories 1** an area of land under the control of a ruler or state **2** a special sphere of thought or experience ♦ *Criminal law was not her territory.* **3** an area which an animal defends against others of the same species **territorial** *adj* **Territorial Army** *n* a trained force of volunteers for use in an emergency

terror *n* **1** extreme fear **2** a terrifying person or thing **3** *informal* a formidable or troublesome person or thing **terrify** *v* **terrifies, terrified, terrifying** to make someone feel terror **terrorism** *n* use of violence and intimidation, especially for political purposes **terrorist** *n, adj* **terrorize** *v* to use terror to coerce people

terry *n* a cotton fabric with raised loops left uncut, used especially for towels

terse *adj* concise or curt **tersely** *adv* **terseness** *n*

tertiary (say ter-sher-i) *adj* coming after something that is secondary, third in rank or order

tessellate (say tess-il-ayt) *v* **1** to cover a floor with mosaics **2** to fit shapes into a pattern without overlapping or leaving gaps

test *n* **1** a short examination, especially in a school, on a particular topic **2** a procedure for finding out how good a person or thing is ♦ *a test of character* ♦ *an eye test* **3** a test match **test** *v* to carry out a test on a person or thing **tester** *n* **test tube** *n* a tube of thin glass with one end closed, used to hold materials for study or experiment in laboratories **test-tube baby** *n* a baby that develops from an egg that has been fertilized outside the mother's body and then placed in the womb

testament *n* **1** a person's will, or other formal statement **2** evidence or proof of a fact or event **Testament** *n* each of the two main divisions of the Bible **testate** *adj* (said about a person) having left a valid will at death

testify *v* **testifies, testified, testifying 1** to give evidence in a law court **2** to be evidence or proof of something

testimony *n pl* **testimonies 1** a declaration or statement, especially one made under oath **2** evidence in support of something **testimonial** *n* **1** a formal statement testifying to a person's character or qualifications **2** a gift or public recognition of a person's services or achievements

testis *n pl* **testes** (say tes-teez) or **testicle** *n* either of the two glands that produce sperm in male mammals, contained in the scrotum behind the penis

testosterone (say test-ost-er-ohn) *n* a male sex hormone

testy *adj* **testier, testiest** easily annoyed, irritable **testily** *adv*

tetanus (say tet-ən-əs) *n* a disease caused by bacteria, which makes the muscles contract and stiffen

tetchy *adj* **tetchier, tetchiest** peevish or irritable **tetchily** *adv*

tête-à-tête (say tayt-ah-tayt) *n pl* **tête-à-têtes** a private conversation, especially between two people

tether *n* a rope or chain for tying an animal while it is grazing **tether** *v* to tie an animal with a tether **at the end of your tether** unable to endure something any longer

tetra- *prefix* four

tetrahedron (say tet-rə-hee-drən) *n pl* **tetrahedra** or **tetrahedrons** a solid with four triangular faces forming a pyramid

Teutonic (say tew-tonn-ik) *adj* to do with the Teutons, an ancient Germanic people, or their languages

text *n* **1** the words of something written or printed **2** the main body of a book or page as distinct from illustrations, notes, appendices, etc. **3** a text message **text** *v* to send a text message to someone **textual** *adj* **textbook** *n* a book of information for use in studying a subject

text message n a message sent from one mobile phone to another and able to be read on the screen

textile n a cloth or woven fabric **textile** adj to do with textiles

texture n the way the surface of something feels to the touch **textured** adj

Thai (say tiy) adj to do with or coming from Thailand in SE Asia **Thai** n pl **Thais** 1 a person born in Thailand or descended from people born there 2 the language of Thailand

thalidomide (say thə-lid-ə-miyd) n a sedative drug that was found to cause babies to be born with malformed limbs when the mothers took it during pregnancy

than conjunction used to introduce the second part of a comparison ♦ She is older than me. or ♦ She is older than I am.

thane n hist a landowner in Scotland or Anglo-Saxon England

thank v to express gratitude to someone for something they have done or said **thankful** adj feeling or expressing gratitude **thankfully** adv 1 in a thankful way 2 fortunately ♦ Thankfully it has stopped raining. **thankless** adj (said about a task) unpleasant or unappealing, and unlikely to win thanks **thanks** pl n an expression of gratitude to someone **thanks to** because of or as a result of ♦ Thanks to their help we can finish the work in time. **thanksgiving** n an expression of gratitude, especially to God **Thanksgiving, Thanksgiving Day** n (in North America) a holiday for giving thanks to God, in the USA on the fourth Thursday in November, in Canada on the second Monday in October **thank you**, n, interjection an expression of thanks

that adj, pronoun pl **those** the one there, the person or thing referred to or pointed to or understood ♦ That book is mine. ♦ Whose is that? **that** adv so or to such an extent ♦ I'll go that far. **that** relative pronoun which, who, or whom, used to introduce a clause that defines or identifies something or someone ♦ The book that I sent you. ♦ The woman that he married. **that** conjunction introducing a dependent clause ♦ We hope that you enjoy your holiday.

thatch n a roof or roof-covering made of straw, reeds, or similar material **thatch** v to make a roof with thatch

thaw v 1 to become liquid or unfrozen after being frozen, or to cause a substance to do this 2 (said about a person) to become less aloof or formal in manner **thaw** n 1 the process of thawing 2 weather that is warm enough for snow or ice to melt

the adj (called the definite article) used before a noun to indicate: 1 a specific person or a thing ♦ the President ♦ the woman in blue 2 something that denotes a class or group ♦ diseases of the eye ♦ the unemployed 3 an occupation or activity ♦ a bit too fond of the bottle

theatre n 1 a building where plays or other forms of entertainment are performed before an audience 2 a room or hall for lectures, with seats in tiers 3 an operating theatre 4 a scene of important events ♦ a theatre of war 5 the writing, acting, and producing of plays **theatrical** adj 1 to do with plays or the theatre 2 (said about a person or behaviour) exaggerated and designed to make a showy effect **theatricals** pl n the performance of plays in a theatre **theatrically** adv **theatricality** n

thee pronoun a form of thou; used as the object of a verb or after a preposition

theft n the act of stealing

their adj of or belonging to them ◊ Do not confuse this word with there or they're, which have different meanings. **theirs** possessive pronoun belonging to them ♦ This luggage is theirs. ◊ It is incorrect to write their's.

them pronoun the form of they used as the object of a verb or after a preposition ♦ We saw them. **themselves** pronoun the form of them used in reflexive constructions (e.g. They hurt themselves.) and for emphasis (e.g. They themselves wanted it. and They did it themselves.)

theme (say theem) n 1 the subject about which a person speaks, writes, or thinks 2 Mus a melody which occurs often in a piece or forms the basis for a set of variations **thematic** adj **thematically** adv

theme park n an amusement park with activities related to a particular theme or subject

then adv **1** at that time **2** next, after that; and also **3** in that case, therefore ♦ *If she said so, then it must be true.* **then** n that time ♦ *from then on*

thence adv formal **1** from that place **2** as a result, therefore

theocracy (say thi-ok-rə-si) n pl **theocracies** government of a country by priests who rule in the name of God or a god

theodolite (say thi-od-ə-liyt) n an instrument used in surveying, with a rotating telescope used for measuring horizontal and vertical angles

theology (say thi-ol-əji) n pl **theologies** **1** the study of religion **2** a system of religion **theologian** n a person who studies theology **theological** adj **theologically** adv

theory n pl **theories** **1** a set of ideas proposed by reasoning from known facts to explain something ♦ *Darwin's theory of evolution.* **2** an opinion or supposition **3** ideas or suppositions in general, as contrasted with *practice* **4** a statement of the principles on which a subject is based ♦ *music theory* **theoretical** adj based on theory and not on practice or experience **theoretically** adv **theorize** v to form a theory or theories

therapy n pl **therapies** **1** a form of medical treatment designed to relieve or cure a disease or disability **2** psychotherapy **therapeutic** adj helping to relieve or cure a disease or disability **therapist** n a medical specialist who treats diseases and disorders by means of therapy

there adv **1** in or at or to that place **2** in that matter ♦ *I can't agree with you there.* **3** used to introduce a sentence when the verb comes before its subject ♦ *There was plenty to eat.* **there** n that place ♦ *We live near there.* **there** interjection **1** used to express satisfaction or dismay ♦ *There! what did I tell you!* **2** used to give comfort ♦ *There, there!* ◊ Do not confuse this word with *their* or *they're*, which have different meanings.

thereabouts adv **1** near that place

2 somewhere near that number or quantity or time, etc. **thereafter** adv after that **thereby** adv by that means, because of that **therefore** adv for that reason **therein** adv **1** in that place **2** in that respect **thereof** adv of that, of it **thereupon** adv **1** as a result of that **2** immediately after that

therm n a unit of heat used especially in measuring a gas supply **thermal** adj **1** to do with heat, or using or operated by heat **2** warm or hot **thermal** n a rising current of hot air

thermo- prefix heat

thermodynamics n a branch of science dealing with the relations between heat and other forms of energy **thermodynamic** adj

thermometer n an instrument for measuring temperature, especially a graduated glass tube containing mercury or alcohol which expands when heated

thermonuclear adj to do with nuclear reactions that occur at very high temperatures

Thermos n trademark a vacuum flask

thermostat n a device that automatically regulates temperature or activates a device when a certain temperature is reached

thesaurus (say thi-sor-əs) n pl **thesauruses** or **thesauri** (say thi-**sor**-iy) a dictionary of synonyms, a book containing words listed in sets according to their meanings

these plural of *this*

thesis (say thee-sis) n pl **theses** (say -seez) **1** a statement or theory put forward and supported by arguments **2** a long written essay based on personally done research and submitted by a candidate for a university degree

thespian (say thess-pi-ən) adj to do with the theatre and acting **thespian** n an actor or actress

they pronoun **1** the people or things mentioned **2** people in general ♦ *They say that wildlife is coming back to the cities.* **3** those in authority ♦ *They are planning to increase fees for students.* **4** used to refer to a person of either sex, instead of 'he' or 'she' ♦ *If anyone has lost an umbrella would they please come to the cloakroom.*

they're v informal they are ◊ Do not confuse

this word with *their* or *there*, which have different meanings.

thiamine (say thiy-ə-meen) *n* vitamin B1

thick *adj* 1 having its opposite surfaces far apart ♦ *The castle's outer walls were thick and massive.* 2 having its opposite surfaces a certain distance apart ♦ *The tree trunk was six feet thick.* 3 dense or crowded ♦ *a thick forest* ♦ *thick fog* 4 (said about a liquid or paste) relatively stiff in consistency, not flowing easily 5 (said about an accent) marked or noticeable ♦ *a thick brogue* 6 (said about a person) stupid 7 *informal* having a close relationship ♦ *Her parents are very thick with mine.* **thick** *n* the busiest part of a crowd or activity ♦ *They wanted to be in the thick of the local musical scene.* **thicken** *v* to become thicker or of a stiffer consistency, or to make something do this **thicket** *n* a number of shrubs and small trees growing close together **thickly** *adv* **thickness** *n* 1 the quality of being thick 2 the distance between the surfaces of something 3 a layer ♦ *The bed had three thicknesses of blankets.* **thickset** *adj* 1 having a stocky or burly body 2 with parts placed or growing close together **thick-skinned** *adj* insensitive to criticism or insults

thief *n pl* **thieves** a person who steals someone else's property **thieve** *v* to be a thief, to steal things

thigh *n* the part of the leg between the hip and the knee

thimble *n* a small metal or plastic cap worn on the end of the finger to push the needle in sewing

thin *adj* **thinner**, **thinnest** 1 having its opposite surfaces close together, not thick 2 made of thin material ♦ *a thin dress* 3 (said about a person) lean and not plump 4 not dense or plentiful ♦ *The audience on the first night was fairly thin.* 5 (said about a liquid or paste) flowing easily, not thick 6 feeble or unconvincing ♦ *a thin excuse* **thin** *v* **thinned**, **thinning** to become thinner, or to make something thinner **thinly** *adv* **thinness** *n*

thine *possessive pronoun old use* yours (referring to one person)

thing *n* 1 something that can be seen or known about 2 an inanimate object as

distinct from something living 3 an act or circumstance, or a task to be done ♦ *That was a funny thing to happen.* **things** *pl n* 1 personal belongings or clothing ♦ *I'll go and pack my things.* 2 circumstances or conditions ♦ *Things began to improve.*

think *v* past tense and past participle **thought** 1 to use your mind to form ideas 2 to have an idea or opinion ♦ *Do you think we will be in time?* ♦ *It is thought to be a fake.* 3 to consider something ♦ *Think how nice it would be.* 4 to remember something ♦ *I can't think where I put it.* **think** *n* an act of thinking **thinker** *n* **think tank** *n* an organization providing advice and ideas, especially on national and commercial problems **to think something up** to invent or produce something by thought

third *adj* next after second **third** *n* 1 a person or thing that is third 2 one of three equal parts of a thing **thirdly** *adv* **third degree** *n* long and severe questioning to get information or a confession **third party** *n* another person besides the two principal ones involved **third person** *n* see *person* **third-rate** *adj* of very inferior or poor quality **Third World** *n* the poorest and underdeveloped countries of Asia, Africa, and South America

thirst *n* 1 the feeling of needing or wanting to drink 2 a strong desire **thirst** *v* to feel a thirst **thirsty** *adj* **thirstier**, **thirstiest** needing or wanting to drink **thirstily** *adv*

thirteen *adj, n* the number 13, one more than twelve **thirteenth** *adj, n*

thirty *adj, n pl* **thirties** the number 30, equal to three times ten **thirtieth** *adj, n*

this *adj, pronoun pl* **these** the one here, the person or thing close at hand or just mentioned

thistle *n* a prickly wild plant with purple, white, or yellow flowers **thistledown** *n* a light fluff on thistle seeds, causing them to be blown about by the wind

thither *adv old use* to or towards that place

thong *n* 1 a narrow strip of hide or leather used as a fastening or as the lash of a whip 2 a skimpy piece of clothing worn as the lower half of a bikini or as underwear

thorax (say thor -aks) *n* the part of the

body between the head or neck and the abdomen

thorn n 1 a sharp pointed growth on the stem of a plant 2 a thorny tree or shrub **thorny** adj **thornier, thorniest** 1 having many thorns 2 causing trouble or difficulty ♦ a thorny problem **a thorn in your flesh** something or someone that gives constant trouble

thorough adj 1 complete in every detail 2 done or doing things with great care or completeness **thoroughly** adv **thoroughness** n **thoroughbred** adj (said about a horse) bred of pure or pedigree stock **thoroughbred** n a thoroughbred animal **thoroughfare** n a public road or path that is open at both ends **thoroughgoing** adj thorough

those plural of that

thou pronoun old use you (referring to one person)

though conjunction in spite of the fact that, even if ♦ We can run for the train, though it may be too late. **though** adv however ♦ They were right, though.

thought n 1 the power of thinking 2 the process of thinking 3 a way of thinking that is associated with a particular time or group of people ♦ in modern thought 4 an idea or piece of reasoning produced by thinking 5 an intention ♦ We had no thought of giving offence. 6 consideration ♦ They will give the proposal serious thought. **thoughtful** adj 1 thinking carefully about what other people need and want, considerate 2 thinking hard and carefully, often absorbed in thought 3 (said about a book, writer, or remark) showing signs of careful thought **thoughtfully** adv **thoughtfulness** n **thoughtless** adj 1 not thinking about other people, inconsiderate 2 not thinking about the possible effects or consequences of something **thoughtlessly** adv **thoughtlessness** n

thousand adj, n the number 1,000, equal to ten times a hundred **thousandth** adj, n

thrall (say thrawl) n old use **in thrall** in bondage

thrash v 1 to beat someone with a stick or whip 2 to defeat an opponent or opposing

side heavily 3 to move around in a violent or uncontrolled way **to thrash something out** to discuss a matter thoroughly

thread n 1 a length of spun cotton, wool, or other fibre used in making cloth or in sewing or knitting 2 the spiral ridge round the edge of a screw 3 a theme or argument running through a piece of writing or speaking ♦ I'm afraid I've lost the thread. **thread** v 1 to put a thread through the eye of a needle 2 to put beads on a thread **threadbare** adj (said about cloth) having a surface worn with age and the threads showing **to thread your way** to make your way carefully through a crowded street or area

threat n 1 an expression of a person's intention to punish, hurt, or harm someone or something 2 a sign of something unwelcome ♦ There's a slight threat of rain. 3 a person or thing that might cause danger or catastrophe **threaten** v 1 to make a threat or threats against someone 2 to seem likely to be or do something unwelcome ♦ The costs are threatening to increase rapidly. 3 to be a threat or danger to someone ♦ Money problems are threatening us.

three adj, n the number 3, one more than two **threesome** n a group of three people **three-dimensional** adj having the three dimensions of length, breadth, and depth, or appearing to

thresh v to beat corn with a flail or a machine in order to separate the grain from the husks

threshold n 1 a piece of wood or stone forming the bottom of a doorway, or (more generally) the entrance as a whole 2 the point at which something begins to happen ♦ Scientists are on the threshold of a new discovery. 3 the point at which something has an effect ♦ a low pain threshold

thrice adv old use three times

thrift n careful management and use of money or other resources **thrifty** adj **thriftier, thriftiest** practising thrift, using money or other resources carefully

thrill n a sudden feeling of pleasure and excitement **thrill** v to feel a thrill, or to give someone a thrill **thriller** *n* an exciting story, play, or film, usually involving crime or espionage

thrive *v* past tense **thrived** or **throve**; past participle **thrived** or **thriven** 1 to grow or develop strongly 2 to prosper or be successful

throat *n* 1 the passage in the neck through which food and air pass into the body 2 the front part of the neck **throaty** *adj* 1 produced deep in the throat ♦ *a throaty laugh* 2 hoarse

throb *v* **throbbed**, **throbbing** 1 to beat or sound with a strong steady rhythm 2 to give pain in a steady rhythm ♦ *a throbbing wound* **throb** *n* a strong regular beat or rhythm

throes *pl n* severe pangs of pain **in the throes of** struggling with ♦ *We are in the throes of moving house.*

thrombosis (say throm-**boh**-sis) *n pl* **thromboses** formation of a clot of blood in a blood vessel or organ of the body

throne *n* 1 a ceremonial chair used by a king, queen, or bishop on formal occasions 2 (**the throne**) the power or position of a sovereign ♦ *the heir to the throne*

throng *n* a crowded mass of people **throng** *v* to come or go or press in a throng

throttle *n* a device that controls the flow of fuel to an engine, or the lever or pedal that operates this **throttle** *v* to strangle someone

through *prep* 1 from one end or side of to the other end or side of ♦ *Cars raced through the tunnel.* 2 between or among ♦ *scuffling through fallen leaves* 3 because of ♦ *We lost it through carelessness.* **through** *adv* from one end or side to the other ♦ *The cat jumped up to the window and squeezed through.* **through** *adj* 1 going through something 2 (said about traffic or passengers, etc.) going all the way to a destination **throughout** *prep*, *adv* all the way through, from beginning to end **throughput** *n* the amount of material dealt with by a process or system

throw *v* **threw**, **thrown** 1 to send something or someone through the air or in a certain direction 2 *informal* to confuse or disconcert someone ♦ *Your question threw me.* 3 *informal* to lose a race or match deliberately, especially by being bribed 4 to put clothes on or off hurriedly or casually 5 to move or turn a part of the body quickly ♦ *He threw his head back and laughed.* 6 to project your voice so that it seems to come from another source 7 to put someone in a certain state ♦ *We were thrown into confusion.* 8 to shape rounded pottery on a wheel 9 to move a switch or lever so as to operate it 10 *informal* to hold a party **throw** *n* the act of throwing **throwaway** *adj* 1 designed to be thrown away after use 2 (said about a remark) said casually or in an offhand way **throwback** *n* an animal or custom having characteristics of an older ancestor or practice **to throw up** *informal* to vomit

thrum *v* **thrummed**, **thrumming** to strum the strings of a musical instrument, to sound monotonously **thrum** *n* a thrumming sound

thrush[1] *n* a songbird with a brownish back and speckled breast

thrush[2] *n* a fungus infection in the mouth or genitals

thrust *v* past tense and past participle **thrust** to push something suddenly and forcibly **thrust** *n* a thrusting movement or force

thud *n* a low dull sound like that of something heavy hitting the ground **thud** *v* **thudded**, **thudding** to make a thud, or to fall with a thud

thug *n* a violent and brutal man, especially a criminal **thuggery** *n*

thumb *n* the short thick finger of the hand, set apart from the other four **thumb** *v* to turn the pages of a book with your thumb **thumbnail** *n* 1 the nail on a thumb 2 a reduced version of a larger digital image **thumbnail** *adj* brief and succinct ♦ *a thumbnail sketch* **thumbs up** a gesture of approval or satisfaction **to thumb a lift** to get a lift by signalling with your thumb, to hitch-hike **under someone's thumb** completely under someone's influence

thump *v* 1 to strike or knock someone or something heavily 2 to throb or beat with a strong pulse **thump** n a heavy blow, or the sound made by this **thumping** adj very large

thunder n the loud noise heard after a flash of lightning during an electrical storm **thunder** v 1 to make the sound of thunder ♦ *It was thundering in the distance.* 2 to make a loud rumbling noise ♦ *The train thundered past.* 3 to speak loudly or angrily **thunderous** adj like thunder **thundery** adj **thunderbolt** n 1 a lightning flash and a clap of thunder occurring together 2 something startling or immensely powerful in effect **thunderclap** n a clap of thunder **thunderstorm** n a storm with thunder **thunderstruck** adj very surprised or shocked

Thursday n the day of the week following Wednesday

thus adv formal 1 in this way, like this ♦ *Hold the book thus.* 2 as a result of this ♦ *He was the eldest son and thus heir to the title.* 3 to this extent ♦ *thus far*

thwack v to strike someone or something with a heavy blow **thwack** n a heavy blow, or the sound of this

thwart v to prevent someone from doing what they want or intend; to prevent a plan from being achieved

thy adj old use your (referring to one person)

thyme (say tiym) n a herb with fragrant leaves, used in cooking

thyroid, **thyroid gland** n a large gland at the front of the neck, which secretes hormones regulating the body's growth and development

tiara (say ti-ar-ə) n a jewelled band worn by a woman at the front of her hair on formal occasions

tic n an involuntary twitching of the muscles, especially of the face

tick[1] n 1 a mark (✓) placed against something written or printed to show that it is correct or that it has been dealt with 2 a regularly repeated clicking sound, especially that made by a watch or clock 3 informal a moment **tick** v 1 (said about a clock or watch) to make a series of ticks 2 to put a tick beside something written or printed **ticker tape** n a paper strip on which

messages are issued from a teleprinter **to tick over 1** (said about an engine) to run slowly without being connected **2** (said about an activity) to continue in a routine way **to tick someone off** informal to scold or reprimand someone **to tick something off** to mark something with a tick to show that it has been dealt with

tick[2] n a mite or parasitic insect that attaches itself to the skin and sucks blood

tick[3] n informal credit ♦ *I bought it on tick.*

ticket n 1 a written or printed piece of card or paper that entitles a person to go into a place or travel on public transport, etc. 2 a label attached to something to show its price or give other information about it 3 an official notification of a traffic offence **ticket** v **ticketed**, **ticketing** to put a ticket or label on something

tickle v 1 to touch or stroke a person's skin lightly so as to cause a slight tingling sensation, usually making them wriggle or laugh 2 to feel this sensation ♦ *My foot tickles.* 3 to amuse or please someone **tickle** n the act of tickling or the feeling of being tickled **ticklish** adj 1 sensitive to tickling, likely to wriggle or laugh when tickled 2 (said about a problem) needing careful handling

tiddly[1] adj **tiddlier**, **tiddliest** informal very small **tiddler** n 1 a small fish 2 an unusually small person or thing

tiddly[2] adj **tiddlier**, **tiddliest** informal slightly drunk

tiddlywink n a small counter flicked into a cup by pressing the edge of it with another counter in the game called **tiddlywinks**

tide n 1 the regular rise and fall in the level of the sea, which usually happens twice a day and is caused by the attraction of the moon and the sun 2 a powerful trend of opinion or feeling ♦ *a tide of excitement* **tidal** adj to do with or affected by a tide or tides **tidal wave** n a huge and powerful wave in the sea, especially one caused by an earthquake **to tide someone over** to help someone through a difficult period by providing what they need

tidings pl n news or information

tidy adj **tidier**, **tidiest** 1 arranged in a neat

and orderly way **2** *informal* (usually said about a sum of money) fairly large **tidy** *v* **tidies**, **tidied**, **tidying** to make something tidy **tidily** *adv* **tidiness** *n*

tie *v* **ties**, **tied**, **tying 1** to attach or fasten something with string, cord, etc. **2** to arrange string, ribbon, a tie, etc. to form a knot or bow **3** in a game or competition, to reach the same score as another competitor or team ♦ *They tied for second place.* **4** to restrict or limit what a person can do or where they can live **tie** *n* **1** (also **necktie**) a strip of material worn round the neck, passing under the collar and knotted in front **2** a string or cord used for tying something **3** something that unites things or people, a bond **4** a result of a game or competition in which two or more competitors have achieved the same score **5** a sports match between two competing teams or players, the winner passing on to the next round **tied** *adj* **1** (said about a house) for use by a person who works for its owner **2** (said about a public house) owned and controlled by one brewery **tiebreak** *n* a means of deciding a winner in a game or competition in which two or more competitors have tied

tier (say teer) *n* each of a series of rows or levels placed one above the other **tiered** *adj*

tiff *n* a brief or minor quarrel

tiger *n* a large animal of the cat family native to Asia, with yellow-brown and black stripes **tigress** *n* a female tiger

tight *adj* **1** fixed or fastened firmly, hard to move or undo or open **2** fitting very closely **3** well sealed against liquid or air **4** severe or strictly imposed ♦ *We are all working to a tight schedule.* **5** (said about a group or organization) well organized and controlled **6** (said about a rope, cord, etc., or a surface) stretched so as to leave no slack **7** not easy to obtain, in short supply ♦ *Money is tight at the moment.* **8** *informal* drunk **9** stingy **tight** *adv* tightly or firmly ♦ *The top is screwed down tight.* **tighten** *v* **tightly** *adv* **tightness** *n* **tights** *pl n* a close-fitting piece of clothing covering the feet, legs, and lower part of the body **tight-fisted** *adj*

stingy with money **tight-lipped** *adj* with the lips firmly closed, not saying anything or showing any feelings **tightrope** *n* a rope stretched tightly high above the ground, on which acrobats perform

tilde (say **til**-də) *n* a mark (~) put over a letter in some languages, for example over Spanish *n* when this is pronounced as in *señor*

tile *n* a thin square piece of baked clay or other hard material, used in rows for covering roofs, walls, or floors **tile** *v* to cover a surface with tiles

till[1] *prep, conjunction* until

till[2] a drawer or box for money in a shop, a cash register

till[3] *v* to prepare and use land for growing crops

tiller *n* a horizontal bar attached to the rudder of a boat, used for steering

tilt *v* **1** to move into a sloping position, or to make something do this **2** to run or thrust with a lance in jousting **tilt** *n* a sloping position or movement **at full tilt** at full speed or with full force

timber *n* **1** wood prepared for use in building or carpentry **2** a wooden beam used in building a house or ship **timbered** *adj*

timbre (say tambr) *n* the characteristic quality of a voice or musical sound

time *n* **1** all the years of the past, present, and future regarded as a whole **2** a particular point or portion of time associated with certain events or conditions ♦ *in Tudor times* ♦ *in times of hardship* **3** an experience or period of activity ♦ *We all had a good time.* **4** a point or portion of time taken or allowed for something ♦ *lunch time* **5** an occasion or instance ♦ *A bus goes to the village three times a day.* **6** a point of time stated in hours and minutes ♦ *The time is exactly two o'clock.* **7** any of the standard systems by which time is reckoned ♦ *Greenwich Mean Time* **8** *Mus* tempo or rhythm depending on the number and accentuation of beats in a bar **time** *v* **1** to choose or arrange the time or moment for something ♦ *The meeting has been timed for Monday afternoon.* **2** to measure the time taken by a person or activity **times** *pl n* used to express multiplication ♦ *Three times four is twelve.* **timeless** *adj* not affected by the passage of time or by changes of taste or fashion **timely** *adj* occurring at a suitable or useful time ♦ *a timely warning* **timer** *n* 1 a device for timing things 2 a device for activating something at a preset time **timing** *n* 1 the choice and control of when something is going to happen 2 a particular time when something happens **time-honoured** *adj* (said about a practice or custom) established and valued because it has existed for a long time **timekeeper** *n* 1 a person who records the amount of time taken by a process or of work done by people 2 a person considered in terms of how punctual they are, or a watch or clock in terms of how accurate it is ♦ *a good timekeeper* **timepiece** *n* a clock or watch **timeshare** *n* 1 an arrangement by which several people own a holiday home and have the right to use it at agreed times each year 2 a property owned and used in this way **timetable** *n* a list showing the time at which certain events will happen, e.g. when buses or trains leave and arrive, or when lessons take place in a school **timetable** *v* to organize events in a timetable **time zone** *n* a region between two lines of longitude, in which a common standard time is used **to do time** *informal* to serve a prison sentence

timid *adj* shy or easily frightened **timidity** *n* **timidly** *adv*

timorous (say **tim**-er-əs) *adj* nervous or timid **timorously** *adv* **timorousness** *n*

timpani (say **timp**-ən-ee) *pl n* kettledrums **timpanist** *n*

tin *n* 1 a silvery-white metal, a chemical element (symbol Sn) 2 an airtight container for preserved food, made of tinplate **tin** *v* **tinned, tinning** to seal food in a tin in order to preserve it **tinny** *adj* **tinnier, tinniest** 1 like tin, especially in not looking strong or solid 2 having a metallic taste or a thin metallic sound **tinfoil** *n* a thin sheet of tin, aluminium, or tin alloy, used for wrapping and packing things **tinpot** *adj* having no real value or power ♦ *a tinpot dictator*

tincture *n* a solution consisting of a medicinal substance dissolved in alcohol

tinder *n* a dry material such as wood or paper that catches fire easily **tinderbox** *n* a metal box containing dry material, flint and steel, and other things used for lighting a fire

tine *n* a point or prong of a fork, harrow, or antler

ting *v* to make a sharp ringing sound **ting** *n* a tinging sound

tinge (say tinj) *v* **tinging** or **tingeing** 1 to colour something slightly ♦ *white tinged with pink* 2 to influence or affect something, especially a feeling, slightly ♦ *Their admiration was tinged with envy.* **tinge** *n* a slight colouring or trace

tingle *v* to have a slight pricking or stinging sensation **tingle** *n* this sensation

tinker *n* a person who travels about mending people's pots and pans **tinker** *v* to work at something casually, trying to improve it or mend it

tinkle *v* to make a series of short light ringing sounds **tinkle** *n* a tinkling sound

tinsel *n* strips of glittering material used for decoration

tint *n* 1 a shade or variety of a particular colour 2 a slight trace of a different colour **tint** *v* to give a tint to something, to colour something slightly

tintinnabulation *n* formal a ringing or tinkling sound, especially of bells

tiny *adj* **tinier, tiniest** very small

tip[1] *n* 1 the part at the very end or top of something, especially something small or tapering 2 a small part or piece fitted to the end of something **tip** *v* **tipped, tipping** to provide something with a tip

tip[2] *v* **tipped, tipping** 1 to tilt or topple, or to make something do this 2 to name someone or something as likely to win or succeed 3 to make a small present of money to a person, especially to someone who has done you a service **tip** *n* 1 a small present of money given to someone who has done you a service 2 a small but useful piece of advice on how to do something 3 a recommendation or piece of information about someone or something that is likely to win or succeed 4 a place where rubbish or refuse is tipped **to tip someone off** to give someone special information about something that is likely to happen **tipper** n **tipster** n a person who gives tips, especially about horse races

tipple v to drink alcoholic drinks **tipple** n informal a spell of drinking alcoholic drinks **tippler** n

tipsy adj **tipsier**, **tipsiest** slightly drunk

tiptoe v **tiptoes**, **tiptoed**, **tiptoeing** to walk very quietly or carefully, with your heels not touching the ground

tirade (say tiy-**rayd**) n a long angry or hostile speech or piece of criticism

tire v to become tired, or to make someone tired **tireless** adj not tiring easily, having a lot of energy **tirelessly** adv **tiresome** adj making you feel impatient, annoying **tired** adj feeling that you need to sleep or rest **to be tired of** to have had enough of something ♦ They were tired of waiting.

tissue (say **tiss**-yoo or **tish**-oo) n 1 the substance forming any part of the body of an animal or plant 2 (also **tissue paper**) very thin soft paper used for wrapping and packing things 3 a piece of soft absorbent paper used as a disposable handkerchief 4 a series of connected things ♦ a tissue of lies

tit n a small bird, often with a dark patch on top of the head

titan (say **tiy**-ten) n a person of great size, strength, or importance **titanic** adj gigantic or immense

titanium (say ti-**tay**-nium or tiy-**tay**-nium) n a grey metallic element used to make light alloys that are free from corrosion

titbit n an attractive or delicious piece of something, especially food or information

tithe (say tiyth) n one-tenth of the annual produce from a farm, etc., formerly paid as tax to support the clergy and church

titillate (say **tit**-i-layt) v to excite or stimulate someone in a pleasant way **titillation** n

titivate (say **tit**-i-vayt) v to smarten something up, or put the finishing touches to it **titivation** n

title n 1 the name of a book, poem, piece of music, or other artistic work 2 a word used to show a person's rank or office

(e.g. queen, mayor, captain) or used to address or refer to a person (e.g. Lord, Mrs, Doctor) 3 the legal right to ownership of property, or a document conferring this 4 a championship in sport **title** v to give a title to a book or other artistic work **titled** adj having a title as a member of the nobility

titular adj 1 belonging to a title 2 holding a title without any real power or authority

title deed n a legal document providing evidence of a person's right, especially to owning a property

titter v to laugh quietly or furtively **titter** n a quiet or furtive laugh

tittle-tattle n idle chatter or gossip **tittle-tattle** v to chatter or gossip idly

tizzy n informal a state of nervous agitation or confusion ♦ in a tizzy

TNT abbr trinitrotoluene, a powerful explosive

to prep used to show 1 direction in relation to a place or state ♦ Shall we walk to the station? 2 extent or degree ♦ Surgery is from 10 to 4 o'clock. ♦ goods to the value of £10 3 comparison ♦ We won by 3 goals to 2. 4 a person or thing affected by an action or feeling ♦ I gave it to Tom. **to** prep used before a verb to form an infinitive or to express a purpose or result ♦ He wants to go. **to** adv in or into the closed position ♦ Push the door to. **to and fro** backwards and forwards

toad n a frog-like animal that lives mainly on land **toady** n pl **toadies** a person who flatters other people and behaves obsequiously towards them in the hope of getting favours **toady** v **toadies**, **toadied**, **toadying** to behave as a toady **toadstool** n a fungus, usually poisonous, with a round top and a slender stalk

toast n 1 a slice of bread that has been warmed to make it crisp and brown 2 a call to a group of people to drink in honour of someone, or the person or thing in whose honour this is done **toast** v 1 to brown the surface of bread by placing it against a source of direct heat 2 to drink a toast to someone or something **toaster** n an electrical device for toasting bread

tobacco n pl **tobaccos** 1 the dried leaves of certain plants, used for smoking or for making snuff **2** the plant that produces these leaves **tobacconist** n a shopkeeper who sells cigarettes, cigars, and tobacco

toboggan n a light narrow sledge curved upwards at the front, used for sliding downhill on snow or ice **tobogganing** n

today n **1** this present day ♦ *Today is Monday.* **2** the present age, nowadays ♦ *The youth of today.* **today** adv **1** on this present day **2** at the present time

toddle v (said about a young child) to walk with short unsteady steps **toddler** n a child who is just beginning to walk

toddy n pl **toddies** a sweetened drink made with spirits and hot water

to-do n a fuss or commotion

toe n **1** each of the five divisions of the front part of the human foot, or each of the divisions of the foot of an animal **2** the part of a shoe or sock that covers the toes **toe** v **toes, toed, toeing** to touch or reach something with the toes **toecap** n the outer covering of the toe of a boot or shoe **toehold** n **1** a slight foothold **2** a small beginning from which progress can be made **to toe the line** to follow instructions or authority, especially under pressure

toffee n a sticky or hard sweet made from heated butter and sugar **toffee-nosed** adj snobbish or pretentious

tofu (say **toh**-foo) n a curd made from mashed soya beans

tog n a unit used in measuring the insulating and warming power of clothing or bedding **togs** pl n informal clothes

toga (say **toh**-gǝ) n a loose flowing outer garment worn by men in ancient Rome

together adv **1** with another person or thing, with each other ♦ *They went to the disco together.* **2** at the same time ♦ *They both cried out together.*

toggle n **1** a fastening for a piece of clothing, made of a short piece of wood or plastic that is passed through a loop **2** ICT a key that switches a function on and off successively with the same action

toil v **1** to work hard and continuously **2** to move with great effort or difficulty **toil** n hard or difficult work

toilet n **1** a large bowl for urinating and

defecating into, usually plumbed into a sewage system **2** a room or compartment containing a toilet **3** the process of washing and dressing yourself **toiletries** pl n things used in washing and caring for the body, such as soap and shampoo **toilet paper** n paper for wiping the body clean after using a toilet **toilet roll** n a roll of toilet paper

token n **1** a sign or indication of something ♦ *a token of our friendship* **2** a voucher or coupon that can be exchanged for goods **3** a piece of metal or plastic shaped like a coin and used to operate a machine or in exchange for goods or services **token** adj serving as a token or gesture rather than for real effect ♦ *The enemy put up token resistance.*

tolerate v **1** to allow something to happen or to be said although you don't necessarily agree with it **2** to bear pain or suffering **tolerable** adj **1** able to be tolerated, endurable **2** fairly good, passable **tolerance** n being tolerant, willing to accept what other people say and do **tolerant** adj **toleration** n

toll[1] (say tohl) n **1** a charge you have to pay to use a public road or bridge **2** the number of deaths or amount of damage caused by an accident or disaster

toll[2] (say tohl) v **1** to ring a bell with a slow sequence of strokes, especially for a death or funeral **2** (said about a bell) to sound in this way, or to indicate a death or funeral by tolling **toll** n the stroke of a tolling bell

tom, tomcat n a male animal, especially a cat

tomahawk n a light axe formerly used as a tool or weapon by Native Americans

tomato n pl **tomatoes** a soft round red or yellow fruit with a shiny skin, eaten as a vegetable

tomb (say toom) n **1** a burial place, especially a large underground one **2** a monument built over a grave or burial place **tombstone** n a memorial stone set up over a grave

tombola (say tom-**boh**-lǝ) n a game played at a fair or fête, in which tickets are drawn from a revolving drum for prizes

tomboy n a girl who enjoys rough noisy

games and activities

tome n a book or volume, especially a large heavy one

tomfoolery adj silly or foolish behaviour

tomorrow n **1** the day after today **2** the near future **tomorrow** adv **1** on the day after today **2** in the near future

tom-tom n a drum beaten with the hands

ton (say tun) n a measure of weight, either 2,240 lb. (**long ton**) or 2,000 lb. (**short ton**) **tonnage** n the amount that a ship or ships can carry, expressed in tons

tone n **1** a musical or vocal sound, especially with reference to its pitch, quality, and strength **2** a manner of expression in speaking or writing ♦ an apologetic tone **3** a tint or shade of a colour, or the general effect of colour or of light and shade in a picture **4** the general character or quality of something ♦ He set the tone with a witty speech. **5** Mus a basic interval, equal to two semitones, separating two notes in an ordinary scale **6** (also **muscle tone**) the normal firmness of a resting muscle **tone** v **1** to give a particular tone of sound or colour to something **2** to be harmonious in colour ♦ The carpet tones in with the wallpaper. **3** to give proper firmness to the body or to a muscle **to tone something down 1** to make something softer in sound or colour **2** to make a statement less strong or harsh **tonal** adj **1** to do with tone or tones **2** said about music written in the conventional system of keys and harmony **tonality** n **toneless** adj **toner** n **1** a liquid put on the skin to improve its condition **2** a powder used to produce tones in photocopying **tone-deaf** adj unable to perceive differences of musical pitch accurately

tongs pl n an instrument with two arms joined at one end, used to pick up or hold things

tongue n **1** the fleshy muscular organ in the mouth, used for tasting, licking, swallowing, and (in humans) speaking **2** the tongue of an ox or other animal as food **3** a particular language ♦ Their native tongue is German. **4** a strip of leather or other material under the laces of a shoe or boot

5 a pointed flame **tongue-in-cheek** adj said or written with irony or sarcasm **tongue-tied** adj too shy or embarrassed to speak **tongue-twister** n a sequence of words that is difficult to pronounce quickly and correctly, e.g. She sells sea shells.

tonic n **1** a medicine that gives strength and vigour, especially after an illness **2** anything that restores people's energy or good spirits **3** Mus the first note in a scale, providing the keynote in a piece of music **4** short for tonic water **tonic** adj having the effect of a tonic **tonic water** n a fizzy mineral water with a bitter taste

tonight n this present or coming evening or night **tonight** adv on the present or coming evening or night

tonne (say tun) n a measure of weight equal to 1,000 kilograms

tonsil n each of two small organs at the sides of the throat near the root of the tongue **tonsillitis** n inflammation of the tonsils

tonsure (say **ton**-sher) n the top part of a monk's or priest's head made bare by shaving the hair

too adv **1** more than is wanted or desirable **2** very ♦ She's not too well today. **3** also, as well ♦ Please take the others too.

tool n **1** a device, held in the hand or in a machine, for performing a particular function **2** a thing used for a particular purpose ♦ An encyclopedia is a useful study tool. **3** a person who is manipulated by another person **tool** v to shape or decorate something by using a tool

toot v to make or cause something to make the short sharp sound of a horn or whistle **toot** n a tooting sound

tooth n pl **teeth 1** each of the hard white bony structures that are rooted in the gums, used for biting and chewing **2** a tooth-like part or projection on a gear, saw, comb, or rake **toothless** adj **toothache** n pain in a tooth or teeth **toothbrush** n a brush for cleaning the teeth **toothpaste** n a paste for cleaning the teeth **toothpick** n a small pointed piece of wood, etc. for removing bits of food from between the teeth

top¹ n **1** the highest part of something **2** the

upper surface of something **3** the covering or stopper of a container **4** the highest position or rank ♦ *She is at the top of her profession.* **5** the utmost degree of intensity ♦ *He shouted at the top of his voice.* **6** a piece of clothing covering the upper part of the body **top** *adj* highest in position, rank, or degree ♦ *at top speed* ♦ *top prices* **top** *v* **topped**, **topping 1** to provide or be a top for something **2** to exceed or be more than something **3** to be the highest in rank or position ♦ *Who topped the list?* **topless** *adj* (said about a woman or her clothing) having or leaving the breasts uncovered

top hat *n* a man's tall stiff black or grey hat worn with formal dress **top-heavy** *adj* too heavy at the top and likely to fall over **topsoil** *n* the top layer of soil, as distinct from the subsoil

top[2] *n* a toy that can be made to spin on its point

topaz (say **toh**-paz) *n* a precious stone, usually yellow or pale blue

toper (say **toh**-per) *n* someone who is habitually drunk

topiary (say **toh**-pi-er-i) *n* the art of clipping shrubs or trees into ornamental shapes

topic *n* the subject of a discussion or piece of writing **topical** *adj* to do with current events **topicality** *n*

topography (say tə-**pog**-rəfi) *n* the arrangement of the features of a place or district, including the position of its rivers, mountains, roads, and buildings **topographical** *adj*

topple *v* **1** to overbalance and fall, or to make something do this **2** to overthrow people in authority, or cause them to fall

topsy-turvy *adj*, *adv* **1** in a muddle **2** upside down

tor *n* a hill or rocky peak

Torah (say **tor**-ə) *n* the revealed will of God, especially the laws given to Moses

torch *n* **1** a small battery-powered electric lamp held in the hand **2** a stick with burning material at the end, used as a light

toreador (say torri-ə-dor) *n* a bullfighter, especially one on horseback

torment (say **tor**-ment) *n* **1** intense physical or mental suffering **2** something causing this **torment** *v* **1** to cause someone intense physical or mental suffering **2** to tease or try to provoke someone by annoying or teasing them **tormentor** *n*

tornado (say tor-**nay**-doh) *n pl* **tornadoes** a destructive whirlwind advancing in a narrow path with the appearance of a funnel-shaped cloud

torpedo *n pl* **torpedoes** a cigar-shaped explosive underwater missile, launched against a ship from a submarine or surface ship or from an aircraft **torpedo** *v* **torpedoes**, **torpedoed**, **torpedoing 1** to destroy or attack something with a torpedo **2** to ruin or wreck a plan or policy

torpid *adj* slow or inactive **torpor** *n* a state of slowness or inactivity

torrent *n* **1** a rushing stream of water or lava **2** an overwhelming flow ♦ *a torrent of abuse* **torrential** *adj* like a torrent, flowing in torrents

torrid *adj* **1** (said about a climate or land) very hot and dry **2** intense or passionate

torsion (say **tor** -shən) *n* the action of twisting, especially of one end of a thing while the other is held fixed

torso (say **tor** -soh) *n pl* **torsos 1** the trunk of the human body **2** the trunk of a statue, without the head and limbs

tortilla (say tor-**tee**-yə) *n* in Mexican cookery, a flat maize cake eaten hot

tortoise (say **tor** -təs) *n* a slow-moving reptile having four legs and a body enclosed in a hard shell **tortoiseshell** *n* **1** the semi-transparent mottled yellow and brown shell of certain turtles, used for making combs and jewellery **2** a cat or butterfly with mottled colouring resembling this

tortuous (say **tor** -tew-əs) *adj* **1** full of twists and turns **2** (said about a policy, argument, etc.) devious, not straightforward

torture *n* **1** the action of inflicting severe pain as a punishment or means of coercing someone **2** severe physical or mental pain **torture** *v* **1** to inflict torture on someone **2** to subject someone to great pain or anxiety **torturer** *n*

Tory *n pl* **Tories** *informal* a member of the Conservative Party **Tory** *adj informal* Conservative **Toryism** *n*

toss v 1 to throw something lightly or casually 2 to throw your head back, especially in impatience or disapproval 3 to send a coin spinning in the air to decide something according to which way up it lands 4 to move restlessly or unevenly from side to side, or to make something do this 5 to shake food in a dressing or liquid to coat it lightly **toss** n a tossing action or movement **toss-up** n 1 the tossing of a coin 2 an even chance

tot[1] n 1 a small child 2 informal a small amount of spirits

tot[2] v **totted**, **totting** **tot up** informal to add up numbers or amounts

total adj 1 including the whole number or amount 2 utter or complete ♦ in total darkness **total** n the total number or amount **total** v **totalled**, **totalling** 1 to reckon the total of something 2 to amount to a certain total **totalitarian** adj to do with a form of government which demands total submission to the state and does not allow rival politics **totality** n **totalizator** n a device that automatically records the number and amount of bets staked, in order to divide the total amount among those betting on the winner **totally** adv

tote[1] n informal a totalizator

tote[2] v **totes**, **toting**, **toted** informal to carry something heavy

totem (say **toh**-təm) n an animal or other natural object adopted in certain societies as an emblem having spiritual significance **totem pole** n a tall pole carved or painted with images of totems

totter v 1 to walk unsteadily or shake as if about to collapse 2 to rock or

toucan (say **too**-kən) n a tropical American bird with a very large beak

touch v 1 to be or come together so that there is no space between 2 to come into contact with something 3 to put your fingers lightly on something 4 informal to eat or drink any of something ♦ She has hardly touched her breakfast. 5 informal to match or equal something or someone in quality 6 to affect someone slightly 7 to rouse a person's sympathy or feelings ♦ He was touched by the generosity people

showed him. 8 informal to persuade someone to give money as a loan or gift ♦ He touched her for a fiver. **touch** n 1 the act of touching 2 the ability to perceive things or their qualities by touching them 3 small things done in producing a piece of work ♦ the finishing touches 4 a special skill or style of workmanship ♦ She hasn't lost her touch. 5 a slight trace ♦ a touch of frost **touched** adj 1 caused to feel warm sympathy or gratitude 2 slightly mad **touching** adj rousing kindly feelings or sympathy or pity **touching** prep concerning **touchy** adj **touchier**, **touchiest** quick to take offence, oversensitive **touchdown** n the act of touching down in an aircraft **touchline** n the boundary on each side of a football or rugby pitch **touchstone** n a standard or criterion by which something is judged **in touch with** 1 in communication with someone 2 having an interest in or knowledge about something **out of touch** no longer in touch with a person or subject, etc. **to touch down** (said about an aircraft) to land **to touch on** to deal with or mention a subject briefly **to touch something off** 1 to make something explode 2 to cause something to start **to touch something up** to improve something by making small alterations or additions **touch and go** having an uncertain outcome

touché (say **too**-shay) interjection used to acknowledge a true or clever point made against you in an argument

tough adj 1 strong enough to endure hard wear ♦ tough leather 2 difficult to break or cut 3 (said about food) difficult to chew 4 (said about a person) able to endure hardship, not easily hurt or injured 5 firm or resolute ♦ a tough policy on fighting crime 6 difficult to do ♦ a tough job **tough** n informal a rough and violent person **toughen** v **toughly** adv **toughness** n

toupee (say **too**-pay) n a small wig or piece of artificial hair worn to cover a bald spot

tour n 1 a journey made for pleasure, visiting several places 2 a series of performances in different places by a theatrical or musical company, or a series of sports fixtures by a travelling team **tour** v to make a tour of an area **tourism** *n* the business of organizing and providing services for tourists **tourist** *n* a person who travels for pleasure

tour de force (say toor də **forss**) *n* an outstandingly skilful performance or achievement

tournament (say **toor** -nə-mənt) *n* a series of contests between a number of competitors

tourney *n pl* **tourneys** a medieval jousting tournament

tourniquet (say **toor** -ni-kay) *n* a strip of material wrapped tightly round a leg or arm to stop the flow of blood from an artery

tousle (say **tow**-zəl) *v* to make someone's hair untidy by ruffling it

tout (say towt) *v* 1 to try to sell something or get business 2 to urge people to buy or use something **tout** *n* a person who sells tickets for a sports match or concert at inflated prices

tow (say toh) *v* to pull something along behind **tow** *n* the action of towing something **towpath** *n* a path beside a canal or river, originally used by horses towing barges **in tow** accompanying someone, or in their charge ♦ *He arrived with his family in tow.* **on tow** being towed

towards *prep* 1 (also **toward**) in the direction of ♦ *She guided them towards the door.* 2 regarding or in relation to ♦ *attitudes towards terrorism* 3 as a contribution to the cost of ♦ *I'll put the money towards a new computer.* 4 near or approaching ♦ *towards evening*

towel *n* a piece of absorbent cloth or paper for drying yourself or wiping things dry **towel** *v* **towelled, towelling** to wipe or dry something with a towel **towelling** *n* thick absorbent cloth used for making towels

tower *n* a tall narrow building standing alone or forming part of a larger building such as a church or castle **tower** *v* to have a great height, to be taller or more eminent than others ♦ *He towered above everyone.*

towering *adj* very tall or high **tower block** *n* a tall modern building containing many floors of offices or flats **a tower of strength** a person who gives strong and reliable support

town *n* 1 a place with many houses and other buildings that is larger than a village and usually smaller than a city 2 the inhabitants of a town 3 the central business and shopping part of a neighbourhood ♦ *Are you going into town?* **township** *n* 1 a small town 2 (in South Africa) a residential area occupied by black people **town crier** *n* an official who formerly made public announcements in the streets **town hall** *n* a building containing local government offices and usually a hall for public events

toxic *adj* 1 of or caused by poison 2 poisonous **toxicity** *n* **toxicology** *n* the study of poisons **toxicologist** *n* **toxin** *n* a poisonous substance of animal or vegetable origin

toy *n* an object for a child to play with **toy** *adj* 1 serving as a toy 2 (said about a dog) of a miniature breed or variety, kept as a pet **toy** *v* **to toy with** 1 to handle or finger something casually 2 to consider an idea casually or intermittently ♦ *We are toying with the idea of going to China.*

trace *n* 1 a mark or indication showing that a person or thing exists or has been present at a place ♦ *There was no trace of the thief.* 2 a very small amount **trace** *v* 1 to follow or discover someone or something by looking for marks, tracks, or other evidence 2 to copy a picture or outline by drawing over it on transparent paper 3 to mark out or form the outline of something ♦ *She traced her signature shakily.* **traceable** *adj* **tracer** *n* a bullet or shell that leaves a trail of coloured light or smoke, so that its course can be followed for aiming **tracery** *n pl* **traceries** a decorative open-work pattern in stone **tracing** *n* a copy of a map or drawing made by tracing it

trachea (say trə-**kee**-ə or **tray**-kiə) *n* the windpipe

track *n* 1 a rough path or road 2 a road or area of ground prepared for something, especially racing 3 a mark or series of marks left by a person, animal, or thing moving along 4 a course of action or procedure ♦ *Are we on the right track?* 5 each of the items on a CD or other recording 6 a set of rails on which a train or tram runs 7 a continuous band round the wheels of a tank or other heavy vehicle **track** v 1 to follow the tracks left by a person or animal 2 to follow or observe something as it moves **tracker** n **track events** pl n (in sports) races as distinct from field events **track record** n a person's past achievements, as a guide to their competence **tracksuit** n a warm loose suit worn when exercising or as casual wear **to keep** or **lose track of** to keep or fail to keep yourself aware of something or informed about it **to track someone** or **something down** to find someone or something after a long or difficult search

tract[1] n 1 a large area of land 2 a series of connected parts in an animal body along which something passes ♦ the digestive tract

tract[2] n a pamphlet containing a short essay, especially on a religious subject

tractable adj (said about a person) easy to control or deal with, docile

traction n 1 the action of pulling something along a surface 2 a medical treatment in which an arm, leg, or muscle is pulled gently for a long period by means of weights and pulleys, especially to set a fractured bone or to correct a deformity **traction engine** n a steam or diesel engine formerly used for drawing a heavy load along a road or across a field, etc.

tractor n a powerful motor vehicle with large rear wheels, used for pulling farm machinery or other heavy equipment

trade n 1 the buying and selling of goods and services 2 business of a particular kind ♦ the tourist trade 3 a skilled job or occupation ♦ He's a butcher by trade. ♦ to learn a trade **trade** v 1 to take part in trade, to buy and sell goods or services 2 to exchange goods in trading **trader** n **trademark** n a company's legally registered name or emblem, used to identify its products or services **tradesman** n pl **tradesmen** a person employed in a trade, especially one who sells or delivers goods **trade union** n an organized association of workers employed in a particular trade or profession, formed to protect and promote their rights and interests **to trade**

on to make use of something for your own advantage ♦ He tends to trade on his good luck. **to trade something in** to give something you have used as part payment for something you are buying

tradition n 1 the passing down of beliefs or customs from one generation to another 2 a belief or custom that has been handed down in this way, especially an established custom or way of doing things **traditionalist** n a person who follows or supports traditional beliefs and ways of doing things **traditionalism** n **traditional** n **traditionally** adv

traduce (say trə-dewss) v to speak badly or untruthfully about someone or something

traffic n 1 vehicles, ships, or aircraft moving along a route 2 trading, especially when it is illegal or wrong **traffic** v **traffics**, **trafficked**, **trafficking** to buy and sell something illegal, especially drugs **trafficker** n **traffic lights** pl n coloured lights used as a signal controlling traffic at road junctions, road works, and pedestrian crossings **traffic warden** n an official who monitors the parking of road vehicles and reports on infringements

tragedy n pl **tragedies** 1 an event that causes great destruction or suffering 2 a serious play with an unhappy ending, especially the death or downfall of the main character **tragedian** n 1 a person who writes tragedies 2 an actor in tragedies **tragic** adj 1 causing great distress or disaster 2 suffering great sadness 3 to do with tragedy **tragically** adv

trail n 1 a series of marks or signs left where someone or something has passed, a trace 2 an improvised path or track 3 a route followed for a particular purpose ♦ Turn left for the tourist trail through the lakes. 4 a line of people or things following behind something **trail** v 1 to follow the trail of someone or something, to track or hunt them 2 to drag something behind along the ground, or to be dragged behind 3 to walk or move slowly or wearily, to lag or straggle 4 to be losing in a game or contest 5 to become less or fainter ♦ The voice trailed away. **trailer** n 1 a truck or other container pulled along by a vehicle **2** a short extract from a film or television programme, shown in advance to advertise it

train n **1** a series of linked railway carriages or trucks pulled by a locomotive or having built-in motors **2** a number of people or animals moving in a line **3** part of a long dress or robe that trails on the ground at the back **4** a series of things ♦ *a train of events* **train** v **1** to give someone instruction or practice in a particular skill **2** to be given instruction **3** to bring a person, team, etc. to the right level of physical fitness, especially for sport **4** to practise in order to come to the right level of physical fitness **5** to teach a person or animal to do something or behave in a particular way **6** to aim a gun or camera at a particular object **7** to make a plant grow in a particular direction **trainee** n a person who is being trained for a particular job or profession **trainer** n **1** a person who trains people or animals **2** a soft shoe with a rubber sole, used for sports or casual wear **3** an aircraft used to train pilots, or a machine simulating an aircraft **trainspotter** n a person who goes to see and record details of railway locomotives as a hobby

traipse v *informal* to walk or wearily, to trudge

trait (say tray) n a distinguishing characteristic

traitor n a person who betrays their country **traitorous** adj

trajectory (say trə-jek-ter-i) n pl **trajectories** the path taken by an object moving under force, especially a bullet or rocket

tram, tramcar n a public passenger vehicle powered by electricity and running on rails laid in the road

trammel v **trammelled, trammelling** to hamper or impede someone

tramp n **1** a homeless person who goes from place to place begging or doing casual work **2** the sound of heavy footsteps **3** a long walk **tramp** v **1** to walk with heavy steps **2** to travel on foot across rough country

trample v to tread on something repeatedly and crush it

trampoline (say tramp-ə-leen) n a piece of gymnastic equipment consisting of a sheet of strong canvas attached by springs to a horizontal frame, used as a springboard for acrobatic jumping

trance n **1** a semi-conscious state of the kind induced by hypnosis **2** a dreamy self-absorbed state

tranquil adj calm and quiet, without disturbance **tranquillity** n **tranquillizer** n a drug used to relieve anxiety and make a person feel calm **tranquilly** adv

trans- prefix across or beyond (as in *transatlantic*)

transact v to carry out business **transaction** n **1** the process of carrying out business **2** a piece of business carried out

transatlantic adj **1** crossing the Atlantic **2** on or from the other side of the Atlantic

transceiver (say tran-seev-er) n a combined radio transmitter and receiver

transcend (say tran-send) v **1** to go or be beyond the range or limits of something ♦ *The experience transcended her wildest expectations.* **2** to surpass something **transcendent** adj **transcendence** n **transcendental** adj belonging to a spiritual or visionary world

transcribe v **1** to copy something in writing, or to write something out in another system of writing **2** to record sound for later reproduction or broadcasting **transcript** n a written or printed version of something originally in a different medium **transcription** n

transept (say tran-sept) n each of the two parts at right angles to the nave in a cross-shaped church ♦ *the north and south transepts*

transfer (say trans-fer) v **transferred, transferring** to move or convey something from one place or person to another **transfer** (say trans-fer) n **1** the process of transferring or being transferred **2** a design that can be transferred from one surface to another, or a piece of paper bearing this design **transferable** adj (said about a ticket or permit) able to be used by another person **transference** n

transfigure v to transform something,

especially to make it nobler or more beautiful **transfiguration** n

transfix v **1** to pierce something with a pointed object **2** to make a person or animal unable to move through fear or wonder

transform v **1** to make a great change in the appearance or character of something **2** to become greatly changed in appearance or character **3** to change the voltage of an electric current **transformation** n **transformer** n a device for changing the voltage of alternating current

transfuse v to transfer blood from one person or animal to another **transfusion** n

transgress v to break a rule or law **transgression** n **transgressor** n

transient (say tran-zi-ənt) adj **1** lasting only a short time, not permanent **2** staying in a place for a short period only **transience** n

transistor n **1** a semiconductor device with three electrodes, used in electronic amplification and control circuits **2** (in full **transistor radio**) a portable radio using circuits with transistors

transit n the process of going or taking things from one place to another **transition** n the process of changing from one condition or form to another **transitional** adj **transitive** adj (said about a verb or a meaning of a verb) used with a direct object, e.g. play in The teams will play each other on Saturday. (but not in The teams will play on Saturday.) **transitory** adj existing for a time but not lasting

translate v to express something in another language **translatable** adj **translation** n **translator** n

transliterate v to represent letters or words in the most closely corresponding letters of a different alphabet **transliteration** n

translucent (say tranz-**loo**-sənt) adj allowing light to pass through without being completely transparent **translucence** n

transmit v **transmitted**, **transmitting** **1** to send or pass something from one person, place, or thing to another **2** to be a medium for a form of energy ♦ Iron transmits heat. **3** to send out a signal or broadcast by telegraph wire or radio waves **transmission** n **1** the process of transmitting a message or broadcast **2** a broadcast transmitted **3** the set of gears by which power is transmitted from the engine to the wheels of a motor vehicle **transmittable** adj **transmitter** n a device or set of equipment for transmitting radio or television signals

transmogrify v **transmogrifies**, **transmogrified**, **transmogrifying** to transform something, especially in a magical or surprising way

transmute v to cause something to change in form or substance **transmutation** n

transparent (say trans-**pa**-rənt) adj **1** allowing light to pass through so that objects behind can be seen clearly **2** easily understood, clear, or obvious **transparency** n pl **transparencies** **1** a state of being transparent **2** a positive photograph printed on film or glass, a slide **transparently** adv

transpire v **1** (said about information) to become known ♦ It transpired that during the war he had been a member of the resistance. **2** to happen ♦ It's hard to know exactly what transpired. **3** (said about plants) to give off watery vapour from the surface of leaves, etc. **transpiration** n

transplant (say trans-**plahnt**) v **1** to remove a plant and put it to grow somewhere else **2** to transfer an organ or living tissue from one part of the body or one person or animal to another **transplant** (say trans-plahnt) n **1** the process of transplanting an organ or tissue **2** something transplanted **transplantation** n

transport (say trans-**port**) v **1** to take or convey someone or something from one place to another **2** to overcome someone with strong emotion ♦ She was transported with joy. **3** hist to deport a criminal to a penal settlement **transport** (say trans-port) n **1** the act or process of transporting people or things **2** a means of transporting people or things ♦ public transport **3** the condition of being carried away by strong emotion ♦ in transports of rage **transportation** n **transporter** n a vehicle used to transport heavy loads

transpose v 1 to cause two or more things to change places, or to change one thing to a different position in a series 2 to put a piece of music into a different key **transposition** n

transsexual n a person who feels emotionally and psychologically that they belong to the sex opposite to their own

transubstantiation n the process of changing one substance into another

transverse adj lying or extending across something **transversely** adv

transvestite n a person who enjoys dressing in the clothing of the opposite sex **transvestism** n

trap n 1 a device for catching and holding animals 2 a plan or trick for capturing or detecting a person unawares or for making a person betray themselves 3 an unpleasant situation from which you cannot easily escape 4 a compartment from which a greyhound is released at the start of a race 5 a two-wheeled carriage drawn by a horse **trap** v **trapped**, **trapping** 1 to catch or hold an animal in a trap 2 to trick or deceive someone into doing something 3 to prevent someone from escaping **trapper** n a person who traps wild animals, especially for their fur **trapdoor** n a small hinged or removable flap in a floor, ceiling, or roof

trapeze n a horizontal bar hanging by long ropes as a swing for acrobatics

trapezium (say trə-**pee**-ziəm) n pl **trapezia** or **trapeziums** a quadrilateral in which two opposite sides are parallel and the other two are not **trapezoid** n a quadrilateral in which no sides are parallel

trappings pl n 1 the clothes and other things that indicate a person's status or position 2 the ornamental harness of a horse

trash n 1 worthless stuff, rubbish 2 worthless people **trashy** adj

trauma (say **traw**-mə) n 1 an emotional shock that leaves a lasting effect on a person's mind 2 Medicine a wound or injury **traumatic** adj

travail (say **trav**-ayl) n literary painful or laborious effort

travel v **travelled**, **travelling** 1 to go from one place to another, to make a journey 2 to journey along or through a region or distance **travel** n the action of travelling, especially abroad **traveller** n a person who is travelling or who travels a lot **travelogue** n a book, film, or illustrated lecture about travel **travel agent** n a business that makes travel and holiday arrangements for travellers **traveller's cheque** n a cheque for a fixed amount of money that is sold by banks and can be cashed for foreign currency abroad

traverse (say trə-**vers**) v 1 to travel across an area 2 to lie or extend across something

travesty (say **trav**-iss-ti) n pl **travesties** a ridiculous or poor version of something worthwhile ♦ *The trial was a travesty of justice.* **travesty** v **travesties**, **travestied**, **travestying** to represent something as a travesty

trawl v 1 to fish from a boat by dragging a large net along the seabed 2 to search a place thoroughly **trawl** n a large net used in trawling for fish **trawler** n a fishing boat used for trawling

tray n 1 a flat piece of wood, metal, or plastic, usually with a raised edge, for carrying a number of small articles such as cups, plates, and food 2 an open container for holding letters and papers in an office

treachery n betrayal of a person or cause, an act of disloyalty **treacherous** adj 1 behaving with or showing deception or betrayal 2 dangerous or unsafe **treacherously** adv

treacle n a thick sticky dark liquid produced when sugar is refined

tread v **trod**, **trodden** 1 to set your foot down, to walk or step on the ground 2 to press or crush something with the feet **tread** n 1 a manner or the sound of walking ♦ *walking with a heavy tread* 2 the top surface of a step or stair 3 the part of a wheel or tyre that makes contact with the ground **treadmill** n 1 a wide mill wheel turned by the weight of people or animals treading on steps fixed round its edge 2 an exercise machine with a moving belt for walking or running on 3 a job or task that is tedious or routine **to tread water** to keep yourself upright in water by making treading movements with the legs

treadle (say tred-əl) n a lever worked with the foot to drive a wheel, especially in a sewing machine

treason n the act of betraying your country, especially by overthrowing the monarch or government **treasonable** adj involving or amounting to treason ♦ a treasonable offence **treasonous** adj

treasure n 1 precious metals, gems, or other valuable objects, or a store of these 2 an object of great worth or value ♦ art treasures 3 a much loved or highly valued person **treasure** v to value something or someone highly **treasurer** n a person appointed to manage the funds of an organization, society, etc. **treasury** n pl **treasuries** 1 a place where money and valuables are stored 2 (**Treasury**) a government department that manages the public finances of a country

treat v 1 to behave in a certain way towards a person or thing 2 to present or discuss a subject ♦ The author treats recent events in detail. 3 to give medical care to a person or illness 4 to put something through a chemical or other process ♦ The fabric has been treated to make it waterproof. 5 to provide someone with food or entertainment at your own expense in order to give pleasure ♦ I'll treat you to a drink. **treat.** n something special that gives a lot of pleasure 2 the act of providing someone with food or entertainment at your own expense ♦ It's my treat. **treatise** n a book or pamphlet on a particular subject **treatment** n 1 the process or manner of dealing with a person, animal, or thing 2 medical care for a person or illness

treaty n pl **treaties** a formal agreement between two or more countries

treble adj three times as much or three times as many **treble** n 1 a treble quantity or thing 2 a high-pitched singing voice, or a singer (usually a boy) with such a voice 3 a high-pitched member of a group of musical instruments **treble** v to make something, or become, three times as much or as many **trebly** adv

tree n a tall perennial plant with a single thick hard stem or trunk that is usually without branches for some distance above the ground

trefoil (say tref-oil) n 1 a plant with three small leaves, e.g. clover 2 an ornament or design having three lobes

trek n a long difficult journey on foot **trek** v **trekked**, **trekking** to go on a trek

trellis n a light framework of crossing wooden or metal bars, used to support climbing plants

tremble v to shake involuntarily, especially from fear or excitement **tremble** n a trembling movement or feeling

tremendous adj 1 very large or immense 2 informal excellent or impressive **tremendously** adv

tremor (say trem-er) n 1 a shaking or trembling movement, a vibration 2 (also **earth tremor**) a slight earthquake 3 a sudden feeling of fear or excitement

tremulous (say trem-yoo-ləs) adj trembling from nervousness or weakness

trench n a long narrow ditch cut in the ground, often used for drainage or to give troops shelter from enemy fire **trench coat** n a belted double-breasted coat with pockets and flaps like those worn by soldiers

trenchant adj strong and effective

trend n 1 a general direction in which something is developing, a continuing tendency 2 a fashion **trendy** adj **trendier**, **trendiest** fashionable, following the latest trends **trendily** adv **trendiness** n **trendsetter** n a person who leads the way in fashion or ideas

trepidation (say trep-i-day-shən) n a state of nervous fear or anxiety

trespass v to enter a person's land or property without their authority **trespass** n 1 the act of trespassing 2 old use a sin or wrongdoing **trespasser** n

tress n a lock of a woman's hair

trestle n a board resting on two sets of sloping legs to form a table or working surface

tri- prefix three or triple (as in tricycle, triathlon)

triad (say **triy**-ad) *n* **1** a group or set of three **2** a Chinese secret organization involved in organized crime

trial *n* **1** the process of examining the evidence in a law court to determine whether an accused person has committed a crime **2** the process of testing the qualities or performance of something by trying it out **3** a person or thing that tests your patience or endurance **trial and error** the process of trying out different methods until you find the one most suitable

triangle *n* **1** a flat figure with three sides and three angles **2** something shaped like a triangle **3** a percussion instrument consisting of a steel rod bent into the shape of a triangle and struck with a small steel bar **triangular** *adj*

triangulation *n* (in surveying) the process of measuring or mapping out an area by means of calculations based on a network of triangles measured from a baseline

tribe *n* a traditional social division in some societies, consisting of a group of families living in one area as a community and sharing a common culture **tribal** *adj* to do with a tribe or tribes

tribulation (say trib-yoo-**lay**-shen) *n* great trouble or suffering, or something that causes this

tribunal (say triy-**bew**-nel) *n* a body of officials appointed to make certain judgements or settle certain disputes

tribune (say **trib**-yoon) *n* an official in ancient Rome chosen by the people to protect their interests

tributary *n pl* **tributaries** a river or stream that flows into a larger river or a lake

tribute *n* **1** something said, done, or given as a mark of respect or admiration **2** payment that one country or ruler paid to another, especially as a mark of dependence

trice *n* **in a trice** in an instant

triceratops (say triy-**se**-re-tops) *n* a large dinosaur with a huge head and two large horns, which fed on plants

trick *n* **1** a clever or cunning action intended to deceive or outwit someone **2** a mischievous or foolish practical joke **3** a deception or illusion ♦ *a trick of the light*

4 a skilful action done for entertainment ♦ *a conjuring trick* **5** a mannerism ♦ *He has a trick of tapping his fingers.* **6** the cards played in one round of a card game such as bridge or whist **trick** *v* to deceive or mislead someone by means of a trick **trickery** *n* **trickster** *n* a person who tricks or cheats people **tricky** *adj* **trickier**, **trickiest** **1** difficult or needing skill ♦ *a tricky job* **2** cunning or deceitful

trickle *v* **1** to flow or cause a liquid to flow in a thin stream **2** to move slowly or gradually **trickle** *n* a slow gentle flow

tricolour (say **trik**-el-er) *n* a flag with three coloured stripes, especially the national flags of France and Ireland

tricycle *n* a vehicle like a bicycle with two wheels at the back and one at the front

trident (say **triy**-dent) *n* a three-pronged spear

triennial (say triy-**en**-iel) *adj* **1** lasting for three years **2** happening every third year **triennially** *adv*

trifle *n* **1** something of little value or importance **2** a slight amount **3** a sweet food made of sponge cake and fruit with layers of jelly, custard, and cream **trifling** *adj* trivial or unimportant **to trifle with** to treat someone casually or without proper seriousness

trigger *n* a lever or catch that releases a spring to activate a mechanism, especially to fire a gun **trigger** *v* **1** to activate a mechanism **2** to cause something to start **trigger-happy** *adj* apt to fire a gun or take other action impulsively

trigonometry (say trig-en-**om**-itri) *n* the branch of mathematics dealing with the relationship of sides and angles of triangles

trike *n informal* a tricycle

trilateral (say triy-**lat**-er-el) *adj* **1** having or to do with three sides **2** between three people or groups ♦ *a trilateral agreement*

trilby *n pl* **trilbies** a man's soft felt hat with a narrow brim and a dent in the crown

trill *n* **1** a vibrating sound made by the voice or in birdsong **2** a quick alternation of two notes in music that are a tone or semitone apart **trill** *v* to sound or sing with a trill

trillion *n* **1** a million million **2** *old use* a

million million million **trillionth** *adj*, *n*

trilogy (say **tril**-əji) *n pl* **trilogies** a group of three novels, plays, or poems about the same people or on the same subject

trim *v* **trimmed**, **trimming** 1 to make something neat or smooth by cutting away unwanted or untidy parts 2 to remove or reduce something by cutting 3 to decorate a piece of clothing by adding decorations such as lace, ribbons, etc. 4 to arrange the sails of a boat to suit the wind 5 to make a boat or aircraft evenly balanced by arranging the position of its cargo or passengers or ballast **trim** *n* 1 how fit or in what condition a person or thing is ♦ *in good trim* 2 extra decoration on a piece of clothing or furniture 3 the colour or type of upholstery and other fittings in a car 4 the cutting or trimming of hair **trim** *adj* **trimmer**, **trimmest** neat and smart, having a smooth outline or compact structure **trimmer** *n* **trimming** *n* something added as an ornament or decoration on a piece of clothing or furniture **trimmings** *pl n* the usual accompaniments or extras

trimaran (say **triy**-mə-ran) *n* a yacht with three hulls side by side

trinity *n pl* **trinities** a group of three people or things **Trinity** *n* (in Christian belief) the three persons of the Godhead: Father, Son, and Holy Spirit

trinket *n* a small ornament or piece of jewellery that does not have much value

trio (say **tree**-oh) *n pl* **trios** 1 a group or set of three 2 a group of three musicians or singers 3 a piece of music for three musicians

trip *v* **tripped**, **tripping** 1 to catch your foot on something and stumble or fall, or to make someone do this 2 to move or dance with quick light steps 3 *informal* to have hallucinations caused by a drug **trip** *n* 1 a journey or excursion, especially for pleasure 2 *informal* an experience of hallucinations caused by a drug 3 an act of tripping or falling over 4 a device for activating a mechanism **tripper** *n* a person who goes on a pleasure trip **to trip someone up** 1 to make someone stumble 2 to show that someone has made a mistake

tripartite (say triy-**par**-tiyt) *adj* 1 consisting of three parts 2 involving three people or groups

tripe *n* 1 the part of the stomach of an ox used for food 2 *informal* nonsense or rubbish

triple *adj* 1 three times as much or three times as many 2 consisting of three things or parts 3 involving three people or groups **triple** *v* to make something, or become, three times as much or as many **triplet** *n* 1 each of three children or animals born at one birth 2 a set of three rhyming lines of verse **triply** *adv* **in triplicate** as three identical copies **triple jump** *n* an athletic event in which competitors make a hop, a step, and a long jump from a running start

tripod (say **triy**-pod) *n* a three-legged stand for a camera, surveying instrument, or other device

triptych (say **trip**-tik) *n* a picture or carving on three wooden panels, usually fixed or hinged side by side and used as an altarpiece

trite *adj* (said about a phrase or opinion) overused and having little meaning

triumph *n* a great success or victory **triumph** *v* 1 to be successful or victorious 2 to celebrate a success **triumphal** *adj* celebrating a triumph ♦ *a triumphal arch* **triumphant** *adj* 1 successful or victorious 2 celebrating a success **triumphantly** *adv*

triumvirate (say triy-**um**-ver-ət) *n* a group of three people having power or authority

trivet (say **triv**-it) *n* an iron stand for a kettle or pot placed over a fire

trivia *pl n* unimportant details or pieces of information **trivial** *adj* having little value or importance **triviality** *n*

troglodyte (say **trog**-lə-diyt) *n* a person living in a cave in ancient times

Trojan *adj* to do with or coming from ancient Troy in Asia minor (modern Turkey) **Trojan** *n* a person born or living in ancient Troy

troll[1] *n* (in folklore) an ugly dwarf or giant living in a cave or under a bridge

troll[2] *v* to fish by pulling a baited line along behind a boat

trolley *n pl* **trolleys** 1 a metal basket

or platform on wheels for carrying or moving things **2** a small table on wheels or castors for carrying food or drink indoors

trolleybus *n* an electrically powered bus with a roof pole that is connected to an overhead wire by means of a contact wheel

trollop *n old use* a promiscuous woman or prostitute

trombone *n* a large brass wind instrument with a sliding tube

troop *n* **1** a moving group of people or animals **2** a cavalry unit commanded by a captain, or a unit of artillery **3** a group of three or more Scout patrols **troop** *v* to assemble or move in large numbers **troops** *pl n* soldiers or armed forces **trooper** *n* a soldier in the cavalry or in an armoured unit

trophy *n pl* **trophies 1** a cup or other object given as a prize for victory or success **2** something taken in war or hunting as a souvenir of success

tropic *n* a line of latitude 23° 26' north of the equator (tropic of Cancer) or the same latitude south of it (tropic of Capricorn) **tropics** *pl n* the hot regions between these two latitudes **tropical** *adj* **1** to do with or located in the tropics **2** (said about the climate) hot and humid

trot *v* **trotted, trotting 1** (said about a horse) to go at a pace faster than a walk **2** *informal* to walk or go ♦ *I'll just trot round to the chemist.* **trot** *n* **1** the action of a horse when trotting **2** a slow gentle run **trotter** *n* **1** a pig's foot used for food **2** a horse of a special breed trained for trotting **to trot something out** *informal* to say something that has been said many times before

troubadour (say **troo**-bə-door) *n* a poet and singer in southern France in the 11th-13th centuries, singing mainly of chivalry and courtly love

trouble *n* **1** difficulty or misfortune **2** something that causes worry or difficulty **3** (often **troubles**) conflict or public unrest **4** (often **in trouble**) unpleasantness involving punishment or rebuke **5** bad functioning of a mechanism or of the body or mind ♦ *engine trouble* ♦ *stomach trouble* **trouble** *v* **1** to cause someone trouble

or difficulty **2** to disturb or interrupt someone ♦ *I'm sorry to trouble you.* **3** to be worried or inconvenienced ♦ *Please don't trouble about it.* **troublesome** *adj* causing trouble or difficulty **troublemaker** *n* someone who constantly causes trouble **troubleshooter** *n* someone employed to deal with faults in machinery or to act as a mediator in disputes

trough (say trof) *n* **1** a long narrow open container, especially one holding water or food for animals **2** a channel for liquid **3** a low part between two waves or ridges **4** an extended region of low atmospheric pressure

trounce *v* to defeat an opponent heavily

troupe (say troop) *n* a company of actors or other performers **trouper** *n* **1** a member of a theatrical troupe **2** someone who is reliable and supportive

trousers *pl n* a piece of clothing worn over the lower part of the body, with a separate part for each leg

trousseau (say **troo**-soh) *n* clothes and household belongings collected by a bride for her married life

trout *n pl* **trout** a freshwater fish that is caught as a sport and for food

trowel *n* **1** a small garden tool with a curved blade for lifting plants or scooping things **2** a small tool with a flat blade for spreading mortar, etc.

troy weight *n* a system of weights used for precious metals and gems

truant *n* a child who stays away from school without permission **to play truant** to stay away as a truant **truancy**

truce *n* an agreement to stop fighting for a time

truck[1] *n* **1** a lorry **2** an open railway wagon

truck[2] *n* **to have no truck with** to refuse to have anything to do with someone or something

truculent (say **truk**-yoo-lənt) *adj* defiant and aggressive **truculence** *n*

trudge *v* to walk slowly and heavily **trudge** *n* a slow heavy walk

true *adj* **1** in accordance with what has happened or is real **2** genuine and proper ♦ *He was the true heir.* **3** exact or accurate

♦ *a true voice* **4** loyal or faithful ♦ *She is a true friend.* **truism** *n* a statement that is obviously true but says very little, e.g. *Nothing lasts for ever* **truly** *adv* **1** in a truthful way **2** sincerely or genuinely ♦ *We are truly grateful.* **truth** *n* **1** the quality or state of being true **2** something that is true **truthful** *adj* **1** (said about a person) always telling the truth **2** true or accurate **truthfully** *adv* **truthfulness** *n*

truffle *n* **1** a soft sweet made of a chocolate mixture **2** a fungus that grows underground and is eaten as a delicacy because of its rich flavour

trug *n* a long shallow basket used in gardening

trump *n* a playing card of a suit temporarily ranking above others **trump** *v* to take a card or trick with a trump; to play a trump **to trump something up** to invent a false excuse or accusation **to turn up trumps** *informal* to turn out much better than expected

trumpet *n* a metal wind instrument with a bright ringing tone, consisting of a narrow straight or curved tube flared at the end **trumpet** *v* **trumpeted**, **trumpeting** **1** to proclaim something loudly **2** (said about an elephant) to make a loud resounding sound with its trunk **trumpeter** *n*

truncate (say trunk-**ayt**) *v* to shorten something by cutting off its top or end

truncheon (say **trun-**chən) *n* a short thick stick carried as a weapon by a police officer

trundle *v* to move along or roll something along heavily on a wheel or wheels

trunk *n* **1** the main stem of a tree **2** the long flexible nose of an elephant **3** a person's body apart from the head, arms, and legs **4** a large box with a hinged lid, used for transporting or storing clothes, etc. **trunks** *pl n* men's shorts, used especially for swimming or boxing **trunk call** *n* a long-distance telephone call within the same country **trunk road** *n* an important main road between large towns and cities

truss *n* **1** a framework of beams or bars supporting a roof or bridge, etc. **2** a padded belt or other device worn to support a hernia **truss** *v* to tie or bind a person or

thing securely

trust *n* **1** a firm belief that a person or thing is reliable, truthful, or honest **2** confident expectation **3** responsibility associated with a trust placed on someone ♦ *a position of trust* **4** a legal arrangement by which a person is given charge of money or property with instructions to use it for another person's benefit or for a specified purpose **5** an organization managed by trustees to promote or preserve something ♦ *a wildlife trust* **6** a large company or association of business firms formed to establish a monopoly or reduce competition **trust** *v* **1** to believe that a person or thing is reliable, truthful, or honest **2** to give something to someone for safe keeping **3** to hope ♦ *I trust you are well.* **trustee** *n* a person who has charge of money or property in trust for another **trustful** *adj* willing to trust people **trusty** *adj* **trustier**, **trustiest** reliable and trustworthy **trustworthy** *adj* worthy of trust, reliable

try *v* **tries**, **tried**, **trying** **1** to make an effort to do something, to attempt something **2** to use or test something to see how effective or satisfactory it is ♦ *Try sleeping on your back.* **3** to be a strain on a part of the body ♦ *Small print tries the eyes.* **4** to examine the accusations against someone in a law court **try** *n pl* **tries** **1** an attempt **2** (in rugby) an act of touching the ball down behind the opposing goal line, scoring points and entitling the scoring side to a kick at goal **trying** *adj* putting a strain on your temper or patience, annoying

tsar (say zah) *n* the title of an emperor of Russia before the Revolution of 1917

tsetse fly (say **tset-**si or **tet-**si) *n* a tropical African fly that transmits sleeping sickness or other diseases by its bite

T-shirt *n* a short-sleeved casual top having the shape of a T when spread out flat

tsunami (say tsoo-**nah-**mi) *n pl* **tsunami** or **tsunamis** a long high sea wave caused by an underwater earthquake

tub *n* a round open container with a flat bottom, used for washing or for holding liquids, soil for plants, etc. **tubby** *adj*

tubbier, tubbiest short and rather fat

tuba (say **tew**-bə) *n* a large brass wind instrument with a low pitch and deep tone

tube *n* **1** a long hollow piece of metal, plastic, rubber, glass, etc., especially for air or liquids to pass along **2** a container made of a flexible material with a screw cap **3** (**the tube**) *informal* the underground railway system in London **tubing** *n* tubes, or a length of tube **tubular** *adj* shaped like a tube or like tubes

tuber *n* a short thick rounded root (e.g. of a dahlia) or underground stem (e.g. of a potato)

tuberculosis (say tew-ber-kew-loh-sis) *n* an infectious disease of people and animals, affecting various parts of the body, especially the lungs, and causing swellings to appear on body tissue **tubercular** *adj*

tuck *v* **1** to put a flat fold in a piece of clothing or other material **2** to put or fold a loose end or edge into something to hide it or hold it in place **3** to put something away neatly or in a small space ♦ *Tuck this in your pocket.* **tuck** *n* **1** a flat fold stitched in a piece of clothing or other material **2** *informal* food, especially sweets and cakes, that children enjoy **to tuck in** *informal* to eat food heartily

Tudor *n* a member of the royal family of England from Henry VII to Elizabeth I **Tudor** *adj* **1** to do with the Tudors **2** imitating the style of houses, etc. of that period

Tuesday *n* the day of the week following Monday

tufa (say tew-fə) *n* **1** porous rock formed round mineral springs **2** rock formed from volcanic ashes

tuft *n* a bunch of threads, grass, feathers, or hair, etc. held or growing close together **tufted** *adj*

tug *v* **tugged, tugging** to pull something vigorously or with great effort **tug** *n* **1** a hard or sudden pull **2** (also **tugboat**) a small powerful boat for towing large ships **tug of war** *n* a contest between two teams tugging a rope from opposite ends until one team manages to pull the other across a line

tuition (say tew-**ish**-ən) *n* the process of teaching, instruction

tulip *n* a garden plant growing from a bulb, with a large cup-shaped flower on a tall stem

tulle (say tewl) *n* a fine silky net material

tumble *v* **1** to fall or roll over suddenly or clumsily, or to make someone or something do this **2** to fall suddenly in value or amount **3** to rumple or disarrange something **tumble** *n* a tumbling fall **tumbler** *n* **1** a drinking glass with straight sides and no handle or stem **2** a part of a lock that holds the bolt until it is lifted by the action of a key **3** an acrobat **tumbledown** *adj* falling into ruins, dilapidated **tumble-dryer** *n* a machine that dries washing by rotating it in a drum through which heated air passes **to tumble to** *informal* to realize what something means

tumescent (say tew-**mess**-ənt) *adj* swollen or swelling **tumescence** *n*

tummy *n pl* **tummies** *informal* the stomach

tumour (say **tew**-mer) *n* a swelling in the body, caused by an abnormal growth of tissue

tumult (say **tew**-mult) *n* **1** a loud confused noise made by a crowd of people **2** a state of confusion **tumultuous** *adj* **1** making a loud confused noise **2** excited or confused

tun *n* a large cask for wine or beer

tuna (say **tew**-nə) *n pl* **tuna** a large sea fish with pink flesh, used for food

tundra *n* a vast level Arctic region of Europe, Asia, and North America, where the soil under the surface is always frozen

tune *n* a pleasant sequence of musical notes, a melody **tune** *v* **1** to put a musical instrument in tune **2** to adjust a radio or television set to receive a certain channel **3** to adjust an engine to run smoothly **tuneful** *adj* having a pleasing tune **tunefully** *adv* **tuneless** *adj* **tuner** *n* **1** a person who tunes a piano or other musical instrument **2** a unit for receiving radio broadcasts **tuning fork** *n* a steel device with two prongs, which when struck vibrates to produce a note of fixed pitch (usually middle C) **in tune** playing or singing at the correct musical pitch **out of**

tune not playing or singing in tune

tungsten (say **tung**-stən) n a heavy grey metal and chemical element (symbol W), used for making the filaments of electric lamps and for making a kind of steel

tunic n 1 a loose sleeveless piece of clothing reaching the hips or knees 2 a close-fitting short coat worn as part of a uniform

tunnel n an underground passage built through a hill or under a building, or made by a burrowing animal **tunnel** v **tunnelled**, **tunnelling** to make a tunnel through something

tunny n pl **tunny** or **tunnies** another word for *tuna*

turban n a man's headdress made by wrapping a strip of cloth round a cap, worn especially by Muslims and Sikhs

turbid adj 1 (said about a liquid) muddy, not clear 2 confused or obscure ♦ *a turbid imagination*

turbine (say **ter**-biyn) n a machine or motor driven by a wheel or rotor that is turned by a flow of water or gas **turbocharger**, **turbo** n a supercharger driven by a turbine that is powered by the engine's exhausts **turbofan** n a jet engine equipped with a turbine-driven fan for additional thrust **turboprop** n a jet engine in which a turbine is used to drive a propeller

turbot n pl **turbot** or **turbots** a large flat sea fish used for food

turbulent (say **ter**-bew-lənt) adj 1 (said about air or water) moving violently and unevenly 2 confused or unruly **turbulence** n

tureen (say tewr-een) n a deep dish with a lid, for serving soup at a table

turf n pl **turfs** or **turves** 1 short grass and earth round its roots 2 a piece of this cut from the ground 3 (**the turf**) horse racing **turf** v to cover a surface with turf **to turf someone** or **something out** informal to get rid of someone or something

turgid (say **ter**-jid) adj 1 swollen and thick 2 (said about language or style) tedious and pompous

Turk n a person born in Turkey in Asia Minor and SE Europe, or descended from people born there **Turkish** adj to do with or coming from Turkey **Turkish** n the language of Turkey **Turkish bath** n a kind of bath in which the whole body is exposed to hot air or steam to induce sweating, followed by washing **Turkish delight** n a sweet made from flavoured gelatine coated in powdered sugar

turkey n pl **turkeys** a large game bird kept for its meat

turmeric (say **ter**-mer-ik) n a bright yellow powder obtained from a plant of the ginger family, used in cookery for flavouring and colouring

turmoil (say **ter**-moil) n a state of great disturbance or confusion

turn v 1 to move or make something move round a point or axis 2 to change or make something change its position so that a different side is on top or in front 3 to take a new direction or make something do this ♦ *Turn left at the lights.* 4 to pass a certain time or age ♦ *She turned eighteen last week.* 5 to change something or become changed in nature, form, or appearance ♦ *The caterpillar will turn into a chrysalis.* ♦ *She turned pale at the news.* 6 (said about milk) to become sour 7 to shape something in a lathe **turn** n 1 an act of turning or of being turned, a turning movement 2 a bend or curve in a road, river, etc. 3 a change of direction or condition 4 an opportunity or obligation to do something that comes to each of a number of people or things in succession ♦ *It's my turn to pay.* 5 a short performance in an entertainment 6 informal a short feeling of shock or illness ♦ *He had a funny turn.* **turner** n a person who makes things on a lathe **turning** n a place where one road meets another, forming a corner **turncoat** n a person who abandons one party or group in order to support an opposing one **turnkey** n pl **turnkeys** old use a jailer **turn-off** n 1 a junction at which a road leaves another 2 something that puts you off; a disincentive **turnover** n 1 the amount of money a business takes in a particular period 2 the rate at which workers leave and are replaced 3 a small pie in which a piece of pastry is folded over a filling **turnpike** n a road on which a toll was charged **turnstile** n a mechanical gate with barriers that revolve to allow people through one at a time **turntable** n a circular revolving platform or support, e.g. for the record in a record player **to turn out** to happen in the end ♦ *We'll see how things turn out.* **to turn someone in** to hand someone over to the authorities **to turn someone on** *informal* to make someone interested or excited **to turn something down 1** to adjust a device to reduce the volume, heat, etc. **2** to reject an offer or application **to turn something off** to use a control to stop a device from operating **to turn something on** to use a control to start a device operating **to turn something out** to turn off an electric light **to turn something up** to adjust a device to increase the volume, heat, etc. **to turn up** to appear or be discovered in the end

turnip n a plant with a round white root used as a vegetable

turpentine (say ter-pən-tiyn) n an oil made from the resin of certain trees, used for thinning paint, cleaning brushes, etc.

turpitude (say ter-pi-tewd) n *formal* wickedness

turps n *informal* short for *turpentine*

turquoise (say ter-kwoiz) n **1** a bright blue precious stone **2** a bright or greenish blue colour

turret n **1** a small tower on a castle or other building or wall **2** a rotating structure protecting a gun and gunners in a ship, aircraft, fort, or tank **turreted** *adj*

turtle n a sea creature like a tortoise, with flippers used in swimming **turtle dove** n a wild dove with a soft cooing call **turtleneck** n a high round close-fitting neck on a knitted top **to turn turtle** (said about a boat) to turn upside down in the water

tusk n a long pointed tooth, one of a pair that project from the mouth of an elephant, walrus, etc.

tussle n a struggle or conflict **tussle** v to take part in a tussle

tussock n a tuft or clump of grass

tut v **tuts, tutting, tutted** to make a sound with the tongue that show that you are annoyed or disapprove of something

tutelage (say tew-til-ij) n **1** guardianship or protection of someone or something **2** instruction or tuition

tutor n **1** a private teacher, especially of one pupil or a small group **2** a university teacher responsible for a number of students **tutor** v to teach or be a tutor to someone **tutorial** n a period of tuition given by a university or college tutor

tutu (say too-too) pl **tutus** a ballet dancer's short skirt made of layers of stiffened frills

TV abbr television

twaddle n *informal* nonsense

twain adj, n old use two

twang n **1** a sharp ringing sound like that made by a tense wire when plucked **2** a nasal intonation in speech **twang** v to make or cause something to make a twang; to play a guitar, etc. by plucking the strings

tweak v **1** to pinch and twist something with a quick sharp jerk **2** to improve something by making fine adjustments **tweak** n a sharp twist or pull

twee adj affectedly quaint or pretty

tweed n a thick woollen cloth, often woven of mixed colours

tweet v to make the chirp of a small bird **tweet** n a tweeting sound

tweezers pl n small pincers for picking up or pulling very small things

twelve adj, n the number 12, one more than eleven **twelfth** adj, n **1** next after eleventh **2** one of twelve equal parts of a thing

twenty adj, n pl **twenties** the number 20, equal to two times ten **twentieth** adj, n

twice adv **1** two times, on two occasions **2** double the amount or degree ♦ *twice as strong*

twiddle v to turn or fiddle with something aimlessly **to twiddle your thumbs** to have nothing to do

twig¹ n a small shoot on a branch or stem of a tree or shrub

twig² **twigged, twigging** *informal* to come to realize what something means

twilight n dim light from the sky after sunset

twill n cloth that is woven to produce a surface pattern of diagonal lines

twin *n* either of two children or animals born at one birth **twin** *v* **twinned**, **twinning** to put things together as a pair

twine *n* strong thread or string made of two or more strands twisted together **twine** *v* to twist or wind one thing round another

twinge *n* a sudden short pain

twinkle *v* to shine with a light that flickers rapidly, to sparkle **twinkle** *n* a twinkling light

twirl *v* to spin round lightly or rapidly, or to make something do this **twirl** *n* a twirling movement

twist *v* **1** to turn the ends of something in opposite directions **2** to wrench something out of its normal shape ♦ *a heap of twisted metal* **3** to wind threads or strands round something, or round each other to form a single cord **4** to take a spiral or winding form or course ♦ *The road twisted through the hills.* **5** to rotate or revolve round something that is not moving, or to make something do this **6** to distort the meaning of something ♦ *Don't try to twist my words.* **twist** *n* **1** the action or movement of twisting or being twisted **2** something formed by twisting, a turn in a twisting course **3** a strange or unexpected development in a series of events **twister** *n*

twit[1] *v* **twitted**, **twitting** *informal* to taunt someone

twit[2] *n informal* a silly or foolish person

twitch *v* **1** to pull something with a light jerk **2** to move with a jerk or series of jerks **twitch** *n* a twitching movement **twitchy** *adj* **twitchier**, **twitchiest** **1** twitching a lot **2** nervous or agitated

twitter *v* **1** to make a series of quick chirping sounds **2** to talk quickly in an anxious or nervous way **twitter** *n* a twittering sound

two *adj*, *n* the number 2, one more than one **twosome** *n* two people together, a couple or pair **two-dimensional** *adj* having the two dimensions of length and breadth **two-faced** *adj* insincere or deceitful **two-time** *v* to be unfaithful to someone

tycoon *n* a wealthy and influential business person or industrialist

tyke *n* an annoying or mischievous person, especially a child

type *n* **1** a class or sort of people or things with the same characteristics **2** *informal* a person of specified character or nature ♦ *brainy types* **3** printed characters or letters **type** *v* **1** to classify people or things according to their type **2** to write something with a typewriter or word processor **typist** *n* a person who types letters and documents, especially in an office **typography** *n* **1** the art or process of printing **2** the style or appearance of printed matter **typographical** *adj*

typecast *v* past tense and past participle **typecast** to choose an actor to play a role that is like them in character **typeface** *n* a set of printing types of one design **typescript** *n* a typed copy of a text or document **typesetting** *n* arranging type for printing **typesetter** *n* **typewriter** *n* a manual or electronic machine with keys for producing characters like print

typhoid fever *n* a serious infectious disease with fever, caused by harmful bacteria taken into the body in food or drink

typhoon (say tiy-**foon**) *n* a violent hurricane in the western Pacific or East Asian seas

typhus *n* an infectious disease with fever, weakness, and a rash on the body

typical *adj* **1** having the usual qualities of a particular type of person or thing ♦ *a typical suburban house* **2** characteristic of a person ♦ *He answered with typical curtness.* **typically** *adv* **typify** *v* **typifies**, **typified**, **typifying** to be a representative specimen of someone or something

tyrannosaurus (say ti-ran-ə-sor-us) *n* a dinosaur (also called *Tyrannosaurus rex*) that walked on its hind legs and fed on flesh

tyrant (say **tiy**-rənt) *n* a person who rules or uses authority harshly or cruelly **tyrannical** *adj* **tyrannically** *adv* **tyrannize** *v* to behave like a tyrant to people **tyranny** *n pl* **tyrannies** **1** government by a tyrannical ruler **2** oppressive use of power, like that of a tyrant

tyre *n* a rubber covering, usually filled with air, fitted round the rim of a wheel to make it grip the road and run smoothly

tyro (say **tiy**-roh) *n pl* **tyros** a beginner or novice

Uu

U[1] the twenty-first letter of the English alphabet

U[2] *abbr* (in film classification) universal

ubiquitous (say yoo-**bik**-wit-əs) *adj* found everywhere

U-boat *n* a German submarine, especially of the kind used in the Second World War

udder *n* a bag-like milk-producing organ of a cow, ewe, female goat, etc., with two or more teats

UFO *n pl* **UFOS** a mysterious object seen in the sky, especially one believed to be a vehicle piloted by beings from outer space

ugly *adj* **uglier, ugliest 1** unpleasant to look at or to hear **2** hostile and threatening; likely to be unpleasant **ugliness** *n*

UK *abbr* United Kingdom

ukulele (say yoo-kə-**lay**-li) *n* a small four-stringed guitar

ulcer *n* an open sore on the surface of the body or one of its organs **ulcerate** *v* **ulceration** *n*

ulterior *adj* beyond what is obvious or admitted ♦ *She had some ulterior motive in coming to see me.*

ultimate *adj* **1** furthest in a series of things; last or final ♦ *Our ultimate destination is London.* **2** being the best or most extreme example of something ♦ *the ultimate accolade* **3** basic or fundamental ♦ *the ultimate cause* **ultimately** *adv*

ultimatum (say ulti-**may**-təm) *n pl* **ultimatums** a final demand or statement of terms, rejection of which will lead to the ending of friendly relations or to hostile action

ultra- *prefix* **1** beyond (as in *ultraviolet*) **2** extremely, excessively (as in *ultra-conservative, ultra-modern*)

ultramarine (say ultrə-mə-**reen**) *n, adj* bright deep blue

ultrasonic (say ultrə-**sonn**-ik) *adj* to do with sound waves with a frequency that is above the upper limit of normal human hearing

ultrasound *n* **1** sound with an ultrasonic frequency, used in medical examinations **2** an examination of an internal part of the body, especially a fetus, using ultrasound; an image produced by this

ultraviolet *adj* (said about radiation) having a wavelength that is slightly shorter than that of visible light rays at the violet end of the spectrum

umber *n* a natural pigment like ochre but darker and browner

umbilical (say um-**bil**-ikəl) *adj* to do with the navel **umbilical cord** *n* the flexible tube of tissue connecting the placenta to the navel of the fetus and carrying nourishment to the fetus while it is in the womb

umbra *n pl* **umbrae** (say **um**-bree) or *pl* **umbras** the dark central part of the shadow cast by the earth or the moon in an eclipse, or of a sunspot

umbrage (say **um**-brij) *n* **to take umbrage** to take offence

umbrella *n* **1** a circular piece of fabric stretched over a folding frame of spokes attached to a central stick used as a handle, or a central pole, which you open to protect yourself from rain **2** a thing that includes or contains many different parts ♦ *an umbrella organization*

umlaut (say **uum**-lowt) *n* a mark (¨) placed over a vowel in German to show a change in its pronunciation

umpire *n* a person appointed to see that the rules of a game or contest are followed and to settle any disputes that arise **umpire** *v* to act as an umpire in a game or match

umpteen *adj informal* very many **umpteenth** *adj*

UN *abbr* United Nations

un- *prefix* **1** not (as in *uncertain*) **2** reversing the action indicated by a verb (as in *unlock*) ◊ The number of words with this prefix is almost unlimited, and many of those whose meaning is obvious are not listed below.

unable *adj* not able to do something

unaccountable *adj* **1** unable to be explained or accounted for ♦ *for some unaccountable reason* **2** not required to account for your actions **unaccountably** *adv*

unadulterated *adj* pure; not mixed with

things that are less good

unanimous (say yoo-**nan**-im-əs) adj with everyone agreeing ♦ a unanimous decision **unanimity** n **unanimously** adv

unassuming adj not arrogant or pretentious

unattached adj 1 not attached to another thing, person, or organization 2 not married or in a relationship

unattended adj (said about a vehicle, piece of baggage, etc.) having no person in charge of it

unaware adj having no knowledge of something **unawares** adv unexpectedly; without warning ♦ His question caught me unawares.

unbalanced adj 1 not balanced 2 mentally disordered or irrational

unbearable adj not able to be endured or tolerated **unbearably** adv

unbeknown, **unbeknownst** adj without someone knowing about or being aware of it

unbelievable adj 1 unlikely to be true 2 extraordinary **unbelievably** adv

unbeliever n a person who has no religious belief

unbending adj inflexible, refusing to alter your demands

unbidden adj not commanded or invited

unborn adj not yet born

unbounded adj having no limits

unbridled adj not controlled or restrained ♦ unbridled rage

unburden v **to unburden yourself** to tell someone your secrets or problems so that you feel better

uncalled-for adj not necessary or deserved

uncanny adj **uncannier**, **uncanniest** strange and difficult to explain **uncannily** adv

unceremonious adj 1 without proper formality or ceremony 2 offhand, abrupt, or rude **unceremoniously** adv

uncertain adj 1 not known certainly 2 not completely confident or sure about something 3 not to be depended on, not reliable ♦ His aim is rather uncertain. **uncertainty** n

uncle n the brother of your father or mother or the husband of your aunt

uncomfortable adj 1 not comfortable 2 feeling or causing unease ♦ an uncomfortable silence **uncomfortably** adv

uncommon adj out of the ordinary, unusual

uncompromising (say un-**kom**-prə-miy-zing) adj not willing to make a compromise, inflexible

unconditional adj not subject to any conditions or limitations ♦ unconditional surrender **unconditionally** adv

unconscionable (say un-**kon**-shən-əbəl) adj formal 1 unscrupulous 2 unreasonable or excessive

unconscious adj 1 not conscious, not aware 2 done or said, etc. without you realizing it ♦ unconscious humour **unconscious** n the unconscious mind, the part of the mind which is not normally accessible to the conscious mind but which affects behaviour **unconsciously** adv **unconsciousness** n

unconstitutional adj not in accordance with the constitution of a country, etc.

uncontrollable adj not able to be controlled or stopped **uncontrollably** adv

uncouth (say un-**kooth**) adj rude and rough in manner, boorish

uncover v 1 to remove the covering from something 2 to discover, reveal, or expose something ♦ They uncovered a plot to kill the president.

unction (say **unk**-shən) n 1 formal anointing with oil, especially in a religious ceremony for consecration or healing 2 pretended earnestness; excessive politeness

unctuous (say **unk**-tew-əs) adj polite and charming in an exaggerated and insincere way **unctuously** adv **unctuousness** n

undecided adj 1 not yet settled or certain ♦ The point is still undecided. 2 not yet having made up your mind

undeniable adj impossible to deny, undoubtedly true **undeniably** adv

under prep 1 below or beneath ♦ Hide it under the table. 2 less than ♦ children under 5 years old 3 lower in rank than ♦ No one under a bishop can attend. 4 governed or controlled by ♦ The country prospered under his rule. 5 undergoing a process ♦ The road is under repair. 6 in accordance with ♦ It is permissible under our agreement.

7 subject to ♦ *He is under contract to our firm.* **8** in view of ♦ *Under the circumstances, I think you had better leave.* **9** known by ♦ *Charles Dodgson wrote under the name 'Lewis Carroll'.* **10** in the category of ♦ *File it under 'miscellaneous'.* **under** *adv* **1** in or to a lower position or subordinate condition ♦ *Slowly the diver went under.* **2** in or into a state of unconsciousness **3** below a certain quantity, rank, or age, etc. ♦ *children of five and under* **under way** in motion or in progress

under- *prefix* **1** below or beneath (as in *underwear*) **2** lower or subordinate (as in *undermanager*) **3** insufficient, incompletely (as in *undercooked*) **underachieve** *v* to do less well than was expected, especially in school work **underachiever** *n* **under age** *adj* not old enough, especially for some legal right; not yet of adult status **underarm** *adj, adv* **1** (in cricket, etc.) bowling or bowled with the hand brought forward and upwards and not raised above shoulder level **2** (in tennis) with the racket moved similarly **3** in or for the armpit **undercarriage** *n* an aircraft's landing wheels and their supports **underclass** *n* the lowest social group in a community, consisting of the poor and the unemployed **underclothes** *pl n* **n** underwear **undercoat** *n* a layer of paint under a finishing coat; the paint used for this **undercover** *adj, adv* done or working in secret, especially when this involves spying or police work **undercurrent** *n* **1** a current that is below a surface or below another current **2** an underlying feeling or influence ♦ *an undercurrent of fear* **undercut** *v* past tense and past participle **undercut**; **undercutting 1** to sell something or work for a lower price than another person does **2** to cut away the part below **underdog** *n* a person or team that is expected to lose a contest or struggle **underdone** *adj* (said about food) not completely cooked throughout **underestimate** *v* to estimate something to be smaller or less important than it really is **underestimate** *n* an estimate that is too low **underfoot** *adv* on the ground,

under your feet **undergarment** *n* a piece of underwear **undergo** *v* **undergoes**, **underwent**, **undergone**, **undergoing** to experience or be subjected to something **undergraduate** *n* a student at a university who has not yet taken a degree **underground** *adv* **1** under the surface of the ground **2** done or working in secret; into secrecy or hiding **underground** *adj* **3** under the surface of the ground **4** secret or hidden; to do with a secret political organization or one for resisting enemy forces controlling a country **underground** *n* **5** an underground railway **6** an underground organization **undergrowth** *n* shrubs and bushes, etc. growing closely, especially under trees **underhand** *adj* done or doing things in a secret or dishonest way **underlay** *n* a layer of material, e.g. felt or rubber, laid under a carpet as a protection or support **underlie** *v* **underlay**, **underlain**, **underlying 1** to lie or be situated under something **2** to be the cause or basis of something ♦ *It is a theme that underlies much of her work.* **underline** *v* **1** to draw a line under a word, etc. **2** to emphasize something **underling** *n* a person working under someone's authority or control; a subordinate **underlying** *adj* basic or hidden ♦ *the underlying reasons for her behaviour* **undermine** *v* to damage or weaken something gradually ♦ *His confidence was undermined.* **underneath** *prep* below or beneath; on the inside of something **underneath** *adv* at, in, or to a position underneath something **underpants** *pl n* a piece of men's underwear covering the lower part of the body and part of the legs **underpass** *n* a road or tunnel that passes under another road or a railway **underpin** *v* **underpinned**, **underpinning 1** to support or form the basis for something **2** to strengthen something from below **underprivileged** *adj* less privileged than others, having less than the normal standard of living or rights in a community **underrate** *v* to have too low an opinion of a person or thing **underscore** *v* to underline something **underside** *adj* the side or surface underneath **undersigned** *adj* who has or have signed at the bottom of this document ♦ *We, the undersigned, wish to protest.* **undersized** *adj* of less than the normal size **underskirt** *n* a skirt worn beneath another, a petticoat **understate** *v* **1** to state a thing in very restrained terms **2** to represent something as being less than it really is **understatement** *n* **understudy** *n pl* **understudies** an actor who learns a part in order to be able to play it if the usual actor is ill or absent **undertake** *v* **undertook**, **undertaken 1** to make yourself responsible for doing something and start to do it ♦ *She volunteered to undertake the mission.* **2** to agree or promise that you will do something ♦ *He undertook to pay all the money back by the end of the year.* **undertaker** *v* a person whose job is to prepare the dead for burial or cremation and make arrangements for funerals **undertaking** *n* **1** a job or task that is being undertaken **2** a promise or guarantee **undertone** *n* **1** a low or quiet tone ♦ *They spoke in undertones.* **2** an underlying quality or feeling ♦ *His letter has a threatening undertone.* **undertow** *n* a current below the surface of the sea, moving in an opposite direction to the surface current **underwater** *adj* situated, used, or done beneath the surface of water **underwear** *n* clothes worn under other clothes next to the skin **underweight** *adj* weighing less than is normal, desirable, or allowed **underworld** *n* **1** (in mythology) the place for the spirits of the dead, under the earth **2** the part of society regularly involved in crime **underwrite** *v* **underwrote**, **underwritten 1** to sign and accept liability under an insurance policy, thus guaranteeing payment in the event of loss or damage **2** to undertake to finance an enterprise

understand *v* past tense and past participle **understood 1** to know the meaning of words or what someone says **2** to realize how or why something happens or why it is important ♦ *Do you understand how computers work?* ♦ *I don't understand what all the fuss is about.* **3** to know what someone is like and why they behave as they do; to

sympathize with how someone feels ♦ *She doesn't understand children.* ♦ *Believe me, I understand the difficulty of your position.* **4** to know the explanation and not be offended ♦ *We shall understand if you can't come.* **5** to have been told something or to draw a conclusion from the information you have ♦ *I understand that you want to speak to me.* **6** to take something for granted ♦ *Your expenses will be paid, that's understood.* **understandable** *adj* **understandably** *adv* **understanding** *n* **1** the ability to understand something **2** an informal agreement or arrangement ♦ *I thought we had reached an understanding.* **understanding** *adj* having or showing sympathy towards other people's feelings and points of view

undies *pl n informal* underwear

undo *v* **undid**, **undone**, **undoing 1** to unfasten, untie, or loosen something **2** to cancel or reverse the effect of something ♦ *She has undone all our careful work.* **undoing** *n* a person's ruin or downfall, or the cause of this **undone** *adj*

undoubted *adj* not regarded as doubtful, not questioned or disputed **undoubtedly** *adv*

undress *v* to take off your clothes or the clothes of another person **undress** *n* the state of being naked or not fully clothed

undue *adj* excessive, more than is appropriate **unduly** *adv*

undulate (say un-dew-layt) *v* to move like a wave or waves; to have a wavy appearance **undulation** *n*

undying *adj* lasting forever ♦ *You have my undying gratitude.*

unearth *v* **1** to uncover or obtain something from the ground by digging **2** to find something by searching or investigation

unearthly *adj* **1** unnatural or mysterious, especially in a frightening way **2** *informal* unreasonably early or inconvenient ♦ *We had to get up at an unearthly hour.*

uneasy *adj* **uneasier**, **uneasiest 1** worried or anxious **2** not comfortable **uneasily** *adv* **uneasiness** *n*

unemployed *adj* without a paid job **unemployment** *n*

unencumbered *adj* **1** not having a burden **2** free of debt or other financial liability

unequivocal (say un-i-**kwiv**-əkəl) *adj* clear and unmistakable, not at all ambiguous **unequivocally** *adv*

unerring *adj* making no mistake ♦ *with unerring accuracy*

uneven *adj* **1** not level or smooth **2** not regular or uniform ♦ *an uneven rhythm* **3** not equally balanced ♦ *an uneven contest* **unevenly** *adv* **unevenness** *n*

unexceptional *adj* not exceptional, quite ordinary

unexpected *adj* not expected **unexpectedly** *adv* **unexpectedness** *n*

unfailing *adj* constant or reliable ♦ *his unfailing good humour*

unfair *adj* not based on or showing fairness; unjust **unfairly** *adv* **unfairness** *n*

unfaithful *adj* **1** not loyal or trustworthy **2** not sexually loyal to your partner **unfaithfully** *adv* **unfaithfulness** *n*

unfeeling *adj* unsympathetic, not caring about other people's feelings

unfit *adj* **1** unsuitable for something **2** not in good physical condition because you do not take enough exercise

unflappable *adj informal* remaining calm in a crisis, not getting into a flap

unfold *v* **1** to open or spread a thing out or become opened or spread out **2** to reveal something or become known slowly

unforeseen *adj* not predicted or anticipated

unforgettable *adj* highly memorable

unfortunate *adj* **1** having bad luck, unlucky **2** unsuitable or regrettable ♦ *an unfortunate choice of words* **unfortunately** *adv*

unfounded *adj* not based on facts

unfurl *v* to unroll something or spread it out ♦ *They unfurled a large flag.*

ungainly *adj* awkward-looking or clumsy **ungainliness** *n*

ungodly *adj* **1** not religious **2** *informal* unreasonably early or inconvenient ♦ *Why are you phoning me at this ungodly hour?* **ungodliness** *n*

ungrateful *adj* feeling no gratitude **ungratefully** *adj*

unguarded *adj* **1** not guarded **2** without thought or caution, careless ♦ *in an unguarded moment*

unguent (say ung-gwənt) *n* an ointment or lubricant

unhappy *adj* **unhappier**, **unhappiest 1** not happy; sad or depressed **2** unfortunate or unsuitable ♦ *an unhappy coincidence* **unhappily** *adv* **unhappiness** *n*

unhealthy *adj* **unhealthier**, **unhealthiest 1** in poor health **2** harmful to health **3** unwise or dangerous **unhealthily** *adv* **unhealthiness** *n*

unheard-of *adj* not previously known of or done

unhinge *v* to cause a person's mind to become unbalanced

unholy *adj* **unholier**, **unholiest 1** wicked or unnatural **2** *informal* very great, dreadful ♦ *Stop making that unholy row.*

uni- *prefix* one; single (as in *unicorn*)

unicorn *n* a mythical animal resembling a horse with a single straight horn growing from its forehead

unicycle *n* a cycle with a single wheel

uniform *n* the distinctive clothing worn to identify the wearer as a member of a certain organization, group, school, etc. **uniform** *adj* always the same, not varying **uniformity** *n* **uniformly** *adv*

unify *v* **unifies**, **unified**, **unifying** to make a number of things into a single unit; to form into a single unit **unification** *n*

unilateral (say yoo-ni-**lat**-ərəl) *adj* done by or affecting only one person, group, country, etc. **unilateralism** *n* **unilaterally** *adv*

uninspired *adj* **1** dull, not imaginative **2** not filled with excitement

uninstall *v* *ICT* to remove an installed program or file from a computer

unintelligible *adj* impossible to understand **unintelligibly** *adv*

union *n* **1** the joining of things together; uniting or being united **2** a whole formed by uniting parts **3** an association of people with a common purpose **4** a trade union

unionist *n* **1** a member of a trade union **2** (in specific uses **Unionist**) a person who wishes to unite one country with another **unionism** *n* **unionize** *v* to organize into a trade union or cause people to join a trade union **Union Jack** *n* the national flag of the United Kingdom

unique (say yoo-**neek**) *adj* **1** being the only one of its kind ♦ *This vase is unique.* **2** *informal* remarkable or unusual ♦ *This makes it even more unique.* **uniquely** *adv*

unisex (say **yoo**-ni-seks) *adj* designed to be suitable for both sexes

unison *n* **in unison 1** speaking, singing, or doing something together at the same time **2** in agreement or concord ♦ *All the firms acted in unison.*

unit *n* **1** a quantity chosen as a standard in terms of which other quantities may be expressed or measured ♦ *Centimetres are units of length.* **2** an individual thing, person, or group regarded as single and complete, or as part of a complex whole ♦ *the family as the unit of society* **3** a piece of furniture as fitting with others like it or made of complementary parts **4** any whole number less than 10 **unitary** *adj* **unit trust** *n* an investment company investing contributions from a number of people in various securities and paying them a dividend (calculated on the average return from these) in proportion to their holdings

unite *v* **1** to join things or be joined together, to make things into or become a single unit or whole **2** to agree or cooperate ♦ *They all united in condemning the action.* **unity** *n pl* **unities 1** the state of being one or a unit **2** harmony, agreement in feelings, ideas, or aims, etc.

universe *n* everything that exists, including the whole of space and all the stars, planets, etc. in it **universal** *adj* to do with, including, or done by everyone or everything **universally** *adv*

university *n pl* **universities** an educational institution that provides instruction and facilities for research in many branches of advanced learning and awards degrees

unkempt *adj* looking untidy or neglected

unkind *adj* not kind, harsh **unkindly** *adv* **unkindness** *n*

unknown *adj* not known, not identified **unknown** *n* an unknown person or thing

unleaded *adj* (said about petrol) without added lead

unleash *v* **1** to set a dog free from a leash **2** to release something so it is no longer under restraint

unleavened (say un-**lev**-ənd) *adj* (said about bread) made without yeast or other raising agent

unless *conjunction* if not, except when ♦ *Don't move unless I say so.*

unlike *prep* **1** not like, different from ♦ *This is unlike anything I've ever read before.* ♦ *Unlike her mother, she enjoys shopping.* **2** not typical of ♦ *It's unlike you to be so gloomy.* **unlike** *adj* not alike, different ♦ *The two children are very unlike.*

unlikely *adj* **unlikelier, unlikeliest 1** not likely to be true ♦ *an unlikely tale* **2** not likely to happen

unload *v* **1** to remove a load from someone or something; to remove goods from a vehicle, ship, etc. **2** to get rid of something **3** to remove ammunition from a gun or film from a camera

unlucky *adj* **unluckier, unluckiest 1** bringing or resulting from bad luck **2** having bad luck **unluckily** *adv*

unmanned *adj* operated without a crew ♦ *an unmanned spacecraft*

unmarked *adj* **1** not marked; with no mark of identification **2** not noticed

unmask *v* **1** to remove a person's mask or disguise **2** to expose the true character of something

unmentionable *adj* too bad, embarrassing, or shocking to be spoken about

unmistakable *adj* clear and obvious, not able to be mistaken for anything else **unmistakably** *adv*

unmitigated (say un-**mit**-i-gayt-id) *adj* absolute, not modified at all ♦ *an unmitigated disaster*

unnatural *adj* **1** not natural or normal **2** artificial, not spontaneous **unnaturally** *adv*

unnecessary *adj* **1** not necessary **2** more than is necessary ♦ *with unnecessary care* **unnecessarily** *adv*

unnerve *v* to make someone lose courage or determination **unnerving** *adj*

unobtrusive (say un-əb-**troo**-siv) *adj*

not obtrusive, not attracting attention **unobtrusively** adv

unorthodox adj not generally accepted

unpack v to open and remove the contents of a suitcase, etc.; to take something out from its packaging or from a suitcase, etc.

unpaid adj **1** (said about a debt) not yet paid **2** not receiving payment for work done

unparalleled adj not paralleled, never yet equalled ♦ unparalleled enthusiasm

unpick v to undo the stitching of something

unpleasant adj not pleasant **unpleasantly** adv **unpleasantness** n

unplug v **unplugged**, **unplugging 1** to disconnect an electrical device by removing its plug from the socket **2** to remove an obstacle or blockage from something

unpopular adj not liked or popular **unpopularity** n **unpopularly** adv

unprecedented (say un-**press**-i-dent-id) adj never done or known before

unpretentious (say un-pri-**ten**-shəs) adj not pretentious, not showy or pompous

unprincipled adj acting without good moral principles

unprofessional adj not worthy of a member of a profession; contrary to professional standards of behaviour **unprofessionally** adv

unprofitable adj **1** not producing a profit **2** serving no useful purpose

unqualified adj **1** (said about a person) not legally or officially qualified to do something **2** not limited or modified

unquestionable adj not questionable, too clear to be doubted **unquestionably** adv

unravel v **unravelled**, **unravelling 1** to disentangle something **2** to undo something that is knitted **3** to investigate and solve a mystery or puzzle **4** to become unravelled

unreal adj not real, existing in the imagination only **unreality** n

unreasonable adj **1** not reasonable in your attitude, etc. **2** excessive, going beyond the limits of what is reasonable or just **unreasonably** adv

unrelenting adj not becoming less in intensity or severity

unrelieved adj without anything to vary it ♦ unrelieved gloom

unremitting (say un-ri-**mit**-ing) adj not relaxing or stopping, persistent

unrequited (say un-ri-**kwiy**-tid) adj (said about love) not returned or rewarded

unreserved adj **1** without reservation or restriction, complete ♦ unreserved support **2** not reserved in advance ♦ unreserved seats **unreservedly** adv

unrest n trouble or rioting caused because people are dissatisfied

unrivalled (say un-**riy**-vəld) adj having no equal, better than all others

unroll v to open something that has been rolled up; to become opened after being rolled

unruly (say un-**roo**-li) adj **unrulier**, **unruliest** not easy to control or discipline, disorderly **unruliness** n

unsavoury adj **1** unpleasant to the taste or smell **2** morally unpleasant or disgusting ♦ an unsavoury reputation

unscathed (say un-**skayth**d) adj without suffering any injury

unscrew v **1** to unfasten something by turning or removing screws, or by twisting it **2** to loosen a screw or lid by turning it

unscrupulous (say un-**skroo**-pew-ləs) adj without moral scruples **unscrupulously** adv **unscrupulousness** n

unseasonable adj unusual for a particular season **unseasonably** adv

unseat v **1** to throw a rider from horseback or from a bicycle, etc. **2** to remove an MP from a parliamentary seat

unseemly adj not proper or suitable **unseemliness** n

unseen adj **1** not seen or noticed **2** (said about translation) done without previous preparation

unselfish adj not selfish, considering the needs of others before your own **unselfishly** adv **unselfishness** n

unsettle v to make someone feel uneasy or anxious **unsettled** adj **1** not settled or calm **2** (said about weather) likely to change **unsettling** adj

unsightly adj not pleasant to look at, ugly **unsightliness** n

unsocial adj **1** (said about hours of work)

falling outside the normal working day, when most people are not working **2 unsociable unsociable** *adj* not sociable, not enjoying the company of other people

unsolicited (say un-sə-**liss**-it-id) *adj* not asked for; given or done voluntarily

unsophisticated *adj* not sophisticated, simple and natural or naive

unsound *adj* **1** not reliable, not based on sound evidence or reasoning ♦ *unsound advice* **2** not firm or strong **3** not healthy ♦ *of unsound mind*

unsparing (say un-**spair**-ing) *adj* giving freely and lavishly ♦ *unsparing in your efforts*

unspeakable *adj* too bad or too horrific to be described in words

unstable *adj* **unstabler, unstablest 1** not stable, tending to change suddenly **2** mentally or emotionally unbalanced

unsteady *adj* **unsteadier, unsteadiest 1** not firm or steady **2** not regular **unsteadily** *adv* **unsteadiness** *n*

unstinting *adj* given or giving freely and lavishly

unstuck *adj* **to come unstuck** *informal* to fail

unsuitable *adj* not suitable **unsuitability** *n* **unsuitably** *adv*

unsuited *adj* not right or appropriate

unsure *adj* not confident or certain

unsuspecting *adj* feeling no suspicion

unswerving *adj* not turning aside, unchanging ♦ *unswerving loyalty*

untapped *adj* not yet made use of ♦ *the country's untapped resources*

untenable (say un-**ten**-əbəl) *adj* (said about a theory) not able to be held or defended against attack

unthinking *adj* thoughtless, done or said, etc. without consideration **unthinkable** *adj* too unlikely or undesirable to be considered

untidy *adj* **untidier, untidiest** not neat or properly arranged **untidily** *adv* **untidiness** *n*

untie *v* **unties, untied, untying** to undo something that has been tied; to release someone from being tied up

until *prep, conjunction* up to a particular time or event ♦ *Until last year we had never*

been abroad. ♦ *Until* is used in preference to *till* when it is the first word in the sentence and also in more formal contexts.

untimely *adj* **1** happening at an unsuitable time **2** happening too soon or sooner than is normal ♦ *his untimely death* **untimeliness** *n*

unto *prep old use* to

untold *adj* **1** too much or too many to be counted ♦ *untold wealth* **2** not told

untouchable *adj* **1** not able to be touched **2** not able to be matched or rivalled

untoward (say un-tə-**wor** d) *adj* unexpected and inconvenient or unfortunate ♦ *if nothing untoward happens*

untrue *adj* **1** not true, contrary to facts **2** not faithful or loyal **untruth** *n* a lie

unused *adj* **1** (say un-**yoozd**) not yet used ♦ *an unused stamp* **2** (say un-**yoost**) not accustomed ♦ *He is unused to such attention.*

unusual *adj* not usual; strange or exceptional **unusually** *adv*

unvarnished *adj* **1** not varnished **2** plain and straightforward ♦ *the unvarnished truth*

unveil *v* **1** to remove a veil or covering from something **2** to reveal or disclose something, to make something publicly known

unwarranted *adj* not justified, uncalled-for

unwary (say un-**wair**-i) *adj* not cautious or careful about danger

unwell *adj* not in good health

unwieldy (say un-**weel**-di) *adj* **unwieldier, unwieldiest** awkward to move or control because of its size, shape, or weight

unwilling *adj* not willing, reluctant to do something **unwillingly** *adv*

unwind *v* past tense and past participle **unwound 1** to draw something out or become drawn out from being wound **2** *informal* to relax after a period of work or tension

unwise *adj* not wise, foolish **unwisely** *adv*

unwitting *adj* **1** unintentional **2** unaware ♦ *She was an unwitting accomplice.* **unwittingly** *adv*

unwonted (say un-**wohn**-tid) *adj* not customary or usual ♦ *She spoke with unwonted rudeness.*

unworldly adj 1 having little awareness of the realities of life; naive 2 not concerned with material things

unworthy adj **unworthier**, **unworthiest** 1 not worthy, lacking worth or excellence 2 not deserving

unwrap v **unwrapped**, **unwrapping** to remove the wrapping from something

unwritten adj (said about a law) resting on custom or tradition rather than on statute

unyielding adj firm, not yielding to pressure or influence

up adv 1 to, in, or at a higher place, level, value, or condition ♦ *Prices have gone up.* 2 to an upright position ♦ *Stand up.* 3 so as to be inflated ♦ *Pump up the tyres.* 4 winning by a specified margin ♦ *United are two goals up.* 5 to the place, time, or amount, etc. in question ♦ *I walked up to one of the boys.* 6 out of bed ♦ *It's time to get up.* 7 into a condition of activity ♦ *She's been stirring up trouble.* 8 apart, into pieces ♦ *I tore up the letter.* 9 completely ♦ *Eat up your carrots.* 10 finished ♦ *Your time is up.* **up** prep 1 upwards along, through, or into; from a lower to a higher point of ♦ *Water came up the pipes.* 2 at a higher part of ♦ *Fix it further up the wall.* **up** adj directed towards a higher place ♦ *an up stroke* **up** v **upped**, **upping** informal to increase something **up against** informal faced with a difficulty or an opponent **up to 1** busy with or doing something ♦ *What are you up to?* 2 capable of ♦ *I don't feel up to a long walk.* 3 required as a duty or obligation from ♦ *It's up to us to help her.*

up-and-coming adj informal likely to become successful

upbeat adj cheerful or optimistic

upbraid v to scold or reproach someone

upbringing n training and education during childhood

update v 1 to make something more modern or up-to-date 2 to give someone the latest information

upend v to set something or be set up on end

upfront adj, adv (said about payments) made in advance, e.g. as a deposit **upfront** adj open and frank

upgrade v to raise something to a higher standard or rank **upgrade** n an upgraded version of something

upheaval n a sudden violent change or disturbance

uphill adv towards the top of a slope **uphill** adj 1 sloping upwards 2 difficult ♦ *It was an uphill struggle.*

uphold v past tense and past participle **upheld** to support or maintain a decision, statement, or belief

upholster v to put a soft padded covering on furniture **upholsterer** n **upholstery** n a soft padded covering on furniture

upkeep n keeping something in good condition and repair; the cost of this

uplands pl n the higher parts of a country or region

uplift v to raise something **uplifting** adj making you feel more cheerful or morally or spiritually elevated

upload v ICT to transfer data to a larger computer system **upload** n the process of uploading, or a file or program that has been uploaded

upmarket adj, adv to do with or towards the more expensive end of the market

upon prep on

upper adj 1 higher in place or position 2 situated on higher ground or to the north ♦ *Upper Egypt.* **upper** n the part of a boot or shoe above the sole **upper case** n capital letters **upper class** n the highest class in society, especially the aristocracy **uppercut** n a punch in boxing, delivered upwards with the arm bent **uppermost** adj highest in place or rank **uppermost** adj on or to the top or the most prominent position **on your uppers** informal very short of money **the upper hand** control or dominance

uppity adj informal self-important

upright adj 1 in a vertical position 2 (said about a piano) with the strings mounted vertically 3 strictly honest or honourable **upright** adv in or into an upright position **upright** n a post or rod placed upright, especially as a support

uprising n a rebellion or revolt

uproar n an outburst of noise and

uproot *v* **1** to remove a plant and its roots from the ground **2** to force someone to leave the place where they have lived for a long time ♦ *We don't want to uproot ourselves and go to live abroad.*

upset (say up-set) *v* past tense and past participle **upset**; **upsetting 1** to make someone unhappy or distressed **2** to knock something over **3** to disturb the normal working of something; disrupt something ♦ *Fog upset the timetable.* **4** to disturb the digestion of someone **upset** *adj* **1** unhappy or distressed **2** slightly ill ♦ *an upset stomach* **upset** (say up-set) *n* **1** a slight illness **2** an unexpected result or setback

upshot *n* the eventual outcome

upside down *adv, adj* **1** with the upper part underneath instead of on top **2** in great disorder ♦ *His flat had been turned upside down.*

upstage *adj, adv* towards the back of a theatre stage **upstage** *v* to divert attention from someone towards yourself

upstairs *adv* up the stairs, to or on an upper floor **upstairs** *adj* situated upstairs

upstanding *adj* respectable

upstart *n* a person who has risen suddenly to a high position, especially one who behaves arrogantly

upstream *adj, adv* in the direction from which a stream flows

upsurge *n* an upward surge, an increase

uptake *n* the action of taking up or making use of something **quick on the uptake** quick to understand

uptight *adj informal* nervously tense or angry

up-to-date *adj* **1** in current fashion **2** containing the latest information or making use of the latest developments ♦ *the most up-to-date edition*

upturn *n* an upward trend in business or fortune, etc., an improvement **upturn** *v* to turn something upwards or upside down

upward *adj* moving, leading, or pointing towards a higher point or level **upwards** or

upward *adv* towards a higher point or level

upwind *adj, adv* in the direction from which the wind is blowing

uranium (say yoor-ay-niəm) *n* a chemical element (symbol U), a heavy grey metal used as a fuel in nuclear reactors

urban *adj* to do with or situated in a city or town **urbanize** *v* to change a place into a town-like area

urbane (say er-bayn) *adj* smooth and courteous in manner, suave **urbanity** *n*

urchin *n* a mischievous child, especially one who is dirty and poorly dressed

Urdu (say oor -doo) *n* a language related to Hindi, spoken in northern India and Pakistan

ureter (say yoor-ee-ter) *n* either of the two ducts by which urine passes from the kidneys to the bladder

urethra (say yoor-ee-thrə) *n* the duct by which urine is passed out of the body

urge *v* **1** to try hard or persistently to persuade someone to do something ♦ *I urged him to accept the job.* **2** to encourage someone to continue ♦ *The runners were urged on by the huge crowd.* **3** to recommend something strongly ♦ *I urge caution in this matter.* **4** to force an animal to go more quickly ♦ *She urged her horse forward.* **urge** *n* a strong desire or feeling that drives you to do something **urgent** *adj* needing to be done or dealt with immediately **urgency** *n* **urgently** *adv*

urine (say **yoor** -in) *n* waste liquid that collects in the bladder and is passed out of the body **urinal** *n* a bowl or trough fixed to the wall in a men's public toilet, for men to urinate into **urinary** *adj* **urinate** *v* to pass urine out of your body **urination** *n*

urn *n* **1** a tall vase with a stem and base, especially one used for holding the ashes of a cremated person **2** a large metal container with a tap, in which tea or coffee is made and kept hot

US *abbr* United States

us *pronoun* the form of *we* used as the object of a verb or after a preposition

USA *abbr* United States of America

use (say yooz) *v* **1** to perform an action or job with something, to put something

of gas or liquid through a pipe or tube **2** a structure in the heart or in a blood vessel allowing blood to flow in one direction only **3** a device for varying the length of the tube in a brass wind instrument

vamp[1] *v* to make or repair something from odds and ends

vamp[2] *n informal* a woman who uses her sexual attractions to exploit men

vampire *n* a corpse that is supposed to leave its grave at night and drink the blood of living people **vampire bat** *n* a tropical bat that bites animals and people and sucks their blood

van[1] *n* **1** a covered vehicle for transporting goods or people **2** a railway carriage for luggage, mail, etc., or for the use of the guard

van[2] *n* the vanguard or forefront

vandal *n* a person who deliberately destroys or damages things, especially public property **vandalism** *n* **vandalize** *v* to deliberately destroy or damage property, etc.

vane *n* **1** the blade of a propeller, sail of a windmill, or other device acting on or moved by wind or water **2** a weathervane ◊ Do not confuse this word with *vain* or *vein*, which have different meanings.

vanguard *n* **1** the leading part of an army or fleet advancing or ready to do so **2** the group of people leading the way in a new fashion, movement, or idea

vanilla *n* a flavouring obtained from the pods of a tropical climbing orchid

vanish *v* to disappear suddenly and completely

vanity *n pl* **vanities** **1** conceit, especially about your appearance **2** futility, worthlessness, something vain

vanquish *v* to defeat someone thoroughly

vantage point *n* a place from which you have a good view of something

vapid (say **vap**-id) *adj* not lively or interesting, insipid

vapour *n* **1** moisture diffused or suspended in the air in the form of clouds, mist, smoke, etc. **2** a substance in the form of a gas **vaporize** *v* to change something into vapour, or to be changed into vapour

vaporizer *n* **vaporous** *adj*

varicose (say **va**-ri-kohs) *adj* (said about a vein) permanently swollen or enlarged

variegated (say **vair**-i-gayt-id) *adj* marked with irregular patches or streaks of different colours **variegation** *n*

varnish *n* a liquid that dries to form a hard shiny transparent coating, used on wood or metal, etc. **varnish** *v* to coat something with varnish

vary *v* **varies**, **varied**, **varying** **1** to make something change or make sure it is not always the same ♦ *Try to vary your diet.* **2** to become different ♦ *His mood varies from day to day.* **3** to be different or of different kinds ♦ *Opinions vary on this point.* **variable** *adj* likely to vary; not steady or regular **variable** *n* something that varies or can vary, a variable quantity **variance** *n* the amount by which things differ **variant** *adj* differing from something or from a standard ♦ *'Gipsy' is a variant spelling of 'gypsy'* **variant** *n* a variant form: or spelling, etc. **variation** *n* **1** a change or slight difference in something **2** a different form of something, a variant **3** a repetition of a melody in a different (usually more elaborate) form **varied** *adj* **variety** *n pl* **varieties** **1** a quantity or range of different things ♦ *for a variety of reasons* **2** the quality of not being the same or of not being the same at all times **3** a thing that differs from others in the same general class ♦ *There are several varieties of spaniel.* **4** a form of entertainment consisting of a series of different types of act **various** *adj* **1** of several kinds, different from one another ♦ *for various reasons* **2** more than one, individual and separate ♦ *We met various people.* **variously** *adv* at variance with in disagreement or conflict with something

vascular (say **vas**-kew-ler) *adj* consisting of vessels or tubes for circulating blood or sap within an organism

vase (say **vahz**) *n* an open, usually tall, container of glass, pottery, etc. used for holding cut flowers or as an ornament

vasectomy (say və-**sekt**-əmi) *n pl* **vasectomies** surgical removal of part of each of the ducts through which semen passes from the testicles, especially as a means of sterilization

vassal n a person in the Middle Ages who gave service to a lord in return for land or protection

vast adj very great in area or size **vastly** adv **vastness** n

VAT abbr value added tax

vat n a tank or other very large container for holding liquids

Vatican n **1** the palace and official residence of the Pope in Rome **2** the papal government

vaudeville (say **vaw**-də-vil) n a kind of entertainment popular in the early 20th century, consisting of a mixture of musical and comedy acts

vault¹ n **1** an arched roof **2** a secure room in a bank for storing money or valuables **3** a burial chamber

vault² v to jump or leap over something, especially while supporting yourself on your hands **vault** n a leap performed in this way

vaunt v to boast about something

VC abbr Victoria Cross

VCR abbr video cassette recorder

VDU abbr visual display unit

veal n calf's flesh used as food

vector n **1** a quantity (such as velocity or force) that has both magnitude and direction **2** the carrier of a disease or infection

veer v to change direction or course suddenly

vegan (say **vee**-gən) n a person who does not eat or use animal products at all

vegetable n **1** a plant or part of a plant used as food **2** informal a person who is not capable of normal physical or mental activity, especially because of brain damage

vegetarian n a person who does not eat meat **vegetarian** adj suitable for vegetarians **vegetarianism** n

vegetate (say **vej**-i-tayt) v to live an uneventful or monotonous life

vegetation n plants collectively **vegetative** adj to do with vegetation

vehement (say **vee**-i-mənt) adj showing strong feeling ♦ a vehement denial **vehemence** n **vehemently** adv

vehicle (say **vee**-i-kəl) n **1** a means of transporting people or goods, especially on land **2** a means by which something is communicated or displayed ♦ The play was the perfect vehicle for this actor's talents. **vehicular** adj

veil n a piece of fine net or other material worn as part of a headdress or to protect or conceal the face **veil** v **1** to cover something with a veil **2** to partially conceal something ♦ a thinly veiled threat

vein n **1** any of the tubes carrying blood from all parts of the body to the heart **2** any of the thread-like structures forming the framework of a leaf or of an insect's wing **3** a narrow strip or streak of a different colour in marble, cheese, etc. **4** a long continuous or branching deposit of mineral or ore especially in a fissure **5** a source of something ♦ a rich vein of satire **6** a mood, quality, or manner ♦ She continued in the same humorous vein. **veined** adj filled or marked with veins ◊ Do not confuse this word with vain or vane, which have different meanings.

Velcro n trademark a fastener for clothes, etc. consisting of two strips of fabric, one covered with tiny hooks and the other with tiny loops

vellum n a kind of fine parchment

velocity n pl **velocities** the speed of something in a given direction

velour (say vil-**oor**) n a thick velvety material

velvet n a woven fabric of silk, cotton, or nylon with a thick short pile on one side **velveteen** n cotton velvet **velvety** adj

venal (say **veen**-əl) adj **1** able to be bribed **2** (said about conduct) influenced by bribery **venality** n

vend v to sell something or offer it for sale **vendor** n Law a person selling something **vending machine** n a slot machine from which you can obtain drinks, chocolate, cigarettes, etc.

vendetta (say ven-**det**-ə) n a long-lasting bitter quarrel; a feud

veneer n **1** a thin layer of finer wood

covering the surface of a cheaper wood in furniture, etc. **2** an outward show of some good quality, concealing your true nature or feelings

venerate v to regard someone or something with great respect **venerable** adj worthy of or given great respect, especially because of age **veneration** n

venereal disease n a disease contracted by sexual intercourse with a person who is already infected

Venetian (say vin-ee-shən) adj to do with or coming from Venice **venetian blind** n a window blind consisting of horizontal strips that can be adjusted to let light in or shut it out

vengeance n punishment or retaliation for hurt or harm **vengeful** adj seeking vengeance **with a vengeance** with great intensity

venial (say veen-iəl) adj (said about a sin or fault) pardonable, not serious

venison (say ven-i-sən) n meat from a deer

Venn diagram n Mathematics a diagram using overlapping and intersecting circles to show the relationships between different sets of things

venom (say ven-əm) n **1** the poisonous fluid produced by certain snakes, scorpions, etc. and injected into a victim by a bite or sting **2** strong bitterness or aggression **venomous** adj **1** secreting venom ♦ venomous snakes **2** full of bitterness or aggression

vent¹ n an opening allowing air, gas, or liquid to pass out of or into a confined space **vent** v to express your feelings freely and openly **to give vent to** to express your feelings freely and openly

vent² n a slit in a piece of clothing, especially a coat or jacket, at the bottom of a back or side seam

ventilate v **1** to let air enter and circulate freely in a room or building **2** to discuss an opinion or issue in public **ventilation** n **ventilator** n **1** a device for ventilating a room, etc. **2** an apparatus for giving artificial respiration

ventral adj to do with or on the underside of an animal or plant ♦ This fish has a ventral fin.

ventriloquist (say ven-tril-ə-kwist) n an entertainer who makes their voice sound as if it comes from another source, such as a dummy **ventriloquism** n

venture n something you decide to do that involves risk, especially a business enterprise **venture** v **1** to dare or be bold enough to do something ♦ No one ventured to tell him he was mistaken. **2** to express something although others may disagree ♦ I wonder if I might venture an opinion.

venturesome adj ready to take risks or do something daring

venue (say ven-yoo) n the place where a meeting, concert, sports match, etc. is held

veracious (say ver-ay-shəs) adj formal **1** truthful **2** true **veracity** n truth, accuracy, or truthfulness

veranda, **verandah** n a roofed terrace along the side of a house

verb n a word used to describe an action, occurrence, or state, e.g. bring, came, exists **verbal** adj **1** to do with or in words ♦ verbal accuracy **2** spoken, not written ♦ a verbal statement **3** to do with verbs ♦ verbal inflections **verbally** adv **verbalize** v to put something into words

verbatim (say ver-bay-tim) adv, adj in exactly the same words, word for word ♦ He copied down the whole paragraph verbatim.

verbiage (say verb-i-ij) n an excessive number of words used to express an idea

verbose (say ver-bohs) adj using more words than are needed **verbosity** n

verdant adj green with grass or other vegetation

verdict n **1** the decision reached by a jury **2** a decision or opinion given after examining, testing, or experiencing something

verdigris (say verd-i-grees) n green rust on copper or brass

verdure n lush green vegetation

verge n **1** an edge or border **2** the point beyond which something will begin or happen ♦ I was on the verge of tears. **verge** v **to verge on** to be very close or similar to something ♦ Sometimes her determination verges on ruthlessness.

verger (say ver-jer) *n* an official in a church who acts as a caretaker and attendant

verify *v* **verifies**, **verified**, **verifying** to make sure or show that something is true or correct **verifiable** *adj* **verification** *n*

verily *adv* old use in truth

verisimilitude (say ve-ri-sim-il-i-tewd) *n* the appearance of being true or lifelike

verity *n pl* **verities** the truth of something; a true principle or belief **veritable** *adj* real, rightly named ♦ *a veritable villain*

vermicelli (say verm-i-**chel**-i or verm-i-**sel**-i) *n* **1** pasta made in long thin threads **2** very small rod-shaped pieces of chocolate used for decorating cakes, etc.

vermilion *n*, *adj* bright red

vermin *pl n* wild animals, birds, and insects that are harmful to crops, food, or domestic animals **verminous** *adj*

vermouth (say **ver**-məth) *n* white wine flavoured with fragrant herbs

vernacular (say ver-**nak**-yoo-ler) *n* the language or dialect spoken by the ordinary people of a country or region

vernal *adj* to do with or happening in the season of spring

verruca (say ver-**oo**-kə) *n* a wart, especially one on the sole of the foot

versatile (say **ver**-sə-tiyl) *adj* able to do, or be used for, many different things **versatility** *n*

verse *n* **1** writing arranged in short lines, usually with a particular rhythm and often with rhymes; poetry **2** a group of lines forming a unit in a poem or song **3** each of the short numbered sections of a chapter of the Bible **versify** *v* **versifies**, **versified**, **versifying** to express something in verse; to write verse **versification** *n* **versed in** experienced or skilled in something; having a knowledge of something

version *n* **1** a form of something that is different from the original or usual form ♦ *the film version of the play* **2** a particular person's account of something that happened

verso *n pl* **versos** the left-hand page of an open book, or the back of a sheet of paper

versus *prep* against

vertebra (say **ver**-tib-rə) *n pl* **vertebrae** (say ver-tib-ree) any of the series of small bones that form the backbone **vertebral** *adj*

vertex *n pl* **vertices** (say **ver**-ti-seez) the highest point of something

vertical *adj* **1** at right angles to the horizontal; upright **2** going from top to bottom, not side to side **vertical** *n* a vertical line, part, or position **vertically** *adv*

vertigo (say **vert**-i-goh) *n* a feeling of dizziness and of losing your balance, usually caused by looking down from a great height

verve (say verv) *n* enthusiasm and liveliness

very *adv* in a high degree ♦ *very good* **very** *adj* **1** exact or actual ♦ *Those were her very words.* **2** extreme, utter ♦ *at the very end*

vespers *n* a service of evening prayer in some Christian churches

vessel *n* **1** a ship or boat **2** a hollow container, especially for liquid **3** a tube in the body of an animal or plant, carrying or holding blood or other fluid

vest *n* a piece of underwear covering the trunk of the body **vest** *v* to give something as an official or legal right ♦ *The power of making laws is vested in Parliament.*

vested interest *n* a strong personal reason for wanting something to happen, usually because you will benefit from it

vestibule (say **vest**-i-bewl) *n* an entrance hall or lobby of a building

vestige *n* a trace or very small amount ♦ *There is not a vestige of truth in it.* **vestigial** *adj* remaining as the last part of what once existed

vestment *n* a ceremonial robe or other piece of clothing, especially one worn by the clergy

vestry *n pl* **vestries** a room in a church where the clergy and choir put their vestments on

vet *n* a veterinary surgeon **vet** *v* **vetted**, **vetting** to make a careful and critical examination of a person or thing

vetch *n* a plant of the pea family, used as fodder for cattle

veteran *n* a person with long experience, especially in the armed forces

veterinary (say **vet**-rin-ri) *adj* to do with

or for the medical and surgical treatment of animals **veterinary surgeon** n a person trained to give medical and surgical treatment to animals

veto (say **veet**-oh) n pl **vetoes** 1 the right to reject or forbid something that is proposed 2 any refusal or prohibition **veto** v **vetoes**, **vetoed**, **vetoing** to use a veto against something

vex v to make someone feel annoyed or worried **vexation** n **vexatious** adj **vexed question** n a problem that is difficult and much discussed

VHF abbr very high frequency

via (say **viy**-ə) prep by way of, through ♦ *from Exeter to York via London*

viable (say **viy**-əbəl) adj 1 able to work or exist successfully ♦ *a viable plan* 2 able to live or grow **viability** n **viably** adv

viaduct (say **viy**-ə-dukt) n a long bridge-like structure for carrying a road or railway over a valley

vial (say **viy**-əl) n a small glass bottle, especially for liquid medicine

viands (say **viy**-əndz) pl n old use items of food

vibes pl n informal (also **vibe**) the atmosphere, place, or mood produced by a person, place, or situation and felt by people ♦ *I get bad vibes from this place.*

vibrant (say **viy**-brənt) adj 1 full of energy or activity 2 bold and strong ♦ *vibrant colours* **vibrancy** n

vibraphone (say **vy**-brə-fohn) n a percussion instrument that gives a vibrating effect

vibrate v 1 to move rapidly and continuously with small movements to and fro; to make something do this 2 (said about a sound) to resonate **vibration** n **vibrator** n a device that vibrates or causes vibration **vibratory** adj

vicar n (in the Church of England) a member of the clergy in charge of a parish **vicarage** n the house of a vicar

vicarious (say vik-**air**-i-əs) adj (said about feelings or emotions) not experienced yourself but felt by imagining you share someone else's experience ♦ *vicarious pleasure* **vicariously** adv

vice¹ n 1 immoral or wicked behaviour 2 a particular form of this, a fault or bad habit ♦ *Smoking isn't one of my vices.* 3 criminal activities involving prostitution, pornography, or drugs

vice² n a device with two jaws that grip something and hold it firmly while you work on it

vice- prefix 1 acting as substitute or deputy for (as in vice-captain, vice-president) 2 next in rank to (as in vice-admiral)

viceroy n a person governing a colony or province as the sovereign's representative

vice versa (say viy-si **ver**-sə) adv the other way round ♦ *Which do you prefer: blue spots on a yellow background or vice versa?*

vicinity (say vis-**in**-iti) n pl **vicinities** the area near or surrounding a particular place ♦ *Is there a library in the vicinity?*

vicious (say **vish**-əs) adj 1 cruel or violent 2 (said about an animal) wild and dangerous **viciously** adv **viciousness** n **vicious circle** n a situation in which a problem produces an effect which in turn produces or intensifies the original problem

vicissitude (say viss-**iss**-i-tewd) n a change of circumstances or fortune affecting your life, usually for the worse

victim n a person who is injured, killed, robbed, etc. as the result of a crime, accident, or disaster ♦ *victims of the earthquake* **victimize** v to single someone out for cruel or unfair treatment **victimization** n

Victorian adj during or to do with the reign of Queen Victoria (1837-1901) **Victorian** n a person living at this time

victory n pl **victories** success in a battle, contest, or game, etc. achieved by defeating your opponent or achieving the highest score **victor** n the winner in a battle or contest **victorious** adj having gained a victory

victuals (say **vit**-lz) pl n old use food and drink

video (say **vid**-i-oh) n pl **videos** 1 the system of recording or broadcasting pictures on videotape 2 a film or other recording on videotape 3 a video cassette or video recorder **video** v **videoes**,

videoed, **videoing** to record something on videotape **video game** n a game in which you use electronic controls to move images produced by a computer program on a monitor or television screen **video recorder** n a device for recording and playing television programmes on videotape **videotape** n 1 magnetic tape suitable for recording television pictures and sound 2 a cassette on which this tape is held

vie v **vies**, **vied**, **vying** to compete eagerly with someone to achieve something ♦ All the reporters were vying for her attention.

view n 1 what can be seen from one place, e.g. beautiful natural scenery ♦ the view from the summit 2 sight, range of vision ♦ The ship sailed into view. 3 an attitude or opinion **view** v 1 to look at or watch something 2 to inspect something; to look over a house, etc. with the idea of buying it 3 to regard something in a particular way ♦ We view the matter seriously. **viewer** n **viewfinder** n a device on a camera by which the user can see the area that will be photographed through the lens **viewpoint** n 1 an opinion or point of view 2 a place giving a good view **in view of** because or as a result of ♦ In view of the excellence of the work, we are not too concerned about the cost. **on view** being shown or exhibited to the public **with a view to** with the hope or intention of

vigil (say **vij**-il) n a period of staying awake to keep watch or to pray ♦ We kept vigil all night. **vigilant** adj watching out for possible danger or difficulties **vigilance** n **vigilante** n a member of a self-appointed group of people who try to prevent crime and disorder in their community

vignette (say veen-**yet**) n 1 a short description or character sketch 2 a photograph or portrait which fades into its background without a definite edge

vigour n 1 physical strength and good health 2 forcefulness and energy ♦ She continued her campaign with renewed vigour. **vigorous** adj **vigorously** adv **vigorousness** n

Viking (say **viy**-king) n a Scandinavian trader and pirate of the 8th-11th centuries

vile adj 1 disgusting or foul 2 morally bad or wicked **vileness** n

vilify (say **vil**-i-fiy) v **vilifies**, **vilified**, **vilifying** to say unpleasant things about a person or thing **vilification** n

villa n 1 a large country house 2 a detached or semi-detached house in a residential district

village n a group of houses and other buildings in a country district, smaller than a town and usually having a church **villager** n

villain (say **vil**-ən) n 1 a wicked person; a person who is guilty of a crime 2 a character in a story or play whose evil actions or motives are important in the plot **villainous** adj **villainy** n

vim n informal vigour or energy

vinaigrette (say vin-i-**gret**) n salad dressing made of oil and vinegar

vindicate (say **vin**-dik-ayt) v 1 to clear someone of blame or suspicion 2 to show something to be right or justified **vindication** n

vindictive (say vin-**dik**-tiv) adj having or showing a desire for revenge; spiteful **vindictiveness** n

vine n 1 a climbing or trailing woody-stemmed plant whose fruit is the grape 2 a slender climbing or trailing stem **vineyard** n a plantation of vines producing grapes for making wine

vinegar n a sour liquid made from wine, cider, malt, etc. by fermentation, used in flavouring food and for pickling **vinegary** adj

vintage (say **vint**-ij) n wine made from a particular season's grapes, especially in a good year **vintage** adj being typical of the best of something from a past period ♦ vintage TV drama

vintner (say **vint**-ner) n a wine merchant

vinyl (say **viy**-nil) n a kind of plastic, especially polyvinyl chloride

viol (say **viy**-əl) n a stringed musical instrument popular especially in the 16th-17th centuries, similar to a violin but held vertically

viola[1] (say vee-oh-lə) n a stringed musical

instrument slightly larger than a violin and of lower pitch

viola² (say **viy**-ə-lə) n a plant of the genus to which pansies and violets belong

violate v 1 to break or fail to follow an oath, rule, treaty, etc. 2 to treat a person or place with disrespect 3 to rape someone **violation** n **violator** n

violence n 1 physical force intended to hurt or damage 2 strength of feeling 3 the strength of a natural force ♦ *the violence of the storm* **violent** adj **violently** adv

violet n 1 a small wild or garden plant, often with purple flowers 2 a bluish-purple colour

violin n a musical instrument with four strings of treble pitch, played with a bow **violinist** n

violoncello (say viy-ə-lən-**chel**-oh) n pl **violoncellos** a formal word for a *cello*

VIP abbr very important person

viper n a small poisonous snake

virago (say vi-**rah**-goh) n pl **viragos** a fierce or bullying woman

virgin n 1 a person, especially a woman, who has never had sexual intercourse 2 a person who is inexperienced in a particular context ♦ *a political virgin* **the Virgin** n the Virgin Mary, mother of Christ **virgin** adj 1 to do with, being, or suitable for a virgin 2 in its original state, not yet touched or used ♦ *virgin snow* **virginal** adj **virginal** n a keyboard instrument of the 16th-17th centuries, the earliest form of harpsichord **virginity** n

Virgo (say **ver**-goh) 1 a group of stars (the Virgin), seen as representing a young woman 2 the sign of the zodiac which the sun enters about 23 August **Virgoan** adj, n

virile (say **vi**-riyl) adj having masculine strength or vigour, especially sexually **virility** n

virology (say viyr-**ol**-əji) n the scientific study of viruses

virtual adj 1 almost or nearly, but not according to strict definition ♦ *His silence was a virtual admission of guilt.* 2 ICT not physically existing as such but made by software to appear to exist **virtually** adv nearly or almost

virtue n 1 moral goodness; a quality

thought to be morally good ♦ *Patience is a virtue.* 2 an advantage or useful quality ♦ *My plan has the virtue of being simple.*

virtuous adj having or showing moral virtue **virtuously** adv **virtuousness** n **by** or **in virtue of** because or as a result of

virtuoso (say ver-tew-**oh**-soh) n pl **virtuosos** or **virtuosi** a person who excels in the technique of doing something, especially singing or playing music **virtuosity** n

virulent (say **vi**-rew-lənt) adj 1 (said about a poison or disease) extremely strong or severe 2 strongly and bitterly hostile **virulence** n

virus (say **viy**-rəs) n pl **viruses** 1 a very simple organism (smaller than bacteria) capable of causing disease 2 a disease caused by a virus 3 (also **computer virus**) a set of instructions hidden within a computer program that is designed to destroy computer data **viral** adj

visa (say **vee**-zə) n an official stamp or mark put on a passport by officials of a foreign country to show that the holder has permission to enter or stay in that country

visage (say **viz**-ij) n a person's face or expression

vis-à-vis (say veez-ah-**vee**) prep in relation to, as compared with

viscera (say **vis**-er-ə) pl n the internal organs of the body, especially the intestines **visceral** adj 1 to do with the viscera 2 to do with deep inward feelings, not the intellect

viscose (say **vis**-kohz) n fabric made of cellulose in a viscous state

viscount (say **viy**-kownt) n a British nobleman ranking between an earl and a baron **viscountess** n

viscous (say **vis**-kəs) adj thick and gluey, not pouring easily **viscosity** n

visible adj able to be seen or noticed **visibility** n 1 being visible 2 the distance you can see as determined by conditions of light and atmosphere ♦ *The aircraft turned back because of poor visibility.* **visibly** adv

vision n 1 the ability to see, sight 2 the ability to think about the future with imagination, insight, and wisdom ♦ *a statesman with vision* 3 a mental image of

what the future could be like **4** something seen in a person's imagination, in a dream, or as a supernatural apparition
visionary *adj* thinking about the future with imagination, insight, and wisdom
visionary *n pl* **visionaries** a person with extremely imaginative ideas about the future
visit *v* **1** to go to see a person or place either socially or on business or for some other purpose **2** to stay somewhere for a while
visit *n* **1** going to see a person or place **2** a short stay somewhere **visitation** *n* **1** an official visit, especially to inspect something **2** trouble or disaster looked upon as punishment from God **visitor** *n*
visor (say **viy**-zer) *n* **1** the movable front part of a helmet, covering the face **2** a fixed or movable shield at the top of a vehicle windscreen, protecting the eyes from bright sunshine
vista *n* a pleasant view
visual *adj* to do with seeing or sight
visualize *v* to form a mental picture of something **visualization** *n* **visually** *adv*
visual display unit *n* a screen that displays data being received from a computer
vital *adj* **1** essential to the existence, success, or operation of something; extremely important **2** connected with life, essential to life ♦ *vital functions* **3** full of vitality **vitals** *pl n* the important internal organs of the body **vitality** *n* liveliness or energy **vitally** *adv* essentially
vital statistics *n* **1** statistics relating to population figures or births and deaths **2** *informal* the measurements of a woman's bust, waist, and hips
vitamin (say **vit**-ə-min or **viy**-tə-min) *n* any of a number of organic substances present in many foods and essential to the nutrition of people and animals
vitiate (say **vish**-i-ayt) *v formal* to spoil something or make it less effective
viticulture (say **vit**-i-kul-cher) *n* the cultivation of grapes for making wine
vitreous (say **vit**-ri-əs) *adj* having a glass-like texture or appearance
vitrify (say **vit**-ri-fiy) *v* **vitrifies**, **vitrified**, **vitrifying** to convert something or

be converted into glass or a glass-like substance, especially by heat **vitrification** *n*
vitriol (say **vit**-ri-ol) *n* **1** sulphuric acid or one of its salts **2** savagely hostile comments or criticism **vitriolic** *adj*
vituperate (say vi-**tew**-per-ayt) *v* **1** to scold someone angrily or abusively **2** to use abusive language **vituperative** *adj*
viva (say **viy**-va) *n* an oral examination, usually for an academic qualification
vivacious (say viv-**ay**-shəs) *adj* attractively lively and high-spirited **vivaciously** *adv* **vivacity** *n*
vivarium (say viy-**vair**-iəm) *n pl* **vivaria** a place prepared for keeping animals in conditions as similar as possible to their natural environment, for purposes of study, etc.
viva voce (say viy-və **voh**-chi) *adj, adv* oral rather than written **viva voce** *n* an oral examination
vivid *adj* **1** (said about light or colour) bright and strong, intense **2** producing strong and clear mental pictures ♦ *a vivid description* **3** (said about the imagination) creating ideas or feelings in an active and lively way **vividly** *adv* **vividness** *n*
vivisection *n* doing surgical experiments on live animals
vixen *n* a female fox
viz. *adv* namely ♦ *The case is made in three sizes, viz. large, medium, and small.*
vizier (say viz-**eer**) *n* in former times, an official of high rank in certain Muslim countries
vocabulary *n pl* **vocabularies** **1** the body of words used in a particular subject or language **2** the body of words known to an individual person ♦ *She has a good vocabulary.* **3** a list of difficult or foreign words with their meanings
vocal (say **voh**-kəl) *adj* **1** to do with, for, or using the voice **2** expressing your feelings freely in speech ♦ *He was very vocal about his rights.* **vocal** *n* a piece of sung music **vocalist** *n* a singer **vocalize** *v* to use your voice **vocally** *adv* **vocal cords** *pl n* two strap-like membranes in the throat that can be made to vibrate and produce sounds

vocation (say və-**kay**-shən) n **1** a strong desire to pursue or a natural liking for a particular occupation **2** a person's job or occupation **vocational** adj

vociferous (say və-**sif**-er-əs) adj expressing your views loudly and forcibly **vociferously** adv

vodka n an alcoholic spirit of Russian origin, distilled chiefly from rye

vogue n the current fashion or style **in vogue** in fashion

voice n **1** sounds formed in the larynx and uttered by the mouth, especially in speaking or singing **2** the ability to produce such sounds ♦ She has a cold and has lost her voice. ♦ The tenor is in good voice. **3** someone expressing a particular opinion about something ♦ Ruth's the only dissenting voice. **4** Gram either of the sets of forms of a verb that show the relation of the subject to the action, either the active voice or the passive voice (see the entries for active and passive) **voice** v to put something into words **voicemail** n an electronic system that can store messages from telephone callers **voice-over** n narration in a film or broadcast by a voice not accompanied by a picture of the speaker

void adj **1** not legally valid or binding **2** empty or vacant **3** lacking something ♦ an act void of all humour **void** n an empty space or hole **void** v **1** to make something legally void **2** to empty the bowels or bladder

voile (say voil) n a very thin, almost transparent, dress material

volatile (say **vol**-ə-tiyl) adj **1** (said about a liquid) evaporating quickly **2** changing quickly and unpredictably **volatility** n

vol-au-vent (say **vol**-oh-vahn) n a small pie of puff pastry filled with a sauce containing meat or fish

volcano n pl **volcanoes** or **volcanos** a mountain or hill with openings through which lava, cinders, hot gases, etc., from below the earth's crust are or have been thrown out **volcanic** adj to do with or from a volcano

vole (say vohl) n a small mouse-like rodent with a rounded snout and small ears

volition (say vəl-**ish**-ən) n using your own will in choosing to do something ♦ She left of her own volition.

volley n pl **volleys 1** a number of bullets, shells, arrows, etc. fired at the same time **2** a number of questions or remarks directed in quick succession at someone **3** hitting the ball in tennis, football, etc. before it touches the ground **volley** v **volleys, volleyed, volleying 1** to hit a ball before it touches the ground **2** to fire or say things in a volley **volleyball** n a game for two teams of players who hit a large ball to and fro over a high net with their hands

volt n a unit of electromotive force **voltage** n electromotive force expressed in volts

volte-face (say volt-**fahs**) n a sudden and complete reversal in your attitude towards something

voluble (say **vol**-yoo-bəl) adj talking very much; speaking or spoken with great fluency **volubility** n **volubly** adv

volume n **1** the amount of space (often expressed in cubic units) that a three-dimensional thing occupies or contains **2** an amount or quantity of something **3** the strength or power of sound **4** a book, especially one of a set **volumetric** adj to do with the measurement of volume **voluminous** adj **1** (said about a piece of clothing) large and loose **2** (said about writings) great in quantity

voluntary adj **1** done or doing something willingly and not because you are forced to do it **2** working or done without payment ♦ voluntary work **3** (said about bodily movements) consciously controlled by the brain **voluntary** n pl **voluntaries** an organ solo played before, during, or after a church service **voluntarily** adv **volunteer** n **1** a person who offers to do something **2** a person who enrols for military service voluntarily, not as a conscript **3** a person who works for an organization without being paid **volunteer** v to give or offer to do something of your own accord, without being asked or forced to

voluptuous (say vəl-**up**-tew-əs) adj **1** giving a sensation of luxury and sensual pleasure **2** (said about a woman) having an attractively curved figure voluptuousness n

vomit v vomited, **vomiting** 1 to bring up matter from the stomach and out through the mouth, to be sick 2 to throw something out violently **vomit** n matter vomited from the stomach

voodoo n a form of religion based on belief in witchcraft and magical rites, practised in the Caribbean and the southern US

voracious (say ver-**ay**-shəs) adj 1 wanting or eating great quantities of food 2 eagerly consuming something ♦ a voracious reader **voraciously** adv **voracity** n

vortex n pl **vortices** (say **vor** -ti-seez) or pl **vortexes** a whirling mass of water or air, a whirlpool or whirlwind

vote n 1 a formal expression of your opinion or choice on a matter under discussion, e.g. by ballot or show of hands 2 an opinion or choice expressed in this way ♦ The vote went against accepting the plan. 3 the total number of votes given by a certain group ♦ Such a policy will lose us the middle-class vote. 4 the right to vote ♦ Today people get the vote at 18. **vote** v 1 to express an opinion or choice by a vote 2 to decide something by a majority of votes ♦ The union voted to accept the deal. **voter** n

votive (say **voh**-tiv) adj given in fulfilment of a vow ♦ votive offerings at the shrine

voucher n a piece of paper that can be exchanged for certain goods or services **vouch** v to vouch for to guarantee that someone or something is reliable, genuine, or true ♦ I will vouch for his honesty. **vouchsafe** v to give or grant something in a gracious or condescending manner ♦ She did not vouchsafe a reply.

vow n a solemn promise or undertaking **vow** v to promise solemnly to do something, to make a vow

vowel n 1 any of the letters of the alphabet a, e, i, o, and u 2 a speech sound made without audible stopping of the breath

voyage n a journey by water or in space, especially a long one **voyage** v to go on a voyage **voyager** n

vs abbr versus

vulcanize v to treat rubber or similar material with sulphur at a high temperature in order to increase its elasticity and strength **vulcanization** n

vulgar adj 1 lacking refinement or good taste 2 rude or coarse **vulgarity** n **vulgarize** v to spoil something by making it ordinary or less refined **vulgarly** adv **vulgar fraction** n a fraction represented by numbers above and below a line (e.g. ¾, ⅞), not a decimal fraction

vulnerable (say **vul**-ner-ə-bəl) adj 1 able to be hurt or harmed 2 unprotected, exposed to danger or attack **vulnerability** n

vulpine (say **vul**-piyn) adj to do with or like a fox

vulture n 1 a large bird of prey that lives on the flesh of dead animals 2 a greedy person seeking to profit from the misfortunes of others

vulva n the external parts of the female genitals

Ww

W[1] the twenty-third letter of the English alphabet

W[2] abbr 1 watt(s) 2 west or western

wacky adj **wackier**, **wackiest** crazy or silly

wad (say wod) n 1 a lump or bundle of soft material 2 a bundle of banknotes of documents **wad** v **wadded**, **wadding** to pad, line, or stuff something with soft material

waddle v to walk with short steps, swaying from side to side **waddle** n a waddling walk

wade v 1 to walk through water or mud, etc. 2 to read through something with effort because it is dull, difficult, or long ♦ I've been wading through his latest novel. **wader** n any long-legged waterbird that wades in shallow water **waders** pl n high waterproof boots worn by anglers

wafer n a kind of thin light biscuit

waffle[1] (say **wof**-əl) n informal vague word, talk or writing **waffle** v to talk or write waffle

waffle² (say wof-əl) n a small cake made of batter and eaten hot

waft (say woft) v to float lightly and easily through the air or over water; to make something do this **waft** n **1** a gentle movement of air **2** a scent carried in the air

wag¹ v **wagged**, **wagging** to move or make something move briskly to and fro **wag** n a single wagging movement **wagtail** n any of several small birds with a long tail

wag² n a person who is fond of making jokes or playing practical jokes **waggish** adj

wage n **wages** pl n a regular payment to an employee in return for work or services ♦ She earns a good wage. ♦ He earns good wages. **wage** v to carry on a war or campaign

wager (say way-jer) n a bet **wager** v to bet

waggle v to move or make something move quickly to and fro ♦ Can you waggle your ears?

wagon, **waggon** n **1** a four-wheeled vehicle for carrying goods, pulled by horses or oxen **2** an open railway truck, e.g. for coal

waif n a homeless and helpless person, especially a child

wail v to make a long sad cry **wail** n a wailing cry, sound, or utterance

wainscot n wooden panelling on the wall of a room

waist n **1** the part of the human body below the ribs and above the bones of the pelvis **2** a narrow part in the middle of something ♦ the waist of an hourglass **waistband** n a strip of cloth that fits round the waist, e.g. at the top of a skirt **waistcoat** n a close-fitting waist-length piece of clothing with no sleeves or collar, buttoned down the front **waistline** n the amount you measure around your waist

wait v **1** to stay somewhere or delay doing something for a specified time or until something happens ♦ We waited until evening. **2** to be left to be dealt with at a later time ♦ This question will have to wait until our next meeting. **3** to be ready for someone ♦ A lovely stew is waiting for you when you get here. **4** to wait on people at a meal **wait** n an act or period of waiting **waiter** n a man who serves people with food and drink in a restaurant **waitress** n a woman who serves people with food and drink in a restaurant **to wait on 1** to hand food and drink to people at a meal **2** to fetch and carry for someone as an attendant

waiting list n a list of people waiting for a chance to obtain something when it becomes available

waive v to refrain from using or insisting upon a right or claim ♦ She waived her right to first class travel. ◊ Do not confuse this word with wave, which has a different meaning. **waiver** n the waiving of a right or claim; a document recording this ◊ Do not confuse this word with waver, which has a different meaning.

wake¹ v **woke**, **woken** (also **wake up**) to stop sleeping, or to make someone stop sleeping **wake** n a watch by a corpse before burial, or a party held after a funeral **wakeful** adj (said about a person) unable to sleep **waken** v to wake up **to wake up to** to become aware of something

wake² n **1** the track left on the water's surface by a moving ship, etc. **2** air-currents left behind an aircraft, etc. moving through air **in the wake of** behind; following after

walk v **1** to move along by lifting and setting down each foot in turn so that one foot is on the ground while the other is being lifted **2** to go over somewhere on foot ♦ We used to walk the fields in search of wild flowers. **3** to go with someone on foot ♦ I'll walk you to your car. **walk** n **1** a journey on foot, especially for pleasure or exercise **2** the manner or style of walking; a walking pace **3** a path or route for walking **walker** n **1** a person who walks **2** a framework that supports a baby learning to walk **walkabout** n an informal stroll among a crowd by an important visitor **walkie-talkie** n a portable radio transmitter and receiver **walking stick** n a stick carried or used as a support while walking **walkout** n a sudden angry departure, especially as a protest or strike **walkover** n an easy victory **walk of life** n a person's occupation or social position

wall n **1** a continuous upright structure forming one of the sides of a building or room, or serving to enclose, protect, or divide an area **2** something thought of as resembling this in form or function ♦ *a wall of fire* ♦ *a wall of silence* **3** the outside part of a hollow structure; tissue surrounding an organ of the body, etc. ♦ *the stomach wall* **wall** *v* to surround, enclose, or block something with a wall **wall-eyed** *adj* having eyes that show an abnormal amount of white, especially because of a squint **wallflower** *n* **1** a garden plant blooming in spring, with clusters of fragrant flowers **2** a shy person who no one talks to or dances with at a party **wallpaper** *n* paper used for covering the inside walls of rooms **to go to the wall** (said about a business) to fail

wallaby (say **wol**-ə-bi) *n pl* **wallabies** a kind of small kangaroo

wallet *n* a small flat folding case for holding banknotes, credit cards, etc.

wallop *v* **walloped, walloping** *informal* **1** to strike or hit someone or something very hard **2** to heavily defeat someone **wallop** *n informal* a heavy blow or punch

wallow *v* **1** to roll about in water or mud **2** to get great pleasure by being surrounded by something ♦ *a weekend wallowing in luxury* **wallow** *n* **1** the act of wallowing **2** an area of mud or shallow water where mammals go to wallow

wally *n pl* **wallies** *informal* a stupid person

walnut *n* **1** a nut containing an edible kernel with a wrinkled surface **2** the tree that bears this nut

walrus *n* a large amphibious animal with a pair of long tusks

waltz *n* **1** a ballroom dance for couples, with a graceful flowing melody in triple time **2** a piece of music for this **waltz** *v* **1** to dance a waltz; to lead someone in a waltz **2** *informal* to move somewhere in a very casual or confident way ♦ *You can't just waltz in and expect a warm welcome.*

wan (say **wonn**) *adj* **1** pale from being ill or tired **2** (said about a smile) faint and strained **wanly** *adv*

wand *n* a slender stick carried in the hand, especially as used by someone performing magic or magic tricks

wander *v* **1** to go from place to place without a settled route or destination or a special purpose **2** to go off course; to stray from your group or from a place ♦ *Don't wander from the path or you'll get lost.* **3** to be distracted or digress from a subject ♦ *He let his attention wander.* ♦ *You're wandering off the point again.* **wander** *n* an act of wandering **wanderer** *n* **wanderlust** *n* a strong desire to travel

wane *v* **1** (said about the moon) to show a gradually decreasing area of brightness after being full **2** to become less, smaller, or weaker **wane** *n* **on the wane** becoming less or weaker

wangle *v informal* to get or arrange something by using trickery, clever planning, or persuasion

want *v* **1** to have a desire or wish for something **2** to require or need something **want** *n* **1** a desire or wish to have something ♦ *a man of few wants* **2** lack or need of something, deficiency ♦ *The plants died from want of water.* **3** being poor and lacking the necessities of life ♦ *Many families here are living in great want.* **wanted** *adj* (said about a suspected criminal) being sought by the police for questioning or arrest **wanting** *adj* lacking in what is needed or usual; deficient

wanton (say **wonn**-tən) *adj* **1** done deliberately without any provocation or motive ♦ *wanton vandalism* **2** sexually immoral or promiscuous **wantonly** *adv* **wantonness** *n*

WAP *abbr* Wireless Application Protocol, a means of connecting a mobile phone to the Internet

war *n* **1** fighting between nations or groups, especially using armed forces **2** a state of competition or hostility between people ♦ *a price war* **3** a strong campaign against something ♦ *a war on drugs* **warring** *adj* **warrior** *n* a person who fights in battle; a soldier **war crime** *n* a crime committed during a war that breaks international rules of war, such as genocide **war criminal** *n* **war cry** *n* **1** a word or cry shouted in attacking or in rallying your side **2** the slogan of a political or other party **warfare** *n* fighting a war; a particular form of this ♦ *guerrilla warfare* **warhead** *n*

the explosive head of a missile, torpedo, or similar weapon **warlord** n a powerful military commander in charge of a region **warmonger** n a person who seeks to bring about war **warmongering** n, adj **warship** n a ship equipped with weapons and used in war **war-torn** adj (said about a place) devastated by war **on the warpath** angry and getting ready for a fight or argument

warble v to sing, especially with a gentle trilling note as some birds do **warble** n a warbling sound **warbler** n any of several small songbirds

ward n 1 a room with beds for a particular group of patients in a hospital 2 an area of a city or borough electing a councillor to represent it 3 a child or young person under the care of a guardian or the protection of a law court **ward** v **to ward someone** or **something off** to keep at a distance a person or thing that threatens danger **warder** n a prison guard **wardress** n **wardroom** n the mess room for commissioned officers on a warship

-ward suffix forming adjectives and adverbs showing direction (e.g. backward, forward, homeward)

warden n 1 an official who supervises a place or procedure 2 the head of certain schools, colleges, or other institutions

wardrobe n 1 a large cupboard where clothes are hung or stored 2 a person's stock of clothes 3 the stock of costumes of a theatre or film company, or the department in charge of this

-wards suffix forming adverbs showing direction (e.g. backwards, forwards)

ware n (used in compound words) manufactured articles of a particular type ♦ silverware **wares** pl n goods offered for sale

warehouse n a large building for storing goods or for storing furniture on behalf of its owners

warlock n a man who practises witchcraft

warm adj 1 fairly hot, not cold or cool 2 (said about clothes, etc.) keeping the body warm 3 friendly or enthusiastic ♦ a warm welcome 4 kindly and affectionate ♦ She has a warm heart. 5 (said about colours) suggesting

warmth **warm** v to make something warm, or to become warm **warm** n 1 a warm place or area 2 an act of warming **warmly** adv **warmness** n **warmth** n 1 the state or quality of being warm 2 friendliness or affection **warm-blooded** adj having a body temperature that remains warm (ranging from 36° to 42°C) permanently **to warm up** 1 to become warm 2 (said about an engine, etc.) to reach a temperature high enough for it to work properly 3 to prepare for athletic exercise by practice beforehand 4 to become more lively or receptive

warn v to tell someone about a danger or problem; to advise someone about what they should do in such circumstances ♦ We warned them to take waterproof clothing. **warning** n 1 something that serves to warn 2 advice to someone that they will be punished if they continue doing something **to warn someone off** to tell someone to keep away or to avoid a thing

warp (say worp) v 1 to become bent or twisted out of shape, usually because of heat or damp; to bend or twist something in this way 2 to distort a person's judgement or principles **warp** n 1 a warped condition 2 the lengthwise threads in weaving, crossed by the weft

warrant (say **wo**-rənt) n written authorization to do something ♦ The police have a warrant for his arrest. ♦ a search warrant **warrant** v 1 to justify something ♦ Nothing can warrant such rudeness. 2 to guarantee or confidently assert something ♦ He'll be back, I'll warrant you. **warranty** n pl **warranties** a written guarantee, especially one given to the buyer of an article by its manufacturer, promising to repair or replace it if necessary within a specified period **warrant officer** n a member of the armed services ranking between commissioned officers and NCOs

warren n 1 a piece of ground in which there are many burrows in which rabbits live and breed 2 a building or place with many narrow winding passages

wart n a small hard lump on the skin, caused by a virus **warty** adj **warthog** n an African wild pig with two large tusks and wart-like

growths on its face

wary (say **wair**-i) *adj* **warier**, **wariest** cautious about possible danger or difficulty **warily** *adv* **wariness** *n*

was past tense of *be*, used with a singular noun and with *I*, *he*, *she*, and *it*

wash *v* 1 to clean something with water or other liquid 2 to be washable ♦ *Cotton washes easily.* 3 to flow against or over something, to go splashing or flowing 4 *informal* (said about an excuse, piece of reasoning, etc.) to seem convincing or genuine ♦ *That argument just won't wash.*

wash *n* 1 washing, or being washed 2 a quantity of clothes that need to be washed or have just been washed 3 the disturbed water or air behind a moving ship or aircraft 4 a thin coating of colour painted over a surface **washable** *adj* **washer** *n* a ring of rubber or metal, etc. placed between two surfaces (e.g. under a bolt or screw) to give tightness or prevent leakage **washbasin** *n* a basin, usually fixed to a wall, for washing your hands and face **washed out** *adj* pale and tired **washing machine** *n* a machine for washing clothes, etc. **washing powder** *n* powder of soap or detergent for washing clothes, etc. **washing-up** *n* the process of washing dishes, etc. after use; the dishes, etc. that are to be washed **washout** *n* a complete failure **washstand** *n* a piece of furniture to hold a basin and jug of water, etc. for washing **to wash something up 1** (also **wash up**) to clean dishes and cutlery, etc. after use 2 to cast something up on shore

washing *n* a quantity of clothes, etc. that is to be washed or has just been washed

wasp *n* a stinging insect with black and yellow stripes round its body **waspish** *adj* making sharp or irritable comments

wassail (say **woss**-ayl) *v old use* to make merry and drink a lot of alcohol

waste *v* 1 to use something extravagantly or needlessly or without getting an adequate result 2 to fail to use an opportunity 3 to become gradually weaker or thinner ♦ *She was wasting away for lack of food.* **waste** *adj* 1 left over or thrown away because it is no longer wanted ♦ *waste products* 2 (said about land) not used, cultivated, or built on **waste** *n* 1 wasting a thing or not using it effectively ♦ *a waste of time* 2 waste material or food; waste products **wastage** *n* 1 loss of something by waste 2 (also **natural wastage**) the loss of employees through retirement or resignation, not through making them redundant **wasteful** *adj* using more than is needed **wastefully** *adv* **wastefulness** *n* **waster**, **wastrel** *n* a person who does nothing useful **wasteland** *n* a barren or empty area of land

watch *v* 1 to look at or observe something for some time, to keep your eyes fixed on something 2 to be on the alert or ready for something to happen ♦ *Watch for the traffic lights to turn green.* 3 to pay careful attention to something ♦ *I'll watch his progress with interest.* 4 to safeguard or take care of something **watch** *n* 1 a small portable device indicating the time, usually worn on the wrist or carried in the pocket 2 the act of watching, especially to see that all is well 3 a fixed period of being on duty on a ship, usually lasting four hours; the officers and crew on duty during a watch 4 a shift worked by firefighters or police officers **watcher** *n* **watchful** *adj* watching or observing closely **watchfulness** *n* **watchdog** *n* 1 a dog kept to guard property 2 a person or committee whose job is to make sure that companies providing a service or utility do not do anything harmful or illegal **watchman** *n pl* **watchmen** a person employed to look after an empty building at night **watchtower** *n* a tower from which a sentry keeps watch **watchword** *n* a word or phrase expressing briefly the principles or policy of a party or group ♦ *Our watchword is 'safety first'.*

water *n* 1 a colourless odourless tasteless liquid that is a compound of oxygen and hydrogen 2 a stretch or body of water, such as a lake, sea, or river 3 a solution of a substance in water ♦ *lavender water* ♦ *soda water* 4 the level of the tide ♦ *at high water* **waters** *pl n* the amniotic fluid surrounding a fetus in the womb **water** *v* 1 to sprinkle something with water 2 to supply something with water; to give

drinking water to an animal **3** to produce tears or saliva ♦ *It makes my mouth water.* **watery** *adj* **water buffalo** *n* the common domestic buffalo of India and SE Asia **water closet** *n* a toilet with a pan that is flushed by water **watercolour** *n* **1** artists' paint in which the pigment is diluted with water rather than oil **2** a picture painted with this kind of paint **watercourse** *n* a stream, brook, or artificial waterway; the channel along which it flows **watercress** *n* a kind of cress that grows in streams or ponds, with strong-tasting leaves that are used in salads **waterfall** *n* a cascade of water where a river or stream flows over the edge of a cliff or large rock **waterfowl** *pl n* waterbirds, especially ducks, geese, and swans **waterfront** *n* the part of a town that borders on a river, lake, or sea **waterhole** *n* a hollow in which water collects, especially one where animals drink **water ice** *n* a dessert of frozen fruit juice **watering can** *n* a container with a long tubular spout, for watering plants **watering place** *n* (also **watering hole**) a pool, etc. where animals go to drink water **2** a spa or a seaside resort **water lily** *n* a plant that grows in water, with broad floating leaves and white, yellow, blue, or red flowers **waterline** *n* the line along which the surface of the water touches a ship's side **waterlogged** *adj* saturated with water **watermark** *n* a manufacturer's design in some kinds of paper, visible when the paper is held against light **watermelon** *n* a melon with a smooth green skin, red pulp, and watery juice **watermill** *n* a mill worked by a waterwheel **water polo** *n* a game played by teams of swimmers with a ball like a football **waterproof** *adj* that keeps out water **waterproof** *n* a waterproof piece of clothing **waterproof** *v* to make something waterproof **watershed** *n* **1** a turning point in the course of events **2** a line of high land where streams on one side flow into one river or sea and streams on the other side flow into another **3** the time after which programmes that are thought to be unsuitable for children are broadcast on television **waterski** *n*

pl **waterskis** each of a pair of flat boards on which someone stands so that they can skim over the surface of water while being towed by a motor boat **waterski** *v* **waterskis**, **waterskied**, **waterskiing** to travel on waterskis **water table** *n* the level below which the ground is saturated with water **watertight** *adj* **1** made, fastened, or sealed so that water cannot get in or out **2** (said about an argument, alibi, agreement, etc.) impossible to dispute; containing no weaknesses or loopholes **water tower** *n* a tower that holds a water tank at a height that provides the pressure needed for distributing water **waterway** *n* a river or canal that ships or boats can travel on **waterwheel** *n* a large wheel turned by a flow of water, used to work machinery **waterworks** *n* a place with pumping machinery, etc. for supplying water to a district **to pass water** to urinate **to water something down 1** to dilute something **2** to make something less forceful or controversial

watt (say wot) *n* a unit of electric power, equivalent to one joule per second **wattage** *n* an amount of electric power, expressed in watts

wattle[1] (say **wot**-əl) *n* a structure of interwoven sticks and twigs used as material for fences, walls, etc.

wattle[2] (say **wot**-əl) *n* a red fleshy fold of skin hanging from the head or throat of turkeys and some other birds

wave *n* **1** a ridge of water moving along the surface of the sea, etc. or arching and breaking on the shore **2** *Phys* the wave-like motion by which heat, light, sound, or electricity, etc. is spread or carried **3** an act of waving your hand **4** a sudden increase in or occurrence of something ♦ *a wave of anger* ♦ *a crime wave* **5** a wave-like curve or arrangement of curves, e.g. in a line or in hair **wave** *v* **1** to move your arm or hand or something held to and fro as a signal or greeting **2** to signal or express something in this way ♦ *I waved him away.* ♦ *We stood on the platform, waving goodbye.* **3** to move loosely to and fro or up and down **4** to make something wave ◊ Do not

confuse this word with *waive*, which has a different meaning. **wavelet** *n* a small wave **wavy** *adj* **wavier**, **waviest**, **wavelength** *n* the distance between corresponding points (e.g. peaks) in a sound wave or an electromagnetic wave

waver *v* **1** to be or become unsteady, to begin to give way or weaken ♦ *The line of troops wavered and then broke.* ♦ *His courage was beginning to waver.* **2** to hesitate or be uncertain ♦ *She wavered between two opinions.*

wax¹ *n* **1** any of various soft sticky substances that melt easily, used for various purposes such as making candles, crayons, and polish **2** a yellow wax-like substance secreted in the ears **wax** *v* to coat, polish, or treat something with wax **waxen** *adj* **1** like wax in its paleness or smoothness **2** made of wax **waxy** *adj* **waxier**, **waxiest**, **waxwork** *n* a lifelike model of a person made in wax **waxworks** *n* an exhibition of waxworks

wax² *v* **1** (said about the moon) to show a bright area that becomes gradually larger until the moon becomes full **2** *literary* to become stronger or more important ♦ *Kingdoms waxed and waned.* **3** to speak or write in a particular way ♦ *He waxed lyrical about his childhood.*

way *n* **1** how something is done; a method or style of doing something ♦ *This is the best way to make scrambled eggs.* ♦ *She spoke in a kindly way.* **2** a habitual manner or course of action ♦ *You'll soon get into our ways.* **3** a road, path, or track **4** a route or direction ♦ *Can you tell me the way to the station?* ♦ *Which way is she looking?* **5** space free of obstacles so that people can pass ♦ *Make way!* **6** a distance ♦ *It's a long way to the summit.* **7** advance in some direction, progress ♦ *We made our way to the front.* **8** a particular aspect of something ♦ *It's a good idea in some ways.* **9** a condition or state ♦ *Things are in a bad way.* **ways** *pl n* parts into which something is divided ♦ *We'll split the money three ways.* **wayfarer** *n* a person travelling on foot **waylay** *v* past tense and past participle **waylaid** to lie in wait for someone, especially in order

to talk to them or rob them **way-out** *adj* unconventional in style **wayside** *n* the edge of a road or path **wayward** *adj* self-willed and unpredictable, not obedient or easily controlled **waywardness** *n*

WC *abbr* water closet (a toilet)

we *pronoun* **1** used by a person referring to himself or herself and one or more other people, or speaking on behalf of a nation, group, or firm, etc. **2** used instead of 'I' by a royal person in formal contexts and by an editor or writer in a newspaper, etc.

weak *adj* **1** lacking physical strength and energy **2** easily broken or bent; not able to withstand rough treatment or great force **3** (said about an argument, evidence, etc.) not forceful or convincing **4** having little power or influence **5** lacking firmness of character; easily led by others **6** lacking intensity ♦ *a weak signal* **7** not functioning well ♦ *weak eyesight* **weaken** *v* **weakling** *n* a weak person or animal **weakly** *adv* **weakness** *n* **1** the state of being weak **2** a weak point; a disadvantage or fault **3** inability to resist something, a particular fondness for something

weal *n* a ridge raised on the flesh by a stroke of a cane or whip, etc.

wealth *n* **1** a lot of money or property **2** the state of being rich **3** a great quantity ♦ *a book with a wealth of illustrations* **wealthy** *adj* **wealthier**, **wealthiest** having wealth, rich

wean *v* to get a baby used to taking food other than milk **to wean someone off** to make someone give up a habit, addiction, or interest gradually

weapon *n* **1** a thing designed or used as a means of inflicting bodily harm or physical damage **2** a means of getting the better of someone in a conflict ♦ *the weapon of a general strike* **weaponry** *n* weapons collectively

wear *v* **wore**, **worn** **1** to have clothes, jewellery, etc. on your body ♦ *He wears his hair long.* **2** to have a certain look on your face ♦ *She wore a frown.* **3** to damage something by rubbing or using it often; to become damaged in this way ♦ *The carpet has worn thin.* **4** to withstand continued

use ♦ *This fabric wears well wash after wash.*
wear *n* **1** clothing ♦ *evening wear* **2** (also **wear and tear**) damage resulting from continuous use **3** capacity to withstand being used ♦ *There's a lot of wear left in that coat.* **wearable** *adj* **wearer** *n* **wearing** *adj* mentally or physically tiring **to wear off** to become gradually less intense or effective **to wear on** (said about time) to pass gradually ♦ *The night wore on.* **to wear someone out** to exhaust someone **to wear something out** to use something until it is no longer usable

weary *adj* **wearier, weariest 1** very tired, especially from exertion or endurance **2** tired of something ♦ *People are weary of war.* **3** causing tiredness ♦ *It's weary work.* **weary** *v* **wearies, wearied, wearying 1** to make someone weary **2** to grow tired of something **wearily** *adv* **weariness** *n* **wearisome** *adj* causing weariness

weasel *n* a small fierce mammal with a slender body and reddish-brown fur, living on small animals, birds' eggs, etc.

weather *n* the condition of the atmosphere at a certain place and time, with reference to the presence or absence of sunshine, rain, wind, etc. **weather** *v* **1** to wear something away or change its appearance by exposing it to the effects of the weather **2** to become worn or altered in this way **3** to come through something safely or successfully ♦ *The ship weathered the storm.* **weather-beaten** *adj* damaged, worn, or tanned by exposure to the weather **weathercock** *n* a weathervane in the shape of a cockerel **weathervane** *n* a revolving pointer mounted in a high place and turning easily in the wind to show from which direction the wind is blowing **under the weather** feeling ill or depressed

weave[1] *v* **wove, woven 1** to make fabric or baskets, etc. by crossing threads or strips under and over each other **2** to put a story together **weave** *n* a style or pattern of weaving ♦ *a loose weave* **weaver** *n*

weave[2] *v* past tense and past participle **weaved** to move from side to side to get round things in the way ♦ *He weaved through the traffic.*

web *n* **1** the network of fine strands made by a spider **2** a network ♦ *a web of deceit* **3** skin filling the spaces between the toes of birds such as ducks and animals such as frogs **the Web** *n* the World Wide Web **webbed** *adj* **webbing** *n* strong bands of woven fabric used in upholstery, belts, etc. **weblog** *n* a personal website on which its creator regularly records events, opinions, and links to other sites **web page** *n* a page on a website **website** *n* a location on the World Wide Web, giving information about a company, subject, etc.

wed *v* past tense and past participle **wedded** or **wed**; **wedding 1** to marry **2** to combine or unite two different things ♦ *We need to wed efficiency to economy.* **wedded** *adj* to do with marriage ♦ *wedded bliss* **wedding** *n* the ceremony and celebration when a couple get married **wedlock** *n* being married **to be wedded to** to be devoted to and unable to abandon an activity or opinion

wedge *n* **1** a piece of wood or metal, etc. thick at one end and tapered to a thin edge at the other, pushed between things to force them apart or to prevent something from moving **2** a wedge-shaped thing **wedge** *v* **1** to keep something in place with a wedge **2** to force something into a narrow space

Wednesday *n* the day of the week following Tuesday

wee *adj* **weer, weest** little

weed *n* **1** a wild plant that grows where it is not wanted **2** a thin weak-looking person **weed** *v* to remove weeds from the ground **weedy** *adj* **weedier, weediest 1** full of weeds **2** thin and puny **to weed something out** to remove people or things that are inferior or undesirable

week *n* **1** a period of seven days, especially from Sunday to the following Saturday **2** the five days other than Saturday and Sunday ♦ *I never go there during the week.* **3** the period for which you regularly work during a week ♦ *a 40-hour week* **weekly** *adj* happening, done, or produced once a week **weekly** *adv* once a week **weekly** *n* *pl* **weeklies** a newspaper or magazine published once a week **weekday** *n* a day

other than Saturday or Sunday **weekend** *n* Saturday and Sunday

weep *v* past tense and past participle **wept** **1** to shed tears, to cry **2** to ooze moisture in drops **weep** *n* a spell of weeping **weepy** *adj* **weepier**, **weepiest** inclined to weep, tearful

weevil *n* a kind of small beetle that feeds on grain, nuts, tree bark, etc.

weft *n* the threads on a loom that are woven under and over the warp to make fabric

weigh *v* **1** to measure the weight of something, especially by means of scales or a similar instrument **2** to have a certain weight ♦ *What do you weigh?* **3** to consider carefully the relative importance or value of something ♦ *Let's weigh the pros and cons.* **4** to be important or have influence ♦ *Her evidence weighed with the jury.* **5** to be a burden ♦ *The responsibility weighed heavily on him.* **weight** *n* **1** how heavy something is; the amount that something weighs **2** a unit or system of units used to express how much something weighs **3** a piece of metal of known weight used on scales for weighing things **4** a heavy object, especially one used to bring or keep something down **5** importance or influence ♦ *The weight of the evidence is against you.* **weight** *v* **1** to attach a weight to something; to hold something down with a heavy object **2** to arrange something in a way that gives someone an advantage or creates a bias ♦ *The test was weighted in favour of candidates with scientific knowledge.* **weighting** *n* extra pay given to compensate for the higher cost of living in a place **weightless** *adj* **weightlessness** *n* **weightlifting** *n* the athletic sport of lifting heavy weights **weightlifter** *n* **weighty** *adj* **weightier**, **weightiest** **1** having great weight, heavy **2** important or influential **3** serious or worrying **weighbridge** *n* a weighing machine with a plate set in a road, etc. on to which vehicles can be driven to be weighed **to weigh anchor** to raise the anchor and start a voyage

weir (say *weer*) *n* a low dam built across a river, serving to regulate the flow

weird *adj* strange and uncanny or bizarre

weirdly *adv* **weirdness** *n* **weirdo** *n pl* **weirdos** a strange or eccentric person

welcome *n* a greeting or reception, especially a kindly one **welcome** *adj* **1** received with pleasure ♦ *a welcome guest* **2** pleasing because it is much needed or wanted ♦ *a welcome change* **3** allowed or invited to do something ♦ *Anyone is welcome to try it.* **welcome** *v* **1** to show that you are pleased when a person or thing arrives **2** to be glad to receive or hear of something ♦ *The decision has been widely welcomed.*

weld *v* **1** to join pieces of metal or plastic by heating and hammering or pressing them together **2** to combine people or things into a whole **weld** *n* a joint made by welding **welder** *n*

welfare *n* **1** people's health, happiness, and comfort; well-being **2** financial support given to people in need **welfare state** *n* a system in which a country's government seeks to ensure the welfare of all its citizens by providing money to pay for health care, old-age pensions, benefits, etc.

well[1] *adv* **better**, **best** **1** in a good or suitable way, satisfactorily, rightly **2** thoroughly or carefully ♦ *Polish it well.* **3** by a considerable margin; very much ♦ *She is well over forty.* **4** with good reason, probably ♦ *It may well be our last chance.* **5** favourably or kindly ♦ *They think well of him.* **well** *adj* **1** in good health **2** in a satisfactory state or position ♦ *All's well.* **well** *interjection* used to express surprise, relief, resignation, etc., or used to introduce a remark when you are hesitating **well-being** *n* good health, happiness, and comfort **well disposed** *adj* having kindly or favourable feelings towards a person or plan, etc. **well-heeled** *adj* wealthy **well known** *adj* known to many people **well meaning** *adj* having good intentions but not having a good effect **well-nigh** *adv* almost **well off** *adj* **1** fairly rich **2** in a satisfactory or good situation **well read** *adj* having read a lot of good books **well spoken** *adj* speaking in an educated and refined way **well-to-do** *adj* fairly rich **well-wisher** *n* a person who wishes another well **well worn** *adj* **1** much worn by use **2** (said

about a phrase or idea) used so much that it is no longer interesting or significant; hackneyed ◊ The adverb *well* is often used in combination with past participles of verbs, e.g. *well advised* and *well known*. It is usual to use a hyphen when the combination comes before a noun (e.g. *a well-known singer*), but not when it comes after a verb (e.g. *a singer who is well known*).

well² *n* **1** a deep shaft dug in the ground to obtain water or oil, etc. from underground **2** an enclosed space in the middle of a building, especially one containing a staircase or lift **well** *v* to rise or flow up ♦ *Tears welled up in her eyes.*

wellies *pl n informal* wellingtons

wellingtons *pl n* rubber or plastic waterproof boots, usually reaching almost to the knee

Welsh *adj* to do with or coming from Wales **Welsh** *n* the Celtic language of Wales

welsh *v* **to welsh on** to fail to honour a debt or obligation

welt *n* **1** a strengthened seam **2** a weal, the mark of a heavy blow

welter *n* a disorderly or confused mass ♦ *welter of information*

welterweight *n* in boxing, a weight (67 kg) between middleweight and lightweight

wen *n* a large but harmless swelling or growth on the skin, especially on the head

wench *n old use* a girl or young woman

wend *v* **to wend your way** to go slowly or by an indirect route

were past tense of *be*, used with a plural noun and with *we*, *you*, and *they*

we're *v* we are

weren't *v* were not

werewolf (say **weer**-wuulf) *n pl* **werewolves** (in legends) a person who at times turns into a wolf

west *n* **1** the point of the horizon where the sun sets, opposite east, or the direction in which this point lies **2** the part of a place or building that is towards the west **the West** Europe and North America seen in contrast to other civilizations **west** *adj*, *adv* **1** towards or in the west **2** (said about a wind) blowing from the west **westerly** *adj* **western** *adj* of or in the west **western** *n*

a film or story dealing with cowboys in western North America **westerner** *n* someone who lives in the west of a country or region **westernize** *v* to bring a person, country, etc. under the influence of ideas, customs, and institutions from Europe and North America **westernization** *n* **westward** *adj*, *adv*

wet *adj* **wetter**, **wettest 1** soaked, covered, or moistened with water or other liquid **2** not yet dry ♦ *wet paint* **3** rainy ♦ *wet weather* **4** *informal* (said about a person) lacking strength of character or firmness of purpose **wet** *v* past tense and past participle **wetted** or **wet**; **wetting 1** to make something wet **2** to urinate in something **wet** *n* **1** liquid that makes something damp **2** rainy weather **3** *informal* a feeble or ineffectual person **wetly** *adv* **wetness** *n* **wet blanket** *n* a gloomy person who prevents other people from enjoying themselves **wetlands** *pl n* swampy or marshy land **wet nurse** *n* a woman employed to suckle another woman's child **wetsuit** *n* a close-fitting rubber suit worn in skin diving, etc. to keep the wearer warm ◊ Do not confuse this word with *whet*, which has a different meaning.

whack *n informal* **1** a heavy resounding blow **2** an attempt ♦ *I'll have a whack at it.* **3** a share or contribution ♦ *Everyone did their whack.* **whack** *v* to hit someone or something hard **whacked** *adj* tired out **whacking** *adj* very large

whale *n* any of several very large sea mammals with a horizontal tail fin and a blowhole on top of the head for breathing **whaler** *n* a person or ship that hunts whales **whaling** *n* hunting whales **whalebone** *n* a horny springy substance from the upper jaw of some kinds of whale **to have a whale of a time** *informal* to enjoy yourself very much

wham *interjection*, *n informal* the sound of a forcible impact

wharf (say **worf**) *n pl* **wharves** or **wharfs** a landing stage where ships may moor for loading and unloading

what *adj* **1** asking for a statement of amount, number, or kind ♦ *What vegetables have we*

got? **2** how great, strange, or remarkable ♦ *What a fool you are!* **3** the or any that, whatever ♦ *Lend me what money you can spare.* **what** *pronoun* **1** what thing or things; the thing that ♦ *This is what you must do.* **2** a request for something to be repeated because you have not heard or understood **what** *adv* to what extent or degree ♦ *What does it matter?* **what** *interjection* an exclamation of surprise **whatever** *pronoun* **1** anything or everything ♦ *Do whatever you like.* **2** no matter what ♦ *Keep calm, whatever happens.* **whatever** *adj* **1** of any kind or number ♦ *Take whatever books you need.* **2** at all ♦ *There is no doubt whatever.* **whatnot** *n* other things of the same kind ♦ *a drawer full of pens, paper, and whatnot* **whatsoever** *adj, pronoun* whatever

wheat *n* **1** grain from which flour is made **2** the cereal plant that produces this **wheaten** *adj* made from wheat flour **wheatmeal** *n* flour made from wheat from which some of the bran and germ has been removed

wheedle *v* to persuade someone to do something by coaxing or flattering them

wheel *n* **1** a circular object that revolves on a shaft or axle that passes through its centre **2** something resembling this or having a wheel as an essential part **3** motion like that of a wheel, or of a line of people that pivots on one end **wheel** *v* **1** to push or pull a bicycle or cart, etc. along on its wheels **2** to turn round quickly to face another way ♦ *He wheeled round in astonishment.* **3** to move or fly in a wide circle or curve **wheelbarrow** *n* an open container for moving small loads, with a wheel beneath one end, and two straight handles (by which it is pushed) and legs at the other **wheelbase** *n* the distance between the front and rear axles of a vehicle **wheelchair** *n* a chair on wheels, used by a person who cannot walk **to wheel and deal** to be involved in business or political activities in an unscrupulous or dishonest way

wheeze *v* to breathe with a hoarse whistling or rattling sound in the chest **wheeze** *n* **1** the sound of wheezing **2** *informal* a clever or amusing scheme or plan **wheezy** *adj*

whelk *n* a shellfish that looks like a snail

whelp *n* a young dog or wolf, a pup or cub **whelp** *v* to give birth to a whelp or whelps

when *adv* **1** at what time; on what occasion **2** at which time ♦ *There are times when joking is out of place.* **when** *conjunction* **1** at the time that, on the occasion that **2** although; considering that, since ♦ *Why risk it when you know it's dangerous?* **when** *pronoun* what or which time ♦ *From when does the agreement date?* **whenever** *conjunction, adv* at whatever time; on whatever occasion

whence *adv, conjunction formal* from where, from what place or source; from which

where *adv, conjunction* **1** at or in what or which place, position, or circumstances **2** to what place **3** in or at or to the place in which ♦ *Leave it where it is.* **where** *pronoun* what place ♦ *Where does she come from?* **whereabouts** *adv* in or near what place **whereabouts** *n, pl n* the place where someone or something is ♦ *Can you tell me his whereabouts?* **whereas** *conjunction* but in contrast ♦ *He is English, whereas his wife is French.* **whereby** *adv* by which **wherefore** *adv* why **wherein** *adv* in what; in which **whereof** *adv, conjunction* of what or which **whereupon** *conjunction* immediately after which **wherever** *adv* at or to whatever place **wherever** *conjunction* in every place that; in every case when **wherewithal** *n* the money or other resources needed for a particular purpose

whet *v* **whetted**, **whetting** **1** to sharpen something by rubbing it against a stone, etc. **2** to stimulate something ♦ *You've really whetted my appetite.* **whetstone** *n* a shaped stone used for sharpening tools

whether *conjunction* used to express a doubt or choice between two possibilities ♦ *I don't know whether to believe her or not.*

whew *interjection* used to express astonishment, relief, tiredness, etc.

whey (say way) *n* the watery liquid left when milk forms curds

which *adj, pronoun* **1** what particular one or ones of a set of things or people ♦ *Which way did he go?* ♦ *Which is your desk?* **2** and that ♦ *We invited him to come, which he did very willingly.* **which** *relative pronoun* the thing

referred to ◊ You use *which* when it begins a clause giving incidental information that you could leave out, e.g. *The house, which is for sale, is round the corner.* You use *that* or *which* when it begins a clause that defines or identifies something and cannot be left out, e.g. *The house that is for sale is round the corner.* **whichever** *adj, pronoun* any which, that or those which ◆ *Get the 45 or 47 bus, whichever comes first.* ◆ *Take whichever one you like.*

whiff *n* **1** a puff or slight smell of smoke, gas, etc. **2** a trace of something ◆ *a whiff of danger*

while *conjunction* **1** at the same time as ◆ *Whistle while you work.* **2** although ◆ *While I admit that he is sincere, I think he is mistaken.* **3** on the other hand, whereas ◆ *She is dark, while her sister is fair.* **while** *n* a period of time, the time spent in doing something ◆ *a long while ago* ◆ *We've waited all this while.* **while** *v* **to while something away** to pass time in a leisurely manner **whilst** *conjunction* while

whim *n* a sudden desire or change of mind **whimsical** *adj* **whimsy** *n pl* **whimsies 1** a whim **2** playful or fanciful humour

whimper *v* to cry or whine softly, to make feeble frightened or complaining sounds **whimper** *n* a whimpering sound

whine *v* **1** to make a long high complaining cry like that of a child or dog **2** to complain in a petty or feeble way **whine** *n* a whining cry or sound or complaint

whinge *v* present participle **whingeing** to grumble persistently **whinge** *n informal* an act of grumbling

whinny *v* **whinnies**, **whinnied**, **whinnying** (said about a horse) to neigh gently **whinny** *n pl* **whinnies** a gentle neigh

whip *n* **1** a cord or strip of leather fastened to a handle, used for urging an animal on or for striking a person as a punishment **2** an official of a political party in parliament with authority to maintain discipline among members of the party **3** a written notice issued by party whips, requesting members to attend on a particular occasion **4** a dessert made by whipping a mixture of cream, etc. with fruit or flavouring **whip** *v* **whipped**, **whipping 1** to beat a person or animal with a whip **2** to beat cream or eggs, etc. into a froth **3** to move or take something suddenly ◆ *He whipped out a knife.* **4** *informal* to steal something **whiplash** *n* **1** the lash of a whip **2** injury caused by a severe jerk to the head, especially in a motor accident **whipping boy** *n* a person who is blamed or punished when someone else is at fault **whip-round** *n* an appeal for contributions of money from a group of people **to have the whip hand** to be in a controlling position **to whip something up 1** to stir up people's feelings ◆ *We've been trying to whip up support for the proposal.* **2** to make or prepare something quickly

whippet *n* a small dog resembling a greyhound, used for racing

whirl *v* **1** to swing or spin round and round; to make something do this **2** to travel swiftly in a curved course **3** (said about the head or mind) to seem to spin round **whirl** *n* **1** a whirling movement **2** frantic or bustling activity ◆ *a mad social whirl* **whirlpool** *n* a current of water whirling in a circle **whirlwind** *n* a mass of air whirling rapidly about a central point **whirlwind** *adj* very rapid and unexpected ◆ *a whirlwind romance*

whirr *v* to make a continuous buzzing or vibrating sound like that of a wheel, etc. turning rapidly **whirr** *n* a whirring sound

whisk *v* **1** to take someone or something rapidly, especially in a vehicle ◆ *A taxi whisked us off to the theatre.* **2** to move something with a quick light sweeping movement **3** to beat eggs, etc. until they are frothy **whisk** *n* **1** a whisking movement **2** a kitchen tool used for whisking eggs or cream

whisker *n* **1** each of the long hair-like bristles growing near the mouth of a cat and certain other animals **2** *informal* a very small amount or distance ◆ *within a whisker of it* **whiskers** *pl n* the hair growing on a man's face, especially on his cheeks

whisky *n pl* **whiskies 1** spirit distilled from malted grain, especially barley **2** a drink of this **whiskey** *n* Irish whisky

whisper v 1 to speak softly, using the breath but not the vocal cords 2 (said about leaves or fabrics, etc.) to rustle softly **whisper** n 1 a whispering tone of voice 2 a rumour 3 a soft rustling sound

whist n a card game usually for two pairs of players

whistle n 1 a shrill sound made by forcing breath through a narrow opening in your lips or through your teeth 2 a similar sound made by a bird or the wind or produced by a flute, kettle, train, etc. 3 an instrument that makes a shrill sound when air or steam is forced through it **whistle** v to make a whistle; to produce a tune in this way **whistle-stop** adj very fast and with only brief pauses ♦ a whistle-stop tour

whit n the least possible amount ♦ not a whit better

white adj 1 of the very lightest colour, like snow or salt 2 having a light-coloured skin 3 (said about coffee or tea) with milk 4 (said about wine) made from pale grapes or skinned black grapes, and yellowish in colour 5 pale in the face from illness or fear or other emotion **white** n 1 a white colour 2 a person with a light-coloured skin 3 the transparent substance (called albumen) round the yolk of an egg, turning white when cooked 4 the white part of the eyeball, round the iris **whiten** v **whiteness** n **whiting** n pl **whiting** a small sea fish with white flesh, used for food **whitish** adj **whitebait** n pl **whitebait** a small silvery-white fish, used for food **white-collar** adj (said about a worker) involved in clerical or professional work done in an office, especially as opposed to manual work **white elephant** n a useless or unwanted possession, especially one that is expensive to maintain **white flag** n a white flag or cloth used as a symbol of surrender or truce **white-hot** adj so hot that it glows white **white lie** n a harmless or trivial lie that you tell in order to avoid hurting someone's feelings **White Paper** n a report issued by the government to give information on a subject **white spirit** n a colourless liquid made from petroleum, used as a paint thinner and solvent **whitewash** n 1 a liquid

containing quicklime or powdered chalk, used for painting walls white 2 deliberately concealing someone's mistakes or faults so that they will not be punished **whitewash** v 1 to paint a wall with whitewash 2 to clear someone's reputation by glossing over their mistakes or faults

whither adv old use to what place or state ♦ Whither did they go?

Whit Sunday n the seventh Sunday after Easter, commemorating the descent of the Holy Spirit on the apostles at Pentecost **Whitsuntide** n the weekend or week including Whit Sunday

whittle v 1 to trim or shape wood by cutting thin slices from the surface 2 to reduce something by removing various amounts from it

whizz, whiz v **whizzed, whizzing** 1 to move or make something move at great speed through the air with a whistling or buzzing sound 2 to move very quickly **whizz** n a whizzing sound **whizz-kid** n an exceptionally brilliant or successful young person

who pronoun 1 what or which person or persons 2 the particular person or persons ♦ This is the man who wanted to see you. **whodunnit** n a story or play about a murder and the attempt to identify the murderer **whoever** pronoun 1 any or every person who 2 no matter who

whoa interjection a command to a horse to stop or slow down

whole adj 1 with no part removed or left out ♦ I told them the whole story. 2 not injured or broken ♦ There's not a plate left whole. **whole** adv 1 in one piece ♦ The snake swallowed the bird whole. 2 completely ♦ a whole new approach **whole** n 1 the full or complete amount, all of something 2 something that is complete in itself **wholly** adv completely or entirely, with nothing excepted or removed **wholefood** n food that has been processed as little as possible and is free of additives **wholehearted** adj without doubts or reservations **wholemeal** adj made from the whole grain of wheat **wholesale** n the selling of goods in large quantities to

be retailed by others **wholesale** *adj, adv* **1** being sold in this way **2** on a large scale ♦ *wholesale destruction* **wholesaler** *n*

wholesome *adj* **1** good for physical health; showing a healthy condition **2** good for moral well-being **on the whole** taking everything into account; in general

whom *pronoun* the form of *who* used when it is the object of a verb or comes after a preposition, as in *the boy whom I saw* or *To whom did you speak?* ◊ *Whom* can sound rather formal. In modern English, especially in speech and less formal writing, it often sounds more natural to use *who*, as in *the boy who I saw* (or simply *the boy I saw*) and *Who did you speak to?*

whoop (say woop) *n* a loud cry of excitement **whoop** *v* to give a whoop **whoopee** *interjection* a cry of wild excitement or joy **whooping cough** *n* an infectious disease that mainly affects children, causing a cough that is followed by a long rasping indrawn breath

whoops (say woops) *interjection informal* an exclamation of apology or dismay

whoosh *v* to move very quickly; to rush

whopper *n informal* **1** something very large **2** a blatant lie **whopping** *adj*

whore (say hor) *n* a prostitute; a sexually immoral woman

whorl *n* **1** a coiled form; a single turn of a spiral **2** a complete circle formed by ridges in a fingerprint **3** a ring of leaves or petals round a stem or central point

who's *v* **1** who is **2** who has ◊ Do not confuse this word with *whose*, which has a different meaning.

whose *pronoun* of whom, of which ♦ *Whose house is that?* ♦ *the boy whose bike we found* ◊ Do not confuse this word with *who's*, which has a different meaning.

why *adv* **1** for what reason or purpose **2** on account of which ♦ *The reasons why it happened are not clear.* **why** *interjection* an exclamation of surprise or indignation

WI *abbr* **1** West Indies **2** Women's Institute

wick *n* a length of thread in the centre of a candle, oil lamp, or cigarette lighter, etc. by which the flame is kept supplied with melted grease or fuel

wicked *adj* **1** morally bad or cruel **2** playfully mischievous ♦ *a wicked grin* **3** *informal* excellent **wickedly** *adv* **wickedness** *n*

wicker *n* thin canes or twigs woven together to make furniture or baskets, etc. **wickerwork** *n*

wicket *n* **1** a set of three stumps and two bails used in cricket, defended by the batsman **2** the strip of ground between the two wickets **wicketkeeper** *n* a fielder in cricket who stands behind the batsman's wicket

wide *adj* **1** measuring a lot from side to side, not narrow ♦ *a wide river* **2** in width, measuring from side to side ♦ *one metre wide* **3** extending far, covering a great range ♦ *a wide knowledge of art* **4** open to the full extent ♦ *She stared at me with wide eyes.* **5** missing a point or target ♦ *His header was a metre wide.* **wide** *adv* **1** widely **2** to the full extent ♦ *Open wide.* **3** missing the target ♦ *The shot went wide.* **widely** *adv* **widen** *v* **wideness** *n* **width** *n* **1** how wide something is; the distance or measurement of something from side to side **2** a wide range or extent **wide awake** fully awake **wide-eyed** *n* **1** with your eyes wide open in amazement **2** inexperienced or innocent

widespread *adj* found or distributed over a wide area or among a large number of people ♦ *a widespread belief*

widgeon *n* another spelling of *wigeon*

widow *n* a woman whose husband has died and who has not married again **widowed** *adj* **widower** *n* a man whose wife has died and who has not married again **widowhood** *n*

wield (say weeld) *v* **1** to hold and use a weapon or tool **2** to have and use power or influence

wife *n pl* **wives** the woman to whom a man is married **wifely** *adj*

wig *n* a covering for the head made of real or artificial hair

wigeon (say wij-ən) *n* any of several kinds of wild duck, the male of which has a whistling call

wiggle *v* to move or make something move repeatedly from side to side **wiggle** *n* a wiggling movement

wigwam (say **wig**-wam) n a hut or tent made by fastening skins or mats over a framework of poles, as formerly used by some Native Americans

wiki n ICT a website developed by a group of users, allowing any user to add and edit comment

wilco interjection used in radio communication to indicate that directions received will be carried out

wild adj **1** living or growing in its original natural state; not domesticated, tame, or cultivated **2** (said about people) not civilized, barbarous ♦ wild tribes **3** (said about scenery) looking very desolate; not cultivated ♦ a wild moor **4** lacking restraint or control ♦ wild behaviour **5** stormy or windy ♦ a wild night **6** very excited, enthusiastic, or angry **7** haphazard ♦ a wild guess **the wild** n a natural environment ♦ a chance to see lions in the wild **the wilds** pl n a remote area, far from civilization **wilderness** n a wild uncultivated area **wildly** adv **wildness** n **wildfire** n **wildcat** adj (said about strikes) sudden and unofficial **wildfowl** n birds that are hunted as game, such as ducks and geese, quail, and pheasants **wildlife** n wild animals collectively **Wild West** n the western states of the USA during the period when they were lawless frontier districts **wild goose chase** n a hopeless or pointless search for something **to spread like wildfire** (said about rumours, etc.) to spread very fast

wildebeest (say **wil**-di-beest) n pl **wildebeest** or **wildebeests** a gnu

wile n a piece of trickery intended to deceive or attract someone **wily** adj **wilier**, **wiliest** crafty or cunning **wiliness** n

wilful adj **1** stubbornly determined to do what you want **2** done deliberately and not as an accident **wilfully** adv **wilfulness** n

will¹ auxiliary verb **1** used to express the future tense ♦ They will arrive soon. **2** used in questions, especially requests ♦ Will you shut the door? **3** used to express a promise, intention, or obligation ♦ I will never let you down. ◊ See the note at shall.

will² n **1** the mental power to decide on and control your own actions or those of others **2** will power **3** a desire; a chosen decision ♦ I wrote the letter against my will. **4** a document containing instructions from a person on how their money and property are to be disposed of after their death **will** v **1** to use your will power; to bring something about by doing this ♦ I was willing you to win. **2** to intend something to happen ♦ God has willed it. **3** to bequeath something in a will **willing** adj ready and happy to do what is wanted **willingly** adv **willingness** n **will power** n strength of mind to control what you do or resist temptation **with a will** with determination

willies pl n **the willies** informal nervous discomfort ♦ This house gives me the willies.

will-o'-the-wisp n **1** a flickering spot of light seen on marshy ground **2** an elusive person, hope, or goal

willow n **1** any of several trees or shrubs with flexible branches, usually growing near water **2** the wood of this tree **willowy** adj (said about a person) tall, slim, and supple

willy-nilly adv **1** whether you want to or not **2** haphazardly

wilt v **1** (said about plants or flowers) to lose freshness and droop **2** (said about a person) to lose your energy because of exhaustion

wimp n informal a weak or timid person

wimple n a cloth headdress folded round the head, neck, and cheeks, worn by women in the Middle Ages and still worn by some nuns

win v past tense and past participle **won**; **winning 1** to defeat your opponents in a battle, game, or contest; to gain a victory **2** to get or achieve something as the result of a battle, game, bet, etc. **3** to gain something as a result of effort or perseverance ♦ Gradually he won their confidence. **win** n a victory in a game or contest **winner** n **winning** adj charming and attractive ♦ a winning smile **winnings** pl n money won, especially in gambling

wince v to make a slight involuntary movement because of pain, distress, or embarrassment **wince** n a wincing movement

winch n a device for lifting or pulling things by means of a cable which winds round a

wind[1] (say wind) n 1 a movement or current of air, especially one occurring naturally in the atmosphere and blowing horizontally 2 breath 3 gas forming in the stomach or intestines and causing discomfort 4 the wind instruments of an orchestra 5 meaningless or boastful talk **wind** v 1 to make someone short of breath 2 to make a baby bring up wind by patting its back **windward** adj situated on the side facing the wind **windward** n the windward side **windy** adj windier, windiest, **windbag** n a person who talks too much **windbreak** n a screen or row of trees shielding something from the full force of the wind **windcheater** n a jacket of thin but wind-proof material fitting closely at the waist and cuffs **windfall** n 1 an apple or other fruit blown off a tree by the wind 2 a piece of unexpected good fortune, especially in the form of a sum of money **wind farm** n a group of windmills or wind turbines for generating electricity **wind instrument** n a musical instrument played by blowing, such as a trumpet or flute **windmill** n a mill worked by the wind turning the arms (called *sails* or *vanes*) that radiate from a central shaft **windpipe** n the tube by which air reaches the lungs, leading from the throat to the bronchial tubes **windscreen** n the glass in the window at the front of a motor vehicle **windsock** n a tube-shaped piece of canvas open at both ends, flown on a mast at an airfield to show the direction and strength of the wind **windsurfing** n the sport of surfing on a board that has a sail fixed to it (called a *sailboard*) **windsurfer** n **windswept** adj exposed to strong winds

wind[2] (say wiynd) v past tense and past participle **wound 1** to go or turn something in a twisting or spiral course ♦ *The road winds through the hills.* **2** to wrap or encircle something ♦ *She wound a bandage round her finger.* **3** to twist or wrap something closely round and round upon itself so that it forms a ball **4** (also **wind up**) to set or keep a watch, clock, etc. going by turning a key or handle **winder** n **windlass** n a device

for lifting or pulling things by means of a rope or chain that is wound round a drum-shaped axle by turning a handle **to wind someone up** *informal* to tease someone **to wind something up** to bring something to an end **to wind up** *informal* to end up in a place or condition ♦ *He'll wind up in jail.*

window n 1 an opening in a wall or roof to let in light and often air, usually fitted with glass in a frame 2 a space behind the window of a shop where goods are displayed 3 a framed area on a computer screen used for a particular purpose 4 an interval or opportunity to do something **window dressing** n 1 the displaying of goods attractively in a shop window 2 presentation of facts in a way that creates a more favourable impression **window-shopping** n looking at the goods displayed in shop windows without necessarily intending to buy anything

windshield n N. Am a windscreen

wine n 1 an alcoholic drink made from fermented grape juice 2 a fermented drink made from other fruits or plants ♦ *ginger wine* 3 dark purplish red **wine** v **to wine and dine someone** to entertain someone with drinks and a meal

wing n 1 each of the pair of parts of a bird, bat, or insect, etc. that it uses for flying 2 one of the pair of long flat parts that stick out from the sides of an aircraft and support it in the air 3 a part of a large building, especially one that extends from the main part 4 the part of a motor vehicle's bodywork immediately above a wheel 5 a section of a political party or other group, usually one with more extreme views than those of the majority 6 the part of a football, rugby, or hockey field close to either of the sides **wings** pl n the sides of a theatre stage out of sight of the audience **wing** v 1 to fly, to travel by means of wings ♦ *a bird winging its way home* 2 to shoot a bird in the wing; to wound a person slightly in the arm or shoulder **winged** adj **winger** n an attacking player on the wing in football, hockey, etc. **wing commander** n an officer of the RAF **wingspan** n the length from the tip of one wing of an aircraft, bird, etc. to

the tip of the other

wink v 1 to close and open one eye quickly, often as a private signal to someone 2 (said about a light or star, etc.) to shine with a light that flashes quickly on and off or twinkles **wink** n 1 an act of winking 2 a brief period of sleep ♦ *I didn't sleep a wink.*

winkle n a kind of edible shellfish with a spiral shell **winkle** v **to winkle something out** to extract or obtain something with difficulty ♦ *I managed to winkle out some information.*

winnow v 1 to toss or fan grain, etc. so that the loose dry outer part is blown away 2 to sift or separate something from the parts that are not wanted

winsome adj charming and attractive

winter n the coldest season of the year, between autumn and spring **wintry** adj **wintrier, wintriest** 1 to do with or like winter, cold 2 lacking warmth or friendliness

wipe v 1 to clean or dry the surface of something by rubbing something over it 2 to erase data from a tape, etc. **wipe** n the act of wiping **wiper** n **to wipe something out** to destroy something completely

wire n 1 metal drawn out into a thin flexible thread or rod 2 a piece of wire used to carry electric current, for fencing, etc. 3 a telegram **wire** v 1 to fit or connect something with wires to carry electric current; to install wiring in a house 2 to fasten or strengthen something with wire 3 to send a telegram to someone **wireless** n 1 old use a radio 2 ICT a link between components by means of radio signals rather than wire or cable connections **wiring** n a system of wires for conducting electricity in a building or device **wiry** adj **wirier, wiriest** 1 like wire 2 (said about a person) lean but strong

wise[1] adj 1 having or showing soundness of judgement and good sense 2 knowledgeable or well-informed **wisdom** n 1 being wise, soundness of judgement and good sense 2 the knowledge and experience that develops within a period or society **wisely** adv **wisdom tooth** n a molar tooth that may

grow at the back of the jaw of a person after the age of 20 **wisecrack** n a witty or clever remark **wisecrack** v informal to make a wisecrack

wise[2] n old use way or manner ♦ *in no wise*

-wise suffix forming adjectives and adverbs meaning 1 'in this manner or direction' (as in *otherwise*, *clockwise*) 2 'with respect to' (as in *price-wise*)

wish v 1 to feel or say that you would like to have or do something or would like something to happen, even though this might be impossible ♦ *I wish I was taller.* 2 formal to want something ♦ *I wish to speak to the manager.* 3 to say that you hope someone will have success, happiness, etc. ♦ *We wish her well.* **wish** n a desire or hope; something wished for **wishbone** n a forked bone between the neck and breast of a cooked bird **wishful thinking** n believing something because you wish it were true rather than because of the facts [about it]

wishy-washy adj weak or feeble in colour, character, etc.

wisp n 1 a small thin bunch or strand of something 2 a small streak of smoke or cloud, etc. **wispy** adj

wisteria (say wis-**teer**-iə) n a climbing plant with hanging clusters of blue, purple, or white flowers

wistful adj sadly longing for something **wistfully** adv **wistfulness** n

wit[1] n 1 the ability to use words or ideas cleverly for humorous effect 2 a witty person 3 intelligence or understanding ♦ *Use your wits.* ♦ *No one had the wit to see what was needed.* **witless** adj foolish or stupid **witticism** n a witty remark **witty** adj **wittier, wittiest** full of wit **wittily** adv **wittiness** n

wit[2] old use **wittingly** adv intentionally **to wit** that is to say

witch n 1 a woman thought to have evil magic powers 2 a person who practises modern witchcraft 3 informal an ugly or unpleasant old woman **witchcraft** n the use of magic, especially for evil purposes **witch doctor** n (among some peoples) a person who is believed to use magic powers to treat illness and to harm people

witch hazel n **1** a North American shrub with yellow flowers **2** an astringent lotion made from the leaves and bark of this plant **witch-hunt** n a campaign to find and punish people suspected of holding views that are considered to be unacceptable or dangerous

with prep **1** in the company of, among ♦ *Come with me.* **2** having, characterized by ♦ *a man with a beard* **3** using ♦ *Hit it with the hammer.* **4** in the care or charge of ♦ *Can I leave a message with you?* **5** employed by ♦ *How long have you been with IBM?* **6** on the side of, of the same opinion as ♦ *We're all with you on this matter.* **7** at the same time as, in the same way or direction or degree as ♦ *She rises with the sun.* ♦ *I was swimming with the tide.* **8** because of ♦ *He was shaking with laughter.* **9** feeling or showing ♦ *I heard the news with calmness.* **10** under the conditions of; in the manner specified ♦ *She sleeps with the window open.* ♦ *They won with ease.* **11** by addition or possession of ♦ *Fill it with water.* ♦ *a woman laden with baggage*

withdraw v **withdrew, withdrawn 1** to pull or take something back or away **2** to leave a place, to retreat **withdrawal** n **1** withdrawing **2** the process of stopping taking drugs to which you are addicted, often with unpleasant reactions **withdrawn** adj (said about a person) very shy or reserved

wither v **1** (said about a plant) to become dried up and shrivelled **2** to become shrunken or wrinkled from age or disease **3** to fade away or fall into decline ♦ *Our hopes withered away.* **withering** adj scornful or sarcastic

withers (say **with**-erz) pl n the ridge between a horse's shoulder blades **withhold** v past tense and past participle **withheld 1** to refuse to give something ♦ *She may withhold her permission.* **2** to hold something back ♦ *We could not withhold our laughter.*

within prep **1** inside, enclosed by **2** not beyond the limit or scope of ♦ *Success is within our grasp.* ♦ *He acted within his rights.* **within** adv inside ♦ *Apply within.*

without prep **1** not having, feeling, or showing ♦ *two days without food* ♦ *They are without fear.* **2** in the absence of ♦ *There's no smoke without fire.* **3** with no action of ♦ *We can't leave without thanking them.*

withstand v past tense and past participle **withstood** to endure or resist something successfully

witness n **1** a person who sees or hears something happen **2** a person who gives evidence in a law court **3** a person who is present at the signing of a document and confirms this by adding their own signature **4** something that serves as evidence ♦ *His tattered clothes were a witness to his poverty.* **witness** v **1** to be a witness to something ♦ *Did anyone witness the incident?* **2** to be the place or period in which something takes place ♦ *The 20th century witnessed a revolution in communications.* **3** to sign a document as a witness

witter v informal to speak at annoying length about trivial matters

wizard n **1** a man with magical powers, especially in legends and stories **2** a person with amazing abilities ♦ *a financial wizard* **wizardry** n

wizened (say **wiz**-ənd) adj full of wrinkles, shrivelled with age ♦ *a wizened face*

woad n a kind of blue dye formerly obtained from a plant of the mustard family

wobble v **1** to rock unsteadily from side to side **2** to make something rock or shake **3** (said about the voice) to be unsteady **wobble** n a wobbling movement or sound **wobbly** adj

wodge n informal a large piece or amount

woe n **1** great sorrow or distress **2** trouble or misfortune **woeful** adj **1** full of woe, sad **2** deplorable ♦ *woeful ignorance* **woefully** adv **woebegone** adj looking unhappy

wok n a Chinese cooking pan shaped like a large bowl

wold n an area of open upland country

wolf n pl **wolves** a fierce wild animal of the dog family, feeding on the flesh of other animals and often hunting in packs **wolf** v to eat food quickly and greedily **wolfhound** n a large breed of dog **wolf**

whistle n a whistle whose pitch rises then falls, used to express sexual attraction or admiration **to cry wolf** to raise false alarms so often that a real cry for help is ignored

wolverine (say **wuul**-ver-een) n an animal that is the largest of the weasel family, common in the north of North America

woman n pl **women** an adult female human being **womanhood** n **womanish** adj (said about a man) effeminate **womanize** v (said about a man) to have sexual affairs with many women **womanizer** n **womanly** adj **1** having the qualities traditionally associated with women **2** suitable for a woman **womankind** n women collectively **womenfolk** n women in general; the women of your family

womb (say woom) n the hollow organ in the body of a woman or female animal in which a child or the young may be conceived and nourished while developing before birth; the uterus

wombat n an Australian marsupial animal resembling a small bear

wonder n **1** a feeling of surprise and admiration **2** something that causes this feeling, a remarkable thing or event **wonder** v **1** to feel that you want to know something; to try to form an opinion or decision about something ♦ We're still wondering what to do next. **2** to feel wonder or doubt ♦ I wonder that he wasn't killed. **wonderful** adj marvellous or excellent **wonderfully** adv **wonderment** n a feeling of awe and admiration **wondrous** adj wonderful **wonderland** n a place full of wonderful things

wonky adj **wonkier, wonkiest** informal faulty, unsteady, or crooked

wont (say wohnt) adj accustomed **wont** n a habit or custom **wonted** adj customary

won't v will not

woo v **woos, wooed, wooing 1** (said about a man) to try to win the love of a woman, especially in order to marry her **2** to try to win someone's favour, support, or custom

wood n **1** the tough fibrous substance that the trunk and branches of trees are made of **2** this substance cut for use as timber or fuel **3** (also **woods**) a small forest **wooded** adj

covered with growing trees **wooden** adj **1** made of wood **2** stiff and awkward in manner, showing no expression or liveliness **woody** adj **woodier, woodiest. woodiness** n **woodcock** n a kind of game bird with a long bill, related to the snipe **woodcut** n **1** an engraving made on wood **2** a print made from this **woodland** n pl n **woodlouse** n pl **woodlice** a small wingless creature with seven pairs of legs, living in decaying wood, damp soil, etc. **woodpecker** n a bird that clings to tree trunks and taps them with its beak to find insects **woodwind** n the wind instruments of an orchestra that are not made of brass, such as the flutes, clarinets, and oboes **woodwork** n **1** making things out of wood **2** things made out of wood, especially the wooden fittings of a house **woodworm** n **1** the larva of a kind of beetle that bores into wooden furniture and fittings **2** the damage done to wood by this larva

woof v to make the bark of a dog **woof** n a barking sound

wool n **1** the fine soft hair that forms the fleece of sheep and goats, etc. **2** thread or cloth made from this **woollen** adj **woolly** adj **woollier, woolliest 1** made of or like wool ♦ a woolly hat **2** covered with wool or wool-like hair **3** not thinking clearly, not clearly expressed or thought out ♦ woolly ideas **woolly** n pl **woollies** informal a woollen piece of clothing, especially a pullover **wool-gathering** n being in a dreamy or absent-minded state

woozy adj **woozier, wooziest** informal dizzy or dazed

word n **1** a single unit of speech or writing expressing an independent meaning **2** a brief conversation with someone ♦ Can I have a word with you? **3** a remark or statement ♦ He didn't utter a word. **4** news or information ♦ We sent word of our safe arrival. **5** a promise or assurance ♦ He kept his word. **6** a command or spoken signal ♦ Don't fire till I give you the word. **word** v to put something into words **wording** n the way something is worded **wordless** adj **wordy** adj **wordier, wordiest** using too many words; not concise **word-perfect** adj

having memorized every word perfectly

word processor n a type of computer or program used for editing and printing text

word-processing n

work n **1** physical or mental effort made in order to do or make something ♦ *His good results are down to hard work.* **2** a task or duty that needs doing, or the materials used for this ♦ *Get on with your work.* **3** something done or produced by work; the result of action ♦ *The teacher marked our work.* **4** what a person does to earn a living, employment **5** a piece of writing, painting, music, etc. **works** pl n **1** a place where industrial or manufacturing processes are carried out **2** operations of building or repair **3** the mechanism of a machine **work** v **1** to do work **2** to be employed or have a job **3** to function or operate properly or effectively ♦ *Is the lift working?* ♦ *It works by electricity.* **4** to have the desired result ♦ *I hope this is going to work.* **5** to cultivate land or extract something from a mine or quarry **6** to shape, knead, or hammer, etc. something into a desired form or consistency **7** to move gradually or with effort into a particular position; to make something do this ♦ *The grub works its way into timber.* ♦ *The screw had worked loose.* **8** to bring someone into a state of excitement, anger, etc. ♦ *She had worked herself into a frenzy.* **workable** adj **1** able to be worked **2** that is likely to work ♦ *a workable plan* **workaholic** n a person who works extremely hard and finds it difficult to stop **worker** n **working** adj **1** having paid employment **2** (said about an animal) used in farming, hunting, etc. **3** adequate for the time being or for normal purposes ♦ *the play's working title* ♦ *a working knowledge of Spanish* **working** n a record of steps taken in solving a mathematical problem **workaday** adj ordinary, everyday **workforce** n the total number of workers in a particular firm, industry, country, etc. **workhouse** n a former public institution where people unable to support themselves were housed in return for work **working class** n the class of people who are employed for wages,

especially in manual or industrial work

working-class adj **working party** n a group of people appointed to investigate and report or advise on something

workman n pl **workmen** a man employed to do manual labour **workmanlike** adj efficient or competent but not outstanding

workmanship n the degree of skill shown in making or producing something **workout** n a session of strenuous physical exercise

workshop n **1** a room or building where things are made or repaired **2** a meeting at which a group comes together to discuss a subject and take part in activities relating to it **workstation** n a computer terminal and keyboard, especially one linked to a network **worktop** n a flat surface for working on, especially in the kitchen

work-to-rule n the practice of following the official rules of your job with excessive strictness in order to cause delay, as a form of industrial protest **the works** everything **to work out 1** to have a particular result ♦ *It worked out very well.* **2** to spend time doing strenuous physical exercise **to work someone up** to excite or arouse someone **to work something out** to solve something by calculation or thinking **to work up to** to gradually progress to something more difficult or advanced

world n **1** the earth with all its countries and peoples **2** a region or section of the earth ♦ *the western world* **3** all the people on the earth; everyone **4** a person's life and activities ♦ *Your world is a lot more exciting than mine.* **5** the people or things belonging to a certain class, historical period, or sphere of activity ♦ *the world of sport* **worldly** adj **worldlier, worldliest 1** to do with material things, not spiritual ones **2** experienced about people and life **worldly-wise** adj having enough experience about people and life not to be easily deceived or impressed **world-weary** adj bored with or cynical about life **worldwide** adj, adv extending throughout the whole world

worm n **1** any of several types of animal with a long soft rounded or flattened body and no backbone or limbs **2** the worm-like

larva of certain insects **3** an insignificant or contemptible person **worm** v **1** to move along by wriggling or crawling **2** to rid an animal of parasitic worms **to worm something out** to gradually get someone to tell you something by constantly and cleverly questioning them ♦ *We eventually managed to worm the truth out of them.* **to worm your way into** to insinuate your way into a person's affections, etc.

wormwood n a woody plant with a bitter flavour

worn out adj **1** exhausted **2** damaged by too much use

worry v **worries**, **worried**, **worrying 1** to make someone anxious or disturb their peace of mind **2** to feel anxious **3** (said about a dog) to chase and attack sheep, etc. **worry** n pl **worries 1** a state of worrying, mental uneasiness **2** something that makes a person worry **worried** adj **worrier** n **worrisome** adj causing worry

worse adj, adv **1** more bad or more badly **2** less good or less well **worse** n something worse **worsen** v **1** to make something worse **2** to become worse **worst** adj, adv **1** most bad or most badly **2** least good or least well **worst** n the worst part, event, situation, etc. **worst** v to get the better of someone

worship n **1** reverence and respect paid to God or a god **2** great admiration or devotion **3** a title of respect used to or of a mayor or magistrate ♦ *his worship the mayor* **worship** v **worshipped**, **worshipping 1** to give praise or respect to God or a god **2** to feel great admiration or devotion for someone or something **worshipper** n

worsted (say **wuu**-stid) n fine smooth yarn spun from long strands of wool; fabric made from this

worth adj **1** having a certain value ♦ *a book worth £10* **2** deserving something; good or important enough for something ♦ *That book is worth reading.* **worth** n **1** value or usefulness **2** the amount of something that a specified sum will buy ♦ *a pound's worth of stamps* **worthless** adj **worthlessness** n **worthwhile** adj important or good enough to deserve the time, money, or

effort needed or spent ♦ *a worthwhile job* **worthy** adj **worthier**, **worthiest** having great merit, deserving respect or support ♦ *a worthy cause* **worthy** n pl **worthies** a worthy or important person **worthily** adv **worthiness** n **worthy of** deserving

would auxiliary verb **1** used as the past tense of *will*[1] ♦ *We said we would do it.* **2** used in questions and polite requests ♦ *Would they like it?* ♦ *Would you come in please?* **3** used to make a polite statement ♦ *I would like to come*, or in a conditional clause ♦ *If they had supported us we would have won.* **4** used to give advice ♦ *I would phone the doctor straight away.* **5** used to express something to be expected or something that happens from time to time ♦ *Occasionally the machine would go wrong.* **wouldn't** v would not **would-be** adj desiring or pretending to be something ♦ *a would-be humorist*

wound (say woond) n **1** an injury done by a cut, stab, or blow **2** a hurt done to a person's reputation or feelings **wound** v **1** to cause a wound to a person or animal **2** to hurt a person's feelings ♦ *She was wounded by these remarks.*

wow interjection an exclamation of astonishment or admiration **wow** n informal a sensational success **wow** v informal to impress or excite someone greatly

WPC abbr woman police constable

wrack n a coarse brown seaweed thrown up on the shore or growing there

wraith (say rayth) n a ghost

wrangle v to have a noisy angry argument or quarrel **wrangle** n an argument or quarrel of this kind

wrap v **wrapped**, **wrapping 1** to put paper or cloth, etc. round something as a covering **2** to arrange a flexible covering or a piece of clothing round a person or thing **3** ICT to make text carry over to a new line automatically; to be carried over in this way **wrap** n a shawl, coat, or cloak, etc. worn for warmth **wrapper** n a cover of paper or other material wrapped round something **wrapping** n material used to wrap something **to wrap something up 1** to enclose something in wrapping paper

2 to finish or settle something **to wrap up** to put on warm clothes

wrasse (say rass) n a brightly-coloured sea fish

wrath (say roth) n extreme anger **wrathful** adj

wreak (say reek) v to inflict or cause something ♦ *Flooding wreaked havoc with the running of trains.*

wreath (say reeth) n pl **wreaths** (say reethz) flowers or leaves, etc. fastened into a ring and used as a decoration or placed on a grave as a mark of respect **wreathe** v **1** to surround or decorate something with or as if with a wreath **2** to move in a curving line ♦ *Smoke wreathed upwards.*

wreck n **1** the destruction of a ship by storms or accidental damage **2** the remains of a vehicle, building, etc. that has been badly damaged **3** a person whose physical or mental health has been damaged or destroyed **wreck** v to damage or ruin something so badly that it cannot be used again **wreckage** n the remains of something that has been badly damaged or destroyed

Wren n a member of the former Women's Royal Naval Service

wren n a small usually brown songbird

wrench v **1** to twist or pull something violently **2** to injure part of your body by making a sudden twisting movement **wrench** n **1** a violent twist or twisting pull **2** pain caused by parting **3** an adjustable tool like a spanner, used for gripping and turning nuts or bolts

wrest (say rest) v **1** to take or pull something away from someone using force **2** to obtain something with effort or difficulty

wrestle v **1** to fight by grappling with a person and trying to throw them to the ground **2** to force someone into a position by fighting them like this ♦ *Police wrestled him to the ground.* **3** to struggle to deal with or overcome something ♦ *I've been wrestling with this problem all week.* **wrestle** n **1** a wrestling match **2** a hard struggle **wrestler** n

wretch n **1** a very unfortunate or miserable person **2** a despicable person **wretched** adj

1 miserable or unhappy **2** of poor quality, unsatisfactory **wretchedly** adv **wretchedness** n

wriggle v to move with short twisting movements **wriggle** n a wriggling movement **to wriggle out of** to avoid a task, etc. on some pretext or by some devious means **wriggly** adv

wring v past tense and past participle **wrung 1** to twist and squeeze a wet thing to remove liquid from it **2** to break an animal's neck by twisting it **3** to squeeze someone's hand tightly **4** to obtain something with effort or difficulty ♦ *We wrung a promise out of him.* **wringer** n

wrinkle n **1** a small furrow or ridge in the skin, especially the kind produced by age **2** a small crease in something **wrinkle** v to make wrinkles in something; to form wrinkles **wrinkly** adv

wrist n the joint connecting the hand and forearm **wristband** n a band worn round the wrist, especially as a form of identification or as a sweatband **wristwatch** n a watch worn on a strap round the wrist

writ (say rit) n a formal written command issued by a law court or other legal authority directing a person to act or refrain from acting in a certain way

write v **wrote**, **written 1** to put letters, words, or other symbols on a surface, especially with a pen or pencil on paper **2** to have the ability to do this ♦ *She couldn't read or write.* **3** to be the author or composer of something ♦ *How many books have you written?* **4** to write and send a letter ♦ *Promise you'll write to me often.* **5** to enter data into a computer memory or storage device; to transfer data from one memory or storage device to another **writer** n **1** a person who writes or has written something **2** a person who writes books, an author **writing** n **write-off** n a vehicle too badly damaged to be worth repairing **write-up** n a published written account of something; a review **to write something off 1** to damage a vehicle so badly that it is not worth repairing **2** to cancel a debt **3** to acknowledge that something is bound to

fail or be lost

writhe (say riyth) v to twist your body about, especially because of pain

wrong adj **1** not correct or true ♦ *the wrong answer* **2** (said about conduct or actions, etc.) morally bad, unfair, or unjust **3** not working properly ♦ *There's something wrong with the engine.* **4** not based on good judgement ♦ *the wrong decision* **5** not what is required, suitable, or most desirable ♦ *That's the wrong colour.* **wrong** adv not correctly or appropriately; mistakenly **wrong** n what is morally wrong or unjust ♦ *They have done me a great wrong.* **wrong** v to do wrong to someone, to treat someone unfairly **wrongful** adj unfair or unjust; illegal ♦ *wrongful arrest* **wrongfully** adv **wrongly** adv **wrongness** n **wrongdoing** n illegal or dishonest behaviour **wrongdoer** n **wrong-foot** v to catch someone unprepared

wrought (say rawt) adj (said about metals) beaten out or shaped by hammering **wrought iron** n iron made by forging or rolling rather than casting

wry (say riy) adj **wryer** or **wrier**, **wryest** or **wriest 1** (said about humour) dry and mocking **2** (said about a person's face or features) twisted into an expression of disgust, disappointment, or mockery **wryly** adv

wt abbr weight

WW abbr World War

WWW abbr World Wide Web

Xx

X 1 the twenty-fourth letter of the English alphabet **2** the Roman numeral for 10 **3** an unknown or unnamed thing or person

xenophobia (say zen-ə-foh-biə) n strong dislike or distrust of foreigners **xenophobe** n **xenophobic** adj

Xerox (say zeer-oks) n trademark **1** a process for producing photocopies without the use of wet chemicals **2** a photocopy

made in this way **xerox** v to photocopy a document by a process of this kind

Xmas n an informal word for *Christmas*

X-ray n **1** a kind of electromagnetic radiation that can penetrate solid things and make it possible to see into or through them **2** a photograph or examination made by passing X-rays through something **X-ray** v to photograph or examine something with X-rays

xylophone (say ziy-lə-fohn) n a musical instrument consisting of flat wooden bars which you hit with small hammers

Yy

Y the twenty-fifth letter of the English alphabet

yacht (say yot) n **1** a sailing boat used for racing or cruising **2** a powered boat used for cruising **yachting** n **yachtsman**, **yachtswoman** n pl **yachtsmen**, **yachtswomen**

yak n a large long-haired Tibetan ox

Yale lock n trademark a type of lock for doors, using a flat key with a toothed edge

yam n an edible starchy tuber of a tropical plant

yank v to pull something with a sudden sharp tug **yank** n a sudden sharp tug

Yankee n informal **1** (also **Yank**) an American **2** N. Am an inhabitant of the northern states of the USA

yap n a shrill bark **yap** v **yapped**, **yapping 1** to give a shrill bark **2** informal to talk at length in an annoying way

yard[1] n **1** a measure of length, equal to 3 feet (0.9144 metre) **2** a long pole stretched horizontally or crosswise from a mast to support a sail **yardarm** n either end of a yard supporting a sail **yardstick** n a standard of comparison

yard[2] n a piece of enclosed ground, especially one attached to a building, surrounded by buildings, or used for a particular purpose or business ♦ *a timber*

yard

yarmulke, yarmulka (say **yar**-mul-kə) *n* a skullcap worn by Jewish men

yarn *n* 1 thread spun by twisting fibres together, used for knitting, weaving, or sewing 2 *informal* a tale or story, especially a far-fetched one

yashmak *n* a veil concealing all of the face except for the eyes, worn by some Muslim women in public

yaw *v* (said about a ship or aircraft) to fail to hold a straight course, to turn from side to side

yawl *n* a kind of sailing boat with two masts

yawn *v* 1 to open your mouth wide and draw in breath (often involuntarily), because of tiredness or boredom 2 to form a wide opening ♦ *a yawning chasm* **yawn** *n* an act of yawning

ye *pronoun old use* you (referring to more than one person)

yea (say yay) *adv, n old use* yes

yeah (say yair) *adv informal* yes

year *n* 1 the time taken by the earth to make one revolution around the sun, about 365¼ days 2 the period from 1 January to 31 December inclusive 3 any period of twelve months 4 a group of students of roughly the same age **years** *pl n* 1 a person's age or time of life ♦ *He looks younger than his years.* 2 *informal* a very long time **yearling** *n* an animal between one and two years old **yearly** *adj* happening or produced once a year or every year **yearly** *adv* annually **yearbook** *n* an annual publication containing current information about a particular subject

yearn *v* to long for something

yeast *n* a kind of fungus used to cause fermentation in making beer and wines and as a raising agent in baking **yeasty** *adj* **yeastier, yeastiest**

yell *n* a loud sharp cry **yell** *v* to shout loudly

yellow *adj* 1 of the colour of egg yolks and ripe lemons 2 *informal* cowardly **yellow** *v* to become yellow, especially with age **yellow card** *n* a yellow card shown by the referee in a football match to a player being cautioned **yellow fever** *n* a tropical disease with fever and jaundice

yelp *v* to make a short sharp cry or bark **yelp** *n* a yelping sound

yen[1] *n pl* **yen** the unit of money in Japan

yen[2] *n* a longing for something

yeoman (say **yoh**-mən) *n pl* **yeomen** (in the past) a man who owned and farmed a small estate **yeomanry** *n* **Yeoman of the Guard** *n* a member of the ceremonial bodyguard of the British monarch

yes *adv* used to agree to or give a positive reply to something **yes** *n pl* **yeses** or **yesses** a positive reply or decision **yes-man** *n pl* **yes-men** a person who always agrees with their superiors

yesterday *n* 1 the day before today 2 the recent past **yesterday** *adv* 1 on the day before today 2 in the recent past

yesteryear *n literary* 1 last year 2 the recent past

yet *adv* 1 up to this time and continuing, still ♦ *There's life in the old dog yet.* 2 by this time, so far ♦ *It hasn't happened yet.* 3 eventually ♦ *I'll get even with you yet.* 4 in addition, even ♦ *She became yet more excited.* 5 nevertheless ♦ *strange yet true* **yet** *conjunction* nevertheless, but in spite of that ♦ *He worked hard, yet he failed.*

yeti (say **yet**-i) *n pl* **yetis** a large animal like a bear, said to exist in the Himalayas, also known as the *Abominable Snowman*

yew *n* an evergreen tree with dark-green needle-like leaves and red berries

Yiddish *n* a language used by Jews of central and eastern Europe

yield *v* 1 to produce something as a crop or other natural product 2 to produce a sum as profit, interest, etc. 3 to give way to pressure or demands **yield** *n* the amount yielded or produced

yippee *interjection* an exclamation of excitement

yob, yobbo *n informal* a bad-mannered or aggressive young man

yodel (say **yoh**-dəl) *v* **yodelled, yodelling** to sing or call with the voice alternating rapidly between a very high pitch and its normal pitch

yoga (say **yoh**-gə) *n* 1 a Hindu system of meditation and self-control designed to produce mystical experience and spiritual

insight **2** a system of physical exercises based on this, practised for health and relaxation **yogi** n pl **yogis** a person who is a master of yoga

yogurt, **yoghurt** (say yog-ert) n a food prepared from milk that has been thickened by the action of certain bacteria, giving it a sharp taste

yoke n **1** a wooden crosspiece fastened over the necks of two oxen or other animals pulling a cart or plough **2** a piece of timber shaped to fit a person's shoulders and to hold a pail or basket hung at each end **3** a part of a piece of clothing that fits over the shoulders and from which the rest hangs **4** something thought of as oppressive or burdensome **yoke** v **1** to harness or join things together by means of a yoke **2** to join two or more things together

yokel (say yoh-kəl) n a simple and unsophisticated country person

yolk (say yohk) n the round yellow part inside an egg

Yom Kippur (say yom kip-oor) n the Day of Atonement, a solemn Jewish religious festival

yon adj, adv dialect yonder

yonder adv old use or dialect over there **yonder** adj situated or able to be seen over there

yonks n informal a long time, ages ♦ I haven't seen him for yonks.

yore n **of yore** literary formerly; of long ago ♦ in days of yore

you pronoun **1** the person or people being spoken to **2** one, anyone, or everyone ♦ You never know when it might come in useful.

you're v you are **your** adj of or belonging to you **yours** possessive pronoun belonging to you; the thing(s) belonging to you **yourself** pronoun pl **yourselves** the form of you used in reflexive constructions (e.g. You've cut yourself and for emphasis (e.g. You told me yourself) **Yours faithfully** a more formal ending to a business letter **Yours sincerely** a less formal ending to a business letter, also used in personal correspondence

young adj having lived or existed for only a short time; not old **young** n young children

or animals **youngish** adj **youngster** n a young person, a child

youth n pl **youths** (say yoothz) **1** the period between childhood and adult age; being young **2** the vigour or lack of experience, etc. characteristic of being young **3** a young man ♦ a youth of 16 **4** young people collectively ♦ the youth of the country **youthful** adj **1** young; looking or seeming young **2** characteristic of young people **youthfulness** n **youth club** n a place providing leisure activities for young people **youth hostel** n a place providing cheap accommodation, especially for young people who are hiking or on holiday

yowl v to make a loud wailing cry or howl **yowl** n this cry

yo-yo n pl **yo-yos** trademark a toy consisting of two circular parts with a deep groove between them, which can be made to rise and fall on a string attached to it when this is jerked by a finger

yucca (say yuk-ə) n a tall plant with white bell-like flowers and stiff spiky leaves

yucky adj **yuckier**, **yuckiest** informal disgusting, revolting

Yule, **Yuletide** n old use the Christmas festival

yummy adj **yummier**, **yummiest** informal delicious

yuppie n a young middle-class person with a well-paid professional job

Zz

Z the twenty-sixth letter of the English alphabet

zany adj **zanier**, **zaniest** crazily funny **zany** n pl **zanies** a comical or eccentric person

zap v **zapped**, **zapping** informal **1** to attack or destroy something forcefully **2** to use a remote control to change television channels quickly

zeal (say zeel) n enthusiasm or energy **zealot** n a zealous person, a fanatic **zealous** adj full of zeal **zealously** adv

zebra *n* an African animal of the horse family, with black and white stripes all over its body **zebra crossing** *n* a pedestrian crossing where the road is marked with broad white stripes

Zen *n* a form of Buddhism emphasizing the value of meditation and intuition

zenith (say **zen**-ith) **1** (in astronomy) the part of the sky that is directly above the observer **2** the highest or most successful point ♦ *His power was at its zenith.*

zephyr (say **zef**-er) *n* a soft gentle breeze

Zeppelin *n* a large German airship of the early 20th century

zero *n pl* **zeros 1** nought, the figure 0 **2** nothing, nil **zero hour** *n* the time at which something is timed to begin **to zero in on 1** to focus your aim or attention on something **2** to go purposefully towards a place

zest *n* **1** keen enjoyment or enthusiasm **2** a pleasantly stimulating quality ♦ *The risk added zest to the whole adventure.* **3** the coloured part of the peel of an orange or lemon, etc.

zigzag *n* a line or course that turns sharply from side to side **zigzag** *adj, adv* forming or in a zigzag **zigzag** *v* **zigzagged, zigzagging** to move in a zigzag course

Zimmer, Zimmer frame *n trademark* a frame that a lame or frail person uses as a support in walking

zinc *n* a white metallic element, used in alloys and to coat iron and steel as a protection against corrosion

zing *n informal* energy or liveliness

Zionism (say **ziy**-ən-izm) *n* a movement for the development and protection of a Jewish nation in Israel **Zionist** *n*

zip *n* **1** a fastening device consisting of two flexible strips of metal or plastic, each with rows of small teeth that interlock when a sliding tab brings them together **2** *informal* liveliness or vigour **zip** *v* **zipped, zipping 1** to fasten or close something with a zip **2** to move quickly with a sharp sound

zircon (say **zer**-kon) *n* a bluish-white gem cut from a translucent mineral

zither (say **zith**-er) *n* a musical instrument with many strings stretched over a shallow box-like body, played by plucking with the fingers of both hands

zodiac (say **zoh**-di-ak) *n* (in astrology) a band of the sky containing the paths of the sun, moon, and main planets, divided into twelve equal parts (called the *signs of the zodiac*) each named after a constellation that was formerly situated in it

zombie *n* **1** (in voodoo) a corpse said to have been brought back to life by witchcraft **2** a person who seems to be doing things without thinking, usually because they are very tired

zone *n* an area that has a particular characteristic, purpose, or use **zone** *v* to divide a place into zones **zonal** *adj*

zoo *v* a place where wild animals are kept for exhibition, conservation, and study

zoology (say zoh-**ol**-əji or zoo-**ol**-əji) *n* the scientific study of animals **zoological** *adj* **zoologist** *n* **zoological garden** *n* a zoo

zoom *v* **1** to move or travel very quickly **2** (in photography) to change smoothly from a long shot to a close-up or vice versa **zoom lens** *n* a camera lens that can be adjusted to focus on things that are close up or far away

zucchini (say zuuk-ee-ni) *n pl* **zucchini** or **zucchinis** *N. Am* a courgette

Quick Language Guide

Misspelled words

In shorter words spelling problems are often caused by vowel combinations and by silent letters. The letters that cause trouble in the list below are in **bold**.

i before **e**	**e** before **i**	words including **'u'**	silent letters
ch**ie**f	**ei**ghth	ga**u**ge	**k**nife
n**ie**ce	h**ei**ght	g**u**ard	**p**sychic
p**ie**rce	s**ei**ze	j**u**ice	recei**p**t
pr**ie**st	w**ei**rd		**w**rite
s**ie**ge			
y**ie**ld			

In longer words problems can be caused by double or single letters, vowel combinations, letters that are not sounded out and silent letters. You need to pay careful attention to the parts of the words in **bold**.

eed or **ede**	**i** before **e**	**e** before **i**	words including **'u'**
prec**ede**	achi**e**vement	dec**ei**ve	g**u**arantee
proc**eed**	misch**ie**vous	for**ei**gn	n**u**isance
supers**ede**	unw**ie**ldy	rec**ei**pt	Portug**u**ese
		rec**ei**ve	pron**u**nciation
			sa**u**sage

double or single letters

a**cc**o**mm**odate	disa**pp**oint	mill**enn**ium
a**cc**o**mm**odation	disa**pp**ointment	mill**i**onaire
a**dd**ress	di**ss**ect	ne**c**e**ss**ary
a**gg**ressive	emba**rr**ass	para**ll**el
begi**nn**ing	emba**rr**a**ss**ment	questio**nn**aire
ca**ss**ette	exa**gg**erate	reco**mm**end
colo**ss**al	ha**r**a**ss**	ski**l**ful
commi**tt**ee	ha**r**a**ss**ment	thres**h**old
disa**pp**ear	insta**ll**	u**nn**e**c**e**ss**ary
disa**pp**earance	insta**l**ment	with**h**old

other difficult spellings

answer	extraordinary	responsible	sergeant
conscientious	extravagant	resuscitate	signature
consensus	February	rhythm	strength
cylinder	government	sandwich	twelfth
desperate	idiosyncrasy	scavenge	unconscious
diphthong	length	secretary	vengeance
ecstasy	library	separate	Wednesday

Common errors

all right / alright
Are you all right? It's cold all right.

The correct spelling is as two words: *all right*. Do not use the spelling *alright*, which is not generally acceptable in Standard English.

behalf
on behalf of means 'for the benefit of' or 'as the representative of': *We are collecting money on behalf of cancer research. I'd like to thank you on behalf of everyone here.* It does not mean 'by' or 'on the part of', and it is wrong to say, for example, *It was a good result on behalf of the visiting side.*

different from / to / than
There are three prepositions that can be used after *different* when it means 'not the same': *from*, *to*, and *than*. The best one to use is *from*, because everyone accepts it: *The new model is very different from the last one.* You can also use *to*, although it is not much used in American English. *Than* is used in American English, but many people dislike it in British English and so you should avoid it.

double negatives
You should never use two negative words together to make a negative statement: *I don't want no more. They never said nothing about it.* (The correct versions are: *I don't want any more.* and *They never said anything about it.*) But you can use a negative word with a word beginning with a negative prefix like *in-* or *un-*, where the two negatives cancel each other out and produce a positive meaning: *The town is not unattractive* (i.e. *it is fairly attractive*).

enormity / enormousness
Enormity means more than just 'huge size'. It means 'great wickedness': *the enormity of the crime.* If you mean 'huge size', use *enormousness*: *the enormousness of the task*, not *the enormity of the task*. (You can also use alternatives such as *immensity* and *vastness*.)

flaunt / flout
To flaunt something is to display it in a showy way: *He bought the most expensive item on the list just to flaunt his wealth.*

To *flout* a rule or instruction is to disobey it openly: *They must avoid flouting the health and safety regulations.*

Take care not to confuse these two words, as they sound similar.

I / me
You use *I* when it is the subject of a verb: *I want to see you.* Strictly speaking you should use *I* also in sentences such as *It is I who saw you*, because what comes after the verb *be* should 'agree' with what comes before, and *it* is the subject of the verb *be* (here in the form *is*). But in informal conversation it is acceptable to say *It is me* (or *It was him*).

You use *me* when it is the object of a verb or comes after a preposition such as *to* or *with*: *Give it to me. He came with me.*

You may be unsure whether to use *you and I* or *you and me* when you have more than one pronoun together. The rule is exactly the same: use *you and I* when it is the subject of the sentence and *you and me* when it is the object of a verb or comes after a preposition

You and I were both there. This is a picture of you and me (not *This is a picture of you and I*). *Between you and me* (not *between you and I*), *I don't think we can win.*

infer / imply
To *imply* something is to suggest it without actually saying it: *Are you implying that I am mad?*

To *infer* something is to draw a conclusion from what someone says or does: *I inferred from the sounds in the house that someone was in.*

Take care not to use *infer* when you mean *imply*: *Are you inferring that I am mad?* means 'have you concluded that I am mad?' and not 'are you suggesting that I am mad?'

it's / its
It is very important to remember the difference the apostrophe makes. *It's* (with an apostrophe) is short for 'it is' or 'it has': *It's [= it is] very late now. I think it's [= it has] been raining.*

Its (without an apostrophe) is a word like *his* and *their* (called a possessive determiner) and means 'belonging to it': *The cat licked its paw. The class wrote its own dictionary.*

who / whom
You use *who* when it is the subject of the sentence or clause: *Who is there? Do you know who that was?*

You use *whom* when it is the object of a verb or comes after a preposition: *Whom do you mean? He invited his friends, most of whom did not know each other. He knew the works of Shakespeare, whom he greatly admired. She was a woman whom everyone liked. This is the person to whom I spoke.*

But *whom* can sound a little formal and stiff. In everyday English, it is acceptable to use *who* instead of *whom* in questions: *Who do you mean?* When *whom* comes at the beginning of a clause without a comma before it, you can leave it out: *She was a woman everyone liked.* With prepositions, you can leave out *whom* and put the preposition at the end of the sentence: *This is the person I spoke to.*

Idioms

Idioms are groups of words that have a meaning that is often impossible to work out on your own. This is frequently because they refer to ideas or beliefs that are no longer current. In a dictionary an idiom will often be listed at the end of an entry of its main word. Below are some interesting examples.

an Achilles' heel a weak or bad point in a person who is otherwise strong or good [from the story of the Greek hero Achilles: his mother Thetis had dipped him in the River Styx because the water would prevent him from harm, but the water did not cover the heel by which she held him. So when the Trojan prince Paris killed Achilles he did it by throwing a spear into his heel.]

have a chip on your shoulder to feel jealous and resentful about life and the way you are treated compared with other people [From an old American custom in which a person would place a chip of wood on their shoulder as a challenge to another person, who would accept the challenge by knocking the chip off.]

in seventh heaven blissfully happy [In some religions, the seventh heaven is the last in a series of heavens that people's souls pass through after death.]

get out of bed on the wrong side to be irritable all day [The idea is that you are irritable from the moment you get up in the morning.]

eat humble pie to have to apologize or admit you were wrong about something [A play on the words 'humble' and 'umbles', which were the inner organs of deer or other animals used in pies.]

once in a blue moon very rarely; hardly ever [A blue moon is a second full moon in a month, which occurs rarely.]

a stiff upper lip you are said to have a stiff upper lip when you are brave and self-controlled when life is difficult or dangerous [Because the upper lip trembles when you are nervous or frightened. The phrase sounds British but in fact it occurs earliest in American writing.]

under the weather feeling unwell or fed up [A ship at sea was under the weather when a storm was overhead, making it uncomfortable for the people on board.]

the spitting image a person who looks exactly like someone else [From a strange old idea that a person could spit out an identical person from their mouth.]

an albatross round someone's neck something that is a constant worry or cause of feeling guilty [An albatross was supposed to bring good luck to sailors at sea. In Coleridge's 1798 poem *The Rime of the Ancient Mariner*, the mariner (sailor) shoots an albatross and this brings a curse on the ship. The crew force the mariner to wear the dead albatross round his neck as a punishment.]

not turn a hair to show no feeling or reaction [Originally used about horses, whose hair becomes ruffled when they sweat.]

out of the blue without any warning; as a complete surprise [Like something coming suddenly out of the blue of the sky.]

back to square one back to the starting point after a failure or mistake [Probably from the idea of going back to the first square as a penalty on a board game. Some people think the phrase is connected with early football commentaries, but this is unlikely.]

go hell for leather at full speed [From horse-riding, because the reins were made of leather, and people thought that going to hell must be very fast and reckless.]

break the ice to make the first move in a conversation or undertaking [From the idea of ships in very cold regions having to break through the ice to pass through.]

let the cat out of the bag to reveal a secret by mistake [Because cats do not like being confined, and it would be hard to keep one in a bag in this way.]

full of beans lively and energetic [Horses used to be fed on beans to make them healthy.]

by hook or by crook somehow or other; by any means possible [From a practice in medieval times of allowing tenants to take as much firewood as they could from the trees by using these two tools.]

like water off a duck's back having no effect on a person; making no impression [Because water runs off the feathers of a duck without soaking through.]

from the horse's mouth you get information straight from the horse's mouth when it comes from the person or people who originated it or who are most likely to know about it [The idea is of someone wanting to make a bet asking the horses themselves which one is likely to win the race.]

a wild goose chase a pointless and hopeless search for something [Originally a kind of horse race in which a leading horse had to run an erratic course which the other horses had to follow: wild geese run about in all directions.]

the lion's share the largest share or part of something [Because lions being very strong and fierce get the largest share of a killed animal's carcass; originally this expression meant 'all of something' as lions were not thought to share.]

have your cake and eat it you say someone wants to have their cake and eat it when they seem to want to have or do two things when only one of them is possible [Because if you eat your cake you cannot still have it: have here means 'keep'.]

come up to scratch to be good or strong enough for what is needed [Scratch is the line marking the start of a race or other sports event.]

on the ball alert and quick to act [A player in a game is on the ball when they have possession of it and are playing it well.]

show somebody the ropes to give someone basic instruction in a task or activity [From the days of sailing ships, when ropes were used to control the ship's rigging.]

hit the nail on the head to say something exactly right or suitable [From the idea of hitting a nail squarely on the head with a hammer, so that it goes in well.]

pass the buck to leave something you should take responsibility for someone else to deal with [In the game of poker the buck was a small piece placed in front of the dealer.]

rain cats and dogs to rain very hard [We cannot be sure where this phrase comes from and it may just be fanciful; originally it was the other way round: rain dogs and cats. One of the earliest uses is by Jonathan Swift, the author of *Gulliver's Travels*, in the 18th century.]

at sixes and sevens with everything very confused and muddled [The phrase is very old; it may have something to do with throwing dice, because there is no 'seven' on a dice and so sixes and sevens would be impossible.]

Proverbs

A proverb is a sentence that gives a piece of advice or says something wise or true.

all's well that ends well If things succeed in the end then it doesn't matter so much about the troubles or difficulties experienced on the way.

an apple a day keeps the doctor away If you eat well you will stay healthy and you won't need to see the doctor.

better late than never Something done at the last moment is better than not doing it at all.

better safe than sorry If in doubt it is better to be cautious than to take an unnecessary risk.

a bird in the hand is worth two in the bush Something you already have is more valuable than something you might get or have been promised.

every cloud has a silver lining Bad situations can often have some benefits.

a stitch in time saves nine If you act promptly you will save yourself trouble later. [From the idea of mending clothes with stitches: nine is used because it makes a good rhyme with time.]

strike while the iron's hot to act at the right moment [From metalwork, in which iron is shaped when hot by hitting it with a hammer.]

don't count your chickens before they hatch Do not assume that something will happen until you are sure about it.

one good turn deserves another If you do someone a favour you can expect another in return.

once bitten, twice shy Someone who has had a bad experience will avoid the same situation another time. [Someone who has been bitten by an animal or insect will stay away from them in future; shy here means 'cautious'.]

every picture tells a story You can often tell what has happened from things you can see. [The idea is of a picture illustrating a story in a book.]

there's no time like the present It is best to get on with a task straight away and not delay.

the proof of the pudding is in the eating You can often only tell how good or useful something is by trying it.

a rolling stone gathers no moss Someone who does not settle down in one place does not become important or wealthy. [Because moss does not start to grow on stones that are moving.]

there's no smoke without fire Rumours and reports usually have some truth about them. [If you can see smoke it usually means there is a fire near.]

two heads are better than one You can usually do things better if you listen to advice.

where there's a will there's a way You often need to be determined to overcome difficulties.

Some phrases seem to contradict one another:

many hands make light work
A job can be done more easily if more people help to do it.

too many cooks spoil the broth
An activity might be badly done if too many people are involved in it.

....

more haste, less speed
If you rush or hurry over a task you will find it more difficult to do well.

time waits for no man
Do not delay in doing things that are important.

....

great minds think alike
Clever people often get the same ideas at the same time (often used jokingly when two people have the same idea or say the same thing).

fools seldom differ
Foolish or silly people will usually act or speak in the same way.

....

absence makes the heart grow fonder
People miss each other when they are apart.

out of sight out of mind
People forget each other or their problems when they are not immediately in front of them.

....

the squeaking wheel gets the grease
You often need to make a lot of noise or fuss to get attention.

silence is golden
It is often best to say nothing and keep quiet.

....

birds of a feather flock together
People of the same kind tend to like each other's company ['Birds of a feather' are birds of the same species.]

opposites attract
People often like other people who are very different in character from themselves.

....

the pen is mightier than the sword
Writing about people or things you do not like is often more effective than attacking them.

actions speak louder than words
It is often better to do something positive rather than just talk or think about doing it.

Foreign words and phrases

ad hoc done or arranged only when necessary and not planned in advance [Latin = for this]

ad infinitum (in-fi-**ny**-tum) without limit; for ever [Latin = to infinity]

ad nauseam (**naw**-see-am) until people are sick of it [Latin = to sickness]

à la carte ordered and paid for as separate items from a menu [French = from the menu]

alfresco in the open air *an alfresco meal* [from Italian *al fresco* = in the fresh air]

alter ego another, very different, side of someone's personality [Latin = other self]

angst a strong feeling of anxiety or dread about something [German = fear]

au fait (oh **fay**) knowing a subject or procedure etc. well [French = to the point]

au revoir (oh rev-**wahr**) goodbye for the moment [French = until seeing again]

avant-garde (av-ahn-**gard**) people who use a modern style in art or literature etc. [French = vanguard]

bête noire (bayt **nwahr**) a person or thing you greatly dislike [French = black beast]

bona fide (**boh**-na fy-dee) genuine; without fraud [Latin = in good faith]

bon voyage (bawn vwah-**yazh**) (have a) pleasant journey! [French]

carte blanche (kart **blahnsh**) freedom to act as you think best [French = blank paper]

c'est la vie (say la **vee**) life is like that [French = that is life]

compos mentis in your right mind; sane (The opposite is **non compos mentis**.) [Latin = having control of the mind]

cordon bleu (kor-dawn **bler**) (of cooks and cookery) first-class [French = blue ribbon]

coup de grâce (koo der **grahs**) a stroke or blow that puts an end to something [French = mercy blow]

coup d'état (koo day-**tah**) the sudden overthrow of a government [French = blow of State]

crème de la crème (krem der la krem) the very best of something [French = cream of the cream]

déjà vu (day-**zh**a vew) a feeling that you have already experienced what is happening now [French = already seen]

de rigueur (der rig-**er**) proper; required by custom or etiquette [French = of strictness]

dolce vita (dol-chay-**vee**-ta) a life of pleasure and luxury [Italian = sweet life]

doppelgänger (doppel-**geng**-er) someone who looks exactly like someone else; a double [German = double-goer]

en bloc (ahn **blok**) all at the same time; in a block [French]

en masse (ahn **mass**) all together [French = in a mass]

en passant (ahn **pas**-ahn) by the way [French = in passing]

en route (ahn **root**) on the way [French]

entente (ahn-**tahnt** or on-**tont**) a friendly understanding between nations [French]

esprit de corps (es-pree der **kor**) loyalty to your group [French = spirit of the body]

eureka (yoor-**eek**-a) I have found it! (i.e. the answer) [Greek]

ex gratia (eks **gray**-sha) given without being legally obliged to be given *an ex gratia payment* [Latin = from favour]

faux pas (foh **pah**) an embarrassing blunder [French = false step]

gung-ho (**gung**-hoh) eager to fight or take part in a war [Chinese *gonghe* = work together, used as a slogan]

hara-kiri (hara-**kee**-ri) ritual suicide by cutting open the stomach with a sword [Japanese = belly cutting]

hoi polloi the ordinary people; the masses [Greek = the many]

Homo sapiens human beings regarded as a species of animal [Latin = wise man]

honcho a leader [Japanese = group leader]

hors-d'oeuvre (or-**dervr**) food served as an appetizer at the start of a meal [French = outside the work]

in camera in a judge's private room, not in public [Latin = in the room]

in extremis (eks-**treem**-iss) at the point of death; in very great difficulties [Latin = in the greatest danger]

in memoriam in memory (of) [Latin]

in situ (**sit**-yoo) in its original place [Latin]

joie de vivre (*zh*wah der **veevr**) a feeling of great enjoyment of life [French = joy of life]

kowtow (rhymes with *cow* (both syllables)) to obey someone slavishly [Chinese = knock the head, from the old practice of kneeling and touching the ground with the forehead as a sign of submission]

laissez-faire (lay-say-**fair**) a government's policy of not interfering [French = let (them) act]

luau (**loo**-ow) a party or feast [Hawaiian *lu'au* = feast]

macho (**mach**-oh) masculine in an aggressive way [Spanish = male]

mano a mano (mah-noh a **mah**-noh) (of a meeting, fight, etc.) between two people only; face to face [Spanish = hand to hand]

modus operandi (moh-dus op-er-**and**-ee) **1** a person's way of working. **2** the way a thing works [Latin = way of working]

nom de plume a writer's pseudonym [French = pen-name (this phrase is not used in France)]

non sequitur (non **sek**-wit-er) a conclusion that does not follow from the evidence given [Latin = it does not follow]

nota bene (noh-ta **ben**-ee) (usually shortened to NB) note carefully [Latin = note well]

nouveau riche (noo-voh **reesh**) a person who has only recently become rich [French = new rich]

objet d'art (ob-*zh*ay dar) a small artistic object [French = object of art]

par excellence (par eks-el-**ahns**) more than all the others; to the greatest degree [French = because of special excellence]

pas de deux (pah der **der**) a dance (e.g. in a ballet) for two persons [French = step of two]

per annum for each year; yearly [Latin]

per capita (**kap**-it-a) for each person [Latin = for heads]

persona grata (per-soh-na **grah**-ta) a person who is acceptable to someone, especially a diplomat acceptable to a foreign government (The opposite is **persona non grata**.) [Latin = pleasing person]

pièce de résistance (pee-ess der ray-zees-**tahns**) the most important item [French]

prima facie (pry-ma **fay**-shee) at first sight; judging by the first impression [Latin = on first appearance]

quid pro quo something given or done in return for something [Latin = something for something]

raison d'être (ray-zawn **detr**) the purpose of a thing's existence [French = reason for being]

rigor mortis (ry-ger **mor**-tis) stiffening of the body after death [Latin = stiffness of death]

RIP may he or she (or they) rest in peace [short for Latin *requiescat* (or *requiescant*) *in pace*]

sang-froid (sahn-**frwah**) calmness in danger or difficulty [French = cold blood]

savoir faire (sav-wahr **fair**) knowledge of how to behave socially [French = knowing how to do]

Schadenfreude (**shah**-den-froi-da) pleasure at seeing someone else in trouble or difficulty [German = harm joy]

sotto voce (sot-oh **voh**-chee) in a very quiet voice [Italian = under the voice]

status quo (stay-tus **kwoh**) the state of affairs as it was before a change [Latin = the state in which]

sub judice (**joo**-dis-ee) being decided by a judge or lawcourt [Latin = under a judge]

terra firma dry land; the ground [Latin = firm land]

tête-à-tête (tayt-ah-**tayt**) a private conversation, especially between two people [French = head to head]

verboten (fer-**boh**-ten) not allowed; forbidden [German = forbidden]

vis-à-vis (veez-ah-**vee**) **1** in a position facing one another; opposite to. **2** as compared with [French = face to face]

viva voce (vy-va **voh**-chee) in a spoken test or examination [Latin = with the living voice]

volte-face (volt-**fahs**) a complete change in your attitude towards something [French]